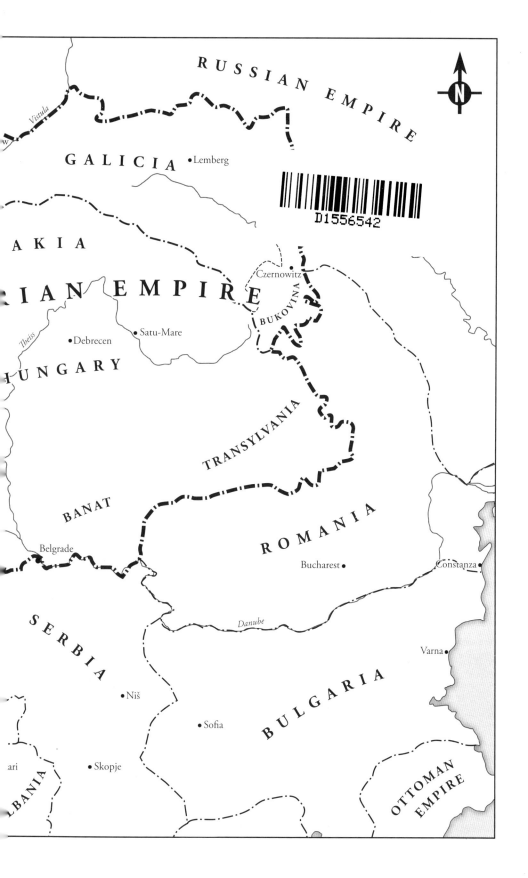

Please return/renew this item by the last date shown
on this label, or on your self-service receipt.

To renew this item, visit **www.librarieswest.org.uk**
or contact your library

Your borrower number and PIN are required.

FOLLY
AND
MALICE

The Habsburg Empire,
the Balkans and the
Start of World War One

John Zametica

SHEPHEARD-WALWYN (PUBLISHERS) LTD

First published in 2017 by
Shepheard-Walwyn (Publishers) Ltd
107 Parkway House, Sheen Lane,
London SW14 8LS
www.shepheard-walwyn.co.uk

British Library Cataloguing in Publication Data
A catalogue record of this book
is available from the British Library

ISBN: 978-0-85683-513-1

Typeset by Alacrity,
Sandford, Somerset
Printed and bound in the United Kingdom
by Short Run Press, Exeter

FOR PETAR AND KONSTANTIN

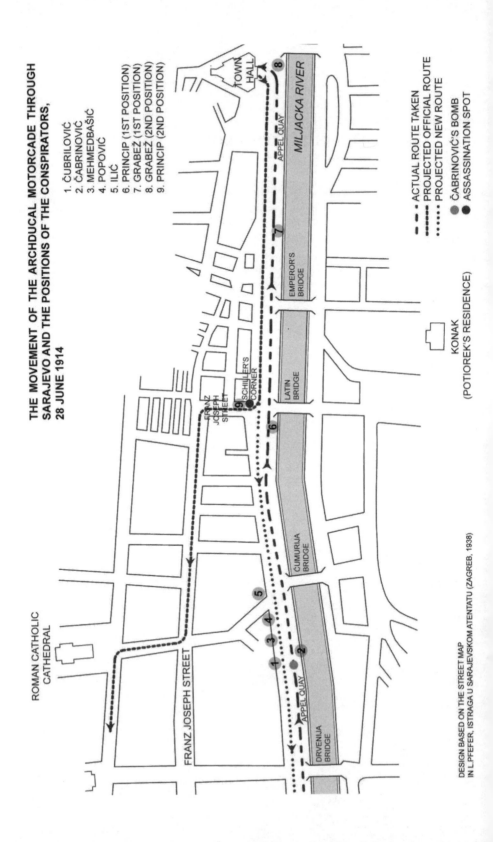

THE MOVEMENT OF THE ARCHDUCAL MOTORCADE THROUGH SARAJEVO AND THE POSITIONS OF THE CONSPIRATORS, 28 JUNE 1914

1. ČUBRILOVIĆ
2. ČABRINOVIĆ
3. MEHMEDBAŠIĆ
4. POPOVIĆ
5. ILIĆ
6. PRINCIP (1ST POSITION)
7. GRABEŽ (1ST POSITION)
8. GRABEŽ (2ND POSITION)
9. PRINCIP (2ND POSITION)

- - - ACTUAL ROUTE TAKEN
—— PROJECTED OFFICIAL ROUTE
········· PROJECTED NEW ROUTE
● ČABRINOVIĆ'S BOMB
● ASSASSINATION SPOT

ROMAN CATHOLIC CATHEDRAL

FRANZ JOSEPH STREET

FRANZ JOSEPH STREET

SCHILLER'S CORNER

TOWN HALL

APPEL QUAY

MILJACKA RIVER

EMPEROR'S BRIDGE

LATIN BRIDGE

ČUMURJA BRIDGE

APPEL QUAY

DRVENIJA BRIDGE

KONAK
(POTIOREK'S RESIDENCE)

DESIGN BASED ON THE STREET MAP
IN L.PFEFER, ISTRAGA U SARAJEVSKOM ATENTATU (ZAGREB, 1938)

Contents

List of Illustrations

Between pages 382 and 383

1. Emperor Franz Joseph
2. Archduke Franz Ferdinand
3. Franz Ferdinand and his wife Sophie
4. Franz Ferdinand with wife and children
5. Alexander Brosch
6. Carl Bardolff
7. Conrad von Hötzendorf
8. Ante Starčević
9. Bishop Josip Juraj Strossmayer
10. Canon Dr Franjo Rački
11. Benjámin von Kállay
12. István Burián
13. Gligorije Jeftanović
14. Ali beg Firdus
15. Josip Stadler, Archbishop of Sarajevo
16. Ilija Garašanin
17. King Milan Obrenović
18. Queen Natalie Obrenović
19. King Alexander Obrenović and Queen Draga
20. Đorđe Genčić
21. Colonel Alexander Mašin
22. The Konak, the old Royal Palace in Belgrade
23. Count Agenor Gołuchowski
24. Alois Lexa von Aehrenthal
25. Ballhausplatz, Vienna
26. King Peter Karađorđević of Serbia
27. Crown Prince Alexander Karađorđević
28. Nikola Pašić
29. Milovan Milovanović
30. Oskar Potiorek
31. Erik von Merizzi
32. Leon von Biliński
33. Miroslav Spalajković

Unless otherwise credited, the images stem from the author's collection.

List of Maps

THE BALKANS BEFORE FIRST BALKAN WAR, 1912

THE BALKANS AFTER SECOND BALKAN WAR, 1913

Preface and Acknowledgements

THIS BOOK explores the Habsburg Empire's entanglement in the Balkans and its interaction with South Slav nationalism during the period leading up to the outbreak of the First World War. As one might expect, different aspects of the rather large subject in question have been much discussed over the years given that the European conflagration of 1914 was occasioned by unresolved problems affecting the Austro-Hungarian state and its relations with Balkan neighbours, primarily Serbia. Even before the Sarajevo assassination of Archduke Franz Ferdinand on 28 June 1914, major diplomatic crises emanating from the Balkans threatened to disturb the peace of Europe. The Sarajevo assassination has of course generated a massive body of literature, but the Bosnian annexation crisis, 1908-1909, and the Balkan Wars, 1912-1913, have also received very considerable attention. Scholarly and popular interest in these themes was renewed in the wake of Yugoslavia's bloody collapse in the 1990s.

In many important respects, however, the story of the clash between Habsburg imperial strategies and South Slav aspirations has been, and continues to be, misunderstood or misinterpreted. Quite a few of the works published in connection with the recent centenary of the outbreak of the First World War betray either startling ignorance of the paramount issues or, in some cases, adjust historical facts to fit a desired narrative. But this book was not conceived as a response to recent interpretations. Ever since the view was established, for example, that Gavrilo Princip, Franz Ferdinand's assassin, was a 'Serb nationalist', or that the Archduke was a peace-loving, reform-minded friend of the South Slavs, or that the so-called Black Hand secret organization of Serbian officers had arranged his killing, the whole subject has, it seems to me, been crying out for revision. The need to revisit it, indeed, is the only apology I offer, if one is required, for writing this book. Perhaps I might add that I have a personal interest and curiosity with regard to the geographic area under consideration and its very complicated political history. All my grandparents were born in the realm of the Habsburgs. For most of my life I have lived and moved in various parts of Central Europe and the Balkans, from Slovenia to Bosnia, from Vojvodina to Montenegro, and from Belgrade to Vienna.

I owe my greatest debt of gratitude for completing this work to Marko Gasic, first and foremost my friend, but also a fellow historian and my literary agent and editor. His deep knowledge of Balkan history enabled him to comment on my work with sharp observations and indeed merciless criticisms, which have had a major impact on the contents and structure of the book. As part of this, he also took great care to make considerable, insightful improvements to the language I employed in draft versions of the book. I am very fortunate to have had his unfailing support and encouragement throughout.

Predrag (Peđa) Petković from Belgrade showed unreserved commitment to my project from the very beginning. Incontestably the greatest bibliophile in Serbia, Predrag responded expeditiously to my countless requests for the often obscure, scarce and normally unobtainable books and pamphlets from Serbia, Croatia, Bosnia-Herzegovina and Montenegro. My work has benefited greatly from the materials that he was able to chase up.

The Duke of Hohenberg kindly allowed me access to Franz Ferdinand's papers, deposited at the Austrian state archive in Vienna (Haus-, Hof- und Staatsarchiv). I am equally grateful to Princess Anita Hohenberg who guided me in the archive of Schloss Artstetten, Lower Austria, where she also oversees a superb museum devoted to Franz Ferdinand. I should also like to thank Gerhard Floßmann and Brigitte Leidwein for their assistance at Artstetten. Jasna Majerle from the Serbian National Library in Belgrade was extremely helpful with regard to the Serbian newspapers from 1914. Jelica Ilić from the Nikola Pašić Foundation in Zaječar, Serbia, provided valuable assistance at short notice.

To Dr Mile Bjelajac, the Director of the Institute for Recent History of Serbia, Belgrade, I am greatly indebted for information and support. Over several years, I spent many hours with him discussing various aspects of my work. His unmatched grasp of issues involving the Serbian Army gave me precious insights into what is a difficult terrain. Dr Michael Stenton, whose work has connections with modern Balkan history, read several versions of this book. I am much obliged to him for his erudite, penetrating comments, and also for suggestions regarding the focus of attention. I wish to emphasize, however, that while others have contributed to my work, its interpretations and conclusions are my own. I bear responsibility for any flaws which it may contain.

I am especially indebted to Branko Ćupić and Jelena Ćupić who played a cardinal role during the entire process of bringing to fruition what turned out to be a very demanding project. Through their companionship they made my work much less solitary than it would otherwise have been, and their many kindnesses greatly facilitated my arduous undertaking. I shall forever be grateful to them.

I wish to acknowledge here my heavy debt to the Reverend Alan Walker, a former colleague, a friend of long standing and a fellow collector of Balkan travel books. An ingenious scholar of the kind that only England produces, Alan offered invaluable guidance, but even more importantly he was a steadfast friend. My sense of gratitude to him cannot be adequately expressed.

My heartfelt thanks are also due to Natalia Bessmertnova, a delightful human being in my life who was there for me when it mattered most.

I should, finally, like to thank the following friends for their support and assistance (listed in alphabetical order): Dragomir Acović, Dr Richard Aldrich, Flavio Caprara, Nataša Ćupić, Predrag Ćupić, Dragan Davidović, David Harland, Gordana Ilic Markovic, Simonida Kordić, Mirjana Kusmuk, Julija Ljubinović, Jean Maughan, Alexandra Moser, Natacha Pejin, Dr Edward Petraitis, Dr Michael Schaude, Milorad (Miša) Suzić, Dr Srđa (Serge) Trifković, Dr Xavier Vicat, Lucrezia Walker, Anthony Werner and Dr Patrick Zutshi. There are a few others whose names are not, and yet should be, on this list. They will know, however, that I think about them. I thank those friends dearly.

Prologue:
Sick Man on the Danube

The Austro-Hungarian 'Anomaly'

AN 'EXPERIMENTAL LABORATORY for the end of the world', was the notorious description of Austria coined by Karl Kraus, Viennese journalist, satirist and culture critic, in his celebrated obituary of Franz Ferdinand, the ill-fated Heir to the Throne. 'A brash messenger' who represented 'old Austria' was how Kraus described the Archduke in his piece for *Die Fackel* on 10 July 1914. Franz Ferdinand was someone who 'wanted to awaken an age that was sick, so that the age would not sleep through its own death. The age is now sleeping through his death'. Clearly, not even Kraus could see that the apocalypse which he so distinctly linked with his country was just around the corner: less than a month later the world was plunged into the unprecedented bloodletting of the Great War. The assassination of Franz Ferdinand in Sarajevo on 28 June provided the immediate background.

What Kraus was lamenting was not an Austrian archduke, albeit one who was meant to reform and rejuvenate the Empire, but Austria itself, in which in his view the general human misery took on 'the hideous visage of a cosy wasting disease'.[1] In the unique intellectual atmosphere of *fin de siècle* Vienna, such gloomy sentiments were commonplace in the fields of philosophy, literature and aesthetics – but also in the field of everyday political discourse. Kraus was merely one of many at the time drawing attention to the looming death of the Austro-Hungarian Empire. And after the war of 1914-1918 other leading personalities who had previously kept faith now saw things in a very different light. Thus the former Austro-Hungarian General Josef Stürgkh reflected with sadness in his memoirs on the institutions to which he had dedicated his life's work and which were no more: the House of Habsburg, its Empire and the Army. 'Like so many of my comrades', he wrote, 'I too came to the bitter realization that we had throughout our lives served a lost cause.'[2]

The belief, within Austria-Hungary itself, that the Empire was a lost cause had begun to circulate well before the 1914-1918 cataclysm. Ironically perhaps, it was to prove a main trigger for the war. The mood of despondency and fatalism prior to 1914 was summed up in the view: 'Better a terrible end than terror without end.'[3] Soon after the outbreak of the war the Hungarian Prime Minister István Tisza admitted that 'for twenty bitter years' he had considered the Monarchy to have been condemned to doom.[4] Ottokar Czernin, who belonged to the circle around Franz Ferdinand, and who rose to become the Foreign Minister during the war, recalled in 1919 that the Archduke's assassination in Sarajevo had been widely perceived as heralding the end of the Empire. Czernin observed, famously: 'Time had run out for Austria-Hungary ... We had to die. We could choose the manner of death, and we chose the most terrible.'[5]

The anticipation of the end was indeed widespread and the malaise was noticeable especially among the elites in the Habsburg state.[6] In the nineteenth century the declining Ottoman Empire had been saddled with the sobriquet 'sick man on the Bosphorus'. By the end of the century, this was being reproduced with regard to the Habsburg state: 'sick man on the Danube'. It was not just the enemies of the Monarchy who used this catchphrase. The 'sick man' analogy was originally expressed by the Austro-Hungarian foreign minister Gyula Andrássy in 1876 when he fearfully considered the prospect of Turkey's disappearance from Europe: for then the Balkan nationalisms would turn against Vienna. By the end of 1912, with this nightmare about an Ottoman collapse becoming a reality in the wake of the First Balkan War, the Austrian statesman Ernest von Koerber echoed Andrássy, despairing that the future was 'hopeless' and that Austria was 'the second Turkey'.[7]

What, then, was so unhealthy about this seemingly thriving empire, containing fabulous cities, making some of the most stunning cultural and scientific advances in the world, boasting a first-class army and building a substantial navy? Vienna alone, in the view of one historian, was the place where 'most of the twentieth-century intellectual world was invented'.[8] Koerber's reference to Turkey meant, of course, that Austria-Hungary's difficulties abroad reflected problems of nationalities at home – for just like Turkey, Austria-Hungary was a polyglot empire. And just like Turkey before 1912, it was a Balkan power. There the parallels ended, but those two states were on the wrong side of history at the turn of the century. By then nationalism had long been the key political gospel in Europe. A few decades earlier Germany and Italy had become shining examples of the struggle for national unification, whereas the Habsburg and Ottoman states, based on dynastic power and bureaucratic-military structures, were medieval creations whose territorial expansion was never guided by any ethnic-national criteria. Lewis Namier noted with regard to the Habsburgs that 'they had a territorial base, but no nationality ... Their instincts were purely proprietary, the one meaning of the Austrian State to them was that they possessed it'. A.J.P. Taylor, similarly, maintained that the Habsburgs were landlords rather than rulers.[9]

Austria-Hungary's nationalities problem appeared in fact more serious than any Turkey had ever had to face. The revolutionary tumult of 1848-49 had already seen Hungarian nationalism come close to destroying the Habsburg Empire. A total of eleven nations lived in the Monarchy (not counting ambiguous groups such as Muslim Slavs, Vlachs, Gypsies and Jews). The Italians, Romanians and Serbs of the Monarchy could all look to adjoining territories in which their co-nationals had independent states. The Italians were the most Empire-hostile. The Polish elites in Galicia, forming the third most privileged group in the Empire after the German Austrians and the Hungarians, were perhaps the most loyal, but nevertheless dreamt of and worked for an independent Great Poland. The Czechs, the Slovaks, the Slovenes and the Croats did not have brothers across frontiers (except when the Croats and the Slovenes saw themselves as being members, with the Serbs, of the same South Slav family), and they all pressed for internal reform. The great mass of Muslims in Bosnia-Herzegovina saw themselves as 'Turks', while their intelligentsia could not decide, with some exceptions, whether they were Serbs or Croats. In any case, their emotional connection was with Istanbul, certainly not with Vienna. The Ukrainians, also known as the 'Ruthenians', were split into Russophiles and nationalists. The latter, although wary of Russia, were increasingly frustrated by Polish hegemony in Galicia. After 1871, when Bismarck founded the Hohenzollern Empire, a considerable number of German Austrians wanted their lands to be joined to the powerful German Reich in the north. The Hungarian ruling classes, wielding disproportionate power after the 1867 settlement made the Monarchy 'dual', were the most comfortable with the state in which they lived – but this did not stop them from provoking serious crises in relations with Vienna in attempts to improve the status of Hungary still further.

Because of its squabbling nations, the Dual Monarchy was also known as the 'Dual Anarchy'.[10] The pre-war pessimism about the prospects of the Habsburg state did in retrospect prove to be well founded given its complete ruination in 1918, the year when the many different nations of which the Monarchy had been composed left to follow their own ways. It was precisely the multi-national structure of the Empire – in the age of nationalism and nation-states – which had widely been seen as the cause of its doom. Towards the end of his life the Emperor Franz Joseph himself remarked that 'anything' was likely to happen in his empire. He explained: 'I have been aware for decades just what an anomaly we are in today's world.'[11] Franz Joseph should certainly have known, not least because he and his state had paid a heavy bill for the Italian and German unifications.

The view that an Austria-Hungary, comprised of so many nations, was an anomaly condemned to death by the progress of history has not, however, gone unchallenged amongst historians contemplating its 1918 collapse. Drawing his sword against such 'misplaced determinism', one historian has argued that had the Central Powers emerged victorious from the war, the Habsburg Monarchy would have remained intact and almost certainly expanded. Another historian put it bluntly: 'What killed the monarchy was the war and the policies ... that led up to it. Why complicate the obvious?' A similar view was held by Hans Kohn, a leading authority: 'The principal cause of the collapse was the foreign policy of the monarchy, which was based upon a false principle of prestige, a *Grossmachtpolitik* which neither the domestic situation nor the economic resources of the monarchy favoured.' A.J.P. Taylor, on the other hand, maintained that, although the impulse which brought down the Habsburg Monarchy had to come from the outside, 'it could never have achieved its tremendous effect had not all been rotten within'. There were no lost opportunities for the Empire in Taylor's opinion: once launched, the national principle 'had to work itself to the finish'.[12]

Interestingly, in 1914 Vienna's German allies also thought that there was something rotten in the state of Austria-Hungary. In a letter to the Foreign Minister in Berlin, only a few weeks before Franz Ferdinand was assassinated, the German Ambassador to Vienna Heinrich von Tschirschky touched on the subject of relations with Austria-Hungary: 'How often in my thoughts have I asked myself whether it is beneficial for us to be hooked up so firmly with this state structure which is cracking at all the seams, and to carry on the tedious work of towing it along.' Tschirschky considered a possible 'decomposition' of Austria-Hungary and even speculated about the desirability of incorporating its German provinces into Germany.[13] A worse prognosis was hardly imaginable, and was in fact fairly accurate. In 1919 the rump Austria ('Deutsch-Österreich' as it officially called itself) wanted to join Germany. Tschirschky's boss in Berlin, Gottlieb von Jagow, shared his view, writing, during the July 1914 crisis, that it was a debatable point whether Germany should hold on to the alliance with the 'increasingly corrosive' state on the Danube.[14] In 1914, the German Chancellor Bethmann Hollweg described the Habsburg Empire as 'crumbling'.[15] Even Kaiser Wilhelm II was not too hopeful about its future. When he tried, early in August 1914, to convince the Crown Prince of Romania that it was in the interest of Romania to be on the side of Germany, he told him that Austria-Hungary 'could not last for more than twenty years', and Germany would then give Transylvania to Romania.[16]

The scepticism about the viability of Austria-Hungary was thus commonplace. 'One lived', the Austrian statesman Rudolf Sieghart recalled, 'in anticipation of an approaching catastrophe'.[17] The mood of despondency among the Habsburg elites was reinforced by the feeling that their multinational empire was inferior in comparison with other Great Powers, particularly the German Reich.[18] Conversing in 1900, the well-connected historian Heinrich Friedjung and the Austrian German politician Joseph Baernreither agreed that a reform from within was unlikely and that an external saviour had to be sought – Germany.[19] But what was the point of saving the Empire? The old mission of the Habsburg state, that of being the bulwark of Christendom, had lost its purpose perhaps as early as during the eighteenth century. In 1930 Robert Seton-Watson wrote that, with Turkey's expulsion and decay, 'the whole *raison d'être* of Habsburg unity has disappeared'.[20] Moreover, the age had also long passed when Austria had actually been seen as a European necessity. Back in 1848 the Czech historian and politician František Palacký had made his celebrated plea in favour of the Habsburg state: 'Certainly, if the Austrian state had not existed for ages, we would be obliged in the interests of Europe and even of mankind to endeavour to create it as fast as possible.'[21] But Palacký also argued that nature knows neither ruling nor subservient nations. The Austrian state that he and many others wanted to see was a federation along national lines – a federation that would ensure national freedom.

Palacký's federalist predilection, in point of fact, figured prominently in the so-called Kremsier constitutional draft (March 1849), freely and unanimously agreed by representatives of different nations in the *Reichstag* (the Imperial Council or parliament). The draft had envisaged a liberal and federal Austrian state, incorporating the ethnic-linguistic principle together with the criterion of historical-political units.[22] It was, as the great historian of the Habsburg Empire Robert Kann noted, 'the only time in Austrian history that such a comprehensive agreement was ever achieved'.[23] But the young Emperor Franz Joseph closed down this assembly and imposed an absolutist constitution instead. In doing so, he dealt what turned out to be perhaps the decisive blow to any meaningful prospect of national harmony in the realm over which he had just begun (in 1848) to rule. Although in the years to come more attempts followed to redesign the Empire along national lines, they were essentially half-hearted. The riddle that was the Habsburg state, the question of how to remove the ever-threatening national frictions, proved beyond the capacity of generations of statesmen and politicians to solve.

Thus a federated Habsburg state never happened. Instead, a compromise was reached between Franz Joseph and the Hungarians in 1867, whereby Austria became Austria-Hungary. This was the famous *Ausgleich* which established the Dual Monarchy and which was to last until the end in 1918. Following the shocking defeat in the Italian war (1859) and, especially, the subsequent debacle in the war against Prussia (1866), which ousted Austria from German affairs (as well from of Italy), the old empire appeared to have run out of steam. Since the end of the revolutionary upheaval of 1848-49 Franz Joseph had held the reins of an authoritarian, centralist state. In order to survive, the Monarchy now had to carry out constitutional reform. But in what direction? Would some kind of constitutional centralism suffice, or would a federalism that would recognize the diversity of the Empire be embraced? The third way, dualism with Hungary, was an option which neither Austria's statesmen nor the Emperor were initially in any hurry to contemplate.

Dualism

Certainly, people in high places in Vienna were toying with the idea of some kind of federalist solution – at least in as much as provincial diets, crammed with aristocrats, would look after business that was not strictly reserved for the imperial centre. The 1860 'October Diploma' was a constitution which contained some such federalist elements. However, it was essentially a sham, designed to restore autocracy under the guise of constitutionalism. As Louis Eisenmann noted, it was certainly not 'made for the nationalities'.[24] Franz Joseph anticipated 'a little parliamentarianism', but not any significant relinquishment of his power.[25] Indeed. In 1865 the Croat politician Ante Starčević remarked that the difference between Austrian federalism and Austrian centralism was the difference between Satan and the devil.[26] Faced with Hungarian hostility, the scheme contained in the October Diploma foundered almost immediately. Then, as in 1848-49, the Hungarians were the most determined and the most articulate opponents of Habsburg power, and they had no time for any federalism, genuine or fake.

What the Hungarians wanted was pure dualism: a minimal constitutional partnership between the Magyars of Hungary and the Germans of Austria. Their attempt in 1848-49 under Lajos Kossuth to break away completely had been defeated. Their statesmen knew better now – outright independence was no longer a serious option, even though Russia, the saviour of the Habsburgs in 1849, was now hostile to Vienna. But any federalist scheme would put Hungary, itself a multinational land, on a guaranteed path to ruin – this, at any rate, was what the Hungarians believed. Equally, Hungary would never agree to a tight centralist system either. So when the Emperor replaced the ill-fated October Diploma with the reversion to centralism that was his 'February Patent' of 1861, this was as such simply ignored by the Hungarians, who, under the able leadership of Franz Deák, began to formulate their dualist demands. In 1865 the Emperor appointed a well-known opponent of this dualism Richard von Belcredi to negotiate with Budapest. Belcredi favoured a five-way federalist division ('Belcredi's Pentarchy') into historical-political units: Austrian-German,

Bohemian-Moravian, Hungarian, Polish-Ruthenian, and South Slav. But this was anathema to Budapest.[27]

Franz Joseph himself, however, treasured nothing except his own position and the glory of the Habsburg dynasty. This monarch, whose popular image to this day is that of an amiable, good-hearted ruler of his nations, could not have cared less for most of them. He genuinely liked only the Italians, appreciating their culture as he did. Franz Joseph was of course a German, even a bigoted German, remarking as late as 1907 that Prague was a predominantly German city – though this had not been the case for a long time. But he would get upset even by his own people if they displayed the black-red-yellow German flag on festive occasions – suspecting in their behaviour a sympathy for the Hohenzollern dynasty. It is in fact pointless to debate this detail about his outlook, for high aristocrats, not nations, were close to his heart.[28] 'His only thought was of dynastic power', A.J.P. Taylor wrote about Franz Joseph. The dynasty was not there to serve the peoples, 'it was for them to be the servants of the dynasty and to sustain its military greatness.'[29] The Emperor's instincts, certainly, were authoritarian. He used to say to General Conrad von Hötzendorf: 'Believe me, one cannot govern the Monarchy constitutionally.'[30]

Franz Joseph ('the most dignified mediocrity of his age', according to one contemporary observer)[31] saw himself as a kind of Roman-German emperor in the tradition of the Holy Roman Empire. To that extent the Habsburgs were German princes and to that extent there existed a German 'slant' in imperial ideology – making the Habsburg universalist claims somewhat hollow.[32] Certainly, burdened by dynastic considerations, he had an interest in German matters that bordered on the obsessive. This led, in July 1866, to a confrontation with Prussia, a genuine German state with no universalist, but with definite German pretensions. The Emperor had stubbornly refused to concede Prussia a position of equality in German lands, and this approach finally produced a conflict.[33]

When, at Königgrätz, Austria had lost that war against Prussia, the Hungarians had got Franz Joseph exactly where they wanted him. With no choice, he soon got rid of Belcredi and brought in Baron Ferdinand Beust to make the adjustment *vis-à-vis* Hungary. Beust, an anti-Prussian politician from Saxony, shared Franz Joseph's overriding concern to stabilise the Empire internally as quickly as possible in order to concentrate on foreign policy and scheme some kind of revenge against Prussia. A war was never that far from Franz Joseph's mind before 1870-71. The Emperor always knew that he had to appease the Hungarians, while hoping that this could somehow be avoided. The Hungarians were definitely hostile. Thus in 1866 a volunteer legion under General György Klapka had been formed in Hungary to fight with the Prussians. Of course, Bismarck's victory over Austria in that year made some kind of compromise with the Hungarians,

8 *Folly and Malice*

the second strongest nation in the Empire, unavoidable. The future of the
Habsburg dynasty was at stake, as was the standing of Austria as one of
the great powers of Europe. Austria, in the view of the German historian
Friedrich Prinz, had already lost the status of a genuine Great Power in
the revolutionary tumult of 1848, or at the latest by 1866; the 1867 deal
with the Hungarians was designed to bring about an 'artificial' prolongation
of the Great Power status.[34]

The Compromise of 1867 was struck between the Emperor and the
leading Hungarian statesmen – Austria had no part in this. The Hungarians,
indeed, saw the *Ausgleich* as a contract with their King (Franz Joseph), not
with Austria.[35] Until 1915 Austria did not, oddly enough, even have an official name, its constitutional existence being acknowledged with the words:
'The Kingdoms and Lands represented in the Reichsrat'. The moment
Franz Joseph realized that the Hungarians would let him retain control of
the army and foreign policy, he even became impatient to finalize the
agreement.[36] To no avail had Belcredi warned of the danger of a dualist
solution that ignored the Slav peoples of the Monarchy.[37] But then, as Robert
Kann suggested, 'the Compromise was never intended to solve the nationality problems of the Habsburg monarchy'.[38] As Franz Joseph said in
February 1867: 'I do not conceal from myself that the Slav peoples of the
monarchy may look on the new policies with distrust, but the government
will never be able to satisfy every national group. That is why we must rely
on those which are the strongest ... that is, the Germans and the Hungarians.'[39] The Slavs, seldom a unified bloc, were already seeking support elsewhere. As the negotiations with the Hungarians proceeded, a delegation
of Czechs, Slovenes, Ukrainians and Croats made a pilgrimage to Russia,
the Czech Palacký among them.[40] In 1865 Palacký had warned: 'The day
of the declaration of dualism will, with inevitable and natural necessity, be
the birthday of Pan-Slavism in its least desirable form ... We [Slavs] were
in existence before Austria and we will still be here after she is gone.'[41]

The essence of the *Ausgleich* was two virtually independent states,
Austria and Hungary, bound in union by the person of the sovereign who
was the Emperor in Austria, and the King in Hungary. Joint institutions
were kept to a minimum: a minister for foreign affairs, a minister of war,
and a finance minister (the currency remained joint). There was, additionally, a joint ministerial council composed of these three joint ministers
together with the Austrian and Hungarian prime ministers. This, however,
did not in any way constitute an Austro-Hungarian Government and there
was no overall head of the ministerial council – the Foreign Minister was
merely entrusted with the formality of presiding over it. The joint ministers had no say in the internal affairs of either state. Both Austria and
Hungary had their assemblies, but there was no joint parliament – the
Hungarians would not hear of it. Instead, two 'Delegations' numbering

60 each (40 from the lower house and 20 from the upper house) would sit alternately in Vienna and Budapest once a year. But they would sit and debate away from each other – their communication was in writing (hence this body of men was known as 'deaf and dumb').

The budgets, of course, were separate except for the War and Foreign ministries, and so the Joint Finance Ministry had little to do. An Austrian contemporary described the Joint Finance Minister as 'a kind of head of an accounts office'.[42] Leon Biliński, who held the post in 1914, recalled that the extent of the joint work on the finances was 'very modest'. The real finances, he pointed out, were in the hands of the two other finance ministers, the Austrian and the Hungarian.[43] In fact the Ministry was largely to busy itself, after 1878, with the administration of the occupied provinces of Bosnia and Herzegovina. Economically, the Hungarians had struck a fantastic bargain in 1867: their contribution towards common expenditure was initially only 30 per cent, and it never rose above 34.4 per cent.[44] The *Ausgleich* was, overall, the goose that laid the golden egg for them. Louis Eisenmann, the unsurpassed authority on the Austro-Hungarian Compromise, provided a famous formula for the system of Dualism: parity of rights, two thirds of joint expenses for Austria, and three quarters of influence for Hungary.[45]

The joint ministers would report to the Delegations, although in practice the real power lay, on the Austrian side, in the hands of the Emperor and, on the Hungarian side, with the Government in Budapest. Franz Joseph had a cabinet office which was divided into Austrian and Hungarian sections. Citizenships were separate – so that, for example, a domestic servant from Slovakia, holding Hungarian citizenship and resident in Vienna, would technically be treated as a foreign citizen.[46] There was a customs union between the two halves of the Monarchy, to be renegotiated every ten years together with other administrative matters – a guarantee for future disputes. The provisional character of the state was thus spelled out in the constitution itself. This became known, Oscar Jászi pointed out, as a system of a '*Monarchie auf Kündigung* [a monarchy at short notice]'.[47] The shambles of the system was revealed, for example, in 1902 when Austria and Hungary signed the Brussels Sugar Convention as separate states. The industrialists in the Austrian half of the Monarchy were to 'constantly complain' that the short term nature of the provision for customs union was a precarious basis on which to maintain the markets. Although the Joint Foreign Minister was supposed to handle commercial matters in relation to foreign countries, he was merely 'an agent' of the two separate governments of Austria and Hungary.[48] Moreover, military budgets for the joint army had to be approved by both sides, and this gave the Hungarians a great deal of de facto control over defence, and hence foreign policy.

Given the weakness of Franz Joseph's position in 1867, the *Ausgleich* was perhaps a predictable outcome, but it was still a remarkable achievement of Hungarian statesmanship. Antonije Orešković, a Croat in the service of Prince Michael of Serbia, met Count Andrássy in 1868 and was struck and revolted by the Magyar's arrogant attitude when they discussed the Balkans. For Andrássy belonged, Orešković wrote, 'to a lonely little nation of 4 million'.[49] As Namier observed, the *Ausgleich* 'made one of the smallest nations in Europe into a Great Power'.[50] It also made any evolution towards federalism most unlikely. Belcredi had naively asked Andrássy whether, if the Hungarian demands were met, it would be alright for Austria to organize its state as it saw fit. 'No,' replied Andrássy, 'Hungary would not be indifferent to that, for Hungary wishes that Austria remains a single state.' He elaborated the Hungarian position: Hungary insisted that Austria should have a unitary constitution and government, and that the Germans of Austria led the Austrian state.[51] Franz Joseph duly obliged. Beust even said to the Hungarians: 'You will keep your hordes, we shall keep ours.'[52]

Those hordes were the non-Hungarians and non-Germans – largely Slavs. Indeed, Beust had envisaged the pact with the Hungarians as being aimed 'against Panslavism'.[53] The Slavs of the Empire formed the majority in both halves of the Empire – the official statistics more or less confirm this but do not give the whole picture. According to the 1910 census, in the so-called 'Cisleithania' (the territories 'this side', i.e., west of the river Leitha, that is, in Austria), the Germans made up 35.5 per cent of the population; in the Hungarian half ('Transleithania' or 'beyond' the Leitha), the Hungarians represented 48 per cent of the population. But these figures hardly reveal the actual national proportions. In the natural melting pot of Vienna, large numbers of Empire Slavs turned into Germans.[54] The statistics should be treated especially carefully with regard to Hungary, in which an untold number of Slavs (the Slovaks in particular) simply became 'Hungarian' in the wake of the aggressive Magyarization policies pursued by Budapest. The state east of the Leitha, certainly, was no melting pot; it was a brutal assimilation machine, even if its work had been facilitated by the non-Hungarians' own aspirations to social mobility. In 1905 a contemporary observer estimated that, out of a population of some 19 million in the Hungarian state, barely 5 million were 'genuine' Hungarians.[55] Franz Ferdinand, admittedly no friend of the Hungarians, told the German Emperor Wilhelm II (shortly before travelling to Sarajevo) that their number had always been falsely represented, and that the actual figure was maybe two and a half million.[56]

In this dualist system there was a kind of sub-division in both halves of the Monarchy. In the Austrian half, the Poles of Galicia, always anti-Russian and therefore pro-Habsburg (as opposed to pro-Austrian), quickly acquired local autonomy after 1867. In 1848-49 they had opportunistically supported the Hungarians against Vienna, but this episode was ignored by Franz Joseph, who set up a curious criterion of monarchic benevolence: the traitors from 1848-49 (Hungarians and Poles) were to be rewarded, the loyal nations (Croats, Serbs, Romanians and Ukrainians) were to be punished. The Poles would be the only Slavonic group in the Empire to profit from it. Their help was needed by Vienna in order to secure a workable majority in the Austrian parliament.[57] In 1869 the Polish language was made official in Galicia, and from 1871 a Polish minister without portfolio would sit in the Austrian cabinets to look after Polish interests. The German language was completely expelled, even from the railways.[58] The number of Poles holding prominent positions in both the Austrian and Austro-Hungarian administrations was testimony enough to their importance. Colonel Carl Bardolff, who was in 1914 the head of Franz Ferdinand's military chancellery, observed in his memoirs that 'no one dared' act against the Poles.[59] This auxiliary master race of the Empire had a free hand to trample on its Ukrainians in eastern Galicia – economically, culturally and politically. The Poles duly informed the Ukrainians that their language was 'too primitive' for use in secondary education.[60] The Ukrainians, a majority in Galicia – though not in the main city, Lemberg (Lvov) – were at one point represented by four deputies in Vienna's *Reichsrat*, whereas the Poles had seventy-five mandates.[61] In 1908 Count Andrzej Potocki, the Polish governor, was assassinated by a Ukrainian student firing from a Browning pistol.

In the Hungarian half, the Croats and the Hungarians had reached a separate compromise, the *Nagodba,* in 1868. Croatia had been tied to the Hungarian crown of St Stephen since the twelfth century: in 1102 Coloman, the King of Hungary, was recognized by Croatia as sovereign. Although this was merely a personal union, the monarch providing the only link between Hungary and Croatia, in practice the latter drifted into a subordinate position – Hungary treated Croatia as an appended part (*pars adnexa*). In 1527, following Hungary's catastrophic defeat by the Turks at the battle of Mohács, the Croatian Diet elected Ferdinand Habsburg as King. He pledged to 'honour, confirm and maintain' Croatia's rights and laws.[62] This, together with, for example, the Croat acceptance of the Pragmatic Sanction in 1712 (well before Hungary followed suit) was indeed proof of Croatia's separate statehood.[63] On paper, the Croats were thus one of the 'historic' nations of the Empire. However, as in the similar case of the Czechs with regard to the Habsburg crown, this status had proved to be of little consequence. In 1848 the Croats had risen against Hungarian hegemony and, under their leader, *Ban* (Viceroy) Josip Jelačić, had done a great deal in that critical year to save the Habsburg dynasty and its state. Franz Joseph thanked them by terminating their self-rule in 1850. An embittered Jelačić commented: 'If in Vienna they continue doing as they have been doing, I give the Monarchy a quarter century of life, and no more.'[64] In 1853, when Franz Joseph survived an assassination attempt against him by a Hungarian nationalist, there was undisguised regret among some Croats that the Emperor had not been killed.[65] Later, Franz Joseph's alleged opinion about the Croats became widely known. He is supposed to have said: 'The Croats – they are rabble.'[66]

The Croat-Hungarian Agreement of 1868 paid lip service to an autonomous Croatia while establishing Budapest's ascendancy. A new, restrictive electoral law had to be introduced beforehand, and a great deal of pressure and corruption was also used in order to secure a pro-Magyar ('Unionist') majority willing to negotiate Croatia into subservience. The key to Croatia's subjugation was its lack of any financial autonomy. Moreover, the appointments of the *Ban* of Croatia were controlled by Budapest: in this matter the Emperor-King had to follow the advice of Hungarian prime ministers. Already in 1871 Eugen Kvaternik, a leading Croat politician, declared Croatia independent and led an armed rebellion during which he was killed. There were bloody demonstrations against Hungarian supremacy across the country in 1883, requiring Army intervention, and again in 1902-1903. It was only the effective, repressive policies of the country's long-ruling *Ban*, the highly able Hungarian Count Károly Khuen-Héderváry (who 'was acquainted with human weaknesses', explained the Croat historian Ferdo Šišić)[67] which prevented Croatia from emerging as the chief internal problem of the Austro-Hungarian Empire. The land was, Baron Károlyi Hieronymi said in 1898, easy to govern: 'In Croatia one simply locks up an inconvenient candidate, he is kept in custody and is released after the elections are over.'[68]

The Croats would regularly refer to the 'state-right' and the 'historic right' of Croatia; the absence in reality of any such rights was best reflected in the fact that Dalmatia and Istria, both predominantly Croat lands, were under the jurisdiction of Austria, not Hungary.[69] Dalmatia, moreover, suffered from catastrophic economic neglect by Vienna – the Croat historian Mirjana Gross called Dalmatia 'the most backward land of the Habsburg Monarchy'.[70] Thus the Croats lived divided in what was for them effectively a prison system cemented by the dualist compromise of 1867. Long before there was any 'South Slav Question' connected with the Serbs and Serbia, a potentially major and purely internal South Slav problem existed in the Monarchy connected with the Croats. Prior to Franz Ferdinand's assassination in Sarajevo, most of the previous South Slav assassination attempts against Austro-Hungarian officials (four out of six altogether) had been carried out by Croats.

Muddling Through

The system of 1867, as Namier observed, was impossible to reform: it, and the Habsburg Monarchy with it, could be destroyed, but 'it did not admit of development'.[71] Excepting an episode from 1905, when the Hungarian Independence Party (leading a coalition of parties previously in opposition) seemed to threaten the whole edifice of the joint empire, the Hungarians were the keenest upholders of the status quo. The Parliament in Budapest was rigged in such a way that, for example in 1913, there were only five Romanian and three Slovak deputies out of the total of 413 deputies in the assembly.[72] Hungary's subject races, the Romanians, the Slovaks, the Croats, the Serbs, as well as some of the Monarchy's Ukrainians and Germans, were all the targets of the policies of Magyarization – above all the Slovaks, but also the Romanians who, like the Croats and the Serbs, had in 1848-49 rendered valuable service to the Habsburgs in their struggle against Hungary. Only Hungary's Jews (numbering close to one million in 1910) had in large numbers opted for voluntary assimilation. The ultimate aim of 'Magyarisation' was the full 'amalgamation' of all the non-Magyar nationalities in the lands under the Crown of St Stephen.[73] The Magyar national aims had been perfectly clear for a long time: one state, one nation and one language from the Carpathians to the Adriatic. Robert Seton-Watson, the acknowledged authority on the nationalities question of the Monarchy, maintained that, until Hitler, 'the Magyar conception of the Herrenvolk was the most thorough-paced in Europe.'[74]

Theoretically, the nationalities in Hungary enjoyed some degree of equality. The Hungarian Nationalities Law of 1868 allowed the non-Magyars the use of their own language in primary and secondary education, in churches, in local administration and communal assemblies, and in local courts of law. This law is almost invariably described in history books as 'liberal', and sometimes even as 'enlightened'. Scholars are careful, however, to note that its provisions were never really implemented. Yet it is difficult to see what exactly was so broad-minded about it in the first place. The Magyar language still had to be used in Parliament and administration, in the justice system, in the county councils and in the single Hungarian University. Robert Kann pointed out that the law was 'tied to the status of the individual and did not acknowledge the existence of national groups as political bodies anchored in public law.'[75] That, indeed, was its whole purpose: to maintain the political integrity of the Hungarian state. It provided a fig leaf of tolerance of the nationalities whilst introducing the rather portentous concept of a Hungarian political nation, to wit: 'all citizens of Hungary constitute a single nation, the indivisible, unitary Hungarian nation, of which every citizen, to whatever nationality he belongs, is equally a member'.[76] But the point of this 'political nation' was that it was Hungarian. Robert Kann also drew attention to the fact that, from the Hungarian nationalist point of view, the term 'Hungarian nation' could actually be interpreted to mean the 'Magyar nation', that is, the ruling group in Hungary.[77] In practice, non-Hungarians in Hungary were treated as political Hungarians, whereas the paper concessions in the 1868 Law were soon allowed to become 'a dead letter'.[78]

The problem with the 1867 Austro-Hungarian Compromise was not so much that the Empire was split into two virtually independent halves – it was much more related to the fact that two national groups, the Germans and the Hungarians, held such privileged positions over other national groups.[79] And whereas the Magyar supremacy was being imposed blatantly and often obnoxiously, the German ascendancy and control in Austria's half seemed more natural – since it had, in most of its lands, been there for a very long time. Some contemporaries, however, did not see much of a difference. Thus in 1912 the Croat poet and political activist Tin Ujević wrote about the Austrian and Hungarian political and state shamelessness: 'cynicism *cis* and cynicism *trans*'.[80] Indeed, while outwardly not as chauvinistic as the Magyars, the Austrian Germans were on the whole every bit as contemptuous of other nations. It is therefore interesting that, hardly had the ink on the 1867 Austro-Hungarian contract dried, than no less a person than Franz Joseph himself appeared ready and willing to redefine the position of the Germans in the hereditary Habsburg territories.

This fascinating effort to re-engineer the structure of the Monarchy happened in the course of 1871 and concerned the Czech question. Two factors made the exercise possible in the first place. The Czechs had been mesmerised by what the Hungarians had achieved in 1867 – their leaders wanted, not unreasonably, the same deal for their nation. Their deputies had been boycotting the *Reichsrat* in Vienna, just to underline this point. Secondly, the Prussian victory over Napoleon III at Sedan, in September 1870, had put paid to any remaining hopes Franz Joseph still entertained that he and his state could play a meaningful role in German affairs. This meant that foreign policy ambitions had to be redirected to the south-east of Europe; which in turn required a strengthening of the domestic political position in the Austrian half of the Monarchy and a curtailing of the newly-acquired power of the Hungarians in theirs. A deal with the Czechs, it was suggested to Franz Joseph, would meet these conditions.

A rather unlikely individual actually whispered ideas along those lines into Franz Joseph's ear: Professor Albert Schäffle, a Protestant German from Baden-Württemberg who had held posts at Tübingen and Vienna universities. He had been noted for his political and ecomomic writings, and managed to get an audience with the Kaiser on 24 October 1870. Schäffle must have known Franz Joseph's main weakness, for he told him that Hungary's 'preponderance' was endangering the country's military strength. The only way to counter the Hungarians was to establish national harmony in the Austrian half, and that meant an *Ausgleich* between the Germans and the Czechs. Even Palacký would then, Schäffle argued, renew his recommendation that if Austria did not exist it would have to be created. Hungary, Schäffle went on, was 'an artificial house of cards', and if justice prevailed in the relations between the Germans and the Czechs the Hungarians would have to cease with the oppression of their Germans, Slovaks, Croats, Serbs and Romanians, and would have to introduce universal suffrage. The centre of gravity would then move away from Budapest, back to Franz Joseph, and the Crown would then be able to carry out, unhindered, 'Austria's oriental mission'. Schäffle emphasized that everything, including relations with Russia, Germany and Italy, thus depended on a compromise with the Czechs.[81]

Slightly fantastic as all this must have sounded even at the time, Franz Joseph called Schäffle again only a few days later, made him minister designate and gave him the go-ahead. 'I can no longer', the Emperor told the Professor, 'lie to my peoples'.[82] This touching remorse was not to be of long duration. A hopeful start had been made, however. In February 1871 a new Austrian government headed by Count Karl Hohenwart took office. Schäffle was given the ministries of commerce and agriculture but was in fact to lead the negotiations with the Czechs. He was, as C.A. Macartney called him, the *spiritus rector* of the whole government.[83] Amazingly, he managed to moderate the Czechs' maximalist demands and came to an agreement with their leaders, Count Heinrich Clam-Martinic and Franz Rieger, Palacký's son-in-law. The 'Fundamental Articles' embodied the deal which, while acknowledging the 1867 Compromise with Hungary, left Bohemia in full control of all the affairs that were not joint – this was the crucial point. The implementation of the agreement would have made Austria a federation and Dualism would have been de facto destroyed. It would have been, Friedrich Prinz maintained, 'Austrian-Czech-Hungarian Trialism.'[84] Another Trialist solution, namely that regarding the South Slav issue, was later to be much talked about when Franz Ferdinand began to throw his political weight around as the Heir to the Throne.

But the Czechs, like the South Slavs, were never going to be allowed to taste Trialism. As might have been expected, Andrássy ('sly as a gypsy', according to Schäffle)[85] and the Hungarians objected rigorously – and justifiably from their point of view – as any Trialist solution would have opened a Pandora's box of various other nationalisms, afflicting Hungary in the first place. Perhaps equally important, the Germans of Bohemia were understandably not enthusiastic to give up their leading role. One of the stipulations of the agreement between the government in Vienna and the Czechs was that officialdom in Bohemia would have be familiar with both languages, Czech as well as German. The message was clear: the

Czechs would not tolerate anything less than total equality with the Germans. But why should the local Germans accept this? They were a formidable element on the ground – a minority overall in Bohemia and Moravia, but a minority confident of itself and not a minority everywhere. When the Prussian Army occupied Prague in 1866, it found that the majority of the population in the city were Germans.[86] The Hohenwart Government's concessions to the Czechs looked to Bohemia's Germans as if they would turn them, the Germans, into a permanently subordinated minority. Their deputies were none too pleased, and walked out of the Bohemian Diet. Elsewhere in Austria, in Vienna in particular, their co-nationals were practically in a state of revolt. 'The whole of the centralistic bureaucracy', Schäffle recalled, 'worked against us together with the parliamentary and journalistic centralists.'[87]

Professor Schäffle, and the Hohenwart cabinet, duly resigned in October 1871 and so ended this Austro-Trialist farce, in which Franz Joseph himself, barely a month earlier, had issued an imperial rescript recognizing the privileges of the Kingdom of Bohemia and declaring readiness to renew that recognition in a coronation oath. This had been meant to be in Prague, where the Emperor had been meant to wear the crown of St Wenceslaus. When he abjectly failed to back his own government, and indeed this scheme to which he himself was a party, a printer in Prague printed the text of the imperial rescript on toilet paper, littering the streets of the city with it.[88] The Czechs were never to forgive Franz Joseph. This whole episode has been described as one of the strangest chapters in the reign of Franz Joseph, though it may be said that his *volte-face* was entirely predictable. When the Hohenwart-Schäfle cabinet resigned the Vienna Opera was performing *Lohengrin*. The crowd went wild at the words: 'For German soil the German sword!'[89]

On the level of theoretical discussion in Austria, however, a lonely but respected voice urged a sensible policy towards the Slavs. This was Adolf Fischhof who in 1869 tackled the question of nationalities in what was probably the most important Austrian treatise of its kind in the second half of the nineteenth century. He was the only authority to recognize clearly the wisdom of making an accommodation with the Slavs of the Empire in a way that would meet their national aspirations and at the same time ensure that they remained loyal subjects. This makes him the most realistic of Austrian political thinkers of the time. 'With the exception of Russia', he wrote, 'no other country counts so many Slavic inhabitants as Austria does.'[90] Fischhof's approach was highly pragmatic. He saw Russia and Panslavism as the inevitable refuge of the Austro-Hungarian Slavs if they felt that they were not being allowed to develop nationally within Austria-Hungary. But he was not obsessed in any way by Panslavism. He thought it was for the time being only a 'fantastic dream about the future'.

What he wanted was to prevent this dream from ever becoming a reality in the first place. He believed in the 'particularism' of Austro-Slavs, that is, their natural tendency to stick to their own languages and cultures. Austria, if it were capable of comprehending its own interest, was therefore 'the natural protector of Slavonic particularism' – as opposed to Russia.[91]

This was far sighted. Fischhof went as far as to say that the particularism of Austrian peoples, 'especially the Slavonic ones', was in fact a guarantee of Austria's existence: to weaken those peoples would be 'self-mutilation' from which only Russia would benefit.[92] He had a slogan encapsulating his philosophy: 'Imperio imperium, regnis regnum' – reign to the empire, home-rule to the lands.[93] It was exactly this advice which was never followed by statesmen of Austria-Hungary – or by the Emperor. From 1867 to 1914 they only managed to antagonize most of the nations under the roof of the Empire, as well as every single one of the neighbours across the southern and eastern frontiers. The point made by Fischhof about 'self-mutilation' was, in retrospect, a most reliable guide to the future. 'Poor Austria', he lamented towards the end of his treatise, 'how deeply you have been hurt by the mistakes of those who had guided your destiny!'[94]

The 1871 Czech fiasco, or any other similar surrender by the Emperor, had already been anticipated in 1867 by Justus Freimund in an influential pamphlet which he had to publish abroad, in Belgium. 'Never can a Habsburg', Freimund wrote, 'be at peace with the spirit of the times.' The title of Freimund's work, *Österreichs Zukunft* (Austria's Future), was probably chosen with sarcastic intent by the author as he made it clear that he saw absolutely no future for the country. A centralised Austrian sate, he thought, could only be upheld 'with millions of bayonets'. A dualist solution would only lead to the destruction of the state as the Hungarians worked for 'an absolute separation' from Austria – dualism was just a detour leading to a break-up. Federalism, finally, was in Freimund's view incompatible with a powerful monarchy – it was only possible in free countries like Switzerland and the United States. 'Does a state have a right to existence', he asked, 'and can it exist divorced from the raw force of the bayonets if it is not built on the foundation of the principle of nationalities? History has given the answer: No.' Thus the break up of Austria, desirable or not, was a 'historical necessity'.[95]

Certainly, Franz Joseph's decision in 1871 to scrap the agreement with the Czechs enshrined the politics of internal paralysis. His pusillanimity on that occasion was to push the Empire yet nearer to its grave along the long funereal path that had begun at the latest by 1867 with the capitulation to Hungary. The Austrian historian Hugo Hantsch considered the endeavour to reach an adjustment with the Czechs 'the last practical attempt' to reconstruct the Monarchy before the World War.[96] From that point on, Austria-Hungary was reduced to muddling through.

The phrase 'muddling through' (*fortwursteln*, that is, 'stretching sausage') is in Austro-Hungarian history most famously associated with Count Eduard Taaffe who as Prime Minister managed to steer Austrian politics for fourteen years. The year 1879, when Taaffe took up office, was significant for two reasons. First, it marked the end of the so-called 'liberal era' in Austrian politics; and second, it was when a treaty of alliance was concluded with Germany. Reliance on Berlin was to become the corner-stone of Austro-Hungarian foreign policy in the years leading up to the outbreak of world war in 1914 – this reliance, indeed, 'barred forever the possibility for a comprehensive settlement of the nationality questions' since the Austro-German and Magyar predominance in the Empire was a prerequisite of the alliance in the first place.[97] The Liberals in Austria (in point of fact centralist-minded, nationalist Austro-Germans) had opposed the occupation of Bosnia-Herzegovina in 1878 which followed the great 'Eastern Crisis' – thereby earning themselves the wrath of Franz Joseph, who tolerated no encroachments into his leadership of foreign policy. As good Austro-Germans the Liberals had every reason to dislike an increase in the Monarchy's number of Slavs. They were of course to be proved right in more ways than one. Their main sin in Franz Joseph's eyes, however, was to even hint that Parliament should have a voice in foreign policy – as Eduard Herbst, one of the Liberal leaders, had suggested.[98] Their almost uninterrupted reign in Austria since 1867 reflected Franz Joseph's own Austro-centralist tendencies, but this alliance was now over.

By bringing in Taaffe, however, Franz Joseph was not in any real sense contemplating federalism again. Taaffe was the Emperor's childhood friend, a nobleman of Irish ancestry, immune to nationalist squabbles. He simply recognized that 'Austria represented a permanent compromise'.[99] The Austro-German Liberal idea that Austria could only be German or it would otherwise simply not exist was soon thrown out as his long admin-istration began. Taaffe managed to bring the Czech deputies back to the *Reichsrat*, constructing together with the Polish and Slovene deputies a solid Slavonic bloc (which admittedly did not include the Ukrainians) in his governmental 'Iron Ring' – as it was known. The Poles in particular supported Taaffe by extracting counter favours 'with fine political *savoir faire*'.[100] The Czechs were temporarily bought off with some language concessions: although their wealth and self-confidence had increased con-siderably since 1871, their demands had curiously become more restrained. The steadfast nature of the Taaffe regime rested on moderate administra-tive decentralization and equally moderate concessions to the nationalities. As Austria stabilized internally, Dualism with Hungary also solidified – there was no question of restructuring the 1867 edifice built with Hungary.

Taaffe's famous formula for the nationalities was to keep all of them in 'a condition of even and well-modulated discontent'.[101]

This, however, could only work for a while. Taaffe had only briefly 'blunted the edge of Slavic discontent'.[102] The Czech-German conflict in Bohemia never went away and in fact had already re-emerged under Taaffe. The so-called 'Young Czech' Party, a radical new formation in the politics of Bohemia, stood in opposition to his coalition – they had 'a sort of spiritual home in the Paris of the Third Republic'.[103] The government that came after Taaffe in 1893 fell in 1895 following a dispute over the proposed building of a Slovene-language school in the predominantly German town of Cilli (Celje). The next government, led by Count Kasimir Badeni (a Pole), was in 1897 having to renegotiate the economic aspects of the *Ausgleich* with Hungary (in accordance with the ten-year stipulation laid down by the Compromise) and required the support of the Czech deputies – in particular the 'Young Czechs' who had come to dominate the politics of Bohemia. A bargain was now made. The government passed decrees to the effect that all German officials in Bohemia and Moravia, irrespective of rank, would have to become competent in Czech. This was a moment of huge crisis for the whole of the Empire. The Austro-Germans were up in arms. Riots took place. Such violence 'Austria had not seen since 1848.'[104] Karl Hermann Wolf, a writer and a German deputy from Bohemia, uttered the words 'Germania irredenta' in the parliamentary debate (he and Badeni were to duel with pistols, and the latter was wounded) – capturing and articulating what had in effect become a wave of Austro-German anti-Habsburg sentiment.[105] Franz Joseph hastily accepted Badeni's resignation. The language decrees were revoked. The judgement of the Slovene historian Fran Zwitter with regard to this episode should perhaps be quoted here: 'The fall of the Badeni government ... proved that, from now on, no important change in Cisleithania was possible against the will of the German parties.'[106]

The Hungarian equivalent of this state of affairs had of course for a long time already held in Transleithania. Unlike in Austria, however, the nationalities in Hungary hardly had a formal political presence. The big, but in practice insignificant, exception were the forty Croat delegates to the Hungarian Parliament who were supposed to look after Croatia's interests there. A Hungarian satirist described the Budapest Parliament thus: 'Below the gallery, in separate sections, sit the belligerent Saxons and the Croats. What can we say about the latter? One Croat, two Croats, three Croats – forty Croats. It doesn't make any difference.'[107] Whereas Austria under Badeni had already considerably increased the franchise, Hungary remained a country ruled by a relatively small circle of landed aristocracy and gentry. On the basis of property qualification only six per cent of its population were entitled to vote – a sure way to suffocate the nationalities.[108] By contrast to Austria's internal disorder, Hungary was to present a very different problem for the stability of the Empire.

For thirty years, from 1875 to 1905, Hungarian politics were dominated by the Liberal Party – 'even more unrepresentative', Robert Kann wrote, 'than its counterpart in Austria'.[109] The governments which it fielded were all loyal to the Dualist system – Hungarian statesmen like István Tisza were fully aware that 'Great Hungary' was inseparably connected with the Austro-Hungarian Monarchy.[110] And yet the party's dissidents were to develop a nationalist wing. Indeed, nationalism was alive and well in Hungary, its targets including the relationship with Austria as much as the subservient nations. The Austrian writer Anton Mayr-Harting considered the notion that Austro-Hungarian relations had been regulated once and for all by the *Ausgleich* as 'pure fiction, repeatedly debunked'.[111] The name of the joint Army, for example, was a bone of contention. Already in 1889 the Hungarians succeeded in getting it renamed from 'kaiserlich-königliche Armee' into 'kaiserliche und königliche Armee' – whereby, as the historian Victor Bibl noted, the inconspicuous conjunction became in fact quite telling.[112] The 'und', of course, reflected the Hungarian obsession with emphasizing the existence of two separate states. A further heated debate concerned the joint coat of arms, agreement on which was reached between Austria and Hungary as late as 1915.

In 1894 Lajos Kossuth, the celebrated leader of the 1848-1849 Hungarian revolt against Vienna, died in exile and was given a grand funeral at home. The opposition Independence Party suddenly received a major injection of support. What this party wanted was complete independence, leaving only one link to Austria: the King-Emperor. To them, the 1867 Compromise was no less than treason. A most serious crisis in relations between Vienna and Budapest began in 1903 when a parliamentary bill on army reorganization prompted the opposition to voice its demand for the introduction of Hungarian as the language of command in Hungary. This was already separatism, pure and simple. Franz Joseph read the signs correctly when, in September 1903, he issued his famous army order from Chlopy in Galicia (where manoeuvres had been held), insisting on the unity of the military.

The Magyar populace had already been demonstrating against the playing of the imperial anthem. Hungarian separatism, in fact, soon triumphed in the formal sense. In January 1905 the opposition parties, in a coalition led by Kossuth's son Ferenc ('the weak son of a great father', is how Robert Kann described him),[113] won the elections handsomely. By April the Army Operations Bureau had plans ready for military action against Hungary.[114] The separation of Norway from Sweden reinforced the crisis psychosis – as did revolutionary upheavals in Russia. Yet there was an important domestic development at the time (discussed in chapter three) that served as a red light against the proposed use of the Army: in October the Croats and the Serbs agreed on a joint front, offering to back the Hungarians against Vienna.[115] Early in 1906, nevertheless, Franz Joseph acted to close the Parliament in Budapest by force. He had appointed the trusted General Géza Fejérváry as Prime Minister and summoned the Parliament for 19 February in order to dissolve it. When the Parliament refused to accept Franz Joseph's letter (in which he announced the dissolution), Army units broke into the hall, chasing out all the deputies and personnel, and sealed the entrance. The Croat politician Ante Trumbić commented later: 'Not a drop of blood was shed by the Magyars in defence of the millenium-old Constitution.'[116] Franz Joseph finally resorted to a clever tactic to end the impasse: he threatened to extend the franchise system in Hungary. The intimidation was successful because a widening of the electorate would have made Hungary far less Hungarian-dominated and possibly even destroyed it. 'Before this threat', C.A. Macartney wrote, 'what courage the Coalition leaders had left collapsed.'[117] Hungary soon went back to normal, but retained its restrictive franchise.

Franz Joseph's action regarding the franchise was no empty posturing: he actually believed in the benefits of universal manhood suffrage. But he had his own specific reason, believing in the extension of the franchise as a way of solving the nationalities problem of Austria-Hungary. Albert von Margutti, who served in his military chancellery, recalled the Emperor's deep conservatism from that period: 'To utter the words trialism or even federalism was already a sacrilege.' Any new restructuring in internal affairs would inevitably make Austria-Hungary a Slavonic state – and from this 'the Emperor Franz Joseph would flinch'. Therefore, according to Margutti, Franz Joseph sought to make harmless the nationalist sources of friction, especially 'the Slavonic danger', by the universal remedy of social-democratic levelling. The panacea was universal franchise.[118]

Already in January 1907 Austria introduced this electoral reform (the new system applied to all males over twenty-four). Experts agree about the conservative background to Franz Joseph's acquiescence to reform in Austria. His view was that the bourgeois classes were responsible for spreading subversive nationalism and that the working classes would save the Monarchy. The suffrage reform, however, was for him just 'an expedient like any other to keep the Monarchy ticking over'.[119] The reform represented a recognition on the part of the Habsburgs of the growing strength of nationalism – a step towards reconciling 'the great contradictions of their empire'. At the same time it was also 'the last of the delaying actions' fought by them since 1848-49.[120] In the event, however, the reform achieved none of the aims of its proponents with regard to solving the nationalities question. The annexation of Bosnia-Herzegovina in 1908 proved that the parliament (*Reichsrat*) in Vienna had no influence over vital matters. There was certainly more democracy after 1907, but the 'Reichsrat did not govern Austria'.[121] Instead of class struggle replacing national conflicts, various nationalisms were merely given more room to play. The parliament building became the scene for deliberate chaos, scandal and obstruction. In March 1914, continued obstructionism by the Czech deputies resulted in the adjournment of the *Reichsrat* – and so in the months before the outbreak of the European war Austria was ruled on the basis of an emergency decree – the famous paragraph 14 of the Constitution.

A very telling episode connected with this state of affairs took place immediately after the assassination of Franz Ferdinand in Sarajevo. The Austrian Prime Minister Count Karl Stürgkh, who had acted to shut down the *Reichsrat* in March, now came under pressure to recall it in order to make possible a parliamentary commemoration for the assassinated Heir to the Throne. However, he refused, insisting adamantly that this would only lead to renewed 'embarrassing scenes' which would reveal to the whole world 'the spectacle of inner disintegration'.[122]

I

Heir to the Throne

The Sorrows of Franz Ferdinand

SO LONG AS the Hungarians did not challenge his sway over the unified Army, whose language of command was German and which, more importantly, served as a decisive factor in propping up his royal clout, Franz Joseph went happily along with Dualism. This was not surprising given his increasingly conservative disposition. Prussia's defeat of France in 1870 had buried his remaining ambitions to play an active role in German affairs. Now he was only interested in stability, both foreign and domestic. The closest he came to contemplating a foreign adventure (excepting the 1878 occupation of Bosnia-Herzegovina) was in 1898 during the Spanish-American War when he got upset with his Foreign Minister Agenor Gołuchowski for not lifting a finger to bring about intervention by European Powers in Cuba. Gołuchowski told him that Austria was better off with a republic in Spain than with a war against the United States.[1] Meanwhile, in domestic affairs, new experiments – at least any far-reaching ones – were also out of the question following the bungled 1871 attempt to replace Dualism with Trialism by bringing in the Czechs. Even with regard to the Austrian half of his Empire, Franz Joseph never had any illusions about trying to create a single multi-lingual nation.[2] He once told Ernest von Koerber that Austria was an old house whose various inhabitants bickered all the time, and that the way to tackle this problem was 'by cautious repairs, because a thoroughgoing reconstruction would be dangerous'.[3]

The Emperor, simply, wanted a quiet life. Paul Nikitsch-Boulles, Franz Ferdinand's private secretary, recalled in his memoirs that the reports submitted to Franz Joseph had to be doctored in order to camouflage any unpleasant news.[4] The Dualism that he and the Hungarian elites were building came to perfectly reflect his beliefs, inclinations and, indeed, selfish interests. Alexander von Spitzmüller, a prominent Austrian banker and statesman, even asserted that the whole system was being kept alive only by the authority of the Emperor.[5] As Rudolf Schlesinger noted, the second part of Franz Joseph's reign (under Dualism) was much more successful than the first.[6]

Franz Joseph, however, was getting old. He was 70 in 1900. What would his successor do? In 1889 his only son, Crown Prince Rudolf, a political liberal, had committed suicide in the hunting lodge of Mayerling – a wretched affair, in which Rudolf's lover, the young Marie von Vetsera, also lost her life. Rudolf and his wife Stéphanie of Belgium only had a daughter. For almost another decade it was not exactly clear who the next monarch was likely to be. Franz Joseph's younger brother Karl Ludwig, next in line of succession, was only three years his junior, and state matters did not interest him. He apparently preferred 'old wines, young women, horses and hunting.'[7] This man who, according to sycophantic accounts, is supposed to have instilled a firm Catholic outlook in the young Archduke Franz Ferdinand, his eldest son, is remembered elsewhere as 'a fat old man of brutish instincts', one of whose chief recreations was ill-treating his third wife, the young Infanta Marie Thérèse of Portugal, Franz Ferdinand's stepmother.[8] Karl Ludwig was never officially declared the Heir to the Throne. He died conveniently in 1896, but well before then attention had understandably turned to Franz Ferdinand as the heir presumptive.

It appeared at the time, however, that the Emperor's nephew was perhaps not such a good bet to succeed him. In 1892 Franz Ferdinand showed symptoms of tuberculosis. He had inherited this, along with a cynical and suspicious frame of mind, from his mother Maria Annunziata of Bourbon-Two Sicilies who had succumbed to the illness in 1870, aged only 28. In 1892, the youngish Archduke (born in 1863) held the rank of a colonel, commanding at the time the 9th Hussars regiment in the small Hungarian town of Sopron (Ödenburg). To his irritation and dismay, his mostly Hungarian officers issued orders in Hungarian rather than in German – paving the ground for the Archduke's ardent hatred for all things Hungarian. However, his anathema was not confined to the Hungarians. By this stage he had already begun to develop an aversion to Jews, liberals, Freemasons and socialists. On learning about his illness, he decided that the best cure would be to travel round the world. The journey which he subsequently made, lasting from December 1892 to October 1893, provided good opportunities for shooting – his favourite pastime – and material for a two-volume travelogue which he subsequently published in Vienna.[9] More importantly, the tour took Franz Ferdinand across the United States where he came face to face with federalism in a multi-ethnic state.

Although his mind was broadened, his health did not improve. Dr Victor Eisenmenger, who examined the Archduke in 1895 and who was to become his personal physician, established that the apex of his right lung had already undergone big changes due to tuberculosis, and the left one was also suspect. The doctor ordered absolute physical and mental rest.

Franz Ferdinand reluctantly obeyed and started a long cure in different health resorts. Eisenmenger considered his patient's condition serious, but also 'quite curable'.[10] The rest of the world thought otherwise. To Franz Ferdinand's great fury, the semi-official Hungarian newspaper *Magyar Hirlap* declared him practically a dead man. Begging to differ, he immediately complained to Franz Joseph about the 'masonic' Hungarian government.[11]

Even more painful than Hungarian opinion, from Franz Ferdinand's point of view, was official behaviour in Vienna itself. This, too, could leave little doubt even to a wider public that he was perceived in the highest quarters as a walking corpse. Evidence of how Franz Joseph rated his nephew's prospects came in 1896 when Franz Ferdinand's younger brother Archduke Otto was given the Augarten palace in Vienna as his official residence. At the same time Otto was officially representing the Emperor at events and ceremonies. The idea to give him a sumptuous palace in Vienna apparently came from the Foreign Minister, Count Gołuchowski, who was acting specifically in the light of Franz Ferdinand's grave illness.[12] But Gołuchowski himself was of course powerless to direct things in the House of Habsburg – the turn towards Otto must have come from Franz Joseph.

Gołuchowski, a Pole, was never forgiven by Franz Ferdinand. The Poles, along with the Hungarians, were now firmly on his list of detested nations – a list that was going to be steadily enlarged. In a letter of February 1897 to his friend, Vienna's great socialite Countess Nora Fugger, he complained bitterly about Gołuchowski and his perceived largesse towards Otto, which included the palace, a royal household complete with cooks, and the Lipizzaner horses.[13] In the same month Otto was being presented at a society ball as the 'presumptive' Emperor of Austria.[14] In April of that year he accompanied Franz Joseph on an official visit to St Petersburg. In May, Franz Ferdinand wrote about the desirability of giving Gołuchowski (and Count Kasimir Badeni, another leading Polish politician) a small dose of 'rat poison'.[15]

Whereas the Emperor did not show any sympathy or affection for the reserved and even haughty Franz Ferdinand, he rather liked Otto. At first sight this might seem strange, for this Archduke (two years junior to Franz Ferdinand) was generally considered to be an embarrassment to the dynasty and the country. 'The handsome Otto [*der schöne Otto*]', as he was widely known, broke many a female heart, but he also broke all the rules of etiquette governing the public behaviour of Habsburg archdukes. Renowned for his 'drunken and obscene orgies', Otto's escapades were legendary.[16] Perhaps the worst incident was when he and his hunting companions (including brother Franz Ferdinand and Crown Prince Rudolf) came across a funeral procession on a road in the country. Otto, according to one account, ordered the priest to halt the procession, so that he could jump over the coffin with his horse. The rest of the party followed his example.[17] On another occasion he paraded, completely drunk and almost completely naked, in the corridors of Vienna's Hotel Sacher – in front of the British Ambassador, his wife and their daughter. Even Otto's otherwise favourably disposed uncle Franz Joseph did not find such behaviour very amusing, and he thought he was punishing Otto when he sent him for two months to a monastery. The monks reported that Otto's stay resulted in a 'drastic depletion' of their wine cellar.[18]

The frolic in the Sacher came at a time when even European diplomats had written off Franz Ferdinand because of his illness, seeing Otto as the next emperor. The Russian Foreign Minister Lobanov-Rostovsky was very apprehensive about the whole situation in Austria-Hungary, believing that Otto's succession would be a 'misfortune' bringing the Empire to collapse.[19] The point about Otto, however, was that though a buffoon, he was at least a pliant one. He had dutifully married Princess Maria Josepha of Saxony, the sister of Mathilde who had been envisaged as a bride for Franz Ferdinand. By all accounts, the sisters were not especially attractive looking. Franz Ferdinand, upon seeing Mathilde, immediately turned down the idea of wedding her. The ensuing, tricky diplomatic situation had to be saved somehow. Admittedly, they had to get Otto drunk before he asked for Maria Josepha's hand, but his act of self-sacrifice for the dynasty had no doubt pleased Franz Joseph.[20] Yet Otto was incorrigible. In a famous episode, he asked his fellow officers (most were drunk) whether they had ever seen how a princess makes love – he actually used a different expression. When they all admitted to not having had such a privilege, Otto said: 'Then come with me, we go to my wife. I will show you then!' It was only the presence of mind and the determination of an aide-de-camp that saved the poor (by all accounts very pious) Maria Josepha from public dishonour.[21]

Unlike Franz Ferdinand, Otto had no will of his own and no political ideas. The Emperor and his ministers could manipulate him as they wished. And, again unlike Franz Ferdinand, Otto was a beloved public icon – despite, or perhaps because of his antics. However, these were to lead him to an early end: he died in 1906 – as a result of syphilis that he had contracted in Monte Carlo.[22] His son Karl was to become the last emperor of Austria-Hungary.[23] By the time of Otto's death Franz Ferdinand had in any case long been the uncontested Heir to the Throne, having fully recovered from tuberculosis and reported back for active military duty in the autumn of 1897.[24]

The new Heir, however, was a bitter man. He had never forgotten how shabbily he had been treated by his uncle and the Court during his battle to stay alive. More importantly, since 1900 the Archduke had new grounds for bearing a grudge against these same people. Having found the love of his life, thirty-two year old Countess Sophie Chotek, he also found her opposed by the royal Court. On 28 June of that year, three days before their wedding, Franz Ferdinand was forced to renounce the rights of succession to the throne of any children born from their upcoming marriage. The renunciation was required to be performed in a solemn ceremony at the imperial Hofburg Palace in Vienna, before the Emperor, members of the Habsburg family, and state and church dignitaries. This was the price he would have to pay for insisting on marrying a mere countess, rather than a member of some royal or otherwise recognised family, as the Habsburg House Law of 1839 demanded of its archdukes. Though her family's aristocratic (Bohemian) credentials dated from the sixteenth century, Sophie Chotek was simply not of blood royal and therefore not 'equal [*ebenbürtig*]'.[25]

Although Franz Joseph had made her the 'Princess of Hohenberg' on the day of her marriage, Sophie was ranked behind the last of the archduchesses.[26] The Emperor had done everything he could to prevent this marriage. But he had not reckoned with his nephew's stubbornness or, for that matter, with Sophie Chotek's ambition. He had asked Gottfried Marschall, the Archduke's former tutor in religious instruction, to dissuade this pious Catholic from marrying his nephew but Marschall had got nowhere. He reported: 'The aspirations of this woman assail the heavens! She says: that's right [*jawohl*], precisely she personally has been entrusted by Providence to carry out a great mission for the Habsburg Empire!'[27] Marschall, who later became auxiliary Bishop of Vienna, would be ever vilified by Franz and Sophie for his intervention.

The lowly official status of his wife was a constant irritation to Franz Ferdinand. Sophie could not sit with him in the imperial box at the theatre or the opera, she could not accompany him to the races or balls (not even the private balls of which he was the patron), she could not ride with him in the Court carriage, etc. No wonder that, when he talked in private about the Emperor, Franz Ferdinand would adopt a 'derisive' stance and make 'vicious remarks'. He would pointedly refer to Franz Joseph as 'the current bearer of the Crown', whilst keeping a register of all the individuals who in his view had not shown his wife sufficient respect.[28]

Perhaps it did not help his wife's status and position that he could 'never' tolerate Prince Alfred Montenuovo, who had since 1907 been Franz Joseph's *Obersthofmeister* (Lord Chamberlain), in charge of Court ceremonial.[29] Those feelings were, it would appear, fully reciprocated by Montenuovo, whom Franz Ferdinand's friend Count Adalbert Sternberg considered 'the real strongman' in the Monarchy and the 'last almighty on the throne'.[30] Montenuovo was 'one of the few' in the Monarchy who did not fear Franz Ferdinand. They had also clashed when the Archduke moved to influence the appointment of clerical-friendly personages at Franz

Joseph's Court – an attempt nipped in the bud by the politically liberal
Montenuovo.[31]

Franz Ferdinand's antagonism towards Montenuovo dated back to 1896
when the latter had become the *Obersthofmeister* to Otto – at that point to
all intents and purposes the Heir Presumptive. But it is simply not true
that Montenuovo had deliberately set out to humble Sophie. He could
hardly alter the fact that Sophie was not an Archduchess. Indeed his office
had absolutely no interest in seeing her embarrassed. From 1910 he worked
to improve her position, not least out of concern for foreign perceptions
of Austria-Hungary. He attempted to ameliorate matters at least 'optically'
in the order of precedence by placing the Duchess ahead of the unmarried
Archduchesses without essentially altering the existing ceremonial
rules.[32] The problem regarding Sophie's standing at the Court was not
Montenuovo, but that Franz Ferdinand wanted to see her treated as a
future Empress.

Countess Sophie Chotek

The romance between Franz Ferdinand and Sophie Chotek – and the ultimate tragedy of the couple – has naturally been the subject of romanticised
interpretation.[33] One of the claims about their liaison, made again and
again, is that the Archduke was hell-bent on making Sophie his wife, dynastically unsuitable though she may have been. The truth is not as simple as
that, not least because the part played by Sophie herself is strangely overlooked. Who was determined to marry whom in this relationship is a question that has perhaps not been fully addressed. Until the Chotek episode
Franz Ferdinand, it has to be said, appeared in every respect a duty-bound,
even fanatical Habsburg, fully conscious of the responsibility entailed by
his position as Heir to the Throne, and of the interests of the dynasty as a
whole. Certainly, his name was being linked to several, respectable candidates for marriage: apart from the Saxon princess, there had also been talk
of a Russian grand duchess.[34] When asked, in 1895, whether it was true that
he was considering for his bride the eldest daughter of Albert Edward, the
future English King Edward VII, he replied that the time had come to 'lift
the prestige of the Imperial House through suitable marriages, and thereby
render a service to the Monarchy.'[35]

What, then, had changed his mind? The answer of course was Sophie.
Austrian statesman Count Erich Kielmansegg wrote in his memoirs that
he had repeatedly observed how Sophie was able to combine modesty with
a 'certain coquetry'. Hinting heavily, Kielmansegg wondered whether
she had used this as a tactic to win Franz Ferdinand.[36] Count Adalbert
Sternberg, who was almost certainly in the know, wrote mockingly that
Sophie would in the presence of the Archduke shut her heavy eyelids 'in

true Christian humility' – something that only spurred him on, as royal highnesses like the unattainable above all. Sophie, Sternberg went on, had put up the greatest resistance, thus arousing in him an 'unappeasable desire'.[37]

Other recollections of this affair are very similar. Juliana von Stockhausen, in her book based on conversations with Stéphanie of Belgium, the widow of Crown Prince Rudolf, depicted Sophie Chotek as a self-controlled, arrogant and calculating woman: 'Her smile was cold, her courtesy was spurious, her warmth was artificial.' According to Stockhausen, Sophie contrived to bind and enthral Franz Ferdinand, without giving herself to him, in order to win him in marriage. Stockhausen concedes that Sophie loved Franz Ferdinand, but adds that she never let her feelings be subordinated to her 'great aim', the marriage itself. Not she, but rather Franz Ferdinand, had to pay the price.[38] The German Ambassador to Vienna noted that Sophie operated with 'humility' and added, maliciously, that she was undecided as to whether she was going to become an empress or a saint.[39]

It is possible, even likely, that the modest material circumstances of Sophie's family played a role in her determination to get on in life by winning the heart of the most eligible bachelor in the Habsburg Empire once such a possibility presented itself. When they first met, in 1892, Sophie was a lady-in-waiting (*Hofdame*) to Archduchess Isabella, the wife of Archduke Friedrich.[40] In the main only young aristocratic women of low pecuniary standing would take up such a post.[41] Sophie's diplomat father, Count Bohuslav Chotek, was by all accounts rather short of money and had many children to feed: seven daughters and one son. Although his diplomatic posts included some important ones like St Petersburg (and Brussels, where he helped arrange the marriage between Crown Prince Rudolf and Princess Stéphanie), no one took this otherwise likeable man seriously. He was the butt of jokes at the Ballhausplatz, the seat of the Foreign Ministry in Vienna. It was said that every now and again he would interrupt his long silence from a diplomatic post, sending a report based on 'reliable sources' after reading the morning edition of the local semi-official newspaper.[42] His daughter Sophie, clearly, proved far more enterprising.

'What, is he not going to make this Chotek woman his mistress?' Otto had wondered about his brother.[43] For a long time during his relationship with Sophie Franz Ferdinand would probably have wanted to do exactly that, for, contrary to the retrospective, widely held view about him, he was by no means a puritan and was indeed in some respects rather similar to Otto. He had already kept a mistress, an actress called Mila Kugler, and one of his affairs had ended up in a court settlement.[44] As one of his fellow archdukes recalled, Franz Ferdinand could get 'heavily drunk' and

had a 'particular weakness' for vulgar, 'harbour pub' humour.[45] Wladimir
Aichelburg, who has devoted many years to researching the life of Franz
Ferdinand, maintains that the Archduke had two illegitimate children.[46]

This man, clearly, was no Catholic prude, and he was as much of a *bon
vivant* as the next archduke. Just like Otto, he liked 'wine, women and song'
– as he himself put it to his political and legal adviser Max Wladimir Beck
in a letter of August 1896, complaining that he had none of them in Lölling,
in the country wilderness of Carinthia, where he was staying.[47] However,
by December 1896, he was boasting to Beck that during his autumn stay
in Meran he had finally been able to enjoy those three good things in life.[48]
In Vienna, Franz Ferdinand resided in the Modena palace which he would
also make available to Otto for his feasts. These tended, 'not seldom', to
degenerate into orgies. Now and again he would take part in the jollities
organized by his brother.[49] Nor was Franz Ferdinand so keen, at this stage,
on the idea of wedded bliss. For in this matter he was, if perhaps not quite
determined to remain a bachelor, then at least a sceptic. In April 1896, and
this was some four years after meeting Sophie Chotek, he wrote to Beck
about his 'anti-matrimonial' feelings. In May 1897, when he was well on the
way to recovery from illness, he was still mocking 'the institution of
the marriage'.[50]

The speculation that Franz Ferdinand had merely been deceiving his
friends and that he was in fact already hopelessly in love with Sophie does
not ring true.[51] His interest in other women had certainly not been killed
by her presence in his life – as his admission to Beck about the merry
goings-on in Meran indicates. The Bavarian envoy in Vienna observed in
1899 that the Archduke loved 'to flirt, to turn the heads of the young ladies
from the aristocracy.'[52] Again in 1899, the German Ambassador to Vienna
reported to Kaiser Wilhelm II that while staying in Budapest Franz Ferdinand had been keen to see all the 'beautiful music hall ladies [*Tingel-Tangel
Damen*]'.[53] The chief problem that he encountered when contemplating
actual marriage was that he could not find an attractive woman of sufficiently high standing. In a very frank letter to Countess Fugger, written in
October 1898, he responded to her earlier suggestion that he should find
a dear, clever, beautiful and good woman: 'Well, tell me,' he wrote, 'where
on earth can someone like that be found?' He went on to complain that
there was no choice among the eligible princesses: nothing but children
of seventeen or eighteen, each one uglier than the next. Better to stay
single, he thought, than create for himself 'life-long misery.'[54]

Franz Ferdinand was approaching thirty-five at the time. He had known
Sophie for a long time now. If he had serious thoughts of marrying her he
was certainly not rushing to bring it about. He had, moreover, fully recovered his health. Sophie was his dear, probably dearest friend. And whereas
he no doubt entertained romantic ideas about her, there was nothing

improper going on. It is reasonably clear that the relationship was not consummated before marriage. In August 1900, less than two months after actually marrying Sophie, Franz Ferdinand wrote a letter to Beck, mentioning his marital bliss. 'I never thought', he wrote, 'that getting married, something on which I had in the past placed so little value, would be so nice and beneficial ... My wife is a treasure and quite the kind that I need, and she is as I had imagined her in my fantasies.'[55] If the Archduke had previously placed 'so little value' on conjugality, why did he suddenly rush into it?

The explanation probably rests on something rather unexpected that happened in 1899. Sophie's employer Archduchess Isabella, who had imagined that the Archduke harboured serious intentions towards one of her numerous daughters, had found out that her lady-in-waiting was the real purpose of Franz Ferdinand's social visits.[56] A scandal ensued. Sophie, fired from her post, now moved to Dresden where one of her sisters was married to Count Karl Wuthenau, a plucky officer in the German Army. According to a German diplomatic source, Sophie was in Dresden in October-November 1899.[57] Franz Ferdinand soon followed her there. But Wuthenau reproached the Archduke for compromising his sister-in-law – either he was going to marry her or he, Wuthenau, was going to challenge him to a duel. The Archduke left hastily for Vienna where he asked the Emperor for permission to make the Countess his wife.[58]

Franz Joseph told his nephew that he should choose between the throne and the woman of his heart. Franz Ferdinand wanted both.[59] And he lectured Koerber, the Austrian Prime Minister, that he could not give up the throne as that would go 'against Divine Right'. This supposedly very religious Archduke also told Koerber that he might have to shoot himself if he could not marry Sophie.[60] Apparently such threats worked on Foreign Minister Gołuchowski who exclaimed to Franz Joseph: 'Majesty, we might have a second Mayerling!' This scenario the Emperor did not wish to see 'under any circumstances'.[61] Gołuchowski actually told the German Ambassador that he believed the Heir to the Throne was suffering from a brain disease caused by tuberculosis.[62] There was always the option of expelling Franz Ferdinand from the ruling house – Franz Joseph had such power on the basis of family regulations and he had exercised it before. But this would have made Otto heir to the throne, and by the end of the 1890s the Emperor had had enough of Otto's scandals.[63] In the recollection of Baron Margutti, Franz Joseph finally capitulated to the Archduke on this matter, following the principle of: 'Anything for a quiet life'.[64]

Whatever precisely motivated Franz Ferdinand to suddenly stick his neck out and fight with the Emperor and officialdom to marry Sophie is not in itself a matter of profound historical interest. The morganatic marriage, however, implied a threat to the dual structure of the Habsburg

Monarchy and possibly even its break-up. The leading Hungarian politicians made it perfectly clear that Hungarian law knew nothing about a morganatic marriage – Sophie, in other words, was in their view a fully legitimate future Queen of Hungary. The Habsburg family statutes of 1839, on the basis of which Franz Ferdinand's marriage was declared morganatic, were not even mentioned in the 1867 constitutional arrangement with Hungary – therefore they could not be binding for Hungary.[65] This meant, theoretically, that Sophie's children with Franz Ferdinand would in Hungarian law be considered the legitimate successors.

There existed, of course, Franz Ferdinand's solemn renunciation regarding the rights of his children. Again, however, the whole of that Hofburg ceremonial in 1900 which the Archduke had to swallow in order to marry Sophie lacked real legal substance – even in Austria. The renunciation was based on Habsburg in-house rules which, moreover, were kept secret. In essence, what the Habsburgs considered admissible with regard to their marriages was their own affair, and it did not amount to law. Corti and Sokol, Franz Joseph's biographers, pointed out that, legally, the renunciation was not necessarily binding, and that it could have been disputed.[66] Even the church had its doubts: Dr Laurenz Mayer, the bishop attached to Franz Joseph's Hofburg Palace, thought that the renunciation was not valid from the point of view of canon law.[67] Edmund Bernatzik, Professor of constitutional law at the University of Vienna, gave his expert opinion that children from the proposed marriage would in fact be entitled to ascend the throne.[68]

Presumably deeply aware of legal loopholes, Franz Joseph pushed a decree through the Austrian and Hungarian parliaments to the effect that any king of Hungary had to be the same person as the Emperor of Austria – thereby barring the possibility that a son of Franz Ferdinand could ascend the Hungarian throne. Interestingly, many Czech deputies in the *Reichsrat* boycotted the occasion on the grounds that the assembly had no right to decide on questions of succession in the lands under the crown of St Wenceslas.[69] In 1902 Franz Joseph admitted to Prince Max Fürstenberg his regret that Austria 'will have no Empress', and he feared embroilments in Hungary.[70] The issue of succession, as Robert Kann remarked, had not really been settled and, indeed could have provoked a crisis in the Empire had Franz Ferdinand not been assassinated in Sarajevo in 1914.[71]

In fact the impression that the Archduke might attempt to secure a better position for his children, born between 1901 and 1904, was never entirely dispelled. Ernest von Koerber, who as Austria's Prime Minister in 1900 was much involved in Franz Ferdinand's marriage negotiations, complained in 1912 that the Archduke was now 'raging' against him for having had to make the renunciation oath in 1900.[72] The whole of that subject seemed to be weighing heavily on the Archducal mind. Professor Heinrich

Lammasch, who from 1910 to 1912 advised the Archduke on constitutional matters pertaining to his ascendance of the throne, had an unpleasant recollection about this. Franz Ferdinand put it to him that, should Sophie die before him, he could marry a woman of his rank and their children would then be able to succeed him (*'sukzessionfähig'*). Lammasch thought to himself that something as obvious as that required no particular emphasis, and wondered whether from time to time the Archduke perhaps regretted marrying Sophie.[73]

No one knew what Franz Ferdinand would do after he ascended the throne – the fear existed that, as the monarch, he could easily modify the Habsburg family law.[74] After all, he had since 1902 been demanding Sophie's rank be raised, despite having earlier promised Franz Joseph, while attempting to persuade him to allow the marriage, that the Countess 'would never show herself at the Court or in high society, and she would never raise any claims or want to play any role'.[75] Albert von Margutti, reporting Franz Joseph's evident relief at the news of the assassination in Sarajevo on 28 June in 1914, also provided an interesting explanation: 'The Emperor, to wit, was continually, seriously troubled by the unresolved situation concerning the future position of the Heir's consort and the children.'[76] It is perhaps also significant that Franz Ferdinand had become guardian to the deceased Otto's son Karl, declaring that he saw it as one of his chief tasks to look after the education of the future heir to the throne and yet, as Count Kielmansegg recalled, doing absolutely nothing in that respect. Kielmansegg speculated whether the Archduke had not privately, 'yielding to the wishes of his wife', hoped to some day secure the Habsburg throne for his eldest son in preference to his nephew.[77] General Conrad von Hötzendorf's view was that Franz Ferdinand had 'deliberately' sought to make Karl 'stupid [*verdummen lassen*]'.[78]

Such suspicions were especially entertained by some of the courtiers around Franz Joseph, and were indeed aimed not so much at Franz Ferdinand as they were at his wife: 'a clever, energetic and high-aiming woman', known to possess a great influence on her husband.[79] Margutti related an episode in which Count Eduard Paar, Franz Joseph's Adjutant-General, had talked about Sophie Chotek, drawing parallels with Countess Mirafiori, the morganatic wife of Italy's King Victor Emmanuel II and his former mistress. Countess Mirafiori never became Queen, and Paar suggested that Sophie would, like her Italian equivalent, ultimately hardly be seen or heard of. Having somehow been informed about Paar's prediction, Sophie told Margutti, looking him straight in the eye: 'I understand that Count Paar compared me with Countess Mirafiori. But he seems to have quite over-looked that I am made of different stuff.' She even talked to Margutti about her aspirations. Margutti provided no details, saying that Sophie related this indirectly, but at the same time 'in no uncertain terms'.[80]

The Duchess of Hohenberg was unpopular not only at Court and in wider aristocratic circles, but also further down the social scale. Heinrich Wildner, from the foreign trade section in the Foreign Ministry in Vienna, wrote in his diary on 30 June 1914 how he had heard from several sources (officials and journalists) that the recently-assassinated Duchess had been 'insatiable' in her craving for power and been 'imbued with boundless ambition'.[81] Ordinary people also viewed her with some hostility. 'The peoples of the Danube Monarchy', Margutti remarked, 'felt no great sympathy for the Duchess, perceiving her as an intruder in the ruling house.'[82] Sources abound concerning her parsimony. No servant spent much time working in the Archduke's household. 'The meanness and the mistrustfulness of the Duchess of Hohenberg', the Austrian politician Josef Redlich recorded an official as complaining in 1912, 'are nothing less than unbelievable'.[83] It was rumoured that she was selling her old costumes and even haggling over prices with second-hand clothes merchants.[84] She and her husband were certainly a well-matched pair. He was constantly telling the staff to save on electricity consumption, took a stable boy to court for allegedly stealing a strap, and actually shot at a poor old woman collecting wood from his forest.[85] In 1896 he horrified the rest of the Habsburg family when, after the death of his father Karl Ludwig, he denied his sister Margaretha her rightful share of the inheritance.[86]

Franz Ferdinand was not the richest Archduke, but nor was he poor. In 1875 he had inherited the estate of the last Duke of Modena-Este. There were two conditions attached by the Duke in his will. One was that Franz Ferdinand should learn Italian – which he did not do. The other was that he should append the title 'd'Este' to his name – which he did, but subsequently arbitrarily changed to 'Österreich-Este'.[87] From the Italian windfall he bought the Konopischt castle and other properties. It is hard to accept the later claims by historians and biographers that the Modena estate was of no real use to the Archduke. Round the same time, and especially after becoming Heir to the Throne, he was receiving a very generous allowance from the Habsburg family fund. From 1904 his annual pay was 950,000 crowns, which made him by far the best remunerated member of the imperial family – and yet he kept making additional demands of the Crown Estate Office.[88] From the Archduke's point of view, Viktor Bibl noted, the state was entirely the property of the Prince: 'unhesitating', he had engineering units build roads to his castles at state cost, and had complete regions closed off – in order to indulge, undisturbed, his passion for hunting.[89]

The Archduke's World View

Those writers who are well-disposed towards the royal couple, bordering at times on the obsequious, like to stress that Franz Ferdinand and Sophie were in their handling of money matters merely trying as parents to make sure that their children, with no future in the ruling house, would be well provided for. Such writings need to be examined with great caution because the real picture was something quite different. Rather than saving for his children, the Archduke was actually spending money as if there were no tomorrow. Alexander Brosch, the head of Franz Ferdinand's military chancellery, remarked privately in July 1910 that, on account of the expenses entailed by his hobbies, the Archduke was 'indebted despite his avarice'.[90] Indeed he died an indebted man: his debts were then taken care of by the Emperor whom he had so hated, and by Archduke Karl Franz Joseph.[91]

And yet there has been no end of retrospective attempts to embellish two rather unlikable characters. The marriage between Franz Ferdinand and Sophie is also presented as a very happy one – as if this should hold off any deeper scrutiny of their characters. Even their model marriage, however, was perhaps not always free of tension. Count Heinrich Lützow, the distinguished Austro-Hungarian diplomat, pointed to where the problems may have existed. In his memoirs he took pity on the Duchess: 'Her life could not have been an easy one, for although the Archduke was a most loving husband, he could not always, with regard to his wife, rein in his passionate temperament.'[92]

Indeed, Franz Ferdinand's touchiness, vehemence and excitability are some of the attributes for which he is chiefly remembered. No doubt his tantrums owed something to the congenital arrogance of a Habsburg prince. And surely his generally inimical attitude to people stemmed at least in part from the bitterness that he had developed when he fought, practically alone, to overcome tuberculosis. His education, or lack of it, is conceivably the third factor that accounts for his brusque manner. Had he had a better education, one designed to prepare him for future rule, he would perhaps have had greater control of his behaviour. But of course it was only Crown Prince Rudolf's suicide that opened up the prospect of power and by then Franz Ferdinand was serving in the military. His previous schooling, like that of most of his fellow archdukes, left much to be desired. In Robert Kann's opinion, his inadequate education, and his shallow knowledge of political and constitutional problems, meant that 'his political prejudices were even more deeply rooted'.[93] The Austrian writer Anton Mayr-Harting used slightly harsher words: the Archduke was 'jam-packed with prejudices', and his ignorance was 'stupendous'.[94]

Assessments of the Archduke's mental ability have differed widely. One contemporary biography of Franz Joseph (from 1909), described his nephew as a man 'of limited brain-power and narrow mind'.[95] But this was rather inequitable. Another view about his mind, much closer to the available evidence about the Archduke, was that it was sharp without being subtle: 'Dominican rather than Jesuit.'[96] As was customary for the Habsburgs, he was educated privately. He and his younger brother Otto were often tutored together, receiving instruction in a number of subjects, from religion to natural science. But this was largely a *pro forma* exercise as both boys were predestined for military careers. Franz Ferdinand himself recognized later the inadequacies of his education, saying that 'we learned everything but knew nothing properly'. Although it has been suggested on his behalf that he subsequently attempted to fill the gaps in his knowledge, there is little evidence for this claim. 'His reading', Eisenmenger observed, 'was limited to newspapers ... to books on castles and forts, gardening and descriptive works on nature in so far as they contained a hunting angle.' Franz Ferdinand could not command a single foreign language. The claim by his biographer Rudolf Kiszling that he 'fully' mastered French is contradicted by Eisenmenger who recalled that the Archduke could converse 'a little' in French and read 'light' French books.[97]

As his Slovak associate Milan Hodža observed in his memoirs, 'Francis Ferdinand was not an ardent student of complicated problems'.[98] Professor Lammasch, when he saw the Archduke in his Belvedere palace in Vienna, could not help observing that his desk in the office 'did not betray much paperwork'. He also could not see on the bookshelves 'any significant works'.[99] Typical of Franz Ferdinand's approach to the study of serious matters is his letter to Baron Beck from February 1902 when he found himself in Venice. He wrote that he had plenty of leisure time which he could use to read books, especially on constitutional matters regarding Austria's relationship with Hungary. Therefore he requested Beck to send him some literature on the subject. 'It goes without saying', he wrote, 'that such a book should be written by an Austrian and not a Hungarian, and it should not be a weighty tome as it would then be too difficult to digest.'[100] But what he lacked in terms of competence, he more than made up for in arrogance. In 1902 he told Karl Gelb von Siegesstern, his new aide-de camp, that he wanted to be advised, not taught.[101] While he assimilated much, he did so 'in passing'; and he did not seek information, it had to be presented to him.[102]

The Archduke's attitude to culture should perhaps not be judged by his comment regarding the monuments to Goethe and Schiller, erected in Vienna in the 1870s: 'Goethe and Schiller get their monuments, while many Austrian Generals, who indebted our fatherland more, get nothing.'[103] There was certainly another side to his understanding of art and culture. Interestingly, he was an enthusiastic collector of art objects. Whether he was a connoisseur is another matter. Edmund Glaise-Horstenau noted that the Archduke's collection included, in addition to some truly valuable pieces, 'quite a lot of kitsch'. An expert opinion from 1928 went further and held that most of his collection was in fact 'junk'.[104] On the day of the assassination, Josef Redlich could not help writing in his diary that the Archduke's 'tasteless art collecting' had long provoked 'the dismay of anti-quarian dealers'.[105] A recent study of Franz Ferdinand's supervision (since 1910) of the central commission for the preservation of cultural heritage takes a more benevolent view of his artistic taste and knowledge.[106] But he certainly disliked modern art. In 1910 he thwarted the appointment of Gustav Klimt as professor at the Arts Academy.[107] He similarly despised the great *Jugendstil* architect Otto Wagner. The Secession movement in art was also an object of his hatred – he used the adjective 'secessionist' as a swear word or simply as a label for things he did not like.[108] March 1914 saw him opine: 'Vienna already leaves the impression of an American city. Poor Vienna!'[109] Bertha Zuckerkandl, the famous Viennese journalist whose villa served as a salon for the city's artistic world, described with horror an occasion in 1912 when the 'Hagenbund' group exhibited paintings – predominantly works by their guest Oskar Kokoschka. Franz Ferdinand ('there was no less popular a figure than this Habsburg', she wrote) suddenly arrived, looked at the paintings and said not a word. The tension was palpable. Then, standing in the middle of the hall, he shouted: 'Disgrace! [*Schweinerei!*]'[110]

Collecting art and being in charge of protecting historic monuments, however, were secondary interests compared to his overriding passion: shooting. His zeal really bordered on mania. He shot his first animal at the age of nine, drawing a congratulatory letter from Crown Prince Rudolf.[111] Before he embarked on his trip round the world in 1892 he made sure to get information from Arthur, Duke of Connaught, about hunting oppor-tunities in India.[112] In March 1893, sailing from Calcutta to Singapore, he wrote proudly to Baron Beck of his successes in India: '7 tigers, 5 panthers, 3 elephants and 1,356 pieces of different types of animals'.[113] The Bosnian Serb politician Danilo Dimović described how Franz Ferdinand killed a hind, and when its young ones came seeking milk shot them as well.[114] Rebecca West gave some examples of this 'capacity for butchery'. Kaiser Wilhelm II had organized a boar hunt, with sixty boars let out: Franz Ferdinand had the first stand and 'fifty-nine fell dead, the sixtieth limped by on three legs'. On another occasion, at a castle in Bohemia, he shot 2,150 pieces of small game in a single day.[115] At Konopischt alone he exhib-ited 30,000 hunting trophies. As the years went on, his hunting passion 'degenerated into mindless, mass shooting spree'.[116] In 1901 the German Ambassador to Vienna wrote to Kaiser Wilhelm that Franz Ferdinand 'loves mass killings above all'.[117] Of course, for the European aristocracy of the day shooting was a sport that went hand in hand with their privileged social status, and it was pursued by many, including Franz Joseph. However, the holocausts inflicted on wild life by Franz Ferdinand on his every shooting expedition were somewhat unusual. It was, Glaise-Horstenau suggested, almost as if the Archduke sought to calm down his all too stormy temperament.[118] Even Franz Joseph found his nephew's passion for mass shooting (*Massenschiesserei*) appalling. He told Kielmansegg: 'The Archduke recently shot several hundred pieces in the Lainz zoo, that's incomprehensible, those are house animals, do you think that's huntsman-like?'[119]

According to one account, the total number of animals killed by Franz Ferdinand was 274,889.[120] An intriguing report exists connected with his passion for shooting and his own death. On 27 August 1913 the Archduke was hunting at Golling, south of Salzburg. The gamekeeper spotted a rare white chamois buck, known in the area by its Slavonic name *zlatorog* (golden horn). Franz Ferdinand shot it immediately. But the legend about this animal, known to the Archduke, went: 'He who kills this creature out of caprice will himself die within the year.' The Archduke boasted to the Duchess about his trophy, but also told her of the legend. 'Why, then', she asked, 'did you shoot the white buck?' His reply was: 'Well, if one has to die, one dies anyway.'[121]

The Archduke used to openly admit that it was a matter of indifference to him whether people liked or hated him, suffice that they feared him.[122] 'Most people are scoundrels!', he once told Prince Konrad Hohenlohe.[123] The circle of friends and companions that he and Sophie had around themselves was quite small. Jews did not figure as their friends. Alexander Brosch, the head of the Archduke's military chancellery, reported his boss's 'ferocious anti-Semitism'.[124] Brosch's successor Carl Bardolff wrote about Franz Ferdinand's 'unshakeable conviction' that the whole of Freemasonry, liberalism and Marxism, as well as the entire big capitalism 'stood under Jewish leadership'.[125] The Heir Apparent chose his intimates almost exclusively from the ranks of high aristocracy, with some clerics and the occasional non-aristocratic outsider thrown in. He felt himself, according to Brosch, 'only as the Emperor of the aristocrats'.[126] Whether someone could gain Franz Ferdinand's trust and confidence depended 'primarily' on the attitude they displayed towards his wife.[127] But the fact that most of those friends were from Bohemia had much to do with the location of Schloss Konopischt (south of Prague), Franz Ferdinand's favourite residence. This did not, as Robert Kann has argued, reflect any genuine sympathy for Bohemia, for Franz Ferdinand was 'a man whose special predilections for certain regions ... were predominantly a function of their potential for hunting terrain.'[128] Among those mingling in his company were Count Ottokar Czernin, Prince Karl Schwarzenberg, Count Heinrich Clam-Martinic and brothers Franz and Jaroslav Thun – the latter had married one of Sophie's sisters. Another member of this circle was Count Ernst Silva-Tarouca, whose estate bordered Franz Ferdinand's Konopischt. Silva-Tarouca, together with Count Augustin Galen, Franz Ferdinand's Benedictine father confessor, appeared to occupy a major position in this social circle. Bishop Marschall complained in 1909 that it was 'always Count Silva-Tarouca and Count Galen ... who exert influence on the Archduke.'[129]

Most of these men were highly conservative, even reactionary characters. Silva-Tarouca wrote to the Archduke in February 1909: 'A bright spot in the political fog is the Shah of Persia, who has my full sympathy: he ordered the slaughter of the head of the Free Masons and had him hung by his feet from the palace gate; he also had his cannons hauled right up to the Persian parliament and had the whole shop shot to bits, just when the worthy members of parliament were in session. Very convenient!'[130] Robert Kann considered that such vulgarities cast a 'regrettable shadow' on Franz Ferdinand and that such men as Silva-Tarouca, Czernin and Count Jaroslav Thun had helped create an 'unwholesome atmosphere', exerting a harmful influence on the Heir Apparent.[131] However, according to Angelo Eisner von Eisenhof, a writer with papal connections, it was only Sophie who exerted 'political influence' on Franz Ferdinand, and she in turn was being guided by her own Jesuit father confessor.[132]

The available evidence does suggest that Sophie was quite interested in politics. Alexander Brosch was convinced that the Duchess, always present when he was reporting on political matters to the Archduke, would take up any such subject with her husband as soon as he, Brosch, left.[133] An early example of Sophie's interest and meddling in politics is from early 1902 when Franz Ferdinand chose Count János Zichy to accompany him to a visit to St Petersburg. This caused a scandal in Budapest as Zichy was a fierce opponent of the Hungarian Government, and the Archduke finally had to give up on him under Hungarian pressure. Alois Aehrenthal, at the time Ambassador to Russia, wrote privately to his mother that the choice of Zichy had been 'completely misguided'. His mother then informed him that Zichy had been Sophie's idea.[134]

Rudolf Sieghart, the head of the office of the Austrian Prime Minister (and, partly on account of his Jewish backround, one of the public figures most hated by Franz Ferdinand) thought in 1909 that the influence of the Duchess on the Archduke was not good: 'She has thrown herself into the arms of the Church, and is mean-spirited and niggardly ... All of this makes a sad prospect for the future.'[135] Francis Pribram, the history professor who had moved in Vienna's high circles before 1914, wrote that Sophie's influence was a factor that helped to make intercourse with Franz Ferdinand more difficult, preventing 'a great many persons holding high positions, social and intellectual, from approaching him.'[136]

To be a friend of Franz Ferdinand, however, also carried certain hazards. Jaroslav Thun noted: 'The poor Archduke has a sick mistrust of all who surround him.' Jaroslav's brother Franz in particular experienced the bitter taste of friendship with the Archduke. Appointed the Governor of Bohemia in 1889, he resigned in 1896 and was then, at the express wish of Franz Joseph, made the *Hofmeister* (Lord Chamberlain) of Franz Ferdinand's establishment. But the Archduke soon turned against Franz Thun, whom he had in the past greatly appreciated as a friend and as a statesman. He would, for example, reproach Thun for wearing a uniform on the grounds that this was a 'masquerade' as Thun was not a soldier – even though Thun held the rank of Major. Their relationship became unbearable, and Franz's brother Jaroslav concluded that 'either the man [Franz Ferdinand] is completely mad, or he is an altogether bad character'. Jan Galandauer, Franz Thun's biographer, has recently written that, in today's terms, Franz Ferdinand would be spoken of as a 'psychopath'. Franz Thun himself wrote to his wife Anna that he hoped, 'for the sake of my beloved Austria', that the Archduke would change, 'otherwise we are moving towards terribly difficult and sad times.'[137]

Apart from his wife, his friends and his shooting (as well as gardening and horticulture) the Heir Apparent had another realm from which he could draw comfort. This was, namely, his Catholic faith. There is hardly a study or biography of Franz Ferdinand that does not emphasize his strong attachment to religion. And yet, as has been seen, religious influences appeared not to have played a role in his life before he married Countess Chotek. Observers noted a marked change thereafter. In 1902 Major Karl Ulrich von Bülow, the German Military Attaché in Vienna, remarked: 'He is not merely imbued with political Catholicism, he is downright fanatically Catholic. His marriage has fortified him in this direction.'[138] Count Kielmansegg even insisted in his memoirs that the Archduke's pronounced clericalism was 'foreign' to his initial, authentic being and could only be attributed to his wife. Earlier, Kielmansegg was adamant, one had 'never' seen this orientation in Franz Ferdinand.[139] Andreas von Morsey, a member of his entourage, also remarked that it was Sophie who had made the Archduke into a 'strongly religious person'.[140]

Sophie's influence in this respect was also clear to Colonel Bardolff, who led the Archduke's military chancellery from late 1911. In his memoirs Bardolff tried to play down the role of the Duchess in politics, whilst nevertheless admitting that she would 'certainly' have taken part in some decision-making.[141] For example, as far as the relationship between Catholicism and the future state headed by Franz Ferdinand was concerned, Bardolff, who was of the view that there should be a church-state separation, thought that on this question the Duchess would have influenced her husband in a 'decisive' manner.[142]

Franz Ferdinand's Catholicism was famously not to remain a private matter. After 1906, when he began to take a close interest in the military and influence appointments therein, promotion became difficult for non-Catholic officers. In 1911 he declared that 'only a good Catholic is also a good soldier'.[143] The atheist Franz Conrad, who became the Chief of Staff with Franz Ferdinand's backing, was the one great exception to this personnel policy practiced by the Heir to the Throne. But he too had a bitter taste of the Archduke's religious ardour in the autumn of 1913 when, during the manoeuvres in Bohemia, he failed to attend a mass to which the other generals had accompanied Franz Ferdinand. 'I am aware of your outlook on religion', a fuming Franz Ferdinand told the astonished Conrad, 'but when I go to the church you too must go.'[144] In his memoirs the General recalled that the Archduke had 'an unmistakeable aversion to non-Catholics', and that capable officers were excluded from certain posts on account of their Protestant faith.[145]

Conrad's appointment in 1906 brought to the fore possibly the most bellicose general in any European army before 1914. His promotion, due solely to Franz Ferdinand, illustrates that the Archduke was by no means averse to contemplating war. When Albert Margutti spoke about Conrad to Alexander Brosch, the head of Franz Ferdinand's military chancellery, the latter told him that Conrad should have complete freedom of action: 'Conrad is simply not the Chief of Staff for peace, but exclusively one for war.'[146] Conrad, the Viennese journalist Heinrich Kanner remarked, never saw his military career as ending in the Austro-Hungarian Army, but rather in world history.[147] It is important to understand this point, for there has been no end of accounts in which Franz Ferdinand has been painted as a pillar of European peace and practically the only man in Vienna in 1914 who would have acted decisively to prevent a continental conflict – the misfortune of his assassination therefore being the greater. Edmund Glaise-Horstenau was already writing in 1926 about the 'tragedy of fate' that Franz Ferdinand was the first to die on 'the battlefield of the World War', the prevention of which had always been his aim.[148]

In Anglo-Saxon academia a full endorsement of this interpretation was to arrive with some delay in 1974 when Samuel Williamson published a major article on Franz Ferdinand's involvement in the policy process. Williamson concluded: 'Alive, Franz Ferdinand had acted as a brake upon the pressures for military action; dead, he became the pretext for war.'[149] Although precious little evidence was provided for the first part, this trenchant summation of Franz Ferdinand has been influencing historians ever since. They have used slightly different words, but expressed the same thought. In 1985, for example, Norman Stone wrote about the 'final irony' to the Sarajevo assassination story: 'a dead Archduke became the excuse for a war that the live Archduke would have stopped.'[150] A recent restatement of this view is similarly confident: 'Sarajevo did not just stir the hawks to war. It also destroyed the best hope for peace. Had Franz Ferdinand survived his visit to Bosnia in 1914, he would have continued to warn against the risks of a military adventure, as he had done so often before.'[151] In fact, current scholarship is just not letting go of this theme. Thus Margaret MacMillan: 'Franz Ferdinand ... had long stood out against those who wanted war to solve Austria-Hungary's problems. His death, ironically, removed the one man who might have been able to prevent his country from declaring war on Serbia and thus setting the whole chain reaction in motion.'[152]

Such sweeping verdicts require not only annotation but also some re-adjustment. Franz Ferdinand's caution in foreign policy (to the extent that he was able to influence it) before 1914 is indeed well documented and indisputable. But he was hardly a pacifist dove. Even viewed in isolation, his enthusiastic backing for the modernization and expansion of the fleet (a policy much approved of by the equally naval-minded Kaiser Wilhelm II) pointed to future trouble with other Mediterranean sea powers – Italy in particular. In Franz Ferdinand the Austro-Hungarian *Kriegsmarine* 'probably enjoyed the most energetic and influential patron in its history'.[153] He even managed to put his anti-Semitism to one side when visiting the head of Vienna's Rothschild dynasty to obtain credits for the navy.[154] Certainly, the British were alarmed by his 'violent anti-Italian, anti-British and pro-German sentiments'.[155] The Foreign Office believed he was more or less an agent of a Germany scheming to use Austria-Hungary in order to weaken Britain's Mediterranean position.[156]

Examples of his combative attitude abound. In August 1900, soon after his marriage, he could not resist complaining bitterly about Austria-Hungary not having sent troops to China to intervene in the Boxer Rebellion – this was a 'scandal' according to Franz Ferdinand, particularly as 'ridiculous states' like Belgium and Portugal were taking part.[157] In 1907 he described the Hague peace conference on the laws of war and limitation of arma-ments as the 'most laughable and stupid of all conferences'.[158] Early in March 1909, at the height of the Bosnian annexation crisis, he spoke to Conrad 'in a completely warlike fashion' regarding Serbia. Also present was Captain Theodor von Zeynek, in charge of planning a strike against Serbia. Zeynek recalled the Archduke stating on that occasion that he was going to command the Serbian operation personally.[159] In Decem-ber 1912 the Joint War Minister Moritz Auffenberg was asked by Franz Ferdinand to hand in his resignation, and when the Minister asked why, he was told it was because he was 'too pessimist and pacifist-inclined'.[160] As will be seen in chapter seven, the Archduke was in late 1912 a most determined advocate of pre-emptive action against Serbia. He would only be restrained by the German Foreign Office and Franz Joseph himself.

And, again in April-May 1913, he was to demand war against Serbia and Montenegro.

With regard to Italy, moreover, a war of conquest was never far from his mind. In February 1913 he told Conrad: 'Our chief enemy is Italy, against which at some point a war will have to be fought, we must regain Venice and Lombardy.'[161] Alexander Brosch had little confidence in the Archduke's statesmanship or his ability to manage a crisis situation. In 1910 he opined about his boss: 'Defiant and obtrusive as he is, he often gets a fright at the last moment.' Brosch therefore believed that it would be typical for the Archduke, when he became Emperor, 'to *provoke*' a war with Italy, and then try at the last moment, 'when it is too *late*' to get out (emphases in the original).[162] Famously, it was Wilhelm II who got cold feet towards the end of July 1914 and tried to pull Germany out of the rapidly escalating conflict situation in Europe – when it was too late. Brosch's insider view of Franz Ferdinand's own likely behaviour in crisis situations is thus somewhat at odds with currently accepted wisdom that the Archduke would have been the only guarantee of European peace in 1914. His 'complicated character', at any rate, did not inspire much confidence at the time. Only a few days before the Sarajevo assassination the distinguished German diplomat Count Anton Monts opined that the Archduke was capable of 'setting the whole of Europe ablaze' in order to make his wife the Queen of Hungary. 'I do not know', Monts said, 'whether this man is more dangerous alive or dead.'[163] Also shortly before 28 June 1914, Sir Louis Mallet, the British Ambassador to Constantinople, gave his opinion about Franz Ferdinand to the Serbian Chargé d'Affaires: 'That man, a bigoted clerical, understands nothing about European politics and is a real danger to European peace.'[164] Carl Bardolff, Brosch's successor as the head of Franz Ferdinand's military chancellery, recalled that one of the Archduke's main doubts (in 1912) about Austria-Hungary getting involved in a war related in fact to money. He had sent Bardolff to Baron Spitzmüller, the Director of Kreditanstalt, to enquire about this matter, and Spitzmüller had told Bardolff that the financial resources could cover, 'at most', only three to four months of war.[165]

Despite everything, it would, nonetheless, probably be safe to argue that Franz Ferdinand would not have rushed into foreign policy adventures – internal consolidation of the Empire, whatever shape that might have taken, was always going to be his top priority. But war also found its place in his order of priorities. Towards the end of February 1913 he told Conrad, who was pressing for military action against Serbia: 'Rest assured, later when our internal political circumstances will be better than they are now – then yes.'[166] He had in the previous month written something similar to Foreign Minister Leopold Berchtold, warning him about premature 'hooray politics [*Hurrah-Politik*]': 'The first thing is to put one's own house in order', for without the unanimous backing of all one's own peoples 'we are in no position to have an ambitious, aggressive foreign policy.'[167] As will be seen in chapter thirteen, however, significant evidence exists that Franz Ferdinand and Wilhelm II had schemed a war against Serbia only a fortnight or so before the Sarajevo assassination. Moreover the very idea of a war of territorial acquisition against Italy demonstrated that the Archduke thought nothing about upsetting the European balance of power. Therefore, while it may be legitimate to argue that a Franz Ferdinand still alive after June 1914 would have successfully worked to stop any warmongers in Vienna, it is equally appropriate to ask what kind of a foreign policy he would have pursued once he had managed to solve the internal affairs of the Empire to his own satisfaction.

For Franz Ferdinand was obsessed about the standing of Austria-Hungary as a Great Power: the whole point about the internal consolidation, the building of a modern navy and the reform and restructuring of the army was to create conditions for the conduct of a robust foreign policy. A recent major survey of the Triple Alliance (Germany, Austria-Hungary, Italy) has suggested that Franz Ferdinand was rejecting risky or belligerent proposals out of such power-political rather than humanitarian considerations – e.g., the army modernization was not expected to be completed before 1919. The same study notes, with regard to Italy, that it is 'questionable' how long the Triple Alliance would have survived after Franz Ferdinand's ascendance of the Throne.[168]

Some expert opinion has generously given Franz Ferdinand the benefit of the doubt with regard to his likely behaviour as Emperor. Robert Kann emphasized the point that the Archduke never overcame his unbridled temperament, but argued in the same breath that 'his misgivings about resorting to drastic actions steadily increased in his years of maturity.' And this, according to Kann, was especially true of foreign policy.[169] Günther Kronenbitter has recently maintained something similar about the Archduke: '... the nearer he seemed to get to his future position, the more political pragmatism he evinced.'[170] But was there really anything stable or tangible in Franz Ferdinand's approach to international affairs? Sir Fairfax Cartwright, the British Ambassador to Vienna, thought in 1912 that the Archduke's views were uncertain.[171] At least one well-positioned contemporary of Franz Ferdinand was also not sure what to make of his views on foreign affairs. This was Milan Hodža, the Archduke's Slovak adviser. In his memoirs he talked about the 'uncertainty' of Franz Ferdinand's associates about his wider foreign policy. 'In fact,' Hodža wrote, 'there was always a cloud of ambiguity screening the international outlook of the man who prepared himself so earnestly for his future task.' With regard to the Balkan policy of the Heir to the Throne, however, Hodža had no doubts, since the Archduke 'never concealed' that he wanted to build up a strong influence for the Empire reaching as far as Salonika.[172]

If so, the Habsburgs' road to Salonika would always have to lead through Sarajevo and Belgrade. Was Franz Ferdinand going to fulfil the oriental 'mission' of the Empire? One of his heroes was Prince Eugene of Savoy who had done much to extend Habsburg power in south-eastern Europe. In his honour, in 1911 Franz Ferdinand had the *Heugasse* (Hay Lane) near his Belvedere palace in Vienna renamed *Prinz Eugen Strasse*.[173] Prince Eugene had in 1717, after a battle that became famous, captured Belgrade from the Turks. Twenty years earlier, in 1697, he had led an Austrian incursion into Bosnia and stopped at the gates of Sarajevo, issuing an ultimatum in which he warned that unless the city surrendered he would destroy everything 'with sword and fire'. When the Turks refused to capitulate his army attacked, burning and pillaging. There was something of a massacre. Only a few of Sarajevo's 120 mosques survived. The Orthodox church was plundered.[174]

Franz Ferdinand, if he had ever read accounts of this campaign, would no doubt have approved – except for the fact that the Catholic church also burnt down. In October 1908, soon after the Austro-Hungarian annexation of Bosnia-Herzegovina, he was in a similarly pugnacious mood. Contrary to the widespread conviction among scholars that he had been totally opposed to the annexation of the provinces, he was in fact delighted when it happened. On 11 October he sent a congratulatory letter to Foreign Minister Alois von Aehrenthal, ecstatically rejoicing in the fact that 'we have shown Europe once again that we are still a Great Power!' The Serbs were, he wrote, 'insolent scoundrels', simply to be ignored. The main thing in Bosnia now was to keep the situation under control with 'iron harshness', and should there be an attempt at a putsch or any crossing of the border by Serbian bands, it should be immediately answered with 'executions by firing squad, hanging, etc. [*mit Füsilieren, Hängen, etc*]'. Commenting on the British displeasure caused by the annexation, he wrote that the wrath of the English was 'hilarious', but that the 'fat' King Edward VII would no doubt calm down after a few bottles of champagne and in the company of 'so-called ladies'.[175]

2

Belvedere 'Reform' Plans

The United States of Great Austria

SO WHAT WAS this *Thronfolger* to do once he ascended the throne? To this day, even among the more disinterested historians, there exists a tendency to look through rose-tinted spectacles at how Franz Ferdinand planned to restructure the Empire once he reached its pinnacle. Only recently, it has been suggested in a major work that he aimed at 'creating a new federated state to include Hungarians, Germans, Czechs, Poles and South Slavs.'[1] This rather implies that Franz Ferdinand was some kind of modern-minded, realistic reformer. As will be seen, however, it is highly problematic to postulate his plans for the future in terms of a 'federated state'. What he intended was something rather different – to the extent, that is, that he actually knew what he was going to do in the first place.

Luigi Albertini, arguably the most influential scholar of the origins of the Great War, was among the initiators of this historiographical *erratum* when he presented Franz Ferdinand's reform plans in surprisingly uncritical light. The Archduke, Albertini wrote, 'greatly disapproved of the repression of the Czechs, Roumanians and Southern Slavs, which alienated them from Vienna.' He claimed that Franz Ferdinand saw Switzerland as a model of conciliation of various peoples: 'Why should not Austria become a greater Switzerland?' But Albertini, failing to back up these assertions with any concrete evidence, was putting words in the Archduke's mouth.[2]

The available documentation, at any rate, shows that the 'new federated state' was in fact to be the old, pre-1867, centralized state, made up of the Crown Lands. These Crown Lands were not mere administrative units, but the original, historic Habsburg acquisitions, which did not necessarily represent compact ethnic areas.[3] And the nationalities, as will also be seen, interested Franz Ferdinand as little as they interested Franz Joseph, though it would of course be true to say that the former saw the non-Hungarians of Hungary as useful tools against Budapest. The principle of parliamentary politics interested him even less. In March 1914 Hans Schlitter, the Director of the *Staatsarchiv* (a post that was of some political significance in those days), put it to him that Parliament should busy itself only with the administration of public funds. The Archduke's response was enthusiastic: 'That is what I think, too. No ministers drawn from Parliament! That has to stop. The state suffers from it.'[4] But even Schlitter, clearly no liberal himself, was uneasy about the Heir to the Throne. He felt the need to recall in his private diary that, back in 1910, Franz Ferdinand 'came up with ideas which bordered on madness'.[5] Schlitter, however, did not elaborate.

Most of the scholars who have busied themselves with Franz Ferdinand's reform plans have carefully noted that those plans were constantly being modified and adjusted. Such caveats, however, have only served to avoid highlighting the essence of those plans, which remained consistent throughout. John W. Boyer is one of the rare historians who has not flinched from spelling it out. He has remarked that the plans developed before the Archduke's death seemed to envisage the state 'as a centralized haven of pure dynastic power'. And he described the ethos of plans developed by or on behalf of Franz Ferdinand as 'semiabsolutist'.[6] In 1899 the Archduke expressed his basic credo: 'I cherish the unity of Austria, and as the unifying means of its peoples I count the Dynasty, the Catholic religion and in particular the German language as the carrier of culture [*Kulturträgerin*] and as the *lingua franca*.'[7] Habsburg, Catholic and German – this was Franz Ferdinand's concept of the Empire, and it never left him. Such a concept could not, even theoretically, be divorced from a centralized power structure. Everything else in his contemplations about the future shape of the state represented half-hearted, and indeed half-baked attempts to reconcile uncomfortable realities with this, his fundamental precept.

In his envisaged scheme(s) of things, the Archduke displayed only a fleeting cognizance of modern times. In 1910 he complained that 'regrettably, the times of feudalism and absolutism are gone'. Despite this reluctant bow to reality, he quickly added: 'the aristocracy, together with the Emperor at the top of the Empire, should act decisively.' Of course, he excluded the Hungarian aristocracy from this on the grounds that it was 'always revolutionary and anti-dynastic'.[8] Austrian statesman Ernest von Koerber told Josef Redlich in February 1912 that Franz Ferdinand was in his ideas closer to the seventeenth century than to the twentieth. He also considered that the Archduke entertained 'very odd notions about the rights of the Sovereign in modern times'.[9]

Some subsequent, albeit isolated, historical judgement of Franz Ferdinand has been similar. Anton Mayr-Harting, for example, wrote very critically (rare amongst Austrian historians) about Franz Ferdinand and his circle being out of touch with the world around them: it required the blind enthusiasm of a powerful but tellingly small circle to overlook the 'hopelessness of Franz Ferdinand's acts and volitions in the face of the claims and objective requirements of the times.' The attitude of the Heir to the Throne, Mayr-Harting argued further, gave rise to a justified fear among observers of the political scene that the autocratic authority he had in mind would, as far as internal policy was concerned, lead back to 'an essentially centralist-absolutist state administration, in which the surviving constitutional features were meant to have a marginal role.'[10]

Whether a centralised and essentially autocratic state was the right solution for the multinational Habsburg Empire in the twentieth century is a question that probably does not even need to be addressed. At the same time, it would be difficult to disagree with C.A. Macartney who pointed out in the late 1960s that 'if there is one lesson which the history of the Monarchy should teach, it is that there was never, at any time, any ideal answer to its problems.'[11] It is, however, one of the contentions of this book that what Franz Ferdinand and his circle were preparing in terms of reorganizing the Empire included measures which, far from strengthening it, would have caused a bloody internal conflict and thus accelerated its demise. These measures had everything to do with the Archduke's obsessive desire to enfeeble Hungary – if necessary by force. For if there existed a single, unambiguous and immutable point in the Archduke's political programme for the Monarchy, then it was to destroy the settlement of 1867.

But could the clock be turned back? The Habsburgs' cardinal experience in the nineteenth century was that a single, centrally-run state had slipped beyond their reach. The 1867 Compromise with Hungary enshrined this realization. The 1871 failed compromise with the Czechs was a reminder of the need for further reform of the Habsburg multinational enterprise. It was only a question of time before nations such as the Croats or the Romanians, along with the Czechs, challenged a system in which they were permanent underdogs. Franz Ferdinand was of course not unaware of the nationalities problem within the Monarchy. But his idea of solving it was to brush it under the worn-out old Habsburg carpet dating from before 1867. To him, the panacea for the national problems, at least in Cisleithania, lay in cutting Hungary down to size. And in Hungary, according to Robert Kann, he was interested in the nationalities 'not because they were socially and politically discriminated against, but because he considered them loyal'.[12]

If Franz Ferdinand's name is associated in historiography with plans to federalize the Empire, it is because he did appear to toy with ideas of federalism. As late as August 1913 he told Albert von Margutti: 'I am and I remain for the Habsburg federal state; Dualism is a folly, a contrivance in a quandary, an anomaly.'[13] But what kind of federalism did he have in mind? Jean-Paul Bled, in his recent biography of the Archduke, drew attention to the fact that in the 1890s he leaned towards the federalist model of the 1860 'October Diploma'.[14] As seen earlier, the constitution of 1860 had been designed to prop up the aristocracy, not the nationalities. Hardly surprising, therefore, that Franz Ferdinand had shown an interest. This was the so-called *Kronlandföderalismus* that he inclined to in the 1890s – that of historic, indeed ancient, political units (Crown Lands) in the Habsburg Empire.[15] But this was no more, as A.J.P. Taylor noted with regard to Franz Ferdinand's reform intentions, 'than an extension of provincial autonomy, a refurbishing of the October Diploma, and not at all a system of national freedom.'[16] József Kristóffy, Franz Ferdinand's loyal Hungarian adviser, recalled regarding his former master: 'He took historic right as not only more valuable, but also stronger than the nationality principle.'[17] This subject, in fact, deserves a little elaboration. For the Archduke also took an interest in the constitution that followed the ill-fated October Diploma. Count Michael Károlyi, of the Hungarian Independence Party, wrote in his memoirs that the 'Belvedere policy' was to grant autonomy to various nationalities, but the idea, in fact, was to strengthen centralism by giving even greater powers to the Emperor and the Vienna bureaucracy along the lines of the February Patent – the centralist constitution of 1861 which had replaced the October Diploma.[18]

In the 1890s, Franz Ferdinand also talked about the federalism that he had seen in the United States. For, as he told Margutti in 1895, he saw 'a striking similarity' with Austria-Hungary in that the United States were not nationally homogenous, either. He asked Margutti whether he thought it was possible to apply the American system in the Habsburg Empire. 'By legislative means alone, certainly not', replied Margutti. 'Then with violence!', countered the Archduke. Margutti put it to him that George Washington had at his disposal a basic unifying element: the predominant and unreservedly recognised Anglo-Saxon culture, the like of which Austria-Hungary lacked entirely. 'What about our Germans?', Franz Ferdinand protested. Whereupon Margutti, sensing that the Archduke was not convinced of his own position, opined that the Austrian Germans, having failed before 1866 to take advantage of being backed by a virtually absolutist government, could hardly expect to attain hegemony almost three decades after the Monarchy had been split into two.[19]

The most celebrated federal scheme associated in historiography with Franz Ferdinand's name has to do with a remarkable book by Aurel Popovici (pronounced: Popović), *Die Vereinigten Staaten von Groß-Österreich* (United States of Great Austria), published in 1906. Popovici, a Romanian from Transylvania, had been a member of the Romanian National Committee in Hungary where he had been persecuted by the Hungarian authorities. He had had to flee to Switzerland and later find refuge in the independent Kingdom of Romania. Above all, however, he was a good Austrian, an Empire loyalist.[20] His work, anti-Hungarian to the bone, specifically anti-Dualist, pro-Habsburg (in a sense even pro-German) and peppered with anti-Semitic remarks, was bound to attract the attention of the *Thronfolger* and his circle. Whether it actually exerted any significant influence on the Archduke – despite the attraction of '*Groß-Österreich*' in its title – is a different matter altogether, notwithstanding big claims made in this regard. Nevertheless, Popovici's book constitutes an important document of its period and deserves a degree of attention in its own right.

One almost does not have to read the book, since one of its main points is contained in a folded colour map attached at the back. The map shows the proposed 'federative' division of Austria-Hungary on the basis of national demarcation. Not surprisingly, therefore, some of the territorial units very much resemble the shape of several existing countries today: Austria, Hungary, Slovakia, Slovenia and Croatia. Save for two German territorial units (German Bohemia and German Moravia), Popovici's suggested unit for the Czechs would also be a close reproduction of today's Czech Republic. In other words, Popovici emphatically rejected the obsolete idea of federalizing the Empire on the basis of any 'historic' principle, arguing that the borders of various 'kingdoms and lands' (nineteen in all) were not at all compatible with the national, ethnographic borders.[21] This was, needless to say, a very bold, almost heretical way of thinking.

Popovici envisaged fifteen territorial units (*Ländern*) in total, each having a pre-eminent language and ethnicity: 1. German Austria, along with the German territories on the western Hungarian frontier, and also the German-inhabited territories in south-west Bohemia and southern Moravia; 2. German Bohemia (north-west Bohemia); 3. German Moravia (together with German-inhabited Silesia); 4. The Czech lands; 5. West Galicia (Polish); 6. East Galicia (Ukrainian); 7. Siebenbürgen (Romanian-inhabited east Hungary, that is, Transylvania); 8. Croatia (with Dalmatia and the port of Rijeka, and with Istria but not its Italian-inhabited coast); 9. Carniola (Slovene); 10. Slovakia; 11. Vojvodina (Serbian-inhabited southern Hungary); 12. Hungary; 13. Seklerland (Hungarian-inhabited parts of Siebenbürgen); 14. Trentino (Italian-inhabited South Tyrol); 15. Trieste (with Gorizia and the Italian-inhabited coastal strip of Istria). Popovici understandably left out Bosnia-Herzegovina (treating the two provinces as *Okkupationsgebiet*), since at that time the Sultan was still the Sovereign.[22]

Theoretically, Popovici's map, and the arguments for it in the book, made a great deal of sense: Dualism to be replaced with federalism, based on a territorial division of the Empire that reflected existing ethnic-cultural, and therefore political, realities. Popovici attacked the system of Dualism relentlessly: its whole fabric was 'totally untenable', it was doomed because the peoples had already emancipated themselves. The time had gone, he argued, when someone like Prince Schwarzenberg could tell the people that they just had to obey and pay their taxes and, 'as an extra treat', they could go to church.[23] Most of Popovici's venom was reserved for the Magyars whose greed 'has for long not known any limits', a people 'pampered for almost forty years'. No one was satisfied in the Empire and all the nationalities were indignant, but it was thanks to the Magyars that one had a situation of '*bellum omnium contra omnes*'. He approvingly quoted Professor Vladimir Lamansky who had written about Austria-Hungary as 'an Empire made up of a whole set of Irelands'.[24]

One factor motivating Popovici to urge a fundamental transformation of the Empire was what he perceived as the Russian danger. To him it was 'the eleventh hour' for reform to be carried out, or otherwise, he thought, 'the whole of the south-east could fall into Russia's hands like a ripe fruit'.[25] He described Russia as posing a mortal threat to Austria-Hungary (and to Germany), but believed that it would be quite wrong to suppress the Slavs of the Monarchy in order to counter the Russian danger. In that context, the idea that Hungarian hegemony (i.e., the system of Dualism) should be allowed to continue because Hungary represented a vital prop of the Triple Alliance, was dismissed by Popovici.[26] Moreover, he argued, the Slavs of the Monarchy were only embracing Pan-Slavism because they were being suppressed. The Czechs and Croats, for example, were turning Russophile thanks to 'our mindless nationalities policy'. Popovici pointed out that even the Romanians – no Slavs – were saying: 'better Russian than Hungarian!' And he fully agreed with Adolf Fischhof's view (discussed in the prologue to this book) that the furtherance and development of Slavonic 'particularisms' within the Empire was the best guarantee for its future. This is not to say that Popovici sympathized with the Slavs – on the contrary. His proposed federalism was, he suggested, the only method of preventing the Monarchy from becoming even more Slavonic in character.[27]

Paradoxically, the great federalist Popovici was in fact quite a centralist. In the 'United States of Great Austria' that he advocated and which would constitute a single customs area, there would be an imperial assembly in Vienna (*Reichsparlament*), consisting of a lower and upper house. There would also be an imperial government (*Reichsregierung*) with an imperial chancellor (*Reichskanzler*), consisting of forty-two members drawn from various nationalities.[28] The competences of this central level would embrace the usual fields: foreign affairs, everything pertaining to the army and navy, common finances, customs, civil and penal law, railways, weights and measures, etc., as well as the governance of Bosnia-Herzegovina.

What Popovici called the 'national states', i.e., the federal units, would have their own parliaments and governments, and would be competent for all affairs not explicitly reserved for and by the central authorities in Vienna. It is difficult to see, however, what this would amount to except for management of purely local affairs, education and the like. To be sure, these would not be insignificant achievements (especially in the light of what had been going on in Hungary with regard to the nationalities), but Popovici's 'states' were in fact local autonomies. He did not envisage a veto power of the individual states as a check on central authority. The constitutions of these states could of course not have any provisions at variance with the imperial constitution and, moreover, any alliances or 'contracts of a political nature' between individual states were 'impermissible'.[29] Therefore, Popovici's proposed overall state resembled much more a voluntary '*Völkerbund*', that is, a union of peoples (a term he himself used), with its individual parts playing almost no role in the Empire except that of sending their representatives to Vienna where they would find themselves pretty much at the whim of the Habsburg Emperor. This was no federalism. Robert Kann described it as 'rather crude federalism', but was surely overly generous, given that Popovici's proposed system, leaving only local and administrative functions available to the individual parts, allocated nearly all state powers to the centre.[30]

The truth is that Popovici – while recognizing that there existed local ethnic and cultural diversities – favoured a strong, Emperor-centred authority in the imperial capital. In his scheme it was the Emperor who would name the governor-general (*Statthalter*) of each state (the governor-general would at the same time be the prime minister of the state). Likewise, the Emperor would name members of local governments at the suggestion of governors – Vienna would thus be fully in control. Needless to say, the Emperor would also name the imperial chancellor, and convoke and dissolve the imperial parliament. Whereas the individual states could use their local languages, Popovici argued strongly for the German language to be employed on the level of imperial bureaucracy and in the armed forces. That this should indeed be German seemed to him 'a matter of course', it being the 'oldest cultural language' of the Empire. The German language could not be compared to Hungarian, and it would always be learned, like French and English, by cultures that seriously cared about themselves.[31]

Accordingly, Popovici's proposals matched several key political prerequisites in Franz Ferdinand's own vision for the Empire: eradication of Dualism and the ensuing establishment of a united, 'Great' Austria; a robust central authority in Vienna controlled effectively by the Emperor; and the unifying bond of German as the intermediary language in transactions across the Empire. The Catholic religion as a further connecting link had no place in Popovici's deliberations, but then this would have been unexpected in such a serious work. Even Franz Ferdinand's close friend Count Sternberg thought that the Archduke was slightly naïve in stressing the importance of Catholicism as a connecting tissue: the real religion of modern people, Sternberg thought, was money ('*die Geldbörse*').[32]

Popovici remarked that such ideas as he was putting forward were opposed by the 'Jewish-liberal newspapers'.[33] But what of the Archduke? He actually showed no eagerness to meet the Romanian. It was only through the personal intervention of Alexander Vaida-Voivod, who was to become one of his Romanian advisers, that Popovici had an audience with Franz Ferdinand, in March 1907. No details about this meeting are known.[34] Nevertheless, the great authority Luigi Albertini would have his readers believe that Popovici's ideas 'won the warm approval of the Archduke'. Franz Ferdinand, Albertini insisted, 'read and approved of Popovici's book'. This claim requires to be addressed head-on. Albertini gave as his source Theodore Sosnosky's biography of the Heir to the Throne.[35] But Sosnosky claimed nothing of the kind. He wrote, on the contrary, that it could not have escaped the attention of the Archduke that Popovici's programme contained 'a vulnerable spot': an all too radical approach in that it recklessly proposed to do away with the centuries-old tradition of the Crown Lands. Having been a member of the Belvedere circle, Sosnosky had known Franz Ferdinand quite well. In his view, the Archduke was such a passionate proponent of historic tradition that he would have felt that Popovici was showing a lack of respect. 'It can hardly be supposed', Sosnosky maintained, 'that he would ever have decided in favour of this intervention.' Sosnosky noted, in addition, that the press ignored Popovici's project, that the Czechs and the Poles would not have been enthusiastic about the division, respectively, of the Sudetenlands and Galicia, and that even Austro-German politicians had all kinds of objections to Popovici on constitutional and administrative grounds. Only the Ukrainians, the Croats and the other nationalities of Hungary could have been expected to welcome the ideas of '*Gross-Österreich*' as a method of freeing them from the Magyar yoke.[36]

It should be mentioned in this connection that Leopold von Chlumecky's famed (though partisan) work on Franz Ferdinand does not even mention Popovici. Robert Kann, by some distance the most authoritative interpreter of Franz Ferdinand, also expressed scepticism that the 'tradition-conscious' Archduke would have followed Popovici.[37] Why, then, is this ultra-reactionary Habsburg repeatedly associated in historical writings with Popovici's (in some respects) radical approach? In part, because influential historians such as Albertini have misread Franz Ferdinand's reform policy. And there are those historians who have perhaps deliberately misinterpreted it. For example in Austria, in 1926, Edmund Glaise-Horstenau led his readers to believe that Franz Ferdinand was a federalist 'to the core [*durch und durch Föderalist*]'. The remark, written almost in passing, was not backed by any analysis or evidence.[38] Even contemporary observers are not blameless. Thus Milan Hodža is in considerable measure responsible for Popovici's fame by having given him much prominence in his memoir and calling his book 'the last attempt to promote workable conditions inside the Habsburg Empire'. However, he did not actually state where exactly Franz Ferdinand stood on the subject.[39] A further reason for Franz Ferdinand's retrospective association with federalism is that the labels of 'Great Austria' and 'federalism' were inextricably linked with Popovici at the time. Thus the idea of 'Great Austria', although it lacked a theoretical elaboration before Popovici (or even a name), appealed to conservative, patriotic Austro-German aristocrats – Franz Ferdinand's natural milieu. Count Ludwig Creneville and Count Alfons Mensdorff-Pouilly, for example, were to publish works, in 1908 and 1910 respectively, in which they expressed a basic sympathy with Popovici.[40] But Mensdorff-Pouilly was also critical, pointing out that the Crown Lands were despite everything 'more than just antiquated memories'.[41]

Perhaps the best explanation, however, of why Popovici has to this day been seen as synonymous with Franz Ferdinand's intentions for the future can be found in the general observation that there has never been a lack of historians attracted to the business of apologia, regardless of subject. Rudolf Kiszling, Franz Ferdinand's influential Austrian biographer, is a case in point. He canonized the Archduke in the concluding passage of his 1953 biography, writing that Franz Ferdinand wanted 'no territorial acquisitions', merely a strong Empire, 'united on a federal basis' and vouchsafing all its peoples the same rights; an 'imposing' European position could thus be attained and peace be maintained; but before it could become reality, this nascent future had been destroyed by the Sarajevo shots.[42] Leaving aside some of these problematic claims, where did Kiszling get his corroboration for the Archduke's federalist plans? In the chapter on Empire reform, he wrote that Popovici's book had aroused in Franz Ferdinand 'the greatest interest'. This claim may well have been true, but Kiszling provided zero evidence for it. He then asserted that the plan contained in *The United States of Great Austria* became 'the central theme [*Leitidee*]' of the Archduke's reform plans, as contained in the 1911 exposé authored (chiefly) by Alexander Brosch and Professor Heinrich Lammasch.[43] This was the famous *Thronwechsel* programme, prepared by his associates for the moment when Franz Ferdinand was to ascend the throne. As will be seen later in this chapter, however, far from being 'the central theme' of that document, federalism was not even mentioned. But only too often such absence of proof for a particular claim has not discouraged historians from making it. Interestingly, in his 1956 article about Franz Ferdinand's reform plans (which with regard to Popovici employed practically the same language as his 1953 book), Kiszling suddenly dropped any reference to Popovici's ideas constituting the '*Leitidee*' of the Brosch-Lammasch *Thronwechsel* memorandum.[44]

Preparing for Power: The Military Chancellery

In his 1945 study of federalism in Central and Eastern Europe, Rudolf Schlesinger remarked that it was 'pure nonsense' to expect the Habsburgs to effect a 'revolution from above' that would bring equality to, and free, the oppressed peoples of Austria-Hungary. This was, Schlesinger insisted, 'especially true of the man upon whom these chimerical hopes were based, Francis Ferdinand'.[45] Similar scepticism was expressed by other distinguished scholars. Thus A.J.P. Taylor wrote that the Archduke 'hated national movements as soon as they became democratic'.[46] What exactly, then, were Franz Ferdinand's by now almost proverbial reform plans? If there is little or no evidence that he was going to federalize the Empire, what was he going to reform? As always with Franz Ferdinand, the answer presents itself through his passionately held beliefs, in this case through his repugnance towards the Austro-Hungarian Dualist system.

Robert Kann noted that the strangest thing about the Austro-Hungarian Compromise of 1867, so obviously prone to attack from various sides, was the fact that it endured, almost unchanged, as long as it did – for more than half a century. He hazarded the guess that foreign policy considerations (the power of Germany in Central Europe, and the increasing friction between Austria-Hungary and Russia), to a great extent determined Vienna's leaving internal matters in the Empire as they had been set up in 1867.[47] A detail that would perhaps usefully add to Kann's interpretation is that the opposition to Dualism was too weak and disorganised to provide a real threat. Although Franz Ferdinand, the greatest opponent of the system, already felt by 1895 that Dualism meant 'altogether the ruin of the Monarchy', he began to be meaningfully active in political affairs only after 1906.[48] And of course he never lived to ascend the throne and mount an assault on the hated system. However, he did prepare, in his lifetime, a detailed plan of action against Hungary, to be used at the first opportunity – immediately upon ascending the throne. This plan, in essence, was all that he intended to do in terms of 'reform'.

Franz Joseph's 'impatient nephew' was widely expected to be the 'deus ex machina' who would do something for the salvation of the Empire.[49] Admittedly, there also existed a view at the time that Franz Ferdinand would within one day make more concessions to Hungary than Franz Joseph had made in twenty years.[50] That, however, seems highly doubtful. His hostility towards Hungary – from its language, history and politics to its ordinary people as well as its political and social elites – was practically absolute. Receiving command of the 9th Hussars in Sopron in 1899, he was already giving his friend Countess Nora Fugger the impression that he 'disliked this land as much as he disliked its inhabitants'. Moreover, he would make this view clear 'at every opportunity, predictably blaming the Hungarians for the events of 1848-49, but also for the disasters of 1859 and 1866.'[51] He even found a way of combining his anti-Hungarian sentiments with his anti-Semitic ones – by referring to Budapest as 'Judapesth'.[52] Indeed, Hungary did not exactly endear itself to the Archduke by the fact that much of its upper bourgeoisie was of Jewish origin, nor by the fact that some of its gentry was Calvinist.[53] He would habitually call the Hungarians 'Huns', and regret their 'bad taste' for having arrived in Europe from Asia in the first place.[54] The Archduke was fond of quoting Cato (by the epithet 'twerp' as he could not actually remember his name) on the necessity to destroy Carthage, evoking him in regard to Hungary: 'ceterum censeo Maggarien esse delendam!'[55] This was pure hatred. Franz Ferdinand did not merely object to the Dualist system, he had a visceral reflex against 'paprika guzzlers' – as he called the Hungarians. Hungary was a 'pig land', and *'every'* (underlined three times) Hungarian, whether a minister or a peasant, was either a 'revolutionary' or a 'scoundrel'.[56] In 1910 the Arch-duke spoke vehemently about 'marching' into Hungary (*'einmarschieren'*) and 're-conquering' the country (*'noch einmal erobert'*).[57]

At Mürzsteg, in October 1903, Franz Ferdinand 'had astonished and even shocked' the visiting Russian Tsar Nicholas II with the kind of language he used about the Hungarians.[58] That was the year when the Hungarians had begun demanding the introduction of the Magyar language for the Army units stationed in Hungary. At this point the Archduke's prejudice and loathing of them was dramatically reinforced. Dualism as a death sentence for the Empire in the long term was one thing (and poten-tially avoidable in his view), but any encroachment on the integrity of the Army represented a far more immediate threat. If the coherence of the Army and its loyalty to the dynasty was under threat, then this put a question mark against the existence of the joint monarchy itself.[59] Like any authoritarian, he understood perfectly well that the Army was in the last analysis a police force, potentially needed to protect his own privileged position. Thus he wrote to his adviser Beck in 1904 that 'now the Army, the last bulwark of the Throne and the Dynasty, is going to be magyar-ised'.[60] In March 1905 he was in near-panic over this matter when he appealed to Beck: 'For God's sake, not the slightest concession in the Army!'[61]

Beyond such entreaties, however, there was not that much that the Archduke could do at this stage. Almost exactly a year earlier, sitting in his Konopischt castle, he had complained to Beck that no one was telling him anything or consulting him over policy – he meant the Emperor and the government institutions in Vienna. 'And so', he lamented, 'I depend solely on newspaper news.'[62] Certainly, Franz Joseph had little time for him. One informed opinion in 1903 held that the Archduke 'gets nothing from his uncle'.[63] They 'detested each other heart and soul', Milan Hodža observed.[64] The Emperor is once supposed to have said: 'I feel tired. I would like to abdicate if I had a son whom I could trust, but never in favour of this dangerous fool.'[65] Franz Joseph's associates did not take kindly to the Heir to the Throne, either. Leopold von Chlumecky, the editor of the *Österreichische Rundschau* and a member of Franz Ferdinand's inner circle of advisers, wrote that practically the whole of 'the old guard' around the Emperor reacted in unison with intrigues and slander against 'the intruder'.[66] As late as 1905 Franz Ferdinand complained: 'I get to know less than the last manservant in Schönbrunn.'[67] However, the palace of Schönbrunn, Franz Joseph's preferred residence in the capital, and Franz Ferdinand's Belvedere Palace soon came to symbolize two rival centres of power in Vienna.

This development owed less to the Archduke's effort or skill and more to his good fortune. To a considerable extent, his frustrated ambition and impotence to influence the affairs of the state (or even to have an insider's overview of what was going on) were down to his own lifestyle. He preferred Konopischt to Vienna; shooting was more important to him, by a clear margin, than political or military questions. Art collecting, too, ranked very high in his order of priorities. He was also very keen on gardening; and, it would seem, his family life mattered to him most of all. Apart from these considerations, however, Franz Ferdinand's position as Heir to the Throne did not represent a platform of any real power and authority – he being restricted to ceremonial functions. His most daring foray into public affairs came in 1901 when he took over the patronage of the Catholic schools association – a move that did not exactly meet with the approval of Franz Joseph who considered it smacked too much of party politics being pursued by a Habsburg.[68] Once Franz Ferdinand had recovered his health (in 1897), and having in the meantime advanced to the rank of *Feldmarschalleutnant*, Franz Joseph and his advisers had no idea what to do with him. Since active military duty was not considered appropriate for the Heir to the Throne, it was decided in March 1898 to place him 'at the disposal of the supreme commander'. The duties of this position were extremely vaguely defined, but they related to his attending of military inspections, manoeuvres and conferences – the intention being that the Archduke should gain a full insight into the workings of the armed forces. He thus became a glorified military (and naval) observer. In retrospect, however, one provision regarding his new function proved not so harmless. For it was also decided that Franz Ferdinand should now have a military staff consisting of two officers, an aide-de-camp and an orderly.[69]

For a long time Franz Ferdinand did absolutely nothing to enhance his single, quasi-institutional office. Since, as the *Thronfolger*, he had no constitutional position except that of some day succeeding his uncle, he might have been expected to make more out of it. Left alone, however, with his various hobbies and a pronounced distaste for desk work, he was rather 'helpless'.[70] It was going to take someone else to make something out of the embryo military chancellery (which officially had no name). From May 1899 it was housed in the Lower Belvedere – a building quite separate, and some distance removed, from the Baroque palace where the Archduke resided (from 1904) when he bothered to come to Vienna.

One person who had definite ideas about what to do with this modest establishment set in the Lower Belvedere's splendid surroundings was Captain Alexander Brosch von Aarenau. The Archduke met him for the first time in the late summer of 1905 following Brosch's brilliant perform-ance at the manoeuvres in South Tyrol. The young Brosch (born 1870) was clever, well-educated and highly ambitious. He had worked for several years in the 5th, by far the most important department of the War Ministry: all the organizational details and armament solutions were prepared there, as well as the papers and documents to be used in the 'Delegations' forum where the Austrian and Hungarian sides would hammer out a mutually acceptable policy.[71] This gave him a unique insight into the military and political transactions in the Monarchy. From such a privileged position he had willingly shared his information with Franz Ferdinand's aide-de-camp, Karl Gelb von Siegesstern. It has been suggested that he might have had an ulterior motive in doing so and that, possibly yielding to 'the fascination of power', he aimed to become the Archduke's next aide-de-camp.[72]

This duly took place in January 1906 – the fascination of power must have been overwhelming. What Brosch (by now a Major) subsequently achieved was quite remarkable: he turned an impetuous, constitutionally impotent and politically incompetent Heir to the Throne into a steady, major political factor, second only to the Emperor, but closely rivalling him. By autumn 1911 when Brosch parted company with Franz Ferdinand in order to return to active military duty, the number of personnel in the chancellery had increased from the initial two to ten, and there had been widespread talk of a *Nebenregierung* (alternative, or shadow government) in the Belvedere. 'Within a short period', Josef Redlich wrote, 'the Archduke's military chancellery evolved towards a central position, quite unknown to the Constitution.'[73] And it was no secret that the occupants of positions such as that of War Minister or Chief of the General Staff were determined in this chancellery.[74] Brosch himself described the actions and attitudes of the Archduke as that of 'His Majesty's most loyal opposition'.[75] Franz Joseph was of course deeply aware of this – as well as of Brosch's very con-siderable personal role. Just before Brosch left the military chancellery, the Emperor told him: 'So, it is now six years that you have fought against me.'[76] There could be no question that Franz Ferdinand, with a great deal of help from Brosch (described by one expert as his 'alter ego'), had in the years after 1906 become a force to be reckoned with – in matters political as well as military.[77] The Austrian statesman Ernest von Koerber summed up the state of affairs in Austria-Hungary: 'Three parliaments, and now even two rulers!'[78]

The view advanced by Samuel Williamson in 1974, that it was Franz Joseph's and Franz Ferdinand's 'shared concern for the dynasty and for the army' which accounted for the Archduke's steadily increasing involvement in the policy process, is therefore problematic: there was practically no cooperation between them, and the insurmountable personal differences between the two men had in fact led to what amounted to warfare between them – as suggested by Franz Joseph himself in his remark to Brosch.[79] There was not a great deal of exaggeration in Koerber's suggestion about two rulers. This was, for example, illustrated in 1910 when Franz Joseph felt the need to let Franz Ferdinand know (through Brosch) that 'for the time being [*vorläufig*]' he was still the Emperor.[80] However, at least with regard to the major imperial appointments, civil as well as military, Franz Joseph had allowed his nephew to either push his choices or bargain over them. In that sense, certainly, he shared power with him.

The name 'military chancellery', which Brosch managed to have officially instituted by the end of 1908 (with a state budget also subsequently secured), was somewhat inaccurate: the Belvedere outfit was admittedly predominantly staffed by military personnel, but it busied itself with every conceivable political and diplomatic issue of the day as well as with Army and Navy matters. A considerable number of external civilian experts were informally brought in by Brosch to advise on aspects of policy, especially with regard to constitutional and nationalities questions. The military chancellery might in that sense be described as a think-tank or a 'workshop' but it was much more than that. In its day-to-day work it was to all intents and purposes an intelligence-collating and assessment centre. At the time, it appeared to many observers as a 'centre of intrigue and troublemaking'.[81] Brosch, certainly, was not above machinations, especially as regarded influencing press opinion. Unusually for an Army officer, he was fully aware of the importance of the press as the only mass medium of the period. He would regularly feed the newspapers with material for articles. More than that, he would cultivate editors and the Archduke could actually count on several papers to support his views, in particular the *Österreichische Rundschau*, *Danzers Armee-Zeitung*, *Das Vaterland* and the *Reichspost*.[82] Friedrich Funder, the editor of the *Reichspost*, described how Brosch, a man with 'uncommon diplomatic talent', had approached him, praising the paper's anti-Hungarian stance.[83]

Some of the individuals involved (directly or indirectly) in the 'Belvedere Party' were selected by Franz Ferdinand himself, but most were picked by Brosch. He even chose his own successor as head of the military chancellery, Colonel Bardolff, when he left in 1911. Brosch was the master-mind, the decisive driving force behind the invigoration of the Belvedere. Referring to his small stature, Funder recalled 'the small Major' directing 'a great game'.[84] With regard to legal and constitutional matters, Brosch enlisted university professors Heinrich Lammasch and Gustav Turba, as well as Johann von Eichhoff from the Austrian Interior Ministry. Those who advised on the nationalities, not surprisingly, had to meet Franz Ferdinand's political criteria: utter loyalty to the House of Habsburg, preferably a Catholic outlook and, more often than not, a grudge against the Hungarians. Thus the Slovak Milan Hodža, actually a Protestant, fitted because of what he thought about Hungarian rule. The Belvedere Roman-ian advisers, similarly, were Orthodox, but thoroughly anti-Hungarian. The Slovenes in touch with the Belvedere, Ivan Šusteršič and Anton Korošec, were good Catholics. The Croats, for example Dr Josip Frank, were Vienna-oriented and blindly loyal to the House of Habsburg. And so on. All the nationalities in the Monarchy were covered by Brosch's network, (including the Ukrainians), except two: there were no obvious individuals in touch with the Belvedere in respect of the Italians and the Serbs. The Muslims as a group did not seem to have attracted the attention of Brosch – in Bosnia-Herzegovina the Belvedere relied on the Bosnian Croat politi-cian Nikola Mandić. There were no formal Czech advisers, either, as the Archduke actually resided in Bohemia most of the time, mixing socially with the local aristocracy.

It has to be said that, with the possible exception of the Romanians and the Slovak Hodža, most of these people were not true representatives of their people. This was particularly the case with the Hungarian advisers: two of them were in fact prominent Germans of Hungary, Edmund Steinacker and (later) Rudolf Brandsch. Although Bishop József Lányi has sometimes been seen as the Archduke's chief Hungarian adviser, this related far more to his futile attempts to teach the latter the Hungarian language – even though he claimed against all evidence that his pupil spoke Hungarian fluently.[85] The Hungarian József von Kristóffy, loyal to the Habsburg dynasty and briefly the Interior Minister in Budapest (1905-1906), was much more of a presence in the Lower Belvedere, but was seen by fellow Hungarians as a renegade: 'the Magyar politician most hated by the gentry and aristocracy'.[86] This was not surprising given that Kristóffy had been used by Vienna to threaten the introduction of universal suffrage in Hungary – a policy typically favoured by Franz Ferdinand in respect of Hungary, but stubbornly opposed by him with regard to Austria.

Indeed, with respect to Hungary Franz Ferdinand's brain trust in the Lower Belvedere was not such a huge success because Cisleithanian official-dom remained cool towards the Heir to the Throne.[87] Not even Brosch could do very much about that. But then again, Brosch shared Franz

Ferdinand's views about the untenable nature of the Dualist system and the dangers that it posed for political relations in the Monarchy.[88] With or without Brosch, however, the Archduke was hopelessly intransigent towards the Hungarians. In 1906 Count Gyula Andrássy (the Younger), at the time Hungary's Interior Minister, told Franz Ferdinand point blank that people in Hungary did not speak well of him: he was snubbing the Hungarians, would visit their land very infrequently, and he communicated with them too little; he was even supposed to have said, Andrássy told the Archduke, that 'one had to march into Hungary'. Franz Ferdinand denied this, but his next reaction was interesting. He disliked going to Budapest, he said, because he loved his wife so much – in Budapest he would have to reside in the Royal Castle, whereas she would have to book herself into a hotel. Not to be outdone, Andrássy put it to Franz Ferdinand that he could build himself a palace in Budapest.[89]

One of Brosch's achievements was to ensure (early on, in March 1906) that copies of decrees and relevant written materials from the War Ministry would be sent to the Belvedere. Additional documents could be requested through Franz Joseph's own military chancellery.[90] Brosch was to use this opening to the full. Relations between Belvedere and Schönbrunn were now placed on an official footing. The resulting bureaucratic traffic between the two chancelleries cut down to the minimum face-to-face encounters between Franz Joseph and Franz Ferdinand. This was perhaps just as well. Alexander Vaida-Voivod, one of Franz Ferdinand's several advisers on Romanian questions, related that the opinionated approach of Franz Ferdinand in his meetings with the Emperor would upset the latter so much that 'a stroke had to be feared'.[91]

To be sure, the success of the military chancellery under Brosch owed not a little to the fact that various soldiers, bureaucrats and politicians of the Empire not unreasonably anticipated that they might soon have to deal with Franz Ferdinand as the Emperor. 'The lot of the ministers', Rudolf Sieghart observed, 'making decisions with one glance at Schönbrunn and another at the Belvedere, was often unenviable.'[92] In a sense, this prospect of imminent change at the top constituted the *raison d'être* of the military chancellery. In turn, planning for the (near) future was always going to be mainly about how to put down Hungary. Since Franz Ferdinand could succeed Franz Joseph any day given the latter's age and frailty, and since he saw Hungary as the chief obstacle to his vision of how the Empire should be run, the Hungarian question was to become the central concern of his associates down in the Lower Belvedere. This is a point that requires, perhaps, some emphasis.

The Lower Belvedere is often, in popular and serious historiography alike, associated with Franz Ferdinand's 'reform plans' for the Empire. In fact, Franz Ferdinand's obsession with the existing system really meant that he was only interested in taking the adjective 'Dual' out of the 'Dual Monarchy'. Only in that sense did he wish to see anything genuinely reformed. In that sense, too, he was a deeply conservative reformer. To him, the destruction of Dualism meant the preservation and enhancement of the two institutions that mattered to him most: the Habsburg dynasty and the Army. Therefore the job of his military chancellery was to prepare for him in advance a set of moves with which he would open up his game on the Austro-Hungarian political chessboard that would emerge following his uncle's death. Specifically, a suitable manifesto by the new emperor had to be prepared as an address to the peoples of the Empire (*An unsere Völker!*) at the moment of the accession to the throne (*Thronwechsel*).

Subduing Hungary: The Brosch-Lammasch Programme

Apart from Brosch, the main, perhaps the crucial role in this exercise was played by the constitutional expert Professor Heinrich Lammasch who was to go down in history as the last Prime Minister (in 1918) of imperial Austria. When the Professor first met the Archduke, in the spring of 1910, he learned that the question preoccupying him most of all was the revision of the *Ausgleich* with Hungary. Lammasch also discovered, very quickly, that Franz Ferdinand's knowledge of legal matters was 'woeful'. By contrast, he thought that Brosch, although no lawyer, possessed an 'extraordinary' familiarity with constitutional issues, particularly those pertaining to the relations between Austria and Hungary.[93] According to Lammasch, there exsisted a specific legal-constitutional problem that greatly exercised the Archduke. The Hungarian Law of 1791 stipulated that the hereditary king should crown himself King of Hungary within six months of ascending the throne – and take an oath at the same time. Doing this meant formally obliging himself to uphold the Constitution of Hungary: something the Archduke was adamantly against – hardly surprising as he would require a free hand to put an end to Dualism. Referring to his 1900 solemn oath of renunciation in Hofburg, he told Lammasch: 'Only once have I sworn in my life ... but in future I shall be on my guard.' Therefore he did not wish to be 'a prisoner of his oath'. The situation was 'either – or': either the Hungarian Constitution would be altered within six months of his ascending the throne, or an attempt would have to be made to obtain an extension of the six-month deadline.[94]

This was child's play for the brilliant Professor. He pointed out to Franz Ferdinand that the Austrian Constitution also required him to swear an oath (something of which the Archduke was completely unaware) and that, furthermore, there existed certain discrepancies between the existing Austrian and Hungarian constitutions. Hence, Lammasch told him, he was not able to give two oaths which in some respects were at variance. To the

Archduke's great delight he cited an example of the contradictory nature of the two constitutions: in the Hungarian oath the new king was obliged to treat Dalmatia as belonging to the Crown of St Stephen, whereas in the Austrian law Dalmatia was a constituent part of the 'kingdoms and lands represented in the *Reichsrat*', i.e., of Austria. 'This moment in particular', Lammasch recalled, 'determined that he went along with my plan.'[95]

And what was the plan? The main idea of all this scheming by Archduke and acolytes was, of course, to put Hungary in its place. Published for the first time in *Neues Wiener Journal* after the Great War, the programme for Franz Ferdinand's accession (*Programm für den Thronwechsel*) was elaborated in the course of 1910-1911 by Brosch and Lammasch.[96] The most authoritative study of Brosch to date names him as the main author of the *Thronwechsel* programme, but ascribes co-authorship in the first place to Lammasch. It also gives 1 September 1911 as the date when Brosch put the finishing touches to the draft programme.[97] One of the issues which the lengthy document suggested for immediate consideration was the 'maintenance' – or 'preservation [*Aufrechterhaltung*]' – of the 1867 Compromise with Hungary. This in the given context, as Robert Kann commented, meant the opposite of what it said: 'namely, not the preservation, but the revision of the Compromise of 1867.'[98] And Lammasch's influence is evident in the accompanying manifesto (*An unsere Völker!*) where there is talk of the need to establish 'full consistency' between the Austrian and Hungarian constitutional provisions.[99] This legal ruse dreamt up by Lammasch was of course never tested in practice, but it is likely that it would have worked as an exercise in quasi-constitutional posturing on the part of the new Emperor: Franz II, as he chose to be called.

The 1911 Brosch-Lammasch memorandum was not a plan for the reform of the Empire. It was actually a monument to Franz Ferdinand's hatred of Hungary. In particular, it provided no answer to the overall nationalities question of the whole of the Empire, referring only to the 'equality of the nations of Hungary'. The implication in the memorandum was that this equality should be achieved through the introduction of universal suffrage (*allgemeine Wahlrecht*) – the only 'instrument of power' available to the Crown against the Hungarians.[100] This, of course, was merely a means to destroy the power of the Hungarian gentry. Non-Hungarian nationalities in Hungary were not there to be emancipated by the new Emperor: they were there to be used, once enfranchised, against the Hungarians. There is a conspicuous absence of any federalist thinking in the Brosch-Lammasch *Thronwechsel* memorandum. Popovici's 'recipe' is admittedly mentioned, but only in a very speculative context. The memorandum touched on it briefly (in half a sentence) as a constitutional idea possibly preferable to Trialism (with Croatia). It interpreted Popovici's proposals in terms of the 'broad autonomy of lands [*weitgehend Länder-*

autonomie]', not of states. And it highlighted the central government, the central parliament and the separation from Hungary of Croatia, Sieben-bürgen (Transylvanuia) and Slovakia – the points in Popovici's programme obviously to the liking of Franz Ferdinand.[101] It has to be emphasized, however, that this was merely a small, meditative digression in the memor-andum, not a constituent part of any concrete steps envisaged within it. The memorandum did not talk about federalism, the term was not used at all in this very long document which otherwise devoted enormous atten-tion to matters such as flags, emblems and titles.

Franz Ferdinand and his associates were apparently not afraid that the introduction of universal suffrage in Hungary would cause more problems than it would solve. 'The claim', the memorandum argued, 'that the Free-masons, socialists, anarchists, Jews, radical Slavs, and irredentist Romanians and Serbs would thereby become the ruling parties and bring the state into even greater quandary ... is groundless.' The explanation was that in Hungary, a predominantly agrarian land, there were few socialists and even fewer anarchists; the Jews were not to be feared since they would always join the strongest party and for business reasons would become 'even anti-Semites'; finally the optimistic claim was made that, for the time being, there were no radical Slavs or irredentist Romanians.[102]

The Hungarians were the problem. And they, it was recognized, would not be so 'silly' as to freely agree to a reform of the electoral system that would take their power away.[103] Therefore the memorandum anticipated the necessity of imposing universal suffrage in Hungary by royal decree (*Oktroi*). Again, however, a rather sanguine scenario was envisaged whereby only the Hungarian gentry would put up determined resistance to such a measure, and they alone could 'not make a revolution.'[104] But it seems that Brosch and his co-authors were not altogether sure about this, for the concluding section of the memorandum considered the use of force as a last resort – the section was entitled, appropriately, 'The Violent Way [*Der gewaltsame Weg*]'. Moreover, the prospect of an armed intervention was presented as a superb opportunity for a radical move: to 'degrade' Hungary to the status of lands such as Croatia or Bohemia by abolishing its min-istries and parliament, and leave it autonomous only in spheres such as local administration and education. In which case, it went 'without saying' that the name of the Monarchy should be 'the Austrian Empire [*Kaisertum Österreich*]' and that a crowning ceremony in Budapest would become superfluous.[105]

These final ruminations in the memorandum perhaps reflected Franz Ferdinand's 'reform' intentions most closely. It is tempting to speculate whether 'The Violent Way' section in the Brosch-Lammasch memorandum was not, in fact, its substance. Realistically, what the Archduke wished to achieve in Hungary was highly unlikely to occur without the use of force.

Contemporaries and historians alike have emphasized his political fixation with Hungary and his determination to drastically reduce its status. The Austrian statesman Ernst Plener succinctly defined the Archduke's chief political ambition as 'a Great Austria, with a rolling back of the power of Hungary's parliament'.[106] A.J.P. Taylor saw the Archduke's hostility to Dualism as the only constant element in his political outlook: 'without sympathy for the peoples oppressed by Magyar nationalism, he had a dynastic jealousy of Hungarian freedom and wished to reduce Hungary to a common subordination.'[107] Of course, the problem with reducing Hungary to a common subordination was that the country's ruling elites would have stood up to any such attempt. And this was something that Franz Ferdinand was deeply aware of. Edmund Steinacker, a leading German from Hungary, reported that the Archduke wanted to 'know nothing' about the 'Magyar oligarchy' and its political leaders, insisting that a reform of Dualism was 'absolutely due'. Franz Ferdinand added, significantly, that this reform would be implemented amicably if at all possible and observing legal norms, 'but if necessary also with violence, with blood and iron'.[108]

One person closely involved with the Belvedere circle was the ultra-conservative Count Ottokar Czernin, a childhood friend of Sophie Chotek, and landowner whose estate in Bohemia bordered the Archduke's own at Konopischt. He also happened to harbour rabidly anti-Hungarian sentiments. In an important article on the relationship between Czernin and Franz Ferdinand, Robert Kann drew attention to several policy papers presented by Czernin to the Archduke in 1908 and 1909. With regard to Hungary, his language was similar and every bit as truculent as that employed by his friend and neighbour in Bohemia. 'The ruler', Czernin wrote in 1908, 'must take up the fight with the Magyars. He must be ready to shoot ... The struggle will not be fought with words or pen, but with blood and iron.' And in 1909 he recommended to His Imperial Highness that during the first years of his reign in Hungary *'the policy must be enforced with bayonets if it is to succeed'*.[109] Whatever differences existed between Czernin and Franz Ferdinand – and they are highlighted by Kann in his article – their views on the Hungarian issue show a meeting of minds.

What, however, would have been the likely response of the Hungarians in the event of an attempt by Franz Ferdinand to tailor-make the Constitution at their expense? The most important person in the 'Magyar oligarchy' was István Tisza, Prime Minister of Hungary from 1903 to 1905, and again from 1913. In the meantime he had founded a political party (the Party of National Work) which had won a clear majority in the 1910 election, and been the Speaker of the lower house of the Hungarian Parliament. He was to become, famously, one of the key men in the 1914 July crisis following the Archduke's assassination. Baron Dezső Bánffy, a Habsburg loyalist and himself a former Hungarian Prime Minister, described Tisza to Friedrich Funder as Hungary's 'smartest man', and someone who represented 'a dreadful menace to our country'.[110] But Tisza likewise saw Franz Ferdinand as a threat. Gábor Vermes, in his major biography of Tisza, emphasizes the latter's determination from 1909 onwards to stabilize the country in order 'to stave off the Archduke's anticipated future aggression'. Tisza, according to Vermes, did not know how far the Heir to the Throne would take his Magyarophobia following his accession. But if Franz Ferdinand failed to display common sense, Tisza was prepared, just like Andrássy (the Younger), 'to go to extremes'. Vermes also points out that in 1911 Tisza warned the Archduke, through Ottokar Czernin, that 'he would fight even against his monarch, should the King violate the constitution.'[111]

The 'wretched' proponents of Great Austria, Tisza was later to remark, would have made Austria very small had they been able to proceed with the realization of their ideas.[112] It is important to note that Franz Ferdinand and Tisza did not have any direct communication. As Colonel Bardolff observed, there was an 'abyss' between them. In 1913, shortly after Tisza became the Hungarian Prime Minister for the second time, Bardolff was walking with the Archduke in the gardens of Konopischt and was suddenly asked whether Tisza should not be given an audience after all. Bardolff's advice to his boss was proof enough of the grudging esteem in which the Hungarian statesman was held: to try and persuade or talk him into anything was pointless, Bardolff said; on the other hand, to reveal a weakness to him would be dangerous.[113]

Clearly, Franz Ferdinand's 'blood and iron' scenario for Hungary was extremely realistic. If nothing else, the Hungarians would have opposed the creation of a central parliament for the Empire based in Austria which, as Lammasch emphasized, the Heir to the Throne 'absolutely wanted'. The Professor also recalled that the Archduke wanted everything to go 'bang-bang [*bums-bums gehen*]' at the moment of accession. There was more than a hint of a martial mindset in all these preparations. But this could have been expected given that Brosch was the man in charge. Edmund Glaise von Horstenau, who had opportunities to meet members of the Belvedere circle, remembered that Brosch stood out for not being pacifist.[114] According to Lammasch, Brosch had planned very carefully for the accession event: 'everything had been set up in detail, like a military campaign'. One detail from the recollections of Lammasch is of notable significance to historiography: there was an ominous anticipation of trouble with the Magyars because Brosch had drawn up a list of the garrisons to be strengthened – 'in particular those in Hungary'.[115]

Among the Archduke's circle of advisers there was a consensus on Hungarian policy. Josef Kristóffy, one of Franz Ferdinand's few Hungarian friends, likewise recommended in a memorandum from March 1912 that one should 'not flinch' from imposing a royal decree on Hungary to change its parliamentary system.[116] A consensus also existed, moreover, that a bloody conflict was practically inevitable in Hungary, with the further anticipation that other parts of the Monarchy could be affected in this violent scenario. Among the papers of the constitutional adviser Johann Eichhoff is a draft addressed to the Foreign Minister with instructions regarding the new imperial constitution. The document envisaged a 'fierce resistance movement' and a 'full rebellion and insubordination', character-ized by conflict with the authorities on the ground, desertions from the joint army, refusal to pay taxes, mutiny of the Hungarian gendarmerie, etc. It predicted at the same time that other disgruntled, 'irredentist' national movements could join in and that extinguishing the whole turmoil would, 'here and there' result in 'rivers of blood.'[117]

In November 1911 Brosch ended his connection with the Belvedere. According to the papers left behind by Leopold von Andrian, Brosch had already by the middle of 1910 persuaded the Archduke to relieve him of his position so that he could resume active military duty. By this stage he had got thoroughly fed up with his job as well as with the Archduke. During private conversations with Andrian in July 1910 he complained bitterly about Franz Ferdinand's 'ingratitude' and 'avarice', but also about his irresponsibility. Alluding to the Archduke's foremost interest, he said: 'One roebuck and the whole political work goes to hell.' The widespread description by the historians of an 'energetic' Franz Ferdinand is actually contradicted by Brosch who repeatedly called his boss 'lazy [*faul*]' and maintained that, at the same time, he was asking 'the impossible' from his people. The aide-de-camp also revealed that Franz Ferdinand trusted absolutely no one, not even him. He, Brosch, 'had to fight, on a daily basis, to win the trust of the distrustful and ungrateful Archduke', and he was 'quite disgusted by the whole business'.[118]

Brosch had the satisfaction of being succeeded by an officer of his choice, Carl Bardolff. His initial preference was one Major Hummel, but Franz Ferdinand turned this proposal down on account of Hummel's Jewish background.[119] Lieutenant-Colonel Bardolff, who also had a doctor-ate in law, assumed his post on 1 December 1911 and was to stay with Franz Ferdinand until the end – he was in the archducal motorcade on 28 June 1914 in Sarajevo. Bardolff's chief achievement was to smooth the passage towards the appointment of Franz Ferdinand, on 17 August 1913, as 'Inspec-tor General of the entire armed force [*Generalinspektor der gesamten bewaffneten Macht*]', a post previously held by the celebrated Archduke Albrecht. This placed both Franz Ferdinand and his military chancellery firmly in the military hierarchy.[120] Bardolff himself was a no-nonsense, firm character. A widower, he asked his boss in the autumn of 1912 for permis-sion to marry again (a woman considerably younger than himself). When the Archduke objected, on the grounds that a young wife would entail social commitments that would impede his work in the military chancellery, Bardolff promptly offered to resign. So Franz Ferdinand simply gave in.[121]

Experts agree that the military chancellery under Bardolff, in contrast to the 'conspiratorial phase' under Brosch, assumed an increasingly bureaucratic face.[122] Some contemporaries, however, took a different view. Rudolf Sieghart, from 1910 the Governor of the Bodenkreditanstalt bank and admittedly no friend of either the Archduke or Bardolff, described the military chancellery after Brosch's departure as a 'mixture of undercover activity and Inquisition': a place that had opened its doors to various 'dilettantes and intriguers'.[123] Be that as it may, the military chancellery under Bardolff did not, so far as future planning was concerned, depart in any significant way from the foundations laid down by the Brosch-Lammasch memorandum of 1911. New, far-reaching blueprints for Empire reform would have meant that Franz Ferdinand's thinking on the subject had matured and evolved beyond the immediate problem of how to deal with Hungary – but there is no evidence for such a contention despite the claims that have been made to that effect.

One such claim was advanced in 1926 by Johann Eichhoff, a constitutional expert from the Austrian Interior Ministry who had been involved with the Belvedere circle since the days of Brosch. In March of that year Eichhoff published an article, splashed on the front page of Funder's *Reichspost*, under the sensational heading: 'The Planned Establishment of the United States of Great Austria'.[124] No less than this had apparently been discussed by the Archduke and Eichhoff on the terrace of the Miramare Castle in Trieste towards the end of April or the beginning of May 1914 – Eichhoff did not give the exact date. Aurel Popovici himself was not mentioned in the article, but its title held obvious associations. Eichhoff bluntly asserted that Franz Ferdinand had planned 'autonomy' for the various peoples of the Empire on the basis of 'carefully demarcated' ethnic separation. For good measure, he added that the fate of any disputed territories would have been settled by plebiscites. He did not elaborate (nor did he use the term 'federalism'), and so his points remain intriguingly fuzzy. 'Great Austria', Eichhoff suggested, would have been a single state as it would have retained a single army, foreign policy, internal market, etc. Bearing in mind Popovici's scheme, this sounds very familiar. Had, then, Franz Ferdinand at long last become a committed Popovician federalist – only weeks before he died?

Given everything that is known about the Archduke's political ideas, this seems highly unlikely. Eichhoff did not provide evidence in his *Reichspost* article that would in any way confirm the existence in 1914 of the grand plan he vaguely wrote about. Later, in 1941, he admitted that there had in fact been no definitive project in place.[125] Historians have dignified Eich-hoff's newspaper article with the label of 'programme' – as if it constituted a planning development somehow separate from, and superseding, the Brosch-Lammasch memorandum.[126] But post-war newspaper rumblings, unaccompanied by hard documentary evidence, cannot be seen as a pro-gramme. What Eichhoff did produce in the *Reichspost* piece was an updated version of the *Thronwechsel* manifesto, presumably from spring 1914. The manifesto stressed that various nations should be able to pursue 'national development' (obviously within the framework of the Monarchy's 'shared interests'). Where this was still not possible the situation should be recti-fied by the introduction of 'just voting laws'. Needless to say, only Hungary could have been meant here. Once again, therefore, the political problem of Hungarian power was at the heart of Franz Ferdinand's preoccupations – not the political inequality of the state's nations, still less remodelling the state along federal lines. The whole business of introducing 'just voting laws' in Hungary was in any case a total charade. In 1943, in his ground-breaking study of Franz Ferdinand's reform plans, Georg Franz supplied evidence to show that Bardolff had issued planning instructions in the Lower Belvedere with the idea of manipulating Hungary's electoral system. The stated aim was to enable the Germans of Hungary to tip the scales in the Hungarian Parliament between the Magyars and non-Magyars.[127]

And just what Franz Ferdinand's military chancellery was all about was spelled out in August 1912 by Captain Erich von Hüttenbrenner who had joined the staff at the Lower Belvedere in the previous year. In a report on the activities of the military chancellery, he described it as 'a kind of *Reich* chancellery', its task being 'to slow down, in timely fashion, possible derail-ments which the national-federalist crumbling could encourage.' In other words, any developments in the direction of ethnic federalism were seen as a threat to the Empire, not its salvation. Hüttenbrenner was very clear on this point: the military chancellery, he wrote, was 'a bulwark against any particular national aspiration [*Bollwerk gegen jede nationale Sonder-bestrebung*]'.[128] It is remarkable, in the light of this elucidation (published as long ago as 1975), as well as all the other available information about the Archduke's stance on the nationalities question, that books are still being written where his so-called federalist leaning is taken seriously. Even recently, Christopher Clark has suggested that, by 1914, Franz Ferdinand was favouring a United States of Austria: 'a far-reaching transformation ... comprising fifteen member states, many of which would have Slav majori-ties.'[129] In fact, Franz Ferdinand's military chancellery was doing the exact opposite of what so much of historiography has claimed to have been its activity: it was actually anticipating and manipulating national movements so that it might hinder them, rather than producing blueprints for the reform of the Empire in order to emancipate those movements.

In the final analysis, of course, the future Franz II was not obliged by anything that his military chancellery drafted on his behalf, and this included the Hungarian policy. Brosch himself noted that the Archduke would 'not for all the world sign anything' and would 'not deliver anything in a written form'.[130] At the same time it is difficult to imagine that his military chancellery did not closely coordinate its work with him. There is a school of thought which has argued that, in the light of the external complications expected after the Balkan Wars of 1912-1913 (i.e., the Russian danger), Franz Ferdinand would have, upon ascending the throne, proceeded very carefully, leaving Dualism in place.[131] But this seems doubtful. If mid-1914 is taken as the last meaningful period for a consideration of the Archduke's political position (since he was killed shortly thereafter), then caution was demonstrably not present in his thoughts. In fact, as will be seen in chapter thirteen, Franz Ferdinand explicitly told Kaiser Wilhelm II at their famous Konopischt meeting (12-13 June 1914) that Russia was internally too weak to pose a danger. So he certainly saw no restraining influences abroad. And it was on the same occasion at Konopischt that the Archduke complained bitterly to the German Emperor about the Hungarians in general and their leader István Tisza in particular. From all the above it is clear that far from being concerned with federal reform, it was Dualism which was, and remained until the end, the Archduke's pre-eminent *bête noir*.

3
Great Croatia: The Trialist Rainbow

The Yugoslav Deliverance

A READER NEW to the subject of Franz Ferdinand's reform ideas will almost certainly be confused by the tendency among historians to present these ideas loosely, almost haphazardly, and in a way which practically conflates the Archduke's 'federalist' plans with his alleged 'Trialist' scheme. This is not a problem caused by the incompetence of reader but by those historians he is reading. For Trialism in Austria-Hungary was a concept born out of the existence of Dualism, and was actually very different from federalism, whether ethnic or that based on historic Crown Lands. In fact, as Robert Kann argued, the very term 'Trialism' ruled out federalism as an overall solution to the Empire problem since Trialism 'recognized, not equality, but a privileged position' of certain nations.[1] The prologue of this book highlighted Franz Joseph's half-hearted and abortive Trialist adventure with the Czechs in 1871. The Trialist tale of Franz Ferdinand concerns the Croats, a people whom he was supposed to have favoured not least because they were Catholic. In countless accounts the Archduke is presented as the would-be father of a Croat-led Yugoslavia which would become the third pillar of the Habsburg Monarchy. This story also relies heavily on the projections of the Archduke as Slav-friendly (*Slawenfreundlich*). So if, as this study has maintained, Franz Ferdinand was no federalist, was he perhaps a trialist, keen to secure a special destiny for the South Slavs?

The people who had plotted to assassinate Franz Ferdinand were South Slavs – Croats and Muslims, as well as Serbs. There is, therefore, an irony here if one were to accept the view that the Archduke had in fact been a friend of the Slavs. Propagated originally by Austrian historians, this proposition has been widely endorsed elsewhere. Thus a recent American work, popular and academically acclaimed at the same time, has described Franz Ferdinand as 'the most pro-Slav member of the Habsburg hierarchy'.[2] Such blank judgements, however, are exceedingly problematic, beginning at the humdrum level of the Archduke's own Konopischt castle, where the personnel were required to speak exclusively in German, with no Slavonic language being tolerated by Franz Ferdinand.[3] The fact that he hated the Poles and had no time for the Slovenes – both nations being Slavonic as well as Catholic – has also been conveniently ignored in attempts to identify Franz Ferdinand with some kind of positive attitude towards the nationalities question. 'Why should I speak Slovene?', he protested to Beck in a letter from 1906, adding for good measure: 'It so happens that we still live in Austria, and here the language ... is German, and only then come these hundreds of hiccup languages like the Slovene.'[4] In reality, the Archduke despised the Slavs. When, in 1913, he urged Foreign Minister Berchtold to support Romania, he remarked that 'thank goodness it is not a Slavic country'.[5]

The narrative about the Archduke's friendliness towards the Slavs is partly inspired by the fact that he had married a Slav woman. In this, however, an important detail has been overlooked. Even though Sophie Chotek (Zofie Chotkova) came from the Czech aristocracy, her Czech credentials were dubious: like many from her Bohemian social milieu, she was hardly 'Czech'. As Glaise-Horstenau reported, she 'barely' spoke Czech.[6] Franz Ferdinand himself stated, almost defensively, that she knew not even fifty words of Czech and that she had almost always lived in a German environment.[7] There was some local history behind this. The Germanization of the Czech aristocracy had begun way back in the eleventh century when the Přemyslid princes and kings began to marry women from German princely houses – to be imitated by scores of Czech nobles.[8] When, during the Thirty Years' War, the old Czech nobility was practically destroyed, its confiscated properties were taken over by immigrant Catholic Germans who then formed a new Czech (Bohemian) nobility. The whole of the Czech nation, in fact, had over centuries become to a considerable degree German. The Czech historian Josef Pekař wrote that at least a quarter of all Czechs had German names, and at least half of the Czechs had German blood flowing in their veins.[9]

Be that as it may, Franz Ferdinand certainly had no sympathy for Czech political and national aspirations within the Habsburg state. In 1899 he warned of the danger of Bohemia becoming fully 'Czechizied', and deplored the possibility that, on top of his 'friends' the Hungarians, the Czechs would have 'the third state'.[10] In March 1901, in an almost hysterical letter, he begged the Austrian Prime Minister Ernest von Koerber absolutely not to yield to the Czechs. 'We know', he wrote, 'how we have already brought our Monarchy to the edge of the grave with Dualism, and now a second, equally eminent danger emerges through the Czechs!'[11] He could not understand, he told Alexander Spitzmüller in 1911, why he was being labelled as 'a friend of the Czechs' when his feelings were with the Germans.[12] For all his social links with the 'Czech' nobility, therefore, the Archduke was politically quite hostile to the Czechs, seeing in them, as his Slovak adviser Milan Hodža reported, only 'Hussite rebels'.[13]

Despite his known opposition to the idea of the Czechs forming 'the third state', the Trialist label has frequently been stuck to the Heir to the Throne with regard to the Croats. In historiography past and present, the discussion around this subject has nourished two separate but connected myths: first, that Franz Ferdinand was going to help the Croats build a Yugoslav state within the Monarchy under their leadership ('Trialism') and, second, that this was the reason for his assassination. The latter thesis, needless to say, is highly relevant to the century-long debate about the origins of the Great War. For the assassination in Sarajevo has been linked directly by some to supposed Serbian perceptions that this purported three-way restructuring of the Monarchy, in which Zagreb would become the capital of the projected third entity, would endanger the idea of a 'Great Serbia'. Certainly, 'Great Croatia' and 'Great Serbia' were mutually exclusive – not least because of competing claims regarding Bosnia-Herzegovina. Thus, in many interpretations of 28 June 1914 (including some Serbian interpretations), Franz Ferdinand was assassinated because his reform plans stood in the way of 'Great Serbia'. In 1929, for example, Oscar Jászi suggested, in his major work on the dissolution of the Habsburg Monarchy, that the Serb nationalist revolutionary organizations hated Franz Ferdinand as the man who was determined to solve the Yugoslav problem 'not on a Great-Serb but on a Great-Croat basis, not outside but inside of Austria'.[14]

Trialism has also been called 'the Austro-Yugoslav idea' – as the influential German historian Ernst Anrich named it in 1931. Anrich defined it as 'setting a Great Croatia against a Great Serbia'.[15] In 1937 the same Anrich argued that Franz Ferdinand was perhaps the only man who would have been able to destroy by peaceful means the Great Serbian movement by reconstructing Austria-Hungary, with Trialism replacing Dualism; Croatia, in this alleged scheme, would have become the third factor in the state, joined by Bosnia-Herzegovina, Dalmatia and Slovenia. The hint as to who therefore stood behind the Sarajevo assassination was more than obvious.[16] But it was Luigi Albertini's seminal work on the causes of the war of 1914 (first published in Italy in 1942-1943) that was mainly responsible for promoting, in no uncertain terms, the view that the Archduke had been eliminated because he had been seen as a supporter of Trialism. Albertini had read Anrich and indeed cited him at great length on this subject. 'Francis Ferdinand', Albertini concluded, 'was sentenced to death precisely because, by upholding the rights of the Slav subjects of the Monarchy, he was undermining the movement which aimed at detaching them from Austria and uniting them with Serbia.'[17] At about the same time as Albertini's work was published, Georg Franz argued in his authoritative work on the reform plans of Franz Ferdinand that Serbian fears concerning the Archduke's intentions had 'significantly' contributed to his murder.[18]

Such speculation – and it was no more than that – has proved attractive to many historians, and the premise that the Habsburg Heir to the Throne fell victim to Serbian anticipation of his reform ideas has persisted to this day. Christopher Clark has written that the Archduke had for a time favoured strengthening the Slavic element in the Empire by creating a Croat and thus Catholic-dominated Yugoslavia. 'It was his association with this idea', Clark has commented, 'that so aroused the hatred of his orthodox Serbian enemies.'[19] The motives behind the assassination of Franz Ferdinand are examined in chapter eleven, together with perceptions of him – it will be seen that the Catholic/Orthodox bad blood, highlighted by Clark, played no part whatsoever in the decision to assassinate the Archduke, and that the assassins had only the vaguest of notions about the Archduke's reform plans.

In any case, what exactly was his 'association' with the Trialist idea? Strangely enough, historians have not exerted any great effort to address this question. Why would a man so consistently opposed to Dualism envisage replacing it with a Trialism which would thereby, in a very real sense, magnify the very evil that he was determined to destroy? Was a Great Croatia as entailed by Trialism really likely in the Archduke's view to solve the problems of the Habsburg Monarchy?

To be sure, some kind of a political synthesis between Franz Ferdinand's anti-Hungarian outlook and the Croat striving for emancipation from Hungarian dominance would have made a great deal of sense in terms of strengthening the state – as long as the Croats felt a strong attachment to the Monarchy. The power of Hungary, so often detrimental to the interest of the Dynasty, would have been curtailed by a new constitutional arrangement, and its territory reduced. If nothing else, a deal between Franz Ferdinand and the Southern Slavs would have addressed directly, and possibly even neutralized, the so-called 'Southern Slav question' which ultimately paved the way for the destruction of the Habsburg Empire. The fact that many Croats had hoped, right up to 28 June 1914, that the Archduke would elevate their lands (and expand them by including Bosnia-Herzegovina) to a status equal with Austria and Hungary is beyond dispute. It is also the case that, perhaps more than any other group in the Monarchy, the Croats were considered *kaisertreu*, a loyal element. But were they really? And, more relevantly, did the Archduke himself perceive them as such? At this point it is necessary to touch on some salient aspects of Croatian history in the late Habsburg period.

Certainly, the Croats had in the past abundantly proved their faithfulness to the House of Habsburg. Along with those Serbs settled in the area of the Austrian military frontier with the Ottoman Empire (known as the 'Krajina', abolished as late as 1881), they had for centuries supplied fierce fighting men to the Habsburg armies. Their warlike character was famous. When regiments from Croatia fought, briefly, for Napoleon, they quickly acquired the reputation for being his best troops.[20] At a decisive moment in October 1848, *Ban* Josip Jelačić helped the Habsburg cause by defeating, at Schwechat, a Hungarian force advancing towards revolutionary Vienna. But this loyalty was not rewarded. With the conclusion of the *Ausgleich* in 1867, Vienna simply delivered Croatia to Hungary. As their national consciousness grew, the Croats began to recognise that fidelity to the Habsburgs was something of a doubtful investment.

And while Hungary was the direct source of their oppression, it was to all intents and purposes the Emperor in Vienna who stood behind it. Even the port of Rijeka (Fiume) became a *corpus separatum* – in reality a Hungarian possession – thus adding to the list of Croat grievances, the main of which concerned the fact that the 'Triune Kingdom' of Croatia-Slavonia-Dalmatia did not in fact include Dalmatia. In 1850 Franz Joseph actually committed himself to reunite Dalmatia with Croatia-Slavonia, but nothing came of it. To make things worse, in 1860 he gave Hungary the Croat territory of Međumurje. After 1868, when Croatia and Hungary made their own Compromise, Franz Joseph treated Croatia-Slavonia, of which he was nominally the King, as part and parcel of Hungary and would never bypass Budapest in Croat affairs. When, following the occupation of Bosnia-Herzegovina in 1878, the Croat Parliament (*Sabor*) asked Franz Joseph that Croatia be included in the administration of the provinces, he refused and reprimanded the *Sabor* for overstepping its competences. Following the abolition of the old Krajina Military Frontier in 1881, the Croats managed only 'with great difficulty' (and only with the help of Hungary) to have that territory incorporated into Croatia.[21] According to Leopold Chlumecky, in 1912 people in Dalmatia were saying: 'The Emperor hates us Croats.'[22] By the turn of the century, in fact, the renowned Croat support for the Habsburgs seemed like ancient history. Alexander von Musulin, the diplomat who became famous for drafting the Austro-Hungarian ultimatum to Serbia in July 1914 and who knew his native Croatia well, wrote that by the 1890s the Croats felt 'Empire disenchantment [*Reichsverdrossenheit*]'.[23] Robert Kann pointed out that in the pre-revolutionary and revolutionary times of 1848-49 Croatian loyalty was considered 'a main pillar' of the unity of the Empire. After this period, however, 'and particularly from 1867 on, this situation was gradually, but radically, reversed.'[24]

The process of radical reversal reflected the fact that Croat nationalism was coming of age. During much of the 19th century Croat national feeling was strong only in Croatia proper, the region around Zagreb. In other Croat lands, particularly in Dalmatia but also in Slavonia, regional loyalty predominated. In Slavonia, for example, people objected to their language being called 'Croat'.[25] No standardized, common literary language existed and differing South Slav dialects were spoken in Croat lands. German was the dominant culture among the intelligentsia. The 'Croat' language (the so-called *kajkavski* dialect) belonged to a minority in and around Zagreb and the term 'Croat' signified the name of a local speech rather than a people.[26] The Croat nobility was cosmopolitan, and unable or unwilling to assume national leadership. Louis Eisenmann emphasized its largely non-Croat, foreign origin.[27] However, the growing assertiveness of Hungary served to accelerate a national awakening of the Croats. By the 1830s, as the historian Wayne Vucinich observed, 'Hungarian nationalism had become a powerful force and threatened the very existence of Croatia as a nation.'[28] The Croat national renaissance in the nineteenth century thus began, and continued, as an exercise in self-preservation.

Bizarrely, the national revival movement in the 1830s and 1840s was called 'Illyrian'. Its leader Ljudevit Gaj, a poet and journalist, believed (and he was not alone in this) that the South Slavs were descended from the ancient Illyrians and he attempted therefore to resurrect this old name. More importantly, and with much greater success, he promoted the so-called 'štokavian' dialect (spoken by most Croats and all Serbs) into the common Croat literary language – the Serbian linguist Vuk Karadžić had already done the same with the štokavian dialect in his reformation of the Serbian literary language. Illyrianism has often been seen as the precursor to the ideology of Yugoslavism: the 'Illyrians' were to Gaj and his followers all the Slavs between Villach in Austria and Varna in Bulgaria. But the Slovenes and especially the Serbs were distinctly unenthusiastic about this ambiguous identity bracelet and so the Illyrian movement remained restricted to Croatia. To the Serbs, 'Illyrian' seemed synonymous with Catholic. Yet the Serbs of the Monarchy were not against the cultural and national unity of the South Slavs and they have been credited with inventing the term 'Yugoslavian' in preference to 'Illyrian'. Thus Jovan Subotić, a leading Serb from Hungary, argued for this name in 1839.[29]

Croat historians point out that 'Illyrian' was just a kind of collective 'neutral surname' for the South Slavs.[30] It is nevertheless clear that there was mixed in with such idealistic South Slav unionism a great deal of down-to-earth Croat nationalism. After all, the only tangible political rationale of the movement was resistance to Hungary – primarily a Croat concern, not a general South Slav one. Indeed, the 'Illyrian' name was banned in 1843 at the insistence of Hungary. C.A. Macartney wrote that nine out of ten nationalist Croats were not actually interested in 'Illyria': what they strove for was 'a Great Croatia'.[31] It is also certain, however, that neither Gaj nor his backers were revolutionaries plotting to destroy or leave the Habsburg Empire. 'In practical terms', Wayne Vucinich noted, 'the Illyrians wanted the unification of Croatian lands within the Habsburg Monarchy, with Zagreb at its center.'[32]

Like so much else in the Monarchy, the Illyrian movement came to a halt with the introduction of absolutist rule from Vienna following the revolutions of 1848-49. By the beginning of the 1860s, with the end of the strict centralist period, an explicitly anti-Habsburg Croat ideology began to develop. In 1861 the Croat Party of Right (*Hrvatska stranka prava*, meaning the Croat state right) came into being. Despite its subsequent fragmentation, the Party of Right was to leave a major imprint on Croatian politics right up to the First World War. As its name suggested, the claims it made related to the ancient rights of the Kingdom of Croatia, that is, they were based on the view that the country had legally never ceased to be independent. Not surprisingly, therefore, it espoused uncompromising Croat nationalism. Ante Starčević, together with Eugen Kvaternik the co-founder of the party (and celebrated in Croatia as *pater patriae*), was in the second half of the nineteenth century the chief ideologue of that, somewhat brazen, nationalism. 'Today, no other nation', he wrote in 1867, 'remember, no other living nation in Europe, has a more magnificent past than the one which the Croat nation has.'[33] He advocated total independence for Croatia, while his more combative party friend Kvaternik actually led a short-lived rebellion for independence in 1871. Obviously, the Croatian separatism which they embraced was 'a concept which was in conflict with the tradition of the nation for over 700 years.'[34] As the Serbian socialist Vitomir Korać observed, the politics of the Party of Right were really 'no politics, but rather a constitutional litigation'. Starčević reluctantly recognized the House of Habsburg as having some legitimacy in Croatia, but recognized nothing else: not the Pragmatic Sanction, not the 1868 *Nagodba* with Hungary, not the Parliament in Budapest and not the Croat *Ban*.[35]

A Serb on his mother's side, Starčević is associated with the idea of an exclusivist Great Croatia whereby all the South Slavs, with the exception of Bulgarians, were seen as Croats: the Serbs were to him 'orthodox Croats', the Slovenes were 'mountain Croats', and the Bosnian Muslims were of the 'purest and noblest Croat blood'.[36] With regard to the Serbs, however, he considered them an 'impure' race and this meant that over time the Party of Right heavily poisoned relations between the Croats and the Serbs.[37] C.A. Macartney described him as a 'fantast'.[38] Interestingly, Starčević saw Vienna, not Budapest, as the root of all evil. And for a while he thought that Russia could be the saviour of the Croats. Erazmo Barčić, a prominent member of the Party of Right, declared, memorably, that the Croat people would 'breathe a sigh of relief when the pavements in Vienna begin to reverberate with the sound of riding Russian horsemen'.[39] Starče-vić did not believe in the possibility of any meaningful reconstruction of the Monarchy, arguing that 'despotisms cannot be repaired, they just fall apart'.[40] Indeed, convinced that nothing could be done, after the 1868 Croat-Hungarian settlement he simply waited for international circumstances to bring about the collapse of the Monarchy.

Starčević is famous for his pronouncement in the Croat Parliament, during a remarkable session in 1861, that 'only God and the Croats' could determine the destiny of Croatia. In a sense he was to be proved right: it was indeed some of his Croat contemporaries (though from a different political party), who propagated ideas which, much later, proved more than contributory in destroying the Monarchy and thus determining the destiny of Croatia. Their programme, if that is the word, was called *Jugoslovjenstvo* – 'Yugoslavism'.[41] Its two creators, incidentally, also happened to be men of God: Canon Franjo Rački and Bishop Josip Strossmayer.

The belief that the South Slavs ('Yugoslavs') were one people had already begun to be proclaimed in the 18th century, but the impact of such a view had been minimal, at least until the Illyrian movement. The Croat historian Jaroslav Šidak argued that the Yugoslav idea was merely an adaptation of Illyrianism.[42] Bishop Strossmayer has traditionally been seen as the apostle of Yugoslavism. The Academy of Science and Art in Zagreb, which carried the name 'Yugoslav', was established with his financial help in 1867. But it was Franjo Rački, a distinguished medievalist (and Strossmayer's intellectual guru), who could be called the true founder of the Yugoslav idea. The essence of the Yugoslavist persuasion was the idea of the basic unity of Serbs and Croats, and Rački emphasized that Serbs and Croats were genetically and linguistically one people, divided by history. Both he and Strossmayer, like Gaj and the Illyrians, included the Slovenes and the Bulgarians in their South Slav conceptions. In line with Illyrianism they believed, not unreasonably, that a single literary language was the chief precondition for unity among these nations. The Academy in Zagreb was meant to further this purpose. Rački even advocated that the Slovenes should give up their language in favour of the more widespread Serbo-Croat.[43]

However, the name of the new ideology was somewhat misleading, for there was a very Croat bent in all of this. It has to be emphasized that Yugoslavism was a specifically Croat construct reflecting Croat needs and fears, and aiming to further Croat ambitions. Rački saw the 'Yugoslavs' of the Empire, i.e., its Croats, Serbs and Slovenes, as the future centre of gravity (*težište*) for those 'brethren' still in the Ottoman Empire.[44] This centre was therefore clearly Croatia – and Rački, no less than Starčević, was obsessed with Croatia's historic state rights. Strossmayer, in turn, was obsessed with establishing Croat cultural superiority, wishing 'Croatia to become Tuscany, and Zagreb to become Florence.'[45] As had been the case with Illyrianism, practical political considerations were also in play in the

Yugoslav thinking of the Croats. As Mirjana Gross pointed out, Yugo-slavism 'was above all an expression of the pursuit to overcome Croat regionalism'. She also argued that the Yugoslav ideology grew out of the Croats' realization that Croatia was in danger without the support of South Slavs elsewhere.[46] Indeed, fear of a Magyar threat continued to play a big role. In 1861 Strossmayer's People's Party (*Narodna stranka*), a major force in Croatian politics, inspired the famous (but futile) Article 42 passed by the Croatian Diet, which stated that all legal ties between Croatia and Hungary had ceased to exist. Behind the Yugoslav façade of Rački and Strossmayer, there was an additional, somewhat megalomaniac motive. They believed that they could reconcile the Eastern Orthodox with the Catholic Church. This meant, of course, the recognition of the Pope by the Orthodox. Mirjana Gross even suggested that the whole ideology of Rački and Strossmayer had in fact been founded on this ambition: their belief that the Yugoslavs were 'chosen by God' to be the intermediaries in the process.[47]

The fact that the 'Yugoslavism' of Strossmayer and Rački was rather Croato-centric was reflected in the uneasiness which the Serbs of Croatia felt towards *Narodna stranka* – they kept away from it. A Serb historian has argued that the Yugoslavism of Strossmayer merely concealed his ambitions for a Great Croatia, and that the Bishop's *Narodna stranka* was just a more subtle version of Starčević's Party of Right – with both parties aiming to assimilate the Serbs.[48] Such were also the suspicions of the Serbs at the time. Svetozar Miletić, the leading Serb politician in Vojvodina, accused Strossmayer's party of using the Yugoslavian ideal to weaken Serbian self-awareness, and of attempting to 'Croatize' the whole of South Slavdom in its drive to create a Catholic Great Croatia.[49] Strossmayer himself wrote to Rački in 1884: 'The Serbs are our sworn enemies.'[50] A recent Croat study has admitted that *Narodna stranka* tended 'above all to affirm the Croat national and political identity'.[51] In her major work on Franjo Rački, Mirjana Gross noted that 'ambiguities were always present in the Yugoslav ideology' and criticized the 1867 conclusion of the Croat Diet that the Serbs in the Triune Kingdom were with the Croats 'one and the same and equal people [*istovjetan i ravnopravan*]'. If, she explained, the Serb people were 'one and the same' with the Croats, then only one people existed, but if the Serbs were 'equal' then two separate peoples existed. Gross blamed Rački for contributing to this equivocal backdrop since he would emphasize that the Serbs and Croats, although they were the same people, had separate state traditions.[52]

Whether those floating Yugoslav ideas in Croatia were genuine in their embrace of South Slav brotherhood or not, the point was that the Habs-burg state was not necessarily their primary frame of reference. In the late 1860s it looked as if the Monarchy could conceivably fall apart and it is therefore not surprising that Strossmayer schemed for a while with the Principality of Serbia to create a federal South Slav state.[53] Though nothing came of this, it showed that Croat political thinking, and not just in Starčević's Party of Right, was looking for a possible outcome outside the Monarchy. In the 1870s Strossmayer and Rački even entertained the hope that Russia would one day defeat Austria-Hungary and thus liberate the Croat people.[54] The Croat historian Dušan Bilandžić best described the opportunistic nature of Strossmayer's *Narodna stranka*, which sought 'to create a space for manoeuvre for all the possibilities which future great events in Europe would open up.'[55]

As will be seen in chapter ten, Yugoslav ideas, and especially the belief in Serbo-Croat indivisibility, would towards the end of the century be taken up by many Croat students at high school and university, and other sections of the young patriotic intelligentsia increasingly frustrated by the inability of previous generations to make significant national headway within the Monarchy. This development was to be of tremendous significance – if only because the Yugoslav orientation in Croatia, manifesting itself in the resistance to Hungary led by rebellious young Croats, was also to decisively influence the youth of Bosnia which carried out the assassination in Sarajevo.

The Party of Right: From Antithesis to Allegiance

The historian Charles Jelavich observed that until 1867 the majority of the political leaders in Croatia were loyal to the Habsburg state and sought a solution to Croat national desires within it; whilst after the 1867 *Ausgleich* they still wished to remain in the Monarchy, (notwithstanding Starčević's Party of Right), but only on the basis of equal status. 'In the period from 1867 to 1903', Jelavich pointed out, 'it became clear that this goal could not be attained.'[56] Indeed – not only was the hope for some kind of equal status being increasingly revealed as a quixotic Croat ideal, but the continuation of even the existing state of affairs was coming increasingly under threat. After 1875 Budapest accelerated its Magyarization drive in Croatia seeking, 'step by step', to curtail and eliminate instances of Croatian autonomy.[57] This process reached boiling point in 1883 when Croat language inscriptions on coats of arms (displayed on joint Croat-Hungarian financial administration buildings) were replaced by bi-lingual, Croat and Hungarian inscriptions – a clear violation of the 1868 Croat-Hungarian Compromise according to which the Croat language was the only official one. Widespread demonstrations and riots ensued, and in this anti-Magyar atmosphere Starčević's Party of Right made considerable advances.[58] Yet the seemingly revolutionary rhetoric of the Party of Right amounted in practice to a lot of hot air – to all intents and purposes it was always going to remain a directionless force under the lackadaisacal and indeed legitimist Ante Starčević.

In the wake of the unrest, 1883 was also the year when Count Károly (Dragutin) Khuen-Héderváry became (at only thirty-three) the new *Ban* of Croatia. His job was to crush opposition in the country and he carried this out brilliantly on behalf of Budapest over his next two decades of rule. In the words of one historian of the period: 'He corrupted those who were corrupt, he rewarded with appointments those who were loyal, and he destroyed the existence of those who could not be broken.'[59] The task of building compliant majorities in *Sabor*, the local parliament, was made easier given that the electoral franchise encompassed only two per cent of Croatia's population.

Croat historians invariably point out another factor facilitating Khuen-Héderváry's rule: the support extended to him by the country's Serb elites. This was certainly true and there was a reason for that. The Serbs were a self-confident, nationally conscious, increasingly prosperous and numerically large communinty – in 1880 their number in Croatia and Slavonia was almost half a million or 26.3 per cent of the population.[60] They were never likely to integrate themselves into the Croat body politic in the way many Croats wanted them to. In his study of Serbian politics in Croatia before the First World War, Nicholas Miller notes that after 1878 the Croat nationalists displayed 'total resistance to granting any recognition to Serbian institutions and cultural characteristics without previous acceptance by the Serbs of the concept that in Croatia the only 'political nation' was the Croatian'. As discussed in the prologue, the concept of the political nation was invented by the Hungarians in their drive after 1867 to assimilate the non-Hungarians. Rightly or wrongly, Miller writes, the Serbs 'feared the loss of their identity in the Croatian political nation'. In this situation Khuen-Héderváry easily bought them off with only minor concessions: in 1887 the use of the Serbian language and Cyrillic alphabet was legalized, and in 1888 Serbian Orthodox schools were authorized in Serbian-majority districts.[61] The hostility displayed against the Serbs by Starčević's Party of Right had of course also played a role. Seton-Watson commented: 'So long as the only serious party of opposition denied the very existence of the Serbs in the Triune Kingdom, the latter had no choice but to accept Count Khuen's friendly overtures.'[62] This was taking place at a time when the independent Kingdom of Serbia under Milan Obrenović was very much in the Austro-Hungarian sphere of influence, and so the Serbs in Croatia had an additional reason to rely on Vienna and Budapest.

But of course Khuen-Héderváry had not come to Croatia to please the Serbs, who he thought combined 'the worst characteristics of East and West'.[63] He was there to Magyarize the land, build Magyar schools, and force the Magyar language on the railways and in secondary education. The 1868 Compromise between Hungary and Croatia had clearly stipulated that the Croats were a separate 'political nation' and had a separate territory. Khuen-Héderváry emphasized, instead, the 'unity of Hungary'. In this he did not necessarily always enjoy the full support of Budapest, but he most certainly had Franz Joseph's backing: the Emperor showed his highest appreciation by awarding Khuen-Héderváry the Order of the Golden Fleece.[64] Already in the late 1880s, however, the great Hungarian statesman Count Albert Apponyi declared that 'the regime of Khuen-Héderváry represents a blemish on Hungary's honourable crest'.[65]

It was not only the skills of Khuen-Héderváry and the Serb collusion with him that benumbed politics in Croatia between 1883 and 1903. The passivity of the Croat political parties also played a role, and in particular the belief within Starčević's otherwise reinvigorated Party of Right that 'internal forces could not by themselves achieve anything', coupled with the expectation that some day a favourable international situation would allow the liberation of Croatia.[66] Bishop Strossmayer had already in 1873 withdrawn from active politics while his *Narodna stranka* had turned pro-Budapest. In 1880 a splinter group formed the *Neodvisna narodna stranka* (Independent People's Party) which continued Strossmayer's Yugoslav orientation, but limited the scope of its practical ambition to uniting all Croat lands within the Monarchy and, indeed, within just Hungary.[67] It and the Party of Right became the chief opposition forces in Croatia. The *Neodvisna narodna stranka* really represented only the free intellectuals while the Party of Right spoke for the broad masses.[68] And whereas the opposition associated with *Neodvisna narodna stranka* was considered moderate, the Party of Right was seen in Vienna and Budapest as the party of high treason – given Starčević's insistence of building a free Croatia on the ruins of the Habsburg Empire. From that point of view, as the Croat historian Josip Horvat noted, Starčević was the leader of a movement, not of a political party, his every speech being 'a prophecy about Austria's downfall'.[69]

Most interestingly, by the 1890s the Party of Right began to modify this approach of waiting for great events to happen – opting instead to abandon Starčević's fundamental hostility to the Dual Monarchy. Having grown into something resembling a petty bourgeois party of small business people, its previous radicalism had to many of its members become an anachronism. This most Croat of political groups was gradually taken over from an ailing and probably senile Starčević by Dr Josip Frank, a well-to-do provincial Jewish lawyer who had converted to Catholicism, but who spoke Croat quite badly. Frank was a man, Josip Horvat observed, prepared 'to walk over corpses' to realize his personal political ambitions.[70] As noted by other Croat historians, Frank's ideas 'had nothing to do with those of the Party of Right'. He had joined the strongest Croat party in order to secure for himself an institutional base, and managed not only to destroy its original ideology, but also simultaneously to convince the majority of its members that he still upheld those 'pure' ideas of Ante Starčević.[71] Frank believed that the Croats should treat the interests of the Habsburg dynasty as their own, that Croatia was important to the Monarchy as a springboard for Balkan expansion, and that the Croats, by helping the Monarchy to consolidate and increase its regional power, would be rewarded by some higher degree of autonomy.[72] Frank also meant to ingratiate himself in Vienna by painting Croatia as a citadel in the struggle against the Hungarians and the Serbs. The fact that the Party of Right was exhausted and demoralized by its struggle against Khuen-Héderváry assisted him to steer it into embracing a 'framework' attitude (*'okviraštvo'*) to the Monarchy: seeking, that is, to attain a Croat solution inside, not outside the framework of the Habsburg state. The idea was to turn the Party of Right into a moderate opposition party that could no longer be accused of high treason. From its previous position of highly principled resistance to any idea of accomodation with Budapest or Vienna, the Party of Right thus changed course in the direction of opportunist Habsburg loyalty.

The Croat politician Frano Supilo remarked that Frank was 'waiting for the solar system to turn upside down, so that the sun begins to orbit the earth and Croatia becomes free'.[73] Josip Horvat put it more bluntly when he wrote that Frank had 'placed Croat nationalism in the service of dynastic politics'.[74] The only area of policy where Frank was to continue the Starčević tradition was in that of animosity towards the Serbs. This made a lot of political sense for the Party of Right if it wished to espouse fidelity: the label of 'high treason [*Hochverrat*]' had to be got rid of by transferring it to the Serbs of Croatia-Slavonia. Certainly, there was now, in terms of their disposition towards the Habsburg state, little difference between the two chief opposition parties in Croatia, the *Neodvisna narodna stranka* and the Party of Right under Frank's de facto leadership. In 1894 these two managed to combine into what they somewhat optimistically called 'United Opposition' (the alliance collapsed almost as soon as it was established), producing a joint programme which constitutes an important signpost in the history of relations between the Croats and the Monarchy. For this is the document that has often been associated with the Croat idea of Trialism, especially as it spelled out the names of the territories which were to be united, as it stated, 'in one independent state body within the framework of the Habsburg Monarchy': Croatia, Slavonia, Dalmatia, Rijeka, Međumurje, Bosnia-Herzegovina and Istria. It also stipulated that the United Opposition would support with all its strength the endeavours of 'Slovene brothers' (previously Starčević's 'mountain Croats') to join the Slovene lands to this state body. On the question of joint affairs within the Monarchy, the programme insisted that the Kingdom of Croatia would as an entity in its own right join in the addressing of these on the basis of 'equality with the Kingdom of Hungary and His Majesty's other lands'.[75]

This, of course, was a blueprint for Great Croatia, but one loyal to the Habsburgs. The 1894 programme was formulated in such a way that it could be interpreted as either Dualist or Trialist, but the fact that the proposed Croat state affected territories in both Cis- and Trans-Leithania pointed towards a restructuring of the Monarchy in the Trialist sense. Certainly in Hungary the programme was seen both as Trialist and treasonable. In point of fact, as Josip Horvat opined in his major work on Croat politics, the 1894 programme looked 'fantastic' against the background of the harsh realities presented by the regime of Khuen-Héderváry. Horvat also emphasized that in their clash with Khuen-Héderváry in the 1890s the Croat political parties nevertheless remained united in their allegiance to the Dynasty – having forgotten the Habsburg lack of gratititude to *Ban* Jelačić after 1848-1849.[76] Thus the Trialist aspirations articulated by the Croats represented, potentially, a threat to Hungary, but not to the Habsburgs. Croat loyalty to Vienna, however, was now conditional, resting as it did on a big assumption: that Croatia would be territorially expanded and constitutionally elevated to a status of equality with Austria and Hungary.

Given that the non-Croat Slovene lands and the largely non-Croat Bosnia-Herzegovina were also included in the Trialist construct, the latter might also be seen as a project for a South Slav state. But Trialism was really no more than an honest, that is, openly Croat version of Gaj's Illyrian proposals or, indeed, of Strossmayer's and Rački's Yugoslavism, with the idea of a Great Croatia being fundamental to it. In the words of Robert Kann: 'Trialism meant, not the equal union of the southern Slav peoples, but the rule of the Croats.'[77] The historic significance of the 1894 document lies in the fact that it remained the official programme of moderate Croat opposition groups right up to the collapse of the Habsburg Empire.[78] It has been suggested that Starčević, by now very much in decline, accepted the programme because he no longer believed that Austria-Hungary was about to collapse.[79] Be that as it may, his party had been transformed beyond recognition – not least because he had been susceptible to Frank's courtship. It soon suffered the first of many cracks which it was to experience in the period leading up to 1914: in 1895 largely personal differences between Frank and senior figures in the Party of Right led him to found the breakaway Party of Pure Right (*Čista Stranka prava*). Starčević supported him in this, but *stari* (the old man) as his acolytes called him, died soon thereafter, in 1896, 'on the ruins of his life's work'.[80]

The Croat hostility towards Hungary reached a new peak in October 1895, on the occasion of Franz Joseph's visit to Zagreb, when Khuen-Héderváry imagined that he would be able to show the Emperor a placid, trouble-free Croatia. Instead, Croat students ostentatiously burned the Hungarian flag in the middle of the city. The political scene in Croatia began at this time to regroup and rejuvenate both its ranks and, with the embrace of Trialism, its outlook. Already in 1897 the *Neodvisna narodna stranka* (Independent People's Party) and the Party of Right (not to be confused with Frank's Party of Pure Right) formed an electoral coalition, and by early 1903 formally merged into a single party. Significantly, the assembly of this new grouping (which insisted that it represented a new party, though it actually called itself the Party of Right), upheld the 1894 Trialist programme.[81] The year 1903 proved quite significant for the Croats: in June Khuen-Héderváry finally left the country, having been appointed by Franz Joseph as the new Prime Minister of Hungary; by then, however, Croatia had already become engulfed in a new anti-Hungarian revolt.

The widespread unrest (often called *narodni pokret* – 'national movement') which began in March 1903 had a great deal to do with the fact that financial relations between Zagreb and Budapest had since 1889 been left unresolved at the expense of Croatia.[82] The long-standing financial exploitation of Croatia by Hungary was reflected, among other things, in the increasing emigration of Croats to the United States. Even someone like Iso Kršnjavi, Khuen-Héderváry's trusted Croat friend and political ally, admitted in his diary in May 1903 that the country was being 'economically ruined'.[83] Disturbances spread from Zagreb and Osijek to the countryside, necessitating Army intervention and, in some instances, martial law. The Croat peasantry, too, proved that it was nationally conscious. Croat politicians from Dalmatia and Istria (where there was much sympathy for the brethren in Croatia-Slavonia) requested an audience with Franz Joseph to voice their concern. Typically, the Emperor refused: he would not allow any meddling from the Austrian into the Hungarian half of the Monarchy.[84] Mirjana Gross wrote in this regard about a belief beginning to take shape among Croats to the effect that 'the Austrian and Hungarian decision-makers, irrespective of their mutual differences, would always jointly oppose the Croats, and that the national question had to be settled outside the Monarchy'.[85] Seton-Watson went as far as to assert that the incident with Franz Joseph's rebuff was 'a turning point in the relations of the Habsburg dynasty and the Southern Slavs'.[86] Wilhelm Schüssler, the respected constitutional expert on Austria-Hungary, also called the episode a 'turning point', and considered it to have been 'disastrous' for the relations between the House of Habsburg and the South Slavs: the dynasty was now seen by them as the 'hangman's assistant' – assistant, that is, to Hungary.[87]

The unrest petered out by June, but one of its important effects was that the Serbs of Croatia-Slavonia, themselves feeling economically squeezed, began to realize the advantages of cooperating with the Croats. The door was thus being opened for a Serbo-Croat *modus vivendi*. On the Croat side, even Frank's Party of Pure Right suspended its anti-Serbian campaign.[88] These developments were taking place at a time when relations between Austria and Hungary had already begun to enter what historians call 'the crisis of Dualism'. As was seen in the prologue, the confrontation between Vienna and Budapest was engineered by Ferenc Kossuth's Independence Party, reaching its climax in 1903-1906. The Hungarian attempt to loosen ties with Austria presented, possibly for the first time since the 1848 Revolution, a great opportunity for Croatia to re-define its own status.

Franz Ferdinand and Croat Trialism

It is perhaps no coincidence Franz Ferdinand voiced his support for a Trialist solution in 1903 – the year in which the Hungarians made their potentially Empire-wrecking demands for a de facto separate Hungarian Army. He was greatly relieved in September when his uncle Franz Joseph insisted, in his spirited Army order from Chlopy in Galicia, on the unity of his armed forces.[89] Shortly thereafter the Heir to the Throne met the Russian Tsar Nicholas II during the latter's visit to Mürzsteg, Styria (30 September-3 October). His anti-Hungarian outburst to the Tsar on that occasion has been noted in the previous chapter. Nicholas II recalled much later, in a 1912 conversation with George Buchanan, the British Ambassador to St Petersburg, some other interesting details from his Mürzsteg encounter with Franz Ferdinand, which Buchanan related in his report to the Foreign Office: 'At that particular moment the Archduke was much concerned with the subordinate position which Austria-Hungary occupied in the Triple Alliance, and had openly complained of the heavy hand with which Berlin kept Vienna in subjection to her. His idea then was to create a Slav kingdom within the Austro-Hungarian dominions and to substitute trialism for dualism ... Since the Bosnian crisis [in 1908-1909], His Majesty continued, the Archduke's views had apparently undergone a complete change: and he was now the devoted friend and admirer of the Emperor William. He was also credited with entertaining anything but friendly sentiments for Italy and of favouring a forward policy in the Balkans.' Just how sceptical the Russian Tsar was about Franz Ferdinand's future intentions is revealed in the concluding sentence of the relevant passage in Buchanan's report: 'So long as the Emperor Franz Joseph lived there was no likelihood of any step being taken by Austria-Hungary that would endanger the maintenance of peace: but when once the aged Emperor had passed away, it was impossible to say what might happen.'[90]

It is not clear from this report which 'Slav kingdom' Franz Ferdinand had intended to promote into the third pillar of the Empire. Given his earlier thundering against the Czechs (and specifically against the idea of a third, Czech unit within the Empire), however, he could only have meant a Slav unit led by the Croats. Mirjana Gross noted that Austria's Christian Social press, which frequently reflected Franz Ferdinand's views, had reported very favourably on the anti-Hungarian Croat movement earlier in the year.[91] It can safely be assumed that Franz Ferdinand had shared those sympathies for the Croats – if only because their wrath was aimed at Hungary. At any rate, his trusted adviser Max Vladimir Beck submitted to him a major memorandum in August, which he had coordinated closely with the Archduke beforehand. Written for the Emperor, it recommended support for non-Hungarian nationalities, 'especially' the Croats.[92] Undoubtedly, in the heated political atmosphere of 1903, Franz Ferdinand, completely obsessed as he was by the problem of Hungary, was looking both for short term allies and long term solutions. His explicit advocacy of Trialism in 1903, as reported by the Russian Tsar, is also, however, the only such recorded instance.

Moreover, it seems very unlikely that Franz Ferdinand had by 1903 thought through the implications of Trialism. Not that it really mattered at the time: it has been seen that his serious involvement in the politics of the Empire only began in 1905-1906. A keen observer of the political scene he may already have been, but until then his pronouncements were of a 'purely academic' character.[93] In any case, in 1905 the Hungarian crisis produced a most unexpected side effect which was to make the Heir to the Throne think twice about pushing for a South Slav kingdom: a pro-Budapest alliance of Croats and Serbs in Croatia. This, of course, represented a radical departure in the politics of the Monarchy's South Slavs. Croat historians call it *Novi kurs* (New Course), and it certainly abounded in political novelties. The immediate background was provided by the electoral victory of the Hungarian opposition Independence Party led by Kossuth at the beginning of 1905. Meeting in Rijeka (Fiume) on 3 October 1905, an all-Croat conference consisting of deputies from Croatia, Dalmatia and Istria passed a resolution which noted that the Kingdom of Hungary was engaged in a struggle to attain 'complete state independence', and that the Croat deputies considered this tendency 'justified' since 'every nation has the right to decide freely and independently on its being and fate'. Promising support for Hungary's fight for 'rights and liberties', the Croat deputies also stipulated their condition for such a favour: the reincorporation of Dalmatia into Croatia-Slavonia.[94]

Soon thereafter, on 17 October, Serb representatives from both Dalmatia and Croatia, passed their own resolution in Zadar (Zara), which also hailed the 'movement of the Magyar nation', and gave support to the Croat demand for the reincorporation of Dalmatia – provided that the Croats 'recognize, without fail, the equality of the Serb nation with the Croat nation'.[95] This stipulation suggested that not everything had yet started to click in Serbo-Croat relations, but there could be no doubting the fact that a massive breakthrough had been achieved. 'The Resolutions of Fiume and Zara', Seton-Watson wrote in 1911, 'mark the beginning of a new era in Southern Slav politics.'[96] The practical consequence of the New Course came rapidly with the birth of the so-called 'Croato-Serb Coalition' in December.

The idea of leaning on Kossuth's Independence Party was perhaps a strange choice given that its chauvinism regarding the Croats had more than matched that of the previous Liberal governments.[97] But the startling aspect of this fresh start in Croatian politics was its antagonism towards Vienna, behind which there also lurked a broader anti-Germanic spirit. The two leading initiators of the New Course, emanating from Starčević's Party of Right, were Frano Supilo and Ante Trumbić, both politicians from Dalmatia under the strong influence of liberal Italian circles forever fulminating about the danger of Germany, Germanism and the so-called '*Drang nach Osten*'.[98] There is a consensus among Croat historians that the New Course reflected a great fear both of Germany and of the Habsburg Monarchy which, despite Dualism, 'remained in essence a German state'.[99] The attempt by Austrian officialdom in Dalmatia, in 1903, to introduce German as the official language seemed to justify such fears. The fact that Russia, the traditional protector of the Slavs, had just been defeated by Japan also played a role in the effort to seek an understanding with Hungary.[100] Besides, many Croat politicians had simply lost all faith in Vienna. Supilo explained this to Josef Redlich in 1909: '[Austria] had never done anything for us and always maintained that the Magyars were preventing it. Very well, we thought, so let us go with the Magyars for a change.'[101]

The other striking novelty of the New Course was the sudden outburst of Serbo-Croat amity. As recently as September 1902, Zagreb had been the scene of major anti-Serb rioting, led by Frank's Party of Pure Right. The 'national movement' of 1903, however, had brought the two sides closer together. Sections of the educated Croat and Serb youth, moreover, had worked together since 1896 on the basis of a shared belief in the unity of the two nations. Svetozar Pribićević, one of the rising Serb politicians from Croatia and a determined advocate of the New Course, had emerged from their ranks. Increasingly, the Serbs of Croatia saw themselves and the Croats as living in a joint fatherland. Pribićević (who became the leader of the Serb Independent Party in 1903) 'accepted the validity of a Croatian state'. He and his followers thus acted as 'political Croats'.[102] Yet the general picture revealed that both the Croats and the Serbs were in fact split over the New Course. On the Croat side, the Party of Right sup-ported the new policy, but Frank's Party of Pure Right doggedly opposed it. Also opposing it was the newly-established (1904) *Hrvatska pučka seljačka stranka* (Croat People's Peasant Party) of Stjepan Radić, an Austro-Slavist and a kind of latter day Palacký who believed that 'Austria was a necessity not only for the European balance of power but also as a guarantor of the national interests of its small nations'.[103] The sceptics on the Serb side included the dignitaries of the Serbian Church in Austria-Hungary.[104] The Serbian Radical Party, which had basically always ignored Croat institu-tions such as *Sabor*, and had emphasized the separateness of Serbs, also had great difficulties in coming to terms with the Serbo-Croat accom-modation. Only Pribićević's Serb Independent Party, with its newspaper *Srbobran*, placed itself firmly behind the New Course.

But what exactly did the New Course stand for, apart from horse trading with Hungary? It seems clear that the maximalist aim was not some kind of Yugoslavia, but rather a Great Croatia that would have the support of the Serbs.[105] In 1905 Supilo wrote that 'the guarantee that we shall not be outsmarted lies ... in the force of our energy, in conjunction with the Serbs'.[106] Supilo himself was hardly known as a friend of the Serbs – on the contrary, his contemporaries called him 'Serb-devourer [*srbožder*]'.[107] Yet in 1907 he was to quote the Dalmatian-Croat patriot Lovro Monti: 'We can achieve a great deal together with the Serbs, only a little without them, and nothing if we oppose them.'[108] Nicholas Miller has advanced the view that the New Course was not meant to reconcile Croats and Serbs, being designed in fact to enable Croatia's progress: 'In other words, this was not a declaration of a new phase in a Yugoslav national movement, it was a Croatian political strategy.'[109] The Croat historian Dušan Bilandžić has desribed Supilo's and Trumbić's New Course strategy as an 'idea of genius', that is: 'how to turn, by adroit manoeuvre, enemies and opponents like the Magyars and their allies the Serbs, into allies who will uphold the Croat national programme'.[110] Indeed. Except that in the end the Magyars did not, despite initial enthusiasm in Ferenc Kossuth's circle, play the game on behalf of the Croats. As was seen in the prologue, the independence movement in Hungary collapsed in 1906, and nothing ever came of the projected Budapest-Zagreb alliance against Vienna. Already defunct because of the ensuing new accommodation between Vienna and Budapest, the New Course crashed completely in 1907 when the Hungar-ians (ironically Kossuth himself) introduced the so-called 'railway prag-matic', making the Hungarian language official on Croatia's railways. Typically, the Emperor supported this further step in the Magyarization of Croatia.[111]

Franz Ferdinand himself, moreover, was never going to remain indiffer-ent to what he must have experienced as being traitorous announcements by the New Course Croats and their Serb supporters in 1905. Rudolf Kiszling, the Archduke's semi-official biographer, wrote that the Fiume Resolution had surprised him 'most embarrassingly', for he had until then considered all Croats to be loyal to the Emperor (*kaisertreu*) as well as antagonistic to the Magyars. His Trialist plans, according to Kiszling, had as a result 'noticeably faded in so far as they had taken any firm shape in the first place'.[112] Moreover, the Croato-Serb Coalition survived despite the immediate setbacks in 1906-1907, and despite some defections (such as the speedy departure of the Serbian Radical Party). Led by Supilo, it did well enough in the elections of May 1906 and formed the government at the end of July. In fact it was to come out top in most of the remaining elections before the First World War.

The Fiume Resolution, oddly enough, could be seen as containing a Trialist logic. Kiszling maintained that it involved a demand for Trialism to be established.[113] The term had not actually been used in the Resolution. It talked, however, about the desirability of 'changing the relationships' between Croatia and Hungary, as well as with the 'western half of the Monarchy', in such a way that the Croat nation would secure an 'independent political, cultural, financial and general economic existence and development'.[114] Mirjana Gross took the view that the signatories of the Resolution were in the short term working for what she called 'sub-Dualism': a Croatia within Hungary, but enlarged with Dalmatia and enjoying the widest autonomy, while joined to Austria, together with Hungary, only through personal union. At the same time she drew attention to a contemporary Croat view that the Resolution could be understood as 'a step towards Trialism'.[115]

In any event Franz Ferdinand, as Kiszling explained, had probably not even gone beyond an initial contemplation of Trialism. And after the shock of Fiume he would certainly not be heard of again as a Trialist champion. The Hungarian historian József Galántai wrote that Franz Ferdinand gave up the policy of Trialism in autumn 1905 under the influence of the Fiume Resolution – but that it was a policy which was in any case 'clearly intended for a transitory tactical solution, expressly for crushing dualism'.[116] Just at a time when most political parties in Croatia, from the Party of Right (and its partners in the Croato-Serb Coalition) to Frank's Party of Pure Right, were on some kind of Trialist trajectory, the Archduke had set himself in the other direction, horrified as he was by the proposed alliance of the Croats with ultra-nationalism in Hungary. He had a name for them, meant to be derogatory: *Resolutionisten* (resolutionists). When he used it on one occasion in July 1907, in a letter to Brosch, it was in the context of his total opposition to the 'aspirations of the *Resolutionisten*' regarding Dalmatia. Those aspirations, he informed Brosch, had to be 'crushed [*vernichtet*]'.[117] His attitude regarding Dalmatia reflected a certain Austrian *raison d'état*.

Dalmatia mattered because of its coastline – not just a status symbol for a self-respecting great power, but a strategic asset. Vienna was never going to give it up – to Croatia or Hungary. And Franz Ferdinand was interested in it, according to Leopold von Chlumecky, not only on behalf of the navy, but also the merchant fleet, especially the Austrian Lloyd.[118] Drawing attention to the danger of Hungary's claim on Dalmatia, Brosch commented in the 1911 *Thronwechsel* Programme: 'Our future, however, lies at least partly on the water.'[119] On land, however, the future appeared less smooth. When Franz Ferdinand visited Dubrovnik in September 1906 he was given a frosty reception by the local populace who had to be urged: '*Rufen sie Živio!* [Shout long live!]'[120] In 1911 he demanded the reinforcement of the state police in Dalmatia and especially in Dubrovnik.[121] The Archduke, perhaps more than anyone, would as Emperor have kept Dalmatia firmly under Austrian control. And yet the return of Dalmatia to the Triune Kingdom was a major assumption behind the Croat embrace of Trialism. Thus the Croat idea of Trialism was incompatible with what the Archduke would ever have allowed.

Five years before he was killed Franz Ferdinand himself provided conclusive proof of his rejection of Trialism. The evidence is contained in a surviving draft letter to Kaiser Wilhelm II which has been dated retrospectively as having been written in July 1909. He wrote it in response to an earlier letter by the Kaiser in which the latter emphasized the Pan-Slav danger to an Austria-Hungary with significant nationalities problems inside the Empire. Wilhelm in his letter had betrayed his insensitivity to the Archduke's anti-Hungarian sentiment, trying to portray the Magyars as useful allies against the Slavs. This drew a predictable knee-jerk reaction from Franz Ferdinand: 'I too consider this Slav advancing and pushing ... most dangerous. Yet, where is the core of the evil? Who has been the teacher of all those elements that succeed by revolutionary pushing and excess? The Magyars.' He continued: 'A few years ago, who had heard anything of Young Czechs or radical anti-militaristic Czechs? Who had heard anything about a Slovene question, about Trialism, about Czech schools, about a Southern Slav question, about the Slavization of whole communities and regions, etc, etc.? ... The Slavs act that way only because they imitate the conduct of the Magyars and because they see how the Magyars get all they want by their shameless tactics.' There was only one remedy according to the Archduke, and that was 'to break the *predominance of the Magyars*' (emphasis in the original). 'Otherwise', he concluded, 'we shall with absolute certainty become a Slavonic empire, and Trialism, which would be a tragedy, is impending.'[122]

Quite apart from the issue of Trialism, this document alone makes nonsense of the Archduke's alleged enthusiasm for the Slavs. But how and why, if Franz Ferdinand considered the possibility of Trialism as a 'tragedy [*ein Ünglück*]', is the relevant historiography replete with assertions of his support for it? Two interpreters in particular are responsible for this state of affairs: Leopold von Chlumecky, and Georg Franz. Chlumecky had since 1906 been one of the editors of the *Österreichische Rundschau*, and a prominent member of the Archduke's circle of advisers. Josef Redlich saw him as a warmonger.[123] In 1929 he published his book on Franz Ferdinand which, because of its wealth of primary material (letters and diary entries), has been one of the most frequently consulted on the subject ever since. Himself a supporter of Trialism, he related that at a dinner with the Archduke, late in June 1911, he and Prince Friedrich Schwarzenberg, another Trialist, spoke in favour of Trialism (Chlumecky provided no details) and that Franz Ferdinand 'nodded approvingly' and 'did not dissent'.[124] Even Mirjana Gross, citing Chlumecky and otherwise sceptical about the Trialist credentials of Franz Ferdinand, described this moment as 'hesitancy' on his part.[125]

In fact there was no vacillation. Only weeks later, on 1 September, the Brosch-Lammasch *Thronwechsel* Programme (examined in the previous chapter) lay ready. Had Franz Ferdinand wanted the Programme to be sprinkled with a Trialist flavour even Brosch would have had to obey his wish. Instead, the head of the military chancellery used the *Thronwechsel* platform to mount a devastating attack on Trialism. To him, Trialism was merely a 'pretty good' means of scaring ('*Schreckenmittel*') the Hungarian chauvinists, without however possessing 'any real advantages for the Dynasty or for Austria.' Warning that the South Slavs were essentially 'unreliable politicians', he asked: 'Now who is going to guarantee that the Monarchy's third state, built out of Croatia, Bosnia and Herzegovina, Dalmatia, and the Austrian Littoral, to which perhaps also Carniola and a piece of Styria would have to be allocated, will always stick with Austria?' He reminded that the Croats, 'much vaunted' for their loyal convictions, had in fact made a common front with Kossuth through the Fiume Resolution. Brosch cautioned, finally, that the existing difficulties could be doubled if there were three governments, three parliaments and three delegations having to work with each other, particularly as the Slav part of the state might 'often find itself on the side of Hungary' against the interests of the Crown.[126]

Georg Franz was another of those responsible for perpetuating the myth of Franz Ferdinand's adherence to Trialism. In 1943 he produced what is still the standard work on the Archduke's plans for reforming the Habsburg Monarchy. In the section on Trialism, however, he claimed that as late as 1913 Franz Ferdinand entertained a 'Trialist plan' which he had elaborated to Colonel Margutti. Yet the latter did not, in his book cited by Georg Franz in this respect, write a single word about Trialism, or report that the Archduke said anything of the kind. Margutti merely related that

Franz Ferdinand had talked about his opposition to Dualism and about his idea of a 'Habsburg federal state', in which context this Habsburg mentioned 'autonomy' for the likes of the Czechs, the Croats, the Slovenes and the Serbs of Hungary.[127] It was seen in the previous chapter that such 'autonomy' was always meant by the Crown Prince to be no more than a minor concession to the heterogeneous nature of a state that he intended to rule autocratically. It is a mystery why Georg Franz, in attaching the label of Trialism to the Archduke's musings, should have in his influential work misinterpreted Margutti so glaringly.

In January 1910, during another bout of problems with Budapest, Franz Ferdinand himself suggested that the Hungarians should be threatened with '*Trialismus*' – clearly, he and Brosch were of the same mind regarding the practical uses of Trialism.[128] His other associates were, just like Brosch, also doubtful about the wisdom of creating a Great Croatia. Professor Paul Samassa argued in his noted work (1910) on the nationalities strife that 'delivering' the Croats to the Magyars would be against the interests of the joint state, but so would a Great Croatia formed by Trialism.[129] Brosch's successor Bardolff was categorical in his judgement of the Trialist idea: it was 'a very dangerous half-measure' in that it would open up the Slovene question with territorial implications for Austria itself in Carniola, Styria and Carinthia. Evidently, Trialism would have been too close for comfort to the Austrian Germans around Franz Ferdinand. Bardolff reasoned in much the same way as Brosch: 'No one could give a reassuring answer to the question whether the South Slavs would in all circumstances reliably stand by the Crown.'[130]

A certain uniformity of reasoning can in fact be discerned in the rejection of Trialism by members of Franz Ferdinand's circle. Theodor von Sosnosky, another of the Archduke's close associates (and his subsequent biographer), tackled the Trialist issue in his major work on the politics of the Habsburg Empire. Writing in 1913, just after the victories of Serbia in the two Balkan Wars, he saw an alarming prospect: if Croatia continued to be exposed to Magyar pressure it could easily happen that, instead of an Empire-friendly Great Croatian movement, a hostile Great Serbian movement would gain the upper hand among the South Slavs. Implementing Trialism to counter this threat, however, seemed to him highly problematic since this would entail territorial sacrifices on the part of Austria, 'above all Dalmatia', but also Carniola and Trieste. And it was 'not in the least so certain' that the third state (Sosnosky called it 'the Kingdom of Illyria') would be loyal to Austria. He too drew attention to the Fiume Resolution and to the possibility of a renewed anti-Austrian combination of the Magyars and South Slavs.[131]

Accordingly, the available evidence demonstrates unambiguously that the Archduke and some of his closest collaborators considered Trialism as being, at best, something of a two-edged sword: it could be used against Hungary, but it could also be turned against Austria. In any case, as Brosch explained to Chlumecky in November 1909, Franz Ferdinand saw the alliance with Germany as the 'pivot' of the Monarchy's policy, and it was a precondition of this orientation that any 'Slavonic ascendancy' be 'absolutely rejected'.[132] The fact that Sosnosky felt compelled to write on the issue of Trialism as late as 1913 merely reflected the continued endurance of the idea in Croatia. To Croats, especially after the annexation of Bosnia-Herzegovina in 1908, i.e., the annexation of lands which had always figured in the Trialist schemes of Croat politicians, Trialism was the 'only possible' legitimate national policy across the domestic political spectrum. It appealed equally to those who saw it as the realization of Great Croatia within the Monarchy, and to those who anticipated it as the first step in the process of joining together the Yugoslav lands inside and outside the Monarchy.[133] Franz Ferdinand, however, considered that the South Slav question could be solved only by factoring in Frank's Party of Pure Right, because it alone had 'an Austro-Slav' approach.[134] This view was certainly understandable on the part of the Archduke. For, as Mirjana Gross showed, Frank had by 1908 in fact abandoned genuine Trialism, satisfying himself with the idea of an enlarged Croatia as a separate admin-istrative unit − not a de facto independent state in the Monarchy along the lines of the Hungarian model. His party was acceptable to Franz Ferdinand's circle because it was the only one prepared to postpone all Croat demands.[135]

   Certainly, as the perception of the South Slav danger grew in Vienna, Croat politicians, and not just Frank, were cultivated by the Belvedere establishment with Trialist promises. This was all the more important because the Slovenes, too, were embracing Trialism in agreement with the Croats.[136] Ivan Šušteršič, the 'uncrowned King of Carniola' and since 1912 the *Landeshauptmann* of the province, was a Trialist and could not be ignored because of his loyalty to the Dynasty. And there was also the Serbian factor. The Serb historian Vladimir Dedijer argued that Franz Ferdinand would tolerate public airing of Trialist plans connected to his name because the idea of Trialism was to him 'a convenient tactical means not only in the conflict between the Magyars and the South Slavs, but also for fomenting the quarrel between the Croats and the Serbs'.[137] Franz Ferdinand was careful never to give an audience to Frank, but he main-tained a network of Croat contacts through Brosch.[138] He did his best to keep alive the hope in Croatia that he was going to be the saviour of the country. In 1909 he told Count Markus Bombelles, his Croat shooting companion: 'Tell your Croats ... I will put right, as soon as I ascend the throne, all the injustice that has befallen them.'[139] In 1911, Seton-Watson, in advocating 'moderate' Trialism, appeared to believe that the policy was favoured 'in the highest quarters'.[140] But all the hints and promises from Vienna failed to impress. The Croat politician Ivan Peršić recalled that the Belvedere had tried to entice the Croats with talk of Trialism, but that their contact with the Archduke's circle only served to undermine their faith in the future ruler.[141]

Frank himself died towards the end of 1911. In that year, after several splits and mergers with other groups, a new, reconsolidated Party of Right emerged. Its delegates, meeting in January 1912 in what they called the 'Trialist Assembly', agreed on a memorandum to be presented to Franz Joseph. This document demanded the 'unification of all Croat lands into a single, independent state body within the framework of the Monarchy'.[142] Of course nothing came of it. Count Ludwig Crenneville, a proponent of Great Austria and close to Franz Ferdinand's circle, reacted on the pages of the *Reichspost* with the reflection that 'in politics, as in human life in general, there are no attainable ideals, and therefore there is also no absolute freedom in Trialism, there exist only greater or lesser evils'. Mirjana Gross wrote that Crenneville thus announced to the Croats that they should give up any idea of attaining Croat statehood within the Monarchy.[143]

Sidney Fay is one of the famous historians of the Anglo-Saxon academic milieu who did his utmost to present Franz Ferdinand in a favourable light, portraying him in glowing terms especially with regard to the nationalities. In the second volume of his hugely influential work on the origins of the World War he wrote suggestively: 'Whether Franz Ferdinand would have actually attempted to replace Dualism by Trialism had he come to the throne, and whether he would have been successful, must remain among the great unanswered questions of history.'[144] But the question does not arise today and it should have been framed in a different way even then. It should have been obvious to Fay already in the late 1920s, when he was writing his book, that the Archduke would have been successful in implementing Trialism only if he had managed to break the resistance of Hungary. The first part of his question, whether Franz Ferdinand would actually have attempted a Trialist solution in the first place, was possibly not so easy to answer at the time because not all the relevant evidence had yet emerged. But even then prominent sceptics existed who had already produced important contributions to the subject. One of them was the German historian Hermann Wendel who wrote, in a celebrated booklet published in 1924, that Trialism was a vague notion and nowhere was it well-defined. 'But so far as it is possible to pass a judgement', Wendel continued, 'Trialism in Franz Ferdinand's sense was anything other than a fulfilment, it was nothing less than a new obstacle to South Slav unity, for the Heir to the Throne proceeded not from the peoples and their needs, but rather from the House of Habsburg and its interests.'[145]

Mirjana Gross, the great Croat historian who researched Trialism more than anyone else, considered that Franz Ferdinand and his circle were only able to have understanding for the political struggle of national movements when that struggle 'was aimed against their own enemies, and to the very modest extent where that struggle would not threaten the Habsburg German state with its centre in Vienna'. She wrote bitterly that the Belvedere circle 'knew nothing about Croatian culture', expecting the Croats to be the bearers of German culture in the Balkans. She concluded her seminal essay on this subject: 'Great Austria only allowed the Croats to be Austrians who speak Croat, and offered only hopes for some provincial autonomy.'[146] In 1929 Theodor von Sosnosky gave perhaps the best brief epitaph. Trialism for Franz Ferdinand was not much more than 'a fling, a flirt: his old, undying love, remained, however, Great Austria'.[147]

4

Bosnia-Herzegovina:
The Gates to the Orient

Occupation 1878

THE WISDOM OF the Austro-Hungarian occupation of Bosnia-Herzegovina in 1878 is easy to challenge in retrospect: as is well known, the move ended up in a world war and the downfall of the Habsburg Empire. 'In the end', wrote the American historian Bernadotte Schmitt, 'the seizure of these provinces against the wishes of the inhabitants was to prove as fatal to Austria-Hungary as the annexation of Alsace-Lorraine did to Germany.'[1] But even at the time some people were able to prognosticate the future with uncanny accuracy. The Russian Chancellor and Foreign Minister Prince Alexander Gorchakov reportedly declared at the Congress of Berlin that Bosnia would become 'Austria's grave'. Also in 1878, the Croat politician Ante Starčević stated in a speech that 'the Habsburgs will be even more sorry for the occupation of Bosnia and Herzegovina' than the Empress Maria Theresa had been for her role in the division of Poland.[2]

Prophecies apart, it should be noted that the general feeling of Austrian and Hungarian party-political elites in the 1870s, backed also by public opinion, was that adding even more Slavs to what was already a Slav-majority Monarchy would not be a good idea.[3] What, then, was so attractive to the decision makers in Vienna and Budapest about a couple of backward, unruly Balkan lands whose Christian population had only recently revolted against Turkish misrule, and whose Muslims also had a record of challenging central authority?

History books explain the expansion of Austria-Hungary to the southeast as a consequence of political and military factors. Politically, after the 1875 uprisings in Bosnia-Herzegovina, which provided the overture to the Great Eastern Crisis, this part of the Turkish Empire was up for grabs. In 1876, Serbia (and Montenegro) had gone to war against Turkey over Bosnia-Herzegovina. And the possibility that the Croats might join the

Serbs could never be excluded – General Stjepan Sarkotić, the last Governor of Bosnia-Herzegovina, noted that the Habsburg occupation had been intended to create 'a separating wedge' between them.[4] Fear of sinister Russian involvement also appears to have helped stiffen political resolve to prevent the creation of a great South Slav state led by Serbia. Historians regularly point out the strength of Pan-Slavist, anti-Austrian ideas in Russia, advanced at this time by General Rostislav Fadeyev and Nikolay Danilevsky – 'There was much talk [in Russia] about the road to Constantinople leading through Vienna.'[5] Militarily, Habsburg Dalmatia, a long, thin strip of coast, was seen as particularly vulnerable to the adjoining hinterland. And there were also considerations of Great Power status relating to prestige: after its defeats in Italy (1859) and against Prussia (1866), the Balkans represented the only area in which the Habsburg Empire could gain compensation through expansion.

Some authorities have questioned the military rationale. The Habsburg monarchy, Robert Kann wrote, 'was strong enough to take care of her interests in Dalmatia without acquisition of new territories'.[6] When the Austrian politician (and Balkan expert) Joseph Baernreither visited its leading city, Split, in 1898 he was appalled that there had still been no rail connection built to Bosnia: 'No place I visited on the Dalmatian coast showed more patently what an empty phrase was the declaration, made at the time of the occupation, that the extension of the coast line of the Monarchy made the possession of the hinterland necessary.'[7] That railway was never built. The Habsburg acquisitive thirst, however, was always strong. In February 1853 an Austrian army of 70,000, commanded by the tried and tested General Josip Jelačić, was assembled on the Croatian-Bosnian frontier. Its purpose was to occupy Bosnia-Herzegovina under the pretext of saving Montenegro from an ongoing Turkish invasion. In the end the Austrians did not move as Turkey settled matters with Montenegro, but the episode revealed a temptation to occupy the lands irrespective of any strategic considerations regarding Dalmatia.[8]

It is true, on the other hand, that concerns were subsequently voiced in military circles about Dalmatia's vulnerability. In 1856 Field Marshal Josef Radetzky wrote a memorandum to draw Franz Joseph's attention to this question. Admiral Wilhelm Tegetthoff voiced the same concern a decade later.[9] But there was always more to this. A detail invariably overlooked in Radetzky's memorandum is that he not only named Bosnia as a 'desirable' Austrian possession, but also Belgrade as the gateway to Serbia, a place from which Austria could effect a connection to the wider Balkans.[10] Count Gyula Andrássy, the Austro-Hungarian Foreign Minister whose efforts to negotiate the occupation of the provinces were crowned at the Congress of Berlin, thought along similar lines. Writing in August 1879 to Duke Wilhelm Württemberg, the then military governor of

Bosnia-Herzegovina, he explained the background to the occupation. One of the main aims was to 'open up' the East to the Habsburg Empire politically and physically; a union of Serbia and Montenegro therefore had to be prevented – their coming together in the form of a 'Slavonic great state' would have cut off Austria-Hungary from the East. The occupation thus prevented Bosnia from becoming a 'cul-de-sac' surrounded by, in Andrássy's view, 'hostile neighbours', which would have entailed adverse military and foreign trade consequences.[11] Friedrich Beck, the head of Franz Joseph's military chancellery, observed in March 1878 that Andrássy was already turning his eyes towards Salonika and Albania.[12]

To Andrássy, however, forestalling the emergence of a 'Slavonic great state' was as much about preserving the Empire as expanding it. He elaborated this point already in January 1875 when he argued that, were it not for Turkey maintaining the status quo in the Balkans, all the nationalistic aspirations of the small Balkan states 'would fall down on our heads'. If, he continued, Bosnia-Herzegovina should go to Serbia or Montenegro, or if a new state emerged there, Austria-Hungary would be 'ruined' and would itself assume the role of the 'Sick Man'.[13] Indeed, this premise about the danger of allowing the rise of a local rival, i.e., 'great Serbia', became the guiding principle of Austro-Hungarian Balkan policy all the way up to 1914.

Article 25 of the Treaty of Berlin, signed on 13 July, 1878, simply stated that the provinces 'shall be occupied and administered by Austria-Hungary'.[14] Andrássy's point about preventing Serbia and Montenegro from uniting referred, however, to a further provision in the Treaty, one which reserved for Austria-Hungary the right to keep garrisons and also to have military and commercial roads in the Sanjak of Novi Pazar – that part of the ancient *vilayet* of Bosnia separating Serbia from Montenegro.

Two weeks later, however, shortly after Austro-Hungarian troops began to move into Bosnia-Herzegovina at the end of July 1878, Andrássy emphasized the expansionist rather than the defensive aspect of this case when he sent Franz Joseph an elated message: 'Now the gates to the Orient are open to Your Majesty!'[15] He had previously argued that acquiring Bosnia would not be just a 'police measure' for controlling insurrections on the border: the real aim being to bring the western half of the Balkans 'permanently under our influence'.[16] And by March 1878 he had already had his eyes set on Salonika and Albania.[17]

Not that the Emperor required any convincing from Andrássy. His military advisors thought much along the same lines. And the thinking at the time was never limited to purely local considerations. General Friedrich von Beck, in charge of the Emperor's military chancellery, contemplated matters well beyond Bosnia-Herzegovina according to his biographer: 'The road from Vienna through Sarajevo to Salonika, predestined by Nature, had to be ... kept open.'[18] This soldier, it should perhaps be pointed out, was also a very close friend of the Emperor. The Austrian statesman Ernst Plener recalled that Beck was the 'chief exponent' of the military-political programme for Bosnia-Herzegovina.[19] Another of Franz Joseph's trusted generals, Anton Mollinary, who had been commanding in Zagreb since 1870, was in favour of blazing a trail right through the Balkans all the way to the Aegean Sea at Salonika.[20]

In fact there exists a fairly solid consensus among historians that Franz Joseph himself greatly encouraged the 1875 uprising in the provinces during a suspiciously long tour of Dalmatia (one lasting an entire month) in the early summer of that year. The man who had masterminded his visit was a friend of General Beck, Dalmatia's Governor General Gavrilo Rodić, a Serb with South Slav sympathies and therefore in the pro-change, occupationist/annexationist camp. According to an account heard by the English travel writer James Creagh, who was in southern Dalmatia later that summer, Franz Joseph had been presenting himself 'everywhere' as a Slav champion, claiming that his 'dearest wish' was to be the King of the Slavs. 'You want a king, my friends', he is supposed to have said, 'I will be your leader.'[21] On hearing of his presence, some Bosnians and Herzegovinians rushed to the border in an act of pilgrimage, carrying the Austrian imperial colours and falling on their knees.[22] No doubt they were Catholics, but it would be difficult to agree with speculation by Austrian historian Helmut Rumpler that Franz Joseph was in 1875 posturing on the borders of Bosnia-Herzegovina to show his support for the idea of a 'United Croatia'.[23] Any such design, whether Trialist or federalist, would have required a re-organization of the Empire which Budapest would have been bound to oppose. And after the Trialist fiasco with the Czechs in 1871, Franz Joseph had no intention of ever again upsetting the internal balance with Hungary established by the 1867 Compromise. What he wanted was Bosnia-Herzegovina for the Habsburgs, not for the Croats.

The Emperor's pronouncements on the subject of the occupation are quite revealing. He would 'never', he told the Austrian diplomat Alexander Hübner in May 1875, agree to the establishment of independent states in Bosnia-Herzegovina on the model of Serbia and Montenegro.[24] This matter really troubled him. In April 1876 he again talked to Hübner about it. 'If an independent Bosnia existed', he told him, 'Croatia and Dalmatia would soon leave us.' The Emperor further insisted that such a thing should never be acceded to since 'we have already lost enough territories'. And his Habsburg rapacity was unmistakeable. 'The western provinces of Turkey', he explained to Hübner, 'are through their geographical position in Austria's sphere of influence, not Russia's. What business does the Tsarist Empire have in Montenegro or in Serbia? ... Central Asia, that is its natural sphere. Do I perhaps control what the Russians get up to in Tashkent or Samarkand? They can do what they like there, I do not care, but Turkey's western lands, that is my business. This clandestine work [of Russia], these affectations of being a protector [of Balkan Slavs] disturb and hurt my feelings. It is unbearable.'[25] The Balkans, in other words, belonged to Franz Joseph according to his deepest conviction. The area was his imperial playground, and no one else's. It was his irritated sense of self-righteousness that led him to assert this principle in 1878 and, by occupying Bosnia-Herzegovina, unwittingly to open Europe's road to 1914. Far from marching into the provinces in order to carry out reforms, or to fulfil a 'civilizing mission' in the East, the occupation was in fact always intended as a sop to Habsburg imperial vanity. The summer of 1877 had already found Franz Joseph prepared to march into Bosnia-Herzegovina for fear that Serbia might get there first. The advice to Vienna from Berlin in March 1878 was that Austria-Hungary should take Serbia as well as Bosnia-Herzegovina.[26]

Austria-Hungary's manifest destiny in the 'Orient' did not get off to a good start. A great deal of imperial hubris was in evidence as the troops prepared to enter Bosnia-Herzegovina to occupy it in accordance with the mandate received at the Congress of Berlin. Andrássy is supposed to have said, famously, that 'a single company, headed by a musical band' would suffice to carry out the task.[27] The Muslim Slavs of Bosnia-Herzegovina, however, had different ideas. Betrayed by the Porte, they took matters into their own hands, overthrowing the Vizier and establishing makeshift governments in Sarajevo and Mostar. In Sarajevo ('this metropolis of fanaticism' as Arthur Evans described it following a visit at the time of the insurrection)[28] one Hadži Hafiz Lojo emerged as the leader of resistance. He printed a proclamation in the Serbian language, appealing to all to fight Austria since the latter, 'the greatest enemy of the people', would bring Western ways and destroy sacred domestic customs. He forced all the Serbs, Catholics and even Jews to wear traditional Bosnian costume. When, in Mostar, some Muslim leaders argued for a friendly reception of the Austrians, they were cut to pieces.[29] In that city Sharia law was introduced.[30]

The Catholics in Bosnia-Herzegovina predictably welcomed the occupation. At the time they were not known as Croats, an appellation that began to gain currency only after 1878. The Orthodox Serbs, the most nationally conscious group in the provinces, were glad to see the end of the Ottomans, but far from exhilarated about the prospect of Austro-Hungarian rule. Yet relatively few of them fought the invaders: those who were given arms mostly ran into woods and villages at the first opportunity.[31] On the other hand the Muslims, with their paramount social and economic position to protect, felt that they had every reason to fight, and put up a stubborn, heroic resistance. The act of occupation turned out to be 'little short of a disaster' for the Austro-Hungarians.[32] General Josip Filipović, the Croat who commanded the invasion force, started at the end of July 1878 with 72,000 troops. Against him was a badly organized and poorly led army of some 79,200 Muslims aided by 13,800 Turkish soldiers, mostly native Bosnians, who had disobeyed instructions from Istanbul. Nevertheless, Filipović had to call for reinforcements, and the number of troops eventually committed was 278,000, which amounted to 'more than a third of the Habsburg Monarchy's ground forces'.[33] In a campaign that lasted almost three months their losses were considerable: 5,198 casualties – killed, wounded and missing.[34] The Austro-Hungarian Army subsequently disgraced itself as it went on an orgy of pillaging, burning and arbitrary murder in the immediate aftermath of the campaign.[35]

When it was all over, General Filipović told the Austrian diplomat Ludwig Przibram: 'Now those gentlemen in Vienna should rack their brains about how to tackle the organization of Bosnia.'[36] In fact, just before the campaign started Filipović had received instructions from Franz Joseph's military chancellery which were to provide the basis of Austro-Hungarian Bosnian policy for the decades to come. Friends and enemies were carefully pinpointed. The General was to pay attention to the 'careful cultivation of the Catholic element which has proved itself reliable and friendly to the aspirations of the Monarchy'. With regard to the Muslims, he was to act protectively towards them, especially as they were 'the biggest land-owners'. Finally, Filipović was instructed to 'bring the Muslims into closer contact with the Catholics', and in particular he was to 'prevent the coming together or an alliance between the Muslim and the Orthodox population', the latter (i.e., the Serbs) requiring 'the strictest supervision given possible hostile aspirations with regard to the occupation'.[37]

The idea of supporting the Catholics, however, was never meant in Vienna, let alone in Budapest, to translate itself into fostering those Croat national ambitions which envisaged Bosnia-Herzegovina's incorporation into an enlarged Croat state. General Filipović, lionized at home in Croatia, deliberately misunderstood this. In the brief time that he controlled the provinces, he employed Croat officials and pursued 'an exclusively Croat course'. The Hungarians intervened in Vienna and he was promptly removed in December 1878.[39] Subsequent imperial bungling resulted relatively soon in the dreaded Muslim-Orthodox alliance becoming a reality. The new masters relied on their own administrative apparatus, stiff and insensitive to local customs. A lot of the imported bureaucrats brought to Bosnia 'nothing other than illustrious titles and a dark past.'[40] More tangibly, the taxation policy which they introduced caused widespread resentment. In 1880 merchants and craftsmen from Mostar complained to the Emperor that the taxes were now four times greater than during the Turkish period.[41] The Orthodox Serbs were in addition unhappy about educational discrimination and, in particular, about the unresolved land reform question.

The Muslims, having been defeated during the occupation and 'having lost their dominant position in the country, withdrew and could not come to terms with the new authority'.[42] For example, there lived in Sarajevo elderly Muslims who, after the 1878 occupation, never emerged from their houses again in order not to have to see the occupiers.[43] The Muslims were especially alarmed by the aggressive attitude of the Catholic Church which manifested itself in a well-publicized case of conversion to the Catholic faith involving a young Muslim woman. Mass emigration of Muslims, mostly to Turkey, began during this period. The last straw for both the Muslims and Orthodox was the introduction, in November 1881, of conscription making all males liable to serve in the Austro-Hungarian Army. Shortly afterward, in Herzegovina in January 1882, an insurrection began. Lacking sufficient external support, it never really spread beyond that region and came to an end in April. But 70,000 Austrian troops were required to put down this joint Muslim-Orthodox Serb revolt by some 5,000 insurgents, which proceeded under the unlikely slogan: 'For the Holy Cross and Mohammed's faith!'[44] The European press interpreted the insurrection as evidence of the inability of Austria-Hungary to carry out the mandate it had received at the Congress of Berlin.[45] Since Turkey had in 1878 been declared to be incapable of controlling anarchy in Bosnia-Herzegovina, it was certainly ironic that Austria-Hungary, the power entrusted with restoring order, appeared equally incompetent. Its Bosnian policies were severely criticized in the Delegations which had to vote money for the increased military commitment, and the suggestion was even made that its mandate should be given up.[46]

A withdrawal, however, was never on the cards. On the contrary, in 1882-1883 serious thought was given in Vienna to replacing the occupation of Bosnia-Herzegovina with annexation. Franz Joseph, it should be noted, had previously 'wanted to annex the provinces outright in full sovereignty'. In face of Turkish opposition at the Congress of Berlin, Andrássy had had to promise the Turks, at the last moment, that the occupation would be temporary and that the Sultan would retain sovereignty over the provinces.[47] However, the subsequent Convention of April 1879 between Austria-Hungary and Turkey dropped any reference to the temporary character of the occupation. And the Turkish sovereignty was in reality a sham: Austria-Hungary chose to interpret it solely in terms of religious matters and 'historic remembrances'.[48] Thus the Sultan's name could be mentioned in mosques on Fridays, but this was pretty much the extent of his sovereignty after 1878. On the other hand, as the 1882 revolt in Herzegovina showed, people could still believe that the Austro-Hungarian presence was of a transitory nature. So for the Monarchy to move the opposite way, from occupation to annexation, was always going to be tricky: unless all the relevant powers agreed, annexing the provinces would entail a breach of the Treaty of Berlin; and, perhaps more importantly, a consensus between Vienna and Budapest would have to be achieved beforehand.

The moving force behind the annexation drive was the would-be imperial superintendent of the Balkans: Franz Joseph. It was no coincidence that in 1882, when the question was aired, he appointed Benjámin Kállay as the Joint Finance Minister. The Joint Finance Ministry had been in charge of administering Bosnia-Herzegovina since March 1879, and Kállay, previously in the Foreign Ministry, was an enthusiastic supporter of annexation. In May 1882 he wrote a memorandum on Bosnia-Herzegovina in which he advocated the annexation of the land as a 'Reichsland'. Franz Joseph then promptly called a meeting of the Ministerial Council to discuss the matter (held on 3 June), but this got nowhere in the light of the difficulties posed by the Hungarian Prime Minister Kálmán Tisza (not to be confused with his son István) who, along with most of the Hungarian political elite, disliked anything smacking of Habsburg centralism. He was therefore keen to shift Bosnian affairs away from the joint institutions of the Monarchy (the Delegations), and on to the separate Hungarian and Austrian parliaments. By the next day, however, Kállay was named as Joint Finance Minister.[49] He was to rule Bosnia for the next twenty years, until his death in 1903.

In October 1882 Franz Joseph renewed his push for an annexation.[50] Very soon, however, Tisza managed to adjourn the project once again. In a confidential memorandum of January 1883 he argued that the only acceptable way to incorporate Bosnia-Herzegovina into the Empire would be by dividing the lands between Hungary and Austria. To annex and leave them as a separate unit would go against the Dualist configuration of the Empire; the danger thus existed that a third, Slavonic, entity would become attractive to other Slavonic lands like Dalmatia and Croatia which would, in turn, bring about Trialism and the Slavicization of Austria-Hungary, making it vulnerable to Pan-Slavic tendencies.[51] This memorandum by the Hungarian Prime Minister underlined just how strongly Budapest felt about the perceived menace of the South Slavs and Trialism. In Austria, on the other hand, there was no enthusiasm for his proposal to divide Bosnia-Herzegovina.[52] There was to be another annexation review in 1896 (when Turkey appeared to be tottering in the wake of the Cretan revolt), but the provinces were not finally annexed until 1908 – thirty years after the occupation and at the cost of creating a major European crisis.

The Uncrowned King of Bosnia: Benjámin von Kállay

Franz Ferdinand regularly referred to Benjámin Kállay as a 'Hun' and sometimes as 'the coarse Gypsy Baron'.[53] The historical profession tends to call him 'the uncrowned King of Bosnia'. Although himself a Hungarian who shared Tisza's fear of the Slavs, Kállay did not believe that Bosnia-

Herzegovina needed to be divided in order that its emergence as a nucleus of Trialism be prevented – provided he could implement his policies instead.[54] One of his policies in particular – the push to create a 'Bosnian' nation – has become famous in South Slav historiography as a political and indeed intellectual fiasco. Both Serb and Croat historians have censured him at length because of this experiment in nation building in a country claimed equally by Serbia and Croatia, but both nations' academics have conceded that he possessed administrative genius and achieved substantial economic and social progress in Bosnia-Herzegovina.[55] Certainly, few in Austria-Hungary were more qualified than Kállay to take charge of the newly-occupied provinces. First and foremost a scholar, he had learned the Serbian language early on (his mother was of Serbian descent) and authored a well-researched and well-received history of the Serbian nation.[56] In 1868, aged only twenty-eight, he became Austria-Hungary's Consul-General in Belgrade, a post which he held until 1875, leaving a very detailed diary from that period.[57] In 1872, at the request of his friend Andrássy, Kállay undertook a study trip to acquaint himself with conditions in Bosnia-Herzegovina. A 'calculating' personality, he worked relentlessly to achieve his aims.[58] 'Doing nothing' he said, 'is the worst thing in politics.'[59] Historians agree that his career ambition was to become Foreign Minister. To his contemporaries, the cerebral Kállay was known as 'the heartless man'.[60]

Kállay's guiding principle in Bosnia-Herzegovina was: 'here we are, and here we shall stay.'[61] A certain 'Orientalist' philosophy defined his approach. In 1892 he spoke about the country he ruled as being largely 'oriental' and explained the difference between 'Orientalism and Westernism [*Orientalismus und Okzidentalismus*]'. The chief characteristic of the East in his view was that it was riven by 'individualism', resulting in petty particularisms and the inability to build something bigger, stronger and more coherent. The spirit of the West, by contrast, was the spirit of old Rome: the idea of the state as wielding total power, 'without consideration of the nationalities' or the 'differences of outlook'. Kállay therefore saw it as his task in Bosnia-Herzegovina to 'awaken' this spirit of the West, that is, this strong feeling of statehood, or – at the very least – to prevent the emergence of 'destructive, corrosive particularism'.[62]

The theoretical foundations for this line of thinking – such as they were – were laid out by Kállay in his 1883 lecture to the Hungarian Academy entitled 'Hungary on the Frontiers of the East and West'. It is noteworthy that he insisted here on the 'political nation' as the chief legacy (along with the rule of law) of the Roman, that is Western spirit. To Kállay even the Greeks were ruled by the spirit of the East, so that the Byzantine Empire, although it had wished to continue the traditions of Rome, had therefore been unable to build a 'political nation' – their Empire had been 'based on a big fallacy'.[63] Of course, the concept of a political nation as some kind of supranational singularity was in fact a Hungarian invention designed to assimilate non-Magyars – in Europe, only the Hungarians, imitated admittedly by the nationalist Croats, talked seriously about it. And Kállay saw Hungary, initially of the East but permeated thoroughly by the spirit of the West, as uniquely qualified to carry out this civilizing mission in the East. 'Our fatherland', he wrote, 'joins up two worlds.'[64]

Needless to say, as far as Kállay was concerned, the abhorrent Eastern particularism which he talked about was to be equated in Bosnia-Herzegovina with the existing Serb and, increasingly, Croat nationalism. The one nationalism which did not exist in the provinces was Bosnian nationalism – or rather the 'Bosnian political nation', a nation that would of course be loyal to the Habsburg Monarchy. And this Kállay intended to put right. His first task, however, was to counter and stifle any local nationalist pretensions. Pre-eminent among these was the perceived Serbian danger. As Robin Okey noted, the Provincial Government was 'paranoid about pan-Serbian nationalism'.[65] But the Croat ambition to include Bosnia-Herzegovina into a Great Croatia was also a major concern. The Muslims, almost by definition, were not seen as representing a threat precisely because they traditionally saw themseves as a religious rather than a national group. Turkey, their natural patron, was increasingly weak. If a meaningful threat associated with the Muslims existed during Kállay's rule, it was that they could succumb to Croat or Serb suggestions that they were in reality Croats or Serbs. If this happened, one or the other group would become the absolute majority. This is clear from the census carried out in Bosnia-Herzegovina in 1879, which revealed the following figures: 496,485 Orthodox (42.88%); 209,391 Catholic (18.08%); and 448,613 Muslim (38.75%).[66]

Kállay clearly recognized that the Serbs constituted the biggest menace. This was reflected in the fact that the first civilian governor (*Ziviladlatus*) for the provinces (appointed in 1882) was Baron Fedor Nikolić, a Serb from Hungary. Although there was also the parallel post of the *Landeschef* (governor), held invariably by a military person who was nominally in overall charge on the ground, the office of the civilian governor proved in practice to be the more important one. Whereas the *Landeschef* was theoretically answerable to the joint Austro-Hungarian government (i.e., the Joint Finance Ministry), as a soldier he was also directly subordinated to the Joint War Ministry. Until the arrival of General Oskar Potiorek in 1911, however, these soldiers really played a secondary role. Kállay, sitting in his Joint Finance Ministry in Vienna (though he did also regularly visit and tour the provinces) conducted most of the business through his *Ziviladlatus* in Sarajevo and the governmental infrastructure that had been set up there, which consisted of three departments: administrative, judicial and financial. This was the *Landesregierung*, the Provincial Government.

Kállay's manoeuvre with Nikolić, however, was not a success, and the latter was removed in 1886. Kállay had hoped that his appointment of a Serb, at a time when official Serbia under Milan Obrenović was dutifully toeing the Austro-Hungarian line, would go some way towards winning the loyalty of the Serbian elites in Bosnia-Herzegovina. These, however, remained sceptical. And just how Serbian Nikolić felt himself to be was demonstrated in November 1882 when he suggested to Kállay settling areas in Herzegovina close to Montenegro with colonists from Tyrol – because the Tyroleans would be a 'good border force'.[67]

The strict control over Serbian schools, the petty persecutions of Serbian teachers, the increasing Catholic propaganda, and the resignation in 1885 of the Serbian Metropolitan Sava Kosanović – all combined to produce disenchantment amongst the Serbs.[68] The authorities in Sarajevo had prevented Kosanović from publicly responding to attacks by Catholic bishops, and had in fact demanded of him that he withdraw his complaints against the proselytizing activities of the Catholic Church.[69] The Kosanović affair was interesting in that it showed how the policy of building local religious leaders into props of the regime could easily back-fire. In his major study of the Kállay administration, Tomislav Kraljačić argued that a main Austro-Hungarian aim in Bosnia-Herzegovina was 'the elimination of the Orthodox Church as a factor of the Serbian people's integration around Serbia'.[70] On paper, this task should have been relatively easy: in 1880 Vienna managed, in a convention concluded with the Patriarchate in Constantinople, to obtain control over appointing Orthodox bishops in Bosnia-Herzegovina. Thus Kosanović was in 1881 the choice of the occupying power, but he nevertheless dared to defend Serbian Orthodoxy, and quite energetically at times. When Kállay began a search for his successor he wrote that the candidate should be 'impervious to Great Serbian as well as to Russian influences'.[71]

The Agrarian Question

The Bosnian Serbs' chief grievance, however, concerned the agrarian question. This was a matter to which the provinces' new authorities had been expected to pay very considerable attention. After all, the great revolt of 1875 had begun in consequence of the unresolved land reform issues – a problem that Austria-Hungary exploited at the time to criticize the Turkish authorities and indeed used as a justification to occupy and administer Bosnia-Herzegovina. The Treaty of Berlin did not impose an obligation on the Monarchy to solve the agrarian question, but its moral obligation was clearly there. What the new occupying power then encountered in the countryside in the relations between land owners and peasants was something close to the feudal system of serfdom: some 85,000

Christian peasant families (60,000 Orthodox and 25,000 Catholic) were cultivating the land of some 7,000 Muslim Slav families. The peasants were known as *kmets* and the landowners as *begs* and *agas* – big and small respectively, a kind of Muslim aristocracy. There were in addition some 77,000 free peasant families, mostly Muslim Slav.[72] Generally, the *kmet* peasants would pay one third of the annual harvest to the landlords – on top of the one tenth to the state. The Ottomans had last regulated these arrangements in 1859. Given the history of the landlords' abuse of the system and the resultant peasant revolts, the unresolved agrarian question in Bosnia-Herzegovina clearly represented an economic, social and political problem of the first magnitude.

As early as 1879 an Austrian administrator demanded a solution to the agrarian question, warning that, otherwise, 'these people will have to be controlled with bayonets and they will never be good subjects'.[73] Yet it was precisely this problem which the Austro-Hungarian rulers chose not to tackle – the *kmet* system was still in place right up to 1918. In his study of the industrialization of Bosnia-Herzegovina, Peter Sugar drew attention to the fact that Serbia (and Bulgaria) had already introduced radical changes in land tenure, involving expropriation and redistribution – something that was well known to the unfortunate Bosnian *kmets*, in whose provinces instead, as Sugar explains, 'the government tried to secure the allegiance of the Muslims, the landowning element. It was obvious that forcible land reform would alienate these people and so no changes were made.'[74] Similarly, Robin Okey has written that 'Kállay saw a role for the Muslim begs as a support of the regime and feared they could not survive to play it if their landed privileges were removed.'[75] There was thus a definite political interest in this policy, although it would also be true to say that, as a Hungarian aristocrat, Kállay had a particularly soft spot for the conservative Muslim *begs*. Certainly, the Magyar gentry as a whole took a lively interest in the Bosnian Muslim upper crust: the more prominent *begs* were often entertained in Budapest.[76]

Perhaps the best moment for dealing with the agrarian question would have been in the immediate aftermath of the occupation: the legal order had in any case been shaken up since 1875 and the Muslim landowners would have been unlikely to offer much resistance.[77] However, this would have required the Austro-Hungarian authorities to finance the reform, as the Bosnian *kmets* did not have the money to buy out the land from their landlords. On the other hand Vienna and Budapest were never going to be so generous even if Kállay had wanted to implement compulsory expropriation. The law of February 1880 stipulated that Bosnia-Herzegovina was to be financially self-sufficient. The exceptions related to expenditure on matters of military-strategic concern such as railways. But the gendarmerie and even the upkeep of the occupying garrisons was to be financed by

Bosnia-Herzegovina.[78] Thus the privilege of having Austria-Hungary carry out its civilizing mission in the east had to be paid for, on the whole, by the local inhabitants.

In any case, given Kállay's anticipation of adverse political consequences, a radical land reform in Bosnia-Herzegovina was never on the cards. He would sometimes try to find excuses for his inaction, for example when he told visiting Belgian scholar Émile de Laveleye that the land question in Ireland showed just how difficult these problems were.[79] But in 1892 the Joint Finance Minister explained publicly his reason for sustaining the old privileges of the Muslim Slav gentry. Addressing the Austrian Delegation, he admitted that he would not be in favour of enforced expropriation even if he had the financial means: 'I say quite openly that I attach the greatest importance to ensuring the lasting survival of the Mohammedan *begs* and *agas*, this state-building element for the land and the people.'[80] What he did not say was that an agrarian reform, stripping the Muslims of their land and income, would have at the same time strengthened the Serbs and the Croats – but particularly the Serbs. Privately, the administrator of Bosnia-Herzegovina was in the habit of raging against the Serbs. 'Le serbisme', he told Leopold von Chlumecky, 'voila l'ennemi.'[81]

Kállay's answer to the agrarian issue was the ineffective voluntary approach: *kmets* and landlords should settle matters among themselves. As a result, during his twenty years of rule the number of *kmets* able to acquire land under their cultivation, in whole or in part, totalled just 17,704; and many of these were in fact ruined as a result because they were subsequently unable to repay the loans they had taken out to buy the land.[82] The Bosnian Serb historian Tomislav Kraljačić pointed out that, politically, Kállay's policy cost him the support of the peasants, while, economically, the agricultural sector suffered, hindering the overall development of capitalism in Bosnia-Herzegovina. Kraljačić also argued that the voluntary expropriation favoured by Kállay was a tactical side-tracking of the issue, which led to the *kmets* exhausting themselves in litigation processes: between 1880 and 1904 there were as many as 200,543 court cases between *kmets* and landlords.[83]

But the main problem for the *kmets* was the taxation system which in many ways made their life even more difficult than during the Turkish period. Following the Habsburg occupation the one-tenth payable to the state had to be paid for with money – previously it had been paid with the *kmets'* produce. Worse, and in another departure from the Turkish practice, the amount would be decided in advance of the actual harvest – by the *desetar* (from *deset*, ten), a kind of auditor who assessed the tax on behalf of the local government. The *desetar* would get a percentage of the assessed sum as his reward, so that unrealistically high assessments were commonplace. The scope for corruption was in fact even greater because the auditors would be bribed by *begs* and *agas* who, in claiming their third of the produce, naturally wished to maximize it. Critically, the one-third payable to the landowners was calculated on the basis of the amount left over once the one-tenth was substracted. Thus the *kmet* was at a double disadvantage. No surprise, then, that *kmets* in their villages might frequently be found burning straw effigies of their auditors.[84] In 1892 Tómaš Masaryk, the Young Czech deputy who had visited Bosnia-Herzegovina, lambasted this state of affairs in a speech about the agrarian policy made to his fellows in the Austrian Delegation. He also observed that the *kmets* tended not to complain to the authorities – because, if their complaints were rejected, they would have to bear the costs incurred by the work of the investigating commissions.[85]

Ferdo Hauptmann, one of Yugoslavia's leading experts on the agrarian question in Bosnia-Herzegovina, was savage in his criticism of Austria-Hungary's policy which, as he put it, 'administratively conserved' the position of *begs* and *agas* despite this being 'politically anachronistic, socially discarded and economically harmful'. In Hauptmann's view, Austria-Hungary had created an absurd situation, in which the occupation brought into play on the one hand a free competition of economic forces, whilst on the other hand social relations in the agrarian sector, the source of income for the vast majority, underwent 'petrifaction'. He also drew attention to the authorities' unwillingness to at least intervene within the existing system which allowed the fragmentation of estates: *kmets* were hereditary tenants who worked as families, and as those families grew, the land which they cultivated would be divided into increasingly smaller and uneconomic units, entailing their 'pauperization'. This meant that, even when the *kmets* somehow managed to buy the land, its small size would condemn them to economic destitution. The failure of the administration to regulate these matters by setting a minimum land area is seen by Hauptmann as an omission even greater than that of not abolishing the *kmet* system itself.[86]

Recent Western writing on the subject has generally glossed over this rather embarrassing chapter of Austro-Hungarian rule in Bosnia-Herzegovina. Thus Noel Malcolm cites the observation made by the British historian William Miller (who had visited Bosnia in the 1890s) that 'the Bosnian *kmet* is 'better off than the Dalmatian or Sicilian peasant' – as if the Dalmatians and Sicilians had known anything other than deep poverty.[87] Essentially the same parallel is produced by Christopher Clark independently (since it does not refer to either Malcolm or Miller) when he writes about 'Serbian *kmets*' who were 'probably more prosperous than their counterparts in Dalmatia or southern Italy.'[88] Such, it seems, is the state of the latest research in the West on these matters. In contrast, Peter Sugar's authoritative 1963 study concluded that the agrarian question 'became the main cause for the Habsburg Empire's failure in Bosnia-Hercegovina'.[89]

Contemporaries, certainly, knew the score: in 1912 an Austrian observer wrote that the agriculture of Serbia, compared with that of Bosnia-Herzegovina, was thirty years ahead.[90] The Bosnian village, the Croat historian Ante Malbaša noted in 1940, faced misery and neglect, while the Bosnian *kmet* became, in time, 'the fiercest enemy of the Austro-Hungarian Monarchy'. Malbaša even went so far as to suggest that the 1914 Sarajevo assassination of Franz Ferdinand was itself 'in the last analysis' a consequence of Kállay's agrarian policy.[91] Certainly, as will be seen in chapter eleven, the assassin Gavrilo Princip spoke at his trial of his outrage regarding the impoverished state of the peasants – and stated that this was the reason why he sought revenge by killing the Archduke.

Contriving the Bosnian Nation

What exactly, then, predicated Kállay's indulgent policy towards the Bosnian Muslim gentry? The wish to prevent the Bosnian Serbs and Croats being strengthened by a liberation of their *kmets* is only part of the answer. The other part has to do with the Minister's scheme to stimulate, in the interests of the Empire, something called the 'Bosnian nation'. His push in this direction is understandable. As a Hungarian, Kállay was perfectly aware of Croat nationalist ambitions regarding Bosnia-Herzegovina and the attendant threat to the Dualist arrangement of the Monarchy; as an Austro-Hungarian Minister, and a former Consul General in Belgrade, he was equally mindful of Serbian aspirations in the provinces. The Muslims, it was true, were emotionally attached to Turkey. But the historian in Kállay had seen just about enough ambiguity in Bosnia's late medieval history to be able to link the *begs* and *agas* with that Christian nobility which had converted to Islam after the fall of Bosnia in the 15th century. The prevalent belief among scholars in Kállay's time was that, before the Turkish conquest, the then Christian Bosnian aristocracy had held on to a Manichean set of beliefs, considered heretical by the Catholic and Orthodox churches alike – and been persecuted for so doing. The adherents to that faith were described as *Bogumils* (dear to God). 'Not Islam so much', Robin Okey has written, 'as the independent spirit of a Bogumil aristocratic elite was what Kállay wished to support.'[92]

In other words, if Bosnia's Muslims, led by their *begs* and *agas*, could be persuaded that they belonged to a nation – the Bosnian nation that was separate from the Catholic Croats and Orthodox Serbs – then the interests of the Monarchy would be served rather nicely. Incidentally, according to Okey, Kállay had even repeatedly expressed the hope that the Muslims would at some distant point in future return to Christianity and, moreover, join the Catholic rather than Orthodox confession.[93]

His logic of nationising from above, moreover, extended to the Serbs and Croats of Bosnia-Herzegovina: the projected nation was meant to be inter-confessional. In 1892 Joseph Baernreither noted that Kállay had been 'obstinately set in his conviction' that there existed in Bosnia 'only Bosnians'.[94] This was rather odd coming from a man who, in his much praised *History of the Serbs* (1878), explicitly maintained that the territory of Bosnia-Herzegovina (with the exception of a small part in the north-west known as 'Turkish Croatia') had since the arrival of the Serbs in the Balkans to 'these days [*heutzutage*]' – been inhabited by the Serbs them-selves.[95] That, however, was the voice of Kállay the historian rather than Kállay the administrator. Moreover, there was also Kállay the Hungarian, who saw the opportunity to introduce the Hungarian concept of the 'political nation' into Bosnian affairs. As Tomislav Kraljačić argued, circumstances in Hungary and Bosnia-Herzegovina were quite different, but the problem was essentially the same: national movements. In Hungary, Magyarization was a policy aimed at attaining a 'Hungarian polit-ical nation'. In Bosnia-Herzegovina Kállay proceeded from the Hungarian model by attempting to create a Bosnian political nation.[96] The Croat historian Zoran Grijak, while noting that the idea was to suppress the development of Croat and Serb national consciousness, is perhaps right in describing Kállay's design as 'some kind of a melting pot'.[97] As will be seen, however, not even the Muslims were ready to be thrown into the Minister's melting pot.

Luka Đaković, another Croat historian, cited a Hungarian document to argue that Kállay had an underlying reason to court the Muslims: Bosnia was 'the starting point for further penetration of the Monarchy in the Balkans once the Eastern Question is fully opened', in which case it would be important to be able to count on 'the sympathies of the Muslim popu-lation in that region'.[98]

But Kállay was also guided by existing political considerations, and they related primarily to Serbia. In 1889 the Austrophile King Milan Obrenović abdicated. Now, after many years, the crowds on the streets of Belgrade could finally shout: 'Long live Russia' and 'Down with Austria'.[99] The Radical Party came into power, implementing the liberal press law granted in the 1888 Constitution – suddenly, the Serbian papers were having a field day as they began to mount attacks on Austria-Hungary and especially its rule in Bosnia-Herzegovina. To Kállay, the challenge associated with the changes in Serbia appeared very serious: in 1891, in a note to Count Gustav Kálnoky, the Austro-Hungarian Foreign Minister, he complained about the increasingly loud clarion call that could be heard in and about Bosnia-Herzegovina: that it contained only Serbs – that the Catholics and Mohammedans were merely Serbs who had accepted another religion and would sooner or later wake up remembering their genuine national identity.[100] Kállay's response was to come up with a counter-narrative, namely that Bosnia's Muslims were a nation, not just a confession. What he now had to do was to convince them.

To achieve this, systematic work was required, and Kállay obliged, beginning in mid-1891, with the founding of a weekly paper *Bošnjak* (The Bosniac), edited and supposedly 'owned' by the pro-Austrian Mehmed-beg Kapetanović Ljubušak. This enterprise was in fact financed by the *Landesregierung*. The paper's view of the nationalities question in Bosnia-Herzegovina could soon be deduced from a poem it published in its second issue, which maintained that there had been no Serbs or Croats in the country even fifteen years earlier.[101] Kapetanović was of the view that the Muslim gentry were the guardians of the state tradition in Bosnia-Herzegovina – the element of continuity with the *Bogumils* of the medieval period – and that they should therefore play the leading role in the future development of the country. And that, just as they had faithfully served the Sultan, they would be equally loyal to the Habsburgs.[102] This position harmonised perfectly with Kállay's own.

Apart from a contrasting history – which the *Bogumil* phenomenon appeared to provide – the projected Bosnian nation would, of course, need some other important badges of identity: a language, a coat of arms and a flag. Kállay generously provided all these. In 1884 Professor Franc Vuletić was tasked by the *Landesregierung* to write a grammar of the local language. However, Vuletić wanted to know beforehand what the language would be called and offered several proposals: 'Croato-Serbian'; 'Serbo-Croatian'; 'Croatian or Serbian'; and 'Serbian or Croatian'. The Joint Finance Ministry rejected all these and accepted the suggestion of the *Landesregierung* that the book should carry the title 'Grammar of the Bosnian Language'. Faced with this title, Vuletić then agreed to write it on condition of strict anonymity.[103] The issues of the coat of arms and the flag were also settled by Kállay although heraldic experts had already established that there was a great deal of uncertainty about the Bosnian coat of arms, and that a Bosnian flag as such did not really exist. In 1889 Kállay pushed through the decision to adopt a red and yellow flag, and also the coat of arms which formerly belonged to the province of Rama (named after a tiny river in Herzegovina), which still existed under the Hungarian Crown, so symbolizing Hungary's rather tenuous medieval association with Bosnia.[104] The Bosnian Muslim historian Mustafa Imamović is convinced that Kállay wished Bosnia to become 'joined to the Magyar nation'.[105]

In his 1892 speech to the Austrian Delegation Tómaš Masaryk remarked that the Bosnian nation had been 'invented', and that it was 'strange' to observe children in schools being given the grammar of a 'Bosnian' language. Masaryk mockingly recommended to the governments in Vienna and Budapest that they should similarly publish grammars of the Siebenbürgen, Tyrolean and Eger languages. He also observed that the religious question in Bosnia-Herzegovina was important because in these provinces religion and nationality were intertwined.[106] And precisely here, it may be suggested, lay the chief flaw of Kállay's nation-building policy: in pushing aggressively a 'Bosnian nation', which through the idea of *Bogumil*-Muslim continuity appeared in any case to be anchored only in the Muslims, a situation was created in which the other two confessions, the Orthodox and the Catholic, felt themselves increasingly Serb and Croat. Paradoxically, therefore, Kállay's effort served to consolidate the very identities that he had hoped to keep within the confessional sphere. Serb and Croat historians are in agreement on this aspect of Kállay's rule.[107] Mustafa Imamović has defended Kállay's inter-confessional 'Bosnian nation' policy, but admits that during the Ottoman rule the term 'Bosnians' (or 'Bosniacs' – *Bošnjaci*) applied in fact only to the Muslims – the Christians were the *raja*, which can be variously translated as 'herd', 'rabble' or 'subjects'.[108] Generally, however, Bosnia's Muslim Slavs were dubbed 'Turks'. James Creagh, who had visited the provinces in the summer of 1875, noted: 'The Bosniac Mussulmans, although the majority of them are ignorant of the Turkish language, are always called Turks.'[109] As late as 1911 the Italian writer Gino Bertolini reported that, when he would ask the Bosnian Muslims (from both the 'bourgeois' and the 'proletarian' classes) to which nation they belonged, they would answer: 'To the Turkish!'[110]

A further paradox was that the Muslims – and particularly the tiny Muslim intelligentsia which might have been expected to form the backbone of the new Bosnian political nation – were at the same time an object of competition between Serbs and Croats. This was the period when Serbs and Croats were laying mutually exclusive claims to Bosnia-Herzegovina, and so winning the allegiance of the Muslims was perceived by both sides as an essential task. To the extent that the Muslims decided to pick either side, the Croats could boast greater successes – not least because Ante Starčević had so positively talked and written about the Bosnian *begs* ('the oldest and purest Croat nobility') in particular, and about Islam in general. The sons of *begs* who studied at Zagreb University, but also Muslim students in Bosnia-Herzegovina's high schools, were attracted to the ideology of the Party of Right in neighbouring Croatia.[111] Bishop Strossmayer also took the view that the Muslims were Croats.[112] The measure of Muslim enthusiasm for the Croats, however, has been a contentious subject. Thus the Croat-American historian Ivo Banac has written that the 'overwhelming majority' of the first Muslim generation emerging from universities saw themselves as Croats.[113] The Bosnian Muslim writer Nijaz Duraković has dismissed this claim as 'certainly exaggerated', arguing that many Muslim intellectuals in fact chose neither the Croat nor the Serb side.[114]

The wider Bosnian Muslim masses, certainly, remained aloof to any proselytizing overtures: be they Croat, Serb or indeed Kállay's Bosnian.

The Bosnian Muslim political scientist Šaćir Filandra has emphasized that their preference for a purely religious identity was their free choice, not imposed by anybody. Thus in 1908 they had 124 clubs and associations, the names of which were all qualified by the term 'Muslim', not 'Bosniac'.[115] By this token alone, Kállay's efforts to subordinate religion to the service of nationhood had not borne fruit. In their souls, moreover, they continued to be attached to Turkey. The seemingly uncertain international status of Bosnia-Herzegovina probably had something to do with this. The Bosnian Serb historian Todor Kruševac noted that as long the Muslims had a glimmer of hope that things would return to the old ways (i.e., Turkish rule) they tended to regard occupation as something temporary.[116] So it was that Bosnian Muslim clerics, for example, demanded that children in schools be taught in Turkish as this was 'the patriotic language'.[117] The Muslims would object if told that they were not 'Turks' but rather Serbs or Croats since, as they insisted, 'our faith is Turkish'.[118]

There existed another important factor behind the collapse of Kállay's Bosnian nation stratagem, and this had to with the fact that the Muslims had for centuries formed the privileged class in Ottoman Bosnia: they found it difficult, in the words of Mustafa Imamović, 'to come to terms with the idea of equality with the other inhabitants of Bosnia'.[119] What they also found quite difficult to accept was that the Kállay regime promoted the expansion of the Catholic Church in Bosnia-Herzegovina. The Bosnian Muslim movement for religious autonomy which began in 1899 – and which is seen by historians as signalling the de facto end of Kállay's one nation scheme – was a direct response to Catholic proselytizing among the Muslims.

Official support for the Catholic Church in Bosnia-Herzegovina was not the same as backing the Croats. Kállay, as Robin Okey observes, and as has already been argued, was not above divide and rule methods, but 'in essence Croat aspirations were no more acceptable to him than Serb ones'.[120] He could hardly have felt otherwise, not least because, since the 1880s, Bosnian Croat political sympathies had lain, overwhelmingly, with Starčević's uncompromisingly nationalist Party of Right. Croat historians have been anxious to list examples of Kállay's hostility to anything Croat. Mirjana Gross stressed repeatedly that he would ban the Croat name until as late as 1899 – even for the singing societies.[121] Ante Malbaša in his study was particularly concerned to dismiss the 'fairy tale' that Kállay had ever favoured the Croats. Malbaša presented Kállay's regime as serving the political and, especially, economic interests of Hungary at the expense of Croat lands. For example, the Hungarians had prevented the building of a railway line between Dalmatia and Bosnia, and all Bosnia's railways and hence its rail traffic had been directed instead to Budapest, with Bosnian exports from the provinces flowing solely through the Hungarian-controlled port of Rijeka (Fiume).[122]

Nevertheless, the Catholics in Bosnia-Herzegovina were Austria-Hungary's 'natural allies' and were treated as such.[123] Before 1878 there were only thirty-five Catholic churches to be found in the two provinces (by comparison the Serbs had 235 churches before the occupation). By 1896 the number of Catholic churches had risen to 188.[124] Some of these were 'in villages in which there was hardly a Catholic to be found.'[125] The official bias was evident. In 1883, for example, the regime spent 162,503 forints on religious establishments, of which 88,878 forints, more than half of the budget, went to the Catholic Church, despite the Catholics comprising only a fifth of the population. This huge disproportion with regard to the other confessions drew Kállay's comment that it would be difficult to find a similar case in any other country of a religious community with such a privileged position.[126]

In 1881 a regular Catholic hierarchy was restored in Bosnia-Herzegovina, with Sarajevo as the seat of a new archbishopric. Vienna had managed to get the Vatican to agree beforehand that the Emperor would name the Archbishop and the bishops.[127] The Habsburgs were not leaving anything to chance in Bosnia-Herzegovina, especially not in matters of church bureaucracy: they were similarly concerned to bring under their control the Orthodox and Muslim religious establishments. For several centuries during the previous Ottoman rule, Catholicism in the provinces had been preserved by the Franciscan order. But the Franciscans, stemming from, and popular among the ordinary people, had first embraced Illyrian ideas from Croatia and then developed pro-Croat sentiments, neither of which had endeared them to the new occupying authorities who simply viewed them as 'politically unreliable'.[128] Franz Joseph himself was sceptical about them.[129]

Josip Stadler, the new Archbishop, had no Bosnian background and was not a Franciscan but a Jesuit. However, Stadler lacked the supposed Jesuit characteristics of elasticity and adaptability, being rigid and tactless instead.[130] His career became famous partly because he waged a war on behalf of the secular clergy against the Franciscans in a relentless dispute concerning mainly the division of parishes. Far more important, Stadler became associated with the highly controversial issue of conversions to Catholicism from the ranks of Bosnia's Muslims. Although he turned out to be a good Croat nationalist (in 1900 he was publicly rebuked by Franz Joseph for advocating the unification of Bosnia-Herzegovina with 'motherland' Croatia), 'his patriotism was always subordinated to his Catholicism'.[131] The Archbishop's slogan was: 'God and faith, and then Croatia.'[132] General Moritz Auffenberg described him as a typical representative of 'Ecclesia militans'.[133] His zeal concerning conversions brought him into conflict with the Provincial Government and the Bosnian Croat lay intelligentsia, both of which 'deplored the damage' thus caused to hopes of building a Muslim-Catholic front against the Serbs.[134]

In May 1899 the case of Fata Omanović, a Muslim girl from the Mostar region who had been kidnapped by some Catholic nuns, provided the spark for a large meeting of Herzegovinian Muslims protesting against increasingly aggressive Catholic propaganda. The protest movement quickly spread throughout Bosnia-Herzegovina. It was led by the conservative Muslim gentry, and supported by the Muslim peasant masses – the nascent Muslim intelligentsia standing aside or even attacking it.

Until then Austria-Hungary had actually believed that it had had the Muslim clergy in its pocket: for in 1882 Kállay had achieved a religious separation of the Bosnian Muslims from the Porte with the establishment for Bosnia-Herzegovina of *ulema medžlis* (a Muslim religious council) along with the office of *Reis-ul-ulema* (the highest Muslim dignitary in the provinces) – all these high appointments naturally having to be confirmed by Emperor Franz Joseph. Thus Austria-Hungary 'transmuted the Muslim religious ministers into its own servants'.[135] As part of these changes, the *vakuf* establishments, Muslim charitable institutions which possessed considerable material means and which financed, for example, Islamic schools, came under the control of the *Landesregierung*. Although the regime did in fact manage the *vakuf* finances admirably, the Muslims were resentful because they no longer had a say in the administration.

The question of who should hold sway over religious appointments was, however, at the heart of this uproar. In December 1900, in a memorandum submitted to Kállay, the protest leaders, while also demanding autonomy in matters dealing with education and the supervision of *vakuf* establishments, pressed for the election by a Muslim assembly of the provinces' Islamic religious leaders who, crucially, would then be approved by the office of *Šejh-ul-islam*, the supreme religious authority in Turkey. Only then was the Emperor to give his own stamp of approval.[136]

Not surprisingly, neither Vienna nor Budapest were ever going to allow the re-establishment of this or any other amount of genuine Turkish sovereignty in Bosnia-Herzegovina – so the negotiations between the Muslim protest leaders and the Provincial Government, which took place between February and April 1901, got nowhere.[137] Ali Fehmiefendija Džabić, the Mufti of Mostar and the leader of the Muslim movement, had been conveniently banned by the authorities from returning home after he had gone to Turkey to seek help. The struggle of the Bosnian Muslims for religious autonomy was to be a long affair, lasting until 1909. But already at its inception in 1899, and even earlier, the Muslims built bridges with the Orthodox Serbs who had in 1896 begun their own campaign for religious and educational autonomy (*pokret za vjersko-prosvjetnu autonomiju*). A key personality behind the movement of the Muslims was Dr Emil Gavrila, a Serb lawyer from Hungary who drafted documents on their behalf and was in a similar advisory capacity also connected with the struggle of Bosnia's Serbian

Orthodox population.[138] In one sense, the Muslims relied on the Serbian experience of bureaucratic battles with the Habsburg state, but in another sense their coming together represented yet another failure of Kállay's policy. For instead of forming a Muslim-Catholic bloc, he was now facing a Muslim-Orthodox one. Šerif Arnautović, one of the leaders of the Muslim movement, even argued that the Muslim-Orthodox alliance should internationalize the dispute: if its reasonable demands were rejected, the Muslim and Orthodox could turn to the Great Powers, thereby proving that the pacifying role of Austria-Hungary in the provinces had failed and that the occupation represented a threat to European peace.[139]

Since the Serb movement did not address the agrarian question, and therefore not affect the interests of the Muslim landowning gentry, the scope for cooperation against Austria-Hungary seemed considerable. In fact, the Serb demands revealed a hankering for the good old Turkish times in one particular respect. Before 1878 their institution of the *crkveno-školske opštine* (church and school communes), run jointly by priests and lay elements, had been allowed an autonomous existence by the Turks. But the activities of those communes went beyond church and educational matters and had, at least on the local level, a quasi-political character. This cosy self-rule was cut short after the occupation, for the new authorities could not tolerate 'a state within a state'.[140] The *Landesregierung*, good police mechanism that it was, wanted above all to control the teachers and the priests. Its resultant, systematic incursions into every detail of the daily running of the Serbian church and school communes became an invitation to resistance. Another source of resentment against the regime was its policy regarding the Orthodox higher clergy: these tended to be brought in by the regime from southern Hungary and Croatia as they were considered loyal. In a series of memoranda submitted to Franz Joseph between 1896 and 1902 the Serbs argued their case for autonomy, but to no effect, and also found themselves diplomatically abandoned by the Patriarchate in Constantinople which valued good relations with Vienna more highly than it did the cause of the Orthodox Serbs.[141] Before this contest could be concluded, however, Kállay died in July 1903.

In his last years this 'masterful orchestrator of events', as Robin Okey has called Kállay, was to be 'everywhere on the defensive'.[142] The title of Okey's important study of Habsburg policies in Bosnia-Herzegovina, *Taming Balkan Nationalism*, is a very appropriate characterization of what Kállay had attempted to do in the occupied territories. From that point of view, however, his effort must be seen as a failure: Serbian national feeling had been strengthened in Bosnia-Herzegovina; Croat nationalism had evolved and embraced Starčević; and the Muslims insisted on being Muslim. By the mid-1890s, the scheme for a Bosnian nation was already lying in tatters. Okey has stated clearly what he sees as 'the bottom line'

of Kállay's 'Bosnianism': it was 'a means to smooth Bosnia's accommodation to the Habsburg state'.[143] But that, it may be suggested, was not
quite the bottom line. The whole point of 'Bosnianism' was to neutralize
Serb and Croat aspirations in Bosnia-Herzegovina and thus thwart any
prospects for a large South Slav state, either inside or outside the Monarchy
– that is, to prevent the emergence either of a Great Croatia in a Trialist
framework, or a Great Serbia in a South Slav framework. So while the exercise was indeed about gluing Bosnia to the Monarchy, its fine print was all
about castrating South Slav national movements.

Towards Constitutionalism

Most Yugoslav scholars have described Kállay's rule in Bosnia-Herzegovina
as 'absolutist'. A British scholar called it 'enlightened autocracy' – and
emphasized its autocratic nature.[144] This chapter has already pointed out
one of Kállay's main failures: his refusal to address the agrarian question,
an omission which, apart from its negative economic impact, entailed grave
social and political consequences. Thus in 1910 the military had to intervene when a local peasant revolt in western Bosnia quickly turned into a
major agrarian insurrection across much of the province. There had already
been peasant rioting in western Bosnia in 1906. The sorry state of the *kmets*
was then brought into sharp focus in 1909 with the famine in Herzegovina.
There were further agrarian disturbances in 1911, both in western Bosnia
and in the Rogatica region, in the east. The *Landesregierung*, which habitually used force to deal with these problems, would regularly explain them
as the work of foreign agents.[145]

To be sure, Kállay's autocracy had achieved a great deal for the
provinces, most notably the beginnings of industrialization, and improvements in the justice and administrative systems. A substantial road and
narrow gauge rail network had also been built, although mainly with an
eye to its military potential. This came cheaply as the labour was unpaid,
thanks to the retention of the *kuluk* (*corvée*) system, dating from the
Ottoman period, whereby peasants had to work on public projects several
days a year. Regarding these Empire railways, Peter Sugar observed that
they were financed indirectly by the taxes of the provinces, emphasizing
that their construction neglected the interests of Bosnia-Herzegovina and
ignored general economic considerations. Furthermore, Hungary's determination, on selfish economic grounds, to protect its port at Fiume and
to prevent Austrian goods reaching the provinces, meant that the economically most important lines were never built.[146]

Perhaps the most widely praised of Kállay's achievements related to the
restoration of law and order and the enhancement of personal security.
In Bosnia-Herzegovina, however, 'law and order' entailed a strict police

regime, and 'personal security' was a doubtful category given that spies and informers were ubiquitous and denunciations commonplace. Practically every owner of a coffee house was seen as an agent of the police. William Le Queux, an Anglo-French journalist and writer who was singularly unimpressed by Austrian rule in Bosnia-Herzegovina (he pronounced Austria 'the Ogre of the Balkans'), visiting Sarajevo in 1906 wrote that in the city 'one half of the population is paid to spy upon the other half'.[147] There was no right of public assembly, no right to form political parties and no constitution. Censorship was massive. A former Bosnian Croat official recalled that not much could be read in Bosnia's Croat and Serb newspapers beyond notices of appointments and details of railway timetables.[148] Serbian newspapers from Serbia, and even those from Vojvodina in southern Hungary, were as a rule banned.

Elsewhere, the record is likewise less than impressive. As late as 1910 there were only 130 doctors in Bosnia-Herzegovina, and almost 90% of the population was illiterate.[149] In 1908 Joseph Baernreither visited the provinces and noted 'this nation of analphabets' who were at the same time 'creatures of most lively political imagination!'[150] Educating the locals had evidently not been a top priority in Austria-Hungary's civilizing mission. Fear of domestic intelligentsia accounted for the slow progress in establishing high schools (*gimnazije*).[151] After the authorities set up the first one in Sarajevo (1879), the next one, in Mostar, was only opened much later (1893), followed by Banja Luka (1895) and Tuzla (1899). There was hardly an educated class to speak of: by 1902 there were only some thirty Serbs and ten Muslims who had completed university education.[152] Thus the imperial bureaucracy recruited overwhelmingly from outside Bosnia-Herzegovina, bringing in people, in effect foreigners, whom the locals contemptuously called *kuferaši* (from the German *Koffer* – suitcase). The law on compulsory elementary education was only introduced in 1912 and even then only a minority of children (26.75%) would attend school.[153]

Kállay's death could not have been much mourned in Bosnia-Herzegovina, especially not by the Serbs. In the spring of 1902, not long before he died, the Minister was seriously concerned that they were preparing an insurrection.[154] In fact they had actually been hoping for his promotion, as it would remove him from the list of their concerns. Thus, some Serb leaders had been greatly encouraged by rumours that Kállay was going to succeed Gołuchowski as Foreign Minister. When they met Jovan Hristić, Serbia's Minister in Vienna, they declared: 'If only we could get rid of him, they can then appoint him wherever they want.'[155]

Stephan Burián, Kállay's successor as the Joint Finance Minister and a fellow Hungarian, must have come as a welcome relief. Yet Burián's desire to frustrate any potentially hostile national movement was the same as Kállay's. He played, moreover, a role in bringing about the annexation of

Bosnia-Herzegovina in 1908 – an outcome which dismayed Serbs and Muslims alike. His approach, on the other hand, was certainly different and he has also been seen as 'Serbophile'. That he never was, but he did say that a 'mild' posture towards the Serbs was 'imperial necessity [*Reichs-notwendigkeit*]'.[156] The greatest compliment to him was paid by Nikola Stojanović, a prominent Bosnian Serb politician: 'Had someone like Burián arrived in 1883 instead of Kállay, who knows how the history of the South Slavs would have developed.'[157] So what exactly did Burián do?

A career diplomat, Burián was no stranger to south-east European affairs, having served in Sofia and Athens. The fact that he became Austria-Hungary's Foreign Minister during the Great War testifies to his ability as well as his ambition. But he also possessed other qualities. Danilo Dimović, another leading Bosnian Serb politician, remembered him as a man with 'a good heart, very religious, and above all honourable and fair'.[158] And perhaps it was just as well that, unlike Kállay, he did not dabble in history. His standpoint was to accept the existing national identities in Bosnia-Herzegovina rather than attempt to create new ones – the Monarchy could live with any ethnocentric expression provided a proper framework was instituted for it. This meant a constitution, a political life and generally an internal policy which, as Burián put it in his memoirs, 'would deprive the discontented nationalities of any occasion, of any wish, and also of any possibility of seeking foreign sympathies'.[159] Of course, this also meant, in practical terms, that the existing occupational *Provisorium* would need to be ended – no constitution was possible without a formal annexation of the provinces. Equally, only annexation looked like it could put the lid on 'seeking foreign sympathies'. But it is difficult to see here anything even remotely resembling a pro-Serbian approach by Burián. He had merely intended to bring the Bosnian Serbs into line with the Habsburg Monarchy by noticing their collective existence. As before, moreover, the Provincial Government's preference remained for 'a Croat rather than a Serb align-ment for Muslims'.[160]

A whiff of liberalism could finally be felt in Bosnia-Herzegovina when Burián abolished, in 1907, the so-called 'preventive censorship'. He also showed some concern regarding the agrarian question, although his effort here did not go beyond a little repair of the taxation system. His major feats lay elsewhere. In the first place, he made possible the organized political activity of the Serbs, Croats and Muslims, in part by bringing an end to Kállay's 'bloodless Bosnianism' – as Todor Kruševac called it.[161] In his 1906 report to the Delegations Burián explained that the notions of nationality and confessionalism had already merged in the pre-Occupation period.[162] From 1907 the name of the language in Bosnia-Herzegovina was 'Serbo-Croat'. The new Minister also settled the Serbs' long campaign for church and school autonomy. In this he was helped by the fact that the rich Bosnian Serb bourgeoisie, which had led the movement, was hardly a revolutionary crew: it gradually reduced its demands until a compromise solution was finally reached in 1905. But Burián had not yielded to the initial Serb demand for the scrapping of the 1880 Convention with the Patriarchate in Constantinople (which had given the state the power to appoint and pay the Orthodox bishops). It was only when he was happy that the *Landesregiurung* had retained sufficient control that he allowed the Serbian autonomy statute to be completed. Those young Serbs who had acquired an education, however, saw the 1905 dealing as a betrayal and urged a stiffening of opposition.[163] A gap had thus opened up between the older and younger generations – the youth rebellion was to last until June 1914.

The parallel struggle of the Muslims for their own religious autonomy took much longer to conclude. It is perhaps not quite the case, as suggested by Robin Okey, that Burián had to some degree considered the Muslims a '*quantité négligeable*', important only in terms of their links with the Serb opposition.[164] In 1910, explaining to Josef Redlich his past policy in Bosnia-Herzegovina, Burián said that apart from the 'the Great Serbian idea' there had been another clear anti-Austrian tendency afoot in the provinces since 1906: namely, the one urging renewal of relations between the Bosnian Muslims and Turkey, with a stronger emphasis on the sovereignty of the Sultan.[165] Indeed this attitude was in full view when the autonomy negotiations between the Muslims and the *Landesregierung*, broken off in 1901, resumed in 1907. The Muslims had fought obstinately against the Emperor's right to appoint their *Reis-ul-ulema*. One of them, Šerif Arnautović, begged to differ with the view expressed by the Habsburg *Ziviladlatus* Isidor Benko, that Franz Joseph was the only ruler of Bosnia and thus had the right to name the *Reis-ul-ulema*. 'On the contrary', Arnautović maintained, the Emperor merely possessed administrative rights and 'His Majesty the Sultan is the genuine sovereign of Bosnia'.[166] In the end another compromise was put together whereby the *Reis-ul-ulema* would be named by the Emperor who would receive a list of three candidates proposed by a Bosnian Muslim spiritual council, after which Turkey would confirm the choice. However, by the time the Muslim autonomy statute was finally approved in 1909, the annexation had already taken place and the matter of religious contact between the Bosnian Muslims and Turkey had lost all political and constitutional importance.[167]

Since late 1906 the Muslims had been waging their autonomy struggle from within the *Muslimanska narodna organizacija* (MNO) – the first political organization in Bosnia-Herzegovina. The MNO was unquestionably representative of all classes of Bosnian Muslim society, from *begs* and *agas* to peasants. The miniscule intelligentsia hardly counted and it was, moreover, supportive of the regime. Mustafa Imamović has pointed out its 'direct hostility' to the MNO.[168] For their part, the MNO leaders thundered against 'absolutist, state police authorities', and would describe Franz Joseph as 'a temporary pacifier'. In September 1907 its paper *Musavat* (Equality) gave perhaps the best description of the Muslim political senti-ment of that time: 'The sons of Bosnia and Herzegovina, condemned by fate not to be touched and fortified by those warm and golden beams which lighten and warm up the hearts of other subjects of the Turkish Empire, have nevertheless not grown feeble, have not become despondent, and have not lost faith in a better and brighter future.'[169] Inasmuch as the MNO had a programme in this direction, it was for an autonomous Bosnia-Herzegovina under the sovereignty of the Sultan.

On paper, at any rate, the Serbs had a similar aim. In 1907 they too had founded a political grouping, the *Srpska narodna organizacija* (SNO) – after their leaders had tracked down Minister Burián on his holiday in Switzer-land and got his permission. The SNO officially spelled out its positions in November that year in the following terms: each nation has the right to self-determination and the source of power in a state is 'popular will'; Bosnia-Herzegovina is an integral part of the Turkish Empire, being 'at present' administered by Austria-Hungary on the basis of the mandate con-ferred by the European Powers; the state constitutional arrangement for Bosnia-Herzegovina should be 'complete autonomy'; Bosnia and Herzego-vina are 'Serb lands' and the official language should be Serbian.[170] The SNO programme also drew attention to the 'vital' agrarian problem which it characterized as a political and social question as well as an economic one.

It is questionable, however, to what extent the SNO really cared about solving the *kmet* problem. Its leaders were affluent individuals, men of the *čaršija* (the town, or its commercial part) known as *gazde* (big bosses). Their 1907 SNO programme merely demanded that the authorities should 'strive' to solve the agrarian question in a 'just' manner and added, amazingly, that in doing so the 'maintenance of social classes' had to be kept in mind.[171] What was important to the SNO was to cultivate the *begs* and *agas*, who held absolute sway among the Muslim masses, in order to present a stronger front against the *Landesregierung*. In this respect, the agrarian question was a nuisance that was best dealt with by merely paying it lip service.

The SNO grandees combined patriotism, political opportunism and business interests. They were, according to Veselin Masleša, 'mostly primitive people, practically-inclined, uneducated and almost without any solid understanding of the politics in the world or even in the Austro-Hungarian Monarchy'.[172] Their economic rise since 1878 had been breath-taking. The Occupation, in fact, was a godsend to them. Masleša, one of the sharpest observers of social and economic conditions in Habsburg Bosnia-Herzegovina, was very interested in the economic upsurge of this Serb merchant class and listed several reasons for it. First, the building of railways and the beginning of industrialization created a proletariat, while

increasing purchasing power in the provinces; second, the new administrative and military apparatus brought in officials and officers who represented 'a very interesting kind of consumer' for the Bosnian traders; third,
Serb merchants participated in the new trade centring on cheap industrial
products suddenly flooding the market; fourth, new roads and railways,
as well as the spread of a money-based economy, increased the size of
the market; finally, the inclusion of Bosnia-Herzegovina into the Austro-
Hungarian customs area meant that exports were now possible: cattle,
plums, jams, eggs, some wheat and maize, etc.[173]

The inert Muslim *begs* and *agas* took no part in these dynamic developments, and the more successful Bosnian Croats ended up mostly as officials
in the Provincial Government. Hence the chief economic beneficiaries of
the Occupation were the Serb merchants. Not surprisingly, they founded
a number of banks and behaved as bankers do – including towards Serb
kmets and their loans. Masleša considered that, particularly as bankers and
merchants, these Serbs had the same exploitative attitude as did the
Muslim landowners. He argued that they had 'abandoned the national
liberation struggle and betrayed national interests'. But he also provided a
superb insight into how this class of Serbs could imagine that they were in
fact good patriots. For 'being a Serb means to be an enemy of Austria, but
being a rich Serb means a stronger enemy of Austria.'[174]

Yet it was precisely these Serbs who steered the SNO and enjoyed, at
least until 1910, massive support – as did their counterparts, the Muslim
gentry in the MNO. Did there exist, then, a basic Serb-Muslim congruence
of aims on the eve of Bosnian annexation? It was true that the agrarian
issue would in principle continue to divide Serbs and Muslims. A more
fundamental difference also obtained between them with regard to where
they saw the future of Bosnia-Herzegovina: ideally, the Serbs would have
wanted the provinces joined to Serbia; whereas the Muslims would have
wanted them returned to Turkey. The autonomist noises made by both
conveniently disguised these diverse desiderata. At the same time, nevertheless, there was an underlying rapport here: Serbs and Muslims both
opposed annexation.

The emerging reality of the Serb-Muslim symbiosis in Bosnia-
Herzegovina in the first years of the twentieth century, based on this joint
interest, has received little attention from historiography. But by 1902
Serbs and Muslims had already negotiated a fundamental cooperation
agreement, signed by their most prominent leaders: Alibeg Firdus and
Bakir-beg Tuzlić for the Muslims, and Gligorije Jeftanović and Vojislav Šola
for the Serbs. Alibeg Firdus had by this time become 'the strongest political
authority among the Muslims'.[175] Some of the provisions of the cooperation agreement may seem astonishing from today's vantage point. 'Serbs
of Orthodox and Moslem faith', so ran the chief passage, 'undertake to

work, and call on the people to do the same, towards Bosnia and Herze-govina acquiring their self-rule under the supreme power of their sovereign the Sultan.' It was agreed that once this objective was attained, there would be alternately a Muslim and a Serb Orthodox Governor of the provinces. The official language would be Serbian and the script would be Cyrillic. It was also envisaged that all the spiritual orders of the Roman Catholic Church except the Franciscans be expelled – the Jesuits were the primary target here. The agrarian question was fudged, since it was to be settled by 'the free will of the people'. The signatories also undertook, 'most solemnly', to 'work against annexation by all possible means'.[176]

Robin Okey has surprisingly chosen to downplay the significance of the 1902 Muslim-Serbian understanding, relying on Bosnian Muslim historians' scepticism about it. Yet Nusret Šehić, one of those historians referred to by Okey, could not disprove that the agreement was relevant. Šehić himself cited Ali Fehmiefendija Džabić, the exiled Mufti of Mostar and one of the chief Muslim supporters of an alliance with the Serbs, as saying that 'there is no salvation without [accord with the Serbs], and nor can we get rid of *Švaba* without [the Serb alliance]' – *Švaba* being the derogatory name used by the South Slavs for the Germans, i.e. Austrians.[177] The fact about the accord which has embarrassed Bosnian Muslim historians is that the Muslim leaders had agreed in 1902 to their people being called Serbs of Muslim faith – as cited above. Adem-aga Mešić, a prominent pro-Croat Muslim politician, even accused the autonomist leadership of wanting to bring Bosnia-Herzegovina 'under Serbia'.[178] This seems implausible – the Muslims simply required strategic partners and were prepared to make tactical adjustments, hence their acceptance of the Serb appellation. In any case, as Mustafa Imamović has argued, modern national ideas were rather 'incomprehensible' to them.[179] Devoid as they were of any national feeling at the time, not even Kállay could convince them that they were Bosnians. Nor, apart from a few intellectuals, were they likely to seriously embrace the Serb identity either. But they did need the Serbs to fight the annexa-tion. Only the post-annexation period would undermine the agreement of 1902.[180]

The Croats, by contrast, had practically nothing to offer to the Muslims. They were, in the first place, the least numerous group in Bosnia-Herzegovina – which was precisely why Burián thought he could not rely on them alone.[181] They were also economically the weakest. The Croat elite consisted largely of a handful of lawyers: in economic terms it was no match for the land-owning Muslim gentry or the wealthy Serb merchant class. The political deficit of the Bosnian Croats was perceived in an inter-esting way by Smajlbeg Džinić, one of the MNO leaders. He explained in January 1908 that the Muslims would perhaps cooperate with them if they enjoyed more favour with the authorities. Zoran Grijak, Archbishop

Stadler's biographer, has pointed to this as evidence of Burián's pro-Serb orientation, but it should in fact be seen as further testimony to the tactical imperative in the politics of the Bosnian Muslims.[182]

In any case, the Croats were to them in key respects the same, or worse, than the occupying power itself. The Bosnian Croat political organization *Hrvatska narodna zajednica* (HNZ) was projected in 1906, but only came into existence at the beginning of 1908. The first point of the HNZ programme claimed Bosnia and Herzegovina as 'Croat lands' by virtue of the tribal origin of the indigenous population and by 'state right'. The second point stressed the 'natural tendency' of the Bosnian Croats to want Bosnia-Herzegovina as joined to the Kingdom of Croatia and therefore also to the Habsburg Monarchy. The third point declared the Bosnian Muslims to be 'indisputably Croats'.[183] At the same time, remarkably, the HNZ hoped to attract 'Croat' Muslims to its ranks as this represented the only means by which it could combat the relative majority formed by the Serbs. Therefore the HNZ did allow for non-Catholics to join, though this move certainly did not result in an influx of Muslims. Its global policy mirrored that of the nationalist parties in Croatia: Bosnia-Herzegovina to be annexed to the Monarchy and joined to a Greater Croatia in a new, Trialist configuration of the Habsburg state. None of this could possibly hold much appeal to most Muslims. Only in the agrarian respect did the HNZ pursue a line of policy designed to meet Muslim approval: just like the SNO Serbs, it had steered clear of the agrarian question in order not to offend its potential allies in the MNO led by the landowning Muslim gentry – the HNZ had therefore done absolutely nothing for the not inconsiderable number of Croat *kmets*.

After almost three decades of Austro-Hungarian occupation, Burián had, in acquiescing to the birth of these party organizations, inaugurated the rudiments of a political framework for Bosnia-Herzegovina. What was needed now was a constitution and a local parliament. Despite the achievements of the Administration, Burián wrote in his memoirs, 'the native population still regarded it as a foreign rule because they had no share in it'.[184] This was rational rather than benevolent thinking by an imperial administrator, though some saw it as weakness. Thus Foreign Minister Aehrenthal privately dismissed Burián in June 1908 as 'well-intentioned', but 'lacking the firm hand with which Kállay had prevailed'.[185] In any case, the annexation of Bosnia-Herzegovina, which was a precondition for Burián's integrationist path, took place in October 1908. Burián had argued for it in a memorandum early in April, with Franz Joseph predictably in favour. By the time Burián met Aehrenthal on 5 August, the latter was also in complete agreement.[186]

Further aspects of the Bosnian annexation crisis are examined in chapter seven. But how did the three groups in Bosnia-Herzegovina react to the annexation? The Croats, of course, welcomed it enthusiastically. In Nikola Mandić, the leader of HNZ, Vienna found a useful ally, notable for his obedience. Franz Ferdinand's circle had demanded of the Bosnian Croats unconditional support for the annexation and 'did not wish to even hear' about a union of Bosnia-Herzegovina with Croatia. Mandić, who was in Vienna at the time of the annexation, duly gave statements to the press praising 'the Habsburg state idea', and said not a single word about the idea of Bosnia-Herzegovina being joined with Croatia. When he was allowed an audience with the Emperor to express his thanks for the annexation, Franz Joseph made not a mention the Croat people to him.[187]

Meanwhile, not to be outdone by Mandić, Archbishop Stadler also hurried to Vienna, heading a 430-strong delegation in two train compositions. Stadler did not say anything to Franz Joseph about his wish to see Bosnia and Herzegovina united with Croatia, but did so when he was subsequently given an audience by Franz Ferdinand. The Archduke merely replied that the Monarchy protected 'cultural and religious interests of all faiths'.[188] Despite widespread jubilation at the annexation by Croats everywhere, the fiasco of their politics within the Habsburg framework was in fact complete. For good measure, Karl Lueger, the Mayor of Vienna, used curious language to praise the Croats at a banquet in honour of Stadler's delegation. The Croats, he said to the consternation of the guests, had always been 'faithful servants' of the Dynasty. In 1910, when Franz Joseph came to Sarajevo to open the new Diet, there was a new twist to this tale of humiliation: the delegation headed by Mandić was not allowed to introduce itself to the Emperor as Croat, only as Catholic.[189]

In the critical days following the official announcement of the annexation on 7 October, the *Landesregierung* could of course count only on the support of the Croats. Not leaving anything to chance, it isolated Bosnia-Herzegovina from the rest of the world: from 7th to 11th October all the provinces' telegraph and telephone lines were blocked. The press was gagged.[190] To the Serbs and the Muslims, four fifths of the population, the annexation represented 'a devastating defeat' for their political movement.[191] Shortly before the event, the Serb representatives from SNO wanted to hold an assembly in Sarajevo, but found themselves banned. They then held it on the train to Budapest where the Delegations were in session. Before they even reached the Hungarian capital they found out from the newspapers that Bosnia-Herzegovina had been annexed. Together with the Muslim representatives, who had also arrived in Budapest, they issued a joint proclamation on 11 October in which they described themselves as 'Serbs, Orthodox and Muslim'. This document, however, urged patience and appealed to the people to stay calm – the struggle would be continued by lawful means, the legal order would be respected.[192]

Such an outcome was, of course, an apparent triumph for Austria-Hungary and also for Minister Burián personally. In 1910 he told Josef Redlich that it was only his much criticized 'Serbophile' policy that had ensured peace and order during the annexation crisis.[193] However, this was perhaps just retrospective braggadocio on his part: for Burián had neither conceded so much to the Serbs, nor had serious disturbances really been likely in the wake of the annexation. The Muslim landowners and the Serb merchants were never going to command their followers to raise the flag of revolution and fight on the barricades in Sarajevo, Mostar and Banja Luka. This was now 1908, not 1878. The Bosnian Muslim historian Hamdija Kapidžić wrote that Serbs and Muslims were 'not certain' about their own strength.[194] Prior to the annexation, they anticipated and feared an imminent change, but lacked a political platform from which to oppose it. In fact, when they saw Burián a month before the annexation, Serb and Muslim leaders petitioned him for the immediate introduction of a constitution, with the appeal that this should be done before any change in the international legal status of the provinces. The idea, clearly, was to fight politically.

In any case, an external stimulus for an insurrection – be it from Serbia, Russia or Turkey – did not materialize in 1908-1909. Serbia's ability to resist Vienna's unilateral action over Bosnia-Herzegovina depended largely on the attitude of Turkey and Russia. But the Young Turk regime, after its initial outrage at the annexation, came to terms with Austria-Hungary in January 1909. Russia's support for Serbia effectively collapsed at the end of February, and Serbia finally capitulated at the end of March. The Bosnian Serbs agitated abroad against the annexation, mostly in Russia, but there were already signs at the beginning of 1909 that its leaders were ready to accept the new situation. As for the Muslims, a report in October 1908 from the *Landesregierung* to Vienna noted that their 'wild joy' at the Young Turkish revolution was followed by incredulity at the annexation which happened afterwards.[195] In February 1909 they submitted a poignant memorandum to the Turkish Parliament, reminding it that the Bosnian Muslims had always been ready to die for the Turkish Empire and asking: 'Is it possible that Turkey ... now as a constitutional state, is to sell its lands to someone who has no right over them?' This was of course more than possible: the loyal Bosnian Muslims were sold to Vienna by the Young Turks for two and a half million Turkish pounds. It was calculated that this came to 96 piastres per head.[196] While some of the most prominent Bosnian Serbs (Gligorije Jeftanović, Vojislav Šola and Danilo Dimović) went to visit Burián in Vienna in early May to recognize the new state of affairs, the Bosnian Muslims kept up their defiance. Only in February 1910, after wide internal consultations, did the MNO leaders (Firdus, Arnautović and others) declare to the authorities in Sarajevo their acceptance of the annexation and express their loyalty to the Dynasty.[197]

Did Austria-Hungary, then, finally succeed in 'taming Balkan national-ism' in Bosnia-Herzegovina? The bitter pill for the Serbs and Muslims of being formally incorporated into the Empire was at least accompanied by two sweeteners from the Emperor: in his proclamation of the annexation, he promised a constitution and a local parliament. This Habsburg largesse towards what was in effect a colonial possession admittedly took a long time to be delivered, with Franz Joseph finally signing the papers on 17 February 1910. The constitutional package, however, was pretty hollow. The provinces remained a separate administrative territory (*corpus separa-tum*) in relation to Austria and Hungary, belonging to neither and depend-ing on both through – as in the past – the Joint Finance Ministry. As Todor Kruševac noted, its people did not even have 'genuine citizenship'.[198] They continued to be treated as subjects of the 'land' (i.e., of Bosnia-Herzegovina), not as citizens of Austria or Hungary.[199] General Oskar Potiorek, the *Landeschef* of the provinces after May 1911, considered that the locals were in effect 'second class' citizens. However, any attempt to equalize the status of Bosnian-Herzegovinian citizenship with Austrian and Hungarian would have invited Hungary's determined resistance given the implication of Trialism that would have arisen.[200] And whereas the Constitution, known as the *Landesstatut*, fully guaranteed the rights of the individual (freedom of movement, religion, etc.), its other provisions were 'a reminder of where power lay'.[201] This was particularly the case regarding the competences, or lack of them, of the new Diet (*Sabor* or *Landtag*).

In the first place, the Provincial Government itself was not in any way accountable to the Diet. It thus operated fully independently of the new legislative body to which, however, it was entitled to send its representa-tives. The Diet could not send its members to the Austrian and Hungarian Delegations which meant that it had no say whatsoever in the business of managing the joint affairs of the Empire. Needless to say, it did not have any powers regarding local military questions, either (such as, for example, approving the number of recruits). Its competences related to playing a role in budgetary matters, and in the spheres of criminal justice, taxation, health, education, agriculture, forestry, etc. The Diet could not choose its rotating three-member Presidency (a Muslim, an Orthodox and a Catholic) – this was named by the Emperor. The latter, moreover, would need to approve any legislative acts passed by the Diet.[202] Which meant, of course, that whatever Sarajevo wished to see legislatively enacted, even within the narrow confines of what was permitted, would require the blessing of parliaments in both Vienna and Budapest. According to Robert Kann, this 'mock constitution' reflected fears of irredentist Serbian activities and it consequently 'reduced the representation of popular liberties to practically nil'. Kann maintained that the Bosnian constitution was in some ways comparable to the new charters for Moravia (1906) and Bukovina (1910), but that it was altogether 'much inferior to either of them as far as the rights of the legislative branch were concerned'.[203] The elaborate electoral system was constructed on the basis of social and confessional divisions – the latter provision favouring the Croat minority. The vote of a Muslim *aga* or a school professor was worth 150 peasant votes. Thus the peasant body could never win in the elections.[204] Nor could any single confession obtain a majority in the new Diet.

Even the *Ziviladlatus* Baron Benko noted the 'unbounded tutelage' of the constitutional system given to Bosnia-Herzegovina where 'in reality a colonial situation exists'.[205] Despite this, it was nevertheless an improvement on what had preceded it, and all the leading politicians and intellectuals treated the Constitution as a 'fait accompli'. The Serb politicians accepted it as a new operative framework.[206] However, the attitude of the youth of the country, or at least that part of it with some education, was going in the other direction and indeed becoming markedly hostile. When a service was held in the main Serbian Orthodox church in Sarajevo just after the annexation, with the Metropolitan blessing the Emperor and the House of Austria, people went down on their knees. But not all. A group of students from the Sarajevo *Gymnasium* kept standing in defiant silence.[207]

Things got worse after Franz Joseph paid a visit to the provinces between the end of May and the beginning of June 1910. During the visit, Bogdan Žerajić, a young Serb ex-student from Herzegovina, shadowed him, armed with a handgun, in both Sarajevo and Mostar. His aim was to assassinate the old Emperor and he did get the chance, having in fact come very close to him.[208] A graduate of the Mostar *Gymnasium* and a former law student at Zagreb University, Žerajić (born in 1887) came from a poor peasant family. It remains unclear why he chose not to shoot the Emperor when he was in a position to do so, but it is generally accepted by Yugoslav scholars that he had probably not had any accomplices. What is beyond doubt is that he had opposed the annexation and had gone to a camp in Serbia where irregulars were trained. His name will be forever associated with the subsequent festive opening of the new Bosnian Diet on 15 June 1910. Having failed to assassinate Franz Joseph, he selected as his next target the Croat military Governor of the provinces, General Marijan Varešanin.[209] As the General left the Diet in his coach, Žerajić fired five shots at him from close distance. All of them missed, but 'only just'.[210] He then used the sixth bullet to commit suicide. The Sarajevo police subsequently cut off his head and kept it as a specimen of an anarchist.[211]

In a draft letter they found after his death, Žerajić described his impressions of Franz Joseph's visit. 'The bishops', he wrote, 'commanded all the priests and church communes to send representatives to greet the Sovereign, and the gendarmes were pushing the people to meet him and to shout long live ... As he was driven the King [Franz Joseph] noticed that there were no peasants to greet him. The peasants had not obeyed the gen-darmes. Our good peasant, he does not like the gendarme.'[212] Indeed. By the autumn of that same year, 1910, there were major clashes between the Bosnian *kmets* and the gendarmes. The unresolved agrarian question had continued to cloud Austro-Hungarian rule in Bosnia-Hezegovina. An agrarian revolt began in August in Šimići – a Croat village in the west of Bosnia.[213] Under the name *štrajk* (strike) it was then taken up by the Serbs around Bosanska Gradiška, spreading rapidly and even encompassing, apart from the Croat and Serb *kmets*, some Muslim ones. All of them had refused to pay the one-third tax normally due to the *begs* and *agas*. These landowners then appealed to the authorities for assistance. The *Landes-regierung* in Sarajevo duly obliged, sending major military formations and gendarmerie to intervene.

In the meantime, wherever the *kmets* moved in the countryside, they were able to recruit new followers for their protest. Much of northern Bosnia was affected, with the revolt poised to spill across the river Bosna to the east and the south. The Army and the gendarmerie thus had to guard the bridges and roads to restrict the movement of the *kmets* who were themselves, despite the peaceful nature of their protests, shot at and generally treated with astonishing brutality. At the beginning of October, when the protests finally petered out, Simo Eraković, a member of the Diet, sent a telegram to the Provincial Government, complaining at the treatment of the *kmets*. He drew attention to an incident when a Habs-burg local government official had inexplicably ordered some protesting peasants to be 'chained', then frog-marched off to prison 'like dogs'.[214] Even *kmet* status had not prepared them for that. As events were to show, the Empire was thus building a rod for its own back.

5

Serbia 1903: Bad King, Bad Blood

Two Kings

IN HISTORICAL writings the year 1903 has become an all-explanatory date for the Balkan background to the origins of the First World War. However, just because a particular date in history seems a good landmark to use does not always mean that the historical events surrounding it are correctly interpreted. Historians sometimes 'pigeonhole' complicated events within definite dates and sweeping thematic categories to make them more easy on the eye to wider audiences. But this can lead to distortion around which a lasting narrative is then established. Such has been the fate of the 1903 events in Serbian history. The events in question relate to the notorious murder in Belgrade of King Alexander Obrenović and his wife Queen Draga on 11 June 1903, and the ensuing re-establishment of the rival dynasty of Karađorđević.

In the case of Belgrade 1903 and Sarajevo 1914, the enticement to thread things together has been, it seems, irresistible. It is by now a very familiar interpretation: Serbia was 'a satellite' of Austria-Hungary under the Obrenović dynasty which had been 'Austrophile'; the bloody removal of the last Obrenović king paved the way for the rival (and 'Russophile') Karađorđević dynasty; the subsequent growth of Serbian, indeed 'pan-Serbian', nationalism brought the small Balkan country onto a collision course with its large neighbour Austria-Hungary, a Great Power tradition-ally competing with Russia in the region; Sarajevo 1914 was thus a culmi-nation of that savage, barbaric night of 11 June 1903 in Belgrade; and finally, to clinch the matter, two Serbian officers involved in the regicide were exactly the two individuals who have been, ever since the 1920s, widely assumed to have organized the 1914 murder in Sarajevo of Franz Ferdinand, the Heir to the Habsburg Throne: Dragutin Dimitrijević 'Apis' and Vojislav Tankosić. Dimitrijević, moreover, is more often than not credited with the leading role in the 1903 conspiracy.

The point about the 1903-1914 continuity of Serbian history appears especially glaring and has been laboured often enough. It is, however, the alleged Austrophile character of Serbia's foreign policy before 1903 and its perceived pro-Russian orientation policy after 1903 which the historical profession has been quick to accentuate, and which, having become one of those received ideas in history writing, has gone largely unchallenged.[1] This version of history has had a fairly universal dissemination from relatively early on. Alfred von Wegerer, who in Germany between the two world wars famously combined scholarship and propaganda, argued that the essential point of the violent change of dynasty in Serbia was ultimately the 'tilting' of Belgrade towards a pro-Russian policy.[2] Sidney Bradshaw Fay, another authority from that period on the origins of the Great War, presented a background to 'a Russophile orientation in Serbian policy' after 1903.[3] Luigi Albertini, who wrote perhaps the most substantial work on the origins of the First World War, highlighted the alleged Russophilia of supposedly key 1903 conspirators in the same breath as he did their connection with Sarajevo 1914.[4]

This rather convenient synopsis of the relevance of Belgrade's 1903 putsch to the catastrophe of 1914 underwent no changes in the decades that followed. Influential works in the 1970s and 1980s, such as those by L.C.F. Turner and James Joll, maintained the narrative.[5] The supposedly manifest and momentous meaning of 1903 was thus retrospectively established, at least in so far as the Balkan origins of the First World War were concerned. To this day the view persists that there was something seminal about the palace coup in Belgrade. A major recent history of modern Serbia by Holm Sundhaussen, a leading German expert, talks of a 'sharp change' in the foreign policy of Serbia brought about by the regicide, and of a subsequent 'dramatic' deterioration of relations between Serbia and the Habsburg Monarchy.[6] Current specialists on the origins of the First World War tend to say much the same thing. Thus Holger Herwig: 'An important Balkan satellite, Serbia, was lost in 1903 as a result of a coup d'état.'[7] By which Herwig is asserting, of course, that Serbia had been an Austro-Hungarian satellite prior to the putsch.

In reality, by the time of the murder of the last Obrenović, Serbia was nobody's satellite. The Austrian historian Hans Uebersberger, writing in 1958, was one of those who recognized that under King Alexander the relationship between Serbia and the Danubian Monarchy would 'never again' be as intimate as that which had existed during the reign of his father Milan. Writing before Uebersberger, Walter Markov, the distinguished German expert on the Balkans, warned in 1934 that 'there can be no talk' of a Russophile Serbian foreign policy replacing an Austrophile one in 1903. Roderich Gooss, the well-known Austrian historian, submitted in 1930 that Belgrade's Austrophile course had already ended in 1889 with Milan's abdication. As far back as 1919 the acclaimed historian Heinrich Friedjung similarly noted that Serbia had been increasingly turning away from the

Monarchy ever since 1889. More recently, in 1972, Francis Roy Bridge remarked that it would involve 'a good deal of hindsight' to see 11 June 1903 in Belgrade as bearing 'the crucial significance for Austro-Serbian relations.'[8]

These scholars, however, have been largely ignored. The erroneous picture of the country as somehow being an Austrian client in 1903 stems in part from too hastily identifying the rule of King Alexander with the rule of his father, Prince and later King Milan. Interestingly, Serbian scholarship has produced very few studies of this ruler, which is probably a reflection of where he stands in the collective national memory. A recent view is that Milan managed to corrupt the political establishment of the country, destroying any free-thinking political opinion in the process.[9] In private life he was notorious for his profligacy, gambling and womanizing. But nearly all the criticism of him has been about his unbending pro-Austrian course.

Initially, however, Milan was by all accounts a genuine Russophile. His wife Natalie was herself of Russian origin. The change in his foreign policy orientation occurred in the aftermath of the Great Eastern Crisis which had in 1875 erupted in Bosnia-Herzegovina. In the following year Serbia embarked on what turned out to be a disastrous war against the Turks, entering the fray in the context of much prompting from unofficial 'Slavophile' circles in Russia. But the Russian government itself had had nothing to do with this decision for war, and had its own, very pragmatic schemes in the Balkans. In March 1878, following its defeat of Turkey, Russia concluded the Treaty of San Stefano which envisaged a huge Bulgarian state largely at the expense of Serbia's interests. The Serbs were horrified by their projected, paltry territorial gains in the south-east and by the fact that under the San Stefano Treaty Bulgaria would take in much of Macedonia. But Russian policy was driven by the idea of closing in on Constantinople, and Serbia, unlike Bulgaria, by virtue of her geographic position could play no role in this. The Russians had in all frankness advised the Serbs to go and seek support on the Austrian side.[10]

San Stefano represented a bold attempt by Russia to solve the Eastern Question unilaterally and inevitably met strong resistance. The scheme for a Great Bulgaria was shattered at the Congress of Berlin (1878), but so was Milan's previous enthusiasm for Russia. Serbia's formal independence was recognized, but its territorial gains were limited, and obtained only with Austrian assistance. Vienna, of course, was to extract a price from its new Balkan client. In an 1881 secret convention with Austria-Hungary, Serbia undertook not to cause trouble in Bosnia and Herzegovina, occupied after the Congress of Berlin by Austria-Hungary – an unequivocal relinquishment of what were considered Serbian lands over which Serbia had only recently fought Turkey. In the absence of Russian support, however, it is difficult to see what choice Milan had other than to follow a policy of leaning on Austria-Hungary. The 1881 arrangement with Vienna gave Milan some compensation for abandoning Bosnia-Herzegovina in the form of a vague backing for Serbia's territorial aspirations in the Turkish-held territories to the south. But this was better than nothing. Perhaps more important to him, Milan extracted what seemed like a clear and firm commitment from Vienna to maintain the Obrenović dynasty.[11] Indeed, soon thereafter Austria-Hungary backed the elevation of Serbia's status: this 'simple and primitive land', as the historian Slobodan Jovanović described 19th century Serbia, became a kingdom in 1882.[12]

So in a way Milan's 'Austrophilia' was dictated by the lack of an alternative. But his principal motivation – in both domestic and foreign policies – was self-preservation. This cannot be emphasized strongly enough. Opportunist that he was, interested before anything else in survival and the good life, Milan was hardly some statesman looking and scheming beyond Serbia's frontiers. Despising Serbia and the Serbs, he once wrote to his wife Natalie, advising her to impress on their son not to trust any Serb.[13] In turn, most Serbs despised him. He feared, correctly, for his own life. In 1883 a large peasant rebellion took place in Timok, eastern Serbia, in protest at the decommissioning of arms. It was soon suppressed by government troops, but behind the peasants had stood the newly-formed, populist Radical Party. Milan had already lost one war (against Turkey in 1876), and when he spectacularly lost another one (against Bulgaria in 1885) the Austro-Hungarian Minister in Belgrade Count Rudolf Khevenhüller had to intervene forcefully to save the day for him. Both those wars had reflected domestic Serbian policy considerations: the first had been a concession to public opinion, and the second a reaction to his shaky political position at home.

At this time Serbia was indeed in Vienna's sphere of influence, and Milan justifiably wore the epithet of Austria's 'satrap'. The Russian diplomat Nikolai Tcharykow related that in those days the Austrians called the Serbian Army their '13th Army Corps'.[14] The Austro-Hungarian Crown Prince Rudolf, on visiting Belgrade in 1884, noted with regret Milan's 'dismissive' attitude towards his own people, and found his professions of loyalty towards Vienna quite embarrassing.[15] But Rudolf could hardly have been surprised. In conversation with him the previous year, Milan had offered to hand his kingdom over to Austria 'with bag and baggage [*mit Sack und Pack*]'.[16] What the King of Serbia really wanted were the privileges of a king without the responsibilities, and so he would indeed have been happy to see his country taken over by Austria-Hungary as long as he could carry on indulging his weaknesses, untroubled by domestic opposition. Serbian politics and Serbian politicians were a tiresome burden to him.

Milan's resolve to abdicate apparently began with his country's defeat by Bulgaria in 1885. Additionally enfeebled by his marital problems with Queen Natalie, and also enormously indebted, he withdrew in 1889 aged only thirty-five in favour of his twelve-year old son, the boy-prince Alexander. But Milan's abdication turned out to be something of a farce as he kept returning to Serbia from his exile in Paris in search of influence, power and, indeed, money. At the same time his very public post-divorce bickering with Natalie created a burlesque image of Serbia internationally.

The abdication also heralded major changes in Serbia internally. The new liberal constitution of 1888 ushered in a parliamentarian era. Serbia, moreover, now had a three-member Regency which represented the young Alexander. The Radical Party, whose leaders had been either in jail or in exile after the 1883 Timok rebellion, had been reconstituted and stood ready for power – which it duly took following Milan's departure. It enjoyed massive support among the peasantry, but was not, as Michael Boro Petrovich argued, a 'peasant party.' Small town merchants and particularly the Party's intelligentsia, educated largely in Germany, Austria and Switzerland, were the most influential within its ranks. Ideologically, the Radicals had socialist roots and stood for self-government at the level of local communities. In practice, however, they soon showed that they were interested solely in power, becoming a deeply conservative force – with the name of the party turning into 'an ironic misnomer.'[17]

Alexander grew up surrounded far more by his tutors than his quarrelling parents. Describing himself as an orphan even though his father and mother were alive, he was seen as a bright and astute child, yet one who was also distrustful and devious.[18] Constantin Dumba, who in 1903 served as the Austro-Hungarian Minister in Serbia, related that Alexander had practiced play-acting from early days: 'It became his second nature, and lying became a daily household remedy.'[19] He entered politics not only early, but also spectacularly. In 1893, at only seventeen, he declared himself of full age for royal duties and had the Regents locked up overnight in his palace – that was the end of the Regency. It is generally agreed that Milan was behind his son's action. Clearly, the ex-King intended to continue to exert influence through his successor – having run out of money. The 1893 coup also revealed the appetite of the Serbian military for meddling in politics, inasmuch as the Army had stood behind Milan's manoeuvring. In May 1894, when Alexander abolished the 1888 Constitution, the Army had again backed this move.[20]

On and off, depending on how close the young Alexander felt himself to his father as opposed to his mother Queen Natalie, 'two Kings' ruled in Serbia during the 1890s. If, however, Alexander was an innocent in politics to begin with, his subsequent career demonstrated an abundance of flair for political machination. Taking over in 1893 was merely the first *coup d'état* of four he was to carry out in his ten years as King. In the course of stormy fluctuations between constitutionalism and authoritarianism, he was to change three constitutions and twelve governments. Slobodan Jovanović, Serbia's greatest historian, maintained that Alexander's idea of a parliamentary system was 'a Parliament without an opposition.' In the manner of British parliamentary chief whips, he would collect information damaging to the deputies, and threaten to use it unless they obeyed his will.[21] In his memoirs, the Liberal Party politician Jovan Avakumović described at great length Alexander's incorrigibly anti-constitutional frame of mind and behaviour.[22]

But was Alexander Obrenović, like his father, an Austrophile? More important, did Serbia under his rule carry on relying unreservedly on Vienna? Much of the non-Serbian historiography on the subject assumes precisely that. A typical recent example is provided by Samuel Williamson and Russel Van Wyk, the editors of a documentary survey of the coming of the First World War. They assert that Dragutin Dimitrijević 'Apis', one of the officers in the conspiracy to murder the King in 1903, 'was appalled by the subservient behaviour of King Alexander toward Austria-Hungary.'[23] As will be seen, however, Alexander's foreign policy was in fact erratic, oscillating between Vienna and St Petersburg. By 1903 he was being cold-shouldered by both. That notwithstanding, for many historians the idea that he had simply continued Milan's pro-Austrian course is essential to their thesis that the year 1903 represented a radical break, setting Serbia on a collision course with the Habsburg Monarchy.

A closer examination of the pre-1903 period, however, reveals a some-what different picture. Serbia's foreign policy had from 1889 (Milan's abdication) to 1903 (Alexander's murder) remained mostly passive in the light of Alexander's domestic preoccupations. This does not mean, as will be seen, that it had remained blindly pro-Austrian. In any case, except for the Greco-Turkish War of 1897, no major Balkan crisis occurred during this period requiring Serbia to take a clear position in foreign policy or to seek to align with a major ally in respect of such an issue. Austria-Hungary and Russia at this time operated a policy of caution and in 1897 reached a 'gentlemen's understanding' to retain the status quo in the Balkans 'as long as circumstances would permit.'[24] And Russia's focus was on the Far East, not Europe. Serbia's activities outside its borders were largely confined to Ottoman-controlled 'Old Serbia' (Kosovo) and Macedonia. On the latter territory, it found itself in competition with Bulgaria with regard to winning over the native, nationally ambivalent population. But if Serbia relied here on any power at all, it was not on Austria-Hungary or Russia, but rather on Turkey – indeed, Serbian historians call this orientation 'Turkophile'. After Milan's abdication, depending on which political group-ing happened to be forming a new government in Belgrade (and also on whether Milan happened to be in Serbia), some effort would be exerted on strengthening relations with either Russia or Austria-Hungary. Despite such occasional efforts it would be wrong to see Serbia in the pocket of either of those two Great Powers at any stage between 1889 and 1903.

The mood among all classes in Serbia in this period was nevertheless pro-Russian. The Radical Party and their leader Nikola Pašić had always seen Russia as Serbia's natural protector. This view had its supporters elsewhere at the top. Jovan Ristić, the grand old man of Serbian politics and the leader of the Liberal Party, was among them. As the head of the Regency Council, he was still one of the most influential figures in the country after 1889, and his position in this matter was unequivocal: 'We may enter into all kinds of relations with the West, receive its culture, send our sons to be educated there, take loans, but there is nothing we can do without Russia to realize our national ideals in respect of unification and the liberation of our tribe. That is the way it has been so far, and that is the way it will remain from now on; it is a historical truth.'[25] The Regency and the Government soon dispatched Nikola Pašić to St Petersburg (February 1890) where he obtained 75,000 rifles, ammunition and a loan for military purposes.[26]

Until then Russia, highly unpopular in Romania because it was in possession of Bessarabia, and squeezed out of Bulgaria by Prince Ferdinand Coburg and Prime Minister Stefan Stambolov, could in the Balkans boast only the doubtful friendship of Prince Nicholas of Montenegro. With Milan now gone, the Serbian opening was therefore eagerly seized by the Russians who had always seen him as incorrigibly pro-Austrian. Indeed, the Tsar provided two million dinars from his personal funds to pay Milan never to return to Serbia again – a deal subsequently ignored by the double-crossing ex-King.[27] Meanwhile, in July 1891 Ristić and Pašić accompanied the new king, young Alexander, on a visit to Russia. The Serbian agenda did not lack ambition. Ristić, keen to secure a dynastic connection, asked Tsar Alexander III to keep in mind that the King of Serbia would some day be getting married. But he also implored the Tsar not to allow the Serbian lands of Bosnia and Herzegovina to be annexed by Austria-Hungary. And whereas the Tsar promised only to consider in due course the matter of Alexander's marriage, he was adamant that Austria-Hungary would not annex Bosnia-Herzegovina: 'That will never happen. They know this in Vienna. Such an attempt would be fatal for the Monarchy!'[28]

In reality, however, the Russians had little appetite for seriously opposing Austria-Hungary in its Balkan backyard. The friendly attitude towards Serbia had been motivated by the need to create a counterweight to Bulgaria – but this was regional politics on a modest scale. Yet it so happened that, at a time when Serbia's relations with Russia were becoming almost cordial, those with Austria-Hungary were taking a turn for the worse, though theoretically Serbia was still bound to Austria-Hungary after 1889. Before abdicating, Milan had extended his secret 1881 convention with Vienna. And although Ristić knew what Milan had done (and was unhappy about the secret convention), Pašić, the Radical Party and the rest of the country were perfectly ignorant about the existence of such an arrangement with Vienna in the first place.[29]

Serbia Between Austria-Hungary and Russia

A problem in the relations between Serbia and Austria-Hungary was caused by the new freedom of the press in Serbia. Article 22 of the 1888 Constitution contained the famous, short provision: 'The press is free.' There was thus no censorship in Serbia.[30] Newly-liberated, the Serbian press then set about attacking Habsburg rule in Bosnia-Herzegovina, to the annoyance of Austro-Hungarian officialdom. Count Gustav Kálnoky, the Austro-Hungarian Foreign Minister, lamented the deterioration in relations and blamed it on the Serbian press, opining that the freedom of the press should only be enjoyed by highly educated nations.[31] Kálnoky himself prized erudition above all: he was a book collector and indeed possessed a library of pornographic books 'unmatched in Europe'.[32]

But the Serbian press was no more than an irritant. The real problem, from the point of view of Vienna, were the indications, however small, that Serbia could be moving towards economic independence from its big neighbour. Late in 1889 the Serbian Government decided to buy salt from Romania – rather than, as in the past, from Hungary.[33] The retaliation which followed combined political and economic elements. The Hungarians in particular, with their own livestock industry and ambitions to dominate the markets of Central Europe, were not going to remain passive. The importation of pigs from Serbia – its chief export to the Monarchy – was abruptly halted in the late spring of 1890, although there were no veterinary grounds for doing so. The ban was lifted by the autumn, but a reminder had been served of who the master was in the relationship.[34] Margrave János Pallavicini, who had been Secretary at the Austro-Hungarian Legation in Belgrade since 1887, described 'with great pleasure' to the Romanian statesman Take Jonescu how, 'whenever the poor Serbian Government resisted any demand of Austria, he would discover that all the Serbian pigs were stricken with sudden illness, and how directly the Serbian Government gave in, the pigs were instantly and miraculously cured, so that their export might be resumed.'[35] Thus the subsequent 1906-1911 customs conflict between Austria-Hungary and Serbia – the famous 'Pig War' – which holds such a prominent place in the historiography of their confrontation prior to 1914, had its first dress rehearsal as early as 1890, many years before the 1903 palace coup in Belgrade – the event which is supposed to have inaugurated such animosity. After 1890, similar bans on the importation of Serbian livestock were also imposed by the Monarchy in 1895-96, 1897-98, 1901 and 1902.[36] In other words, the 1889-1903 period was one long 'Pig War'.

The importance to Serbia of its livestock exports, and of the Austro-Hungarian market for them, is illustrated by the fact that as late as 1905 Austria-Hungary was taking 89.8% of Serbia's exports, of which 98% was livestock.[37] Economically, Austria-Hungary was thus absolutely dominating its small Balkan neighbour. In 1881 Serbia had been forced, in order to avoid a customs war, to conclude a very unfavourable trade agreement, giving Austria-Hungary privileged trade terms without any reciprocity. The next agreement, concluded in 1892 and lasting until 1906, was no better: Serbian livestock exports were subject to the Veterinary Convention (1892), which meant that they depended on the good-will of Austria-Hungary. The latter also enjoyed a virtual monopoly over Serbian imports because of low tariffs for its products. It acted, moreover, as the intermediary for the sale of Serbian goods elsewhere in Europe and it controlled, at the same time, Serbia's railway tariffs. Furthermore, Serbia's credit lines for its import and export trade depended on the financial institutions of Austria-Hungary.[38] Chronically and exorbitantly indebted as a state, Serbia was able to borrow money only in Austria-Hungary, a state of affairs that imposed obvious restrictions on the country's freedom of action.

There were occasions when Vienna anticipated that the Serbs would simply crumple under the weight of their economic problems. In December 1893, for example, Foreign Minister Kálnoky seemed convinced that Serbia, then facing possible bankruptcy, was about to collapse internally.[39] No wonder that the Serbian Government tried to wriggle out of this situation. In 1895-96 it attempted in vain to find alternative markets for the sale of livestock via the port of Salonika. While Serbia struggled, in Vienna and Budapest pigs were being seen and used as an economic weapon even to achieve political aims of a relatively trivial character. When Belgrade protested at the proposed display of the Serbian flag (along with those from lands under the Crown of St Stephen) during the Hungarian millennium celebrations of 1896, Count Agenor Gołuchowski, Kálnoky's successor as Foreign Minister, was incensed, threatening the Serbian Government that he would no longer mediate with the Hungarian Government to facilitate the passage of Serbian exports.[40]

This tension in relations with the Monarchy had led a crowd in Belgrade to burn a Hungarian flag and then proceed to the Russian Legation where it shouted ovations.[41] The Government headed by Stojan Novaković, in power since mid-1895, had already begun to turn towards Russia. That this course is associated with Novaković is interesting because scholar, diplomat and founder of the Progressive Party, Novaković had long been a convinced Austrophile. However, during his time as the Serbian Minister at Constantinople (1885-1892) he had observed how Austria-Hungary showed little enthusiasm for advancing Serbia's interests in European Turkey and how the only diplomatic support had come from Russia. Before accepting King Alexander's suggestion to form a new government, he drew up a memorandum for him, rejecting the idea that Serbia should have a secret convention with any foreign power – he meant, of course, Austria-Hungary. What he wanted was a free hand for Serbia to pursue a policy of relying on Russia. Alexander accepted this memorandum and Novaković became Prime Minister.[42]

Lasting almost eighteen months, the Novaković Government was one of the longest during Alexander's mercurial reign. And although this period was not long enough for it to accomplish anything major, internally or externally, it nevertheless decisively shattered the notion that Serbia was in foreign policy a satellite state of Austria-Hungary. A recent Serbian judgement about Novaković as Prime Minister is that he was 'the greatest possible nationalist in Serbia'.[43] He told Franz Schiessl, the Austro-Hungarian Minister in Belgrade, that, while Serbia wanted to cultivate equally friendly relations with all the Powers, 'Slavonic identity' was a strong unifying factor.[44] To be sure, although the Russian press welcomed the change of direction in Belgrade, official Russia did not rush to embrace a Serbia which, with its unsettled internal political scene, disastrous finances and a weak Army, inspired little respect.[45] When, in October 1896, the Serbian Government attempted to obtain 100,000 rifles from Russia, the Finance Minister Sergei Witte told the Serbian Minister at St Petersburg: 'You shouldn't be buying rifles if you don't have the money.' The Serbian effort thus ended in a fiasco.[46] Meanwhile, by early 1896 a *rapprochement* had been effected between Russia and Bulgaria – Serbia's rival in Macedonia. But Russia, with an eye on influencing regional developments, also wished the Balkan states to turn to each other. This corresponded to Novaković's own views on the necessity of Balkan cooperation. A Russian orientation in Belgrade, at a time when Austria-Hungary had renewed the squeeze on Serbian livestock imports, appeared all the more justified.

Mihailo Vojvodić, a noted authority on Serbia's foreign policy at the close of the nineteenth century, has drawn attention to the existence, by the mid-1890s, of an important consensus in the Serbian political establishment: all three of Serbia's political parties – Progressive, Liberal and Radical, considered Serbia's national interests to be best served by relying on Russia.[47] For the time being at least the consensus also included King Alexander, because he now listened more to his pro-Russian mother Natalie than to his father, ex-King Milan. The administration which succeeded Novaković in early 1997 has been seen as her creation. In particular, she wanted Alexander to cooperate with the Radical Party, seeing in such an alliance the best guarantee for the Throne given the strength of the Radicals – several of whom now became ministers.[48] The new Prime Minister was Đorđe Simić, until recently Serbia's Minister in Vienna and a man with strong sympathies for the Radicals.[49] And although there was concern in St Petersburg (and some relief in Vienna) at the departure of Novaković, the Simić Government made sure to reassure the Russians that it would 'not be Austrophile oriented.'[50]

Simić thus continued what Slobodan Jovanović termed 'nationalist' foreign policy, which really amounted to attempts at protecting and extending Serbian church and cultural interests in Macedonia.[51] Although Serbia had wanted to get Bulgaria to agree to a division of spheres of influence in Macedonia, Bulgaria, eying the whole of Macedonia, had successfully resisted this. But a de facto delineation had existed as Russia, balancing between Belgrade and Sofia, had been thwarting Bulgarian ambitions (e.g., the appointment of its bishops) across the right bank of the Vardar river where Serbia wished to establish its own influence. Such Russian support of Serbia, however, ended with the downfall of the Simić Government in early autumn 1897. By now Alexander had again become receptive to his father, who had long been regarded in Russia as a mere instrument of Austrian policy, the ultimate aim of which – it was believed in St Petersburg – was to annex Serbia.[52] But Milan had had a personal reason to bring about the change: the Simić Government, just like that of Novaković beforehand, had been against his return to Serbia.[53] It would also seem that Milan had convinced his son about a plot, supposedly hatched by the Radical leader Nikola Pašić, to replace him on the Serbian Throne with a Russian Grand Duke. Therefore Milan considered it his 'duty' to return to Belgrade, to be, as he put it, 'at the post of danger', in order to help his son preserve his throne.[54]

The new government came into being in October 1897. Headed by Milan's devoted friend Vladan Đorđević (who had until then served as Serbia's Minister at Constantinople), it is normally described as being in the service of King Aleksander's 'personal regime'. Its foreign policy orientation has almost universally been seen among Serbian historians as breaking with the pro-Russian course established by the Novaković and Simić governments and reverting back to the old reliance on Austria-Hungary. However, in her recent biography of Vladan Đorđević, Suzana Rajić has argued convincingly that the Prime Minister had in fact seen the folly of tying Serbia's destiny to just one Great Power (i.e., Austria-Hungary), showing that he had actually bent over backwards to retain Russia's friendship.[55]

The problem which had caused a massive deterioration in Russo-Serbian relations after 1897 was not Đorđević's foreign policy, but rather the fact that Milan had returned to Serbia. Not long thereafter, the Russian

Tsar Nicholas II ostentatiously received Peter Karađorđević, the pretender from the rival Serbian dynasty – a move widely interpreted as indicating Russia's complete abandonment of the House of Obrenović. Russia also reduced the level of diplomatic representation in Belgrade, leaned on France to prevent Serbia obtaining a loan in Paris, and insisted that its own loans to Serbia be immediately repaid.[56] In Vienna, by contrast, Joint Finance Minister Kállay had acted quickly to force the Unionbank into giving Serbia a much-needed loan. There was a further sign of Austro-Hungarian approval. 'Our pigs', Slobodan Jovanović wrote, 'which at the time of the Novaković and Simić governments were at every moment sick, became during Đorđević's government unexpectedly healthy.'[57]

King Alexander, just like his Prime Minister Đorđević, was unhappy about the rift with Russia. Significantly, he had not renewed the 1881 secret convention with Austria-Hungary before its expiry in 1895. As Michael Boro Petrovich has argued, Alexander was not 'a confirmed Austrophile', and wished to balance between St Petersburg and Vienna.[58] But this was not possible as long as Milan continued to play a role in Serbia. That role, indeed, soon became even more important: in early January 1898 Alexander appointed his father Commander of the Active Army. For Serbia, this turned out to be a stroke of luck. With unbounded energy, the ex-King threw himself into the pressing task of reforming his country's Army. Its state in 1897 was pitiful: the artillery was antiquated and most of the rifles were in poor working order; the officer corps was too small even for peace-time conditions, while the non-commissioned officer structure was also far too small with the NCOs themselves badly trained; and the training of Army recruits likewise required modernization.[59] In his reform drive, Milan increased the size of the regular Army dramatically, creating a new organizational formation of twenty regiments, each with four battalions; the Belgrade Military Academy produced 500 new officers within four years; the building of new barracks improved conditions for both officers and men; and, new weaponry, in the form of rifles and heavy cannon, was obtained, although not in sufficient quantities, from Germany and France respectively. The colossal financial expenditure for all this was only possible because of Milan's exceptional drive and authority as 'co-ruler'. The Government and the Assembly were made to approve the budgets without a murmur, and any opposition to Serbia's military build-up would be branded as unpatriotic.[60] Significantly, the military profession had begun to attract the flower of the young Serbian intelligentsia – before which Milan would, 'like a magician, unfold the national banner'. The ex-King made every effort to create a military caste on the Prussian model.[61]

Thus the modern Serbian Army, which was to fight with such distinction from 1912 to 1918, was unquestionably Milan's creation. The youth and professionalism of its officers and non-commissioned officers stemmed directly from the period of Milan's Army reforms. Slobodan Jovanović remarked that the Army, spending a third of the state budget, looked better organized than the state itself.[62] Ironically, Milan had intended it to fight Russia. He had disapproved of the 1897 agreement between Austria-Hungary and Russia to maintain the status quo in the Balkans: he wanted Austria-Hungary to completely eject Russia from the region, believing that this was the only way for Serbia to obtain Macedonia which Russia had earmarked for Bulgaria; and that this, too, was the way to ensure the survival of the Obrenović dynasty, threatened and undermined as it was by Russia. Convinced that some day there would be an Austro-Russian war, he had intended the Serbian Army to take part – as fully prepared as possible.[63] Another irony, as subsequent events were soon to demonstrate, was that the Serbian officers' corps had under Milan's stewardship developed loyalty to him personally rather than to the dynasty.

Caesar's Wife

Russian displeasure with Serbia became particularly noticeable following Milan's appointment as Army Commander. The Serbian diplomat Čedomilj Mijatović even asserted that the Russian secret police had organized the assassination attempt on Milan, which then occurred in the middle of Belgrade, on 6 July 1899. Certainly, the assassin, a young Bosnian Serb, claimed to have been recruited and paid by a Russian person in Bucharest.[64] If so, the *Ivandanjski atentat* (St John's Day Attempt) backfired terribly: not only did Milan escape practically unhurt, but Russia's friends in the Radical Party leadership, whose involvement in the assassination attempt Milan had alleged, were now locked up, put on trial and sentenced to heavy prison terms. Nikola Pašić, the Radical leader, was among those imprisoned, though there is no evidence that he or his fellow Radicals had had anything to do with plotting against Milan's life. He escaped execution thanks to Russian and Austro-Hungarian representations in Belgrade. Ignorant at the time about his life having been spared, he had made grovelling confessions about his 'objective' responsibility in the assassination attempt – a cowardly and despicable act which, implicating as it did some of his friends in the Party as 'anti-dynastic' elements, had brought him a pardon, but also resulted, temporarily at least, in his political demise. People would now avoid Pašić 'as if he were a leper'.[65]

What Milan had done was to exploit the opportunity provided by the failed assassination to destroy his old enemy the Radical Party – irrespective of who had been involved in the conspiracy. Interestingly, he later told his faithful friend Vladan Đorđević, the Prime Minister in 1899, that it had actually been his own son, King Alexander ('little Nero', as he called him) and his mistress Mrs Draga Mašin, who had stood behind the St John's

Day Attempt. He explained at great length to Đorđević how he had opposed Alexander's liaison with Draga, and how they had concluded that he had to be 'got rid of'. In this, so Milan claimed, the couple knew that they could rely on the help of his sworn enemies, the Russians. Moreover, Draga was according to Milan 'a mere agent of Russia'.[66]

Who, then, was Draga Mašin (née Lunjevica)? This supremely ambitious woman, who in August 1900 married Alexander and thus became the Queen of Serbia, managed to jolt Serbian history largely by virtue of her dubious reputation. To most of those opposed to her marriage with Alexander – and they probably formed the vast majority of the adult population, women as well as men – she was just a 'slut [*drolja*]'. Similar or worse appellations about her were widely circulated. Yet she stemmed from a solid bourgeois family, her father Pantelija Lunjevica having held important administrative posts. She had received a good education and had a flair for foreign languages.[67] In fact, she attained the height of respectability by becoming a *dame d'honneur* to Queen Natalie, which is how the young Alexander met her in the first place. Apparently, however, there was another side to her. She had married young, and her husband, Svetozar Mašin, an engineer of Czech descent, died early. Most historians link his death to alcohol abuse, but a well-informed contemporary German source gives an expanded, though unsubstantiated rendition: Mašin had died of 'sorrow' because his hot-blooded Draga had had many lovers.[68]

Be that as it may, the years between the death of her husband (1886) and the beginning of her service with Queen Natalie (1891) have been seen as Draga's 'dark period', during which her moral downfall is supposed to have taken place. All accounts agree that, newly-widowed with meagre income, she had faced a very difficult situation. But Ana Stolić, Draga's able biographer – though at times an uncritical one – points out only one relationship which Draga had pursued at this time, unsuccessfully with a French engineer working on the Oriental Railways in Serbia.[69] By contrast, Slobodan Jovanović, an authority on modern Serbian history greater than which is hard to imagine, maintained that Draga went from one 'friend' to another – mostly well-to-do men – in search of marriage and material security. In this respect, the episode with the Frenchman is historically interesting because, as Jovanović commented, she had faked pregnancy in order to get him to marry her.[70] As will be seen, possibly similar behaviour by Draga and her inability to conceive a child was to play a role in the downfall of the Obrenović dynasty.

Those historians who have defended Draga have argued that Queen Natalie would never have selected a woman with a bad reputation to be her lady-in-waiting. On the other hand, Jovanović maintained that Natalie had taken Draga into her service out of 'sheer pity.'[71] At that time (1891) Natalie had already gone through a messy divorce with Milan and had actually been expelled from Serbia. Pašić's Radical Government, fearing Milan's detrimental influence, had agreed to his proposals whereby, in return for his promise not to return to Serbia until Alexander came of age, he would receive a large financial compensation and Natalie would also leave the country. Pašić thus sacrificed Natalie, a popular figure who was forcibly and scandalously removed from Serbia amid public protests in May 1891. She then set up her residence in exile, in Biarritz. Draga joined her there and this is where, in 1894, Alexander met his future wife for the first time.

Draga is said to have been something of a beauty in her youth, but all the available photographs only show a pudgy, unalluring creature. Just what had so attracted the King to her remains a matter for speculation. It would appear, however, that she was able to overcome and exploit to her advantage Alexander's anxieties about his sexual adequacy.[72] Significantly, this woman was much older than Alexander. Ana Stolić gives her year of birth as 1866 (Alexander was born in 1876), but most other accounts maintain that she was twelve years his senior. The Russian diplomat Alexander Savinsky, who met her in 1902, described her appearance as 'rather plain than pretty, no longer in her first youth and inclined to be stout.'[73] Constantin Dumba, who became the Austro-Hungarian Minister in Belgrade in February 1903, wrote that she showed 'no trace' of her former attraction and assessed her age as forty.[74] Irrespective of her fading looks, or her age, she captivated the young King completely and she knew perfectly well what she was doing – the idea of course was to marry him. The Serbian historian Andrija Radenić has scoffed at the recent attempts to portray Draga in a favourable light, arguing that she had abused her influence on the young Alexander, whom he describes as 'a sick man'.[75] Queen Natalie had no hesitation about what to do once she found out about the seriousness of the liaison between her monarch son and her lady-in-waiting: Draga was dismissed in autumn 1897 and had to leave Biarritz. Undeterred, Alexander set her up in a comfortable house not far from the Royal Palace in Belgrade. Here, she left nothing to chance, quickly creating her own intelligence/police apparatus. According to Tasa Milenković, the famous Serbian police chief, she was better informed about what was going on in the ministries and in town than Alexander himself.[76]

Although everyone knew that she was the King's mistress, members of the diplomatic corps went to Draga's weekly receptions and would invite her to their own functions.[77] She had become the 'Serbian Pompadour' – as Vladan Đorđević called her in his memoirs.[78] Without doubt, it was precisely her blatant and significant role in Alexander's life which had attracted the attention of the resident diplomats. In plotting her path to royal consort status, she could also rely on some powerful friends from within that community – the Russians. As has been seen, the aim of

Russian policy in Serbia was to remove Milan (who had returned to Serbia to take charge of the Army), as an exponent of Vienna. According to the Obrenović loyalist Čedomilj Mijatović, the well-informed Serbian diplomat who had until 1900 served as the Minister in London, Draga could play a useful role in this. He wrote in 1906 that 'unofficial Russia', as he described it, was 'terribly unscrupulous' and bent on ousting Milan; that Milan 'hated' Draga; that Alexander was madly in love with his mistress; and that the latter was known to be very ambitious. 'Could this woman', Mijatović suggested, 'not be used as wedge between the son and father, to separate them for ever?'[79]

Practically all the important Serbian historiography on the subject, from Jovanović in the 1930s to Vojvodić in the 1980s, has recognized Russia's machinations in bringing about the marriage between Alexander and Draga. In the 1950s, Wayne Vucinich, the respected Serbian-American historian, also devoted considerable attention to this matter.[80] More recently, Vasa Kazimirović attempted a loose general defence of Draga ('She was, in the first place, an educated woman ...'), but admits that since early 1901 the Tsarist secret police had been 'practically camping in the Serbian Royal Palace.'[81] Whether Draga was 'a mere agent of Russia' – as Milan was to claim – is questionable since she clearly pursued her own agenda. From 1899 at the latest, certainly, she was in close touch with the Russian Legation in Belgrade, initially with the Military Attaché Baron Taube and then with the Chargé d'Affaires Paul Mansurov. In a private letter from 1901, Queen Natalie maintained that her son had been the victim of a political intrigue and that Draga had been directed from the Russian Legation.[82] Ana Stolić has used Russian documents to demonstrate conclusively that Mansurov in particular had worked with Draga backstage. In October 1900 he proudly wrote to St Petersburg that 'Russia had brought Queen Draga to the Serbian throne.'[83]

This would obviously not have been possible had Alexander not likewise been keen to make Draga his wife. Cleverly, however, he had struck a bargain with the Russians before announcing his engagement. Anticipating strong resistance to Draga throughout Serbian society, he desperately needed to cover the whole wretched affair with the fig leaf of respectability which only a major foreign power could provide. The Russian agenda in Serbia included, in addition to getting rid of Milan, the return to political grace of the Russia-friendly Radicals, most of whose leadership was in jail following the St John's Day Attempt on Milan. But this was a small price to pay as far as Alexander was concerned. A rehabilitation of the Radicals and a breach with Milan over Draga would bring Serbia nearer to Russia, which in any case suited his objective of cultivating Russian friendship: he knew that his father's very presence in Serbia was a provocation to Russia.[84] According to Slobodan Jovanović, only three days before the announcement of the royal engagement, Mansurov had stipulated to Alexander that Russia's attitude towards the proposed marriage would depend on whether the Radicals would be pardoned; Alexander, opportunist to the core, in turn asked that the Russian Tsar be his best man at the wedding.[85]

It was a deal. And for Alexander it was the best possible one in the circumstances. His matrimonial plan could certainly find no approval anywhere else. When, on 21 July 1900, the betrothal was announced, he not only alienated his father forever, but also annoyed the Austrian Emperor. A master at double-dealing, Alexander had authorized Milan to seek on his behalf a princess in Western Europe while in reality he had already decided on Draga. Milan, ignorant about his son's real intentions, was of course keen to ensure the continuation of the dynasty and took the whole matter very seriously.[86] But he was also anxious to ensure that Serbia would be anchored to the Triple Alliance, and so he enlisted the help of the Austrian Foreign Office in his search for a future Queen of Serbia. In the end both Franz Joseph and Wilhelm II were personally engaged in this farcical exercise. The German Emperor actually found a suitable bride, Princess Alexandra von Schaumburg-Lippe who was 'beautiful, highly-cultured, and closely connected with several great Courts.'[87] Arrangements had already been made with the Princess, and Milan left Serbia for Carlsbad to apply the finishing touch: to prepare the ground for her meeting with Alexander. Soon, however, the sensational news broke out that he would actually be marrying Draga Mašin. The celebrated Montenegrin diplomat and statesman *Vojvoda* Gavro Vuković commented on this occasion: 'Serbia is a land of surprises, the like of which happen nowhere else.'[88] Franz Joseph, who had kindly received Alexander in audience as recently as December 1899, was by all accounts furious.[89]

Franz Ferdinand, on the other hand, was apparently delighted. Among the first telegrams of congratulation that Alexander received following the engagement was one from the Archduke.[90] This was hardly surprising as the latter, himself only recently wedded with his Sophie in the teeth of Court opposition, would have sincerely welcomed Alexander's determination to marry a woman of his heart's choice. The Austrian writer Karl Gladt, who produced a substantial work on the Obrenović dynasty, speculates that Franz Ferdinand's marriage with Sophie must have encouraged Alexander to make his own, similar decision.[91] It was indeed a bold step, bordering on reckless. In Serbia, the news of the royal engagement was received with utter consternation. Vukašin Petrović, the acting Prime Minister (in the absence of Vladan Đorđević who had gone abroad), tried to talk the King out of the proposed marriage, listing some formidable objections: Draga was infertile; she was considerably older than Alexander; in any case she enjoyed, rightly or wrongly, a bad reputation; the rival

Karađorđević dynasty would suddenly receive massive support; the royal couple would never be received at any European court; the Serbian educated classes would never come to terms with such a marriage; finally, Petrović warned, Serbia would become the subject of derision and contempt around the world.[92]

What Petrović did not articulate was the thought probably on the minds of most Serbs: Draga was just an ordinary woman and she was actually Alexander's mistress – a widely known and problematic fact for patriarchal Serbia. But the main problem was the prevalent belief that she had also been the mistress of quite a few other men. By the time of her engagement to Alexander, Belgrade was awash with rumours that Draga had slept with, among others, Ludwig von Wäcker-Gotter, the German Minister in Belgrade, and the aforementioned Paul Mansurov, the Russian Chargé d'Affaires, as well as Baron Fedor Taube, the Russian Military Attaché.[93] Unlikely as these liaisons were, the gossip would not go away. Attempting to dissuade the King from marrying Draga, his relative Colonel Alexander Konstantinović told him that he had slept with her himself and for ten dinars.[94] Ex-King Milan later claimed that Draga's tariff had subsequently gone up to five hundred dinars.[95] Đorđe Genčić, the Interior Minister, kept a list of Draga's supposed lovers.[96] But was his own name also on that list? For according to Herbert Vivian, a contemporary British observer of Serbia, Genčić had told the King with regard to the proposed marriage with Draga: 'Sire, you cannot marry her. She has been everybody's mistress – mine among the rest.'[97] Possibly Alexander believed him, for he went red in the face, raised his arm and, all trembling, struck the Interior Minister on the cheek with full force. As the King displayed every intention to continue his assault, Genčić took him by the arms. The appearance of other Ministers then put a stop to this unseemly scene in the Royal Palace.[98]

While Genčić would later conceive and lead the conspiracy to topple the royal couple, opposition to the proposed marriage was fierce from the start. The Đorđević Government promptly resigned after failing to change the King's mind. The Liberal Party politician Živan Živanović remarked at the time that, 'physically and morally', as well as dynastically, such a wedlock would stand out in Europe as a 'monstrosity'.[99] It is important to note that disapproving of Draga was seen as a requisite act of patriotism. What was at stake was the reputation of the country. As the Liberal Party leader Jovan Avakumović put it, Alexander's marriage with Draga would not only be demeaning for the King, but also 'disgracing for the fatherland.'[100] This view has reverberated in many writings. 'By the people of Serbia as a whole', wrote the British historian Harold Temperley, 'the match was resented as a national humiliation.'[101] Whether Draga had in reality led a loose life is a matter of very slight historical interest – the point is that, at the time that she became the Queen of Serbia, this had been a broadly accepted proposition.

With the Government incapable of influencing Alexander, the only power player in Serbia that could have stopped him from carrying out his plan was the military. As the King, Alexander should theoretically have enjoyed the loyalty of the officer corps, but the latter was loyal in the first place to Milan, the commander-in-chief who had done so much for the Serbian Army. A widespread belief existed among officers that Milan would return to the country to lead a revolt against his son – in which case they would have obeyed his orders. Admittedly, there were those among the senior commanders who did not wish to lead the Army 'down the path of revolution', but in informal consultations the vast majority of officers declared themselves against the King marrying Draga.[102] However, this time they waited in vain for Milan: he was never to return to Serbia. Having resigned as the commander of the Active Army, he wrote a short letter from Vienna to his son which was then widely circulated in the European press. In it, he warned Alexander about the *'impossible* wedlock', arguing that it would lead Serbia directly into ruin and that the dynasty would never recover. He ended his missive: 'I would be the first to salute that Government which would expel you from the land after such a feather-brained act.'[103]

In his dismay and exasperation, Milan had admittedly not been content to draw the line at writing angry letters. During the night of 24/25 July 1900, only days before Alexander's wedding with Draga, a group of high-ranking officers met with Jovan Avakumović, the former Prime Minister who had been close to Milan. The officers included three generals, four colonels and a lieutenant colonel. They were led by General Vasa Mostić who had received a message from Milan, conveying to Avakumović his demand that the marriage with Draga (he called her 'a tart') be prevented. Milan had left it to Avakumović to choose the way in which this could be achieved, but also expressed his consent, 'if it cannot be done in any other way', for his son to be killed. Of course, this was a very grave message and Avakumović, otherwise a fierce opponent of Draga, had quite a job trying to persuade the officers that no action should be taken. What is quite interesting is that several of them, albeit a minority according to Avakumović, were in favour of killing Alexander.[104] As will be seen, the same sentiment was rather widespread among the lower officer ranks in the Serbian Army. As for Avakumović, despite his nonviolent disposition, he would soon find himself in a conspiracy against the King and the Queen – although he would not admit this in his memoirs. Indeed, he was to be the Prime Minister of the first post-regicide Serbian Government.

Pregnant Anticipation

Shocked by Alexander's announcement, the political class in Serbia was in disarray. And Milan, potentially the greatest threat to Alexander, did not venture out of Vienna. Possibly, he feared for his life. So determined was his son the King to legalise his union with Draga that he was quite ready to use force against Milan in the event that the latter returned to Serbia.[105] Draga was now given the ludicrous official title of 'Serene Fiancée', and Royal Guards were posted at her house. All of Serbia observed these events with stupefaction. A delegation of prominent merchants begged the King, practically 'on their knees', not to marry Draga.[106] But Alexander would not be embarrassed. His chief concern, after the resignation of the Đorđević Government, was to form a pliant new cabinet to help him navigate through this stormy period – for without a Government in place, his marriage would be even less defensible. Politician after politician, however, refused to lead such an administration despite his pleas, bribes and threats. One of them, Steva Popović, told the King openly in Draga's presence: 'You wish to marry Draga – you must be joking! Draga – really? God be with you!'[107] Some politicians found Alexander's pressurizing tactics almost impossible to bear. After more than an hour of being bullied by the King to join a new government, Živan Živanović cried out: 'Leave me alone, for God's sake! Or I'll open the window and jump ... I don't care what happens to me.'[108]

In the end, the infatuated and tenacious young King managed to cobble together a government of non-entities, the so-called *svadbeno ministarstvo* (wedding cabinet). The Prime Minister became Aleksa Jovanović, the President of the Court of Appeal who took the Foreign Ministry portfolio at the same time despite speaking no foreign language.[109] Few people had heard of this quiet judge. Even fewer had heard of the rest of his team, who were mainly anonymous, lower-level bureaucrats. As no Army General wished to be placed in charge of the War Ministry, Alexander appointed his own aide-de-camp, Lieutenant-Colonel Miloš Vasić. Even such as it was, this Government nevertheless represented a success for the King. Significantly, he had also broken the resistance of the Church – though Metropolitan Innocentius, in giving his blessing to the marriage, also made sure to cite reasons against it.[110]

But it was the Russian blessing which, as it turned out, provided the sugar-coating that ultimately made the marriage with Draga palatable to an otherwise disbelieving and scoffing Serbian public. The ensuing support from the Radicals, made possible only by Russian enterprise in the whole affair, was also of inestimable value to Alexander. On 22 July it was announced that the Russian Tsar would be the best man (*kum*) at the wedding – by Orthodox tradition the *kum* being one who is, as Rebecca West put it, 'as

it were a godparent of the marital tie'.[111] Admittedly, the Tsar would not
attend in person, he would be represented by the Chargé d'Affaires Mansurov. Still, given the huge importance that the Serbs have always attached
to the institution of *kumstvo*, the Emperor's gesture extended much-
needed legitimacy to the whole shoddy-seeming business with Draga.

Alexander's Russian gambit, it has to be said, was simply brilliant. For
inevitably, the official involvement of the Tsar himself added a political
dimension. Astutely, Alexander allowed the news to filter through that
Milan had stood behind the effort to bring a German princess to Serbia.
The question now being asked among the people was: are you for Russia
and Draga, or are you for Austria and Milan?[112] In this way, Jovanović
pointed out, those opposing Milan and Austria – the greater part of Serbian
public opinion – were reluctantly shifting themselves to Draga's side.[113]
Already on 25 July the official gazette announced the decree pardoning the
Radical Party members who had been jailed in the aftermath of the failed
assassination on Milan.

The elaborate royal wedding took place soon thereafter, on 5 August
1900, in Belgrade's Cathedral Church of St Michael the Archangel. Alexander had indeed triumphed over his opponents, although all he had really
demonstrated was that purely personal considerations were more important to him than those of the state. But in his mind, he had identified
himself – and his wife – with the state. A massive purge began in Serbia
even before the wedding ceremony: all those who had opposed the
marriage with Draga were pushed out of the way, beginning with Palace
personnel. Members of the Đorđević Government were vilified and some
of them, like Genčić, sought refuge in Vienna. The Army represented a
main target, given that so many of its officers, especially the high-ranking
ones, were known for their personal loyalty to Milan. Four of Serbia's six
generals were now pensioned off. Milan's supporters in the officers' corps
were 'systematically' removed and the most important appointments went
to those who were the quickest to adapt to the new situation – in which
what counted most of all was allegiance to Queen Draga. As for Milan, the
Russian secret police kept a watch on his residence in Vienna's Johannes-
gasse, while two cavalry regiments patrolled along the banks of the Sava
and Danube rivers with orders to use force if the ex-King attempted to
return to Serbia.[114]

A possible explanation for Alexander's hubristic behaviour is that he
apparently believed his wife was pregnant. A royal baby, clearly, would have
strengthened the dynasty and silenced all the critics of his marriage. On 7
September 1900, i.e., barely a month after the royal wedding, it was officially announced that Queen Draga was expectant. According to a report
from the Austro-Hungarian Legation, Alexander stated shortly before
marrying Draga: 'This woman has already risked her life for me twice, I

am not going to allow a third time!"[115] Ana Stolić admits that on two occasions before they got married Draga had persuaded Alexander that she was expecting his child.[116] Thus it may be assumed that Alexander had now rushed into marriage partly on account of a genuine desire not to have a third pregnancy terminated. From Draga's point of view, certainly, such concern for her well-being could only facilitate her ascent to royal status.

In fact, Draga never carried an unborn young. What was born, instead, was a European scandal of the first order. Eugène Caulet, the French doctor who in September established Draga's pregnancy, later admitted that he had not properly examined the Queen.[117] Caulet's role remains murky, but it is most unlikely that Draga, given her previous manipulations, actually believed herself to be carrying a child. 'Once she began to lie', Slobodan Jovanović wrote, 'she had to lie more and more.'[118] Alexander and Serbia had been fooled into accepting the certainty of the postulated 'blessed condition'. But what was the idea behind this madness? Was there anything to the rumours about an intention, as the London *Spectator* put it in May 1901, 'to foist a supposititious child upon the people'?[119] This, certainly, was what Queen Natalie suspected and she warned the Russian Court about it. Jovanović suggests that Draga had been under the strong influence of her sister Christine, who happened to be pregnant at the time, and that the idea of sneaking in someone else's baby had originated with her. Christine's own pregnancy, however, ended with a miscarriage. Draga then 'lost her head entirely and let matters take their course'.[120] The whole plot, as the contemporary Balkan pundit Mary Edith Durham put it, was 'worthy only of a second-rate cinematograph'.[121]

The happy royal event was supposed to take place in the second half of April 1901. In the meantime, Draga had in consequence began to gain popularity. The Royal Palace was inundated with gifts of infant clothes and cradles, some of the latter very elaborate. An Austrian midwife had duly taken up residence in the Palace. Of course, everything would have been forgiven had the Queen given birth to an heir. But the month of April came – and nothing was happening. Dr Caulet was summoned back to Belgrade and established 'immediately' that the Queen was not pregnant. He later defended himself by saying that he had in the previous year informed the royal couple only about what he saw as 'indications' of expectancy.[122] More importantly, the Russians had sent their own gynecologist, Dr Vladimir Snegirev, who arrived accompanied by a fellow Russian specialist. According to Jovanović, both the Russian Legation in Belgrade and the Russian secret police had demanded this. On 29 April Snegirev examined Draga – he reportedly declared that Draga was as capable of giving birth as he was.[123] Together with Caulet, he signed a protocol stating that the Queen was not pregnant. Alexander's initial reaction was to demand that Snegirev be 'whipped senseless' and then dumped over the border.[124]

In the circumstances, however, the authorities in Belgrade had to publish the expert finding. The European press enjoyed a field day in the light of this debacle. Draga was mercilessly ridiculed, but so was Alexander. 'With such a royal couple', Jovanović wrote with disgust, 'the Serbian state looked like the last among the states, its history being no more than a chronicle of scandals.'[125] And although many in Serbia had always had their doubts about Draga's fertility, the whole episode was now seen by all and sundry as a massive, inexcusable hoax. The reputation of the Queen had been dealt the final, mortal blow. By all accounts, however, Alexander's loyalty and affection for her remained undiminished. In fact, she had become his co-ruler and possibly more than that. Already during the crisis caused by the resignation of Đorđević's Government, she had used her connections to help Alexander construct the so-called 'wedding cabinet', two members of which were her relatives.[126] After becoming Queen, she had moved fast to consolidate her power. In November 1900 the Serbian politician Mihailo Vujić told his Montenegrin friend Gavro Vuković that 'everything' in Serbia depended on the 'energetic' Draga: 'The King and the Government unconditionally execute all her wishes.'[127]

The same perception of Draga's power and influence was recorded by Constantin Dumba, the Austro-Hungarian Minister in Belgrade. Not only, he wrote, had the police become the Queen's arbitrary instrument, but also the appointments and promotions in both the civil and military branches of the state, however minor, depended 'solely' on her caprice.[128] Jovanović suggested that the King saw her as 'the epitome of wisdom and goodness' and would do nothing in politics without consulting her.[129] But this was a most contradistinctive relationship. Vlaho Bukovac, the artist who made portraits of the royal couple, recalled that Draga would treat Alexander as if he was a 'baby'. The King, in his childhood much neglected by his parents, must have loved it. Indeed, he imposed his obsession with Draga on the whole of Serbia: regiments, schools and villages were named after her. This crafty woman came to be a 'state cult'.[130]

King Alexander's Foreign Policy Fiasco

Interestingly, the Russians were unimpressed. Having played such an important role in bringing about the royal marriage, the Russian Imperial Court refused to receive the Serbian royal couple at St Petersburg – something which, Tcharykow, their Minister in Belgrade, considered to have 'destroyed their prestige among the Serbian people.'[131] For the Tsar made various excuses in order not to grant the new royal couple an audience. As it turned out this was a matter of some consequence: it isolated Alexander internationally and thus eased the way to his bloody end – one which provoked little regret.

An obvious question regarding Russia's policy towards Serbia imposes itself: why did the Russian Tsar agree to be the best man (*kum*), albeit by a proxy, at Alexander's wedding? The desire to get rid of Milan has already been discussed, but surely the Tsar must have been informed about rumours concerning Draga's history – could he knowingly have stooped so low as to publicly endorse Alexander's utterly inappropriate choice of Draga for queen and fellow royal in the interests of Russian *realpolitik*? The Montenegrins, who had been carefully observing the developments in Serbia, were also discussing this question. Prince Nicholas of Montenegro, who clearly recognized Alexander's folly, was also delighted by it, as he now considered his way to the Serbian throne open – since he was always scheming to install himself in Belgrade as the leader of all Serbs. Simo Popović, his able secretary, put it to him: 'It is amazing, my Lord! Draga being what she is, she is a woman with a past, so how come the Tsar agreed to be *kum*?' The Prince replied: 'Well, that's the Russians for you. They have never known what they are doing. Tea and vodka have scorched their brains.'[132] This was, however, an unfair assessment. In fact, Mansurov, the Russian diplomat in Belgrade, knew perfectly well what he was doing, but St Petersburg did not, having not been properly informed – about Draga.

Initially, to be sure, everything went well for the Serbo-Russian relationship in the wake of the royal marriage. Alexander's foreign policy was 'simple and clear' according to Jovanović: 'he gave himself up entirely to the Russians.'[133] It is just not true, as Albertini maintains, that Alexander fell under Russian influence only after Milan died in 1901.[134] A pro-Russian course had been determined in 1900, immediately after the royal wedding. The King personally picked Stojan Novaković, the former Prime Minister who had pursued a pro-Russian course, to be Serbia's Minister in St Petersburg. Novaković was told that Serbia's friendly policy towards Russia would not be some kind of temporary political manoeuvre, but rather an orientation 'on a firm and permanent basis.'[135] The Russians, for their part, sent to Belgrade Nikolai Tcharykow, one of their best diplomats from the younger generation, to fill the long-vacant Minister's spot – a sure sign that Serbia was being paid great attention.[136] Tcharykow later described the time of his arrival, at the end of February 1901, as 'the heyday of renewed Russo-Serbian friendship'. This was a consequence, he wrote, 'of the love match of King Alexander with Madame Draga.'[137]

But Madame Draga, as Tcharykow was soon to discover, was precisely the problem. Reacting to the complete flop of the royal pregnancy, Alexander sought to improve Draga's standing by trying to get her, and himself, received by the Tsar – in fact, he was desperate to make this public relations exercise happen. As noted above, however, Queen Natalie had by now warned the Russian Court about Draga's infertility and the possible scheme to sneak in someone else's child. As a result, doubts concerning the respectability of the Serbian Queen began to emerge in St Petersburg. Tcharykow keenly supported the proposed visit, but was 'surprised at receiving dilatory answers' from Count Vladimir Lamsdorff, the Russian Foreign Minister, and blamed 'irresponsible feminine influences' directed against Draga.[138] Indeed, a feminine antagonism towards Draga did exist at the Russian Court, but it was calculated rather than irresponsible. The person in question was Princess Stana (also known as Anastasia), the daughter of Prince Nicholas of Montenegro. Married to the Russian Prince George of Leuchtenberg, she could exert considerable influence at the Imperial Court.[139] Her wily father Nicholas now used her to prevent Alexander's and Draga's projected visit to St Petersburg. According to his secretary Simo Popović, he worked 'most energetically' on this matter: 'Anything disgusting and ugly that he could hear or think of concerning Draga, he would pass on to Stana of Leuchtenberg, so that she would announce it to the Tsar and Tsarina and thus convince them that they could not receive Draga without humiliating themselves.'[140]

It worked. Count Sergei Witte, the Russian Finance Minister, confirms in his memoirs the impact of the Montenegrin 'intrigues' in preventing the Serbian royal visit.[141] Jovanović maintains that, apart from the Montenegrin intervention in St Petersburg (and that of Queen Natalie), Austrian diplomacy had also worked to enlighten the Tsar about Draga's 'true and complete history'. Originally, it would appear, the Tsar believed that Draga, as a former lady-in-waiting, was at least a woman of 'impeccable repute' – Jovanović blames the Russian Chargé d'Affaires Mansurov, a man of 'reckless Cossack daring', for involving the Tsar in the first place.[142] Be that as it may, the Serbian royal couple never made it to the Russian Imperial Court despite Alexander's repeated and increasingly agonized requests. According to the Montenegrin statesman Gavro Vuković, so 'embittered' was the Tsar by Alexander and Draga that no one would now dare ask him to be a godfather or the best man at a wedding.[143]

It is therefore ironic that Tcharykow's initial instructions, as he was about to take up the post in Belgrade, were to cultivate Draga because of her influence on the King and her perceived pro-Russian sentiment.[144] The Russians, certainly, had no reason to swear by Alexander, whose foreign policy direction appeared to move entirely in line with his personal circumstances. The only people they trusted in Serbia were their friends the Radicals. However, only gradually, and reluctantly, did Alexander let the Radicals back into power. What he wanted, as with any other set of politicians, was to manipulate them and rule arbitrarily under a guise of constitutionalism. But the Russians were keen to see genuine constitutional government in Serbia in order for the Radical Party, by far the strongest in the land, to exercise real power. Alexander had no choice but to begin to yield to this pressure. Aleksa Jovanović's 'wedding cabinet' was reconstructed in February 1901 to include two prominent Radicals, Mihailo Vujić and Milovan Milovanović. (Nikola Pašić had at this stage still not recovered politically from his betrayal of party comrades in the wake of the St John's Day assassination attempt on ex-King Milan.) In March, Vujić formed a new government which included both the Radicals and the Progressives. This was the so-called 'midwife cabinet' – as the people called it, since at this time the imminent birth of a royal baby was expected. The Radicals, or to be more precise, members of the Party's old guard, had been softened up by years in opposition (and indeed in jail) and were now perfectly happy to work with the King. They had also been advised by the Russians to show moderation and come to terms with him.[145] When Avakumović, the Liberal leader, put it to Vujić that he should not allow Draga to plant a false baby, the Prime Minister commented: 'That is none of my business. I shall not be in the room'.[146]

Vujić's 'midwife' Government is also known for introducing a new Constitution in 1901 (the 'April Constitution'), which has generally been seen in a positive light since it allowed secret ballot and guaranteed freedom of assembly and freedom of the press. On the other hand, it also represented Alexander's renewed attempt to control politics in Serbia. The new Constitution introduced the Senate, an institution which Serbia had never had in the past. Alexander clearly hoped that a bi-cameral legislature would help him manipulate the political process – he himself would appoint most of the Senators. But there may have been something else on his mind. Živan Živanović, who had closely observed these events and wrote a substantial account about them, pointed out that Article 6 of the new Constitution provided for female succession in the House of Obrenović – in the event that there was no male heir. This, surely, is further evidence that Alexander had at this point genuinely believed his Draga to have been pregnant – and had even been ready to have a daughter as his heir. Živanović also drew attention to Article 21, dealing with a situation in which the Monarch might have died before his successor had come of age, which in those circumstances provided for the elevation of his widow (i.e., Draga) to the position of Regent. It is not clear whether this provision was the idea of Alexander or Draga herself, but Živanović himself had no doubts. 'The plans of a *parvenu*', he wrote, 'are always large and brazen.'[147]

The price which the Radical Party had to pay for its cooperation with the Crown was the acceleration of a developing split in its own ranks: its younger and more combative members, highly mistrustful of Alexander and critical of the opportunistic old guard, were soon to establish their own party, the *Samostalna radikalna stranka* (Independent Radical Party). In fact, at this time all three political parties in Serbia, the Radicals, the Liberals and the Progressives, were experiencing internal dissensions. Always on the lookout for servile politicians, the King was in this situation able to form, unofficially at least, what people called the 'Fourth Party' or the 'Court Party' – made up of opportunists and sycophants from all three parties.

He was naturally pleased. Yet although it must have seemed to him that he had the domestic situation firmly in his grip, there was not a great deal that he could boast of in his foreign policy. Reliance on Russia, it was true, did confer some benefits for Serbia. Thus the Government was in the spring of 1901 able to secure its much-needed loan in Paris – given the previous Russian-influenced French policy, this would have been inconceivable when Milan was still playing a role in Serbia. Also, in September 1901, Russia's diplomatic intervention at Constantinople forced Turkey to introduce protective measures for the Serbs exposed to violent attacks by the Albanians in Kosovo.[148] Of course, for Alexander the ultimate accolade from Russia would have been the granting by the Tsar of an audience to him and Draga – his efforts to achieve this goal were what Serbia's foreign policy had actually amounted to since the royal wedding. 'His foreign policy', Walter Markov observed, 'made for grotesque statecraft, revolving only around rehabilitating Draga.'[149] Only in October 1902 with Tcharykow's explanation that, due to the Tsarina's illness, no reception was possible, was it finally accepted in Belgrade that nothing would come of the proposed Russian trip. Alexander was livid. The Vujić Government had no choice but to resign.[150]

In the meantime, relations with Austria-Hungary had deteriorated. The very fact that Alexander had duped Franz Joseph over the projected marriage with a German princess was bad enough – the Serbian King would henceforth never be trusted in Vienna. And Serbia's ensuing pro-Russian orientation was markedly more fervent than it had been during the Novaković and Simić governments. In January 1901 the President of the Assembly publicly stated that the Serbian people expected Russia's help in the task of Slavonic unification. The Radical Party press, moreover, soon unleashed blistering attacks on Austria-Hungary.[151] Further deepening the Austro-Serbian antagonism was the sudden death in Vienna (February 1901) of ex-King Milan, aged only forty-six. A broken man since his son's marriage to Draga, Milan was set not to return to Serbia even as a dead man – literally. Some months before he died, he deposited his request at the Foreign Ministry in Vienna (the 'Ballhausplatz') that he be buried in one of the Serbian monasteries in Srem, on Hungarian territory. Although Alexander appeared determined to have his father buried in Belgrade and had sent his Adjutant General to Vienna to make the arrangements, Franz Joseph was resolved to respect his friend Milan's last will. In the end, Alexander was completely side-lined. On 17 February the Emperor attended the benediction for Milan in a packed Serbian church off Renweg and then, in bitter cold, walked behind Milan's coffin, flanked by troops, as it proceeded to the railway station.[152] Milan was buried in Krušedol monastery on Mt Fruška Gora – not inappropriately perhaps with Habsburg military honours and at Habsburg state expense.

Alexander hardly regretted the passing of his father, but he was furious at this turn of events, ordering the Serbian press to write abusively about the neighbouring Monarchy.[153] In fact, it could be argued that Austria-Hungary had, in burying Milan in accordance with his wishes, finally given up on his son, the only remaining Obrenović.

Austro-Serbian relations, bad as they now were, proceeded to suffer further setbacks. Between August and September, 1901, both the Hungarian and Austrian Governments banned the import of Serbian livestock from the Belgrade district on flimsy veterinary grounds.[154] The Serbian royal couple was spoken of in a derogatory manner at the Ballhausplatz, and by September 1901 Foreign Minister Gołuchowski considered Alexander's reign as 'unsalvageable [*unrettbar verloren*]'.[155] Towards the end of the year he was expressing his private opinion that Serbia was heading for a catastrophe: 'politically, financially and dynastically'. His view was that Alexander's governing methods, his despotism and his dishonesty alienated all the reputable people in Serbia. Significantly, the chief point of concern for Gołuchowski was that, if Alexander disappeared from the scene, a Montenegrin prince could ascend the Serbian throne and the possibility of a union between Serbia and Montenegro could open up – something that Austria-Hungary would 'never allow'.[156]

In other words, the main thing really to be feared from such a disappearance was a process leading to the establishment of a Great Serbia. Neither the House of Obrenović nor even Serbia's general internal situation were in themselves particularly important as far as Vienna was concerned. Gołuchowski even considered Serbia at this time to be a 'quantité négligeable', and had a ready-made policy in case the country misbehaved. 'We shall simply crush Serbia', he told Prince Eulenburg, the German Ambassador to Vienna, 'if the situation in the Balkans becomes serious and Serbia pursues a policy different to the one we want.'[157] In truth, there was little prospect of this scenario ever taking place as the 1897 Austro-Russian understanding on the Balkans (i.e., maintaining the status quo) held firm. Margrave Pallavicini, the Austro-Hungarian Minister in Bucharest, told the Romanian Foreign Minister in 1901 that, given its good relations with Russia, Austria-Hungary was not frightened by the idea of King Alexander throwing himself into Russian arms.[158]

This basic apathy towards Serbia was in fact shared by Russia. In the light of Far Eastern developments, Foreign Minister Lamsdorff wanted 'peace and quiet and nothing but peace and quiet' in the Balkans. His policy towards Austria-Hungary was conspicuously friendly.[159] In December 1902 Lamsdorff actually paid a visit to Serbia and Bulgaria having become alarmed by assessments that these countries could take some action against Turkey. After meeting Alexander and Draga in Niš, his impression of the Serbian Queen 'was not favourable'. His chief instruction to Tscharykow was 'not to meddle with the internal affairs of Serbia' and only to make sure that its foreign policy was in harmony with that of Russia. Tcharykow described this directive as 'the death warrant of King Alexander and Queen Draga.'[160] Indeed, given the earlier decision not to receive the royal couple at the Russian Court, this disinterested approach towards Serbia by Russia could only entail Alexander's further isolation.

It speaks volumes about Alexander's despair, and not just his undependable character that, having apparently committed himself so deeply to the Russians, he thought nothing of turning to Vienna once his expectations about a reception in St Petersburg were finally disappointed in autumn 1902. Not long before, he had described Austria-Hungary to a journalist as Serbia's 'arch-enemy'.[161] Now Alexander was to adopt a new diplomatic position. But some domestic political manoeuvres came first. Following the fall of the Vujić Government (over the failure to realize a visit by the Serbian royal couple to the Russian Court), a new administration was formed in October 1902. Headed by Pera Velimirović, it was really no more than the King's obedient instrument, heralding his return to personal rule and his jettisoning of the Radical Party – and thus also of the Russian alliance. Velimirović's cabinet lasted only a month, to be replaced early in November by that of General Dimitrije Cincar-Marković. This was to be the twelfth and the last Government thrown together by the volatile young King of Serbia. Its official programme announced the aim of changing the (April 1901) Constitution – yet again. Having only recently instituted the Senate, Alexander now wanted to get rid of it as the Senators were becoming increasingly independent-minded. This was a significant development: 'The King had lost much of his authority, the fear of him was not the same as the fear of Milan had been.'[162]

At the same time, Alexander wished to rebuild his bridges with Austria-Hungary – to compensate for the Russian setback and to regain some badly needed legitimacy for his tottering regime. Investing this effort with a symbolic stamp, in February 1903 he and Draga crossed into Hungary to visit Milan's tomb in Krušedol monastery on the second anniversary of the ex-King's death. In the words of Živanović, having contributed so much to his early demise, theirs were 'crocodile tears' for Milan. Of course, what Alexander was seeking, apart from repairing relations with Vienna, was a kind of rehabilitation for Draga on foreign soil. Suspicious of his motives, Franz Joseph sent him his personal train and even his personal cook, but not his personal representative. The Serbian royal couple were received by Khuen-Héderváry, the *Ban* of Croatia-Slavonia, whereas Alexander had hoped for an Archduke and was furious that one had not come.[163]

What is perhaps startling, even taking into account Alexander's protean mindset, is the sheer extent to which he was ready to change his foreign policy course. Vienna was informed that he would revert to the pure Austrophile orientation that had been pursued by his father, that Milan's supporters would be re-appointed, and that the Serbian railways would be handed over to Austria-Hungary. He offered a military convention and a customs union, even suggesting that he bring Serbia into the kind of position *vis-à-vis* the Habsburg Monarchy which Bavaria and Saxony held within the German Reich. What he wanted in return was Austro-Hungarian backing for Serbia's territorial expansion to the south at the expense of Turkey, i.e., in Kosovo and Macedonia.[164] Some authorities, including Jovanović, have left open the possibility that Alexander, in seeking such a far-reaching *rapprochement* with Austria-Hungary, had acted for patriotic reasons, concerned as he apparently was at this time that Bulgaria might under the Russian aegis obtain more than its fair share in Macedonia in the event of a carve-up of European Turkey. Yet it is difficult to imagine him turning to Vienna if he had been successful in getting his Draga received and thus approved of by the Russian Court.

The Ballhausplatz, however, lacking any belief in his trustworthiness, remained entirely cool towards the overtures coming from Alexander. His offer, moreover, was not particularly enticing: supporting Serbia's territorial ambitions would have wrecked the 1897 Balkan entente with Russia. The fiasco of Alexander's foreign policy was now on full view. Draga, who had fundamentally dictated this policy, had become an albatross around the King's neck. One of his last major initiatives shortly before he was murdered in the Royal Palace came towards the end of May 1903 when he asked whether Franz Joseph would receive him on the occasion of the Austro-Hungarian autumn military manoeuvres at Temesvár, close to Serbia. But by the next day he was additionally asking whether he and now Draga could on some other occasion hope to be officially received in Vienna or Budapest. Constantin Dumba, the Austro-Hungarian Minister in Belgrade, had no doubts as to who had stood behind this widening of the request. 'Already after 24 hours', he wrote, 'the influence of the ambitious woman had prevailed, enticing the King to take a step that ruled out a possible success of the first request.'[165] Indeed, Franz Joseph now let the Austro-Hungarian Legation in Belgrade know that he did not contemplate a Serbian royal visit either on the field of manoeuvres or in one of the two capital cities of the Monarchy.[166]

Ironically, by this time – May 1903 – Alexander had actually decided to get rid of Draga. Something of a consensus exists among Serbian historians on this subject. Živan Živanović speculated in the mid-1920s that the new Government, headed by General Cincar-Marković, had been formed with the intention of presiding over the King's divorce. Certainly, Cincar-

Marković himself, the members of his cabinet, and other recently promoted public figures were not known for supporting Draga. Rather, they
had been the ex-King Milan loyalists. General Jovan Belimarković, the new
President of the Senate, was famously refusing to kiss the Queen's hand.[167]
While Jovanović could in the early 1930s only assert that a royal separation
had been on the cards, Ana Stolić in her recent biography of Draga demonstrates beyond any doubt that Alexander had indeed schemed a divorce.
His plan, apparently, was to send Draga to spa Franzensbad in Austria from
which she would then be forbidden to return to Serbia as the divorce
proceedings got under way. The King's infatuation was over.

Significantly, Alexander began corresponding with his mother again.
The celebrated *Vojvoda* Živojin Mišić wrote that he had in April 1903 been
told by the King to expect an important event which, Mišić later found
out, concerned the expulsion of Draga.[168] The former Prime Minister
Vujić recalled in 1908 that Alexander had even sent his secretary to see
Gołuchowski in Vienna, with the request that the Austrian authorities
should prevent Draga's return from Franzensbad to Serbia.[169] Whatever
else may be said of Alexander, neither his contemporaries nor the historians
of his reign considered him stupid – at the very least, he must have become
concerned that Draga's infertility had brought the survival of the dynasty
into question. To her mortification, Draga found out that Alexander had,
without even mentioning her, declared to the correspondent of London's
Daily Mail that he thought he could still have an heir because he was only
twenty-seven.[170] At the end of May 1903, in a report to Vienna, Dumba
gave credence to the information he had received about 'endless differences
of opinion' between the King and Queen, and about a 'cooling' of their
relations.[171]

The inability of the Serbian Queen to ensure the continuation of the
Obrenović line had in fact highlighted wider political issues. The question
of succession, for example, inevitably involved the rival Karađorđević
dynasty. In February 1902, in a bizarre episode, a Karađorđević supporter
by the name of Rade Alavantić crossed into Serbia from Hungary. Wearing
a Serbian general's uniform and accompanied by a small entourage, he was
in the process of taking over the border town of Šabac before being shot
dead. His last words were: 'Long live Karađorđević!' Jovanović maintains
that the Russian secret police, and possibly the Austrian authorities too,
had known about Alavantić's intentions. The idea, apparently, was to
test the popular reaction.[172] Alexander, however, was not intimidated by
this challenge. What really worried him was the prospect, as he saw it,
of the incurably pro-Montenegrin Russians helping to install as his successor the Montenegrin Prince Mirko, Prince Nicholas' second son who had
married a member of the Obrenović clan. In reality, this was always a
non-starter as the Habsburg Empire would not tolerate a Montenegrin

successor given the inherent likelihood of a union of Serbia and Montenegro resulting from such an event. At the same time there had been some
talk in Belgrade that a Russian candidate could become the next King
of Serbia.[173] Just in case, Alexander had his own plan, and he passed it
on to the Austrians: he was ready to adopt a male child from the female
Obrenović line (two daughters of Miloš, the founder of the dynasty, and a
daughter of Miloš's brother Jovan) that had settled in Austria-Hungary
having married Hungarian citizens. He was also ready, moreover, to let
Austria-Hungary participate in the choice of his successor. As with his
other overtures to Vienna, however, this one was also ignored.[174]

It was to be expected that Draga would have her own ideas regarding
the succession. Since it had become known in 1901 that she could not conceive a child, this enterprising woman now sought to secure her imperiled
position by encouraging the idea that her younger brother, Nikodije Lunjevica, could become the heir to the Serbian throne. She had in fact already
saddled Alexander with the whole of her large family – sisters, brothers
and cousins – much to the dismay of Serbian society. Thanks to Draga, the
Lunjevicas found themselves in the lap of luxury, enjoying sycophantic
attention and deference. They were ever-present in the Royal Palace, and
the rules of Court protocol did not exist for them – thus they would be
positioned immediately behind the royal couple on festive occasions, with
Alexander meekly tolerating the inflated status of his wife's family.
However, when persistent rumours begun to circulate, in the second half
of 1901, that Nikodije had been chosen to succeed to the Serbian throne,
Alexander publicly denied them in September 1901. Despite this, the
rumours were believed because Draga had been doing so much in pushing
for the Lunjevicas to become to all intents and purposes members of the
House of Obrenović. It looked very much to observers at the time that
she had been busy creating a 'Lunjevica dynasty'.[175]

Like the rest of her family, the Queen's two brothers, Nikola and
Nikodije, were not exactly beloved in Serbia. Both were junior officers, but
their haughty behaviour and scandalous drunken sprees barely qualified
them for, as Jovanović observed, the rank of non-commissioned officers.[176]
Tcharykow described Nikodije as 'merely a third-rate officer in the Serbian
Army.'[177] Being complete nobodies before their sister became the Queen,
the brothers now embraced privilege, sometimes in the most primitive
manner. On one occasion, Nikola entered the famous Belgrade coffee
house 'Kolarac', demanding the orchestra play the national anthem because
he was a member of the ruling dynasty. That evening he went in and out
of 'Kolarac' seven times, with the orchestra having to play the anthem each
time and those present having to stand to attention. In the end, the public
reacted with rage and Nikola had to be rescued by gendarmes.[178] The
younger brother Nikodije, Draga's favourite sibling, was by all accounts no

better than Nikola, throwing tantrums and insulting his fellow officers. But being the Queen's brother and the reputed Heir to the Throne he could and did get away with a great deal.

The assessment of Draga made shortly after her death by James Bourchier, celebrated Balkans correspondent of *The Times*, seems rather accurate. She had not, he wrote for his paper, shown herself alive to the responsibilities of her position. Instead, she used her unbounded influence on Alexander 'for the satisfaction of private animosities' and for 'the advancement of her friends and relations'.[179] The Italian Chargé d'Affaires in Belgrade reported in October 1901 that Draga had been openly endorsing Nikodije and thereby deepening the resentment of the officers' corps and the people.[180] Draga as the Queen had already been taken as a gross insult by the officers. Their outrage was further aroused by her alleged remark that she could buy any officer for two napoleons – which, they felt, was a little rich coming from someone who had not long ago been selling herself for the same sum.[181] And now, the prospect of one of her overweening brothers becoming the Crown Prince served to increase their bitterness enormously.

Scheming Revenge: Đorđe Genčić

This bitterness was to culminate in one of Europe's most brutal palace revolutions. Serbian officers were to carry out the act of regicide in the early hours of 11 June, 1903. But did they in any meaningful sense hatch and lead the conspiracy? The historiography of the event has on the whole not bothered to explore this question. The military provenance and character of the entire action has been routinely asserted by Serbian and non-Serbian historians alike – with the role of civilians commented on only in passing. What is also striking, especially in non-Serbian accounts, is the inclination to exaggerate the role in the 1903 regicide of Dragutin Dimitrijević Apis, later the head of Serbian military intelligence who supposedly masterminded the 1914 assassination of Franz Ferdinand in Sarajevo. In 1989, for example, the American historian David MacKenzie, a recognized expert on Serbia, claimed that the military coup of 1903 had been 'organized chiefly' by Apis.'[182] Other historians have recently been describing Apis's role in similar terms. Three examples are typical. In 2007 Holm Sundhaussen, another recognized specialist, claimed in his history of Serbia that Apis was 'Führer der Putschisten'. Sean McMeekin writes that 'in 1903 a clique of hypernationalist military officers led by ... Dragutin Dimitrijevitch ... had murdered Serbia's own king and queen to protest their insufficient devotion to the Serbian cause'. And Christopher Clark submits that a military conspiracy had in 1901 'crystallized' around Dimitrijević, describing the latter as the 'chief architect of the regicide'.[183]

It is true that Dimitrijević Apis had played a significant part among the conspiring officers, particularly in terms of recruiting new conspirators, but contrary to the above claims his role in the undertaking was not even remotely a leading one. In 1985 the eminent Serbian historian Milorad Ekmečić expressed his puzzlement that Apis should be so consistently portrayed as the leader of the conspiracy when in fact no evidence supported this.[184] What also needs to be appreciated with regard to the regicide of 1903 is that Apis and his friends actually belonged to a wider conspiracy, organized and coordinated by civilians. Admittedly, the idea that the Serbian royal couple should be killed had already been entertained in the second half of 1901 by a small circle of officers gathered around Lieutenant Antonije Antić who was serving in the Cavalry Guards. During August and September Antić was in contact with six other junior officers, among them his friend Lieutenant Dimitrijević Apis. But Antić's group must rank as one of the most inept in the history of Serbian complots. Apis for example suggested a plan whereby Alexander and Draga would be killed with cyanide-poisoned daggers during a forthcoming celebration of the Queen's birthday (23 September) at the Belgrade cafe 'Kolarac'. In fact, the conspirators had no idea whether the royal couple would even attend the festivity. Their plan envisaged cutting off the electricity, burning the drapery and stabbing Alexander and Draga in the general chaos. In the event, the officers failed to cut off the electricity and the royals failed to turn up. Beforehand, however, the dagger with cyanide had been successfully tried on a cat. One dead cat was thus the result of this grand conspiracy.[185] The next plan was similarly ludicrous. The King and Queen were expected to attend the autumn manoeuvres south-west of Belgrade and were supposed to use a tent. The idea was to hit the royal tent with an artillery projectile. To their credit, the conspirators soon abandoned this particular scheme.[186]

In any case, by Antić's own admission, his group had not even tackled the question of the post-assassination period.[187] But there were those who had. It so happened that Antić's uncle was Đorđe Genčić who, as the Interior Minister, had been involved in a Royal Palace fracas with Alexander over Draga. Genčić subsequently withdrew to exile in Vienna where he gave a statement to the *Neue Freie Presse,* warning against the 'fatal, Byzantine new course in Serbia.' However, he soon got bored with exile and sent letters to Alexander, requesting unimpeded return to Serbia. His wish was granted, but Alexander quickly changed his mind, and Genčić was tried and sentenced to seven years in prison for crimes which included his statement to the Austrian press. He actually served only eight months: Alexander pardoned him in the belief that the former Minister would in future behave like a repentant sinner. In fact, when Genčić left prison in December 1901, he was an unrepentant conspirator, firmly determined to do away with the last Obrenović and became the central figure in conspiring against him.[188] He may even have stood behind Antić's circle of officers in 1901. In his important study of praetorian tendencies in Serbia, Radovan Drašković suggests that Genčić had been instructing Antić to recruit his fellow officers for a plot against the King even before he, Genčić, ended up in prison.[189] And Colonel Dragutin Mićić insisted that civilians headed by Genčić were the initiators of the conspiracy of 1903, with Antić and Apis merely being 'given directions'.[190]

Đorđe Genčić is one of the more colourful and interesting figures from turn of the century Serbia. He came from a wealthy family in the east of the country, possibly of Tatar or Circassian origin. On the face of it, he was just a dandy. Tall and lean, he had an immaculate taste in attire and was arguably the best dressed man in Serbia. King Milan himself would describe Genčić's appearance as 'tiré à quatre épingles'. Herbert Vivian, who knew Genčić, commented on his 'inordinate vanity', especially with regard to his personal appearance. Genčić also had an interest in horse breeding and hunting game animals – including bears, a pastime which he would pursue together with Milan. As a young man he spent some time at a merchant school in Vienna but ended up in Russia after meeting General Mikhail Chernyayev who helped him enrol into a military academy. He had advanced to the rank of a Guards Captain when Jovan Ristić, his father's friend and the leader of the Liberal Party, persuaded him to return to Serbia. His progress in the Liberal Party and in Serbian politics was due to a combination of opportunism and ruthlessness. He had allied himself with ex-King Milan, earning the latter's gratitude for his bellicosity towards the Radicals. As Governor of the city of Niš, Genčić once managed to track down and arrest a notorious Russian nihilist. And it was Genčić who, as Interior Minister, visited the Radical leader Pašić in jail to cajole him into making a confession following the assassination attempt on Milan. Pašić did not know that his life had already been saved thanks to Russian and Austro-Hungarian interventions, and Genčić intimidated him with the threat that twelve Radical heads would roll. In 1901 Serbia's veteran police chief Tasa Milenković described Genčić to King Alexander as a courageous man with that 'revengeful oriental blood' – someone who could become 'dangerous'.[191]

This is precisely what Genčić did become. Perhaps Alexander should have listened to his experienced policeman. Once out of jail, Genčić initiated conspiratorial meetings between several prominent people: Jovan Avakumović, the Liberal Party leader; Dragomir Rajević, a former Minister; General Jovan Atanacković, the former War Minister in the Đorđević Government, who had been pensioned off following Alexander's marriage with Draga; and Aleksa Novaković, a prominent Belgrade lawyer and Genčić's father-in law. This group also included Nikola Hadži-Toma, the richest man in the country and a friend of the Karađorđević dynasty.

He was the 'fat cat' described in various accounts as the financier of the conspiracy. Among those who subsequently joined this group were Vukašin Petrović, another former Minister, and the industrialist Georg (Đorđe) Weifert, governor of the Central Bank of Serbia since 1890. They were united in the belief that Alexander and Draga had to be removed. And there was something else that united them: they were mostly in the Liberal Party. The Radicals were conspicuous by their complete absence in the ranks of the conspirators.

A further point deserves to be emphasized here: these people, almost to a man, were friends of the Habsburg Monarchy – hardly surprising since they were Milan's partisans. Vasa Kazimirović has, for example, described Genčić as 'a leading Austrophile in Belgrade'.[192] This fact – that the conspiracy against King Alexander originated in Serbia's Austrophile camp – was pointed out as early as 1934 by historian Walter Markov, who has since been ignored by generations of historians wishing instead to paint the putsch of 1903 as some kind of pro-Russian enterprise.[193] And a new, puzzling interpretation has recently been added. Christopher Clark writes, in the context of the regicide, that among powerful mercantile and banking families in Serbia there were those 'who saw the pro-Vienna bias of Obrenović foreign policy as locking the Serbian economy into an Austrian monopoly and depriving the country's capitalists of access to world markets'. The authority cited by Clark is the Serbian historian Branislav Vranešević, but Clark has failed to notice that Vranešević in his references to the pro-Vienna bias of Obrenović foreign policy is actually discussing the situation prevailing in the 1880s, under the previous King – Milan – not the state of affairs in 1903 under regicide victim Alexander.[194] By getting his facts and kings confused, Clark has also led himself into an error of analysis by suggesting that there was an anti-Austrian economic rationale for the regicide, whereas its Austrophile leaders obviously had no such motivation.

Genčić was the heart and soul of the cabal. Aca Novaković, a prominent Jewish lawyer and Genčić's father-in-law, himself deeply involved in the conspiracy, subsequently stated that Genčić was not only the soul of the conspiracy, but also its 'begetter and chief organizer'.[195] Antić, who in his memoir notes goes out of his way to praise his friend Apis, admits nevertheless that several members of his group asked him to contact his uncle, Genčić: what they wanted was leadership from a resolute political figure who could prepare the ground for the post-assassination stage. However, Radovan Drašković has argued convincingly that this whole scenario in which the officers ended up asking for guidance from the politicians had been pre-planned by Genčić himself, then implemented by him through Antić and Apis. Genčić, according to Drašković, had become disturbed by what he had learned from Antić about the officers' amateurish schemes to kill Alexander and Draga, fearing that their youth and inexperience could ruin everything. But he wanted the officers to believe that they had themselves, 'spontaneously', arrived at the conclusion that politicians too should get involved. Genčić's aim, Drašković maintains, was to create the impression that the Army was taking on, on behalf of the people, the responsibility for an action against the King and Queen.[196]

In any case, Slobodan Jovanović writes, Genčić had made 'a strong impression' on the officers, who were now ready to follow his leadership.[197] Irrespective of who was the begetter of the whole plot, the officers had accordingly realized that they could not really act without the civilians. One reason for this was no doubt because the vast majority of them, a group that numbered perhaps a hundred and twenty, were very junior in rank – lieutenants and captains. The absence of senior military figures among the conspirators also posed problems for the recruitment of new members. Among those few with a higher rank was Colonel Damjan Popović, who was envisaged to lead the military wing of the conspiracy, but was hardly a luminary among Serbian officers. Alexander Mašin, another Colonel and interestingly the brother of Draga's deceased husband, was to play a crucial part in the planning and execution of the regicide. Although better known, he had in fact been pensioned off in 1900 – for criticizing Draga.[198] General Jovan Atanacković, also retired for opposing Draga, was the highest ranking Army conspirator, but he had been recruited by the civilians and then refused to coordinate anything with the officers – curiously on the grounds that soldiers should not meddle in politics. He was keen, however, to make himself available should someone else do the dirty work. On the strength of his name and reputation many other officers joined the secret plotters.[199]

But what exactly motivated these two disparate groups, civilian and military, to get involved in the dangerous business of plotting the removal of Alexander and Draga? As far as the civilian conspirators were concerned, Radovan Drašković has emphasized that they were hardly known for their love of constitutional order and parliamentary government. They were mostly Alexander's former servants who had been helping him sustain his authoritarian regime – Genčić was the prime example – and were now against him simply because they had fallen out of favour. So, concludes Drašković, it was revenge that drove them.[200] But this assessment is somewhat unfair. With the exception of Genčić, who had actually been jailed by Alexander, no civilian conspirator can be said to have harboured deeply personal grudges against the royal couple. And people like Avakumović, for example, were clearly not supporters of despotic rule. The civilian conspirators may not all have been genuine democrats, but this is immaterial. The issue in 1903 was perceived to be the honour, dignity and, indeed, the whole future of Serbia. It would be difficult to deny that a strong, public-spirited impulse had influenced the behaviour of the civilians, even someone like Genčić. After all, by the time the latter began to form his conspiratorial network, Serbia had become the laughing stock of Europe because of the scandal with Draga's pregnancy. Perhaps crucially, it appeared that things could only get worse – as they did when the rumours concerning her brother Nikodije began to circulate. So most of the civilians in the conspiracy acted not because the King had humiliated them personally, but rather because they believed he had humiliated and retarded the whole country.

A patriotic impulse to an awful act can also be ascribed to the officers. It would be wrong to see their action as being connected with the deterioration of material conditions in the Army – which most accounts of 1903 point out as a root cause of disaffection among them. It is of course true that in the post-Milan period the Army was no longer being indulged. Milan had paid tremendous attention not only to its equipment and training, but also to its material well-being. Once he left, Alexander neglected the officers, whose pay would often arrive with several months delay, forcing them to borrow money at exorbitant rates in the meantime. Such a state of affairs, certainly, increased their resentment, but they did not then decide to kill the King and Queen in order to get paid regularly. As the Balkan Wars were to show, most of them were dedicated soldiers and patriots who fought and died bravely for their country. In 1904, in his influential book on Serbia, Herbert Vivian called the officers in the conspiracy 'a small clique of criminals' and 'bloody murderers'.[201] In the minds of the officers, however, the evildoers were the King and Queen. Antonije Antić relates in his memoir notes how he and his fellow officers had heard that female cabaret singers in Vienna and Budapest were trumpeting the line: 'If there were another Serbia in the world, I too could become a Queen.'[202] It was this kind of opprobrium attached to the Serbia of Alexander and Draga that touched the raw patriotic nerve of many officers.

Viennese Blessing for the Putsch

Genčić had two main tasks to perform: first, to ensure that there would be no international intervention in the event of an overthrow in Serbia, which meant non-interference by Austria-Hungary and Russia; and second, to line up a pre-arranged successor to the Serbian Throne, which again entailed the consent of Austria-Hungary and Russia. The choice of the new Sovereign, however, also required consensus amongst the conspirators themselves. It is almost universally assumed that they immediately opted for Peter Karađorđević, who did eventually ascend the Throne. But this appears not to have been a pre-ordained matter at all. According to Colonel Mićić, who in 1913 talked to Antić about the events of 1903, the conspirators had convened a meeting to debate the issue, inviting only Antić and Apis from the officers' group (Mićić gives no date). There were those, including Genčić, who advocated someone from Russia (specifically Grand Duke Konstantin Konstantinovich), but also those who argued for a West European prince. Interestingly, Apis was in this second camp, declaring himself in favour of the Prince of Connaught – presumably Queen Victoria's grandson Prince Arthur. In the end, however, the meeting opted for a Russian candidate – it is not clear whether a Karađorđević, or for that matter a Montenegrin Petrović succession, had been considered at all. Genčić was authorized to travel to Vienna to negotiate with Count Pyotr Kapnist, the Russian Ambassador in Austria-Hungary, and his personal acquaintance.[203]

But Kapnist, who was told 'everything' by Genčić – according to Antić's testimony as related by Colonel Mićić – advised against a foreign prince on the grounds that things would then acquire an international character leading to possible complications. Austria, he said, would not tolerate a Russian Grand Duke. He suggested, instead, the candidature of Prince Peter Karađorđević, for Russia would in that case be able to extend full support to Serbia given that the matter would then be a purely internal Serbian one. Genčić asked him whether he was speaking personally or as the Russian Ambassador. Kapnist replied that he was expressing his opinion as the Russian Ambassador. The conspirators, 'lacking an alternative', decided to establish a connection with Peter Karađorđević, who at the time lived in Geneva, and for this task chose Vukašin Petrović, the former Minister in the Đorđević Government. Petrović passed on to the conspirators his judgement on Peter: 'Taking everything into account, I believe that he will be a good constitutional ruler.'[204]

The initial decision to seek a Russian prince may well have reflected a concern to assuage the Serbian public, pro-Russian as it mainly was, after what was inevitably going to be a very nasty overthrow of an admittedly unpopular royal couple. It has to be remembered that the fear of a civil war was always present in the minds of the conspirators. In particular, what they could not be sure about was just how the rest of the Army would react. As Jovanović observed, while the officers may have abandoned the King, the rank and file had by and large remained loyal.[205] Colonel Mašin even considered a possible failure of the whole plot, in which case, he said, 'I suggest a retreat from the town towards Topčider hill [in the vicinity of Belgrade]. On that hill we shall raise the flag and call on the people to make a revolution.' His proposal was accepted.[206] It was precisely this prospect of a civil war which apparently influenced the conspirators not to spare the lives of Alexander and Draga. For there were indeed those among them in favour of merely expelling the royal couple from Serbia. According to Constantin Dumba's information, the decision to opt for murder was taken in the interest of avoiding a bloody internal conflict because Alexander would inevitably attempt a restoration.[207]

Obviously, the significance of the Kapnist-Genčić meeting in Vienna had not so much to do with the fact that the Karađorđević dynasty was brought back into play, but rather that the Russians had full knowledge of what was afoot. Tcharykow practically admits this in his memoirs: 'Signs of growing unrest and of approaching attempts on the King's life became more and more frequent.' He does not say, however, that he warned the King about the approaching danger.[208] But then, as seen above, his instructions had since December 1902 been not to stick his nose into Serbia's internal affairs. In his memoirs, Dumba goes out of his way to defend his colleague Tcharykow, writing that the Russian Legation in Belgrade played absolutely no part in the whole conspiracy. Tcharykow, despite his 'addiction to intrigues' was nevertheless 'a gentleman' in Dumba's judgement: someone who would never, not even in a passive role, participate in such a murder plot. But while Dumba is quite right in suggesting that Count Lamsdorff in St Petersburg wanted stability rather than risk anarchy and civil war in Serbia, the inference that the Russians had no idea of what was being prepared does not ring true.[209]

What about the Austrians – what did they know? In his unpublished memoir, Colonel Mićić mentions briefly that in Vienna Genčić had, apart from meeting Kapnist, also visited Franz Schiessl, Franz Joseph's cabinet secretary, formerly Austria-Hungary's Minister to Belgrade in the 1880s.[210] This tallies with what Nikola Pašić told Lloyd George in August 1917. He said that Genčić had told him about a trip to Vienna, undertaken before the regicide on 11 June 1903 for the purpose of establishing whether Austria-Hungary would intervene if 'a revolution cost King Alexander his head.' Genčić and his (unnamed) colleagues had requested an audience with the Emperor, but were received by Schiessl who told them: 'These are your internal affairs, we have no reason to interfere.' Then, Pašić related, they went to see Foreign Minister Gołuchowski who commented in much the same manner. 'When they got this', Pašić told the British Prime Minister, 'they carried out the assassination.'[211] And just like the Russians, the Austrians were in favour of a Karađorđević succession. At the Ballhausplatz Genčić talked about the possibility of some German Prince becoming the King of Serbia since, he said, Romania, Greece and Bulgaria also had German rulers. But he was told by 'a high-ranking functionary' that Russia would not swallow a fourth German ruler in the Balkans. 'However', this man continued, 'if your dynasty should become extinguished, you have another one, outside the country.'[212]

In 1936 Fritz von Reinöhl attempted to discredit the notion that Vienna was in any way privy to the conspiracy against the Serbian King.[213] But there can be absolutely no doubt that Habsburg officialdom was in the know about it. In an article published in 1985, the historian Milorad Ekmečić showed that Austro-Hungarian intelligence had learned about the existence of a movement against King Alexander. Ekmečić also pointed out that the Joint Finance Minister Benjámin Kállay had his own agents engaged in monitoring the situation.[214] It would appear that some of Kállay's close associates were even actively involved. Henry Wickham Steed, who was *The Times* correspondent in Vienna, recalled that in March 1903 Kállay had told him: 'Keep your eyes on Belgrade. Master Alexander has got an awful fright.' After the regicide took place, in fact later in the course of 11 June, Steed went to see Kállay again. The latter appeared delighted by the possible effects of the event: 'Alexander was doomed', he said, 'and the intrigues of Nicholas of Montenegro have been nipped in the bud.' Steed learned later that Kállay had been kept informed about the conspiracy by one of his officials, a Hungarian, 'who attended the meetings of the Vienna section of the conspirators at the Café Imperial on the Ringstrasse.'[215]

The 'Vienna section' consisted primarily of Vukašin Petrović and Jakov Nenadović. Petrović, the Finance Minister in the Đorđević Government, took up residence in Vienna in the wake of Alexander's engagement with Draga. A businessman in private life, he was not particularly attached to any group in Serbia, and was consistent only in promoting an Austrophile orientation for his country. But he was in the conspiracy while maintaining contacts with both Kállay and Gołuchowski.[216] Nenadović, also a resident in Vienna, was a cousin of Peter Karađorđević and his representative in that city. He later boasted to Dumba that he had been one of the chief conspirators.[217] Certainly, he was the main conduit between them and Peter Karađorđević in Geneva. As for Kállay's official who kept company with these two conspirators at the Café Imperial, Steed named him in 1917 as Ludwig von Thallóczy, a section chief in the Joint Finance Ministry.[218] Thallóczy was a distinguished scholar and perhaps the foremost Austro-Hungarian expert on the Balkans. Another, and possibly more important high-ranking official in Vienna who appears to have been in frequent touch with Petrović and Nenadović was Heinrich Müller, the head of the Press Bureau at the Ballhausplatz.[219]

According to most accounts, Peter Karađorđević was hesitant and sceptical at first about the offer of the Throne, and accepted only when he learned that officers, and not just politicians, were involved in the conspiracy. For he did not like or trust politicians. But was he also indirectly responsible for the terrible demise of the Obrenović line? Miloš Bogićević, the former Serbian diplomat, wrote to Robert Seton-Watson in 1927 about what he had heard from Nenadović: that Peter insisted he would not ascend the Serbian throne 'so long as a single member of the Obrenović dynasty is alive'.[220] Perhaps not surprisingly, this declaration has attracted the attention of Serbian and non-Serbian historians alike, but it is impossible to verify. However, the question of whether Peter had accepted to wear the Serbian Crown on condition that Alexander be killed is in some ways superfluous: since he welcomed the involvement of the officers, he must have anticipated the use of violence in the removal of Obrenović. In that sense, he was always going to have blood on his hands.

Moreover, it would seem that this pretender was exceedingly keen to become King. Vukašin Petrović wrote that in October 1902 his co-conspirator Nenadović had gone to the Ballhausplatz with Peter's statement in which he renounced any claims to Bosnia-Herzegovina in the event of ascending the Throne. Peter would have been happy, in other words, for Austria-Hungary to annex the provinces in exchange for its recognition of his claims in Serbia. While careful not to commit himself with regard to the veracity of Petrović's account, Peter's latest biographer Dragoljub Živojinović has nonetheless opined: 'This was something remarkable.'[221] The former Serbian diplomat Bogićević wrote that he had been told something similar by Petrović: that Peter had promised Vienna not to tolerate any agitation regarding Bosnia-Herzegovina.[222] No wonder, then, that some three months before the regicide Petrović could relate to Genčić what he had been told at the Ballhausplatz: 'We shall recognize Peter Karađorđević within 24 hours.'[223]

Domestic Turmoil

The international outlook was thus hardly promising for Alexander. By the end of 1902 at the latest both Russia and Austria-Hungary had given up on the shifty, completely untrustworthy Serbian King. It would therefore be difficult to disagree with Mihailo Vojvodić's judgement that the June 1903 overthrow had been made possible by the external factors.[224] But it may also be argued that domestic developments had speeded up the *denouement* in Serbia. In particular, two events in spring 1903 cast dark shadows over the existing regime. The first was the so-called 'March demonstrations' (according to the old calendar) in Belgrade. And the second was Alexander's exceptionally brutal manner of tinkering with the Constitution soon thereafter.

In fact, the demonstrations of 5 April (23 March under the old calendar) grew out of the popular anticipation, indeed apprehension, that the King was going to do away with the liberal Constitution of 1901 and replace it with something tyrannical. On that day Belgrade's Grande École students held a meeting which, steered by young socialist agitators, quickly turned into a protest against Alexander's policies. In the afternoon hours the students were joined by workers, apprentices and many bystanders. As this coalition advanced towards the *Konak* (as King Alexander's royal residence was known) it was stopped by the gendarmerie. Božo Maršićanin, the Prefect of Belgrade and Queen Draga's trusted man, warned his gendarmes that the protesters could be allowed to approach the *Konak* 'only over your dead bodies'.[225] Unable to break through, people turned back and began smashing the windows and ransacking the offices of several pro-regime newspapers. The demonstration then appeared to be over, but a late scuffle resulted in the use of arms by the gendarmerie. Matters got totally out of control and four protesters were in the end killed, including a student and a woman – a house maid. Dozens were wounded. In panic, the authorities had sought the help of the Army. But when a cavalry unit reached the scene, its commander – who happened to be a conspirator – famously ordered his men: '*Pazi, ne gazi!* [Be careful, do not squash!]' Sensing bene-volence, the crowd went wild, shouting heartily: 'Long live the Army!'[226]

By all accounts the protest in Belgrade had given Alexander a genuine fright. The mood of the people had found expression in several slogans: 'Down with absolutism! Down with Alexander!' But also: 'Down with the Queen!' and 'Long live Republic!' The acclamation of the Army, at the same time, was highly worrying. Indeed, Alexander had received information that some officers had been protecting the protesters from the gendarmes. He also heard that there had been whisperings about a conspiracy in the 6th Regiment.[227] It was absolutely certain that he was going to act now. For this was a King who once said that 'if five or ten thousand heads need to roll to defend the Throne, then let them roll!'[228] So his reaction was swift. At 11:15 p.m. on 6 April (24 March, old calendar) he suspended the Constitution of April 1901, only to bring it back into force forty-five minutes later, i.e., on 7 April. In the intervening brief space of time, that is, during this forty-five minute constitutional vacuum, he got rid of the elected and appointed Senators as well as the members of the State Council; he dissolved the lower Assembly; and he nullified all the laws introduced on the basis of the 1901 Constitution, including the law on the press. Hardly had the burgers of Belgrade had the time to digest the King's first proclamation (about suspending the Constitution) from the placards which the police had been putting up around the town, when new placards, announcing the return of the Constitution, began to appear in the early morning hours on 7 April. All this was not just *sui generis*, as Živan Živanović was to remark, this was naked dictatorship.[229]

Alexander's action was aimed primarily at the Radical Party. Its leading positions in the Senate, the Assembly, in the courts, and in the municipal structures, were wiped out at a stroke of the King's pen. New Assembly elections, held on 1 June (19 May, old style), were boycotted by the Radicals and produced one hundred and thirty pro-Government deputies – out of one hundred and thirty available mandates. While lip service was still being paid to the principle of secret voting, the electoral process was in reality grossly manipulated, with the deputies' list being determined in the Royal Palace in Belgrade.[230]

Needless to say, the King's unpopularity now reached new lows. The real danger to him, however, was never the Radical Party which, opportunist to the core, could always be accommodated. Ironically, as has been seen, his real enemies were the friends of the Obrenović dynasty. Most actors in the civil-military conspiracy against him – the leading officers included – had some kind of affiliation with the Liberal Party, on which he and his father had so often relied.[231] The question arises: how ripe was their conspiracy now in the spring of 1903? Fragmentary as it is, the evidence suggests that Genčić had by mid-March 1903 secured Russia's and Austria-Hungary's tacit sanctification of a putsch. A Karađorđević succession was also in the bag. It was only a question of time now before the conspirators would act. The April demonstrations in Belgrade had the effect of providing new members, but they also injected a new urgency into the whole enterprise. The commander of the 6th Regiment, the unit which had come under suspicion, was replaced – although the new man in charge, Lieutenant-Colonel Petar Mišić, happened to be a conspirator. Far more worrisome was the arrest, in the wake of the disturbances, of two conspirator officers from that regiment. They were released thanks only to their courageous bearing during a three-day investigation. This episode, however, served to remind everyone in the conspiracy that they could become exposed at any time, especially as there existed a list with signatures of those officers who had joined. The list had been Genčić's idea: by making the officers sign it, he intended to reinforce their commitment.[232]

In truth, by this time the conspiracy was hardly a well-kept secret. Belgrade was a small place. The number of those who had learned of a plan against the royal couple, but who were themselves not actively involved, must have been considerable. Certainly, two of Alexander's fellow Balkan rulers had gleaned some information: both Carol, the King of Romania, and Prince Ferdinand of Bulgaria alerted him about a conspiracy. It is hardly surprising that Carol had learned about it from the Austrians and Ferdinand from the Russians.[233] Alexander also received letters of warning from anonymous persons. For a long time, however, he refused to believe that anyone in the Army was seriously scheming against him. He feared civilians from the opposition rather than his officers. As late as 23 April 1903, after hearing about yet another tip-off, he asked Maršićanin, the Prefect of Belgrade: 'So where is this conspiracy' ... Who knows anything positive about it? Give me something concrete and not just mere talk that something is brewing among the officers.'[234]

Alexander's incredulity was bolstered by some of those closest to him: the Prime Minister (and General) Cincar-Marković and the first adjutant

General Lazar Petrović. These soldiers, committed to an Army ethos instilled by Milan, thought an officers's conspiracy to be 'morally impossible'. Still, the King and Queen were becoming increasingly nervous. Alexander would try to avoid engagements in town and Draga likewise preferred to stay in the Royal Palace. The number of guards posted in and around the Palace was doubled. Both Jovanović and Dumba write that the King may have had a confrontation with Cincar-Marković only hours before he was murdered on 11 June. For he is supposed to have been given the names of many officers involved in the conspiracy – Dumba mentions a list containing up to sixty-two names. Alexander reportedly demanded from Cincar-Marković the introduction of courts-martial in Belgrade. This General in the shoes of the Prime Minister, however, is said to have defended his fellow officers and even offered his resignation.[235]

In the meantime the conspirators had a new, urgent reason to act. For they are supposed to have found out from Živan Živanović that the King was about to expel Draga. Živanović had recently been appointed Education Minister, but according to Radovan Drašković he was in fact a supporter of the conspiracy – his wife was the sister of Dragutin Dimitrijević Apis. Although Živanović says not a word about such a role of his in the major work he published on the political history of modern Serbia, Drašković argues convincingly that the Minister had found out about Alexander's divorce plan from Cincar-Marković and passed this information on to the conspirators.[236] Now, rumours about a possible royal split had already been circulating in Belgrade and had, according to Antonije Antić, greatly worried the conspirators because many people had greeted those rumours with approval. In other words, much of the *raison d'être* of the conspiracy would have been removed following Alexander's divorce from Draga. 'Those rumours', Antić writes, 'influenced us decisively'.[237] If so, information from an insider like Živanović confirming an imminent breakup signalled that there was no time to lose. All of which would give the 1903 overthrow a most cynical nuance: there was a rush to murder the royal couple because they would soon not be a couple.

At the same time – and it is important to be reminded of this – the conspiracy was never aimed so much against the Queen as it was against the King. In the eyes of those who plotted against him, especially the younger officers, Draga was merely one outrageous, spectacular proof of his many shortcomings as a monarch. Antić says as much. He writes that Genčić, too, had received information about a possible expulsion of Draga, which accelerated the conspirators' preparations 'because for us, the younger ones, the main thing was to remove him [Alexander], as we considered him the chief culprit. Draga, an ambitious and rotten woman, wanted to become the Queen and succeeded in this. But he was the one who should not have allowed it.'[238] Genčić evidently shared this view. In other words, even if Alexander appeared ready to mend some of his ways, he was never going to be given the benefit of the doubt. His fate was sealed.

Murder in the Palace

The conspirators swung into action shortly before 2 a.m. on 11 June (29 May, old calendar). Colonel Mašin had planned the whole operation. Although retired from the Army, he wore his uniform on that night. He, not Captain Dimitrijević Apis, was in charge. The classic account by Dragiša Vasić, in which Apis is otherwise praised at every turn, admits that Mašin was 'the chief commander'.[239]

On paper, this should have been an easy putsch. For by now, the support of an important individual had been enlisted: Lieutenant-Colonel Mihailo Naumović, an adjutant of the King. In most accounts concerning the timing of the strike Naumović is placed at the forefront – the night of 10/11 June had been chosen because he would then be on duty in the Royal Palace. Critically, he would have the keys of the so-called Arab salon, a chamber which led to the royal bedroom on the first floor at the far end of the Palace. Another insider secured for the conspiracy was Lieutenant Petar Živković who would unlock the main iron gate. Moreover, there would be plenty of soldiers to back up the officers: units from the 6th and the 7th Regiment, who would actually be told that they were coming to protect the King. An artillery battery and a company of cavalry would also be at hand. The Palace would be blocked from all sides. Separate detachments were meant to occupy the post and telegraph offices and the city Prefecture, while others were going to surround the private residences of the Prime Minister, the War Minister and the Interior Minister.[240]

Even the best-planned operations, however, can go wrong. The main strike group of twenty-eight officers emerged from the Officers' Club, not far from the Palace, expecting a battalion from the 6th Regiment, commanded by Lieutenant-Colonel Petar Mišić, to join them as a protection force. But Mišić and his troops were nowhere to be seen. Dragiša Vasić wrote that Mišić had initially got cold feet, which infuriated Lieutenant Milan Marinković, who then led his detachment on his own. Marinković was one of the most determined officers that night. As he set off with his troops, he told a second lieutenant: 'I am going, and you join me. Should this bastard [Mišić] not follow us, kill him and lead the battalion.'[241] In the meantime, the twenty-eight officers had run towards the Palace – to the amazement of street cleaners on their job. They reached the gates where Lieutenant Živković let them in. Several guards were immediately disarmed. One group, which included Apis, managed to get inside the Palace itself. However, Lieutenant-Colonel Naumović, who was supposed to unlock the Arab salon, proved completely useless as he had got drunk that night. One conspirator officer, who had not been told about Naumović's role, actually shot him dead. That would not have been a problem in itself had the keys been found. But they were never found. So the doors to the Arab salon were now blown up with dynamite cartridges.

The troops and gendarmes guarding the King did resist. Captain Jovan Miljković, on duty that night, knew about the conspiracy but had refused to join it. He bravely fought the intruders before he was killed. Lance Sergeant Velimir Milojević, one of the Palace guards, suddenly appeared before the conspirators but was mown down in a hail of fire. Apis himself was knocked out of action when hit by three bullets in an exchange with the guards – he would barely survive. But all resistance was quickly overcome when Lieutenant-Colonel Mišić finally arrived with his battalion. Colonel Mašin also appeared on the scene with the 7th Regiment.[242]

Alexander and Draga, however, had still not been found. As they entered the royal bedroom, the conspirators found it empty. The bedding was still warm. A French novel lay on the bedside table, opened on page eighty. Its title was *La Trahison*. And indeed, one officer now shouted: 'Treason!'[243] He meant of course that the conspiracy had been betrayed. The royal couple appeared to have escaped. Hardly surprisingly, the conspirators became tense and volatile. Various accounts have stated that at some point Draga had appeared at the window of the Palace calling for help – and even that she was then shot at, sustaining a wound in the left shoulder. This seems unlikely because if the royal couple had already hid themselves from the assailants, amid explosions and shooting, then they would hardly have wanted to draw attention to themselves in these moments of horrific uncertainty. Without doubt, in this pandemonium, they would not have been able to distinguish between friend and foe.

Following the bedroom fiasco, a frenzied search got under way, but the lack of electric lighting was a major problem. The electricity was apparently short-circuited by dynamite explosions, but several sources maintain that General Lazar Petrović ('handsome Laza'), the King's first aide-de-camp who resided in the palace complex, had ordered that it be turned off. Be that as it may, the conspirators were tottering in darkness and their putsch began to look like a total shambles. Candles had to be obtained from people living in houses nearby. The Palace was searched from top to bottom, at first hectically, but then systematically. An axe was used to bang against the walls of various chambers. All over the Palace, shots were fired indiscriminately and furniture was smashed. It was a race against time: if the royal couple could not be found by dawn, the troops led by the conspirators might perhaps turn their weapons against them. Lieutenant Antić, hugely frustrated, appeared at one of the windows of the royal bedroom, shouting to the artillery officer in the garden: 'Shoot! Tear down!'[244]

The destroying of the Palace by artillery fire – while many conspirators were still inside – was about to begin when Colonel Mašin, utterly calm, arrived and ordered that this action be stopped. On arrival, he had taken command of the operation. With daylight approaching and the royal couple still not found, he held a council of war in the front courtyard. He had asked that Genčić also be present. The two of them decided to announce to the troops that Alexander had been overthrown and that Peter Karađorđević had been proclaimed the new King. Genčić then went to the Interior Ministry to take it over. The decision had also been made to kill the Prime Minister, and the ministers of War and Interior. Mašin later explained that such a step was necessary as these people could get hold of some telephone to alert the authorities in the interior of the country – in which case the result would be a bloody civil war.[245]

Mašin then ordered that General Petrović, who had in the meantime been taken prisoner, be brought to him. 'Where are the King and Queen?', he asked him. Petrović replied that he did not know. Mašin's rejoinder was brusque: 'You have got to know where they are, and if you don't find them within ten minutes you will be killed.' Ten minutes, indeed, was about the length of time that it now took to ferret out the royal couple. Unknown to the conspirators, but in all probability obvious to Petrović, Alexander and Draga had hidden themselves in a narrow alcove adjoining their bedroom. Draga used it as her wardrobe. This recess in the bedroom was accessed by a door which was almost invisible because it was covered by the same green wallpaper as the rest of the walls. Taking General Petrović with them, three officers now returned to the bedroom: captains Ilija Radivojević and Mihailo Ristić, and Lieutenant Velimir Vemić. The first two were later described by Colonel Mićić as 'the most determined extremists among the conspir- ators.' But it was Vemić who apparently had the best eyesight because he spotted the door of the alcove and called for an axe to be brought.[246]

It is impossible to establish whether it was Vemić who made this discovery, or whether Petrović actually led the conspirators to Alexander's and Draga's hiding place.[247] According to most accounts, Petrović had remained loyal to the very end. Having realized that the game was up, however, he is supposed to have shouted: 'Majesty! I am, your Laza. Open the door to your officers!' Now came Alexander's reaction. He asked, in a calm voice: 'May I count on my officers' oath of allegiance?' Vemić was the first to reply; 'No, no way!' At that moment another conspirator, Lieutenant Petar Marković, entered the bedroom and shouted: 'You may!' The door opened and the royal couple appeared, huddling together. He was wearing a red silk shirt and she was covered only with a *peignoir*. Ristić was the first to shoot with his revolver, then Vemić, then Radivojević. Alexander was killed with the first bullet, but Draga was apparently still alive even after being hit ten times. It was 3:50 a.m.[248]

As the shooting began, General Petrović, who had managed to hide a pistol, now tried to use it against Ristić, but the latter dispatched him with a bullet to the head.[249] A little later the royal corpses were thrown out of the first floor window into the courtyard – for the benefit of the increasingly impatient, potentially rebellious troops. But the corpses were not naked as is often asserted. Tcharykow, who had observed events from the Russian Legation located on the main street exactly opposite the Palace, wrote that the bodies were wrapped in the window-curtains as they fell down. He also wrote that the body of the Queen had already been 'horribly mutilated by the swords of the conspirators'. While it is incontestable that Draga's body had been cut up, there is reason to doubt that this had been done by 'the conspirators', i.e., by the officers – or for that matter that swords had been used.[250] On 13 June the Austro-Hungarian Minister Dumba wrote a report to Vienna, in which he passed on the confidential information obtained from a doctor who had taken part in the autopsy. According to this doctor, Alexander's body had been hit by thirty bullets, but showed no signs (*'keine Spuren'*) of sword wounds or bayonet stabs. Draga's corpse, on the other hand, showed eighteen bullet wounds and was clearly mangled by bayonets (*'von Bayonetten förmlich zerfleischt'*). Dumba added, intriguingly, that the autopsy revealed venereal disease on both bodies (*'waren beide Körper venerisch gewesen'*).[251]

The autopsy findings are interesting because they contradict the reports, subsequently widely circulated, that Alexander's body had been hacked and his fingers cut off (thus: 'The King had only one thumb left').[252] As for Draga, the ghastly deed on her corpse seems to have been caused by bayonets rather than swords – this would implicate ordinary soldiers and not the officers. Unsurprisingly, all kinds of fantastic stories were told about the putsch. Antonije Antić complained in his memoir notes that he himself had been accused of shooting the King and Queen, and then piercing them with his sword – although he had not fired a single shot that night and had not even carried a sword.[253] Be that as it may, the terrible end of Alexander and Draga shocked the rest of Europe. And with good reason. At the same time, however, there was something ineluctable about the night of 11 June 1903. As the Serbian philosopher and historian Lazar Vrkatić put it, 'Serbia's entire hatred, its sense of helplessness and shame, exploded in that crime.'[254]

6

The Rise of Austro-Serbian Antagonism

Republic Scare

THE KILLINGS did not stop at regicide. Also murdered by the conspirators in the early hours of 11 June 1903 were the Prime Minister Dimitrije Cincar-Marković and the War Minister Milovan Pavlović. The Interior Minister Velimir Todorović, shot several times and left for dead lying in a pool of blood, did somehow survive. Less lucky were Queen Draga's two brothers, Nikola and Nikodije, executed that night apparently on the whim of Second Lieutenant Vojislav Tankosić – the officer whose actions in 1914 would acquire world significance following the assassination of Franz Ferdinand in Sarajevo.

Yet despite its bloody and grim nature, the putsch in Belgrade had not turned into a wholesale massacre of the loyalists of the late King. The changeover in Serbia was rapid and generally uncomplicated. A Provisional Government was promptly set up, and the Constitution of 1901 fully restored. By 5 a.m. 11 June, Constantin Dumba, the Austro-Hungarian Minister, had already managed to meet Colonel Mašin, who as one of the leading conspirators assured him that he and his friends were 'absolutely the masters of the situation'.[1] And so they were. A civil war was never on the cards once the last Obrenović was no more. A joint meeting of the Assembly and the Senate, as they were composed in 1901, convened on 15 June to elect Peter Karađorđević as Serbia's new Monarch. The garrisons all accepted the new state of affairs. Merchants and other wealthy people in Belgrade immediately notified the Provisional Government that they would lend it substantial amounts of money if that were required.[2] Peace and order reigned everywhere. In fact, a wave of relief passed over the country at the news of the putsch – a collective feeling, Nikolai Tcharykow noted, 'as of relief from an impending general catastrophe'.[3]

Those two pivotal diplomats in Belgrade, Dumba and Tcharykow, now found themselves in secondary roles because their governments had already decided on their Serbian policies. Both Austria-Hungary and Russia were happy to accept, in the first place, what seemed to them the cardinal result of Alexander's bloody removal: the accession of Peter Karađorđević. On 16 June Franz Joseph sent a telegram to Peter, at the time still in Geneva, in which he took care to condemn the crime of regicide in Belgrade, but at the same time expressed his full sympathy and best wishes to the new Monarch. 'I have to admit', Dumba wrote later, 'that I had not reckoned with such a swift and unconditional recognition'.[4] In fact, as Hermann Wendel emphasized, His Apostolic Majesty from Vienna's Hofburg was the first to accept Peter Karađorđević on his 'bloodstained Throne'.[5] Indeed, Dumba was the first foreign representative to present his letter of accreditation to the new king and thus become the doyen of the diplomatic corps in Belgrade.[6] Without a doubt, this swift recognition reflected the belief in Vienna that Peter would be a pliant instrument. When Joseph Baernreither ran into Gołuchowski at the Sacher Hotel on the day after the murder, he put it to him that: 'Excellency, now is a great moment for Austria' – implying, of course, that it was an opportune moment for a military intervention in Serbia. But the Foreign Minister countered: 'What on earth are you talking about, they already have another king and he is a good man!'[7]

The idea that the putsch provided a unique – and missed – opportunity for Austro-Hungarian troops to barge into Serbia has been laboured by many of those indulging in Habsburg nostalgia following the collapse of the Empire in 1918. But what is interesting is that three different and quite respectable Austrian sources went further – claiming that St Petersburg had even indicated to Vienna its willingness to go along with such an intervention. Alexander Hoyos, who had served as a diplomat in Serbia and was later, famously, Count Berchtold's *chef de cabinet* in 1914, wrote that the Russians would have agreed to a 'permanent' Austro-Hungarian occupation of Belgrade in return for concessions elsewhere. According to Prince Liechtenstein, Franz Joseph turned down the idea. The diplomat Heinrich Lützow recalled that the Russians would have raised no objections had Austria-Hungary marched in to restore order ('*Ordnung machen*').[8] Of course, as the Austro-Hungarian Legation in Belgrade knew and reported, order in the country had been preserved following the putsch. This story, nevertheless, has attracted some scholarly support.[9] However, in reality, the Russians, who must have heard about the wild interventionist talk in Vienna, were actually alarmed by it. As a result, on 2 July Foreign Minister Lamsdorff warned Baron Aehrenthal, the Austro-Hungarian Ambassador to St Petersburg, that any Austro-Hungarian military action in Serbia could create complications and necessitate a Russian counter-intervention.[10] The available evidence, in any case, indicates that Austro-Hungarian policy did not contemplate anything beyond the imperative of maintaining regional stability. Meanwhile, the Russians, just like the Austrians, played the Karađorđević card, calculating that Peter would be a malleable new actor. Two days after the coup in Belgrade, Lamsdorff told Aehrenthal that Peter would be 'a docile element in our hands', someone unlikely to cause difficulties to their 'great work' of pacifying the region.[11]

But Peter Karađorđević had yet to be elected — and there was actually something of a problem with this in Belgrade. The issue was not so much the proposed Karađorđević succession, but rather the much larger question of whether Serbia should be a monarchy or a republic. Joseph Pomiankowski, the Austro-Hungarian Military Attaché, reported on 12 June that enthusiasm for Karađorđević was 'nowhere noticeable', and on the following day he drew attention to the growth of republican tendencies in the population and the press.[12] After the putsch the Russians, too, appeared concerned about the risk of republicanism in Serbia. Instructions were dispatched to Tcharykow to urge the Provisional Government to counteract republican agitation. Of course, the prospect of a republican Serbia could only be viewed with aversion by the conservative Tsarist regime. Tcharykow even demanded of the new authorities that the Assembly should elect Peter unanimously.[13] The British information at St Petersburg was that Lamsdorff was not going to incur 'the risk of seeing a Republic proclaimed'.[14]

Another telegram by Pomiankowski on 13 June informed the War Ministry in Vienna that the officers were determined to push through a Karađorđević succession — or else they would 'blow up' the Assembly.[15] Such a drastic idea would suggest that some serious opposition to Peter existed in the ranks of Serbian politicians. But it would also suggest that the conspirators were inordinately zealous in backing this aspirant to the Serbian throne. Why? In these first days after the putsch, the rationale for their behaviour was simply self-defence. On 11 June they declared Peter the new King even though the old monarch was actually still alive. Insisting on Peter was important since Austria-Hungary and Russia had consented to him. Official international recognition of Peter, they also hoped, would whitewash their crime. Besides, a monarch who had been championed by the conspirators was unlikely to turn against them for murdering his predecessor. Also important was the appearance of legality; as the former Prime Minister Đorđe Simić observed, the conspirators realized the negative ramifications if Peter was seen as having been imposed by the Army.[16] So they included non-conspirators in their Provisional Government. Except for the Progressive Party, all the other political parties were represented in the 'revolutionary government' — as it was christened by Belgrade press.

The Serbian political class, in other words, had to be co-opted because legitimacy was now required. The civilians in the conspiracy had successfully argued against the desire of some officers to form a purely military administration.[17] Among the civilian conspirators, Jovan Avakumović and Đorđe Genčić now insisted that the Radical Party be represented in the

Provisional Government.[18] The Radicals, by far the largest political party, were only too keen to join the new regime although they had played no role in the conspiracy. But now their man Stojan Protić received the Interior Ministry initially earmarked for Genčić, who became the Economics Minister, with Colonel Alexander Mašin taking the Public Works portfolio. The conspirators Avakumović and General Atanacković became Prime Minister and War Minister respectively, while non-conspirators were given the portfolios of foreign affairs, finance, justice and education, as well as the Interior Ministry.

The next question to decide was whether the state would be a monarchy or republic. On 15 June the Assembly and Senate voted 'unanimously' to proclaim Peter Karađorđević King of Serbia. This appeared a formality, but some hard work behind the scenes had been needed to make it happen. Jovan Žujović, a prominent politician from the Independent Radical Party had apparently, with a group of other intellectuals, negotiated with the conspirators for the introduction of a republic, but found his proposal 'categorically' rejected.[19] A 'stormy', five-hour meeting took place on 14 June, in which Assembly and Senate members clashed with the conspirators. Dumba reported that, 'without a doubt', Peter Karađorđević had relatively few supporters and that the majority of Independent Radical deputies favoured a republic. It was Đorđe Genčić who pointed out that such a republic would not be recognized by either Austria-Hungary or Russia. However, the main argument to sway what Dumba called this 'Congress' in favour of Karađorđević seems to have been the physical presence, in the immediate neighbourhood, of large numbers of troops.[20] Indeed, the Assembly building had been surrounded by a whole battalion. Similarly, on 12 June, when the Belgrade *Dnevni list* published a pro-republican piece, soldiers appeared in its offices to prevent further distribution of the newspaper.[21] Rumours that a republic was being schemed by some politicians had led, Antonije Antić recalled, to 'a certain nervousness' amongst the conspirators, especially the older ones. At a meeting of their number they decided that a republic 'should not be allowed under any circumstances'.[22] Appropriate action followed. According to Radovan Drašković, in the lead-up to the vote on 15 June the conspirators exerted pressure on individual deputies and senators to vote for the Karađorđević succession. One officer, Lieutenant Todor Pavlović, duly visited a leading politician of the Radical Party, Aca Stanojević. Pavlović told Stanojević that he was under authority to remind him of the recent events in the Royal Palace. As the building could be seen from the window of Stanojević's office, the Lieutenant actually pointed his finger at it. Stanojević was informed that the Army would 'remain in readiness' until Peter Karađorđević was elected King.[23]

In the end, on 15 June, a joint session of the *Skupština* (Assembly) and the Senate did elect Peter unanimously.[24] As has been seen, however, he got to become the new King of Serbia against all the odds. The Serbian politician Jaša Prodanović, himself a republican, later recalled that in 1903 one could count the supporters of the Karađorđević dynasty 'on the fingers of one hand'.[25] The conspirators, in search of someone to replace a King whom they were about to murder, picked Peter purely because the Austrians and the Russians had proposed him. To the Austrians he was the least objectionable choice and had at the same time the reputation of an Austrophile.[26] To the Russians he looked innocuous enough and his accession would frustrate republican tendencies in Serbia; while to the Serbian political class, finally, there seemed no choice other than to accept him because the conspirators had seized power and demanded his election in no uncertain terms – he had become quite simply *their* man.

On that day, before the joint session, the Assembly passed a rather important motion, read out first by a deputy: 'The National Assembly gives full acknowledgement to the Army and its conduct and, perceiving its work and action in this instance as an outcome of difficult and critical moments, the National Assembly approves it. The Serbian Army has always been and remains the shield of the fatherland, the mainstay of law and order, and the guarantee for the bright and splendid future of Serbia.' Minutes later the Senate was presented with an identical motion. Both chambers immediately adopted it.[27] Thus the officers were not going to be brought to trial for the murder of the King and Queen, and were even thanked for it. But Christopher Clark has in his recent book rendered the matter somewhat differently: 'Apis, still recovering from his wounds, was formally thanked for what he had done by the Skupština and became a national hero.'[28] Clark does not cite any sources for this assertion, which is a most perplexing one given that Apis was not named in the Skupština motion.

Another important step taken by the new authorities was to rush through a new constitution, before the new King arrived to take power. The 1901 Constitution, functioning once again as it had before Alexander's manipulations in April, was liberal but nevertheless controversial. Serbia's Independent Radicals particularly resented the arbitrary manner in which King Alexander had simply imposed it. They therefore pushed for the restoration of the Constitution of 1888 (1889 new calendar) – that Alexander had abolished in his first royal coup back in 1894. On the eve of the joint session on 15 June, Jovan Žujović argued forcefully that the 1888 Constitution was perhaps not the ideal one, but that it nevertheless represented a legally created instrument. 'Gentlemen', he said, 'we wish that tomorrow's day brings not only the restoration of the first people's dynasty, but also the restoration of strict lawfulness, democratic constitutionalism and genuine parliamentary government.' When the objection was raised that restoring the 1888 Constitution before the arrival of the new King would betray a lack of confidence in him, Žujović replied that every written constitution stems from distrust, and continued: 'If you wish to give the King, in advance, every proof of boundless fidelity, you may as well do away with all constitutions.'[29]

These arguments carried the day. The Constitution of 1903, as it was to be called, was simply a moderately modified Constitution of 1888. The Senate, of course, was now abolished. More significantly, the powers of the Monarch were reduced in several areas.[30] By the time Peter Karađorđević arrived in Belgrade on 24 June, Serbia had a constitution which waited not on the new King's signature, but rather for his solemn oath of allegiance to it. The next day in the New Palace – built by Milan of the rival dynasty of Obrenović – Peter took his oath. The Palace stood right next to the old Palace, the *Konak*, where Alexander and Draga were murdered just a fortnight earlier.

Peter's proclamation to his people (*Mome dragom narodu*) was distributed that same day (25 June), having been written for him by Avakumović, the conspirator heading the Provisional Government. In this document the new King promised to be a genuinely constitutional monarch, declaring that the Constitution was to him sacred. He had thus been, as his biographer Živojinović observed, presented with a *fait accompli*, and the victory of parliamentary government over the Monarchy looked complete, 'to an extent that had been inconceivable in the Obrenović era'.[31]

Serbia's 'Secret Plan': Načertanije

If there is anything seminal about the palace coup against King Alexander, it is that Serbia did indeed become a truly constitutional monarchy after 1903. Peter Karađorđević did not disappoint the hopes that he would reign rather than rule. In truth, he had little choice. While still in Geneva, he had, in the description of the former Prime Minister Vladan Đorđević, agreed to a Constitution that tied 'his hands as well as his legs'.[32] The young, autocratic, capricious and in many ways unhinged Alexander was thus replaced by an elderly, restrained, French-educated Karađorđević exile who had, in 1868, translated John Stuart Mill's essay 'On Liberty' into Serbian. But this was a change of dynasty accompanied by an abatement of royal power – not, as has been argued *ad nauseam*, 'a major realignment' of policies.[33] For the same politicians, bureaucrats and diplomats who made up Serbia's elite before 1903 continued to be active after 1903 – and only a handful of them had had anything to do with the coup. It is of course true that in the initial phase of Peter's reign some of the military conspirators possessed power and influence. However, they possessed neither the ability nor the imagination to steer Serbia in any particular direction. In any case, Alexander was killed because of the overall 'bankruptcy of his rule', and not for pursuing this or that specific set of objectionable policies.[34] The changes resulting from 1903, in other words, represented adjustment, not revolution.

The removal of Alexander meant, of course, that the country could now pursue its national programme in conditions of greater internal stability. So what was this national programme? Apart from the usual references to the need for material and civilizational progress, the Serbian political and intellectual classes also talked, somewhat loosely, about national unification, that is, the liberation of Serbs living outside Serbia – no mean task as this meant those Serbs in the Ottoman and Habsburg empires. In practice, this could only apply to the patently crumbling, increasingly chaotic European part of the Ottoman Empire. The realm of the Habsburgs, despite its internal weaknesses, was still that of a formidable Great Power. This was understood in Serbia by peasants and politicians alike. To the extent that Serbia had at this time a foreign policy at all, the same aspirations towards Old Serbia and Macedonia, as had already been evident during the reign of King Alexander, would continue under King Peter.

Yet the subject of Serbia's pre-1914 plans to expand its borders has generated perhaps the most enduring furore in the historiography of southeastern Europe. Moreover, it seems that no discussion of this theme is possible without going back in time to an alleged Serbian secret plan from 1844, the *Načertanije* ('outline' or 'draft'), which supposedly contained a blueprint for sweeping expansion, and which is normally attributed to Ilija Garašanin, at the time the country's Interior Minister. The controversy regarding *Načertanije* began seventy years later, in the aftermath of the Great War when Serbia's role in the events leading up to the war was placed under scrutiny. Similarly, at the time of Yugoslavia's wars in the 1990s, which were themselves to attract considerable attention around the world and produce an army of instant experts on the country, a trend emerged seeking to explain Serbia's foreign policy in terms of a grand design. Today, a broad academic and journalistic consensus exists outside Serbia that Belgrade had ever since *Načertanije* pursued aggressive policies against neighbouring states, and against non-Serbs, designed to bring about a 'Great Serbia'. The historic significance of *Načertanije* is thus rarely questioned. On the contrary: 'It would be difficult to overstate', Christopher Clark writes, 'the influence of this document on generations of Serb politicians and patriots; in time it became the Magna Carta of Serb nationalism.'[35]

In fact, the importance of *Načertanije* has not only been grossly overstated, but its content has been and is routinely misrepresented. Firstly, one should note that this document originally lacked any Serbian input. *Načertanije* was actually a diluted version of a Balkan political project initially dreamt up by a Paris-based Polish exile, Prince Adam Czartoryski. The latter, working for the restoration of Poland, had created in his headquarters at the Hôtel Lambert a kind of foreign office in exile. Backed by France and Britain, his organization was not without importance. An indefatigable opponent of Russia, he had played quite a role in Serbian politics: in 1843 his agents had persuaded the Serbs to elect as their Prince the pro-Western, that is, the pro-French and pro-British, Alexander Karađorđević. In 1844, Tsar Nicholas I complained that all the difficulties he had in Serbia were due to Czartoryski.[36] The British diplomat David Urquhart, a most illustrious figure and a friend of Karl Marx, had apparently stimulated Czartoryski's interest in the affairs of Serbia which Urquhart had visited several times in the 1830s. Prince Miloš Obrenović, the country's ruler at the time, had told him about his wish to get rid of Russian influence. Urquhart shared with Czartoryski a general obsession with Russia.[37] Serbia's attraction for Czartoryski was as the nucleus of a future big Balkan state that would be pro-Western and anti-Russian – as well as anti-Austrian. In January 1843 he wrote and sent to the Serbian leaders his *'Conseils sur la conduite a suivre par la Serbie'* in which he advocated Serbia's territorial expansion and urged that it should take a lively interest in its fellow Slavs in the Turkish and Austrian Empires. He was as hostile to Austria as he was to Russia, warning the Serbs that Austria intended to swallow up their country. He even recommended to them that they try to get on with the Hungarians in order to weaken Austria.[38]

In 1844 Czartoryski's agent in Belgrade František Zach, a Czech, decided to use this memorandum to make Serbian-language proposals of his own. The 'Zach Plan', as it became known', could actually in many ways be seen as a blueprint for a Great Serbia. It opens with the idea that the medieval Serbian Empire of Tsar Dušan which had been destroyed by the Turks could see a 'renaissance', now that the power of Turkey was on the wane, something that 'the other South Slavs' would welcome 'with joy', for nowhere else in Europe was remembrance of glorious past so strong as with the Slavs of Turkey. Zach then specifically mentions a 'new South Slav, Serbian state [*nova južnoslavenska, srbska država*]' and repeatedly points to the old Serbian Empire as the foundation on which to build it. In the section on Serbia's relations with Croatia, he considered Serbs and Croats 'one and the same people, speaking the same language', with the Croat literary language 'becoming increasingly Serbian'. He even suggests that the 'Illyrian' movement in Croatia was given its name because, under Austrian rule, the Croats would not have been allowed 'to raise the flag of the Serbian name and Empire'. So while Zach may have been imagining a state of the South Slavs, it would clearly have been one in which the Serbs and their history towered above the rest. A key concept contained in his Plan is that of historic right. 'You Serbs', Zach wrote, 'will appear before the world as the rightful inheritors of a glorious past, as the sons of great fathers, who are merely reclaiming ancestral lands ... and so Serbdom, its nation and the affairs of its state stand under the protection of holy historic right'. It is simply not the case, as Christopher Clark maintains, that Zach had in his plan 'envisaged a federal organization of the South Slav peoples'. On the contrary, in his discussion of Bosnia, Zach recommends that awareness be spread among the people of Bosnia of 'all the fundamental laws, the constitution and all the main regulations of the Principality of Serbia'.[39] But then, Clark does seem anxious to fashion out of nothing 'Zach's cosmopolitan vision' – as he describes it – in order to contrast it with 'a more narrowly focused Serbian nationalist manifesto'.[40]

Such a manifesto is supposed to have been penned in 1844 by Ilija Garašanin, the Serbian statesman with whom Zach maintained contact in Belgrade. But interestingly, Garašanin, who is often accused of having transformed the Zach Plan into a master plan for a 'Great Serbia' (*Načertanije*), did precisely the opposite: the change he made was to replace the megalomaniac ideas of Czartoryski and Zach with something more realistic. In this vein, Garašanin cut out in its entirety Zach's section on relations with the Croats, for he was interested in the Turkish, not the Habsburg Empire. Where Zach had written 'new South Slav, Serbian state', Garašanin replaced this with 'new Serbian state in the South [*nova srbska država na jugu*]'.[41] The territories to which he paid attention in the *Načertanije*, apart from Montenegro, were Bosnia, Herzegovina and 'Northern Albania', i.e., Kosovo and Metohija or 'Old Serbia'. At this time, of course, these were all part of the Ottoman Empire and Serbia itself was still its vassal state. It must have been clear to Garašanin that what in Zach's plan amounted to a Great Serbia, envisaged to incorporate Habsburg as well as Ottoman territories, was an objective hopelessly beyond the means of the tiny Serbian Principality. Garašanin's vision was that of a future Serbian state made up basically of the Serbs of Turkey. His programme was 'Serbian, not Great Serbian'.[42] He nevertheless retained Zach's suggestions about Serbia's possible South Slav cooperation with the Serbs and Croats in the Habsburg Empire, and the Bulgarians outside it. Clearly, though, this was to him of secondary importance, a project perhaps for some distant future.

A hypothetical court case on authorial rights between Garašanin the politician and Zach, Czartoryski's agent, would have no difficulty in deciding that descriptions of Garašanin as the author of *Načertanije* are entirely exaggerated: most of the time, he copied Zach's Plan word by word, sentence by sentence, passage by passage. All the key inputs by Zach, and especially the references to the medieval Empire of Tsar Dušan and the Serbs' historic rights arising from it, were left untouched by Garašanin. The often cited message of *Načertanije* that Austria must be seen as a 'permanent enemy' is also Zach's. Garašanin's few original additions were insubstantial. It would be much more accurate to describe him as *Načertanije*'s editor. His cuts and modifications, however, were significant in that they reduced the Zach Plan to a more realistic scope. Charles and Barbara Jelavich, the noted authorities on Balkan history, described Garašanin's programme as laying emphasis 'on the acquisition of lands that were Serbian and Orthodox in population'.[43]

But Garašanin did not write, and nor did Zach, that 'Where a Serb dwells, that is Serbia'. Those words are simply not there. Such non-existent content, bewilderingly supplied in this case complete with quotation marks (but without a reference) by Christopher Clark, might leave an erroneous impression in the minds of non-specialist readers who are hardly likely to have the text of *Načertanije* lying around.[44] Persistent attempts to present it as a toxic instrumentality at the heart of Serbia's foreign policy have necessitated here a closer scrutiny of this otherwise inconsequential mid-nineteenth century piece of work. For *Načertanije* is neither a bona fide Serbian document nor has anyone been able to demonstrate its impact on Serbian policy after 1844. It is in fact a classic example of a historiographical straw man argument. Ivo Pilar, the Bosnian Croat nationalist who under the pseudonym von Südland published in 1918 *Die südslawische Frage*, one of the most sustained attacks ever on what he saw as plans for a 'Great Serbia', says nothing about it and does not even mention Ilija Garašanin. The respected Serbian historian Andrija Radenić has drawn attention to the fact that the importance of *Načertanije* has – retrospectively – been vastly exaggerated. According to Radenić, no one among the rulers and leading personalities in Serbia had used it for guidance; it had got no mention in the programmes of political parties; not a single word had been uttered about it in the sessions of the National Assembly or at the meetings of other state and social institutions; only historians and later, publicists, took a great interest in it.[45] To this may be added that *Načertanije*, first published in Belgrade in 1906, had not been particularly 'secret', either: in 1893, in his famous study of Serbia's Balkan policies, Vladislav Karić paid it a warm tribute. But contrary to the mythology about *Načertanije* supposedly illuminating Serbia's path, Karić complained bitterly that Serbian statesmen had actually been ignoring it.[46]

Just what exactly Serbia's foreign policy amounted to was at times not clear even to those in charge of it. Two years after the 1903 coup, the lack of direction was so conspicuous that the acting Foreign Minister Jovan Žujović felt the need for a brainstorming event. In August 1905 he staged a conference of Serbia's diplomatic representatives abroad, attended also by several political figures, to discuss the priorities of the country's foreign policy. In the first session of the three-day conference the complaint was heard that 'our foreign policy has no clearly formulated direction.' Another view expressed was that, since the Congress of Berlin, 'we have been drifting, trying to find a path'. No one brought up *Načertanije*. Czartoryski, Zach and Garašanin must have been turning in their graves. What is quite striking – in the light of so much cock-sure modern historiography about Serbia's purported expansionist drive after 1903 – is that the conference very nearly failed to discuss Bosnia-Herzegovina at all. The matter was only addressed belatedly when General Sava Grujić noted that a record about the work of the conference would survive in the Foreign Ministry, and that 'it would not look good' if Bosnia-Herzegovina were not to have been mentioned. So the participants then addressed this question, but merely agreed that Serbia's work should steer the various religious groups in Bosnia-Herzegovina towards getting ready to put forward a demand for autonomy 'at an opportune moment'.[47]

It is therefore odd that things are now presented as having been exactly the opposite. 'After the regicide of 1903,' writes Christopher Clark, 'Belgrade stepped up the pace of irredentist activity within the empire, focusing in particular on Bosnia-Herzegovina'.[48] Just what this 'irredentist activity' consisted of Clark does not clarify. In reality, in December 1906 Burián stated in the Austrian Delegation as the minister responsible for Bosnia-Herzegovina that he was not aware of any centrifugal tendencies among the Serbs (or the Muslims) of Bosnia.[49] As late as December 1907 he was explaining to his fellow ministers in the Joint Ministerial Council that the Serbian autonomist endeavours in Bosnia-Herzegovina were occurring 'only in the framework of the Occupation concept' (i.e., within Habsburg rule), that a tendency towards outside (i.e., towards Serbia) did not exist, and that the danger of a revolutionary movement among Serbs or any other population group in Bosnia-Herzegovina was likewise non-existent.[50]

After 1903 Serbia did stage significant, albeit sporadic, cross-border activities, but they related to Macedonia, not Bosnia-Herzegovina. The Serbian Army, certainly, did not think that the country was implementing some lofty national project. In his confidential report of November 1906, criticising the weakness of the Serbian Army, Colonel Mašin wrote: 'In the last decades we have lived, and still live today, without a national programme. We have talked a great deal and felt the need for a grand national policy, for the unification of dispersed Serbs, for the creation of Great Serbia. Such a policy can only be realized by relying on an Army as ready and as large as possible, but we have not achieved that.'[51]

The Conspirators Question

Far from pursuing some kind of grand design, after 1903 the leaders of Serbia were faced with the more pressing and immediate problem of having to deal with the international consequences of the putsch against King Alexander. Although Austria-Hungary and Russia had been quick to recognize the new regime, regicide did not go down well with Edward VII, the King of England. No Court mourning had been ordered in England following the murder of the Serbian royal couple – unlike in Russia, Spain, Bulgaria and Romania – but the English Monarch was able to influence a far more effective response: on 19 June diplomatic relations between Britain and Serbia were suspended. There can be little doubt that he was behind this gesture. The Austro-Hungarian Ambassador in London had already informed Vienna on 13 June about the idea circulating in London of withdrawing the British representative in Belgrade, ascribing it to Edward VII's wish to show his 'revulsion over the ghastly slaughter'.[52] The position of the Foreign Office would henceforth be that the regicides should be punished before normal relations could be restored.

Those relations would not be re-established until 1906. The consequent absence of a British Minister in Belgrade was more than just an irritant – because Serbia's politicians and diplomats had increasingly seen 'Engleska' as a valuable potential ally. Britain's reaction to the regicide in Belgrade highlighted the so-called 'conspirators question [*zaverenićko pitanje*]' in post-1903 Serbian politics. In this context, the 'conspirators' are normally taken to be the officers – as opposed to the civilians. Their importance in the affairs of Serbia for a period of some three years after the putsch cannot be denied. Although they did not quite run the country after 1903, for several years they did hold sway over the King, control the Army, and, occasionally, make or break a government. They were the dubious heroes of 11 June, but after the event their clout was due primarily to their thriving relationship with King Peter. The latter has often been seen as the 'prisoner' of the conspirators. This he may well have been if it is true that they held proof of his foreknowledge about the plan to murder King Alexander. Count Michael Muraviev, the Russian Chargé d'Affaires in Belgrade, claimed to his Austro-Hungarian colleague Ludwig von Flotow that he had seen written evidence about Peter's 'active involvement' in the plot to murder King Alexander.[53]

Even without such compromising material, however, the King had good reasons to be on good terms with the officers. He could not rely on any political party in the country, and nor did he have the skills or inclination to manipulate politicians as Alexander Obrenović had done. Having left Serbia for exile at an early age, he was very much a foreigner in his own country. His French was superior to his Serbian.[54] In October 1903 he told Dumba: 'Sadly, I lack the initiative and also I do not know the people in Serbia ... I am a novice in the business of government'.[55] He thus became an instrument in the hands of the leading officers from the conspiracy, seeing in them a guarantee for his own and his dynasty's survival. The alliance between Peter and the officers, however, represented a natural political symbiosis. Like the King, the officers could not count on any political party for support. Their 'revolutionary' Government, in any case, was of short duration because their civilian accomplices in the putsch turned out to be, in effect, the godfathers of constitutional government in Serbia. Elections in September 1903 produced an overwhelming majority of Radicals and Independent Radicals who then joined forces to put together a new administration. The former, Pašić's party, were traditionally suspicious of the Army. Given these circumstances, the leading officers associated with 11 June, concerned as they were to retain influence, extracted the maximum from the King: at the Court they provided his adjutants and ordnance officers; divisional commanders and other impor-tant military appointments, as well as promotions, were under their strict control; and, critically, the War Minister always had to be their man. Signi-ficantly, many officers who had had nothing to do with the plot against Alexander became for opportunistic reasons the allies and defenders of the relatively small group of conspirators.[56] It was small wonder then that the conspirator officers felt themselves to be in the saddle and that they acted arrogantly, even towards their King. The latter, shocked by the rude manner of Lieutenant-Colonel Miloš Božanović, his adjutant, asked him: 'In what relationship, then, do we actually find ourselves, if you allow your-self such behaviour towards me?' Božanović reportedly replied: 'Your Majesty, we are companions'.[57]

The privileged position of the chief conspirator officers caused much resentment elsewhere in the Army. Their closeness to the King was seen as a conduit for moral and material corruption – quite a few of the con-spirator officers were beneficiaries of financial backing from the King.[58] Soon there emerged a 'counter-conspiracy' – as it is called in the literature on the subject. Captain Milan Novaković, who had been in Paris at the time of the putsch, was appalled by the state of affairs he encountered on returning to Serbia. Some of his officer friends estimated the number of conspirators at no more than eighty, telling Novaković, as he noted in his diary: 'We have got rid of two Lunjevicas [Queen Draga's two officer brothers], and now we have eighty of them.' One officer complained: 'I did not wish to serve the whore [Draga], but now we have corruption from above ... The whore was better'.[59] In August 1903 in Niš, where he had been posted, Novaković began circulating a proclamation to the Serbian officer corps in which he demanded the dismissal of the conspirators from the Army as they had broken their oath of allegiance to King Alexander. An honourable man, Novaković appeared interested solely in restoring moral integrity to the Serbian Army. He was quickly arrested and tried, together with more than two dozen of his fellow officers who had signed the procla-mation. The dirty work of investigating this dissent in the Niš garrison had been entrusted to Captain Dragutin Dimitrijević Apis. After serving two years in prison, Novaković emerged to continue his campaign against the conspirators as a civilian, ending up once again in prison – where he was murdered in 1907, probably on the order of the conspirators.[60]

Although much discussed in the relevant historiography, the 'counter-conspiracy' was of little consequence, for though it cost a man his life it never really amounted to more than a protest. Novaković had merely articulated the moral outrage felt by many officers outside the 1903 conspiracy. Belatedly, the standards of right and wrong also began to be perceived by the Belgrade diplomatic corps. In November 1903 Constantin Dumba initiated a boycott of the Serbian Court. Around the New Year many foreign diplomats left Belgrade in an attempt to pressurize King Peter into removing the conspirator officers from the Court. Kajetan von Mérey, Gołuchovski's right-hand man at the Ballhausplatz, took a dim view of this action. He complained privately that six months after allowing the new regime to consolidate itself, and after acquiescing in King Peter becoming fully a prisoner of the military clique, 'we now suddenly remind ourselves that we should actually be scandalized by the murderous deed'.[61]

Indeed, as events were to show, this whole international indignation over the conspirator officers was somewhat spurious. For example, Russia had, despite its early recognition of Peter, subsequently demanded that he order an investigation and punish those responsible for Alexander's murder. By July 1903, however, Lamsdorff was only talking about a 're-establishment of discipline' in the Serbian Army, while in February 1904 he demanded no more than the removal of conspirator officers from the Court.[62] Yet Austria-Hungary was to surpass Russia in this exercise of moral and political flexibility: as will be shown below, in 1906, when it was keen to secure artillery orders from Serbia, it actually enlisted the support of the conspirator officers. Even Britain, which had after the putsch immediately withdrawn its Minister (though its Chargé d'Affaires remained at his post) and demanded that the officers with blood on their hands be punished, began to adjust its position in 1906. Its principled stand in 1903 was made easier given that it had virtually no interests in the affairs of Serbia at the time. By 1906, however, when it looked like Germany, in combination with Austria-Hungary, would push eastwards through the Balkans, the Foreign Office hurried to resume full British presence in Belgrade and was happy to settle for the retirement of five leading conspirators. As Foreign Secretary Edward Grey succinctly explained to King Edward VII, the restoration of diplomatic relations with Serbia was desirable for 'political reasons'.[63]

It is quite wrong to suggest, as Christopher Clark has done, that only Austria had in 1903-1904 'joined the British in imposing sanctions on the Karadjordjevic court'. With the exceptions of Greece and Turkey, all the powers, including Russia, had withdrawn their representatives from Belgrade as well. However, Clark is also keen to make a different, far more important point: 'Hoping to profit from this loosening of the Austro-Serbian bond, the Russians moved in, assuring the Belgrade government that Serbia's future lay in the west, on the Adriatic coastline, and urging them not to renew their long-standing commercial treaty with Vienna'.[64] Now, even non-specialists may be aware of the existence at this time of the Austro-Russian Balkan entente and the utter determination of the two foreign ministers, Gołuchowski and Lamsdorff, not to do anything that would jeopardize it. Is it really likely then, that the Russians, increasingly busy as they were in the Far East, would suddenly decide to make trouble in the Balkans by inciting anti-Austrian behaviour in Belgrade? Clark gives F.R. Bridge's *From Sadowa to Sarajevo* as his source. This standard work on Austro-Hungarian foreign policy does indeed mention the points which Clark makes, but gives no reference.[65] The only Austrian documents that appear to be relevant to this question, in any case, tell a very different story. On 10 July 1903 Gołuchowski received a report from Belgrade, in which Dumba informed him about a conversation he had held with Jakov Nenadović, King Peter's *chef de cabinet*. Nenadović had related to him how Tscharykow, the Russian Minister, had during a *déjeuner* with King Peter's French friend, the Marquess de Rose, told the latter about the 'possibility of Serbia's economic emancipation from Austria-Hungary' and expressed the view that Serbia would be making a grave mistake if it concluded a trade agreement with Austria-Hungary 'at any price'. Though he did also say that Serbia should consider transporting its exports down the Danube, he was definitely not reported as saying that Serbia's future lay in the west.[66]

From the dinner table context and level of the participants, it is clear anyway that this was just diplomatic small talk which Bridge appears to have raised to the level of official Russian policy. It did not even take place with a representative of the Serbian Government. Tscharykow, for his part, was known for his solo excursions, something of which Foreign Minister Lamsdorff was aware and definitely disapproved of. Gołuchowski reacted to Dumba's report by asking Baron Aehrenthal, his Ambassador in St Petersburg, to take the matter up with Lamsdorff. When, at the end of July, Aehrenthal then complained to Lamsdorff, the latter used 'very disparaging words' about Tscharykow, while stating his intention to recall the Minister from his post in Belgrade.[67] This was actually done several months later. There is thus no basis for the claims that Russia intended to profit from the loosening of ties between Austria-Hungary and Serbia.

By the end of March 1904 the diplomatic boycott was already over. King Peter had helped to ease the situation by agreeing to remove from his entourage all the conspirator officers. Yet he had remained loyal to them: they had simply left the Court to assume influential positions elsewhere. Thus Colonel Mašin became the Chief of General Staff.[68] Nevertheless, by the time of Peter's coronation in September 1904 Serbia had escaped international isolation. That said, the affair regarding the conspirators dragged on because they had not retired from the Army.

By 1906, when the restoration of relations with Britain came to be seen as a priority in Serbia's foreign policy, the matter was finally fixed and without too much acrimony when five leading conspirator officers were retired. Group cohesion among the officer class had, in any case, already broken down. The younger ones, fed up with the bickering generated by the conspirators question, had held a meeting which sent a message to King Peter, urging him to sacrifice the five officers in question.[69] This society of 'companions in fate', as Walter Markov called the officers from the 1903 conspiracy, was now no more.[70] None of which really meant that the Serbian Army had been removed from the political scene. After 1911, following the establishment of the notorious 'Unification or Death' organization, also known as the Black Hand, praetorian tendencies in Serbia would manifest themselves with renewed vigour. The conspirators question, however, was in mid-1906 put *ad acta* at least as far as its international implications were concerned.

Pragmatic Patriot: Nikola Pašić

The person primarily responsible for this elimination by retirement of the leading conspirators was Nikola Pašić. Who exactly was this man? Despite his pivotal role in Balkan events leading up to the start of World War One, little is known about Pašić outside narrow academic circles in the West.[71] At first glance, over the past decades he has certainly featured as one of the 'established' figures of the July 1914 crisis. Photographs of him, along with those of Moltke, Grey, Berchtold, Sazonov and other key personalities in 1914, are regularly included in the photo-sections of books on the subject. They show an elderly man with a long white beard, and an expression both calm and stern. Would this man contemplate provoking a world war, with all its accompanying risks, in order to achieve the goal of national unification? This is the hypothesis put forward by Christopher Clark who, admittedly, is careful to write that in 1914 Pašić did not 'consciously' seek a broader conflict. Nevertheless, Clark sees Pašić as someone perhaps anticipating and at least toying with the idea of accepting a European war for the sake of dislodging 'the formidable obstacles' standing in the way of Serbian reunification.[72] In the light of such speculation it might be useful to take a closer look at Pašić.

It was seen in the previous chapter how Pašić had disappeared into the political wilderness as a consequence of his ignominious conduct following the attempt at assassinating ex-King Milan in 1899. For Pašić had both betrayed his party colleagues and confessed that the work of the Radical Party had been anti-dynastic. Craftiness, not courage, was Pašić's strong point. And he knew that his was not an easy profession. 'In politics', he is quoted as saying, 'everyone can make a mistake, even the cleverest, the strongest and the best. For politics is the most difficult business of all.'[73] After a period of self-imposed exile in Trieste, he returned to Serbia when Alexander married Draga and when, as a result of Russian support of this marriage, life became more tolerable for the Radical Party. In 1901, after Alexander had imposed a new constitution with a new, bicameral chamber, Pašić became a Senator. This did not complete his political comeback, however, and he remained careful not to expose himself unnecessarily. Thus, having been told about the impending putsch against Alexander, he immediately left for the Austrian Adriatic sea resort of Abbazia – just in case the putsch did not succeed. Gradually, with the help of some remaining political friends, he clawed his way back to the leading position in the Radical Party. By February 1904 Pašić was Foreign Minister in the cabinet of General Sava Grujić, and by the end of the year he was already the Prime Minister. In the decade leading up to the outbreak of the Great War, he was incontestably the pre-eminent Serbian politician.

Except that, strictly speaking, Pašić was not Serbian. This matter would perhaps not in itself be noteworthy were it not for the fact that his biographers tend to skirt over the issue.[74] Pašić was born in 1845, in a deeply provincial little town in eastern Serbia called Zaječar, a place dreaded by Serbian officialdom as 'Serbia's Siberia'.[75] The population included, in addition to the Serbs and Bulgarians, a substantial *Cincar* (Tsintsar) element. The Cincars (or Vlachs or Aromanians, as they are also called), represented an indigenous but subsequently romanized Balkan people who spoke a kind of Latin.[76] Racially, therefore, they have nothing to do with the Slavs of the Balkans.[77] Pašić's real surname was Pasku, and he came from a Cincar family originally resident in western Macedonia. A mysterious nation without much of a written history, they have certainly not lacked in individual success. Eminent Cincars include Herbert von Karajan and Mother Theresa. In pre-1914 Serbia they made up much of the country's elite in arts, commerce and politics. Lazar Paču, Pašić's Radical Party friend and Serbia's distinguished Finance Minister, was a Cincar. So was Alexander's last Prime Minister, General Cincar-Marković (as the surname makes obvious), as was his longest-serving Prime Minister Vladan Đorđević. So, too, was Colonel Dragutin Dimitrijević Apis, one of the most notorious Serbs ever.[78] For these people were indeed Serbian – by assimilation. While the multinational character of the Habsburg Empire is widely understood, it is often forgotten that national Balkan states contained significant minority populations. And although Serbia was something of a melting pot, everybody knew who was who. When General Jovan Belimarković, Milan's and later Alexander's loyal soldier, found out the names of the principal figures involved in the 1903 conspiracy, he declared that at least he had the satisfaction of knowing that it was not the Serbs who had murdered the King, but rather 'Cincars, Bulgars, Czechs, Vlachs and Jews'.[79]

In any case, Pašić has been seen by his many hagiographers as one of the greatest-ever Serbs. So it perhaps of interest that his contemporaries considered his Serbian ungrammatical and generally quite poor. His foreign language skills, reportedly, also left something to be desired. Although he had studied at the Zurich Polytechnic, 'he did not fully command' the German language according to Baron Giesl, the Austro-Hungarian Minister in Belgrade in 1914; his French was 'abominable' according to Hamilton Fish Armstrong, the editor of *Foreign Affairs*; and as for his Russian, Dimitrije Popović, the long-serving Serbian diplomat in St Petersburg, recalled that Pašić 'could not even speak Serbian properly, let alone Russian'. Constantin Dumba maintained, similarly, that Pašić could not speak any language correctly, 'not even Serbian'.[80] Be that as it may, Pašić's name, among ordinary people in Serbia (he is often referred to by his nickname 'Baja'), is today, as in the past, a synonym for unflinching patriotism and plucky statesmanship. He is a household name in Serbia where he is celebrated rather as is Churchill in Britain. A main square in central Belgrade is named after him, complete with a massive bronze statue. His perceived qualities of pragmatism, patience and self-control are seen as amounting to political genius.

It has to be said, however, that several contemporaries have painted rather unflattering portraits of Nikola Pašić. One of his most savage critics was his Radical Party colleague Kosta Stojanović, Serbia's able Economics Minister between 1906 and 1908. More than any other man, Stojanović managed during that period to free Serbia from economic dependence on Austria-Hungary. In his fragmentary memoirs, he could not hide his bewilderment and bitterness that practically the whole of Serbia had come to view Pašić as a man whom 'Providence had sent to direct the affairs of the state'. For Pašić, according to Stojanović, sadly lacked both the intellectual and moral qualities of a statesman, imposing 'despotism' on the Radical Party and removing from it all those who could think or who held high principles. Foreign powers, according to Stojanović, believed that Pašić mattered in his own country, whereas Serbia believed that Pašić enjoyed prestige abroad. 'On the basis of these two fallacies', Stojanović writes, 'Pašić grew in stature, becoming indispensable – at the expense of Serbia'. Internationally, he managed to make Serbia look brazen, made possible the suspicion that it had provoked a European war, and was responsible for the belief abroad that the Serbs were 'the biggest megalomaniacs'. Stojanović insists that Pašić was 'the sworn enemy of progress, culture and morality', and also 'one of the greatest opportunists I have ever seen or heard of'. Not exactly mincing his words about Pašić's corruption, he calls him 'the central figure among the profiteers, vultures and that scum of the earth which had brought the Party and the country to ruination'. By 'ruination' he meant Serbia's catastrophic defeat in 1915.[81]

Even Vasa Kazimirović, Pašić's sympathetic, far too uncritical biographer, admits that his subject was 'to a certain extent a Machiavellian, not respecting at all times the prevailing norms, either ethical or political'.[82] The corruption issue, in particular, seems to have dogged Pašić for most of his career. For example, it was pointed out to Josef Redlich when the latter arrived in Belgrade in November 1912, at the height of the Austro-Serbian crisis generated by the First Balkan War. Redlich was briefed on Pašić by Stephan von Ugron, the Austro-Hungarian Minister in Belgrade, who told him that the Serbian Prime Minister was 'the true King of Serbia' and had 'earned' 10 million francs, an enormous sum for the time. Interestingly, Ugron contended that Pašić was keen to maintain peace precisely because of his fortune.[83] Assessments of Pašić as a crooked politician, by Serbs and foreigners alike, are in fact too numerous to ignore. In 1908 the Independent Radical Jovan Žujović remarked that the main charge against Pašić was not that he had become a conservative, but rather that he had become 'the soul of corruption in Serbia'.[84] Within his own Radical Party, Pašić was seen by the able diplomat and statesman Milovan Milovanović as holding on to power by means of a slush fund and the help of a group of 'contractors and entrepreneurs'.[85]

In 1927, soon after Pašić's death, Jaša Prodanović, an Independent Radical Party politician before 1914, wrote: 'Nikola Pašić loved, above all, two things: power and money.' As character assassinations go, Prodanović's effort, published in Belgrade's prestigious literary magazine *Srpski književni glasnik*, is utterly devastating. Pašić was not, according to Prodanović, a thinker, an orator, or a writer; he was unfamiliar with both Serbian and foreign history; constitutional questions did not interest him and he did not burden himself with political theory. In fact, to Prodanović Pašić was a politician entirely devoid of principle. Initially a supporter of the parliamentary system, he ended up serving King Alexander's autocratic personal regime; he had criticised bureaucracy, but no one had bureaucratized the state as much as he and his friends had done; from the original Radical Party programme he realized 'not one bit'. Prodanović writes, in a reference to Thomas Macaulay, that Pašić's programme was as adjustable as 'the tent of the fairy Paribanou'. Prodanović also dwelt on Pašić's corruption, drawing attention to his mining concessions and manipulation of land purchases in the territories gained by Serbia in the First Balkan War.[86]

Finally, with regard to Pašić's foreign policy contribution, Prodanović held that the attainment of national liberation and unification – the monumental feats widely ascribed to Pašić – were ones of which he was 'completely innocent'. Prodanović emphasized that the Balkan Alliance of 1912, which resulted in a major territorial aggrandizement of Serbia, was not Pašić's work, but rather that of his Radical Party colleague Milovan Milovanović; that prior to the war which Bulgaria had started in 1913, and in which the Serbian Army was again victorious, Pašić had wanted to resolve differences with that country (through the arbitration of the Russian Tsar) in a way which would have entailed a loss of the gains made in 1912; and that the war of 1914 likewise had nothing to do with him, being moreover a conflict which his Government initially called a defence of threatened territories. So national unification with other Serbian territories, Prodanović argued, was in the end brought about despite, and not because of Pašić.[87]

It is perhaps worth bearing in mind that all these recollections of Pašić by his contemporaries do very convincingly show him as a corrupt, unprincipled opportunist, concerned mainly with maintaining himself in power. It will also be shown on the pages below that Pašić's alleged Russophilia, invariably interpreted as constituting part and parcel of his Serb patriotic orientation, was in fact something of a spurious affair. All of this, of course, does not mean that Pašić was not a nationalist politician – such were the times that practically every politician in Serbia was a nationalist, for no one could aspire to power or hold power without being seen as a defender of national interests. But the question here is: what were his priorities? In the light of everything that is known about Pašić, it is difficult to imagine him as a reckless Serbian patriot burning with the desire to attain national unification and ready to risk everything in that process: including the peace of Europe, the destiny of Serbia and, in particular, his own career and even his wealth. For one of his guiding tenets was: 'It is preferable to proceed at a slower pace, always and only along a safe path.'[88] This chimes with another contemporary view of Pašić as being one of those statesmen who would never 'run ahead of events in order to steer them in a desired direction'. Rather, he was a pronounced representative of the 'laisser-allez' philosophy: one who would 'put off all the difficult questions, until events themselves would impose solutions'.[89]

The Mürzsteg Agreement and the 'Drang nach Saloniki'

February 1904 saw Pašić appointed Foreign Minister of Serbia. By this time, two recent developments were affecting the course of politics and diplomacy in the Balkans. The first was the October 1903 Mürzsteg Agreement between Austria-Hungary and Russia on reforms in European Turkey. In essence, Mürzsteg represented a continuation of Austro-Russian efforts to keep the Ottoman Empire alive and to 'keep the Balkans on ice'.[90] In practice, Austria-Hungary was to play the leading role in overseeing the Mürzsteg reform process. For the second development was the outbreak, on 8 February 1904, of war between Russia and Japan. Russia's consequent involvement in the Far East, its defeat in the war and resultant turmoil at home, would make it for some time a more or less a passive onlooker regarding the affairs of Europe.

The Mürzsteg Agreement came in the wake of a major, indigenous (Slavonic) revolt against Turkish rule – the so-called *Ilinden* (St Elijah's Day) uprising of August 1903 in the region loosely called Macedonia. Badly planned and lacking external support even from Bulgaria, it was quickly and bloodily suppressed by the Turks. The leaders of the Internal Macedonian Revolutionary Organization (IMRO – as opposed to the external one, controlled by Bulgaria) which organized the action, had been working for an autonomous Macedonia and hoped to bring about European intervention. The only intervention, however, was a programme of reforms, agreed by foreign ministers Gołuchowski and Lamsdorff at a hunting lodge near Mürzsteg, Styria, and imposed on the predictably reluctant Turkey. The project envisaged ameliorating the situation in the *vilayets* (provinces) of Salonika, Kosovo and Monastir by reorganization, supervised by the Great Powers, of the gendarmerie and police, and of administrative and judicial institutions.[91] But there was potentially more to the agreement. Article III demanded the Ottoman Government modify 'the territorial delimitation of administrative units' to reflect the population concentrations of different nationalities.[92] Bulgaria, Greece and Serbia would now send their irregular bands into Macedonia because 'all factions tried to seize the largest possible areas in anticipation of a future partition'.[93]

The turn of events in the Balkans that began with the Macedonian trouble in 1903 proved of particular significance for Austro-Serbian relations which, almost imperceptibly, began to deteriorate in the second half of that year. But this had had nothing to do with the change of dynasty in Serbia or some consequent 'major realignment' of policies. Paradoxically, in the light of so much historiography which concentrates on the perceived threat posed by Serbia to Habsburg territories (i.e., to Bosnia-Herzegovina), something of the opposite was in play. The post-1903 worsening of relations between Belgrade and Vienna arose in part because, after Mürzsteg, Serbia perceived what it considered *its* territories in Old Serbia (i.e., Kosovo and Metohija) and Macedonia to be threatened by Austria-Hungary. The latter's overall threat in the region, imagined or real, was labeled '*Drang nach Saloniki* [drive to Salonika]' – not to be confused with, but complementing Germany's famous *Drang nach Osten*.

Were Serbia's fears justified? Certainly, Serbian diplomats were furious that Balkan states had not been consulted before Mürzsteg, and this resentment was as much against Russia as against Austria-Hungary.[94] But there was now also a new perception – of discrepancy in the regional capabilities of those two Powers. In November 1903 Milovan Milovanović, Serbia's Minister in Rome, argued that Russia's position in the Balkans was weak, resting as it did on only the traditional religious and tribal sympathies of Balkan Christians. Austria-Hungary, on the other hand, was always able, by virtue of its occupation of the Sanjak of Novi Pazar, to send its

Army to Kosovo ('the strategic key to the whole western half of the Balkan peninsula') and to develop its influence among the Albanians, a people both armed and willing to cooperate militarily. And whereas Russia had important interests elsewhere, especially in Asia, it was only in the Balkans that the Habsburg Monarchy could 'contemplate an expansionist policy'.[95] Moreover, as Dumba informed Vienna at this time, a widespread belief existed in Serbia that Russia had sold Serbia out ('*ausgeliefert*'), and that Austria-Hungary would 'undoubtedly' act from Novi Pazar in spring 1904 and would, if strategically necessary, occupy the Kingdom of Serbia.[96]

The Serbs were certainly right to suspect Russia. In February 1904, for example, the Russian Ambassador to Vienna Count Kapnist, talking to his German colleague Count Wedel, suggested without batting an eyelid, that Austria-Hungary could occupy Belgrade if it wanted to 'rein in' Serbia. Notifying Berlin about this conversation, Wedel could not hide his amazement.[97] As late as October 1906 Prince Lev Urusov, Kapnist's successor in Vienna, tried to convince the Serbian Minister Mihailo Vujić that his country did not require armaments – Serbia's arming was 'unnecessary', he said, since it was not Serbia that would be solving the problems of the Balkans. Thoroughly appalled by what he had heard, Vujić remarked to Urusov that, at a time when even Switzerland was arming itself, the Balkan countries could hardly be expected to neglect their own armaments.[98] Not surprisingly, the Serbs, as Dumba observed in December 1904, expected no support from Russia in the next five to ten years.[99]

To the Serbs themselves, the prospects for their country looked bleak. In February 1904 Austria-Hungary's Military Attaché Pomiankowski reported that all the talk in Belgrade coffee houses, restaurants and private conversations was about an impending Austro-Hungarian occupation. He wrote about the 'bitter feeling' among the Serbs that Russia was always treating Serbia like a 'trading commodity' – in accordance with its egoistic aims. There existed 'a mood of resentment against Russia' and, with increasing fatalism, the Serbs had begun to reconcile themselves to the idea of being occupied by the Monarchy. Many Serbian officers, according to the Military Attaché, actually denied the right of Serbia to build an independent state, wishing instead 'an administration of the land through Austria-Hungary'. Pomiankowski added, for good measure, that those officers would, in the event of an armed intervention by Austria-Hungary in Macedonia, 'directly support' rather than oppose the marching-through of its Army.[100]

Such assessments of the Serbian Army by Pomiankowski may have been somewhat exaggerated, but even if the mood of the country was less resigned than he painted it, there can be no doubt that genuine dread existed about possible aggressive inroads by Austria-Hungary deep into the Balkan peninsula. Moreover, at this time Serbia was by no means isolated in fearing Vienna's intentions. Mürzsteg, and Russia's subsequent embroilment in the Far East, set alarm bells ringing throughout the region. In December 1903 the Italian Foreign Minister Tommaso Tittoni felt it necessary to tell the Austro-Hungarian Ambassador to Rome that there existed in Italy – 'and not only in Italy' – an anxiety that Austria-Hungary would move south to occupy the regions *au delà de Mitrovitza* – that is, beyond Mitrovica in Kosovo, bordering on the Sanjak of Novi Pazar.[101] In Montenegro, as the Austro-Hungarian Minister at Cetinje informed the Ballhausplatz in March 1904, the 'generally prevalent' thinking was that Austria-Hungary possessed aspirations towards Salonika, and that it might avail itself of the opportunity presented by the Russo-Japanese war to march through Sanjak.[102] Much the same view was also held in Bulgaria, from where Vienna's diplomatic representative János Forgách wrote about the 'ineradicable fear' existing in the country that the Monarchy, with Russia busy in East Asia, would exploit the flimsiest complication in the Balkans to push to Salonika and occupy 'Bulgarian Macedonia'.[103] In Greece, too, newspapers were attacking Austria-Hungary, accusing it of harbouring designs for a descent to Salonika.[104] The Turks, for their part, also saw the Mürzsteg reform process as merely a 'mask' for Austria-Hungary's 'conquering plans'.[105]

Thus apprehension about a 'Drang nach Saloniki' was fairly widespread. Austro-Hungarian diplomats would regularly deny any such intentions. Given that trouble had begun to brew in Hungary in 1903 (discussed in chapter two), it was indeed the case that Vienna could hardly contemplate a major push south. In any case Gołuchowski was temperamentally not the type to break the Balkan entente with Russia as any advance to Salonika would entail. But this does not mean that the Ballhausplatz had no schemes in the region. The above-mentioned Article III of the Mürzsteg Agreement is particularly interesting in this connection. On 19 November 1903 the Joint Ministerial Council met in Vienna under Gołuchowski's chairmanship to discuss Mürzsteg. The Foreign Minister dwelt on the stipulation regarding the new delimitation of *sanjaks* (districts), based on the national character of the population – 'Bulgarian, Serbian, Greek, Albanian', he said, and chose rather revealingly to talk about the Albanians. Pointing out that there co-existed in some *sanjaks* Slavic and Albanian populations, it was in the Monarchy's 'eminent interest' to 'consolidate the *purely Albanian* districts' (emphasis in the original). For it was precisely the Albanian nation, Gołuchowski explained, which formed a dam against 'the Slavonic torrent' threatening Turkey's possessions in the Balkan peninsula.[106] This, it may be suggested, was hardly a policy of inactivity or indifference.

A Slav himself, Gołuchowski was also a Catholic and had little liking for the Christian Orthodox Slavs of the Balkans. But personal sympathies were not at issue here. Strengthening the Albanians was meant to put obstacles in the way of Serbia's expansion in European Turkey. Certainly, retaining the option to create an Albanian state was a major element in Austria-Hungary's Balkan policies after Mürzsteg. This option, indeed, would be put into practice in 1912-1913. Gołuchowski was apparently also keen to prevent Bulgaria's expansion, and was therefore against giving Macedonia an autonomous status. As he elucidated to Wilhelm II in September 1903, an autonomous Macedonia would in time be annexed by Bulgaria – this would disturb the Balkan equilibrium, which had to be maintained 'under all circumstances'. He also emphasized to the German Kaiser the importance of keeping Russia out of Constantinople because the alternative would entail Russia's 'absolute supremacy over all the South Slavs', and Austria-Hungary's freedom of action would then be 'halted at Budapest'.[107] Meeting separately with Prince Bülow, Gołuchowski likewise argued that Russia could not be allowed to settle in Constantinople, but also told the German Chancellor that Austria-Hungary would not permit 'the formation of a Great-Serbia'. His policy, as surmised by Bülow in his memoirs, was to uphold the *status quo* in the Balkans for as long as possible and try and solve 'the Oriental question' slowly, by degrees. The idea was to have 'a Greece as large as possible, a large Bulgaria, a strong Rumania, a weak Servia, a modest, because small, Montenegro, an independent Albania'.[108] It can only be speculated whether he really meant 'a large Bulgaria' in the light of what he had told the Kaiser about the undesirability of Macedonia being swallowed up by that country. Be that as it may, he certainly meant to keep Serbia as weak as possible.

Guns and Pigs

Gołuchowski quite liked – for he would do it often – referring to Serbia's 'catalogue of sins [*das Sündenregister Serbiens*]'.[109] One of those sins was committed by Serbia in the matter of its proposed purchase of modern artillery. The alarm bell regarding its armaments had sounded in 1903 when it was realized that the Bulgarian Army was better equipped.[110] This was at a time when the whole regional outlook was looking most uncertain. Andra Nikolić, Pašić's predecessor in the Foreign Ministry, admitted that Serbia needed peace on its borders, but expressed his doubts that the Mürzsteg process would succeed in pacifying Macedonia. Montenegrin Foreign Minister Gavro Vuković, writing from Cetinje at the end of 1903 on behalf of 'the second Serbian state', sent an impassioned plea to Belgrade for a military alliance, drawing attention to Austro-Hungarian military measures and suggesting that war was 'inevitable'. From Vienna, Minister Vujić wrote privately to Pašić in February 1904 that secret military preparations were being made there for a possible Austro-Hungarian action in Kosovo. In

Rome, a highly depressed Milovanović told Tittoni that, should Austria-Hungary establish itself in Kosovo, the Serbs might as well surrender to the Habsburg Monarchy – as the Croats had already done.[111]

Such, then, was the atmosphere towards the end of 1903 and the beginning of 1904. Adding to the bleak picture were Serbian consular reports from Kosovo and Macedonia which at this time regularly dwelt on the atrocities committed by the Albanians against the Serbs. But what particularly worried Pašić were signs that Austria-Hungary would resist the implementation of Mürzsteg reforms in Kosovo, parts of which, he expected, would form a new *sanjak* where Turkish officers would be left in charge of the gendarmerie. This, he thought, would perpetuate the existing anarchy, forcing the Serbian population to continue to emigrate under Albanian pressure. Echoing Milovanović, he warned that the project of Serbian unification was 'doomed if Austria-Hungary consolidates itself in Old Serbia'.[112] In mid-March 1904 he even contemplated a scenario whereby Serbia would in alliance with Montenegro, Greece and Turkey fight an Austro-Hungarian attempt to occupy Kosovo.[113]

Except that the Serbian Army was not really ready to fight. Although ex-King Milan had done a great deal to reform it, he had not quite managed to re-equip the Army. It had received only 90,000 quick-firing rifles whereas more than 300,000 were required. The situation was particularly critical with regard to artillery. At the end of 1904 an expert Army commission produced a programme calling for the procurement of 416 artillery pieces of various calibres (field and mountain guns, howitzers, and siege guns).[114] Serbia's railway network, constructed largely for transit purposes, also left much to be desired in terms of its potential for military use. There was also a great need for local railways. The building of some 600 km of additional railway was at this time envisaged.[115] Indeed, the Government had already announced in September 1903 that it would tackle the questions of armaments and railway expansion. However, with inadequate domestic sources of finance for such massive projects, this could only be done by raising a loan abroad. Given the fact that several countries, including Austria-Hungary, could supply both the armaments and the railway materials, the whole subject of Serbia's loan and its choice of equipment developed into a tremendous foreign and domestic policy issue.

When, in spring of 1904, the Government of General Sava Grujić began negotiations for a loan in Paris, the Ballhausplatz was immediately alarmed. Dumba wrote to Gołuchowski, questioning whether Austria-Hungary could afford to observe this development with stoic calm. Gołuchowski did react, but Austrian capital was not really in a position to compete with French and German.[116] Besides, it was not in the least certain that Serbia would order its artillery from the Austrian, or rather Bohemian, Škoda works anyway. Of course, the whole point about the Ballhausplatz effort to mobilize Austrian banking in this matter was to secure the orders for its domestic industry. The Škoda works were desperate for orders at this time, and it was also rumoured that several Austrian archdukes, and possibly Franz Joseph himself, had personal stakes in the success of the factory. Škoda's main competitors for the artillery order were Schneider-Creusot from France and Krupp from Germany. It was generally held that the guns of both Schneider and Krupp were superior to those of Škoda. King Alexander Obrenović had in 1903 actually ordered a battery of Škoda guns, but the Serbian Army had not been happy with their performance. Even Dumba admitted that those artillery pieces from Škoda required improvements.[117]

The quality of weapons, however, was hardly likely to play a determining role in a matter so heavily dominated by political calculation. Of course, if Serbia wanted to create more economic and political freedom for itself *vis-à-vis* the Habsburgs, it could never consider taking a loan and ordering its artillery from Austria-Hungary. Most Serbian accounts of the 'Guns Question', as it is called, emphasize precisely this point. But Dimitrije Đorđević has in his authoritative work drawn attention to an episode from the beginning of December 1904 when Nikola Pašić, the then Foreign Minister, sought to strike a deal with Austria-Hungary: letting Dumba know that Serbia would accept an Austrian loan and order Austrian artillery if Vienna made certain political concessions in return. He meant by this Austro-Hungarian support for Serbian aspirations in the south, i.e., in European Turkey.[118] It will be remembered that in 1903 King Alexander had likewise offered Vienna a very close alliance in return for getting support over Kosovo and Macedonia.

Indeed, it was a case of *plus ça change, plus c'est la même chose*: Dumba relates that in the spring and summer of 1904 the ostensibly Russophile Pašić had on three separate occasions made overtures to Vienna, calling for a closer relationship between Serbia and Austria-Hungary. Each time Pašić argued that Serbia could expect nothing in Bosnia-Herzegovina, and that its future 'lay in the south'. What Pašić wanted from Austria-Hungary, in the first place, was that it ensure the extension of the Mürzsteg programme to Kosovo in order to protect the Serbians from the Albanians. But he also talked to Dumba about a future division of Macedonia, in which he hoped that Vienna would award territories to Serbia on the principle of nationality. He even suggested, as a *quid pro quo*, that he would promote 'an Austrophile Party in Serbia'. Dumba was personally keen on such ideas – provided the loan and artillery orders were immediately settled – but in Vienna 'they did not show an interest in my reasoning'.[119]

This, undoubtedly, was an opportunity missed. And since Gołuchowski showed no interest in cultivating Serbia in the proposed fashion, the Government which Pašić formed in December 1904 decided to go for the

French loan (offered, in fact, by a Franco-German banking consortium) and French artillery.[120] The previous administration had included the Independent Radicals, but now Pašić was heading a pure Radical Party cabinet. On 6 May 1905, in Paris, Finance Minister Lazar Paču signed terms for a loan of 110 million francs – which represented about 150 per cent of Serbia's annual budget.[121] This still had to be passed in the Serbian Assembly. But Austria-Hungary had in the intervening months put up a most determined fight to secure at least the artillery order from Serbia. Minister Dumba in particular distinguished himself in what became a no holds barred contest for the Serbian orders. In January 1905 he wrote to Gołuchowski that 'if we are to do anything on behalf of Škoda, we must first bring down Pašić'.[122] To begin with, however, he decided to bribe the King of Serbia. Peter Karađorđević was chronically indebted: a fact which, incidentally, was most welcome to Serbian politicians who could always bend his will by increasing his grant in the civil list.[123] Aware of the King's weakness, Dumba arranged for him a loan of one million francs with the Viennese Länderbank – on most favourable conditions and without a provision for repayment guarantees.[124] He also had on his side the two key men at Peter's Court: cabinet secretary Jakov Nenadović and private secretary Živojin Balugdžić. Both of them were not only Austrophiles, but also Pašić's sworn enemies. Balugdžić, a Serb of Armenian origin, also happened to be in charge of the Foreign Ministry's press bureau and, amazingly, a correspondent of Vienna's highly influential *Neue Freie Presse*. To all intents and purposes he was an Austro-Hungarian agent, informer and propagandist at the heart of Serbian politics.

In order to maintain Škoda in contention, Dumba insisted on comparative testing of guns – something to which Pašić, with his mind set on the French loan and French equipment, was quite opposed. Behind the scenes, he had already struck a deal with the French.[125] The King, who had initially favoured the French guns, now came onto Dumba's side, as did several Belgrade newspapers – bribed by the Škoda works. Balugdžić for his part was conducting his own campaign in the press in favour of comparative tests. His Court colleague Nenadović did not lag behind in endorsing Škoda, nor apparently in ensuring some material interest would accrue on his own behalf. But the French firm Schneider-Creusot was also active in lubricating its case in Serbia, especially among Army officers. As for Pašić, Dumba suggests in his memoirs that he had arrived at his own arrangements with Schneider-Creusot and the French banks.[126] Charges and counter-charges of corruption were widespread. The conspirator officers, concerned to prop up the King in order to retain their influence in Serbian politics, joined in the demand for comparative testing, as did the Independent Radicals, by far the most serious opposition to Pašić's Radical Party.

In this highly charged situation, plenty of political maneouvring was taking place, with alliances made, then broken. 'Belgrade is a madhouse', wrote Dumba to Gołuchowski in February 1905, 'yesterday the Government made peace with the King, and today it submitted its resignation to him.'[127] The stakes were getting high. On 8 February Gołuchowski told the Serbian Minister in Vienna that Austria-Hungary's behaviour in the forthcoming talks on a new trade agreement between their countries would depend directly on the extent of 'consideration and agreeability' shown by Serbia towards the Monarchy when placing its orders abroad.[128] Conversely, although Pašić had under pressure agreed that comparative tests be conducted, he subsequently did everything to prevent them. In this he succeeded because he obtained the support of Radomir Putnik, the Chief of the General Staff, and otherwise a friend of the conspirator officers – but only because Putnik in return extracted from Pašić a Government commitment to greater military expenditure. Having mobilized Putnik, Pašić also managed to eliminate Balugdžić by having him tried and sentenced for his slanderous writings in the press and revealing of state secrets.[129] Together with Finance Minister Paču, Pašić argued that time was running out, as any comparative testing of guns would be a protracted affair and the Paris group of bankers was losing patience. But the King, reluctant to strain relations with Austria-Hungary, maintained his resistance. It was only when Pašić threatened him with yet another cabinet resignation, at the beginning of April, that the King finally capitulated.[130]

But it was Pašić who would soon be forced to buckle under. The loan which Paču concluded in Paris turned out to be financially unfavourable and was as a result greeted with hostility by much of Serbia's public opinion. There were signs of dissent even within Pašić's own Radical Party. In May, sensing that he could not get the loan passed by the Assembly, Pašić offered his government's resignation and this was accepted by the King. The French loan was now a dead duck. Elections in August produced a victory for the rival Independent Radical Party – only just, since its majority in the Assembly consisted of a single deputy. Nevertheless, the Independent Radicals now formed the new administration, headed by their leader Ljubomir Stojanović.

What did these Independent Radicals stand for? A brief reference was made in the previous chapter to the split in the Radical Party which had developed in the aftermath of Alexander's marriage to Draga. At that time the old guard of the Party happily cooperated with the autocratic King, becoming in essence a conservative force. Those in the Party, mainly younger members, who desired a return to the original liberal-left ideology of Serbian radicalism eventually established themselves as the Independent Radicals in 1904, but were active under that name even before then. Some of their leaders, Stojanović and Žujović in particular, leaned towards republicanism. The Independent Radicals also talked about the need for a 'moral renaissance' of Serbia.[131] In practice, however, there was not a great deal of difference between the two parties. They were also roughly equal in terms of electoral strength. With the Liberal and Progressive parties fading after 1903, the two Radical blocs absolutely dominated the Serbian party political scene until 1914.

Interestingly, the Independent Radicals were the only political party in Serbia emphasizing the need to 'nurture the Yugoslav spirit'.[132] In foreign policy, they were supposed to be just as suspicious of Austria-Hungary as the old Radicals. Stojanović himself was described by Dumba as 'one of the fiercest Austrophobes'.[133] Yet his Government ended up concluding a new loan in the Dual Monarchy. This was not quite as surprising as it seems. The Independent Radicals had in their opposition to the Radical Party over the loan and armaments question emphasized the importance of the financial conditions attached to the proposed loan, as well as the technical quality of the weapons to be purchased – irrespective of where they came from. In principle, then, they were after the best possible deal. But their room for manoeuvre was limited. Stojanović's Government initially tried, and failed, to raise money in London. Moreover, the Paris group of banks no longer seemed interested. The Unionbank of Vienna then stepped in – just when the time was fast approaching for Serbia to negotiate a new trade agreement with Austria-Hungary (the old trade agreement was expiring in March 1906). Maintaining good relations with the Monarchy was now a first concern. It seemed desirable, therefore, to resolve the loan issue with the Unionbank given the overwhelming importance to Serbia of negotiating favourable trade arrangements with the Monarchy.

The loan deal which the Stojanović Government clinched in November 1905 with a consortium led by the Unionbank was both smaller than the previous one (70 million francs as opposed to the 110 million negotiated by Paču) and carried better financial conditions. Its terms, however, were such that the banks could withdraw from the whole business if they were unhappy about the allocation of Serbia's industrial orders. What this implied, of course, was that Serbia would have to purchase its guns from Škoda. That was too much for some. Quite apart from the ensuing attacks on the loan deal by Pašić and his Radicals, a major revolt against it also developed in Stojanović's Independent Radical Party itself.[134]

But what really killed off this second loan proposal was the sudden deterioration in Austro-Serbian relations caused by a rather unexpected turn of events. Late in December 1905 it was revealed that Serbia had entered into a customs union with Bulgaria. The news of this Balkan arrangement immediately led to attacks on Serbia in the Austrian and Hungarian press.[135] Gołuchowski promptly suspended the trade agreement talks with Serbia which had been going on in Vienna since November. Yet the exchange of goods between Serbia and Bulgaria was negligible and likely to remain so. Why, then, were they so upset in Austria-Hungary? Officially, the Ballhausplatz declared that the Serbo-Bulgarian customs union made nonsense of the most favoured trading status granted by the Congress of Berlin to the Great Powers themselves. The real reasons for alarm, however, lay elsewhere, as Gołuchowski admitted in a meeting of the Joint Ministerial Council early in February: Serbia and Bulgaria, he said, might establish 'an even closer association' which would, he added, be 'very worrying' from the point of view of the Monarchy's political interests.[136]

Without suspecting it, the Austro-Hungarian Foreign Minister was more in the right than he could imagine. Although it was King Peter who had initially expressed the desire for a Serbo-Bulgarian *rapprochement*, it was actually Bulgaria's Prince Ferdinand who had, early in 1904, pushed for a concrete agreement. What was involved here, however, was much more than a customs union. Of course, the conflicting aspirations of Bulgaria and Serbia towards Macedonia had for a long time been the stumbling bloc in preventing closer relations between the two countries. After Mürzsteg, however, this problem was for the time being entirely academic, for the aspirations towards the region of a different Power were now centre stage. Or, as Prince Ferdinand's emissary put it to Pašić that February, a Serbo-Bulgarian agreement was necessary in order to resist 'any foreign foray' into Macedonia.[137] By this he could only mean an Austrian foray. By mid-April 1904 Sofia and Belgrade had duly negotiated a Friendship Treaty as well as a Treaty of Alliance. The latter called for resistance to any 'hostile action' or occupation attempts – 'irrespective from which state' – in the *vilayets* of Salonika, Monastir, Kosovo and Edirne. The supplementary final protocol, signed on 13 April, emphasized that the *sanjak* of Novi Pazar, at the time garrisoned by Austria-Hungary, belonged to the *vilayet* of Kosovo. This meant, as Ernst Helmreich observed, that 'Bulgaria pledged herself to oppose an Austrian annexation of a region which at that time was occupied by the forces of the Dual Monarchy'.[138]

Obviously, the Treaty of Alliance was kept secret. And so was the Treaty of Friendship which called for the opening of borders by Serbia and Bulgaria to products of domestic origin – a policy that, it was hoped, would eventually lead to a customs union (*Zollverein*, as the Treaty spelled out in German).[139] In July 1905 a customs union was indeed concluded, with effect from March 1906 and projected to operate until March 1917. In the light of the approaching trade negotiations with Austria-Hungary, the Serbian side was careful to stipulate that the customs union would be non-binding in the event that it led to difficulties in concluding or ratifying trade agreements with other states. The Bulgarians agreed. But without asking the

Serbs, they formally disclosed its existence early in January 1905 when it was passed in the *Sobranie* by acclamation.[140]

The Stojanović Government was at this point already facing fierce domestic opposition because of the Unionbank loan. In addition, it was unable to solve the 'conspirators question', i.e., the removal from the Royal Court of the officers involved in the putsch against Alexander. And now the trade agreement with Austria-Hungary was under threat because of the Bulgarian indiscretion. On 17 January 1906 Gołuchowski sent instructions to Baron Moritz Czikann, Dumba's successor in Belgrade, to notify the Serbian Government that trade talks would not continue unless it: (1) gave written assurances that during the period of those trade negotiations it would refrain from submitting to the Assembly for consideration the customs union agreement with Bulgaria; and (2) committed itself, in writing, that it would, in the event of a trade agreement with Austria Hungary being concluded, make any modifications to the customs union agreement with Bulgaria demanded by Austria-Hungary.[141] By any standards, these would have been formidable encroachments on the affairs of a sovereign state. Nevertheless, there were those in Serbia, including the King and his Court, who did not think it wise to resist Austria-Hungary. The Government, however, did not yield. So it was that on 22 January, 1906, Gołuchowski announced to the Serbian Minister in Vienna the end of trade talks, adding that measures would also be taken to stop the importation into Austria-Hungary of Serbia's livestock, which he duly declared to have become 'sick'.[142] This, in effect, was the informal start of the tariff war against Serbia.

Squeezed from all sides, the Government first dropped the Unionbank loan and then, after unsuccessfully trying to come to terms with Vienna over trade agreement issues, resigned on 7 March. By this time, their country targeted by Austria-Hungary's coercive measures, the Serbian public felt a rising sense of indignation. Among the main political parties, a consensus on the need for economic independence from Austria-Hungary now came into existence.[143] No one, however, be it in Belgrade or in Vienna, was considering a complete break. The Bulgarian connection was actually quietly dropped by the Serbs. The new Serbian Government appointed that March was again made up of the Independent Radicals, but headed this time by their sympathizer General Sava Grujić. It quickly concluded a stopgap agreement (*Provisorium*) with Austria-Hungary because the previous trade agreement had expired on 1 March. The tariff war was temporarily suspended as a result, but already on 5 April Gołuchowski, was talking to the Serbian Minister in Vienna 'quite bitterly' and in no uncertain terms, making the future trade agreement conditional on Serbia purchasing its guns from Austria-Hungary. On the same day the Serbian trade negotiators in Vienna received an official *pro memoria* to that effect.[144] In Belgrade, the Austro-Hungarian Military Attaché Major Pomiankowski verbally informed Serbia's Prime Minister, Grujić, about the choice he was being given. Grujić, otherwise 'one of the mildest mannered of men', had difficulties restraining himself from showing Pomiankowski the door.[145]

But Gołuchowski was quite resolute. 'I am going to show these gentlemen', he told the British Ambassador, 'that they can't play fast and loose with Austria. No contract for guns – no Commercial Treaty.'[146] The old conspirators question was now exploited by the Ballhausplatz not only to secure armament orders from Serbia, but also to frustrate the latter's objective of re-establishing full diplomatic relations with Britain. For, as long as the conspirator officers were in influential positions at King Peter's Court, the Foreign Office would not be sending a minister to Belgrade. It was clearly in Austria-Hungary's interest to postpone the return of a British Minister to Belgrade who might strengthen Serbia's resistance to the Ballhausplatz demands on the question of the commercial treaty.[147] At the same time, the officers themselves could be be persuaded to argue Vienna's case in Belgrade on behalf of Škoda guns. Franz Joseph himself was reportedly willing to receive King Peter 'and all the regicides'.[148] For their part, since the Grujić Government was prepared to sacrifice the officers as the price of restoring relations with Britain, the officers themselves welcomed the new complication regarding the guns purchase in order to topple Grujić. With both the King and Austria-Hungary on their side, they did indeed manage to bring down the Government on 17 April 1906, a month and a half after it had taken office.[149] The conspirators had thus become the protagonists of Austria-Hungary, which was 'the only Power' whose protection they could seek against all those demanding their removal.[150] The King, their chief domestic guardian angel, was at this time himself also behaving like the extended hand of the Ballhausplatz.[151]

The new cabinet (of 30 April 1906) was formed by Nikola Pašić. Interestingly, at this point he too was in a pro-Austrian frame of mind. Shortly before the fall of the Stojanović Government he called a meeting of some of the most prominent Radical Party politicians to discuss 'an important and urgent matter'. Nastas Petrović, one of those present, later recorded how Pašić astonished his colleagues by arguing that the Party should 'begin to shift from our present policy in terms of leaning on Russia and that we should begin to get closer to Vienna, to Austria'. Such a new orientation of the Radical Party, Pašić further explained, would be well received by Vienna, and he had positive assurances about that. From this proposed new course he expected, he said, 'enormous benefit' both for the Party and for the country. His party, however, was less than impressed. Petrović related how the rest of the Party leadership reacted immediately by warning Mihailo Vujić, the Serbian Minister in Vienna, who then acted behind the scenes to stop Pašić from being received by Gołuchowski – Pašić had indeed arrived in Vienna early in March, but the Austro-Hungarian Foreign Minister just ignored his presence. It is not clear how Vujić had been able to achieve this, but whatever he had done proved effective. In recalling these events, Petrović could not hide his utter contempt for Pašić: 'His Slavophilia and his supposed devotion to Russia were just a façade', something he was quite ready to ditch if an Austrophile orientation brought him 'back to power'.[152]

Indeed, Pašić's enormous lust for power had been on full display in that April of 1906 as he manoeuvred to become Prime Minister once again. Following the resignation of the Grujić cabinet, King Peter and the conspirator officers around him intended to set up a new government under Vukašin Petrović, the loudly pro-Austrian civilian conspirator from 1903 who had been residing in Vienna ever since falling out with King Alexander because of Draga. Pašić, however, stepped in with his own candidacy, making attractive promises both to the Court camarilla and to Austria-Hungary: assuring King Peter that he would put off solving the conspirators question, and sending messages to the Škoda works that they would be receiving substantial armament orders – for more than half of Serbia's artillery requirements. It all worked out rather wonderfully for this crafty politician. In the end, Pašić became Prime Minister on 30 April with the blessing of the monarch and the backing of Austria-Hungary.[153]

Far from postponing the conspirators question, the month of May found him already moving quickly to tackle it in order to restore full relations with Britain. One officer after another came to him for one-to-one talks. Typically for Pašić's method, the five most prominent conspirators (Mašin, Mišić, Colonel Damjan Popović, Lieutenant-Colonel Luka Lazarević and Major Ljubomir Kostić) were simply bought off with pensions equal to their salaries and additional substantial sums (60,000 dinars each) in return for 'voluntary' retirement.[154] This was the end, at least internationally, of the conspirators question. Even though prominent civilian conspirators, notably Đorđe Genčić, were both conspicuous and influential at the Serbian Court after 1903, no one abroad ever raised this issue.

But Pašić was unable to solve the huge matter of the trade agreement with Austria-Hungary, complicated as it was by the question of Serbia's artillery orders which Gołuchowski insisted had to be part and parcel of the next commercial treaty between the two countries. Having promised Vienna quite a few artillery orders in order that he might sit again in the prime ministerial chair, Pašić now held back and pretended that he had never given such assurances. It is difficult to say whether he had by this stage got cold feet over allying Serbia to the Dual Monarchy. He was certainly aware that the Serbian Assembly would never approve a humiliating trade agreement with Austria-Hungary which imposed the purchase of the

Škoda guns.[155] But he sought to avoid a confrontation by offering Vienna 26 million dinars worth of business. Crucially, however, artillery and artillery materials were excluded from this proposal.[156] Pašić may have been playing for time here as he had some grounds at this point to anticipate or at least hope for an enforced and early depature by Gołuchowski from the Ballhausplatz. Reports from the Serbian Consul in Budapest, and from the Minister in Vienna, spoke of the increasing Hungarian hostility towards Gołuchowski.[157] And although agrarian interest groups in Hungary were firmly opposed to a reasonable Austro-Serbian trade treaty, there also existed industrial circles who were upset by Gołuchowski's intransigence towards Serbia because Hungarian munitions factories would have benefited from Pašić's offer of 26 million dinars.[158] In their eagerness to vilify the Foreign Minister, members of the Hungarian Delegation had even requested the Serbian Government to supply them with materials on Austro-Hungarian policies in Turkey, Serbia and Bosnia which they could use against him. Pašić was only too happy to oblige.[159]

The Hungarians, in the end, did get rid of Gołuchowski – he had, among other things, repeatedly attacked the demands of the Hungarian nationalist coalition, in power since early 1905. Their Prime Minister Sándor Wekerle worked actively to oust him.[160] Franz Ferdinand, too, was very much against Gołuchowski – this hostility dating back to the 1890s when, during the Archduke's illness, Gołuchowski had appeared to treat Archduke Otto as the Heir to the Throne. In fact, except for Franz Joseph, everybody seemed to be against Gołuchowski. The military circles grumbled that his Balkan policy was far too passive at a time when Russia's absence in the region was presenting new opportunities.[161] He finally resigned in October 1906. Before then, however, he managed to declare economic war on Serbia. On 30 June Belgrade received what amounted to an ultimatum: the provisional trading arrangement would not be extended unless the Serbian Government gave a written and binding statement that it would, during the duration of the extended trading period, do nothing to prejudice Austria-Hungary's demands with regard to orders of artillery and other industrial materials. Or to put it another way, buy Austrian or don't buy at all. Pašić did not budge and so on 7 July 1906 the long tariff war began between Austria-Hungary and Serbia.[162] This, undoubtedly, was a defining moment in post-1903 Austro-Serbian relations.

As has been seen, however, the rise of antagonism between Vienna and Belgrade had nothing to do with the change of dynasty in Serbia, nor with any pro-Russian course pursued by the Serbs, nor indeed with some fundamental realignment of policies following the putsch. On the contrary: the King and his camarilla were decidedly on Austria-Hungary's side in the 'guns' affair; Russia, after 1904, played practically no role in Serbian calculations; and both the Stojanović and Pašić governments had gone far to avoid confrontation with Vienna – Pašić had privately even contemplated arriving at a far-ranging political and economic accommodation with the Monarchy. The worsening of relations had even less to do with any 'Great Serbian agitation' in the Habsburg territories, for there was none. And if anybody saw themselves directly threatened in the Austro-Serbian relationship, it was, as discussed above, post-Mürzsteg Serbia. The problem between them was simply that for Vienna Serbia's actions had become a touch too independent. Its customs union with Bulgaria was bad enough from Gołuchowski's point of view. But its intention to buy artillery outside Austria-Hungary was just too much for him. Nor did it help that he, the aristocratic, snooty Gołuchowski 'utterly despised the Serbs'.[163] The end result of the increasing antagonism was that the Pašić Government took the decision in October 1906 to buy French guns from Schneider – 49 field and 15 mountain batteries. In November, Paču concluded a loan in Geneva with a Franco-Swiss consortium for 95 million dinars, though the Swiss participation was minor.[164] Economically at least, France had suddenly become the lynchpin of Serbia's international position.

It lies beyond the scope of this book to review in detail how Serbia succeeded in winning the so-called 'Pig War' which, for Austria-Hungary, proved 'a disaster in every respect'.[165] The key, of course, was obtaining new markets. They were found, mostly, in Germany, Belgium, France, Turkey and Italy. But Serbian pigs and cattle also ended up in some surprising places, such as the British garrisons in Egypt and Malta. The river Danube proved of great importance for transportation purposes, both upstream and downstream.[166] The harbour of Salonika, thanks to an agreement with Turkey, played an even bigger role. Far from moving towards economic collapse, as Gołuchowski had expected, Serbia just a few months after the outbreak of the tariff war had already begun to record export successes.[167] At the same time, foreign investments stimulated industrial development in the country. Germany in particular was more than happy to fill the gaps created by Gołuchowski's economic war against the Serbs. By 1911, when the conflict ended, Serbia had attained economic independence. In Austria-Hungary itself, this *Schweinekrieg* led to a rise in the cost of living as foodstuffs became more expensive. And instead of pork, the Emperor's subjects now ate more horseflesh.[168]

7

From the Bosnian Annexation
to the Balkan Wars

Baron Alois Lexa von Aehrenthal

IN 1906, after Germany's clash with France at the Algeciras Conference on Morocco, Kaiser Wilhelm II's telegram famously described Gołuchowski as the 'brilliant second on the duelling ground'. No doubt Gołuchowski could have done without a compliment which implied, quite unfairly, a degree of servility to Germany. Retrospectively, however, it is his mismanagement of Balkan affairs which has caused far more damage to his reputation, and justifiably so. His Serbian policy in particular, according to Holger Afflerbach, was 'a downright failure'.[1] Serbian diplomats at the time kept wondering why, with regard to the trade treaty, he had turned this purely economic issue into a political one. The rise of Austro-Serbian discord, it has to be said, was very much his deed. His bullying tactics were unnecessary at a time when carrot could have done so much more than stick: all the relevant factors in post-1903 Serbia, from the Court camarilla to Pašić himself, were quite flexible in their foreign policy orientation. As has been seen, the conspirator officers, who ran the Army, were actually embracing Vienna. Even on the artillery question, Pašić was willing to buy from Škoda if he could obtain Austria-Hungary's backing for Serbia's ambitions in Kosovo and Macedonia. As Wayne Vucinich observed with regard to Pašić's attempts in 1904 at a *rapprochement* with Vienna, Serbia's friendship 'would obviously go to the highest bidder'.[2]

Russia, preoccupied in the Far East, was certainly not doing any bidding in the Balkans at this time. Moreover, Gołuchowski was getting reports from Belgrade indicating that displeasure with Russia – indeed despair of the big Slavonic brother – was widespread from the top down. But negotiating a *modus vivendi* with the Serbs was the last thing that the imperious Gołuchowski felt it necessary to do. Instead, he waged a trade war on the Monarchy's small neighbour. Up until 1906, Serbia had been almost totally dependent economically on Austria-Hungary. Gołuchowski's policy, however, made it economically and therefore also politically independent. Little wonder, then, that in March 1907 Edward Goschen, the British Ambassador in Austria-Hungary, recorded hearing some Viennese diplomatic conversation about the tariff war to the effect that Serbia 'had won all along the line – and that Golu[chowski] was the hero of the hour in that country – as his absurd policy had made her find out she could do without Austria'.[3]

Gołuchowski's successor at the Ballhausplatz was *Freiherr* (Baron) Alois Lexa von Aehrenthal, formerly the Minister in Bucharest and, since 1899, Austria-Hungary's Ambassador at the pivotal post in St Petersburg. Among students of the late Habsburg Empire, Aehrenthal is famous for his active, bold, and above all optimistic foreign policy – as opposed to the passive, timid and pessimistic approach adopted by his predecessor Gołuchowski. As Solomon Wank has argued, however, the differences between the two men were in reality insubstantial: they were both painfully aware of the internal weaknesses of the Empire and their different tactics merely reflected 'varieties of political despair'.[4] Aehrenthal, of course, is a more controversial figure than Gołuchowski, and also infinitely better known given that his name is forever associated with his annexation of Bosnia-Herzegovina in 1908. This event caused a diplomatic storm across Europe at the time and has long been a compulsory subject for academics investigating the origins of the First World War.

Although he actually died in 1912, quite a few contemporaries subsequently burdened Aehrenthal with heavy responsibility for 1914. 'Without exaggerating,' wrote the Romanian statesman Take Jonescu, 'one may say that he was to a great extent the author of the war'.[5] The Austrian banker and statesman Rudolf Sieghart noted that, in practice, Aehrenthal's annexation of Bosnia-Herzegovina brought 'not a single square metre' to the Empire and possibly led to its final liquidation.[6] Scholarly opinion has sometimes been similarly harsh on the Foreign Minister. Eurof Walters, for example, has maintained that 'by a policy of expediency and of adventure Aehrenthal personally did more than anyone else to prepare the way for the break-up of the empire'.[7] G.P. Gooch, one of the foremost authorities on pre-1914 Europe, also saw Aehrenthal as the man who set in motion forces which were ultimately to destroy the realm of the Habsburgs: 'For the world war grew directly out of the quarrel between Vienna and Belgrade, a quarrel which he had done more than any other man to foment'.[8]

And yet Aehrenthal had initially approached Serbia in what seemed to be a spirit of goodwill. Moreover, he was a severe critic of his predecessor's Balkan management. As the Serbian Minister Vujić reported from Vienna, Aehrenthal took a dim view of Gołuchowski's 'petty politics' over the guns question. Vujić's first impressions of Aehrenthal were on the whole quite favourable. The new Foreign Minister told him that he had genuine sympathies for Serbia and, more to the point, that he would keep economic and political matters strictly separate.[9] Indeed, in June 1907 negotiations resumed between Vienna and Belgrade on a new trade treaty. In October Aehrenthal declared to the Joint Ministerial Council: 'Our policy of making Serbia economically and politically dependent and treating it as a *quantité négligeable* has foundered.'[10] The main obstacle to now re-establishing trade relations with Serbia was represented by agrarian interests in Hungary, but also those in Austria. Aehrenthal, however, keen to attain economic hegemony for the Monarchy in the Balkans, intervened with the Hungarian and Austrian governments, to help bring a new treaty into being in March 1908, one ratified in August by the Serbian Assembly. It reflected a compromise all round and, not surprisingly, was immediately attacked both in Austria-Hungary and Serbia. In any case, soon thereafter, in October, came the annexation of Bosnia-Herzegovina and the accompanying deterioration in Austro-Serbian relations. As a result, by early January 1909 the trade treaty was dead in the water.[11]

But was there really ever a chance for an Austro-Serbian reconciliation under Aehrenthal? Soon after becoming Foreign Minister, he was to privately tell his friend the historian Heinrich Friedjung that Gołuchowski's insistence on getting the Serbian artillery orders was 'excessive', and something that should not be imposed on a sovereign state.[12] It is difficult to believe, however, that he was greatly concerned about the sovereignty and independence of the small Balkan states. As the Hungarian historian István Diószegi remarked, Aehrenthal was 'a forceful adherent of the Austrian Great Power idea'.[13] He wanted to see the region divided into two spheres of Great Power influence: with the West Balkans as the Austro-Hungarian sphere, and the East Balkans as the Russian. While still serving in St Petersburg in 1899-1900, he began expounding these views both officially and unofficially. Interestingly, in sharp contrast to Gołuchowski, he would make the point that it was to no avail to try and keep Russia out of Constantinople; at the same time, he saw Salonika as the end point (*Endpunkt*) of Vienna's Balkan efforts.[14] For him, the Western Balkans was the area 'from Serbia as far as Salonika'. What he envisaged for both the Austrian and the Russian spheres of influence was a form of 'protectorate' or rather 'the establishment of over-lordship' through alliances, trade agreements, military conventions, and other arrangements.[15] As will be seen, in the case of Serbia he had even more radical solutions in mind.

It is not surprising, then, that Pašić could not arrive at a far-reaching political understanding with Aehrenthal, though not for wont of trying. Dimitrije Đorđević, the great authority on Austro-Serbian relations during this period, has shown that Pašić's desire to renew trade relations with Austria-Hungary was for political rather than economic reasons. When he met with Aehrenthal in September 1907, he laid out the same outline for a deal that he had already sought to achieve with Gołuchowski: Serbia had no aspirations in Bosnia-Herzegovina; it would be accommodating on questions of trade; but it wanted the Monarchy's support in Macedonia. Aehrenthal, however, stuck to trade issues, refusing to discuss such political matters. Had Aehrenthal chosen to accept Pašić's proposals instead, in the view of Đorđević, it would have 'fundamentally altered Austro-Serbian relations'.[16]

On the face of it, Aehrenthal's ideas concerning Balkan policy amounted to soft penetration rather than outright conquest. Some historians, in fact, have gone so far as to argue that the annexation of Bosnia-Herzegovina 'was essentially a conservative move, and anything but a forward thrust into the Balkans'; that in annexing the provinces, Austria-Hungary was 'voluntarily setting a limit to its own frontiers'.[17] Unfortunately for Aehrenthal's defenders, there is substantial evidence to disprove such claims. Thus, in December 1907, the Foreign Minister himself explained to Conrad, the Chief of General Staff, that the aim of his Balkan policy was the annexation of Bosnia-Herzegovina and the 'incorporation of non-Bulgarian parts of Serbia'.[18] Even if he had let the Bulgarians define the non-Bulgarian parts, this incorporation would have encompassed at least half of Serbia. In August 1908, when the decision to annex had already been reached, he also composed an important memorandum which, according to Joseph Baernreither, remained the outlook of the Ballhausplatz 'right down to the outbreak of the war'.[19] In this policy paper (*Denkschrift*), Aehrenthal supported the idea of creating, 'at Serbia's cost', a 'Great Bulgaria'. Given 'a favourable European constellation', he wrote, Austria-Hungary would then be able to lay its hands on 'what still remains of Serbia'. In this way, he thought, the Monarchy would secure its borders, by means of an 'Albania becoming independent under our aegis, a Montenegro with which we maintain friendly relations, and a Great Bulgaria which owes us a debt of gratitude'.[20]

In other words, Aehrenthal's Balkan schemes would have amounted to the destruction and disappearance of Serbia. Moreover, these were plans he had entertained for quite some time. Back in 1895, he approvingly quoted Foreign Minister Kálnoky when the latter wrote that 'the pivot of our power position [*Machtstellung*] towards the South East lies in *Belgrade*'. In order to secure a dominating position in the Balkans, Aehrenthal also argued, the Monarchy would have to incorporate Serbia.[21]

That said, he did seem to oscillate between incorporating Serbia into the Monarchy and giving it to Bulgaria. In September 1908, in Berchtesgaden, he told Wilhelm von Schoen, the German State Secretary for Foreign Affairs, that the aim of his Balkan policy was 'the complete removal of the Serbian revolutionary nest', and that Serbia could be 'awarded [*vergeben*]' to Bulgaria.[22]

Either way, Serbia's prospects never looked particularly good with Aehrenthal. On the eve of the Bosnian annexation, he met with the Austrian statesman Ernst Plener. The latter was doubtful about the proposed action and rather shocked when Aehrenthal suggested that the road to Mitrovica in Kosovo lay through Belgrade. Such a march, Plener objected, 'would be tantamount to war'. Aehrenthal made no reply.[23] Far from pursuing a 'conservative policy', he waited like a predator for an opportunity to pounce. 'The time for an energetic intervention will arrive', he reassured his friend Friedjung in November 1907. At the beginning of 1908 he told him that Austria-Hungary's interest in supporting the *status quo* in the Balkans was not as great as Germany's. In November 1908, after he had spectacularly proved this point by pocketing Bosnia, he changed tack somewhat, saying that ripping off a part of Serbia was far from his thoughts and that, in the event of an armed conflict, the Serbs would be chastised and rendered harmless by having to pay war reparations.[24] Yet in August 1909, in a secret *pro memoria*, he returned to his old theme, arguing that some day, and under certain circumstances, 'we could, or we should, think about incorporating part of Serbia'. For Austria-Hungary could not allow, he insisted, that 'this small state on our border becomes a focus of attraction'.[25]

Attraction, that is, for the South Slavs living in the Habsburg Empire. The Croat historian Mirjana Gross suggested in 1960 that Aehrenthal was the first Austrian minister to really understand the meaning of the South Slav question for the Monarchy. In her ground-breaking study of the politics of the Croato-Serb Coalition in Croatia, she brought to attention and analysed two memoranda, written by Aehrenthal in February 1907, on the relationship between the South Slav question and the internal structure of the Habsburg Empire.[26] In 1963 Solomon Wank published these secret *mémoires* (in their original German) and included a third one, also from February 1907.[27] They reveal in the first place, according to Wank, that Aehrenthal saw himself more like an imperial chancellor than just another of the Habsburg foreign ministers who had, since 1867, had no constitutional competences in the internal affairs of the Monarchy. Indeed, his February 1907 memoranda make sweeping proposals for internal reorganization in the light of the benefit, as he saw it, of grouping together the South Slavs of the Empire to make them into a viable counterweight to the attraction of the 'the Great Serbian idea'.[28]

One must bear in mind that Aehrenthal wrote these memoranda at a time when relations between Austria and Hungary left much to be desired, and when their negotiations for a new ten-year economic arrangement, involving the vexed question of common tariffs, had yet to be concluded: Hungarian nationalism, both political and economic, was alive and well, and that is what Aehrenthal was addressing. He now proposed that a new South Slav group be formed within the realm of the Hungarian Crown of St Stephen. It would consist of Dalmatia (which would be gifted to Hungary by Austria), Croatia, Slavonia and Bosnia-Herzegovina. This group would have its gravitational centre in Agram (Zagreb). Austria, by way of compensation for Dalmatia, would in return receive Hungary's consent to a tariff union that would last twenty-five years, as well as a new Army law of the same duration.

It is fairly clear that Aehrenthal was concerned less with the South Slav question as such, and much more with the need to repair and enhance imperial unity. For without internal political and economic stability Austria-Hungary could not behave like a Great Power. So the immediate problem for him was Budapest, not Belgrade. In fact, he himself frankly admitted that the power of Great Serbian propaganda 'is certainly not to be overestimated'.[29] One thing the Foreign Minister may, however, have overestimated was the feasibility of his own stratagem. His proposed Southern Slav group would, in his view, exert 'such power of attraction that, in the end, Serbia itself would not be able to elude it'.[30] This prognosis, at a time when Serbia had begun to taste economic and political independence following the outbreak of the 'Pig War', sounds somewhat sanguine. Furthermore, his plans for the Southern Slavs of the Monarchy would have amounted to the creation of a Catholic-dominated, Zagreb-centred Great Croatia – hardly a tempting prospect for Serbia. His subsequent suggestions about partitioning Serbia with Bulgaria, discussed above, actually made much more sense: by 1907, after Gołuchowski had done so much damage to Austro-Serbian relations, a Habsburg Yugoslavia that included the Serbs from the Kingdom of Serbia was probably only possible by force.

Although Aehrenthal's idea of creating a Southern Slav unit under the Hungarian Crown would have left the Dualism of the Empire intact, being by definition sub-dualist, he did see the logic of his project in terms of 'the path to Trialism [*die Bahn des Trialismus*]'.[31] It is of course highly doubtful that Budapest would ever have consented to such a Great Croatia within its own borders, let alone outside them. Moreover, as seen in chapter three, Archduke Franz Ferdinand would have been opposed to Austria giving up Dalmatia. Interestingly, Aehrenthal argued that Hungary, as a defender of the Dalmatian coast, would then pay much more attention to the Navy than it had done hitherto.[32] Mirjana Gross considers that Aehrenthal made this point precisely for the benefit of the Archduke, the chief supporter of the Austro-Hungarian Navy.[33]

Needless to say, nothing ever came of the proposals by Aherenthal contained in the three secret *mémoires*. According to Solomon Wank, however, the latter are 'crucial for an understanding of Aehrenthal's diplomacy. Taken together, they explain his long-range plans and reveal the substance behind the much-heralded policy of action'.[34] There is certainly something to be said for Wank's viewpoint, but the emphasis must be on 'long-range plans'. The short-term action plan was annexation: for if the provinces of Bosnia and Herzegovina were to become part and parcel of the projected South Slav, Habsburg entity, they would first have to be annexed. In this light, the *mémoires* indeed confirm that Aehrenthal was conducting an aggressive foreign policy (i.e., annexation) in order to prepare the ground for internal consolidation and thus augment Austria-Hungary's position as a Great Power. As has already been suggested, however, the obstacles to the kind of internal reform advocated by Aehrenthal would have been formidable. The late Professor Wank, indisputably the greatest authority on Aehrenthal, referred to 'the blend of reality and unreality which characterises the *mémoires*'.[35]

In the meantime, the annexation of Bosnia-Herzegovina seemed both realistic and desirable as an immediate boost to the Great Power prestige of Austria-Hungary. The Austrian statesman Ernst Plener left a valuable recollection of his encounter with Aehrenthal after the annexation. Plener had himself taken a position resembling the one Aehrenthal had advocated in the three *mémoires*: annexing Bosnia and Herzegovina would only make sense if these lands were then joined with Croatia and Dalmatia into a single body to form the basis for a 'purposeful' South Slav policy. Yet when they met Aehrenthal told him that he did not want to be 'burdened' with this matter, and would in any case be unable to overcome the 'obdurate' opposition of the Hungarians. Plener concluded that Aehrenthal had been interested only in the 'momentary success' of his diplomacy, and that, as a result, the annexation remained 'a half-measure, without real benefits for the position of the Monarchy towards the South Slav movement'.[36]

Whatever his motives, Aehrenthal's push to annex Bosnia-Herzegovina was bound to lead to renewed complications with Serbia. In the meantime he announced, in January 1908, the Sanjak of Novi Pazar railway project. This was for a railway to link the existing line ending in eastern Bosnia with the Turkish line ending in Mitrovica (Kosovo). Its construction would have established a direct connection between Vienna and Salonika. Solomon Wank suggested that this railway plan of Aehrenthal's was an integral element of his foreign policy. The project was part of a programme of economic imperialism designed to penetrate the Balkan countries, 'making them economically and diplomatically dependent on Vienna, ultimately leading to Austro-Hungarian political hegemony in the region'.[37] Aehrenthal also envisaged additional railway projects, two of which would link the Serbian rail system with Bosnia and Dalmatia, while a third would link Dalmatia with Lake Scutari by way of Montenegro. The idea was, according to Wank, 'the subordination of the transport system of the entire western half of the Balkan peninsula to Austro-Hungarian control'.[38]

Aehrenthal's railway programme was greeted with hostility by nationalist and Pan Slav circles in Russia. Alexander Izvolsky, who had in 1906 succeeded Lamsdorff as Foreign Minister, did not belong to those circles, but was left no less aghast by Aehrenthal's scheme. Austro-Russian relations were suddenly in a crisis. The Gołuchowski-Lamsdorff partnership had been stable and had kept the Balkans reasonably quiet. Aehrenthal, rather arrogant, vain and excitable, and Izvolsky, every bit as arrogant, vain and excitable, were about to wreck the Austro-Russian pact dating from 1897. It did not help this relationship, or indeed the peace and security of Europe, that both these men were at the same time inveterate and accomplished liars. To the reactionary Aehrentahl, Izvolsky was suspect because of his liberal tendencies and, more importantly, because he had begun to steer Russia towards Britain with the 1907 Anglo-Russian agreement over Persia. This had created profound European consequences by giving birth to the Triple Entente of France, Russia and Britain. Izvolsky, on the other hand, was offended for not having been briefed by the Ballhausplatz in timely fashion and saw Aehrenthal's announcement as undermining Russia's Balkan position. And so, 'a personal estrangement began which was to leave its mark on the history of Europe'.[39]

In Serbia, the railway project was seen as a threat to Salonika – the country's trade gateway to the West – and as an overture to the complete Austro-Hungarian occupation of the Sanjak of Novi Pazar. 'Across the cemetery of Serbia to the Aegean Sea', screamed a headline in a Belgrade newspaper.[40] Hysterical as this may sound, it should be borne in mind that Serbia and Austria-Hungary were in the middle of a tariff war. The Government in Belgrade quickly dusted off plans for the construction of a railway line between the Danube and the Adriatic which it had been seriously considering in the first half of 1907. Under these, the Turkish port of San Giovanni di Medua (today Shëngjin in Albania) was meant to become Serbia's new point of commercial escape from the Monarchy's clutches. For his part, however, Aehrenthal had actually miscalculated badly with regard to the financial viability of his own planned railway through the Sanjak of Novi Pazar. So he was most probably bluffing when he announced the project in January 1908. For he had already the previous year learnt about a damning feasibility study which stated that the narrow-gauge Bosnian lines would need to be widened at enormous cost, and that even then there could be no real competition to the Belgrade-Salonika railway line. Told about this study, Aehrenthal turned 'deathly pale'.[41]

None of these Balkan railways were ever built. In announcing his project, Aehrenthal may have simply wanted to break with Russia.[42] It may also have been conscious bravado. As G.P. Gooch noted, the project had placed Aehrenthal on the centre stage of European affairs, whereas until then he had played a secondary role.[43] Be that as it may, he certainly managed to upset Izvolsky and public opinion in Russia as well as that of Serbia. At a time when the Great Powers, Britain above all, were seeking to continue the reform process in Macedonia, particularly in the judicial field, Aehrenthal was consigning to history the entire Mürzsteg programme from 1903 and with it a decade of Austro-Russian camaraderie in the Balkans, begun in 1897. What is also significant is that immediately afterwards, in February 1908, Dimitrije Popović, the Serbian Minister at St Petersburg, asked Izvolsky for Russia's help to stand up to this 'Germanic *Drang nach Osten*' since, he said, Serbia could not prevent it alone. In other words, this was the very first time, following the putsch of 1903, that Serbia actually turned to Russia for assistance in foreign policy. It had therefore taken the supposedly 'Russophile' post-1903 Serbian regime almost five years to start considering a Russia option. A rather 'reserved' Izvolsky did promise backing for the Adriatic railway provided Serbia solved the technical and financial questions.[44]

Nevertheless, Serbia was now backed by Russia. And not just Russia. Aehrenthal's Sanjak railway proposals had only boosted Serbia's international position. Suddenly, Serbia had important friends in Europe: in Italy, France and even in Britain. All these Powers were ready to line up behind Serbia's alternative scenario of an Adriatic railway. Tittoni was disgusted by what he called Aehrenthal's 'double-faced policy'. Stéphen Pichon, the French Foreign Minister, talked about the need '*de la liberation de la Serbie*'. In Britain, Foreign Secretary Sir Edward Grey was upset by Aehrenthal because, he thought, to press for railway concessions just when the reform process in Macedonia was at a standstill, 'would produce the very unfavourable impression that the Powers were abandoning the reforms in order to pursue their own interests'.[45] From now on, Christer Jorgensen has argued, 'the Monarchy which had been trusted to keep the peace and ensure stability in the Balkans was a force for turbulence and insecurity herself'.[46]

Tales, Lies and Great Serbian Propaganda

Although the diplomatic history of the Bosnian annexation crisis is well known, the relevant Serbian documents have only recently been published, the last two tomes as late as 2014.[47] This body of evidence demonstrates that, prior to annexation, Serbia's chief foreign policy effort consisted of reacting to the perceived threat of Vienna's Sanjak railway project. Gathering international support for the rival Danube-Adriatic railway remained a major preoccupation for Belgrade right up to October 1908.[48] In 1907-1908 considerable attention was also paid to Kosovo and Metohija ('Old Serbia'), to Macedonia and, most importantly, to the growing prospect of a war against Bulgaria. Relations with Montenegro also came under considerable strain at this time. It is striking how little Bosnia and Herzegovina figure in the Serbian documents for 1907 and most of 1908. This is an important point to emphasize because Aehrenthal and his diplomats were to claim that Belgrade-directed Great Serbian 'agitation' in the provinces necessitated their annexation – a piece of propaganda which is echoed even today in some literature.

One of the problems for Serbia's foreign policy during 1907-1908 came from an unexpected direction: Montenegro. The Montenegrins were furious with Serbia for projecting its Adriatic railway to end up in a Turkish, Albanian port, rather than their own port of Bar. They conveniently ignored the fact that Bar was within easy range of Austro-Hungarian artillery, and even of rifle fire. However, what really poisoned relations was the so-called *bombaška afera* (Bombs Affair). In October 1907 the Montenegrin police discovered seventeen bombs and arrested scores of students. There was a connection to Serbia in both cases: the bombs were of Serbian manufacture, and the students had spent time in Serbia. They were accused of plotting to assassinate Prince Nicholas and planning to overthrow the dynasty.[49] Whether there existed an actual assassination plan is very doubtful. But the whole affair was exploited – and to some extent staged – by the Montenegrin authorities in order to create an excuse for stepping up the persecution of domestic political opponents.[50] Particularly glaring was the appearance in court, during the trial of the students, of one Đorđe Nastić, a journalist from Sarajevo, already suspected at that time of being an agent of the Bosnian *Landesregierung*. Nastić was in fact chief witness for the prosecution. Even Lazar Tomanović, the Montenegrin Prime Minister, admitted later that Nastić was Austria's man.[51]

Nastić alleged that the supposed plot had been prepared in Belgrade, and hinted broadly at the involvement of King Peter and Crown Prince George. The students, he said, were merely obedient tools in the hands of the true organizers.[52] In June 1908 the Serbian Minister in Cetinje, who had closely observed the trial, broke off diplomatic relations, telling Tomanović that practices in Montenegro were 'reminiscent of Africa'.[53] The Montenegrin historian Novica Rakočević was to conclude that no one from Serbian officialdom was planning or instigating a revolution in Montenegro.[54] Serbo-Montenegrin relations were quickly patched up in the wake of the Bosnian annexation, and although some of the accused had received death sentences, all were pardoned by 1913. There is a consensus among Yugoslavian historians that Austria-Hungary was involved in the 'Bombs Affair', out of a desire to set Montenegro and Serbia against each other as it prepared to annex neighbouring Bosnia-Herzegovina, while being anxious at the same time that Serbia be seen as the aggressive, sinister, expansionist state.

Apart from the ongoing tariff war with Austria-Hungary, Serbia's most serious foreign policy problem for quite a time before the Bosnian annexation concerned relations with Bulgaria. As seen above, the Serbo-Bulgarian friendship and customs union treaties concluded in 1905-1906 were of short duration. The main issue between the two countries remained Macedonia. Bulgarian irregular bands' activities in the province had begun in 1897 and were then emulated by Greece and Serbia. These bands (*čete* in Serbian), occasionally fought the Turkish Army, but they mostly attacked each other and also, as a rule, targeted each other's teachers and priests because education and church propaganda activities were viewed as the most potent tools in this struggle. After 1903, with the introduction of the Mürzsteg reform programme for Macedonia, the fighting came to be seen as a serious obstacle to the work of the Powers involved in the reforms. The Serbs were anxious to try and keep the Bulgarians completely out of the *vilayet* of Kosovo. However, the latter included the *sanjak* of Üskub (Skopje), a region that happened to be of great interest to Bulgaria, so all attempts by Belgrade to convince Sofia to agree to a division of spheres of influence fell on deaf ears.

That Serbia should be so preoccupied with events across its southern frontiers was hardly surprising, for dangerous escalations always appeared very likely. Thus in April 1907 Pašić was tipped off by Italy's Foreign Minister Tittoni about an imminent Bulgarian attack on Serbia. This turned out to be a false alarm, but the atrociously bad relations with Bulgaria justified Pašić in immediately warning Britain, France and Russia – he did not bother with Germany, let alone Austria-Hungary.[55] The Serbian Prime Minister was incidentally far more interested in Kosovo and Macedonia than he would ever be in Bosnia-Herzegovina, and was jumpy if anything looked like threatening the Serbian position in those lands. That position was actually quite weak. As the Serbian diplomatic agency in Sofia admitted, the Serbs had made little impression in the *vilayet* of Salonika, equally little in the *vilayet* of Monastir (Bitolj), and were inferior to the Bulgarians even in the *sanjak* of Skopje.[56]

A further concern in this region related to the Albanians. Report after report from consulates in Skopje and Priština talked about the terror to which the Serbian population was being subjected at the hands of the Albanians – a terror which led many Serbs to migrate to the United States of America.[57] In 1914 Professor Masaryk estimated that, since the eighteenth century, under Albanian pressure, half a million Serbs had been forced out of Old Serbia and northern Macedonia.[58] The main danger that Pašić perceived here was the failure of the Great Powers to extend the Mürzsteg reform action to Kosovo (especially the reform of the gendarmerie), a failure that would, in effect, deliver the remaining local Serbians to the Albanians. In March 1908 he was so upset by what he saw as the embryo Albanian region being created in Old Serbia that he decided to blackmail the Russians, sending them the message that 'such prospects for the future could force the Serbs to seek their salvation within the framework of the Austro-Hungarian Monarchy'.[59]

The main worry, nevertheless, was Bulgaria. News of Bulgarian atrocities against the Serbs multiplied in the second half of 1907. And whereas Serbia got no sympathy from Izvolsky over this issue, Aehrenthal, while not directly criticising Bulgaria, did tell the Serbian Minister in Vienna that Serbia's conduct in Macedonia was 'correct and loyal'.[60] The Serb *četnik* bands, however, also committed atrocities. One of these took place in the village of Stracin, in May 1908, when six civilians were killed, including a woman. The action was led by Vojislav Tankosić, the officer who had taken part in the 1903 palace putsch against King Alexander, and who had commanded the execution of Queen Draga's two brothers. In Bulgaria, not surprisingly, the press launched a furious campaign against Serbia over the Stracin incident, accusing it at the same time of colluding secretly with Greece. Sveta Simić, Serbia's Diplomatic Agent in Sofia, warned on 4 June that relations could be broken off at any time and that Bulgaria was contemplating war against Serbia. A week later, Stefan Paprikov, the Foreign Minister of Bulgaria, confirmed this view by openly talking to Simić about the possibility of war.[61]

In the end, Russia acted swiftly and decisively to prevent a conflict. Izvolsky, committed to the reform process in European Turkey, but also fearing wider consequences, was not going to allow this *'folie furieuse'*, as he called it, to happen, and he intervened forcefully in both Belgrade and Sofia. Just in case, however, fifteen ships from the Russian Black Sea fleet, including three cruisers, suddenly appeared at the Bulgarian port of Varna. This naval demonstration reportedly produced a 'heavy impression' on Prince Ferdinand of Bulgaria.[62]

Accordingly, for many months before October 1908, Serbia did not and could not think about Bosnia-Herzegovina. The future of the provinces was not even remotely on the agenda of Serbian foreign policy at this time. Some historians say otherwise. 'Agitators from Serbia', writes Margaret MacMillan, 'were already busy in Macedonia and, after 1900, they increasingly moved into Bosnia-Herzegovina'. She adds: 'The Serb-language press in both Belgrade and Sarajevo denounced Austria-Hungary's tyranny and called on the peoples of the provinces to rise up'.[63] Now, if true, this sounds like a dangerous pre-revolutionary situation. Yet, as seen above, Burián, the Minister for Bosnia since 1903, was of the firm and repeated view that the Bosnian Serbs were not to be feared. Though some in the Habsburg establishment did not share Burián's view, it has been seen in chapter four that the Bosnian Serb leadership was anything but rabble-rousing. To be sure, inflammatory articles against Austro-Hungarian rule did on occasion appear in the Bosnian Serb press during the Burián regime. In May 1908, for example, the Banja Luka Serb paper *Otadžbina* (Fatherland) published a particularly fiery piece, in connection with Aehrenthal's Sanjak railway project, which, anticipating a war, called on the Serbs of the provinces to be ready to fight together with their brothers in Serbia. Significantly, however, the Bosnian Serb leaders distanced themselves from the article and the rest of the Bosnian Serb press condemned it.[64] Another Bosnian

Serb anti-Habsburg article, from March 1908, is cited at some length in a memorandum by Conrad, the Austro-Hungarian Chief of General Staff.[65] Yet though Conrad saw the 'Serbian agitation' in the Habsburg Monarchy in terms of a grand conspiracy, an irredenta 'fomented from the outside' (i.e., from Serbia), such occasional instances of writings as exist should not lead historians into following him (or indeed their fellow historian MacMillan) by lumping together the press in Belgrade and the Bosnian Serb press.[66] For even Conrad could not cite any evidence from the Belgrade press in support of such a scenario, let alone provide evidence of any connections with the Serbian Government, though one presumes he must sorely have wanted to do both.

The truth is that any articles in the Serbian press calling for the overthrow of Habsburg rule would have immediately provoked the reaction of the Ballhausplatz. Both Gołuchowski and later Aehrenthal would never fail to bring to the attention of the Serbian Minister in Vienna even the most trifling Belgrade press items that had annoyed them. Yet there is no trace in Austrian documents, or for that matter in Serbian ones, of any complaints by Vienna about the grave matters indicated by MacMillan. An Austrian doctoral dissertation from 1971 which looks specifically at the writing of the Serbian press in relation to Austria-Hungary from 1903 to 1914, diligently lists all its main lines of attack until 1908 – which were the Mürzsteg Programme, the tariff war and the Sanjak railway project – but does not mention any calls to the peoples of Bosnia-Herzegovina to 'rise up' against the tyranny of Habsburg rule.[67]

The first time that Đorđe Simić, Vujić's successor as the Serbian Minister in Vienna, reported to Belgrade on the possibility of annexation was in early December 1907 – but he had only read about it in newspapers. Later that month Simić looked into the matter again and, having got his information from a 'very reliable' source, triumphantly concluded that 'we should in the near future not fear an annexation of Bosnia and Herzegovina by Austria-Hungary'.[68] Thereafter, from the end of 1907 until mid-May 1908 there is nothing in the Serbian documents that relates to Bosnia-Herzegovina in any significant way. Then, on 13 May 1908, Popović reported from St Petersburg on a meeting with Izvolsky. The latter said that he had received information about a 'certain tension' in Austro-Serb relations over Bosnia-Herzegovina. Austria-Hungary, Izvolsky explained, was 'complaining' that Serbia was agitating in the provinces and 'stirring up' the people. Clearly surprised, Popović expressed his private opinion that such complaints were 'absolutely unfounded' and designed to provide justification for Vienna's 'egoist' plans in Bosnia-Herzegovina.[69]

What Izvolsky told Popović is quite important because it points to the beginning of Aehrenthal's effort to create the right climate for the eventual annexation. Interestingly, Aehrenthal had seen Đorđe Simić on 5 May, but said not a word about Bosnia-Herzegovina. Their next meeting took place on 13 May (the day when Izvolsky talked to Popović), but again the Austro-Hungarian Foreign Minister found it unnecessary to draw attention to any supposedly subversive action by Serbia in Bosnia-Herzegovina.[70] In fact, when he did mention the subject to others, Aehrenthal talked about it in the most general terms. At a meeting with Tittoni in Salzburg on 5 September, he complained about the 'Great Serbian movement in Bosnia' and about the Serbian Government which was 'aiding' that movement.[71] Towards the end of September he told Tschirschky, the German Ambassador in Vienna, that the annexation would be Austria-Hungary's 'answer to the Great Serbian propaganda' which was being 'driven from Belgrade', adding, amazingly, that the situation in the provinces had become 'untenable [*unhaltbar*]'.[72] This was at a time when, as seen in chapter four, the leaders of the Bosnian Serbs, Orthodox and Muslims, representing four fifths of the population, had fully expected annexation and had actually demanded of Burián an assembly for Bosnia-Herzegovina, that is to say, had indicated their willingness to work constitutionally within Bosnia-Herzegovina.

Not only was the Serbian Government in the first half of 1908 more than busy with foreign policy issues unrelated to Bosnia-Herzegovina, it was also engrossed in domestic political problems. Because of parliamentary obstruction by the Independent Radicals, Finance Minister Paču was unable to get his budget passed, while the trade agreement with Austria-Hungary, concluded in March 1908, came under sustained opposition attack. Pašić's administration finally collapsed after early elections in June weakened the Radical Party to such an extent that a coalition with the Independent Radicals was the only way forward. Negotiations about the formation of the new government, however, lasted well into the summer. The Independent Radicals agreed in the end to form a government with the Radicals, but only on condition that Pašić, Protić and Paču, the most prominent and hated Radical leaders, were excluded from it.[73]

The new Prime Minister, taking office on 20 July, was Pera Velimirović, a Radical. As was Milovan Milovanović, the new Foreign Minister, until recently the head of the Serbian Legation in Rome. Milovanović, a Paris-educated constitutional lawyer, was perhaps Serbia's most talented and sophisticated statesman of that period. He enjoyed a high reputation in Europe's diplomatic circles, one which, Slobodan Jovanović noted, 'bore no relationship to Serbia's reputation at the time'.[74] His biographer Dimitrije Đorđević cites an assessment of Milovanović as the 'the greatest European of the Balkans'.[75] He was actually supposed to be a Russophile, but because he did not view Russia as particularly powerful, he believed that Serbia should tie itself to Russia only if France had already done the same. As for his country's future shape, Milovanović was 'not a fanatic', and 'did not carry in his head a geographic map of Serbia'.[76]

Milovanović's major concern, on becoming Foreign Minister, was to try and repair ties with Vienna. Unlike Pašić, he had no illusions about Austria-Hungary and knew just how dangerous it could become. However, he opposed the tariff war, convinced that a trade agreement with the Monarchy was a pre-condition for Serbia's economic progress – as the country could not, he thought, find a better market for its exports than that of Austria-Hungary. Slobodan Jovanović, who knew him well, repeatedly emphasized in his essay on Milovanović that he was a man of compromise, one who would avoid confrontation if at all possible.[77] It is interesting to note just how anxious he was in the weeks before the annexation not to allow anything that could upset Austro-Hungarian sensitivities. In August a large group of Serbs from Belgrade arrived in Skopje where they were cordially received by Young Turk officers – those being the early days of the new, constitutional regime, when much fraternization occurred between different national groups in the Ottoman Empire. At a banquet held for the visiting Serbs there were loud calls of 'Freedom for Bosnia and Herzegovina' and shouts of 'Down with Austria!' As soon as he was informed of this by the Serbian Consul in Skopje, Milovanović sent instructions demanding that all talk about Bosnia and remonstrations against Austria-Hungary should cease.[78]

Like Pašić, however, Milovanović was unable to make any headway with Aehrenthal when they met on 14 September in Vienna. According to the relatively scant Austrian record of the meeting, Milovanović immediately revealed his intention to work for the betterment of relations between their two countries. Putting Serbia in a position of permanent opposition to its 'powerful neighbour', he said, would be 'downright lunatic'. Aehrenthal, however, replied that, since the new Serbian Government had only been in power for a short time, he had to remain sceptical. He described the policy of the previous cabinet in Belgrade as 'hazardous', one that had made enemies of all of Serbia's neighbours. With regard to Austria-Hungary, Aehrenthal continued, that policy had fostered and fomented 'every hostile agitation'. This, he warned, could be 'nothing less than dangerous' for Serbia. It is not clear from the record of the meeting whether Milovanović had reacted to these charges, and if so how. But he was clearly infuriated, in early October, by articles in the Vienna and Budapest press alleging Great Serbian agitation, articles he succinctly described as 'tendentious fabrications'.[79] At any rate, Aehrenthal concluded their meeting by saying, significantly, that there now existed between Austria-Hungary and Russia 'a complete harmony of views' regarding the Near East, i.e., the Balkans.[80]

All of which represented a declaration of scarcely concealed hostility towards Serbia. Milovanović must have left the meeting a rather worried man. He already knew, before seeing Aehrenthal, that the annexation of

Bosnia-Herzegovina was very much on the cards. At the beginning of September, at Karlsbad, he had met with Izvolsky who had told him that Aehrenthal wanted to annex Bosnia and Herzegovina. 'That has to be prevented at any cost!' Milovanović protested. 'Impossible!', insisted Izvolsky and suggested that 'compensations' be demanded instead.[81]

What Milovanović did not realize at the time was that Izvolsky was about to sell Bosnia-Herzegovina down the river. On 6 July the Russians had presented the Ballhausplatz with an *aide mémoire*, dated 2 July, in which they declared readiness to discuss the status ('annexation') of Bosnia-Herzegovina and the Sanjak of Novi Pazar, together with the question of Constantinople and the Straits.[82] This was the prelude to perhaps the greatest diplomatic fiasco of the twentieth century. On 16 September, two days after he had talked to Milovanović, Aehrenthal met with Izvolsky at Schloss Buchlau (Buchlovice), the splendid Baroque country seat of Count Berchtold, Austria-Hungary's Ambassador in St Petersburg. It is entirely immaterial whether, at this famous meeting, Izvolsky was somehow misled by Aehrenthal into believing that the annexation of Bosnia-Herzegovina would not proceed as quickly as it ultimately did. The point is that he was ready to bargain with the occupied provinces in return for what really mattered to him: the unrestricted passage of Russian warships through the Straits. Of course, with the possible exception of Slavic Orthodox solidarity, Russia owed nothing to Serbia and had every right to put its own interests first. Incredibly, however, in the *aide mémoire* of 2 July Izvolsky stipulated that the Sanjak of Novi Pazar could also be annexed by Austria-Hungary. 'Izvolsky', Aehrenthal later told Friedjung, 'had himself made us the offer to annex not just Bosnia but also the Sanjak'. Friedjung was 'amazed' and he wanted to hear that again. 'What, also the Sanjak?', he asked. 'Yes', replied Aehrenthal, 'also the Sanjak'.[83] Needless to say, Izvolsky's gratuitous offer would have entailed a permanent Habsburg wedge between Serbia and Montenegro. In his classic account of Austro-Russian relations in the pre-annexation period, W.M. Carlgren commented on Izvolsky's largesse regarding the Sanjak: 'No Russian Foreign Minister had after the Congress of Berlin offered as much as Izvolsky'.[84]

With such friends in Russia, Serbia hardly needed any enemies elsewhere. As it turned out, Aehrenthal was not in the least interested in the Sanjak and actually wanted to get the garrisoning troops out of there as fast as possible. He had received military opinion that cast doubts on the value of the Sanjak for the Austro-Hungarian Army and saw it rather as a *cul-de-sac*. From then on he tended to describe the Sanjak as a 'deathtrap [*Mausefalle*]'. This did not, however, mean that Vienna was now giving up the option of moving further south into the Balkans – a claim Aehrenthal was to trumpet with much smug moralism following the annexation. In private, as seen above, he told Ernst Plener that Mitrovica in Kosovo could be better reached via Belgrade. That, certainly, was also the view of Conrad and the Army General Staff. Pulling out of the Sanjak thus conveniently enabled Aehrenthal to profess to Turkey, Italy and others that annexation had fully satisfied the Balkan ambitions of the Habsburg Monarchy.

At the same time Aehrenthal was promoting the story about Great Serbian agitation to explain what had impelled him to act in the first place. On 7 October Count Lajos Széchényi, the Austro-Hungarian Chargé d'Affaires in London, presented a note at the Foreign Office, announcing Vienna's step. He said that 'the real reason' for acting speedily to annex the provinces 'was the Serbian propaganda that was being carried on there, in which King Peter himself was implicated'.[85] Towards the end of the month the Austro-Hungarian Ambassador, Count Albert Mensdorff-Pouilly, similarly attempted to convince Foreign Secretary Grey that a main reason for the annexation was the 'agitation driven from Serbia'. Grey commented that he knew 'next to nothing' about this propaganda and that, since so little had been heard about it, one was not expecting it to be a motive for Austria-Hungary's sudden decision to annex.[86]

The truth was that Aehrenthal required for the annexation of the occupied provinces a modicum of apologia, and for that reason he peddled his tales about Great Serbian agitation instigated from Belgrade. Charges of subversive Serb activities before the annexation actually emerged not in Bosnia but rather in Croatia. There, the new *Ban* (Viceroy) since the beginning of 1908 was Baron Rauch, a determined opponent of the Serbs. When the Croat politician Iso Kršnjavi put it to him that the Serbs of Croatia should be made politically harmless, he agreed. 'Yes', he said, 'we cannot exterminate 700,000 Serbs'.[87] Rauch's main task in Croatia was to destroy the Croato-Serb Coalition. The latter had in the February elections gained a majority in the *Sabor*, whereas the Rauch (i.e., government) party failed to win a single seat. The aims of Budapest and Vienna happened to coincide for once: the Hungarians were worried about the Croato-Serb Coalition as a force driving towards Trialism, with the Serb Independent Party being the main prop of the Coalition. Meanwhile, Aehrenthal, by now already pursuing a forward policy in the Balkans, was keen to promote the image of subversive Serb activities within the Empire.[88]

And so, in July 1908, the Austro-Hungarian agent Đorđe Nastić, of Montenegrin 'Bombs Affair' fame, suddenly re-emerged in Budapest where he published a pamphlet entitled *Finale*.[89] Here, Nastić named prominent Serbs of Croatia, connecting them to *Slovenski jug* (The Slav South), an allegedly Pan Serbian organization in Belgrade, suggesting they were planning terrorist activities on Austro-Hungarian territory. The whole pamphlet is riddled with contradictions and unlikely constructions. *Slovenski jug*, which also published a journal under the same name, had indeed existed and Nastić had known the people around it from his *agent provocateur* days

in Serbia. But judging by the articles in its journal, *Slovenski jug* was a platform for idealist, Yugoslav-oriented young intellectuals advocating 'a union
of Serbia, Bulgaria, and Montenegro' which would then be joined by 'all
South Slavs'.[90] This was no Pan Serbian agency. Interestingly, the journal
was frequently attacked by *Samouprava*, the mouthpiece of Pašić's Radical
Party, and even had to close down on one occasion.[91] The whole outfit
existed on a town council subsidy. At any rate, soon after the publication
of Nastić's *Finale*, many leading Croatian Serbs from the Croato-Serb
Coalition were locked up and held for months before being tried for high
treason in 1909. At the court in Zagreb (Agram) the pamphlet was used as
cardinal evidence against fifty-three accused Serbs, thirty-one of whom
received sentences. Political bias on the part of the court at the expense
of the accused was clearly visible. Europe was scandalized, and eventually
the Emperor was to pardon all those who had been imprisoned. But the
Ballhausplatz likewise used Nastić's material: only days before the annexation, the prestigious *Österreichische Rundschau* published an article about
'King Peter and the Great Serbian Movement', basing itself on Nastić.[92]
In the absence of better material, Nastić's pamphlet would have to do.

It was Aehrenthal who was also reponsible for the next and easily the
greatest embarrassment to the Habsburg Monarchy during his time in office.
At the height of the annexation crisis, he supplied his friend Friedjung with
some documents from Serbia and let him publish, on 25 March 1909, an
article in the *Neue Freie Presse*. This incendiary piece accused the Croato-
Serb Coalition of receiving money from the Government in Belgrade
(Friedjung named Miroslav Spalajković, Secretary General of the Serbian
Foreign Ministry) and from *Slovenski jug*, and painted Serbia as a state
which, 'through conspiracies, dynamite and dagger', worked to destroy the
work of the Congress of Berlin.[93] This was rather rich coming from an
ardent supporter of the annexation which had just months earlier torpe-
doed the Treaty of Berlin. In any case, Aehrenthal was at this stage determined to wage war on Serbia if the latter did not recognize the annexation,
and the Friedjung article did indeed sound like 'a prelude to an Austro-
Hungarian declaration of war'.[94] Poor Friedjung did not know that the
documents were forgeries, supplied by János Forgách, the head of the
Austro-Hungarian Legation in Belgrade.[95] The leaders of the Croato-Serb
Coalition promptly sued for libel. The ensuing 'Friedjung Process' in
Vienna (December 1909) clearly revealed that the documents on which
the article was based were falsifications. In one instance Friedjung said
that he had minutes of a subversive meeting in Belgrade presided over by
Professor Božidar Marković in November 1908. Marković, however,
pointed out that he was actually in Berlin at the time – and this was duly
confirmed by the Berlin police. Spalajković himself volunteered to testify
and proved a most eloquent witness.[96] The trial attracted great attention

in the Monarchy and indeed in the whole of Europe. A compromise was reached in the end whereby charges were withdrawn, but the damage had been done. Friedjung subsequently broke off all relations with Aehrenthal.[97]

Serbia in the Bosnian Annexation Crisis

The decision to annex Bosnia-Herzegovina was sealed at two meetings of the Joint Ministerial Council, firstly on 19 August 1908 in Vienna and then on 10 September in Budapest.[98] Of course, the international legal character of Bosnia-Herzegovina was subject to the 1878 Treaty of Berlin. Any changes, therefore, would require the collective approval of the Great Powers. But Aehrenthal argued in those two ministerial meetings that other Great Powers were not likely to challenge annexation and that the moment was now favourable to proceed. Conversely, on 10 September he warned of the danger that the Turkish Parliament could in November take its own decision on Bosnia-Herzegovina. The Young Turk revolution, which had begun in July and which seemed to promise a new era of constitutionalism, is normally seen as the reason why Aehrenthal hurried to bring about the annexation. The Turks, according to F.R. Bridge, 'were planning to summon representatives from Bosnia and the Herzegovina to the new Ottoman parliament'.[99] It seems doubtful, however, that this was seriously contemplated by the Young Turks. The Bosnian Muslims, certainly, were hoping for such an end result, but the Young Turk regime itself did not raise the issue.[100] In his detailed study about Austria-Hungary and the Young Turks, the Serb historian Đorđe Mikić shows that the Young Turkish press, voicing the views of the new rulers, went further and rejected any suggestions about taking away from Austria-Hungary its mandate for Bosnia-Herzegovina, contending that 'no man with a sound mind' could contemplate something that would only complicate Turkish foreign policy at a time when the country was facing burning internal questions.[101] Markgrave Pallavicini, Aehrenthal's Ambassador in Constantinople and an opponent of annexation, made sure of sending Aehrenthal a translated article about Bosnia-Herzegovina taken from a paper close to the Young Turks, its main conclusion being that Turkey, busy as it was with internal reforms, was merely hoping for the retention of the *status quo*.[102]

Be that as it may, the establishment of the Young Turk regime certainly provided Aehrenthal with a useful rationale to proceed apace with the annexation. Significantly, the Hungarians only agreed to it on condition that it would not threaten the Dualist system of the Monarchy.[103] The annexation of Bosnia-Herzegovina was announced on 6 October. A day before, in a coordinated move with the Ballhausplatz, the Turkish vassal state of Bulgaria declared its independence from Turkey. This, as Aehrenthal had correctly anticipated, was a far bigger blow to the Young Turks than the formal loss of Bosnia-Herzegovina. What he did not foresee was that the annexation would cause a storm of protest in Europe. In Russia, Prime Minister Pyotr Stolypin was fuming at Izvolsky for giving away two Slavic provinces and even the Tsar, 'who was no Panslav', stated that their absorption by Austria 'sickens one's feelings'.[104] Public opinion and the press in Russia turned against both Austria-Hungary and Izvolsky. The latter, as is well known, was unable to drum up support in Paris and London for the opening of the Straits to Russian warships – but had already bargained away Bosnia and Herzegovina, which put him in an impossible position. In the salons of St Petersburg he was now mocked as 'The Prince of Bosphorus'.[105]

Elsewhere, Foreign Minister Tittoni came under savage attack in Italy for agreeing to annexation without any compensations, and in France Prime Minister Clemenceau roundly condemned Austria-Hungary's unilateral action.[106] France would actually do no more than protest, but the reaction in London was quite severe. Britain would as a result of Aehrenthal's annexation become a major player in the Balkans. The view of the Foreign Office was mainly shaped by the fact that the Young Turks were enthusiastically Anglophile – Turkey's previous pro-German course seemed to have been abandoned by the new regime. What worried the British was the damage which the Young Turks sustained by Bulgarian and Austro-Hungarian action. As a result, Britain commenced a policy of championing Turkish interests.[107] It did not help Aehrenthal's image among British statesmen and diplomats that he had shortly before the Bulgarian declaration of independence lied shamelessly to Goschen, the British Ambassador in Vienna, in pretending he knew nothing about it. Prime Minister Asquith later described Aehrenthal as 'perhaps the least scrupulous of the Austrian statesmen of our time'.[108] Only Germany, otherwise the Sultan's great friend, provided support for Austria-Hungary – in what looks, retrospectively, like a *Nibelungentreue* rehearsal for July 1914. Even so, Kaiser Wilhelm II was enraged by Aehrenthal's 'shocking foolishness'. For, as he commented on a telegram from Prince Bülow on 7 October, 'my Turkish policy, constructed so painstakingly over twenty years, bites the dust!'[109]

Predictably, the most furious reaction to annexation came from Serbia. In 1876 Serbia had fought Turkey because of Bosnia and Herzegovina. It cannot be emphasized too strongly that the Serbs considered the two provinces as Serb lands. So too, incidentally, did many foreign travellers, linguists, ethnologists and historians – at the very least they thought those were Serb-speaking lands.[110] Maximilian Schimek's history of Bosnia, the first ever published, drew attention to its Serbian character in the medieval period.[111] The 1910 Austro-Hungarian population census for Bosnia-Herzegovina (the very last), recorded 1.898,044 souls, of which there were 825,918 (43.49 %) Orthodox, i.e., Serbs; 612,137 (32.25%) Muslims; 434,061 (22.87%) Catholics (mostly Croats); and 26,428 (13.9%) 'others'.[112] At the time of the annexation, as seen in chapter four, the Bosnian Muslim leaders called their people 'Serbs of Muslim faith'. The best summary of how the Serbs in Serbia itself felt about Bosnia-Herzegovina was given in 1909 by Jovan Cvijić, the Serb geographer and ethnologist with a European reputation for scholarship. 'These provinces', he wrote, 'are not for Serbia what Alsace and Lorraine are for France, or Trent and Triest for Italy, or the Austro-Alpine regions for Germany. They represent rather what the Muscovite province is to Russia and what the most integral parts of Germany and France are to those two countries, that is those parts most strongly representative of the French and German races'.[113] To others, of course, the annexation just looked like a formalization of an existing state of affairs. To the Serbs, however, the removal of Turkey as sovereign Power in Bosnia-Herzegovina also meant the removal of even a theoretical chance that the provinces would some day join Serbia following a partition of Turkey in Europe. A new, and for Serbia seemingly hopeless situation had been created by the annexation: despite its internal problems, the Habsburg Empire did not look in 1908 as if it was going to collapse any time soon.

Once it became known that annexation was about to happen, all hell broke loose in Serbia. The Belgrade daily *Politika* carried the news on 5 October, a day before the act itself, and massive demonstrations immediately erupted. The next day saw 20,000 people gather at a meeting in central Belgrade –roughly a quarter of the entire population of the city. Protest meetings broke out all over the country. In Šabac the enraged crowd wanted to kill the Austro-Hungarian Vice Consul. In Montenegro, the Army had to intervene when the protesters were about to pull down the building accommodating the Austro-Hungarian Legation. About this time news arrived that Crete would finally be joining Greece. Coupled with Bulgaria's declaration of independence, this produced a feeling among the Serbs that they were the only ones left empty-handed. Serbia's *vox populi* now demanded war. Volunteers flocked to enlist in the patriotic, paramilitary *Narodna Odbrana* (National Defence) organization which had been hastily organized. Referring to the river Drina which formed a natural border with Habsburg Bosnia, people shouted: 'To the Drina! War on Austria!'[114]

Slobodan Jovanović has pointed out that no one in Serbia actually believed in the success of a military confrontation with Austria-Hungary – war was demanded 'without faith in victory'. Apart from being seen as the *finis* of Serbian dreams about national unification, the Bosnian annexation, moreover, was also perceived as a prelude to the destruction of Serbia's own existence as an independent state. Therefore the view became widespread that it was better for Serbia to go down in a blaze of glory than face a 'gradual and shameful' ruination.[115] Interestingly, this was precisely the kind of logic, mixed with sentiment, which was to emerge in Austria-Hungary even before the assassination of Franz Ferdinand in Sarajevo on 28 June 1914.

The Serbian Government, and Milovanović in particular, proved more rational in 1908 than the Serbian public. It understood that nothing could be done to oppose annexation without massive external support. However, as much as the chancelleries across Europe were unhappy about Vienna's breach of international law, Serbia in fact stood alone on the question of whether something should be done about it. Tcharykow, who had since his Belgrade days advanced to become Izvolsky's deputy, told the Serbian Minister in St Petersburg: 'No one will help you. The whole world wants peace'.[116] Izvolsky himself was equally blunt when he met Milenko Vesnić, the Serbian Minister in Paris. 'You Serbs', he said, 'could not contemplate throwing Austria-Hungary out of Bosnia and Herzegovina by force of arms. And we Russians cannot go to war with her because of these provinces.' That was fair enough, but Izvolsky lied through his teeth when he told Vesnić that Austria-Hungary was only withdrawing from the Sanjak of Novi Pazar because he, Izvolsky, had demanded this withdrawal in return for his agreement to the proposed annexation of Bosnia-Herzegovina. Austria-Hungary, he said, 'gains nothing' with the Bosnian annexation, whereas its abandonment of Novi Pazar opened up the possibility of Serbia and Montenegro pushing their frontiers towards each other. As seen above, it was precisely Izvolsky who had only recently been offering Aehrenthal both Bosnia-Herzegovina and the Sanjak of Novi Pazar on a silver platter.[117]

Milovanović realized from the beginning that he could only conduct a damage limitation exercise. Even before the annexation took place, he had asked the Army Chief of Staff about Serbia's military strength. The answer he was given was that no more than 40,000 soldiers could be armed and that they could not wage war for more than fifteen days.[118] It is true that, in emergency session, the Serbian Assembly voted to allocate 16 million dinars on armaments, but this was more a step to placate bellicose public opinion. It did, however, leave the Russian Foreign Minister unimpressed. 'Presumably you do not believe', a contemptuous Izvolsky put it to the Serbian Minister in London, 'that you can go to war on 16 million dinars?'[119]

It has already been pointed out, in chapter four, that the Bosnian Serbs themselves were not keen on a fight. Todor Petković, Serbia's Consul General in Hungary, had been in contact with the Bosnian Serb leaders who had arrived in Budapest where the Delegations were meeting. He reported back to Belgrade that in Bosnia-Herzegovina 'there is no enthusiasm for war' and that one should not count on an insurrection. The prevailing feeling in the provinces was that any insurrection would be unsuccessful and that it would only 'bring misery on to the people'.[120] In Vienna, Minister Simić was carefully monitoring the situation in Bosnia-

Herzegovina and passed on his assessment that, while both the Orthodox and the Muslims were keeping quiet, it was the Muslims who were more likely to offer armed resistance to Austria-Hungary.[121] If Belgrade had conducted so much agitation and spread so much propaganda as Aehernthal and his envoys abroad were alleging, it seems to have had remarkably little effect on the Bosnian Serbs.

The only thing that Milovanović could do was to cry foul. He certainly did so in the protest note of the Royal Serbian Government, dated 7 October, which he had personally put together and which demanded the restoration of Bosnia's status within the provisions of the Treaty of Berlin. However, the weakness of the Serbian position was revealed in the first sentence of the note which invoked 'incontestable Serbian national rights'. Although the 'principle of nationality' was talked about in Europe, 'national rights' were not recognized in international law. Austria-Hungary may have displayed utter contempt for an international treaty (to which it was itself a signatory), but Serbia, a non-signatory Power, had no *locus standi*.[122] Nevertheless, Serbia had every right to put its case to the Great Powers, since it was they who were mandated to decide, collectively, on the fate of Bosnia-Herzegovina. Milovanović's protest note actually offered a way out: if the restoration of Bosnia's pre-annexation situation proved impossible, it demanded that Serbia be given 'corresponding compensation'. What this demand meant was that Belgrade was in principle ready to accept the annexation.[123]

The protest note severely undermined Milovanović's position in Serbia, inviting attacks on him from nationalist circles: 'Instead of demanding the maximum, he set out with the minimum'. The Foreign Minister's critics argued, for example, that Cavour did not seek compensation, telling the Austrians instead: 'Get out of Italy!' But Milovanović was totally opposed to war over the issue and successfully resisted suggestions that the Serbian Army should attack in the Sanjak of Novi Pazar. 'We have to preserve our strength', he wrote at the time, 'for the decisive, great conflict'.[124] The compensation that he had in mind was a strip of Bosnian (i.e., Austro-Hungarian) territory linking Serbia with Montenegro which could serve a corridor for the construction of the Adriatic railway line. James Whitehead, the British Minister in Belgrade, reported that this proposed compensation would only cover some 800 square miles – out of the 20,000 square miles which Austria-Hungary had gained through annexation.[125] A physical link between Serbia and Montenegro, however, was anathema to Austria-Hungary.

Milovanović's alternative to territorial compensation was 'Bosnian Autonomy'. He meant by this not just administrative autonomy, but rather political or 'international-political' as he called it, which would give Bosnia the right to regulate independently its relations with Serbia and Montenegro.[126] These demands, whether territorial or political, were never likely to be seriously considered at the Ballhausplatz, and Milovanović knew it. What was realistic, however, was that a conference of the Great Powers would be staged to address the fallout from Vienna's illegal action. Such a conference could conceivably bring some benefits to Serbia. Following the annexation, quite a few chancelleries in Europe were anticipating the possibility of some kind of new Congress of Berlin. It was even speculated that this would take place in Rome. But Aehrenthal would only go to such a conference provided the annexation was accepted beforehand as a *fait accompli*. So he refused to discuss the annexation (*'indiscutable'*, he said), and he was equally against territorial or political compensations. At most, he might consider some economic concessions to Serbia.[127]

That same month of October, Milovanović organized a three-pronged action. Stojan Novaković, the former Prime Minister, was sent to Constantinople to negotiate a military convention with Turkey, though after many weeks it became clear that nothing would come of this because the Turks had decided not go to war against Bulgaria and to negotiate their own deal with Vienna. Also in October, Milovanović sent Crown Prince George, accompanied by Pašić, to St Petersburg, while he himself embarked on a West European tour to plead Serbia's case. He should not perhaps have bothered with the Crown Prince, a problematic young man. The Russian Empress was succinct about him, and in English: '... as for the Crown Prince, I am afraid that his case is a hopeless one'.[128] And so it was: in 1909, after he had beaten his valet to death, he was made to renounce all his rights to the succession in favour of Alexander, his younger brother. It was in any event Pašić, with his Russian contacts and good standing at the Russian Court, who mattered on this visit. What emerged from it was that Russia supported Serbia's demand for territorial compensation in theory only, and even this level of support was at best half-hearted. Izvolsky, moreover, was cagey about whether or not he would recognize the annexation. One thing, however, was quite clear: Russia would not fight. As the Tsar put it to Pašić on 30 October: 'Russia cannot wage war at the moment'.[129] By 6 November Pašić had essentially given up on his Russian friends, informing Belgrade that Russia was reluctant to pursue 'a firm foreign policy', and advising that the Serbian Army should get ready – 'just in case'.[130]

Indeed, the likelihood of armed conflict seemed very high. Serbia mobilized its first reserve, while Austria-Hungary poured reinforcements into Bosnia-Herzegovina and Dalmatia. Simić reported from Vienna as the crisis began that Aehrenthal was irked against Serbia and 'ready for anything'.[131] In this war psychosis the Serbian Government moved the state archive to the southern city of Niš.[132] After the initial 16 million dinars approved in October, further war credits were voted through by the Serbian Assembly in December. The third prong of the diplomatic offensive, Milovanović himself, though averse to war, nevertheless warned

Foreign Secretary Grey, at their meeting on 28 October in London, that Serbia would be preparing itself to fight. War was 'inevitable', he insisted, if Serbia's demands for territorial compensation were not satisfied. Grey did promise him Britain's support for territorial compensation ('so long as Russia maintained it', he said), but made it very clear that Britain could not be expected to 'push matters to the point of provoking a conflict'.[133] Only days before, in Berlin, Milovanović had been told by Wilhelm von Schoen, the State Secretary for Foreign Affairs, that Germany stood 'completely' behind Austria-Hungary.[134] In Rome, Tittoni informed his old friend Milovanović that, while Italy had much sympathy for Serbia, it was 'not ready for war'.[135] If there was to be conflict, it seemed clear that Serbia would have to fight it alone.

Serbian historiography pertaining to the Bosnian annexation crisis has repeatedly stressed that, if nothing else, Milovanović had during his West European peregrinations succeeded in placing the Serbian question on 'the agenda of Europe'. But this is a rose-coloured perspective. Even relatively friendly countries could not wait to get Serbia off the European agenda. As the crisis dragged on into 1909, what was worrying the foreign ministries in London, Paris and St Petersburg was the increasingly likely prospect that Austria-Hungary would decide to crush Serbia militarily, thereby creating the risk of a wider war. The French were the first to lose their nerve, and late in February 1909 they complained to Izvolsky about the Serbian insistence on territorial compensations which, in their view, 'are difficult to justify'.[136] Izvolsky, too, in a major turnabout, now urged Serbia to abandon territorial claims because, he insisted, they 'must lead to an armed conflict with Austria'.[137] The Serbs were at this point quite resigned about the Russians. 'No reasoning here', Popović wrote from St Petersburg, 'can overcome the fear of war, which has been the key to the whole conduct of the Russian Government since the beginning of the crisis.'[138]

Concurrently with Izvolsky's urgings from St Petersburg, the Foreign Office in London was also advising Belgrade to drop its demands for territorial compensation.[139] Keen to end the Balkan wrangle, Britain had two months previously suggested to Aehrenthal that he make Turkey 'a generous pecuniary offer' to compensate it for the loss of sovereign right over Bosnia-Herzegovina.[140] On 26 February, only a day or so before Serbia began to be pressed into abandoning its territorial claims, Vienna and the Sublime Porte finalized a deal whereby the latter would receive two and a half million Turkish pounds. This settlement with Turkey was a major boost for Aehrenthal. Having flagrantly violated international law by the act of annexation, he now began to lay down the law on a new relationship between great and small Powers. This became evident despite Belgrade surprisingly agreeing, in a note presented to the Powers on 10 March, not to claim from Austria-Hungary 'any compensations, whether territorial, political or economic'. The note had been drafted by Izvolsky and it repre-sented, needless to say, a massive climb-down by Serbia.[141] Sergeyev, the Russian Minister in Belgrade, reported that Milovanović was able to get his colleagues on board 'only with the greatest difficulty'.[142] Yet the Serbian note was still not good enough for Aehrenthal. For he wanted to force the Government in Belgrade to be dealing directly with Vienna, instead of addressing itself to all the Great Powers. Moreover, the Serbs had in their note of 10 March declared that the annexation of Bosnia-Herzegovina was 'a European question' to be settled by the Powers – in other words, they had still not recognized the annexation. Having himself recently reached agreement with Turkey, Aehrenthal now insisted that Serbia acknowledge the annexation as a settled matter 'no longer open to discussion'.[143]

This was a moment of profound crisis, when it looked as if diplomacy could easily give way to warfare. In the previous few weeks the Foreign Ministry in Belgrade had been receiving alarming reports about Austro-Hungarian military preparations on Serbia's borders. On 21 February the Russian Military Attaché in Vienna even predicted to Simić the date of the Austro-Hungarian attack as being between 1st and 3rd of March.[144] Although no attack was launched, Milovanović had every reason to be concerned since he also heard from St Petersburg that Austria-Hungary was amassing troops towards Russia.[145] For the time being, however, he remained defiant. On 17 March, in a circular to the Serbian legations abroad, Milovanović still maintained that Serbia could not give up its national aspirations, 'nor can it abase itself by playing the role of Austria-Hungary's assistant in speedily and successfully solving the Bosnian question'.[146]

Very soon, however, a major change occured. The Serbs had known for a long time that Izvolsky was of little use to them. He confirmed this most emphatically on 10 March when he said that Russia would not go to war even if Serbia were occupied by Austria-Hungary.[147] But at least he was still giving assurances that Russia would not recognize the annexation. On 4 March, for example, Popović reported him as declaring that he would 'never put his signature to it'.[148] On 11 March, however, Count Berchtold, the Austro-Hungarian Ambassador in St Petersburg, walked into Izvolsky's office, looked him in the eye and informed him that if Russia did not act to make the Serbs recognize the annexation, Aehrenthal would reveal to Belgrade, and possibly also to London and Paris, the contents of the Austro-Russian exchanges from the summer of 1908 which had preceded the annexation. As he looked back at Berchtold, Izvolsky must have felt that his own duplicity had finally exploded in his face: he could no longer oppose the annexation which he had done so much to facilitate. Certainly, the blackmail had the desired effect on the Russian Foreign Minister who, Berchtold reported, appeared 'eminently taken aback'.[149]

Things now moved rapidly. In his desperation, Izvolsky turned for help
to the Germans, asking Chancellor Bülow to extricate him from his 'very
painful situation'.[150] Berlin had played second fiddle to Vienna from the
beginning of the crisis, but this was an opportunity to take the initiative.
Izvolsky was told that Germany wished to bring about 'a clear situation'.
What this meant was that the Powers would recognize the annexation and
the proposed conference would merely register this fact – 'or it would not
take place at all'.[151] Izvolsky, in his reply of 20 March, accepted that the
Powers should recognize the annexation through an exchange of notes,
but he would still not 'exclude the necessity of the meeting of a European
conference'.[152] Now it so happened that State Secretary von Schoen was
not well at this time, and the German Foreign Office was being run by
Alfred von Kiderlen-Wächter, an energetic diplomat who 'thought of
himself as a second Bismarck'. No more keen on Balkan entanglements
than his hero, he thought it would be just too stupid (*trop bête*) to have a
European war because of 'those pigs, the Serbs'.[153] But as for the Russians,
he had an aversion to Izvolsky.[154] It was Kiderlen who now drafted on
Chancellor Bülow's behalf the famous *ja oder nein* de facto ultimatum to
Russia. Dated 21 March, it instructed Count Pourtalès, the German
Ambassador in St Petersburg, to clarify with Izvolsky whether Russia
would declare, 'without any reservation', its formal agreement to the
annexation. Germany expected 'a precise answer – yes or no; we shall have
to consider any evasive, conditional or unclear answer as a *refusal.*' As for
the question of a conference, that was a separate matter and subject to 'an
exchange of views among the Powers'.[155]

The collapse in St Petersburg was total. In its reply of 23 March Russia
gave 'unconditional assent' to the German *démarche.*[156] Izvolsky had thus
dragged himself and his country into a humiliating surrender. But it was
worse than that. On 24 March Popović reported to Belgrade on the sudden
importance of the German Ambassador in St Petersburg: 'Izvolsky does
practically nothing without prior agreement with him'.[157] The Russian *volte
face* infuriated Britain, which was still refusing to recognize the annexation,
and was the only Power genuinely concerned that an Austro-Hungarian
diplomatic victory over Serbia should not expose the latter to subsequent
bullying. In the circumstances, however, Foreign Secretary Grey joined the
other Powers in the effort to persuade Belgrade that the game was up. The
Serbian Government, indeed, decided on 30 March to give way, submitting
on the following day a *pro memoria*, every detail of which had been dictated
by Aehrenthal. Not only did this document recognize the annexation, it
also emphasized 'changing the course' of Serbia's policy towards Austria-
Hungary and promised to maintain good neighbourly relations.[158]

The British had attempted to moderate the final text in Serbia's favour,
but Aehrenthal would have none of it, secure as he was of Izvolsky's

backing. Sir Charles Hardinge, Permanent Under-Secretary at the Foreign Office, complained bitterly about Izvolsky's subservient conduct towards Aehrenthal in the drafting of the *pro memoria* which Belgrade would be required to sign on the dotted line.[159] Soon after Russia's capitulation to Germany, Popović mentioned to Sir Arthur Nicolson, the British Ambassador in St Petersburg, that Izvolsky was justifying his policy as having been motivated by his desire to help Serbia. Nicolson 'laughed' and commented: 'That's nice of him.'[160]

The Serbo-Bulgarian Alliance

In annexing Bosnia-Herzegovina and – with a little help from Berlin – diplomatically defeating all opposition in Europe, Baron Aehrenthal certainly did a great deal to rescue the ailing prestige of the Habsburg Empire. In August 1909, Emperor Franz Joseph duly made him a Count. Shortly before the conclusion of the crisis, however, the Foreign Minister himself predicted that his victory would be an empty one. 'What's the use', he complained to the German Ambassador, 'if the existing antagonisms between Austria-Hungary and Serbia are now bridged over by patched up, basically worthless Serbian declarations'. There would be, he thought, no definitive stability on the south-eastern borders of the Monarchy, and one would still, in a few years' time, have to march into Serbia. That is why, indeed, he had 'silently' hoped until the last moment that 'England' or Serbia would do something to wreck the ongoing diplomatic effort.[161] It is interesting that he had supplied Friedjung with forged documents about 'Great Serbian' activities precisely because he thought war was just round the corner. But when push came to shove he could not quite summon up the courage to provoke one.

War or no war, the year 1909 in Austro-Serbian relations suggested, perhaps for the first time, that any armed conflict with Serbia would also serve the cause of domestic Habsburg politics. The annexation of Bosnia-Herzegovina represented a step in the direction of imperial consolidation and little independent, protesting Serbia had thus been sucked into the internal affairs of its large neighbour. The idea was simple: revitalization at home through military success abroad. Thus the Austrian-Bohemian statesman Count Clam-Martinic argued, in March 1909, for a military solution to the Serbian question on 'internal grounds'.[162] As will be seen, the same clamour for war against Serbia as a means of resolving in-house issues of the Empire would be much in evidence among imperial elites in 1912-1914.

Belgrade did try to improve relations with its powerful neighbour soon after the Bosnian crisis. However, when, in November 1909, Milovanović came to Vienna hoping for a 'fundamental change' in Austria-Hungary's policy towards Serbia, Aehrenthal was non-committal. Like Pašić before

him, Milovanović had assumed that he might, in some *quid pro quo* negotiations, get Habsburg backing for Serbian interests in Macedonia. Aehrenthal's refusal to even consider the matter left Milovanović 'fully in the dark
about Austria's intentions'.[163]

In retrospect, 1909 would have been a very favourable moment for
Austria-Hungary to strike. Russia was still in bad shape, and Britain and
France quite determined not to be dragged into an Austro-Serbian quarrel;
before the Balkan Wars (1912-1913), Serbia was a small country with less
than three million inhabitants; moreover, the Bosnian Serbs and Muslims
were docile. Furthermore, it was perfectly understood in Berlin that
Austria-Hungary had to be backed or it would be lost as an ally. Also, at
this time (March 1909), Franz Ferdinand not only approved of military
preparations, he actually wanted to take command of any operation against
Serbia.[164] But the person who would have been the most glad to give
Aehrenthal a war against the Serbs was Conrad von Hötzendorf, the Chief
of the General Staff. When it did not happen, Conrad concluded that the
Habsburg Empire could no longer be saved. 'You will see', he announced
prophetically to his assistant Theodor Zeynek, 'in ten years the Monarchy
will be reduced to the size of Switzerland.'[165]

It was not a scenario which Aehrenthal would live to see. The most
important event which took place during the remainder of his life was the
Italo-Turkish war over Tripoli, which began in September 1911 when Italy
invaded this North African possession of Turkey's. Three years earlier,
while preparing the Bosnian annexation, Aehrenthal had hinted to Tittoni
that Austria-Hungary stood 'in obligation' towards Italy with regard to
Tripoli.[166] Little did he anticipate at the time that he was encouraging the
Italians to start a war that would lead to a fundamental weakening of the
Habsburg position in the Balkans. When Italo-Turkish hostilities commenced, and the Italian Navy engaged some Turkish torpedo boats off the
coast of Albania, he was suddenly rather upset at the prospect that the
conflict would not stay localized and that it could threaten the Balkan *status
quo*.[167] Not that he was concerned about maintaining Balkan peace, he just
did not wish to see the regional situation develop beyond his control.

Aehrenthal's fears were entirely justified. Almost as soon as Italy and
Turkey began fighting, Balkan politicians naturally saw new, attractive
possibilities. However, they also feared Vienna's intentions, and understood
that no Balkan country could take proper advantage of the new situation
if it acted alone. The initial overture for an alliance of Balkan states came
in the end from Bulgaria. Here, apart from King Ferdinand (who was
actually 'Tsar' Ferdinand, as the Bulgarian language has no word for 'King'),
the chief actors were now Stojan Danev, the President of the National
Assembly, and Ivan Gueshoff, the Prime Minister and Minister for Foreign
Affairs. Significantly, both men represented the Russophile current in

Bulgarian politics. No one, however, expected Russia to be more than a diplomatic Great Power protector of the interests of small Slavic nations in the Balkans. Any fighting would have to be done by the Balkan states themselves. Danev and Gueshoff realized that, in practical terms, only an alliance with old rival Serbia could generate enough force to stand a chance against either of the two likely enemies: the Ottoman Empire or the Habsburg Empire. It should perhaps be emphasized here that the agenda of the Balkan League of 1912 was not connected exclusively with plans to divide up Turkey-in-Europe: fears about Vienna's intentions in the region also played a role.

Indeed, Habsburg predatory instincts were very much on the minds of the Bulgarians. Danev was on 30 September already suggesting to the Serbian Chargé d'Affaires in Sofia that Serbia and Bulgaria should start talking. What made him want to talk was the Austrian threat: 'If Austria-Hungary intends to descend down to Sanjak', he said, 'she will not stop there. Inevitably, she would have to continue on the road to Salonika'.[168] Salonika, of course, was very much a Bulgarian objective. Gueshoff was similarly concerned about Aehernthal's plans. 'Aehrenthal', he told Spalajković who had become the Serbian Minister in Sofia, 'wants to create an anti-Slav state in the Balkans. Austria is working to establish a great, autonomous Albania which would encompass the greater part both of Old Serbia and Macedonia, as well as Epirus. Austria wants to reach Salonika, that I know for sure.'[169] In Serbia, where Milovanović had remained the Foreign Minister and had also in June 1911 become the Prime Minister, such thinking was well received. In September Milovanović, fearing just such an Austro-Hungarian thrust, decided to impress on Nicholas Hartwig, the Russian Minister in Belgrade, the need for a Serbo-Bulgarian agreement, 'with Russia as its witness and guarantor'. Hartwig agreed and promised to report to St Petersburg.[170] The Russians did not need a great deal of convincing. 'Our policy', declared Anatole Nekludov, the Russian Minister in Sofia, 'is to arrive at an agreement between Serbia and Bulgaria.'[171] Such a new Balkan configuration was intended by the Russians to be a force for maintaining the status quo or, to be more precise, preserving it from Austrian encroachments. Nekludov did gloat, however, that 'Austria-Hungary can allow anything in the Balkans except an agreement between Serbia and Bulgaria'.[172]

It goes without saying that any agreement between Serbia and Bulgaria had to tackle their differences over Macedonia. Early in October 1911 the Bulgarian emissary Dimitri Rizov approached Milovanović, asking for an alliance, the need for which he assessed as 'urgent', and expressed for the first time Bulgaria's willingness to divide Macedonia with the Serbs, as part of which Bulgaria would be willing to sign over the city of Skopje to Serbia in advance. Milovanović could hardly believe what he was hearing. But there was a snag: a large strip of Macedonia, from the town of Veles south of Skopje, and extending all the way to the northern shores of Lake Ohrid, was claimed by both sides. So Rizov suggested that the matter could be resolved later, through the arbitration of the Russian Tsar. Milovanović accepted this formula partly because he believed that Russia 'feels a moral obligation towards us after the annexation of Bosnia and Herzegovina'.[173]

Both the Bulgarians and the Serbians were in a hurry. 'Everyone in Bulgaria', a Bulgarian diplomat told the Serbs, 'wants a war' – against Turkey, that is.[174] The Serbs, for their part, were increasingly apprehensive about Austria's next move. Milovanović had been told by Fairfax Cartwright, the British Ambassador in Vienna, that Austria-Hungary was rapidly preparing the ground for an autonomous Albania, 'which will be the first manifestation of her conquest of Balkan land up to Salonika'. The Serbian Prime Minister had no doubt that an alliance with Bulgaria was an urgent necessity. 'Without an agreement with Bulgaria', he wrote, 'Serbia stands helpless *vis-à-vis* Austria-Hungary.' Without it, he inferred dramatically, 'Serbia will have no choice but to lay down its arms before Austria-Hungary and become her servant.'[175]

Adding to the sense of urgency in Belgrade was unease about the increasing likelihood of an improvement in Austro-Russian relations, particularly after Aehrenthal's death in February 1912.[176] There was no time to lose: on 13 March Serbia and Bulgaria signed their friendship alliance and a secret annex in which they undertook, in the event of a territorial dispute, to accept the Tsar's decision on the matter. Two months later, on 12 May, the parties also concluded a military convention which, on paper, contained some very serious provisions: if Austria-Hungary attacked Serbia, Bulgaria was bound to help Serbia with at least 200,000 troops; and if Romania attacked Bulgaria, Serbia was obliged to send at least 100,000 troops to Bulgaria's aid.[177] Although it seems quite doubtful that King Ferdinand of Bulgaria would have consented to fighting Austria-Hungary, it has been seen how wary, ever since Mürzsteg, Bulgaria's politicians had been of Vienna's designs on Salonika and Macedonia.[178] Prime Minister Danev, for example, was terrified at the prospect that Serbia could drift into Austria-Hungary's orbit.[179] It is also a fact that in November 1912, after the Balkan War had begun, Bulgaria let the Russians know in no uncertain terms that it would 'go to war' on behalf of Serbia's right to acquire a port on the Adriatic.[180]

Be that as it may, it became increasingly clear that the Balkan Alliance would actually be fighting the Turks. Towards the end of May the Serbo-Bulgarian combination was in effect joined by Greece when the latter signed a treaty with Bulgaria. Russia, it should perhaps be emphasized, had done nothing to encourage Greece's accession to the Balkan League. Serbia and Greece were still conducting their separate negotiations right up to the outbreak of the Balkan War in October 1912. Greece, like Bulgaria, wanted to fight Turkey. So too did Montenegro. In August, Montenegro and Bulgaria concluded a military convention verbally by which, typically, Montenegro would receive a Bulgarian financial subsidy. Finally, on 6 October, an alliance was concluded between Montenegro and Serbia.[181] Whatever other plans Milovanović may have had, a coalition had emerged by the autumn of 1912 which intended to destroy the remnants of Turkish power in Europe. The Russians were powerless to stop it. Sergey Sazonov, who had in 1910 succeeded the hapless Izvolsky as Foreign Minister, was initially delighted by the Serbo-Bulgarian Alliance, believing that it gave Russia control over Serbia and Bulgaria and provided at the same time a bulwark against Austria-Hungary.[182] When, however, he saw that the Alliance plan was to wage a war against Turkey, his attitude quickly changed and he started issuing threats, both to Bulgaria and Serbia. Gueshoff, the Bulgarian Prime Minister, was quite amused by this, asking Nekludov, the Russian Minister in Sofia, whether Sazonov's intent to stop an action in the Balkans would involve enlisting the help of Austria or Romania.[183]

It has to be said that Russian input into the creation of the Balkan League has in any case been vastly exaggerated in the relevant historiography. In particular, historians like to focus on Hartwig, the Russian Minister in Belgrade, and portray him as some kind of viceroy of Serbia and the ultimate arbiter of the country's domestic and foreign policies. 'Hartwig', according to Christopher Clark, 'pushed the Serbs to form an offensive alliance with Bulgaria against the Ottoman Empire'.[184] In fact, as has been seen, the initiative for an alliance came from Bulgaria. Milovanović, who was far more concerned about the Austrians than the Turks, accepted the overtures from Sofia and merely sought Hartwig's, that is, Russia's, retrospective blessing – since neither the Serbs nor the Bulgarians needed to be 'pushed' into a mutually beneficial alliance. This has been well understood by some. In 1965 the American historian Edward Thaden argued convincingly that the Balkan alliance 'was originally conceived by the Balkan peoples themselves, not Russia'. Thaden also pointed out that, after 1908, Russia was consistently avoiding military and diplomatic adventures in the region. 'This caution', Thaden noted, 'is at odds with the common view that the tsarist government repeatedly and energetically tried to create a Balkan alliance directed against either Turkey or Austria-Hungary.'[185]

Milovan Milovanović was not able to see the fruits of his work because he died on 1 July 1912. A Serbo-Bulgarian alliance had been his *idée fixe*.[186] Nikola Pašić, his party colleague and greatest rival on the Serbian political scene, had taken part in the negotiations with Rizov and initially been quite unbending in his maximalist territorial demands in Macedonia, before reluctantly accepting Russian arbitration. As Dimitrije Đorđević has argued, Pašić did not trust the Russians. Đorđević also suggests, however, that though Pašić was not strong enough to dethrone Milovanović at this time, he wished nevertheless to make known his opposition to a deal with the Bulgarians over Macedonia.[187] In Western literature Milovanović is invariably portrayed as a 'moderate' and Pašić as a 'nationalist'. This distinction, it may be suggested, is not particularly helpful. In 2000, Richard Hall wrote in his study of the Balkan Wars: 'Six weeks after his [Milovanović's] death, the ardent nationalist Nikola Paschich became prime minister and minister for foreign affairs.'[188] In his recent and more widely read book, Christopher Clark writes: 'Six weeks after his [Milovanović's] death, the ardent nationalist Pašić took office as prime minister and minister for foreign affairs'.[189] What is noticeable here is not just the remarkable coincidence in expression of these two historians, but also their insistence on Pašić being an 'ardent nationalist'. Had it been left to Pašić, it is doubtful that Serbia and Bulgaria would have reached agreement. Had it not been for Milovanović, there would probably have been no Serbo-Bulgarian Alliance which was to enable Serbia to achieve that most eminent of nationalist goals: territorial aggrandizement.

Reluctant Bear: Russia, Serbia and the Balkan Wars

With Milovanović dead, it was then Pašić who led Serbia through both the Balkan Wars. Although he had only grudgingly accepted Milovanović's legacy of an alliance with Bulgaria, he was nevertheless prepared to exploit it for what it was worth. This meant joining Bulgaria in a war against Turkey. The Serbian Army, no less than popular sentiment, was impatient for action, especially after the Bosnian annexation crisis. Even if he had wanted to, Pašić would not have been able to resist the pressures to go to war. Keen as he was for Serbia to gain as much as possible in Macedonia, he was perhaps even more anxious to extend Serbia's territory in order to secure an Adriatic commercial port on the Albanian coast. Serbian documents for 1907 and 1908 reveal his absolute dedication to Serbia's Adriatic Railway Project, a desire which had nothing to do with Macedonia. Strategically, an Adriatic port looked like the more important objective. Now, in 1912, came the opportunity.

By now, however, Pašić's famous Russophilia – if it had ever existed – had evidently deserted him. In September 1912, he argued against informing Hartwig, the Russian Minister in Belgrade, about the Serbo-Bulgarian resolve to go to war, for 'he would be duty-bound to report this to his Government, and the latter would do everything to prevent us'.[190] So much for Pašić's reliance on Russia and his confidence in its policies. In the light of the July Crisis of 1914, it is important to understand how the Russian position was really perceived by Pašić and his diplomats in the run up to the Balkan Wars. Their perspective, it should be noted, did not reflect some minor tactical concern *vis-à-vis* Russia. Milovanović, as seen above, believed in a Serbo-Russian partnership only if Russia had powerful friends, such as France. Pašić's outlook was similar, but he also made sweeping proposals about what should be done if allies did not deliver. After once again becoming Prime Minister and Foreign Minister, he wrote to his friend Vesnić, the Serbian Minister in Paris: 'We have gone along with Russia and the Triple Entente, and should they be unable to restrain Austria and Germany, it would then be better if we come to an agreement with our enemies as soon as possible since we would be getting no help from where we were expecting it.'[191]

Serbian thinking in 1912 about ditching Russia and the Triple Entente has hardly figured in the voluminous literature on the Balkan Wars. But then, the prevalent assumption among historians continues to be that Serbia was a Russian client state.[192] This assumption flies in the face of the fact that ill-disposed Russian diplomacy made such a Serbian alignment with Russia and the Triple Entente impossible. For little had changed since 1908-1909. At the end of September 1912 Sazonov flew into a hysterical rage at a meeting in London with Grujić, the Serbian Minister. The Russian Minister repeatedly described as 'mindless' the intentions of Serbia and Bulgaria to attack Turkey, warning that Austria would 'immediately' attack Serbia. He added for good measure that Serbia and Bulgaria wanted to 'hoodwink' Russia with their Alliance, insisting that Russia needed 'at least ten years' to complete its economic, financial and military renaissance.[193] His unambiguous message was that the South Slavs had no basis on which to ask for help from St Petersburg – nor any basis on which to expect it. In the British Foreign Office the view was expressed that the Russians 'have got themselves into an equivocal position in the Balkans, for, having made the marriage, they are compelled to urge divorce for fear of its first fruits'.[194]

In Sofia, the Serbian Minister Spalajković, appalled by Russia's pressure to prevent the outbreak of war against Turkey, told his British colleague that the Serbs and Bulgarians were thoroughly 'embittered' by Russia and the Triple Alliance.[195] In St Petersburg, Popović concluded: 'It seems to me that current Russian diplomacy, out of weakness and fear of war, takes greater care about the interests of other states than about its own and that of Slavonic states.'[196] In Paris, Russia's great friend and ally the French Prime Minister and Foreign Minister Raymond Poincaré tried to intimidate Vesnić by pointing out the danger from Austria. The Serbian Minister calmly suggested that, since Europe was so convinced of Austria-Hungary's omnipotence, it should not be surprised if Serbia were some day to seek an arrangement with Vienna. Vesnić added, for good measure, that the Triple Entente would never achieve anything if it worked only to avoid war.[197]

In fact, there was initially no danger whatsover that Austria-Hungary would attack, because it was anticipating that Turkey would easily defeat

Serbia. Austria-Hungary, according to the Vienna correspondent of *The Times*, 'welcomed the prospect of a Balkan war in which the Turks were expected to smash Greece and, particularly, Serbia, however successful the Bulgarians might be'.[198] But it is also true that the Austrians had been caught napping: their Military Attachés in Belgrade and Constantinople were on holiday as the war approached.[199] And so was Stephan von Ugron, the Austro-Hungarian Minister in Belgrade. A messenger reached him in Hungary where he was shooting, and gave him the news: 'There is a mobilization in Serbia. Belgrade is full of soldiers.' Whereupon Ugron protested: 'That is not possible. For I would have known something about it.'[200]

He was soon to know much more. Keen to be the first in the field, tiny Montenegro declared war on Turkey on 8 October 1912 – King Nicholas had apparently sensed that he could make money by 'bearing' the Viennese and other stock markets.[201] Serbia, Bulgaria and Greece declared war on 17 October. Most observers had expected the German-organized Turkish Army to defeat the forces of the Balkan states. But the latter recorded one stunning victory after another over the Turkish adversary. 'To no class', Winston Churchill wrote, 'had the crushing Turkish defeats come with more surprise than to the military experts.'[202] The Bulgarian Army, having smashed the Turks in Thrace, soon stood at the gates of Constantinople. Meanwhile the Serbian Army, having brushed aside the Turks in Macedonia, stood on the shores of the Adriatic Sea. The Russians were appalled at the prospect of the Bulgarians taking Constantinople. Sazonov had previously asserted that Russia's only interest in the Balkans was to ensure that the Straits remained in the Turkish hands.[203] But in Vienna they were equally horrified at the sight of the Serbian Army in the port of Durazzo. Supported by Italy, Austria-Hungary led a sustained drive to force Serbia away from the Albanian coast. The London Conference of the Ambassadors was set up, a main aim of which was to bring into existence an independent state of Albania, which duly took place at the end of July 1913.

The First Balkan War had experienced a temporary standstill from 3 December 1912, the date an armistice was declared on all the fronts, with the Turks still holding Edirne, besieged by the Bulgarians, Yanina, besieged by the Greeks, and Scutari, besieged by the Montenegrins. Hostilities resumed following the Young Turk coup in January 1913. Yanina and Edirne surrendered in March, but Scutari held on. The Montenegrins finally took the town late in April, but an Austrian-led international action coerced them to withdraw early in May. Earlier, in January 1913, Austria-Hungary had undertaken a series of mobilization measures designed to put pressure on the Serbs to withdraw from Northern Albania. The First Balkan War was finally ended by the so-called London Settlement on 30 May 1913. But the Second Balkan War quickly followed only a month later. Forced away from the Adriatic by Austria-Hungary, the Serbs decided they should keep most of their gains in Macedonia instead, proposing to the Bulgarians a revision of their treaty concerning the division of this land. While it is true that the Serbian Army had helped the Bulgarians to take the city of Edirne, that the Bulgarians had made massive gains in the east, and that they had done nothing to help the Serbs in Macedonia, the Serbian position constituted a clear-cut breach of the Serbo-Bulgarian Treaty of 1912. Without waiting for any arbitration by the Russian Tsar, at the end of June 1913 the Bulgarians attacked the Serbs as well as the Greeks who, for their part, had in the previous campaign taken the contested port of Salonika. The attack was repelled, however, and now both Romania and Turkey joined this war against Bulgaria, ensuring its complete defeat. The Treaty of Bucharest (August 1913), while excluding Turkey as a participant, was an all-Balkan affair which formalized the new order on the peninsula without the patronage of the Great Powers. Serbia emerged from these conflicts with its territory almost doubled. At the same time it was bitterly antagonized by the Austro-Hungarian action which had denied it its principal war aim of a port on the Adriatic.

This was indeed Austria's objective. Once it was understood in Vienna that Serbia would emerge victorious from the Balkan conflict, the chief concern was to keep it away from the Adriatic Sea. The official reason that Austro-Hungarian diplomacy put forward for objecting to the Serbian presence in northern Albania was that it was inhabited by Albanians. Borrowing the slogan that had been current in the Balkans for several decades, Vienna argued for 'The Balkans to the Balkan peoples!' This was of course somewhat cynical coming from a Power that had, back in 1878, conquered Bosnia-Herzegovina with blood and iron and which, thirty years later, annexed the provinces against the wishes of four fifths of the local population. Besides, the nationality principle was not exactly a holy precept in the Habsburg Monarchy. To the official argument was added a kind of semi-official one opposing a Serbian port on the Adriatic. Such a port, it was suggested, could be turned into a stronghold of the Russian Navy. This, however, was a fanciful fable dreamt up at the Ballhausplatz. Russia's naval construction programme was proceeding very slowly before 1914. In the Baltic Sea, the Russians faced the vastly superior German Navy, while any meaningful operations from the Black Sea required the physical possession of at least one side of the Straits. Any kind of Russian naval threat in the Mediterranean was years away.[204]

The real reasons for wishing to throw the Serbs out of the Adriatic area in Albania were the old ones, those formulated by Gołuchowski: building a Vienna-controlled Albanian entity as a non-Slav barrier to Serbia's expansion; preventing Serbia from securing its commercial independence by denying it an Adriatic port; and generally keeping Serbia as small and as weak as possible so that it would lack any power of attraction for the South

Slavs of the Monarchy. Admittedly, there were those in the Habsburg elite who took a somewhat different view. Thus General Moritz von Auffenberg, who was until December 1912 the Joint War Minister, believed that it would have been better to leave the Serbs with the Albanians, for 'the Albanian morsel' was quite tough and it might take Serbia ten to twenty years to digest it.[205] Interestingly, Aehrenthal's successor Count Berchtold did initially want to talk to the Serbs. Early in November 1912 he sent Professor Josef Redlich to Belgrade to explore the possibility of an Austro-Serbian customs union – which would, of course, coupled perhaps with a military convention, have been the easiest way to control Serbia. General Oskar Potiorek, who in 1911 became the *Landeschef* in Bosnia-Herzegovina, was to advocate similar ideas. But Berchtold made clear in advance to Redlich that the Albanian region had to be preserved and that the Serbs would not receive a port, that is to say, would be getting nothing from Berchtold. Redlich was thus predictably unsuccessful in Belgrade. Pašić thought a customs union achievable at some point in future, but he insisted on the Adriatic port. Significantly, however, he offered to Redlich that Serbia would not trespass the Bosnian line. Conditions, he said, could be different in a hundred years' time when perhaps the whole of Europe would constitute a 'single realm'.[206] This was not the first time that Pašić had promised the Austrians Serbia's passivity towards Bosnia, and it would not be the last time, either. But no one was impressed in Vienna.

In Budapest, on the other hand, they did not even want to hear about a customs union with Serbia. As he stopped in the Hungarian capital on his way back from Belgrade, Redlich found that no less a person than Tisza was against it.[207] This Austro-Hungarian comedy about an accommodation with Serbia then quickly gave way to war planning against Serbia. For quite apart from the Serbian Army's march towards the Adriatic, the impermissible joining of the Serbian and Montenegrin forces in the Sanjak had already taken place. Decades of Austro-Hungarian policy towards Serbia had been shattered in just a few weeks. To the Austro-Hungarian military, according to Germany's Military Attaché in Vienna, it was now a question of maintaining one's prestige as a Great Power. 'We are ashamed', is what the officers were saying at the General Staff Headquarters. 'We have begun to feel ashamed of ourselves', was how the mandarins felt at the Ballhausplatz.[208]

Inevitably, however, there existed a degree of concern in Vienna about a possible Russian intervention in the event of a war against an otherwise completely unprotected Serbia.[209] Such fears were unfounded. Although a vocal military party existed at St Petersburg, Russia was in fact not ready or willing to fight. On 8 November Sazonov informed Popović that Russia and France would not go to war over Serbia's port on the Adriatic. And he was furious when he heard that Miloš Bogićević, the Serbian Chargé d'Affaires in Berlin, had talked to diplomats there about the certainty of

Russian military support for Serbia.[210] On 23 November, when the Tsar wanted the precautionary measures of reinforcing Russia's frontier against Austria-Hungary to be considered, the Russian Prime Minister Vladimir Kokovtsov famously disagreed even with this, for 'mobilization remained a mobilization, to be countered by our adversaries with actual war'. Sazonov, also present at this meeting, fully backed Kokovtsov.[211] Christopher Clark's assertion that in the winter crisis of 1912-1913 'Sazonov supported a policy of confrontation with Austria' is a most puzzling endeavour to ignore evidence to the contrary.[212] At the height of the Albanian crisis in December 1912 Sazonov told Popović that, if it were up to him, he would give Serbia the whole of Albania, but that if Serbia wanted to go to war with Austria-Hungary on the matter, it alone would have to bear the consequences as Russia would not help it.[213] Early in January 1913, the Russian Foreign Minister declared point blank to an amazed Popović that 'Russia has no interests in the Balkans'.[214]

On the other hand, the Austro-Hungarian Chief of General Staff *Feldmarschalleutnant* Blasius Schemua (in fact Blaž Žemva, a Slovene name) was demanding war against Serbia and assessing, on 9 November, that the chances of success were not unfavourable even if the Monarchy had to go to war alone.[215] But as his *incognito* visit to Berlin on 22 November testifies, it was still important to him to know what the German ally would do. And although both the Kaiser and the Chief of the General Staff Helmuth von Moltke promised him Germany's support 'under any circumstances', this pledge proved to be quite misleading. As in 1909, Kiderlen-Wächter, who had in the meantime become Foreign Secretary, once again acted decisively in the European arena. Upset at this time that the Ballhausplatz had been giving him almost no information about its intentions, and keen also to maintain good relations with Britain, he arranged for the publication in a semi-official German newspaper of an article whose main message was that the Serbian-Albanian question would be tackled jointly by the Great Powers. In Vienna, this had the effect of a 'cold shower'.[216]

Very soon, however, Serbia definitively reconsidered its own position on Albania. On 1 December 1912 Pašić called a meeting of leaders of all political parties to tell them that, in the light of advice from St Petersburg, Serbia could no longer insist on a direct outlet to the Adriatic.[217] The absence of Russian support had indeed led to this climb-down. Meeting with Foreign Secretary Grey, the French Ambassador Paul Cambon commented that this was good news, showing that 'Russia had been acting energetically'.[218] The Serbian Government's decision, however, was not made public in order to avoid a humiliating capitulation. The crisis thus continued, but Pašić had found an exit strategy in accepting the mediation of the Great Powers.[219] On 20 December the Serbian Chargé d'Affaires handed to Grey an *aide-mémoire* in which the Serbian Government formally

consented to the question of its access to the sea being decided by
the Ambassadors' Conference convening in London.[220] The focus of the
wrangle between Austria-Hungary and Serbia now shifted to the question
of Albania's northern frontiers. In particular, the Serbs were keen to retain
the town of Đakovica in Kosovo which Vienna wanted to allocate to the
future autonomous Albania. Once again, Belgrade found little support in
St Petersburg. 'We are not', Sazonov told Popović, 'going to war over
Đakovica'. Pašić was appalled, and minuted: 'We now realize, with horror,
that Russia cannot defend us.'[221]

Franz Ferdinand in the Fighting Camp

Meanwhile, in Austria-Hungary during this period, one of the chief advocates of the war option was Franz Ferdinand. On 18 November 1912, he
instructed Colonel Bardolff, the head of his military chancellery, to hand
the Chief of Staff Schemua a most warlike memorandum calling for an
immediate reinforcement of the Galician front against Russia and the
sending of a 'sharp protest note' to Serbia and Montenegro, demanding, *inter
alia*, that their troops clear out of the Albanian region. Should the protest
note be ignored after forty-eight hours, the memorandum demanded an
'ultimatum' and 'mobilization'.[222] Franz Ferdinand, too, was in Germany
around the time of Schemua's visit (on 22 and 23 November) and spoke to
Wilhelm II who assured him that, 'if the prestige of Austria-Hungary was
at stake', he would 'not be afraid of a world war' and was ready to enter
into a conflict with the Triple Entente. For his part the Archduke insisted
that Austria-Hungary would 'under no circumstances' allow Serbia an Adriatic port. After the meeting, a rather delighted Archduke sent a telegram
back to Vienna about the 'splendid' meeting he had had with the Kaiser.[223]

Soon thereafter, on 24 November, the Archduke received some counsel
that must have dampened his enthusiasm for war somewhat. His trusted
adviser Heinrich Lammasch had submitted to him a memorandum on
Balkan affairs which, as Lammasch himself knew, 'did not at that time
correspond to the disposition of the Heir to the Throne'. The memorandum argued that a fully independent Albania was not in Austria-Hungary's
interest as it would actually gravitate to Italy; that a Serbian port at
Durazzo presented 'no particular danger'; that a war against Serbia would
turn the South Slav population against the Monarchy; and that an annexation of Serbia would simply add a further two million hostile South Slavs
to those already in the Monarchy, creating thereby 'a new Lombardy'.[224]

It would appear that Lammasch was successful at least in slowly persuading Franz Ferdinand that annexing Serbia would probably be a blunder.
For by February 1913 the Archduke was declaring that he did not wish to
take 'a single plum tree' from Serbia.[225] This statement has been endlessly

paraded by those historians wishing to present the Archduke as a man of peace. The problem with their presentations is that the context is always lacking. When Russia did not look particularly threatening, he would invariably leave open the possibility of military action against Serbia in order, as he put it to Conrad towards the end of that same month of February 1913, 'to chastise it'.[226] And in November-December 1912, despite Lammasch's memorandum, he was certainly still hoping for a military solution to the crisis. For this reason he was at that point intent on bringing back Conrad to replace Schemua as Chief of General Staff. Conrad had previously fallen out with Aehrenthal for advocating a preventive war against Italy. This got him the sack early in December 1911.[227] In addition, his affair with Gina von Reininghaus, a married woman and mother of six, did not exactly endear him to the Kaiser. But in the crisis atmosphere prevailing in Austria-Hungary towards the end of 1912, Franz Ferdinand managed to restore him to his old post on 12 December: if there were to be a war effort, it had better be led by the man who had talked so much about it.

A day before, in the Belvedere Palace, Berchtold had an audience with the Archduke who told him that things did 'not look good in the Balkans', and that timely military preparations with regard to Serbia and Montenegro had to be made instead of waiting until it was 'too late'. There was a danger, he continued, not only of losing influence in Albania, but also of losing 'our South Slav lands'. As things stood, Austria-Hungary could count on Germany, and Russia would not move in any case because it was 'not fully prepared'. In vain did Berchtold point out that the German Government did not share Kaiser Wilhelm's fighting élan and, moreover, that it had stated pretty clearly it would not participate in an aggressive policy. The two men were then chauffeured off to a crisis meeting called by Franz Joseph at Schönbrunn Palace. Among others, the Joint Finance Minister Biliński and the Austrian Prime Minister Count Karl Stürgkh were also there. The Emperor spoke in favour of keeping the peace, the Archduke in favour of making military preparations, and Berchtold to express his misgivings about adopting a combative policy at a time when the London Ambassadors' Conference was about to start its work. The other ministers supported Berchtold. Franz Ferdinand was 'obviously not a little taken aback' at being overruled.[228]

The Archduke again showed his bellicose inclination a few months later, at the height of the Scutari crisis in April 1913. The Montenegrins had shown gross inefficiency in their previous attempts to take the town. The Serbian Army was now helping them – with artillery, troops and even aircraft.[229] To Austria-Hungary, Scutari was hugely important not only as a vital part of a future Albania, but also as its main Catholic stronghold. In March the Russians agreed that the city should go to Albania. The forces of Montenegro and Serbia nevertheless kept up the siege. Early in April a naval demonstration arranged by the Great Powers took place off the coast of Montenegro: three Austro-Hungarian warships, two Italian, and one each from France, Britain and Germany. Sazonov could not quite bring himself to send a Russian warship. At this time, a demonstration in St Petersburg, numbering some 50,000, demanded: 'Scutari to Montenegro, the Holy Cross on St Sophia'.[230] On 10 April Pašić decided, 'with wrath and pain in the soul', to withdraw the Serbian forces.[231] The Montenegrins, however, continued the fight defiantly. By this time starvation and disease had considerably weakened the defenders inside the city. It finally surrendered on 24 April after King Nicholas and Essad Pasha, the Albanian commander of the Turkish forces, had made an inglorious arrangement involving money.

A Serbian intelligence report from Vienna passed on an assessment from circles hostile to Franz Ferdinand that the fall of Scutari was primarily his defeat.[232] Certainly, as General von Auffenberg recalled, the Archduke had been a leading force behind the Albanian project.[233] On 26 April, immediately after the Montenegrins had entered Scutari, he went to see Franz Joseph to argue in favour of 'the great action [*der großen Aktion*]' because what was at stake now was 'the prestige of the Throne'.[234] Significantly, the Russians had in March agreed with the Austrians that Scutari should not go to Montenegro. Against the background of this Great Power consensus, Franz Ferdinand felt quite free to advocate war. In those days after the fall of the city he was 'constantly conferring' with Conrad and War Minister Krobatin.[235]

Berchtold, too, was in a warlike mood. At a Joint Ministerial Council meeting on 2 May he told those present that Montenegro would probably be giving Serbia the nearby port of San Giovanni di Medua, and then went so far as to state that Scutari was the 'key to our Balkan programme' – there could be no viable Albania without it.[236] Given that the fall of Scutari was being taken so tragically at the highest levels of Habsburg hierarchy, there was now no doubt that Austria-Hungary would intervene militarily. The only dilemma faced by Vienna's decision-makers was whether such an operation would be restricted to ejecting the Montenegrins from Scutari, or whether it should be a much wider one, aimed at both Montenegro and Serbia. The latter course was unsurprisingly favoured by Conrad.[237] It seems, however, that this view was widely shared at the time. According to Biliński, there had existed in Vienna, in April and May 1913, a firm resolve to make the proposed campaign against Montenegro the starting point for a final reckoning with Serbia.[238] The only reason that nothing came of these Austro-Hungarian war plans was that the Montenegrins, under tremendous pressure, announced their withdrawal on 5 May.

The Scutari commotion demonstrated once again Franz Ferdinand's readiness to back military action. Significantly for July 1914, this was also true of Berchtold. For all his caution and hesitancy, the Foreign Minister was in the last analysis a closet advocate of violent solutions. His many conversations with Conrad, recorded in the latter's extensive memoirs, reveal a frustrated figure who, for example, complained in March 1913 that he had support only in military circles.[239] Nor had Berchtold's diplomacy sought to exploit opportunities to improve relations with Serbia. When, for example, the Czech politician Tomáš Masaryk, a member of the Austrian Parliament, visited Belgrade and talked to Pašić on 10 December about Austro-Serbian relations, Pašić begged him to convey to Berchtold that, while Serbia wished to retain economic and political independence, it also wished 'most friendly' relations with Austria; that Serbia would accept an autonomous Albania, but wished a harbour and a connecting strip of territory to it, even the narrowest one; that the harbour would never be fortified and 'all possible guarantees' could be given, including the Serbian Government's commitment not to place the harbour at the disposal of any other Power; and that, finally, Serbia was ready to extend to Austria-Hungary first consideration in all economic matters, including railway materials and all the necessary loans to be obtained exclusively from Austria-Hungary. To indicate his seriousness, Pašić offered to come to Vienna and discuss these questions with Berchtold.[240] Masaryk duly informed Berchtold, but the latter 'would not hear of a reconciliation'. The Czech statesman later recalled: 'More than ever did I become convinced of the superficiality and worthlessness of the Viennese Balkan policy.'[241]

Important figures in Vienna, such as Joseph Baernreither and Ottokar Czernin, were highly disappointed by Berchtold's refusal to talk to Pašić, and they told him so.[242] Joint Finance Minister Biliński, responsible for Bosnia-Herzegovina, soon adopted a similar view and took up the matter with the Foreign Minister. To his astonishment, the latter told him that Masaryk's motive in mediating had been to 'earn a provision'.[243] Berchtold's biographer Hugo Hantsch has defended the Count's decision to ignore the overture by Pašić on the grounds that Serbia was offering 'no concrete concessions' and that Pašić was hardly a reliable partner.[244] But Pašić's suggestions could hardly have been more conciliatory and indeed concrete given that Austria-Hungary had since 1906 been doing its best to strangulate Serbia economically. Also, if Pašić was such an unreliable partner, why had Berchtold only recently sent Professor Redlich to Belgrade to offer a far-reaching customs union which would tie Serbia economically to the Monarchy? This proposal had not been accepted by Pašić. The truth was, as Berchtold himself told the German Ambassador on 6 December, Serbia was not willingly going to make itself economically dependent on Austria.[245] In that sense, there was indeed nothing that Berchtold could discuss with Pašić.

The Strange Case of the Disappearing Consul

Equally foreboding was the behaviour of the Ballhausplatz in the so-called 'Prochaska Affair' of November-December 1912. This, in fact, is perhaps the most famous episode in Austro-Serbian relations during the Balkan Wars, a protracted incident that contributed enormously to the war psychosis in Vienna. Oskar Prochaska was a Czech and a Habsburg loyalist in the Austro-Hungarian consular service. At the outbreak of the First Balkan War he was serving in Turkey as Consul in the town of Prizren, Kosovo. Late October saw the town captured by the Serbian 3rd Army. On 6 November Crown Prince Alexander, who was commanding the 1st Army, sent a telegram to Pašić, informing him that the Austro-Hungarian Consul in Prizren had been inciting the Turks and Albanians against the Serbian troops, encouraging them not to surrender. The Crown Prince requested that the Consul should leave Prizren, otherwise he might find himself in difficulties. Pašić then contacted Minister Simić in Vienna, to suggest that the Ballhausplatz recall its Consul so as to avoid 'unpleasant incidents'.[246] On 8 November Simić duly acted at the Ballhausplatz on the basis of this instruction.[247]

Prochaska, for sure, was no Serbophile. In one of his reports, which the Serbian Army seized at a local post office, he wrote of the Serbs as 'savages'. His job, according to the Belgrade correspondent of the Viennese *Telegraphen-Korrespondenz Burau*, was to organize and set the Muslim and Catholic Albanians against the Serbian population.[248] It also happened that he was on very bad terms with the Russian Consul in Prizren, Nicholas Emilianov. The latter may have painted a very negative picture of the Austro-Hungarian Consul to General Božidar Janković, the Commander of the 3rd Army. Janković, in turn, was quite upset at the fact that Prochaska was ignoring his presence in town and being 'openly hostile'.[249] The General posted sentries at the Austro-Hungarian Consulate – which really irritated Prochaska, though it should be mentioned that the Consul's freedom of movement was in no way restricted by this, and nor had people been prevented from entering and leaving the Consulate. Finally, on 17 November Prochaska actually visited the General to announce that he wanted to leave for Skopje because, he alleged, restrictions had been placed on him. His wish was granted. On 24 November, the Consul, his mistress, and the personnel of the Consulate, left the town.[250] As his carriage drove out, flanked by a military escort, some children ran behind him, he later reported, throwing 'tin pots, copper kettles, sticks, stones, cabbages and similar'.[251] It would appear that the son of the Russian Consul was the ringleader.[252]

However, apart from '*dieser Skandal*', as Prochaska wrote, he had not been subjected to any mishandling or physical abuse. Yet in the meantime he had been pronounced probably dead by the Austrian and Hungarian press. How had this come about? Being in the middle of the war zone, the town of Prizren found its communications with the rest of the world cut off during those days in November, so Prochaska was unable to report to Vienna. Following Simić's demand for the Consul's recall, the Ballhausplatz wanted to send its own man to investigate the matter. A consular official, Theodor Edl, was picked and permission requested from the Serbian Government for his journey to Prizren. Belgrade agreed straight away, but because the matter also involved the military authorities, it took five days before the formalities were cleared.[253] It was during this period, when all contact with Prochaska had been broken, that the press in Austria-Hungary engaged in an orgy of anti-Serb hysteria. Depending on which newspaper one read, Prochaska had been abducted, castrated or even killed by the Serbs. The *Reichspost*, which often reflected the views of Franz Ferdinand's circle, claimed on 19 November that Prochaska, while not dead, had suffered 'bayonet stabs'. In its leading article (entitled 'How much longer...') the paper commented: 'If the Monarchy now allows its patience to be perceived as weakness, then soon every goat herder in the whole of the Balkans will have the audacity to preach war against Austria-Hungary.'[254]

Prochaska reached Skopje on 25 November – the Ballhausplatz was immediately informed by its Consul in the city.[255] In his brilliant short study of the Prochaska affair, Robert Kann draws attention to 26 November as a rather important date in the whole story – for that was the day when, at the very latest, the Ballhausplatz found out that Prochaska was alive and well. And yet, it was not until 17 December that the Foreign Ministry's Press Bureau finally issued a *communiqué* declaring the whole matter to be closed as all the rumours about Prochaska's fate were 'completely unfounded'. The statement even praised the Serbian Government for having been 'perfectly accommodating' towards the emissary Theodor Edl.[256] General astonishment greeted this announcement. For three weeks the Ballhausplatz had kept the great Austro-Hungarian public – and the world at large – in complete ignorance of the true facts in the affair of the Consul Prochaska. Admittedly, on 6 December Berchtold did 'confidentially' inform the German Ambassador that there was 'nothing very incriminating' for Serbia in the Prochaska case. But the same German Ambassador found it necessary to complain to Berchtold a full week later about the continued warmongering in the Austrian and Hungarian press. Germany, of course, had a vital interest in being fully acquainted with the Balkan aims of its Austro-Hungarian ally. Yet shortly before his death at the end of December 1912, Kiderlen-Wächter protested that Vienna had kept Berlin in the dark about what exactly it knew and intended to do in the Prochaska affair.[257]

There can be no doubt that a kind of war fever was being encouraged and promoted by Habsburg official circles. Robert Kann points to Kálmán von Kanya, the head of the Press Bureau at the Ballhausplatz, as the direct instigator of the Prochaska-related press campaign.[258] When the Austro-Hungarian diplomat Baron Julius Szilassy expressed his misgivings to von Kanya about the effective concealment of the facts of the Prochaska affair, he was told that 'the whole country wants war'.[259] It is almost certain, however, that Conrad too, as well as the circle around Franz Ferdinand, had also made patriotic contributions to this exercise.[260] Berchtold's role remains unclear. His biographer Hugo Hantsch absolutely glosses over the whole episode.[261] The Foreign Minister made no reply when he was asked, later, whether the Prochaska affair had been manipulated so as to serve eventually 'as the excuse for a conflict with Serbia'. And he tried to justify not clearing things up on the implausible grounds that 'the matter had been overlooked, in the pressure of other business'.[262]

Christopher Clark describes the Prochaska affair as 'a modest but inept exercise in media manipulation'.[263] In fact, it was neither modest nor inept: for weeks it kept the whole of Europe on edge. It was a highly successful ploy to precipitate war, which only turned into a farce in December 1912 when, lacking German support, Vienna finally decided against the military solution. Clark also writes that Prochaska had been 'illegally detained' by the Serbs. Yet the Consul had not been detained at any point. Had he been, he would most certainly have mentioned it in his exhaustive report to Vienna of 26 November.[264] Such details, surely, are easier to check today than they were in 1912. In the immediate aftermath of the admission by the Ballhausplatz on 17 December that no harm had come to Prochaska, the witty, sarcastic Viennese provided their own assessment of the whole affair. Because so much had in the previous weeks been made of the Consul's testicles, they would now go to restaurants and enthusiastically order 'omelette à la Prochaska'.[265]

8

Quo vadis Austria?

The Shock of Balkan Wars

IN OCTOBER 1912, the frustration was enormous in Vienna as the Ottoman Empire began to suffer defeats at the hands of its Balkan neighbours. 'We have been Turkophile for decades', Berchtold fretted, 'and we have nothing to show for it!'[1] Towards the end of the year, with the spectacular collapse of Turkey-in-Europe, the writing was on the wall for Great Austrians like Berchtold. The fact that an alliance of small Balkan countries, consisting of Bulgaria, Serbia, Greece and Montenegro, had managed to vanquish the Ottoman armies in such convincing manner caused consternation among these imperial patriots. One of them, Colonel Alexander Brosch, formerly the head of Franz Ferdinand's military chancellery, wrote privately on New Year's Eve: 'We have abdicated as a Great Power because our Eastern policy, the only area of pursuit left to us for the future, is now blocked.'[2] This did not yet amount to an obituary for the Empire, though there were certainly those who felt it was the right time to prognosticate a bleak future. Thus in early January, 1913, Hans Schlitter confided to his diary: 'In circa four to five years – maybe even earlier – the war will break out between us and Russia/Serbia, but the constellation will not be as favourable as it is today.' Bemoaning the fact that the Dual Monarchy, having been expelled from Italy and Germany, had now also lost influence in the Balkans, Schlitter knew exactly at which door to lay the blame. 'When are we going to throw Dualism on to the scrap heap', he asked, 'for we may thank it for all the misfortunes in our internal and foreign policies?!' A month or so later he was thrown into despair again as he had heard of the conviction prevailing among officers that the Army was 'incapable'.[3]

Yet it was precisely the military option which, increasingly, came to be seen in both Vienna and Budapest as the panacea for what the Monarchy perceived as its Balkan predicament. As was shown in chapter seven, Franz Ferdinand had in November and December 1912 led a determined, if ultimately unsuccessful, initiative to launch a military campaign against Serbia. He had even brought back Conrad in anticipation of such an enter-prise. Conrad's first memorandum to the Archduke, on being re-appointed, emphasized that: 'Serbia as an independent state was and is a danger for the Monarchy.'[4] In those days, other members of the Habsburg military establishment queued up to call for war against Serbia. In December 1912, just after his resignation as Joint War Minister, General Auffenberg told Heinrich Friedjung that he had proposed the summer of 1914 as the time to carry out an attack on Serbia – by which time Austria-Hungary would be in a better state of military readiness. He added: 'It does not matter where the pretext for war comes from.'[5] General Alexander Krobatin, Auffenberg's successor as War Minister, was less patient. At a dinner in Vienna's Hotel Sacher at the end of January 1913, he thundered that a war of conquest against Serbia should already be waged in spring in order to secure the southern borders.[6]

What is striking about some of these bellicose calls is the domestic political rationale frequently attached to them. Thus Krobatin also told Josef Redlich that such a war was required in order to overcome the inter-nal problems of the Empire, and Conrad admitted to Redlich that, without a war, an improvement in the internal position would be very difficult to achieve.[7] Prominent members of the civilian elite shared this view. The historian Alfred Přibram, as well as Michael Hainisch, who was to become the first President of the Austrian Republic, desired war against Serbia 'on the grounds of internal politics'.[8] According to the Austro-Hungarian diplomat Baron Szilassy, there existed in Vienna at this time a large party in favour of 'smashing or annexing' Serbia, some members of which declared to him that this course provided the only 'salvation' for the Monarchy.[9] And after the war had broken out in July 1914, Berchtold declared that it represented the best solution in the light of the Monarchy's 'dismal position'.[10]

In the wake of the Balkan Wars the Serbian issue had for many in the Habsburg establishment fully coalesced with the Monarchy's South Slav issue. As Berchtold put it in August 1913: 'the South Slav or, better said, the Serbian question'.[11] Even a liberal German-Austrian politician like Joseph Baernreither would contemplate a war against Serbia – and not just that. When, on a visit to Berlin in March 1913, he was asked by the German Foreign Secretary von Jagow what Austria-Hungary could hope to achieve in the event of a successful war against Serbia, Baernreither replied that Serbia would then 'have to be annexed'.[12] In other words, defeating Serbia would never be enough: it would have to cease to exist in order not to constitute a threat.

General Oskar Potiorek, the Governor of Bosnia-Herzegovina, was also quite explicit on this point. In a major memorandum from spring 1913 he argued that concessions to the South Slavs of the Monarchy might not provide a permanent solution to the South Slav problem. Only a 'radical measure' would deliver such a result: 'the erasure of Serbia from the map'.[13] Indeed, by this time the top brass of the Austro-Hungarian military were consistently advocating doing away with Serbia once and for all. In November 1912 Colonel August Urbański, the head of the *Evidenzbüro* (the military intelligence), suggested marching into Serbia with four army corps and then, 'hopefully', annexing the land permanently.[14] It was high time, as Conrad told Berchtold in September 1913, to create order down south ('*endlich Ordnung zu machen*'). Berchtold then asked Conrad whether, after a successful war, Serbia should be reduced in size. 'No', replied the Chief of General Staff, 'it should be annexed to the Monarchy'.[15] In October, in a Joint Ministerial Council meeting he argued for Serbia's future relationship with the Monarchy to be based on the model of Bavaria's status within the German *Reich*.[16] Otto Gellinek, the Austro-Hungarian Military Attaché in Belgrade, admitted in January 1914 that the only hope for improving relations with Serbia lay through the 'annihilation of the existing Kingdom as an independent state'.[17]

There was, in 1913-1914, no end of official and unofficial proposals by Austro-Hungarian military men, diplomats and politicians for liquidating Serbia in this or that manner. The emergence of an enlarged, triumphant Serbia was seen as a catastrophic development, a decisive step towards the formation of a Great Serbia – obviously at the expense of Austria-Hungary. Some of the results of the First Balkan War, especially the establishment of contiguous territory between Serbia and Montenegro, were bad enough; however, the subsequent defeat of Bulgaria, Serbia's sole regional rival, made the situation look infinitely worse. At the same time Habsburg officialdom was obsessed about the international reputation of the Monarchy. Emanuel Urbas, a Ballhausplatz mandarin, wrote later that the doubling of Serbia's size, against the publicly announced wishes of the Government in Vienna, had entailed 'such a great loss of prestige' that it was doubtful whether the Empire could in the long term retain the status of a Great Power.[18] No wonder that towards the end of the Second Balkan War Redlich remarked in his diary on the 'deep depression' reigning in Vienna's official circles.[19]

By contrast to Conrad and others, Franz Ferdinand's friend Ottokar Czernin did not wish to annex Serbia. But, from his post as the Austro-Hungarian Minister in Bucharest, he also argued in March 1914 that 'we must do away with the present-day Serbia'; Serbia was an 'appendix' – to be operated upon and removed; and while it was undesirable to have even more Serbs within the Monarchy, Serbia could be reduced to a minimum by giving some of its territories to Bulgaria, Greece and Albania. This could be done following a successful '*Feldzug* [military campaign]'.[20] Count Karl

Stürgkh, the Austrian Prime Minister, had already argued along these lines, except that he had gone a step further, saying in October 1913 that any Austro-Hungarian mobilization would have to be followed by a 'spectacular' military success against Serbia which, once defeated, should, he thought, be reduced in size and its dynasty replaced with a 'reliable' one.[21] Thus, whatever the specifics of various quick fix ideas for dealing with the Serbian menace, they all presupposed a fighting *modus operandi*.

What is extraordinary, however, is the sheer abandon of these proposals for dealing with Serbia. In his short 1928 memoir Berchtold's *chef de cabinet* Alexander Hoyos spelled out candidly the basic thinking of the Habsburg establishment since the end of the Balkan Wars: 'From the day of the conclusion of the peace in Bucharest', he wrote, 'it was clear to all well-informed Austrian and Hungarian statesmen that it must come to a world war unless something happened to offset the sinister impact of that peace.'[22] The 'sinister impact' of the Treaty of Bucharest, however, was actually the apocalyptic interpretation it generated in Vienna – the blasé contemplation there of 'a world war' to undo a local Treaty. Franz Joseph himself, according to Géza von Daruváry who had worked in his cabinet, had since the Balkan War of 1912 been increasingly convinced that it would come to a war with Serbia.[23] He was, to be sure, slightly more concerned than others in his own risk assessment, but equally appalled by the outcome of the Balkan Wars. In November 1913 he told Ottokar Czernin: 'The Peace of Bucharest is untenable, and we are heading for a new war. God grant that it remains confined to the Balkans.'[24]

Brigadier-General Christopher Thomson, who had worked for the Balkan Service of the British War Office, spent some time in Vienna during the spring of 1914 and recorded what he had heard being said about Serbia: 'Many serious people frankly expressed the hope that some incident would occur which would provide a pretext for taking military action against the Serbs.'[25] Conrad, who never bothered to seek such a pretext and was always quick to berate the pusillanimity of his superiors for blocking his proposed war path, noted a significant change after the Balkan Wars: 'Now, when years had passed away and the chances had decreased appreciably, it began all of a sudden to dawn on the hitherto disapproving statesmen of Austria-Hungary that the Serbian question had to be solved, and that it could hardly be solved by means other than war.'[26] János Forgách, the *éminence grise* at the Ballhausplatz, told the German Foreign Secretary in September 1913 that Serbia was 'our deadly enemy'. Early in October he declared himself in favour of 'a violent intervention' against Serbia.[27] The same view was held by Hoyos, who advocated a march on Belgrade.[28] Berchtold himself, generally seen by historians as a highly cautious Foreign Minister, in fact never excluded the war option. 'We are, after all, still here', he told Redlich early in November 1912, 'and if necessary we shall wage war to preserve our integrity in political and economic policy respects.'[29] As shown in the previous chapter, by early in July 1913 he had already begun to toy with the idea of dealing militarily with the Serbs. By August he was convinced that the differences with Serbia were 'lasting and insurmountable' and that only a 'successful military campaign' by Austria-Hungary might convince the Serbian people to give up the dreams of a Greater Serbia and become loyal to the Monarchy.[30] In November he was even more categorical: the solution to the South Slav question existing between the Monarchy and the Serbian state could only be a 'violent' one, and there could be 'no talk [*davon kann … keine Rede sein*]' that the enmity could, in time, be allayed or made good.[31]

Of course, in the days following the assassination of Franz Ferdinand no options other than the military one were even contemplated in Vienna and Berchtold was a leading hawk. The Sarajevo assassination, however, was hardly some kind of transformative eye opener since it merely reinforced the previous radical attitudes. Yet despite this, historian Alma Hannig, who has written a fair amount on Austro-Hungarian involvement in the Balkans, has recently drawn attention to the 'remarkable fact' that the Austro-Hungarian Balkan policy initiatives coming from the civil servants and diplomats of the Ballhausplatz 'did not contain aggressive war plans against Serbia'. There were, moreover, 'no war aims either'. The Austro-Hungarian plan, she contends, was really 'a typical plan of classical diplomacy, with the final objective of preserving the peace and status quo'.[32] What is in fact 'remarkable' about her assertions is that they fly in the face of the overwhelming evidence to the contrary. Habsburg civil servants and diplomats not only talked about military action against Serbia long before the Sarajevo assassination, they also had in mind, as has been seen, a very clear war aim: the destruction of Serbia as an independent state. It did not matter whether this was to be done by annexing Serbia or by making it harmless in some other way, for example by reducing its territory. Whatever the final political solution, such an aim could only be achieved by war, and there was certainly no room here for the peace-oriented 'classical diplomacy' posited by Alma Hannig.

By contrast, the renowned Austrian historian Fritz Fellner has commented that, after 1912, the servants of the great Habsburg state could envisage no other response to the danger represented by Serbia 'than a warlike action aiming at the total annihilation of this small state', and has seen such thinking as reflecting a lack of confidence in the Monarchy's 'own capacity for a constructive internal policy or a coherent foreign policy'.[33] Fellner's referral in the same breath to the Dual Monarchy's internal and foreign policies underlines the complexity of its predicament. But what did the Serbian part of that predicament really mean in 1913-1914? How did relations between Austria-Hungary and Serbia develop in the aftermath of the Balkan Wars? Was the Sarajevo assassination just some latest, shocking act of unmitigated Serbian hostility?

Surprisingly perhaps, historians investigating Austria-Hungary's pre-occupations during 1913-1914 have scarcely dealt with these questions, focusing, instead, on the wider regional picture, and concentrating on what has been seen as the crumbling of its diplomatic and political standing in South-Eastern Europe. The keynote themes here are Romania's apparent drift away from the Triple Alliance and towards the Triple Entente; the inherent difficulties of any attempt to draw Bulgaria closer to the Triple Alliance; the ill-starred birth of Austria-Hungary's protégé state of Albania; the nightmarish prospect of a union between Serbia and Montenegro; and, increasingly during the first six months of 1914, the spectre of a new, Russian-backed alliance of Balkan states to be unleashed – so the Ballhaus-platz would argue – against the Habsburg Monarchy. The nature of the relationship between Austria-Hungary and Serbia after the Balkan Wars is examined further below. As for the regional issues elsewhere, they certainly presented the Monarchy with uncertainties and potential complications, some of which – especially Romania – would, on the eve of the 1914 July Crisis, appear to loom on the Balkan horizon even larger than Serbia.

Local Difficulties: Romania, Bulgaria and Albania

The greatest uncertainty for the Ballhausplatz did, indeed, concern Romania. Essentially a Francophile country, Romania was on paper part and parcel of the Triple Alliance, having signed a treaty with Austria-Hungary in 1883, which Germany joined soon thereafter with a statement of accession.[34] This treaty, engineered by the German Chancellor Otto von Bismarck, obliged the parties to come to each other's assistance in the event of unprovoked attack (by Russia, though this had not been spelled out). The treaty had been kept secret, and was only known on the Romanian side to the Hohenzollern King Carol and a few of his ministers. Yet although it was renewed as late as February 1913, the treaty was by this time hardly in tune with Romanian sentiments or, indeed, interests. Only the ageing Carol still seemed to provide some degree of comfort and assurance to Vienna, for he had remained, as Berchtold observed, 'a German from tip to toe'.[35]

Serious territorial or political issues existed between the Kingdom and all its neighbours except Serbia: with Russia, which had since 1878 been in possession of Bessarabia; with Austria-Hungary, which held Transylvania (Siebenbürgen) with its large Romanian population living under Magyar domination; and with Bulgaria, which after the First Balkan War looked as if it was going to be the dominant Balkan power, and against which Romania had had competing claims on Dobruja. Indeed Bulgaria was soon to become an actual foe. Significantly, however, public opinion in Romania had increasingly been turning against Austria-Hungary, for whom the advantage of having a treaty with Romania was obvious: it provided a most welcome degree of military assistance on the eastern flank in the event of a war with Russia. Remarkably, this did not stop Austria-Hungary from bullying Romania, against whom it waged a tariff war from 1886 after Romania had tried to protect its industry and agriculture. Ending only in 1891, its most enduring result was, according to Keith Hitchins, political: 'it reinforced the underlying hostility the majority of Rumanians felt for Austria-Hungary'.[36] The intolerant treatment meted out by Budapest to the Romanians of Hungary was the primary source of this hostility. Already in 1891 the '*Liga Culturală*' had been established in Bucharest with the aim of promoting cultural unity of all Romanians, but the political aim, of course, was national unification. At the top of the tree, King Carol (stemming from the Swabian and Catholic Hohenzollern-Sigmaringen dynasty) may have been pro-German and pro-Austrian, but he was certainly not pro-Hungarian and would warn Berlin and Vienna that Hungary's draconian 'Magyarisation' assimilation policy was eroding what little support existed in Romania for the Triple Alliance.[37]

The Balkan Wars provided additional grounds for Romania's alienation from the Monarchy. Romania was a neutral during the first phase of the conflict, but an increasingly nervous one in the wake of Bulgaria's successes in the First Balkan War. What really appalled the Romanian political establishment was Berchtold's more or less openly Bulgarophile policy. This inevitably reduced Vienna's capacity to uphold Romania's compensation claims – directed, as they were, against Bulgaria and concentrating on frontier rectification around the Southern Dobrujan town of Silistra. In the end, Romania obtained a much bigger slice of territory after it joined Serbia and Greece against Bulgaria in the Second Balkan War. Although the Romanian Army had advanced across the Danube into Bulgaria practically without firing a shot, its intervention had been militarily decisive and the final peace terms were dictated in Bucharest – without the participation, or rather, tutelage of the Great Powers. Suddenly, Romania emerged as the arbiter of the Balkans.

Germany supported the Treaty of Bucharest (10 August 1913) in part because of Kaiser Wilhelm's sympathy for King Carol (and his pronounced antipathy for King Ferdinand of Bulgaria), but also because of his Greek brother-in-law, King Constantine. Austria-Hungary, on the other hand, was a horrified bystander in this re-structuring of South Eastern Europe. Suspicions soon arose elsewhere that Ballhausplatz wished to see a revision of the Treaty of Bucharest – a revision in favour of Bulgaria. At the end of August Berchtold complained bitterly about the Treaty to the Serbian Minister in Vienna.[38] Of course, what he wanted was to keep Bulgaria big and Serbia small. Romania, however, had its own agenda. King Carol later related to Mihailo Ristić, the Serbian Minister in Bucharest, that he had during the Balkan Wars been receiving messages from Vienna about how it was not in Austria-Hungary's interests to have a Great Serbia in its neighbourhood. His reply, he told Ristić, was that, 'on the other hand, it was not in Romania's interests to have a Great Bulgaria in its neighbourhood.' In trying to be friendly to both Romania and Bulgaria, the King said, Austria-Hungary wanted to 'sit on two chairs'.[39]

The liberal Austro-German politician Joseph Baernreither was among those who were convinced that, in Romania, Berchtold's pro-Bulgarian policy 'cut the ground from under us'.[40] Ottokar Czernin's main point in his famous report to Berchtold from Bucharest, sent on 11 March 1914, was that the Austrian-Romanian alliance represented 'a worthless scrap of paper'.[41] Czernin, Austria-Hungary's Minister in Bucharest, was almost entirely right: this alliance was effectively being kept alive solely by the aged Romanian King, who, while pursuing an independent Balkan policy, had remained personally attached to Vienna and Berlin. He was indeed the guarantor that a definite defection would not take place so long as he ruled. In March 1914, during his short stay in Vienna, Kaiser Wilhelm assured Berchtold of King Carol's loyalty, prompting the Foreign Minister in turn to send the following reply of reassurance to his rather sceptical Minister in Bucharest: 'King Carol feels himself fully the master of the situation, the Army obeys only him, and he is unswervingly determined to fulfil his obligations towards the Triple Alliance whenever it proves necessary.'[42]

Admittedly, the Balkan interests of Austria-Hungary and Romania had clashed significantly. Prominent Romanian politicians were quite happy at this turn of events, with Take Jonescu declaring, during a visit to Athens in November 1913, that Romania had freed itself of Austro-Hungarian influence.[43] Worsening relations had also led to some wild talk by Romanian officials. Thus Ballhausplatz learned about a statement ascribed to Romania's Consul-General in Budapest that 'Austria will only come to its senses when a Serbian-Romanian Army stands in front of Vienna.'[44] With Carol on the throne, however, there was not the remotest chance of the Romanians assailing Vienna, for Romania remained under a degree of Austro-Hungarian influence. In April 1914, Carol himself assured Czernin that, as long as he lived, Romania would never march against Austria-Hungary. 'After my death ...', the King said but did not continue – gesturing with his hand instead to suggest no one could know what would happen then.[45] And that indeed was the problem: Vienna could be reasonably confident of Romania's neutrality for the time being, but the political battle had been lost. The apparent reality that Romania and Serbia had become de facto allies added at the same time a massive dose of apprehension to the calculations at the Ballhausplatz: in a future war with Russia, Vienna might discover both Romania and Serbia on the opposing side. And as Conrad told Franz Joseph in October 1913, the Monarchy was militarily 'no match' against a coalition of Russia, Serbia and Romania.[46]

Should the crisis in Austro-Romanian relations be ascribed to foreign influences? In the literature about the immediate origins of the First World War much has been made of the visit paid by the Russian Tsar to King Carol at the Romanian port of Constanza on 14 June 1914. This event, certainly, can be seen as a continuation of the tremendous efforts being made at the time by Russian diplomacy (fully supported by France) to woo Romania away from Berlin and Vienna. Some historians, however, have gone further. Thus Christopher Clark sees the Constanza royal get-together as having led to no less than a 'restructuring of Balkan geopolitics'.[47] But that had already happened at the end of the Second Balkan War. The acknowledged expert Samuel Williamson, for his part, has contended that King Carol had 'assured' the Tsar that 'Bucharest would under no circumstances enter a war on Austria-Hungary's side'.[48] No evidence, however, exists that anything of the kind had actually been said. On the contrary, in his detailed internal report on the visit, Russia's Foreign Minister Sazonov, who had also been present, emphasized that Carol had 'not even once' mentioned Austria-Hungary. Having also talked to the Romanian Prime Minister Ionel Brătianu, Sazonov's overall impression was that, in the event of a war between Russia and Austria-Hungary, Romania would join the side that looked stronger.[49] Indeed this was also the view of Ottokar Czernin, Berchtold's or rather Franz Ferdinand's man in Bucharest, who reported in early April 1914 that there were two camps in Romania: a small Austrophile one around King Carol, and an opposing one which 'calculates quite differently'. The latter, Czernin thought, was convinced that a war between Austria-Hungary and Russia would break out sooner or later, and its tactics would be to wait first before joining the winning side – so as to take either Transylvania or Bessarabia.[50] In 1975 Paul Schroeder warned against attaching undue weight to the Constanza visit, for 'one should not really speak of a triumph of Russian diplomacy in Romania. Russia had not produced the Austro-Romanian break, only profited from a situation not of her making.' Schroeder also emphasized that Russia's final diplomatic goals in Romania had by no means been achieved by July 1914.[51]

That Romania would keep its options open had also been abundantly clear to Franz Ferdinand. In a letter to Berchtold, dated 12 April 1914, he wrote: 'The Romanians are realists in their policies; they want to have two irons in the fire and are always spying ahead to see whether in the distant future Bessarabia or Transylvania will fall into their lap.'[52] As is well known, the Archduke had played a crucial role in Czernin's appointment as

Minister in Romania. The idea behind it had as much to do with the Monarchy's internal politics as it had with attempting to improve relations with a neighbouring state: Czernin had been chosen precisely because he was known to hold, just like Franz Ferdinand, strong anti-Hungarian views, a fact which made him a palatable figure in Bucharest. At the same time a hope existed in Vienna that Budapest would finally make some concessions to the Romanians of Hungary. Indeed, Czernin, as he commenced his Romanian mission in October 1913, was himself convinced of this, assuring Take Jonescu that those concessions would be made 'whether Budapest liked it or not'. As Jonescu noted, however, it later became clear even to Czernin that such an idea about Magyar concessions amounted to 'an Arabian Nights' romance'.[53] In October 1913 the Hungarian Prime Minister Tisza did actually initiate talks with the local Romanians, but they had broken down by February 1914: for whereas he was ready to consider yielding on ecclesiastical, cultural and educational issues, Hungary's Romanians wished to extract administrative and political concessions leading to de facto autonomy. Tisza returned their proposals with the comment that the 'Magyar stomach cannot digest these.'[54] All of which, inevitably, led to a worsening of relations with Romania.

Paul Schroeder goes so far as to present the difficulties which Austria-Hungary had encountered in its alliance with Romania as the cardinal influence on its decision to go to war in July 1914. 'It was the loss of Romania', he writes, 'more than the assassination of Francis Ferdinand, which made the decisive difference for Austria between further postponement, living with the Serbian challenge and hoping somehow to outlive it, and the determination to settle the problem once and for all, at all costs.'[55] This sounds strange in light of the fact that, far from fawning over such an important country, Vienna and Budapest had in their different ways done a great deal to alienate it. To the extent, however, that Austria-Hungary perceived Romania's apparent defection from the Triple Alliance as yet another huge blow to its Balkan *Machtposition*, Schroeder is quite right to point it out as a factor in the Ballhausplatz calculations during the July Crisis. The famous Matscheko Memorandum of 24 June, to be discussed in chapter thirteen, was to tackle the subject of Romania at great length, but its assumption throughout would be that the country had indeed been lost.

Was Bulgaria a feasible alternative to Romania? The Ballhausplatz did not actually view the matter in those terms, for it wished to gain benefit from both countries, i.e., to build bridges with Bulgaria, while simultaneously retaining Romania within the orbit of the Triple Alliance. Already in March 1913 Berchtold was writing to his German colleague von Jagow that no sources of friction existed between Austria-Hungary and Bulgaria – on the contrary, there being many joint interests. 'Bulgaria', he was certain, 'represents the strongest and the most promising factor on the Balkan peninsula.'[56] Even the comprehensive drubbing suffered by Bulgaria in the Second Balkan War had not caused Berchtold to question the country's potential usefulness to Austria-Hungary. Thus, at the beginning of August, he assured his Ambassador in Berlin, Szögyény, that Bulgaria, despite recent defeats, would according to expert opinion recover quickly, and was militarily 'the most capable' among the Balkan states. What he wanted to see was a Balkan 'configuration' to prevent Serbia from pursuing, unimpeded, its Great Serbian plans. Bulgaria was 'a natural ally' that could serve as a counterweight to Serbia.[57] And that, of course, was what had fascinated Berchtold about Bulgaria: for Austria-Hungary was not the only power obsessed by Serbia. On the face of it, therefore, Vienna and Sofia seemed destined to waltz together. Certainly, the Russophobe Radoslavov Government was keen to enter into a formal political arrangement with Austria-Hungary. So was King Ferdinand. When, however, the latter came to Vienna in November 1913, he was told by Berchtold that an Austro-Bulgarian understanding was desirable, but that any road to it would need to pass across Romania.[58]

Here lay a massive problem: Berchtold's Balkan 'configuration' was based on the optimistic assumption that relations between Bucharest and Sofia would improve. But to King Ferdinand the Peace of Bucharest represented '*cette boucherie cruelle*', and he pointed out to Berchtold that Romania was 'cool and reserved' towards his own country.[59] A further fanciful premise in the Foreign Minister's scheme was that Germany could be persuaded to see the wisdom of incorporating Bulgaria within the Triple Alliance. A big problem here was that Kaiser Wilhelm II held the lowest possible opinion of the Bulgarian King, but there was certainly more to Austro-German differences than that. At the time the exchanges between Vienna and Berlin on Balkan policy resembled a dialogue of the deaf. Thus, at the beginning of November 1913, Ambassador Szögyény dined with Chancellor Bethmann Hollweg, who had been briefed by Wilhelm II about his recent visit to Vienna. Bethmann outlined to Szögyény the Kaiser's position on the Balkans: only through a reliance on Romania and Greece could the Slavic danger in the Balkans be successfully confronted, and such a policy could even lead to the establishment of a beneficial *modus vivendi* with Serbia. According to Bethmann, the Kaiser had received the impression that Berchtold shared this outlook.[60] But Berchtold, once the discussion was reported to him, made clear that he most certainly did not share anything of the kind. Reacting to Szögyény's post-dinner telegram immediately, almost furiously, he wired back to his Ambassador, asking him to emphasize the following to the German statesmen: that Greece was in an alliance with 'hostile' Serbia, and so a pact with Athens was at the very least 'premature'; that, in the light of the 'alarming' behaviour of Romania, the best thing for the Triple Alliance was to build a good relationship with Bulgaria; and that it was desirable, in the interests of both Austria-Hungary and Germany, for Bulgaria to reach an understanding with Turkey.[61]

Clearly, German and Austro-Hungarian Balkan policies had been any-thing but closely coordinated. In a further dispatch from Berlin, Szögyény reported Wilhelm II as emphasizing that the primary objective should be to cultivate the non-Slavic states of Romania and Greece, a combination which Serbia would then adhere to *'nolens volens'*. The Kaiser had claimed that Franz Ferdinand had endorsed his view – which may well have been the case given the Archduke's sympathy for Romania, as well as his detes-tation of Bulgaria's King Ferdinand.[62] But this was not the view of the Austro-Hungarian foreign office. Szögyény, at any rate, dutifully carried out Berchtold's instructions, meeting with Bethmann on 6 November and reciting to him the deductions of the Ballhausplatz about the Balkans – particularly with regard to Bulgaria. Bethmann, however, was totally unim-pressed. He had to, he said, 'again and always' point out that the alliance relationship with Romania necessitated 'great care' to be taken when considering relations with Bulgaria. His information from Romania was that the Bulgarians, who had only 'teeth-gnashingly' accepted the Peace of Bucharest, had already begun preparing themselves to extract a *revanche* by force of arms.[63]

Berchtold, on the other hand, kept hoping for a *rapprochement* between Romania and Bulgaria, explaining that only a Romania unhindered in the south would be able to fulfil its military obligations (*casus foederis*) to the Triple Alliance.[64] Hugo Hantsch considers that an alliance with Bul-garia was Berchtold's *'Herzenswunsch* [heart's desire]', for it would have provided a counterweight to Serbia.[65] But the Germans kept emphasizing that the Bulgarians could hardly wait to exact a 'bloody revenge' from Romania. At the same time, anticipating a future continental conflict and mindful of Serbia's military capability, they pestered Vienna to settle the existing differences with Belgrade.[66] Nevertheless, the Germans can hardly be blamed for this shambles by the Triple Alliance in the Balkans. For Berchtold was wanting the impossible: a miraculously faithful Romania, despite the Transylvanian problem, to help Austria-Hungary fight a war against Russia; and an allied Bulgaria, hopefully on friendly terms with Romania, to help against Serbia. It was an absurd wish, assuming a unity of interests where almost none existed. In practice, Bulgaria, which was actively seeking a formal arrangement with the Triple Alliance, was being kept at bay in order not to offend Romania, which was actively distancing itself from the Alliance. Berchtold himself recognized the problem when he admitted to Wilhelm II that trying to co-opt Bulgaria without affecting relations with Romania was a bit like 'squaring the circle'.[67] He was never to square that circle.

By contrast, Albania presented a very different problem for the Ballhausplatz. This was a country without settled frontiers, without a capital, without a central government and, until March 1914, without a ruler. Many observers at the time also believed that it was a country without a future. 'I do not think', Sir Arthur Nicolson wrote in 1913, 'that this somewhat artificial creation will have a very long life.'[68] The American journalist Herbert Adams Gibbons went to Albania in July 1913 and could not help observing that the place had neither a national spirit nor a national past. As for the aspirations of the Albanians, Gibbons remarked: 'What the Albanians really wanted, none could guess, much less they themselves!'[69] A British manual from 1916, prepared for the Admiralty and the War Office, described Albania as a state whose population, especially in the north, knew no such thing as government: 'Nothing like these North Albanian Highlanders has survived in Western Europe since the pacification of the Scottish Highlanders after 1745.'[70] Count Lützow, who visited Albania in spring of 1914 with a party of fellow Austrian aristocrats, described the conditions in the country as being not so much 'medieval, but rather downright Adamic'. Only someone like Cecil Rhodes, he opined, could maybe create something lasting there.[71] Berchtold, to be sure, was no Cecil Rhodes, yet Albania was in a sense his greatest success. For the decision by the London Ambassadors' Conference at the end of March 1913 to set up Albania as an independent state had blocked Serbia's access to the Adriatic, thus subverting its principal war aim of obtaining a sea port which had been seen as the key to commercial freedom. This, indeed, was the whole point of a so-called independent Albanian state. In the words of Theodor Wolff, the editor of the *Berliner Tageblatt*, it had sprung from Berchtold's head 'as Athene sprang from the head of Zeus', setting the stage, before the tragedy, for 'the last Viennese operetta'.[72]

But what exactly did Berchtold's operatic Albania amount to? Certainly, it presented a chaotic picture, though not perhaps a jolly one. In the course of 1913 there were at least four governments in the country. First, there was the 'provisional government' in the southern port city of Valona, led by the pro-Austrian Ismail Kemal who had spearheaded the Albanian independence movement in November 1912. However, no one, not even Vienna, recognized his government which, most of the time, did not exercise much power outside Valona. The second authority was established by the Great Powers to the north, in Scutari, following the Montenegrin withdrawal in May 1913. But the international force based in the city never controlled more than a 10-kilometre radius around it. In fact, even the region of Alessio, not far from Scutari, had under the leadership of Ded Zogu managed to establish a kind of autonomy.[73] Moreover, large mountainous areas in the north, inhabited by the Mirdite and Malissori Catholic tribes, recognized no one. Bib Doda, the Mirdite leader, was in mid-1913 looking to set up a separatist Mirdite duchy under a Serbian and Monte-negrin protectorate.[74] The third government was based in the coastal city of Durazzo. Led by Essad Pasha Toptani, the dubious hero of the siege of Scutari, it controlled central Albania with its overwhelmingly Muslim population, and was constantly at loggerheads with the government in Valona. Essad Pasha, though feared and unpopular, may have come closest to being a national leader and certainly possessed the ambition to be such. The fourth authority was in fact a Greek one: the Greek Army having during the Balkan Wars taken possession of Northern Epirus (i.e., Southern Albania), where the population, if not Greek, had at least been Christian Orthodox and hellenized. The Greeks, however, had not managed to take Valona. Nevertheless, their presence in the area had alarmed the Italians, obsessed as they were by the naval consideration that a foreign power, possibly Greece's friend France, could install itself at Valona and thus control the straits of Otranto.[75]

Indeed, Professor Edward Capps pointed out the cynical view that 'the discovery of the Albanian question was due to the existence of two harbors on the Albanian coast: Durazzo and Valona.'[76] An 'independent' Albania was from that point of view a sensible Austro-Italian collaborative project to keep the Serbs away from the Durazzo area in the north, and the Greeks away from the bay of Valona in the south. However, the fixing of the northern and southern boundaries of Albania proved quite a challenge. The six Great Powers had appointed two boundary commissions, northern and southern, which began their work in October 1913 and soon degener-ated into Great Power elbowing. In the south, Italy and Austria-Hungary predictably resisted the Greek claims, whereas in the north Russia and France backed the Serbian claims. The southern commission did success-fully conclude its work towards the end of the year, but only because Venizelos, the Greek Prime Minister, was willing to sacrifice Northern Epirus in order to secure the Aegean islands. The northern commission, however, had still not finished by August 1914.[77]

The anarchic conditions in Albania looked like coming to an end in October 1913 when an international control commission, appointed by the London Ambassadors' Conference, arrived in Valona to oversee the transition period until the arrival of a new ruler. But in Durazzo at almost exactly the same time Essad Pasha had proclaimed the 'Republic of Central Albania' with himself as President. After two months in office, the commission was really no more than just another government in Albania, and it could do nothing to alter the increasingly volatile situation on the ground.[78] Ismail Kemal, the leader of the unrecognized provisional government in Valona, had in the meantime conspired with the Young Turks to bring a Muslim prince to the Albanian throne and align Albania with Turkey against Greece and Serbia. The attempted putsch, however, was foiled in January 1914 by the international control commission which had at its disposal a local gendarmerie force commanded by Dutch officers. Kemal was forced into exile and his government ceased to exist.[79]

The long-awaited arrival of Albania's new ruler finally took place on 7 March 1914 when the German Prince Wilhelm of Wied reached Durazzo on the Austro-Hungarian yacht *Taurus*. This reflected a consensus among the Great Powers to install a European and Christian sovereign into the predominantly Muslim Albania – for there had indeed been Muslim candidates, three from Turkey and one from Egypt. Admittedly, Kaiser Wilhelm II, who otherwise considered Austria's Albanian project a nonsense (*Blödsinn*), favoured a Muslim ruler.[80] Being a Protestant, Wied seemed a sensible, neutral choice for a country which also had considerable Catholic and Orthodox Christian communities. Yet his elevation (if that is the right word) to the Albanian throne owed a great deal to the romantic enthusiasm of two slightly dotty, extravagant women: Elizabeth, the Queen of Romania, whose nephew he was, and his own ambitious wife Sophie, the Queen's adored protégé. Elizabeth, also a woman of letters better known by her *nome de plume* Carmen Sylva, had brought about Sophie's marriage with her nephew Wilhelm. The two women 'sang, painted, composed, wrote poetry, played the harp and piano together'.[81] When the Albanian opening arose, they successfully schemed to make Wilhelm the Prince of Albania. The Queen had got the Romanian Foreign Office to make noises on his behalf. When the German Foreign Secretary Kiderlen-Wächter was approached, he did not waste words on Wilhelm of Wied: '*C'est un idiot*'.[82] The latter, admittedly, had not been too keen on the proposed new job himself. As Marie, the Crown Princess of Romania at the time, wrote in her wonderful memoirs, 'Sophie was full of excited anticipation, but it seemed to me as though quiet William was a little less enthusiastic'.[83]

His misgivings, as it turned out, were to be entirely justified. The principal local player in Albania was undoubtedly Essad Pasha. Prince Wied appeared to recognize this, choosing for his princely seat Essad's base of Durazzo, much to the annoyance of the burgers of Scutari, Albania's largest city, as well as those of Valona.[84] He also gave Essad the key portfolios of War and Interior Minister in an eight-member government formed in Durazzo after the control commission had handed its powers over to him. By all accounts, however, Essad had entered into a tactical alliance with the Prince, while permanently plotting to make himself the ruler of Albania. A Serbian Foreign Ministry circular from early April 1914 informed its diplomats abroad that Essad Pasha really took 'no notice' of Wied.[85] Heinrich von Löwenthal, the Austro-Hungarian Minister in Durazzo, thought that Wied lacked energy, did basically nothing, had no opinion of his own, and saw himself as a constitutional monarch.[86] And while the Prince behaved passively, Essad ran everything. Prime Minister Turkhan

Pasha was just a figurehead, most of whose cabinet members did not even have their own offices. Rudolf Nadolny, a councillor at the German Legation in Durazzo, reported that they would assemble at Essad's house, just chattering and drinking coffee '*alla turca*'.[87] Interestingly, at the insistence of Austria-Hungary and Italy, the new government could have no diplomatic representatives abroad as Albania was deemed only half-sovereign.[88] The question of sovereignty, in fact, also extended to the south of the country at the time of Wied's arrival. At the end of February an autonomous (Greek) republic of Northern Epirus had been proclaimed despite the fact that the Greek Army had in great part withdrawn. A proclamation of independence followed shortly after. Clashes broke out between Albanian guerrilla bands and the Epirotes. Hardly surprising, then, that Kaiser Wilhelm II was to remark sarcastically only days after Wied's landing at Durazzo: 'Above all, he is still there!'[89]

The Northern Epirus issue was briefly settled by the end of June with the granting of a wide autonomy, but the advent of war in Europe brought back the anarchy.[90] In the meantime, in May, Wied had to face a much more formidable challenge in the form of a Turkish-backed and directed rebellion in central Albania. What had begun as peasant discontent was channelled by the Young Turks into an anti-European revolt with Wied being targeted as a Christian Prince. Led by some two hundred and fifty Turkish officers, the rebels demanded a Muslim ruler and carried Turkish flags as they advanced towards Durazzo. Whether Essad Pasha had covertly supported the rebellion in order to destabilize Wied cannot be established with certainty.[91] What seems clear is that a major conflict had developed between Essad and the Dutch officers commanding Wied's gendarmerie: the Dutch, loyal to Wied, had demanded that Essad put his own armed force under their command, which the latter had refused.[92] At dawn on 19 May, using a hundred Albanians recruited from the south of the country and hostile to Essad, a Dutch Major named Sluyss surrounded Essad's house in Durazzo and employed artillery to force his surrender. Panta Gavrilović, Serbia's diplomatic representative at Durazzo, reported that the Austro-Hungarian Legation was 'the soul' behind this action and that the Italians had been kept in ignorance.[93] Essad was placed under arrest on an Austro-Hungarian warship. The Italians, furious at this turn of events, succeeded in having Essad released and brought him to Italy. To them, the Austro-Hungarian involvement was obvious. Nadolny, the German diplomat on the spot in Durazzo, felt much the same, informing Bethmann Hollweg that the Austro-Hungarian Legation was a big opponent of Essad Pasha because it saw the latter as Italy's steadfast supporter. He pointed out that the Legation had made three Austro-Hungarian artillery officers available to Major Sluyss – officers who were then used to direct fire from Austrian guns on to the roof of Essad's house.[94]

The Italians and Essad were generally believed to be allies.[95] In October 1913 Berchtold suggested that Essad should be 'bought', but the Italians had clearly been faster.[96] Baron Carlo Aliotti, the Italian Minister in Durazzo, was a particular *bête noire* to the Austrians because he worked relentlessly to extend Italy's influence in Albania and seemed to have developed a close relationship with Essad. When Kaiser Wilhelm visited Franz Ferdinand in June at Konopischt castle, the Archduke complained bitterly about Aliotti. Essad was certainly not dancing to Vienna's tune and, in Pašić's view, had for that reason been removed by Austria.[97] The suspicion that he was in the pay of Belgrade is contradicted by Serbian documents which show that he was mistrusted by Pašić.[98] In any case, Vienna had achieved nothing by ousting Essad, whose supporters now joined the rebels. The Government had resigned. Suddenly, Aliotti, who had been in Italy during the coup against Essad, returned to mastermind one of the most effective pieces of skullduggery in twentieth-century European history. On 23 May he told Wied to abandon Durazzo because a major rebel force was about to invade the city. In fact, at the time no real danger existed, but Wied was not to know. Amid scenes of chaos, the ruler of Albania, with his wife Sophie and their two children, promptly fled to the Italian ship *Misurata*. The fact that Wied hoisted an Albanian flag on the ship did not lessen the humiliation of his departure. Although he remained on the ship for only one night, it was an action which, as H. Charles Woods wrote in 1918, 'was sufficient to seal his fate in a country where, to say the least of it, cowardice is not one of the faults of the people'.[99]

And so Prince Wied came to be seen as a traitor to his people, becoming at the same time the laughing stock of Europe. The Austro-Italian rivalry in Albania had by now completely overshadowed their initial joint interests. Germany's Ambassador to Rome reported that Italian public opinion saw the Albanian rebellion as an Italian triumph over Austria.[100] The turmoil in Albania thus completed a picture of what can only be described as complete disarray in Austria-Hungary's Balkan policies in the first half of 1914. Conrad had as recently as January written to Berchtold, proposing that an Albanian Army of 80,000 should be built up in order to tie up Serbian and Montenegrin forces.[101] Given the prevailing chaos in the country, this was always going to be a tall order. No less fanciful was Berchtold's August 1914 proposal to Wied to side with Austria and proceed 'aggressively' with his Albanians against Serbia. The Prince, however, refused. Entrapped by the rebels in Durazzo, he hardly had any Albanians he could count on, but he was also sufficiently sensitive to the issue of Albania's neutrality, established by the London Conference, to engage in such an adventure.[102] In any case, he was not to last for long: early in September 1914 he left Albania for good, ingloriously ending 'The Six Month Kingdom'.[103]

The Crisis of October 1913

Even a cursory examination of Austro-Hungarian documents from the 1914 July Crisis will immediately reveal a torrent of official, and often hysterical, appraisals of the apparently supreme and ongoing threat to the Habsburg Empire posed by the little Kingdom of Serbia. A random selection provides a flavour of these evaluations: 'the machinations of Serbia'; 'revolutionary propaganda from Serbia hostile to the Monarchy'; 'Serbia, the root of dangers'; 'subversive movement from the centre in Belgrade'; 'an anti-Austrian crusade embracing the whole Serbian nation'; 'the Great Serbian subversive activities'; 'an intolerable state of affairs', and so on. One might, on this basis, easily conclude that Serbia had been waging a relentless war of sedition against Habsburg Monarchy. Of course, the outpouring of such anti-Serbian sentiment in July 1914 stemmed to some extent from the suspected involvement of official Serbia in the Sarajevo assassination. It has been seen, however, that identical views were held by Habsburg officialdom long before Sarajevo: the flow of bitter hatred and accusation from Vienna can be traced at least as far back as the Bosnian annexation crisis. And although there was no love lost between Austria-Hungary and Serbia, it is still important to ask the question: did the assassination of Franz Ferdinand merely confirm, albeit in spectacular fashion, the 'intolerable' nature of the relations between the two countries? For quite apart from the important matter of whether any official Serbian structures stood behind the assassination plot, the evidence suggests that, far from being intolerable, relations between the two had been entirely civil in the months prior to the assassination.

It cannot be emphasized strongly enough that, following the Balkan Wars, there was in fact only one crisis in Austro-Serbian relations prior to Sarajevo. Lasting from September to October 1913, it concerned Albania and therefore had nothing to do with any supposed Serbian-inspired movement aimed at 'disjoining the South-Slav portions of Austria-Hungary from the monarchy' – as Berchtold put it in his famous dossier of 25 July 1914, listing Serbia's alleged wrongdoings preceding the assassination of the Archduke.[104] The Albanian crisis in question was really just a leftover from the Balkan Wars: neither the Albanian tribes living in the north and north-east, nor the Serbian Government were happy with the borders envisaged by the London Ambassadors' Conference. The Serbian Army had never completely evacuated the whole of Albanian territory: Belgrade, waiting for the final decisions of the boundary commission kept two regiments, some two thousand men, in the disputed border area, strategically positioned and spread out along a hundred kilometre line.[105] In late September 1913 these troops were actually being withdrawn at the insistence of the Great Powers when, possibly not by coincidence, a major incursion into

Serbian territory took place. Albanian guerrilla bands, numbering between ten and twenty thousand (estimates vary) pushed north into Kosovo, and in the south into west Macedonia. They scored significant successes, taking the towns of Đakovica, Ohrid, Struga and Debar. The town of Prizren was surrounded and a republic proclaimed at Debar. Two hundred Serbian soldiers were captured as well as seventeen pieces of artillery. The Albanian onslaught, occurring only eleven days after Serbia had completed its demobilization following the Balkan Wars, forced Belgrade to re-mobilize two of its divisions. These forces then launched a counter-offensive and expelled the guerrillas. The trouble was, at least from Vienna's standpoint, that the Serbian Army's drive took it deep into Albania – all the way, by way of Tirana, to the Adriatic Sea at Durazzo, with some units even reaching Elbasan in the heart of the country.[106]

What did the Serbs aim to achieve? At the Serbian War Ministry, the Austro-Hungarian Military Attaché in Belgrade was told that the idea was to give the Albanians such a lesson that they would not, 'for years to come', dare repeat anything similar.[107] There was, of course, more to it. As the Serbian historian Dragoslav Janković pointed out, Pašić's Government had never sincerely accepted the idea of an independent Albania and hoped to regain access to the Adriatic by exploiting the opportunity provided by the Albanian foray.[108] Berchtold, just back from holiday, was furious. But who stood behind the well-led, well-armed and, apparently, well-financed Albanian guerrillas? Essad Pasha, the strongman of central Albania, had definitely had nothing to do with them. In fact, he sought to make political capital out of the crisis, asking the Serbian Government to make an announcement that it would be withdrawing its forces at his request. According to Serbian documents, Bulgarian officers had joined the Albanian guerrillas, and Jovanović, the Serbian Minister in Vienna, had been to tell Berchtold so.[109] The Serbian Government also quickly learned that at least two members of Valona's provisional government were involved, and that a major accumulation of arms and ammunition had taken place in Albania over the previous three months.[110] Essad Pasha informed the Serbs that Ismail Kemal, the head of the provisional government, had supplied the warlords with money to finance their bands – Essad did not know the origin of the money, except that it had not come from Albania. The suspicion in Belgrade, of course, was that Austria-Hungary had engineered the Albanian guerrilla raid, and this was also the belief in the Greek Foreign Office. Later, in December 1913, Philip Nogga, a leading Albanian politician, told the Serbian Minister in Bucharest that Austria had known about it.[111] From Belgrade, Dayrell Crackanthorpe reported to London at the beginning of the crisis that Austrian influence had been at work to 'stir up' the Albanian tribes against Serbia – partly with a view to creating obstacles to the latter's work of internal consolidation.

Crackanthorpe also reported that modern Austrian Mannlicher rifles had recently been taken in considerable quantities from the Albanians.[112]

Serbian documents contain an interesting piece of evidence about what Austro-Hungarian diplomacy may have been scheming in the region. In April 1913 Ismail Kemal had visited Vienna, protesting at the Ballhausplatz that the Albanian-populated towns of Prizrcn, Peć, Đakovica and Debar had not been assigned to Albania. He also talked to the Serbian Minister in Vienna, who then passed on to Belgrade what Kemal had told him: those towns, according to the Ballhausplatz, had been left outside Albania in order to create a *'foyer d'agitation'*, with a view to generating events that could provide the Monarchy with the right to intervene.[113] Indeed, as the Albanian crisis developed in the autumn of 1913, Conrad predictably saw it as an opportunity to conduct a win-or-bust war against Serbia (*'den Krieg bis zur äussersten Konsequenz zu führen'*).[114] In his major study of the Austro-Hungarian Army before 1914, Günther Kronenbitter amply documents Vienna's efforts to furnish the Albanian tribes with arms and ammunition.[115] Major Kageneck, the German Military Attaché in Vienna, reported in January 1913 on the calculations of the Austro-Hungarian Chiefs of Staff that the Albanians, supplied with arms and ammunition, could be used as trusted allies in a future war against Serbia.[116] The question of 'the right to intervene' was also considered at the highest levels in the Austrian capital during the autumn 1913 crisis. On 29 September Conrad urged Berchtold that an ultimatum be given to Serbia, followed by a mobilization if the latter did not evacuate Albania within twenty-four hours. Berchtold said his heart was for it, but not his head as he was not sure about the support from above. He did, however, go to see Franz Joseph on that day and met again with Conrad late in the afternoon, informing him that the Emperor was 'not a bit averse' to an energetic action against Serbia, but only concerned that a 'legal basis' for it should exist.[117]

In the end, such niceties were dispensed with. On 3 October, at a session of the Joint Ministerial Council in Vienna, Berchtold suggested that the choice was to either accept a Serbian *fait accompli* or to issue an ultimatum to Serbia to evacuate northern Albania. The participants were generally bellicose – and not just Conrad, who thought that the moment for action was 'most favourable'. The Hungarian Prime Minister Tisza was also in favour of delivering an ultimatum, as a prelude to inflicting on Serbia either a diplomatic or a military defeat. Stürgkh, the Austrian Prime Minister, even suggested that a humiliation for Serbia was a 'condition for life [*Lebensbedingung*]' for the Monarchy.[118] Another meeting, possibly informal, took place in the Schönbrunn Palace on 13 October, with Berchtold declaring himself 'convinced' of the necessity to proceed against Serbia.[119] This meeting was decisive. The participants, Berchtold, Tisza, Burián, Biliński, Conrad and Karl von Macchio (from the Ballhausplatz) agreed on an 'energetic' course of action. Conrad demanded 'total mobilization', and expressed his wish – backed by Stürgkh – to 'provoke' a war with Serbia.[120] Finally, on 18 October, Wilhelm von Storck delivered the Austro-Hungarian ultimatum to the Foreign Ministry in Belgrade: Serbia was given eight days to clear out its troops from Albania, failing which the Imperial and Royal Government would, to its 'great regret', resort to appropriate means to ensure the realization of its demand.[121] By 20 October Storck could elatedly report that Serbia had given in.[122]

Nine months later another ultimatum was to result in a world war. The difference in July 1914 would be that the decision makers in Vienna and, for that matter, in Budapest, would not be satisfied with a diplomatic triumph over Serbia. But there can be no doubt that there already existed, in October 1913, a determination to pursue war if necessary. Franz Joseph himself was to express his opinion to Burián on 15 October that 'he hardly thought it possible to have a third mobilization and remain inactive'. On the very day of Serbian capitulation, 20 October, he was 'entirely in favour of mobilization'.[123] Habsburg military and civilian leaders alike were now resolved that yet another expensive mobilization should not end with an empty diplomatic success but would actually need to be followed by warfare. In fact, even a conflict beyond the Balkans had been contemplated. Admittedly, Berchtold seemed pretty certain that Russia and France were not keen on war and that Serbia's 'bluff' could be called.[124] Nevertheless, the Hungarian Prime Minister Tisza, whom historians have endlessly celebrated for his alleged resistance to war in July 1914, stated at the Schönbrunn meeting on 13 October that if it had to come to a war with Russia, it was, ultimately, 'better now than later'.[125] Tisza, while he would rather not have a war, was prepared to risk it. The same could be said of Berchtold in 1913.

Had they become blinded by considerations of prestige? Samuel Williamson has suggested that, in October 1913, the Habsburg statesmen had replaced interest politics with prestige politics.[126] Yet at the outset of the Albanian crisis Austro-Hungarian prestige was in no way involved. Serbian troops in Albania, after all, had been sitting there for a long time. The crisis itself, which began with the Albanian sortie into Serbian territory, had in no small measure been manufactured with Vienna's connivance. Moreover, waging war on Serbia by proxy, weakening it militarily and financially, was an obvious Austro-Hungarian interest. The issue of prestige undoubtedly emerged once this game began to backfire, but hard calculations were still in place. As Berchtold told Prince Stolberg on 15 October, the Serbs, in attempting to achieve modifications of the frontier with Albania in their favour, would actually be making the first step in pressing forward to the Adriatic.[127] Containing Serbia, in other words, had remained the chief fixation.

Curiously, many accounts of the October 1913 Albanian crisis omit to mention that it began with a massive Albanian incursion into Serbian territory in the first place. Hugo Hantsch writes not a word about it in his biography of Berchtold. Even Galántai and, more recently, Kronenbitter, have nothing to say on the subject. Other, highly regarded works on Austro-Hungarian policy are also silent on this point. F.R. Bridge, whose 1972 book *From Sadowa to Sarajevo* remains standard reading on the foreign policy of the Dual Monarchy, argues that the crisis was 'provoked by Serbia' which pleaded the necessity of 'suppressing disorders' – Bridge does not say where exactly, and indeed whether, those disorders were taking place and whether Serbia actually had a case or not – his definition of the crisis is from Vienna's perspective.[128] Similarly, Samuel Williamson totally ignores the Albanian invasion. He gives the origins of the crisis in one sentence: 'Reports reached Vienna that Serbia had not only failed to evacuate Albanian territory, but had in fact expanded into new Albanian areas.'[129] In a like manner, Christopher Clark writes that Albanians 'near the frontier' had only responded to 'Serbian provocations', and then the 'Serbian units pushed back even further into Albanian territory'.[130] A reader of such lines could be forgiven for concluding that the whole episode had occurred entirely within Albania's frontiers and at Serbia's instigation. In this sense, much of the historiography of the October 1913 crisis, whatever the motives of the Serbian Government may have been afterwards in re-conquering portions of Albania, seems ill-informed by virtue of being incomplete.

As was to be the case in July 1914, Vienna had made sure of obtaining Germany's backing. On 15 October Berchtold told the German Chargé d'Affaires in Vienna that this time Austria-Hungary was determined not to give in and that he hoped for Germany's moral support. Evidently calibrating his message for German ears, he said that the existence of Albania was threatened and a stop had to be put in the way of the Slavs; Germany, he suggested, also had an interest in opposing the 'Slavonic tide'. On the following day the German Foreign Office duly instructed its Minister in Belgrade to line up behind Austria-Hungary.[131] Certainly, Kaiser Wilhelm II stood on this occasion most enthusiastically behind his ally. When, on 18 October, he read a telegram from Vienna which related Berchtold's confidence that it would not come to war, he famously wrote in the margin: 'That would be very regrettable! Now or never!' That same day, at Leipzig, he saw Conrad at the centenary celebration of the victory against Napoleon. 'I go along with you', he told Conrad, adding that the other Powers were 'not ready' and urging him to take Belgrade 'in a couple of days'.[132] This time, according to Fritz Fischer, Germany assisted the Monarchy because it did not wish to 'put undue strain' on their relationship.[133] However, Italy, the other ally in the Triple Alliance, was only half-hearted in its support for Austro-Hungarian representations. Moreover, San Giuliano, the Italian Foreign Minister, was quick to point out that 'Greece was as recalcitrant in Southern Albania as Serbia was in the North'.[134]

And while the Triple Alliance had not been split by the crisis of October 1913, Austria-Hungary's determination to oust the Serbs from Albania did manage to break the Concert of Europe. The latter of course consisted of the six Great Powers which, in theory, were supposed to jointly manage the affairs of Albania. But what Berchtold really hated, as he explained to Redlich on 16 October, was to have immediate, regional Austro-Hungarian interests treated as affairs of Europe. 'What business has for example England', he asked, 'to interfere in this whole thing?'[135] Thus it was that Vienna did not even consult Russia, France and Britain over the proposed step in Belgrade. The reaction in London was incredulity. Eyre Crowe, Assistant Under-Secretary at the Foreign Office, thought that Austria was doing wrong 'to precipitate a conflict without even telling the other Powers. This is not straight-dealing.' Foreign Secretary Edward Grey was prepared to support the frontier established by the Ambassadors' Conference, but he, too, had been taken aback by Vienna's unilateral action. Besides, he believed that Serbia had a case in that the Powers had not established a settled government in Albania, and the Albanians had been the first to violate the frontier.[136]

A peaceful outcome of the crisis was always on the cards: still bleeding from the Balkan Wars, Serbia was hardly likely to defy Austria-Hungary and risk being attacked. The Government in Belgrade knew, moreover, that Russia was most unlikely to prop it up. As Dimitrije Popović, the Serbian Minister at St Petersburg, was to report, Sazonov showed 'an absence of any interest for Albanian affairs'.[137] In fact, the Serbian Army completed its evacuation of Albania well before the eight-day deadline. However, in Vienna, Conrad was predictably unhappy about Serbia's compliant climb-down and told the Emperor so.[138] Berchtold, on the other hand, was delighted by his diplomatic success – as was Franz Ferdinand who sent a letter of congratulations to the Foreign Minister. The Archduke's position in October 1913 has often been seen as proof of his peaceful approach to foreign affairs. On 12 October, right in the middle of the crisis, he wrote from Konopischt castle to Berchtold that he doubted the truth of the reports about the assault by the Serbs on Durazzo. He continued: 'I am firmly *opposed* to an armed intervention on our part as long as this is halfway feasible; to begin with, we have no soldiers available now, just recruits, so we would have to mobilize, that is, mobilize in full, and then war would be inevitable ... And what would be the upshot? A winter campaign, and how will Russia respond, given our very weak and shaky footing with our allies ... I would definitely avoid belligerent action now, because I am absolutely convinced that it is not necessary and that this pressure emanates entirely from elements that are wittingly or unwittingly seeking to harm the monarchy.'[139]

This, clearly, was not a principled anti-war stance, but rather a sober consideration of the circumstances at hand – entirely in keeping with the Archduke's generally pragmatic philosophy regarding peace and war. Interestingly, Franz Ferdinand had his own secret little plan for Serbia. Its details remain unknown, but in a letter to Berchtold, dated 24 July 1913, he did reveal a kind of skeleton: 'With respect to Serbia, I have a new and, I believe, excellent idea, which would help surmount all difficulties and which would surely meet your approval, but I must communicate it to you in person. I believe that it is a veritable egg of Columbus, which would produce a wonderful gain for the monarchy with one blow. But for this a strong Romania and a Greece that we have not alienated by bad treatment are prerequisites. Then my scheme can be carried through and I can guarantee a brilliant outcome.'[140] What could this 'egg of Columbus' scheme have possibly been? Apparently, the Archduke did inform Berchtold about it in person because on 21 October 1913, in the letter of congratulations to the Foreign Minister on the success of the ultimatum to Serbia, he wrote: 'And so I assured Your Excellency [in Vienna] that I am *convinced* that we can get rid of these pigs without striking a blow and without recourse to Conrad's bravado policy!'[141]

By 'these pigs' Franz Ferdinand meant the Serbs. Evidently, what he had in mind was some kind of regional policing by Romania and Greece. A few months earlier, on 24 July 1913, he urged Berchtold to '*support Romania from now on, make it great, very great*, and attach it to us with the firmest ties by our love and unconditional support, no matter how hard these fine Hungarians try to hamper this policy ... Romania and Greece are the only two non-Slavic states, they hate the Slavs, and will always side with us, if they are treated right.'[142] And in a previous letter, dated 6 July, he wrote that 'with these two states Austria could keep the Balkans checkmated'. In this letter, apart from amply demonstrating his anti-Slav prejudice ('I would do all I could to stem the pan-Slavic tide'), he also lambasted the Bulgarians and their King, Ferdinand. Of the Greeks he did not have a high opinion either ('a cowardly people'), but he thought their King was 'a decent ruler who thinks like a German', so that his advice to Berchtold was to grant the Greek King ' a few more square metres of Albania and a few islands, thus tying him to the Triple Alliance'.[143]

However, the Archduke's 1913 proposals for neutralizing Serbia were highly unrealistic, running as they did against aspects of Austro-Hungarian and, especially, Hungarian policy. A 'great' Romania was the last thing Budapest wanted, and as has been seen both the Ballhausplatz and the Hungarian statesmen were keen to keep the Bulgarian option alive – thus alienating both Romania and Greece. Greece, in turn, could not really be accommodated for fear of alienating Italy. Franz Ferdinand's ideas, including the anti-Slav sentiment, were in perfect harmony with Germany's take on the Balkans, but they hardly corresponded to the dynamics of the existing situation. Moreover, the Archduke certainly did not wish to annex Serbia – at least not in early 1913. On this point he was very explicit in his letter to Berchtold of 1 February 1913: 'And God save us from annexing Serbia: a country over its head in debts, brimming with regicides and scoundrels ... We can throw away billions there and still be faced with a terrible irredenta.'[144] His 'egg of Columbus' was probably just a hypothesis that Serbia could be kept permanently isolated and weak by what he imagined would be a loyal Romanian-Greek outpost of the Triple Alliance, reinforced possibly by the Albanians. Whatever the precise idea may have been, Berchtold must have responded to it with polite evasion. In any case, as will be seen in chapter thirteen, for all his Romanophilia and Bulgaro-phobia, Franz Ferdinand would in fact shortly before his assassination acknowledge the view long held at the Ballhausplatz that, since Romania was actually unreliable, the Triple Alliance should court Bulgaria.

Austria-Hungary and Serbia, 1913-1914

On 3 October 1913, as the Austro-Hungarian Joint Ministerial Council was deliberating the situation in Albania, Serbia's Prime Minister Nikola Pašić was passing through Vienna and Berchtold found the time to receive him. It was, in the circumstances, a reasonably successful meeting even though it began with an exchange of insincerities: Pašić assured his host that Serbia was not contemplating any conquests of Albanian territory, while Berch-told maintained that the provisional government in Valona had nothing to do with the uprising. Strangely, the two statesmen did not then discuss the burning Albanian issue any further. Instead, they reviewed economic matters: customs, revising the existing trade agreement, the import of live-stock into the Monarchy, the renewing of the Shipping Convention of 1911, railway links and the future ownership of that part of the Eastern Railways track located on territory that had become part of Serbia after the Balkan Wars. It was a thoroughly business-like meeting, free of any tension. Towards the end, however, Pašić made a significant, even startling announcement. He told Berchtold that whatever internal methods of government Austria-Hungary employed towards its South Slavs, Serbia categorically did not wish to influence the latter and would strive to cultivate 'absolutely correct conduct'. He added: 'You can give the Croats and the Serbs either more or fewer freedoms, that will not concern us and also our relations with the Monarchy will not be affected thereby.' In his account of the meeting with the Serbian Prime Minister, Berchtold did not record his reaction to this extraordinary olive branch offer.[145]

It is, however, of the greatest importance to emphasize that this was the moment, on 3 October 1913, when Austro-Serbian relations could have been placed on an entirely normal footing: what Pašić was promising Berchtold was no less than Serbia's cool indifference to events in Austria-Hungary – even if the Monarchy chose to treat its South Slavs reprehensibly. Later in the day Berchtold informed the participants in the Joint Ministerial Council that Pašić had talked about 'decades' of friendly relations.[146] The Serbian Prime Minister may have been less than honest with Berchtold about his country's intentions in Albania, but he had been quite candid with regard to the much more substantive matter of policy towards Austria-Hungary. Dayrell Crackenthorpe, the British Chargé d'Affaires at Belgrade, had already written to the Foreign Office the previous month that Pašić had made known in political and journalistic circles Serbia's readiness to receive favourably any advances by Austria. He also reported on the assurances given by Pašić that it would not be part of Serbia's policy to agitate in Bosnia. The British diplomat believed those assurances to have been 'quite genuine' because any forward policy, at a time when the country was exhausted by war, would be prejudicial to the task of internal reorganization.[147]

Indeed, whatever territories Serbia might ideally wish to wrest from the Dual Monarchy, any such ambition amounted for the time being to pure fantasy – for no one knew when an actual opportunity would arise. The facts in the autumn of 1913 were plain: Serbia could perhaps hope to extract something in Albania, but it was far too weak to directly challenge a Great Power like Austria-Hungary. At the same time Belgrade had its plate full simply amalgamating its newly-acquired territories. This point, noted by Crackanthorpe, was also being made repeatedly by King Carol of Romania to all the Austro-Hungarian statesmen he would meet: that 'Austria is in the wrong when it opposes the enlargement and progress of Serbia which, preoccupied with its tasks in the south, will not be able to carry out in the north and the west that which Austria is accusing it of.'[148]

Even before the Pašić-Berchtold meeting, non-interference in the Monarchy had already become Serbia's state policy. In July, Pašić had sent out an important circular telegram to all of Serbia's legations abroad. While noting that Austria was working 'everywhere' against Serbia's interests, he actually wondered about its conditions ('which and what kind') for friendship, 'for we wish to coexist in friendship and in our behaviour take pains to facilitate the offer of that friendship'.[149] By 'friendship', which was a rather ambitious aim regarding relations with the Dual Monarchy, Pašić probably meant the elimination of avoidable conflict points. An example of this is his reaction, in mid-October 1913, to Berchtold's concern, expressed to Jovanović in Vienna, about Serbia's likely treatment of its new Catholics, i.e., those Catholic Albanians who found themselves inside

Serbia's borders after the Balkan Wars. On receiving Jovanović's report, Pašić minuted that the authorities in the new territories should 'proceed heedfully and in a friendly way with the Catholics, any complaints should be staved off'.[150] There can be little doubt, therefore, that from mid-1913 to mid-1914 the attainment of unruffled relations with Austria-Hungary was a major strategic rather than just a short-term tactical objective of Serbian policy. The great Romanian statesman Take Jonescu had been appraised of this attitude by his friend Pašić at the height of the Albanian crisis in October 1913. Soon after the Austro-Hungarian ultimatum to Serbia, Ristić, the Serbian Minister in Bucharest, had communicated to Pašić Jonescu's private and personal recommendation that Serbia should adopt a conciliatory position over Albania. In his reply to Ristić, Pašić remarked that he had wanted to 'soften and improve' relations with Vienna, but that the 'Austrian war party' had been against improving those relations and had 'forced' Berchtold to issue the ultimatum. 'Assure Mr Take', Pašić concluded, 'that I am guided by the policy of peace.'[151]

In this, however, the Serbian Prime Minister was not going to get much reciprocity from Vienna. For Berchtold, far from having been 'forced' by anyone to adopt a tough line with respect to the Serbs, was utterly convinced that he could do no business with them. This is apparent, for example, in his August 1913 reaction to a telegram from Prince Karl Fürstenberg, Czernin's predecessor as Austro-Hungarian Minister in Bucharest. Fürstenberg had reported on a conversation between King Carol and Miroslav Spalajković, at the time Serbia's Acting Minister for Foreign Affairs. The King had pleaded that Serbia should improve its relations with Austria-Hungary if it wished to pursue its great tasks undisturbed. Spalajković quite agreed with him, stressing that a friendly policy *vis-à-vis* Austria-Hungary would be 'essential' in future.[152] Berchtold, however, wrote back to Fürstenberg that he entertained the 'utmost scepticism' about the success of any efforts to get Serbia to pursue a friendly policy towards the Monarchy. The Serbian people, he insisted, were unable to come to terms with the annexation of the Bosnian provinces, and the 'unshakeable' aim of Serbian policy was to detach them from the Monarchy and unite them with Serbia. This antagonism was 'permanent and unbridgeable'. It would thus be a 'disastrous mistake' to let oneself be deceived by Serbia's temporising or by its complaisance in the economic sphere. In short, Serbia had to be recognized as a 'tenacious and purposeful opponent'.[153]

Berchtold's remarks went to the heart of the Austro-Serbian issue: was it worthwhile for Austria-Hungary to strive for peaceful coexistence with Serbia on the basis of a mere hope that the ambitious little Balkan Kingdom would simply give up its pretensions to Habsburg territories inhabited by the South Slavs, particularly Bosnia-Herzegovina? Evidently, few people in the Habsburg hierarchy believed that such a course was desirable. But there were some exceptions. In his memoirs, Biliński regretted that an opportunity had been lost in the spring of 1913. At that time, he wrote, it was still possible to bind with Serbia which would only 'gladly betray' Russia. Biliński also drew attention to the person of Jovan Jovanović, the Serbian Minister in Vienna whom he had known so well. Jovanović supported 'out of conviction' a policy of working with, not against, the Monarchy. Moreover, he belonged to that group which, in order to unite the Serb lands, was ready to 'exchange the Karadjordjević dynasty with the Habsburgs'.[154] What this illustrates, of course, is that there existed forces in Serbia which, while not losing sight of the ultimate aim of national unification, were quite flexible as to the method of attaining it. As far back as 1909 the Bosnian Serb leader Jeftanović was sending messages to Vienna that 'there were Serbians in the Kingdom and in Bosnia who cherished the notion of uniting all the Serbs under the Habsburg sovereignty'.[155] In other words, Serbia had its definite goals regarding Austria-Hungary, but was not necessarily, as Berchtold painted it, an implacable foe bent on destroying the neighbouring Monarchy. Serbia, moreover, was hardly a marionette of Russia. After it failed to extend support over Scutari in the spring of 1913, Russia lost much of the esteem it had previously enjoyed in Belgrade – even in Pašić's eyes. Commenting on the Russian diplomacy which had threatened Serbia with 'heavy consequences' unless it withdrew from the siege of Scutari, Pašić wrote in April 1913: 'Our friends are loath to go to war for reasons inconceivable and unknowable to us.'[156] In 1930 Count Carlo Sforza, who knew Pašić well, wrote about a 'legend': Pašić, for all his visits to St Petersburg, 'was far less under the sway of Russian influence and admiration than has been said, and will still be said'.[157]

There can be no doubt, on the other hand, that the Serbian Prime Minister did nevertheless anticipate an armed conflict with Austria-Hungary at some point in future and that he envisaged Russian support in such a context. On 9 June 1914, he wrote an important minute in response to a dispatch from Ristić in Bucharest. Ristić had reported on a conversation between Take Jonescu and Markgrave János Pallavicini, the Austro-Hungarian Ambassador to Constantinople. Pallavicini had complained about some statements concerning Bosnia-Herzegovina which had allegedly been made in Serbia. But he had also suggested that Serbia planned to reach an agreement with Bulgaria by ceding Macedonia and would then declare war on Austria-Hungary. This report immediately provoked Pašić to write instructions to Ristić, in which he informed his Minister in Bucharest about what would happen if the Balkan situation remained peaceful: 'We shall have time to improve the financial situation and ready the Army, while awaiting the development of that big event which is being prepared [*da čekamo razvoj velikog događaja, koji se sprema*].

Romania, Serbia and Russia are supposed to work on this (Montenegro will join us).' Lest these remarks by Pašić be understood, on a cursory reading, as some kind of ill-intention by Romania, Serbia and Russia to attack Austria-Hungary at some stage, one should point out that, by the 'big event', Pašić simply meant a European war, the likelihood of which was being talked about across the continent ever since the Triple Alliance and the Triple Entente had come to be seen as rival power blocs. It is entirely in keeping with his passively-inclined 'laissez-aller' philosophy that awaiting this conflict (*da čekamo*) was his chosen position. Pašić's minute suggests that Romania, Serbia and Russia were supposed to be preparing and presumably coordinating their defences in anticipation of the 'big event'. The Serbian language words '*koji se sprema*', 'which is being prepared' or 'which is being readied', can equally be translated as 'which is being cooked up', and, being wise to some of the views in Vienna on war with Serbia, he certainly did not mean that the Entente Powers were cooking up the 'big event'.[158]

Even though Pašić did not provide further details, his references to Romania, Russia and Montenegro make it crystal clear that he had meant a future confrontation with Austria-Hungary. Significantly, however, he added: 'Tell Jonescu for his information: I am making sure to well assuage rather than offend Austria-Hungary, although there are great difficulties. She is working constantly on all sides against us. About Bosnia and Herzegovina I had said nothing and done even less. In order to satisfy her, all her spies, more then ten of them, have received a pardon – and there has not been even a thank you. The thought of attacking Austria-Hungary never crosses our minds. Relations with Bulgaria could not be worse.'[159]

The least that can be said is that, whatever its ambitions for the future, Serbia was not, in 1913-1914, set on a war path against Austria-Hungary. Interestingly, this was also the view of the Austro-Hungarian diplomats in Belgrade. After Pašić's meeting with Berchtold in Vienna, even the Serbophobe Legation Councillor Wilhelm von Storck considered the Serbian Prime Minister sincere in his desire for improved relations – at least for the near future. Otto Gellinek, the Military Attaché, reported in December 1913 that the Serbian press campaign against the Monarchy had noticeably decreased.[160] From Bucharest, Ottokar Czernin passed to Ballhausplatz in February 1914 his information that Pašić had during a recent visit used 'very friendly' expressions when speaking about the Monarchy.[161] Later that month Wladimir Giesl, the Austro-Hungarian Minister in Belgrade since December 1913, presented Vienna with another reassuring assessment of Serbian foreign policy. The existing military and financial conditions in the Kingdom, he reported, precluded automatically and effectively the pursuit of an 'adventurous policy', and this alone made Pašić's friendly utterances 'credible'.[162]

Giesl's memoirs contain a brief passage about his activities in Belgrade from the beginning of his appointment to the Sarajevo assassination – a passage quite revealing in its casualness. He writes that from the end of 1913 he was mainly occupied with the Oriental Railways (*Orientbahnen*) negotiations – concerning that stretch of the network located in Serbia's newly acquired southern territories. He also mentions a Serbian ministerial crisis in the first half of June 1914, but notes its short duration and Pašić's reappointment. The remaining ongoing affairs, Giesl remarks, 'were of such trivial nature that they do not deserve a mention'.[163] Indeed, Giesl thus confirms that from the end of the October 1913 Albanian crisis to the assassination of Franz Ferdinand, Austro-Serbian relations were remarkably free of any tensions. Far from being 'intolerable', those relations had become so routine that Giesl was able to leave Belgrade for a holiday in France on 16 June.[164]

Negotiations on ownership of the Oriental Railways in Serbia, as Giesl suggested, constituted easily the lion's share of the diplomatic traffic between Vienna and Belgrade in the six to seven months before Sarajevo. Any researcher examining Jovan Jovanović's reports and telegrams from Vienna during this period will be struck by the overwhelming dominance of the Oriental Railways theme. Though the points at issue carried strategic and economic implications, at no stage were the negotiations really under threat. The Oriental Railways Company (*Die Betriebsgessellschaft der Orientalischen Eisenbahnen*), which owned large tracts of the only line between Central Europe and Constantinople (known, famously, as the 'Orient Express') was effectively controlled by German banks. After the First Balkan War, Serbia was predictably keen to acquire ownership of that stretch which passed through its new territories in the south. Vienna, however, acted to buy control of the Company from the German banks, accomplishing this via an Austro-Hungarian banking consortium in April 1913. As Herbert Feis noted in his important 1930 study of the connection between world finance and diplomacy before 1914, Vienna had planned to include long stretches of the Oriental Railways passing through Serbia in the route of an envisaged Vienna-Salonika line. A further reason for not letting the Serbs acquire ownership arose when France proposed a plan to internationalize the Railway. Austria-Hungary went along with the idea, largely because it saw in it the possibility of gaining access to the French money market. Nothing came of this because Serbia, after initially flirting with the scheme, renewed its insistence on direct purchase.[165] In May 1914, however, Vienna and Belgrade appeared to be quite close to an agreement whereby Serbia could purchase the Railway if in return it bought all the rolling stock for that line from Austria-Hungary, and in addition granted a concession to the Monarchy to build inside Serbia a connecting line with Bosnia.[166] The assassination in Sarajevo, however, put an end to these talks.

'Poetic Blooms': Union of Serbia and Montenegro

Historians of the origins of the First World War often refer to another of Vienna's Balkan preoccupations at this time, namely the rumours about a proposed union of Serbia and Montenegro. The Ballhausplatz, certainly, was always going to be rather jittery at the idea of the two independent South Slav states merging into one. Constantin Dumba recalled in his memoirs the only instruction he had received from Foreign Minister Gołuchowski before taking up his post, in 1903, as Minister in Belgrade. 'We could under no circumstances tolerate', Gołuchowski insisted, 'a union of the Kingdom of Serbia and the Principality of Montenegro; we would prevent it even at the cost of a war.'[167] This policy had not changed a great deal in the subsequent years and remained fully supported by Franz Joseph himself. In March 1914 he told the visiting German Emperor that, while he wished the international situation to remain peaceful, he could nevertheless 'not allow a union of Serbia with Montenegro'.[168]

The reason why the Habsburg statesmen were so adamant on this point had of course to do with their fear of a large and strong Serbian state acting as a magnet to the Monarchy's own South Slavs. But another reason emerged following the creating of Albania – by which act Serbia had been denied access to the Adriatic. Reacting in November 1913 to what he termed 'indications' about Serbia and Montenegro moving towards a union, Berchtold instructed his Ambassador in Rome on the Austro-Hungarian position: a Serbian advance to the coast would upset the equilibrium in the Adriatic and could not be allowed. Moreover, he suggested, if the union became a fait accompli, 'the least' upon which Austria-Hungary should insist should be that the whole of the Montenegrin coast, including the ports of Dulcigno (Ulcinj) and Antivari (Bar) be joined to Albania.[169] Just how this could be done without recourse to war was not explained by Berchtold.

Unquestionably, however, the Ballhausplatz was treating the matter with utmost seriousness and making its concern clear to the Russians. Early in March 1914 Count Friedrich Szápáry, Austria-Hungary's Ambassador at St Petersburg, told Sazonov that, should a union take place, his country could not remain a passive bystander.[170] Its ally Germany, however, was hardly on the same track. Only days later the Kaiser remarked that the union could absolutely not be prevented. And if Vienna were to try and prevent it, it would be engaging in 'a big stupidity', risking a war against the Slavs 'which would leave us quite cold'.[171] The same view about the certainty of the union had already been expressed in October 1913 by San Giuliano, the Italian Foreign Minister. In marked contrast to Vienna's position, he told Vladimir Kokovtsov, the visiting Russian Prime Minister, that the union of Serbia and Montenegro was not only inevitable but also 'necessary', for Montenegro in his view had no possibility of surviving and progressing as an independent state.[172]

But how much substance was there to these speculations about a Serbia-Montenegro union? Perhaps the most important point to be emphasized here is that all the initiatives in 1913-1914 for such a union came from Montenegro – not from Serbia or, for that matter, Russia. It is also important to bear in mind that King Nicholas of Montenegro likewise had nothing to do with those initiatives. Autocratic as this ruler may have been, the small political elite also counted for something, as did the intelligentsia – educated largely in Belgrade. Public opinion began increasingly to assert itself after the Balkan Wars. For Montenegro, one of the victors on paper, had in fact emerged as something of a cripple from the conflagration. The casualties it had sustained, over ten thousand, were massive for such a small country. Led by a badly trained officer corps, its Army had performed poorly during the siege of Scutari – an episode greatly affecting the self-esteem of the proud Montenegrin warrior people. The failure of King Nicholas' diplomacy in the spring of 1913 to retain a city won at such high cost in blood added to the sense of failure, but also decreased the prestige of the dynasty and state. 'The question of Scutari', the leading Montenegrin historian Novica Rakočević observed in 1981, 'was taken tragically'. The picture of Montenegro emerging at the end of the Balkan Wars wars was rather grim. The treasury was empty and there had even been famine at the end of the Scutari crisis. The realization of a new international loan was proceeding very slowly. Montenegro possessed neither the finances nor the personnel to administer the newly acquired territories. In foreign policy, quite apart from a hostile Austria-Hungary, the traditional Russian ally had shown great displeasure over King Nicholas' independent posturing during the Scutari episode – an issue giving rise to question marks over any future military aid from Russia.[173]

Modernizing the country on the cheap, as it were, and setting it on a path to progress seemed possible only in a joint state with Serbia. The popular mood in Montenegro at the beginning of 1914 was strongly against King Nicholas and increasingly in favour of uniting with Serbia. It did not help the image of the Petrović dynasty that Danilo, the Crown Prince, was considered 'daft', whereas Mirko, Nicholas' second son, was seen as morally 'depraved'.[174] In the Assembly elections in January the conservative political grouping that had previously formed the government and backed the King was soundly defeated and now replaced by unionists. The new Government's programme pointed clearly towards integration in the military, customs and diplomatic spheres.[175] Deputies in the Assembly competed in who would be seen as the greater champion of convergence with Serbia.[176] On the other hand, the very idea of a union provoked 'mortal fear' at the Montenegrin Court and among its supporting circles who viewed the project as leading to the loss of their positions and material privileges.[177] A tie-up with Serbia, however, was something that the King himself was reportedly not averse to contemplating – if it took place on his own terms. Thus the Ballhausplatz learned in January 1914, and then again in March, that Nicholas might play his 'last card': to bring about, together with political allies in Serbia, the fall of the Radical Party and thereby, so the King's supporters hoped, an 'automatic' overthrow of the Kardjordjević dynasty. He would then head a united Serbia-Montenegro that would, interestingly, become a part of a restructured, trialist Habsburg Empire. His allies in Serbia reportedly included Vladan Đorđević, Serbia's Austro-phile Prime Minister during the reign of King Alexander Obrenović.[178]

Fantastic as these schemes sound, one has to bear in mind the point brought up by the historian Rakočević: that there existed among the Montenegrins a strongly held belief that their country represented the continuation of the Serbian medieval state, and was therefore the successor of that state.[179] But Nicholas, who had been genuinely popular among all the Serbs in the 1870s and 1880s, could by 1914 hardly expect to unify the two Serbian states under his own dynasty. Belgrade, for its part, was highly cautious about the whole issue. Sentiment in Serbia was, as in Montenegro, very much in favour of a merger. The Government, however, had to consider the sensitivities of Austria-Hungary as well as those of Russia – the latter had no desire to find itself in a war against Austria-Hungary on account of Serbia and Montenegro coming together.[180] Nor would Pašić at this stage risk a conflict with the Habsburg Monarchy for the sake of absorbing Montenegro – sooner or later such an outcome seemed certain anyway. Nevertheless, he was fully aware that the Serbian public had different expectations. In January 1914 he explained to Lazar Mijušković, the Montenegrin Minister in Belgrade, that it was very difficult indeed for his Government to hold off a public debate about the 'delicate' question of union; that Serbia could not be the first to propose a union since it would look as if a stronger country was pressurizing a weaker one; that, in any case, the Government could not be sure about the response of King Nicholas, without whose backing any agreement would be worthless; and that any proposal by the Montenegrin Government would receive a sincere welcome in Belgrade. The Serbian Prime Minister added, when pressed by Mijušković, that such a proposal would have to be based on complete equality of the two states, with a guarantee of the independence of both dynasties and states – for which course of action, he said, there were 'many reasons internal and external'.[181]

To the Russian Tsar, who was less than happy with the Montenegrins, Pašić presented essentially the same elucidation of Serbia's policy when he was granted an audience early in February.[182] With Belgrade so guarded, the impetus to move towards a union came in the end from Montenegro.

On 15 March, relentlessly urged to act by his Government, Nicholas sent a letter to his son-in-law, King Peter of Serbia. The most important passage in the letter, while mentioning the need to define mutual obligations in military, diplomatic and financial matters, emphasized at the same time the desirability of reaching an agreement about the 'independence and equality of our states and dynasties'.[183] This kind of playing it safe corresponded exactly to Serbia's own approach and it hardly heralded an immediate union. As Hartwig commented to Sazonov, the letter contained 'brotherly outpourings and poetic blooms' rather than real proposals.[184] And this was hardly a surprise to anybody who knew the Montenegrin King. The German Minister at Cetinje reported towards the end of February that Nicholas had 'not the slightest' intention of allowing a fusion between Serbia and Montenegro.[185]

The play-acting about a union continued when the Serbian Government, in consultation with Hartwig, put together a reply to Nicholas on behalf of King Peter. The two kings, incidentally, could not bear each other. The letter sent by Peter to Nicholas on 2 April vaguely mentioned the creation of 'strong ties', and pointed out that a similar project 'had been so happily concluded in Germany'. The Serbian King merely asked that just one person on each side should be involved in further talks and named Pašić as his delegate.[186] The negotiator on the Montenegrin side became Mijušković, who was genuinely in favour of a speedy union. The Serbian Prime Minister, however, was certainly not. Hartwig's reports to Sazonov from this period are full of praise for Pašić's 'statesmanlike experience and prudence' which guaranteed that no careless step would be taken in the direction of a union with Montenegro.[187] As for King Nicholas, Mijušković complained to Alexander Giers, the Russian Minister at Cetinje, that after the exchange of letters he was using various excuses to place obstacles in the way of the envisaged agreement with Serbia.[188] As a result, the talks about a union, apparently such a concern for Vienna, had got nowhere by the time of the assassination in Sarajevo. The Ballhausplatz, in fact, knew full well that a joint Serbo-Montenegrin state was not about to emerge. As late as 13 June 1914 Giesl informed Berchtold about a conversation with Mijušković, in which the latter had insisted that King Nicholas would not give up even 'an ounce' of his sovereignty – the realization of efforts at union was 'at present not on the cards'. Mijušković had added, significantly, that there existed in Serbia little inclination to tackle the matter because of the awareness of 'possible consequences and complications'.[189]

On the eve of the Sarajevo assassination, in other words, there was not a single issue making waves in Austro-Serbian relations. While never amicable, those relations had since the ending of the October 1913 Albanian crisis not even remotely hinted at an apocalyptic upshot. On 10 April Giesl sent a report to Vienna, in which this absence of sore points was given a sensible clarification and commentary – at least as far as Serbia's behaviour was concerned. Explaining that Serbia, given its precarious financial position, had as yet done almost nothing to raise living standards in its new territories, the Austrian Minister inferred that it wanted peace since it was in the circumstances unable to wage war; for the time being at any rate, Serbia's love of peace was 'sincere', and this feeling dominated the entire population as well as the Army; in fact, Giesl concluded, Serbia had been weakened militarily and economically by its territorial expansion, and would 'for years to come' have to expend major military and financial resources to assert itself in the new provinces – all these factors being 'reassuring moments in the assessment of Serbia's present position'.[190]

But Berchtold clung obstinately to his line about the impossibility of friendly coexistence with Serbia. Irritated in mid-May by renewed German promptings for the establishment of better Austro-Serbian relations, he wrote to Szögyény in Berlin about the 'deep-rooted animosity against the Monarchy in the Serbian national soul', as well as the 'blatant' Serbian aspirations towards Austria-Hungary's integral parts. The whole thing, he thought, was 'hopeless'. Berchtold's conviction had apparently been strengthened by a report which had arrived from Otto Gellinek, the Austro-Hungarian Military Attaché in Belgrade. In that report Gellinek had provided a cursory review of the writings in the Belgrade newspapers (for the main part the gutter press) on the occasion of Orthodox Easter celebrations in Serbia. He had highlighted those passages which talked about the 'resurrection' of the Serbian nation following its successes in the Balkan Wars and the unhappiness of those South Slavs still ruled by Austria-Hungary. He had not referred to *Samouprava*, the mouthpiece of Pašić's ruling Radical Party and the only yardstick for official thinking. Berchtold sent this 'estimable' report to his Ambassador in Berlin, asking him to make it known to the leading statesmen in Wilhelmstrasse.[191]

This was curious behaviour on the part of the Austro-Hungarian Foreign Minister – not least because he should have been far more concerned by ominous developments in Romania. The Serbian press writing about their brethren in the Monarchy may indeed have been irksome, but it was nothing compared to what the Romanian King and his Government were tolerating right in the heart of Bucharest. Towards the end of March Czernin reported on the demonstrations in the city against Austria-Hungary. Organized by *Liga Culturală*, the crowd had shouted in front of the royal palace: 'Down with Austria, down with Hungary ... long live Russia'. Czernin subsequently informed the Ballhausplatz that the attitude of the Romanian Government towards the demonstrators had been 'passive'.[192] Nothing of the kind had happened in Belgrade for quite some time. In a pamphlet entitled *Quo vadis Austria?*, published in Germany in 1913, the former Serbian Prime Minister Vladan Đorđević, in all other repects an incorrigible Austrophile, asked: 'Why is it that for the last two hundred years the Austrian Government has hated all the Balkan peoples and especially the Serbs? Why is it maltreating its own Serbs, Croats and Romanians? Why is it hell-bent on creating a Serbian and a Romanian irredenta on top of an Italian one?'[193] Indeed, the ill will of the Monarchy was a source of genuine bafflement for some of the leading Serbs. After the Balkan Wars, at a meeting between Crown Prince Alexander of Serbia and King Constantine of Greece, the latter recommended that Serbia should reach an understanding with Austria-Hungary. While agreeing with this advice, Alexander asked: '*Mais dites-mois comment?*'[194]

9
General Oskar Potiorek

The Aspiring General

THE IDEA that Archduke Franz Ferdinand, the Heir Apparent to the Habsburg throne, should attend military manoeuvres in Bosnia-Herzegovina in June 1914, and subsequently pay an official visit to the capital city of Sarajevo, was one which originated in the headquarters of General Oskar Potiorek, the *Landeschef* (Governor) of Bosnia-Herzegovina. In inviting the Archduke, Potiorek was pursuing the purely personal ambition of trying to secure the position that had eluded him for so long: that of the Chief of the General Staff of the Austro-Hungarian Army. The manoeuvres would give him a unique opportunity to impress Franz Ferdinand by staging a dazzling display of military flair and organizational competence in this highly sensitive border region – for at the time the Balkans looked likely to decide the future of the Austro-Hungarian Empire. The concluding parade through the streets of Sarajevo would then convince the Archduke that Potiorek was governing over a loyal population. Theodor von Zeynek, the General Staff officer who knew Potiorek well, insisted that such self-promotion was his hidden agenda: the *Landeschef*, pursuing his aim of becoming the Chief of the General Staff, had invited the Heir to the Throne to attend the manoeuvres 'in order to attain this aim'.[1] The extent of his ambition surrounding the Archduke's visit is revealed by the fact that, as Colonel Bardolff reported, he had initially envisaged the programme to last for as long as ten days.[2] Thus the stakes were high for the General. In the end, however, he blundered repeatedly, the Archduke and his wife were killed in front of him, and the final result was a world war.

Potiorek's trajectory before 1914 had been impressive. When the question arose, in 1906, as to who would succeed the long-serving Friedrich Beck as the Chief of the General Staff, there were two exceptional candidates for this post: Potiorek and Franz Conrad (from 1910: von Hötzendorf). Various other names were bandied about, but in terms of military renown and distinction, those two men were the only serious contenders. As it turned out, when the acid test of war finally arrived in

1914 Conrad spectacularly mismanaged Austria-Hungary's mobilization, while Potiorek led his forces to a humiliating debacle in Serbia. In 1906, however, they enjoyed tremendous reputations: Potiorek as a strategist and logistician, and Conrad as a tactician.[3] At the time, the 'crown prince' to Beck was undoubtedly Potiorek, his actual deputy. Beck wanted him as his successor and Potiorek for his part was convinced that he would indeed take over. This in fact was a widespread belief: for many years he had been seen as the 'coming Chief of Staff'.[4] Even Conrad, who apparently did not want the job, put Potiorek's name forward as the 'obvious' one.[5] Hardly surprising, for Potiorek was in leading military circles considered to be nothing less than a 'genius'.[6] The old Archduke Albrecht, famous victor of the second battle of Custoza, saw in him a bright hope for the future.[7] General Moritz Auffenberg described Potiorek as a man animated by 'consuming ambition', but noted that 'being praised to the skies' from youth onwards had bred the megalomania which was his misfortune and his doom.[8]

Oskar Potiorek was born in 1853 in Kreuth near Bleiburg in Carinthia, today the region of southern Austria on the border with Slovenia. His father Paul was a mining superintendent who had moved from Silesia to Bleiburg, a mixed German and Slovene speaking town. The family was of Czech origin, but there has been a fair amount of confusion regarding his ethnicity. Perhaps because he grew up among Slovenes some of his officer colleagues mistakenly thought he was a Slovene. The eminent Serbian historian Vladimir Ćorović likewise maintained that Potiorek was of Slovene descent. But despite growing up among them, his Slovene was only 'passable'.[9] Jovan M. Jovanović, who was in 1914 the Serbian Minister in Vienna, thought that Potiorek was by origin a Croat.[10] In fact, thoroughly Germanized, he felt himself to be first and foremost an Austrian – in the then not unusual way that many Slavs of the Empire had become, over generations, loyal German-Austrians. He was not a Slav renegade, though this label was later pinned on him. To betray anything, one has to belong to it in the first place, and he could not have properly belonged to some-thing so outside his experience and education.

Potiorek was a product of the *Technische Militärakademie* in Vienna, from which he graduated in 1871. His subsequent progress was rapid. At the War College, he was General Ferdinand Fiedler's best student.[11] Then, as a troop commander, he won praise from his superiors for his sharp vision, self-confidence and thoroughness, as a result of which he was put in charge of the *Operationsbüro*, the all-important planning section of the General Staff, a post he held from 1892 to 1898.[12] However, his loftiness and forbidding demeanour hardly made him popular among fellow officers. One of them wrote of his 'complicated nature' and 'remoteness'. His sense of self-importance apparently had no bounds. There was an episode in 1913 when he was observed assuming a pompous posture towards the Emperor himself.[13] And his leadership potential did appear doubtful at times, such as when he greeted a suggestion about the importance of good food provisions for the troops with the following remark: 'To wage war means to go hungry! If today I start an operation with 250,000 men, I know that I shall reach the objective with only 100,000!'[14] Yet he also possessed plenty of élan. Arthur Bolfras, the head of Franz Joseph's military chancellery, wrote to him in September 1914 that it would be a matter of 'luck' if the Monarchy emerged undiminished from the war that had just begun. 'Oho!', replied Potiorek, 'Much more than that! What is the point of conducting war if we do not wish our fatherland to emerge from it considerably enlarged, and its power and reputation vastly strengthened?'[15]

It has to be said that Potiorek was revered only by few and feared or disliked by many. All those who left written recollections of him are unanimous in their assessment that he was aloof, vain and arrogant. His biographer sees him as a textbook example of a pathological narcissist.[16] One contemporary observed that he was mercilessly sarcastic towards those with lesser intellects. Another remembered him as uncommunicative, withdrawn and unapproachable.[17] Nevertheless, even when he was frowned upon, no one could deny his ability. In 1906, when the question of Beck's successor was being decided, he was the great luminary of operations planning. When, in 1905, it had looked as if the independent-minded politicians in Budapest were threatening the very existence of the dual state, Potiorek was one of three officers entrusted with drawing up plans for a military invasion of Hungary.[18] He seemed to dazzle everyone with his knowledge of military matters. During a reconnaissance trip in Dalmatia, Theodore von Zeynek was flabbergasted by Potiorek's depth of knowledge. He considered him, after Conrad, 'the Army's most interesting personality'.[19] Radiating a 'mystic' intelligence, Potiorek appeared predestined to become the Chief of Staff.[20]

But it was not to be. Archduke Franz Ferdinand, the increasingly assertive heir to the Habsburg throne, was hell-bent on securing the appointment for Franz Conrad. The leadership qualities that the enterprising and charismatic Conrad had exhibited in the previous year during manoeuvres in south Tyrol had greatly impressed him. And in any case he knew Conrad much better than he knew Potiorek.[21] Another important factor in Franz Ferdinand's decision appears to have had to do with Conrad's politics. When the Archduke talked to him at length in the autumn of 1901, on the occasion of the *Kaisermanöver* in southern Hungary, Conrad advocated a solution of the 'South Slav question' in favour of the Croats – and hence at the expense of Hungary. It will be recalled that the Archduke still imagined at this time, i.e., before the 'New Course' in Croat politics which turned Croatia towards Budapest in 1905, that he could use the Croats against Hungary. Conrad's well-known, indeed notorious hostility towards Italy must also have been greeted with warm approval.[22]

It is true that Potiorek had highly influential friends, for example Arthur Bolfras, the head of Kaiser Franz Joseph's military chancellery. Albert Margutti described at some length how Bolfras would treat Potiorek with 'veneration'.[23] But this did not in the end make any difference. It has recently been suggested that Potiorek was seen as a disciple of old Friedrich Beck, and that Franz Ferdinand, who had engineered Beck's downfall, was not going to promote anyone who had been under the wing of the old Chief of the General Staff.[24] However, in view of the fact that the *Thronfolger* and his circle did subsequently endorse Potiorek elsewhere, the situation in 1906 must be seen simply in terms of Conrad presenting a far more dynamic image at the time. Thus it was that Franz Ferdinand pushed obstinately for Conrad who, perhaps against his better judgement, yielded to the Archduke's pressure and was appointed *Chef des Generalstabes* in November 1906. Although he was removed from his post in December 1911 – as the price for meddling in foreign policy – Conrad was reinstated as the Chief of Staff only a year later – during the First Balkan War, a conflict that was redrawing the map of south-eastern Europe and causing much alarm in neighbouring Austria-Hungary. Franz Ferdinand, once again, was instrumental in Conrad's re-appointment.

The Heir to the Throne, indeed, was constantly encroaching on the old Emperor's beloved territory of military affairs, an area the latter had for so long treated as his exclusive domain. And Conrad was just one prominent example. Another one was Moritz Auffenberg, who had commanded the 15th Corps in Sarajevo and whom the Archduke and his military advisers managed to put in charge of the War Ministry at the end of 1911 – much against the wishes of Franz Joseph. But Franz Ferdinand was not content just to control appointments at the highest level. In July 1914, just after the Sarajevo assassination of the Heir to the Throne, the *Danzer's Armee-Zeitung* stated that 'not a single Austro-Hungarian colonel was in charge of a regiment without having previously been approved by the Archduke'.[25] Increasingly losing control over the army, and also his previous joy in running it, the Emperor gave up in the end: in August 1913, he named his nephew as the Inspector-General of the armed forces, a role that would also make him the Commander-in-Chief in wartime.[26] The last military manoeuvres that the Emperor had attended had been those in Carinthia – as far back as the summer of 1907. As he relinquished control, Franz Joseph was in any case disgusted with the Army in the wake of the Colonel Alfred Redl espionage affair.[27] So in June 1914, in his new capacity of Inspector-General, it was Franz Ferdinand who was to attend the manoeuvres south-west of Sarajevo, the capital of Bosnia-Herzegovina. His host there was to be General Oskar Potiorek, the Governor of the provinces since 1911.

The fact that Potiorek had advanced to one of the pivotal positions within the Empire was again due in no small measure to Franz Ferdinand. In the course of 1910 a consensus was emerging that any new military governor of Bosnia-Herzegovina would have to have a strong political role.[28] This view was shared by Franz Ferdinand and his circle of advisers at the Belvedere palace in Vienna. In June 1910 the military governor, General Marijan Vorešanin, narrowly escaped an assassination attempt by the Bosnian Serb Bogdan Žerajić, a student who had initially schemed to kill Franz Joseph – the Emperor having shortly beforehand paid a visit to the provinces. Verešanin, who had also been Franz Ferdinand's choice for the Bosnian post, had during his tenure generally disappointed the expectation that he would govern assertively. The annexation period, moreover, was internationally a very turbulent affair, and it was reasonable to anticipate further complications. There was thus a growing realization in Vienna that someone particularly energetic and resourceful was required in the tricky environment of this 'Quasi-Reichsland'.[29] As early as January 1909, Potiorek's name was being mooted as a candidate for the Sarajevo job.[30] He may have lacked, as Archduke Friedrich observed, the necessary 'knowledge of people and manners', but he more than made up for it in energy and loyalty.[31]

The choice of the decision makers in Vienna in 1910 did indeed fall on Potiorek. His failure in 1906 to obtain the top military post must have been a bitter blow to him at the time, but he had never given up hope of becoming the Chief of Staff, and was always working to accomplish this aim. This is the context in which his acceptance of the Sarajevo posting must be seen. Far from being a forgotten figure, he was doing well in his military career and had indeed absolutely shone during the manoeuvres of 1907 in Carinthia.[32] Promoted to *Feldzeugmeister*, the second highest rank in the Austro-Hungarian army, in 1908, he became Army Inspector in 1910. Potiorek was in Graz commanding the 3rd Corps when, late in 1910, the Bosnian opening arose. He grasped the opportunity immediately.

Sarajevo was certainly preferable to Graz for an officer as aspiring as Potiorek – even though it was a place where, as his biographer put it, one could not just 'win everything, but also lose everything.'[33] Writing about Potiorek's career-oriented nudge towards Bosnia, the Austrian chronicler of the era Karl Nowak pointed out that 'Sarajevo was perhaps the most important, and certainly the most critical place in the Monarchy. It was no small matter to deal with the orthodox Serbs and the Mohammedans, and with the Mohammedans and the Catholics. Whoever commanded in Sarajevo had to show the kind of skill required when walking on the parquet floor in the Imperial palace.'[34] No doubt Potiorek had a good idea of the challenges before him. Irrespective of its potential pitfalls, however, the Bosnian station was the next best thing to being the Chief of Staff, and possibly a stepping stone to it.

But not everyone was keen on Potiorek. Stephan Burián, the Joint Finance Minister who was in overall charge of Bosnia-Herzegovina, reportedly feared Potiorek and tried to sabotage his appointment as Governor. Foreign Minister Aehrenthal was also against him.[35] And although Potiorek was *'persona gratissima'* with Franz Joseph, the latter was said to have considered his 'abrupt manner' rather unpromising for the Sarajevo post.[36] Critically, however, the General had the support of Franz Ferdinand and his military advisers. Burián was a Magyar, and the deep-seated anti-Hungarian sentiment of Franz Ferdinand had predictably translated itself into backing Potiorek. The General's candidacy had also been 'massively supported' by the Emperor's military chancellery, i.e., by Bolfras.[37] Baron Bolfras, showing 'infatuated worship' for Potiorek, did his part by exerting his influence on an otherwise sceptical Franz Joseph who kept delaying the matter for months.[38]

What is noteworthy is that Conrad von Hötzendorf, too, argued in favour of Potiorek. The Chief of General Staff, unhappy about what he saw as the neglect by the civil administration of military concerns in the provinces, had been arguing since 1907 for an extension of the Governor's competences. In 1910 he repeatedly intervened with Franz Joseph to that effect. In December of that year he had recommended the 'energetic' Potiorek to the Emperor for the Bosnian post.[39] It has been speculated that Conrad, keenly aware of Potiorek's thirst for his own job as the Chief of Staff, deliberately steered his rival's career towards a place where, given the accompanying difficulties of the assignment, he could easily make grave mistakes.[40] Certainly, he had no illusions about him. Only weeks after he had recommended him, he revealed bitterly in a private letter that Potiorek had been opposing him on all fronts: 'this man whom I treated four years ago in such a friendly and gentlemanlike manner!' Conrad's impression was that Potiorek was still striving, 'and now perhaps more than before to replace me in my post'.[41] If Conrad had indeed thought that Potiorek would end up in a snake pit, such anticipation was to prove correct – albeit in ways quite unexpected. In May 1911 Potiorek was formally named the *Landeschef* of Bosnia-Herzegovina.

In what was, as will be seen, the reasonably benign political environment presented by Bosnia-Herzegovina in mid-1911, the new Governor could in the initial phase afford to pay little attention to the concrete problems of the lands he was in charge of, and pursue instead his personal plan to construct a position that would allow him to rule as absolutely – and as independently of the Joint Finance Ministry – as possible. He was to be hugely successful in this. As if he did not already know the limitations of his initial power, the press in Sarajevo greeted the new *Landeschef* in June 1911 with comments about the superfluous nature of his post: the real boss in Bosnia-Herzegovina, it was suggested, was the *Ziviladlatus*. Since 1882 the *Ziviladlatus* had acted as the chief political representative of imperial authority in Bosnia-Herzegovina — whilst the military commander, who was the nominal *Landeschef*, had taken a back seat. Both Kállay and Burián had in effect ruled Bosnia-Herzegovina through these civil servants on the spot. So what was the point of retaining a military governor who never governed? A Muslim paper commenting on Potiorek's arrival argued that a military governor had only been necessary at the time when shooting was still going on. A Croat paper demanded that the office, costing the provinces 10,000 crowns, be abolished.[42]

Potiorek, however, had not come to fill a redundant post. This soldier proved very adept in bureaucratic battles: within a year of arriving in Sarajevo he had managed with the help of his influential connections in Vienna to reform much of the previous system of governing the provinces to his own advantage. Count Kielmansegg recalled that Potiorek, 'in his megalomania', wished to get rid of the *Ziviladlatus* in order to fully seize the reins of the government.[43] It was also a case of egomania. When initially approached about the post in the autumn of 1910, Potiorek stipulated as a condition of his acceptance that the powers of the Governor be widened.[44] Interestingly, he then went to Sarajevo without in advance securing an extension of his powers. This was perhaps a sign of his self-confidence, but in any case the time was not yet ripe. The Joint Finance Minister Burián, predictably opposed to changing the status quo, had in any case opposed Potiorek's appointment. Franz von Schönaich, the Joint War Minister since 1906 and Potiorek's ally, urged Burián in 1911 to see the wisdom of boosting the position of the *Landeschef* since Bosnia-Herzegovina would certainly become a battlefield in the event of war, and therefore war preparations should have 'the decisive role.' Burián refused to alter anything, insisting especially on the retention of the post of *Ziviladlatus* which was such a thorn in Potiorek's side.[45]

But Burián was to his astonishment and great disappointment soon ousted from office. As Foreign Minister Aehrenthal lay dying early in 1912, Franz Joseph was hell-bent on ensuring that the Minister's successor should be Count Berchtold — a holder of both Austrian and Hungarian citizenships who spoke little Hungarian, but who was considered by the Emperor to be Hungarian. Since, however, the practice of Dualism did not permit two out of three joint ministers to belong to the same nation, Burián became the surplus Hungarian and had to give way in this very Austro-Hungarian farce.[46] His replacement as the Joint Finance Minister was Leon von Biliński, appointed in February 1912. Franz Ferdinand, delighted at the turn of events, though not necessarily by the advancement of this Austrian Pole, told Biliński of his happiness that Burián, whom he described as a 'rogue and scoundrel', had finally been removed.[47] The Archduke had already in 1908 qualified Burián's rule in Bosnia-Herzegovina as 'disastrous'.[48]

Potiorek now wasted no time and submitted to Biliński a memorandum detailing his reform proposals. Biliński offered no resistance and by the decree of 1 April 1912 the General got everything that he demanded.[49] The previous power relationship between the *Landeschef* and the *Ziviladlatus* was now reversed. The function of *Ziviladlatus* was abolished and replaced by that of *Stellvertreter* (deputy): henceforth Potiorek was to have civilian control in addition to his military prerogatives. The new deputy was to be Potiorek's mere executive attendant. Also henceforth subordinate to his whims would be the local bureaucracy. Article 1 of the decree stated: 'No other functionary of the Provincial Government is authorised to do in political matters anything other than carry out the orders of the *Landeschef*.'[50] Isidor Benko, the long-serving *Ziviladlatus* whom Potiorek had been side-stepping from the beginning, duly resigned.

Moreover, the *Landeschef* was also given greater freedom of action in relation to his bosses at the Joint Finance Ministry in Vienna. Potiorek had already complained that the Provincial Government was merely a mouthpiece of the Ministry.[51] Now it was to be his own mouthpiece: except for business relating to the railways, forestry and mining (over which the Joint Finance Ministry retained overall control), the Provincial Government was essentially given independence of action and could even conclude contracts to the value of 20,000 crowns.[52] In the military sphere Potiorek answered directly to the Emperor. He commanded the troops in Bosnia-Herzegovina (15th Corps, Sarajevo), but also those in Dalmatia (16th Corps, Dubrovnik). Such was his appetite for regional power that in the autumn of 1911 he revealed his hankering to have the 13th Corps, headquartered in Zagreb, added to his military dominion. But this was blocked by the men of Franz Ferdinand's military chancellery, for it smacked too much of an embryo South Slav entity for their liking.[53] Even before the formal announcement of his new status, the local press sensed that Potiorek had begun to initiate major changes. When, in March 1912, he called a meeting of the Provincial Government – something previously always done by the *Ziviladlatus* – the Bosnian Serb paper *Otadžbina* commented: 'Until now every *Landeschef* would treat his post as a well-paid honorary one. They would not exert any influence on the administration itself. Now everything is different!'[54]

The changes of April 1912 made Potiorek a formidably strong governor of Bosnia-Herzegovina. Karl Nowak wrote that only in India did the English viceroy have such an abundance of control.[55] The General had of course received important backing from Conrad – although probably for mendacious reasons, as seen above. But his accumulation of power would not have been possible without the support of Franz Ferdinand and his circle of advisers. In January 1912 Colonel Bardolff agreed with the Governor's suggestion that the powers of the *Ziviladlatus* be quashed – as did Franz Ferdinand.[56] Politically, Potiorek seemed to them exactly the right type of governor for the job in the Balkans. Thus his protests during 1911 about 'Hungary's paralysing influence' in Bosnia-Herzegovina could not have gone unnoticed and would have resonated with the Archduke's military chancellery. Similarly, he was entirely in tune with the Lower Belvedere when he wrote in his annual report for 1911 that relations between Croatia and Bosnia-Herzegovina could potentially lead to Trialism and therefore constituted a 'danger for the Empire'.[57]

The idea behind the fusion of military and civilian competences was not, of course, to reward Potiorek's politics, but rather to have someone on the spot who would, generally, prioritize the military frame of reference with regard to Austro-Hungarian actions in Bosnia-Herzegovina. Specifically, a governor was required who would rule with an iron fist in the event of the anticipated Balkan tumult.[58] This was the flip-side of the constitutional period that had only just begun. General Moritz Auffenberg described the system of enhanced control in Bosnia-Herzegovina – coexisting with the constitutional forms of governance – as 'disguised absolutism.'[59] Bosnian Serb and Bosnian Muslim historians have tended to call it 'the military course'.[60]

A Brilliant Surrogate: Erik von Merizzi

For all of Potiorek's ostentation and disdain for others, there is, strangely perhaps, a real sense in which he voluntarily shared his power in Sarajevo – at least on the military side. When he arrived there in 1911 to take up his new post, he came accompanied by only two officers: Major Erik von Merizzi, his aide-de-camp, and Senior Lieutenant Baron Moritz Ditfurth, his personal adjutant. Those two were still with him on 28 June 1914, holding the same positions, only with higher ranks. Merizzi was, famously, to be wounded that day by an assassin's bomb – thrown at the motorcade proceeding through Sarajevo and intended to kill Franz Ferdinand – while the Archduke's attempt to then visit Merizzi in hospital was to end in a second assassination attempt, this time deadly, and a world war. That much is widely known about Merizzi, but there has been little interest in him beyond the incidental role that he played on that fateful Sunday.

Born in Ljubljana (Laibach) in 1873, Erik was the son of Carl Merizzi, a veteran officer of the Italian campaigns of 1859 and a volunteer in the Mexican adventure of Franz Joseph's younger brother Maximilian. In Slovenia and Trieste Carl Merizzi had served with the 17th 'Carinthian' infantry regiment. Through this regiment he had met and befriended Potiorek, a company commander at the time. On retirement in 1890 he became a minor noble with the title 'Edler von'. His son Erik excelled at his secondary school, where he was a 'model pupil'. He received from his parents a very attentive home upbringing, apparently against a strong Catholic background: his mother in particular was very pious. In 1894, Erik graduated from Vienna's technical military academy (which Potiorek, too, had attended), and authored a study on military horses which received an award from the War Ministry. In 1910 Potiorek took on this son of his comrade as his aide-de-camp.[61]

Of Potiorek's two adjutants, Ditfurth and Merizzi, the latter was by far the more important to the Governor. It was rumoured that Merizzi had great influence on Potiorek, who viewed him with 'special favour'.[62] The most detailed picture that there exists of this officer is provided in the memoirs of Alfred Jansa – the man best known for his role as Austria's Military Attaché in Berlin (1933-1935) and subsequently the Chief of the General Staff of the country's armed forces. But for his retirement in 1937, he might have led an armed resistance to Hitler's Germany. Having been in Bosnia since 1910, Jansa was in 1914 serving as a captain at Potiorek's headquarters. When he reported to Potiorek for the first time the latter, typically, merely extended his hand towards him, without saying a word, and dismissed him with a nod of the head.[63] Jansa loved Bosnia, Herzegovina and Dalmatia, their scenery and their people. His observations about fellow officers are crisp and illuminating. He was never overawed by Potiorek, but he was manifestly mesmerised by Merizzi: 'His brilliant mind makes him the most fascinating man that I have ever met in my life.'[64]

In fact, Jansa had a love-hate type of relationship with Merizzi – as his memoir makes fairly clear. As much as he admired Merizzi's 'superior intellect', he retained a critical attitude, describing him as 'Machiavellian', a man of 'great ambition', who wasted no time in Sarajevo in making sure that no one but himself could influence Potiorek. Merizzi, according to Jansa, worked systematically to keep the command posts of the Sarajevo 15th Corps and Dubrovnik 16th Corps at arm's length from Potiorek. Their previous powers and competences were now taken over by Potiorek's headquarters, that is to say, by Merizzi. The fact that the *Landeschef* would spend considerable amounts of time in the Provincial Government on a daily basis was used by Merizzi to take care of the military side of his boss's business. Everything had to go through Merizzi, and this soon caused resentment. Even General Eduard Böltz, the Chief of Staff to Potiorek, was pushed aside by this aide-de-camp. While Potiorek expended his time and energies on the civilian apparatus, Merizzi was given licence to become the de facto military governor of Bosnia-Herzegovina. Even Jansa himself, in charge of the border area with Serbia and Montenegro, as well as of intelligence matters, was not allowed direct access to the Governor and had to report to Merizzi. Interestingly, when Merrizzi's boss Potiorek had been in charge of the Operations Bureau, he had behaved in much the same way towards the old Friedrich Beck, always seeking to monopolize access to him.[65]

But the net result of the adjutant's urge to control all the avenues to his superior was that, in the *Konak* – the Governor's residence where they worked, ate and slept – Potiorek, Merizzi and Ditfurth were, according to Jansa, 'fully closed off from the surrounding world'. Jansa was not the only one to have remarked on Potiorek's isolation. In another recollection by a contemporary, 'Potiorek, withdrawn and taciturn, lived in Sarajevo quite secluded and was almost nowhere to be seen.' General Auffenberg wrote, similarly, that Potiorek had lived 'the life of a hermit' in Sarajevo and thus lost touch with reality. And Major-General Leopold Kann wrote after the war that Potiorek was 'so hermetically secluded from the external world that in this respect he presented heavy competition to the Dalai Lama of Tibet. The godlike feeling, which had already been dormant in him, had woken up fully and demanded worship.'[66]

In the same vein, General Michael Appel expressed the view that Potiorek 'lived on Mars'. Appel, in charge of the 15th Corps in Sarajevo, was according to Jansa 'a great grumbler' regarding the whole of Potiorek's headquarters. But it was Merizzi who was Appel's main target of complaint. In March 1914 he wrote bitterly, in a private letter, that Merizzi was 'quixotic', that he shied away from troops and that Potiorek allowed himself to be informed exclusively by Merizzi who was 'a pure theoretician and bureaucrat'. The two of them, Appel noted, 'live in the *Konak*, in their self-constructed world'. In April he restated his complaint about Potiorek's undivided reliance on Merizzi. His principal onslaught, however, was reserved for the aide-de-camp: 'I know of no officer in the whole of Sara-jevo – and neither do I know anyone from among the better civil servants – who does not want to send Merizzi to hell, or does not find in him the cause of so many frictions.'[67]

Regardless of what others thought of them, Potiorek and Merizzi were perfectly congenial to each other: Potiorek had no intention of letting near him someone with greater formal authority, whereas Merizzi reaped bene-fits in terms of power and influence over and above what his rank would otherwise have permitted.[68] But was there perhaps something more to this relationship than met the eye? Merizzi was, in the view of a contemporary, the Governor's 'preferred confidant, the only one with whom Potiorek also got together off-duty'. A short memoir of Sarajevo 1914, by staff officer Friedrich Bauer, stressed that Potiorek had closer contact 'only with his aide-de-camp ... who also lived in the *Konak*, and dined mostly with him'.[69]

Whether the two shared anything more than the roof of the *Konak* and its dining table is something upon which one can only speculate. According to the British historian Norman Stone, Potiorek was 'a neurotic homo-sexual'. Theodor von Lerch recalled that, 'rightly or wrongly', Potiorek's reputation among the officers was that of a 'misogynist'.[70] Heinrich von Lützow, the distinguished Austro-Hungarian diplomat, wrote suggestively in his memoirs that Potiorek had a protective 'warm friend' in the military chancellery – the head of the chancellery was of course Potiorek's great admirer Baron Bolfras.[71]

In his biography of Potiorek, Rudolf Jeřábek tackles this subject towards the very end, pointing out the closeness of the Potiorek-Merizzi relationship, and even referring to Freud's observation that narcissistic homosexuals choose partners who mirror aspects of themselves. He takes the view, however, that Potiorek's 'enormous self-discipline' alone, quite apart from his awareness of career-ending scandal, would, as he puts it, 'seem' to preclude any 'corresponding sexual behaviour'.[72]

Be that as it may, Potirek and Merizzi were certainly bed-fellows in the metaphorical sense. They combined their skills to play a tactical game from Sarajevo with regard to the flavour of their reports to the two different and in many ways opposed power centres in Vienna: the Schönbrunn and the Belvedere. Those reports were, in a sense, made-to-measure. Jansa noted the 'eagerness' of Potiorek and Merizzi to please equally the old Emperor and his military chancery on the one hand, and the Archduke and his own military chancery on the other: 'In the light of the poor relations between the Heir to the Throne and the Emperor, Potiorek and Merizzi did not balk at feeding different reports. I could not under-stand this double-dealing, it was simply repugnant to me.' Certainly, Potiorek knew that he could not ignore Franz Ferdinand: he made it his practice, for example, to check all the sensitive appointments in Bosnia-Herzegovina with the Belvedere.[73] Whereas his wish to sit on two chairs might be comprehensible and indeed logical given that he was the Gover-nor, Merizzi's very active role in this endeavour must be seen in the context of his own, not inconsiderable appetite for success.[74]

Staff officer Jansa also identified another instance in which, much to his aggravation, Potiorek and Merizzi conspired to join forces. And this was aimed against no less a person than the Chief of the General Staff, Conrad von Hötzendorf. The latter was 'adored' by officers in Sarajevo – a sentiment which, not surprisingly, was not shared by Potiorek. In Jansa's eyes, the Governor's attitude to Conrad was 'depressing'. The specific matter which arose in the first half of 1914 was the urgent need to replace the old mountain artillery available to the Austro-Hungarian forces in Bosnia-Herzegovina: they still had guns from 1875, with a range of 3km, whereas the Serbian Army possessed the modern French artillery, made by

Schneider, with a range of 7.5km. The energetic Conrad had succeeded in getting the Škoda works to produce an equivalent and have it ready for trials. The new batteries were successfully tested at Kalinovik in Bosnia, but Potiorek and Merizzi objected on what Jansa described as 'senseless and silly' grounds: the new gear, the heavy 7.5cm mountain gun, would have to be drawn by seven horses (as opposed to three for the old guns), which increased the possibility of a horse falling over. It is not hard to imagine that the initiator of this sabotage was Merizzi, the author of a study on military horses. So Potiorek and Merizzi demanded that the whole system be redesigned so that only five horses would be required to pull the gun. The end result was that this weapon was not introduced until 1915. Jansa, beside himself with fury, decided to protest over this matter to Merizzi – an officer otherwise schooled in artillery. He told him that 'the whole thing would be an irresponsible hold-up of the efforts of the Chief of the General Staff'. Jansa slammed his reports folder on the table in disgust as Merizzi, 'smiling smugly', commented with not a scintilla of guilt: 'So indeed it should be.'[75]

The role played by Erik von Merizzi in the genesis of the idea to invite Franz Ferdinand to the June manoeuvres in Bosnia-Herzegovina is a matter of legitimate conjecture. For it seems most unlikely that this man of 'Italian intrigue', as Jansa described him, would have had nothing to do with the initial thinking about a possible visit. It is even probable that he originated the entire enterprise. In a whole army of Austro-Hungarian civil administrators and military personnel in Sarajevo, only two people actually mattered: Potiorek and Merizzi. This is abundantly clear from all the relevant memoir literature. In the light of his ability to control all the channels to the Governor, however, Merizzi was perhaps the most important officer in Bosnia-Herzegovina, and he was no less ambitious than his boss Potiorek.

One of the more revealing details about Merizzi in Jansa's memoir concerns his attempt to ingratiate himself with the Archduke through an ostentatious display of religious ardour: a Franciscan prior would often receive so much attention on his visits to Merizzi that everyone else would be kept waiting for a long time. The reporting of even the most urgent matters would be stopped when this Franciscan appeared at the headquarters. Merizzi would hurry towards him to kiss his hand, making a deep bow. Jansa received the impression that Merizzi's humility was deliberately overemphasized 'in order that his pious Catholicism would be reported to the Archduke-Heir to the Throne, whose devotion to the Catholic church was well known'.[76]

That Merizzi should wish to get noticed by the Archduke is not in the least surprising. Potiorek's own 'ambitious plans' to have Franz Ferdinand come to Bosnia were known to contemporaries, as Count Kielmasegg for example noted in his memoirs.[77] But Merizzi shared that ambition for his own reasons. Not only was Franz Ferdinand going to be the future Emperor: he was already making or breaking military careers. Merizzi had perhaps excellent reasons to believe in his own ability as a soldier and in his good prospects for advancement – he was not a mere protégé of Potiorek's, and his professional background was anything but routine. Before Potiorek made him his aide-de-camp in 1910, he had already served as an orderly officer to Friedrich Beck at General Staff headquarters, and later spent seven years in the the so-called 'Op.B.': the Operations Bureau, the brain centre of the Army.[78] This was a distinguished record. In Jansa's judgement Merizzi was a highly capable military planner.[79] Certainly, Potiorek backed him to the hilt. Thus in 1911 he declared that Merizzi 'possesses excellent aptitude for the head of a chiefs of staff bureau, or the chief of staff of a higher command, as well as for a military attaché and for difficult special missions'.[80]

Being in such a privileged position at Potiorek's side, in the politically and militarily pivotal part of the Empire, he could be justified in thinking that his talents would be taken note of by Franz Ferdinand were the latter to come to Bosnia. The point about the summer 1914 manoeuvres is that their planning had been entrusted to Merizzi. During the actual manoeuvres Potiorek himself would have overall supervision while Merizzi was to be entrusted with the operational side.[81] Thus Merizzi had every reason to view the whole exercise as potentially enhancing his career: if the war games went well, Potiorek would receive the acclaim, but he would share some of it. And if Potiorek succeeded in becoming the Chief of the General Staff, so much the better.

Bosnia-Herzegovina After 1910

The political situation prevailing in Bosnia-Herzegovina at the time of General Potiorek's arrival in June 1911 had of course been affected by the introduction in 1910 of the Constitution and the local Diet. It was shown in chapter four that the Serb and Muslim leaders (of the SNO and MNO respectively) had, albeit reluctantly, accepted the annexation and then, curiously, even welcomed the impotent Diet bestowed subsequently on Bosnia-Herzegovina. The SNO and MNO were the two main political groupings of the Serbs and Muslims, but they were certainly not the only ones. Before the annexation the Serbs had also had the *Srpska samostalna stranka* (Serb Independent Party), and the Muslims the *Muslimanska napredna stranka* (Muslim Progressive Party). The former was concerned mainly with the agrarian issue and yet it was Monarchy-oriented, while the latter was a Croat-leaning and likewise Empire-friendly party. But neither enjoyed significant support. The SNO and MNO had easily maintained their pre-eminent positions.

The Bosnian Croats, although united in their support for the annexation, were the ones who were otherwise the most seriously split. The leaders of their party, the HNZ, were supremely aware that, owing to the numerical inferiority of the Bosnian Croats, the party had to remain open to, and try to win over the Muslims, whom it treated as Croats of Muslim faith. Yet Archbishop Stadler, who had been keen to take over the leadership of the HNZ, wished to see the Bosnian Croat political organization established on a strict national-confessional basis. He saw it as his duty, he explained, to fuse Catholicism with Croat patriotism.[82] The Muslims could only have a subordinate place in this scheme of things. Unable to impose his line in the HNZ, Stadler established a clerical party in January 1910, the *Hrvatska katolička udruga* (HKU) – Croat Catholic Association. Much of his support was based on the Catholic immigrant element in Bosnia-Herzegovina. Unlike HNZ, moreover, the HKU was rabidly anti-Serbian, believing that the Serbs were more dangerous to the Croats than either the Magyars or the Austrian Germans.[83]

Apart from dividing the Bosnian Croats over what the character of their national party should be, however, the HKU stood firmly on the positions developed in Croatia since the mid-1890s by the successors of Ante Starčević: a Great Croatia to include Bosnia-Herzegovina, but within a reformed Habsburg framework, i.e., within a new, Trialist configuration.[84] In this key policy orientation the HKU did not differ from its HNZ rival. All the politically organized Bosnian Croats, in other words, shared with their brethren in Croatia-Slavonia the optimistic expectation that the Habsburg Empire would actually reform in line with Croat national aspirations. As was seen in chapter three, Croat loyalty to the Monarchy was thus conditional, save for that of the Pure Party of Right whose leader and political fortune-hunter Dr Josip Frank had since 1908 practically, given up on the Trialist scenario, and embraced instead the obedient 'Austro-Slav' approach beloved by Franz Ferdinand. Although quite close to Frank, Stadler was on the other hand never going to abandon the idea of Bosnia-Herzegovina together with other Croat lands forming a new unit in a re-designed Monarchy. A main consideration behind his founding of the HKU was the fear that the HNZ would cooperate with the Croato-Serb Coalition in Croatia – in Stadler's view a dangerous step that could in turn lead to a Croat-Serb alignment in Bosnia-Herzegovina and thus also to a possible abandonment of the cardinal Croat demand that these provinces be joined to Croatia.[85]

The May 1910 Diet elections had produced sweeping victories for the established parties. Interestingly, voter turnout was massive, especially among Serbs and Muslims. The SNO won all thirty-one of the Serbian ethnic/confessional mandates, while the MNO won all of the twenty-four reserved for the Muslims. The HNZ won twelve out of the sixteen Croat seats, leaving Stadler's newly-formed HKU with only four – and the Archbishop 'exceptionally disappointed and bitter'.[86] All these different parties, however, quickly found common cause. On 23 June 1910, just days after the opening of the Diet, the deputies unanimously passed a joint resolution demanding a revision of the Constitution. A main complaint was that the governments of Austria and Hungary had unlimited powers to determine the administrative direction in Bosnia-Herzegovina; another was that the Provincial Government lacked any responsibility towards the Diet. The deputies pointed out that legislative control by their representative assembly was thus 'fully illusory'.[87]

Nevertheless, on 4 August 1910 the majority of deputies duly approved the Government's budget, adopting the standpoint – according to one interpretation – that it would be wrong to create a constitutional crisis at the very beginning of the constitutional era.[88] Todor Kruševac best described the background of the prevailing, forward-looking mood: the pleasing novelty of free public assembly; the holding of elections without any interference by the Provincial Government; the opening of the Diet with the introduction of parliamentary practices hitherto unknown; and, finally, the voicing by the deputies of sharp criticism of foreign absolutist rule – all these combined to create the impression that, outwardly at any rate, the political situation in Bosnia-Herzegovina had changed a great deal.[89]

The Bosnian *kmet* rebellion in the west and north (discussed in chapter four) which began soon thereafter was to have important repercussions on political alignments within the Diet and on the politics of the Muslims in particular. The Serb SNO had in its election platform emphasized the importance of the agrarian question and demanded a solution on a compulsory basis. This demand had been a token one, as has already been argued in this book, for the affluent merchant class (the so-called *čaršija*) leading the SNO had been less concerned with improving the position of the Serbian *kmets*, than it had been about maintaining its ties with the Muslim MNO. It seems that official Serbia had also been hinting to the SNO leadership that it should treat the strategic alliance with the Muslims as its priority.[90] However, internal pressures for a radical solution of the agrarian problem remained quite strong. The most prominent champion of the *kmets* was the writer Petar Kočić, himself a deputy and the editor of *Otadžbina* (Fatherland), a paper based initially in Banja Luka before it moved to Sarajevo. Kočić and a powerful group of like-minded SNO deputies could not be ignored by the leadership, but soon the incongruities in Serbian policy programmes were to be on full view in the Diet.

The *kmet* rebellion that took place in summer-autumn 1910 had a decisive influence on Muslim opinion: uniting it in the belief that the turmoil had been no spontaneous affair and that it had been deliberately instigated by the Serbs – by Kočić and his group in particular. It was even believed that the events signified the 'beginning of terror' by means of which the Orthodox Serbs intended to drive out the Muslim landowners from their possessions. Mustafa Imamović assessed that such fears were 'definitely exaggerated', but sufficient for the Muslim MNO bosses to jettison their previous alliance with the Serbs and seek a new one with the HNZ Croats.[91] The latter now welcomed the opportunity to build an alliance with the Muslims – this, after all, had always been the aim of the HNZ. Equally, a Muslim-Croat coalition had been the preference of the Austro-Hungarian administration since its arrival in 1878. Continuing its policy of upholding the privileges of *begs* and *agas*, the *Landesregierung* introduced in July 1910 a bill on the agrarian question – proposing it be solved on the basis of optional, that is voluntary, rather than compulsory purchase of the land cultivated by *kmets* – an option based of course on the assumption that the *kmet* and the landlord had already reached an agreement about the transaction. This had in any case been the practice in the past – the novelty was that the Provincial Government was now ready to provide the necessary loans. The snag was that the proposed law envisaged the purchase of land only if the *kmet's* enterprise was economically viable, and only the Provincial Government, as the intermediary, could be the judge on this matter.[92]

The bill was eventually passed in the Diet in April 1911, predictably through the support of the Muslims and their new Croat allies. Significantly, twelve Serb deputies from the *čaršija* group also voted for it, including the prominent SNO leader and multi-millionaire Gligorije Jeftanović. He was privately quite pleased that the press in Belgrade had supported him on this.[93] In all likelihood, therefore, official Belgrade had in this instance been behind what amounted to support of Austro-Hungarian policy in Bosnia-Herzegovina. Petar Kočić and his agrarian group had already left the SNO in 1910, thus dealing the first official blow to Serb unity. It seems that those Serbs voting for the agrarian bill had hoped to make the HNZ Croats look a little unnecessary to the Muslims in the light of the newly-forged alliance between the two.[94] Indeed, the old Serb leadership, the *čaršija* grandees who had led the struggle for church and school autonomy, had never abandoned their policy of wooing the Muslim patricians.

By the time of Potiorek's arrival in Bosnia-Herzegovina the organized political forces representing the Serbs, Muslims and Croats had thus become much less of a threat to the Monarchy. The annexation had not resulted in any internal unrest, and the attempted assassination by Bogdan Žerajić on Governor Varešanin had in fact been a lonely protest. The 1910 *kmet* rebellion had been directed against an ancient system of taxation and had had little to do with Austro-Hungarian rule as such. Perhaps the most important change since the annexation was in the attitude of the Muslims. Before 1908 there existed a joint Muslim-Serb interest in preventing the provinces being annexed to the Monarchy; after the annexation conflicting Muslim and Serb interests regarding the *kmets* gradually emerged into the forefront.[95] The Muslim landowning class could now finally be brought into line with Austro-Hungarian interests in Bosnia-Herzegovina.

The Serbs, on the other hand, were internally split and outmanoeuvred in the Diet by the post-1910 Muslim-Croat combination. The conservative leadership of the *čaršija* faction, in any case, wished to be seen as a loyal rather than a radical opposition. The Croats, divided between the HNZ and Stadler's HKU, had begun to heal their split from early 1911, a process which was to lead in 1912 to the fusion of the two parties.[96] However, the Croat strategem of 'Croatizing' the Muslims into then supporting a Trialist reconstruction of the Monarchy had always been a pipe-dream. The idea presupposed, of course, Bosnia-Herzegovina joining the Croat lands. On 2 May 1911 the Muslim deputies issued an unambiguous statement: 'We Muslims uphold the autonomy of Bosnia and Herzegovina, whatever the constitutional shape of the Habsburg Monarchy.'[97] As Mirjana Gross noted, the Muslim *begs* could now feel confident that they were a factor of extraordinary importance: favoured by the regime and an object of Serbo-Croat competition, they could always tip the scales.[98]

The Biliński-Potiorek Partnership

Even before the Balkan Wars had begun in the autumn of 1912 Potiorek thought that the vital nerve, as well as the future, of the Monarchy lay in the Balkans, and that any war embroilments would begin there.[99] For the time being, however, there was no sign of any major trouble. On 2 October 1911 the *Landeschef* opened the new, second, session of the *Sabor* (Diet) with a short speech which, according to the local press, he delivered 'as if he wanted to make fun both of the Sabor and of the language in which he spoke'.[100] Alfred Jansa recalled that Potiorek had 'studied Serbian very diligently', but noted also that learning the language was no light task for a man of his age.[101] Potiorek's priorities at this point, in any case, were neither the local politics nor the local language. Apart from building the case for the enlargement of his authority, he was anxious in the initial phase of his rule to ascertain the military situation in the provinces. He spotted the main problem immediately: poor transport links with the rest of the Monarchy and an almost complete absence of standard-gauge railways. This was bad news in the event of a war in the south-east. Potiorek suggested the construction of a standard-gauge line through western Bosnia 'at least to Mostar', another line through east Bosnia to Sarajevo, and a cross connection, also standard-gauge, between those two. As he was to find out, however, railway planning for Bosnia-Herzegovina presented a typical Austro-Hungarian quagmire: the two partners, Austria and Hungary, had different ideas about the routes. Moreover, there existed no clarity regarding the costs, nor was it clear which lines the Monarchy should finance and which lines should be financed by the provinces themselves.[102]

As a former Director-General of Austrian State Railways, the new Joint Finance Minister Leon Biliński also took an interest in the Bosnian railways – indeed this was to be the chief element of his ambitious investment programme for Bosnia-Herzegovina. So in this aspect Potiorek could feel that he had an ally rather than a rival in Vienna. And despite his successful power grab in Sarajevo, he still had to report to the Joint Finance Minister in Vienna and co-ordinate policies with him – especially with regard to the railways. But should Biliński be dismissed as otherwise irrelevant? Robin Okey has suggested that, in the light of Potiorek's seizure of overall civil-military control, Biliński's role 'was clearly intended to be technocratic in character, and he developed no distinctive strategy for Bosnia'.[103] Yet, as can be seen in contemporary diplomatic reporting, Biliński's Bosnian policy was identified as the indirect cause of the 28 June assassination in Sarajevo. Thus the French Ambassador to Vienna, Alfred Dumaine, wrote in a telegram dated 2 July 1914: 'General Potiorek ... has established that, in the past months, none of the rigorous measures he has been calling for to curb Pan-Serbian party propaganda have been approved in Vienna. Responsibility for this falls to M. de Bilinski ... who was experimenting with conciliation and appeasement methods.'[104] Given that such assessments of the Joint Finance Minister pervaded much of the subsequent historiography, it would seem relevant to ask: what were his broad objectives in Bosnia-Herzegovina? How did he get on with Potiorek?

As is well known, the Biliński-Potiorek relationship came under severe strain, amid mutual recriminations, following the assassination of Franz Ferdinand. Later, in his memoirs, Biliński painted a most unflattering picture of Potiorek, whereas the Governor's apologists attempted to discredit the Minister. One of them was Josef Brauner who in 1929 wrote a long article on pre-1914 Bosnia-Herzegovina for the influential *Berliner Monatshefte* (formerly *Die Kriegsschuldfrage*). Brauner, while grudgingly acknowledging Biliński's loyalty to the state, nevertheless accused him of having pursued a policy which was 'at heart Slavonic', and actually spelled out what this meant in the Bosnian context by referring to 'Biliński's sympathies for the Serbs'. In 1964 Potiorek's first biographer Franz Weinwurm made the same point.[105] Biliński's predecessor Burián had also been accused of Serbophilia. On a superficial reading, then, it would appear that the Bosnian policies of Benjámin Kállay's two successors at the Joint Finance Ministry had, paradoxically, been guided by pro-Serb sentiment for more than a decade prior to the assassination of Franz Ferdinand.

However, it has been seen in a previous chapter that Burián can hardly be considered in that light. So what about Biliński?

Biliński's personal loyalty to Franz Joseph has never been disputed, but it must be made clear here that he was at the same time profoundly supportive of the Habsburg state itself. His Polish background has to some suggested otherwise. However, Rudolf Sieghart, who knew him well, recorded his own impression that, as the Monarchy fell apart at the end of the war, Biliński was one of the 'genuinely grieving' Poles. And more than that: 'He [Biliński] was the type of the Austrian, indeed Viennese Poles, who felt himself at his most comfortable in the balmy, gentle air of Austrianism.' It is true that he had after the war been called by Józef Piłsudski to come to the new Polish state, and he did serve briefly in 1919 as Finance Minister in the government of Jan Paderewski. However, as Sieghart noted, he became 'disgruntled' in Poland and soon returned to Austria, living mostly in Vienna and Bad Ischl.[106]

Jovan M. Jovanović, the Serbian Minister in Vienna who had dealt with Biliński far more than with the Foreign Minister Berchtold, provided interesting insights into the outlook of this Austrian Pole. He emphasized that Biliński had favoured a peaceful resolution of differences between Austria-Hungary and Serbia, 'not because he was a Slav, a Pole, but because he had deeply believed that Austria-Hungary, in its struggle with Serbia, had to be stronger. His mind, his Austrian mentality, could not contemplate any other end result.' Moreover, Biliński left Jovanović in no doubt about his Habsburg orientation: 'When we discussed the Yugoslav problem, he would always persevere in maintaining that, sooner or later, all the Slavs outside Russia would unite, indeed under the Habsburgs and against Russia.' The Joint Finance Minister was thus hardly a closet anti-Habsburg, or a Slav subversive. As for his supposed sympathies for the Serbs, Jovanović could detect only flexible tactics designed to produce an ultimate Habsburg success: 'Biliński believed that, through his conciliatory policy of concessions of every kind in Bosnia, he would succeed in forcing first the Serbs in Bosnia, and later Serbia, to give way and meet final doom in some distant future.'[107] Obviously, what was meant by 'final doom' was the collapse of the idea that Bosnia-Herzegovina would leave the Monarchy to join Serbia.

Even Brauner admitted in his 1929 article that, 'until the unfortunate 28 June 1914', the relationship between Biliński and Potiorek had been perfectly amicable and that any divergences would have been eliminated through mutual understanding and accommodation.[108] Biliński favoured, as Jovanović reported, a peaceful approach towards Serbia – and yet, as is well known, in July 1914 he was to advocate war. What is less known is that he had already urged war against Serbia in the spring of 1913. Potiorek, on the other hand, has generally been seen as an uncompromising opponent of the Serbs – the Austro-Hungarian General second only to Conrad in his dogged resolve to settle the South Slav question by force of arms. The *Landeschef*, however, began to display this attitude only with the onset of the Balkan Wars in October 1912. Even in early 1913 he was still capable of arguing what would today be called a 'soft power' approach. Thus, in a private letter to Biliński, he wrote that Sarajevo should be a spiritual centre to rival Belgrade, a seat of excellence especially in the field of Balkan research: 'the whole world', he wrote, should see that Sarajevo was the 'undisputed' leader.[109] This was both statesmanlike and entirely consistent with Biliński's line of reasoning.

It is also questionable whether any major disagreement existed between Biliński and Potiorek on the *modus operandi* to be employed towards the Bosnian Serbs – or rather the Serb deputies in the Provincial Diet. In his memoirs Biliński accused Potiorek of nurturing political and personal hatred of the Serbs. He went on to write that he, Biliński, could not, in the administration of Bosnia-Herzegovina, ignore the Serbs who were the strongest of the three groups, not only numerically but also in terms of 'wealth, political aptitude, energy, ability, church and school organization, etc'. Significantly, however, he added that he had conducted his administrative policy in agreement with Potiorek who had always offered him 'help and almost friendship' and whom he had always supported with the Emperor.[110] This would point not only to a cosy working relationship between the Joint Finance Minister and the *Landeschef*, but also to their basic consensus about the Serbs. It is simply not the case, as Vladimir Dedijer asserted, that Potiorek 'completely opposed' Biliński's efforts to build bridges with Serb bourgeois groups in Bosnia-Herzegovina.[111]

The truth was that neither Biliński nor Potiorek were interested in being either courteous or horrible to this or that side in Bosnia-Herzegovina. What they were interested in was getting things done, which is the key to their essentially harmonious relationship. This is illustrated, for example, by their dealings with the Bosnian Diet in the course of 1912 when they sought approval for the annual budget and, more importantly, the railways investment programme which had by then been coordinated with the governments of Austria and Hungary. Biliński and Potiorek, working closely together, were now keen to secure a pro-Government majority – with or without the Serbs. In the first half of 1912 the Muslim-Croat majority in the Diet had become unstable. Some Muslim deputies, led by Derviš beg Miralem, had deserted to the Serbs.[112] And although the Serb SNO contained a cooperative group fluctuating between seven and sixteen deputies (*arbeitswillige Serben*) around Gligorije Jeftanović and Vojislav Šola, the party (always a 'loose alliance' according to the Bosnian Serb historian Milorad Ekmečić) had by spring effectively ceased to exist in the aftermath of major defections.[113] It was in this fluid state of affairs that Biliński, during his first visit to the provinces in June 1912, sounded out all parties to ascertain their position on his investment programme which, apart from railways, also envisaged improvements in agriculture, health, etc. By 19 June an ad hoc Government majority was in place, consisting of Serbs, Croats and Muslims. But when these deputies demanded alterations and attached conditions to Biliński's proposals, he told them, before leaving Sarajevo, that unless they agreed to the whole of his programme, unaltered, he would bring it about without the Diet – a telling comment on how much impor-tance the Minister from Vienna attached to the Bosnian parliament.[114]

The Muslim-Croat bloc agreed later to accept the programme in its entirety. This bloc was then joined by pro-Government Serb deputies who became known as the 'business group'. On 3 December 1912 all of them together, forming a majority, voted both for the budget and the investment programme.[115] In retrospect, however, the whole furore turned out to be a waste of time because delays in the construction of the financial package, as well as in getting the approval of the Austrian and Hungarian parlia-ments, meant that the programme was never realized. At the time, how-ever, such was the keen anticipation of the promised investments that the pro-Government deputies dropped at the last moment their previous opposition to the use of the German language on the railways – agreeing to treat the matter as a separate issue.[116] The Serb deputies in this coalition represented in part the interests of the more prosperous Serbs who had accumulated capital and in some cases owned banks – for them the lure of the various economic opportunities presented by the railways project was difficult to resist. However, before the Serbs had decided to lend a hand, Biliński, viewing the Serb deputies in general as obstructive and even describing them as 'childish', had been happy to accept Potiorek's proposal that they could be left out if the effort to build a Muslim-Croat majority should succeed.[117]

Neutralizing the Serbs of Bosnia

By the time that the Bosnian deputies had voted for the investment programme, Potiorek had already had to busy himself with more pressing matters. The Balkan War broke out in October 1912 and was not surpris-ingly to claim most of this soldier's attention. Sharing the widely-held expectation that the Serbian forces would be defeated by the Turks, and convinced that those Serb deputies still hesitant to join the Government bloc would overcome their doubts once this happened, the politician in him initially actually welcomed the conflagration on the south-eastern borders of the Empire.[118] Very soon, however, his tone changed markedly. When the Serbian Army entered Skopje in Macedonia, all the Serb groups in the Bosnian Diet, divided as they otherwise were, wrote a congratulatory

telegram to Prince Alexander. Since Bosnia-Herzegovina's postal and telegraph services were in the hands of the military, the telegram was never
sent, but Potiorek, of course, had read it. Tellingly, he commented to Biliński on 28 October: 'The incident shows quite clearly how it is with the
dynastic feelings of our Serbian intelligentsia. For the time being there is
nothing to do except wait patiently, until the hour of reckoning strikes.'[119]

By now, what primarily worried the *Landeschef* was the potential impact
of the Balkan conflagration on the internal political situation in the
provinces. Interestingly, in October he still believed that 'the bulk of our
Serbs are undoubtedly not hostile to the Empire'. But he drew attention
to individual 'machinations', coordinated with Serbia, aimed at getting
those Serbs liable for military service in Bosnia-Herzegovina to desert
across the border. Such activities in his view would soon be successful and
would then require repressive measures – something that would damage
the internal political situation far more than 'preventive measures,
deployed in a timely manner'.[120] If anything, however, Potiorek had
underestimated the popular mood in Bosnia favouring Serbia during the
First Balkan War. Hamdija Kapidžić, in his important essay on Austro-
Hungarian policies in Bosnia-Herzegovina during 1912, reminded that only
the Bosnian Muslims were on the side of the Turks; the Bosnian Serbs were
helping Serbia by 'all possible means' – with volunteers, with help to the
Serbian Red Cross, etc; and 'a significant part' of the Bosnian Croats had
begun to sympathize with the Balkan allies in their war against Turkey.[121]

The tremors were felt regionally: for example, Serbian victories led to
anti-Habsburg demonstrations in several towns in Dalmatia, garrisoned by
the 16th Corps and therefore within Potiorek's military domain. Some
8,000 came to a meeting in Split on 10 November – more than a third of
the entire population. Vinko Katalinić, the Mayor, told the crowd: 'We
Croats rapturously salute the sound of our national resurrection.'[122] At a
parallel meeting in Šibenik, people shouted: 'Down with Franz Joseph! ...
Down with Hungary! Down with Austria!'[123] When a group of Montenegrins stopped over in Split on their way from Germany to Montenegro,
the Mayor gave them a jolly welcome, distributing a hundred crowns to
each. The Montenegrins thought that the whole Monarchy was supporting
Montenegro in the war against Turkey, so they began to acclaim Franz
Joseph – and then found that the burghers of Split were not joining in.[124]
Alarmed by the unrest, Potiorek had hurriedly left for Split to assess the
situation. During his absence, on 16 November, some five hundred Serbs
and Croats marched through the streets of Sarajevo, chanting songs and
expressing support for the Balkan allies.[125]

On the same day there was a further shock for Potiorek when all the
Serb deputies, as well as most high dignitaries of the Serbian Orthodox
Church in Bosnia-Herzegovina, signed a declaration which was published

in the leading Serb papers. At a time when Austria-Hungary and Italy were supporting the establishment of an independent Albanian state – and thus denying Serbia its gains on the Adriatic coast – the declaration stated: 'The behaviour of Austria-Hungary, which is demanding autonomy rights for the uncivilized Albanians even though it is denying the same rights in its own state to the South Slavs ... is provoking the greatest bitterness in all sections of the Serbian people in Bosnia-Herzegovina.' The Serb deputies expressed, as an act of 'holy duty', their 'admiration for the brethren in the Kingdom of Serbia and in Montenegro'.[126] Potiorek was furious, as indeed was Biliński who even demanded that the deputies apologize in the form of a communiqué.[127] A counter-measure of a kind ensued swiftly, on 18 November, when some 3,000 Muslims assembled at Potiorek's residence to demonstrate loyalty to the Emperor and shout anti-Serb slogans. According to Hamdija Kapidžić, this event had in all probability been staged in cooperation with the authorities.[128]

Yet it would be wrong to conclude that the complete Bosnian Serb elite had suddenly become traitors. It is true that only the ultra loyal Metropolitan Evgenije Letica had refused to sign their declaration. However, the opportunist leaders from the Serb *čaršija*, among them Gligorije Jeftanović and Vojislav Šola, were simply anxious to keep their political careers alive and professed astonishment that their signatures should have been construed as indicating a lack of loyalty to the state. Even the agrarian champion and confirmed oppositionist Petar Kočić said that he could not grasp why the declaration should throw doubts on the dynastic fidelity of the Serbs. Potiorek, puzzled, commented: 'In Serbian heads the world certainly reflects itself somewhat differently than in those of the West Europeans.'[129] In fact, hard calculations were in play. When Potiorek asked Šola to explain his signature, the latter replied at length about his initial unwillingness to sign. But he also pointed out that the Slav members in the Delegations and the Vienna *Reichsrat* had already made their sympathy for the Balkan allies known – it was only the Bosnian Serbs who had until then kept quiet; some Serbian deputies had threatened to brand him 'a traitor of the nation' unless he signed; and even Muslim and Croat leaders had told him that signing was 'the lesser evil'. As Jeftanović subsequently explained, if he and his reluctant colleagues had not signed the declaration, 'we would have been finished for good, and this way we could still have opportunities to work for the people and the state'.[130] He meant the Habsburg state.

In late 1912 the problem of Bosnia-Herzegovina for the Monarchy was not the loyalty, or lack thereof, of the Bosnian Serb elite. The problem was that the Habsburg state seemed to be offering nothing to its Serbs or to the South Slavs in general, whereas at the same time the Kingdom of Serbia was with its allies ousting Turkey from the Balkans. The effects of the Balkan War were mesmerizing. Provincial Government reports talked about Bosnia's peasants rejoicing that Serbia would take Bosnia and 'immediately liberate the serfs'.[131] Serbia's *Anziehungskraft* (drawing power), as it was to be called in Vienna, was clearly recognized by Potiorek when he wrote on 24 December to Baron Bolfras, his friend and protector in Franz Joseph's military chancellery: 'What I fear, however, is the increasingly pervasive opinion among the local civil population that the Kingdom of Serbia, in a similar manner to what it is now doing with the Turkish land, possesses the power and the will to annex Bosnia-Herzegovina within a short space of time.' The *Landeschef* advocated as a solution that Serbia and Montenegro be, as he put it, 'chained' to the Monarchy through a customs union. But first they had to be beaten. And here, again, Potiorek was concerned about domestic political perception. Since, he explained, the Serbs of Bosnia could now see Serbian and Montenegrin troops in the areas which had only recently been garrisoned by Austria-Hungary (i.e., Sanjak), their conviction about the weakness of the Monarchy could only be dispelled if their South Slav neighbours were removed from there. But the Bosnian Serbs would actually have to 'see it' happen – because 'that is the only way in the East'.[132] This was a good point, but of course it implied a military intervention in the Balkans. It also spoke volumes about how the Monarchy perceived war as an instrument necessary to solve its internal nationalities problems. The same reasoning was to play a part in Vienna's decisions in July 1914.

During these weeks and months of heightened regional tensions Potiorek was not only worrying about the Serbs. Casting a glance at neighbouring Croatia early in December, he noted that the Croats, under the regime of *Ban* Slavko Cuvaj, felt themselves persecuted, abandoned by the Dynasty, and delivered to their mortal enemy, Hungary. He also perceived the spread of Yugoslav ideas amongst them, but what bothered him most was the fact that the Bosnian Croats were taking their instructions from Zagreb – conditions in Croatia were thus having a direct impact on the political climate in Bosnia-Herzegovina.[133]

At the outset of the crisis in October 1912, Potiorek sought to have the troops under his command placed on a war footing (*Kriegsstand*). His plea fell on deaf ears – with Franz Joseph turning down his request – and Vienna's approval of some additional border units was scant consolation.[134] Characteristically, however, the *Landeschef* did not give up. On 19 October, in a letter to Bolfras, he reasoned that the way to avoid internal unrest in the coming months was through a 'display of military power' and the introduction of a state of emergency (*Ausnahmezustand*).[135] On 4 December, despite his earlier rebuff on this matter, he formally requested permission from the War Ministry in Vienna to place his troops on a war footing – 'to show the Muslims and Croats that the Monarchy was at all times anxious to protect Bosnia-Herzegovina'. This was granted on 8 December, the measure covering the entire 'BHD' zone – i.e., Bosnia, Herzegovina and Dalmatia, the lands garrisoned by the 15th and 16th Corps.[136] Potiorek also made sure that he transmitted his views to Conrad, who had been rein-stated as Chief of General Staff on 12 December, writing to him on the 21st: 'Spirit and discipline leave nothing to be desired, and the troops are yearning to be allowed to show what they are worth.' The last thing he wanted was a peaceful outcome that brought no obvious and lasting success. 'But for God's sake', he therefore urged Conrad, 'just no phoney peace.' If the current 'malady' were treated only with 'palliatives', he suggested, the next crisis in two or three years' time would have to be managed under even worse circumstances; the popular mood in Bosnia was already sceptical about the power of the Monarchy to impose its will. So an 'illusory success' now, that is to say one based on diplomacy and not on force, would actually entail 'disastrous consequences' for the internal political situation in Bosnia-Herzegovina and cause 'irreparable damage' to the morale of the Army.[137]

Of course, Potiorek was knocking at an open door here. Conrad is famous for his unremitting advocacy of a war against Serbia, with modern historians competing to work out the exact number of his many proposals to that effect in the period between 1906 and 1914. Conrad's attitude is best summed up by his reaction to Franz Joseph telling him that Austria had never instigated a single war: 'Regrettably, Your Majesty', quipped the General.[138] When Potiorek requested the call up of all the reserve troops in Bosnia-Herzegovina and Dalmatia, Foreign Minister Berchtold con-vened a meeting on 23 December, with Conrad, Biliński and the Joint War Minister Krobatin present. Those three lined up entirely behind Potiorek. Biliński argued that they would be burdening themselves with 'heavy responsibility' if the Governor, on whose shoulders lay peace and security in Bosnia-Herzegovina, were not supported. But Berchtold, fearing international isolation, refused to back the proposed mobilization.[139] It was hardly surprising that the new Joint War Minister General Alexander Krobatin, Conrad's friend, had backed Potiorek and that, with his appoint-ment, 'it now appeared that the war party was in the ascendancy'.[140] But Potiorek could rely just as much on Biliński and his Joint Finance Ministry to argue the case for tough policies in Bosnia-Herzegovina and action to be taken against Serbia and Montenegro. It is wrong to describe the views of the Joint Finance Minister during the crisis as 'pacific'.[141] It was thanks to Biliński that the *Landeschef* managed to obtain, on 8 January 1913, the Emperor's approval for the introduction of emergency measures in Bosnia-Herzegovina. The emergency measures – suspending constitutional pro-visions, banning various societies and assemblies, restricting freedom of movement, etc. – could now be activated as soon as Potiorek telegraphed

Vienna a request to that effect.[142] Indeed, they were to come into force a few months later, at the height of the Scutari crisis.

It was seen in a previous chapter that Montenegrin forces had captured Scutari on 23 April 1913, prompting Austria-Hungary to threaten the use of force if they did not withdraw. Potiorek now used these tensions to ask for his emergency measures which were duly introduced on 3 May. Once again, Biliński was quite cooperative. And more than that: at a Ministerial Council meeting in Vienna on 2 May, with Berchtold presiding, the Minister was every inch as hawkish as any of the generals in the 'war party'. He could not understand, he said, why one should wait when there was no time to lose. The 'fact' was that 'there remains for us nothing other than war.' Echoing Potiorek, he argued that in Bosnia the belief was taking hold about 'an entirely powerless' Monarchy which would acquiesce in anything. In the event of war, he advised, not only Montenegro, but also Serbia should be fought: Serbia as an independent state should 'cease to exist', while the Serbian people should, as an equal member, be annexed to the Monarchy where it should find 'its national and political home'. Predictably, the Hungarians present did not like the sound of this. The Hungarian Prime Minister László Lukács stated that the crisis was not about who took possession of Scutari, but rather about the South Slav question. 'It is however certain', he continued, 'that if Mr Biliński's idea is realized, Trialism will be the outcome. We would then have a Slav majority and this means the end of Dualism.'[143]

The spectre of Trialism obviously continued to exercise the minds of Hungarian statesmen. The debate between Biliński and Lukács in fact highlighted the quandary of Austria-Hungary's domestic and international positions: unless the Monarchy took on Serbia, the simmering South Slav problem would destroy it; but should it successfully abolish the Serbian state and then incorporate its people, it would change beyond recognition.

With the emergency measures approved by the Emperor on 1 May, Potiorek must have thought that a military showdown with Serbia was just round the corner. If he is remembered for anything other than his role on 28 June 1914, and his army's subsequent, disastrous campaign in Serbia, it is for the brief episode of emergency rule from 3 to 15 May 1913 when Bosnia-Herzegovina experienced the full weight of his disciplinarian methods. In 1914 the memory of this episode was still very fresh: Gavrilo Princip and Nedeljko Čabrinović, two of the Sarajevo assassins, were to declare that they had acted against Franz Ferdinand in the belief that he had instigated the emergency measures. During this period of virtually unrestrained dictatorial power available to him, Potiorek not only suspended the Diet (6 May), but also those provisions of the Constitution guaranteeing citizens' rights. He introduced military trials. He dissolved or suspended, in addition to socialist societies, practically all Serbian associations and organizations – religious, educational, gymnastic, singing, temperance, etc. The ban on newspapers was so comprehensive that it included *Gostioničar* (The Innkeeper), the paper of the hotel and restaurant trade.[144] The *Landeschef* also called up the reservists – thus bringing about a de facto mobilization in Bosnia-Herzegovina.[145] He had already for some time been organizing the *Schutzkorps* auxiliary units from which the Serbs had been excluded.

Joseph Baernreither described this state of affairs as 'a militarist-police *régime*', comparing it to what was once a similar case in Lombardy. He wrote in his diary that the Government had thus started a 'war' against the Serbs, who represented forty-three per cent of the population: 'In the eyes of the world, they were to be stigmatised as traitors.'[146] Some Bosnian Croat leaders also felt uneasy about this, like those in Banja Luka who let it be known that they were 'ashamed' because the emergency measures had not touched them.[147] In his analysis of domestic reaction to the new measures, the Government Commissar for Sarajevo Baron Carl Collas reported on 7 May that the Muslims wanted war, that the Serbs feared it, and that the Croats could not summon up any enthusiasm for it.[148]

In the end, no war broke out – Montenegro, yielding to enormous international pressure, announced on 4 May that it would withdraw its forces from Scutari. Even Biliński now realized that the maintenance of the state of emergency would be politically counterproductive and suggested to Potiorek, on 7 May, that it should be lifted once the Montenegrins were out. Potiorek resisted on the grounds that the danger of war still existed, and that the Serbian Army had not demobilized. And on 9 May he admitted to Biliński quite openly that he would view it as 'a misfortune for the Monarchy if the current crisis ends without a resort to arms.' Franz Joseph, however, decided otherwise: on 14 May he authorized the lifting of the state of emergency and Potiorek was informed the following day.[149] To the Bosnian Serbs, the culprits for May 1913 were the Joint Finance Minister and the *Landeschef* in equal measure. Now that the press could breathe again, a Serbian paper in Sarajevo commented: 'Biliński and Potiorek are the best Serbian agitators, for they have opened the eyes of the Serbs'.[150]

Nevertheless, reporting to Biliński on the reactions that followed the lifting of the emergency measures, Potiorek was quite unperturbed by such attacks in the local press.[151] The situation did, indeed, quickly return to business as usual. This was helped by the fact that, as always, the Bosnian Serb elite contained a significant bloc anxious to reach accommodation with the Provincial Government – in order to better pursue the economic interests of the Serb *čaršija*. Now, in the second half of 1913, this bloc consisted of about a dozen deputies in the Diet. It included such grandees as Gligorije Jeftanović and Vojislav Šola, and historians normally identify it as being grouped around the Sarajevo newspaper *Srpska Riječ*, owned by Jeftanović. In July 1913 it held secret negotiations with Potiorek about joining the pro-Government bloc, i.e., the Muslim-Croat coalition, and in September it made this intention public, its members referring, suddenly, to Serbo-Croat unity, whilst conspicuously failing to mention the agrarian question – thereby playing up to the Croats and Muslims. The Serbian overtures, however, were rejected by the *Landesregiurung*. Unable to reach a deal and compromised in the eyes of the more numerous Serb deputies who formed the main opposition, twelve of this pro-accommodation grouping resigned from the Diet on 22 September.[152] Robin Okey remarked that 'they could no longer balance their Serb nationalism and their prudence.'[153]

This moment represented a victory for Habsburg rule and ambitions in Bosnia-Herzegovina: the Bosnian Serb political class had in effect been neutralized. Out-manoeuvred in the parliamentary game, it was also divided within itself on the issue of whether to opt for opportunist collaboration or passive resistance to Habsburg rule. Its deputies in the Diet could either co-operate or be ignored, and by now it did not really matter to the Provincial Government which of the two courses the Serbs chose. It is also true, however, that the Bosnian Serbs had not placed too many obstacles in the way of this Habsburg victory. For, in retrospect, Bosnian Serb nationalism had only locked horns with Habsburg rule until 1905, when its long campaign for church and state autonomy had ended with the granting of some limited concessions. What followed after 1905 was essentially the politics of assent: with hardly a protest, the leading Bosnian Serbs swallowed the annexation and then even welcomed a pseudo-constitution. The essentially docile acceptance of the annexation by the bulk of the Bosnian Serb political elite reflected, of course, regional and international realities – it certainly did not reflect the general opinion of Serbs in Bosnia. What is perhaps more surprising is the massive failure, post-annexation, of the Bosnian Serbs within the newly created arena of constitutional politics: they did not properly address, let alone force, the longstanding agrarian issue; they lost, after 1910, their erstwhile Muslim allies anyway; the idea of approaching the Bosnian Croats instead, to possibly construct a Bosnian version of the Croato-Serb Coalition that existed in Croatia, came as an afterthought; and even the reasonably pliant bunch of Serb deputies still wishing to work with the Provincial Government were in the late summer of 1913 being rebuffed.

Indeed, Biliński and Potiorek could by this time afford to dump those Serbs who were merely cooperative, as they had recently found some Serbs whose loyalty to the Habsburgs seemed beyond any doubt. These were led by Danilo Dimović, a lawyer originally from Croatia. The other prominent member of this group was Milan Jojkić, a doctor, and likewise an immigrant from Croatia. Both of them were to figure on the list of potential assassination targets discussed by the rebellious youth of Bosnia-Herzegovina. In Vienna they and the group of followers around them were known as the 'Biliński–Serben' even in 1915.[154] Dimović had previously taken part in the preparations aimed at getting the Bosnian Serbs to accept the annexation, whereas Jojkić had tried to get a declaration of loyalty to the Habsburg state into the programme of the Serb SNO Party.[155] In the by-elections that took place (8-10 December 1912) after the resignation of the twelve Serb deputies in September, the Dimović group won as many as nine seats in the Diet. It was to call itself *Srpska Narodna Stranka* (SNS) – the Serb People's Party – though it never formally constituted itself as a political party.[156] Biliński congratulated it on its 'splendid' electoral success.[157] Dimović, meanwhile, was clever, explaining to Biliński that a 'realistic' Serb political party would be anchored to the Pragmatic Sanction – that holy document for the Habsburgs, tying the lands over which they ruled to the Dynasty. Franz Joseph was most appreciative, telling Dimović in January 1914: 'You have done a great deal for my House, that is why I see you as one of its supporting pillars.'[158]

Of course, Dimović and his SNS had extracted a price: their loyalty was not unqualified. On 8 November 1913 in Vienna he and Jojkić had negotiated a deal with Biliński and Potiorek. The Dimović group, universally belittled in Serb historiography as 'opportunist', had in fact pushed some burning Bosnian Serb interests to the forefront of the agenda, primarily the agrarian question. Dimović and colleagues advocated the compulsory expropriation of the lands worked by the *kmets*, and this was also the line they took in their newly-founded paper *Istina* (The Truth). In the Vienna agreement with Biliński and Potiorek, however, a compromise had been reached whereby the voluntary purchase of land would continue, but with the Provincial Government undertaking to pay off one half of the interest rate on the loans taken by *kmets* to buy the land. It was stipulated that the measure would start to be implemented by 1 January 1915 at the latest.[159] Interestingly, both Biliński and Potiorek had already seen the basic wisdom of tackling the agrarian question in Bosnia-Herzegovina head on, i.e., by compulsory expropriation. In May 1913 Biliński had written to Potiorek to that effect. The *Landeschef*, in his reply, agreed but cautioned against a hasty decision on the grounds of finances and the continuing crisis on the borders.[160] By November, however, he was telling the local politicians that Serbia and Montenegro would soon implement a radical solution of the agrarian question on the territories taken from Turkey, and that the Monarchy could not be seen to be lagging behind the neighbours.[161]

Things were on the whole going quite well for Potiorek as the year 1914 approached. The turbulence brought about by the Balkan Wars of 1912 and 1913 had now given way to a more settled period. The Bosnian Diet began its fourth (and last) session late in December 1913. Muslims, Croats (with only three deputies in the opposition ranks) and, critically, Dimović's men provided a solid working majority for the Provincial Government – a respectable bloc of Serbs were thus on board. Admittedly, when the *Landeschef* appeared at the opening of the Diet, on 29 December, he was greeted with shouts from the opposition of: 'Down with Potiorek!'[162] His emergency measures in May had certainly left a bitter aftertaste. But otherwise the Diet worked in businesslike fashion. It voted in the new agrarian law, as well as the language law. The language question, in which the Muslims were not in the least interested, had caused one or two problems in the past: Vienna had insisted that, for military reasons, the German language should be retained on the Bosnian railways. All the groups in the Diet had already agreed that the mother tongue should be called 'Serbo-Croat' and that it should also be employed on the railways. Biliński and Potiorek, overcoming the objections of the War Ministry, solved this problem with a vague but elegant formula: they agreed to the use of Serbo-Croat language in the internal transactions of the railways 'to the extent that the military interests allow it'.[163]

All of which suggested more than just a return to normality after the Balkan Wars: Austria-Hungary actually appeared to have tamed nationalism in Bosnia-Herzegovina by 1914. Even the agrarian issue had finally been addressed in a sensible fashion. In his study of Bosnian Serb politics, Karl Kaser concluded that at this point the Serbs posed 'no danger whatsoever' to the Provincial Government.[164] Robin Okey wrote about Bosnia-Herzegovina in 1914 as being 'far from the point of ungovernability' and commenting that, in hindsight, 'Habsburg Bosnia in 1914 looks no less stable than the Monarchy as a whole'.[165] Biliński and Potiorek, moreover, even entertained lofty schemes for the future development of Bosnia-Herzegovina within the Monarchy. Biliński wanted to found philosophy and law faculties in Sarajevo, and he also talked about a gradual recruitment of local personnel into the top administrative posts of Bosnia-Herzegovina.[166] Potiorek was sceptical about establishing higher education institutions ('we would be saddled, on top of undisciplined secondary school students, with analogous higher education students'), but he backed Biliński's proposal that Bosnia-Herzegovina should in future gain a voice in the Monarchy's joint affairs. The concrete idea here was that the provinces should be represented in the Austrian and Hungarian Delegations with three members in each.[167] The proposed innovation might of course have added to the schizophrenic quintessence of the Dual Monarchy, but Bosnia-Herzegovina would have, through direct representation, become its indubitable, integral part.

Therefore, had it not been for the June 1914 assassination of Franz Ferdinand in Sarajevo, the Biliński-Potiorek partnership might have succeeded in welding the provinces solidly to the Habsburg state. But the durability of such an attachment would of course have depended on the staying power of the Monarchy itself. When considering its long-term prospects, even the loyalist Dimović was sceptical. His private view at this time was that within 'fifteen to twenty years' Serbia would 'arrive here'. And he was convinced that during that period it was 'useful and necessary' that there existed in Bosnia-Herzegovina 'a Serb opportunist party' to protect Serb national interests.[168] Dimović had maintained contacts with the Serbian Government through Zagreb where he had friends in the Croato-Serb Coalition. The view in Belgrade was identical to his. Nikola Pašić, the Serbian Prime Minister, even advised Jovo Simić, one of those Bosnian Serb deputies who had resigned in September 1913, to join the Dimović party which, in his view, could serve as a defensive bulwark in those 'difficult times'.[169] Pašić was thus hardly someone plotting the immediate overthrow of the Austro-Hungarian Empire. To Serbia's Prime Minister, just as much as to the Bosnian Serb political class, the Monarchy was, in the words of Robin Okey, 'a going concern'.[170]

But not everybody possessed the virtue of patience. Potiorek had mentioned to Biliński in the spring of 1914 the 'undisciplined secondary school students' of Bosnia-Herzegovina. As the next chapter will show, many students had already given him good cause to do so when they had in February 1912 staged a major demonstration in the centre of his fiefdom, the Bosnian capital itself. Their passionate manifestation on the streets of Sarajevo was the defining event in the rise of a nameless and practically leaderless movement which had little idea about how to overthrow foreign rule in Bosnia-Herzegovina, but which wanted, nevertheless, to make a political statement that would be heard far and wide. In this ambition, it would succeed all too well.

10

South Slav Student Nationalism

The Croat Connection

IN 1911 WHEN Robert Seton-Watson published his seminal work on
the problems of the Habsburg Monarchy, he called it *The Southern Slav
Question*. Between the Bosnian annexation crisis and the outbreak of the
war in 1914 this question came to be seen in almost apocalyptic terms by
loyalists inside the Habsburg state contemplating its future. Before 1914,
however, the Yugoslav, or Southern Slav, idea was just that – a desire, a
hypothesis, and only a very vague scheme in the heads of dreamers rather
than politicians. It was in one sense a panacea for Southern Slav identities,
so often contested and confused. At the same time it carried major political
implications: a Southern Slav state, in whatever shape and under whatever
leadership, entailed the end of Austro-Hungarian Dualism and possibly the
end of the Monarchy itself. 'Every politician' in Austria-Hungary spoke
before the war about the '*südslawische Frage*', and about the 'necessity of
solving it'.[1] In the event, despite so much talk about it, this question which
was to instigate the destruction of Austria-Hungary was never even close
to being seriously tackled by Vienna and Budapest.

In Bosnia-Herzegovina, it was not some 'Serb nationalists' but young,
student adherents of the Yugoslav idea who conceived and carried out the
assassination of Franz Ferdinand. Moreover, the aspirations for a Yugoslav
state and the ambitions for a 'Greater Serbia' stood in fundamental
contradiction. In the Western world this is one of the least understood
aspects about the background to the Sarajevo assassination. Sean
McMeekin – to take one example from a wave of recent First World War
historians – states that Princip was 'a radical Serb nationalist'. He is
expressing a widely held assumption which, remarkably, is almost never
examined.[2] Decades ago Luigi Albertini wrote without any supporting
argument that Princip 'had conceived the idea of doing something big for
the Pan-Serb cause'.[3] Time and again, the assassins have been presented
as members of a Great Serbian conspiracy.[4] However, this explanation is
a mistake – floating on blunders, distortions and even fabrications – a

mistake which has perverted the historiography of 1914 for a century. Princip was a genuine Yugoslav.

Many, perhaps most of his fellow students in Bosnia-Herzegovina did not, even in 1914, share such a perception of themselves as 'Yugoslav' or 'Serbo-Croat nationalists'. However, a great many did. How did this come about and what exactly did it mean? Closer examination reveals a twisted, but very Austro-Hungarian affair. The Yugoslavian outlook in Bosnia-Herzegovina evolved as an interaction between the specifically local and the wider Austro-Hungarian contexts. To the extent that it was imported, it arrived from Croatia, not from Serbia. Indeed, the Yugoslav orientation among Bosnian high school pupils owed much to a movement which began in the mid-1890s among students in neighbouring Croatia. Croat students, in turn, had formed their political ideas in Prague under the influence of that exceptional thinker and politician, Tomáš Masaryk, who was later to become the first President of Czechoslovakia.

A chance event had played a role in the early history of Yugoslavism among the young South Slavs. Their unrest began in October 1895 when Franz Joseph visited Zagreb to witness the triumph of Croatia's *Ban* Khuen-Héderváry 'in transforming Croatia into a submissive Hungarian province'.[5] In reality, the occasion actually turned into a show of defiance against Hungary. With an eye for symbolic choreography, demonstrating Croat students burnt a Hungarian flag in front of Josip Jelačić's equestrian statue in the main square of Zagreb – while the statue itself, in the spirit of 1848, pointed its sword at Hungary. These Croat students who had in the past always stood behind Ante Starčević, did, however, hail Franz Joseph at least with: 'Long live the Croat King!' The historian Josip Horvat considered the event as 'a prologue to a great drama in Croat politics'.[6]

The academic youth of Croatia had previously been enthused by Starčević's teaching that all South Slavs belonged to one nation – the Croat nation.[7] But in that respect at least, change was under way, a change which began when a group of Zagreb students was expelled from the University for showing lack of respect during the Emperor's visit. Continuing their studies in Prague, they came under the wing of Professor Masaryk.[8] The importance of this Slavonic get-together cannot be exaggerated. Unfolding in Bohemia at this time was the Czech-German conflict over language and local administration. Masaryk's rejection of Czech 'romanticism', his anti-clericalism and his emphasis on realistic political work which should occur in 'small steps' found a profound, positive response among the Croat students, who had been disappointed by the fruitless efforts of the older generations in Croatia, with their empty rhetoric based on an ancient past and disconnected from the wider mass of the population.[9] Critically, for the first time they observed in Prague the effort of the German '*Drang*' and saw a similar danger for the South Slavs. Masaryk, who thought Serbs and Croats were the same people, instilled into them the idea of Slav solidarity. Recently a British scholar described the Czech influence as 'a key building block' in the creation of progressive young South Slav student nationalism.[10] Increasingly attracting Serb and Slovene students as well, the University of Prague thus became, at the turn of the century, a focal point for young South Slavs and the birthplace of a fresh approach to the Yugoslav idea.[11]

One of the journals started by the Croat students in Prague, *Hrvatska Misao* (Croat Reflection) described Croatia as 'practically a Hungarian province', and saw its 'state and historic rights' as existing 'on paper only' while at the same causing conflicts with the Serbs. *Novo Doba* (New Age), another publication founded by the Croats in Prague, emphasized the 'national unity of Croats and Serbs'.[12] Even a 'Serbo-Bulgarian Association' was set up in Prague. Masaryk's apostolic stature clearly mesmerised the South Slav students, who particularly liked his practical philosophy course 'How to work? [*Jak pracovat?*]'[13] Many would arrive in Prague as narrow nationalists, only to return 'baptized' into broad-minded Yugoslavians.[14] Pero Slijepčević, an eminent student leader from Bosnia-Herzegovina, recalled that practically all the notions and watchwords he and his friends had used had come from Masaryk: education of the people, sobriety, passion for action and hatred of empty phrase, abruptness towards the Church, the need for an 'internal religion', all-Slav solidarity, and ridicule of romanticism.[15]

The sentiments at Zagreb University did not lag far behind those in Prague. In 1896 the 'United Croat and Serb Youth' came into being. In the spring of 1897 Croatian and Serbian students pooled their efforts to produce an almanac *Narodna Misao* (National Idea), with texts printed in both Latin and Cyrillic scripts. The students grouped round *Narodna Misao* sought opinions regarding Serbo-Croat relations from a great number of prominent South Slav personalities in both Austria-Hungary and Serbia, including Bishop Strossmayer and Serbian Metropolitan Mihajlo. The idea of brotherhood and unity received strong commendations as a result, which were printed in the almanac and found a widespread echo among South Slavs attending universities. Apart from Zagreb and Prague, these were chiefly those of Vienna, Graz and Innsbruck, all of which witnessed increasing cooperation amongst Serbs and Croats. From 1897, the politically active students in Croatia became known as the 'Progressive Youth [*Napredna omladina*]' and were to play a role in the formation of the 'New Course' in Croatian politics. Elsewhere, students in Belgrade (where in 1905 the city's *Grande École* became a university) founded a club in 1902 which they called *Slovenski Jug* (Slavonic South) and also a journal in 1903 (under the same name) which carried the rallying cry: 'South Slavs, unite!'[16]

The Yugoslav ideas taking shape, however, suffered from a great deal of political imprecision. Even *Slovenski Jug* envisaged only a Balkan confederation – the talk was about four distinct South Slav nations or 'tribes': Serbs, Croats, Slovenes and Bulgarians. The discourse at the time about South Slav 'cultural unity' really meant cultural cooperation rather than cultural integration.[17] What *Slovenski Jug* advocated was 'an alliance of Serbia, Bulgaria and Montenegro, and then all the South Slavs' – but this was merely a cry for some kind of a defensive posture to be adopted in the face of the 'deceits and political lies of the Great Powers'.[18] As late as 1908 the Croatian writer Antun Matoš, hugely popular among Croatian youth, called the Yugoslav political idea 'an absurd Utopia', and compared the idea of Yugoslav cultural kinship to the existence of a European cultural community.[19] Although lofty student idealism seemed to be overcoming previous dissension and hostility, not everything was flourishing in Serbo-Croat affairs. In 1899, at a celebration in Zagreb honouring the Serbian poet Jovan Jovanović Zmaj, things turned ugly and degenerated into demonstrations against the Serbs. The height of Croat resentment of the local Serbs – who were both annoyingly Serb and provokingly loyal to the Dynasty rather than pleasantly Yugoslav and anti-Hungarian – was reached at the beginning of September 1902 when anti-Serb riots took place over three days in Zagreb. The authorities appeared indifferent.[20]

The September 1902 tumult in Zagreb was the last incident of its kind – for quite a while. Deteriorating relations between Vienna and Budapest in the meantime opened up new possibilities for the Monarchy's South Slavs. In 1903 Count Khuen-Héderváry finally left Croatia after twenty years (having been promoted by Franz Joseph to the post of Prime Minister of Hungary so as to manage the Dualist crisis). In 1905, moreover, the Croato-Serb Coalition in Croatia was born, winning the elections the following year. Glaise–Horstenau considered Masaryk to be one of its 'spiritual fathers'.[21] Old enmity now gave way to a period of opportunist positioning. However, in the eyes of the older generations of Serbs and Croats, the bad blood never disappeared. This was demonstrated soon enough in 1908-1909 during the Bosnian annexation crisis when many Croats rejoiced (and staged yet another anti-Serbian pogrom) amid widespread Serbian protests and consternation. In addition, while that part of Croatia's younger generations still faithful to Starčević's conception of the South Slavs being Croats had indeed 'crossed the Rubicon' in 1912 to join the rest of the 'Progressive Youth' and embrace the Yugoslav 'nationalist' idea – it did so in the belief that this idea was merely a 'higher level' of the old Great Croatia gospel.[22]

Nevertheless, there can be no doubt that, at least during the period from 1908 to 1914, the belief in a common Yugoslav destiny and, in particular, the acceptance of the theory that the Serbs and Croats were one people, had come to dominate the thinking and actions of a very wide portion of South Slav academic youth in Austria-Hungary. Croatia and Dalmatia had led the way, with Bosnia-Herzegovina eventually following. Political conditions in Croatia served to place it in the vanguard of this development. Between 1908 and 1910 the *Ban* of Croatia was Baron Pavao Rauch. Even before Rauch's appointment, Foreign Minister Aehrenthal had known that Croatian public opinion held him in low esteem.[23] By the spring of 1908 Rauch's methods had already produced a conflict with Zagreb University students, resulting in a second 'exodus' to Prague University.[24] Rauch's tenure in office was to be most associated, and notoriously, with the Zagreb high treason trial the following year. However, for the young students of Croatia, both Croat and Serb, it was 1910 which proved decisive. Rauch's successor as *Ban* that February was Nikola Tomašić, a friend of Khuen-Héderváry who had again become Prime Minister in Hungary and with whom Tomašić and his wife conducted a happy *ménage à trois*.[25] The leaders of the Croato-Serb Coalition decided to enter into a pact with Ban Tomašić in order to extract from him a widening of the electoral franchise – at under 49,000 the narrowest in Europe.[26] But this pact, born of opportunism, caused widespread disappointment among the younger generations and a loss of faith in the gradualist approach towards solving the national question or, indeed, of solving it within the confines of the Habsburg Monarchy. The growing Yugoslav sentiment among the young Croats thus reflected a frustration with Vienna and Budapest as well as with local politicians in Zagreb. It also conflicted with the Hungarian attempt at this time to accelerate the Magyarization of Croatia, especially in schools.[27] In the words of the Croat historian Mirjana Gross, now had come the age of revolution and assassins.[28]

Between June 1912 and May 1914 there were four assassination attempts in Croatia. The first, and certainly the most spectacular of them, took place in Zagreb on 8 June 1912 when law student Luka Jukić tried to kill no less a person than the *Ban* of Croatia, the highly unpopular Slavko Cuvaj. As Cuvaj's car slowed down in a steep street, Jukić fired his revolver three times. His bullets missed Cuvaj, but did hit one of the officials with him in the car – the man died a few days later. The assassin now began to escape down the street. A policeman, his sword drawn, tried to stop him, but Jukić fired again, killing him on the spot, jumping over his body and continuing to run. He was to wound another policeman before finally being overpowered and taken to a police station.[29] As will be seen below, Jukić had only a few months previously played a significant role in a major student riot in Sarajevo, organized in solidarity to protest against Cuvaj's authoritarian rule in Croatia-Slavonia. Condemned at his trial to death by hanging, Jukić became an instant hero throughout Croat lands. Young women threw roses at him in the courtroom, for which act they received prison sentences.[30]

Governor Cuvaj was the target once again, in a bizarre episode on 30 October 1912, when Stjepan Planinšak, another law student, climbed a telegraph pole opposite Cuvaj's residence in Zagreb. As Cuvaj appeared at the window, Planinšak fired but missed and then committed suicide.[31] Another assassination attempt took place in August 1913, after Stjepan Dojčić, a young *émigré* in the United States, returned to his native Croatia, also intending to kill Cuvaj. In fact, Dojčić had to be content with shooting Ivan Skerlecz, Cuvaj's successor. As *Ban* Skerlecz emerged from Zagreb's Roman Catholic cathedral on 18 August (Emperor Franz Joseph's birthday), Dojčić shot him with his large revolver, wounding him in the arm. Immediately after firing, he shouted so that everyone could hear him: 'Long live Croatia! I shall in this way shoot everybody who comes to oppress Croatia!'[32] The last of the Croat assassination deeds almost took place on 25 May 1914. That evening the Zagreb Opera was staging *Tosca*, a performance attended by Skerlecz and Archduke Leopold Salvator. The two men left the theatre early, after act one, only to be greeted outside by student Jakob Schäffer, armed with a revolver. Before Schäffer could unleash a bullet, however, a detective standing nearby intervened, and successfully. The student was stopped. His mentor is supposed to have been Rudolf Hercigonja, another student, accused of trying to talk young men into assassinating Archduke Franz Ferdinand or indeed other Habsburg dignitaries, such as the Hungarian Prime Minister István Tisza.[33]

The first assassin among the South Slav students was actually a Serb from Herzegovina, Bogdan Žerajić. His suicide, after he attempted in June 1910 to kill the Bosnian Governor Marijan Varešanin, left a profound impression on South Slav youth throughout the region. But the idea of self-sacrifice was not confined to the Serbs. Mirjana Gross pointed out that about this time the younger Croats began to embrace the cult of Eugen Kvaternik, the leader of the failed bid for independence in 1871 who had paid with his own life. Since Žerajić's intended target General Varešanin was considered in Croatia to be precisely the man responsible for Kvaternik's death in 1871, Žerajić was post-humously doubly 'popular' on the Croat side.[34] Contemplation of self-sacrifice had been further promoted by the Croat sculptor Ivan Meštrović, a convinced Yugoslav, who in his artistic interpretation of the Battle of Kosovo (1389) presented the Serbs as martyrs for heaven and thereby 'undoubtedly contributed to the conviction that violence, too, was justified in bringing about Nation as a divine creation'.[35] As Robin Okey has observed, it was actually the Croat Meštrović who was, before 1914, the 'greatest exponent of the Kosovo myth'.[36] The young Croat intelligentsia was also fired up by the first Russian revolution, which suggested to them that only 'direct action' could be effective against tyrannical rule.[37]

The most rebellious young Croats were those from Dalmatia, and they emphasized the need for 'revolution and terror', as well as 'the state and national unity of Serbs and Croats'. To them the existence of a Serbo-Croat 'Yugoslav' nation was already a reality, and their preference was to see the names 'Serb' and/or 'Croat' wiped out in favour of 'Yugoslav'.[38] Their spokesmen and leaders constituted an illustrious group of able agitators and talented literary figures: Oskar Tartaglia, Vladimir Čerina, Tin Ujević, Milostislav Bartulica and Matej Košćina. These Dalmatians founded *Val* (Wave), a publication that was 'full-blooded and pugnacious, nationalist and revolutionary'. The first issue of *Val*, printed in 2,000 copies, quickly sold out. Not surprisingly perhaps, the paper approvingly quoted the Russian anarchist Pyotr Kropotkin that liberty had to be seized, not begged for.[39] Although the paper was founded in Zagreb, some of its main ideologues and drive came from the city of Split in Dalmatia. Oskar Tartaglia wrote in his memoirs that Split was the 'Piedmont of nationalism and Yugoslavism'. He may not have been exaggerating: when, in August 1910, the Serbian Heir to the Throne Alexander Karadjordjević stopped briefly in Split, the crowds hailed him: 'Long live the future Yugoslav King!'[40] Discussing in 1937 this period, Ferdo Šišić, the Croat historian of the Yugoslav idea, remarked: 'And so the Croat question gradually began to transform itself into the Yugoslav question in the Austro-Hungarian Monarchy'.[41]

The unitary Yugoslav ideology propagated by *Val* came as a 'shock', but was read 'breathlessly', and it seems that the paper circulated in Bosnia-Herzegovina as well as Croatia.[42] Matej Košćina, one of the leading lights of the *Val* circle, argued in 1911 on the pages of Belgrade's *Slovenski Jug* that the Serbs should lose themselves among the Croats and that the Croats should disappear among the Serbs. This was too much even for the Yugoslav-oriented Serbs in *Slovenski Jug*. The paper distanced itself from such radicalism, especially since 'the greater part of the Croats' was still 'negating the Serbs and serving Rome and Vienna'.[43] Indeed, before the First Balkan War in 1912 the enthusiastic evangelism for an integrated South Slav nation was maintained predominantly by young Croat intellectuals who believed they had seen a new horizon. One of them was the gifted poet Tin (Augustin) Ujević, a former Croat nationalist. Along with his philosopher friend Krešimir Kovačić he thought that the difference between Greater Croatia and Yugoslavia was in name only – because the South Slavs were one nation. This 'illusion', Mirjana Gross remarked, exerted 'a strong influence' on some young Croats.[44] Serbia was idolized by them – in the spirit of perceived South Slav universality. In April 1912 Kovačić wrote in *Slovenski Jug*: 'The Croats must never forget that there exists a free Croat state – Serbia, just like Serbia should never forget that there exists a Serbian state not yet liberated – Croatia.'[45] Niko Bartulović, the Yugoslav-oriented Croat writer, observed in 1929 that the pre-war Croat students were highly uncritical towards Serbia, to the point that there existed amongst them 'a fetishism of everything emanating from Serbia'.[46]

The Birth of 'Young Bosnia'

Undoubtedly, even before the Balkan Wars, the young Croat intelligentsia was increasingly entranced by a sweeping Yugoslav orientation. One Croat historian noted that the Yugoslav elation among the Croat youth was created and maintained by hatred of the Habsburg authorities and their anti-Croat behaviour: 'The youth of Croatia believed that there existed no place worse than the Monarchy.'[47] The older Croat generations were equally preoccupied with the national problem, but the annexation of Bosnia-Herzegovina in 1908 had encouraged many of them to believe that this act was a prologue to the creation of a Great Croatia (to include Bosnia-Herzegovina) within the Habsburg Monarchy – the Croat hope in Trialism had never died in the run-up to 1914. Meanwhile, the Monarchy's Serb students were lagging somewhat behind their Croat counterparts in embracing the idea of Serbo-Croat unity. Early in 1910, some of those studying in Vienna founded, the journal *Zora* (Dawn) which did drift towards the position of Serbo-Croat 'nationalist' youth, but only gradually, and under the influence of *Val*.[48] Even then, there were those in *Zora* who maintained that Serbo-Croat unity had yet to be attained.[49]

In Bosnia-Herzegovina itself, the Yugoslav ideology had also begun to make inroads, especially among young Bosnians – irrespective of religion or ethnicity. This process, admittedly, was a little slow. Unlike Croatia and Serbia, Bosnia-Herzegovina could not boast a university.[50] In this situation Zagreb University was increasingly becoming a natural destination for the academically-inclined youth of the two provinces: between 1905 and 1910 the number of students from Bosnia-Herzegovina at the University of Zagreb rose rapidly from 65 to 139.[51] By contrast, even by 1914 Belgrade University attracted only a handful students from Bosnia-Herzegovina. Dragoslav Ljubibratić, who knew the scene in Belgrade, wrote that there were few students from Bosnia-Herzegovina at Belgrade University, and 'fewer still' in Serbia's secondary schools.[52] Bosnia-Herzegovina's high schools, the *gimnazije*, existed in Sarajevo, Mostar, Tuzla and Banja Luka. The Jesuits ran a *gimnazija* in Travnik and the Franciscans had one in Visoko. There was also a teachers' training college in Sarajevo (the so-called *preparandija*), along with 'technical' and 'commercial' schools. At the turn of the century the situation in those schools was a predictable one. In the words of Pero Slijepčević: 'Serbs and Croats disputed every day to whom the Muslims and Bosnians belonged. The Serbs were in favour of unification with Serbia and Montenegro, the Croats favoured uniting with Croatia, the Muslims were for autonomy, and there was no compromise here given our temperaments.'[53]

When Cvetko Popović, later one of the six Sarajevo assassins, came to the city from his native Prijedor in 1911, the situation had not changed a

great deal. In 1928 he wrote a memoir about that pre-1914 period in Sarajevo. He found out on arrival that secret student societies existed in all the
schools, but these reflected national divisions. If a common denominator
existed, then it was hatred of state authority. Popović enrolled into the
teachers' training college and there joined a secret society made up of
Serbs. He also discovered sub-divisions in the national student bodies.
Some Serbs would not even want to hear about any joint work with the
Croats, considering them 'the greatest enemies'. Others, the majority in
Popović's view, were more 'moderate', arguing for 'concord [*sloga*]' with the
Croats. The latter were also divided. Most of them agreed with the nation-
alist line that had been pursued by Dr Josip Frank in Croatia (*frankovci*),
negating the very existence of Serbs in the Monarchy. 'For them', Popović
recalled, 'the Serbs existed only in Serbia and Montenegro! Those were the
Croats to the liking of Austria'. But there were also more 'progressive'
Croat students who did not care for Vienna, or Budapest or Rome –
Popović thought they were 'distinctly anticlerical'. The Muslims, too, were
split. Some considered themselves Serbs, others saw themselves as Croats,
and a good proportion was just 'Muslim'. But there was nothing firm,
according to Popović, about the orientation of those Muslims who described
themselves as Serbs or Croats: 'Yesterday's passionate Serb became, lo and
behold, today's freshly minted Croat and the other way round.' Popović
was of the view that, with honourable exceptions, most Muslims 'traded'
their nationality.[54]

The one national group that Popović had never heard of before and
now, in 1911, encountered 'for the first time' in Sarajevo were the 'Serbo-
Croats'. It was, he emphasized in his memoir, a very small group of
students, in his view numbering only about ten before the (First) Balkan
War. They maintained that they were neither Serb nor Croat, but rather
both. They were not only the object of peer curiosity, but targets for vitriol,
as Popović explained: 'We, Serbs and Croats, all of us together, would
attack them as traitors to their people.' These Serbo-Croats used to wear
a badge combining Serb and Croat tricolors: red-blue-white-red. 'Hence
we called them chameleons', Popović commented. He also remembered
that Gavrilo Princip belonged to this small group.[55]

By 28 June 1914, when he lined up with Princip and others along the
Appel Quay in Sarajevo to wait for Franz Ferdinand, Popović too was a
Serbo-Croat. The reference in his memoir to the First Balkan War touched
on what was of course the defining event in the development of 'Serbo-
Croat' or 'Yugoslav' consciousness. Volunteers from Bosnia-Herzegovina
rushed to cross the border in an attempt to join the Serbian Army. Most
were returned because they were under age. Although there were also some
Bosnian Muslim volunteers fighting with the Turks, the majority of South
Slavs were enthralled by Serb victories in the autumn of 1912. When Skopje

was taken there were all-night celebrations in Sarajevo's centrally located caffe 'Evropa'.[56] Significantly, *La Marseillaise* was sung in those days.[57] Student manifestations in the city would now regularly turn into demonstrations against Austria-Hungary and 'very quickly' a significant number of secondary school students ended up in Sarajevo police jails. 'The Croats too', Popović noted, 'ceased to view Serbia as a small and insignificant state which represented nothing compared to Austria-Hungary ... They too began to feel that Serbia was a natural centre around which all the Slavs from the south of the Monarchy should rally if they wished to become independent.'[58]

Yet it was the impulses coming from Croatia, rather than developments concerning or stemming from Serbia, that had already been forging the political consciousness and actions of young Serbs, Croats and Muslims in Bosnia-Herzegovina. At the beginning of 1912 Slavko Cuvaj, a Budapest loyalist although he spoke no Hungarian, became the new *Ban* of Croatia. At the time, he was described to Josef Redlich in Vienna as 'a beast, a former sergeant!'[59] The distinguished Croat historian Josip Horvat wrote that Cuvaj's regime made Croatia 'the most anachronistic part of the Habsburg Monarchy'.[60] Cuvaj quickly dissolved the Croat Assembly (with its majority made up of parties opposing Budapest), and followed up by banning newspapers and arresting politicians. His spies were everywhere. 'Walls grew ears', Tin Ujević wrote, 'in this espying Monarchy.'[61] By inclination Cuvaj was perhaps more of a stern imperial bureaucrat than a tyrant, but his moves served to increase the bitterness in Croatia over the arbitrary rule which had already existed for years. His policies merely confirmed the widespread impression that not even 'the most moderate pseudo-constitutional regime' was possible in Croatia.[62]

A revolt against Cuvaj promptly followed, led by the young students of Croatia. On 1 February the students staged an anti-Cuvaj public assembly in front of the University of Zagreb building, during which the police charged the participants with swords drawn. Blood was spilt and the disturbances spread across the city and late into the night. Policemen on horses were attacked with stones. The demonstrators barricaded themselves in the University building the following day and hoisted a black flag. Oskar Tartaglia gave 18 speeches within 36 hours. Strikes in secondary schools across the country followed day after day, lasting until April and spreading beyond Zagreb and indeed beyond the Kingdom of Croatia to Istria, Dalmatia and Slovenia.[63] Significantly, the Serbian students in Croatia gave full backing to these protest movements. A new Serbo-Croat solidarity, born not of theory but of action, took the Yugoslavian idea to new heights.

Perhaps the most enthusiastic response to the Zagreb protests, however, came from students attending secondary schools in Sarajevo. On

18 February young people in the city staged a demonstration that became legendary – not so much as a valiant gesture in support of fellow students in Croatia, but more as a formative moment in the development of youth rebellion against foreign rule. Typically, Tartaglia had arrived in Sarajevo from Zagreb to orchestrate the Sarajevo protest. In his entourage of 'delegates' was also one Luka Jukić, a Bosnian Croat graduate of the Sarajevo *Gymnasium* and former law student at Zagreb. Jukić would gain fame among the South Slavs only a few months later for his attempt to assassinate Slavko Cuvaj in Zagreb.

Tartaglia and his colleagues did not have to over-exert themselves to persuade the Sarajevo student leaders to take action. Ivan Kranjčević, a Bosnian Croat with South Slav sympathies, later to be involved in the Sarajevo assassination of June 1914, recalled in his memoir that a protest had been much discussed before Tartaglia's arrival. He also wrote that, in addition to the Socialists, the nationalist Serb students had promised to take part out of solidarity with the other students even though con- ditions in Croatia, they said, were none of their business. Kranjčević explained that there was a general perception in Sarajevo at the time about an anti-Slav policy being pursued by Vienna and Budapest, and that the news about the bloody clashes in Zagreb 'heightened the revolt to extreme limits'.[64]

An important event had taken place in Sarajevo shortly before the city's February 1912 demonstration. Towards the end of 1911 one key element of the city's student body had founded the 'Serbo-Croat Progressive Organization [*srpsko-hrvatska naprednjačka organizacija*]', thus merging the hitherto separate Serb and Croat 'progressive' groupings. This, too, represented an influence from Croatia, and especially the influence of the journal *Val*.[65] Miloš Pjanić, the Secretary of the new organization, recalled that the pupils forming it represented a 'minority'.[66] However, the move somewhat clarified and simplified the complex political scene among students in Bosnia-Herzegovina: the 'progressives' were 'Serbo-Croats' or 'Yugoslavs' from all three religions – they later called themselves by the informal name 'nationalists'. By 'nationalist' they meant Yugoslav. Lazar Đukić, one of the defendants at the October 1914 trial of the assassins of Franz Ferdinand, was asked to define 'nationalism'. He replied: 'The idea of the unity of Serbs and Croats.'[67] The majority at the time, the nationally-exclusivist Serbs (*radikali*) and Croats (*frankovci* and *klerikalci*) were in their own separate organizations; and the Muslims were to be found in all of the groupings. The first President of the newly-established Serbo-Croat 'progressive' combination was Ivo Andrić, a Bosnian Croat who later declared himself as a Serb and who would win the Nobel prize for literature in 1961. Commenting in his diary on the attempt by Luka Jukić to assassinate the repressive Cuvaj, Andrić wrote: 'How wonderful that the secret threads of action and revolt are being tightened. How elatedly I anticipate the days of great deeds.'[68]

By all accounts the 18 February protests in Sarajevo constituted quite a battle. Tartaglia wisely avoided taking direct part and so Luka Jukić, 'a man of wild temper', became the unofficial commander-in-chief.[69] At the preparatory pre-protest meeting with the Sarajevo Serbo-Croat Progressive Organization he swore that he would travel to Zagreb and kill Cuvaj.[70] At seven in the evening students gathered on the square in front of the Catholic Cathedral. Heavy police units had already arrived. A Hungarian flag was torn and burnt as the demonstrators sang the anthem '*Hej Sloveni*'. The police, on foot and horseback, surged forward, hitting everybody in sight with their swords and also firing shots, one of which seriously wounded Salko Šahinagić, a Muslim firmly in the Croat camp, in the head. According to Lavoslav Klofač, a Czech student at the teachers's training college, there were about a thousand pupils taking part. The police commander who had ordered the shooting, a Hungarian, was thrown into the river. Some policemen were disarmed by the demonstrators.[71]

The ranks of the students were considerably strengthened by workers from socialist organizations. The battle moved to side streets where the demonstrators picked up stones and forced the police to beat a retreat. A nearby Hungarian elementary school had its windows smashed. Here, another Hungarian flag, brought to the scene by Luka Jukić wearing a fez, was burnt by Džemal Drljević, a Muslim schoolboy. Only the arrival of Army infantry and cavalry units, rushed to the scene to reinforce the hard-pressed police, brought the protests to an end.[72] One of the 'most active' participants in the fight with the police was Gavrilo Princip, whose clothes were torn in the fracas.[73]

The February 1912 clashes in Sarajevo constituted perhaps the symbolic birth of what became known, retrospectively, as the 'Young Bosnia' movement, which espoused the shared nationhood of the Serbs and Croats ('Yugoslavs'). This, though, is somewhat paradoxical. For, in fact, there was not all that much that was 'Serbo-Croat' or 'Yugoslav' about the demonstration. Thus Luka Jukić, such a prominent participant, was at the time a supporter of the exclusivist Croat nationalism that had been preached by Ante Starčević. The existing national divisions in the student body were highlighted by the attendees and absentees on the day: despite their leaders' promise, most Serb nationalist students failed to show up – only the day before there had been a quarrel in the Sarajevo *Gymnasium* between Serbs and Croats over what the Serbs considered to be an offensive song sung by the Croats during a break between lessons.[74] Before the demonstration, the Serb students had demanded that the Austrian flag be burned along with the Hungarian one, but after several meetings this had not been agreed to by the Croats.[75] Even though the demonstration was supported by Serbs belonging to or sympathising with the Serbo-Croat Progressive Organization, the occasion was to a considerable degree an anti-Hungarian display by Sarajevo's Croat youth and its Muslim student Croatophiles. Following the uproar, over twenty Croat and Muslim pupils were expelled from the city's schools, but not a single Serb.[76] Bosnian Serb politicians condemned those Serb pupils who had joined in on the grounds that the demonstrations were in favour of Trialism. Some of the shouting on 18 February ('Long live Trialism!'; 'Bosnia is not Hungarian, Bosnia is Croat!' and 'Long live the Croat King Franz Joseph I!') would seem to corroborate such misgivings.[77] Risto Radulović, a leading Bosnian Serb intellectual, sharply criticized the demonstrations and wrote in his paper *Narod* (The People) that 'children' had been instrumentalized to put forward demands for 'Trialism and Great Croatia'.[78] Gavrilo Princip, accused by some historians of killing Archduke Franz Ferdinand to stop Trialism was, therefore, a demonstrator in a pro-Trialist demonstration avoided by alert Serbian nationalists.

Whatever its exact political content on the day, the 18 February demonstration had a measurable, significant impact not only on the student movement in Bosnia-Herzegovina, but also on that in Croatia. Sarajevo had not seen such street violence since the 1906 workers' agitation in the city. According to Ferdo Behr, a Croat student who was to play a role on 28 June 1914, the wounding of Salko Šahinagić and the brutality of the police 'united' the whole of the high school youth. Indeed, the initial news about Šahinagić was that he had been killed – which sparked off a new wave of student unrest in Croatia, turning into a general strike by high school pupils.[79] In Sarajevo itself there were already further protests the following day, 19 February, and a school strike was called. As the historian Vladimir Dedijer remarked, 'for the first time in Bosnian history, Croats, Serbs and Muslims took part together'. Gavrilo Princip in particular was active in inciting new protests, going from class to class, even threatening the wavering pupils.[80] There followed wholesale expulsions of students from the city's schools. Drago Ljubibratić, Princip's biographer and a student contemporary, considered that the demonstrations had increased the 'revolutionary temperature' and revived the memories of the example that had been set by Bogdan Žerajić.[81] In a letter to his former tutor Princip described the differences between the Yugoslav-oriented Serbs and the nationalist Serbs (who had stayed away from the protest) as a 'horrendous schism'. But he proudly noted that, 'with an enthusiastic manifestation', he and his friends 'gave expression to a feeling of solidarity'.[82] Writing later in 1912 about this 'red and bloody' event (in the journal *Zora* which had moved from Vienna to Prague), student Miloš Pjanić noted the absence of most of the 'radical' (nationally exclusivist) Serbs, but nevertheless expressed satisfaction with 'the first act by the pupils, the first demonstration which bore the badge of our Serbo-Croat nationalism'.[83]

And thus a movement, much later known as 'Young Bosnia', came into being – nameless, unstructured and leaderless throughout. It would be utterly meaningless to talk about its existence before February 1912. It is equally meaningless to assert, as has been done in a German academic account, that 'Young Bosnia' had a 'radical wing'.[84] Without a body there could be no wings. Predrag Palavestra, indisputably the greatest authority on 'Young Bosnia', wrote about the 'militant part of the prewar nationalist youth grouped in Young Bosnia'. This is far more accurate.[85] There was only one grouping that could possibly be called a 'Young Bosnia': the Sarajevo-based, Serbo-Croat and Yugoslav-oriented youth. Inasmuch as this grouping carried out the assassination of Franz Ferdinand, it was certainly 'radical' and 'militant'.

The 'Serbo-Croat nationalism' referred to by Miloš Pjanić suddenly appeared as something of a force to be reckoned with across the whole region. March 1912 saw students in Serbia organize a big meeting to condemn the conditions in Croatia brought about by the policies of Governor Slavko Cuvaj. Tin Ujević from Zagreb University was one of the speakers in front of a crowd numbering some 5,000.[86] The Croat students returned the compliment, and in April some 160 of them, representing the entire spectrum of political persuasions in Croatia, paid a visit to Serbia where they were received with a degree of pomp and ceremony. Croat students who formerly denied the very existence of 'Serbs' were now kissing the Serbian flag. There was a sense in which Croatia's internal difficulties were thus internationalized. Oskar Tartaglia again led the way with his homage to Belgrade, 'the Piedmont of Serbdom and Yugoslavism'.[87]

In fact, the Serbian Government was deeply embarrassed by the whole episode. Apart from the reception at Belgrade University, the only other semi-official greetings of the guests were extended by the Serbian Army which also supplied the military musical bands. King Peter had turned down the suggestion that he should grant the visitors an audience. His son, Crown Prince Alexander, failed to appear at a pre-scheduled private meeting with the students from Croatia.[88] Foreign Minister Milovan Milovanović told Stephan von Ugron, the Austro-Hungarian envoy in Belgrade, that he had observed the Army encroachment with 'great discomfort', and that he would have a serious talk with the War Minister. Ugron himself, in his report to the Ballhausplatz, drew attention to the information at his disposal to the effect that 'sober-minded' Serbs disapproved of the excess in the 'artificially beefed-up enthusiasm' for the Croats.[89]

Dimitrije Mitrinović: 'Liberty Smells of Blood'

Shortly before the trip by the young Croats to Serbia, three different student tracts were printed (all in Belgrade, within the space of just a few weeks) which, taken together, have been seen by some historians as constituting the programmatic framework ('fundamental programmatic texts') of subsequent activity by the rebellious South Slav students in general and by the 'Young Bosnia' movement in particular.[90] These were: (1) *Smrt jednog heroja* (Death of a Hero) by Vladimir Gaćinović; (2) *Hrvatska u borbi za slobodu* (Croatia in the Struggle for Freedom) by Tin Ujević, and (3) *Narodno ujedinjenje* (National Unification) by Dimitrije Mitrinović. This was a highly distinguished group of authors. All three, young as they were, had already become well-known for their political activism and literary merit. They have been venerated ever since: Gaćinović as the godfather of the revolutionary spirit among Bosnia's youth, Ujević as Croatia's best avant-garde poet, and Mitrinović as a mystic of genius and one of the forerunners of the European Union idea.

Of the three tracts, Gaćinović's *Death of a Hero* is by far the most frequently mentioned in the world literature on the Sarajevo assassination – or at least in its more specialist branch.[91] Yet it may also have been, for Princip, the least influential. The reason for its renown is easy to establish: Gaćinović has been widely seen as the chief ideologue of the 'Young Bosnia' movement. In addition, his mysterious journeying, his membership of the Black Hand organization, his links with Trotsky and other Russian revolutionaries, and his early death in Switzerland (under allegedly mysterious circumstances), present him as a colourful figure, eagerly embraced by historians trying to make sense out of a 'Young Bosnia' which had neither a formal structure nor a particular leader. *Death of a Hero* is Gaćinović's reverential tribute to Bogdan Žerajić, the failed assassin of 1910. The two had known each other from their time in the Mostar *Gymnasium*. The 16-page pamphlet (which Gaćinović had written in Vienna and then sent to Belgrade) was of course circulated among the Sarajevo students, and, on the face of it, had a powerful impact. Cvetko Popović wrote that it had 'fired' and 'enthralled' them – although they had no idea about the identity of its author, concealed behind the pseudonym *Osvetnik* (Avenger).[92] Later, during the archducal assassination trial Nedeljko Čabrinović, one of the assassins, confirmed that *Death of a Hero* had been 'of decisive importance' (those words were used by the judge) in his decision to carry out the assassination. The foreword to the pamphlet was actually read to the court, and when the judge asked whether anyone had any remarks to make, Princip exclaimed: 'Glory be to Žerajić!'[93]

However, a distinction should be made at this point between Žerajić as a paragon and a subsequent pamphlet championing him. Princip told the court that Žerajić had been his 'first role model'. He added that he would, already aged 16 (in 1911, the year before Gaćinović's tract), visit Žerajic's grave and swear to emulate him – Princip clearly did not require additional inspiration from Gaćinović's pamphlet.[94] Čabrinović, too, stated in court that Žerajić had been his 'role model [*uzor*]', which makes his earlier confirmation about the importance of *Death of a Hero* merely a clumsy re-statement of a pre-existing attitude toward a contemporary.[95] Undoubtedly, however, Gaćinović had successfully revived the memory of the lone assassin. In 1910, only a few days after Žerajić had committed suicide on the Emperor's Bridge, Sarajevo's pupils would take off their caps while walking past the spot.[96] But group worship did not then develop and, as Cvetko Popović recalled, he had by 1912 become a forgotten figure.[97] Princip and Čabrinović were among the few who had really remembered his act. In that sense, the appearance of *Death of a Hero* was naturally welcomed by Sarajevo students, arriving as it did just at the time when many of them were becoming thoroughly radicalised.

In February 1912, when Gaćinović published his celebration of Žerajić, there already existed a firm 'Serbo-Croat'/'Yugoslav' orientation in a section of Bosnia's high school studentry – the one which took part in Sarajevo's anti-Cuvaj demonstrations and to which Gavrilo Princip belonged. By June 1914 practically all the assassins and their accomplices were in this camp: Serbs, Croats and Muslims. But Gaćinović's *Death of a Hero* says not a word about Serbo-Croat unity or about Yugoslavs. Addressed to 'young Serbdom [*mlado srpstvo*]', his pamphlet describes Žerajić as a 'young Serbian hero', specifies the 'Serbian revolutionary' and talks of 'Serbian liberation'.[98] In other words, the politics of Gaćinović's pamphlet did not accord with the ideology of Young Bosnia, though its advocacy of direct action resonated with student feelings at the time. If one is to believe some of the post-1945 Yugoslav historiography on the subject, Gaćinović eventually evolved from a Serb to Yugoslav nationalist.[99] In 1912, however, his views and his pamphlet had fallen behind the rapidly evolving South Slav spirit of the times.

Much in *Death of a Hero* reads like a passionate wake-up call to the entire Serbian youth of Bosnia-Herzegovina (interestingly, Gaćinović specifically addressed young Serbian women several times in the pamphlet). He justifies the pamphlet on the grounds that the memory of Žerajić was fading just at the time his case should have been serving as a guide against indolence. Paraphrasing Žerajić himself, Gaćinović writes: 'We have to wage deadly warfare against the pessimism of dispiritedness and languor, we the heralds of new generations and new people.' Indeed, Gaćinović is very keen on what he calls 'the new type' – people who would 'prepare direct action and shake up the Serbian present'. Unquestionably, *Death of a Hero* attempted to incite a revolutionary spirit, but it did so in rather vague, indeed practically meaningless terms. For example: 'The whole of society needs to be reorganized from top to bottom and be joined in a great conspiracy for freedom.' Just how this was to be done was not explained. Moreover, some of Gaćinović's musing constitutes incomprehensible gibberish. Thus: 'Revolution never arises, as is wrongly believed, out of despair, but out of the revolutionary idea which grows in the spirituality of the people, bursting with enthusiasm and internal life, and with the gestures that exist in the mystic psychology of the masses.'[100]

Death of a Hero has recently been described in Clark's *Sleepwalkers* as 'one of the key cult texts of the pan-Serbian terrorist milieu'.[101] The problem with this view is twofold: not only did such a 'pan-Serbian' terrorist milieu not exist anywhere in the Monarchy, but it is also easy to exaggerate the impact of Gaćinović's dogmatically Serbian broadside on the pro-Yugoslav activist youth seeking a general settlement of the entire South Slav question. The truth of the matter is that *Death of a Hero* has over the decades come to be seen as 'one of the key cult texts' only because Gaćinović himself was built up, after 1918, into a 'Young Bosnia' cult figure. The latter movement, it has been asserted, was Gaćinović's 'baby [*čedo*]'.[102] Unfortunately, this claim has been uncritically accepted in the West.[103] It may have something to do not only with the notoriety of *Death of a Hero*, but also with a 1910 article that Gaćinović authored under the title 'Young Bosnia' – where he talked about 'the young Bosnian movement for the renewal of the land'. Yet in the first sentence of that article he stated: 'Bosnia is an old Serbian land.'[104] A new book on Young Bosnia, published in Serbia, uncritically calls Gaćinović its 'founder and ideological leader' – but then, the book was written by a relative of Gaćinović.[105]

It is indeed difficult to reconcile Gaćinović's Serbian bent with his supposed ideological tutelage of Princip and his Serbo-Croat 'nationalist' comrades in 'Young Bosnia'. To Gaćinović, as he himself said, the Serbo-Croat or Yugoslavist ideology was like 'pouring water into Serbian wine'. Although he admired the Croat Eugen Kvaternik (and the latter's associate from 1871, Vjekoslav Bach), he was described by Tin Ujević as being distrustful towards the 'Croat brothers'.[106] Cvetko Popović, the young assassin of 1914 and later probably the best judge of the Bosnian student scene from that period, categorically rejected the view that Gaćinović was the 'leading personality' of their 'Young Bosnia' movement and the 'most authentic interpreter of its ideas'. Inasmuch as 'Young Bosnia' was a part of the Yugoslav nationalist movement, Popovic pointed out, Gaćinović could not be regarded as its leading personality. Popović insisted that Gaćinović was 'not at all' Yugoslav-oriented in the national sense and had not, 'until his death', accepted the Yugoslav national ideology.[107] When Drago Ljubibratić, a 'Serbo-Croat' participant at the February demonstration in Sarajevo, subsequently met Gaćinović, the latter seemed impressed only by the fact that the workers' had joined in.[108] In his 1929 article on the ideology of 'Young Bosnia', Pero Slijepčević, a very close friend, admitted that Gaćinović, along with Žerajić, had talked mostly about 'Serbdom'.[109]

Tin Ujević's pamphlet *Croatia in the Struggle for Freedom*, the second of the three texts considered to have been pivotal in the revolutionary shift of the South Slav students of the Monarchy, was by contrast completely on the lines of the emerging Yugoslav sentiment.[110] It circulated in both Croatia and Bosnia-Herzegovina.[111] Ujević addressed it to the Croat youth (*omladina hrvatska*), but wrote in no uncertain terms that the people of Croatia were the 'Serbo-Croat' people (*njena naroda srpsko-hrvatskoga*). And, in his enthusiastic Yugoslavism, he went a step beyond demanding Serbo-Croat unification by also adding the Slovenes: 'unification is only a genuine unification when the complete unification of all Slovenes, all Croats, and all Serbs is envisaged.' *Croatia in the Struggle for Freedom* is without doubt a ferociously combative document. Croatia could only gain freedom, Ujević argued, if foreign dynasties were overthrown. He appealed: 'We need a revolution. We cannot attain anything in the Austro-Hungarian Monarchy by peaceful means ... In a plundering state the first right and the ultimate reason is force, and we shall have to use it.' Convinced about the 'futility' of mere parliamentary struggle within the Monarchy, and emphasizing the 'most radical methods', Ujević urged 'the youngest Croat generation' to act in a fashion that was 'the most determined and the most self-sacrificing'. In its national ideal this youngest generation had to be 'irreconcilable and absolute'; it had to serve the national ideal 'to the full extent' and it had to begin implementing it with 'iron logic'.[112]

Croatia in the Struggle for Freedom thus makes Gaćinović's *Death of a Hero* look like a gospel of pacifism. 'It is better', Ujević pointed out, 'to deliver blows than to take them'. For good measure, he reminded his readers to keep in mind that 'anti-Habsburg idea' for which Eugen Kvaternik had sacrificed his life in the independence bid of 1871. However, it is not just these fighting messages which make Ujevic's pamphlet a remarkable document. In his Yugoslav zeal, he lumped together Ljudevit Gaj, Bishop Strossmayer and Ante Starčević as the advocates of Serbo-Croat unity: 'That idea of ... Serbo-Croat unity, which Gaj disseminated under the Illyrian name, Strossmayer under the Yugoslav name, and Starčević under the Croat name itself, should give us strength and confidence.'[113] Whereas it was possible to view Gaj and Strossmayer as champions of Serbo-Croat unity (albeit from positions of Croat interest), to involve Starčević with them probably made the latter turn in his grave, given his persistent and ugly denial of the very existence of 'Serbs' in Croatia or Bosnia.

Clearly, therefore, in those days the spirit and élan among Yugoslav agitators knew no bounds. Even in Serbia, where the political circles stood somewhat aloof from the idea of Serbo-Croat unity, there existed a towering intellectual figure who supported it. This was Jovan Skerlić, literary critic and editor of *Srpski književni glasnik*, the respected literary periodical. He was an incorrigible Yugoslav. In 1909 he argued that 'not a single South Slav tribe has sufficient political or cultural power to assimilate the other tribes. Reality itself directs the South Slavs towards a grouping, on the basis of full religious and national equality, into one great national unit.'[114] Writing in February 1912 about Ante Starčević (only weeks before the appearance of Ujević's pamphlet) he claimed, astonishingly, that Starčević had not negated the Serbs – only their name. 'The Great Croatia of Ante Starčević', Skerlić suggested, 'is in fact the same as the Great Serbia of our patriots. The difference is formal, in name only.'[115] This was touchingly generous – to both sides. Whereas Skerlić would not have supported Ujević's advocacy of the use of force, he nevertheless legitimised the latter's overall argument for an integrated South Slav nation, complete with an apologia for Starčević.

Historians in both Serbia and Croatia have expressed bewilderment at such fast-moving developments in Yugoslav ideology before 1914. A recent Serbian study maintains that the South Slav intelligentsia was a prisoner of a certain 'intellectualist' approach to reality: it believed it could form nations through sheer will.[116] In the late 1960s Mirjana Gross wrote that no theoretical basis existed to support the integral Yugoslav idea preached by the young radicals. Everything rested on a 'moral imperative', whereby the events which occurred in the South Slav lands of the Monarchy supported the thesis that the South Slavs could only flourish within their own state.[117]

Dimitrije Mitrinović's *National Unification*, the third document from this period associated with the turbulence amongst the South Slav students, is not as explicitly militant as Ujević's *Croatia in the Struggle for Freedom*, but is equally uncompromising in its insistence on Serbo-Croat unity.[118] In contrast to the pamphlets by Gaćinović and Ujević (both of whom were Mitrinović's friends) the impact of *National Unification* can more easily be documented. Printed as a leaflet for distribution rather than as a publication, its full title was *The First Draft of a General Programme for the Youth Club National Unification*. The youth club in question was founded in Belgrade in connection with the April 1912 visit of the Croat students to Serbia.[119] Thus it was not a Serbian club, but rather a kind of overarching roof structure for South Slav youth. Mitrinović wrote the programme in Zagreb and brought it to Belgrade shortly before the arrival of the Croat students.[120]

In comparison with Gaćinović, Mitrinović is perhaps surprisingly little-known in Western accounts of the Sarajevo assassination. His British biographer concentrates on Mitrinović's work in London (from 1914 until his death in 1953) in the *New Age,* the Adler Society and the New Britain

Group. This is the period of Mitrinović's career which earned him the reputation of a mystic and messianic figure – in 1933 he called for the establishment of a European and ultimately world Federation.[121] Before 1914, however, he was busy calling for the formation of the Yugoslav state.

A graduate of the Mostar *Gymnasium*, Mitrinović was a Herzegovinian Serb. His family background was petty bourgeois rather than peasant in that both his father and mother were school teachers. Mitrinović studied at the universities of Zagreb, Vienna, Belgrade, Munich and Tübingen. As a very young man on the South Slav intellectual scene, he was already a pioneer of the modernist approach to art and literature. His talents were recognized early on by his appointment to the editorial board of *Bosanska vila*, the Bosnian-Serb literary journal in Sarajevo which he did a great deal to regenerate. Fascinated by the civilization of Western Europe, he advocated borrowing from it, or else 'uncultured and non-modern as we are, the vibrant and strong West will run over us by the force of its culture'.[122] For all his involvement with artistic and literary matters, Mitrinović never shied away from political commitment. He was even briefly arrested by the Zagreb police on suspicion that he had been involved in the assassination attempt made by his friend from Mostar, Bogdan Žerajić.[123] As a child, Mitrinović grew up hating the Habsburgs. He would later relate how in church during prayers for the royal family he and other school children would kneel on one knee only – in the hope that their prayers would thus be rendered ineffective.[124] His Yugoslav orientation apparently owed not a little to the celebrated Croat sculptor Ivan Meštrović, whose work he often interpreted on the pages of literary journals. The Yugoslav idea to Mitrinović was 'the supreme moral dogma' and he expounded the 'trinity' of nationalism, modernism and culture.[125] Along with the ever-present notion of 'Serbo-Croat unity', in his writings he used the terms 'modernism', 'culture' and 'radical democracy' almost in the same breath.

This is evident, for example, in the first sentence of his 1912 programme *National Unification*, in which he writes about the ideological basis of the club: 'The fundamental and central task of the club is the *propagating of the philosophy of nationalism* in general, particularly propagating *radical democratic political doctrines*: all of this for the purpose of strengthening the Serbo-Croat national soul and ... the creation of a modern and national Croato-Serb national culture.' In the second section of the programme, concerning the political orientation of the club, Mitrinović defined the 'Yugoslav idea' in the sense of '*complete Serbo-Croat and Slovene equalization and unification* and in the sense that there is a need to create a new and great, modern and national Yugoslav culture'. As has been seen, the same position with regard to the Slovenes was taken up by his friend Ujević. Mitrinović also spelt out what all this was meant to lead to: 'The central nationalist *dogma of the club is the idea that a national culture is impossible without a national society, and a national society is impossible without a national state.*' And this state, expressing the 'sovereignty of the Serbo-Croat people', was going to be 'founded on liberal principles'. (All emphases in the original.)

What Mitrinović meant by 'radical democratic political doctrines' is explained in the section of *National Unification* which deals with 'the concrete programme of the club'. He stood for a thoroughgoing opposition to clericalism, the expropriation of property belonging to the church and the great landowners, the abolition of the prerogatives of nobility and more generally of all social privileges. He was also anxious to underline the financial aspect of the proposed enterprise, recommending the establishment of a 'Croat-Serb national Fund for the material basis of the struggle' and the 'centralization' of economic resources in the fatherland. Practical and far-sighted, he wanted to see a society established for the allocation of scholarships to help students study abroad. The material component was additionally important to him because he also envisaged an effort to spread 'nationalist propaganda in Europe'.

On the one hand, *National Unification* proposed seemingly harmless methods of work: public lectures, discussions, meetings and publications. On the other hand, Mitrinović, just like Ujević, made clear that a parliamentary struggle in a 'non-parliamentary state' (i.e., Austria-Hungary) was 'futile'. In his view the main thrust of the effort had to be outside parliament, conducting 'national self-defence' by means of 'work, suffering and self-sacrifice'. The last section of the programme, concerning the duties of the club's members, commanded the latter to arouse everywhere a 'chivalrous spirit and fighting joy', and to work on improving themselves in the sense of 'self-education for national self-sacrifice'.[126]

If the rebellious part of the South Slav youth in the Monarchy had an action programme before 1914, one which they themselves acknowledged as such, then it was without a doubt Mitrinović's *National Unification*. In April 1912 the visiting students from Zagreb received copies of it in Belgrade. In fact, it was Mitrinović's friend Tin Ujević who handed some thirty of these over to the Croat students.[127] Apart from Croatia, the programme also reached Dalmatia and Bosnia-Herzegovina. According to Ljubibratić, it had 'great propaganda value' in all the South Slav lands.[128] Oskar Tartaglia and his friend Vladimir Čerina, after their return from Belgrade, organized their Serbo-Croat student sympathisers in Croatia and Dalmatia on the basis of Mitrinović's programme. This soon gained even more renown when it was read at the trial of Luka Jukić after the latter's attempt, in June, on Governor Cuvaj's life. In August Tartaglia even printed it in the paper *Sloboda* (Freedom). He recalled that the Belgrade trip yielded new people, 'a new generation that took a new, but shorter route: through evolution to revolution'.[129] In Sarajevo, the members of the 'Serbo-Croat Progressive Organization' also accepted the document which had reached them from Belgrade via their Secretary Miloš Pjanić. Explaining the local student goings on to his former tutor, Gavrilo Princip wrote in April 1912 that they were 'adhering to Mitrinović's revolutionary programme'.[130]

Mitrinović was indeed a revolutionary. But in contrast to the narrowly Serbian agenda of Gaćinović, Mitrinović's agenda in the wider Austro-Hungarian and Balkan context was Yugoslavian. And so it was Mitrinović, as the author of *National Unification*, who came nearest to being a kind of leader of like-minded students throughout the region, and not just of 'Young Bosnia'. He also commanded great respect as an intellectual in touch with the rest of the world. Ivo Andrić recalled how Mitrinović would press the youth in the Sarajevo *Gymnasium* to open up their horizons and read works in German, English and French. One day Andrić was reading some domestic author when Mitrinović approached him, pulled the book away from him and threw it on the floor, then producing a volume of Walt Whitman's verses. 'Read this', he told Andrić, 'and not that rubbish!'[131]

According to Predrag Palavestra, Mitrinović 'possessed not just literary, but also revolutionary authority' as a result of writing the programme.[132] In late summer 1912, not long before the First Balkan War broke out, he wrote an article for *Slovenski jug*, entitled 'At the Crossroads [*Pred raskrsnicom*]'. This piece of work provides an insight into how he (and presumably the youth he inspired across the South Slav lands within the Monarchy) viewed the regional and European picture. Here, he predicted correctly that war was going to engulf the Balkans as well as Europe, assessing the political scene in Europe as an 'enormously entangled' situation that was 'ripe and seeking a solution'. He commented on Austria-Hungary's troop concentrations along the border with Serbia, and on the bad state of Anglo-German relations. Italy's war against Turkey met with his approval since it was justifiable that 'a stronger culture finishes off cultural cripples'. Austria-Hungary he called an 'anti-national state without a historic moral sense, which continues to shame modern civilization by its existence'. And whereas Franz Joseph was to him a picture of the 'compromised impotence of an old and inveterate ruler without a national heart', he took Franz Ferdinand much more seriously. The Habsburg Heir to the Throne was seen by Mitrinović as possessing a 'tyrannically energetic, gendarme-like steely and adventurously militaristic nature'. Not only was Franz Ferdinand about to occupy the throne that would soon be empty, he was also about to begin his 'anti-Hungarian and especially anti-Serb exploits'.

Turning to Croatia and lamenting its 'miserable' revolutionary dynamic, Mitrinović considered that it was at a crossroads: the land could choose between 'the burial of its honour' (which he thought could only mean the fate of a Silesia), or 'an honourable and powerful liberating endeavour'; something that would demand the sacrifice of 'boiling national blood and bodies raised for the last and final struggle for liberation and unification'.

He warned that a Croat state could not be created in any 'hideous' Trialism within Austria-Hungary, but could only be built on the ruins of everything that the black-yellow Monarchy had built 'on our Croat territory'. Croat culture, moreover, established on the basis of 'Serbo-Croat ethno-physical unity', could only exist in a freely based Serbo-Croat society. For good measure, he added: 'A state cannot be created by meaningless parliamentary efforts alone: liberty smells of blood, and it craves its precious red smell'.[133]

II

Gavrilo Princip and Friends

A Newspaper Cutting

IN 1910, GAVRILO PRINCIP, the young man from Bosnia who was to shoot his way into historical renown, said to a friend: 'There is a certain restlessness inside me, some sense of mission, or is it a curse?'[1] Dobroslav Jevđević, a contemporary, wrote that Princip had not even seen a locomotive when he was ten, but had set the world aflame when he was nineteen. Writing his memoir in 1934, Jevđević also noted that the vast size of the world literature on the Sarajevo assassination was matched only by the enormity of its ignorance.[2] Today, as in Jevđević's time, there is still a great deal of superficial enquiry regarding Princip and his fellow assassins. During the run-up to the 100th anniversary of the Sarajevo assassination, for example, a polemic took place in the Balkan media as to whether Princip was a 'terrorist' or a freedom fighter.[3] It was a debate reflecting less an interest in history and far more the ethno-political prejudices in the region, whereby Princip's South Slav (i.e., Yugoslav) orientation was largely ignored and his Serbian ethnic background emphasized by Serbs and non-Serbs alike. At the same time, a Western historian could not resist joining in: comparing the Young Bosnians with the fundamentalists of twenty-first century Al Qaeda.[4] This is less history than melancholy proof that the stock pot of rhetoric can always take another stirring.

If terrorism is a means to a political end, Princip was by his own admission a terrorist. He was asked at the trial how he imagined to free the Yugoslavs from Austria and unite them in a single state. 'By terror', he replied, and elaborated that this meant 'killing people at the top, removing those evil-doers standing in the way and hindering the idea of unification'.[5] The term 'terror', as can be seen, had a different meaning at the time, targeting key individuals rather than landing indiscriminate blows. Initially, however, Princip did not describe his act of assassination in any rational political terms. When questioned on 4 August 1914, he said: 'I carried out the assassination mainly out of revenge and hatred against Austria. Austria was always unjust towards the Yugoslavs whom it oppressed ... whoever possesses a soul and feels for the suffering people has to protest or do whatever, for revenge is sweet and bloody.'[6] These words, 'revenge', 'hatred', 'protest', speak more readily of a grand gesture than of precise political calculation. They reveal a state of revolt, which was the essence of 'Young Bosnia'. '*Après moi, le déluge!*', Princip said defiantly only a few days before 28 June in response to a last minute effort to dissuade him from going ahead with the assassination.[7]

After many decades, attempts are now being made again to identify Princip, a Yugoslavian as opposed to Serbian nationalist, with the 'Unification or Death' organization, better known as the Black Hand, the Serbian society said to have schemed the creation of a Great Serbia and masterminded the assassination of Franz Ferdinand. Princip was according to Christopher Clark a member of the Black Hand.[8] This is a rather startling contention, but Clark does not supply a footnote to justify such conjecture. A casual reader might assume Princip's membership of the Black Hand to be an accepted matter of fact. In a variation on Clark's claim, Sean McMeekin has recently written that Princip, and Čabrinović (who as one in the team of assassins in Sarajevo on 28 June threw a bomb at Franz Ferdinand's car) 'were not active members of the Black Hand'.[9] Does he mean that so much is known about the Black Hand that he can assess the status of its members? Or perhaps he is admitting, obliquely, that one does not really know such things but that the Black Hand, at one or more removes, *ought to be seen* through the fog of rumour. All claims, if backed by evidence, that Princip and Čabrinović were members of this group would of course be a sensational revelation, for if true it would, once and for all, prove the involvement of the notorious Black Hand (notorious in history books, that is) in the assassination of Franz Ferdinand – an involvement from conception and plotting to organization and execution.

Yet, few before Clark have actually claimed that Princip belonged to the Black Hand. In 1927, Miloš Bogićević, a pro-German ex-Serbian diplomat, was one, asserting that Princip, along with Danilo Ilić and Muhamed Mehmedbašić (two other conspirators in the group of seven who waited for Franz Ferdinand on the streets of Sarajevo on 28 June 1914), were all members of the Black Hand. But Bogićević, who had fallen out with the Serbian Prime Minister Nikola Pašić, was being used by the Germans in the 1920s to write propaganda about Serbia's role in 1914 – having already defected to Germany during the war itself. Crucially for the credibility of his assertion, Bogićević failed even to provide the conspirators' entry numbers within the organization, entry numbers such as are invariably found in other lists of Black Hand members.[10] Experts, including David MacKenzie, the leading authority in the West on the Black Hand, have dismissed Bogićević.[11] On the basis of research by Drago Ljubibratić, himself a Young Bosnian, MacKenzie explicitly stated in connection with

Princip's February 1914 arrival in Belgrade: 'Neither he [Princip] nor his comrades ... joined the Black Hand which barred minors and was no longer recruiting members.'[12] It is any case highly doubtful in the first place that someone like Princip, with his staunch Yugoslav convictions, would even have wanted to join the Black Hand – an organization dedicated to promoting exclusively Serbian aims.

In the past, the only historian of repute who had ever linked Princip with the Black Hand was the indefatigable Luigi Albertini. He had talked to Colonel Čedomir Popović, the former Secretary of the Black Hand, and to Oskar Tartaglia, one of the few Croat members of the organization who was, as was seen in the previous chapter, one of the most zealous anti-Habsburg activists among the South Slav students. Both of them, Albertini wrote, had 'assured' him that Princip, along with Danilo Ilić, belonged to the Black Hand.[13] It is therefore odd that the names of Princip and Ilić do not appear on the list of members which Tartaglia himself had provided in his 1928 memoir. He explained there that his own name did not figure on the list and nor did the names of any members from outside Serbia lest the Austrian authorities found out. But this is demonstrable nonsense: at least two Bosnian Serb names are included in the list supplied by Tartaglia – those of Vladimir Gaćinović and Milan Ciganović (the latter was to play an important role in the preparations for the Sarajevo assassination).[14] It is also curious that Colonel Popović, in several articles about the Black Hand which he published after the war in the Zagreb journal *Nova Evropa*, does not mention Princip as a member.

But then, as has already been seen in this book, Albertini is not always a reliable interpreter of events. He even suggested, in the absence of any evidence whatsoever, that Trifko Grabež, another assassin on 28 June 1914, might have been a Black Hand member.[15] Moreover, the entire thrust of Albertini's early chapters in the second volume of his massive work is to argue in a highly speculative manner the existence of a wide conspiracy on the Serbian side and even the involvement of Russia in the Sarajevo assassination. These chapters read as if Albertini had a preconceived thesis, the credibility of which he tried to sustain by mixing a *soupçon* of fact with a surfeit of opinion.

Much the same can be said about the approach now being adopted by recent historians supporting the Black Hand hypothesis. Why should Clark, against evidence and the scholarly trend accumulating since 1914, see Princip acting as a member of the Black Hand? An answer suggests itself. In the more recent debates about the genesis of the First World War, there has been a reversion to polemic. Even if the evidence has been mined out long ago, a junior generation can still kick around the conclusions. Too many writers want to bring back the blame-game for the conflict – or to start a new one by shifting the focus away from Berlin and Vienna. The complex causes of the war are less compelling than they once were.

But one of the *simplifying* pieces of the narrative in the whole otherwise complicated story is the assumption that the Black Hand did indeed stand behind the assassination. This was often taken as an axiom in the less specialized accounts, even in the majority of Yugoslav and Serbian inter-pretations – a classic *argumentum ad infinitum*. Therefore it seems only a small step to link Princip with the Black Hand as a fully paid up member – the lack of credible evidence seems irrelevant given the sheer abundance of historiographical assertions alleging the involvement of the Black Hand in his assassination of Franz Ferdinand. As this and the next chapter will show, however, the role of the Black Hand organization in the events leading up to 28 June 1914 was practically non-existent – claims to the contrary about it constitute one of the most perennial but fatuous myths of twentieth century historiography, now spilling into the twenty-first.

Gavrilo (Gabriel) Princip, the man in question, was born on 25 July 1894, on the feast day of Archangel Gabriel, in Veliki Obljaj, a village near Grahovo, western Bosnia. His family, originally called Jovićević, was of Montenegrin stock, from a little town there also called Grahovo. By the eighteenth century at the latest the family had moved to northern Dal-matia and from there to Bosnia. Princip's great-grandfather Todor was a fierce man armed with a short rifle and a long knife, who would invariably ride his white horse while wearing a resplendent costume with silver decorations. The Italians in Dalmatia called him *Il principe bosniaco* and the name stuck. Great-grandson Gavrilo was very keen on learning and completed the four years of elementary school with excellent results. His family intended him to become an officer in the Austro-Hungarian Army. Indeed, in 1907 they sent him to Sarajevo to enrol at the officers cadet school. His elder brother Jovo happened to reveal this plan to a Serbian friend of his in Sarajevo, a well-to-do merchant. Appalled by the prospect that the boy could become an enemy of his own people, the man advised that Gavrilo be enrolled in the city's commercial school instead, and this was done on the same day.[16]

In 1910 Princip decided to switch to *Gymnasium* (high school). This was not to get better career opportunities – he actually despised careerists and simply needed the *Gymnasium* as a badge of prestige, so that his peers, dealing with abstract ideas, would not look down on him.[17] His move to high school took him to the town of Tuzla (where he passed additional qualifying exams which included Latin), before returning to Sarajevo to continue in the *Gymnasium* there. Princip tried his hand at poetry, indulged in a bit of billiards in the coffee houses of the capital, but refused the suggestions of his friends to attend a school of dance. Tidy and 'well dressed' – with different contemporary sources agreeing that he paid attention to his external appearance – he was persistent rather than stubborn, though somewhat 'boastful' in discussion. Detecting in him a rebellious spirit, his school mates nicknamed him 'Gavroche' – a reference to Hugo's character in *Les Misérables*.[18] Other observers viewed him as perfectly harmless. Krešimir Kovačić, one of the young Croat rebels who met Princip in the summer of 1912, wrote that he was 'good-natured' and that one could 'never have anticipated the assassin in him'.[19] In the Sarajevo *Gymnasium* Princip founded a secret literary organization '*Nada* [Hope]'. The aim of the proposed organization, he said, would not be 'purely literary'. He was chosen to be its president.[20] During this period (1911-1912) he would pay visits to the grave of Bogdan Žerajić – often, interestingly, in the company of Croat activist students Karlo Brkić and Alexander Odić. But then, many young Bosnian Croats were scheming to assassinate the *Ban* of Croatia, and so Žerajić had multi-ethnic appeal.[21]

The previous chapter has examined how Princip took part in the formation, early in 1912, of the combative Serbo-Croat student movement subsequently going under the name of 'Young Bosnia'. By this time he had dropped out of the *Gymnasium*, having both fallen ill and failed in maths. Becoming a *privatni djak* (private student), he moved to Belgrade at the end of May 1912 with his friend Borivoje Jevtić to take his exams there. He was in any case disappointed with the native Serb political establishment's 'miserable policy and particularism', which he viewed as having brought dissent and hatred into relations between Serbs and Croats after the February demonstrations in the city.[22] This had given him further motivation to leave Sarajevo for Belgrade. He was, as Jevtić wrote, 'fed up with Sarajevo which he afterwards always hated'.[23]

Writing to Jevtić from Sarajevo in June 1912, his friends Miloš Pjanić and Drago Ljubibratić asked: 'How is Gavro [Princip]? Is he shouting: Long live the revolution!'[24] So what kind of a revolutionary firebrand was Princip? Stemming from an impoverished background, he and most of his friends in Young Bosnia associated the spartan social conditions in Bosnia-Herzegovina with foreign rule. National emancipation was therefore in their eyes intended to be combined with a social and economic revolution. To this end, they pored over the writings of Russian anarchists and socialists: Bakunin, Chernyshevsky, Stepnyak, Herzen and Kropotkin among others. Jovan Kršić, who studied the reading habits of the Sarajevo assassins, emphasized that their world view was not 'singularly nationalist', and drew attention to the fact that Princip and his fellow assassin Čabrinović had, for example, thoroughly absorbed and discussed between them *News From Nowhere* by the English utopian socialist William Morris, which had been translated into the Serbian in 1911.[25]

Yet for Princip the national component of the struggle was a clear priority. In 1916, in a document submitted to Dr Martin Pappenheim, the psychiatrist who observed him in jail, he wrote that he and his friends had studied Kropotkin's writings as expressed in Vienna's anarchist paper *Wohlstand für Alle*. This was apparently just before the assassination of Franz Ferdinand. Princip's circle agreed that a social revolution was possible. Nevertheless, added Princip, 'before that, a state of affairs in the whole of Europe should be created whereby the differences between nations should be evened out; although we read socialist and anarchist literature, as nationalists we did not busy ourselves too much with this question since we maintained that each one of us has another duty, the national duty.'[26]

Princip was a great fan of Friedrich Nietzsche and would often, and 'with particular pleasure', recite in his halting German the lines from *Ecce homo*: '*Ich weiss woher ich stamme!* ... ['I know where I come from!]' As insatiable as a flame, I glow and consume myself. All that I touch turns to light, all that I let go turns to coal: surely I am a flame!') He also liked to read Walter Scott and Alexandre Dumas (*père*), though he was not too keen on Tolstoy. When Dobroslav Jevđević, carrying a Tolstoy book, initially met Princip in Sarajevo's city park, the first words he heard from him were: 'All of Tolstoy's works should be burnt, he is an advocate of the peaceful endurance of evil.'[27] That was in 1910. It would appear that Princip's sense of 'national duty' had matured in him by the first half of 1912. Shortly after he was arrested on 28 June 1914, one of the first pronouncements he made in the police station was that he had already decided, two years earlier, 'out of nationalist feeling', to carry out an assassination against any high person representing the official Austria.[28]

This would coincide with the time of his radicalization within the Serbo-Croat and Yugoslav-minded student circle in Sarajevo which had taken part in the demonstrations of February 1912, as well as with Luka Jukić's assassination attempt in Zagreb (June 1912) which had had such a profound impact on South Slav youth. And although at the time Princip did not have a specific person in mind for assassination, some of his friends most definitely did. In fact, there was no shortage of ideas about who should be killed, and there was no lack of volunteer assassins either. Vladimir Dedijer listed some of the conspiracies from that turbulent year of 1912. One of the envisaged targets was the Joint Finance Minister Biliński. Dragutin Mras, a Slovene, offered to shoot him, as did Vladeta Bilbija, Princip's relative from Grahovo, and Ibrahim Fazlinović, a Muslim. Nothing came of this. The same Fazlinović also came forward when his Muslim friend Đulaga Bukovac suggested that no less than Emperor Franz Joseph should be assassinated. The two of them went to Belgrade to obtain weapons, but they gave up their plan with the outbreak of the First Balkan War in the autumn of 1912. Finally, Srećko Džamonja, a Croat attending the teachers training college in Sarajevo, decided he would kill Foreign

Minister Berchtold, but travelled in vain to Zagreb and Belgrade in search of support for his scheme.[29]

The stories behind these conspiracies show up some fairly absurd and whimsical assumptions. Thus Srećko Džamonja imagined that there was a hotel right opposite the Ballhausplatz in Vienna where he could book himself a room facing Berchtold's office and shoot him from there with a carbine.[30] And Đulaga Bukovac, who was later to play a role in the Sarajevo assassination, thought that Franz Joseph should be killed by a Muslim – although a Muslim himself, he did not volunteer as he considered himself to be a Croat.[31] But these stories also demonstrate that members of all South Slav nationalities were scheming one or the other assassination aimed at Austro-Hungarian officialdom. It is conspicuous, though unsurprising, that at this stage Governor Potiorek did not figure on the would-be assassins' list of targets. Biliński, Berchtold and of course the Emperor himself were clearly seen as the more spectacular victims. This was soon to change. Once Potiorek introduced, in May 1913, his emergency measures in Bosnia-Herzegovina, he became the most hated figure in the eyes of revolutionary South Slav youth. 'It can be asserted with certainty', Cvetko Popović wrote, 'that had the Heir to the Throne Ferdinand not come to Sarajevo in 1914, an assassination on Potiorek would have been carried out in the course of that year. For not one but dozens of young men dreamt about that assassination.'[32]

In the period 1912-1914 one of the focal points of the conspiratorial activity of these young Bosnian men was in Belgrade, in the area round *Zeleni Venac* (Green Wreath) market square just beneath the central plateau of the city. And while *Zeleni Venac* with its coffee houses was typically Balkan, it also had, as the Serbian writer Bora Ćosić recently remarked, its own *genius loci*.[33] One of the favourite venues was the unassuming *kafana* (coffee house, restaurant) *Zlatna Moruna* (Golden Sturgeon). This was the meeting place for 'emigrants' (as they called themselves) from Bosnia-Herzegovina. Princip was a frequent visitor to this establishment where coffee was cheap and no one was under any pressure to order anything.[34] There, he would meet other students from his generation who began to arrive in Belgrade in greater numbers after 1912 – many of them having been expelled from Bosnian schools. Croat and Slovene students were also frequenting the *Zeleni Venac* area.[35] However, another category of Bosnian 'emigrants' visiting the coffee house were not men of learning, but men of violence, the so-called *komite* or *četniks*, the irregulars who had fought the Turks and who preferred to steer clear of the Austro-Hungarian authorities in their native Bosnia-Herzegovina. They, too, liked coming to the Golden Sturgeon where the students would give them news from the home land. 'It was a peculiar world', Borivoje Jevtić recalled, 'restless, always in some kind of anticipation ... Smooth student faces alongside bearded, knife-carrying *komite*; rough and difficult types, accustomed to outrage and blood, side by side with the dreamy countenance of youth.'[36]

Ideologically, too, these two groups stood in stark contrast. Whereas the irregulars thought that the aim of the national struggle was the unification of the Serbian people, the students were generally in favour of Serbo-Croat unity and a South Slav orientation. What attracted the students to the irregulars was the contact with 'revolutionary practice'.[37] But who did they intend to subject to their own practice? It is quite interesting that, excepting Potiorek and, as has been seen, some big names in Vienna, they trained their sights mostly on the opportunist local politicians and dignitaries of Bosnia-Herzegovina. Moreover, those whom they identified as collaborators were predominantly of Serbian nationality. In his interrogation Čabrinović identified some of those 'to be removed': Danilo Dimović, Milan Jojkić, Gligorije Jeftanović and the Serbian Metropolitan Evgenije Letica.[38] Princip was certainly not alone in despising the Bosnian Serb elite.

The student emigrants 'lived more on illusions than on bread'.[39] Princip's own material circumstances were never great although his entrepreneur brother Jovo would normally send him sufficient funds. But there were also times, especially in 1914, when he could not afford to feed himself.[40] In 1912, with the approach of the First Balkan War, he enlisted as a volunteer and went to Prokuplje in the south of Serbia where Major Voja Tankosić ran a training camp. Tankosić, a founding member of the Black Hand, was to be famously involved in providing the arms for the assassination of Franz Ferdinand in Sarajevo. There is a legend, frequently retold in the historiography of Sarajevo 1914, that Tankosić, upon seeing Princip at the training camp, sent him away because of his weak appearance and small stature. In one of the widely read accounts, Gordon Brook-Shepherd maintained that the rejection had a profound impact on Princip, so much so that he was now set 'to find personal glory in some private act of revenge'.[41] In fact, Princip was rejected, along with scores of other students, for a very different reason: it was not the policy of the Serbian Army to take under-age volunteers – and he was only sixteen at the time. Drago Ljubibratić, among the volunteers at Prokuplje along with Princip, wrote that a speech was given to the students to tell them that they were too young for war and had better get on with their education.[42] Dobroslav Jevđević (who knew him in Belgrade), related that Princip had only volunteered because he did not want to come across as a 'coward'. He was against the Turkish war, 'seeing in Austria the only enemy'. Jevđević also provided important evidence of Princip's strictly Yugoslav ideology: when in 1913 the Serbs fought the Bulgarians, a fellow South Slav nation, Princip, being 'a convinced supporter of Yugoslav unity', took this conflict 'tragically'.[43]

Between May 1912 and May 1914 Princip spent most of his time in Belgrade, returning twice to Sarajevo for extended periods – from October 1912 to March 1913, and October 1913 to February 1914. The third time he returned to Sarajevo, at the end of May 1914, he was of course a man on a mission to kill Franz Ferdinand. And he was not alone in this, travelling to Sarajevo with two co-conspirators: Trifko Grabež and Nedeljko Čabrinović. Interestingly, he had actually worked hard in Belgrade on preparing for his exams, especially during 1913-1914. One of his constant friends (and also a room-mate) during that period was Grabež. Princip had known him in the Sarajevo *Gymnasium* which Grabež had left in order to continue in Tuzla, but there he had slapped his professor and been expelled from the school, ending up, like Princip, as a private student at the 1st Belgrade *Gymnasium*. The son of a Serbian Orthodox priest, he was the only one of the assassins who declared at their October 1914 trial that he was a believer in God. At the same time Grabež was no less than Princip a firm believer in the need for South Slav unity. And it was Princip's 'enthusiasm', Grabež later explained, that converted him to the idea of assassinating the Austrian Heir to the Throne.[44] He was, according to Ratko Parežanin who knew them both in Belgrade, 'noble, well brought-up, modest' and 'equally as firm, serious and stable as was Princip'.[45] Parežanin recalled that Princip and Grabež had from early spring 1914 been preparing for exams, with days when they had worked 'from dawn to dusk'. But then, around the beginning of May 1914, Parežanin noted that 'Princip and Grabež were no longer learning. They had given up on the books.'[46] What, then, had turned them from studying to something else?

At the time, Princip and Grabež had been in frequent contact with Nedeljko Čabrinović, a typesetter from Sarajevo who had found employment in a state-owned printing press in Belgrade. A born rebel with socialist and anarchist leanings, Čabrinović had been expelled by the police from Sarajevo for taking part in a print workers' strike. What had especially irritated him on that occasion was that a foreigner working as a Bosnian government official had given him a moral sermon on the matter. In a sense, this was a perfect illustration of what the Young Bosnians were against: the perceived arrogance of foreign rule. Čabrinović recalled this episode with great bitterness during his interrogation on 28 June 1914: 'He, a foreigner, had the nerve to lecture me, a native.' Had he had a weapon on him, Čabrinović said, he would have killed the man on the spot.

It would appear that under the influence of Princip and his friends (such as Borivoje Jevtić), Čabrinović subsequently embraced their Serbo-Croat and Yugoslav outlook. But he really required no ideological fine-tuning because at the time of his expulsion, in 1912, he had already decided that the way to resolve these matters was by throwing bombs.[47] Apart from the fact that he did actually hurl a bomb at Franz Ferdinand's car on 28 June

1914, and possibly because his reputation had preceded him, Čabrinović's other claim to fame is to have been anonymously sent a newspaper cutting which announced that very visit by the Archduke to Bosnia in the first place. Someone had typed on the envelope: 'To Čabrinović, Belgrade, Coffee House Golden Sturgeon, Zeleni Venac.' The cutting was glued to a piece of paper.[48]

Research carried out in the 1930s by Vojislav Bogićević established fairly conclusively that the newspaper item was from *Hrvatski Dnevnik*, the Sarajevo Croat daily, which on 17 March 1914 reproduced a brief piece of news that had already been printed in the city's German language *Bosnische Post*. It talked about 'well informed Viennese circles' according to whom there existed a 'prospect' that Franz Ferdinand would towards the end of June visit Bosnia on the occasion of the 15th Corps' upcoming military manoeuvres in the province. Bogićević established that three men in Sarajevo, Jovo Varagić, Jovan Šošić and Mihajlo Pušara, were involved in the sending of this cutting to Čabrinović in Belgrade. The fact that Čabrinović, a worker, had been chosen to receive it rather than any of the emigrant students was later explained by Šošić on the grounds that they had not known the addresses of the students who, being private students, were moving all the time between Belgrade and Bosnia.[49] Čabrinović had, on the other hand, been known to Varagić and his friends. In order to cover their tracks, Pušara posted the cutting from the town of Zenica rather than Sarajevo.

Predrag Palavestra, the great authority on the literary activity of the Young Bosnians, was of the opinion that the initiative to send the newspaper item may well have stemmed from Jovo Varagić.[50] The latter, a poet, was the literary editor of *Srpska riječ* (Serbian Word) where he ran a secret *kružok* (i.e., circle, cell, group). Pušara, a municipal clerk in Sarajevo, also a poet, and Šošić, a lawyer, were members. Varagić may have worked for a paper which had 'Serbian' in its title, but he and his friends were ideological Yugoslavs. The influence that had been exerted on them by Dimitrije Mitrinović was quite extraordinary. Borivoje Jevtić, another member, recalled: 'Mitrinović would open up to us the horizons of great world literatures and would teach us about mutual tolerance, about the need for mutual national heedfulness, about the great idea of brotherhood and unity of Yugoslav peoples.'[51] But there was something else as regards Varagić. His late-romantic, pessimist poetry, as Palavestra noted, contained much on the necessity for sacrifice.[52] Varagić wrote at the beginning of 1914 that a 'new age' was approaching and that it demanded new people. 'We are preparing the ground for new events', he continued, 'and we have been chosen for the honourable task of clearing the path at the price of us ourselves, of our peace and our happiness.'[53] Indeed: in picking that news item about the Archduke, Varagić did much to prepare the ground for new events.

Assuming that Pušara sent the cutting on 17 March or, more likely, a day or so thereafter, and that the letter would have travelled several days to Belgrade, Čabrinović would still have received it by the last week of the month.[54] As is well known, by 28 May Princip, Grabež and Čabrinović were on their way to Bosnia, laden with four Browning pistols, eight magazines for those pistols, five boxes of ammunition, and six bombs.[55] What exactly happened in Belgrade in the preceding two months represents one of the most obscure chapters in the events leading to the assassination of Archduke Franz Ferdinand and the outbreak of the war in Europe.

Target Franz Ferdinand

Čabrinović, upon receiving the newspaper cutting, did not just show it to Princip. In fact, he paraded it practically everywhere he went in Belgrade, first brandishing it to his colleagues at the printing press where he worked. Among those present was an elderly man called Nikola Novaković who, Čabrinović recalled, 'immediately shook his head as he saw it'. In the afternoon Čabrinović went to the coffee house *Zeleni Venac* on the square bearing the same name. There, he sat with a group of people among whom was also a certain Đoka Bajić, widely suspected by Bosnian emigrant youth of being an Austrian spy. This possibility was also known to Čabrinović, but it did not stop him talking carelessly about wishing to go to Vienna to kill Đorđe Nastić, the well-known Austrian *agent provocateur*. Bajić, in all probability playing just such a role himself, suggested that it would be a better idea to kill Franz Ferdinand. 'I laughed', Čabrinović recalled, 'and showed him the letter I had received that day.'[56]

If Bajić was working for the Austrians, he would no doubt have reported this encounter with Čabrinović. Be that as it may, Princip was also informed on that day about the content of the envelope, though he later claimed that he had already read 'ten days' beforehand in 'newspapers' about the arrival of the Heir to Throne. The cutting produced by Čabrinović indicated to him, said Princip, that Franz Ferdinand was 'definitely' coming, and it was then that he and Čabrinović decided to assassinate the Archduke.[57] They went to a park in central Belgrade, *Obilićev venac*, where the 'definitive' decision was made, and they gave each other word of honour to that effect.[58]

So, the information was there and the determination was also there. The only problem was how to do it: the would-be assassins had no weapons nor sufficient funds to buy them privately. Subsequently Princip visited a shop selling handguns in Belgrade where he saw one (9 mm) which he thought would have 'suited' him, but it cost sixty dinars.[59] This childlike reconnaissance of a weapons store alone would suggest that Princip had not received instructions from some powerful or professional conspiratorial centre in Belgrade, for any such promptings would surely have been accompanied by some pledge regarding the availability of weapons.

But why Franz Ferdinand? Was he the target simply because he was going to make himself available in Sarajevo? It does appear that the practicality of eliminating him on home ground and his perceived importance combined to produce a death sentence. This is illustrated by the strange coincidence that, in June 1914, the Young Bosnians had the unique opportunity to choose between two Austrian archdukes visiting Sarajevo: Franz Ferdinand and Leopold Salvator. The latter was in town between 7 and 13 June and was, incidentally, an important military figure in his own right: Inspector General of the Artillery since 1907, he had devoted his energies to the build-up and modernization of the Austro-Hungarian artillery.[60] This Archduke came to Bosnia (together with the War Minister Alexander von Krobatin) to observe artillery tests at Kalinovik. Accommodated at Hotel Evropa, he would have been an easy target, with the local press reporting in great detail on all his movements, and even taking part, on 12 June, in the Corpus Christi procession through the centre of the city.[61] According to Cvetko Popović. 'the spirit of assassination' was much in evidence during the visit of Leopold Salvator, with many students protesting that it was 'shameful' to allow the Archduke to provoke with his walkabouts.[62] Certainly, some in Sarajevo thought this was an opportunity not to be missed. Mihajlo Pušara's brother Vido, a well known brawler, was keen to shoot him with his Mauser revolver, but brother Mihajlo and Jovo Varagić (the same Varagić who was behind the idea of sending the newspaper cutting to Belgrade), argued that Leopold Salvator was no military strategist and finally convinced Vido to give up his intention so as not to spoil 'the main thing'.[63]

Franz Ferdinand, 'the main thing', was, on the other hand, very much seen as a strong military figure. Čabrinović, when asked why he and his friends had chosen to kill the Archduke, went so far as to describe him as 'a man of genius' who would have been 'a second Napoleon' for Austria.[64] Čabrinović may have been prone to hyperbole, but Princip had told Grabež that Franz Ferdinand was 'a powerful military factor in Austria'. There was, however, much more to this. In their opinion, Grabež stated to the interrogators, 'the Heir to the Throne was altogether an enemy of the Slavs'. Grabež explained that they had formed their opinions about Franz Ferdinand reading Serbian as well as Croatian newspapers.[65] 'We heard about him', Čabrinović stated in court, 'that he was an enemy of the Slavs'. But he added that no one had told them directly: 'Kill him'.[66]

The evidence that the assassins had considered the Archduke a threat because they thought he had some Trialist or some other supposedly Slav-friendly reform schemes that would have rendered impossible a 'Great

Serbia' is extremely thin. Nevertheless, some historians, among them Christopher Clark, have jumped to this conclusion. Clark has argued that the Archduke was not 'targeted on account of any alleged hostility to the Slavic minorities', but 'on the contrary' because of his reputed support for more autonomy to the Slavic lands. This is, at best, labyrinthine history. Princip himself testified that one of his motives to target the Archduke was to take revenge for the parlous poverty of the peasantry and for the repressive measures taken against them, declaring the Archduke to be the source of this evil. Oblivious to the clear evidence in the assassins' testimony that they had seen Franz Ferdinand as an enemy of the Slavs, Clark cites something else Princip said about the Archduke at the trial on 12 October 1914, namely that 'as future Sovereign he would have prevented our union by carrying through certain reforms'.[67] But Princip did not actually say 'prevented our union', he used the verb '*smetati*' (i.e., be in the way, hinder, interfere with) and, more importantly, qualified his remarks with the words that such reforms, 'it goes without saying [*razumije se*]', would be harmful 'over here [*kod nas*]'. This rather suggests that Princip worried less about Trialism in particular, and more about the overall effect ('over here') on the South Slavs of the Archduke's general competence and policies as a ruler in revitalising and strengthening the Habsburg state at the expense of an imagined South Slav alternative.[68] Clark passed over, moreover, what Princip said immediately beforehand about some of his motives for killing Franz Ferdinand: 'I knew that he was an enemy of the Slavs ... I thought that he would hinder and damage the Slavs.'[69] Nikola Stojanović, writing in 1929, explicitly rejected the notion that the younger generations saw the Archduke's alleged Trialism as a genuine prospect: 'The youth did not believe in it.'[70] Princip may or may not have been alluding to Trialism when he mentioned 'certain reforms', but he was evidently concerned about all the South Slavs, and not just the Serbs. To paint him as an exponent of Great Serbian ambitions is to be blind to Princip's profound Yugoslavism. Whilst they were supportive of a free Serbian state, the assassins never mentioned a 'Great Serbia'. Their obsessive talk was only about a Yugoslavia.

Clark's observations on this subject only amount to a re-statement of what the Austrian historian Glaise-Horstenau argued in 1929: that the Archduke had been killed because of his perceived ability to successfully solve 'the Austrian problem' and thereby rob the Serbian '*Irredentismus*' of its *raison d'être*.[71] It was seen in chapter three that Albertini was to employ the same argument. Addressing this issue in 1936, the Serbian historian Vladimir Ćorović warned against ascribing to the young assassins any far-reaching political calculations when they were in fact looking for the first possible target of distinction. Ćorović also pointed out that Trialism was only conceivable in the context of Franz Ferdinand embarking on a collision course with Hungary. In this scenario, those Yugoslavs wishing a union would have more reason to celebrate such a Trialist attempt than to fear it, since the resultant struggle against the Magyars 'would undoubtedly weaken the power of the Monarchy', thus giving the Yugoslav tendencies a welcome opportunity.[72] It is also highly unlikely that the Black Hand organization (had it really it stood behind the Sarajevo assassination, which this book disputes in the next chapter) would have seen Franz Ferdinand's alleged Trialist outlook as a real threat and decided in consequence to have him out of the way. As will be shown, Jovan M. Jovanović, in 1914 the Serbian Minister in Vienna, was very close to the Black Hand and would presumably have been consulted before any such conclusion about the Archduke was reached. Whereas Jovanović, as he wrote soon after the Sarajevo assassination, believed that it would be 'groundless [*bez prava*]' to ascribe to Franz Ferdinand a supposed desire to create a third, Trialist state. 'His intentions', Jovanović suggested, 'were to tighten up the Dual Monarchy as best he could rather than create a third, let alone a Yugoslav state.'[73]

Čabrinović was the only one of the assassins to reveal something specific about what they knew of the Archduke's future plans: he had read somewhere, he said, that Franz Ferdinand was contemplating a federalist Austria to which Serbia and Montenegro would be 'joined'.[74] But this obviously had nothing to do with Trialism – it concerned, in the eyes of the assassins, the clear and present danger of Austrian expansion in South-Eastern Europe led by an anti-Slavonic Franz Ferdinand. It would, therefore, be somewhat misleading to conclude that Franz Ferdinand was killed because the assassins had decided, reading newspapers, that this or that of his alleged plans for the reorganization of the Empire was not to their liking. They saw in him, above all, an enemy of the Slavs, and what they believed or guessed about his future intentions could only be of secondary importance in this context. To the extent, however, that a direct motive for the assassination can be identified, it had the flavour of local revenge. Grabež related during his preliminary questioning that Princip had considered the Archduke to have 'inspired' the high treason trials (in Croatia) as well as the introduction of emergency measures (in Bosnia).[75] Čabrinović even said that he had decided on the assassination 'chiefly' in revenge for the Archduke's 'instigation' of the emergency measures.[76] Such perceptions of Franz Ferdinand show that the assassins were perhaps less concerned with what he was likely to do with the South Slavs of the Monarchy, than with what they thought he had actually been doing to them.

Indeed, searching for some elaborate political background or high-flown strategic purpose to the assassination betrays an ulterior motive among historians who do so, for there is more than sufficient evidence that the assassins saw the Archduke in the simple moral category of an evil man. At the trial Princip actually said so: 'I am convinced that I removed an evil ... He [Franz Ferdinand] did evil things to everyone.' Confirming what Grabež had already told the investigators, Princip said on the same occasion that Franz Ferdinand was 'the initiator of the emergency measures and the high treason trial'. But he added something else. It was seen in chapter four that the agrarian question in Bosnia-Herzegovina was perhaps the single most vexing issue during Austro-Hungarian rule – and Princip appeared to be extremely sensitive to this question. The 'people suffer [*narod trpi*]', he said. Asked by the presiding judge what he meant, he answered: 'Because they [the people] have been completely impoverished, because they treat them [the people] like cattle. The peasant is impoverished, they have ruined him completely. I am a villager's son and I know what it is like in the villages. That is why I wanted to take revenge, and I am not sorry.'[77]

A Major for All Seasons: Vojislav Tankosić

Early in April, Princip and Čabrinović discussed whether it made sense to approach the *Narodna Odbrana* (National Defence) for assistance with weapons. This was later of great interest to the Austro-Hungarian officials interrogating the assassins: to establish the latter's link with official Serbia would have represented a major coup for Vienna.[78] The Austrian obsession with the *Narodna Odbrana* is plain to see in the interrogation record of practically all those arrested after the assassination. But statements by both Princip and Čabrinović make it clear that they did not mind mentioning their initial thinking about the *Narodna Odbrana* since nothing had come of it and no one there had been approached by the students. Princip said that he knew no one in that organization.[79] However, he did know of someone else: Milan Ciganović, an employee of the Serbian state railways, a former *četnik* irregular and a member of the Black Hand. A native of western Bosnia, Ciganović (born 1888) began but soon abandoned the study of theology at Prizren, Kosovo. He moved to Serbia in 1908 and joined the *komite* training camp in Ćuprija under the command of (then) Captain Voja Tankosić. Princip, and then Čabrinović separately, both contacted Ciganović. This is a point that needs, perhaps, to be emphasized in the light of frequent and unsubstantiated assertions that the young Bosnian assassins had been 'recruited' in Serbia: the entire assassination saga had begun with those two young men seeking assistance in Belgrade from their fellow Bosnian Ciganović rather than the other way round. Their choice of Ciganović had a great deal to do with his reputation for privately hoarding bombs left over from various Balkan conflicts – some eighty or so according to Čabrinović.[80]

Although Princip had two years previously lived at the same Belgrade address as Ciganović (where he had seen some of those bombs), he felt that he did not know him well enough for a direct approach and decided to enlist the good offices of Đulaga Bukovac. The latter, as has been seen, was the Muslim who felt himself to be a Croat, and who had been involved in a plot to assassinate Emperor Franz Joseph. Having been one of the leaders of the Sarajevo students' strike which followed the demonstration of February 1912, Bukovac had been banned from all schools in Austria-Hungary. He then moved to Serbia where his education continued in a different manner when he attended the *komite* training course at Prokuplje. Bukovac knew Ciganović quite well – so much so, according to Nikola Trišić, a contemporary and a chronicler of Young Bosnia, that he had planned the assassination of Franz Joseph together with Ciganović.[81] These two, clearly, had much in common although it is unlikely that Bukovac, given his tender age (born, like Princip, in 1894), would also have been a member of the Black Hand.[82] Bukovac was, it seems, very much into bombs. Čabrinović, who also knew him, described in great detail during his interrogation how Bukovac had already been instructing him around January 1914 in the art of detonating and throwing bombs.[83]

Princip stated later that Bukovac was the second person whom he had told, after Čabrinović, about the idea of assassinating Franz Ferdinand.[84] Because he needed bombs, he asked Bukovac to talk to Ciganović. At this stage there was no talk about handguns because it was the bomb which enjoyed something of a cult status at the time. The historian Novica Rakočević, writing about the Montenegrin revolutionary youth of that period, noted that the bomb was considered 'the most efficient revolutionary implement. Ignorant people thought it a terrible weapon.'[85] The bomb expert Bukovac had moved quickly: Ciganović met Princip 'soon thereafter'. However, Ciganović was also 'somewhat reserved' about Princip's plan. This Bosnian brigand said, as Princip recalled, that he would 'think it over'.[86] It is impossible to determine when exactly the initial meeting with Ciganović took place, but Princip stated during his interrogation that it was 'towards Easter' that he thought of approaching Ciganović.[87] In 1914 the Orthodox Easter fell on 19 April. Despite his hesitation, Ciganović was obviously interested in the scheme since, as Princip told his interrogators, the two of them would from then on get together 'almost every day'. Probably near the end of April, Ciganović finally promised Princip the weapons. Princip stated that he had received this promise before his friend Grabež returned from Bosnia where Grabež had been staying over Easter with his parents before heading back to Belgrade.[88] In one of his interrogations Grabež recalled that he had returned to Belgrade 'towards 1 May'.[89]

Čabrinović had in the meantime independently talked to Ciganović. Predictably enough, he showed him the newspaper cutting, whereupon Ciganović commented: 'That would be an opportunity if only we had the people.' Čabrinović assured him that finding people would not be a problem if weapons were available. When Ciganović said that they could get the weapons 'easily', Čabrinović asked him to provide bombs. Afterwards, he told Princip about this meeting, to which Princip commented that he had already talked to Ciganović.[90] From these separate contacts, the latter, no doubt, must have received the impression that there existed in Belgrade at least two young men very keen to assassinate the Archduke.

But what did Ciganović do with this information? It is widely assumed that he had gone to his *komite* boss Major Voja Tankosić to seek both the blessing and the bombs for the proposed assassination of Franz Ferdinand by Princip and Čabrinović. Practically the entire historiography of the Sarajevo assassination further assumes that Tankosić then sought and received the go-ahead from Lieutenant-Colonel Dragutin Dimitrijević Apis, the unofficial leader of the Black Hand. Typical of this certitude among historians is the recent unsupported contention by Christopher Clark: 'Ciganović reported to Tankosić, who in turn reported to Apis.'[91] However, there is no evidence – none whatsoever – that Ciganović went to see Tankosić in connection with the requests made by Princip and Čabrinović. But there is evidence that he went to see someone else. That someone was Đuro Šarac, a friend of both Ciganović and Princip, and an enigmatic figure in the available history of the Sarajevo assassination.

Đuro Šarac was another Bosnian Serb who had crossed over to Serbia to join the *komite* under Voja Tankosić. In fact, he was to stay with his leader until the very end: Tankosić, mortally wounded in October 1915 by German shrapnel, died in Šarac's arms. Šarac buried him.[92] This irregular (born in 1889) had, unlike his friend Ciganović, completed his training for priesthood at the Prizren seminary before turning to guns, knives and bombs. Although he never actually took up priesthood, he was seen, in the words of Dobroslav Jevđević, as one of those 'bloody Bosnian priests'.[93] More interesting than that, however, Šarac may be described as one of the precursors of Young Bosnia. He had attended the Sarajevo *Gymnasium* where he was a leading light in a student revolutionary organization called *Jafetovci*, founded in 1905, which preached resistance to Austro-Hungarian rule.[94] He spent two months in prison for saying, at the time of the Bosnian annexation, that 'annexation was simply a robbery of someone else's property'.[95] Princip knew him in Sarajevo, and they met again in Belgrade.

It would appear that Šarac had plotted something even before it became known that Franz Ferdinand was going to come to Bosnia. His close friend Dušan Slavić, a Herzegovinian bookseller in Belgrade, left behind (in 1928) a short account of the preparations for the Sarajevo assassination. In this document Slavić mentioned that on 31 March 1914 Šarac had acquainted him (and Ciganović) about his 'secret intentions', but that both he and Ciganović had thought the plan was 'unworkable'. Slavić revealed no details, but he wrote that 'several days' later, when the press announced Franz Ferdinand's forthcoming arrival, Šarac came up with a new plan which now met with the approval of his two friends.[96] The only exact date provided here by Slavić – the 31 March one – would suggest that Ciganović had at the time not yet been approached by either Princip or Čabrinović, but that Šarac had only 'several days' later developed his new scheme following the news that Franz Ferdinand would pay a visit to Bosnia-Herzegovina. This time scale reflects the likely period when the press cutting from Bosnia reached Belgrade and produced the commotion among the activists referred to earlier. In his account Dušan Slavić presented Šarac as the true organizer of the assassination, for the purpose of which he established a secret organization called 'Death or Life [*Smrt ili Život*]'. First Čabrinović and then Princip were sworn into membership at midnight ceremonies in a Belgrade cellar (there is no mention of Grabež). Sworn members also had to sign a statement that they would be committing suicide – presumably after carrying out whatever dangerous tasks were assigned to them.

Whether Šarac had learned about the Archduke's proposed visit to Bosnia from Ciganović (to whom Čabrinović had shown the newspaper cutting), or perhaps from some other source, must remain a matter for conjecture. Be that as it may, it seems likely that Šarac and Princip had independently of each other come up with the idea of killing Franz Ferdinand, but that their two separate initiatives were now morphing into one, with Ciganović playing godfather by bringing together these two acquaintances from Sarajevo. A famous photograph, dated May 1914, shows Grabež, Šarac and Princip sitting on a bench in the Kalemegdan park in Belgrade. What were they doing together? Mere coincidence seems out of the question.

However, both during his interrogations and at the trial Princip stubbornly insisted, a little too much perhaps, that he and he alone had conceived the idea to kill Franz Ferdinand. This was understandable and chivalrous: in assuming the primary responsibility Princip wanted to conceal any other spiritual fathers of the conspiracy. He was to display a characteristic concern to minimize the number of those who could be implicated. For example, after his arrest he repeatedly professed his distrust of Mihajlo Pušara even though he knew perfectly well that Pušara had been in the conspiracy from start to finish.

With regard to Šarac, it should be pointed out that Čabrinović, the most talkative of the defendants, named him at the trial as one of the three persons in Belgrade, along with Ciganović and Bukovac, who had influenced Princip.[97] Typically, Princip was to protest when interrogated: 'No one influenced me.'[98] Šarac figured only sporadically otherwise in the interrogations after the assassination and during the trial itself. But Čabrinović also named him as one of perhaps half a dozen people in Serbia who were in the know about what was being planned for Sarajevo.[99] Significantly, Princip later pretended that he could not remember whether Šarac had been present on the day (28 May) he, Čabrinović and Grabež left Belgrade for Sarajevo – but Čabrinović confirmed that he had. Significantly, too, Grabež tried to hide the fact that Šarac knew about the assassination plot.[100] Not surprisingly, however, the interrogators and the court showed far more interest in Major Tankosić, an officer in the Serbian Army, than in Šarac, a mere Bosnian irregular.

But when and how did Tankosić get involved? In May 1916 Princip related to Dr Pappenheim that Tankosić had been told 'at the last moment, when we were inwardly ready'.[101] Just when this 'last moment' came is impossible to determine, but it was probably in the second half of May 1914 since, as will be seen, Princip and Grabež had their first (and only) weapons training session as late as 25 May. Princip's perspective on events, however, was not the only one. It was not just a matter of acting when the youths felt ready in principle, for things had also needed to be made ready for them in practice. It was after having given up on the idea of obtaining weapons for Princip and his friends from his fellow *komite* in Macedonia, that Šarac had made the decision, according to Slavić, to turn to his contact Tankosić.

This was the point at which the handguns entered the picture. Šarac and Slavić went to see Tankosić (Slavić did not mention a date), with Šarac explaining the 'purpose of the visit'. It will be seen shortly that Tankosić was to claim in 1915 that he had thought the weapons were meant against Potiorek or some other high-ranking Austro-Hungarian official – not against Franz Ferdinand. In any case, he was more than forthcoming. 'So far', he said, 'I have given away for similar purposes plenty of weapons, and not only was there nothing done, but not even a shot was heard. When you say that the matter is on a safe course, I will give not only the weapons but also myself.' They then discussed handguns and Tankosić produced one from his cupboard ('as if designed for secret revolutionary organizations', he said). He also promised a safe passage for the assassins and their weapons through 'channels' known to his 'comrades and friends' on the border.[102]

If Slavić is to be believed, then, it was not Ciganović, but rather Šarac who made the crucial contact with Tankosić regarding the logistics of the assassination. This, certainly, should not be surprising given the close, comrades-in-arms relationship between Šarac and Tankosić. On the evidence available, Šarac comes across as a major player in the conspiracy and possibly its fulcrum, whereas Ciganović does not seem to have been anything other than an errand boy. Now, Ciganović was a member of the Black Hand, but Šarac was not. No one, not even Albertini, has ever suggested that Šarac was a member.[103] It is indeed impossible, therefore, to see any involvement by members of the Black Hand in the origin of the idea to assassinate Franz Ferdinand – or to see just how the assassins are supposed to have been recruited by the Black Hand to do so. The next chapter will show that neither the Black Hand as an organization, nor any of its members individually, had anything to do with conceiving the plot.

The basic credibility of Slavić's account about the role of his friend Šarac in the conspiracy was affirmed not only by Drago Ljubibratić (who had discovered it), but also by Vladimir Dedijer in his classic work on Sarajevo 1914.[104] There also exists, in this connection, an interesting testimony by Šarac himself, hitherto neglected by historians – possibly because it is to be found in a most unlikely place. Dr Milovan Grba, a well-known Serb politician from Croatia, met Šarac in Geneva towards the end of the war and wrote an article about their encounter in July 1924 – in *Prager Presse*, the German-language daily published in the Czechoslovak Republic during the interwar period. Grba was curious about the background to the Sarajevo assassination, which Šarac 'portrayed as the fruit of an exclusively Bosnian conspiracy to which belonged predominantly the Bosnian Serbs, but also Muslims and Croats.' They were organized, Šarac said, on the basis of a Russian-style *troika* system, with Princip, Čabrinović and Grabež constituting the first *troika*. The whole business with Tankosić and the weapons, Šarac explained, 'took place without many words spoken'. Most important of all, however, Šarac also stated to Grba that Tankosić had no idea that the weapons he had 'approved' were meant to kill Franz Ferdinand. Šarac insisted on this point: he said that Tankosić himself explained in the course of the war, 'in front of him [Šarac] and others' that he had given the weapons in the belief that 'the assassination was directed at Potiorek or some other Austro-Hungarian dignitary, he had not thought about Franz Ferdinand.'[105]

This, of course, must be seen as a contentious point. For it is at first difficult to accept that someone like Tankosić would not have known, in May 1914, that the Habsburg Heir to the Throne was about to visit Bosnia and would not have established by enquiry that the weapons were meant for him. But then, from everything that is known about Tankosić, it is also difficult to believe that he had had much contact with external realities. Whatever the truth, his famous friend Dragutin Dimitrijević Apis was said to have contemptuously dismissed him as a 'drunkard and a good for nothing type'.[106] So who was he, this Serbian officer who in 1914 played what turned out to be such an important incidental role in European history? To describe him as reckless or irresponsible would be putting it very mildly. Robert Seton-Watson wrote that 'behind his calm and even insignificant exterior', Tankosić 'hid a savage and ill-disciplined nature'. This British historian had conducted interviews with former members of Tankosić's band and they were 'far from regarding him as a heroic figure'.[107] No hero on a white horse perhaps, but Tankosić was any-thing but a coward. A propensity to brutality and violence is what defined him from early on. One of his recent biographers has written that Tankosić (born 1880) was the kind of restless child about whom the Serbian people had a saying: 'He will live to attain great glory unless he ends up on the gallows beforehand.'[108]

Holding the rank of second lieutenant in 1903, Tankosić took part in the bloody overthrow of King Alexander Obrenović. It is said that the execution of Queen Draga's two brothers was on his command yet without orders from above.[109] There is a piece of Belgrade gossip from this period that Tankosić roughed up Winston Churchill when the latter stopped over in Belgrade while travelling on the Orient Express from Istanbul. Tankosić had allegedly been mad at Churchill for writing an anti-Serbian article in reaction to the Serbian sympathy for the Boers in their war against Britain.[110] The story is probably apocryphal, but it reflects well the fierce and turbulent character of the young officer. Much of Tankosić's career was spent in clandestine, military intelligence activities south of the border in Turkish-ruled Kosovo and Macedonia. But as a *komite* he also took part in guerrilla clashes with the Turks, Albanians and Bulgarians. In April 1905, he fought against the Turks and Albanians in the famous, and for the Serbs victorious, battle of Čelopek, which was a defining moment for the entire Serbian *Četnik* movement. His methods were ruthless and arbitrary. In Skopje he organized the assassination of a Turkish officer who was about to take up a diplomatic post in Serbia. The man had apparently had Serbian blood on his hands and Tankosić, who had him blown up with a bomb, commented: 'If those people in Belgrade can watch this man parading his immunity around, I certainly can't!'[111] It was seen in chapter seven that, in 1907, his attack on a Bulgarian village and the accompanying atrocity nearly provoked war between Bulgaria and Serbia.

He had absolutely no respect for anyone. When Crown Prince George swore at him (cursing his mother), Tankosić used his fist to hit him in the mouth and said: 'Who are you to swear at my mother?!' In 1908, on a different occasion, he even challenged the Prince to a duel, but was not given this satisfaction[112] Also in 1908, during the Bosnian annexation crisis when Serbia began to slowly give in to Austro-Hungarian pressure, Tankosić spotted, in the heart of Belgrade, the carriage (*fiaker*) of the Foreign Minister Milovan Milovanović. Jumping on to the running board, he shouted so that everyone could hear him: 'Watch out, Milovan, or dark-ness will swallow you up!' On the eve of the First Balkan War in 1912, as the Prime Minister Nikola Pašić was negotiating with the Bulgarians, Tankosić took him by the throat and threatened to kill him if he 'sold out Macedonia'.[113] The list of such deeds by patriot Tankosić is rather a long one and it includes his threat against the Interior Minister Stojan Protić, his slapping of the face of the Serbian Minister in Athens, Živojin Balugdžić, and other similar behaviour.[114]

But his greatest act of personal assertion and defiance is related to the outbreak of the war with Turkey, in October 1912. It would not be a great exaggeration to say that Tankosić started the war almost single-handedly. He and his *četnik* irregulars had been given orders to cross the frontier unnoticed and act behind enemy lines – but only once the Serbian Army commenced hostilities. This caveat was ignored by Tankosić who commanded his unit to attack two border posts straight away. His action alerted the Turks and their Albanian allies who took up the fight, creating a major obstacle in a sector of the front where the Serbian Army had not yet positioned itself adequately and so suffered great casualties as a result. An official Yugoslav history of the First Balkan War blamed Tankosić for his 'irresponsible act'. The Serbian Army division commander on the front demanded that Tankosić be made answerable, but nothing happened.[115] What is really interesting about this episode is that Tankosić had displayed insubordination even towards Dimitrijević, whose 'right-hand man' he was supposed to be. The truth is that Tankosić was nobody's man. Apis, wanting a war against Turkey and fearing that the pusillanimous politicians in Serbia might at the last moment try to avoid the conflict, had instructed his officer friends on the border, including Tankosić, to provoke some incident 'at his prompting'. But Tankosić did not wait even for Apis to give him the green light before taking matters into his own hands.[116] The official declaration of war followed only after Tankosić had made it inevitable. He emerged from all this, in early 1913, as the youngest Major in the Serbian Army.[117]

For quite a few weeks in April-May 1914 the situation with the three would-be Bosnian assassins in Belgrade (Princip, Čabrinović and Grabež) was that they had decided to act, but had no idea whether they would actually have the opportunity to do so because obtaining weapons had been left to others. Ciganović's promise of weapons to Princip in the second half of April was probably just make-believe at that stage. Čabrinović stated in court that it was 'a long time' (he then specified that it was perhaps a month) between his own initial approach to Ciganović and the day when the latter finally gave the green light by showing him a box of ammunition.[118] There was a further question mark hanging over the whole enterprise. The European press was widely reporting at the time that the ageing Franz Joseph was not well. Ciganović told Princip that 'nothing' would now happen in the light of the Emperor's illness since Franz Ferdinand was going to be ascending the throne rather than coming to Bosnia.[119] On around 18 May, however, Tankosić let it be known through Ciganović that he wanted to meet one of the students. Princip (the 'dictator', as Čabrinović called him) thought that he could not go himself as he was 'weak and small', and that Čabrinović was 'loose-tongued' – so the order to present himself to Tankosić was given to Grabež, who, according to Čabrinović, had the advantage of looking 'sinister'.[120] This was a useful attribute since the Major apparently wished to convince himself that the students were up to the job.[121] On Sunday 24 May, Grabež, accompanied by Ciganović, made the journey to see the Major at his house. It was the shortest of meetings. Tankosić simply asked him: 'Are you the one? Are you resolved?' When he then asked him whether he could shoot, Grabež had to admit that he could not. Tankosić, instead of drawing the conclusion that his young guest was clearly not up to the job, merely turned to Ciganović saying that he would give him a handgun and that they should practice shooting for a day. He then left in a hurry.[122]

The Major could not have made a good impression on Grabež who told Princip that 'this Tankosić is a very naïve person' and added that only a few words had been spoken.[123] This, however, must have been a matter of indifference to Princip who could now at least be reasonably sure that the weapons would be delivered to his group. And indeed, shooting practice did take place the following day, Monday 25 May, in the Topčider park – with the aid of a Browning pistol. This was, however, something of a charade. Only Princip and Grabež took part (Čabrinović was at work), managing to fire some fifty rounds between the two of them before a policeman chased them away because it was a park, not a shooting range.[124] There was to be no further practice before the students departed on 28 May. The much-trumpeted, indeed insistent claims that the assassins had been given weapons training by Belgrade, amount to just this farcical, single session.

But who was instructing Princip and Grabež on that Monday, 25 May? Grabež said it was Ciganović. Dušan Slavić, however, asserted emphatically that Đuro Šarac was the instructor.[125] It is of course possible that both were present. Be that as it may, the highly improvised nature of the preparations cannot be denied. Princip, Čabrinović and Grabež gave inconsistent accounts as to when exactly the weapons were handed over to them, but they certainly had them by the evening of 27 May. Ciganović had according to Princip initially tried to collect the four Browning pistols from a Belgrade weapons store, but got nothing and had to return to the store with a 'piece of paper' (probably a bill of exchange) from Tankosić.[126] It remains an open question whether Tankosić had also facilitated the supply of six bombs or whether those came via Ciganović or perhaps Šarac. But more interesting than the weapons is the financial aspect of the undertaking. The assassination that sparked the First World War was very low-budget. On the day before departure Ciganović gave Princip 130 dinars, apologising that he did not have more at his disposal. Princip immediately protested that the sum was insufficient and so Ciganović returned later with another thirty dinars and the comment that he could not 'scrape up' any more.[127] The sum of 130 dinars in 1914 would be worth some 400 euros in 2017. The students were also supplied with cyanide in a small glass tube, in all probability procured by Šarac, for as has been seen, members of his 'Death or Life' organization had to sign suicide declarations. On that last evening, according to Dušan Slavić, the conspirators held a joint farewell dinner, with himself and Šarac also present. Towards the end of the event someone in the group said pointedly: 'God forbid that we should ever see each other again!' Princip responded briefly: 'I understand!'[128]

The 'Mystic' Journey

Practically all the details concerning the preliminaries to Sarajevo 28 June 1914 point to the lack of any serious planning and reveal some strikingly casual improvisations. Princip maintained in his interrogation that Major Tankosić did not give them 'any instructions as to how to carry out the assassination'.[129] As for Ciganović, Grabež recalled that he had told them 'nothing' about the manner of going about their enterprise – 'that was left to us'.[130] It is not known whether Đuro Šarac, as a godfather of the conspiracy, had given any specific guidelines. Of course, none of these people in Belgrade could have been very helpful as the programme of Franz Ferdinand's stay in Bosnia had in late May not yet been published. As will be seen, no scenario had been analysed, not even in terms of logistics.

At seven in the morning on Ascension Day, 28 May, the Belgrade *troika* boarded a steam boat for Šabac, a Serbian town on the Sava river close to the frontier with Bosnia.[131] Thus began the 'mystic journey' as Princip was to describe it. Šarac was there to see them off, but not Ciganović. The latter had merely instructed them that they were to go to the town of Tuzla in Bosnia, via the Serbian towns of Šabac and Loznica. On the other hand, he had 'expressly ordered' them not to talk to anybody about the assassination plan – for in Serbia they would be 'quite certainly arrested' if the civil authorities got wind of the plot.[132] Ciganović mentioned Tuzla because, as he told Grabež, if they could not get the weapons to Sarajevo, they could deposit them in Tuzla with, 'he believed', a certain Miško Jovanović whom he had 'heard' was a 'good man'. In Šabac beforehand they were to contact one Captain Popović who would help them get to Loznica.[133]

This, then, was the famous 'channel' which the Black Hand is supposed to have set up for the assassins to get them and their weapons safely to Bosnia. In reality it was hardly the smooth, well-organized passage that many historians have cracked it up to be. Sidney Fay, for example, imagined that it had been 'long prepared' by Serbian officials and 'had worked to perfection'.[134]

In fact the journey began to look more like a farce as soon as the assassins reached Šabac, where they found Captain Rade Popović in a coffee house playing cards. Grabež handed him Ciganović's visiting card whereupon Popović took them to his office. There, they told him that they wanted to cross into Bosnia, to which he declared: 'I have not been informed about this'. Nevertheless, he did finally promise to help them get to Loznica and gave them railway passes as well as a letter for the border officer in which he wrote: 'Receive these people and help them further as best as you can.' The officer in Loznica, Captain Jovan Prvanović as it turned out, was as little *au courant* as Popović when he met the students the following day, 29 May. 'What should we do now?', he asked as he read Popović's brief request. Princip had to explain to him, without however mentioning their weapons, that he and his friends could not cross legally. Somewhat more in the picture following this explanation, Prvanović commented that it would be 'difficult' to assist them in this manner.[135] It was only on the next day that the Captain brought into play three customs officials to see if they could assist with an unobserved crossing. Two of them said that this would be impossible from their posts, but the third expressed readiness to find someone who would be able to conduct them to Bosnia. Luckily for the students, this third person, one Sergeant Rade Grbić was the local contact man for intelligence reports from Bosnia and an expert at covert activities. So he understood what was needed much better than Captain Prvanović.[136]

But this was no prearranged 'channel' since Grbić, regardless of his competences, was there only by improvised, spontaneous invitation. All else now also proceeded on a similar basis of ad hoc arrangements – mostly with peasants, a total of eight of whom were to be involved from the border to the town of Tuzla. In the meantime Princip and Grabež had become furious with Čabrinović because the latter had in their view been too indiscreet in the way he talked during casual encounters with people on their journey. They took away the weapons he was carrying, leaving him only with the glass tube containing cyanide. Grabež gave Čabrinović his passport which he then used to enter Bosnia legally at Zvornik. They all agreed to meet in Tuzla.

Princip and Grabež crossed the Drina river late on 1 June, from the island of Ada Isakovića between the villages of Lešnica on the Serbian side and Janja on the Bosnian. Two Bosnian Serb peasants recruited by the resourceful Sergeant Grbić led them across a river ford and a swamp. One of these, Jakov Milović, was a smuggler but also a courier for the *Narodna Odbrana* (National Defence) – the para-military organization that sprang up in Serbia immediately after the annexation of Bosnia-Herzegovina, but which became a passive patriotic society following the Serbian Government's capitulation to Austria-Hungary in March 1909. The *Narodna Odbrana* did maintain, however, a network of confidants and couriers in Bosnia-Herzegovina. Along the way Milović enlisted the help of a third peasant to help with the carrying of weapons.

Milović knew that the students wanted to reach Tuzla, but he led them instead to a man named Veljko Čubrilović, a teacher in the small town of Priboj near Tuzla. No one in Belgrade had ever mentioned Čubrilović to the assassins and he was indeed unknown to them.[137] Yet bringing them to Čubrilović was logical for Milović: the teacher was an important local confidant of the *Narodna Odbrana*. Luigi Albertini made what he could out of this: 'here appears the link between *Narodna Odbrana* and *Black Hand*'.[138] But this crossing of the Drina was improvised. Ordinary Serbs on both sides of the border, regardless of their political persuasion, hated Austria-Hungary. The 'link' suggested by Albertini did not exist and, moreover, was most unlikely to have existed: Grabež related to the court his conversation with Ciganović in which the latter had told him that Tankosić was 'the greatest enemy of the *Narodna Odbrana*'.[139] This was hardly surprising in the light of the hostility of Tankosić and his friends in the Black Hand to the Serbian Government – given that the *Narodna Odbrana* was controlled by the Pašić Government. Vladimir Dedijer writes that Milović, apart from being a *Narodna Odbrana* courier, also 'performed services' for Serbian military intelligence.[140] This may have been the case, but he most certainly saw only the Šabac-based Boža Milanović as his boss and indeed protector. Milanović was the local head of the *Narodna Odbrana* in this Serbian border town. After 28 June Milović fled to Šabac, where he sought refuge with Milanović. The latter, furious because of the assassination, told him to go back to Bosnia: 'Let them hang you if you did not prevent a thing like that.'[141] Milović did return to Bosnia, was imprisoned and died in jail.

Veljko Čubrilović, the teacher in Priboj, was also to pay dearly for his encounter with the assassins: he was executed in February 1915. Princip told the court that Čubrilović was 'candidly surprised' by their arrival. He saw the weapons and he was told who they were meant for. Princip thereafter threatened Čubrilović that his family would be killed if he did not keep everything to himself.[142] This threat was unnecessary – Čubrilović knew Jakov Milović's connection with the *Narodna Odbrana* and assumed – the first to make this error but certainly not the last – that the students were 'somehow' connected with Božo Milanović in Šabac.[143] In this tragi-comic circle Čubrilović knew Miško Jovanović in Tuzla, a fellow confidant of the *Narodna Odbrana* and the only Bosnian point of contact for the assassins actually mentioned by Ciganović in Belgrade. Čubrilović therefore laid on more peasants and a cart to help his unexpected guests proceed to Tuzla. Thus the *Narodna Odbrana* did play an accidental part on the logistics side of the Sarajevo assassination, but without knowing what was afoot.

Miško Jovanović, the wealthy Serb entrepreneur in Tuzla, likewise paid with his life (hanged in February 1915 as well) for assisting the assassins. Čabrinović was already waiting in town when Princip and Grabež arrived there early on 3 June. Before Jovanović had even seen them, their weapons were brought to him by the peasants. Shortly thereafter, Princip and Grabež appeared, handed him a short letter from Čubrilović and asked him whether he would be so kind to take the weapons to Sarajevo because they had no identity papers and because they thought the police would be on a higher state of alert in the light of Franz Ferdinand's forthcoming visit. Jovanović refused point blank. Faced with his refusal, they asked him to keep the weapons for a few days until someone came to collect them. This he agreed to, but Princip nevertheless felt it necessary to speak to him threateningly, saying that he would 'destroy' him and his whole family should he betray anything.[144]

Now, the case of Miško Jovanović opens up interesting questions. He was of course the person recommended by Ciganović. But both during his interrogation and trial he denied knowing Ciganović, protesting that he had not even heard of him.[145] Of course, he could have lied to protect himself and others. Did there exist, after all, a wider conspiracy? For Jovanović was not just a confidant of the *Narodna Odbrana*, he also maintained links with the Black Hand. Vaso Ristić, who knew him well and who was in 1914 the director of the Serbian Bank in Tuzla, believed that Jovanović had been in touch with Rade Malobabić who was no less than Serbia's chief clandestine operative on Austro-Hungarian territory and Lieutenant-Colonel Dimitrijević's favourite spy. Ristić presumed that Jovanović had through Malobabić also maintained links with Dimitrijević. Indeed Jovanović used to ask Ristić to give him political information and intelligence about the Austro-Hungarian Army.[146] As is well known, in 1917 Dragutin Dimitrijević Apis claimed in a written submission at his trial in Salonika that he had conceived the assassination of Franz Ferdinand and that Malobabić had organized and executed his order.[147] Surely, in that case, Malobabić would have alerted Jovanović, their collaborator in Tuzla and the contact man for the assassins suggested by Ciganović, about what was being prepared?

But nothing could be further from the truth: Jovanović had been completely in the dark. As soon as Princip, Čabrinović and Grabež left Tuzla for Sarajevo, on the evening of 3 June, he met with his friend Vaso Ristić and asked him to go for a walk outside the town because he wanted to discuss something. He then revealed to Ristić that the students had left weapons with him – weapons meant for the assassination of Franz Ferdinand. Jovanović, according to Ristić, 'was very worried and I concluded from his demeanour that the matter had come unexpectedly to him. The students had tried to reassure him, he said, by swearing that they would not betray anything and that he would suffer no consequences.'[148]

What this suggests, of course, is that the Black Hand did not inform Jovanović about anything simply because it was not involved. The point here is this: if Malobabić had been the person who organized the assassination (as claimed by Apis) how was it possible that he had not consulted and prepared Jovanović whose good offices had been explicitly recommended to the assassins by Ciganović? The case of Miško Jovanović alone makes it fairly clear that Colonel Apis and Malobabić, his top spy in Austria-Hungary, had nothing to do with the organizing of the Sarajevo assassination. Ciganović was working with Tankosić, but evidently not with Apis and Malobabić. Tankosić, moreover, was not representing the Black Hand, but only himself. And it is almost certain that Jovanović spoke the truth when he said that he knew nothing about Ciganović – the latter had simply told the students that he had 'heard' that Jovanović was 'a good man'.[149] Relying, clearly, on nothing more than Jovanović's reputation for patriotism, Ciganović had mentioned him to the students as the person who would help them with the weapons.

Travelling from Tuzla by train, and carrying no weapons, Princip, Grabež and Čabrinović finally reached Sarajevo on 4 June. At this point, they had no idea whether Franz Ferdinand had already come to Bosnia or whether he was still about to do so. The garrulous Čabrinović sat down in a Tuzla coffee house and found out the precise date of the Archduke's planned arrival (25 June) during a chat with a police detective.[150] By this time another *troika* of assassins had been recruited in Sarajevo. It is not entirely clear exactly whose idea this was. In Sarajevo Princip had a long-standing friend (since 1908) in Danilo Ilić, a former teacher. Ilić (born 1890) was something of a socialist, but was at the same time a convinced Yugoslav. As a member of Jovo Varagić's *kružok* in Sarajevo he was informed about the newspaper cutting that had been sent to Čabrinović and 'quietly approved'.[151] In his recent work Christopher Clark names Ilić, along with Princip, as a member of the Black Hand. And just as with Princip, no supporting evidence is provided.[152] In 1969 Cvetko Popović felt compelled to dismiss the identical claim about Ilić made by the American writer Roberta Strauss Feuerlicht.[153]

Often described (especially by Serbian and Yugoslavian historians) as the organizer of the Sarajevo assassination, Ilić was never more than second fiddle in the whole business. As will be seen, he in fact tried in the end to stop it. Although five years older than Princip, Ilić was, Princip maintained in prison, 'under his influence'.[154] During the trial, Princip said that he had sent Ilić a letter from Belgrade, 'in some allegorical form', informing him 'around Easter' (i.e., around 19 April) about the idea of an assassination.[155] Although there is no conclusive proof that Princip had asked Ilić to recruit more assassins, he had almost certainly done so, since it was precisely this which Ilić set about doing. Of course, at the time Princip could not yet have been sure about obtaining weapons: his enthusiasm and optimism must have been remarkable. But he was also very impatient and wished to share his secret with friends. Thus on 25 May, one day after he had practised shooting, he sent a message to another member of Varagić's *kružok*, Borivoje Jevtić in Sarajevo, via Ratko Parežanin who was returning to Bosnia from Belgrade. In the message Princip wrote that he had found 'those books' and would soon bring them to Sarajevo. After the war Jevtić confirmed to Parežanin that by 'books' Princip meant weapons.[156]

The circle of people in Sarajevo who thus knew in May-June about the assassination plan was therefore not inconsiderable: one must assume that it was known to practically everyone grouped around Varagić in the newspaper *Srpska riječ*. In addition, as has been seen, Mihajlo Pušara's brother Vido was also in the picture, as was Vido's Croat friend Tonči Osana – both Vido and Tonči volunteered to take part.[157] The number of those in the know grew further still once Danilo Ilić started his recruitment drive for the second *troika*. Borivoje Jevtić wrote, however, that Ilić was now acting independently of the Varagić circle.[158] He initially contacted Lazar Đukić, a student at the teachers training college – Đukić specified the period as 'the beginning of May'. Đukić did not wish to get 'involved', but Ilić kept pestering him, asking him to find someone who would be 'capable' of carrying out an assassination.[159]

In the end two rather young men were found. One of them was Vaso Čubrilović, only seventeen and the younger brother of Veljko Čubrilović from Priboj – the teacher to whom the peasants had led Princip and Grabež from the Serbian border. Vaso, when approached by Đukić, immediately expressed readiness to take part in the assassination.[160] Whether he was actually 'capable' of doing so was a different matter. Marko Perin, who knew Vaso in the Sarajevo *Gymnasium* and had learned about the plot from him, described him in the preliminary investigation as 'a total windbag', and as someone who was always full of self-praise. 'I did not believe in the slightest', Perin declared, 'that Čubrilović seriously intended to carry out the assassination, and I would sooner have believed my grandmother that she would do it.'[161] Perin's assessment was to be proved entirely correct. In the weeks before Franz Ferdinand's arrival Vaso displayed all the hubris of an excited teenager, going round Sarajevo and telling student friends that an 'anarchist party' had been formed, and would they join it to participate in the assassination of the Heir to the Throne.[162] At least five students were told by Vaso about the plot.[163]

Danilo Ilić had thus managed to enlist an irresponsible adolescent. Vaso Čubrilović's single credential in subversion was that he had been expelled from the Tuzla *Gymnasium* for walking out when the imperial anthem was played.[164] Like Ilić and the Belgrade trio of assassins, however, he did hold to a Yugoslav orientation. He had progressed, as he stated under interrogation, from a 'radical' (i.e., exclusivist Serb) to a 'Serbo-Croat'.[165]

Cvetko Popović, the other recruit who joined Ilić's group in Sarajevo, was a Serbo-Croat both politically and by family background: his father was Serbian and his mother Croatian. Aged eighteen, he attended the teachers training college. It was Vaso who found him: since Ilić wanted an additional assassin he actually entrusted Čubrilović to look for one. On 22 May, when Čubrilović let him into the secret, Popović agreed without hesitation to 'await' Franz Ferdinand. He was, admittedly, an altogether more serious character than Čubrilović and had already been detained in prison for suspected activity against the state. However, he too talked about the conspiracy, revealing 'everything' to his female student friend Dragica Đaković.[166] Furthermore, his short-sightedness (out of vanity he refused to wear glasses) did not exactly qualify him for an assassin's role.[167] In any case, the young Popović and even younger Čubrilović were to receive a risible amount of weapons training: on 27 June Ilić showed them how to unscrew the cap of a bomb and then fired a round himself from the Browning pistol which he then gave to Popović. The latter subsequently stated under interrogation that he had had no idea how to load or unload the handgun.[168]

Muhamed Mehmedbašić, the man who completed Ilić's *troika* in Sarajevo, seemed by contrast a seasoned revolutionary. His case is quite interesting. A Muslim carpenter from the small Herzegovinian town of Stolac he was, paradoxically, the most Serbian of all the assassins. Whereas the other five (or six if Ilić is counted) all had a Serbian ethnic background, they were 'Serbo-Croats' or 'Yugoslavs' to a man. Mehmedbašić (born 1886) said in 1938 that he felt himself to be a Serb because of the Serbian mother tongue. In Stolac he had joined the 'Serbian Falcon' association. During a visit to Belgrade in 1912, his friend from Stolac, Mustafa Golubić (another Serbian of Muslim faith), introduced him to Vladimir Gaćinović, the ardently Serb rabble-rouser. From that moment, Gaćinović became his 'idol and spiritual guide'. He gave Serbian names to all four of his children.[169] Ilić described him as a 'Serb, through and through'.[170] Colonel Apis, whom he met in 1915, defended him in 1917 as 'the *only* Serb-Muslim' who had taken part in the Sarajevo assassination.[171]

Mehmedbašić figures prominently in a bizarre episode early in 1914 concerning a plan to assassinate Governor Potiorek. In 1913 Gaćinović moved to Lausanne in Switzerland to continue his studies, whereas Mustafa Golubić ended up in Toulouse, France, also as a student. Golubić sent a letter to Mehmedbašić, asking him (without an explanation) to come to Toulouse. Mehmedbašić stopped everything, raised the money and reached Toulouse in mid-January 1914. Gaćinović arrived subsequently from Paris. Mehmedbašić was told that he was the most suitable person to kill the hated Potiorek who, in the event of a war against Serbia, would lead the Austrian army. He was further informed that the best occasion to carry out this assassination would be during the ceremony of installing, in Sarajevo, the new *Reis-ul-ulema* Čaušević. The whole idea of using a Muslim to kill Potiorek belonged to Mustafa Golubić who thought that in this way Muslim discontent would receive publicity.[172] For this purpose Gaćinović and Golubić gave Mehmedbašić a 'Swedish knife' ('like a dagger'), indented at the top so that it could hold 'poisonous powder'. Even though Mehmedbašić himself related some of these details in 1938, it all sounds a little bizarre.[173]

Be that as it may, the rest of the story is that Mehmedbašić returned with his curious killing instrument, but panicked and threw it away when his train was searched by gendarmes near Dubrovnik. Undeterred, however, he got a Browning pistol from a friend and proceeded to Sarajevo where Čaušević was to be installed in a mosque as *Reis-ul-ulema* on 26 March, an occasion Potiorek was expected to attend. In Sarajevo he got in touch with Danilo Ilić through Nikola Trišić, a mutual friend – Golubić had at their meeting in Toulouse vaguely mentioned Ilić.[174] This is the point at which Luigi Albertini brings his energy to construct yet another facet of his favourite theory that there had been a huge Serbian conspiracy behind the Sarajevo assassination. He writes that Mehmedbašić and Ilić had a meeting during which the latter stated that the removal of Franz Ferdinand would be most useful 'for the realization of Jugoslavism'. Albertini gives no reference (or date for the meeting) but writes that Ilić had deposed this at the preliminary investigation.[175] Yet whoever reads the record of Ilić's preliminary questioning in *Prozess in Sarajevo* will find no such statement. One can only conclude that Albertini became confused.[176] But how or why? Albertini's point here about Ilić was that 'he expressed himself in this way before knowing that the Archduke was to visit Sarajevo'. He elaborated that, consequently, 'the first threads of the conspiracy had already been spun before the press announcement of Franz Ferdinand's impending visit to Bosnia'. The 'point of great importance', according to Albertini, is that 'Princip already knew' and 'probably Ilić also' that the Archduke was visiting even before this had been announced in the press.[177]

Albertini, quite apart from the confusing clumsiness in his remarks about Ilić (who, according to him, talked about eliminating Franz Ferdinand 'before knowing' about the press announcement, and yet 'probably' knew in advance about the visit) was suggesting clearly enough that Princip in Belgrade and Ilić in Sarajevo possessed some kind of foreknowledge. And who might have told them? Why, no less a person that Apis. 'Now who better than Dimitriević', Albertini wrote, 'the head of Military Intelligence of the Serbian General Staff, was in a position to know beforehand that the Austrian manoeuvres were to be held in Bosnia and that the Archduke was to attend them?'[178] But all this, on close inspection, proves to

1. Emperor Franz Joseph

2. Archduke Franz Ferdinand
© Artstetten Castle/Lower Austria

3. Franz Ferdinand and his wife Sophie
© Artstetten Castle/Lower Austria

4. Franz Ferdinand with wife and children
© Artstetten Castle/Lower Austria

5. Alexander Brosch, the head of Franz
Ferdinand's military chancellery
© Artstetten Castle/Lower Austria

6. Carl Bardolff, Brosch's successor at
the Archduke's military chancellery
© Artstetten Castle/Lower Austria

7. Conrad von Hötzendorf, the Chief of
the Austro-Hungarian General Staff

8. Ante Starčević, the father of Croatia's independence movement

9. Bishop Josip Juraj Strossmayer, the apostle of 'Yugoslavia'

10. Canon Dr Franjo Rački, the guru of 'Yugoslavism'

11. Benjámin von
Kállay, the
uncrowned
King of Bosnia

12. István Burián,
Minister in
charge of Bosnia-
Herzegovina from
1903 to 1912

13. Gligorije Jeftanović, leader of the Serbs of Bosnia-Herzegovina

14. Ali beg Firdus, leader of the Muslims of Bosnia-Herzegovina

15. Josip Stadler, the Archbishop of Sarajevo and a Bosnian Croat leader

16. Ilija Garašanin, the Serbian statesman alleged to have produced a programme of Great Serbian expansion

17. King Milan Obrenović

18. Queen Natalie Obrenović

19. King Alexander Obrenović and Queen Draga

20. Đorđe Genčić, the leader of the civilian wing of the conspiracy to murder King Alexander and Queen Draga

21. Colonel Alexander Mašin, the officer leading the military wing of the conspiracy

22. The Konak, the old Royal Palace in Belgrade where Alexander and Draga were murdered in June 1903

23. Count Agenor Gołuchowski,
Austro-Hungarian Foreign Minister,
1895-1906

24. Alois Lexa von Aehrenthal,
the man who annexed
Bosnia-Herzegovina

25. Ballhausplatz, Vienna, the seat of the Austro-Hungarian Foreign Ministry

26. King Peter Karađorđević of Serbia

27. Crown Prince Alexander Karađorđević

28. Nikola Pašić, Serbia's
Prime Minister

29. Milovan Milovanović, a key creator
of the alliance of Balkan states

30. Oskar Potiorek, the Governor
of Bosnia-Herzegovina

© Artstetten Castle/Lower Austria

31. Erik von Merizzi, Governor's
brilliant aide-de-camp

© Artstetten Castle/Lower Austria

32. Leon von Biliński, the Minister for
Bosnia-Herzegovina

33. Miroslav Spalajković, the Serbian Minister in St Petersburg

34. Count Alexander Hoyos, the man who brought the 'blank cheque' back from Berlin

Österreichische Nationalbibliothek, Bildarchiv

35. Count János Forgách, the grey eminence of the Austro-Hungarian foreign office in 1914

Österreichische Nationalbibliothek, Bildarchiv

36. Vladimir Gaćinović, Serbian nationalist and advocate of individual action

37. Tin Ujević, poet, rebel and Yugoslavian nationalist

38. Dimitrije Mitrinović, the father of 'Young Bosnia'

39. Bogdan Žerajić, the first of the South Slav assassins

40. King Nicholas of Montenegro

41. King Carol of Romania

42. King Ferdinand of Bulgaria

43. William of Wied, Prince of Albania

44. Jovan M. Jovanović, the Serbian
Minister in Vienna

45. Baron Giesl, the Austro-Hungarian
Minister in Belgrade

46. Sergey Sazonov, Russia's
Foreign Minister

47. Count Tisza, the Prime Minister
of Hungary

48. Count Berchtold and Chancellor Bethmann Hollweg in November 1912

49. Ilija Jukić, the first of the
Croat assassins

50. Gavrilo Princip, the assassin
who looked away as he fired

51. Trifko Grabež, the 'sinister
looking' assassin

52. Nedeljko Čabrinović,
the bomb thrower

53. Danilo Ilić, the
reluctant assassin

54. Cvetko Popović, the
short-sighted assassin

55. Vaso Čubrilović, the
youngest assassin

56. Muhamed Mehmedbašić, the
Muslim assassin

57. Lieutenant-Colonel Dragutin Dimitrijević Apis, the leader of the Black Hand, sitting in the middle

58. Major Vojislav Tankosić, the man who armed the Sarajevo assassins

59. The emblem of Unification or Death, aka 'Black Hand'

60. Franz Ferdinand arrives at the Sarajevo Town Hall, 28 June 1914

© Artstetten Castle/Lower Austria

61. Sarajevo Town Hall building

62. The arrest of Nedeljko Čabrinović

63. The arrest of Ferdo Behr. Many descriptions of this photo wrongly suggest that the man being led to the police station is Gavrilo Princip.

64. The archducal car, about to turn right from Appel Quay
into Franz Joseph Street.

65. In the background, the Konak building where Franz Ferdinand
and the Duchess of Hohenberg died.

66. The unveiling of the Gavrilo Princip memorial plaque in Sarajevo on 2 February 1930. This occasion was boycotted by the Yugoslav Government. The inscription reads: 'At this historic spot Gavrilo Princip heralded freedom on St Vitus's Day, 15 (28) June 1914'.

67. German officers presenting the Princip memorial plaque to Adolf Hitler in April 1941.

be tendentious poppycock. Firstly because Ilić did not require any such intelligence from Belgrade when he initially talked to Mehmedbašić. By the time he met him, in the third week of March, the Archduke's arrival had already been announced in the press, and he already knew from his friends in Jovo Varagić's *kružok* of the 17 March newspaper cutting to that effect which had surreptitiously been sent to Čabrinović. In one of his recollections, Mehmedbašić's friend Nikola Trišić insisted that Ilić had known this at the time.[179] Mehmedbašić, who had come to kill Potiorek, was therefore told by Ilić that the moment was not opportune, and was sent back to Herzegovina to await further instructions. Any attempt on Potiorek would of course have compromised the more ambitious scheme aimed against Franz Ferdinand. But Ilić did not tell Mehmedbašić at this stage anything about plans regarding the Archduke.[180] Poppycock secondly, because, by the time he did inform him about it, at a meeting in Mostar, it was already early June: by then the archducal plans were known, and Ilić was now actively seeking another assassin.[181]

Accordingly, with the recruitment of Mehmedbašić and Popović, and with the arming of the Belgrade *troika*, all the fundamental preparations were completed during the last two weeks of May and the first days of June.

12

Black Hand – Red Herring

'Unification or Death'

IN OCTOBER 1908, amid widespread protest and revolt in Serbia over Austria-Hungary's annexation of Bosnia-Herzegovina, a nationalist association called the *Narodna Odbrana* (National Defence) was improvised almost overnight. Its openly stated purpose was to resist the annexation by force. It signed up volunteers for auxiliary units and quickly established over 220 local committees in Serbia. But as the annexation crisis ended with Serbia's capitulation at the end of March 1909, so the para-military *Narodna Odbrana* ended its own ambitions in this respect, morphing into something of a placid cultural society.[1] Its practical recommendations henceforth amounted to 'small deeds' designed to boost national consciousness.[2] General Božidar Janković, the President of the *Narodna Odbrana* in 1914, told the Russian Military Attaché in Montenegro after the outbreak of the war that the programme of the organization excluded any 'violent or terrorist actions'.[3]

As is well known, however, Vienna's notorious ultimatum to Serbia, delivered on 23 July 1914, declaring that the weapons used by the Sarajevo assassins had been given to them by Serbian officers and officials of the *Narodna Odbrana*, demanded that the latter be dissolved 'at once'.[4] From Sarajevo, *Landeschef* Potiorek had been bombarding Vienna since early July with unverified information about the heavy involvement of the *Narodna Odbrana* in organizing the assassination.[5] The ultimatum made no mention of the so-called Black Hand, the not-so-secret Serbian society which subsequently became the persistent, indeed obligatory point of reference in the massive historiography of the Sarajevo assassination and of the origins of the Great War in general. Barbara Jelavich, who researched the information about the Black Hand available to the Austro-Hungarian authorities before Sarajevo, concluded that the incoming military and diplomatic reports from Belgrade, concentrating as they did on the internal role played in Serbia by the Black Hand, failed to make the connection between that organization and possible actions against the Habsburg Empire.[6]

What, then, was this legendary Black Hand all about? The immediate association, of course, is with 'political black arts' and, in particular, the murder of Franz Ferdinand.[7] Generations of school children have been taught by their history teachers that this organization, with its fittingly sinister unofficial name, had masterminded the Sarajevo assassination of the Archduke, an event that sparked off a chain reaction leading to the outbreak of the First World War.

Though the Black Hand came to be seen as a junta of Serbian officers, its chief architects were in fact two civilians. Kick-starting a secret nationalist society was Bogdan Radenković from Kosovo, a former student of theology – who would, interestingly, become in 1912 the Serbian Government's official nominee for the post of Metropolitan of the Raška-Prizren Eparchy, i.e., Kosovo, only to be beaten by a candidate from Montenegro. Following the Bosnian annexation, Serbia had in the light of its weak international position practically ceased its previous sponsorship of the irregular, *četnik* action in Macedonia. At the same time the Young Turk regime was conducting a policy of terror and murder of prominent local Serb leaders. In late 1910 Radenković headed a strong bloc of Macedonian Serbs who demanded the resumption of *četnik* action. Having got nowhere with his pleas to the Government in Belgrade, he turned to the veterans of the struggles in Macedonia, his friends Voja Tankosić and Velimir Vemić, both captains in the Army, and Ljubomir ('Ljuba') Jovanović, also known as 'Čupa', a civilian who had been a *četnik* volunteer. Radenković believed that the proposed organization should be a movement, even a political party – at any rate a grouping that would not work against the Government but rather try to influence it in the desired direction.[8] While he quickly convinced his three friends, he also insisted that Major Ilija Radivojević and Major Dragutin Dimitrijević Apis should be lined up in support.[9] Radenković did not personally know those two, but their reputation was of course considerable. Apis had since the 1903 putsch against King Alexander built a solid following among officers, whereas Radivojević, along with Vemić and Mihailo Ristić, was one of the three officers who had actually murdered Alexander and Draga.

Radivojević and Apis agreed to join, as did four other officers. The Black Hand was founded in Belgrade on 22 May 1911 when eight officers and two civilians signed its statute. The official name of the society was *Ujedinjenje ili smrt* (Unification or Death). Radivojević was chosen as President and Vemić became the Secretary. It was Ljuba Jovanović-Čupa, the other civilian in the founding group, who did the main work in drawing up the Black Hand's statutory provisions and rules of procedure. Jovanović-Čupa was one of the leaders of the student protests against King Alexander in March 1903 and one of the founders, also in 1903, of the weekly *Slovenski jug*. He was, according to Vladimir Gaćinović who knew him well, 'a fanatic-agitator' and one of the central figures in the movement for 'the liberation and unification of our tribe'. To Gaćinović, who would join the Black Hand, Jovanović-Čupa was no less than 'the Mazzini of Young Serbia'.[10] His ideas about the proposed project, however, differed somewhat from those of Radenković. A subversive spirit, he studied as a postgraduate in Brussels where he may have picked up the ideas of Buonarotti and Blanqui. He was also a Freemason.[11] Thus the Black Hand under his aegis became 'a sort of Serbian Carbonari'.[12]

The mysterious rituals that Jovanović-Čupa stipulated for the initiation of new members also betrayed a touch of the Illuminati. Each member was supposed to bring into the society five new members. The setting for the swearing-in ceremony was a dark room, lit only by 'a small wax-candle'. In the middle of the room was a table covered with a 'black cloth'. On the table were a cross, a knife and a revolver. Once the new members agreed to join and just before the swearing-in ceremony, 'a completely disguised and strictly masked man' would 'suddenly' enter the room. He would remain silent throughout.[13] The subsequent sworn declaration was something of 'a pagan oath of fidelity and sacrifice' as new members pledged themselves to the secret society 'by the sun which warms me, by the earth which feeds me, by God and by the blood of my forefathers, by my honour and by my life'.[14] Jovanović-Čupa, who must have thoroughly enjoyed his role as the mastermind of Black Hand scenography, also devised the logo for its seal: a flag held by a hand, featuring a skull and crossbones, to the left of which were a bomb, a dagger and a flask containing poison.

To be sure, the subversive character of the whole enterprise was spelled out in Article 2 of the statute: alluding implicitly to the failings of the *Narodna Odbrana*, it stated that the organization 'subordinates the cultural to the revolutionary struggle', for which reason it had to remain 'absolutely secret'. The purpose of its existence was the fulfillment of the national ideals: the 'unification of Serbdom' (Article 1). In order to bring this about, the organization would influence all the social strata and all the official factors in Serbia, 'as the Piedmont'; and outside Serbia's borders, it would fight 'by all means' against the enemies of Serbian unification (Article 4). The excessive Great Serbian tone regarding the objectives to be pursued was revealed in the explicit denotation of 'Serbian' lands outside Serbia: '1. Bosnia and Herzegovina, 2. Montenegro, 3. Old Serbia and Macedonia, 4. Croatia, Slavonia and Syrmia, 5. Vojvodina and 6. the Littoral' (Article 7). Indisputably, there were Serbs living in all these lands, but they were also minorities in some of them.

'Unification or Death' had barely been founded before everybody learnt about the existence of a mysterious Black Hand (*Crna ruka*). Several Belgrade newspapers were already writing about it in mid-1911.[15] The popular Black Hand sobriquet for this secret society was based on the title of a crime fiction novel being serialised at the time.[16] Soon the organization's fame spread abroad. Early in 1912 the *Daily Chronicle* and the *Pall Mall Gazette* in London carried stories about it, much to the dismay of the Serbian Minister at the Court of St James's.[17] But what were the real intentions of this much talked-about society? On inspection, it becomes clear that liberating the Serbs outside Serbia represented only the second phase of the business envisaged by the Black Hand. The main obsession of the organization was domestic politics. It had its own newspaper, *Pijemont* (Piedmont), the chief editor of which became Jovanović-Čupa. This paper could not wait to declare war on Serbia's entire political establishment. Its very first issue (3 September 1911) declared: 'Neither with these governments, nor with these opposition parties.' Criticizing Serbia's foreign policy for proceeding 'aimlessly', it demanded the creation of a new party, with 'a purely *étatiste* programme', and went on to pontificate that 'parliamentary government does not constitute the ultimate in political wisdom'. The authoritarian and militarist essence of its orientation was blatantly acknowledged. 'Only such a movement', it was emphasized, 'sufficiently *étatiste* and national-militarist, will gratify the people.' Later, in 1912, the paper would thunder that 'militarism is the token and the measure of the patriotism of a people'.[18] And it would approvingly quote Herbert Spencer's famous sentence from *The Man versus the State*: 'The great political superstition of the present is the divine rights of parliaments.'[19]

Whatever the motives of members such as Radenković, and whatever its statute declared, the Black Hand project was less about a crusade to unify the Serb-inhabited lands – an aspiration shared by everyone in Serbia – and more about who was going to be in charge of this enterprise. But most of all it was about what kind of state Serbia itself should be. The aim of the Black Hand, as its mouthpiece *Pijemont* spelt out, was no less than the establishment of a military dictatorship. In his major study of the Black Hand, Vasa Kazimirović concludes that such a dictatorship was meant to be 'camouflaged' – implemented through some political party in which the officers would have the upper hand. He emphasizes that *Pijemont*, while heaping praise on German militarism, was at the same time very reserved towards Russia. He also writes that Apis was primarily interested in internal matters.[20] In November 1911, Austria-Hungary's Minister in Belgrade reported that the Black Hand had 'a decidedly political tinge' and that it was working against the Radical Party. In May 1912 the Minister assessed that the organization had become a power factor which the Serbian Government had to reckon with, 'a kind of augmented, military *Narodna Odbrana*'.[21] Radovan Drašković has in his work on militarism in pre-1914 Serbia called attention to a *četnik* camp in Serbia, controlled by the Black Hand, where young men from Bosnia-Herzegovina received military training. Although they thought they were some day going to fight against the Austrians, the idea, according to Drašković, was to employ them, 'at a decisive moment', in the overthrow of the regime in Serbia. The Bosnians were considered a better option than the domestic element which 'did not look sufficiently reliable'. Indeed, they were kept in Serbia right up to the outbreak of the war in 1914.[22]

Dragutin Dimitrijević Apis had quickly emerged as the unofficial leader of the Black Hand although as late as August 1912 an Austro-Hungarian confidant was reporting that it was Jovanović-Čupa who was the boss.[23] The latter, certainly, was the chief ideologue. However, it was Apis who, by all accounts, possessed natural leadership qualities. This youngish officer (born in 1876) was a rather large man, so much so that while still at school he had been nicknamed 'Apis' – after the sacred bull of the ancient Egyptians. Slobodan Jovanović recalled that Apis gave the impression of a ringleader, not only because of his physical appearance, but also by his entire demeanour.[24] He had a way of captivating people, often holding court in his favourite Belgrade coffee house 'Kolarac', while sitting at the table always reserved for him there. An unmarried teetotaller, Apis was a chain smoker and 'a genial host' who cast 'a virtual hypnotic spell over friends and comrades'.[25] Politically, his direction seems to have been defined by his hatred of the Radical Party. Antonije Antić, his fellow regicide from 1903, noted that Apis became a sworn enemy of the Radicals whilst observing their corruption and dirty deeds.[26]

The politicians of the Radical Party justifiably saw Apis and the Black Hand as a threat. With most of the War Ministers between 1911 and 1914 – invariably military persons – sympathetic to it, the influence of the organization made itself felt.[27] Although he was later to distance himself from the Black Hand, Crown Prince Alexander initially also showed interest and contributed 25,000 francs to the setting up of the *Pijemont* newspaper.[28] Whatever its clout, however, the Black Hand remained no more than a small pressure group – instead of the wide movement envisaged by Radenković. The great authority Vladimir Ćorović mentions the figure of 517 as the maximum number of Black Hand members, whereas one list from within the organization has only 172 names.[29] To suggest that the Black Hand was 'a government within the government', as Samuel Williamson has recently done, is a little far-fetched.[30] Despite its intentions in this respect, no dazzling figures from Serbia's intellectual, political, commercial or even military elite ever joined its ranks. The Black Hand was throughout its life composed mainly of junior officers and controlled principally by a bunch of regicides.

In the second half of 1911 and the first half of 1912, in any case, the Black Hand leadership, rather than making a decisive bid for power, found itself having to wait. During this period, it was of course Serbia's despised political establishment that was working on the Serbo-Bulgarian alliance which was to lead to the Balkan War against Turkey. Apis, Jovanović-Čupa and their cronies observed these developments and could only try to influence them. Needless to say, the Black Hand was very keen on war. In September 1912 *Pijemont* warned Pašić not to remain passive and not to listen to Russia which had 'sold out' Serbia several times in the past and was probably doing it again.[31] Even though people like Tankosić held a poor view of Milovanović's nationalist credentials, Apis at Čupa's suggestion went to see the Foreign Minister. During their meeting, Apis confirmed the existence of the Black Hand to Milovanović and it would seem that the latter then decided to cultivate this group in order to secure Army support for any future clashes with his Radical Party rival Pašić.[32] But Vasa Kazimirović has shown that the role of the Black Hand in the preparation and conduct of the ensuing Balkan Wars was practically non-existent – the organization was not even given the details of the alliance treaty with Bulgaria.[33]

In 1912, the Black Hand did appear to have scored an important success when Major Milan Vasić, a founder-member, managed to infiltrate his way into the *Narodna Odbrana* as its Secretary. This might in time have become useful to the ambitions of 'Unification or Death' given that the *Narodna Odbrana*'s work in the Habsburg Monarchy did have one non-cultural aspect – a network of confidential agents among the South Slavs who were meant to obtain 'information on any Austro-Hungarian military preparations which threatened Serbia'.[34] It is doubtful, however, that this was ever a particularly efficient structure or that Vasić did anything to improve it. Apis later declared that, on becoming the head of the intelligence section at the Serbian General Staff in August 1913, he found 'no organization whatsoever' in Austria-Hungary (*'nisam zatekao nikakvu organizaciju'*).[35] Be that as it may, Vasić was in any case killed shortly afterwards, during the Balkan Wars. Several other prominent members of the Black Hand also found death on the battlefield, including Ilija Radivojević, the President of the society, who had commanded a regiment – this Black Hand vacancy was never filled again. Prematurely gone, too, was the Mazzini of Serbia, Jovanović-Čupa, the editor of *Pijemont*, who had volunteered to fight, been wounded, but then died of typhus contracted while in hospital.

Thus the Black Hand had by 1914 been considerably weakened. Colonel Radoje Lazić, a prominent member, went so far as to state in 1917 that the organization 'de facto did not exist' in 1914. Similarly, Colonel Čedomir ('Čeda') Popović, one of its founding fathers, wrote in 1932 that 'as a totality and as an organization' the whole outfit had ceased to function after the Balkan Wars.[36] However, the Army's successes in those wars had bestowed such great prestige on the Serbian military class that many officers, and not just those in the Black Hand, felt the merit and relevance of the Army far exceeded that of the political parties. Unsurprisingly, faced with these self-appointed guardians of the national interest, especially those in the Black Hand, the ruling Radical Party attempted to control the situation. When General Miloš Božanović, the War Minister, demanded an increase in the military budget, he was promptly rebuffed by the Government. Božanović had been blatantly acting before that on behalf of the Black Hand to which he stood in close proximity. He had for example secured an amnesty and even a decoration for Major Velimir Vemić who had during the Balkan Wars murdered a Serbian soldier for insubordination – after lining up his entire unit to watch. After taking three bullets, the soldier, a father of two, was still able to beg Vemić to spare his life. But Vemić, a Black Hand luminary, fired twice more and killed the man.[37] His amnesty and decoration caused a major scandal. Božanović was promptly removed in early January 1914. The new War Minister became Colonel Dušan Stefanović, a man much more to the liking of Pašić and his Radical Party: he was an opponent of the Black Hand and had set no conditions before accepting the appointment. The Radicals could breathe a sigh of relief, for some thirty officers previously approached by Pašić had already refused this cabinet post.[38]

The stage was now set for civil-military relations in Serbia to enter a critical phase – which was to end just days before the Sarajevo assassination. Just how tense the situation was had already become clear towards the end of 1913 in the reaction of some officers to the rumour that the Government was contemplating replacing Božanović as War Minister with a civilian – specifically the Black Hand's bogeyman, the Interior Minister Stojan Protić. This aspirant was soon stopped in the street by Major Tankosić and two fellow officers, who warned him 'not to play with fire', or else he would be 'blown up', along with his house and his whole family.[39] Though it was in the end Stefanović not Protić who got the post, the British Minister in Belgrade still assessed Božanović's forced removal as providing the first evidence of the Government's desire to rid itself of Black Hand influence.[40] Alarmed by the loss of their man as War Minister, Apis and other members of the Black Hand, together with some officers from outside the organization, conferred during the night of 15-16 January in the seat of the Danube Division in Belgrade. Pašić and his colleagues had got wind of this meeting and, fearing a military takeover, they kept police and gendarmerie forces in a state of readiness over the next two days. Nothing happened in the end, but thereafter the Government began to bring into the capital city those officers whom it did not suspect of being subversive.[41]

In the meantime, a major conflict was brewing between civilian and military authorities in the newly-acquired territories of Kosovo and Macedonia. The constitution of Serbia was not applied to these lands on account of their backwardness. Instead, their administration was based on a series

of Government decrees. The problem here was to do with the administrators. Most civil servants in Serbia worth their salt resisted being sent to
work in the primitive south. So, the ruling Radical Party recruited officials
from the ranks of 'peasant bureaucrats, half-educated apprentices and
problematic intellectual proletariat' instead. Many of these people also
happened to be supporters of the Radical Party, which hoped to advance
its party's interests in the new territories. Quite a few of them had criminal
records connected with commercial and financial malpractice. Lawlessness
and corruption was the result.[42] The quality of police personnel was
similarly poor. The former Minister Kosta Stojanović wrote later: 'Murder,
theft, plunder, humiliation – all that and more – was carried out in the
name of the most hallowed ideals of our state and our people.'[43]

Behind these abysmal occurrences lay the uneasy coexistence of parallel
civilian and military authorities. The Army wanted the new territories to
remain under military rule for a period of several years, but the Radical
Party would not hear of it. Tensions between civil officials and Army
officers were becoming commonplace. News about civilian misrule in the
south initially reached the rest of Serbia through Army channels.[44] Major
Alexander Blagojević, a Black Hand member, reported a police official who
had engaged in theft and then transported his plunder on fifty horses.
However, Interior Minister Protić dismissed the report as 'insolent'.[45] On
the other hand, Vasa Kazimirović has pointed out that the behaviour
towards the local population of some Army officers, especially those
belonging to the Black Hand, also left much to be desired.[46] Things came
to a head after Protić issued the so-called 'Priority Decree' of 21 March
1914 – whereby civil servants, irrespective of their rank, took priority over
senior Army officers at official functions and festivities.[47] This was perhaps
an unnecessary reminder from the Interior Minister that the state stood
above the military. For what was essentially a trivial issue of protocol
suddenly became a huge bone of contention between the Army and the
Government. In previous months, Army officers had not insisted on being
accorded precedence over the civilian authorities. In the light of Protić's
decree, however, Damjan Popović, the Skopje-based General commanding
the Serbian forces on the new territories, decided to upset this applecart:
making the Prefect stand behind him and his suite of officers during a
church ceremony. Popović, a prominent regicide from 1903 and a member
of the Black Hand, was promptly pensioned off.[48]

There followed what Vladimir Dedijer called 'the fateful weeks before
June 28, 1914'.[49] With Protić's 'Priority Decree', the Radicals managed
'to unify against themselves the entire officers' corps'. Even Popović's
successor in Skopje, General Petar Bojović, who had no connection with
the Black Hand, criticized the decree once he found out that all the
officers under his command were opposed to it.[50] In the meantime, the

Government acted to discredit the Black Hand by revealing financial irregularities in the affairs of the Officers' Cooperative which had transferred funds to the *Pijemont* newspaper.[51] Gloves were off. On 15 May *Pijemont* carried a big article on its front page about War Minister Stefanović, entitled 'Portrait of a Government's Lackey'.[52] For Apis, the whole situation looked like a golden moment to act. He was, according to Colonel Victor Artamonov, the Russian Military Attaché in Belgrade, 'a strong, ambitious man who aimed at gaining complete and unconditional command of the State'.[53] The Black Hand had of course already favoured having a military regime in Serbia's new provinces, where, incidentally, Protić had banned the distribution of *Pijemont*. The stakes, however, were now much higher. The opportunity had suddenly opened up to bring down the hated Radical Government and replace it with the Black Hand in the driving seat. On 28 May *Pijemont* called the Radical Party 'a living corpse'.[54]

But how was such a *coup d'état* to be achieved? Apis had on his side his own Black Hand organization, the Chief of General Staff *Vojvoda* Radomir Putnik and, potentially, a very considerable body of Army officers who felt humiliated by Protić's Priority Decree. He could at the same time try and influence three other power factors: the King, the Crown Prince and the opposition parties. The Black Hand duly put enormous pressure on the King to make Pašić withdraw the Priority Decree. What this really meant was that he should get rid of the Radical Government. This put the old man in quite a dilemma: if he supported the officers, he would contribute to the fall from power of the Radicals and thereby bring about a serious internal crisis; if, on the other hand, he backed the Government, he would alienate the Army which had always enjoyed his sympathy. In the circumstances, he tried to mediate between the parties. This proved a waste of time, which became apparent when General Damjan Popović sent him a blunt message: there was more likelihood, Popović submitted, that the King's head would 'roll in the streets of Belgrade' than that the Black Hand would make peace with the Pašić Government.

This particular instance of Black Hand scare tactics had reportedly so angered Crown Prince Alexander that he decided there and then to destroy Apis and his organization.[55] Having successfully commanded one of the Serbian armies during the Balkan Wars, Alexander had become an important figure of power in Serbia. He had also gathered around himself a potent coterie of officers known as the 'White Hand', a group which included regicides from 1903, mostly those who had fallen out with Apis. The latter could only hope to neutralize his royal opponent by threats. Aware of Alexander's standing, but probably overestimating his own, he warned the Crown Prince not to meddle in the Priority Decree question. Branislav Gligorijević, Alexander's biographer, believes that the warning was worded in brutally explicit terms: 'We have brought you to where you are, and we can also remove you.' By all accounts, however, Alexander was in 1914 impatient to reign and unwilling to live in Apis's shadow. An autocratic type himself, he replied to one of Apis's emissaries that 'he wants to be the ruler, and does not acquiesce to being ruled'.[56]

In spring 1914, the prospect of power was also being eyed by Serbia's opposition parties. Exploiting the discontent and the restlessness in the Army over the Priority Decree, the opposition, particularly the Independent Radicals, used the floor of the Assembly to launch blistering attacks on the Government. A collusion now occurred between the opposition and the Black Hand. By mid-May at the latest, Apis was assiduously cultivating the leading opposition politicians, principally the Independent Radicals' Milorad Drašković and Ljuba Davidović. This was an unholy alliance, for in the past, Serbia's opposition parties had severely criticised the Radicals under Pašić for tolerating the continued presence of the regicides from 1903 – and the Black Hand was of course swarming with them. For its part, the Black Hand fulminated through *Pijemont* that 'all parties of today have proved their lack of morality, of culture and of patriotism'.[57] Notwithstanding these postures, the opposition parties and the Black Hand clearly intended to use each other in order to see the back of the Radical Party. Meanwhile, Interior Minister Protić attacked the Independent Radicals in the Assembly, accusing them of providing support to the 'Praetorians' (i.e., the Black Hand officers).[58]

It is surprising indeed, that the opposition was prepared to go along with Apis's drastic methods. Jaša Prodanović, a prominent Independent Radical, admitted later that he had met with Bogdan Radenković, representing the Black Hand, to discuss 'the violent overthrow of the Radical Government'.[59] Interior Minister Protić stated privately that there existed 'a written pact between the Independent Radicals and the Black Hand'.[60] At the very least, the flirtation between the opposition and the officers from 'Unification or Death' did not represent a good omen for parliamentary government in Serbia. Vojislav Vučković, an authority on the subject, emphasized the portentious aspect of the pact between the opposition and the officers: 'It is not clear how those officers could have contributed to the fall of the Radical Government other than by overthrowing it.'[61]

By April-May, the opposition parties, in cahoots with the Black Hand, were obstructing the work of parliament by walking out of the Assembly prior to voting. The Government, with its wafer-thin majority, could not pass legislation without the necessary quorum. On 29 May Pašić asked the King to dissolve the Assembly, but this was refused. On 2 June Pašić resigned. It looked as if the Black Hand was winning. According to Slobodan Jovanović, in this crisis situation the King leant more towards the Army than to the Government.[62] He now began consultations with the opposition parties. But Apis was leaving nothing to chance, for he knew that it could all end up with Pašić being re-appointed. And so he finally decided that if the Radical Party did remain in power he would strike.

At some stage after Pašić's resignation, probably on 8 or 9 June, Apis wrote a letter to his friend Colonel Dušan Glišić, a senior officer in Macedonia and a fellow regicide from 1903. The letter, in a sealed envelope, was given by Apis to Colonel Milovan Plazina who was also serving in Macedonia at the time and was only briefly in Belgrade. Plazina, about to return to his post, was to hand the envelope over to Glišić. Revealing the main contents of the letter to Plazina, Apis said that he was instructing Glišić, together with several other trusted officers, to 'remove the police authorities in the new territories and to report to him by dispatch about it'. Apis also told Plazina that he, Apis, would then make sure of doing 'what needs to be done' in the old territories – i.e., in Serbia. When Plazina remarked that 'this should not be done' and that the officers in Skopje would not agree to carry out the instruction, Apis countered: 'They will, they will!'[63]

But they did not. What Apis's plan amounted to was a military putsch in Macedonia followed by one in Serbia. Slobodan Jovanović, who knew Apis well, wrote that he had reckoned on the Macedonian population to 'greet' and 'support' the putsch.[64] According to Antonije Antić, Apis had intended that the troops in Macedonia should thereafter march on Belgrade.[65] Serbia was on a knife-edge. However, Colonel Glišić and the other Black Hand officers in the region supposedly loyal to Apis drew back from the brink. Plazina, who had duly returned to Skopje, wrote to Apis on 10 June that he had met with Glišić and three other officers, to tell them what they were required to do after the receipt of 'the official report that the Government remained the same one', i.e. that Pašić and the Radicals would carry on. Plazina then explained how the officers felt: 'They are, to the man, against the Army taking power'. Glišić himself wrote to Apis on the same piece of paper: 'There is not a single man here who would agree with your proposed action in the given case.' Lieutenant-Colonel Milutin Lazarević, another of the officers in Macedonia whom Apis had counted on, wrote the final part of their response to Apis: 'What you asked for cannot be carried out.'[66]

And so Apis's dream of taking power in Serbia lay in tatters. In the meantime, sensing trouble, the Government had rushed additional gendarmerie troops to Belgrade from the interior. Their officers had orders to kill all the ringleaders of any putsch.[67] Antonije Antić, who was at the time serving as an adjutant to King Peter, noted later that in the spring of 1914 Serbia's civil-military conflict threatened to turn into 'a serious civil war'.[68] Apis's anticipation that the Radicals would stay in power proved correct, for on 11 June the King asked Pašić to form the next cabinet.

Much has been written about the role and influence exerted in those days by the Russian Minister Hartwig. The generally held view is that Hartwig, keen to retain Pašić at the helm of Serbia, had pressurized King Peter to support the old Radical. But King Peter's biographer Dragoljub Živojinović doubts the importance of foreign policy considerations on the King's decisions in the crisis.[69] Be that as it may, on 23 June the Assembly was dissolved and new elections were called for 14 August. On 24 June the King issued a proclamation to the people, announcing that he was being prevented by illness from carrying out his royal duties and that, for the duration of his illness, the Crown Prince would rule. This, in effect, was an abdication.[70]

It will be remembered that in the middle of all this the three Sarajevo assassins had left Belgrade on 28 May and two of them, Princip and Grabež, had illegally crossed into Bosnia during the night of 1-2 June. Apis's name is invariably linked to their act of assassination at Sarajevo. The question which begs to be asked here is how likely it would have been that Apis, in the midst of his frenetic efforts to bring down the Radical Government through an open military *coup*, would have simultaneously been scheming to assassinate Archduke Franz Ferdinand? Or, to put it in a different way: what possible benefit could Apis have hoped to gain from assassinating the Archduke at the exact time when he was expecting to take power in Serbia? Would Apis really have wanted his intended new Serbian government to be immediately confronted by the (avoidable) wrath of an enraged Austro-Hungarian Empire? How would a dead Archduke help him attain or retain power? Vasa Kazimirović's major and exhaustive work on the Black Hand says a great deal in saying almost nothing about the claim that this organization played a role in the assassination. It seems that, to Kazimirović, this idea is a non-starter. He does write, however: 'All these claims in connection with the assassination in Sarajevo must be taken with great reserve. As for the claim that Apis had in spring 1914 been concentrating more on the murder of Ferdinand than on bringing down Nikola Pašić's Government, it is entirely unconvincing.'[71]

Lieutenant-Colonel Apis and the Sarajevo Assassination Plot

What knowledge, then, did Lieutenant-Colonel Dimitrijević Apis really have of the plan for the assassination of Franz Ferdinand? As will be seen, he was to take a great interest in the whole matter – but only in a desperate attempt to stop it. Contrary to what he later said on the subject – and contrary to what a legion of scholars and writers have been asserting over the decades – the hand of Apis in the Sarajevo assassination is conspicuous only by its absence. Of course, Apis himself boasted about his role in the event that sparked off a world war, most famously in his written submission at the 1917 Salonika Trial. Apart from that submission, there exist two records of his musings about the assassination in Sarajevo. Surprisingly, all of this evidence – such as it is – has hardly been subjected to even a brief comparative analysis, let alone a deep enquiry. Faced with what amounts to 'The Confessions of Apis', a rip-roaring good story about the Black Hand and the Sarajevo assassination, the historical profession, normally sceptical by vocation, has reacted by suspending disbelief.

It lies outside the framework of this book to scrutinise the Salonika Trial (2 April-5 June 1917) which resulted in the execution, on 26 June 1917, of Colonel Apis and two of his associates (Rade Malobabić and Major Ljubomir Vulović). Suffice to say that the charges against Apis and others belonging to the Black Hand – to the effect that they had attempted an assassination in September 1916 against Regent Alexander – were trumped up; that not only the Regent (and his coterie of officers), but also the leading Radical Party politicians stood behind this legal farce; and finally, that the overall consequence of this trial was to make Apis into a martyr – which was to have its own important repercussions on the historiography of the Sarajevo assassination. Regent Alexander had obsessively viewed Apis as a threat to his control over the Army, whereas some high-ranking officers around him held personal grudges against the Colonel and his followers in the Black Hand. 'The Salonika Trial', David MacKenzie observed, 'revealed the unfortunate Serbian penchant for bitter factional and personal feuds and the desire to wreak bloody vengeance upon opponents.'[72]

For any interpretation of the Sarajevo assassination, however, the evidence which Apis provided during the Salonika Trial is obligatory reading. Sensing the mortal danger in which he and his comrades found themselves, on 10 April he submitted his 'confidential report [*poverljiv raport*]' to the court. This is the cardinal passage:

> As the Chief of the intelligence section of the General Staff, I engaged Rade Malobabić to organize the intelligence network in Austria-Hungary and he took on the task. I did this in agreement with the Russian military attaché Artamonov who would personally meet with Rade in my presence. After Rade began his work, feeling that Austria was preparing for a war against us, I thought that with the disappearance of the Austrian Heir to the Throne, the military party and tendency which he headed would lose its strength and that the danger of war for Serbia would in that way be obviated or at least postponed for a while. Hence I engaged Malobabić to organize the assassination on the occasion of Ferdinand's scheduled arrival in Sarajevo. I decided on this definitively only after Artamonov gave me the assurance that Russia would not leave us without protection if Austria attacked us. I did not on this occasion relate to Mr Artamonov anything about my intention regarding the assassination. The reason for seeking his opinion about the attitude of Russia was that our intelligence activity might

be observed [*što se naš rad na izveštajnoj službi mogao osetiti*] and so this too could become a pretext for Austria to attack us. Malobabić carried out my order, he organized and carried through the assassination.[73]

Just how an Austrian detection of routine Serbian intelligence activity could become a pretext for war was not explained by Apis. Be that as it may, his written submission, he imagined, was his trump card: surely, no Serbian court could continue to try, let alone condemn, a Serbian patriot with such a distinguished record. Or, as he put it towards the end of his confidential report, giving the reason why he had to write it: 'I would not rest in peace even in the grave at the thought that a Serbian officers' military court could complete and wrap up the verdict of the Austrian court in Sarajevo.'[74] Cvetko Popović, the former Sarajevo assassin, remarked that this sounded almost like 'blackmail'.[75]

It was not until 1953, when the communist regime in Yugoslavia staged a retrial (which rehabilitated Apis and his comrades) that the confidential report was published. However, the fact that Apis had signed a statement in which he talked about organizing the Sarajevo assassination was disclosed as early as 1922 in *Radikal*, the paper of the then ruling Radical Party – in an article most probably penned by former Interior Minister Stojan Protić.[76] More evidence came in 1932 when Colonel Čedomir Popović published his recollections of what Apis had told him about the Sarajevo assassination when they met during the war in 1915. Popović quoted him at length:

I was convinced that the projected manoeuvre in Bosnia was a pretext for Austria's invasion of Serbia, headed by the commander-in-chief of the Austrian Army, the Heir to the Throne Franz Ferdinand ... Before our troops could arrive from the southern territories Serbia would be run over ... And therefore, when one day Tankosić came to my office and said: 'There are some Bosnian youths who have been pestering me, asking me to allow them to go to Bosnia – should I let them go?' – I indeed said at that moment, not thinking any further: 'Well, let them go!' Tankosić told me on that occasion that those youths, in agreement with comrades in Bosnia, wished to attempt something against Ferdinand. To tell you the truth, I thought at that moment that it would be impossible for such an assassination to succeed, and that maybe it would not even take place. I assumed that the Austrian Heir to the Throne would be so guarded and protected that nothing could happen to him; at most, that there would be some incident which would serve as a reminder to him and the people surrounding him for them to realize that it was dangerous to attack Serbia. In any case, I could not even in my wildest dreams suppose [*nisam mogao pretpostaviti ni u snu*] that such an assassination could prompt a war against Serbia ... Still, when after a while I thought a little more about the matter, I resolved to try and bring back the youths and that the assassination be by all means prevented. That attempt was conducted through the *četnik* Đuro Šarac. It was too late. The assassins, those two who had left from Serbia, as well as those already in Sarajevo, did not want to hear of it ...[77]

Now, the discrepancy between the two testimonies above is astonishing. Whereas Apis, in his 1917 Salonika submission, claims to have decided 'definitively' on the assassination only after Artamonov had given him assurances of Russia's protective stance towards Serbia, he had previously claimed to Popović in 1915 that he had not initially thought the matter through ('Well, let them go!'). In his Salonika statement Apis presented himself as a careful planner who had consulted the Russian Military Attaché about the possibility of an Austrian attack, but in a free conversation with Popović he had said that an Austrian attack, following from the assassination, did not figure even in his 'wildest dreams'. What, then, is to be believed here? Also, the naiveté of the view expressed by Apis at Salonika that killing the Austrian Heir to the Throne would obviate or at least postpone an attack on Serbia defies belief. Equally, his suggestion to Popović in 1915 that an incident in Sarajevo would frighten and deter Franz Ferdinand from attacking Serbia is simply too childish to believe. What military strength or other capabilities did Serbia possess with which to frighten or deter a Great Power like Austria-Hungary? It could not have escaped Apis's attention that the Habsburg leadership had in 1912-1913 been itching to have a military showdown with Serbia. The 'military party' in Vienna, whose existence he himself mentioned, could only be strengthened, not weakened, by the Archduke's assassination. Even without firm proof of Serbian complicity in such an assassination, Vienna would have no qualms about attacking Serbia – which is precisely what happened in 1914.

Apis's basic rationale for the assassination of Franz Ferdinand, as related to Popović, was his fear that 'the projected manoeuvre in Bosnia was a pretext for Austria's invasion of Serbia'. This, too, should be dismissed straight away. On 26 May 1914 Colonel Lešjanin, the Serbian Military Attaché in Vienna, reported that the manoeuvres would be held south of Sarajevo in the direction of Mostar – i.e., not even close to the border with Serbia. Lešjanin commented that there was no reason to view the manoeuvres with disquiet and that no need existed for Serbia to take any preventive military measures.[78] This report would have automatically landed on Apis's desk. As Vojislav Vučković has argued, any significant Austro-Hungarian movement of troops towards Serbia could not have remained unobserved by the Serbian General Staff. The transport of just a single division would have required some thirty train compositions, and this would have been impossible to conceal.[79]

Apis, in his conversation with Popović, did not even seem to know how many Bosnian assassin youths had left Serbia for Sarajevo: he said two. This would all be mind-boggling from the former head of Serbian military intelligence if it had truly been his operation. As will be seen, the only true piece of information that Apis related to Popović concerns the attempt to stop the assassins through Đuro Šarac.

Further material regarding Dimitrijević's baffling reflections on the Sarajevo assassination is provided by Antonije Antić in his memoir, published for the first time in 2010 (but available to researchers for years beforehand). Antić, a key officer participant in the 1903 plot to murder King Alexander and Queen Draga, tends to mess up his dates, and so his account, written probably in the 1930s or even later, is not always reliable. Nevertheless, the abundance of credible details make it a document of great historical interest. In 1914 Lieutenant-Colonel Antić was serving as an orderly to the old King Peter. What he heard from Apis was a similar, and yet in some details different, story from the one recorded by Popović. Arriving in Belgrade from the south of the country, he met Apis on 24 July – or so it would appear from the context of his memoir – the day after the presentation of the Austro-Hungarian ultimatum to Serbia. Apis explained to him that he had received reports that Austria had been preparing to invade Serbia from Bosnia where manoeuvres were to take place. 'I was the first to receive that report from the Russian military envoy Artamonov', he maintained, 'that is, that this was discussed on the occasion of the meeting of [Kaiser] Wilhelm and Franz Ferdinand at Konopischt. After-wards our confidant Malobabić also reported to me about the talk in the Austro-Hungarian officer circles that they would attack us across the Drina during the manoeuvres.' Apis assured Antić that General Putnik, the Chief of the General Staff, had beeen notified about all this by him and that Putnik then informed the Prime Minister Pašić – but Pašić did not believe it and was busy preparing for elections. 'What could I do in such a situation?', Apis asked Antić. He then said that he had asked his confidant Malobabić what he thought should be done. Malobabić apparently had had no doubts: 'Franz Ferdinand', he said, 'should be killed.' He also said that he had 'some youths from Bosnia'. So Apis asked his confidant to 'bring them' to him and when this was done he called Tankosić, ordering him to train the youths in shooting. Finally, Apis told Antić what he was to repeat, essentially, to Popović in 1915: that he did not believe Franz Ferdinand would be killed, but only frightened so that he would not 'dare' come to Serbia out of fear of an assassination there.[80]

The Konopischt meeting mentioned by Apis to Antić is discussed in the next chapter, but it needs to be emphasized here that it took place on 12 and 13 June. As has been seen, the assassins had already left Belgrade on 28 May. So, whatever information Lieutenant-Colonel Dimitrijević may have received from attaché Artamonov following Konopischt could clearly not have played any role in the initiation of the Sarajevo assassination plan. Apis, evidently, lied through his teeth to Antić. It is also noteworthy that he told him that Malobabić had lined up the Bosnian youths, but a year later he told Popović that this had been done by Tankosić (who, in the Antić version, is relegated to the role of a mere shooting instructor). As for Radomir Putnik, the Chief of the Serbian General Staff, it is difficult to believe that he had intervened with Prime Minister Pašić with regard to the imminent danger from Austria allegedly reported by Artamonov. The measure of Putnik's concern is illustrated by the fact that on 27 June, day two of Austria's military manoeuvres, he left Serbia for a cure in Bad Gleichenberg, Austria.[81] Artamonov himself had already left Belgrade on 19 June for a holiday in Switzerland.[82]

The sheer depth and scale of contradictions, implausibilities and downright absurdities contained in the three available narratives by Apis would necessitate his instant dismissal as a credible source on the background to the Sarajevo assassination.[83] The question imposes itself, however: why did Apis consistently take credit for Sarajevo 1914 when the nonsense his statements constitute indicates that he had nothing to do with it? Two factors must be borne in mind here. The first is that the elimination of the Habsburg Heir to the Throne was seen as a brave patriotic deed across wide sections of Serbian society – in the light of all the hostility displayed by Vienna and the humiliations which Serbia had suffered since 1908, such an act was saluted by many. In that context, for anyone to be associated with it was laudatory. And second, the chattering classes of Belgrade, that grapevine beast called the *čaršija* (the town), assumed immediately after the assassination that someone organized and powerful must have stood behind those green young men in Sarajevo. Apis himself, with his endless coffee house sessions, was a main prop of Belgrade's gossip and rumour industry. A recollection typifying the goings on is that by Milan Stojadinović, the Prime Minister in the Kingdom of Yugoslavia who was in 1914 a junior official in the Ministry of Finance. 'It was clear to us in Serbia straight away', he wrote in his memoir, 'even before any court investigation in Sarajevo, that both assassins [Čabrinović and Princip] must have had connections with our *Narodna Odbrana*, or with the *Četnik* Association, or with the Black Hand. Only Belgrade could have given the bombs and the weapons.[84] In fact, the spectrum of guesswork was quickly narrowed down to the Black Hand, and new evidence would suggest that Apis himself played a role in this.

The new evidence, hitherto overlooked by historians, comes from the 1924 article by Dr Milovan Grba in the *Prager Presse* (to which a reference was already made in the previous chapter) about his meeting with Đuro Šarac in Geneva.[85] Grba put to him the 'explicit question' of whether Apis had been privy to the conspiracy ('*in die Verschwörung eingeweiht war*'). Šarac gave a very clear, arresting answer. He said that 'in the first few days after the assassination, various self-imagined Belgrade leviathans of national propaganda showed no slight inclination to intimate pompously that Princip and his comrades had in fact only done the deed under the influence of their own significant personalities.' Characteristically perhaps for Serbia and for Belgrade in particular, people boasted and lied about their association with an event which the whole world was talking about and which had the Serbs in a leading role. But where was Apis in all this? It would appear that his name was rather prominent in the Belgrade chatter and rumours following the Sarajevo assassination. For Šarac added, significantly, that 'in reality the assassination had been prepared without the involvement and knowledge of one Belgrade man.' By 'one Belgrade man [*eines Belgraders*]' Šarac meant Apis. This becomes clear as Dr Grba continues his account of what Šarac had told him: 'When, in the well-known Salonika Trial, Colonel Dimitrijević-Apis attempted to rehabilitate his patriotism by claiming that he was the initiator of the Sarajevo assassination, Šarac and Ciganović let him know that unless he withdrew his claim, they would, along with other Bosnian emigrants, prove indubitably [*klipp und klar*] before the Court that Apis had not had a clue [*keine Ahnung gehabt habe*] about the conspiracy against Franz Ferdinand.'[86]

This testimony by Šarac constitutes to date the most compelling corroboration that all the stories about Apis, the Black Hand and the Sarajevo assassination amount to fantastic hogwash. What makes it particularly credible is that Šarac (who died in Switzerland towards the end of the war) spoke to Dr Grba in 1918 – in other words, well before any of the controversies surrounding Serbia's role in 1914 began in the 1920s. One small, key detail from the Salonika Trial also significantly supports the Šarac testimony. At the start of his questioning on 8 May 1917, Apis was asked whether he still intended to use in his defence the confidential report which he had submitted on 10 April. He replied, interestingly, that he no longer considered it necessary to use it.[87] Šarac, Ciganović, Đulaga Bukovac and other Bosnian emigrants were all present in Salonika in 1917 and they could indeed have testified, and contradicted Apis, on what happened in 1914. Why would the Colonel otherwise have given up on using a report which he initially reckoned would save his life?

Anticipating Disaster

What Šarac did not, apparently, mention to Dr Grba was that Apis had actually sent him on a mission to make the assassins abandon their plan. This episode, of course, confirms the fact that the chief of Serbian military intelligence had initially had no idea about what was being prepared right under his nose. As has been seen, he told Čedomir Popović in 1915 that he had had second thoughts about the asasassination and tried to stop it through Đuro Šarac. But there were no second thoughts: only a realization, once he found out about the conspiracy, that it would be complete madness for Franz Ferdinand to be shot or blown up by weapons from Serbia wielded by assassins travelling from Serbia. Moreover, as discussed earlier in this chapter, Apis was in May-June 1914 preparing a *coup d'état* in Serbia. The very last thing he would have wanted at that time was an Austro-Hungarian invasion. Svetozar Pribićević, the Serbian politician from Croatia who knew Apis, wrote in his memoirs: 'Dimitrijević would have had to be mad to desire a war with Austria-Hungary at that moment. And mad he certainly was not.'[88]

It would seem, from evidence that has subsequently emerged, that Colonel Popović did not tell the full story in his 1932 account of what he knew about the background to the Sarajevo assassination. In 1987 the Belgrade journalist Stevan Zec published the recollections of Josif Protić, the deputy prison commander in Salonika where Apis and his friends were held. Zec was Protić's son-in-law and had inherited his papers. Lieutenant Protić had known most of the prisoners and they used to confide in him. One of them was Čedomir Popović, who told him: 'Protić, I will tell you the truth: if Tankosić were still alive, had he not died in battle, Alexander's bullet would now be awaiting that hothead and not us or at least not many of us ... Voja [Tankosić] was pigheaded. I know: a trusted man had arrived from Belgrade, from Apis, bearing a secret message ... And the man says: 'Apis has ordered Voja to stop his lions ...' But too late, they'd crossed the Drina! I sent a man who reached them and passed on the message.' This account by Popović to Protić makes clear that at this stage Apis had not yet confronted Tankosić in person. For the latter's reaction in the meantime, as related by Popović to Protić, was to say: 'Push off! I don't believe it has been decided not to shoot. And even if it has been decided, I am not reversing course ...'[89]

If Protić is to be believed, Tankosić thereby displayed yet again his violent nature and his insubordination even to Apis. It is by no means clear from these jailbird elaborations by Popović whether the man Apis sent to intervene was Đuro Šarac. And the identity of the person then sent by Popović to the assassins will probably forever remain a mystery, though it is likely that this was merely a local courier. Certainly, in June 1914 Popović was serving as a battalion commander in Valjevo, in an area adjoining the border with Bosnia, and he was therefore in the right location to take further action. Besides, he had had experience of clandestine work in the region as a member of the specialist Army 'Officers Border Service', an institution that was officially abolished at the end of 1913 because it served the purposes of Apis and the Black Hand rather than the Army, but which in reality continued to function.[90] Thus the 'channel' which historians like Albertini and Fey touted so much as the Black Hand's logistical avenue for the Sarajevo assassination was in fact used to try and stop it. Given the overwhelming likelihood that Tankosić had kept Apis in the dark about his private enterprise in Bosnia, it has to be assumed that it was this mechanism made up of officers and confidants along the border which alerted Apis to the fact that there had been a crossing of armed youths.

But when and why, in the first place, did scholars, and the world, begin to talk about an involvement of the Black Hand in the Sarajevo assassination? Oddly enough, almost nothing had been heard about Apis and the Black Hand in this regard before the 1923 publication of a booklet by Serbian historian Stanoje Stanojević, entitled *The Murder of the Austrian Heir to the Throne Ferdinand.*[91] Here, however, Stanojević was not writing as an impartial historian, but as someone close to Pašić's Radical Party, at a time when Apis's supporters had begun to raise demands for the retrial of Salonika, especially actively on the pages of the influential Zagreb periodical *Nova Evropa*. Stanojević's booklet, without any footnotes or supporting material, was clearly written with political objectives in mind, the main one being to present Apis as the single person responsible for what happened in 1914 as well as to paint him as an incorrigible conspirator who had even dreamt up the plot to assassinate Crown Prince Alexander in 1917 – thus justifying the role of the Radical Party's politicians in the judicial murder of Apis. The unintended end result of this postwar bickering among Serbs, however, was that it decisively influenced international historiographical interpretations of the start of the Great War.

In his pamphlet, Stanojević wrote that Apis had received information from the Russian General Staff that, at the Konopischt meeting, Franz Ferdinand and Wilhelm II had agreed on an Austrian attack on Serbia; that Apis believed only the elimination of the Archduke could prevent such an attack; and that he got Tankosić to instruct 'two youths' in the handling of weapons. It would appear from this that Stanojević, looking for some material, had talked to Popović as well as to Antić since the story contains elements which would feature in the subsequent writings of both men. What is distinct in his account, however, is the claim that on 15 June Apis had convened a meeting of the 'main board [*glavni odbor*]' of the Black Hand, telling it that people had been sent to Bosnia to kill Franz Ferdinand. 'Practically all the members of the board', Stanojević wrote, 'rose against the implementation of this plan' – and Apis was finally persuaded to send a message to Sarajevo that the assassination should not be carried out. But 'it was either too late or the assassins did not want to listen'.[92]

Interestingly, however, when the Serbian historian Vladimir Ćorović talked after the war to Colonel Grgur Milovanović, a member of the main board, the latter emphasized that the Black Hand organization had had nothing to do with any aspect of the matter and that it had 'never' been in session to take a decision on it in the first place.[93] Highly problematic as it is, however, Stanojević's pamphlet attracted world-wide attention and, more importantly, received almost uncritical acceptance. Some scholars, admittedly, were sceptical. In 1925 Robert Seton-Watson wrote that Stanojević had exalted 'out of all proportion' the importance of the Black Hand. And in 1930 Bernadotte Schmitt warned that Stanojević 'has to be treated with great caution'.[94] But this work was immediately translated in Germany where the 'war guilt' revisionists could hardly believe their luck: here, finally, was proof that Serbia had, through its head of military intelligence, unleashed the terrible war of 1914-1918.[95] As late as 1958, the Austrian historian Hans Uebersberger maintained that Stanojević was 'the official Serbian historian of the Sarajevo assassination'.[96] In fact, as noted above, his pamphlet represented just a continuation of agenda-ridden, internal Serbian political squabbling.[97]

Stanojević's little brochure nevertheless proved to be something of a historiographical game changer. Quite apart from placing Apis at the centre of the Sarajevo assassination plot, Stanojević in the same pamphlet also created a dazzling picture of him as a master-assassin specializing in crowned heads. Thus, according to Stanojević, Apis was one of the chief organizers of the conspiracy against King Alexander in 1903; then in the summer of 1911 he 'sent a man' to kill either Franz Joseph or Franz Ferdinand; in February 1914 he was plotting together with a secret Bulgarian revolutionary committee to kill King Ferdinand; in 1916 he 'sent a man' from Corfu to kill the Greek King Constantine; and finally, in 1917, he was seeking to establish contact with the 'enemy' (i.e., Austria-Hungary and Germany) and, 'it would seem', organizing an assassination attempt aimed at the then Crown Prince Alexander of Serbia.[98] Not surprisingly, then, Joachim Remak wrote of Apis in 1959: 'He was, quite possibly, the foremost European expert in regicide of his time.'[99] This is hyperbole worthy of Conan Doyle or Anthony Hope. Apis's only documented regicidal case relates to his 1903 role in the removal of King Alexander Obrenović. It has long been established, for example, that the alleged assassination attempt on the life of Crown Prince Alexander, at Salonika in 1917, was a concoction created by Apis's enemies. And it would have been a bizarre and pointless enterprise, to say the least, to have schemed the assassination of King Ferdinand in February 1914 – given that Serbia had already defeated Bulgaria by that time. Yet historians have rarely questioned the fine terrorist pedigree that Stanoje Stanojević had in 1923 constructed for Apis. An exception was David MacKenzie, Apis's biographer, though he was content simply to remark that Stanojević's account of Apis as a professional assassin was 'surely a gross mischaracterization'.[100] One wonders why, if Apis had time, motivation and resources to scheme assassinations of more distant figures such as the Bulgarian and Greek kings, he did not first of all eliminate Pašić and Interior Minister Protić, by far his most dangerous and immediate opponents.

Given the man's established reputation, post-Stanojević, as the doyen of terrorist action in the early 20th century, it may be appropriate here to pose this question: what as a matter of objective fact was the attitude expressed by Apis to terrorist action and assassination abroad? As far as action in Austria-Hungary was concerned the evidence suggests that Apis was actually highly circumspect. It is illuminating to read what Krešimir Kovačić wrote about Apis and Tankosić. As seen in chapter ten, Kovačić was one of the young, Yugoslav-minded Croat activists, a philosopher and a friend of the strident Serbo-Croat nationalist, poet-rebel Tin Ujević. He knew the leading lights of the Black Hand, including Ljuba Jovanović-Čupa and Bogdan Radenković, as well as Apis. He and Tin Ujević also got to know the mercurial Tankosić who, Kovačić revealed, 'did not, in regard of some actions in Austria-Hungary, agree either with Čupa [Jovanović] or with Apis.' What Tankosić wanted, Kovačić pointed out, was to create *četnik* irregular units for Austria-Hungary – on the Macedonian model. Tankosić even attempted to train Kovačić and Ujević in the use of bombs and weapons, and gave them some written material on how to blow up bridges and the like. But Apis warned Kovačić about Tankosić: 'Leave him alone, he is crazy, he thinks that Austria is Turkey, whereas Austria cannot wait to declare war on us before we settle accounts with Turkey.'[101] Kovačić also wrote that 'people in Belgrade' were actually 'against assassinations [*protivili su se atentatima*]' because 'Austria should not be prematurely provoked into war'. And he named some of them: 'Ljuba Jovanović-Čupa, director of *Pijemont* and Apis Dimitrijević, Major Vasić, and Vemić and some other members of the Black Hand'.[102]

The fact that Apis considered Tankosić to be 'crazy', especially with regard to the latter's injudicious attitude towards Austria-Hungary, hardly suggests that the Chief of Serbian Military Intelligence would have backed Tankosić's incalculable adventure across Serbia's western frontier. Kovačić related what he knew in 1912. But Apis's fundamentally cautious line was still there in 1914 – for after the bloody, exhausting Balkan Wars this would be an even worse period than 1912 to be provoking the powerful neighbour. His view about Austria-Hungary was that it should be gradually weakened rather than suddenly confronted. In 1912 he told the Croat sculptor Ivan Meštrović to 'be patient', and that Austria should be undermined 'from inside'.[103] In a 1913 conversation between Svetozar Pribićević, the Serbian politician from Croatia, and Rade Malobabić, the latter was asked how the representatives of the Serbian Army viewed the general situation. Malobabić, himself from Croatia, related to Pribićević what Apis had told him that he feared most of all, namely that 'Austria-Hungary might attack Serbia before it recovered'. Apis had, according to Malobabić, added: 'We require several more years of peace, and thereafter we shall come to you.'[104]

The problem was that Tankosić, Serbia's most dangerous loose cannon, was clearly as 'crazy' in 1914 as he had always been. Apis therefore directed an interventionist action from Belgrade to stop Tankosić's perilous enterprise. Evidence for this is provided through the case of Danilo Ilić. On 15 June Ilić went to Tuzla from Sarajevo in order to collect the weapons Princip and Grabež had left behind with Miško Jovanović. As instructed by Princip, he had to identify himself to Jovanović by showing a packet of 'Stefanija' cigarettes. Yet just a day later, on 16 June, Ilić left Sarajevo again by train for Bosanski Brod. He had obviously had a pre-arranged meeting there. Following his return to Sarajevo, late on the same day, he suddenly began to talk against the wisdom of the planned assassination – though he had never previously spoken against it.

In his interrogation Princip stated that Ilić had 'in the last ten days' before 28 June 'repeatedly' argued that the time was unfavourable and that there would be no 'use' in the proposed action.[105] This timetable corresponds closely with his mysterious trip to Bosanski Brod. Who did Ilić meet there? He himself did not reveal the identity of his interlocutor either in the investigation or during the trial – but then, strangely, he was not pressed to do so. Ljubibratić and Dedijer, the two chief Yugoslavian specialists on Sarajevo 1914, both assumed that the person Ilić had met was Đuro Šarac although direct evidence for this is lacking.[106] However, it was certainly a logical assumption on their part given that in 1915 Apis told Čedomir Popović that he had used Šarac when attempting to prevent the assassination. Ilić's itinerary is indicative. He went all the way to Tuzla and then back to Sarajevo on 15 June, then went out again on 16 June in the same direction as he had just done the previous day, only further this time, to Brod. Logistically, it would have been easier to go to Brod first, then circle back round to Tuzla and then complete the circle by returning to Sarajevo. The fact that he did not supports the idea that he had at some point agreed a meeting with someone in Brod for that specific day of 16 June. It also suggests a consequent decision on his part to collect the weapons from Tuzla and bring them to Sarajevo before that meeting – so that this weapons collection would be a fait accompli by the time he spoke to his interlocutor in Brod. It is reasonable to conclude that at this point he still believed in carrying out the assassination and might have been afraid of being pressured not to proceed.

The apparent oddity that Ilić and Šarac met in Bosanski Brod rather than Sarajevo is explained by the fact that Šarac did not wish to risk going to Sarajevo just before the manoeuvres when stronger police measures could be expected.[107] In any case, the effect of whatever Šarac told Ilić must have been very considerable. From a determined assassin Ilić suddenly became an enthusiastic peace broker. On returning to Sarajevo he attempted, unsuccessfully, to dissuade Princip from going ahead with the assassination on the grounds that it would be, as he put it, 'more damaging than useful to the Yugoslavs'.[108] Grabež related that Ilić spoke 'energetically against the assassination' three days before 28 June, trying to convince him not to participate. So confident was Ilić that he had converted Grabež that the latter was not even given cyanide to have ready on the day.[109] Ilić even wrote to Mehmedbašić to tell him not to trouble to turn up in Sarajevo, but the latter came nevertheless.[110] Right at the last moment, on the morning of 28 June, Ilić was still busy agitating against the assassination, telling Grabež that it was pointless as the Slavs would only suffer damage as a result. Grabež admitted during his interrogation on 16 July that he had been persuaded by Ilić, which was the reason why he failed to throw his bomb at the Archduke's car when it was leaving the Town Hall.[111]

The decision made by Apis to send Šarac as the messenger to warn the assassins about the consequences of what they were about to do might appear quite strange: Šarac was more Tankosić's than Apis's man and he had, moreover, been at the very heart of the conspiracy. Once he found out about it, however, Apis must have confronted Tankosić who then revealed Šarac's involvement – no evidence whatsoever is available with regard to this and so one can only speculate. But it does stand to reason that Apis had demanded of Tankosić to see Šarac, and that the latter was first berated and then sent to put things right precisely because of his central role in the affair. It also made sense to aim at Ilić, both because he was senior in age to the other assassins and because he was personally known to Šarac.[112]

But Princip, the true head of all the conspirators in Sarajevo, ignored Ilić's pleas that he should give up on the assassination. Ilić was in a most difficult situation: the instructions from Belgrade were clear and he no doubt believed them to be judicious; on the other hand, his sense of shame in the light of Princip's determined stand influenced him at least to the extent that he reluctantly went along, distributing the weapons in the end to five of the assassins – Princip, who had lodged in Ilić's house, simply helped himself to his own Browning and a bomb.[113] Just how awful Ilić felt is illustrated by his remark to Grabež on the morning of 28 June as the latter was given his weapons: 'Take away these things', Ilić said with disgust, 'so that they are no longer with me'.[114]

Ilić must already have notified Šarac about Princip's obduracy, for Šarac then wrote Princip a series of letters – five or six in June, according to Milan Šakota to whose address in Sarajevo (left behind in Belgrade by Princip) those letters were sent. It is possible, even probable, that some of these letters reached Princip even before Šarac met Ilić on 16 June. The last letter, received between 20 and 25 June, also contained a money order for eighty dinars. According to Šakota, Šarac urged Princip to return to

Belgrade and abandon the scheme 'as it would be gravely damaging for Serbia'. The money was presumably sent to cover his return trip. When Princip read this letter, he got angry, cursing Šarac's parents.[115]

Some evidence exists that Apis had tried a further avenue of dissuasion. During the investigation no less than four pupils from the Tuzla *Gymnasium* stated that they had seen Grabež in Tuzla seven or eight days before 28 June. One of them said that Grabež was together with some man. Grabež, of course, had attended the high school in Tuzla and so was known to those pupils. At the trial he denied that he had gone to Tuzla but, as Ljubibratić argued, four of his fellow pupils could not have been wrong. Ljubibratić also speculated that the man Grabež had been seen with was probably Rade Malobabić, Apis's chief operative in Austria-Hungary, and that, on account of Grabež's meeting with Tankosić in Belgrade, Grabež had been seen as the leader of the Belgrade *troika*. According to Ljubibratić, Rade Malobabić was staying in Tuzla during that period.[116] The fact that Malobabić was active in the area at the time is confirmed by the testimony of Vaso Ristić – the director of the Serbian Bank in Tuzla and the person who was told by Miško Jovanović early in June about the arrival of the assassins in town. Ristić recalled that on either 1st or 2nd of July Malobabić came to his bank 'unusually distraught and nervous'. This, of course, was soon after the Sarajevo assassination and Ristić had no doubt that Malobabić had arrived from Sarajevo. 'The situation is very critical', Malobabić told him, 'I have to cross immediately to Serbia and I have come to you to recommend to me the safest passage.'[117] If Malobabić had really – as asserted by Apis in 1917 at Salonika – organized the the Archduke's elimination, then why should he, given the successful outcome, suddenly be so agitated and troubled? His attitude is more consistent with his having been sent to stop the assassins: and having failed to do so, seen at first hand the resulting pogroms against the Serbs and heard all the bellicose talk against Serbia. All this would have given him every reason to believe that the situation was 'very critical'. It would appear that Malobabić was indeed in Sarajevo at the time of the assassination.[118] In the 1978 revised edition of his classic work on Sarajevo 1914, Vladimir Dedijer wrote cautiously but still pointedly: 'It cannot be excluded that Malobabić had gone to Sarajevo to prevent the assassination, and not to organize and carry it through, as claimed by Colonel Apis.'[119]

What did Pašić Know?

In the long list of unresolved issues concerning the immediate origins of the First World War there is also one that may well be connected with Apis's dismay at the prospect of uncontrollable fallout if Franz Ferdinand tempted fate by visiting Bosnia. This is the famous 'Serbian warning' to

Austria-Hungary, issued at a meeting in early June between the Serbian Minister in Vienna Jovan M. Jovanović and the Austro-Hungarian Joint Finance Minister Leon Biliński. Much has been written about this encounter, not least by Jovanović (but almost nothing, intriguingly, by Biliński). Even after a hundred years it remains a perplexing episode. Did Jovanović go to see Biliński on the instructions of the Government in Belgrade, or did he do so on his own initiative? The question is certainly not without importance. For if Jovanović had been directed by the Government to take such a step, then Nikola Pašić and his colleagues must have possessed some fairly accurate foreknowledge of the plot. If, on the other hand, Jovanović had made his own decision to go to Biliński, without such instruction – as he later repeatedly insisted – then what possible information could he have had sitting in his office in Paulanergasse no.4, 4th *Bezirk*, Vienna?

Thus the whole of this question rests on assessments of who among the leading Serbs knew what about the assassination plot. Those historians and writers wishing to burden Serbia with responsibility for the outbreak of the war made a great deal of an article written by Ljuba Jovanović, the Education Minister in 1914. Entitled '*Posle Vidova dana 1914. godine* [After St Vitus's Day, 1914]', it appeared as the leading piece in a collection of articles published in 1924.[120] A German translation duly followed in *Die Kriegsschuldfrage* in February 1925.[121] An English translation was published by Chatham House in March 1925.[122] The relevant passage ran as follows:

> I do not remember whether it was at the end of May or the beginning of June, when one day M. Pašić said to us (he conferred on these matters more particularly with Stojan Protić, who was then Minister of the Interior; but he said this much to the rest of us) that there were people who were preparing to go to Sarajevo to kill Francis Ferdinand, who was to go there to be solemnly received on *Vidov Dan*. As they afterwards told me, the plot was hatched by a group of secretly organised persons and in patriotic Bosno-Herzegovinian student circles in Belgrade. M. Pašić and the rest of us said, and Stojan agreed, that he should issue instructions to the frontier authorities on the Drina to deny a crossing to the youths who had already set out from Belgrade for that purpose. But the frontier 'authorities' themselves belonged to the organisation and did not carry out Stojan's instructions, but reported to him (and he afterwards reported to us) that the order had reached them too late, for the young men had already got across. [...] Thus the endeavour of the Government to prevent the execution of the plot failed, as also did the endeavour made on his own initiative by our Minister in Vienna, M. Joca Jovanović, in an interview with the Minister Bilinski, to dissuade the Archduke from the fatal journey which he contemplated.[123]

Alfred von Wegerer, the editor of *Die Kriegsschuldfrage*, noted triumphantly that members of Pašić's cabinet knew about the intended murder and 'let things take their course after a failed attempt to stop the murderers at the border'. The suspicion entertained by the Austro-Hungarian Government in July 1914, Wegerer added, 'is hereby fully validated'.[124] In Britain, the Serbophobe travel adventurer and publicist Edith Durham wrote that, although Pašić and his colleagues knew 'the murderers were on their way, they simply sat down and waited to see what would happen, and by this inaction became accomplices to the plot'.[125] In the United States, the historian Sidney Fay concluded much the same: 'From this it appears that members of the Serbian Cabinet knew of the plot a month or so before the murder took place, but took no effective measures to prevent it. The Serbian Government was thus criminally negligent, to say the least.'[126] Luigi Albertini wrote that 'Ljuba Jovanović spoke the truth in disclosing that Pašić knew of the plot'.[127] More recently, citing Jovanović's 'most eloquent testimony', Christopher Clark has considered it as 'virtually certain' that Pašić knew about the plot 'in some detail'.[128]

But how much detail did Pašić really have? The crucial evidential document here is a report that reached the Government in Belgrade some time in June. As recounted in the previous chapter, the man who led Princip and Grabež to Veljko Čubrilović, the teacher in Priboj near Tuzla, was Jakov Milović, a peasant and a courier for the *Narodna Odbrana*. He subsequently talked about it to Boža Milanović, his *Narodna Odbrana* boss in Šabac, Serbia, close to the border with Bosnia. Milanović, obviously alarmed, then notified Belgrade, but it is not clear when exactly. Vladimir Dedijer, who has provided an exhaustive analysis of this episode, suggests that the report on the matter (undated and unsigned) was written on 5 June or even a day or two later.[129] Ljuba Jovanović's recollection that Pašić had talked to his cabinet colleagues towards the end of May or the beginning of June would have been based on the old style calendar which, with the thirteen-day difference, places the events he described in the second week of June.

What did the report say? It was not written by Milanović himself, but rather by someone, probably in Belgrade, who had received information from Milanović. The latter had related what Jakov Milović had told him: that two high school students, one of whom was called 'Triša' (presumably Trifko Grabež) had on 2 June been led by Milović to Veljko Čubrilović in Priboj, from where they were meant to be taken to 'M.J.' (presumably Miško Jovanović) in Tuzla and on to Sarajevo; that the students carried six bombs and four revolvers; and that he, Milović, did not know the purpose of their mission. According to Dedijer, there can be no doubt about the authenticity of the document, especially because there also exists a handwritten short note (five lines, undated) by Pašić, which contains short excerpts based both on the report itself and on what must have been a running commentary by his associates as they studied the report. Thus

Pašić's note contains the name 'Triša' (Trifko Grabež), but also 'Tankosić' – whose name does not otherwise figure in the report.[130]

Princip was not mentioned in any way nor, more importantly, was Franz Ferdinand. The fact that Pašić had jotted down Tankosić's name is ascribed by Dedijer to the suggestion that Pašić must have heard from someone about Jakov Milović being a confidant of both the *Narodna Odbrana* and of Major Tankosić. Yet, despite Tankosić's name, so closely associated with mischief and the Black Hand, Pašić had very little to proceed on. Ljuba Jovanović was in his memoir embellishing the level of detail concerning the plot available to the Prime Minister. The identity of the students was by no means clear, nor was that of 'M.J.' in Tuzla. Pašić had undoubtedly conferred with his colleagues, and in his memoir Ljuba Jovanović connected this with the Prime Minister's concern that 'there were people who were preparing to go to Sarajevo to kill Francis Ferdinand, who was to go there to be solemnly received on *Vidov Dan*'. But some of this was Jovanović's *ex post facto* construction: as will be seen, the assassins themselves had no idea, to begin with, on which day they were going to attempt the assassination of the Archduke – so how could Pašić know? The itinerary of the Archduke's visit was not published until shortly before his arrival in Bosnia-Herzegovina.

Vladimir Dedijer considers that, in writing down excerpts from what he had heard about the crossing into Bosnia of two armed youths, Pašić showed that he was taking the matter 'seriously'. Just how seriously, however, remains open to question. Ljuba Jovanović admitted after the war that Pašić had brought up the subject outside, not inside, the cabinet forum.[131] Vladimir Ćorović, one of the most authoritative Serbian historians, is sceptical about Jovanović's claims and draws attention to the fact that Velizar Janković, the Economy Minister, was happily travelling in Austria-Hungary on the day of the Sarajevo assassination with his entire family.[132] Ćorović also points to a consideration which he believes must have been important at the time: that had the Serbian Government warned Vienna with some vague information, this could have been interpreted as an attempt by Serbia to prevent Franz Ferdinand's visit to Bosnia. A government, Ćorović argues, can only warn about such matters if it possesses credible intelligence about certain persons and preparations – which the Serbian Government did not possess.[133] Discussing this very issue in the 1920s, the German historian Hermann Kantorowicz suggested much the same political consideration: unless a government is on the friendliest of terms with another government, it cannot possibly tell it that its future head of state had better take care not to show himself before his own subjects.[134]

In a sense, there was little new about Milanović's information. This was exactly the period – June 1914 – when similar reports from the border with

Bosnia were arriving in Belgrade. Thus Kosta Tucaković, the Prefect of the Šabac region, notified Protić on 4 June that he had received a report about a planned attempt by frontier officers to send 'bombs and weapons' to Bosnia. Protić reacted immediately with orders that this be prevented. Pašić minuted that the War Minister be notified to stop 'every such activity because it is very dangerous for us'.[135] The War Minister Stefanović intervened on 14 June, demanding a detailed investigation.[136] But Putnik, the Chief of General Staff, claimed on 18 June that he knew nothing about weapons transfers to Bosnia.[137] It can only be speculated what members of the Government privately thought, especially because the name of Rade Malobabić figured prominently in some of the reporting from the border areas. He was supposed to have been the recipient of the weapons from Serbia referred to by Tucaković. But Malobabić, a Serb from Croatia and Apis's chief operative across the border, was strongly suspected by the Government of being an Austro-Hungarian spy. The memory of Nastić was still fresh. From Šabac, Tucaković wrote that Malobabić was known for his links with the Austro-Hungarian military authorities and that there could be 'new affairs *à la* Nastić'.[138] In June 1917 Malobabić was executed at Salonika together with Apis.

Apis himself was forced by Pašić to make a statement.[139] On 21 June he submitted a report to Putnik, vigorously defending Malobabić. He disputed that any weapons were being sent to Bosnia for the purpose of arming the local population, but admitted that he had, at Malobabić's suggestion, agreed to send four revolvers for couriers and confidants, i.e., non-assassins, to use in self-defence. It transpired later that these were indeed revolvers, the Russian Nagant M1895, not the Browning pistols that Tankosić had supplied to the Sarajevo assassins. But Apis denied any knowledge of a transfer of bombs.[140] Dissatisfied, Pašić ordered the War Minister to proceed with an investigation. This was then duly undertaken by Colonel Stanko Cvetković, but his report has never been found.[141] What this episode shows, at any rate, is the sensitivity and even dismay of the Pašić Government that couriers used for routine operations by Serbian military intelligence in Austria-Hungary should be armed.

In other words, only days before the Sarajevo assassination the Serbian Prime Minister was trying to get to the bottom of various disturbing reports emanating from the Serbian civilian authorities in the area adjoining Bosnia. In part, those reports reflected the tensions in civil-military relations which had culminated in Protić's Priority Decree and which had just brought Serbia to the brink of a bloody civil war. Indeed, Pašić was in May-June 1914 so preoccupied with staying in power and beating the challenge from the military that it is a wonder he could still find time to deal with weapons smuggling issues. He certainly possessed bits and pieces of information that suggested some kind of roguish conduct by the officers, but this was far from having a clear picture of an assassination plot. Pašić therefore did not warn Vienna because he himself was fundamentally in the dark as to what was going on.[142]

The Serbian Warning to Vienna

Who, then, warned Vienna? In June 1924, in a letter to *Neues Wiener Tagblatt*, the Serbian Minister in Vienna Jovanović gave his account of the June 1914 meeting ('around 5 June') with Biliński which, he wrote, 'arose from my initiative'. He told the Joint Finance Minister about his concern that the projected manoeuvres would take place on the Drina river, right across from Serbia, and that they would be directed by Franz Ferdinand. 'If this is true', Jovanović said, 'I can assure Your Excellency that it will cause the greatest unrest among the Serbs who would have to consider it as an act of provocation. Under such circumstances the manoeuvres are dangerous. Among the Serbian youths there could be someone who could put a live cartridge in his rifle or in his revolver instead of a blank one and then fire it. And this bullet could strike the provocateur [*Herausforderer*].' Jovanović therefore advised that the Archduke should not go to Sarajevo. Biliński responded that he 'took note' of those words and would notify Jovanović what effect his intervention was going to have on the Archduke, although he himself did not think that the manoeuvres could have the kind of effect envisaged by the Serbian Minister. His information was that the Serbs in Bosnia were 'perfectly calm'.[143]

Further details about the Biliński-Jovanović meeting are discussed below. Its most controversial aspect, however, should be pointed out straight away: those historians pronouncing the Serbian Government complicit in the Sarajevo assassination have understandably claimed it to have been Pašić who had acted to warn Vienna through Jovanović, claiming also that he would not subsequently admit it for fear of revealing his and his government's knowledge of the plot. Pre-eminent among such historians was of course the relentless Albertini who considered it 'practically certain' that Pašić had initiated the contact with Biliński. One of the major pieces of evidence submitted by Albertini is a note (dated 1 July 1914) by Abel Ferry, the Under Secretary at Quai d'Orsay, concerning his conversation with Milenko Vesnić, the Serbian Minister in Paris. In the note Ferry reported Vesnić as saying that the Serbian Government 'had actually warned the Austrian Government that it had got wind of the plot'.[144] Albertini's implication is that Vesnić knew about the warning because he was presumably reading some confidential telegrams from the Serbian Foreign Office. Christopher Clark has recently re-launched the story, apparently independently of Albertini, as he does not acknowledge him, declaring Ferry and his note the 'most unimpeachable source' regarding the Serbian warning to Vienna.[145]

Neither Albertini nor Clark appear to have considered, or even known about, the newspaper reporting at the time. In its morning edition of 29 June 1914 the Budapest German-language daily *Pester Lloyd* carried a piece of news from Vienna, dated 28 June. 'Rumours are being spread here', it reported, 'that the Serbian Minister at the Court in Vienna had some days ago warned against the trip to Bosnia by the Heir to the Throne, invoking information received from the Serbian Government.'[146] In other words, the whole of Vienna was talking about Jovanović and his warning only hours after the Archduke and his wife had been killed in Sarajevo – and days before Ferry had his *tête à tête* with Vesnić. But who was the source of the reports? No doubt Biliński was busy on the telephone already in the afternoon hours of Sunday 28 June, telling his officials in the Joint Finance Ministry to spread the word worldwide that the Austro-Hungarian Government had been warned in advance. This was the best way to counter the expected avalanche of charges against his Ministry given that it was formally in charge of Bosnia-Herzegovina. Responsibility for the disastrous archducal visit, which had proceeded despite the warning, could thus be spread to embrace the highest levels of the Habsburg state: Franz Ferdinand himself, possibly the Emperor, and certainly Berchtold and his Ballhausplatz. And no doubt, too, Biliński sincerely believed that Jovanović had come to see him on behalf of the Serbian Government – anything else would hardly have made any sense. Hence the reference in the *Pester Lloyd* report to 'information received from the Serbian Government'.

Similar reports appeared elsewhere in the world press on 29 June and so these rumours had already become common knowledge before Vesnić had his conversation with Ferry.[147] Vesnić, unlike Albertini and Clark, would certainly have been aware of those reports coming from Austria-Hungary. And so would Miroslav Spalajković, the Serbian Minister at St Petersburg who, according to Seton-Watson, either 'on 30 June or 1 July' gave an interview to *Novoye Vremya*, also suggesting that there had been a warning to Vienna.[148] But there is no evidence whatsoever that those two diplomats had read anything other than articles appearing in the press on 29 and 30 June. At a difficult moment for their country, when the whole of the Austro-Hungarian press was otherwise already in full swing calling for revenge against Serbia, they felt compelled to make statements on the basis of hearsay – critically, however, this hearsay had emanated in Vienna itself.

The proof that Serbian diplomacy was in this instance acting without instructions from Belgrade can be found in the telegram, dated 30 June, to the Foreign Ministry in Belgrade from Milan Vl. Đorđević, the Serbian Chargé d'Affaires at Constantinople. Đorđević reported: 'All our friends in the embassies of Powers favourably inclined towards us were gladdened by the news that Mr Jovanović, our Minister in Vienna, notified the Austrian Government in timely fashion about the dangers facing the Heir to the Throne if he went to Bosnia, and that he advised vigorously that he should not go there.' Đorđević then continued: 'I do not know whether that news is correct, but I acted everywhere as if I believed in its accuracy and I myself propagated it.'[149] Vesnić and Spalajković, at their own diplomatic posts, had clearly also been doing the same on the basis of the same press reporting. Đorđević's telegram alone proves that, as far as the warning was concerned, there had been no guidance from the Serbian Ministry for Foreign Affairs to its diplomats following the assassination, and for a very good reason: the Pašić Government could not have issued a warning as it was a mere spectator of events.

Back in Belgrade, Pašić himself was not a little puzzled. He sent a brief telegram to Jovanović in Vienna on 4 July: 'Some foreign newspapers have reported that before the assassination you had drawn to the attention of the Austro-Hungarian Government the dangers of the Sarajevo trip. Please let me know by dispatch what in fact is the case.'[150] But Jovanović, in his reply that same day, was extremely evasive and even specious. He wrote only that he had at the end of May talked to 'some Ambassadors and circles close to the Government', telling them that the manoeuvres scheduled in Bosnia seemed like 'a demonstration against the Serbs' and that this would cause 'bother [*uzbuđenje*]' in Serbia given that the Albanians were in a state of anarchy at the time and there were rumours that Austria-Hungary would occupy Albania.[151] Thus Jovanović did not even tell Pašić the most basic fact that he had seen Biliński. On 7 July the Serbian Prime Minister denied in the Budapest paper *Az Est* that a warning had been sent to the Austro-Hungarian Government.[152] The reasons for Jovanović's obfuscation to Pašić shall be examined later in this chapter.

Returning to the subject of the Biliński-Jovanović meeting itself: the historiography of Sarajevo 1914 has consistently asserted that Jovanović's counsel against the archducal visit was somewhat vague. Only recently, Samuel Williamson has suggested that the warning to Biliński 'was so obscure that the Habsburg official did not grasp the full import of the communication'.[153] Jovanović's words, T.G. Otte believes, 'were deliberately Delphic, and scarcely constituted a clear warning'. According to this historian, the whole purpose of the visit to Biliński was to make Franz Ferdinand abandon the Bosnian trip so as to provide further evidence of the Dual Monarchy's decay.[154] However, the warning was in fact quite clear and, coming from the Serbian Minister, a startling tip-off: he had left nothing to imagination about whom a live cartridge might strike and had explicitly recommended that the Archduke should therefore not go to Sarajevo. The simple fact that Jovanović was in Vienna as Serbia's official representative could not have left any Habsburg bureaucrat indifferent to his words of caution. Biliński, indeed, does appear to have taken immediate action, despite later suggestions to the contrary. One such is by Christopher

Clark, who writes that it was 'clear' that Biliński had not taken the warning seriously because 'it was couched in such general terms', and so he did not pass the message to Berchtold.[155] Gordon Martel maintains with similar assurance that Biliński decided not to pass on the warning.[156] The confidence is thus great amongst historians that the Joint Finance Minister had taken no action. Where does it come from? Much of it rests on what Paul Flandrak, the head of the press bureau at the Joint Finance Ministry who had been told about the meeting (having not been present at the meeting himself), wrote in 1925 for *Neues Wiener Journal*: 'I believe that he [Biliński] did not even inform Count Berchtold'. This 1925 speculation by him, widely publicized subsequently, has misled many writers, who used it out of context. In the continuation of the same sentence Flandrak told his readers that Biliński would otherwise report to Berchtold 'about all his meetings with the Serbian Minister'. Flandrak, moreover, opined that Biliński must have, 'deep in his heart' even agreed with Jovanović about the danger to Franz Ferdinand.[157]

Why on earth, then, should Biliński have remained passive in this particular instance, as Flandrak hypothesized? Biliński himself denied in his memoirs that he had ever warned Franz Joseph as he, Biliński, had no competences to interfere in the strictly military visit being undertaken by Archduke Franz Ferdinand.[158] But this is a ridiculous claim: information coming from Serbia's official representative in Vienna that the Archduke's life was possibly in danger would have nullified any such bureaucratic considerations. Implicitly, moreover, Biliński thus acknowledged in his memoirs that he had indeed received a warning. As has been seen above from Jovanović's 1924 letter in *Neues Wiener Tagblatt*, Biliński had promised him he would act. Indeed, towards the end of his letter Jovanović wrote that a few days after meeting Biliński he visited him again (no exact date was supplied) with regard to the same issue, and learned that the original archducal programme would be maintained and that nothing would be changed – 'despite my warning'. Franz Ferdinand, Jovanović observed, 'listened only to himself'. It seemed to the Serbian Minister that his warning, instead of making the Archduke waver, 'only confirmed' him in his decision to take part in the manoeuvres.[159] Clearly, Jovanović was relating his impressions here on the basis of what Biliński must have told him.

It is certain, however, that the Joint Finance Minister, viewed with hostility by Franz Ferdinand, had not gone directly to him after hearing Jovanović's warning – the only audience the Archduke had ever granted Biliński was in 1912.[160] The point, however, is that Biliński had evidently acted after meeting Jovanović on 5 June – he had passed on his information and then been told, as he in turn told Jovanović, that there would be no change so far as the visit was concerned. What will probably forever remain a mystery is the exact address to which the Joint Finance Minister had turned in between the two meetings he had with Jovanović on the matter.[161] But there can be no doubt that Biliński would have immediately taken some action. In any case, it is unimaginable that he would not have reported further on his extra-ordinary meeting with the Serbian Minister. As Biliński's trusted colleague in the Finance Ministry Božo Čerović revealed in 1929, it was actually Biliński's job to maintain contacts with Jovanović – at the request of Foreign Minister Berchtold and with Franz Joseph's knowledge.[162]

Flandrak's public conjecture in 1925 – about what Biliński may or may not have done following Jovanović's visit – was in subsequent years blatantly co-opted to favour the Austrian side of the story concerning the origins of the war. It should be remembered that in 1925, when Flandrak chose to present his perspectives, the controversy over the 'war guilt' question was in full swing: already in July 1923 the Germans had launched their *Kriegsschuldfrage* revisionist journal, a publication with a wide international readership. In 1973 the same Flandrak was still alive. Interestingly, in that year he chose to relate to the Austrian writer Hellmut Andics a more credible version of the famous meeting. In contrast to his earlier exposition which had so influenced perceptions of the July crisis, Flandrak now gave what amounted to a personal confession and a professional admission. 'Flandrak confirmed', Andics noted, 'that the Serbian Minister's warning had been taken altogether seriously' in the Finance Ministry (*'durchaus ernst genommen wurde'*). Flandrak additionally 'confirmed the dispatch of the letter from Biliński to Berchtold, which the Foreign Minister did not mention later.'[163] The letter in question concerned, of course, Jovanović's warning. This particular testimony by Flandrak sets the historical record straight, making it clear that the Austro-Hungarian Foreign Ministry knew of Serbian unease at the proposed archducal trip to Bosnia-Herzegovina – and failed to act. The Austrian historian Glaise-Horstenau even wrote in a 1924 newspaper article (which historiography has largely ignored) that 'various indications' existed to the effect that Biliński had not gone to Berchtold after meeting Jovanović, but passed the information 'directly to Kaiser Franz Joseph'.[164] It is extremely doubtful, however, that Archduke Franz Ferdinand ever found out about any of this. The Ballhausplatz predictably denied, on 1 July, that a warning had been issued.[165] In this, at least, Austria-Hungary and Serbia had a common position.

If, on the other hand, as seems far more likely, the Ballhausplatz and possibly the Emperor himself knew about the warning, then questions arise about their responsibility for the death of the Heir to the Throne. Assuming that it existed in such quarters, the information about Jovanović's warning would also have been shared with Conrad in his capacity as the Chief of the General Staff. Of course, conjectural shots in the dark by historians are always based only on fragments of evidence, but such fragments can be rather compelling. For example, Professor John Röhl, the great authority on Kaiser Wilhelm II, has been repeatedly stating, at least since 1995, that the German military may have had foreknowledge of the Sarajevo assassination plot: 'Indeed it is not impossible', he wrote in 2007, 'that some of the Army leaders had wind of the planned outrage before the event.' He has based his carefully worded suggestions to that effect on the instruction issued on 16 June 1914 by Georg von Waldersee, the Quartermaster-General of the German General Staff, to the military plenipotentiaries of Bavaria, Saxony and Württemberg to cease all written reporting to their war ministries until further notice.[166] This, needless to say, is an extraordinary little piece of history for anyone interested in the immediate origins of the First World War. Now, if the German generals had indeed got wind of the plot, the bellicose Conrad, who had by this time fallen out with Franz Ferdinand, may well have been their source (and it is difficult to see who else could have been), telling them what he had learned about Jovanović's visit to Biliński. But this, of course, is no more than a hypothesis.

The question, however, remains: on whose behalf, then, had Jovanović really been sticking his neck out when he had gone to the Joint Finance Ministry? The bizarre nature of his intervention has, of course, been noted and commented upon. Bernadotte Schmitt described Jovanović's warning as being 'of a peculiar kind'.[167] Sidney Fay wrote, in the 1930 edition of his major work on the origins of the world war, that it seemed 'strange that he [Jovanović] should take such an important step without authorization or instructions from the Serbian Minister of Foreign Affairs'.[168] This, it might be suggested, was a perfectly appropriate observation: the step taken by the Serbian Minister was more than strange. Jovanović's claims that he was using his own initiative led Fay to ask the logical question: 'If he really acted on his own initiative ... why did he wait until the beginning of June?' Fay pointed out that the announcement of the archducal trip had been made already in March. And so this American historian concluded, long before Albertini, that Jovanović had acted on instructions from Belgrade.[169]

There is reason to believe that those instructions had indeed come from Belgrade – but clearly not from the civilian administration of Pašić. From which source, then, did this key intelligence emanate? This source must have been so credible as to impel Jovanović to act immediately on this information at the highest level in Vienna, while hiding from his own Prime Minister the fact that he had acted in his formal capacity with the Habsburg Government. Clearly, Jovanović wanted to avoid the embarrassment of being quizzed by Pašić as to the source of his warning (and his mandate to warn Vienna in the name of the Serbian Government).

The logical conclusion can only be that the source of the intelligence was an important enemy of Pašić (outside the government) who was simultaneously a credible major player in Belgrade's intelligence community; and moreover, one who had access to Jovanović. This description points unerringly to the head of Serbia's military intelligence: Lieutenant-Colonel Dragutin Dimitrijević Apis.

How so? With no direct evidence available, dates are very important here. Princip, Grabež and Čabrinović left Belgrade on 28 May. The first two youths, laden with with four pistols and six bombs, crossed into Bosnia during the night of 1-2 June, while Pašić was surely meditating on his government's resignation which he submitted the following morning. Meanwhile, Apis was preparing his putsch in Macedonia, to be followed by one in Serbia. He would have been notified almost immediately by his agents on the border about the crossing of some armed youths. At some point after 2 June, perhaps even on that same day, Apis, using the information he had to hand, would have have sent a man by train from Belgrade to Vienna to alert his friend: Minister Jovan Jovanović. The latter saw Biliński on 5 June or so (he wrote 'around 5 June'). In his dismay at this interruption to his own plans, Apis thus made an attempt to stop the Archduke from even coming to Bosnia in the first place. Jovanović was the obvious, indeed the perfect man for the job.

Apart from the fact of their friendship, not a great deal is known about the relationship between Apis and Jovanović. It is not inconceivable that Jovanović was a member of Apis's Black Hand, especially as he seemed to like backdoor activities, being for example identified as a Freemason in a recent Austrian collection of documents.[170] Early in 1912, when Jovanović was Secretary-General in Serbia's Foreign Ministry, the Italian Minister in Belgrade Nobile Baroli questioned him about the Black Hand organization. Jovanović talked about it 'in such a positive way' that Baroli gained 'the firm belief' that the Secretary-General himself belonged to it or at least maintained relations with it.[171] Be that as it may, Jovanović was in June 1914, when Apis was busy trying to bring down the Pašić government, the candidate of the Black Hand, that is of Apis, for the post of Foreign Minister. According to Léon Descos, the French Minister in Belgrade, Jovanović was 'the diplomatist it [the Black Hand] trusts'.[172] A major biography of King Aleksandar Karađorđević has also suggested that Jovanović's name had been put forward by the Black Hand.[173] A recent study of the 1914 civil-military conflict in Serbia states more precisely that the Black Hand proposed Jovanović for the post of Foreign Minister after Pašić's resignation on 2 June.[174] Vasa Kazimirović, Serbia's leading expert on the Black Hand, wrote that Jovanović was 'close' to the Black Hand.[175] Jovanović and the Black Hand had already worked together, before the First Balkan War, over the question of winning the cooperation of the Albanians.[176] In 1978 Vladimir Dedijer wrote that relations between Pašić and Jovanović were 'strained' in 1914, and that the latter had had 'some links' with members of the Black Hand.[177]

It would appear that those links were very solid indeed. They would certainly have facilitated communication between Jovanović and Apis. But in his postwar recollections about what exactly preceded his meeting with Biliński, Jovanović was careful not to publicly reveal anything ticklish. In a lecture that he gave in Belgrade in 1926, he emphasized repeatedly that everywhere, in Belgrade and in Vienna, in Sarajevo, Budapest and Zagreb, there was 'whispering and talk' about what might happen in Bosnia when the Archduke went there. Referring to himself in the third person, he stated: 'Such rumours about it [the archducal visit] also reached the Minister in Vienna, and so the step taken by the Serbian Minister Jovanović with regard to the Joint Finance Minister Biliński took the form of a friendly warning rather than a note, but still a timely warning.'[178] Yet only a year or so earlier, in a private letter to Robert Seton-Watson, Jovanović himself provided a most important clue that he had received information and instruction from Apis. In this letter he did not mention any whispers or rumours – on the contrary. Referring to himself in the third person, as was, it seems, his custom, he wrote to the British historian: 'Jovanović had to know something in the capacity of the Serbian Minister when he went to see Biliński to inform him about such an important matter.'[179]

In other words, no hearsay, no rumours, no gossip and no whispers made Jovanović go to Biliński, for to do so Minister Jovanović *had to know something*. And since, as has been seen, he did not ascertain anything from Pašić, it is reasonable to conclude that the only other person capable of enlightening him about such a confidential matter was no less a person than Lieutenant-Colonel Dimitrijević Apis. It is the ultimate irony of the entire historiography of Sarajevo 1914 that this fairly obvious explanation for the warning to Vienna has never even been hinted at: namely, that Apis, the man so widely seen as the architect of the Sarajevo assassination, was the man who had actually taken measures in Vienna to try to prevent it.

All of Jovanović's postwar writings and pronouncements on the subject were designed in part to disguise the embarrassing fact that Apis had alerted him. Jovanović, therefore, was not obscuring the non-existent warning from Pašić – he was concealing his own foreknowledge about the planned Sarajevo assassination. For in the postwar circumstances when Serbia's role in 1914 had begun to look increasingly controversial, it would have been rather inconvenient both for himself and for his country to reveal such knowledge. Already in 1923 Stanoje Stanojević's booklet, a by-product of Serbian politics and mutual recriminations following the Salonika trial, had saddled Apis with the role of the begetter of Sarajevo. And Jovanović, who knew better, felt the need to defend the man, but without compromising himself. So in that 1926 lecture, he made a very explicit point that Apis and Pašić would never have contemplated or approved the assassination of Franz Ferdinand. What is interesting here is not only his placing of Apis ahead of Pašić in the hierarchy of importance in 1914, but also his implication that Apis was equal to Pašić in soberly and responsibly appraising the position of Serbia. 'Was it really the case', Jovanović asked, 'that the then Chief of the Intelligence Section of the General Staff, as well as the head of the Serbian Government, could not possibly be aware of the effect of such an action? It would be clear even to a child that such an assassination, successful or unsuccessful, would mean war between Serbia and Austria-Hungary.'[180]

13

The Secrets of Konopischt

Succession Fever in the Belvedere

IT IS CLEAR that, in the weeks before he set out on his journey to Bosnia-Herzegovina, Franz Ferdinand had expected to become Emperor fairly soon. Such anticipation was not unreasonable. In April, Franz Joseph's serious pneumonia condition had caused widespread concern both at home and abroad. His nephew had indeed been preparing to ascend the throne for some time. In 1910, when he first met Heinrich Lammasch, his constitutional adviser, he would speak about the Emperor's demise in terms of 'what God may prevent for as long as possible', or 'when the misfortune arrives'. To Lammasch it was obvious that such 'empty phrases' were not seriously meant by the Archduke, who later dropped them. Recalling further a conversation with Colonel Brosch, in which the latter had cited the Hofburg doctor Professor Neusser, Lammasch also related that medical opinion in 1910-1911 gave Franz Joseph one or two years at most.[1]

The Emperor did eventually recover from his illness, but in the light of his advanced age in 1914 (he being in his eighty-fourth year) the outlook was justifiably pessimistic. On learning of his uncle's poor health, Franz Ferdinand reacted immediately. The 'workshop', as Milan Hodža called the Belvedere circle of associates and advisers, was 'hurriedly summoned to meet and to prepare all details of procedure and action'. Members of the group drafted and revised texts of a manifesto, and also worked on the wording of an appropriate Bosnian title for the next Emperor. He was to be 'König und Herr von Bosnien und Herzegovina'.[2] Early in May Franz Ferdinand's friend Count Adalbert Sternberg told Josef Redlich that Franz Joseph's days were 'numbered', and that the Archduke had long ago completed his plans for the succession, but kept them secret.[3] In mid-May Paul Samassa revealed to Redlich that various drafts of these were held by Baron Johann Eichhoff. The plan was, according to Samassa, to cancel Franz Ferdinand's crowning in Hungary, replacing it instead with the imposition (*Oktroyierung*) of universal suffrage on the country.[4] This, certainly, was very much in line with the Brosch-Lammasch

Thronwechsel assumptions elaborated in 1911, as discussed above in chapter two.

On 28 May Hans Schlitter noted in his diary that Franz Joseph was 'furious' with Franz Ferdinand because the latter had already begun to behave as the supreme commander during the Emperor's illness.[5] Further evidence of the take-over fever in those days is provided by Andreas von Morsey in the unpublished sections of his memoir. The young Morsey was Franz Ferdinand's *Dienstkämmerer*, a kind of all-purpose personal secretary and equerry. An employee at the *Staatsarchiv* in Vienna, he had been allocated to Franz Ferdinand's office at the beginning of 1914. On 20 June the Archduke and his entourage moved from Konopischt to his estate in Chlumetz (Chlumec) east of Prague where they expected, on 23 June, the arrival of Russia's Grand Duke Cyril. This was to be a secret visit. According to Morsey, the Belvedere had received reliable information about the Russians indicating their wish to move closer to an Austria under Franz Ferdinand; such a rapprochement was for them out of the question while Franz Joseph still lived (because of memories stretching back to the Crimean War), but they had nothing against the person of Franz Ferdinand. 'At this time the old Emperor was dangerously ill', Mosley wrote, 'a calamity was not impossible, and this placed Cyril's arrival in a special light.' The Grand Duke never arrived, however, and there was speculation in Franz Ferdinand's circle that the visit might have been stopped by an intrigue from Berlin or by the Pan-Slavists in Russia.[6]

Be that as it may, Franz Ferdinand was showing every sign of anticipating a speedy accession, wondering aloud how Karl, Otto's son, would manage as his *Thronfolger*, and telling Morsey that he wanted to get rid of, among others, Prince Montenuovo and Rudolf Sieghart. His special contempt was reserved for the Hungarian Prime Minister István Tisza who, he said, considered himself 'We, by the Grace of God, the uncrowned King of Hungary'. And he raged against his uncle, asking an embarrassed Morsey whether he thought that under Franz Joseph any reform in any area, even a modest reform, was imaginable at all in the 'Great Austrian sense'. The Emperor had, Franz Ferdinand thundered, 'surrendered, step by step, every power anchor [*Machtposition*] of the Dynasty'. The reference to reforms '*in grossösterreichischem Sinne*', together with his concern for the Dynasty, do incidentally provide the last recorded evidence about where Franz Ferdinand stood with regard to his internal restructuring plans for the Empire just before he was killed.[7]

And whereas the old Emperor was not so well at this time, neither was the Heir to the Throne himself – at least not according to some observers. In fact an abundance of reports and rumours exists about the Archduke's worsening state in 1913-1914, but there is little agreement on the cause of his condition. In March and again in April Hans Schlitter was writing in his diary about Franz Ferdinand's renewed suffering from tuberculosis.[8] Early in August 1914 Julius Szeps, editor-in-chief of the semi-official *Fremdenblatt*, told Sir Maurice de Bunsen, the British Ambassador to Vienna, that Franz Ferdinand had had something seriously wrong with his bladder and only one year to live.[9] Henry Wickham Steed, until 1913 the Vienna correspondent of *The Times*, maintained in May of that year that Franz Ferdinand had contracted syphilis twenty years previously, now leading to 'progressive paralysis which is already so far advanced as to cause grave doubt whether the brain is not on the point of being affected'. The historian John W. Boyer has suggested that Steed's information came from Tomáš Masaryk and others.[10] An Austrian study from 1970, hostile to Steed, also named Masaryk as Steed's source on the Archduke's state of health.[11] In 1913 Franz Ferdinand himself told Kristóffy that he was not well and that he feared he would not live to ascend the throne.[12] In his diary entry for 7 May 1914 Josef Redlich made only brief mention of the illness of Emperor Franz Joseph, dwelling instead on the Archduke and the rumours of him as suffering from paralysis. The Senate President Miroslav Ploj told Redlich that for the past year and a half the Archduke had been having 'fits of raging madness' and had nearly strangled a servant. 'It will be a tragedy', Redlich opined, 'when Franz Ferdinand ascends the Throne, but it will not last long.'[13]

Whatever his future, the Heir to the Throne could hardly complain about a surfeit of official engagements before the Bosnian manoeuvres of June 1914 (and the concluding procession through the city of Sarajevo). In mid-April he paid a visit on behalf of Franz Joseph to the Bavarian Court in Munich. Given his reforming intentions he was seen there as an 'interesting puzzle', embodying an almost un-Austrian toughness. Bavaria's Crown Prince Rupprecht was apparently sceptical about the Archduke's chances of bringing about an organic transformation and consolidation of Austria-Hungary. Twenty years earlier Rupprecht had travelled in the south-eastern parts of the Empire. Now he noted in his diary that there was always a lot being said about the Habsburg's state-building formula of *divide et impera*, but so much was being divided in Austria-Hungary that there would be little left for *imperare*.[14]

Early on the morning of 29 April the *Thronfolger* arrived in Budapest to address the Delegations on behalf of the still-recovering Emperor, only to leave the hated Hungarian soil just a few hours later as fast as he could. Such was his aversion to that country that he would lower the curtains in the compartment while his train was travelling through Hungary.[15] In the weeks before he left for Bosnia by far the most important event in Franz Ferdinand's engagements book was his meeting with the German Kaiser, Wilhelm II, which took place at Konopischt over two full days, on 12 and 13 June. Given the assassination in Sarajevo soon thereafter and the world war which followed several weeks later, the meeting has figured considerably on the pages of history. There is enough documentation about it to suggest that even if the assassination had not taken place the Konopischt episode would still have formed an outstanding short chapter in international affairs regarding developments in south-eastern Europe at an important moment: with Russia's Tsar Nicholas expected to visit the Romanian King at Constanza on 14 June.

The Konopischt meeting has in the past been presented as no less than a 'war council' by some and vehemently denied as such by others. Thus in 1925 Robert Seton-Watson described as 'credible' the assumption that, at Konopischt, 'Franz Ferdinand had propounded a scheme for Serbia's overthrow, and that William II had promised Germany's support'.[16] In 1953 Rudolf Kiszling, Franz Ferdinand's deferential biographer, described the whole idea as 'the worst slander'.[17] What is the truth?

A Stroll in the Rose Garden

Much has been made in many accounts of the Konopischt meeting about the informal character of the occasion. Von Jagow, Germany's Foreign Minister in 1914, wrote soon after the war that Franz Ferdinand had invited Wilhelm II to Konopischt because he wanted to show him the rose blooms on his beloved estate – the visit was of a 'purely friendly' nature.[18] Such a view has prevailed to this day. However, Prince Lichnowsky, Germany's Ambassador to London, recorded in his memoirs: 'I do not know whether the plan of an active policy against Serbia had already been decided on at Konopischt.'[19] It seems, at the very least, that he did not think the Konopischt meeting to have been merely about inspecting blooming roses. In his recent work on the Imperial Austrian Army, Richard Bassett also takes a dissenting view when he writes that the horticultural theory about the Konopischt meeting 'simply does not stand up to close scrutiny'.[20]

Certainly, Franz Ferdinand's famous rose garden, on which he had spent a massive amount of money, had been presented in the press as the object of the visit. Yet Paul Nikitsch-Boulles, Franz Ferdinand's secretary, clearly remembered that in June 1914 'not a single rose bloomed in the whole of Konopischt'. Nikitsch-Boulles even spelt out the purpose of the Kaiser's arrival: 'to discuss the important political questions of the day', safely removed from the bustle of a big city and its prying journalists.[21] True, as Morsey recorded, artificial means were used to force the roses to bloom, such as watering them with water warmed to the correct temperature. Morsey also suggested that Grand Admiral Alfred von Tirpitz, accompanying Wilhelm II, had been invited by the Archduke because he was a well-known lover of flowers, especially roses. Yet Tirpitz himself recognized the farcical aspect of whitewashing the rationale for the visit in this way. He could not imagine, he told Morsey jokingly with regard to the inspection of roses, 'what the English would make of it'.[22] Indeed. The Admiral noted a day or so after the visit that Wilhelm II had talked with Franz Ferdinand about the desirability of moving the whole of the German fleet to the Mediterranean where, the Kaiser said to his host, 'united with the Austrians and the Italians we can jointly strike [*schlagen*].'[23] There was, clearly, more to the Konopischt meeting than just a pleasant stroll through the rose garden. 'It is a curious thing', Theodor Wolff noted, 'that neither William II in his *Erinnerungen* nor Admiral von Tirpitz in his big volumes devotes a single syllable to this last visit to Franz Ferdinand's palace.'[24]

At least some of what was discussed at the Bohemian castle can be ascertained from the record in the *Grosse Politik*, Germany's official collection of documents. Carl-Georg von Treutler from the German Foreign Office had been brought along for the trip by the Kaiser, and he subsequently wrote a report (in the form of a private letter to Under-Secretary Arthur Zimmermann), partly on the basis of his own brief attendance during one of the exchanges between Franz Ferdinand and Wilhelm II, and partly on the basis of what the latter chose to relate to him the following morning.[25] Whether Treutler can be seen as a reliable chronicler is very much open to question. In his fragmentary memoirs he claimed that Ottokar Czernin had also been present at Konopischt, and that he had seen Czernin walking with Wilhelm II in front of himself and Franz Ferdinand, who had described Czernin as 'my future minister for foreign affairs'.[26] All of which is rather remarkable because Czernin was at this time at his post in Romania as his telegrams to Vienna from Bucharest-Sinaia dated 12 and 13 June attest.[27]

Be that as it may, according to Treutler's report Franz Ferdinand was sceptical about the Italians, telling the Kaiser that in the long term a relationship with Italy was 'impossible'. He pointed out, for example, that in Albania the Italians were acting in bad faith, with Baron Carlo Aliotti's continued presence in Durazzo being a case in point. Wilhelm II, for his part, tried to put a more positive light on Italy's attachment to the Triple Alliance. The Archduke further fulminated against the Hungarians, describing conditions in Hungary as 'anachronistic and medieval' – ironically perhaps, given the absence of any progressive ideas in his own political outlook. But it was important to Franz Ferdinand that he make his points against Hungary: for the German Kaiser, despite his pro-Romanian line, had taken a liking to the Hungarian Prime Minister Tisza. The two had first met a short time previously, in Vienna on 23 March – and the very fact of this meeting seems to have greatly upset Franz Ferdinand.[28] Indeed, according to Paul Samassa who was closely involved in the Archduke's circle, the Konopischt meeting was all about making sure that the German Kaiser properly understood the situation in Hungary – since the Archduke, when he ascended the Throne, intended to get rid of Tisza.[29] The relevant report in *Grosse Politik* supports this interpretation of the meeting to some extent. Franz Ferdinand described Tisza to the visiting German Emperor as being 'already a dictator' in Hungary, and aiming to become the same in Vienna. What was particularly alarming, he went on, was that Tisza made no secret of his view that a separate Hungarian army was something to be strived for. Wilhelm II, however, interrupted his host to argue that Tisza should not be thrown overboard, for he was an 'energetic' man whose estimable talents should be utilized. Undeterred, the Archduke went on to criticize Tisza's policy of suppressing the Romanians of Hungary at the precise time when it was necessary to cultivate the neighbouring state of Romania, and even asked the Kaiser to instruct the German Ambassador to Vienna to constantly remind the Hungarian Prime Minister about this problem.[30]

This attempt by Franz Ferdinand to get a foreign power to influence the internal affairs of the Habsburg Empire evidences the extent of his impotence with regard to Hungary. But Treutler's report provides strange reading. One would expect to find references in it to Serbia, to the rumours about an impending union between Serbia and Montenegro and, especially, to the speculation about a new, Russian-backed Balkan alliance directed at Austria-Hungary and thus also at Germany. There is none of that in the report although these were all hot topics in June 1914 – at least in Vienna. Most surprising of all, Russia is only mentioned in one sentence. This in itself is proof that the *Grosse Politik* record of what went on at Konopischt is very incomplete. A wider discussion must have taken place. In fact, that single sentence is the concluding one in Treutler's report and also perhaps the most significant: 'In the opinion of the Archduke Russia is not to be feared [*nicht zu fürchten*]; the internal difficulties are too great to allow an aggressive foreign policy to this country.'[31]

Not to be 'feared' in what context? Was Franz Ferdinand, a fortnight before he was killed, contemplating with the German Emperor a war in the Balkan theatre (with, realistically, only Serbia and Montenegro as possible targets) and dismissing the chance of a Russian reaction? Of course, the objection may be raised that something as specific as that should not be inferred from what would have been a perfectly normal and sensible review of the general international situation on the part of Franz Ferdinand and Wilhelm II – during which the position of Russia would inevitably have been discussed. On the other hand, the question of Austro-Hungarian and German designs in the Balkans at this time is a necessary one to raise in the light of what Conrad disclosed about the Konopischt meeting in the fourth volume of his memoirs. On 5 July 1914 he had an audience with Franz Joseph. The Chief of General Staff had come to press for war against Serbia in the wake of the Sarajevo assassination. 'Quite right', Franz Joseph commented, 'but how are we going to wage war if then everybody pounces on us, Russia in particular?' Conrad protested that Germany provided the backing. 'Are you sure of Germany?', the Emperor asked. He then explained that he had asked Franz Ferdinand to clarify at Konopischt with Wilhelm II whether Austria-Hungary could in the future 'unconditionally [*unbedingt*]' reckon with Germany's support. But, according to Franz Joseph, the German Kaiser 'had evaded the question, giving no answer'.[32]

Needless to say, the enquiry about Germany's unconditional support could only have related to support for Vienna's intentions in the Balkans – Austria-Hungary was hardly going to act unilaterally against Italy, let alone Russia. Since 1878 its 'Great Power' radius had not extended beyond South-Eastern Europe. Conrad went back to the office after the audience and informed Colonel Josef Metzger, the head of the Operations Bureau, about his talk with the Emperor. When he came to the point about Franz Joseph's doubts as to whether Germany would come along in the event of a war 'imposed' on Austria-Hungary, Metzger suddenly remembered something important. Interjecting, he said that on the evening of 27 June, at the Ilidža hotel outside Sarajevo, Franz Ferdinand had asserted to him that, at Konopischt, with regard to this particular question the German Kaiser had said: 'If we did not get going [*losgingen*], the situation would get worse.'[33] The implication of German backing, indeed encouragement, of an Austro-Hungarian strike in the Balkans was fairly clear, and a war 'imposed' on Austria-Hungary would have been its war against Serbia.

Why, then, did Franz Joseph tell Conrad on 5 July that Wilhelm II had been evasive at Konopischt about guaranteeing unconditional future support to Austria-Hungary? Either the old Emperor had not been accurately informed by his nephew on what had been said at Konopischt with regard to German support or, much more likely, he wanted to keep Conrad on the leash while awaiting news from the mission he had sent to Berlin to extract a renewed pledge from Germany's Wilhelm II that very day, 5 July. Be that as it may, the records of the Konopischt meeting appear to have been heavily censored or destroyed. Robert Seton-Watson concluded that von Treutler's report 'may be presumed not to be complete'.[34] In 1927 historian Hermann Kantorowicz expressed his incredulity at the idea that, in conversations which had encompassed all issues relating to the Balkans, not a word had been said about Serbia. Ironically, Kantorowicz's work on the question of war guilt was itself suppressed and did not see publication until 1967.[35] Meanwhile, Alfred von Wegerer's postwar claim that von Treutler had written 'an extensive report' was an attempt to convince the world that the talks at Konopischt 'involved neither Serbia, nor were any warlike intentions and plans mentioned'.[36] Yet at the time, Franz Ferdinand told Foreign Minister Count Berchtold soon after the Kaiser had departed that they had 'thoroughly' discussed 'all possible questions' and had in every respect found themselves in full agreement.[37] In fact, when Colonel Bardolff published his memoirs in 1938, he stated, without elaborating, that the German Kaiser and Franz Ferdinand had discussed at Konopischt the Monarchy's relations with Serbia and Montenegro.[38] This makes it even odder that there is no mention of it in the available record.

The evidence stemming from the Konopischt meeting, fragmentary as it is, thus points to the conclusion that three key players (Franz Joseph, Franz Ferdinand and Wilhelm II) were in mid-June 1914 mulling over the scenario of an Austro-Hungarian move against Serbia. Theodor Sosnosky, Franz Ferdinand's biographer, argued rather unconvincingly that Colonel Metzger had on 27 June at Ilidža either 'misunderstood' the Archduke, or that the latter had 'wrongly expressed' himself. Interestingly, however, Sosnosky did not try to dispute that Franz Joseph had asked Franz Ferdinand to quiz Wilhelm II at Konopischt about the kind of support the Monarchy could expect of Germany.[39] Albertini, on the other hand, maintains that Metzger had probably understood correctly, but that the Archduke, who did not believe in the desirability of an attack on Serbia, had not been frank with Franz Joseph. However, Albertini does not address the question of why, at this stage, the Emperor and his nephew would have been interested in ascertaining Wilhelm's position in the first place.[40] Sidney Fay relegates the whole Metzger–Conrad episode to a footnote – merely quoting Conrad, but without even beginning to discuss the implications.[41] Bernadotte Schmitt, by contrast, gives the matter his full attention, considering it as 'evident' that the question of an early strike had been raised at Konopischt.[42] In his 1928 study of the 1914 war guilt, H.W. Wilson wrote that action against Serbia 'must have been examined' by Franz Ferdinand and the German Kaiser, 'but Treutler, in his very incomplete report on the meeting, is entirely silent on the subject.'[43]

Kaiser Wilhelm's Volte Face

Indeed, Conrad's writings indicate that Franz Joseph and Franz Ferdinand had undoubtedly conferred on Balkan issues and decided that Wilhelm II should be sounded out at Konopischt. This step of consulting the ally was necessary in any case: all the more so because Wilhelm II had in the past revealed himself to be a highly inconsistent ally. But Franz Joseph and Franz Ferdinand were now knocking on an open door: Colonel Metzger's talk with Conrad makes it fairly clear that the German Kaiser was at Konopischt even urging a timely action. Hermann Kantorowicz has chronicled the bewildering swings in choice of policy displayed by Wilhelm II when replying to Austria-Hungary's requests that Berlin back its various Balkan entanglements – from his bombastic expressions of *Nibelungentreue* during the Bosnian annexation crisis to his enthusiastic support for the Balkan

League against Turkey. However, the respected German scholar maintained that, from October 1913, the Kaiser adopted a hostile attitude towards Serbia that was still there in July 1914.[44]

Yet this development did not occur as early as October 1913. It may be said that the German Emperor in fact never had any strong feelings about the Serbs – except, possibly, that he could not forgive them for being Slavs. What really concerned him was to ensure that the Serbian Army should not be an opponent in any future war with Russia. Serbia should therefore be tied to the Triple Alliance – by stick or carrot – preferably the latter. So it was that, soon after declaring support for Austria-Hungary in October 1913 at the time of the Albanian imbroglio he was telling Berchtold over a cup of tea at the German Embassy in Vienna that everybody in Serbia, beginning with King Peter, could be had for money. He also suggested Austria-Hungary should provide military training to the Serbs and offer trade privileges. In return, Serbia should be 'submissive' and its troops, which had shown that they were capable, should be placed at the disposal of Austria-Hungary. But if the Serbs refused, Belgrade should be 'bombarded' and held until the will of the Austrian Emperor was fulfilled.[45] According to Tschirschky's report to Bethmann Hollweg on this meeting between Berchtold and Wilhelm II, the latter stated that: 'Austria-Hungary must do everything to establish, if at all possible *à l'amiable*, an economic and political understanding with Serbia, but if that could not be achieved by peaceful means more energetic methods must be employed. Somehow or other Serbia must *in all circumstances* be made to join forces with the Monarchy, particularly in the military sphere; so that *in case of a conflict with Russia* the Monarchy will not have the Serb army against it but on its side.'[46]

And this was not just Wilhelm II advocating an Austro-Serbian rapprochement – it was official German policy. For example, in November 1913 both Behmann Hollweg and Arthur Zimmermann, Under-Secretary at the Foreign Office, were insistently telling the Austro-Hungarian Ambassador in Berlin that it would be to Vienna's great advantage if the differences with Serbia could be somehow ironed out.[47] And it has to be said that the German Emperor himself was consistent in backing such an approach to Serbia. In December 1913, in Munich, he continued on this theme to Ludwig Velics, the Austro-Hungarian Minister in Bavaria. One way or another, Serbia had to be attached to the Monarchy, he said, and then suggested eminently sensible policies: for example major financial investment in Serbia, and opening to the Serbs ('wide open') Austria's academies and institutes, including the leading secondary school in Central Europe, Vienna's Theresianum *Gymnasium*. The Germans, he explained, meaning also the Austrian Germans, could not be unconcerned about whether or not in the event of a conflict (he meant a European war), 'twenty of their divisions' were earmarked to march against South Slavdom.[48]

The Kaiser's position was to change dramatically, however, not very long before the Konopischt meeting. On 23 May he announced to Szögyény, the Austro-Hungarian Ambassador to Berlin, a stunning about-face. Though he considered the establishment of friendly neighbour relations with Serbia 'extremely desirable', he said he fully realized that the attitude of Serbia's Government, and public opinion, was causing Austria-Hungary 'virtually insuperable difficulties' in this regard. Szögyény provided no elaboration in his report to Vienna, and perhaps there was nothing to elaborate. Suddenly, Wilhelm II had adopted a point of view on relations with Serbia practically identical to that held by Berchtold and his mandarins. Only a few weeks earlier, at the beginning of April, he had still insisted that: 'For Serbia a tempting *modus vivendi* with the Dual Monarchy must be found.'[49]

The German Emperor's change of direction was extraordinary, but what is also notable is the curious fact that historiography has paid it no attention whatsoever.[50] After all, the support extended by Germany to Austria-Hungary at the beginning of the July Crisis was to entirely determine its outcome, i.e., a Balkan war leading to a European one, and the importance of Wilhelm's personal role in this cannot be exaggerated. Quite simply, Austria-Hungary would never have declared war on Serbia in 1914 had it not been sure of the support of the German Kaiser and his Government. The question of how and why he had come to view Austro-Serbian relations from the Ballhausplatz perspective is in fact one of the more interesting regarding the immediate origins of the war of 1914. Within some three months, he had transformed himself from an impatient advocate of Austro-Serbian *rapprochement* to a protagonist, early in July, of a confrontation with Serbia. The question of why will probably remain an unresolved one. Certainly, the reasons given by the Kaiser (the attitude of the Serbian Government and Serbian public opinion) could not possibly have played a role, for, as seen in previous chapters, the Serbian Government was at the time at its most conciliatory towards Vienna and, in any case from spring 1914, entirely absorbed with the Army and the Black Hand over the so-called Priority Decree. It is true that Serbian public opinion had always been hostile, but no more so than that of Romania, and nothing had occurred in the spring of 1914 to make it raise its voice in a manner louder than usual.

It is possible, on the other hand, that the Kaiser's new line of thought reflected the influence which István Tisza had recently begun to exert on him. The Hungarian Prime Minister had by all accounts captivated Wilhelm II at their meeting in Vienna on 23 March. Tschirschky wrote two days after the meeting that the Kaiser 'now stands completely under Tisza's impact'. A member of his entourage noted that 'Count Tisza had made an extraordinary impression on His Majesty'. For the first time, according to this report, the Kaiser had heard in Vienna 'a positive programme, instead of complaints and resignation'. In reality, he had been the subject of a highly successful brainwashing operation. What Tisza had done in that meeting was to carefully guide the German Emperor towards the Austro-Hungarian, and more specifically Hungarian, understanding of the Balkans, making sure all the time not to challenge any of his well-known views on the region. The key here was to take into account Wilhelm's soft spot for Romania. Thus Tisza lied shamelessly about progress being made in the talks with the Romanians of Hungary – despite the fact that, as has been seen, those negotiations had already broken down in February. Pursuing his pro-Bulgarian line and knowing what his interlocutor thought about the Bulgarian King, Ferdinand, he stated judiciously that he did not wish to draw the King's person into the debate, but was arguing that the Bulgarians were a 'strong people' whose future had to be reckoned with. Cleverly, he painted a bleak picture of a devious Russian plan for the Balkans: to build up an anti-Austrian grouping of Serbia, Bulgaria and Romania. Whether by guessing or by knowing Wilhelm's view, Tisza additionally asserted what Wilhelm also believed in: that the union of Serbia and Montenegro was 'inevitable'. But here he employed Berchtold's argument that Serbia, as an outpost of Russia, should be kept away from the Adriatic, and if the union did materialize then the Montenegrin littoral should be assigned to Albania. Amazingly, he added that, 'as a compensation to Bulgaria', the latter should be given the Serbian-held districts of Ischtip (Štip) and Kotschana (Kočani) in eastern Macedonia – presumably as a compensation for the enlargement of Albania. For good measure, the Hungarian Prime Minister emphasized that the Balkan policy of the Monarchy had to be conducted in mutual understanding with Romania.[51]

What is surprising is that Wilhelm II bought into this scenario. As noted above, at the beginning of April he was still insisting that a *modus vivendi* be found between Austria-Hungary and Serbia – this was after his meeting with Tisza. He had apparently been upset by what he heard in Vienna from Berchtold and Franz Joseph about not letting Serbia unite with Montenegro even at the price of war. On 5 April, anticipating that Vienna would make such bellicose noises at first and then accept a Serbo-Montenegrin union anyway, with the inevitable loss of prestige, he backed Tisza's suggestion that the Montenegrin coast be allotted to Albania as compensation, arguing that Tisza's 'sensible estimation' should be adopted.[52] Yet the implementation of Tisza's proposals would have meant provoking major trouble in the Balkans anyway – one war or more. For it is inconceivable that Montenegro and Serbia would have stood idly by as some of their territories were grabbed up; and horrendous complications would assuredly have arisen with Italy and Russia, creating an accompanying European diplomatic crisis of the first order. The Kaiser had clearly been mesmerized by Tisza. At their meeting in March he told him that Hungary had every reason to stand fast with '*Germanentum*' against the 'Slavonic tide'. The best way to combat the latter was, he said, 'a German Austria and a Magyar Hungary'.[53] No wonder Tisza was delighted. 'In an East European war', he wrote subsequently, 'we can reckon with almost half of German armed forces.'[54]

Whoever or whatever it was that influenced the German Emperor to consider Austro-Serbian differences as irreconcilable may remain a matter of debate. But there can be little doubt that by the time he arrived in Konopischt to meet Franz Ferdinand he was no longer preaching *rapprochement* between Vienna and Belgrade. It is also important to emphasize that the Kaiser did not fear that Balkan adventures might lead to a European war since, in his view, Russia was still weak. Thus in March 1914 he assured the Austro-Hungarian Ambassador to Berlin that Russia could not think about a war 'for some considerable time [*für geraume Zeit*]'.[55] In October 1913 he had been very specific regarding this length of time, telling Berchtold that one did not need to worry about Russia for the next six years.[56] His Foreign Minister von Jagow was also convinced of this, telling. János Forgách in September 1913 that the power of Russia was 'in every respect overrated'.[57]

Austro-Hungarian statesmen, diplomats and soldiers also thought along such lines. The idea that an opportunity for action against Serbia existed as Russia was still weak was already being expressed at the beginning of 1914 by a person well placed to make such an assessment: Count Friedrich von Szápáry, the Austro-Hungarian Ambassador to St Petersburg. On 17 January, in Vienna, Szápáry talked privately with Hans Schlitter, who noted Szápáry's words in his diary: 'Russia could not wage any war, and we would certainly be able to see the Serbs off.'[58] Only a few weeks earlier, in December 1913, Baron Julius Szilassy, the Austro-Hungarian Minister in Athens, had visited Prime Minister Tisza who told him that 'a war with Serbia was unavoidable, but on account of internal reasons Russia would not and could not intervene under any circumstances.'[59] Franz Ferdinand, evidently, was not isolated in his view about Russia's weakness. It is noteworthy that both Szápáry and Tisza talked about it in the context of envisaging a war against Serbia. This belief that Russia was fragile was in any case widely shared in 1914 at the top of the Austro-Hungarian state. In August 1914, shortly after the war broke out, Biliński maintained that it was wrong to overestimate Russia as its Empire was politically 'in complete disintegration'.[60] Soon after the Sarajevo assassination, Prince Franz von Hohenlohe, the Austro-Hungarian Military Attaché in St Petersburg, told Nicolas de Basily of the Russian Foreign Office: 'Do you understand that you cannot go to war? If you do, you will expose yourself to revolution and to the ruin of your power.'[61] Already in February 1913 Conrad questioned, in a letter to Berchtold, whether an action against Serbia would necessarily involve a Russian intervention.[62]

There may have been an element of wishful thinking in such prognoses and calculations. Yet it cannot be said that either the Kaiser or the Archduke had at Konopischt completely dismissed the danger of a general conflict. A European war had been anticipated by them, though they talked about it in rather hypothetical terms and also differed in their predictions. According to Jaroslav Thun, the German Emperor said: 'If – God forbid – we should ever have a war against France and Russia, then Italy will be with us.' Predictably, Franz Ferdinand commented: 'If – God forbid – we should ever have a war against Russia, then Italy will be *against* us!'[63] One particular scenario leading to a European war was definitely discussed at Konopischt. In the unpublished part of his memoir, Andreas von Morsey relates what he had heard being discussed by the Archduke and his guest: 'As a result of the turmoil in Albania, one feared that there would be a Serbo-Greek attack on Albania, which would then make Bulgaria march and without fail also Romania, leading inevitably to the outbreak of a European conflagration.'[64] Just how this would have worked out to such a culmination is not explained by Morsey, but presumably he meant that Austria-Hungary and Germany would at some stage intervene. It is at least clear that Franz Ferdinand and Wilhelm II had been considering worst-case eventualities.

The Konopischt meeting, Samuel Williamson insisted in 1991, had been 'quite prosaic and humdrum'.[65] Curiously, some historians have been hard at work even quite recently to deny that anything of any importance happened at Konopischt.[66] 'It had all been very innocent', maintains another new book about Franz Ferdinand.[67] However, it is worth noting how Franz Ferdinand's Slovak adviser at the Belvedere, Milan Hodža, recollected Konopischt: 'It was not an improvised exchange of views. Carefully prepared memoranda had been dispatched from Belvedere and Berlin, and were treated on the same level as certain Austro-Hungarian military problems which at that time attracted the attention of Berlin and Vienna.'[68] Baron Eichhoff wrote in 1926 that, two months before the Kaiser's arrival in Konopischt, Franz Ferdinand (staying at Miramare near Trieste at the time) was already busy preparing for the visit.[69] The fact that the Konopischt meeting was no ordinary social get-together of royals is also confirmed in Burián's diary. Burián was at the time Tisza's official representative in Vienna and would make it his business to pry into everything. He recorded (on 17 June) his disappointment at what he saw as the 'very weak' result of the meeting: 'weak interrogation [of Wilhelm II], unsatisfactory answer on Romania and Bulgaria, pussyfooting around'. It would appear that Burián (intensely disliked by Franz Ferdinand) had only heard a watered-down account of the meeting – for if Conrad, who had himself admittedly fallen out of Archducal favour by this time, only found out from Colonel Metzger on 5 July that Wilhelm II had at Konopischt recommended speedy action, there is no reason to suppose that Burián would have been better informed. But his diary observations do at least demonstrate that there had been high expectations surrounding the German Emperor's visit.[70]

Was, then, the mid-June 1914 meeting at a Bohemian castle meant to coordinate sinister plans for war? The thesis that Konopischt was a 'council of war' for a general European conflict is certainly incorrect. Even Professor Fritz Fischer, arch proponent of German guilt for World War One, rejected this thesis about Konopischt. He maintained, however, that 'it is correct as far as the preparations for a war between Austria and Serbia were concerned'.[71] That is to say, for a localised European war. Graydon Tunstall, a noted authority on Austro-Hungarian and German military planning before 1914, notes briefly that the Konopischt meeting was meant 'to reaffirm Germany's unconditional support for Austria-Hungary'.[72] An obvious question arises here: why would Franz Ferdinand, given his known preference for sorting out domestic matters before embarking on an aggressive foreign policy, contemplate a hostile action against Serbia in June 1914? After all, as he so vigorously stated to Berchtold in a letter of 1 February 1913, the first thing was 'to put one's own house in order'. He wanted external peace in order to be able to carry out 'an energetic internal clean-up', and only then 'the time will come to pursue a vigorous foreign policy'.[73] For the Archduke, this concern over domestic affairs meant above all the abolition of Dualism. But the Emperor, after what the Belvedere circle had in spring assumed to be his last days, continued stubbornly to live on. Franz Ferdinand thus had to postpone his showdown with the Hungarians. Would he therefore not oppose rather than support a risky foreign adventure given that nothing had yet changed at home?

As discussed in the foregoing pages, however, by mid-1914 much had changed for the worse in Austria-Hungary's Balkan position. And some impetus for an active Balkan engagement may well have come from Franz Joseph himself rather than his nephew. According to the testimony of Géza von Daruváry who had worked in the Emperor's cabinet, Franz Joseph had since the Balkan War of 1912 become increasingly convinced that it would come to an armed conflict with Serbia.[74] It was seen in a previous chapter that during the October 1913 crisis concerning Serbian troops in Albania he was prepared to go all the way along a military path, and that he even envisaged circumstances in which he himself would initiate a war against Serbia (i.e., that he would not allow a Serbo-Montenegrin union). Certainly, Franz Joseph was by mid-1914 highly concerned about the Balkan situation in general. Burián's diary supplies evidence that he was especially worried about Romania. On 8 June Burián had a long meeting with the Emperor who told him that he had 'lost all confidence in Romania'.[75] His instruction to Franz Ferdinand to investigate with Wilhelm II at Konopischt whether Austria-Hungary could count on Germany reflected these concerns and could only have been related to the idea of a pre-emptive strike.

Some experts, it should be emphasized, have emphatically argued that no Konopischt scheme against Serbia existed in the first place. Thus Samuel Williamson: 'At no point, however, had the archduke and the German Kaiser discussed any military action against Serbia.'[76] But Williamson does not address some relevant points made by József Galántai, the Hungarian historian on whose work he does sometimes rely. In 1979 Galántai published, in German, his book on Austria-Hungary and the World War, an *oeuvre* which stands out because of its mastery of important Hungarian sources. With regard to Konopischt, Galántai notes the position agreed there by Franz Ferdinand and Wilhelm II, whereby 'Austria-Hungary should stand up to Serbia – the sooner, the better – even if that provokes Russia's intervention which Kaiser Wilhelm guaranteed to shield.' And then Galántai continues with reference to the Archduke's well-known fondness for an alliance of the three conservative Empires (Austria-Hungary, Germany, Russia): 'At this time Franz Ferdinand's preferred foreign policy conception had already been shaken, and he no longer believed that a revival of the Three Emperors' League was still relevant to actual situation.'[77] If so, and if the Archduke, as will be seen below, had also come round to the Ballhausplatz (and Hungarian) view that Romania was defecting and that Bulgaria should be cultivated instead, then the idea of crushing Serbia must have become quite appealing to him.

For with one blow the regional strategic picture could be enormously altered to the advantage of Austria-Hungary. Serbia was the military-strategic key to the whole of the Balkans: with Serbia out of the way, Romania's Balkan position would collapse in the face of a revisionist Bulgaria to the south and a Dual Monarchy threatening from the west. And if, as everyone in Vienna and Budapest reckoned, a war with Russia was inevitable at some point, proceeding against Serbia certainly made a great deal of sense in order to secure the all-important south-eastern flank before any such general conflict became reality. Franz Ferdinand's view, expressed to the German Kaiser at Konopischt, that Russia would for the time being remain inactive on account of internal exigencies, underlined the need for timeliness in such bold forward planning. A regional strike at Serbia therefore carried wider geostrategic benefits for Germany and Austria-Hungary in terms of the overall European balance of power.

Wickham Steed on Konopischt

While a historiographical consensus about what took place at Konopischt may never emerge, one particular *vignette* spun about the meeting at the Bohemian castle and relating to the idea of a general war is no longer seriously discussed, as historians generally agree that it rested on pure fiction. The matter in question is a startling article published in 1916 by Henry Wickham Steed, the former Vienna correspondent of *The Times*. Here he quoted information that he had received to the effect that the Kaiser had come to Konopischt proposing a dramatic transformation of Europe after a European war that Germany would begin by provoking Russia: following a German victory, the old Polish state, also comprising Lithuania and the Ukraine, would come to life again – a kingdom for Franz Ferdinand, to be inherited by his eldest son, Maximilian; whereas the Archduke's second son, Ernst, would become the king of a new realm that would include Bohemia, Hungary, most of Austria's Southern Slav lands, Serbia and Salonika. German Austria would come under Archduke's Otto's son, Karl, but it would be, with Trieste, brought into the German Reich – so Germany would become an Adriatic power. This enlarged Germany would enter into a close and perpetual military and economic alliance with the proposed two new states, making the new power constellation 'the arbiter of Europe', commanding the Balkans and the route to the East. Berlin could then at will bring, say, Holland and Belgium, into 'the Great Confederated German Empire'.

Steed presented his information in the context of the parental concern felt by Franz Ferdinand and Sophie for the future position of their children. Whatever scheme that may have entailed for the post-accession period, the second person in line to the Habsburg succession could not be ignored: Karl, born in 1887 to Otto and a certain unfortunate Maria Josepha. In 1911 he married Zita von Bourbon-Parma who in the following year gave birth to their son Franz Josef Otto (later known as Otto von Habsburg) – thus strengthening the legitimate line of succession. This was the background to Steed's sensational wartime account which, he admitted, was merely a 'remarkable hypothesis'. Though he did not suggest in his article that Franz Ferdinand had accepted the Kaiser's proposals, Steed nevertheless christened the episode 'The Pact of Konopisht'.[78]

Quite a few historians have enjoyed attacking Steed, seeing his 1916 article as a piece of wartime propaganda. There was 'not a shred of evidence', thundered Sidney Fay, that the Archduke was plotting at Konopischt. Similarly, Luigi Albertini maintained that Steed's story 'is not authenticated and finds no credence among historians'. Interestingly however, Alfred Dumaine, France's Ambassador to Vienna in 1914, did not question in his memoirs the credibility of Steed's account.[79] In 1916 Robert

Seton-Watson thought that Steed's article was 'extremely important', deserving of 'the most serious consideration', though he was to adopt a more guarded attitude after the war.[80] Bernadotte Schmitt, in his major work on the origins of the war, noted that Steed's account was 'discredited', and yet added: 'But the fact that it is not mentioned in the official reports of the Konopischt conversations proves nothing, as is often asserted to the contrary, for if the two august persons did discuss any such wild scheme as that alleged, they would in all probability keep the secret to themselves.'[81] Steed himself summarized his article again in 1924, revealing that his source had been an Austro-Polish aristocrat and that the Vatican had initially got hold of the sensational Konopischt story via the Papal Nunciature at Vienna. Its contents did not seem inherently impossible to him 'given the semi-madness of the Archduke and the ambitions of the German Emperor'.[82]

It so happens that there now exists some corroboration for Steed's claims about Konopischt. In 2009 the memoirs of Vasily Strandtmann were published for the first time in Serbia after lying neglected for decades at the University of Columbia. Strandtmann was the Russian Chargé d'Affaires in Belgrade in 1914, who had in June that year gone to Venice for a health cure. Much of the diplomatic corps from Rome was also in Venice at that time of the year, and Strandtmann naturally tried to obtain political information from those sources. Intrigued by the news about the visit of Wilhelm II to Konopischt, he mentioned the subject to 'Baroness' Ambrózy (she was in fact a Countess), the wife of Count Ludwig Ambrózy, a counsellor at the Austro-Hungarian Embassy in Rome. Smiling, she told him that the Konopischt meeting had to do with a covert 'plot' against Serbia. Strandtmann allowed himself a show of surprise, whereupon the Countess added that the talk had also been about 'the creation of an independent Poland, as well as about wider plans for a re-composition of Europe, in which there would also be room for Maximilian and Ernst, the sons of Archduke Franz Ferdinand.' Strandtmann concluded this brief paragraph in his memoirs: 'Sensing that her openness had gone too far, my interlocutor added that these were rumours without any foundation since they emanate from people who are very sceptical towards the Duchess of Hohenberg.'[83]

Strandtmann does not give the precise date of the conversation, but it is clear from the context that it took place several days before the assassination in Sarajevo. The casual manner in which he mentions this encounter with the Countess, and the otherwise great depth and reliability of his memoir, remove any grounds to imagine that he might have wanted to fabricate evidence to support Steed's disclosures. If the Konopischt story (as recounted by the Countess and by Steed) indeed originated in circles hostile to Franz Ferdinand's wife, it could demonstrate that those circles were on permanent alert to identify and expose any conniving by the royal couple. However, the significance of Countess Ambrózy's fascinating tittle-tattle, which she had probably gleaned from her diplomat husband, is not whether it authenticates in any way the existence of a plan for Franz Ferdinand's children. Particularly of interest here is that she also talked about some kind of a 'plot' against Serbia concocted at Konopischt – this obviously had nothing to do with any schemes, fantastic or not, on behalf of the children. The latter may indeed have been unfounded rumours generated by the enemies of the Duchess of Hohenberg, but the simultaneous mention of a Konopischt plan regarding Serbia tallies, intriguingly, with the sketchy and yet compelling evidence presented by Conrad.[84]

Wilhelm II was racing in his yacht *Meteor* at Kiel when the news reached him that the Archduke and his wife had been assassinated. Prince Lichnowsky, Germany's Ambassador to London, was staying with Wilhelm II on his yacht on the day of the Sarajevo assassination, and related the Kaiser's reaction to the event: 'His Majesty regretted that his efforts to win the Archduke over to his political ideas had thus been rendered in vain.'[85] Edward Goschen, the British Ambassador to Berlin, was also one of Wilhelm's guests. On Monday 29 June Goschen was at the railway station as the Emperor was departing from Kiel. The Ambassador recorded him in his diary as saying what a 'dreadful blow' the assassination had been to him: 'both because it was only a fortnight ago that he had been staying with them and seen their happy family life – and because it was such an upset of everything they had planned and arranged together.'[86]

The Matscheko Memorandum

The German Kaiser left Konopischt late on 13 June. Just a day later, Foreign Minister Berchtold arrived at the Bohemian castle. Morsey speculates that Berchtold may have been kept away during Wilhelm's stay because the Emperor was supposed to dislike him. But Morsey also gives what was probably a more important reason: Berchtold's presence would have sent alarm signals to the outside world, and one did not wish to 'make Europe twitchy'.[87] The Foreign Minister came accompanied by his wife Nandine. Again, however, this was to be more than a social occasion. True, Berchtold did have the opportunity to inspect the rose garden and look at the Arch-duke's weapons and art collections, but the two men then got down to a 'confidential talk.'[88] This must have been very confidential indeed, because when on 17 June Berchtold talked to Tschirschky, the German Ambassador to Vienna, the latter was told next to nothing about the Konopischt meeting. Franz Ferdinand, Berchtold said, had been 'supremely' satisfied by Wilhelm's visit (*'im höchsten Masse befriedigt über den Besuch'*). But the only matter specifically mentioned by the Foreign Minister, as reported by Tschirschky to Chancellor Bethmann Hollweg in Berlin, was the Archduke's complaint to the Kaiser about Tisza and his treatment of Romanians in Hungary. Significantly, however, Berchtold did say that the royals had 'thoroughly' discussed 'all possible questions', and that they had reached full accord 'in every respect'.[89]

Now, the fact that Berchtold had been briefed by Franz Ferdinand immediately after the meeting with Wilhelm II has been linked by some historians with the genesis of a famous document produced in Vienna on the eve of the July Crisis, named after Franz von Matscheko, the Ballhausplatz mandarin who had drafted it. Following the assassination in Sarajevo the revised version of this so-called 'Matscheko Memorandum', sent to Berlin, became famous as part and parcel of the so-called 'Hoyos Mission' that was to obtain Germany's notorious 'blank cheque' for action against Serbia. It is therefore a paradox that the analyses and recommendations of the original, pre-assassination version of the document, which dealt with issues in the Balkans, are alleged, at times emphatically, to constitute proof of Austria-Hungary's peaceful foreign policy intentions. If for no other reason, therefore, this document requires a detailed examination.

According to Manfried Rauchensteiner, it was Franz Ferdinand who had suggested to Berchtold during the latter's visit to Konopischt that a detailed memorandum be prepared on the Balkan situation, and that this Austrian assessment should then be used for an intensive exchange of views with Berlin. 'The Ballhausplatz', Rauchensteiner writes, 'went to work immediately.'[90] Whether the idea to produce a thorough appraisal of challenges facing Austria-Hungary in South Eastern Europe had indeed come from the Archduke cannot be established with certainty. But given that Franz Ferdinand had just had wide-ranging talks with the Emperor of Germany on precisely that subject, that he had summoned Berchtold to Konopischt immediately thereafter, and that a draft memorandum lay completed in the Ballhausplatz by 24 June, it is entirely feasible that the whole exercise had originated during Berchtold's meeting with Franz Ferdinand on 14 June. Berchtold's biographer Hugo Hantsch implies strongly that this was indeed the case. A memorandum was needed since it was not really certain whether, as Hantsch suggests, the Archduke had managed to educate the Kaiser about 'the importance of Balkan problems for the Monarchy' – problems important also for the alliance between Austria-Hungary and Germany.[91] It is also entirely possible, however, that the Kaiser required no further education or convincing. As Berchtold had made clear to Tschirschky, full accord had been established at Konopischt 'in every respect' and the Archduke had pronounced himself extremely happy about the visit. If so, the Kaiser did not need a Ballhausplatz memorandum, but his advisers presumably did – people like Chancellor

Bethmann Hollweg, and Jagow, the Foreign Secretary – especially if a forward policy in the Balkans had been agreed on at Konopischt. For this reason, it could at Konopischt quite possibly have been Wilhelm II who suggested to Franz Ferdinand that such a memorandum be put together for the benefit of his Government – which could account for Berchtold's presence in Konopischt so soon after the German guests had departed. In other words, complete agreement regarding Balkan policy had yet to be reached. What became known as the 'Matscheko Memorandum' was certainly supposed to lead the way, that is, to convert Berlin's possible sceptics into supporters of Vienna's vision of what needed to be done in the Balkans.

Historiography, however, has pointed out some deeper roots regarding the provenance of the Memorandum. Some scholars have traced it back to Tisza's own '*Denkschrift*' of mid-March 1914. Sidney Fay called this 'Tisza's Peace Program', and A.J.P. Taylor maintained that the Ballhausplatz memorandum of 24 June 1914 'had originated with Tisza'. Fritz Fischer went so far as to assert that the Memorandum handed to the Germans on 5 July had been 'compiled by Tisza'.[92] So what had Tisza been urging? In his analysis of 15 March he attacked the 1913 Peace of Bucharest for having created a situation which could not bring genuine, lasting peace. His concern related primarily to the danger, as he saw it, of Bulgaria coming to terms with Romania, Serbia and Greece – under Russian patronage. This, he argued, would tilt the military balance in Europe and provide the Russian-French combination with the necessary superiority to attack Germany. Europe's centre of gravity should thus be seen as lying in the Balkans, and Germany should understand that the region was of decisive importance to its own interests and not just those of Austria-Hungary. 'The Triple Alliance', Tisza warned, 'could not make a greater fatal error than to push Bulgaria away.' His analysis assumed throughout that Serbia was an enemy. Without offering any concrete proposals to placate Romania, he saw an improvement in relations with the latter only as a consequence of a stronger Austro-German affiliation. The task of Austria-Hungary was to work, together with Germany, on disentangling Romania and Greece from Serbia and getting those two reconciled with Bulgaria, which should be enlarged at Serbia's expense.[93] Implying a war against Serbia, this was hardly a peace programme. Tisza's biographer Gábor Vermes has observed that, although the memorandum did not mention territorial conquest, its goals 'carried serious implications, because they involved reversing dominant trends in the Balkan peninsula'.[94]

As will be seen below, a great deal of Tisza's reasoning would indeed be echoed in the Matscheko Memorandum of 24 June. A further forerunner of Matscheko was undoubtedly the position paper prepared in May by Ludwig von Flotow, a Ballhausplatz expert on the Balkans who had served in Bucharest and Belgrade.[95] Flotow was concerned by a public opinion in Romania increasingly inimical to Austria-Hungary, pointing out that 'in the event of a war with Russia' the Monarchy would not only be unable to count on Romania's help, but would also have to take into account its possible hostility. Like Tisza, Flotow saw a danger of a new, Russian-backed alliance of Balkan states emerging: Romania, Turkey, Greece and Serbia – a grouping aimed against Austria-Hungary, which Bulgaria might have no choice but to join. And, like Tisza, he viewed it as a great menace to the Triple Alliance. What he recommended was a 'clarification' of relations between Vienna and Bucharest, to be achieved through a public acknowledgment by King Carol or his Government that Romania actually had a treaty with the Triple Alliance. Realizing that there would have to be some *quid pro quo* for this, Flotow thought some concessions should then follow to Romania – to be precise, only two. One of them, he suggested, might be a guarantee of its existing border with Bulgaria. Flotow did not explain how this could be sufficiently attractive to Bucharest when the main problem between Austria-Hungary and Romania in fact concerned the position of Romanians in Transylvania. But his other proposed 'concession' was genuinely bizarre. Given the friendly relationship between Romania and Serbia, he pointed out, it could be left to Romania to work for a *rapprochement* between Vienna and Belgrade – in which case Austria-Hungary would demonstrate an accommodating approach towards Serbia. Flotow did not specify, however, what inducements Vienna was ready to offer to Belgrade. In other words, Romania, a country up in arms because of the treatment of its co-nationals in Transylvania, should try and convince Serbia, a country stifled at every turn by Vienna, that the Habsburgs were not so bad after all. Moreover, Bucharest was even supposed to be grateful for being entrusted with such a task.

This absurd game plan for winning over Romania betrayed perhaps the absence of any belief at the Ballhausplatz that anything could still be rescued in relations with that country. Flotow, certainly, had alternative proposals ready in the event that Bucharest did not play along: a diplomatic effort to bring about a Bulgarian-Turkish alliance; then, a drawing in of Bulgaria by treaty, to Austria-Hungary and the Triple Alliance; and, significantly, military fortification works to proceed along the frontier with Romania. There was a note of urgency in Flotow's reflections on the existing Balkan situation. In 'this critical moment', when Russia and France were so intensively at work, all the indicators were pointing towards the destruction of the Monarchy's position, and it would be 'ruinous' to allow such developments to mature through passivity. Flotow also deployed what had at the time already begun to figure as characteristic language with regard to Austria-Hungary's possible involvement in a war, for he wrote about such a war '*in dem wir gezwungen wären*' ('into which we would be forced', or 'which would be imposed on us').[96] Austro-Hungarian diplomatic and military reports from the first half of 1914 are peppered with this kind of virtuous wording.

Interestingly, the Matscheko Memorandum, or rather the famous draft of it that had materialized by 24 June, is based largely on the assumption that a war was approaching between Austria-Hungary and Serbia. The exact opposite interpretation, it should be noted straight away, has been put on the Memorandum by some recognized specialists. According to F.R. Bridge, it 'contained not the slightest hint of war'. What it represented, in Bridge's view, was 'still a long-term policy, an attempt to solve the problem by patient and persevering diplomacy.' Alma Hannig, similarly, sees the Matscheko Memorandum in the context of a consistent Balkan strategy formulated by the Ballhausplatz – a policy 'without any war plans against Serbia'.[97] A closer reading of this rather lengthy document, however, reveals an entirely different picture.[98]

What is strange in the Matscheko Memorandum, with its detailed review of the Balkan situation, is the near-absence of an obvious theme: Serbia. The country which had during the Balkan Wars so obsessed the Habsburg establishment hardly gets a mention. Matscheko considers Serbia only in passing, in the introductory section which draws a balance sheet between positive and negative developments in the region over the previous two years. Serbia, according to Matscheko, stood entirely under Russian influence; its policy had for years been inspired by hostility against Austria-Hungary; and, given the 'general strengthening of the Great Serbian idea', its recent additions of territory and population looked like becoming even greater because of the possibility of a union with Montenegro. That was the sum total of analysis of this dangerous neighbour in the south-east. The implication was that Serbia was an implacable foe – certainly not an object for 'patient and persevering diplomacy'. It seems reasonable to suppose that had a diplomatic approach towards Serbia been on the Habsburg list of options then the Memorandum would have brought this out. The other negatives in Matscheko's audit of assets and liabilities were the practical disappearance of Turkey-in-Europe and, in particular, Romania's shift towards Russia. Echoing Flotow's memorandum, he wondered whether Romania would not, 'in a given moment', act as an enemy rather than as a friend of the Triple Alliance.

On the plus side, according to Matscheko, Albania had been established as an independent state and thus served as a counterweight to Serbia's encroachments. It could even, in time, be included as a 'military factor' in the calculations of the Triple Alliance. Looking at the map of South-Eastern Europe almost as if he was a General Staff officer, Matscheko counted Greece among the positives in his survey, noticing that its gradually improving relations with the Triple Alliance meant the country should not necessarily be seen as 'an adversary [*Gegner*]' despite its alliance with Serbia. Bulgaria, finally, had woken up from its 'Russian hypnosis' and its Government was seeking a closer relationship with the Triple Alliance. On the whole, however, Matscheko saw the situation as 'anything but favourable', and he was anxious to draw attention to Russia and France. Those two Powers, far from satisfied with what they had already achieved in the region, were pursuing an 'aggressive', indeed 'decidedly offensive' policy. Matscheko was also keen to make the point that the only reason why European peace had remained intact in the face of Franco-Russian interferences (*Störungen*) was the military superiority of the Triple Alliance, and in the first place the combination of Austria-Hungary and Germany – for which the alliance with Romania was a highly valuable factor.

Probably borrowing from Tisza's memorandum of 15 March, Matscheko painted Russia as planning to build an alliance of Balkan states by means of which the military superiority of the Triple Alliance would be eliminated. Such an alliance, he insisted, could only be directed against Austria-Hungary. Russia's plan, he believed, was to direct its Balkan coalition westwards. Such a fragile and complicated grouping of states could only be brought about by the expectation of each member that its territorial cravings would be satisfied – e.g., Bulgaria's in Macedonia and Serbia's in Bosnia. Matscheko blithely asserted that Serbia, under Russian pressure, would give up Macedonia to Bulgaria. It should 'not be doubted', Matscheko wrote, that Serbia would 'pay an appropriate price' in Macedonia – on the basis that this sacrifice would bring Bulgaria into a Balkan alliance also directed at the conquest of Bosnia. On this point, it should be noted, Serbia did not yield even in 1915, when the Allies badly wanted to prevent Bulgaria from joining the Central Powers and when their pressure on Belgrade to cede Macedonia was enormous. Matscheko of course knew that his audience was in Berlin and that Kaiser Wilhelm's well-known dislike of the Bulgarian King Ferdinand had to be borne in mind. Hence he emphasized that Russia and France were busy working to diplomatically isolate Bulgaria and thereby make it more receptive to their offers to join their coalition directed against Austria-Hungary and indeed the Triple Alliance. He urged that 'action' be taken to strengthen Bulgaria's 'spine', thus helping it to avoid isolation and resist Russian 'threats and baits'.

The perceived need in Vienna to impress on the Germans the urgency of the Balkan situation is also apparent in Matscheko's treatment of the Romanian issue. Here, he expanded on Flotow's arguments about Romania's essential unreliability: despite King Carol's loyalty to the secret alliance, wide sections of the Romanian Army, intelligentsia and people had been won over to support an anti-Habsburg programme for 'the liberation of brothers beyond the Carpathians', that is to say in Hungary. In the event of 'a Russian attack on the Monarchy', it was 'unthinkable' that Romania would side with Austria-Hungary – at best it offered only neutrality, one which depended entirely on King Carol and his ability to control foreign policy; if an armed conflict with Russia broke out 'now', Russia would hardly need to field a single soldier against Romania, whereas Austria-Hungary could not be sure of Romania's neutrality and would need to fortify the border areas of Transylvania. Matscheko warned, pointedly, that Romania's change of direction threatened not only the security of Austria-Hungary, but also the Triple Alliance system itself (in a 'very sensitive point'), as well as 'the stability of the existing political relationships in Europe'.

All of which sounded more like a study emanating from the Operations Bureau of the Austro-Hungarian Army than a Ballhausplatz assessment of diplomatic hurdles to be overcome. F.R. Bridge's insistence that the Matscheko Memoprandum 'contains not the slightest hint of war' is practically impossible to reconcile with the actual document. Time and again Matscheko argues from the position of 'what if?' – emphasizing that events in the Balkans could at 'anytime [*jederzeit*]' force Austria-Hungary to come up with a response (*Stellungnahme*). And he named such eventualities: tensions between Greece and Turkey, the 'danger' of a union between Serbia and Montenegro, and the critical situation in Albania. The fact that he was contemplating military rather than political responses is evidenced by the following sentence in the Memorandum: 'Such a response [*Stellungnahme*] would however be exceedingly aggravated if the crucial decisions would have to be reached on the basis of a political calculation in which Romania represents an unknown quantity.' That is to say, it would be very difficult for the military to allocate troops to a war in which they did not know whether their Romanian neighbour would be an ally, an enemy, or something in between.

For Matscheko, there was no time to lose. Thus, 'in case of a European war', the Monarchy had to make, 'immediately', military provisions for the defence of the border with Romania. Matscheko demanded, along the lines of Flotow's memorandum, that action be taken, 'without delay', to press Romania to get off the fence and openly declare its allegiance to the Triple Alliance. However, if Romania did not give such guarantees and opted for Russia instead, it was 'urgently necessary' for the Monarchy to assess the military consequences. Explaining that the considerable preparatory period demanded by border fortification works was the reason why the matter was so pressing, Matscheko even attached to his Memorandum a separate document dealing with proposed measures for the military protection of the Transylvanian region – i.e., protection from a Romanian attack.

Indeed, contrary to the claims of F.R. Bridge, there is practically nothing in the Matscheko Memorandum that would indicate a 'long-term' policy direction or demonstrate a commitment to 'patient and persevering diplomacy'. Its recommended diplomatic approach to Romania, moreover, can only be described as preposterous. Matscheko, like Flotow before him, suggested that Bucharest should be offered two inducements to make it choose the Triple Alliance: a guarantee of its territories *vis-à-vis* Bulgaria; and the giving of a green light to Bucharest to mediate between Vienna and Belgrade. As noted above, these proposed inducements were hardly meant to be serious. Paul Schroeder pointed out that the offer of a guarantee *vis-à-vis* Bulgaria would not have impressed Romania, for it already enjoyed such a guarantee through the support of France, Russia, Serbia and Greece – and the sympathy of Germany and Britain. As for Vienna's promise regarding improving relations with Serbia, 'nothing' was likely to come out of it since everyone, including the Austrians, knew that 'what Austria and Romania meant by good Austro-Serbian relations were two different things, and that what Serbia meant was yet another'.[99]

Even Matscheko drew a line in his potty pretense at diplomacy. With those two favours, he wrote, the Monarchy's fund of concessions would be 'exhausted [*erschöpft*]'. It was therefore 'self-evident [*selbstverständlich*]' that the subject, for example, of internal political relations in Austria or Hungary was no business of the Romanian Government. This exclusion of the Transylvanian issue represented, probably, a Hungarian input into Matscheko's Memorandum, but is in any case proof enough that the Ballhausplatz did not think Romania could – or should – still be courted. Not just in Budapest, but also in Vienna powerful voices were against an accommodation with the Romanians in Hungary. In November 1913 the counsellor at Austria-Hungary's Bucharest Legation, Franz von Haymerle, had suggested that, unless the Romanian national question in the Monarchy were settled, relations with Romania would continue to deteriorate and lead to dangerous, Bucharest-sponsored agitation in Hungary. This had drawn an angry response from Alek Hoyos, Berchtold's influential *chef de cabinet*. Any concessions, he argued, would merely open the 'doors and gates' to the Romanian irredenta in Hungary and would ultimately lead to the demise of the Monarchy.[100]

Towards the end of the Romanian analysis in his paper, Matscheko could only offer wishful thinking and distinctly undiplomatic solutions. He considered that even those Romanians most fervently opposed to their country's association with Austria-Hungary and the Triple Alliance might in the end find it 'highly dubious' to definitively destroy the existing bridges, as this would make the country completely dependent on Russia. 'The more categorically' Romania was confronted with the choice between the Triple Alliance and its opponents, 'the greater are the chances that Romania will sober up ... and decide in favour of the first alternative'. One wonders whether this was just a facetious suggestion to be read by the naïve Germans.

A sense of urgency pervades the whole of Matscheko's Memorandum. Following Flotow, he proposed that the Monarchy should respond to Bulgaria's overtures and enter into a treaty with it – as a counterweight to Romania. At the same time, and again along the lines of Flotow's recommendations, he urged that an alliance also be established between Bulgaria and Turkey. But he warned that, in the light of Franco-Russian activity in the region, it was 'uncertain how much longer the road to Sofia and Constantinople will remain open.' Appropriately for a memorandum conceived for German consumption, a concluding observation was that Russian hostility was not aimed at Austria-Hungary as such, but rather against the most exposed part of 'the Central European bloc' which barred Russia's from realizing its 'world-political plans'. Breaking the military superiority of Germany and Austria-Hungary by enlisting 'auxiliary Balkan troops' was the Franco-Russian aim, but it was not the ultimate Russian aim. Russia, in essence cut off from the open seas, was pursuing an aggressive policy in Europe and in Asia, and doing so in the knowledge that it would harm Germany's important interests and provoke its resistance. Accordingly, the manifested tendency to encircle Austria-Hungary was designed to make impossible Germany's resistance to a Russia which was determined to attain 'political and economic supremacy'. It was 'short-sighted', Matscheko protested, to describe specific Austro-Hungarian interests as being far removed from those of Germany's own, or to see Germany's support for them as arising merely out of loyalty to an ally. Finally, 'at this stage of the Balkan crisis', it was in Germany's interest, no less than that of the Monarchy, to act energetically and in a timely manner to counter Russia's advancement, for later it would perhaps be 'impossible to reverse it'.[101]

Christopher Clark has seen the Matscheko Memorandum much as F.R. Bridge before him, since 'there was no hint in it whatsoever that Vienna regarded war – whether of the limited or the more general variety – as imminent, necessary or desirable'. He regards its focus as, 'on the contrary', being 'firmly on diplomatic methods and objectives'.[102] Again, as with Bridge, this is a baffling interpretation. Even a superficial reading of the Memorandum reveals that the Ballhausplatz considered some kind of conflict as at least likely in the short term. Its hypothesis of a war with Russia 'now' ('a Russian attack on the Monarchy'), its emphasis on the 'decidedly offensive' Franco-Russian policies in the Balkans, its questioning of what Romania might do 'in a given moment', its warnings about the looming threat to the military superiority of the Triple Alliance, its reference to the possibility of 'a European war' – all these, and indeed all its proposed 'diplomatic methods and objectives', as mentioned by Clark, assumed and anticipated war. In fact, Matscheko had proposed almost no diplomacy. Serbia was to him a hopeless case and Romania was practically in the same category, except that – and this cannot be emphasized strongly enough – given the pro-Romanian sentiment of Wilhelm II and his Government, the Ballhausplatz felt obliged to rehearse a semblance of an Austro-Hungarian diplomatic effort to keep Romania tied to the Triple Alliance.

As is well known, a somewhat shortened and modified Matscheko *Denkschrift* was presented to Wilhelm II on 5 July in the context of the so-called Hoyos mission which sought to obtain German backing for an Austro-Hungarian strike against Serbia.[103] Much of the relevant historiography considers the discrepancies between the two versions as evidence of a fundamental transformation of Austro-Hungarian foreign policy in the Balkans: from intending to pursue firm but non-belligerent methods just before Sarajevo, to embracing the war option just after Sarajevo. A great deal of such scholarly confidence rests on the work of H. Bertil Petersson who published, in 1964, an exhaustive, compare-and-contrast type of study about the two memoranda with parallel texts and commentary. He admitted that the two documents were surprisingly identical, but then zoomed in on Romania, arguing that the Matscheko Memorandum of 24 June envisaged 'important concessions' to Romania and that, in the light of Romania's good relations with Serbia, Austria-Hungary was hoping it could relax tensions with Serbia by enlisting Romania's help. Petersson's influential study thus concludes that Matscheko's appraisal was 'obviously' a step in the direction of developing a long-term peace policy (*'einer langfristigen Friedenspolitik'*), whereas the updated variant taken to the Germans was its 'diametrical opposite'.[104]

This, however, is a serious blunder on the part of Petersson who takes the pre-Sarajevo document at face value. As discussed above, Matscheko's proposed stimulants would probably have been seen as depressants in Bucharest. Moreover, the emphatic refusal to put the nationalities (i.e., Romanian) question in Hungary on the agenda testified to the fact that Vienna was not serious about achieving a diplomatic recovery in Romania. Petersson does not even attempt to show how Matscheko's 'important concessions' would actually have been concessions at all, let alone important ones. His is a close analysis of two texts, but it lacks historical context. Paul Schroeder, by contrast, argues persuasively that the idea of forcing Romania to make public its adherence to the Triple Alliance or, should this fail, to prepare militarily against it, was 'an admission of defeat, a declaration of diplomatic bankruptcy'. Even more importantly, according to Schroeder, 'the June 24 diplomatic offensive had no chance of success, as Austrian appraisals of the situation made clear'.[105] The truth is that the only meaningful diplomatic offensive envisaged by the Matscheko paper of 24 June was aimed at Berlin and not anywhere in the Balkans. On 26 June Hoyos wrote privately to Pallavicini in Constantinople, informing him that a long memorandum for Berlin had been prepared and that Berchtold was in the meantime doing his utmost to 'open the eyes' of Tschirschky, the German Ambassador.[106] And it is quite wrong of Petersson to suggest that, in trying to clear up its relationship with Romania, the Habsburg Monarchy was seeking to establish a 'secure foundation for a long term Balkan policy'.[107] The Matscheko Memorandum does not betray at any point a concern for the pursuit of a stable, long term Balkan policy. It talks, instead, about the 'important interests of imperial defence [*die wichtige Interessen der Reichsverteidigung*]'.[108]

Moreover, the policy paper of 24 June assumed, to all intents and purposes, the loss of Romania. Berchtold, it should perhaps at this point be emphasized, had as far back as August 1913 pointed out to Franz Joseph that the newly-established solidarity of interests (*Interessengemeinschaft*) between Romania and Serbia was 'for the time being' directed against Bulgaria, but could also be turned against Austria-Hungary.[109] Nothing had happened by June 1914 to remove this anxiety. In the Matscheko paper, the only diplomacy that could really be conducted concerned Bulgaria and Turkey. Bringing these recent foes together seemed in 1914 to be a perfectly feasible project. As Matscheko himself noted, 'favourable dispositions' for it existed in both states.[110] In the light of the entire tone of his Memorandum, however, this would have been no Bismarckian endeavour to prevent war but rather to prepare for it. As for the proposal to make Bulgaria an ally of the Triple Alliance, the main obstacle would have been in Berlin because the Kaiser took a dim view of King Ferdinand. On the other hand Franz Ferdinand, another sharp critic of the Bulgarian King, had by the summer of 1914 begun to see the usefulness of Bulgaria. In an important disclosure about what the Archduke had discussed at Konopischt with Wilhelm II, József Galántai cites from Burián's letter to Tisza, dated 16 June: 'According to Berchtold – and this would be an achievement – the Heir to the Throne now recognizes the necessity that we keep Bulgaria warm and should support it politically as a counterweight to Romania's possible trespasses in the future'.[111] No wonder, then, that Matscheko had felt so free to question Romania's loyalty.

It will be remembered, however, that Franz Ferdinand had at Konopischt also said that Russia was not to be feared (*nicht zu fürchten*) because its internal difficulties were too great to allow 'an aggressive foreign policy'. Yet the Matscheko Memorandum stands in astonishingly sharp contrast to this assessment, for it is bristling with denouncements of aggressive Russian action already taking place in the Balkans – a prelude to no less than a 'political and economic supremacy' that Russia was purportedly trying to achieve. Moreover, leading Austrian authorities (Hantsch, Rauchensteiner) agree that the Memorandum had been coordinated between Franz Ferdinand and Berchtold at their meeting on 14 June. Is it really possible that Matscheko's major policy review should contain an assessment so much at odds with the view held by the Archduke? The latter was still alive and well on 24 June. If Russia was internally too weak to afford an aggressive international posture, who would start the European war being anticipated by Matscheko? It has been shown in this chapter that the German Kaiser, too, did not think Russia was yet fully prepared for war. One must therefore emphasize that this seemingly glaring contradiction between expert and Archduke disappears if one interprets Franz Ferdinand's words to mean that, in the event of an Austro-Hungarian action against Serbia, Russia would not move.

The Matscheko Memorandum only makes sense if it is seen as a discussion of issues that would become hugely important if Austria-Hungary were to move to knock out Serbia. That, surely, had been a main subject of discussions at Konopischt. The telling absence of references to Serbia in the surviving records of the Konopischt meeting is matched only by Matscheko's studied inattention to this pivotal country. The elimination of Serbia – the elephant in the room – was the unspoken assumption in Austro-Hungarian planning just days before the Sarajevo assassination. In his important 1975 article Paul Schroeder stated as much. The Matscheko Memorandum, he wrote, 'even though it did not explicitly envision a resort to violence in order to regain a lost position of strength, paved the way for it and logically required it. Had the assassination not intervened, and had the Austro-German political offensive been tried [i.e., in Romania] its failure would quickly have compelled the Central Powers to seek the sort of ground for preventive war that the assassination gave them.'[112] Habsburg Minister to Bucharest Ottokar Czernin had by early June 1914 got a pretty good idea that Austria-Hungary had set itself on a collision course. He himself had by now come round to the view that the Monarchy should try and reach a settlement with Belgrade. 'If we cannot smash Serbia', he told Baernreither, 'we should abandon all prejudices.' But coming to terms with the Serbs, he said, was a view which could get 'no hearing either in Vienna or in Budapest'.[113]

14

Warnings, Misgivings and the Last Supper

Intelligence and Security

MADAME DE THÈBES, the celebrated French clairvoyant, wrote in her almanac for 1914: 'He, who believes that he will become the ruler, will never become that, and a very young man will become the ruler instead. Before six months of the year transpire, the one who believes that he will become the ruler will fall victim to an assassination. The same will happen to his wife.'[1] The subjects of this prognostication were presumably Franz Ferdinand and his wife Sophie, as well as his nephew Karl, the future, and final, Emperor of Austria-Hungary. Of course, at the time the annual book of prophecies by Madame de Thèbes first came out, no one took any notice of this — as it transpired — remarkably accurate piece of foretelling. However, in the days after the Sarajevo assassination, the Parisian press, followed by that in London and Vienna, quickly latched on to Madame's prophecy.

Certainly, Franz Ferdinand did not need a clairvoyant to tell him that the trip to Bosnia-Herzegovina could be a risky affair. In fact, the situation in 1914 must have been a familiar one to him. He had already lived with the danger of death by assassination for some time. Thus, in the summer of 1906, while staying with his family in Lölling (Carinthia) he had learned that the Italians were preparing to assassinate him during his forthcoming visit to Trieste. The Archduke, 'very disturbed', summoned the local priest and told him: 'I have to represent His Majesty in Trieste, and our lives are never safe, I have to reckon with death.' Following which, kneeling down in his gala general's uniform, he made his confession.[2]

Attempts to make the Archduke refrain from the journey to Bosnia had undoubtedly been made and can to some extent be documented. Gottlieb von Jagow, who was the German Foreign Minister in 1914, wrote as early as 1919 that Franz Ferdinand had been warned before the trip, but that Potiorek had vouched for its security.[3] The most famous warning of all, that by Jovanović, the Serbian Minister in Vienna, has been discussed in detail in chapter twelve. It is doubtful, however, that the Archduke had been told about it. So what was the nature of the warnings that Franz Ferdinand himself received? This is one of the murkiest parts of the history of the Sarajevo assassination. The Heir to the Throne, as will be seen, went to Bosnia most unenthusiastically.

August Urbański, between 1909 and 1914 the head of Austro-Hungarian military intelligence, the *Evidenzbüro*, recounted in a 1926 article how 'signs' of a Serbian action to negate the effect of the Archduke's Bosnian journey had increasingly been reaching his office. The incoming information had suggested that the Serbs would not be 'deterred by anything'. These reports left 'no doubt' that Franz Ferdinand's life was in danger. If true, these revelations by Urbański are of great historical interest. However, Urbański provided no details, moving on instead to the claim that, in consequence of this intelligence, Conrad von Hötzendorf then tried in vain to make the Archduke abandon the idea of visiting Bosnia-Herzegovina. In 1929 Urbański again asserted that Conrad had 'repeatedly' expressed himself against that journey. In 1938, when he published his biography of Conrad, he made this point once more, merely adding that internal political considerations in favour of the visit had prevailed. But the forceful way in which he insisted that Conrad had intervened is remarkable: 'As a witness of those events, as well as someone knowledgeable about the background to the fateful journey of the heir to the throne, I must declare that the Chief of Staff had decidedly spoken against it.'[4]

It is therefore odd that Conrad himself in his very detailed memoirs did not say anything about trying to stop Franz Ferdinand from going. What he writes, in fact, conflicts sharply with Urbański's subsequent account. To Conrad, the Archduke's proposed visit to Bosnia-Herzegovina was understandable and in the interest of the dynasty.[5] Urbański's account is also contradicted by a significant colleague, for apart from Urbański the *Evidenzbüro* had another master-spy: Major Maximilian Ronge. The latter was in charge of the counter-espionage section, the *Kundschafts-gruppe*. According to Ronge, the Archduke had repeatedly expressed interest in the activities of this branch of the service. In line with the usual practice when it came to manoeuvres, Ronge suggested that safety measures be put in place for the Archduke during his stay in Bosnia-Herzegovina: the assignment of competent Vienna detectives and police officers with local knowledge to cordon him off. Such measures, says Ronge in his memoirs, had in the past always led to the removal of numerous suspect individuals. And it seemed to him that there was a particularly strong requirement for preventive action in the politically malign environment of Bosnia-Herzegovina. Ronge relates how he was therefore rudely surprised when the Archduke turned down his suggestions. 'It has remained a puzzle to me', he writes, 'what or who had moved him to do that.'[6]

Ronge may have been puzzled, but what is significant about his recollections is that they emphasize only the routine measures that had been proposed for the Archduke's visit – unlike Urbański, Ronge mentions no intelligence reaching Vienna about possible attempts to kill Franz Ferdinand. It is unlikely that Urbański would know more about such intelligence than Ronge. In fact, Urbański's postwar claims tend also to be discredited by Captain Alfred Jansa who had been receiving intelligence on the spot in Sarajevo and who is very clear on this subject: 'Although the intelligence service reported from Serbia persistent statements of hate against our Monarchy, there was no specific intelligence about assassination plans or planned demonstrations against the visit of the heir to the throne.'[7]

Recent scholarly studies of the Austro-Hungarian General Staff and its secret service have failed to throw more light on this subject.[8] Both Urbański and Ronge omit to mention that, together with their boss Conrad von Hötzendorf, they had already in 1913 lost much of Franz Ferdinand's respect. In the wake of what became a famous espionage scandal involving Colonel Alfred Redl, the Archduke's relationship with the *Evidenzbüro* in 1914 was not exactly a shiny one.[9] The fact that Redl had been selling Austro-Hungarian military secrets to the Russians – as well as to the French and the Italians – for several years was one thing; to the strictly Catholic Archduke this Army intelligence disaster was compounded by the fact that Conrad and his top intelligence officers then proceeded, in May 1913, to limit the fallout by goading Redl into committing suicide. Urbański and Ronge were both in the four-man *Kommission* in Vienna's Hotel Klomser where Redl was given a pistol to do the deed. Franz Ferdinand, not amused by these events, responded by having Urbański suspended, and his ties with Conrad were heavily damaged.[10] It is possible that the Archduke was simply outraged by the fact that Redl's suicide had prevented a thorough investigation of the case.[11] Although Conrad writes that the Archduke was quite friendly towards him during the Bosnian manoeuvres, the damage was in fact permanent.[12] An Austrian historian has noted that neither Conrad nor Ronge were particularly moved by the death of the Archduke.[13] Admittedly, Conrad did in his memoirs pay handsome tribute to Franz Ferdinand, pointing out among other things that the Archduke had perceived 'the growing power of international Judaism'.[14]

There is nothing to suggest that Franz Ferdinand had actually been warned on the basis of specific intelligence, directly and in no uncertain terms, to think twice about his Bosnian trip. Attempts at dissuading him from going did take place, but were couched in general terms. One such effort was by Bishop Emmerich Bjelik who pleaded with the Archduke to avoid that 'volcanic ground' where everything was undermined. In the presence of Baron Bolfras, the head of Franz Joseph's military chancellery, the Bishop told him: 'Your Highness owes it to yourself, to your family and to the Empire not to travel down there.' To which Franz Ferdinand responded: 'We shall see.'[15] There were other warnings of this kind. Heinrich Wildner, from the foreign trade section at the Ballhausplatz had towards the end of April 1914 met Colonel Bardolff, who asked him about conditions in Bosnia. Wildner wrote in his diary that he had 'warned' the head of Franz Ferdinand's military chancellery that those conditions left something to be desired as Belgrade, in his view, had just then 'flung itself with all force at Bosnia'.[16]

Whilst various stories also exist suggesting that there had been more direct warnings, they are of dubious value. One of these, told to Margrave Béla Pallavicini, is about a native of Bosnia-Herzegovina, an unnamed captain in the Austro-Hungarian army, who, having picked up rumours about an assassination plot, turned up on 23 June at the Archduke's residence in Chlumetz to sound the alarm. However, an unperturbed Franz Ferdinand responded by producing and reading to this officer a report from Leon Biliński, in which the Joint Finance Minister mentioned numerous threatening letters and warnings, but downplayed them all on the grounds that predicted assassinations never take place in practice. What is interesting (and gives this story some credence) is that Biliński does actually use similar language in the section of his memoirs which addresses the assassination issue, writing that when anonymous threats and warnings began to arrive no one paid any attention to them because the least dangerous revolutions are those that are announced in advance.[17]

Though there is no real proof that Franz Ferdinand had received any concrete indications himself about the dangers of his Bosnian expedition, there is sufficient circumstantial evidence to suggest that what vague warnings he did hear made him travel only most reluctantly. At the very least, there is a clear record of an attempt by him to wriggle out of the trip. The pretext that he had found was not a bad one: in April 1914 the old Emperor looked as if he was not going to last all that long as he had fallen ill with pneumonia. Accordingly, the following month Franz Ferdinand sent Baron Rumerskirch, his Lord Chamberlain, to explore with Prince Alfred Montenuovo the idea of dropping the Archduke's Bosnian commitment in the light of the Emperor's illness. It made a lot of sense to take this up with Montenuovo as the latter was Franz Joseph's right-hand man, seen by many as the most powerful behind the scenes actor of the Empire. The result of Rumerskirch's visit was amusing, but probably not to Franz Ferdinand. For Montenuovo declared himself privately against the visit on the grounds that 'these Oriental peoples' would not be overly impressed by something lacking the 'great pomp and ceremonies' that had accompanied Franz Joseph in 1910 during his tour of the provinces. The Archduke would be going merely as Inspector General of the armed forces. On the other hand, Montenuovo made it clear that the Emperor was recovering nicely from his illness, so that his state of health could not play a role in Franz Ferdinand's 'doubts' about travelling.[18]

The discussion between Rumerskirch and Montenuovo on 21 May constitutes the clearest evidence that the Archduke had indeed experienced very serious misgivings about attending the manoeuvres. Subsequent claims to the contrary by his son Max appear to be without foundation.[19] Also in May, a telegram was sent to Sarajevo from Konopischt. Indicating the dithering position of the Archduke, it left the local authorities by no means sure that he would arrive.[20] In the end, an increasingly nervous Franz Ferdinand took matters into his own hands by intervening with the Emperor himself. This episode is related by Conrad, who on 4 June had his own audience with the Emperor. As he was waiting to be received, Prince Montenuouvo told him that the Archduke had been to see the Emperor. For reasons of health, according to Montenuovo, Franz Ferdinand was not keen to travel – the problem was the great heat. 'Do as you wish', had been Franz Joseph's comment to his nephew. This must have sounded like a negative reaction to the request. What Franz Ferdinand did extract from the Emperor, however, was permission that the Duchess could accompany him – a consolation prize. A week after the assassination, on 5 July, the Emperor confirmed this exchange to Conrad: 'I blame myself', he told him. 'He had asked me whether he should perhaps abandon the journey.'[21]

Franz Ferdinand is known to have had asthma problems, and it would not have been altogether unreasonable of him to seek to avoid the summer heat of Bosnia-Herzegovina because of personal health issues. What seems more likely, however, is that he had been influenced both by considerations of the manifest dangers entailed in an official visit to Bosnia-Herzegovina, and by the fears and anxieties expressed by his wife in that regard. In advance of the journey he told Dr Eisenmenger that he would have far preferred it if the Emperor had entrusted the mission to someone else. Significantly, although he was his physician, Eisenmenger did not report any health issues that could have swung the decision in that direction. But he stated decidedly that the Duchess of Hohenberg had been greatly fearful for her husband's life. She had even shared those apprehensions on the telephone with Eisenmenger's wife.[22] The Duchess, indeed, seemed concerned for her husband throughout. Arriving separately and in advance of him at the spa of Ilidža on the morning of 25 June, she sent a telegram to her son Max, breathing a sigh of relief: 'Thank God I have good news from him.'[23]

A defamatory leaflet against the Duchess herself had already emerged before she set off, calling her a 'Bohemian beast of a whore' who deserved to be murdered. It ended with the call: 'Down with the Este dog [meaning Franz Ferdinand] and the filthy Bohemian swine!' The facsimile of this leaflet (typewritten in German) is contained in a 1919 booklet by Janez Žibert, who had known the royal couple and who suspected a Hungarian involvement in the Sarajevo assassination.[24] It is extraordinary that Gerd Holler, in his biography of Franz Ferdinand, ascribed the authorship of this hate spurt to 'fanatics' in the Serbian-Orthodox parishes in Bosnia-Herzegovina – a pure invention by Holler given that Žibert whom he cites had written not a word about the Serbs being responsible and had in fact pointed to a member of staff in the Belvedere as the actual author. Historians get away with such demonstrably false constructs only too often: they attach a footnote to a story, referring to a source (in this case Žibert), and such false footnoting makes the story look like a fact.[25] Thus, in his book on the Sarajevo assassination Gordon Brook-Shepherd duly repeated this footnoted fantasy.[26] Neither he nor Holler asked themselves why the Bosnian Serbs should be distributing to Serb parishes in Bosnia materials written in German. A recent English-language biography of Franz Ferdinand also cites Holler's concoction, but takes it further by telling the reader that the 'pamphlets were distributed in Orthodox churches throughout Serbia' – not even Holler claimed that.[27]

Nevertheless, the sheer number of the various general warnings against the Bosnian trip had clearly alarmed Franz Ferdinand and his wife. The assertion by Wladimir Aichelburg that the Archduke had no premonition of death is open to doubt.[28] Shortly before he left for Sarajevo, the Heir Apparent was a guest of Count Franz Harrach. The latter was the owner of the Gräf & Stift car in which the Archduke and his wife rode on 28 June. Indeed, Harrach was with them on that fateful day. Harrach's wife Icy (Alice) wished Franz Ferdinand a good journey, to which he replied: 'As the whole matter is not particularly secret, I would not be surprised if over there a couple of Serbian bullets were waiting for me.'[29] The Duke of Braganza related later what his nephew Franz Ferdinand had told him shortly before the trip: 'I know that the bullet intended for me has already been cast, but duty demands that I go to Bosnia.'[30] Princess Alexandrine Windisch-Grätz, a friend of the Archduke, reportedly stated that he had 'anticipated the worst'.[31]

Hardly surprising, then, that a few days before his departure, he repeatedly expressed within his circle 'an inexplicable, strange trepidation', wishing that some obstacle would materialize to prevent him from making the trip to Sarajevo. This information was passed on to the *Reichspost* soon after the assassination by an anonymous person close to the Archduke. On Friday 19 June, still at Konopischt, he attended mass at eight in the morning and, 'as if he could not leave', stayed for the next mass at nine. In the afternoon, accompanied by the whole family, he went to the Sacred Heart chapel (which he had had built) and there prayed 'long and fervently'. And in Vienna, before taking the train for Trieste on the evening of 23 June, he prayed in the chapel of the Belvedere Palace, staying there for so long that his associates thought he would miss the time set for the train to depart.[32]

The role of Colonel Bardolff in the story of the Sarajevo assassination has not attracted a great deal of attention, but is an interesting one. Aide-de-camp to the Archduke, the head of Franz Ferdinand's military chancellery (and Hitler's future General) was of course included in the archducal party for Bosnia. He had previously arranged with Potiorek the most minute details of the trip, including (and especially) the menus and musical programmes during the visit. The problem, as it turned out, was that the two men were not quite as interested in the security arrangements.[33] In his memoirs Bardolff stated that, soon after Franz Ferdinand's visit to Bosnia had been arranged and approved of by Franz Joseph (at the beginning of 1914), 'misgivings' began to emerge from 'various sides'. Bardolff claimed to have personally informed the Archduke about such doubts (without however specifying their exact nature) and to have also informed Potiorek in writing. He added that Franz Ferdinand ignored such warnings (they 'fell on deaf ears') and that Potiorek took responsibility for the security of his guest.[34]

Whether Bardolff told the true story is open to doubt. Just before he left for Bosnia the Archduke, while still in his residence at Chlumetz, spoke to Franz Janaček, the head of his household: 'What do you think J. [Janaček], if Brosch were still here, would he also advise and persuade me to travel down there. Bardolff is hustling me into death.'[35] Why, then, was Bardolff so keen that the Archduke should go to Bosnia? The explanation may well be that Bardolff and Potiorek were good friends. As Theodor Zeynek recalled in his memoirs, Bardolff came from 'Potiorek's school' – referring, presumably, to his period with the Chiefs of Staff. Elsewhere, Zeynek described Bardolff as '*ein Anhänger Potioreks*', which may be translated as Potiorek's 'disciple' or 'devotee'.[36] Perhaps, keeping this powerful Bardolff-Potiorek combination in mind, the Archduke never stood a chance of dodging the Bosnian trip. Soon after the assassination, Franz Ferdinand's friend Count Adalbert Sternberg sent a letter to Bardolff, pointing out the latter's personal responsibility, as well as that of Potiorek. Criticising the security measures, Sternberg wrote: 'One can behave in such manner in an operetta, but not in a state where supposedly well-ordered standards are in place.'[37]

In retrospect Franz Ferdinand's fervent prayers in the Belvedere Palace chapel on 23 June were more than justified. The security fiasco on 28 June has not surprisingly been debated for a whole century. The role of the Sarajevo police in particular came under heavy attack immediately after the event and is even today the subject of scathing criticisms. A characteristic judgement of 28 June among historians refers to 'the failure of the Austrian authorities to adopt elementary precautions in a hostile environment'.[38] Of course, from Potiorek's perspective the whole point of the tour around Sarajevo was to demonstrate to the Archduke a friendly environment. And it has been clear for a long time that many of the security shortcomings stemmed from petty bureaucratic and political rivalries in Vienna and Sarajevo. Bosnia and Herzegovina was officially run by the Joint Finance Ministry, headed by Biliński. Franz Ferdinand, however, was quite hostile to Biliński and had, with regard to his Bosnian journey, 'refused any involvement of the civilian authorities'.[39] In doing so, he certainly played a big personal role in his own demise. Having excluded Biliński and his Ministry from the whole affair, he was going to have to rely just on Potiorek.

The latter, however, had his suspicions about the Finance Ministry. He thought, for example, that Biliński's closest associate in the Joint Finance Ministry, Božo Čerović, was a Serbian spy.[40] In any case, the Archduke's arrival in Bosnia was to Potiorek a great opportunity and he was determined to shut out the Ministry in Vienna in order to control the proceedings himself. The programme of the visit is often presented in history books as being of a purely military character. Potiorek had repeatedly stressed this aspect before 28 June. But matters did not stand in quite that way. The post-manoeuvres tour around Sarajevo on 28 June, prominently featuring as it did the presence of the Duchess of Hohenberg, had an emphatically civilian flavour. Biliński was certainly right to point this out in his memoirs, complaining that 'the extension of the journey into the civil sphere had been permitted without myself being asked and without my knowledge'.[41] On the face of it, however, a genuine administrative problem did not really exist: although the headquarters of the 15th Corps were entrusted to deal with security arrangements, the police would play its role. Baron Carl Collas, formerly the Government Commissar for Sarajevo and in 1914 the civilian head of the government of Bosnia-Herzegovina (*Präsidialchef des Landesregierung*), explained later: 'Given the dual, civil and military positioning of the *Landeschef*, this measure in no way entailed a complete exclusion of the civilian apparatus, but only a subordination to the military directives.'[42] What Collas did not say was that he was among those, on the civilian side, being quite happily subordinated to the military. He was, his contemporary Władysław Gluck, wrote, 'Potiorek's favourite' and had owed his position to Potiorek.[43]

Collas is perhaps an undeservedly obscure figure in the history of the Sarajevo assassination. Given his position, and his relationship with

Potiorek, his recollections merit some attention. He stemmed from an old, aristocratic French family which had during the French Revolution emigrated first to Germany and then to Hungary. Before becoming the *Präsidialchef* in 1913 he had been in charge of the police. According to Gluck, his influence under Potiorek was so great that he 'practically governed Bosnia'.[44] This man certainly had strong political views. In his 1929 memoir he dwelt on a conference he had attended in Vienna, in May 1914, at which Conrad, Potiorek and Biliński were also present. He described Biliński as someone who looked at everything 'in the rosiest colours', and who 'raved' about the loyalty of the Bosnian Serbs and the correct behaviour of Belgrade. More importantly, Collas, a Hungarian, did not admire the Archduke either, seeing in his behaviour 'a cautionary example of volatility and petulance'. Franz Ferdinand, in his view, regarded any weakening of Dualism as a personal triumph, diligently sawing off, with a 'Czech saw' the only branch on which the Habsburg Monarchy was still able to sit – an unmistakeable reference to the Duchess and her Bohemian friends.[45]

He described how, at the May 1914 conference in Vienna, he took a very different view from that of Biliński, to the extent of warning that every Serbian schoolboy in Bosnia was in the service of Belgrade propaganda and that Bosnia and Herzegovina was faced with a 'volcano about to erupt'. This was a remarkable announcement in the light of what took place only weeks later. What, then, did Collas do when he returned to Sarajevo where the news had arrived that the Heir to the Throne had confirmed his attendance at the manoeuvres? Interestingly, despite his alarmist official attitude, Collas did not privately think anything would happen to Franz Ferdinand. He believed that the Archduke, supported by the Duchess of Hohenberg, was undertaking a mission to woo 'the South-Slavdom', whereby a blow would be struck against Hungary. 'I personally held the erroneous opinion', he wrote, 'that the Archduke ... would be spared by the Belgrade circles.' His view was that those (unnamed) circles in Belgrade might be held back by an 'instruction' from Prague, and that they were just waiting for Franz Joseph to die, in the expectation that an 'aggressive' Franz Ferdinand would then bring about 'a catastrophic collapse' of the Monarchy from within.[46]

Collas's memoir (revealing some fantastic assumptions and prejudices) thus provides a useful insight into how the internal politics of Austria-Hungary – reflected in this case in the personal political outlook of a leading individual in the administration of Bosnia-Herzegovina – fitted into the background of the Sarajevo assassination. Collas, the most important civilian official in the land, was never likely to lift a finger for Franz Ferdinand's safety. His only proposal in the debate concerning archducal security was a suggestion, rejected by the Archduke, that, following the example set during Franz Joseph's visit to Bosnia-Herzegovina in 1910, Franz Ferdinand should ride through Sarajevo *à la Daumont* – in a horse-driven carriage flanked by Horse Guards. But the Archduke ordered '*das Auto*'.[47]

Franz Joseph's 1910 tour of the provinces was accordingly already being mentioned as a model in 1914, and it has also been highlighted by historians ever since as a successful security operation that had strangely not been replicated for the visit of Franz Ferdinand. The measures taken in 1910 were indeed impressive. Before the Emperor's arrival scores of suspect persons were deported to Pale, outside Sarajevo; the city itself swarmed with agents and confidants who would report anything suspicious to the police; all foreigners coming from Italy, Turkey, Russia and Serbia were subjected to special monitoring; border and gendarmerie troops were transferred from their normal duties in order to strengthen security for the Emperor's visit; and, famously, in every Sarajevo street where Franz Joseph moved there was a double cordon of troops to guard him.[48] The Emperor for his part was not happy about such massive security. He was 'furious' as he left, remarking that 'I see plenty of uniforms and tailcoats in Vienna every day, I wanted but couldn't see the population'. No one from the provincial authorities subsequently received what should have been customary decorations.[49]

What is being overlooked in comparisons between 1910 and 1914, however, is the simple fact that Franz Joseph had paid a visit as the Emperor whereas Franz Ferdinand was coming as the Inspector General of the Armed Forces. The difference in status was always clear: Montenuovo had, after all, advised Rumerskirch against the trip as it would lack pomp and ceremony. Moreover, by insisting that the Bosnian visit was of a purely military character, the Heir to the Throne had voluntarily diminished the status of his trip. In any case, even the 1910 police and intelligence effort was in a sense a failure and could have ended in disaster: although the authorities had had a hunch about Bogdan Žerajić, he was close to assassinating Franz Joseph in Mostar, and soon thereafter did attempt to assassinate Governor Varešanin.[50]

The case of Žerajić should have served as a warning, and probably did, but there was a much more recent one, directly relevant to Franz Ferdinand. In August 1913 Luka-Lujo Aljinović, a Croat from Dalmatia, was arrested in Zagreb, and charged with preparing to assassinate the Archduke. Aljinović saw in him an enemy standing in the way of 'the unification of the South Slavs'.[51] After Sarajevo, the case of Aljinović was deemed important enough for Foreign Minister Berchtold to mention it in his circular *Memoire* of 25 July 1914, published subsequently in the Austro-Hungarian *Red Book*.[52]

The available evidence concerning security measures for the archducal trip demands that, Baron Collas apart, a sharp distinction be drawn between the military and civil authorities in Sarajevo. The Interior Minister for Bosnia-Herzegovina in 1914 was Teodor Zurunić, a Serb and an appointee of Biliński. He controlled all the police and gendarmerie forces in the provinces. In Sarajevo itself, the Government Commissar for the city was Dr Edmund Gerde, a Hungarian and a friend of Collas. Gerde's function entailed responsibility for the city police force. Subordinated to Gerde in the city police structure was Petar Maksimović (another Serb) as chief of detectives. Gerde's second deputy was Władysław Gluck, a Pole. Ironically, it was these four individuals, stemming from the nations so despised by Franz Ferdinand (Gerde also had a Jewish background), who did their best to make sure that no harm should come to him.

Maksimović was well-versed in local affairs and in fact his brief was to report to Gerde on political matters. As soon as he heard about the archducal visit 'he drew attention to the great danger that the Archduke faced', and Gerde was left in no doubt that the visit 'should be prevented'.[53] Zurunić, too, was concerned. A few weeks before the Archduke's arrival he went to see Potiorek to ask him about security measures for the visit, and to his 'amazement' the *Landeschef* replied: 'The Archduke is coming to Bosnia in the capacity of a General, and it is not the business of the government to concern itself with it.' Despite this rebuff Zurunić did not give up and 'considered it his duty' to approach Potiorek again. Several days before 28 June he told Potiorek that, given the length of the archducal route through the city, the Sarajevo police was 'absolutely not in a position' to keep order in the streets and ensure safe passage. But Potiorek was adamant and oblivious: 'I am telling Your Excellency once again that His Imperial Highness is arriving in the capacity of a General, this is not at all the business of Your Excellency, it is an Army concern.'[54]

In the second half of May *Kommissar* Gerde was invited to attend a conference at the military headquarters to consider the programme of the visit. The idea of cancelling it, as Maksimović had recommended, could not be for the officers present 'even a subject of discussion'. Gerde then demanded that the Army should provide cordons of soldiers along the procession route. He also stated that the police should have unlimited authorization to carry out house searches during this period. He was told: 'You are seeing ghosts [*Herr Regierungskommissar, sie sehen Gespenster*]'. Gerde then insisted that a record of the meeting be made. Władysław Gluck had several times 'pressed hard' on Gerde regarding the security measures, deeming them insufficient and anticipating that Franz Ferdinand's journey would 'end tragically'. Gluck's subsequent interpretation of Potiorek's reluctance to involve the civilian authorities in a meaningful way is that this would have entailed asking Biliński for additional finances, thus bringing the Joint Ministry in on the act – one which, for purposes of due acclaim, the *Landeschef* preferred to be his and his alone.[55] After the war

Biliński described as a 'blatant lie' Potiorek's claim that Sarajevo had been denied credits for security measures surrounding the Archduke's visit.[56]

The most damning piece of evidence against Potiorek comes from Zurunić. In 1919 Dr Milovan Grba met him in Zagreb and 'asked him openly' whether the Sarajevo police had had any inkling about the preparations for the assassination. Zurunić told him that 'some two weeks' before the arrival of the Archduke a meeting of the civil and military authorities had taken place. According to Zurunić, Gerde announced on this occasion that he had 'got on to the track of a conspiracy against Franz Ferdinand [*er sei einer Verschwörung gegen Franz Ferdinand auf die Spur gekommen*]'. This is the only piece of evidence, hitherto completely neglected, that the Sarajevo police knew at least something about preparations to assassinate the Archduke. But Potiorek replied that the officers corps would protect its high guest. Thus Gerde felt 'free of any liability'.[57] It can only be speculated as to just what Gerde (or his people) had come up with in their investigations, but whatever they may have had could obviously not have been hot leads. Nevertheless, even when Potiorek's arrogance is taken into account, it is astonishing that Gerde's announcement about the existence of an actual conspiracy was so lightly brushed off.

Gerde, although in Gluck's view inexperienced in police matters, was perfectly well aware of the 'dangerous terrain', and had sought advice among the seasoned Serbian officials in Sarajevo. But the whole situation was now, as Gluck observed, in the hands of 'Providence'. The Sarajevo police force numbered 112 in total, including five detectives. Before 28 June extra detectives were brought into the city, but it is not clear how many. Gluck maintains that only six came: four from Budapest and two from Vienna.[58] However, local policemen subsequently talked of 15 extra detectives that Gerde had ordered from Budapest, and corroborating evidence exists that this was indeed the case. The problem was that most of those detectives understood neither Serbo-Croat nor the local milieu. They were, moreover, allocated the most sensitive sectors along the archducal route.[59] The historian Vladimir Dedijer wrote that fifty gendarmes were additionally employed on 28 June, although Gluck asserted that there were only 'a few'.[60] If the figure of fifty gendarmes is correct, and if the figures for the extra detectives are also taken as correct (fifteen from Budapest and two from Vienna), then some 179 security personnel altogether were in place on 28 June. An unknown number of Army confidants was also on the streets – Potiorek's single active measure. The length of the route to be guarded was seven kilometres, but Gluck pointed out that, in effect, the length was only four kilometres as some policemen could be transferred from one street to another. However, this still meant that policemen would be separated by some fifty metres from each other, standing in zig-zag fashion on both sides of the route.[61] Meeting Gerde on the morning of

28 June, minutes before Franz Ferdinand was to arrive in town, Gluck was told by the Government Commisar that, as he had closed the door of his apartment, he had been overcome by the thought that 'he would not return to it alive'.[62]

The Journey and the Manoeuvres

In 1909 General Emil Vojnović, the former head of Austro-Hungarian military intelligence, suggested to Franz Ferdinand that it would be in the interests of the Empire's Balkan policy if one of the archdukes went to Sarajevo and took up residence there. The Archduke had laughed and answered with the question: 'Well, which Archduke would do *that*?'[63] Perhaps this was more of a comment on what the Heir Apparent thought about Bosnia-Herzegovina than about his fellow archdukes. Now, in June 1914, a few days' residence for him in the provinces was an inescapable duty, however much he disliked the whole idea. And dislike it he very much did, exploding with anger, cursing the 'Bosnian journey', and first crumpling then tearing up a handkerchief, simply because Bardolff notified him about a train timetable change for the return trip.[64]

On 21 June, having moved the previous day from Konopischt to Chlumetz, Franz Ferdinand was to fire his last shot in life. He was in a car, inspecting the woods around Chlumetz which he himself had cultivated. A cat appeared on a meadow. The Archduke positioned himself on the back seat of the car and, shooting offhand, still managed to kill the cat.[65] Though it was a good shot, it was not exactly a glorious finale to a distinguished shooting career, but the Archduke was of course not to know it. His mind was already preoccupied with what he would do immediately after returning from Sarajevo. On 23 June (just before departing) he told Morsey to prepare materials concerning joint Finance Minister Biliński about whom he was going to complain to Franz Joseph. Biliński, he said, 'immediately telephones and telegraphs everything to Budapest'. Moreover, in Bosnia, he thought, the Hungarians were being difficult and protecting the 'Empire-hostile' Serbs.[66]

The journey from Chlumetz to Sarajevo went well – on the whole, after an initial mishap at the Chlumetz railway station, when the news was telephoned that the Archduke's private salon coach was overheating. 'Well, that's a really promising start to the trip', he commented.[67] In the evening, having reached Vienna, he parted with Sophie at the Belvedere Palace – for during the official military stage of the trip he was to travel down the Adriatic on a warship whereas she was to follow an overland route by train across Hungary and Croatia. At Vienna's Südbahnhof station he and his party were given the coach normally used by the Austrian Prime Minister Count Karl Stürgkh. This coach also had problems – with its electricity –

and the party was forced to make do with candle light. The flickering interior of the coach made it appear like a 'death chamber'. To the Archduke this was 'another omen'.[68]

At Trieste, in the morning hours of 24 June, the Heir to the Throne embarked on *Viribus Unitis* (with united strength) the pride of the Austro-Hungarian navy: in service since 1912, this 20,000-ton battleship had twelve 12-inch guns and was the first in the world to have triple-gunned turrets. Having seen the special accommodation for Wilhelm II on battleship *Deutschland*, Franz Ferdinand had arranged a similar treat for himself on *Viribus Unitis*.[69] As the ship steamed south along the Istrian coast he stood on the bridge, observing the islands of Brioni where he and his family had spent many happy days. Much of the talk on *Viribus Unitis* concerned its return to Trieste a few days later: a test run was planned, doing the whole stretch at full speed.[70] In the event it was rather a different journey with two coffins on board.

Very early on 25 June the mouth of the river Neretva was reached. Here the Archduke and his party transferred to the *Dalmat*, a small steamer yacht that took them up the river to Metković. Potiorek was on the yacht to greet his much-expected guest. Crowds lined both banks of the river to greet him, wearing their colourful costumes, with men, young and old, shooting into the air from their incredibly long muskets.[71] In Metković they got on a train to Mostar, arriving at the capital of Herzegovina basking in the summer sunshine. Here, a big reception was held. The City Council had at the end of May completed a new public bath, naming it the 'Franz Ferdinand Municipal Bath' – its inspection was in the programme of the Archduke's brief visit. On 3 June, at the festive opening of this new addition to the city, a telegram by Mayor Mujaga Komadina to Franz Joseph was read out. It stated that Bosnia and Herzegovina was 'the youngest, but the most devoted daughter of the Habsburg Monarchy'. The same Komadina (a Muslim) now greeted Franz Ferdinand with similar words of loyalty, and wished him 'a long and happy life'.[72]

The Heir Apparent's train reached the small railway station at Ilidža, some nine kilometres west of Sarajevo, shortly before 3 p.m. This spa resort had been very successfully modernized and built up during the period of Kállay's administration. Heinrich Renner, a German travel writer who visited Ilidža in the late 1890s, wrote that the place stood 'confidently' shoulder to shoulder with the better European spas.[73] It was raining when the Archduke arrived, but a relatively large crowd was there to welcome him. Also present was Conrad, accompanied by Colonel Metzger and Major Kundmann, as was Count Franz Harrach with his chauffeur Leopold Lojka. Conrad considered the security measures in place to be thorough without being blatant.[74] As the train approached, a military band played '*Gott erhalte*'. The Archduke emerged and duly inspected the guard of honour. According to Ivan Kranjčević, a friend of the conspirators, everywhere in Sarajevo the talk subsequently was that Franz Ferdinand had, on arriving in Ilidža and seeing various national flags on display, ordered that all flags other than 'Austrian' ones be removed, since in 'Austria' he knew no other nationality than 'Austrian'. It is very unlikely that he ever ordered anything of the kind, but there is no reason to disbelieve Kranjčević that the story had indeed circulated in Sarajevo.[75]

In fact the Archduke was in a very good mood. He was soon reunited with his wife who had arrived in the morning and was waiting for him in the Hotel Bosna. The good, fresh air had also cheered him up; he described it as 'very much like Upper-Styria'.[76] The Duchess had had plenty of time to admire the new surroundings in which she was to reside over the next few days. The Hotel Bosna had been thoroughly adapted and prettified for the sojourn of the high guests. The Bosnian Land Government's architect Knopfmacher had been entrusted to lead all the works. He had already distinguished himself in 1900 when he prepared the Bosnian pavilion for the Paris world exhibition. Sumptuous flower decorations were to be seen all around. Even palms from the Italian Riviera had been specially imported. The royal couple had at their disposal a big salon with a veranda, a bedroom and a bathroom. The Archduke had a dressing room, whereas the Duchess had a boudoir and her own small salon. Everything was arranged and decorated in oriental style, giving the archducal accommodation the appearance of 'a real fairy-tale from the Thousand and One Nights'.[77]

Particularly enhancing the overall appearance were the many colourful and luxurious rugs and carpets, some of them being local Bosnian products. Along with oriental furniture, these were provided by the firm of Elias B. Kabilio (*Orientalisches Teppich-Haus und Bosnische Kunst-u. Hausindustrie*) which had its shop in the centre of Sarajevo. Kabilio also had branches in Constantinople and Damascus. So enchanted were Franz Ferdinand and Sophie (the Duchess in particular) by what they saw in their rooms that they decided, towards evening on the day of their arrival, to pay an impromptu visit to the Kabilio establishment, together with some members of their entourage. When the column of three cars reached it in Rudolfgasse, opposite Hotel Zentral, there were hardly any people around, and Kabilio himself had only been informed about the visit shortly beforehand. In order to play things down, the local police only sent two detectives in civilian clothes and two policemen who stood around at a discreet distance. Franz Ferdinand, with wife and a small entourage 'entered the shop without practically anybody noticing them'. The royal couple, much enthused with the wares on display, spent more than an hour with Kabilio and his wife, buying among many other items, three blankets, two cushions, an expensive, embroidered portiere curtain, six prayer mats and three copies of the Koran. In the meantime a big crowd had assembled on the street, and when the Archduke appeared briefly on the balcony there were one or two calls of '*živio!* [long live!]' which he acknowledged by bowing. There was no commotion.[78]

In an interview given after the assassination, Potiorek complained bitterly that Franz Ferdinand had told him 'not a word' about wanting to make this visit, and that he only found out about it once the Archduke's party had left Kabilio's premises.[79] But the *Landeschef* was at this point conducting a damage limitation exercise following his spectacular mis-management of 28 June. Given that the excursion to Sarajevo on 25 June was a spontaneous matter quite outside the official programme, no real danger existed. According to Borivoje Jevtić, Gavrilo Princip stood outside the shop ('by chance') and had seen the Archduke clearly, while aware that a police agent was observing him from behind. Although Jevtić did not write that Princip had been armed, many subsequent accounts basing themselves on Jevtić assumed so and thus made a fanciful addition to the history of the assassination – it was most unlikely that Princip would have been walking around the city armed three days before the planned assassination.[80] He himself said nothing about this subject in the long interrogations after his capture.[81] A further story about this day, recently restated, that the royal couple had visited 'the Sarajevo bazaar, where they had walked unmolested in the narrow crowded streets' constitutes another false legend – they were not even close to the bazaar and they never walked in the streets.[82] Not surprisingly, however, one of the detec-tives accompanying the shopping party was 'intensely apprehensive through-out'. And on the way back to Ilidža, the police agent Chalupski told Morsey that he was 'mortally terrified' about the upcoming visit to Sarajevo on 28 June.[83]

On 26 and 27 June, with her husband away at the military manoeuvres, the Duchess visited various schools and religious establishments. She had come well equipped for this purpose. Just before the Bosnian journey she had sent her lady-in-waiting Countess Vilma Lanjus to Vienna to buy 'heaps of holy pictures and other devotional objects', as well as 'whole mountains of bonbons'.[84] Along with this, however, came a further component of the public relations exercise envisaged for the Sarajevo trip: according to a Slovene newspaper, the Duchess brought along 2,000 photographs of herself with her family to distribute among children.[85]

Meeting the local Catholics was clearly by a long way at the top of Sophie's Sarajevo agenda. On Friday 26 June she and Countess Lanjus began by visiting the Sarajevo cathedral, moving on to the convent of St Augustin (where a choir sang *Hoch Habsburgs Thron*), and then to the *Jugendheim* for Croat Catholics, an establishment run by the Jesuit Anton Puntigam. There followed a visit to the convent of St Vincent.[86] Everywhere she went she handed out photographs, *Zuckerln* and cash donations. Back in Ilidža in the afternoon, she walked with Franz Ferdinand in the park. Four young bears were running around quite free and, as the Archduke carelessly attempted to stroke one of them, his finger was bitten.[87]

On 27 June the Duchess called on Archbishop Dr Josip Stadler and subsequently went to a Muslim girls' school, following that with visits to a Muslim orphanage and the Franciscan monastery. She rounded off the official part of the day with a short stay at the local carpet-weaving works, ordering one example of each product that was shown to her. The Duchess did not visit a single Serbian school or church.[88] According to Morsey, the Serbian schools were closed because of an epidemic of scarlet fever.[89] The local papers, however, carried no such information, and the Serbian church and its dignitaries were also ignored. On 26 June, the Duchess asked: 'What, are there no Catholic Serbs whatsoever in Bosnia?'[90] In fact, there were some. The most prominent Catholic Serb in Sarajevo was Stjepo Kobasica, the chief editor of *Srpska Riječ*. Of course, given the occasionally critical attitude towards the Habsburg Empire taken by his newspaper he would never have been seen as appropriate company for the Duchess. Soon after the assassination, Kobasica was unceremonously expelled from Bosnia without having been in any way involved in the events of 28 June.

During those two days the Archduke was in the hills south-west of Sarajevo inspecting the progress of the manoeuvres. Much has been made in the literature of apologia for Austria-Hungary and Franz Ferdinand that the June 1914 manoeuvres in Bosnia had nothing to do with Serbia since they took place relatively far from the Serbian (and Montenegrin) borders.[91] This was certainly true as far as geography was concerned. The war games were in the area of Pazarić, Tarčin and Bradina, close to Herzegovina, a difficult terrain of mountain ridges and *Karst* limestone plateaus. But this was precisely the military point: the idea was to have an exercise in mountain warfare. Against whom potentially? The answer was spelled out in *Bosnische Post* on 19 May after the paper received an update on the forthcoming manoeuvres from Potiorek's headquarters. Since in the event of a war the troops of the 15th and 16th Corps would be called upon to advance towards 'the south-eastern front of the Empire', the projected mountain manoeuvres would be 'a good preparation' for such an event ('*eine gute Vorschule*').[92] A south-eastern advance of the kind hypothesised by Potiorek's headquarters would lead these soldiers of the Empire straight into Serbia and Montenegro.

The weather in and around Sarajevo had been quite bad since Tuesday, 23 June, with thunderstorms and even hail. The troops of the 15th and 16th Corps, assembling that day for the forthcoming manoeuvres, had 'had a bad night'.[93] Conditions had not improved by the time the exercises officially began at 2 p.m. on 25 June. Apart from the 15th and 16th Corps, some units of the border infantry also took part, totalling some 22,000 men and officers. The 16th Corps (the 'red' or 'south' party), led by Lieutenant-General Wenzel Wurm, had a simple *ordre de bataille*: to advance from Herzegovina towards Sarajevo across the Ivan-sedlo pass, attract to itself and 'destroy' the opposing 15th Corps. The latter, (the 'blue' or 'north' party), commanded by General of the Infantry Michael von Appel, was to counteract this threat by moving across the same area of Ivan-sedlo and destroying the enemy in the valley of the Neretva. As the Archduke arrived on the scene by train and horse, on the morning of 26 June, it was raining incessantly ('Heavens have no mercy', wrote the special correspondent of the *Bosnische Post*).[94]

For Potiorek, of course, this whole business was less about preparing for a war against Serbia and more about preparing the ground to succeed Conrad. Things looked good for him. He and Merizzi accompanied Franz Ferdinand and Conrad round different sectors of mock battles, visiting both Wurm and Appel. Everywhere, Captain Jansa wrote later, the Archduke was praising the troops. The next day, Saturday 27 June, the sunny weather that had materialized allowed at long last for a superb overview of the area. The Archduke was 'in a radiant mood', Jansa recalled, while 'Conrad spoke very little and remained very grave the whole time; his personal relationship with the Archduke appeared as cool as that with Potiorek'. Jansa had received 'the grim impression' that the brilliant relationship which the Archduke and Conrad had enjoyed for years 'must have cooled off very considerably'. By ten that morning General Appel had already managed with an enveloping movement of his defending forces to make the position of the 16th Corps untenable. At eleven o'clock Franz Ferdinand gave the call-off signal.[95]

This was Potiorek's moment of triumph. Manfried Rauchensteiner, a leading Austrian historian, has written that Franz Ferdinand, in the light of his disharmony with Conrad, wanted to see Potiorek perform in the context of great manoeuvres, 'in order to test him, after a fashion, and then reach his final decision'.[96] The Archduke could not have been far from making a decision in favour of Potiorek. Theodor Zeynek recalled that, in order to become the *Chef des Generalstabs* (which he had missed becoming back in 1906), Potiorek had invited Franz Ferdinand to attend the manoeuvres in 1914. The *Landeschef* finally 'stood close to fulfilling his ambitious desire', Zeynek wrote, 'when on 28 June the murder ensued, which carried the whole world to destruction.'[97] Indeed, in his Army order issued on 27 June, Franz Ferdinand stated that his expectations had been in every respect 'fully confirmed' by the excellent accomplishments he had been able to observe. He further stated that he would report on this to the Emperor. And he expressed his thanks, first of all, to '*Herrn Armee-Inspektor*' (Potiorek), and then to all the officers and the troops of both

Corps.[98] Franz Joseph, in Bad Ischl since 27 June, was duly informed by his nephew about the success of the manoeuvres. At 11 a.m. on 28 June – about the time Franz Ferdinand was killed – the Emperor sent him a telegram which concluded: 'One can confidently look forward to [*Feldzeugmeister*] Potiorek's leading role in the future.'[99]

27 June 1914: *The Penultimate Chance*

Now that the military part of the the Archduke's visit was successfully out of the way, it was time to relax and, in a sense, to celebrate. A gala dinner had been organized at Hotel Bosna in Ilidža on 27 June at 7 p.m. The top-notch of the local establishment were invited to attend, along with Potiorek's imperial-administrative pack, which actually ran the country. The native political elite was represented by the President of the Bosnian Diet, Dr Safvet-beg Bašagić (a Muslim), and his two vice-presidents: Danilo Dimović (a Serb) and Dr Josip Sunarić (a Croat).[100] Bašagić was a man of literary inclinations, the author of a history of Bosnia-Herzegovina in which he argued, somewhat unpersuasively, that the country had not really lost its independence and freedoms when it fell to the Turks in the 15th century.[101] Dimović's political rise has been discussed in chapter nine. A lawyer, he was one of those opportunist Serbian leaders who took a loyal line, even arguing that Bosnia-Herzegovina should be tied to the Habsburg dynasty on the basis of the Pragmatic Sanction of 1713.[102] Sunarić, another lawyer, was someone with whom Franz Ferdinand was already familiar, having in 1911 advised the Archduke to abandon his plan to visit Bosnia that year on the grounds that the Serbs would 'lie in ambush' to murder him. True to form, Sunarić had unsuccessfully tried to stop this visit too, by sending Biliński an urgent telegram in which he warned of the 'Great-Serbian Irredenta' which was determined and capable of anything.[103]

The native religious elite was of course also represented at this dinner which really resembled an Austro-Hungarian commonwealth in miniature. For Sarajevo was as cosmopolitan as any other part of the Empire. The growing and thriving Jewish population in Sarajevo was represented by the young rabbi Dr Moritz Levy on behalf of the long-established Sephardic community. But chief rabbi Dr Samuel Weszel, a theologian as well as a historian of repute, was also there on behalf of the minority Ashkenazic community.[104] The Muslims had their *Reis-ul-ulema*, Džemaludin Čaušević, in attendance. This Reis, though loyal, was an incorrigible Muslim funda-mentalist who had only a few years earlier invented the so-called 'arebica' script, which as the name suggests was Arab, though adapted to the Serbo-Croat language. It proved a success, especially since the Muslims of Bosnia-Herzegovina, or at any rate those who could read, considered both the Latin and Cyrillic scripts to be 'repulsive'.[105]

The Serbian religious leader, sitting at the table next to the Duchess on her left, was the Metropolitan Evgenije Letica. A former reserve officer in the Austro-Hungarian army, Letica was a model of dependability: after Austria-Hungary annexed Bosnia-Herzegovina in 1908, with all the Serbs up in arms, he had held a church service during which he blessed the Emperor Franz Joseph and his family. To the right of the Duchess sat the Croat religious leader, Dr Josip Stadler, since 1881 the first Archbishop of Sarajevo. His political activity has been discussed in chapter four. It was thanks to Stadler that Sarajevo got its Catholic cathedral, built in the 1880s. This turbulent priest subsequently managed to antagonize everybody: primarily the powerful and popular Franciscans of Bosnia-Herzegovina, but for different reasons also Vienna and Budapest. Potiorek himself worked to get rid of the man, who nevertheless stayed obstinately afloat owing to Pope Pius X. Like many other Croats, Stadler dreamed of a Greater Croatia encompassing Bosnia-Herzegovina under the Habsburg dynasty – and he was pinning his hopes on Franz Ferdinand to bring this about. Another Croat religious dignitary present for the occasion was Lovro Mihačević, the Franciscan Provincial of Bosnia (as opposed to Herzegovina). This man would, the following morning, administer the last rites to Franz Ferdinand and the Duchess of Hohenberg as they lay dying in Potiorek's residence.

On the evening of 27 June, however, the atmosphere was very jolly at Ilidža. The *K. und k. Garnisons-Musik* from Sarajevo played pieces by Béla Kéler (a Slovak by birth), Strauss (*An der schönen blauen Donau*), Puccini, Bellini, Schumann and Lehár.[106] It is not known whether the Archduke enjoyed drinking the Hungarian wines – Tokaji *szamorodni* (from 1901) was one such served during the meal, along with other drinks that included (for dessert) the dry, slightly acidic Žilavka from the Mostar region – this wine, chosen from the Gjorjo and Jelačić cellar, had figured two years earlier on the wine list of the *Titanic*.[107] What is of course well-known is the Archduke's deep antipathy towards the Magyars. Hence it is perhaps not surprising that his last recorded political pronouncement should be an uncontrolled outburst on this subject. Danilo Dimović related how in the course of the evening Franz Ferdinand approached him and his two colleagues in the presidency of the Diet, Sunarić and Bašagić. 'Straight after the conventional niceties', Dimović wrote, 'he switched to politics. He talked in sharp terms against the Magyars. He emphasized how everything could be achieved in Vienna and through Vienna, and that nothing could be done in Budapest.' Potiorek was present during the conversation. As soon as the Archduke finished and left this group, he told the three politicians that such statements could not be regarded as official, and asked them to keep quiet about what they had heard.[108]

Accounts of the dinner speak of forty-one persons present, which is indeed the number on the official *Sitzliste*, but there were additional visitors. For example Conrad, whose name does not appear on the list, also arrived at some point, together with his aide-de-camp Major Rudolf Kundmann and Colonel Josef Metzger, the head of operations planning – as seen in chapter twelve, the latter was to be told that evening by Franz Ferdinand that the German Kaiser had, while at Konopischt, recommended to him an early strike. Those three high officers, however, had to leave by 9 p.m. as Conrad was hurrying to Karlovac in Croatia. Conrad wrote later that the Archduke and the Duchess presided over the dinner in a most amiable way.[109] Certainly, there existed good reasons for the couple to be in a buoyant mood. The Duchess had just been informed on the telephone that Maximilian, the elder son, had done well in his entrance examination at the famous *Schottengymnasium* in Vienna. During the informal after-dinner circling, a smiling Duchess saw Sunarić from a distance and made with her finger a mockingly threatening gesture towards him. She was clearly aware of the warning Sunarić had sent to Vienna to try and stop the Archduke's visit, for she told him: 'Dear Dr Sunarić, you were mistaken after all, things are not the way you always depict them. Everywhere we went here, the people, including without any exception the Serbian population, have greeted us in such a friendly way, with such cordiality and unfeigned warmth, that we are very happy about it.' To which Sunarić replied, famously: 'Your Highness, I pray to God that, should I have the honour of seeing you tomorrow evening, you will be able to repeat those same words to me. A burden, a great burden will then fall off my chest.'[110]

But the Duchess was in a superb mood and was actually looking forward to the next day. She spoke to Sarajevo's mayor Fehim Effendi Ćurčić and expressed to him her desire to meet Muslim women during the planned visit to the Town Hall. The *Bürgermeister* naturally replied that her wish would be accommodated.[111] She and her husband would have been surprised to know that Ćurčić was a member of the first Bosnian Masonic lodge and had, according to some accounts, become the mayor of Sarajevo thanks to that.[112] The Archduke, too, was in genial mood, smoking his *Regalia Media* Havana cigar, and talking about his favourable impressions of the country and its people. Such 'remaining, minor prejudices' that he may have had against Bosnia (he did not elaborate which) had now disappeared. Much progress had been made, he said, since his last trip to Bosnia in 1899 – on that occasion he shot a bear in the Kupres region.[113]

The joviality, however, did not last all night. Later on, with many of the guests already departed, a most remarkable debate developed among the remnants of the company. The subject of this urgent ad hoc conference was whether the Archduke should abort the final day's programme which envisaged him visiting Sarajevo in the morning – and simply leave Bosnia immediately instead. It is not clear what exactly gave rise to such a dramatic turn of discussion after what had by all accounts been a most pleasant and relaxed festivity. Sources differ in important details, and scholars have only added to the confusion. According to Paul Nikitsch-Boulles, the Archduke's private secretary, Franz Ferdinand remarked after dinner: 'Thank God that this Bosnian journey is now over.' Whereupon Karl von Rumerskirch, his chamberlain (although Nikitsch-Boulles was not quite sure, he thought it may have been Rumerskirch, but in any case someone from the Archduke's entourage), proposed that he should simply cancel tomorrow's visit and embark on his return journey that same night. Nikitsch-Boulles wrote that there now followed 'from all sides' a lively coaxing of the Archduke to agree to the proposal – and he 'almost' gave in, but some 'military' voices were then raised, arguing that a cancellation would amount to a 'direct insult' of General Potiorek. Nikitsch-Boulles did not give the names of any of those who objected to the proposal, but wrote that they 'badgered' the Archduke with arguments until in the end the programme remained unchanged. In fact, as will be seen, the decisive voice was that of Potiorek's aide-de-camp Erik Merizzi. Potiorek himself had apparently already left by that stage.

What, it may be asked, was the sudden hurry to just cut everything and run? Nikitsch-Boulles speculated that the entourage may have had a premonition of the next morning's tragedy. He added that people around Franz Ferdinand knew only too well his distaste for the whole Bosnian journey.[114] Carl von Bardolff, the head of the Archduke's military chancellery and another important source for this episode, provided a possible clue. He stated in his memoirs that after the festivities were over Franz Ferdinand assured him how 'extraordinarily' contented he was with the progress of the journey hitherto. 'Nevertheless', Bardolff continued, 'the anxieties stemming apparently from uncontrollable rumours had not been fully disposed of among the gentlemen in the entourage'. Unfortunately, Bardolff said nothing about the nature of those 'uncontrollable rumours', but in the light of his testimony it would not be pure conjecture to say that the rumours, which evidently existed, must have related to the safety aspects of Franz Ferdinand's stay in Bosnia. Nor did Bardolff volunteer any information about where exactly he had stood in this debate.

Soon after the assassination the *Reichspost* reported that the Serbs had had criminal plans, about which 'it had been rumoured in Sarajevo for weeks already'.[115] In his 1934 memoir Dobroslav Jevđević wrote of the 'general conviction' in Sarajevo that the Heir to the Throne was exposing himself to an assassination, and that there had been 'public talk about some conspiracy against Ferdinand'.[116] Of course, the kind of stories picked up in Sarajevo by army or police informers about a possible threat to the Archduke could only have been extremely vague – otherwise there would have been no assassination on 28 June. It was seen earlier in this chapter how in 1919 Teodor Zurunić recalled Edmund Gerde's warning to Potiorek that the Sarajevo police were on the tracks of a conspiracy. It is entirely possible that one or more of Potiorek's officers may have been conscientious enough to pass this on to Franz Ferdinand's entourage – this could account for the drama emerging in Hotel Bosna towards midnight on 27 June.

Rumours and whispers undoubtedly circulated, and must have reached someone in that entourage – they must also have been either sufficiently persistent or sufficiently alarming to provoke the startling proposal to cut the visit short. But who proposed this? Whereas, as has been seen, Nikitsch-Boulles opined that this person may have been Rumerskirch, Bardolff named him as Major Paul Höger. This officer had served with the Chiefs of Staff, before being transferred to Franz Ferdinand's military chancellery. Bardolff related that Höger put forward ('for consideration') a proposal whereby the official visit to Sarajevo should perhaps be abandoned and the journey home be undertaken 'swiftly' that night. But the suggestion, according to Bardolff's account, was rejected in a friendly way by a smiling Archduke.[117] Other accounts do not mention a smiling Archduke.

Interestingly, Höger himself wrote not a word about this event in his published memoir (1924) on the *Todesfahrt* (death journey). He merely stated that the possibility of 'incidents' had not been overlooked, and that there had been no shortage of 'warnings'.[118] There exists a third source, however. This is Andreas von Morsey. He recounted that after dinner an intimate circle had formed around the Archduke. They stayed together until midnight. Morsey emphasized the Archduke's 'particularly good mood' that evening. And it was Rumerskirch, according to Morsey, who aired the following plan: now that the manoeuvres were over, next morning's planned programme of a trip around Sarajevo should be dropped, and the shortest route via Mostar should be taken 'immediately [*gleich*]' to reach the battleship *Viribus Unitis*. Morsey believed that Major Höger 'supported' this proposal which was then considered 'in all seriousness'. He then continued, dramatically: 'The cancellation of 28 June came to within an inch, and it was not excluded that the Archduke would acquiesce.' But then there were objections. Morsey named Lieutenant-Colonel Erik von Merizzi as the person who quashed the plan: 'Merizzi expressed serious misgivings and thought that a cancellation of the reception in Sarajevo would be a slight against the absolutely Monarchy-loyal Croatian population, and would be regarded as an affront.' The account by Nikitsch-Boulles, mentioned earlier, adds a significant detail to this picture in talking of the 'direct insult' to Potiorek which would ensue if the visit were cancelled. So the group went along with Merizzi's view. It was already 28 June, Morsey writes, when they dispersed.[119]

Merizzi's decisive intervention towards midnight on 27 June thus ensured, if not the death of the Archduke, then at the very least the possibility that he was going to be facing death the following morning. Two out of three accounts of the late night consultation in Hotel Bosna on 27 June (Nikitsch-Boulles and Morsey) agree that matters stood on a razor's edge. The third account, that by Bardolff, also hints at a drama. Merizzi may or may not have cared about the sensitivities of the Sarajevo Croats when he persuaded Franz Ferdinand to continue with his visit to the city on Sunday – it is rather more likely that the Italian in Merizzi held the Croats in disdain. But he cared about his boss Potiorek. A cancellation of the visit on security grounds would have been a damning comment on Potiorek's competence in Bosnia-Herzegovina. A triumphal parade through the streets of Sarajevo, on the other hand, would have brought him nearer to becoming Conrad's successor. Merizzi, in opposing those members of the Archduke's entourage seeking a premature end to the visit, certainly thought he knew what he was doing.

15

Assassins' Avenue:
Sarajevo 28 June 1914

The Motorcade

AFTER BREAKFAST on Sunday 28 June Franz Ferdinand dictated a telegram to Baron Morsey for his daughter Sophie in Chlumetz: 'Myself and Mummy feeling quite good. Weather warm and nice. Yesterday we had a big dinner and this morning there will be the big reception in Sarajevo. In the afternoon again a big lunch and then the journey back on *Viribus Unitis*. I embrace you dearly. Tuesday. Daddy.' Tuesday was the day the Archduke expected to be seeing his daughter again. Another telegram was composed for Dr Horak, his secretary at Konopischt. In the event, neither of those telegrams was ever sent.[1]

Good Catholic that he was – at least since marrying Sophie Chotek – Archduke Franz Ferdinand began his day at 9 a.m. by attending mass in Hotel Bosna – in a room on the first floor serving as private chapel for the occasion of his visit. General Potiorek had spared no expense to create a proper place of worship here, complete with coloured windows to darken the daylight. The service was conducted by Johann Hromadka, the *Feld-superior* attached to the 15th Corps. In this rather restricted space, the strong smell of flowers combined with palpable heat to produce an oppressive atmosphere.[2] A little later mass was said separately for the Duchess of Hohenberg, accompanied only by Countess Vilma Lanjus, her lady-in-waiting.[3] The Duchess, known for her at times excessive religiosity, took communion – which, as Rebecca West noted, she would do 'so extremely often that she was constantly at odds with the Bishop who guided her spiritual life'.[4]

It was a fine day. The burgers of Sarajevo later recalled it as one full of gentle warmth and flickering light.[5] Making their way out of the Hotel Bosna, the Archduke and the Duchess, together with their entourage, also all staying at the hotel, walked the short distance across the park to the small Ilidža railway station and climbed onto the *Hofsonderzug* for Sarajevo.

On this, his last day, Franz Ferdinand was resplendently attired in the parade uniform of a General of Cavalry: a light blue *Waffenrock* – the subsequently famous blood-stained tunic with its raised collar through which the assassin's bullet was to enter; black trousers with a double line of broad red stripes; a gold-braided waist belt; a helmet with its distinctive plume of fluffy, pale-green rooster feathers; and a sword with two large tassels hanging down from its handle. As always on such occasions, the Archduke was sporting a row of decorations, with the highest, the Order of the Golden Fleece, around his neck.

The Duchess, for her part, wore a long white silk dress, a red sash around her waist, decorated with flowers; ermine tails hung from her shoulders. A broad-brimmed hat with black ostrich feathers and a veil completed her outfit. Anticipating strong sunshine and heat, she carried a parasol and a fan.

A minor delay now ensued in the proceedings. Although the train's departure had been scheduled for 9.25 a.m., it actually left at around 9.42, arriving at a tobacco factory on the western edge of Sarajevo at 10.07.[6] That is to say, the train did not bring its passengers to the Sarajevo railway station, as has been claimed in numerous accounts of 28 June 1914. The reason the train took its royal passengers and their entourage to the tobacco factory was that their programme envisaged a short visit to the Filipović barracks, which were close to the factory. From the barracks, their journey into town would continue in a motorcade of cars. Despite his cavalry rank, the Archduke actually disliked riding horses. But he rather liked cars: 'I am an admirer of the automobile', he once said, 'it is a most marvellous thing.'[7]

As the train departed from Ilidža a 24-gun salute was fired. There was a further gun salute when the train crossed the city boundary, and one more when it arrived at the tobacco factory. So far, Potiorek had organized things splendidly. As the Archduke entered the barracks, the imperial flag was hoisted. Completed in 1901, the *Phillipoviclager* barracks had been named after Baron Josip Filipović who had, in 1878, led the Austro-Hungarian armies to subdue stiff, largely Muslim, local resistance to the occupation of Bosnia-Herzegovina.

The Archduke was received by Michael von Appel, who had as a young lieutenant fought with distinction and been wounded in the 1878 Bosnian campaign. Now a general, and since 1911 the commander of the Sarajevo-based 15th Corps, he and his officers formally greeted Franz Ferdinand in the presence of Potiorek. Apart from the guard of honour for the Archduke, the barracks was empty. As Appel complained bitterly afterwards, Potiorek had ordered the Army to remain outside Sarajevo on completion of the manoeuvres – the troops were not to return to the city before 29 June. This had been done, Appel wrote, 'without us even being asked about it'. All that had remained in Sarajevo were two depleted companies of the 92nd Regiment and three equally under-strength companies from 12th Regiment – some 250 men altogether.[8]

During the short stopover at the Filipović barracks, the Duchess waited outside in the company of Count Franz Harrach and local dignitaries from Sarajevo. Seeing Mayor Ćurčić among them, she sent Harrach to check with him whether he had arranged the meeting with the Muslim ladies for later that morning in the Town Hall. On hearing of the Mayor's confirmation that all had been prepared, the Duchess looked over at him with a contented smile.[9] Then, with the inspection of this military establishment complete, the Sarajevo visit was able to proceed towards its next port of call – the Town Hall. It was about 10.17 a.m.

At this point, the historical picture of what happened next gets completely confused about something which turned out to be rather important: namely, how many cars there were in the archducal convoy, and who was in each. Different scholars have given different numbers. Kiszling, Remak, Dedijer, Würthle and Galántai have six cars. Aichelburg, Brook-Shepherd, Cassels, Holler, Sösemann, Weissensteiner and Grgić, however, have seven cars.[10] An American historian recently identified only three vehicles.[11] Fay, Schmitt and even Albertini mentioned only four cars.[12]

To some extent the confusion among experts reflects an inconsistency in the way the witnesses recounted their stories: many of them, particularly those in the entourage, in their mind's eye placed the archducal car at the head of the column, counting it as the leading car and deferentially ignoring any vehicles in front of it. The perceived number and order of the cars thus depends on how they were being counted. This is not in itself important with regard to the journey to the Town Hall, but it does become a factor in the narrative about the return journey from the municipal head-quarters. Sarajevo 1914 is popularly seen as a farcical, indeed tragicomic affair, whereby someone 'forgot' to inform a chauffeur about an amended itinerary, resulting in the most disastrous 'wrong turning' in history. If so, who exactly was that chauffeur, which car was he driving, and who were the people sitting in the car?

There were in fact eight cars waiting for the train passengers from Ilidža. On the basis of contemporary and memoir accounts it is possible to reconstruct the following order and composition of the motorcade:

Car No. 1: Karl Mayerhoffer, Dr Josef Troyer von Monaldi and (presumed) local chauffeur.

In all the countless chronicles of 28 June 1914 Mayerhoffer is hardly ever mentioned, and Troyer has never before been named. These people have somehow remained obscure and their car scarcely figures on the pages of history. Yet their front car was guiding not only his Royal and Imperial

Highness but also, in retrospect, the destiny of the world. Mayerhoffer was the commander of the Sarajevo police force, and Troyer was in charge of the security bureau of the Provincial Government. Just a few days later, in his press statement of 3 July 1914, Mayor Ćurčić, who had on 28 June been in the car behind, clearly identified Mayerhoffer and Troyer as leading the way.[13] Their car was actually the most distinctive one in the convoy, as it was the only one with a hard top, all the others being convertibles with roofs folded back.[14]

This car probably fails to figure in the recollections of some of the witnesses because, as one bystander, Dr Max Bernstein, testified, it was some distance ahead of the second car and therefore not obviously part of the procession.[15] At one point during the drive it was so far ahead of the others that it stopped and even reversed in order to reconnect with the rest of the motorcade.[16] It is likely that Mayerhoffer and Troyer were being driven by a chauffeur, but no one else is named in contemporary accounts with regard to this car. In 1971, Friedrich Würthle, an Austrian writer, placed police inspector Władisław Gluck, of Polish nationality, and detective inspector Petar Maksimović, of Serb nationality (along with a local chauffeur) in this car. However, Würthle does not even mention Mayorhoffer or Troyer, and his assertion about Gluck and Maksimović is not accompanied by any documentary corroboration.[17]

Car No. 2: Fehim Effendi Ćurčić, Dr Edmund Gerde and local chauffeur.

This is the famous *Bürgermeisterwagen* (mayoral car) which the vast majority of Sarajevo 1914 narratives have as leading the way both to and from the Town Hall. In this distorted context, the archducal car moves up the claimed order to second place, just behind the mayoral car. Many accounts place an unnamed 'chief of police' in this car with Mayor Ćurčić. The most celebrated account of Sarajevo 1914, that by Dedijer, actually names him – as Dr Edmund Gerde, and gives his rank as 'Chief of Police'.[18] Yet, strictly speaking, Gerde was the deputy government commissioner for Sarajevo, and it was Mayerhoffer who was in charge of the police (*Polizeikommandant*). This slightly confusing designation of Gerde has arisen because Mayerhoffer answered to Gerde in the Sarajevo administrative structure. Technically, therefore, Gerde was in charge of the police. But the narrower police apparatus was actually in Mayerhoffer's hands.[19] So to call Gerde 'chief of police' is somewhat misleading, as he was a bureaucrat, not a policeman. Still, however described, Gerde was indeed in this second car, together with Ćurčić – as many witnesses testified. The car was a 'Landes Auto Nr. 5', a Bosnian Government car, its registration plate simply displaying the number 5.[20] Because of their rank and status, Ćurčić and Gerde had a local chauffeur driving them – a photograph clearly shows a uniformed (though non-military) chauffeur leaning on this car soon after the arrival of the motorcade at the Town Hall.[21] No one else has ever been mentioned as riding in this car.

Car No. 3: Archduke Franz Ferdinand, Duchess Sophie Hohenberg, General Oskar Potiorek, Count Franz Harrach, Gustav Schneiberg and Leopold Lojka (chauffeur).

The third car, possessing the Viennese number plate A III-118, was a 'Doppelphaeton', a 28/32 PS-type touring car with a folding top, manufactured in Vienna in 1910 by the renowned firm of Gräf & Stift.[22] Its bodywork was decked out separately by Carl Czerny & Co. – in accordance, as was the custom, with the owner's specifications. Made of wood covered by sheets of aluminium, its fine leather upholstery left bystanders in no doubt that this was indeed a luxury car. On 28 June 1914, proudly fastened on its left side was the Habsburg imperial ensign.

Count Harrach, the car's owner, was Franz Ferdinand's friend from Bohemia. He sat on one of the two auxiliary seats in the back – these seats were supported by just one prop in order to provide maximum leg space for the back seat passengers.[23] Harrach was a member of the Austrian Volunteer Automobile Corps, founded in 1906, and commanded in 1914 by Prince Alexander Solms-Braunfels. The Archduke's military chancellery had asked the Volunteer Automobile Corps to provide cars for the use of the Archduke and his entourage during the Bosnian trip – it was the usual practice for the Automobile Corps to drive the royals around at various manoeuvres.

The *Leibjäger*, or bodyguard, was Gustav Schneiberg. A photograph shows him sitting in front next to the chauffeur as the motorcade left the Filipović barracks. On that day of 28 June, he was in uniform, probably that of a reserve officer, and was to play his own small part in the momentous events of the morning.[24]

The driver, Lojka, in some accounts mistakenly named Sojka, was a 28-year old, Vienna-based Czech from Moravia, *en route* to becoming the most talked about chauffeur in history. His role did not go unappreciated at the time: Lojka received from Franz Joseph (on 27 July 1914) a gold watch, engraved with the imperial eagles, as a reward for 'services rendered' in Sarajevo on 28 June 1914.[25]

In this car Potiorek did not, as is almost always stated, sit 'across' or 'opposite', that is, facing the Archduke and the Duchess. That would have been quite impossible as the two auxiliary collapsible folding seats faced forwards. What Potiorek did was to push down the folding mechanism meant to support the back of the passenger, and sit rather uncomfortably on the seat nearest to the Archduke, with his back leaning on the inside left door of the car, thus looking sideways at Franz Ferdinand and the Duchess.

Car No. 4: Baron Karl Rumerskirch, Countess Vilma Lanjus, Lieutenant-Colonel Erik von Merizzi, Count Alexander Boos-Waldeck and Karl Divjak (chauffeur).

Boos-Waldeck, a reserve Senior Lieutenant, was the owner of this vehicle, a Mercedes Knight.[26] Like Harrach, he was a member of the Austrian Volunteer Automobile Corps. His father, Count Hugo Boos-Waldeck was a teammate of designer Ferdinand Porsche in the Austro-Daimler racing team. Divjak, aged 24 and from Trieste, was in all the relevant testimonies identified as the chauffeur of this car, but after the war he made the fantastic claim that it was he who in fact had driven Franz Ferdinand's car.[27] Boos-Waldeck sat next to Divjak in the front of the car. Merizzi sat on the auxiliary seat in the back. It was a matter of protocol that Countess Lanjus, as the lady-in-waiting to the Duchess (sitting on the right), and Baron Rumerskirch, as the Archduke's chamberlain, were placed together in the main seats at the back. The Countess was the daughter of Admiral Karl Lanjus von Wellenburg.

Car No. 5: Colonel Dr Carl von Bardolff, Major Paul Höger, Dr Ferdinand Fischer, Senior Lieutenant Adolf Egger and Max Thiel (chauffeur).

Egger was the director of the Fiat works in Vienna. He too was a member of the Austrian Volunteer Automobile Corps and this was his car – which, predictably, was a Fiat.[28] He sat in front next to Max Thiel, the chauffeur. Bardolff was the senior figure in this car and he was placed in the back with Höger on his left. On the auxiliary seat in front of Höger sat Dr Fischer who was a Court doctor in Vienna. His services were to be required in the course of the morning. Dr Victor Eisenmenger, Franz Ferdinand's personal physician, had fallen ill and had not accompanied him to Bosnia-Herzegovina.

Car No. 6: Count Josef Erbach-Fürstenau, Baron Moritz von Ditfurth, Major Erich von Hüttenbrenner, Lieutenant Robert Grein and Eduard Grein (presumed chauffeur).

Robert Grein was an industrialist and a reserve lieutenant from Graz. Yet another member of the Volunteer Automobile Corps, he was the owner of this car. His brother Eduard, who is mentioned in several witness accounts but never under his first name, had accompanied Robert on the Sarajevo trip. Eduard was a 'Reserve-Kadett' in the artillery, but wore civilian clothes on 28 June.[29] The two brothers and their car had been at the disposal of the Duchess during her Sarajevo excursions on 26 and 27 June.

It is doubtful that this car was driven by Robert Grein himself on 28 June – as Wladimir Aichelburg claimed in his 1984 book.[30] Baron Morsey who that day had been in the car behind, wrote in his 1934 memoir that the brothers Grein were both in this vehicle, while Hüttenbrenner was already suggesting on 29 June that Robert Grein may have had his own chauffeur – by which Hüttenbrenner probably meant Grein's brother Eduard.[31] Indeed, on the way back from the Town Hall, Robert Grein switched to car no.4 in the restructured cortege, which would suggest that someone else like Eduard, rather than Robert, had been driving this car.

Major Hüttenbrener, formerly a General Staff officer, had been serving in Franz Ferdinand's military chancellery since 1911. The count from Vienna, Josef Erbach-Fürstenau, held the rank of *Garderittmeister* (colonel in the Imperial Horse Guards). Baron Ditfurth was Potiorek's personal adjutant, not to be confused with Merizzi who was Potiorek's *Flügel-adjutant* (aide-de-camp).

Car No. 7: Baron Andreas Morsey, Captain Gustav Pilz, Dr Heinrich Starch and (presumed) local chauffeur.

It is not clear who drove this car and who its owner was. None of the three passengers was likely to have been the owner. Bosnia-Herzegovina had its own automobile club in 1914 with headquarters in Sarajevo (*Bosnisch-Hercegowinischen Automobil-Club*), and it may have supplied this car and a chauffeur, or this could have been done by the government in Sarajevo. Captain Pilz, although he was described by Baron Morsey as Franz Ferdinand's orderly, was in fact a liaison officer from the 92nd infantry regiment in Sarajevo, and had been allocated to the Archduke for the duration of the visit. Dr Starch, a German from Bohemia, was an official in the Provincial Government, and had as a local expert been accompanying the Duchess around Sarajevo over the previous two days. Baron Morsey, in his statement on 28 June, could not remember whether he had travelled in the 'fourth or the fifth' car – but like several other members in the entourage of Franz Ferdinand, he was counting the archducal car as the first, neglecting the two cars in front.[32] Morsey was therefore in what he would count as the 'fifth' car, but which in reality was car no.7.[33]

Car No. 8: This was the reserve car, and as events unfolded it was to prove its worth in the convoy. History books, strangely, have taken no note of this last car. But Morsey mentions it in three separate published accounts (in July 1914, in 1924 and in 1934). In the rendition of 1934 he explicitly stated that 'a special reserve car completed the column'. In 1924 he wrote that this car was 'empty', which – apart from the driver – it would have been as a reserve car.[34]

Colonel Bardolff, in his 3 July report on the assassination written at Conrad's explicit request, stated that the passengers of Boos-Waldeck's car, which had been incapacitated by the effects of the exploding bomb, had switched to Lieutenant Grein's car (No. 6) – highly improbable, given that Grein's car only had one spare seat.[35] In fact, Countess Lanjus confirms in her unpublished memoir that, after the bomb attack, the passengers in her car had actually gone to the reserve car (*'Wir bestiegen ein Reserveauto und fuhren zum Rathause'*).[36]

There are a number of seriously misleading legends concerning the motorcade. One of these, often repeated by historians, was originated by the great authority Vladimir Dedijer. On this occasion misreading his source (the Polish-language memoirs of Leon Biliński) Dedijer writes: 'The first car was reserved for the special security detectives, but an initial slip in the program occurred when only their chief officer climbed in with three local police officers, leaving behind all the others, who were in Sarajevo specifically to guard the Archduke.'[37] Dedijer gives no names, and the minimum of four passengers in the front car of the motorcade, which his assertion entails, was never reported in any witness accounts. Other writers and historians, however, have been mesmerised by this attractive yet entirely unauthenticated story – so much so that, as is explained in the footnote to this passage, some of them appear to have, for reasons best known to themselves, carelessly dropped Dedijer as the true source of their accounts and instead embraced Biliński – Dedijer's source. The farcical aspect of this is that Dedijer had badly misread Biliński and even cited the wrong page number of Biliński's book when referencing it. A comedy of errors has since ensued, as some other historians have repeated Dedijer's blunders while claiming that their source was Biliński, and have even cited the same wrong page in the Minister's memoirs – which also seems to indicate that they went no further than reading Dedijer or each other on this matter.[38]

Already in 1914 there had been a similar kind of story about a security lapse, mentioned in the diary of Ludwig Thallóczy, of the joint Finance Ministry. According to this, a detective who had been allocated to the Archduke, together with the Archduke's butler, had both had to wait the whole time at the Museum near the Filipović barracks because no car was available for them.[39] Vienna, however, was in the days after 28 June full of post-assassination tales of this kind. In truth there was no special security policeman waiting at the barracks. Those who had been brought in from outside Sarajevo (from Vienna and Budapest) had already taken up their posts in the city.[40] As the Sarajevo police knew only too well, detectives were in short supply that day, and they would have been fairly useless riding in cars.

The fact that the Archduke was moving in an open car was something that had not been planned. On the contrary, it had been stressed that it was 'absolutely necessary' that he should ride in a closed vehicle (*'unbedingt erforderliche geschlossene Wagen'*). Colonel Bardolff, Franz Ferdinand's aide-de-camp, wrote to this effect to Count Harrach on 22 June when he found out to his embarrassment that Harrach's car was an open tourer. The problem was that Harrach, as the highest ranking member of the Volunteer Automobile Corps in Sarajevo, had been designated to have the Archduke in his car. Bardolff therefore politely asked Harrach to swap cars with Boos-Waldeck whose vehicle, he believed, matched the security requirements. In a country where the officialdom was obsessed with rank and status, Harrach accordingly could and should accompany Franz Ferdinand – provided he took Boos-Waldeck's car.[41] It transpired, however, that Boos-Waldeck also had an open touring car. In the end, therefore, the Archduke and his wife climbed into Harrach's vehicle: full etiquette was thus maintained, but security had been sacrificed. The famous Austrian *Schlamperei*, that notorious sloppiness, was alive and well in Sarajevo on 28 June.

This, then, was the procession of motor vehicles, with Mayerhoffer and Troyer leading, Ćurčić and Gerde following, the Archduke and the Duchess in the third car, and behind them five more cars, including the reserve car, setting off in an easterly direction towards the Town Hall. In accordance with the rule of the road of the time they were driving on the left.

The Hunter Hunted: Čabrinović's Bomb

Journeying along the Bahnhofstrasse, the cars turned gently into Mustafa-bey Street, soon emerging at the beginning of the long Appel Quay running alongside the Miljacka river to their right. Appel Quay was Sarajevo's main avenue, named not after General Michael Appel mentioned earlier, but rather after Johann von Appel, the Military Governor of Bosnia-Herzegovina from 1882 to 1903.[42] This Appel had, like his boss, the Joint Finance Minister Kállay, argued for the creation and promotion of a specific Bosnian-Herzegovinian identity to counter Serbian and Croatian political and cultural influences, and proposed the creation of a specific 'Bosnian' language.[43] Appel Quay, in the memorable description of Archbishop Stadler, was shortly to become better-known as the 'avenue of the assassins'.

As they entered the town, the Archduke and the Duchess could see the houses and buildings on their route decorated in their honour. Mayor Ćurčić had already issued a proclamation to his fellow townsmen on 23 June that they should prepare an 'imposing' welcome so that the Heir to the Throne could be assured of their 'immense love', and also take home memories of the well-known 'Slavonic hospitality'. The Mayor was particularly keen that houses and shops be adorned with flags, rugs, flowers and other decorative objects.[44] Indeed, by 27 June, the local *Bosnische Post* was able to report that wherever one looked there were flags on display: those of the Empire, Bosnia-Herzegovina, the Serbian and Croatian tricolors, as well as the 'green flags of the Prophet'.[45] A special accolade *en route* for the Archduke had been prepared by the city authorities on 23 June, when they renamed a section of the central Ćemaluša Street into 'Franz-Ferdinand-Strasse'.

But there was a further, invisible and unreported measure to prettify the place. Sarajevo's dregs of society, its criminal and anti-social elements, had been picked up from the streets by the police and imprisoned for the duration of the Archduke's stay. Following the assassination, they were released and unleashed against Sarajevo's Serbian population.[46]

With the motorcade now in the town, Potiorek's role was that of a tourist guide. He was drawing the attention of the Archduke and the Duchess to anything interesting along the way.[47] Franz Ferdinand had asked that the speed be reduced so that he could observe the sights at leisure. No doubt he was enjoying all the visible and audible honours around him. Cannon salutes were being fired with attendant noise, and military music was to be heard playing somewhere in town. Rows of people were cheering along the side of the road. Sarajevo's Croats were perhaps the most delighted by the visit. They were shouting: 'Long live the future Croat King!'[48] Apart from the fact that many men, and not just the Muslims, wore the fez, the Archduke could see they were dressed in much the same way as anywhere else in Austria-Hungary on a festive occasion: tails and top hats and plenty of uniformed men, including those wearing veterans' and fire brigade uniforms.[49] In the bright June sunshine, all of Sarajevo's different denizens appeared to have come together to give the royal couple a warm welcome. Potiorek must have felt very gratified.

An alternative welcome had of course also been prepared along the Appel Quay – the famous 'avenue of the assassins'. That designation, however, is somewhat overblown, for the assassins did not represent a single, integrated team. Princip, Grabež and Čabrinović knew each other of course, and they all knew Danilo Ilić, but they did not know Mehmed-bašić, Čubrilović and Popović – the troika put together by Ilić at Princip's request from Belgrade. Princip had known of its existence, but not the identity of its members. Whilst Čubrilović and Popović did know each other, they did not know anyone else except for Ilić. Mehmedbašić for his part knew only Ilić. And not all of them, in fact, could properly be described as assassins, least of all the youngest two, Čubrilović and Popović, who had received no weapons training. Ilić, the central coordinating figure, was pacing up and down Appel Quay unarmed. His heart and mind, as has been seen, were no longer in the conspiracy, and he had already persuaded Trifko Grabež that the assassination of the Archduke was a bad idea. But on 28 June he was still going through the motions, probably in deference to Princip's grim determination. The question now was just how determined the other conspirators would be.

At the Appel Quay there was a very brief stop at the imposing main post office, during which Count Harrach and bodyguard Schneiberg apparently switched their positions in the archducal car, with Harrach now sitting in front next to Lojka, and Schneiberg on the reserve seat next to Potiorek. The stop at the post office was just a courtesy call to allow the Archduke to express a few words of appreciation to Emil Gaberle, its able Polish director. One of Gaberle's officials then handed the Archduke a telegram that had just arrived from his children at Chlumetz. In front of the building the commander of Sarajevo's cadet school had lined up some of his young uniformed pupils to give the visitors a brisk salute. The sight of these boys made the Archduke enquire as to their identity, while the Duchess waved at them, 'visibly' and 'pleasantly surprised'.[50] Very soon thereafter, a most unpleasant surprise followed.

It was about 10.30 – Vojislav Bogićević, a witness, recalls hearing the bells of the Catholic cathedral. Another estimate put the time at between 10.26 and 10.30.[51] Around then, according to a postwar Bosnian Serb account, a big black and yellow Habsburg flag, hanging from the Racher & Babić locksmiths store near the Catholic cathedral, suddenly swayed and fell to the ground.[52] If true, it was a most allegorical scene on a day which was to presage so much change in Europe.

At about this time the motorcade passed the first of the six armed conspirators: Vaso Čubrilović, armed with a bomb and a Browning. A minor fallacy has since been perpetuated in the more detailed analyses of the assassination to the effect that the first in the row of the assassins was Muhamed Mehmedbašić. His fellow-conspirator Ilić had indeed told Mehmedbašić to stand at the Austro-Hungarian Bank (erected in 1912), a placement that would have enabled him to inaugurate the hostile reception. The rest of the team was due to be positioned, in a kind of zig-zag fashion, further down the Appel Quay towards the Town Hall. In the books reconstructing the event, every single map of this area of Sarajevo (showing where the motorcade moved as the assassins waited) has Mehmedbašić in position no. 1.

In fact, Mehmedbašić was in position no. 3. Waiting for the motorcade before him were Čubrilović at no. 24 Appel Quay and, in spot no. 2, Nedeljko Čabrinović, who stood on the riverside almost opposite building no. 24. When, according to Ilić's instruction, Mehmedbašić arrived to take his place at the Bank, he realized that there were no people in the immediate vicinity. So in order not to draw attention to himself, he decided to move up towards the Town Hall instead, where he could mingle with the crowd. As he himself stated in 1938, he had walked past Čabrinović by 'some thirty steps'.[53] That put him in the third ambush spot in relation to the approaching motorcade. Another mistaken belief about Mehmedbašić is that he was on 28 June armed with only a bomb. It has already been mentioned in chapter eleven that Mehmedbašić had in March 1914 obtained a Browning pistol from a friend for the purpose of the planned (and later abandoned) assassination of General Potiorek. According to his own testimony, he had arrived in Sarajevo in June carrying this weapon and Ilić had additionally given him a bomb – as well as poison.[54] In other words, of the six assassins, only Čabrinović did not have a handgun.

Very close to Mehmedbašić, though unknown to him at the time, was assassin no. 4, Cvetko Popović, waiting on the corner of Ćumurija Street at a kiosk contained inside the corner building. This was at the point of Appel Quay level with the Ćumurija bridge – the Jewish Temple and the headquarters of the 15th Corps across the river already being behind. The crowd, in order to avoid the strong sunshine, had chosen to wait for the visitors under the shades of the chestnut trees lining that side of the avenue with its buildings facing the river. No one, except for Čabrinović and an acquaintance he was using for cover, stood across the road on the sunny side of the street. Danilo Ilić, unarmed, was also nearby, so that this area was absolutely crowded with conspirators. Gavrilo Princip, in position no. 6, was a considerable distance further up, standing on the riverside near the Latin bridge, whereas the sixth and last assassin, Trifko Grabež, was at the next bridge towards the Town Hall, the Kaiser bridge.

As the cars approached hats were flung into the air, accompanied by cheers of 'Long live!' – '*Živio!*' in Serbo-Croat and '*Hoch!*' in German: both languages could be heard. Some people had stepped onto the road and the police, visibly nervous, started pushing them back onto the pavement. In the third car the Archduke had just taken an interest in the Prince Eugen barracks, a new, yellow bastion sitting atop a hill in the distance straight ahead, whereas Potiorek was trying to draw his attention to the seat of the 15th Corps on the right.[55] At this moment Vojislav Bogićević, standing on the pavement close to his friend Cvetko Popović (but otherwise uncon-nected with the assassination plot), recognised Mayerhoffer in the first car because of his red hair, and he also saw 'someone else' in the same car – this was Troyer von Monaldi.[56] The first two cars in the motorcade had driven past building no. 24 on Appel Quay, only a few metres from the Ćumurija bridge. The building housed the residence and offices of Danilo Dimović, the Serbian vice-president of the Bosnian Assembly, who had attended the gala dinner in Ilidža the previous evening. On the ground floor was the Miotto gas, water and electric installations workshop. Dimović's wife Slava was watching from the window of their apartment on the second floor. She was a few days later to give a very detailed witness statement.

Unknown to Mrs Dimović, Vaso Čubrilović, the youngest of the conspirators at only seventeen, was on the pavement underneath. He had initially positoned himself close by at the women's college. Like Mehmed-bašić, however, he had moved on so as to be within the crowd. When questioned on 6 July about his part in the assassination, he stated: 'As the Archduke drove past me I did not reach for either the bomb or the revolver, for when I saw the Archduke I felt troubled about killing him [*war es mir leid, ihn zu töten*]'.[57] The softheartedness on the part of Čubrilović, if that is what it was, thus left everything undisturbed and shifted matters, and the initiative, to the second assassin: Nedeljko Čabrinović.

Mrs Dimović could from her privileged position observe very precisely what was happening on the other side of the avenue, separated from the river below by a low stone wall – especially since there were no trees in front of her building to block her view. In her deposition of 2 July 1914 she stated that about a quarter of an hour before the cars arrived she watched two young men as they came from Ćumurija bridge and then sat on the stone wall. They spoke quietly and gesticulated with their hands. One of them – it turned out to be the assassin Čabrinović – wore dark clothes and a cap, the other wore a fez. Čabrinović later explained that the man he was with was Moric Alkalaj. The latter was deaf, dumb and spiritually disturbed. He was well known in Sarajevo and therefore good cover. The two young men stood out, as Mrs Dimović explained, because along this whole stretch of the road on the sunny side she could see no one else.

As the motorcade approached, Čabrinović, with his right hand by now in his trouser pocket, stepped slightly forward and suddenly produced an 'object' which, according to many accounts, he slammed against an iron lamp-post in order to detonate. However, eyewitness Dr Max Bernstein stated three times in his deposition that he had seen Čabrinović hit the object against the embankment stone wall.[58] Be that as it may, Čabrinović then released the bomb in the direction of the Archduke's car. Flying through the air, it landed on the car's folded roof before bouncing down onto the road. From her flat above, Mrs Dimović saw quite clearly how the Duchess suddenly 'jumped up' in the car and then, standing, turned towards the assassin 'as if she wanted to shield the Archduke'. Still in his seat, the Archduke, meanwhile, shifted and turned back to look. Dr Bernstein, who was below in the crowd with his son, noted: 'I saw exactly that Her Highness the Duchess of Hohenberg raised herself and lent forward, whereas His Imperial and Royal Highness the Heir to the Throne lifted himself only a little and made an instinctive hand movement, seemingly to push away an object.'[59]

There is a myth that Franz Ferdinand had gallantly pushed away, or deflected, the bomb onto the street – a myth repeated in innumerable histories of 28 June 1914. Austrian historians in particular are keen on rehashing this legend.[60] But it flies in the face of all the witnesses who saw and subsequently described the bomb coming down onto the roof without being deflected in any way, and then, as Harrach precisely observed, skidding off in an elliptical movement.[61] A version of this myth is that the bomb had actually landed inside the car. After the event the investigating judge asked Vojislav Bogićević if he would be prepared to testify that the Archduke had thrown the bomb out, as such a heroic gesture would reflect well on 'the pride and honour of Austria-Hungary'. Bogićević refused because to do so would be 'untrue and tendentious'.[62] His principled position did not, however, prevent the story from taking hold.

Similarly, there is a piece of fiction, endlessly retold by historians presumably because of its amusement value, to the effect that Čabrinović had with supreme nonchalance asked a policeman on the street to kindly point out the Archduke's car as the motorcade approached, and the man duly obliged. In fact, no witness had ever reported a policeman, or a detective, anywhere near Čabrinović at the time, and had there been one around he would have pounced on the bomber straight away following the loud detonation.[63] Another unlikely story about Čabrinović, reported in the Vienna press, was that he tossed his cap up into the air and cried '*Živio!* [long live!]' before he flung the bomb at the car.[64] However, two recent additions to the corpus of folk tales about what went on along the Appel Quay that day, intriguingly unsourced, are possibly the wildest yet. Robert Donia writes about the moments as the motorcade approached the Ćumurija bridge: 'Someone in the crowd hurled two bombs at the archduke's car. The first missed the car and fell behind it; the second bounced off the back of the car and exploded under the following vehicle, injuring two passengers.'[65] Did the alleged first bomb also explode? – the reader is left wondering. Donia is regarded as an expert on the history of Bosnia-Herzegovina, but it is difficult to see how his extra bomb can be anything other than the product of some serious confusion on his part. Geoffrey Wawro, another American historian, has provided a slightly more dramatic variation with regard to those moments on the Appel Quay: 'The seven Serbian assassins were strung out at intervals along the route. The first fired his Browning pistol at a range of thirty feet and missed ... The second assassin threw a hand grenade, but the archduke's driver accelerated under it and it exploded beneath the next car ...'[66] The breathtaking jolt of this new revelation about an assassin hitherto unknown to history, shooting and missing – and from *exactly* 'thirty feet' – is however quickly allayed by Wawro's lack of source. Certainly, none of the witnesses at the time, and none of the myriad of historians since, ever recorded a gunman springing into action at this point *à la* Wawro.

Another spurious tale about Sarajevo 28 June 1914 relates to the brief space of time during which the bomb was flying through the air. The story here is that the chauffeur Leopold Lojka, supposedly fully alert at just the moment when he needed to be, suddenly speeded up as he saw something being thrown and thus saved the lives of his passengers. When Wawro writes that the Archduke's driver had 'accelerated' under a bomb he is restating a widely accepted canard. Describing this scene in 1959 Joachim Remak wrote that the car's owner Count Harrach 'had heard the detonating sound made by Čabrinović's knocking off the cap of the bomb. His instinctive reaction was to think that a tyre had blown out ... The driver, more quick-witted than Harrach, also had heard the sharp, cracking sound, and had seen a black object hurling through the air. Rather than following the Count's instructions and stopping, he did precisely the right thing under the circumstances, pressed down on the accelerator, and drove on at full speed.'[67] Lojka himself claimed later that day, as he gave evidence, that he had started driving at greater speed seconds before the bomb actually exploded. Harrach also stated that his chauffeur had taken such action. But Lojka had initially done nothing of the kind. There were at least three witnesses who saw something very different. Mrs Dimović, continuing her depiction of the scene when the Duchess had stood up in the car, observed the following: 'The Duchess seated herself again and the automobile, which had very briefly stopped, started moving again and drove further at the same moderate speed with which it had arrived.'[68] So the car *had very briefly stopped*. This was just moments before the explosion.

Another witness, Josip Vrinjanin, confirmed that the Archduke's car, as well as those behind him, had indeed stopped just before the bomb went off.[69] Indeed all the cars had come to a halt except for the first two, which had already passed, and Baron Rumerskirch, sitting in the car just behind the Archduke's, even jumped out briefly to check out what was happening up front. As did Baron Morsey, further down the motorcade in car no.7, except that he had seen Čabrinović try to get away and so he got out of the car with his sword drawn. Rumerskirch had at this point observed several policemen wielding their swords, running towards the embankment wall along the river where Čabrinović was attempting to escape. Mrs Dimović related that Boos-Waldeck's car, immediately behind the archducal vehicle, had also briefly stopped.[70] Meanwhile, Čabrinović's bomb, after he had detonated it, took anything between 10 and 13 seconds to explode. It is not clear just how long he held it before releasing it. Bogićević saw him actually holding on to the bomb for a while, with it 'hissing' in his hand, after he had activated it.[71] At some point, as those seconds ticked away before the bomb's explosion, the motorcade was at a standstill.

Far from keeping cool and accelerating at this point, chauffeur Lojka had in fact got alarmed and had stepped on the brake for what might have seemed a good reason: he had heard a noise which his boss Count Harrach, sitting next to him, immediately commented on as being a burst tyre.[72] A driver does not start speeding up if he is told that a tyre has burst. Harrach's remark also suggests that neither he nor his driver had actually seen anything flying through the air. Of course, the noise had nothing to do with tyres. For as Čabrinović activated the bomb, a sound resembling a pistol shot was produced, and heard. At the same time the detonating cap of the bomb whizzed towards the Duchess and ever so slightly grazed her neck. This may explain why she suddenly stood up. Lojka did accelerate rapidly but, contrary to his later claims uncritically accepted by historians, this acceleration only took place once the bomb had come down on the roof and then fallen off – and then most probably only after the explosion itself. For, as has been seen, Mrs Dimović was categorical that the arch-ducal car, having stopped briefly, then continued at the same leisurely speed at which it had arrived. The car had stopped, of course, *after* the bomb had been activated and in reaction to the sound of that happening. Bogićević, who was on the spot, observed that the car 'swiftly accelerated' after the actual explosion, i.e., not before it.[73] Certainly, the archducal car was near enough to the scene when the bomb exploded for several pieces of shrapnel to hit its back. In any case, whether at the moment when Čabrinović propelled the bomb, or just a few seconds beforehand when he noisily activated it, the archducal car became stationary for a very short while. This may be the reason why Čabrinović neither 'threw' nor 'hurled' his bomb – but rather, as Bogićević described the scene, flipped it from underarm (*'ispod ruke'*) in the way done by children playing with coins – precisely because he could do so at leisure.[74] In her statement on 28 June Countess Lanjus emphasized that 'in the critical moment the drive was proceeding at a very slow speed'.[75] So slow, in fact, that the first two cars, carrying police commander Mayerhoffer and Mayor Ćurčić, even stopped for a while at the building of the *Prosvjeta* Serbian cultural society to wait for the rest of the motorcade.[76]

Čabrinović thus had all the time in the world. All the same, the bomb landed not in the car but rather on the middle part of the folded roof behind the Archduke and the Duchess. According to Count Harrach it sat there for about two to three seconds.[77] As it fell on the side of the road nearer to the buildings on the left, the spectators could see smoke and hear a sharp hissing sound. Mrs Dimović described it as a rectangular object, the size of a battery torch, giving off smoke like a 'cigarette'. Soon there was a terrific explosion. Car no. 4 was passing by the bomb at that very moment. The pressure of the explosion caused all the oil from the car to burst out, drenching a sizeable part of the road.[78] Many depictions of this event have suggested that the bomb went off very close to the back left wheel of Boos-Waldeck's car (car no.4). In reality, it exploded on the left side of the road in front of the car, with the Count subsequently identi-fying 70 holes on the body of his vehicular pride and joy.[79] The two glass panels on the car, in front of and behind the driver, were shattered, and the roller shutters on the shops nearby were pelted with fragments from the explosion, which had produced a big plume of powder, rising some ten metres high, accompanied by red and yellow flame.

'I have always expected something like this'

Pandemonium ensued: women screamed and men shouted, parents with their children crying were running away from the spot. Some women fainted and collapsed on the pavement. Policemen were blowing their whistles. Two children were injured by the bomb. Estimates of the number of spectators wounded by shrapnel vary between fifteen and twenty. Several of the victims were put on a *fiaker* (carriage) – with the coachman seen furiously beating the horses as he drove away. People poured water over the big pools of blood, which made everything look even worse.[80] The fact that no one was actually killed by the blast was less a matter of miracle and more because people had already begun to flee as soon as they saw the bomb lying on the road, hissing loudly and giving off smoke.[81] The bomb was of the type which the Austrians called '*Flaschenbombe*', filled with nails and chopped lead.[82]

Next after Čabrinović in the zig-zag line of unofficial archducal welcome was Mehmedbašić, armed with a bomb and a pistol. As the only one of the seven Sarajevo conspirators who managed to escape after 28 June (to Montenegro and then to Serbia), he was never interrogated by the Austro-Hungarian authorities. In the critical moments he stood on the pavement between Čubrilović to his right and Popović on his left. Those were the moments when Franz Ferdinand's car had briefly stopped and then slowly begun moving again. After the war Mehmedbašić explained to his friend Nikola Trišić that before he could act Čabrinović had already swung into action – thus confirming his own position as the third of the assassins.[83] This, however, does not explain away his own inaction: Mehmedbašić could see that no harm had come to the Archduke whose car was there, moving at almost snail's pace right in front of him. His record as an assassin, it has to be said, was not exactly a fearsome one. It was seen in chapter eleven how, earlier in the year, when gendarmes had climbed on the train in which he was travelling from Dubrovnik, he had panicked, throwing away the poisoned dagger he had been meant to use against Governor Potiorek. Following his further fiasco on the streets of Sarajevo with his weapons remaining silent, he subsequently stated that he had retreated to a reserve position on Franz Joseph Street.[84]

Another would-be assassin stood on the pavement only slightly further to the right from Čabrinović, but across the road from him. This was Cvetko Popović, equipped like his young friend Čubrilović with a bomb and a Browning. Popović, who survived war and imprisonment and subsequently wrote many thoughtful articles about 28 June 1914, was yet another actor in the Sarajevo drama not exactly cut out for his designated role. He was short-sighted, refusing to wear glasses out of vanity, and far too excitable – even by his own admission. 'I was in a peculiar state of mind, in a kind of hypnosis', he wrote years later, describing the seconds as the motorcade approached.[85] This youngster, just like Čubrilović, was never going to do anything. When Čabrinović's bomb exploded he thought that Čubrilović had thrown it. 'At this moment', he told the investigators on 8 July, 'the Archduke's car drove past me quite slowly, someone had got up in it and, had I wanted to, I could have thrown the bomb in quite easily.' Popović then admitted frankly: 'I lacked the energy to do it; I do not know why I lacked it.'[86] So it was that each member of the second troika of assassins – Čubrilović, Mehmedbašić and Popović – had passed up his own opportunity to change the course of history.

Popović's statement about Franz Ferdinand's car driving quite slowly *at the moment* of the explosion is further contradiction of the widespread retrospective claims that Lojka had accelerated beforehand. According to Potiorek, the car behind him and the Archduke, which bore the brunt of the explosion, kept moving forward for a while and then stopped, some of its passengers stepping out.[87] However, two of them, Boos-Waldeck himself and Erik von Merizzi remained seated, for they had sustained wounds. Though Boos-Waldeck's left shoulder had been hit and required bandaging, the matter was relatively insignificant. Merizzi, on the other hand, looked seriously wounded. This was the very person who had in Ilidža the previous night argued against cancelling the archducal visit to Sarajevo on 28 June. Now, in the centre of the city, he was bleeding severely from the back of the head. Countess Lanjus, herself very slightly injured in the face, rushed to Merizzi's aid, duly producing a handkerchief to try and stem the streams of blood. Merizzi was soon given medical attention at the nearby residence of Dr Löffler. The garrison hospital was immediately notified by telephone, and four army doctors led by Colonel Gottlieb Arnstein, rushed to the scene in an ambulance. Merizzi, accompanied by Dr Fischer from car no.5, was then taken to that military hospital by the same ambulance.[88] And yet Potiorek's aide-de-camp and close friend was still to play a major role in the subsequent events of that morning.

In the meantime, amidst all this commotion, the chase had got under way to catch Čabrinović. Having sent the bomb in the direction of the Archduke's car, he at first made as if to go towards Ćumurija bridge. Two or three steps later, however, he took a step back, jumped up onto the stone embankment wall and from there down into the shallow Miljacka river, a reckless dive of several metres.[89] Indeed, he injured his leg as he landed, yet then managed nevertheless to proceed towards the bank opposite. But now he was moving very slowly, as if perplexed and disoriented, without any thought of escaping. Hardly surprising, for he thought he was about to die. In the pocket of his waist-coat he had carried a small bottle containing cyanide dissolved in water.[90] This he had already swallowed after releasing the bomb, before jumping into the river. However, contrary to his expectation, the dose turned out to be completely ineffective, with vomiting its only consequence. Meanwhile, as he stumbled along, up above him shouts could be heard: 'He is below, he is below!' Baron Morsey, seeing Čabrinović in the river, screamed to a policeman in his broken Serbo-Croat, mixed with some Czech: 'Shoot him in the head!' Morsey had thought, mistakenly, that Čabrinović had a revolver which he was about to use.[91]

One of the most alert persons in the crowd was Károly Marossy, a Hungarian barber in Sarajevo. His other job was as a 'confidant' to the Headquarters of the 15th Corps, a fact known to the police in Sarajevo. The next day he was to be in the forefront of anti-Serbian demonstrations in town.[92] As soon as Marossy saw Čabrinović launching an object at the Archduke's car, he rushed towards him, telling the press later that Čabrinović must have noticed this and as a result chosen to plunge into the river. Marossy followed him there, complete with his white fedora hat, and was joined by detective Zejnolović who, on reaching Čabrinović, was about to fire from his revolver. 'Don't shoot,' Marossy warned him, 'we must get the man alive.' Soon other policemen were on the scene in the middle of the shallow river and Čabrinović, unsuccessful with his bid for suicide by cyanide, surrendered without offering any resistance. Nevertheless, as he was taken to the bank under the bridge opposite Appel Quay, policemen clobbered him with swords. One well-dressed man charged at Čabrinović, hitting him with his walking stick.[93] Many others from the crowd soon arrived and the police now had to make an effort to save Čabrinović from a lynch mob. Observing this scene, Franz Ferdinand turned to Potiorek and remarked: 'Why don't the security men allow those people to club him to death? The court will as usual only condemn him to four or five years and then, furthermore, soon pardon him.'[94]

Whilst bewailing the imagined vagaries of the Habsburg justice system in this manner, Franz Ferdinand was once again sitting in a stationary car. After chauffeur Lojka had accelerated – immediately following the explosion – he had slowed down again. This had been done by order because his passengers were naturally wanting to see what was happening behind. So he drove, as Josip Vrinjanin reported, 'very slowly' at this point. Having then observed that Boos-Waldeck's car had come to a halt, Franz Ferdinand now ordered that his own car should stop. Demonstrating his military upbringing, he asked Count Harrach to go back and see whether there had been 'dead or wounded'. He stood in the car staring towards the Ćumurija bridge, his face 'bloodless' – a strange sight, according to Vrinjanin, when juxtaposed with the fluttering green feathers on his helmet. The Duchess held his hand, looking 'remarkably pale and frightened'.[95]

According to an Austrian version of what happened during these moments, the Archduke and the Duchess quickly got out of the car. Franz

Ferdinand's voice could clearly be heard as he asked his wife (*'liebes Sopherl'*) to return directly to Ilidža and wait for him there. He was said to have been calm and collected. But the Duchess, with a melancholy expression on her face, replied: 'I shall stay with you, Franz, I am not going to leave you. Wherever you are, I wish to be there too.'[96] Baron Morsey was to note a similar exchange taking place between them minutes later in the Town Hall – Franz Ferdinand, by now no doubt perfectly aware of what kind of welcome Sarajevo had prepared for him, not surprisingly sought to place at least his wife out of the danger zone. Potiorek reported him as saying at this stage: 'I have always expected something like this.' The Archduke then turned his attention to his wife who had noticed her neck injury. 'Only a small scratch', he said.[97]

By the time Harrach returned with his casualties report, car no. 5 with Colonel Bardolff, Major Höger and Senior Lieutenant Egger had left Boos-Waldeck's crippled vehicle behind it and moved on to join the Archduke's car, thus becoming car no. 4 in the motorcade. Its glass protection screen had been hit, and Egger inside had had a narrow escape when his cap was brushed by a bomb fragment. The other cars followed on behind and this recomposed procession proceeded towards the Town Hall. Höger stated that his car had quickly rejoined the Archduke's so that the latter would not drive alone – as if this were some kind of security measure.[98] A security measure of a kind, however, was taken when Gustav Schneiberg stepped on the running board of the car, next to the Archduke, to protect him with his own body for the rest of the journey to the Town Hall – it is not clear on whose initiative Schneiberg did this.[99] By now, Baron Morsey and Captain Pilz from the car that was originally no. 7 (and now no. 6) had left the motorcade, staying on the Quay to observe the arrest of Čabrinović. They then walked to the Town Hall. Dr Fischer was likewise absent as he had gone to hospital with Merizzi. The latter was transported there in the ambulance which had brought Dr Arnstein and his three colleagues from the military hopital to the scene of the attempted assassination. Dr Arnstein joined Dr Fischer in accompanying Merizzi back to the hospital while his three colleagues stayed behind to look after the wounded on the street.[100]

Historians have drawn attention to those moments, or perhaps minutes, when the Archduke's car stood there in the middle of the road unprotected, while he himself observed Čabrinović's capture in the manner of a bystander. A 'perfect target' and 'sitting ducks' are some of the descriptions that have been used.[101] Several accounts have focused on the fact that Baron Rumerskirch had then come running to the Archduke's car, supposedly to point out the perils of the car being stationary. But this was not the purpose of his quick arrival. Rumerskirch, as he stated in his deposition, had merely wanted to check that no one was hurt.[102] Even so, he would have been entirely justified had he also urged getting a move on. For, according to Harrach, the pause on the road may have lasted as long as five minutes.[103] This was probably an exaggeration, but even five seconds here, between the Ćumurija and Latin bridges, could potentially have been fatal.

Franz Ferdinand, however, after escaping the bomb attack, was lucky again. In this 'avenue of the assassins' there were by this stage only two left, and they were not near enough to strike. Trifko Grabež, the last of the assassins, was far out towards the Town Hall and Gavrilo Princip, though nearer, did not arrive quickly enough to make use of what would have been an unexpected opportunity. Moreover, he was somewhat confused. Having heard the explosion from his post at the Latin bridge, he had hurried towards the Ćumurija bridge, a little over two hundred metres away, wondering who had carried out the assassination attempt, while having no idea whether it had succeeded. Unaware also that, as he walked towards Ćumurija bridge, the Archduke, still alive, was a sitting duck immediately ahead of him on the same short stretch of road. But even this short distance proved enough for the Archduke to escape Princip's attentions at that point between the bridges. Princip was still only half-way down the road when the motorcade, now moving again, drove past, with the would-be assassin then unable even to spot the Archduke. So he returned to the Latin bridge, without knowing the outcome of events, to pace up and down until, minutes later, he learnt that the bomb attempt on the life of Franz Ferdinand had been a total failure.[104]

Municipal Make-Believe

Franz Ferdinand's arrival and reception at the Town Hall in Sarajevo represents one of those fantastic and bizarre moments in world history when the actors themselves are supremely aware of the irony of their own affectations in the face of reality. A future emperor, on a ceremonial drive through a town with his wife, has just survived a bomb attack on his life to reach the Town Hall where the town's Mayor, undeterred by his near-demise, municipal officials lined up behind, is preparing to give a flowery, pre-scripted speech of welcome to him, their almost-assassinated guest, on behalf of the city. Even more grotesque, the script of this play demands the Archduke respond with an equally euphemistic and purple speech of his own, complete with an upbeat concluding sentence in Serbo-Croat.

Many scholars of Sarajevo 1914, among them Kiszling, Remak, Dedijer and Holler, have maintained that the dignitaries waiting on the steps of the Town Hall, the Mayor included, had no idea what had happened just minutes earlier on the Appel Quay.[105] In fact, nothing could be further from the truth. Firstly, the Mayor was initially not even present. Some thirty officials had assembled long before 10.00, the most senior of them being the two deputy mayors, Josip von Vancaš, a Croat, and Risto Hadži Damjanović, a Serb. Fehim Effendi Ćurčić, the Muslim Mayor, had of course been part of the motorcade and had not yet arrived. Hearing the explosion, those present initially assumed it was just another cannon salute. But then, as Vancaš told the *Bosnische Post* on 2 July, running messengers began to arrive with the news of what had taken place. Ćurčić appeared soon thereafter, and he confirmed to them that there had been an assassination attempt. 'The impact was dreadful', said Vancaš, 'we all stood there as if paralysed.'[106]

It was probably a little after 10.30 when the Archduke and his party finally reached the Town Hall themselves. They had been scheduled to arrive at 10.10, but the initial seventeen-minute delay at Ilidža had been supplemented by a delay of several more minutes caused by the matter of Čabrinović. In a newsreel showing the arrival of the archducal car, Gustav Schneiberg (who had stood on the left running board of the car following the bomb episode) can be seen jumping off the car as it slowed down in front of the Town Hall. Schneiberg then opened the door of the car.[107] Mato Dabac, a police detective of Croat nationality, recalled that the Archduke was 'pretty upset', his face 'as white as a wall'. Similarly, *Bürgermeister* Ćurčić was 'as pale as a corpse' according to Władysłav Gluck[108] The Mayor waited at the bottom of the steps, his fez on his head, with his two deputies, Vancaš and Damjanović, both in tails, standing just behind him. Other officials stood on the steps in two lines, forming a tunnel through which the guests were to ascend into the Town Hall. There is absolutely no evidence for the assertion of Gerd Holler that religious notables had also showed up, supposedly including Archbishop Stadler, representatives of the two Jewish communities and the Greek Catholic community, as well as a Serb Orthodox Archimandrite and a Muslim Hafiz.[109]

Some of the other cars in the motorcade now started arriving. A big crowd was already assembled in front, made up predominantly of Muslims, but also of the less well-to-do Serbs from the upper parts of the town. The narrow streets towards Baščaršija, the old Turkish bazaar, had become crammed with curious onlookers. The police began to react with alacrity, and the masses were seized by excitement.[110] Among them was Trifko Grabež, armed with a bomb and a Browning, but hemmed in from all sides – and in any case, as explained in chapter eleven, having succumbed to Danilo Ilić's anti-assassination talk in the previous days he was never likely to do anything.

Franz Ferdinand was clearly not in the mood to put up with the pre-scripted etiquette. When the hapless Mayor began to read his speech of welcome ('Highly delighted are our hearts over the most gracious visit ...'), the Archduke stopped him abruptly: 'That's enough! Thank you very much, Mr Mayor! This is outrageous, a disgrace, bombs have been thrown. Is that what one comes to Sarajevo for?' The Duchess, standing to his right, tried to calm him down: 'Franzl! Franzl! Please, Franzl!' The intervention apparently worked because the Archduke then said: 'Now you may speak.'[111] In what is probably the more correct recollection of his words, the sailor in him actually used naval jargon: 'So, now you may launch your speech.'[112] As might be expected, there are several versions of what exactly Franz Ferdinand said, but all the versions agree that he savaged Ćurčić pitilessly. The Mayor himself, when he talked to the press, recalled an only slightly milder outburst by the Archduke: 'Mr Mayor, this is outrageous. Bombs were thrown. One comes to Sarajevo, and is received in this manner.' Ćurčić admitted that he was 'distraught', but that he managed to collect himself and deliver his speech without pausing. Yet he did so in a dry and frightened voice.[113]

So the Mayor was allowed to carry on, but what he said must have further tested, and severely, the frayed nerves of the almost-assassinated Archduke. Ćurčić himself noted that during his entire address Franz Ferdinand 'stood stock-still, rage glinting in his eyes'. Given the circumstances, it was most unfortunate that the whole speech was peppered with phrases such as: 'the feelings of our love and devotion'; 'all the citizens ... greet with the greatest enthusiasm your Highnesses'; 'deep gratitude and loyalty', etc. The Archduke smiled sarcastically at the mention of a cordial welcome.[114] When the Mayor finished, Franz Ferdinand could not immediately respond: the text of his reply was with Rumerskirch, his chamberlain who had been lagging behind. At this stage something happened to lift his mood somewhat. According to the *Neue Freie Presse,* the crowd, upon learning about the failed bomb attempt, began to acclaim him with loud '*Živio!*' cheers. And the *Reichspost*, admittedly a paper very supportive of the Heir to the Throne, even reported 'stormy ovations'.[115] Rumeskirch finally made the scene, jumping out of the car and handing the Archduke two sheets of paper. Afterwards, Ćurčić said in his press statement that he had seen blood stains on the paper – Rumeskirch having of course been in the luckless car no.4 when his fellow passenger Merizzi was wounded by the exploding bomb.

Whether because of the tributes of the crowd, or the calming presence of his wife, Franz Ferdinand managed to make a masterful impromptu start to his response. In his thin voice, he addressed the Mayor: 'It is with special pleasure that I accept the assurances of your unswerving loyalty and devotion to His Majesty, our most gracious Emperor and King, and I thank you, Mr Mayor, dearly glad for the exultant ovations given to me and my wife by the population, especially as I also see in them an expression of joy over the failed assassination.' The formal, pre-written part of the speech then followed, consisting of only two sentences. In the first the Archduke talked of his sincere satisfaction at the gratifying progress in the development of

the provinces. And then, notoriously bad at foreign languages, he concluded in what may have only with some difficulty passed as Serbo-Croat:
'I ask you to convey my cordial greetings to the inhabitants of the beautiful,
great [*Šeher*] city of Sarajevo, and I assure you of my steadfast grace and
goodwill.'[116]

Franz Ferdinand's goodwill, of course, was by now under a big question
mark. For he had lost any illusions he may have had about where he was –
remarking to Harrach once inside the Town Hall: 'Today a couple of bullets
are in store for us.'[117] This proved to be a remarkably accurate forecast. But
poor Effendi Ćurčić should perhaps have been spared the initial tantrum
since the man responsible for the Archduke's security stood right behind
him: Oskar Potiorek. In all probability the fury was indeed directed at
Potiorek, with the Mayor merely a convenient scapegoat. Apart from
expressing to the *Landeschef* his wish that the lynch mob around Čabrinović
should be allowed to club the would-be assassin to death, it is not known
what else Franz Ferdinand said to Potiorek before they reached the Town
Hall. A Serbian source claimed that after the bomb episode Franz Ferdinand barely said a word to the Governor who for his part was now reduced
to suggesting that the assassin was a mercenary and a foreigner, unlike the
population itself, which was loyal and Austrophile.[118] Words from Potiorek
to that effect would have been very likely and indeed typical. What else
could he have said to Franz Ferdinand? This Sunday parade through the
streets of Sarajevo had been meant to demonstrate to the Archduke
the support and loyalty of the population to Habsburg rule, a manifestation
which would in turn have demonstrated Potiorek's unique competence in
being able to bring about such a satisfactory state of affairs in this potentially troublesome land. His success would have been highlighted and
presumably noted by the Archduke. But the bomb had changed all that,
Potiorek's entire conception was now shattered. His personal failure
was colossal. He, Potiorek, one of the most arrogant men in the Austro-
Hungarian Empire, was facing the most difficult moments of his life – with
even his beloved Merizzi now in hospital, quite possibly on the brink of
death. It had been a pretty bad morning altogether for General Potiorek.
The resultant state of mind of the Governor of Bosnia-Herzegovina is the
key to comprehending what took place next at Sarajevo Town Hall – some
ten to fifteen minutes of confused decision making that was to change the
course of human history.

Following the acrimony and charade at the steps of the Town Hall,
the normal programme resumed. Going up the steps, the Duchess was
greeted at the entrance by Razija, the daughter of a local Muslim grandee,
Hilmi Bey Kapetanović, who handed her a bouquet of flowers. Razija's
mother was waiting upstairs on the first floor – she was one of those
'Mohammedan' or 'Turkish' women, as the Austrian guests called them,

who had been hurriedly put together by Ćurčić at the request of the Duchess the previous night in Ilidža. If nothing else, Ćurčić deserves credit and praise for this organizational feat. Not surprisingly, he included his own wife in the select group of women. Accompanied by Countess Lanjus, the Duchess proceeded upstairs to meet them in the salon of the Presidency of the Assembly – since the local parliament was housed in the Town Hall. This episode therefore represented a minor, last-minute addition to the programme. Rebecca West noted, somewhat harshly perhaps, that the Duchess had wanted such a meeting with the Muslim women 'in order that she might condescendingly admire their costumes and manners, as is the habit of barbarians who have conquered an ancient culture'.[119]

Government Commissar Gerde and Mayor Ćurčić accompanied the Duchess and Countess Lanjus as they went upstairs. According to a Serbian source, Gerde was so shaken by Franz Ferdinand's outburst at Ćurčić that he had difficulty climbing the stairs.[120] As it would have been inappropriate for the two men to be present during this get-together of females, they soon withdrew. Although she was at first still 'somewhat troubled' by the impact of the bomb assault, the Duchess quickly relaxed in the company of the patrician Muslim ladies, splendid in their oriental costumes, wearing their gold, pearls and precious stones. Countess Lanjus recalled 'twelve ladies from the Turkish aristocracy'.[121] They kissed the hand of the Duchess and sat chatting with her on silk cushions. In such comfort, she could have been forgiven had she felt like an empress already. But she remembered that she was also a mother. As her eyes fell on the 'Turkish' daughter of one of the women (presumably Razija, who had handed her the bouquet), she said: 'You see, this child is almost the same height as my Sophie', adding: 'We have never left our children alone for so long ...'[122]

Downstairs, Franz Ferdinand asked the Deputy Mayor von Vancaš, otherwise an architect, whether it was he who had built the Town Hall. Vancaš was probably pleased he could give a negative answer – the unsightly building, completed in 1894, had been designed in the pseudo-Moorish style by the Austrian architect, Alexander Wittek, who had gone to Cairo specifically to find inspiration. During Kallay's rule, buildings throughout Bosnia-Herzegovina had been erected in this style to flatter the province's Muslims. Vancaš had in fact designed Sarajevo's Catholic Cathedral – unfortunately not a pretty sight, either. This brief exchange with the Deputy Mayor is the only recorded piece of small talk involving Franz Ferdinand during his short stay at the Town Hall. Thereafter he began to confer 'exclusively with his suite', according to Vancaš, about the assassination attempt that had just taken place. The Archduke was 'quite composed', and the discussion went on in the 'calmest of ways'.[123]

One of the group clustered round Franz Ferdinand, Andreas von Morsey, later related that the Archduke, having entered the vestibule of the Town Hall, immediately proceeded to address the issue of the bomber's attempt on his life. With Morsey's assistance a text was put together for a telegram, addressed to Franz Joseph's cabinet office in Bad Ischl (where the Emperor had just begun to enjoy his summer break) so as to pre-empt any misleading alarm in newspapers. And then, according to Morsey, 'came the most important part, a discussion about an immediate change of the programme, in order to make a decision in the light of a possible repetition of the danger that each of us instinctively recognised as not having gone away'.[124]

Merizzi, Potiorek and the Telephone Call

At that point, a piece of information, seemingly inconsequential, may have just arrived: with someone supposedly telephoning the Town Hall to say that Lieutenant-Colonel Merizzi's wound was of a light nature. That, at any rate, is what Potiorek later claimed to have happened. If true, it is unclear as to who exactly in the entourage received this news and how widely it was shared, but Potiorek would have been the first to have been told. He mentioned such a call and its substance in his statement later that day, implying that at the very least the Archduke had also been informed.[125] A further ambiguity concerns the place from where the call might have originated: Potiorek does not name it, but in 1959 the historian Joachim Remak quite logically suggested that the call had come from the garrison hospital.[126] Whether Potiorek had in his statement given the truth about the seriousness of Merizzi's wound, or whether he somehow twisted the information conveyed on the telephone, or whether, indeed, there had ever even been this telephone call, are compelling historical questions. Whatever the case, the Archduke was soon to express his desire to visit Merizzi in hospital, and by all accounts to insist on doing so. A general consensus has existed since then that with this decision Franz Ferdinand signed his own death sentence.

Thus it is that the telephone call concerning Merizzi's condition constitutes perhaps the most important single detail in the whole story of the Sarajevo assassination. But Potiorek's claim that there had been such a call is most problematic. In the first place, it seems very unlikely that any doctor or doctors in the hospital could have established so rapidly, and so confidently, that Merizzi was out of danger. Even more so since Merizzi and the doctors accompanying him had probably not even reached the hospital gates by the time the alleged telephone call was supposedly made to the Town Hall, just moments after the archducal party had itself entered this building. Following the explosion on the Appel Quay Merizzi had initially been brought to Dr Löffler's apartment where a bandage was applied. This must have lasted minutes rather than seconds. And then he still had to be driven to the hospital, located in the western outskirts of Sarajevo, at least five minutes away. A preliminary medical examination would have also taken more than just a few minutes – by which time the visitors would already have left the Town Hall.

Did Dr Löffler perhaps make that call – and not someone at the hospital? This seems most unlikely. It would have been highly presumptuous and professionally irresponsible of Löffler to make such a call regarding the condition of a high ranking officer who, having been hurriedly bandaged, was about to be moved from a private practice to a proper military hospital. On the other hand, Joachim Remak's suggestion that the call had come from the hospital is quite difficult to accept because, as discussed above, even the most charitable time estimates cannot accommodate it. A contemporary news item proves as much. On his way to the hospital Merizzi had been accompanied by Dr Arnstein as well as Dr Fischer from car no.5. A report in the *Neue Freie Presse* on 29 June stated: 'The chief physician Dr Arnstein and Lieutenant-Colonel v. Merizzi had scarcely reached the garrison hospital before the news about the second attempt came.'[127] The *second* attempt – in other words, the telephone call existed solely in Potiorek's imagination. Significantly, Potiorek is the only source to mention a telephone call reaching the Town Hall detailing Merizzi's condition – certainly no other source concerning the proceedings in the Town Hall ever included learning of such a call in the discussions they described. That is to say, none of them recorded Potiorek mentioning such a call, or such content, at the time that they were actually in the Town Hall.

It is both necessary and legitimate to labour this point a little further, particularly because a consensus has long existed among historians that an intended hospital visit eventually led to the outbreak of the First World War. Clearly, doctors Arnstein and Fischer did not even have time to examine Merizzi properly, for after arriving at the military hospital they had to immediately head back to town – to Potiorek's residence in the *Konak*, where the unfortunate Archduke and Duchess were brought after the second and successful assassination attempt.[128] In any case, just how serious Merizzi's wound was could not be ascertained straight away. The medical report, signed on 1 July by doctors Zahradka and Bayer, talked of a lacerated wound at the back of the head that had required a probe and an x-ray to establish whether any foreign body (bomb fragment) was present. Although no fragments were found, the doctors warned that in cases of injury caused by an explosion there was a strong possibility of heavy infection 'whereby life would be directly threatened'.[129] This was hardly the minor affair described by Potiorek in his summary of the supposed telephone call. On 3 July a Slovene newspaper carried a short article entitled 'The third victim of the Sarajevo assassination', reporting that Merizzi was 'dying' owing to infection of the wound and that the doctors had lost all hope of saving his life.[130] This was subsequently denied, but on 8 July Potiorek's personal adjutant Baron Ditfurth was forced to intervene in the press to counter the persistent rumours about Merizzi's condition. The point, however, is that the patient had remained in hospital.[131]

Why, then, did Potiorek apparently lie in his statement of 28 June about a telephone call, concocting a story about the light nature of Merizzi's wound? The answer, as always with Potiorek, has to do with his stupefying ambition: after the first assassination attempt, and with Franz Ferdinand alive and well, his own career was as good as dead; following the second, successful assassination and the death of the Heir to the Throne, however, his career could still be rescued from the abyss. But this could only be achieved if he pushed through a half-sanitized and half-manufactured account of what had taken place in the Town Hall minutes before Franz Ferdinand was shot dead – an account that would present him in a reasonably favourable light and, critically, in a fairly minor role. His claims regarding Merizzi's supposedly light wound and the Archduke's supposedly unshakeable wish, *despite the supposedly light wound*, to visit him at the hospital were meant to draw attention away from his own responsibility. However, during those dramatic minutes in the Town Hall it was Potiorek, not Franz Ferdinand, who was the key decision-maker: being, after all, the host who was supposed to possess local knowledge, it was he who had been asked all the relevant questions, and it was he, by all accounts except his own, who decisively influenced the course of deliberations in the Town Hall.

The Four Chronicles

Four different versions by contemporaries exist about what was said there, in Sarajevo's *Rathaus*. The first three, by Colonel Bardolff, Baron Morsey and Potiorek himself, are well known to professional historians without necessarily having been subjected to intense scrutiny. For all their superficial similarity, these three versions constitute distinct and even, to a considerable extent, conflicting accounts. The last, by Władysław Gluck, a police functionary of Polish nationality in Sarajevo, is almost completely unknown even though it was published as long ago as 1935. The fact that this account was written in the Polish language cannot be an excuse for neglecting it. For it will be seen that of all the accounts Gluck's version is in passages perhaps the most revealing, given that it is the only one that actually provides some otherwise missing background and an explanation as to why the first two cars in the motorcade turned right from the Appel Quay into Franz Joseph Street, an intersection at which Princip, the assassin, awaited.

Bardolff Version. Colonel Bardolff, in his report to Conrad von Hötzendorf of 3 July 1914, provides what must be described as a somewhat fragmentary and, to that extent, also somewhat misleading picture of what took place. The report was published in 1923, in the fourth volume of Conrad's memoirs. Perhaps because of its easy accessibility, most historians have relied on Bardolff.

The Archduke, Bardolff reported, spoke about the failed assassination attempt and asked Potiorek 'whether or not the journey should be continued, and whether or not things with the bombs will carry on'. Potiorek replied that he was convinced 'nothing more will happen', but he added that there were two alternatives to consider: that either they should go directly to the *Konak* (his residence just across the river), or drive to the Museum (the next stop on the day's official programme) by a route avoiding and thus 'punishing' the town. Now, going to the *Konak* was already in the official programme of the Archducal party, as a reception and a *déjeuner* had been planned there, starting at midday. By mentioning the possibility of going straight to the *Konak* from the Town Hall, Potiorek was in effect suggesting a shortening of the official programme, but in proposing at the same time the alternative of driving to the Museum (albeit by a route different from the one that had been published), he was also encouraging its de facto full continuation. In either case, the General evidently saw no further danger.

According to Bardolff, the Archduke then asked Gerde, who had just joined them, whether the drive (*'die Fahrt'*) could be continued, to which Gerde answered 'affirmatively'. His Imperial Highness thereupon declared 'in the most decided manner' that he wanted, 'categorically', first to visit Lieutenant-Colonel von Merizzi in the garrison hospital, and then to continue to the Museum. Rumerskirch thereupon asked where the hospital was located and whether it could be reached without driving through the town, to which Potiorek gave a positive answer, explaining that it could be reached by driving straight down Appel Quay. At this point, Bardolff claims to have summed things up for those present: the decision was to drive to the hospital along Appel Quay, thus avoiding the town, and then continue to the Museum. He added that the Duchess now also changed her own original programme, according to which she had been meant to go from the Town Hall straight to the *Konak*, asking Franz Ferdinand for permission to join him on his planned journey instead. This request was granted by the Archduke without objection.[132]

However, there had in reality been no change to the Duchess' original programme. The Duchess had always been meant to accompany the Archduke to the Museum and indeed had been meant to be with him throughout the day in Sarajevo during all the official receptions. That, from Franz Ferdinand's angle, was precisely the point of bringing her to Sarajevo: for her to be seen as the wife of the future Emperor. Even a cursory glance at her own and the Archduke's programmes for the day easily establishes the fact that they had a joint programme requiring them to be together the entire day.[133] Whereas if, as Bardolff says, she was supposed to have gone straight to the *Konak* from the Town Hall, what was she meant to be doing there for some eighty minutes while her husband was at the Museum? Bardolff had made this up, and this little fiction in his report has been widely accepted in historical works. His story is of course an attractive one in that it portrays a wife determined to stay together with her husband at difficult moments. This she actually did – not, however, by changing her programme, but rather by sticking to it.

What is of far greater interest in the Bardolff version is his repeated mention of the Museum being next on the revised schedule following the proposed hospital visit. This meant, of course, that the official programme would be resumed. Such confidence on the part of Franz Ferdinand and his Town Hall circle is astonishing given the bomb attack that had just taken place on the Appel Quay. Indeed, this decision defies belief: the assurances and guarantees given to Franz Ferdinand at this point about the safety of not just the route, but also of Sarajevo in general, must have been very convincing indeed. And yet Bardolff says nothing on this subject, in effect playing down the role of his friend Potiorek, and possibly that of himself, in creating a blasé atmosphere, to say the least – despite the fact that one assassination attempt had already taken place. Certainly, this whole episode caused puzzlement among the officials at the Foreign Office in London. 'We never understood', Lord Vansittart wrote later, 'why Austrian officialdom, after the first abortive bomb-attack, again sent the doomed pair forth, with renewed lack of precaution, to be finished off with a revolver.'[134]

Bardolff, in addition to composing the report for the benefit of Conrad von Hötzendorf, appears also to have sent a message about the assassination to the Joint War Minister, Alexander von Krobatin, who showed some passages from the message to selected officials in Vienna. Ludwig Thallóczy, an official at the Joint Finance Ministry, was apparently one of those who saw Bardolff's message, referring to it in his diary entry for 4 July 1914. He relates that after the first assassination attempt Franz Ferdinand asked Potiorek whether more bombs would be thrown and whether the route was safe, whereupon Potiorek answered 'he was absolutely sure' that it was. The Archduke reportedly repeated the question to Government Commissar Gerde who expressed the same view about the safety of the route. It was after this that Franz Ferdinand made his decision to go to the hospital. Potiorek then allegedly had second thoughts about the whole matter and sought to dissuade the Archduke, but the latter resolutely stated that 'if you say the route is safe, then I shall go to the hospital to visit the wounded aide-de-camp.'[135]

Morsey Version. In his *Konopischt und Sarajewo*, the 1934 variant of his memoir which is also the longest one of the three that he published, Andreas von Morsey provides important details which Bardolff's report never mentions. This Morsey material, however, should be combined with that in the 1924 article which he wrote for the *Reichspost* and also with his unpublished memoir deposited in the Schloss Artstetten archive.

Morsey was with the Archduke and his group in the vestibule when Franz Ferdinand instructed him to take the Duchess, accompanied by the bodyguard Schneiberg, either to the *Konak* or back to Ilidža in Lieutenant Grein's car. Morsey duly left the group and went upstairs to where the Duchess was meeting the Muslim ladies in order to ask her to join him as the Archduke had instructed. Men not being allowed inside, he had to wait outside the closed door, till the Duchess emerged. On hearing about her husband's instructions, she told him: 'If the Archduke is to be appearing in public today, then I shall not be leaving him.' Morsey bowed in silence and returned downstairs to inform the Archduke. Those were, he says, the last words that he heard the Duchess speak.

It also emerges from Morsey's account that Franz Ferdinand and his circle initially decided to give up the rest of the official programme altogether. This, in retrospect, is a startling piece of evidence, and it is odd that it is not even mentioned in Bardolff's version. The advice from the entourage (Morsey gives no names) was to go directly first to the *Konak* and then to Ilidža, avoiding a drive through the town. 'The further programme', writes Morsey, 'was abandoned.' If so, this is a most intriguing piece of the jigsaw puzzle of goings on in the Town Hall – for very soon the decision was inexplicably reversed. As Bardolff likewise reported, the programme was to be continued by going to the Museum after first visiting Merizzi in the hospital. What caused this change of mind? Prudence and level-headedness had initially prevailed, only to be thrown to the winds in no time at all. Admittedly, this revised official programme now envisaged driving to the hospital along only a short stretch of the original Appel Quay route, but this was still foolhardy given that the stretch in question was also known to possible assassins as part of the programme.

The 'fatal moment' according to Morsey (writing in his 1924 *Reichspost* article) came immediately after the early consensus that the rest of the programme in Sarajevo should be discarded: the Archduke then insisted he would pay a visit to Merizzi in the hospital. Neither in the *Reichspost* article nor in the 1934 *Berliner Monatshefte* variant of his recollections, does Morsey explain what caused the Archduke to be so adamant about going to see Merizzi – the person who had the previous night so successfully countered the proposal that the Sarajevo visit be scrapped altogether. However, Morsey's unpublished account preserved at Artstetten does contain an explanation of a kind. The Archduke, Morsey writes, stated that

Merizzi had been wounded 'on his [the Archduke's] account [*seinetwegen verwundet worden war*]'.[136] No doubt Franz Ferdinand must have said something to that effect. But did someone else, perhaps Potiorek himself, suggest the hospital visit? Certainly, the explanation that the Archduke had simply decided out of gallantry to pay a courtesy visit to a wounded officer whom he hardly knew is difficult to accept in the light of the events in Hotel Bosna the night before when the question of whether to proceed with the visit to Sarajevo stood on a razor's edge, and when the very same Merizzi had been instrumental in persuading him not to abandon the programme.

In the Morsey version Rumerskirch asked Potiorek whether getting to the hospital was possible without entering the town, which Potiorek confirmed. This information actually tallies with Bardolff's. Gerde, according to Morsey, also attested to the safety of the route indicated by Potiorek. The most sceptical person here was Major Paul Höger. He advised, Morsey says, that they should stay in the Town Hall until at least two companies of soldiers were brought in from the manoeuvres area. The streets should then be cleared, and in the meantime no one should show himself at the windows of the Town Hall because of the danger of being shot at. This plan was 'unfortunately' rejected – no explanation is given by Morsey for the rejection. Bardolff, according to Morsey, then re-stated the route suggested by Potiorek, presumably to the hospital, before asking Gerde to repeat the whole thing after him. But Commissar Gerde, Morsey claims, headed for the door instead and towards his car, merely saying in a cursory manner: 'Yes, yes, certainly.' Morsey had no doubts as to who to blame for what happened soon thereafter: 'This disregard has stuck in my memory as that decisive moment which, ultimately, shaped the external conditions for the possibility of an assassination.'[137] Gerde may indeed have mumbled something along the lines described by Morsey, but it will be seen below that he had already, by now when the party was leaving the Town Hall, received from Potiorek a very clear instruction to keep to the original route and so may well have paid scant attention to any subsequent exchanges from other functionaries. In any case, he was hardly a decision-maker. The 'external conditions' for the assassination were enabled, in the first place, by the decision to drive from the Town Hall along part of the previously scheduled route – without implementing additional security measures in order to guarantee safety. Even Morsey, in the unpublished part of his memoir, specifically identified Potiorek as being responsible, 'above all', for the tragedy which then took place. 'Had Potiorek', Morsey wrote, 'decidedly explained to the Archduke that he would not allow any further drive before the enactment of security measures, the Archduke would have acquiesced.'[138]

Potiorek Version. Substantial parts of Potiorek's version of what had gone on in the Town Hall on the morning of 28 June (including before, during and after this episode) were immediately passed by the General himself to the press in Vienna in the form of an anonymous official report (*von offizieller Seite*). Shaping public opinion was clearly of paramount importance to him after his high guests were shot dead in the middle of a town where he was supposed to be in charge and which was meant to greet the guests with pro-Habsburg jubilation. Thus an article which appeared in the *Neue Freie Presse* on 30 June with the details of the assassination was copied with only minor modifications from Potiorek's long, 29 June telegram to the Austrian Prime Minister Count Karl Stürgkh (this telegram itself being a reproduction of an earlier one he had sent to the Hungarian prime minister István Tisza at the latter's request).[139]

At some point during the afternoon or in the later hours of 28 June Potiorek had given a witness statement about the events of the day, but this statement (*Wahrheitserinnerung*) was not countersigned by any court official as was the case with the depositions of other witnesses. In his memoir of Sarajevo 1914, the investigating judge Leo Pfeffer writes that Potiorek had been 'interrogated' for the witness statement by Theodor Davidzak, a court counsellor of Polish nationality. Pfeffer gives here a telling picture of the awe in which Potiorek was held by local officialdom. Wondering why the first (police) car in the archducal column had not been immediately notified to drive straight down the Appel Quay, Pfeffer opines that Davidzak 'either forgot, or dared not ask Potiorek'.[140]

Indeed it is doubtful whether any real interrogation took place at all. Friedrich Würthle has remarked that its contents give the impression of a statement dictated rather than produced in answer to questions posed by a court person, and that Potiorek may not yet, at this stage, have overcome the shock he had suffered in the Archduke's car.[141] Potiorek's deposition does, indeed, bear all the hallmarks of a dictated note, but, rather than betraying any mental trauma, it also appears to have been carefully designed to deflect suspicions about his own culpability: 'Before the journey continued', Potiorek stated, referring to the stay in the Town Hall, 'His Imperial Highness asked me ... whether something similar was to be feared. I answered that I did not think so. However, despite all the security measures that had been taken, it was not entirely impossible that something could be done from close range and therefore, if His Imperial Highness agreed, I would propose either to go directly to Ilidža by the Appel Quay, or immediately to the *Konak* and, after a short stop there, to the Bistrik railway station.'

The Bistrik station, small and local, was close to Potiorek's residence in the *Konak*, itself just across the river from the Town Hall – a route ensuring the Archduke's safety. It is of course indicative that Potiorek was anxious in his above statement to imply that he had taken security measures. These were in reality almost non-existent. What is also interesting is that he avoided any reference to the decision, taken after the first attempt on the Archduke's life, to continue with the planned visit to the Museum, a decision which Bardolff explicitly mentions. Potiorek's acquiescence in this decision would in retrospect have looked very bad. At this crucial juncture for his career, required to explain the turn of events, Potiorek also placed full responsibility for the decision to visit the hospital on Franz Ferdinand, without providing any details as to who had influenced his view and how: 'His Imperial Highness declared that he definitely wished to visit von Merizzi who had been taken to the garrison hospital, notwithstanding that the telephone message had reached the Town Hall that his injury was quite light.' As has already been seen, however, the supposed telephone call was in all likelihood another piece of history engineering by Potiorek, designed to draw attention away from any role he may have had in encouraging the Archduke to make the hospital visit, and also to present Franz Ferdinand as reasoning in a highly contrary manner.

Potiorek's biographer Rudolf Jeřábek has not expressed any scepticism about the existence of the telephone call, but has made an important suggestion as to why Potiorek may have wanted the Archduke to make the hospital visit: 'This new decision', Jeřábek writes, 'which would in future always be bandied about as being exclusively the Heir to the Throne's own idea – as Potiorek indeed repeatedly suggested – became an integral part of the tragedy of a humane prince who had to die in the course of a staunch performance of duty, carrying out a chivalrous hospital visit.' Jeřábek continues: 'In reality, however, it may well have been Potiorek who had at least strengthened the Archduke's decision to take on this new risk in order to salvage matters by staging his own and Merizzi's hero drama, after the setback of the first assassination attempt which may have lost him the longed for favour of the Heir to the Throne.'[142]

That Potiorek at the very least reinforced the idea of going to the hospital is clear even from his own statement. In response to the Archduke's declared wish to make the visit, he said that the town population 'absolutely' required a 'punishment' after the assassination attempt. Therefore the route envisaged by the programme should be abandoned, and the hospital should be reached by the somewhat longer direction of driving along the same Appel Quay by which the party had arrived at the Town Hall. (Lying on the western outskirts of the city, the hospital could be reached by either of the two routes.) 'I added', Potiorek stated, 'that I was recommending this because the second, unprogrammed drive along the long Appel Quay would be absolutely safe as no one would have reckoned with it.' In other words, nothing could be safer. Somewhat defensively,

Potiorek also explained that 'naturally, until the turnoff to Franz Josef Street, a short stretch of the Appel Quay would again have to be used. But nothing happened along this short stretch.'[143] In fact, everything was to happen precisely because of that short stretch of the Appel Quay.

Potiorek's statement of 28 June is repeated, in a somewhat abbreviated form, in his telegram to Prime Minister Stürgkh of 29 June. This telegram, too, is notable for its concoctions and omissions about what had gone on in the Town Hall. Apart from omitting to state that he had actually agreed to resume the official programme in Sarajevo after the hospital visit by continuing to the Museum (as Bardolff's account makes clear), there is a further omission in Potiorek's story: he never mentions Major Paul Höger's advice that the party should stay in the Town Hall until the soldiers cleared the streets. He kept quiet about this because Höger's proposal would of course have been the correct way to proceed after Čabrinović with his bomb had made it obvious that some in Sarajevo had prepared an alternative kind of welcome for the Heir to the Throne. Franz Ferdinand's secretary Paul Nikitsch-Boulles related with much revolt and revulsion how Potiorek turned down the suggestion that troops should be brought in on the 'peculiar' grounds that the soldiers were still in their field uniforms and therefore inappropriately attired to line the streets. 'As if', Nikitsch-Boulles commented, 'the beauty of the street appearance was in this case of greater importance than the safety of life of his future monarch!'[144] Theodor von Sosnosky, one of Franz Ferdinand's biographers, does not consider this story a credible one, but he criticizes Potiorek for not keeping the Archduke inside the Town Hall until safety could be ensured by bringing enough troops by car into Sarajevo.[145] Indeed, this would have taken only a few hours: General Appel wrote that the first troops, the 49th and 84th regiments, had already arrived in Sarajevo by 3 p.m. following a forced march. Sadly for the Archduke and the Duchess, they had been given orders to march after the second, not the first, assassination attempt.[146]

Gluck Version. Władysław Gluck, a police official in Sarajevo, is an indispensable source for the events of 28 June and particularly for the Town Hall episode. His Polish father, a doctor, had settled in Sarajevo. Gluck grew up there and became a deputy police commissioner. Fluent in Serbo-Croat as well as German and Polish. Gluck is better known to historians in ex-Yugoslavia than in the West – although Vladimir Dedijer practically ignores him in his acclaimed *The Road to Sarajevo*. In the 1930s he made several contributions regarding the assassination to the Sarajevo literary periodical *Pregled*, as well as to Belgrade's daily *Politika*, and subsequently cooperated with Vojislav Bogićević for the latter's important documentary source *Pisma i saopštenja* (Letters and Notices) about Sarajevo 1914.

In 1935 Gluck published in Cracow his *Sarajewo* (*Historja zamachu sarajewskiego*). The subtitle, 'A History of the Sarajevo Assassination', is somewhat misleading in that the scope of the book is far greater, dealing with Bosnia-Herzegovina from the period of the Turkish conquest onwards. Thus the book is not strictly a memoir, although Gluck was in Sarajevo on 28 June and would have discussed all the events with Edmund Gerde, his superior, and with his friend and colleague Petar Maksimović, the Serbian police inspector.

In his book Gluck confirms the observation of Deputy Mayor von Vancaš that Franz Ferdinand, his military entourage and Potiorek kept away from the 'civilians' in the Town Hall. According to Gluck, it did not occur to any of some ten officers clustered around the Heir to the Throne to consult the government officials about the safety of continuing the journey. They were, he commented with unconcealed disdain, 'all very arrogant people, confident in the knowledge that they would be around the future Emperor Francis II'.[147]

Both Bardolff and Morsey, as has been seen, allocate a significant role to Dr Edmund Gerde – who had, according to their two accounts, vouched for the safety of the newly proposed route from the Town Hall. The fact that Gerde was a 'local' man and, furthermore, in charge of the police, would tend, in retrospect, to give even greater weight to the advice he gave at the Town Hall. But was Gerde really the black sheep of 28 June as Morsey would have it? Why, then, does Potiorek not even mention Gerde? Gluck's record of this episode casts serious doubt on whether Bardolff and Morsey ever really grasped what had been going on during those fateful moments.

Immediately notable in Gluck's account is that there was more than one convocation happening in the lobby of the Town Hall. While Franz Ferdinand and his circle deliberated on what to do next, a parallel group composed of local officials and presided over by Gerde was doing the same. 'Commissioner Gerde', Gluck writes, 'frantically took counsel with the surrounding circle of officials.' And all of them were of the same opinion: the further drive envisaged by the programme should be abandoned – because the next stage, with its narrow, winding streets requiring a slower speed, would be the most dangerous one. The consensus among the officials was that the guests should stay in the Town Hall while mounted police emptied the Appel Quay. The party should then cross the river by the Kaiser Bridge, located close to the Town Hall, from where Potiorek's *Konak* was only a short distance away. What Gluck meant by emptying the Appel Quay related only to a short section of the embankment – a few hundred metres – to ensure the safety of the archducal passage across the Kaiser Bridge. He noted that the programme had in any case envisaged lunch for the guests at the *Konak*, after which they were meant to return to Ilidža from the nearby Bistrik station. 'This undertaking', writes Gluck, 'was not beyond the capacity of the Sarajevo police force.'

A similar course of action had of course been proposed by Major Paul Höger. Ironically, it was a Serb, inspector Petar Maksimović, who now urged Gerde to inform Potiorek about the locals' proposal. This Gerde did – and Potiorek was 'of the same opinion' as the local officials. But, Potiorek told Gerde, the final decision would be made by the Archduke. Gluck then relates that after this Franz Ferdinand, in separate conversation with Potiorek, asked the *Landeschef* whether, in the light of the bomb assault, something similar could again be expected. But at this point Potiorek, instead of feeding back for the Archduke's consideration Gerde's advice that the party should wait in the Town Hall until the surrounding area was cleared, ignored it totally, proposing instead that they should either drive to Ilidža by Appel Quay 'at the greatest speed', or go straight to the *Konak*. A minor modification of the former course was recommended by Potiorek when the Archduke 'persisted' with visiting Merizzi at the hospital: namely that as a 'punishment' for the city, the Archduke's programme should be discontinued, and that they should drive to the hospital along the Appel Quay and then via Mustafa-bey Street – 'no one' would be expecting such a change of route. Franz Ferdinand agreed to this. This decision to discontinue the visit, as will be seen below, was subsequently changed, bar one element – the use of one section of the Appel Quay.

In relating as above what was being said by the Archduke's inner circle, Gluck seems to be acting purely as a historian restating Potiorek's own version – which he could have read in the eighth volume of the official Austrian documents published in 1930. For neither he nor Gerde could have been privy to the discussion in the 'military' circle. Indeed, Gluck says so: 'Meanwhile, the government commissioner [Gerde], standing a few steps away ... could not have heard what was being advised, nor could he take a position in relation to the plan which by no means excluded the danger of an assassination.'

The main weight of Gluck's description of these scenes comes immediately afterwards: 'Seeing the Duchess already descending from the second floor to the lobby, Gerde asked Potiorek about the decision and to his horror he received in response these three German words: '*Programmässigen Weg einhalten* [Maintain the route in accordance with the programme]'. Potiorek's instruction was very clear and, as it transpired, carried fatal consequences. It was the reason why, only minutes later and as originally planned, the first two cars in the motorcade did indeed turn right at the Latin bridge into Franz Joseph Street, on the corner of which Franz Ferdinand and his wife were to be shot. There was no mistake, the cars had been ordered to do so. But why? What was Potiorek planning here?

Gluck insists that at the Town Hall Potiorek did not 'say a single word' to Gerde about changing this route. Thus, according to this account, the man in charge of the Sarajevo police had been left ignorant about a major decision concerning the movement of the motorcade – the one Potiorek had just taken with the Archduke. Gerde therefore repeated to his police officials (Mayerhoffer and Troyer) riding in the first car the instruction he had received from Potiorek – to stick to the original route. In Gluck's assessment, Potiorek apparently calculated that 'it would be best if Dr Gerde, not knowing anything about it, went in the direction originally intended, and in consequence the Archduke, going another way, would be safer.'[148] In other words, a diversionary manoeuvre – and perhaps a lack of faith in the locals.[149]

Gluck's attempt at explaining what was probably in Potiorek's mind makes a lot of sense. As has been seen, Potiorek, in his official statements about the assassination, was anxious to emphasize that his proposed route to the hospital, back along the Appel Quay, would have been unknown to any potential assassins. Moreover, by keeping the first two cars to the original route he must have intended to sow confusion among potential assassins as to the Archduke's whereabouts. Critically, of course, the execution of this plan depended entirely on a simple instruction being given to – and being understood by – the archducal chauffeur, Lojka: to keep driving straight on, that is, ignoring Gerde's car in front of him when the latter made the scheduled right turn from the Appel Quay having driven the few hundred metres down it from the Town Hall.

These Town Hall deliberations could not have lasted longer than about ten minutes. Sketchy as it is, the evidence of the discussions inside it does highlight the central role played by General Oskar Potiorek. Comparing and contrasting the four versions of what exactly was said and decided in the Town Hall reveals a rather telling detail about Potiorek's attempt to subsequently cover things up: Bardolff relates that Potiorek had proposed a drive to the Museum, whereas Potiorek, offering half the story, claims he had suggested a drive to Ilidža – but does not mention the Museum. Bardolff must be seen as the more credible source because other accounts apart from his own state that the Museum was chosen to be the next stop after the hospital visit. Bardolff even claims to have summed-up to that effect at the Town Hall – a summing-up during which Potiorek must have been present. Rumerskirch's deposition of 28 June, for example, is similarly unambiguous when he speaks of the decision to 'drive directly to the Museum' after visiting Merizzi. Deputy Mayor von Vancaš also confirmed that the intention was to drive to the Museum following the hospital visit.[150] Subsequently, only Potiorek was to keep quiet about this.

The significance of this projected return to the official programme, which Potiorek apparently encouraged, relates to the amount of persuading that must have occurred to convince the Archduke that everything was safe in Sarajevo – even after a bomb had been thrown at him. This is indeed a very important detail in the story of 28 June. The Bardolff and Potiorek versions agree that it was Franz Ferdinand who had raised the question of how safe it was to proceed further through the city. Morsey's account reinforces the impression that security was a paramount concern for the Archduke: the latter had asked Morsey to tell the Duchess that she should leave separately and thus skip the Museum visit. But within some ten minutes he had changed his mind, apparently persuaded that Sarajevo was free of risks, and even thought nothing of allowing his wife to accompany him on the journey to the hospital and for the rest of the official programme.

So who persuaded him? Was it just Potiorek, or was he joined in this by Commissar Gerde – as both Bardolff and Morsey suggest? The role of Dr Edmund Gerde is presented in starkly different lights: Bardolff and Morsey claim that he had confirmed Potiorek's soothing assurances about the harmlessness of proceeding further through Sarajevo. Morsey even goes as far as identifying Gerde as a main culprit for the Sarajevo murders by virtue of his apparently nonchalant attitude when asked by Bardolff to repeat the agreed arrangements for driving from the Town Hall. But Gluck maintains the exact opposite: saying that Gerde was the leading proponent in the alternative group – the local officials – which argued for staying put in the Town Hall until safety was re-established. These are irreducible discrepancies. Who should be believed?

It should also be emphasized at this point that Gerde was not asked to give any evidence in the preliminary investigation conducted after the assassination. Indeed, for some curious reason no one from the first two cars of the motorcade was questioned after the event. The massive (503 typewritten pages) *Prozess in Sarajevo*, the relevant record deposited among Franz Ferdinand's papers in the Haus-, Hof- und Staatsarchiv in Vienna, contains testimonies from most members of the archducal party, including Merizzi who was questioned in the military hospital. It is therefore extraordinary that there are no testimonies from Mayerhoffer, Troyer and their driver (car no. 1), and Gerde, Mayor Ćurčić and their driver (car no. 2). Why had some of the most relevant witnesses of the events surrounding the assassination in Sarajevo been left out of the investigation? The only possible explanation is that Potiorek, the all-powerful Governor of Bosnia-Herzegovina, had seen to that.

Such further evidence as does exist tends to confirm Gluck's representation of Gerde as a man sceptical about the wisdom of continuing the journey, and of Potiorek as one gambling recklessly. In his memoirs Leon Biliński writes that he and the Hungarian Prime Minister Tisza had seen an official letter on the events of 28 June from Baron Rumerskirch to War Minister Krobatin. 'It is clear', Biliński says, 'that the Heir to the Throne did not, especially because of the presence of the beloved wife, wish to assume the role of a fearless hero. Rather, he wanted as an ordinary mortal to adjust to the given circumstances.' Biliński claims that Gerde, when asked by Franz Ferdinand whether they could continue ('What about those bombs?') began to show 'fear and misgiving'. On the other hand Potiorek, whom Biliński calls a 'megalomaniac', exclaimed: 'Your Imperial Highness can drive safely, I take the responsibility.'[151]

A similar version of events was being circulated by Biliński's officials in the Joint Finance Ministry. Josef Redlich recorded in his diary a conversation about the assassination he had had with Paul von Kuh-Chrobak, a section chief at the Ministry. Kuh-Chrobak told him that Franz Ferdinand, following the bomb attack, had been fully conscious of the dangers of Sarajevo. But Potiorek theatrically put his hand on his heart, bowed, and said to the Archduke: 'I take responsibility.' Moreover, there exists the evidence of Countess Lanjus. In her unpublished memoir she quotes Potiorek's answer to Franz Ferdinand when the latter asked about what was likely to happen next: 'Imperial Highness, we live in a civilised land, this is the act of an individual, I guarantee that nothing else will happen.'[152] In the operations planning section of the Austro-Hungarian General Staff it was reported that Potiorek confidently commented after the first assassination attempt: 'There is no second murderer in Sarajevo.'[153]

The second murderer – Gavrilo Princip as it turned out – was by now apprehensively anticipating the kind of security measures for Franz Ferdinand which the local officials and Major Paul Höger had separately advanced in the Town Hall: he thought that the streets would be emptied after Čabrinović's attempt with the bomb, so that the way for the Archduke's return to Ilidža would be clear of danger. Princip related his fear to Mihajlo Pušara as they walked from the vicinity of the Cathedral towards the Appel Quay along Franz Joseph Street. Pušara was of course in the know about the assassination plot. Indeed, as has been seen, he was the person who had in March anonymously sent a newspaper cutting to Čabrinović in Belgrade to alert him of the forthcoming visit to Bosnia-Herzegovina by Franz Ferdinand. As he and Princip reached the Schiller delicatessen store at the corner of Franz Joseph Street and the Appel Quay, he assured Princip that 'there will be no emptying of streets because, had they thought of doing this, they would already have begun'. So Princip and Pušara stood there on the corner, waiting for the motorcade at the spot where it was due to make the turning, in accordance with the published programme. After all, as Princip said at the trial, he had read about the Archduke's route in both the *Bosnische Post* and the *Sarajevoer Tagblatt*.[154]

Of course, the whole point about such detailed pre-event publicity being given to the Archduke's sojourn in Sarajevo on 28 June had been to do with Potiorek's ardent desire to produce welcoming crowds on the streets, loyally cheering the Habsburg Heir to the Throne. The success of the visit would be the Governor's own, personal success: and perhaps the decisive step towards his promotion to Chief of Staff at the expense of his great rival Conrad, an outcome that, in 1914, depended almost wholly on Franz Ferdinand. Considerations relating to his career, or at the very least to his reputation, also account for Potiorek's post-assassination pronouncements. His testimony about what had been discussed in the Town Hall is proof of this. For he kept quiet about several crucial matters. Firstly, that after the unsuccessful bomb attack there was initially a consensus to abandon the official programme altogether (as reported by Morsey). Secondly, that reassurances must then have been given to the Archduke about the safety of conditions in Sarajevo (with Potiorek involved, according to several witnesses) because Franz Ferdinand soon agreed to resume the official programme and even took his wife along after having initially been concerned for her safety. Thirdly, that Major Höger had actually proposed (as stated in the Morsey memoir) staying put in the Town Hall until the streets were cleared and made safe by soldiers brought in from the area of the manoeuvres. And, finally, that the official programme had indeed been resumed (a truth Potiorek smothered by simply omitting to mention it) with the visit to the Museum restored to the schedule, as reported by Bardolff and two other witnesses (Rumerskirch and von Vancaš). Instead of dwelling on these, the *Landeschef* attempted to obfuscate everything by drawing attention to another proposed visit: that to Merizzi as he lay wounded in the Sarajevo military hospital. The visit to the hospital, it is true, was indeed decided on at the Town Hall, but so was the visit to the Museum – immediately afterwards – demonstrating that, with or without the hospital visit, a decision had been taken under Potiorek's leadership to send the Archduke back into the non-safety of the city with no additional security precautions other than had already failed him.

In addition to these sins of omission, Potiorek's testimony also contains a fascinating sin of commission, for he had almost certainly invented a telephone call to the Town Hall supposedly informing him of the light nature of Merizzi's wound. This was a pivotal element in his story to his superiors in Vienna about who was really to blame for what subsequently happened in Sarajevo. Potiorek's message to Vienna was thus: Merizzi's injury, given its light nature, was not one with which anyone should have been overly concerned, least of all the Archduke, and yet Franz Ferdinand had been hell-bent on going to the hospital nevertheless. In this way, the Governor presented the Archduke rather than himself as the crucial yet illogical decision-maker in what happened, perfidiously shifting blame on to the victim of his serial incompetence – the one man not alive to contradict him. Simple and brilliant, this deception by Potiorek has worked for a hundred years.[155] Today it would be called 'spin'.

The 'Wrong' Turning

At the Town Hall the archducal party was preparing to leave. Count Harrach had established that there were five bomb fragments in the back of his car. He showed one of them to the Duchess. 'Thank you very much,' she said, taking the fragment, 'I shall have it set in a medallion as a memory of our fortunate rescue.'[156] The general mood among the guests, however, was less than celebratory. Deputy Mayor von Vancaš recalled that the Arch-duke and the Duchess left the Town Hall without saying goodbye to the officials of the city council who had greeted them there on their arrival.[157]

One of the people in the entourage most concerned about what might yet happen was Count Franz Harrach. Opening the door to his car, he helped the Duchess climb in. After everyone was seated, an unerring instinct drove him to forsake his own seat next to the chauffeur Lojka, and to step on to the left running board of the car instead, where his body would protect the Archduke. Later in the day, he was to explain that he had done so because he had been 'convinced that a new assassination would take place'.[158]

In a further demonstration of his imperious loftiness, Potiorek, obser-ving Harrach's behaviour and perhaps needled by the Count's obvious disregard for his own reassurances, responded by airing his doubts about the usefulness of Harrach's precautionary step.[159] Little did he realize, of course, that Harrach, with his contrary view, was soon to be proved right. Once this truth had sunk in, however, it did not stop the Governor, in his official version of events, omitting to report his own comment in this con-nection, highlighting instead how His Imperial Highness had made some 'remark' regarding Harrach's gesture. According to Morsey, the Archduke tried to laugh away the whole thing, but Harrach was insistent.[160]

It was in all likelihood between a quarter and ten to eleven when the guests left. The municipal officials had again lined up on the steps before the Archduke and the Duchess descended down the red carpet runner. The photographs of this scene show some of the officials saluting the couple. But the facial expressions on others betray a peculiar resignation. 'The tension was great', Paul Höger wrote later, 'as the Heir to the Throne and his wife stepped out over the threshold of the Town Hall ... at any moment a new assassination could take place.'[161] Höger and Harrach were not alone in thinking that something could happen again. The son of one of the muni-cipal officers, present in the Town Hall with his father, told Rebecca West that 'we knew that when he went out he would certainly be killed. No, it was not a matter of being told. But we knew how the people felt about him and the Austrians, and we knew that if one man had thrown a bomb and failed, another man would throw another bomb and another after that if he should fail. I tell you it gave a very strange feeling to the assembly.'[162]

As it departed from the Town Hall, the composition of the motorcade was as follows:

Car No. 1: Mayerhoffer, Troyer and local chauffeur.

Car No. 2: Gerde, Ćurčić and local chauffeur.

Car No. 3: Franz Ferdinand, Duchess of Hohenberg, Potiorek (and Harrach, standing on the left running board). Chauffered by Leopold Lojka.

Car No. 4: Rumerskirch, Countess Lanjus, Robert Grein and Gustav Schneiberg. (Chauffeur unknown.)

Car No. 5: Bardolff, Höger, Egger and Max Thiel (chauffeur).

Car No. 6: Hüttenbrenner, Erbach-Fürstenau, Ditfurth and Eduard Grein (chauffeur).

Car No. 7: Morsey, Pilz and Starch. (Chauffeur unknown.)

Wladimir Aichelburg has been the only historian to have reconstructed the archducal motorcade with a reasonable degree of detail and accuracy. In that respect his 1984 study of 28 June 1914 stood head and shoulders above any other account of the assassination day. However, in his recent (2014), massive, three-volume compilation taken from various sources regarding the life of Franz Ferdinand, he reconstructed the motorcade again – making at least one surprising change. In the 1984 study, having previously correctly identified the car leading the motorcade as the police car, and the second as the mayoral car, he has the archducal car as the third in the motorcade to leave the Town Hall.[163] However, in his 2014 version Aichelburg explicitly states that, from the Town Hall on, the leading police car was 'no longer' engaged. A few pages down, he repeats that the leading police car had stayed behind at the Town Hall and speculates, with a touch of irony: 'or, more likely, it had been entrusted with other duties'.[164] By 2014 Aichelburg may have decided to become more critical of the Sarajevo police force. But he provides no supporting evidence whatsoever for his new assertion.

Since Aichelburg also fails to take into account the reserve car, his 2014 version of the motorcade leaving the Town Hall has only five cars: stripped of the police car and ignoring the reserve car. On the whole, he correctly identifies the passengers in his first four cars, but with regard to his last, fifth car, he only mentions Morsey together with a (nameless) chauffeur, meanwhile failing to account for the following seven passengers: Hüttenbrenner,

Erbach-Fürstenau, Ditfurth, Eduard Grein, Pilz, Starch and Schneiberg – these nine men could not all have been riding in just this car.[165] As for the newly-missing police car, it certainly figures in the recollections of several witnesses. Mato Dabac, the Sarajevo policeman on duty at the Town Hall, reported two cars preceding the archducal car as the motorcade left.[166] Milan Drnić, waiting to greet the Archduke at the corner of Appel Quay and Franz Joseph Street, stated that cars were arriving, 'one after another', before the archducal car appeared.[167] Mihajlo Pušara, who was with Gavrilo Princip at the same corner, saw 'the first car, and then the second and the third, which carried Ferdinand and Sophie'.[168] In other words, the leading police car was still doing its duty and there were seven, not five cars in the motorcade that had departed from the Town Hall.

One car carrying four persons from the original cortege was neverthe-less absent: Boos-Waldeck's car having been knocked out by Čabrinović's bomb. But this was no problem as the reserve vehicle was available. Boos-Waldeck himself was among the absent because the wound he had sus-tained in the bomb attack, though minor, had nevertheless required him to stay behind to be bandaged. Karl Divjak, his driver, was also left behind with the crippled car. Merizzi and Dr Fischer, its other passengers, were of course in the hospital. The Archduke's bodyguard Gustav Schneiberg was almost certainly amongst the motorcade passengers once again, but it remains unclear in which vehicle that might have been – circumstantial evidence points to car no.4, possibly the original reserve car.[169] Apart from the absentees, the only change that had now taken place was that Lieutenant Robert Grein, originally with his brother Eduard, and with Hüttenbrenner, Erbach-Fürstenau and Ditfurth, had switched company so as to be with Rumerskirch and Countess Lanjus – in the car immediately behind the Archduke's own vehicle.

The big crowd that had greeted Franz Ferdinand on his arrival at the Town Hall was still there as he was leaving. Again there arose shouts of '*Živio!*' The motorcade left in no great hurry. Trifko Grabež, his Browning in his right trouser pocket, observed the departure. He was, indeed, merely an observer since he had been persuaded by Danilo Ilić not to act. He stated later that the cars drove past him 'slowly', and the opportunity was 'very favourable', but that he had nevertheless had no intention of carrying out an assassination.[170] By all accounts, however, the cars quickly gathered speed as they drove down the Appel Quay towards the Latin bridge. This was the only stretch of the new route, some 370 metres long, which corres-ponded to the old one.

It has to be emphasized once again that the new route did not entail an abandonment of the official programme – visiting Merizzi at the hospital was merely an ad hoc addition to it. The idea was to resume the programme after the hospital stopover by going to the Museum. Potiorek's diversionary manoeuvre to send the first two cars in the motorcade along the officially published route, while driving to the hospital with the Archduke by the unheralded route along the Appel Quay, was intended to provide a degree of security. Yet for all the *Landeschef* knew, there might have been one or several assassins waiting for the party at the Museum, ready to hurl bombs. Despite this, he had consented to, and indeed helped develop this plan. The fact that he had suggested a route to the hospital which was to take along 370 metres of the published route was bad enough, but that he should then so confidently plan to continue with the programme by carrying on to the Museum was an unfathomable decision to tempt fate. Of course, the whole brave or foolhardy scheme with the Museum was never put to the test because Franz Ferdinand was assassinated within the next few minutes.

Historians of 28 June 1914 have, over and over again, maintained that someone 'forgot' to inform the chauffeur that there had been a change of route, and a world war broke out in consequence. This has been asserted with such frequency and with such confidence that it has become perceived as gospel truth. However, this easy and somewhat farcical explanation has in fact never itself been subjected to scrutiny. The whole episode, in fact, represents one of the more important unanswered questions about the Sarajevo assassination. And the question here is certainly not whether Mayor Ćurčić and Commissar Gerde, or Mayerhoffer and Troyer in the leading car, had been informed about the change of plan. For these people were unwitting players in Potiorek's deception manoeuvre: they had been explicitly told by him that there was to be *no* change of plan, and that they should stick to the original route. Władysław Gluck is categorical on this point, and he also clearly states that Gerde had passed on Potiorek's instruction to the first car – to Mayerhoffer and Troyer. There was accordingly no 'blunder' when the first two cars in the motorcade turned right into Franz Joseph Street. The blunder concerns only the movement of the third car. What remains to be answered is whether Potiorek told his fellow Czech Leopold Lojka that his route had been changed and that he should now drive straight on along the Appel Quay – or indeed whether he forgot to do so.

Accounts by Potiorek and Harrach make it possible to reconstruct a reasonably clear picture of what happened just seconds before Princip fired his shots. As Lojka drove them down the Appel Quay, Potiorek was talking to the Duchess and Franz Ferdinand. The latter made a remark concerning the bomb attack. This prompted Potiorek to say that he himself would on a daily basis have at the back of his mind the possibility of an assassination, whilst being driven to the government building from his residence in the *Konak*. Both the Archduke and the Duchess smiled at this, commenting that there was nothing left other than to 'put one's trust in God'.[171]

But matters were not in God's hands. They were literally in Lojka's hands as he approached the Latin bridge and turned the steering wheel of the Gräf & Stift to the right, thus angling the archducal car into Franz Joseph Street. Hundreds, perhaps thousands of accounts have described what followed next, and they all say that Potiorek, noticing the mistake, ordered Lojka to stop and reverse back into Appel Quay. Potiorek himself repeatedly claimed that he did so. In his statement on 28 June he said that he 'noticed' how the car carrying Gerde and Ćurčić had turned right 'despite' the earlier decision taken by His Imperial Highness: 'Therefore I shouted to Count Harrach's driver not to follow the car in front, but to drive on along the Appel Quay.' In his telegram to Karl Stürgkh on 29 June Potiorek repeated this account, except that he now stated he had shouted to 'Count Boos-Waldeck's chauffeur' – a driver not even in the convoy at this point. This error about the identity of the chauffeur driving him and the Archduke was a measure of Potiorek's confusion about what had taken place the previous day. It was also a measure of the superficiality of his previous communications with the Archduke's actual chauffeur, Lojka, which as will be seen below, may well have been the precise cause of the events he regretted. Nevertheless, he was at least consistent in asserting that, on observing what the driver was doing, he had immediately commanded him to go back.[172]

In fact, it did not happen quite that way. Harrach in his diary tells a somewhat different story. He relates how the car in front (the mayoral car) 'wrongly' turned into Franz Joseph street and, after 'ten metres', Potiorek exclaimed to Lojka: *'du fährst ja falsch!* [you are driving the wrong way!]' In this context the German particle *'ja'* is significant: it was used by Potiorek to accentuate his realization that Lojka had done something wrong. Moreover, it implies surprise on the part of Potiorek, and hence a more faithful translation would be: 'Why, you are driving the wrong way!' This was heard by Harrach, standing on the running board of the Archducal car, who then then asked Potiorek: 'Should we reverse?' Potiorek replied: 'Yes.' Only then was Lojka given the command 'Lojka, reverse' – and not by Potiorek, but by Harrach. So Lojka stopped and prepared to drive backwards to the Appel Quay.[173] It was at this moment that Gavrilo Princip saw his opportunity to act.

Potiorek's stupefaction was clearly related to what Lojka was doing and not to the fact that the two cars in front had turned right. He knew that this was no mistake on their part because only minutes earlier in the Town Hall he himself had instructed Gerde to stick to this same original route. His problem now was that Lojka was continuing to follow Gerde's car. Potiorek knew he had to stop this – having promised the Archduke a safe route along the Appel Quay which would avoid the old town. The point here, however, is that Potiorek did not halt the car as energetically and briskly as he later claimed – his order was delivered indirectly, via an intermediary, Harrach. Earlier events may still have been playing on his mind, and he was rattled, indeed dumbfounded, to find the archducal car at the top of Franz Joseph Street – things were going from bad to worse that morning.

The great question remains: why did Lojka follow the two cars ahead of him into Franz Joseph Street? In his deposition of 28 June he said: 'I was under orders to always follow the Mayor's car, and that is the way that I drove my car on the occasion of the second assassination as well.' This statement would suggest, of course, that Lojka had never been told anything other than to remain behind the car in front. Whether Lojka's evidence can fully be trusted is however open to question. For it is clear that when he talked to the investigating court officer on 28 June he was at sea as to what had gone on, that is to say, he was entirely confused about the nature and number of instructions he had received and who from. He declared that, as they reached the place where the assassination was about to take place, Potiorek ordered him not to follow the car ahead and instead to 'go over a bridge [*über eine Brükke einzubiegen*]'. This was presumably the nearby Latin bridge leading to Potiorek's residence at the *Konak*. Potiorek, however, could not have been ordering Lojka to go over a bridge because the route to the hospital did not require crossing the river. Lojka declared further that he then halted the car and, 'as I was about to turn back', a young man fired two times in succession. But the instruction he had received to drive across the bridge came after, not before the shots were fired – and it came, moreover, not from Potiorek who, as will be seen, was in those moments after Princip had fired his shots stunned and incapable of any decision making, but from Rumerskirch who came running to the Archduke's car after the motorcade had stopped and the shots had been fired. Reaching the car, as he later testified, 'I screamed at the chauffeur at the top of my voice to reverse quickly back towards the bridge, and this was done.'[174] Thus in his statement Lojka conflated Rumerskirch's instruction to go to the bridge (given after the shots), with Potiorek's instruction to stop and reverse out of Franz Joseph Street (given before the shots), as communicated to him by Harrach. The veracity of his account may have been fatally undermined by the sensory overload caused by being plunged suddenly into a living nightmare. His evidence that day, in other words, is practically worthless.

Troubled and upset though he undoubtedly was because of the bomb attack, it is nevertheless inconceivable that Potiorek, having in the Town Hall thought up a ruse to divert the first two vehicles on the way to the hospital, somehow forgot to speak to the chauffeur. For the discussion at the Town Hall demonstrated Potiorek in full damage limitation mode with the Archduke. Desperate to rescue his cause, he was keen above all to restore an impression of control and competence. His alternative security scenario, resting on the diversion to be created by the first two cars in the motorcade, would allow, he believed, for the programme to be resumed in conditions of greater security by confusing any potential enemies as to the Archduke's intentions and whereabouts. And if there was just one single action that he absolutely had to take in order to restore some of his battered reputation, it was to instruct the Archduke's driver to go straight down the Appel Quay. Issuing an instruction so crucial to him would have been an absolute priority for the self-seeking, monumental egoist that was Oskar Potiorek. An important corroboration that he indeed did so was read at the trial of the assassins, in Sarajevo on 21 October 1914. The court heard Potiorek's witness statement that Franz Ferdinand had consented to a drive along the Appel Quay to visit the wounded Merizzi in the military hospital: 'In line with this, the chauffeur, too, was issued an order [*Dementsprechend wurde der Auftrag auch dem Chauffeur erteilt*]'.[175] The statement added that, when the Archduke's car turned right from the Appel Quay into Franz Joseph Street, this was 'evidently by mistake of the chauffeur [*offenbar aus Versehen des Chauffeurs*]'. Potiorek was thereby asserting unequivocally that he had ordered the chauffeur to go straight on, but that his instruction had not been followed. From all that is known about him, it is extremely probable that this particular assertion was indeed true. The Austrian writer Fritz Würthle has cast doubt on the authenticity of this witness statement, but provides no convincing argumentation to invalidate it.[176]

Moreover, there exists a very telling piece of evidence that the convoy's departure from the Town Hall had been carefully planned and organized, and that someone must have been in charge of doing that. In his deposition of 28 June, Baron Rumersckirch stated that he and Countess Lanjus had got into the car immediately behind Franz Ferdinand's, 'with the instruction [*Auftrage*] to follow it at a very close distance.'[177] Someone was clearly handing out instructions, and that could only have been Potiorek – Rumerskirch was evidently not in charge, and it is difficult to conceive of Bardolff as replacing Potiorek in matters of command and control. Bardolff was admittedly the most senior member of the Archduke's entourage, but he was neither the host, nor did he possess local knowledge.

It should be pointed out here that Potiorek appears not to have talked to Lojka's boss Harrach about the change of course. Harrach had not been part of the Archduke's inner circle inside the Town Hall – he had merely heard that there had been some talk of 'possible changes to the programme'.[178] From Potiorek's point of view, there had been in any case no need to involve Harrach, especially if he was not even fully aware that Lojka was Harrach's personal driver, and it would have been inconvenient and perhaps demeaning to have to explain to a non-driver the new stratagem of letting the first two cars follow the original route. The same applied to Lojka, indeed even more so, for Potiorek must surely have viewed chauffeurs as being there to obey orders, not to think about them. But Lojka was doing the driving, and he did have to be told something – at least something. And it had to be by Potiorek because it was his plan and he knew how he wanted to execute it. Since he was hardly likely to omit its key element, it seems apparent that before the motorcade set off from the Town Hall Potiorek merely gave a curt command to Lojka to keep driving straight on down the Appel Quay – but did not bother to tell him that those in front of him would still be turning off it, for it would have been entirely out of character for the *Landeschef* to let Lojka, a lowly chauffeur, in on the details of his ruse when a simple command would do. A haughty and arrogant man like Potiorek who treated even high-ranking officers with disdain, was not likely to demean himself by sharing his judgement and logic with a mere driver.

Therein lay the seeds of an event which was to lead to a world tragedy. Lojka had been briefed, but inadequately. Indirect as it may be, the evidence that Potiorek really had briefed Lojka at the Town Hall does exist. His exclamation of astonished bewilderment ('Why, you are driving the wrong way!') suggests strongly that he had informed Lojka what the right way was and, in line with this, expected him to continue straight on along it – whereas, Lojka had frustrated his anticipation. Had he forgotten to give Lojka a clear instruction at the Town Hall it is likely that he would instantly have realized the missing cog in his plan and immediately ordered appropriately. For his part Lojka had misunderstood the command because it had not been elaborated upon, and, as he saw the convoy begin to turn right, he was not even in a position to double-check the matter with his boss Harrach since the latter was by now behind him on the running board. Driving straight down the Appel Quay was in any case what the first two cars also did for the first 370 metres. When they turned right, Lojka naturally followed.

In the dark about Potiorek's tactical scheme to let the cars in front act as decoys, Lojka must have assumed that the cars in front knew what they were doing. Indeed, it would have been surprising had he not followed them by turning right. Yes, Potiorek had told him to drive straight on, but Lojka acted on the premise that any movement of the motorcade would have been synchronized with the leading cars – a most reasonable supposition. When Potiorek protested that Lojka, following the first two cars, was driving the wrong way, the Governor's evident astonishment at his hapless chauffeur was related to Lojka's disregard of the instruction he had issued. But the instruction was being ignored precisely because it was flawed: Lojka drove contrary to his new instruction, but not contrary to the logic of the situation.

Black Ink and Blue Blood

Gavrilo Princip did not go to Moritz Schiller's delicatessen shop on 28 June. The story that after the bomb incident he entered the premises of this establishment on the corner of Franz Joseph street and Appel Quay to seek refreshment ('a sandwich', 'coffee', 'sustenance' etc.) is an appealing one, but is not supported by any evidence. The only thing that Princip intended to swallow that morning was cyanide. In fact, to the nationalist and revolutionary youth of Sarajevo the Schiller establishment was actually quite loathsome because its signs were in the German language – a fact which would regularly prompt the schoolboys to deface the shop with black ink. In that street – Franz Joseph Street – they much preferred a nearby coffee house called 'The Titanic'.[179]

At the entrance to Franz Joseph Street from the Appel Quay a large crowd awaited, especially thick on the corner opposite Moritz Schiller's. Princip initially moved to that side, to stand outside a store belonging to a Greek, Gorgoliatos. However, the police there were constantly pushing people back onto the pavement. It was not a good place from which to attempt an assassination, so Princip crossed the street to position himself on the opposite corner, right in front of the door of Schiller's shop. Mihajlo Pušara was just a few steps away, as was another friend of Princip's, a Croat of Czech descent, Ferdo Behr. Suddenly news spread that the Heir to the Throne was about to arrive. At this moment, as Ferdo Behr recalled, 'the mass of people began to shift and the police apparently lost their heads. The commotion was indescribable.' Princip moved a few steps forward towards the corner, still on the pavement, and stopped. The excited crowd around him was getting bigger, the motorcade was approaching and the citizens were greeting it with loud 'ovations'. It was at this point, as the archducal car came to a halt right in front of him, that Princip took out his gun, releasing the safety catch, and opened fire.[180]

There followed 'a moment of silence' before tumult began.[181] The exact number of rounds that Princip fired is by no means clear. Although many witnesses reported having heard only two shots, just as many thought the number was three or even four. Princip himself was subsequently not sure – he thought it possible that he had fired more than twice. He was precise, however, when he stated that the number of bullets in his Browning, which he had stuck inside the belt at the back, was initially seven. The morning and evening editions of the Budapest *Pester Lloyd* of 29 June revealed that following the arrest of Princip five bullets were found in the magazine of his weapon, Yet Andreas Morsey in his 1934 memoir asserted that when Princip's Browning was opened only four bullets were still in it.[182]

Whatever the number of rounds fired, the more interesting aspect of the shooting is the question of Princip's targeting – or lack of it. For

Princip was rather agog at the prospect of what he was about to do. Or as he described it soon after his arrest: 'I was overcome by a strange feeling.'[183] Such feelings had also assailed some of the other assassins. However, in Princip's case he opted to continue with the plan regardless. The luxurious archducal car had now arrived right in front of where the educated peasant boy stood; the Archduke, seated together with his wife and Potiorek, was clearly visible inside the vehicle. Lojka, having received Harrach's instruction to go back to the Appel Quay, had stopped the car in order to start reversing it. Observing the tableau in front of him, Princip at first thought of using the bomb he was carrying inside his belt, at the back on the left side. But, as he stated on 3 July, he quickly decided against doing so, as he felt that the cap of the bomb had been tightly screwed and that he would therefore have found it hard to unscrew; he also believed that the presence of so many people around him would have made it very difficult to throw the bomb. 'So I drew the revolver', he continued, 'and raised it towards the car, without aiming. As I shot I even turned my head away.' He was, by his own admission, 'very uptight'.[184]

Gavrilo Princip, arguably the most famous assassin in world history, thus looked away as he carried out his act, without even trying to aim. In all probability, he did not have to load the chamber of his semi-automatic Browning 9 mm by pulling back the slide and releasing it – an action that would have been seen and heard. The weapon must already have been loaded: the magazine carried six rounds and the seventh had been inserted into the chamber at some stage earlier that morning. Soon after his arrest Princip stated he had loaded the pistol with seven rounds.[185] All he then had to do was to flick the manual safety lever (blocking the slide) with his thumb and press the trigger. Mihajlo Pušara reported that, as Princip pulled out the gun, he deblocked it and fired (*'otkočava i puca'*).[186]

Although Pušara also talked about Princip's 'incredible presence of mind' in those moments, there was in fact absolutely nothing cold-blooded about the manner in which he managed to kill Franz Ferdinand and his wife. A young man of nineteen, practically still a schoolboy, understandably became too agitated to be able to look straight down the barrel of his gun. A myth subsequently emerged that one of the bullets had been meant for Potiorek, but had somehow killed the Duchess. Princip himself claimed so months later, in October 1914, at his trial in Sarajevo. His declaration that he had 'deliberately' aimed at Franz Ferdinand and Potiorek appears to have been just an absurd, retrospective creation on his part.[187] In the light of what he himself testified soon after his arrest, he clearly had not been aiming, at any stage, at anyone in particular. On the other hand, there can be no doubt that he never intended to kill the Duchess and would have much preferred to have eliminated Potiorek. In December 1914, as he was transported by train to the prison in Theresienstadt, Princip remarked to his guard: 'Who would want to kill a mother? I know what a mother means to children, for I too have a mother. It was a chance event. A bullet does not always fly in the direction one wants it to, and she was the first to be hit.'[188]

And yet, despite his failure to aim, Princip's shots were deadly. One witness, a policeman, who was very close by, reported that Princip, as he fired, could not have been more than two and a half metres from the car.[189] However, the most that can be said for the assassin's target identification is that it successfully encompassed the large car right in front of him. For that is exactly what the first bullet hit: the car. It struck the back door, on the side where the Duchess was seated, but then continued onwards, tearing through ten centimetres of door, first penetrating the sheet aluminium and then the wooden construction, before ripping through the leather upholstery on the other side and coming out at an angle of forty-five degrees to the entrance hole. Almost as an afterthought, this 'dumdum-like' projectile, as Count Harrach described it, ended up in the lower abdomen of the Duchess, cutting the main artery.[190]

The next shot was likewise a fluke. Princip held the pistol in just one hand: had he held it with both hands he would have had more control – although he was looking away in any case. As a result of his one-handed grip, the recoil lifted Princip's hand upward, taking his weapon with it. When in his paroxysm he pressed the trigger again, it was no longer the car, but rather the Archduke himself who was now in the field of fire.[191] This bullet hit Franz Ferdinand in the neck, penetrating the right side of the collar, severing the jugular vein and coming to a halt in the spine. A report in the *Neue Freie Presse* on 1 July, based on 'an absolutely reliable source', described how the Archduke had leant towards the Duchess after the first shot, and suggested that it was for that reason only that the second bullet found its way into his neck. Baron Morsey claimed that at least one more bullet was fired: this one is supposed to have gone through the plume of feathers on the Archduke's helmet, tearing them to shreds. A heap of green feathers was later seen lying around in the car.[192]

On 1 July two military doctors, Paul Kaunitz and Richard Pollak, who had embalmed the bodies of the Sarajevo victims, gave statements about the highly accidental way in which the couple were killed. Dr Kaunitz spoke of 'an appalling chance' which led to the Archduke's death: 'Had the bullet gone right or left by a hair's breadth the injury would not have been fatal.' Dr Pollak, speaking both as 'a soldier and a doctor', stated that 'Princip was not able to aim', something which was obvious, he said, by the very fact that the first bullet hit the side of the car before hitting the Duchess.[193]

Such was the assassination in Sarajevo on 28 June 1914 – amateurish in planning, haphazard in execution and fortuitous in outcome. A suggestion that Princip succeeded because he had been helped at a crucial moment by his friend Mihajlo Pušara is an old inaccuracy, recently rehashed. Thus Clive Ponting has written: 'As Princip took aim a policeman tried to knock the revolver out of his hand, but a bystander, Mihajlo Pušara, kicked the policeman in the knee and he lost his balance.'[194] Yet nothing in the quoted sentence actually happened except that the policeman may indeed have lost his balance: he did not even see Princip as the latter 'took aim'; the policeman in question, Smail Spahović, moved only after he had heard the shots fired; and it was only then that Pušara took action – and then not by kicking Spahović in the knee, but rather by pushing him with both hands in the stomach.[195]

What this intervention by Pušara did achieve, however, was to give Princip a few moments in which to do several things. Firstly to thump Spahović on the head with his Browning. Secondly to swallow his poison, though as in the case of Čabrinović, Princip's chemical only made him sick – the doses of cyanide taken by the Sarajevo assassins must have been two of the most benign ever concocted. Finally, Princip almost had enough time to make sure that he really would die. Immediately after swallowing the poison he started raising his hand up to shoot himself – at which point he was seized, as he stated, by officers and policemen.[196]

In fact, the first person to seize Princip was a civilian, a Croat theology student named Daniel Pusić, who jumped on Princip and grabbed his neck, at first wanting to 'strangle' him, but then stopping on the thought that the 'eternal judge' would surely not fail to punish the assassin. Another civilian, a tramway conductor called Suljo Mrzić, a Muslim, was second on the scene, running from across the street, just when Spahović was recovering from the head blow he had sustained. Mrzić grabbed the assassin's hands. He, Spahović and Pusić, were then assisted by Alois Fordren, a locksmith. There was still no one else in the immediate vicinity at that moment – the crowd having scattered in a flash when Princip's shots rang out.

But the public quickly returned, and began to shout repeatedly: 'Slay him! Kill the monster!' By now some officers and policemen had finally appeared, drawing their sabres. They started to hit out at Princip furiously, but also indiscriminately. Pusić, Mrzić and Spahović, the trio that had apprehended the assassin, or was still trying to do so, were themselves exposed to this savage assault and absorbed a fair share of it. Those three also had to suffer the punches and kicks of the crowd which was now actively participating.[197]

Princip had defended himself 'fiercely', but of course was soon knocked down, bleeding profusely. And yet, as both Morsey and Harrach observed, he still had his Browning in his hand, pressed tight between his knees – and was not letting it go. Morsey, the most combative person in the Archduke's entourage, had on hearing the shooting leapt out of his car at the tail end of the convoy and hurled himself at Princip whose smoke-stained pistol muzzle left black marks on his parade trousers. Two other members of the entourage also attacked Princip – Lieutenant Grein and Captain Pilz. Morsey struck Princip with two heavy blows to the head with his ceremonial sabre.

But not everybody in the crowd thought that Princip had done even remotely a bad thing, and Morsey himself was soon in trouble. Someone with a short iron instrument attacked him from behind with heavy blows to his helmet which became twisted in the process. Indeed, the sympathy on the street for the assassin was not inconsiderable. Several people were brave or foolish enough to warn Morsey, in German, that he should just go away. Moreover, a police guard came up to Morsey, saying: 'Move on, this is none of your business.' It must have been all too much for the imperial sensitivities of the young Morsey. With 'indescribable fury' he began striking the policeman with his sabre until he 'rolled' to the ground.

All those who were hostile to Morsey's intervention spoke German. Ferdo Behr could not remain indifferent to the vicious onslaught on Princip as the latter lay on the ground – 'At that point something broke inside me', he recalled. He grabbed Morsey by the arm and shouted: '*Lassen sie ihn!* [Leave him!]' Morsey felt compelled to swing his sabre and threaten: 'Whoever touches me will die.' In no time at all Behr was splattered by blood as he began to sustain knocks and strikes from the police and the crowd. Thus he paid for his audacity, but in a curious manner also gained a certain fame which has lasted to this day. He was taken by three policemen who, holding their man by the arms and neck, pushed him towards the prison, located in a narrow street directly across from the Town Hall. On the way there this scene was photographed. The resulting picture, capturing the drama of the day, has been widely publicized as the arrest of Princip. The confusion arose, Behr later explained, because he had actually been led to the prison minutes before Princip.[198]

In the face of the overwhelming odds, Princip himself was quickly overpowered. At some point – it is not clear exactly when – he had dropped his bomb. In contradiction to what the assassin himself later said about not having prepared the bomb, Pušara was to declare that the cap of the bomb had been unscrewed, and that Princip, preferring to use his pistol, had let it fall just before he began shooting. This would indicate that he had been standing very close to the edge of the pavement, because the bomb did not fall on the pavement but on to the street. Morsey, when he realized that the police had not even seen the bomb, was appalled. Daniel Pusić also drew attention to this new danger, which caused a 'tremendous panic' in the crowd: 'It was terrible to watch this desperate and frightened mass of people; some ran around, others stood petrified, not knowing whether to run away or to stay.' Someone then had the bizarre idea of using a wet sack to cover the bomb. An expert commission later attended the scene and disarmed it.[199]

As for Princip's other weapon, the deadly Belgian Browning, one Ante Velić claimed at the trial that he had jumped on Princip just as the latter was about to shoot himself: 'I took him by the arm and snatched his revolver ... He had pointed the revolver against himself.' But Morsey and Harrach had seen Princip still holding the pistol – squeezing it between his knees – and therefore Velić's evidence is questionable. Indeed, Morsey wrote in 1924 that he and Lieutenant Grein had tried to wrest the pistol away from Princip. Be that as it may, it was the policeman Smail Spahović who, together with his squad commander, managed to pull Princip out of the scuffle with the crowd. They brought him to the Appel Quay, where Spahović, still in great pain after Pušara's blow to his stomach, had to ask Alois Fordren, the locksmith who had been at the scene, to take over from him. Meanwhile, Princip's defiance was astounding. A witness reported that as he was led to the police station, 'members of the public repeatedly spat at him, and each time he spat back'.[200]

Death in the Konak

Count Franz Harrach has gone down in history as the man who stood on the wrong running board of a car. Joachim Remak has paid tribute to this aristocrat, and part-time poet, who insisted on shielding the Archduke with his own body: 'Harrach's gesture was a wonderfully Austrian one – kind, impulsive, brave, chivalrous, and ineffectual.'[201] What in retrospect deserves perhaps greater emphasis is the fact that Harrach was the one person in Franz Ferdinand's entourage who, without even participating in the post-bomb discussion at the Town Hall, had instinctively felt more than any other that there was something rotten about Potiorek's safety measures in Sarajevo. In the circumstances, moreover, his decision to stand on the left-hand side, with his back towards the river and immediately next to Franz Ferdinand who was sat on the left in the car, was the correct one: it was on the river side that Čabrinović had stood when attempting the first assassination; and with the car driving on the left Harrach was protecting the Archduke from any potential assassin on the pavement nearest to him.

But the logic of Harrach's decision to stand on the left was rendered invalid by his own chauffeur Lojka committing something of a traffic offence when he turned into Franz Joseph Street – manoeuvring the car nearer to the right-hand pavement, when it was expected and would have been proper for him to have continued to drive on the other side, closer to the left-hand pavement. Thus, as Friedrich Würthle calculated, instead of the car being five or six metres away from the assassin, Lojka's corner-cutting had inadvertently reduced this distance to just two or three metres.[202]

In his diary, Harrach described dramatically the moments after Princip had fired his shots. Immediately, blood spurting from the Archduke's mouth splashed his cheek. 'For God's sake', the Duchess exclaimed to the Archduke, 'what has happened to you?!' – but then collapsed towards her husband herself, her head sinking onto his thighs. '*Und es war vorbei* [and it was over]', Harrach wrote, in brackets, implying that the Duchess was already dead. 'Sopherl, Sopherl, do not die on me, live for my children', cried the Archduke. He never said, as is so often stated, '*our* children'. Harrach, observing the blood streaming out of Franz Ferdinand's mouth, put it to him: 'Your Imperial Highness must be suffering terribly?' To which the Archduke replied: 'Oh no, it is nothing', and then, his throat rattling: 'it is nothing, nothing ...'[203] All this was happening as the car was reversing rapidly. In the statement he gave on 28 June Harrach said that the Heir to the Throne, losing consciousness, repeated six or seven times, his voice gradually diminishing in strength: 'It is nothing.' Then he stopped – gasping out heavily as the blood came pouring out.[204]

Given that the bullet had ripped the jugular vein, mangled the thyroid gland and shattered the trachea – leading to such massive internal bleeding that no person with this kind of injury could have uttered a single word – doubts have been expressed as to whether the Archduke was able to say anything at all. And yet, if Harrach had for some reason invented the last words of the couple in his official statement to the investigating judge, why would he have repeated the same in his private diary? Rumerskirch also stated that the Archduke had 'murmured' some words which he could not understand. For his part, Potiorek, in his own diary, wrote that he believed he had heard Franz Ferdinand say: '*also doch noch einmal* [so, once again after all]'.[205] One wonders what the Archduke would have had to say to the Governor on the matter had he survived.

Potiorek, of course, when reporting about this episode, presented himself in the best possible light. He had heard, he stated, some 'weak' shots: 'two, maybe three or four' – he was not sure. But then he continued, suddenly imbued with military precision: 'I had, on this occasion, straight away the indubitable impression of an assassination, but was initially convinced that it was luckily once again unsuccessful, for I saw Her Imperial Highness, as well as His Highness to the right of me, sitting calmly upright. It was immediately clear to me, however, that in these circumstances a further drive along the right bank of the Miljacka river was out of the question, and I shouted to the chauffeur to reverse the car, which had in the meantime been stationary, to the left bank across the Latin bridge directly behind us, in order to reach the *Konak* which lay in the immediate

vicinity."[206] Ironically, therefore, the journey to the hospital was being abandoned just when it was finally looking like a very logical destination.

Whether anything was 'immediately clear' to Potiorek is of course very
much open to question. The person who commanded Lojka to drive over
the Latin bridge was Rumerskirch, not Potiorek. Rumerskirch was in the
car just behind. Seeing the motorcade halted and hearing the shots, he
jumped out, sprinting towards the Archduke's car. Interestingly, he first
heard 'three-four' shots, and then, as he ran, 'another two-three'. As seen
earlier in this chapter, Rumerskirch, reaching the car, screamed at Lojka
to reverse quickly back towards the Latin bridge.[207] In other words, Lojka
was now taking orders from Rumerskirch.

There is nothing about this in Potiorek's statements. Officially, he saw
almost nothing and heard almost nothing: he did not see the blood which
spurted out of the Archduke's mouth immediately after he was shot, and he
did not hear the screaming of Rumerskirch. According to his account, he
only heard some 'weak' shots, saw the couple 'sitting calmly upright' and
thought all was well. In fact, when Princip fired from his Browning the
sound was so loud that Mayor Ćurčić and Dr Gerde, driving well in front,
immediately halted their car and jumped out.[208] Officially, too, however,
Potiorek made it look as if he, not Rumerskirch, had ordered Lojka to
reverse. In truth, the Governor of Bosnia-Herzegovina just sat in the car
paralysed with disbelief and horror, utterly incapable of taking command.

In addition to Rumerskirch, Major Hüttenbrenner, aged thirty-six, also
showed presence of mind in these moments. He too had run forward and,
amid loud calls for medical help, quickly recruited two military doctors
who stepped forward, packing them into his car and ordering them to
follow the archducal vehicle. Potiorek's subsequent claim that medical
assistance was already at hand on arrival at the *Konak* is another claim that
does not fit the facts. Hüttenbrenner had initially stayed behind, but then
jumped into the next car heading for the *Konak*. When he got there, the
Archduke and the Duchess were already being carried from the car into
the building, but the two doctors had still not arrived – they were having
difficulty finding the entrance to the secluded mansion, surrounded as it
was by its own park. So Hüttenbrenner ran back, found them and helped
them get in. Senior Lieutenant Adolf Egger also managed to collect two
doctors and an emergency medical orderly on the street, and together they
followed the other cars.[209]

Farcical scenes had already taken place as Lojka rapidly reversed his car
to the *Konak*. Some men in the public, not knowing about what had
just happened, were taking their hats off, hailing the dying couple with
loud and enthusiastic cries of 'Long live!'[210] Both the Archduke and the
Duchess were still alive – just. Major Höger had seen the Duchess when
she had originally fallen towards the Archduke – as if 'seeking protection'.

But she was, even now, still breathing. The car was speeding backwards so fast that Morsey thought it was actually moving forward. Franz Ferdinand's helmet with its attendant feathers had fallen off his head.

Rumerskirch, Bardolff and Höger had stepped onto the running boards of the car. Harrach does not actually clarify – either in his diary or in his deposition – whether he too had continued to stand on the step platform, but other witness accounts confirm that he had. Thus there were now four men hanging on to the car from its running boards as it reversed. Bardolff, on reaching the car, had tried to unbutton the Archduke's tunic. Höger had observed that the Duchess, with her head on the Archduke's lap, was motionless, whereas he remained sitting in his seat, the expression in his eyes becoming 'increasingly withdrawn'. His blood gushed again as the car crossed the Latin Bridge.[211]

It is clear from Höger's deposition that only now, with the car already in backward motion, was Potiorek able to regain some command of his senses, at least managing to direct Lojka to the park gate entrance outside the *Konak*. The drive from what became known as 'Schiller's Corner' to Potiorek's mansion across the river could not have lasted more than two minutes. The *Konak* building (*konak* means 'residence' or 'overnight stay') dating from 1869, had been built for Osman Pasha by Dalmatian architects from Split. From it Potiorek's Turkish predecessors had ruled the sometimes turbulent country. For a while it was the only three-storey building in Sarajevo. During his 1910 Bosnian visit the Emperor Franz Joseph had stayed there, using among others the room in which his nephew was going to die. This room, on the first floor, was now Potiorek's study.

An article in the *Pester Lloyd* on 1 July reported that as they reached Potiorek's residence both the Duchess and the Archduke had slumped from their seats to the floor of the car.[212] The Duchess, unconscious, was the first to be lifted from the vehicle. This was done by Bardolff and Rumerskirch and not, as the incorrigible Potiorek related, by his 'quickly summoned servants'. Those two were then helped to carry the Duchess upstairs by Countess Lanjus, Baron Ditfurth and Lojka.

It is as if Potiorek had made a deliberate effort in his official outpourings to eliminate from the record as many witnesses from the Archduke's entourage as possible – witnesses to his incompetence and what must almost have been his nervous collapse. Leon Biliński in his memoirs goes so far as to assert that Potiorek was so out of touch with reality in those moments that, on arrival in the *Konak*, he asked the Archduke and the Duchess to step out of the car in order to go inside and have the planned *déjeuner*.[213] There also exists a variation on this story. Henry Wickham Steed, the former correspondent of *The Times* in Vienna, writing later in his memoirs, by contrast related an account that stressed Potiorek's cynical conduct. Once the couple were brought to his the study on the first floor, according to Steed, Potiorek emerged from the room, saying: 'Gentlemen, this is a terrible misfortune. Nevertheless, one must eat. Let us go to luncheon.'[214]

Practically all the newspaper reports, as well as most first-hand accounts, maintained that by the time of the arrival in the *Konak* the Duchess was already dead. They also agreed that the Archduke was still alive. Höger, Hüttenbrenner and Erbach-Fürstenau joined Bardolff and Rumerskirch to carry him inside. As they did so, Höger noted with horror that Franz Ferdinand's tunic was 'completely covered in blood.'

The couple were at first brought to the Turkish salon on the ground floor, and then taken upstairs. As the Archduke was carried up the stairs he batted his eyelids several times and kept moving his arms in the air, 'as if searching'. He was placed on an ottoman in Potiorek's study, while the Duchess was put on the Governor's bed in an adjacent room. Together with Lojka and a doctor, Countess Lanjus attended to the Duchess. Bardolff and Rumerskirch were with the Archduke, trying to undo his garments. Rumerskirch was struggling to unfasten Franz Ferdinand's waistband, 'desperately shouting for help', until Morsey used a pen knife to cut it.[215]

What exactly Potiorek himself was doing during the last moments of this drama is a matter of conjecture because little evidence is available – reliable or otherwise. All that exists in this connection is a statement, contained in a report in the *Neue Freie Presse* of 3 July, and attributed to a direct witness who had shared his observations with the Korrespondenz Wilhelm press agency. According to this, 'Potiorek ... had been seized by a heavy nervous shock, and he collapsed, unconscious. The doctors struggled hard to bring him back to awareness.' Practically identical reports also appeared, on the same day, in *Reichspost* and *Pester Lloyd*.[216]

Indeed, it seems likely that the Governor had been stupefied by the events of the morning to the point of nervous collapse. The newspaper dispatches to that effect were certainly not being dismissed in Vienna's high circles. When Ludwig Thallóczy met with the War Minister Krobatin on 4 July, they discussed the matter, and agreed that, if the newspaper stories were true, 'it was hardly a good omen' for Potiorek as a leader.[217] The news about the Governor's dramatic breakdown may have been just a wild rumour, but the subsequent denials in the press were not convincing.[218] It is quite conceivable that, at his fairly advanced age, and given the grievous shocks to the system suffered by him that morning, he may indeed have required some medical help. Dr Paul Flandrak, the head of the Press Section in the Joint Finance Ministry, described Potiorek after 28 June as 'spiritually disturbed' from then on.[219]

If he himself did require medical help, there was certainly no shortage of doctors around the place. At least four of them materialized in the mansion soon after the royal couple had been brought there. Wladimir Aichelburg writes that doctors Arnstein and Fischer – both of whom had been involved in Merizzi's medical case – had come accompanied by doctors Polazzo and Hochmann. This was thanks to Major Höger who, on arriving in the *Konak*, had rushed to telephone the military headquarters and ask for doctors to come. But it took Arnstein and his colleagues some fifteen minutes to get to the *Konak*. It is almost certain that Hütten-brenner's two street recruits, doctors Peyer and Wolfgang, were the first to offer medical assistance, along with the two additional doctors who had been collected by Egger, likewise on the street.[220]

Spiritual sustenance had also been recruited. On seeing the Franciscan Provincial Mihačević in the courtyard, Morsey made sure to 'drag him upstairs'.[221] But the doctors had not given up yet on either the Duchess or the Archduke. An attempt was made to revive the Duchess with ether. This was unsuccessful. Some of those present had initially believed that she had merely fainted as there was no visible wound. Countess Lanjus placed wet bandages on her forehead, but could not help noticing her 'lemon yellow face'. On doctor's instructions, the lady-in-waiting removed the clothing of her mistress and only then was a small brown-red mark detected in the groin area, 'without any trace of blood'.[222]

In the meantime Dr Peyer was attending to Franz Ferdinand as others struggled with his tunic and shirt to ease his breathing. The garments he wore had to be cut with scissors. The decision was then made to place him in an upright position. This produced an outpouring of blood from his neck wound, though the breathing could suddenly be heard again and Hüttenbrenner sprang to his feet to fetch ether.

However, the moment of hope regained was to be brief. Dr Peyer, who wanted to operate on the Archduke, was at the same time highly sceptical, saying that it would be sheer luck if they managed to bring him alive to the garrison hospital. Holding his left hand, Morsey asked the Archduke: 'Your Imperial Highness, should I say something to the children?' But no answer came. Franz Ferdinand merely leant backwards, by now almost lifeless.[223] Soon it was all over. At just before 11 in the morning Dr Peyer announced: 'Any further human help is in vain here. His Imperial Highness is suffering no more.' Morsey recalled that imme-diately thereafter he turned towards Bardolff and said to him: '*Finis Austriae!*'[224]

Bardolff and Rumerskirch reportedly broke down in tears. Morsey put a cross against the Archduke's lips. The story subsequently circulated in Vienna society that, as Morsey did this, the Archduke moved his lips 'as if he wished to kiss the cross'. But he was dead. Members of the entourage now kissed the hand of the deceased Heir to the Throne. Rumerskirch closed the eyes of his master.[225]

Two priests now appeared in the *Konak*, one after the other, in an episode which has confused historians. First, the Franciscan Provincial

Lovro Mihačević, and then a Jesuit, Father Anton Puntigam – each of whom is said to have administered the last rites. Mihačević had been brought by Morsey – and he gave absolution to the couple. As this was taking place, Father Puntigam was making his way to the *Konak*. He had heard about the incident and wanted to offer words of comfort to the Duchess who had two days earlier visited the 'Jugendheim' he was running in Sarajevo for Croat Catholic youth. Potiorek's residence was cordoned off by soldiers, but the officers let the Jesuit through. On the steps he ran into Mihačević who was already leaving. The Franciscan told him: 'Both are dead, I gave them absolution. The Duchess was still moving her lips; I did not see the Archduke's face, it was veiled.'

His words and the veil imply that the Duchess was showing signs of life at least for a time after the Archduke had died – quite the opposite of the widely held view, then and now.

Puntigam hurried to the first floor where he came across the Duchess first, 'her face and hands as white as lilies'. Crying, the Jesuit knelt down and spoke the words of the absolution again. He later described his action as a conditional absolution ('*die bedingungsweise Absolution*') because, of course, Mihačević had already performed the rite. Puntigam then moved to the next room. At his request Franz Ferdinand's face was uncovered: it was pale and quite shrunken, the neck and the mouth bloody. The Archduke, too, was given the absolution *sub conditione*.

Why did Puntigam give these 'second' absolutions? Mihačević's departure suggests he was certain the royal couple were dead, but Puntigam might have taken his words to imply that they had only just died. Finding himself now the only priest present in the terrible circumstances he did what was expected of him and what was natural for him to do.

When someone present then asked whether their highnesses should not also be anointed, he replied: 'Certainly, if it has not been done already'. He then hurried to the nearby Franciscan chapel to get the holy oil. Again, Puntigam may simply have been doing what he could to console those present, perhaps justifying his actions to himself on the basis that there might be some difference between 'medical' death and less identifiable 'theological' death – the separation of the soul from the body. Mihačević may not have considered this extreme unction appropriate because he knew – certainly in the case of the Archduke – that by now a certain time had elapsed since death.

Morsey assisted the Jesuit to perform the anointing, first of the Archduke and then of the Duchess. Countess Lanjus had taken off the Duchess's gloves and shoes, and placed roses – those which the little Muslim girl had given to the Duchess at the Town Hall – 'on the dead body of my gracious mistress'. The first floor of the *Konak* was by now crowded. Army chaplain Canek was saying prayers for the departed. Archbishop Stadler had also arrived, accompanied by another bishop and the papal delegate. 'Every-body was sobbing', recalled Puntigam, and a crying Rumerskirch fell onto Stadler's chest. Everywhere, people knelt and prayed: Rumerskirch and the rest of the entourage, and 'scores of generals and doctors'.[226]

The priests, and especially Puntigam, accordingly did a far more con-scientious job at steering the Archduke and the Duchess out of Sarajevo and this world than Potiorek had done when escorting them in the city. Had the Governor opted to take no risks, there would probably have been no need for any priests.

The evidence about Potiorek's mental state and behaviour for the rest of that day of 28 June is conflicting. Alfred Jansa was returning to Sarajevo that morning from the manoeuvres area, riding his horse at a slow pace. When he heard about the assassination he headed straight for the *Konak* to find Potiorek dictating at his desk, displaying his 'customary calmness'. But when the investigating judge Leo Pfeffer encountered the Governor that evening, he saw a very wretched creature: 'his head was down and he was totally dejected, his arms dangling, pale and with unkempt hair, and with his tunic unbuttoned – he looked like some desperate man.'[227]

The position was certainly not an easy one for Potiorek. On 30 June the press in Vienna reported that 'in society circles' charges were being levelled against both him and Gerde over the inadequate security meas-ures. On the same day the *Pester Lloyd* carried the text of a telegram that had arrived from Sarajevo, whereby Potiorek, according to 'well-informed' sources, was about to resign.[228] This rather alarmed Safvet-beg Bašagić, the Muslim president of the Bosnian Diet, who, when he came to Vienna in early July, threatened the Joint Finance Minister Biliński that if Potiorek went, 'the Mohammedans would then emigrate'.[229]

Potiorek of course had no intention of resigning. Luckily for him, he had a very solid reputation as an opponent of the Serbs – and general anti-Serb hysteria had already begun that afternoon throughout the Austro-Hungarian Empire. On the other hand, Biliński's policy was seen as Serbophile, and he thus became an easy target for the Viennese press, par-ticularly the *Reichspost*, run by Franz Ferdinand's friend Friedrich Funder. This certainly helped Potiorek – the *Reichspost*, never keen on Biliński, ironically now defended the Governor.[230] Privately, however, some of the Archduke's closest associates had a very different opinion. Colonel Alexander Brosch wrote to Auffenberg on 1 July: 'Heavy is the respon-sibility that weighs on ... Potiorek; I would have shot myself after this misfortune – he is obviously too much of a coward for that!'[231]

Quite. In marked contrast with Brosch's ambitions for him, and indeed with his own assurances to the Archduke, Potiorek was soon to display plenty of concern for his own safety – barricading himself in the *Konak* and venturing out of his mansion only twice more prior to the beginning of the war with Serbia. The first time was the day after the assassination of his guests – in the evening when, amid heavy military security, the coffins of the Archduke and the Duchess were taken to the small Bistrik railway station, to be transported to Metković on the Adriatic coast – and from there by dreadnought *Viribus Unitis* to Trieste, and by train on to Vienna. The second time was a few days later, on 3 July, when a requiem for the victims was held in Sarajevo's Catholic cathedral. Potiorek, followed by officers, moved through a double cordon of soldiers. On this occasion, the shops and gates had to be closed. While people were allowed to be on the streets, they were forbidden to appear at the windows, and the shutters had to be lowered. Alfred Jansa recalled the 'peculiar' sight of troops positioned 'with their faces towards the partaking populace'.[232]

16

Austria-Hungary in the July Crisis

Up in Arms: The Ballhausplatz Juniors

ON THE DAY of the assassination in Sarajevo, Franz Joseph was enjoying himself at his beloved Kaiservilla in the spa resort of Bad Ischl, set in the spectacularly beautiful region of Salzkammergut, east of Salzburg. He had an interesting neighbour there: Ernst August, the exiled Crown Prince of Hanover, who, owing to a blood connection with the British Royal House, also held the title of the 3rd Duke of Cumberland. When he heard about the assassination, 'Herzog von Cumberland' jumped into a car and was reportedly the first to reach Franz Joseph with the news. Although, according to the Duke, the Emperor expressed his dismay, he remained 'calm' and said that he could draw comfort from the fact that the Archduke and his wife had been 'an embarrassment [*eine Verlegenheit*]' for the Imperial House.[1]

So much for the uncle's sympathy. Sources are not unanimous on the identity of the first person to tell Franz Joseph about the assassination, but most of them agree that his reaction was one of relief. 'For me', he told his daughter Marie Valerie, 'it is one big worry less'.[2] Biliński, who saw Franz Joseph soon after the event, reported him as being 'almost relieved'.[3] It would seem, from the account by Count Paar, his Adjutant-General, that the Emperor also took something of a metaphysical view of the matter: 'A higher power', he murmured to himself, 'has re-established that order which I sadly could not preserve'.[4] However, it is not the case, as is often claimed, that Franz Joseph and Prince Montenuovo, the master of Court ceremonies, had contrived to demean the royal couple, evincing deliberate pettiness and malevolence with regard to the funeral arrangements. The coffins holding Franz Ferdinand and Sophie, having been transported to Trieste by sea on *Viribus Unitis*, were put on a special train which reached Vienna's Südbahnhof station on the night of 2 July. They were then brought to the *Hofburgkapelle*, the Habsburg family chapel. Austrian scholarship has exploded the myth that there was anything disrespectful about the details in these proceedings. On the contrary, what took place was a 'generous interpretation' of strict royal protocol. The Duchess was accorded the treatment reserved for members of the Imperial House. It is simply not true that her coffin, lying in state in the chapel, was placed lower than that of the Archduke; and the pair of white gloves, displayed together with a fan in front of her coffin, were not put there as a reminder of her former status of lady-in-waiting, but rather placed there as symbols appropriate to a female member of the Imperial House.[5] Nevertheless, the occasion did perhaps require more attention and greater sensitivity, for the impression became current that Franz Ferdinand and Sophie had been buried 'with undeserving haste'.[6] On 4 July, in accordance with the Archduke's will, he and the Duchess found their final resting place in the family vault beneath Schloss Artstetten, Lower Austria.

As with Franz Joseph, not many people in the Empire were particularly distressed by the news of the assassination. Sigmund Freud, the celebrated Viennese founder of psychoanalysis, remarked on 29 June that if Franz Ferdinand had come to power there would probably have been a war between Austria and Russia.[7] Ludwig Thallóczy of the Joint Finance Ministry wrote in his diary on 28 June that the Archduke's death spared the Monarchy, and Hungary, from the shocks which his ascendance of the Throne would certainly have entailed.[8] War Minister Krobatin admitted that his ministry now felt 'freed' from a certain pressure.[9] The Austrian writer Stefan Zweig described how he had on 28 June found himself in the lovely spa resort of Baden near Vienna, sitting in a park, reading while listening to music being played by a band nearby. Suddenly, the music stopped. A crowd gathered round the bandstand to read why, for a placard had just been put up. This announced that Archduke Franz Ferdinand had been assassinated, and also his wife. 'But to be honest,' writes Zweig of the crowd, 'there was no particular shock or dismay to be seen on their faces, for the heir-apparent was not at all well liked.' He lacked, according to Zweig, everything that counted for popularity in Austria: 'amiability, personal charm and easy-goingness'. The music later resumed.[10]

Politically, however, it was a different story. In Sarajevo the authorities released the criminals from the prisons and put them under the command of well known city ruffians. The resultant mob, mostly Croat, embarked on a savage anti-Serb pogrom, burning and looting. Ivan Kranjčević, a Croat and friend of the Sarajevo assassins, recalled that 'a well-dressed man' walked in front of the 'demonstrators', holding a list of Serb houses and shops to be attacked and their contents demolished. Behind them moved the police, tasked with protecting this 'patriotic work'.[11] Bizarrely, all Roma musicians from Serbia ('*Zigeunermusikanten*') were arrested by the police and expelled.[12] Following the assassination, vicious anti-Serb violence also took place in Zagreb and elsewhere in Croatia, Slavonia and Dalmatia. From the outset, both the Austrian and the Hungarian press pointed their accusing fingers at Belgrade. In Vienna's 4th *Bezirk*, there were daily demonstrations around the Serbian Legation in Paulanergasse, near Favoritenstrasse, but here the police held off the crowds, though they numbered hundreds, even thousands. Particularly active were young members of Catholic associations who blew whistles to make a deafening noise. The revolted crowd burned the Serbian flag and sang the patriotic repertoire: '*Wacht am Rhein*', the '*Kaiserlied*' and the '*Prinz Eugen-Lied*'. Showing political awareness, it shouted: 'Long live Bulgaria!' outside the nearby Bulgarian Legation, and 'Down with Russia!' at the Russian Embassy in the neighbouring 3rd *Bezirk*.[13]

In the wake of the murders in Sarajevo, the emerging reflex in the Habsburg establishment was pretty much in tune with the sentiments displayed by the crowds besieging the Serbian Legation. Following the assassination of the royal couple it took less than forty-eight hours for most of the Empire's small decision-making elite to decide that Austria-Hungary should go to war against Serbia. Count Alexander ('Alek') Hoyos, Berchtold's *chef de cabinet*, related in a private conversation with Hans Schlitter on 24 July that war had been decided upon 'immediately after the arrival of the news about the assassination'.[14] This was an exaggeration, but only a slight one. On 28 June Berchtold was on his estate in Moravia, shooting ducks. On hearing the news, he took the first train to Vienna. That night he was already holding meetings at the Ballhausplatz.[15] The crucial days, nevertheless, were those from Monday 29 June to Wednesday 1 July.

Who were the chief players pushing for war? The Emperor himself, according to Biliński, was 'determined on war from day one'.[16] He may otherwise have just wanted a quiet life but, as seen in chapter seven, he was in 1913 quite clear that he would wage war rather than watch Serbia and Montenegro merge into one state. It is obvious from his conversation with Conrad von Hötzendorf on 5 July 1914 that he had decided on war and was merely waiting for assurances of German support.[17] Had he wanted to prevent a war against Serbia in July 1914, he could easily have done so, even though the Habsburg establishment was in July 1914 teeming with combative jingoists. Predictably, one of those most vehement after 28 June in demanding a war against Serbia was *Feldzeugmeister* Potiorek in Sarajevo. Of course, he would have been a hawk in any confrontation with Belgrade, but now he had even more reason, for the assassination had showed up his incompetence and he wanted to 'wash it off with blood'.[18] Equally predictably, Conrad now moved to exploit the new opportunity opened up by Sarajevo. The Chief of General Staff saw Berchtold on 29 June, to energetically demand action against Serbia. Berchtold, however, appeared to him undecided. Although he said that the moment had arrived for 'the solution of the Serbian question', he also talked, to Conrad's horror, about the need to await the results of the enquiry into the Sarajevo assassination and about the possibility of making certain demands on Serbia, for example that it should abolish certain associations and dismiss the Interior Minister.[19]

But the diplomat Berchtold soon turned into a most tenacious advocate of the military option. In fact, his declared position in the crisis proved crucial to the fateful decisions that followed in the course of July. Yet on the face of it, he was the most unlikely of warmongers. This self-effacing, fabulously rich aristocrat was above all a *bon vivant*, with an interest in arts, apparel, horse racing and women. It was said of him, as Redlich noted in his diary, that he was very much 'in need of love' and was on the lookout everywhere for attractive prostitutes (*'gefällige Frauenzimmer'*).[20] Legendary was the meticulous attention Berchtold paid to his attire. On one occasion, a visitor at the Ballhausplatz was amazed to spot in the ante-chamber to his office four overcoats, four hats, four pairs of hand gloves and four canes. The guest was later told that the Minister always had those ready, so that he could choose when going out, whatever best suited the weather conditions, the clothes he happened to be wearing and his own mood. Berchtold had reportedly also installed a wonderful system of secret bells for dealing with difficult questions raised by his visitors. Concealed push buttons for different foreign policy areas were electrically connected to the offices of the relevant Ministry experts: a Berchtoldian push of the appropriate button and the specialist official would soon turn up by apparent chance to help out his Minister.[21] Count Berchtold was 'a frivolous aristocrat, but the Foreign Minister of Austria-Hungary', according to A.J.P. Taylor.[22] 'Fop, dandy, la-di-da', is how Winston Churchill described him. Berchtold was, in the opinion of the British statesman, 'one of the smallest men who ever held a great position'.[23] In his memoirs, the former German Chancellor Prince Bülow wrote of 'Count Leopold Berchtold, whose frivolous incapacity far exceeded even Austrian standards'.[24]

Although he was a competent enough Ambassador at St Petersburg, almost no one took Berchtold seriously. When, however, his name began to be mentioned among the candidates to succeed Aehrenthal, some of his colleagues were suddenly alarmed. Julius Szillasy, who worked for him at St Petersburg, as well as Pourtalès, the German Ambassador in Russia, thought initially that press speculation about his candidacy for the post of Foreign Minister was 'a bad joke'. Szillasy even predicted that if Berchtold ever became Minister, it 'could result in world war'.[25] Popović, the Serbian Minister at St Petersburg, reported in March 1912 that Berchtold's appointment at the Ballhausplatz had caused great surprise both in Russian society and in the diplomatic corps because it was considered that he 'was not up to the job'.[26] Early in 1912, as he lay dying, Aehrenthal recommended three names as his possible successor: Burián, Miklós Szécsen (the Ambassador to France) and Berchtold – in that order. The first two, however, being genuine Hungarians, differed from Berchtold who held both Austrian and Hungarian citizenship. Burián, in particular, could never gain Franz Ferdinand's approval. The new chief at the Ballhausplatz would have to be the least objectionable candidate, not necessarily the ablest. Under pressure from the Heir to the Throne, but also from the Emperor, Berchtold eventually and reluctantly accepted the post.[27]

Berchtold, indeed, knew his limitations and became Foreign Minister in February 1912 only out of loyalty to the old Emperor. As to the extent to which he then formulated foreign policy, especially in 1914, this remains open to question. For there are just too many appraisals by contemporaries to the effect that it was actually János Forgách who ran the Ballhausplatz in the first half of that year. After his controversial period as Minister in Belgrade, from where his Legation sent the forgeries that later led to the Friedjung trial, Forgách had been moved as Minister to the quiet diplomatic backwater of Dresden, Saxony. Berchtold then brought him back to the Ballhausplatz in August 1913, and in October promoted him to Second Section Chief (political) in the Ministry. In this position he was able to influence, as Ludwig Bittner wrote, 'the most important foreign policy decisions'.[28] This may actually have been an understatement, for it seems to have been much more a question of control than mere influence. Count Anton Monts, the distinguished German diplomat, related in his memoirs that, once Forgách got to the Ballhausplatz, he in fact 'usurped' many functions that should have been managed by Berchtold.[29] Thallóczy noted during the July crisis that Forgách behaved as if he, not Berchtold, was the Foreign Minister.[30] Everybody knew, according to the Ballhausplatz mandarin Emanuel Urbas, that Berchtold was 'interested only in women', and not in his office business which was conducted by would-be Foreign Minister Forgách.[31] The latter was by all accounts very adroit and diligent, but also disdainful of his boss and other colleagues. When a diplomat from the French Embassy mentioned to him a conversation he had had with Berchtold, Forgách immediately complained: 'For God's sake, why do you go to Berchtold and [Karl von] Macchio, they don't know what they are talking about, you just come and talk to me.'[32]

The significance of Forgách wielding so much power at the Ballhausplatz in July 1914 is that he was fanatically anti-Serbian, telling Szilassy, his fellow Hungarian, that he would like to see the inscription '*delenda est Serbia*' hung on the walls of every office at the Ballhausplatz. To Forgách the destruction of Serbia was the 'fundamental condition' for the continued existence of the Habsburg Monarchy.[33] King Carol of Romania, always well-informed, spoke very disparagingly of Berchtold at the height of the July 1914 crisis, accusing him of falling under the influence of the 'mighty' Forgách, whom he described as Serbia's 'personal enemy'.[34] However,

Forgách was a Slavophobe not just a Serbophobe, and many historians are quite wrong to see his hostility to the Serbs as stemming from the period when he was Minister in Belgrade between 1907 and 1911. He did, admittedly, have a difficult time there following the scandal with the forgeries, but his anti-Slav reputation had been established and talked about long before that. In January 1907, while serving in Athens, Jovan Jovanović found out that Forgách would be the next Austro-Hungarian Minister in Belgrade, and having known him from their days in Sofia, he immediately raised the alarm. Describing Forgách as 'very nasty', Jovanović pleaded that his appointment be prevented if at all possible, and quoted what the Russian Military Attaché in Bulgaria had told him in 1903 about Forgách: 'Be careful with him. He is the greatest enemy of Slavdom, he is ready for anything'.[35] In July 1914, Forgách was not only ready for anything, he was also supremely confident. 'The premier military power in the world', he told Alexander Spitzmüller, 'is our ally!'[36]

One of the reasons why Forgách had become so important at the Ballhausplatz was his friendship with the Hungarian Prime Minister Tisza. Karl von Macchio, Berchtold's deputy, emphasized in his short memoir devoted to the July crisis that 'without Tisza, one could not make foreign policy', and that Forgách for his part was the 'indispensable intermediary' between Vienna and Budapest. Forgách, according to Macchio, pushed after the Sarajevo assassination for a policy that did not repeat Austria-Hungary's 'inglorious' crisis handling of the Balkan Wars. This could itself only mean war. Apart from Forgách, Macchio named Alexander von Hoyos and Alexander von Musulin as the two other Ballhausplatz mandarins forming part of the inner circle of Berchtold advisers.[37] Among the Ballhausplatz hawks from July 1914, Count Hoyos is perhaps the best known because he was the man with the mission to Berlin; a mission crowned by Germany's so-called 'blank cheque' of support to Austria-Hungary. As pointed out in chapter eight, he had in October 1913 advocated marching on Belgrade, and was at the time, according to Emanuel Urbas, 'the most resolute' advocate at the Ballhausplatz for an immediate intervention.[38] Musulin, for his part, is widely credited for drafting the notorious Austro-Hungarian ultimatum to Serbia of 23 July 1914, a task entrusted to him because of his stylistic mastery of the French language.[39] Always described as a Croat in world literature on the July crisis, he had in fact a Serb background, his ancestors stemming from the village of Musulinsko near Gomirje, Croatia, an area settled by Serb families and forming a part of the *Militärgrenze* against the Turks. But those ancestors had at some stage embraced the Catholic faith and so their branch of the Musulin tribe became 'Croat'. In any case, meeting at the Ballhausplatz on 29 June, with Forgách and Hoyos also in attendance, Musulin was already arguing that this was 'the last moment' to win the Croats over to the idea of a war against Serbia.[40]

Forgách, Hoyos and Musulin were by no means the only ones at the Ballhausplatz advocating a settling of accounts with Serbia. Prince Gottfried Hohenlohe, only recently designated as Austria-Hungary's next Ambassador to Berlin, was equally hawkish.[41] So was Count Friedrich ('Fritz') Szápáry, the Ambassador in St Petersburg, who happened to be in Vienna at this time. And so, too, must have been Macchio who wrote an apologetic article for the *Berliner Monatshefte* in 1936, but who, in 1909, fumed that 'the Serbian ulcer' had to be 'squeezed out [*muß ausgequetscht werden*]' either by war or revolution.[42] In the 1970s and 1980s, the Austrian historian Fritz Fellner and the British specialist on the late Habsburg Empire John Leslie documented how these mostly younger officials and diplomats, all of them Aehrenthal's disciples and admirers of his forward foreign policy, worked to steer Berchtold towards war against Serbia.[43] They formed a 'fronde of diplomatic cadets' who, according to Leslie, 'welcomed, even deliberately provoked' war.[44] Certainly, after the fighting began, while the going was still good, Musulin boasted that he had been the initiator of the war. On the other hand, just after the war Hoyos seriously considered suicide because he felt so burdened by his 'historic responsibility'.[45] Leopold von Andrian-Werburg, the Austro-Hungarian Consul General in Warsaw who had been summoned to Vienna in mid-July, left a very revealing short record of his impressions from that period. 'We started the war,' he wrote, 'not the Germans and even less the Entente – that I know.' Specifically, he thought that it was his friends Hoyos, Forgách, Musulin and possibly Szápáry who had 'made the war'.[46]

Count Hoyos in Berlin

It seems that it did not take Berchtold's colleagues a very long time to persuade him what needed to be done after the assassination in Sarajevo. On 1 July the Hungarian Prime Minister Tisza wrote to Franz Joseph, complaining that he had learnt from Berchtold of his intention to use the Sarajevo outrage as the occasion for settling accounts with Serbia.[47] In other words, some forty-eight hours after the assassination at the latest, the Foreign Minister of Austria-Hungary was set on a Balkan collision course. A very important document confirms this. By 1 July a re-worked, shortened version of the Matscheko memorandum of 24 June (discussed in chapter thirteen) was ready. Together with a handwritten letter from Franz Joseph to Wilhelm II, dated 2 July, it was to be taken to Berlin to enlighten and warn the German ally about the impending catastrophe for the Habsburg Empire, and indeed for Germany, if nothing was done in the Balkans.[48] Of course, those two documents, associated with the so-called Hoyos mission in Berlin of 5-6 July, were thereby meant to secure Germany's cover for a violent, military *finale* to the differences between Austria-Hungary and Serbia.

The person chosen by the Foreign Minister to liaise with the Germans was his *chef de cabinet* Count Alexander Hoyos, an Englishman on his mother's side. Hoyos was well connected in Germany, but more importantly he was one of the principal warmongers at the Ballhausplatz. In the evening hours of Saturday, 4 July, he boarded a train for Berlin. Franz Ferdinand and Sophie had been entombed at Artstetten earlier in the day. Berchtold's emissary carried in his briefcase two documents prepared at the Ballhausplatz: a letter from Franz Joseph to Wilhelm II, which Hoyos had drafted himself, and the Matscheko Memorandum, adapted by Berchtold, Matscheko and himself. In addition, Hoyos carried in his head Berchtold's verbal instructions which emphasized Vienna's assessment that the moment for settling scores with Serbia appeared to have arrived.[49] This youngish diplomat, as it turned out, had embarked on a dramatically fateful diplomatic assignment. The ill-famed result of his journey was the extraction of a 'blank cheque' from Wilhelm II on 5 July, officially confirmed on 6 July by his Chancellor Bethmann Hollweg. Austria-Hungary received, in the words of Konrad Jarausch, 'one of the most momentous assurances in European history'.[50]

Wilhelm II talked to Count Szögyény, the serving Austro-Hungarian Ambassador to Berlin, on 5 July over a *déjeuner* at the New Palace in Potsdam. Hoyos had previously handed the Ambassador the paper work from Vienna and was not present at the meeting – on that day he was conducting informal talks with Under Secretary Zimmermann at the German Foreign Office. In the evening hours of 5 July Szögyény informed the Ballhausplatz that Wilhelm II had in his presence read 'with the greatest attention' the documents brought by Hoyos. This must have taken a while. Franz Joseph's personal letter to the German Kaiser was admittedly relatively short. But the new rendition of the Matscheko Memorandum was still a heavy-going piece of analysis of considerable length: eight densely printed pages in the Austrian collection of documents as opposed to the ten pages taken up by the original of 24 June. At any rate, the German Emperor certainly grasped the gravity of the moment. He told Szögyény that he had to bear in mind the possibility of 'a serious European complication' and could therefore not give a definitive answer before consulting with Chancellor Theobald von Bethmann Hollweg. However, in his view Russia was 'not remotely' ready for war and would think twice before resorting to arms. And he would 'regret' it, he said, if Austria-Hungary did not use the existing favourable moment to proceed against Serbia. As far as Romania was concerned, he would see to it that King Carol and his advisers behaved correctly. And although he had not 'the slightest confidence' in King Ferdinand of Bulgaria, he would 'not in the least' object to an Austro-Bulgarian pact as long as it contained nothing directed at Romania.[51]

Clearly, the German Emperor was ready to back Austria-Hungary against Serbia. But then, he had made up his mind even before Hoyos had arrived. 'Now or never', he commented on the margin of a report his ambassador Tschirschky had sent to Bethmann Hollweg on 30 June, informing the Chancellor about the widespread fervour in Vienna to square things with the Serbs. Tschirschky, however, added that he had been warning the Austrians against taking 'hasty steps'. Here, Wilhelm II scribbled what became one of his famous pieces of marginalia: 'Who authorized him to do that? That is very foolish! ... The Serbs must be put away *and* right *now*.'[52] Only a few days earlier, on 21 June, the Kaiser talked to the Hamburg banker Max Warburg, expressing his concern about Russia's rearmament programme and prioritisation of its railway construction. He was 'more nervous than usual', anticipating that Russia's preparations might lead to war by 1916, and wondering whether it would not be better 'to strike out, instead of waiting'.[53] This was certainly in keeping with his pronouncements at Konopischt, but if he wanted to take on Russia the best way was firstly to create security on Germany's south-eastern flank.

The encouragement, however, that Wilhelm II extended to Szögyény on 5 July was unofficial. As he indicated to the Ambassador, Bethmann Hollweg would also need to be consulted. Unfortunately for the peace of Europe, the *Reichskanzler* now chose to accept the risk of continental war entailed by an attack on Serbia. In the afternoon hours of 5 July, Wilhelm II told him about the meeting with Szögyény. By this time Bethmann Hollweg had already read the two documents brought by Hoyos. It was not Germany's business, the Emperor said, to be telling the Austrians how to respond to the bloody deed in Sarajevo; Germany should strive by all available means to stop the Austro-Serbian quarrel turning into an international conflict; but Franz Joseph should know that Germany would not abandon Austria-Hungary in its hour of need, as Germany's vital interest was the preservation of an intact Austria; finally, the idea of attaching Bulgaria to the Triple Alliance was 'good', though this should not be done at the cost of alienating Romania. 'These opinions of the Kaiser', the Chancellor recalled later, 'corresponded with my own.'[54]

On 6 July, accompanied by Zimmermann, he met with Szögyény and Hoyos to give them the official German position. Hoyos must have been overjoyed as he listened. According to the report of the meeting bearing Szögyény's signature, Bethmann Hollweg accepted the basic premise of the Matscheko Memorandum: that Russia's plan to build a Balkan League posed dangers not just to Austria-Hungary but also to the Triple Alliance itself. He only stipulated that Bulgaria's adherence to the Triple Alliance should not prejudice obligations towards Romania. The latest events, he said, made him realize that Austro-Serbian harmony, which he had previously advocated, was now 'virtually impossible'. And 'whatever' Austria-Hungary decided to do, it could rest assured that Germany would stand behind it as friend and ally. An 'immediate intervention' against Serbia was the 'most radical and best solution' to Austria-Hungary's Balkan problems. From the international point of view, the Chancellor considered the existing moment for such an intervention as more favourable than a future one.[55]

This was outright incitement. Not that Berchtold and his bellicose coterie of Aeherenthal adherents at the Ballhausplatz needed any real encouragement – all they needed was assurance of Germany's certain support. That support, however, was absolutely decisive. Hoyos, in his 1922 booklet, referring to this mission in Berlin, claimed that Berchtold would have been prepared to pull back from a confrontation with Serbia had Germany advised him to do so.[56] There is every reason to believe him: Austria-Hungary was simply too weak to risk a war against Russia without Germany's secondment. Little did the Ballhausplatz think that the Germans would in the end be so forthcoming. In a brief memoir dealing specifically with his Berlin assignment (first published by Fritz Fellner in 1976) Hoyos further disclosed a remarkable detail from his meeting with Bethmann Hollweg on 6 July. On this occasion, he told the Chancellor that, although Austria-Hungary considered a military clash with Serbia unavoidable sooner or later, it was prepared to content itself for the time being with closer ties to Bulgaria – 'in case Germany believed that a later moment would be more favourable from a European point of view'. Hoyos was thereby passing on the message of the Austro-Hungarian leadership that it would not attack Serbia without German approval. This would have meant no war at all, local or otherwise, in the summer of 1914, but Bethmann Hollweg reacted immediately to squash this option, promising Germany's 'entire might' if Austria-Hungary deemed it necessary to proceed against Serbia.[57] It was the moment when one person, and one person alone, Bethmann Hollweg, could have stopped war from breaking out, but chose not to, indeed chose to encourage it instead. Clearly, then, although there was no shortage of war enthusiasm in Vienna, the German leaders were dashing ahead. Hoyos later told Luigi Albertini that Bethmann Hollweg had on 6 July 'twice over' urged 'immediate action against Serbia', the international situation being 'entirely in our favour'.[58]

The Calculations of Bethmann Hollweg

Bethmann Hollweg gained much notoriety after he had, on 4 August 1914, declared the Belgian neutrality treaty to be just a 'scrap of paper'.[59] And his shocking September 1914 programme, first revealed by Professor Fritz Fischer, envisaged a sweeping reshuffle of the existing European system in order to make way for German hegemony.[60] But his pre-war reputation was that of a responsible statesman. The British in particular had a good opinion of him. At the height of the July crisis Hoyos sent a long letter to Lord Haldane, whom he knew from the period when he had served at the Austro-Hungarian Embassy in London. The letter, sent with Berchtold's approval, suggested that Russian intrigues stood behind the Sarajevo assassination. 'Englishmen should realise', Hoyos wrote, 'what the whole world would look like ... if Russia held the Balkans and Constantinople.' For good measure, Hoyos warned that Russia might turn its eyes 'towards India'. Haldane noted that the letter 'is an attempt to scare us into neutrality with the Russian bogey. The one hope is that Bethmann-Hollweg's influence in Berlin will prevail.'[61]

This hope, as it turned out, was utterly misplaced. Yet a little earlier that year the Chancellor would probably have been a good receptacle for it. Like Wilhelm II, Bethmann Hollweg had not long previously been counselling Vienna to be nice to the Serbs, warning Berchtold in February 1913 in very sharp terms that if Austria-Hungary should wage war on Serbia, he would consider it 'a mistake of immeasurable consequence'. But Bethmann Hollweg was only urging restraint for tactical reasons: out of belief that cracks had begun to appear in the Triple Entente and that Britain was slowly moving away from it. He therefore wanted this process to be given a chance to 'ripen'.[62] The subsequent course of British policy, however, was to disappoint his expectations. By July 1914 he was highly pessimistic with regard to Germany's overall international position and worried, in particular, by recent Anglo-Russian naval discussions. He considered Russia's military strength to be 'growing fast', whereas Austria-Hungary was increasingly 'weak and inert'.[63] Russia, in fact, was his obsession. The German Chancellor perceived it as the main enemy and, together with other Slavonic nations, as the greatest future threat.[64]

On 8 July Bethmann Hollweg's private secretary Kurt Riezler noted in his diary some details in the Chancellor's thinking: 'If war does not come about, if the Tsar does not want it or if France, dismayed, counsels peace, so we still have the prospect of taking apart the Entente.'[65] What was on the Chancellor's mind? Serbia abandoned by Russia really meant Russia abandoned by France. For one would not wage war without the other and differing views on whether to defend Serbia could split the unity of their alliance. And if it was the Tsar himself who desisted from war, Russia would still end up humiliated. Indeed, Bethmann Hollweg allowed himself to imagine that, by unleashing the Austrians against Serbia, he could pick up major winnings on the cheap. Riezler related in 1915 that his boss believed Russia might 'swallow a slap in the face', namely the occupation by Austria-Hungary of Belgrade together with a part of the Serbian state.[66] This was the concept of the so-called 'limited war' – one limited to Serbia. V.R. Berghahn's account of the July crisis points out that the advantages of the plan to proceed against Serbia seemed eminently obvious to the Chancellor:

'the strengthening of the Central Powers, the weakening of Russia and of Pan-Slavism, the soothing of the Right at home'.[67]

Bethmann Hollweg's name will forever be associated with the premise of 'calculated risk'. Interestingly enough, in spring of 1914 his right-hand man Riezler published a book which elaborated this concept within a theory of deterrence. To Riezler, wars in modern times were on their way out because they had become 'an antiquated form of fighting'. By contrast to the not so expensive conflicts in previous centuries, modern states would now, if they wished to wage wars, have to incur massive financial expenditure and set in motion armies numbering millions. 'The risk', according to Riezler, 'has become greater than the benefit.' In these circumstances, wars would be conducted only if the chances of success were very high, and the risk of defeat was very low. Wars would 'no longer be fought but calculated'. Armaments thus served an important purpose: 'Guns do not fire, but they have a say in the negotiations.' However, Riezler also pointed out that the element of bluff had become 'the chief requisite of the diplomatic method': if two parties confront each other, the victor will not always be the one who is the more powerful, but rather the one who can longer sustain his claim that he will strike out.[68]

The whole point, however, about Bethmann Hollweg in July 1914 is that he was not bluffing. On 7 July he told Riezler: 'An action against Serbia could lead to a world war.' Then on the following day he opined: 'Should war come from the east, so that, namely, we fight for Austria-Hungary and not Austria-Hungary for us, we have a chance of winning it.'[69] He meant that, in a war against Serbia started by Austria-Hungary and provoking a Russian response, Germany could at least count on the support of its ally. In other words, the scenario of a wider war had been taken into account by the *Reichskanzler*. Even with France at Russia's side, he thought, the Central Powers were in a good position, for he and those surrounding him were convinced that 'England did not want war'.[70] In 1917 the newspaper editor Theodor Wolff, critical of the Chancellor's conduct in 1914, put it to him that an arrangement to prevent war would have been possible at Austria's cost. But Bethmann Hollweg snapped back: 'Who can say that? And if war had come after Russia had rearmed – where would have that left us?'[71] In 1916, Riezler related to Wolff the estimate of the German General Staff in 1914 that the war against France would last 40 days. 'Bethmann', Riezler said, 'had pondered the risk very carefully.'[72]

Bethmann Hollweg's musings on the relationship between Germany and Austria-Hungary, related to Riezler on 7 July, focused on 'our old dilemma' whenever Austria conducted an action in the Balkans: 'If we encourage them, they say we pushed them into it; if we discourage them, they say we let them down. Then they draw closer to the open arms of the

Western powers and we lose our last passable ally.'[73] As it transpired, it was
the Chancellor's own 'open arms', extended towards Vienna, which made
all the difference between war and peace – at least in the Balkans. He must
have been excited by the panorama that opened up after the Sarajevo assassination. Certainly, he wanted to be in charge of it, making sure, on 6 July,
to send Wilhelm II on a cruise off Norway, for he did not want to risk any
interference from the bumbling Emperor.

Quite possibly, Bethmann Hollweg may have believed that Russia would
not act in the event of an Austrian step against Serbia. In a letter to Theodor
Woff, written in 1930, Riezler pointed out that the German military had
in 1914 underestimated Russian preparedness for war, and that the German
political leadership could only have based its policy on those military
assessments.[74] If so, the First World War broke out because of the failure
of German military intelligence. A realistic assessment of Russian military
capabilities in the summer of 1914 might have persuaded Germany not to
issue its 'blank cheque' to Austria-Hungary. Be that as it may, the hoped
for scenario in which Russia did not intervene still required, from the
German point of view, a swift Austro-Hungarian action against Serbia. As
Bethmann Hollweg explained to Riezler, he needed 'a quick fait accompli'
in Serbia. Once this 'shock' had passed, the Entente could be talked to in
a 'friendly' way.[75] No one knew, of course, how the situation would develop
– whether Russia and Britain would go to war – and in mid-July Bethmann
Hollweg himself confided to Riezler that he saw the whole action as 'a leap
in the dark [*Sprung ins Dunkle*]'.[76] Under Secretary Zimmermann, however,
apparently had a much clearer picture. He told Hoyos on 5 July that there
was a 90 per cent chance of 'a European war' if Austria-Hungary moved
against Serbia.[77] It is difficult to believe that he was the only policy-maker
in Berlin with such an assessment.

It falls outside the scope of this book to dwell on the subject of German
motives and calculations in July 1914. But even the brief examination above
shows that a preventive war was very much contemplated – there would
be no bluffing *à la* Riezler. Discussing German policy in July 1914, Christopher Clark contends that there was 'nothing' in the reaction of the German
leaders to suggest that they 'viewed the crisis as the welcome opportunity
to set in train a long-laid plan to unleash a preventive war on Germany's
neighbours'. Their own contribution to the unfolding of the crisis, according to Clark, was 'their blithe confidence in the feasibility of localization'.[78]
It may reasonably be argued, however, that even such a 'localization', i.e.,
a war limited to the Balkans, was entirely within Germany's power to
prevent – what was the point of the Hoyos mission if not to get permission
from Berlin to start a local war? The smoking gun, denied by Clark, in the
story of July 1914 is to be found in Bethmann Hollweg's refusal to even
consider the scenario put to him by Count Hoyos that Austria-Hungary

would desist from attacking Serbia if Germany considered the moment to be unfavourable.[79]

In that fateful month of July 1914, as Professor John Röhl has argued, Germany pursued a 'twin-track policy'. Its minimum aim was the elimination of Serbia, 'thereby improving the starting position for the Triple Alliance in a war that might be brought about against Russia later'; its maximum aim was 'the immediate unleashing of a continental war' against Russia and France in conditions deemed to be favourable.[80] Everything in July 1914, however, stemmed from Bethmann Hollweg's blank cheque to Vienna. In the words of Professor Hew Strachan, 'it was indeed blank'.[81] The crisis was not made in Germany, but Germany's role was decisive given that it had a de facto veto over Austria-Hungary's proposed course of action. The Habsburg lap dog was unleashed on 6 July 1914.

Tisza and the War

Yet one of the most powerful persons in the Dual Monarchy did not appear particularly enthusiastic about a war in the Balkans. As has been seen, Tisza wrote to Franz Joseph on 1 July to denounce Berchtold's plan for a reckoning with Serbia. His initial opposition to the war option forms a prominent chapter in the mammoth historiography of the July crisis. Historians are fascinated by this strongman who was both constitutionally and politically in a position to prevent what became the greatest bloodbath in human history. Wilhelm Fraknói, who wrote a short study of Tisza just after the Great War, levelled a charge against him for not having resigned and continued his 'peace policy' as a leader of a mighty opposition.[82] In fact, Tisza, despite being a Calvinist and a 'deeply religious man',[83] never had a genuine peace policy, only a refined grasp of tactics.

Franz Ferdinand's death must have come as welcome news to the Hungarian Prime Minister who, soon after the assassination, told the Bosnian Serb politician Danilo Dimović: '*Der liebe Herrgott, hat es so gewollt, und dem lieben Herrgott müssen wir für alles dankbar sein!* [Dear God has so willed it, and we must be grateful to dear God for everything!]' He had, Dimović wrote, emphasized the last words 'in a strange way'.[84] Prince Ludwig Windischgraetz, who arrived in Budapest on the day of the Sarajevo assassination, recalled soon after the war: 'I found the whole political world of Buda Pesth as though freed from an incubus. Tisza's party made no attempt to conceal their joy.'[85] In keeping with this, one of Tisza's main concerns immediately after the assassination was to prevent members of Franz Ferdinand's military chancellery from connecting with Archduke Karl, the new Heir to the Throne.[86] The Hungarian Prime Minister wanted no polluted ideological legacy bequeathed to the new Heir to the Throne. But no sooner had Franz Ferdinand, the greatest threat to Hungary's privileged position in the

Habsburg Empire, been eliminated, Tisza now also found himself opposing the settling of accounts with Serbia because he could see in the proposed action a new threat to Hungary – not from Serbia, but rather from Romania. As he told Berchtold on 30 June, his fear was that a war against Serbia would invite a Romanian invasion of Siebenbürgen (Transylvania), an area of east Hungary heavily populated by ethnic Romanians. The Hungarian historian Galántai lays great emphasis on this point in Tisza's calculations.[87]

Nevertheless, in July 1914 Tisza was not against the war as such, only against its proposed timing. When he objected to a military solution, in his appeal to Franz Joseph on 1 July, he drew attention to what he saw as a very unfavourable regional picture: Romania was as good as lost, and Bulgaria, the only state in the Balkans which could be counted on, was 'exhausted'. What Tisza wanted to see was a more favourable 'diplomatic constellation' whereby Bulgaria would be drawn to the Triple Alliance without, however, such a development antagonizing Romania. Bulgaria was to Tisza the key state in the Balkans. He argued that if Germany could not ensure an open declaration of loyalty by Romania to the Triple Alliance, then at least Bulgaria should be secured, something that should not be put off 'out of love for Romania'. This ambiguous regional picture was the only thing Tisza wanted to clear up before proceeding against Serbia. 'In the present Balkan situation', he wrote candidly to Franz Joseph, 'it would be my least bother to find a convenient *casus belli*'.[88]

Indeed. Back in October 1913, at the height of the crisis over the Serbian Army's operation in Albania, Tisza spoke of 'inflicting a military defeat' on Serbia, should the latter not withdraw its forces from Albania. 'One must here not waver or prolongate', he said at the Ministerial Council meeting on 3 October.[89] In chapter thirteen mention was made of Tisza's pronouncement to Baron Julius Szilassy in December 1913, that a war with Serbia was unavoidable and that Russia would for internal reasons not intervene under any circumstances. Historians of the July crisis, however, have generally paid much more attention to Tisza's fear of the consequences of annexing Serbia, that is to say, of the ensuing increase in the number of Slavs in the Monarchy. Yet the historian József Galántai believes this much discussed aspect of his conduct during the July crisis played only a secondary role for the Hungarian statesman. What really concerned him was the risk of a Romanian incursion into Hungary, and he argued against war merely because he believed that a later juncture would be more favourable for the Central Powers.[90] This point is also stressed by Tisza's biographer Gabor Vermes: in early July 1914 the dividing line in the Habsburg establishment 'lay not between hawks and doves in a sharply polarized sense', but rather between those, like Berchtold and Conrad, who pushed for immediate action, and those, like Tisza and Burián, who wanted to delay it in order to manoeuvre diplomatically.[91]

The meeting of the Joint Ministerial Council on 7 July is one of the most discussed episodes in the run up to the outbreak of the First World War – largely because Tisza stood alone against a united front of Habsburg ministers clamouring for war. But it was something of a non-event. By this time, of course, the 'Hoyos mission' had secured the backing of Germany for an Austro-Hungarian attack on Serbia. Indeed Hoyos was also present, entrusted with the task of recording the minutes of the proceedings. Berchtold, presiding, advocated making Serbia 'forever harmless'; the Austrian Prime Minister Stürgkh thought that any action against Serbia should end up in war; the Joint Finance Minister Biliński opined that a Serb understood 'only force'; and the Joint War Minister Krobatin asserted that if nothing was done the South Slav provinces would see it as a sign of weakness. Tisza tried cleverly to exploit the success of the Hoyos mission – one aspect of it, that is. Surely, he argued, now that Germany had agreed to the idea of drawing Bulgaria into the Triple Alliance, one could follow up by creating a Bulgarian-Turkish counterweight to Romania and Serbia which could force Romania to return to the fold. But he also barked against Germany: 'It is none of Germany's business to judge whether or not we should strike out at Serbia now.' He proposed that Serbia should be presented with tough (but not 'unacceptable') demands and then with an ultimatum if those demands were not fulfilled. What he wanted to see was a diplomatic effort that would lead to Serbia's 'heavy humiliation'. Berchtold, however, along with the other ministers, dismissed a purely diplomatic victory over Serbia as 'worthless'. The meeting thus ended inconclusively.[92]

Of course, in permitting the idea of an ultimatum to Serbia, the logic of Tisza's position had begun to move towards war. Indeed, once he learned over the next few days that Romania would in all likelihood remain neutral and, moreover, that Germany considered the moment for war as being possibly the best from the point of view of the prevailing power relations in Europe, his position evolved accordingly.[93] As Galántai remarked, had Tisza been fundamentally against war, there would have been nothing for him to adjust in his attitude.[94] John Leslie suggests that it was Forgách and, even more decisively, Burián, who helped to move Tisza to the immediate war option.[95] By 14 July, in a meeting with Berchtold, Stürgkh and Burián, Tisza was no longer an opponent of war, insisting only that there should be no acquisition of Serbian land save for minor frontier modifications. He even boasted to Ambassador Tschirschky that he had sharpened some points in the ultimatum to Serbia which was being prepared. The explanation he gave to Tschirschky – that he had found the pronouncements of the Serbian diplomats and the Serbian press 'unbearable' – is hardly credible.[96] What may have swayed him, in addition to the attitude of Germany, was the fear that the substantial Serb population in southern Hungary could, with Serbia's backing, pose a significant threat sooner rather than later. More importantly perhaps, he must also have realized that Serbia's defeat would bring Romania back into line and thereby remove the support which the Romanians of Transylvania had hitherto been receiving from their brethren. As for his opposition to annexing Serbian territory, he was, by November 1914, proposing, because of 'very important strategic concerns', the annexation of north-western Serbia (Mačva), Belgrade, and the area around Negotin in north-eastern Serbia. These were, as Marvin Fried has observed, 'by no means minor frontier rectifications'.[97] In the final analysis, Tisza's change of direction at the end of the second week of July should be ascribed to his Hungarian nationalist instinct. He knew, as Gustav Erényi wrote in 1935, that the notions of 'Great Hungary' and the 'Austro-Hungarian Monarchy' were inseparable.[98]

The way was now clear for an attack on Serbia. In mid-July Tisza told Danilo Dimović: '*Wir gehen sehr bewegten Zeiten entgegen!* [We are heading for very eventful times!]'[99] Of course, the Ballhausplatz had anticipated this somewhat earlier. Already on 11 July Karl von Macchio went to see Hans Schlitter, the Director of the State Archive, with a 'strongly confidential' request for copies of the war manifestos of 1859 and 1866, which he needed as models.[100] On that same day the text of the ultimatum to Serbia was also being discussed in Vienna, with Burián present as Tisza's representative. Present, too, was Conrad who argued that Serbia should be given a maximum of forty-eight hours to reply to the ultimatum. On 14 July, at the meeting in Berchtold's 'Strudlhof' Vienna residence which saw Tisza line up behind the Ballhausplatz position, the Hungarian Prime Minister also endorsed a draft of the ultimatum containing several deliberately 'unacceptable' points which moreover imposed a forty-eight hour time limit for the reply. At Burián's suggestion it was agreed at the same time that the ultimatum should be delivered only after the French President Poincaré had ended his visit to the Tsar at St Petersburg.[101] Later that day Tisza talked to the German Ambassador, informing him that the ultimatum would be formulated in such a way as to make its acceptance as good as 'impossible'.[102] On the following day, 15 July, Tisza spoke in the Hungarian Parliament. 'War', he said, 'is a very sad *ultima ratio*.' However, he then added that every nation and state, provided it wished to remain a nation and a state, must be able and willing to resort to war after all other possibilities of solution had been exhausted.[103] As will be seen, Tisza's speech would be noted with great apprehension by the Serbian Prime Minister.

The Wiesner Report

Although everybody now wanted war, finding a good excuse for it proved
somewhat elusive. On 13 July Berchtold made a remarkable admission
while meeting Ludwig Thallóczy, one of Biliński's closest associates at
the Joint Finance Ministry. Talking to this Balkan expert, the Austro-
Hungarian Foreign Minister complained 'that only scant information exists
in the records about the Great Serbian movement [*daß es in den Akten nur
sehr wenige Daten über die großserbische Bewegung gibt*]'. For his part, the Balkan
specialist was unable to help. Thallóczy could only assuage the Foreign
Minister that the Great Serbian idea lived 'in the souls' of the Serbs.[104]
Nothing, it may be observed, better illustrates the weakness and absurdity
of the Austro-Hungarian case against Serbia in July 1914 than this exchange
between Berchtold and Thallóczy. The person at the Ballhausplatz who
had been charged on behalf of Berchtold with the task of searching the
documentation to establish a connection between Great Serbian propaganda and the assassination was the legal expert Friedrich von Wiesner.
He had commenced work on this over a week earlier, on 4 and 5 July, in
the Foreign Ministry, but been unable to find 'much useful material'. On
7 July Wiesner found himself digging away in the Joint Finance Ministry,
but here too the materials were 'sketchy and inadequate'. Having found
nothing terribly helpful on the Great Serbian movement in either the
records of the Ballhausplatz or the Joint Finance Ministry, he was then
ordered, on 9 July, to travel to Sarajevo in order to liaise with the local
authorities there and, as he understood it, to look for 'conclusive evidence'
of a linkage between the murders in Sarajevo and the Serbian Government.

But this was a hurried exercise, meant to follow the timetable already
set in Vienna. Wiesner was given until 13 July to complete his work. He
arrived in Sarajevo on the 11th and duly reported on the 13th, the day of
Berchtold's conversation with Thallóczy. As Wiesner himself wrote in 1928,
'time was pressing', since the ultimatum to Serbia would probably have to
be delivered on 25 July: by which day, the Ballhausplatz 'itinerary' (as
Wiesner called it) foresaw that the French President would end his visit
to St Petersburg. This meant that Austria-Hungary's missions abroad would
have to be instructed by 20 July 'at the latest' in order to make diplomatic
preparations; and this, in turn, made 19 July the last possible date to hold
the next Joint Ministerial Council meeting. Before then, however, a few
days had to be allowed for the Foreign Minister to hammer out a consensus
between the Austrian and Hungarian prime ministers, beginning with an
initial meeting due to be held on 14 July. So it was that Wiesner had to file
his report by 13 July.[105]

If this is what Berchtold meant by an 'enquiry into the Sarajevo assassination' – which, as seen above, he mentioned to Conrad on 29 June –

then it was a complete farce, designed to produce a specific conclusion to fit in with and underpin the whole mechanism of steps already taken to confront Serbia – for the 'itinerary' of the road to war had been set in motion, with the clock already ticking away. Unfortunately for this scenario, the conscientious lawyer Wiesner, who had worked very intensively in Sarajevo, failed spectacularly to provide the appropriate decorum for this exercise. His report of 13 July on the result of his efforts spelt out with devastating pithiness that: 'There is nothing to show the complicity of the Serbian Government in the directing of the assassination or in its preparation or in the supplying of weapons. Nor is there anything to lead one even to conjecture such a thing. On the contrary, there is evidence that would appear to show that such complicity is out of the question.'[106]

Wiesner subsequently complained that this paragraph had been 'torn out of its context' when used at the 1919 Paris Peace Conference to saddle Austria-Hungary with the responsibility for war. But was it? In his rather brief report, he wrote of the 'conviction' of the authorities in Bosnia-Herzegovina that 'Pan-Serbian propaganda' was taking place with the encouragement of the Serbian Government. But such a 'conviction', as he knew, was of course no proof of anything. His report frankly admitted that the pre-assassination material contained 'no evidence' of propaganda being encouraged by the Serbian Government. So what was the 'context' of his report? Presumably his remark that 'sparse' but sufficient material existed to show that propaganda efforts had proceeded 'with the toleration of the Serbian Government'. And his statement that a Serbian state official, Ciganović, and a Serbian officer, Major Tankosić, had provided the bombs, ammunition and cyanide. But he was careful to observe that the bombs may have belonged to irregulars rather than have come straight out of a Serbian state armoury. He did also add that three assassins were secretly smuggled from Serbia into Bosnia with the assistance of Serbian frontier officers who may or may not have been aware of 'the purpose of the journey', but who must 'surely' have been cognizant of the 'mysterious nature of the mission'. Finally, Wiesner described the material on the *Narodna Odbrana* organization as 'valuable', although it had yet to be 'carefully examined'.[107]

Such, then, was the 'context' of the Wiesner report: propaganda had been taking place with the 'toleration' of the Serbian Government, and some Serbian officers and state officials were involved in the arming and smuggling of the assassins. The report's key point, however, was that there was nothing to show or even hint at the complicity of the Serbian Government in the Sarajevo assassination. Of course, this main conclusion of his investigations into Sarajevo was never going to be taken into account by the Ballhausplatz which was for its part preparing, as has been seen, an 'impossible' ultimatum to Serbia. 'I never believed', Hoyos admitted in his

1922 memoir, 'that the murder of the Archduke Franz Ferdinand had been prepared or intended by authorities in Belgrade or Petersburg.'[108] Presumably, in July 1914 Hoyos must also have conveyed this belief to his colleagues and to his boss Berchtold. In a sense, therefore, Wiesner had been sent on a wild-goose chase. To establish some connection between the Belgrade Government and the Sarajevo assassination would have been nice to have, but ultimately this did not matter given that the decision for war had already been taken.

This farce about an 'enquiry' into the Sarajevo assassination deserves a more prominent place than it has hitherto been accorded in the historiography of the July crisis. Samuel Williamson, in his widely read study of Austria-Hungary and the origins of the First World War, makes no mention of Wiesner, but writes that 'the evidence from Sarajevo, buttressed by information coming from Belgrade, correctly reinforced Vienna's initial assumptions that some elements of the Serbian government had been involved in the assassination plot'. It seems not to have occurred to Williamson, when he advanced this unsupported claim, that had Vienna really been in possession of any such information, it would have made sure the whole world knew about it.[109] Less surprising is that Berchtold's biographer Hugo Hantsch chooses to ignore the Wiesner report.[110] Manfred Rauchensteiner, the leading Austrian expert, does at least cite the relevant passage from the Wiesner report, but fails to convince with his claim that Wiesner 'had left everything open' – for there was precious little left open in Wiesner's categorical conclusion concerning the paucity of evidence to link the Government in Belgrade with the assassination in Sarajevo.[111]

Remarkably, however, new attempts have recently been made to turn the Wiesner report into a strong suit of Austria-Hungary's July 1914 policy. Sean McMeekin describes it as 'welcome news' for Vienna because it established that the assassination plot had been hatched in Belgrade. While admitting that the report 'all but ruled out' the complicity of the Serbian Government, he fails to quote the relevant passage directly, focusing instead on that part which talks about the assassins being armed and assisted to cross into Bosnia by Serbian officers. So, according to McMeekin, Berchtold was happy with the report because it had 'reassured' him 'that a proper dossier outlining Serbian guilt would be ready in time to make Austria's case for war'.[112] The problem for this view of McMeekin's is that no evidence exists for it. Indeed the evidence points to the contrary, including the fact that Berchtold had decided on war within forty-eight hours after the Sarajevo assassination. Clearly he felt no need for the kind of reassurance hypothesized by McMeekin. Even Sidney Fay, the American historian sympathetic to the case of the Central Powers, wrote that Berchtold appeared to have made 'little or no immediate use' of the Wiesner report.[113] Had it been positive it is difficult to believe he would not have done so.

No less perplexing is Christopher Clark's treatment of this particular episode from July 1914. He writes: 'Wiesner dispatched a report concluding that there was as yet no evidence to prove the responsibility or complicity of the Belgrade government.'[114] But Wiesner did not say there was no evidence as yet, he said there was no evidence ('nothing'). He had in fact made his determination and concluded that there was no evidence even to imagine that the Serbian Government might be guilty. The fact that Wiesner had in fact also mentioned evidence which suggested such complicity to have been 'out of the question' is not addressed by Clark, whose emphasis is clearly on there having existed 'as yet no evidence'. This was certainly not how Potiorek in Sarajevo had understood Wiesner's findings. Before sending his report to Vienna, Wiesner had shown it to the *Feldzeugmeister* who then furiously wrote to Conrad on 14 July, protesting that he could not let the matter pass 'without comment'. What the Bosnian Governor objected to in the report was precisely that 'Wiesner considers the connivance of the Serbian Government in the assassination as out of the question'.[115] Interestingly, therefore, whereas Potiorek at the time called a spade a spade, objecting to Wiesner having unequivocally cleared the Serbian Government, Clark somehow interprets the summary of the Wiesner report as inconclusive. Back in 1930, by contrast, the significance of Wiesner's pronouncements was certainly not lost on Bernadotte Schmitt, who is to this day one of the most highly regarded authorities on the origins of the Great War. 'Count Berchtold', Schmitt observed, 'would have been in a stronger position *vis-à-vis* the European Powers if his agent [Wiesner] had not exculpated the Serbian Government from direct complicity in the crime of Sarajevo'.[116]

Austria-Hungary's War Aims

Much as the Wiesner report and other post-Sarajevo issues between Vienna and Belgrade are important in any discussion of the July crisis, one should note that the sudden, unique opportunity of 'settling accounts with Serbia' opened up by Franz Ferdinand's death was not the only issue on the agenda of the Habsburg establishment in July 1914. However, the overwhelming focus of most historical accounts of Vienna's post-assassination policy rests precisely on this Austro-Serbian antagonism and the desire of Austria-Hungary's officialdom to solve, once and for all, what it described as the 'existential threat' to the Monarchy posed by the South Slav, that is, the Serbian question. It may perhaps be a self-evident truth, but the point nevertheless needs to be made that the Monarchy did not, in July 1914, consider its Great Power position purely in terms of its relations with

Serbia. Assassination or no assassination, Serbia was seen as a constituent part of a complex, indeed grim, regional predicament.

Hence there can indeed be no proper understanding of Vienna's decision for war without taking into account its view of developments on the wider Balkan front: Romania, hitherto a key ally of the Triple Alliance in South Eastern Europe, now appeared increasingly unreliable; Bulgaria, on the other hand, a would-be ally, could not join the Triple Alliance as long as its differences with Romania persisted and as long as Berlin continued to prefer Romania; while Albania, which both Conrad and the Ballhausplatz were hoping to turn into a militarily valuable regional ally, was in fact hopelessly ungovernable. Most important of all, Vienna believed that Russia was building a new Balkan league, aimed at the Monarchy itself. As seen in chapter thirteen, just days before the Sarajevo assassination, the Matscheko Memorandum drew attention to a highly dangerous situation that Austria-Hungary was supposedly facing in the Balkans. The Memorandum was basically a plea for assistance addressed to Germany, contending as it did that Russia and France were working away in the Balkans to fatally undermine the Triple Alliance. This book has argued that, contrary to the established view, the Matscheko Memorandum was not a scenario for patient, long-term diplomatic action, but rather a game plan for short-term, indeed urgent, responses to perceived threats and challenges in the region. The Memorandum's chief underlying assumption, as has also been argued, was a pre-emptive strike against Serbia. The crucial frame of reference, however, was not the Serbian danger in itself, but rather a dreaded, Russian-organized Balkan league. The assumed enmity of Serbia and the perceived loss of Romania naturally led the Ballhausplatz to anticipate a hostile combination that could also include Bulgaria and Greece. This concern about such a Balkan bloc was the starting point not only of the Matscheko Memorandum, but also of Tisza's paper from March and Flotow's from May.

It has been a profound historiographical misjudgement to see the Matscheko *Denkschrift* as an analysis espousing patient diplomatic solutions when its entire message was that the time for diplomacy had practically run out. The assassination in Sarajevo had conclusively strengthened this view in Vienna. Now, surely, was the moment to deal with Serbia. But no such action in the Balkans would be possible without a firm pledge of German support. The 'Hoyos Mission' was meant to obtain this insurance from Berlin, a stark testimony to the fact that Austria-Hungary, on paper a Great Power, could not in practice act alone. Admittedly, it was facing formidable hazards in July 1914, and it was not just the Russian reaction that the Habsburg decision-makers were worried about. As has been seen, Romania, too, was now a grave concern in both Vienna and Budapest. Tisza's initial objections to war against Serbia rested on his fear of

Romania's possible intervention on Serbia's side. On 1 July Berchtold instructed Conrad to prepare a *mémoire*, to be sent to Berlin, detailing the military implications of Romania's neutrality or, conceivably, hostility, in the event of 'a European war'.[117] Conrad responded quickly. He delivered his thoughts the next day, warning that the mere fact of Romania staying neutral would free up at least three Russian corps for deployment against Austria-Hungary. However, should Romania actually become hostile, it could, together with the forces of Serbia, press forward into 'the centre of the Monarchy' and put the Austro-Hungarian Army in such a difficult position that it would be unable to score a decisive victory over the Russians.[118]

Accordingly, Berchtold's shopping list in Berlin included not only military cover against Russia, but also Germany's diplomatic assistance in Romania. It is not clear whether this *mémoire* of Conrad's was also in Hoyos's briefcase as he travelled to Berlin. Either way, the revised Matscheko Memorandum he was carrying concentrated just as heavily on the Romanian problem as had the original paper of 24 June. The question needing to be asked here is whether there was any meaningful difference between the two versions. Or, to put it differently: given that many historians see the Matscheko Memorandum as having proposed long-term diplomatic responses to Austria-Hungary's Balkan problems, could it then really have been possible to change it so quickly and smoothly, into an argument for a short-term Austro-Hungarian military response – that is to say, into a case for Berlin to back Vienna in an immediate war against Serbia? T.G. Otte, one of those historians, is content to explain this seeming contradiction in terms of an 'ironic twist' – since the Memorandum 'was to furnish the strategic rationale for a war against Serbia after Sarajevo'.[119] Leading expert Samuel Williamson, who likewise subscribes to the view that Matscheko had initially put forward a programme of assertive diplomacy, simply says that Berchtold 'polished' the Memorandum after Sarajevo.[120] Surely, students of history wishing to understand whether the Hoyos Mission, one of the chief episodes of the July crisis, represented continuity or departure in Austro-Hungarian foreign policy, will be more than baffled by such perfunctory explanations of the document that underpinned it.

In fact, as indicated in chapter thirteen, the initial Memorandum of 24 June had already anticipated a war in the Balkans. In as much as it said anything about Serbia, it presented the latter as an implacable enemy; and in placing so much emphasis on the danger to both Austria-Hungary and Germany from a new Balkan alliance, sponsored by Russia, it presupposed that Serbia, as the pivot of that assumed alliance, would have to be knocked out. The revised Matscheko Memorandum, brought by Hoyos to Berlin, merely amplified and, where necessary, spelt out this basic message. In that sense, indeed, the document of 24 June only needed to be 'polished'.

Just like its predecessor, the revised document argued for the necessity of an alliance with Bulgaria. A notable difference relates to Romania. Whereas the 24 June analysis suggested a last-ditch attempt to clarify and even flush out Romania's position *vis-à-vis* the Triple Alliance, the new evaluation declared that the possibility of securing a reliable alliance with that country should practically be 'ruled out'. The 24 June paper had effectively also written Romania off – except that, mindful of the German Kaiser's soft spot for King Carol, it had professed that one last attempt should be made to reclaim the country for the Triple Alliance.

In any case, much of the emphasis in the version delivered by Hoyos to the Germans is on a hypothetical Balkan league, presented as the spearhead of a sinister Russian plan (supported by France) to shatter the Balkan position of Austria-Hungary, and thereby decidedly affect the position of Germany itself. Just to make Berlin even more uneasy, the revised piece included a reference to French '*Revanchebestrebungen* [revanchist ambitions]' which, it was elaborated, would be boosted by the weakening of the Habsburg Monarchy. As for Serbia, it received almost as little attention in the post-Sarajevo variant as it did in the original analysis of 24 June: its intrinsic hostility was taken for granted. Unsurprisingly, however, the main addition was the mention of the murder act in Sarajevo, described as 'the indubitable proof of the insurmountable differences between the Monarchy and Serbia'.[121]

What of Franz Joseph`s handwritten letter, also delivered by Hoyos? This is possibly the most interesting single item in the gigantic body of documentation concerning the immediate origins of the First World War. As with the revised Matscheko paper, Serbia is not at the centre of its observations. The focal point is Romania, but the fundamental misgivings expressed by the Austrian Emperor relate to Russia. To begin with, he links Russia with the Sarajevo assassination of his 'poor nephew'. This act, he claims, was 'a direct consequence of the agitation fuelled by the Russian and Serbian Panslavists, whose sole aim is the weakening of the Triple Alliance and the destruction of my Empire.' Not even the Austro-Hungarian press had after 28 June suggested a connection with the Russian Panslavists. But then, Franz Joseph's letter to Wilhelm II was drafted at the Ballhausplatz (by Hoyos) and it reflected the Ministry's fixation, shared by Tisza, about Russia's aggressive Balkan diplomacy. With regard to Romania, the letter drew attention to the friendly relationship between Bucharest and Belgrade, to the 'hateful agitation' against the Monarchy tolerated by the Romanian Government, and to King Carol's recent pronouncements that, in the light of his people's hostile mood towards Austria-Hungary, he would not be in a position to fulfill alliance obligations in an emergency. The most important comment in the letter, however, was that the Romanian Government was striving, 'with Russian help', to establish a new Balkan league, directed against the Habsburg Empire. The only way to keep Romania within the Triple Alliance, the letter suggested, was to prevent the formation of a Balkan league under Russian patronage. This could be achieved, on the one hand, if Bulgaria were to be won for the Triple Alliance and, on the other, if Romania were to be clearly told that 'Serbia's friends cannot be our friends'.

Unlike the revised Matscheko paper or, for that matter, its original of 24 June, Franz Joseph's letter actually sketched a way forward, offering a vision of how things should be ordered in the Balkans. It envisaged the 'isolation and diminution' of Serbia; the strengthening of the Bulgarian Government (to save it from a 'return to Russophilia'); the encouragement of a Bulgarian-Romanian understanding based on Bulgaria's guarantee of Romania's territorial integrity; and, finally, the 'reconciliation' of Greece with Bulgaria and Turkey. The idea here was, as the letter explained, to create 'a new Balkan league', under the patronage of the Triple Alliance, the objective of which would be to stop the forward push of the 'Panslavist flood'. There was one impediment, however. 'But this will only be possible', Franz Joseph wrote towards the end of his letter, 'if Serbia, which is currently the lynchpin of Panslavist policy, is disabled [*ausgeschaltet*] as a power factor in the Balkans.' Without employing the term 'war', the Austrian Emperor thus made it abundantly clear that the road to salvation and success was through military action. 'You too', he concluded his letter to Wilhelm II, 'will be convinced after the latest terrible events in Bosnia that a straightening out of differences which separate us from Serbia is no longer conceivable, and that the existing peace policies of all European monarchs will be at risk so long as this fulcrum of criminal agitation in Belgrade remains unpunished.'[122]

So, it was punishment time – except that punishing Serbia was really a way of confronting and expelling Russia from South Eastern Europe. And this could be done just by knocking out Serbia. The Sarajevo assassination thus offered a wonderful opportunity to Austro-Hungarian statesmen and soldiers to cut the Gordian knot in the Balkans. Defeating Serbia would effectively destroy what Vienna saw as a potentially menacing, Russian-inspired Balkan league, because such a league without Serbia would simply be a non-starter. The prizes would be rich and plentiful: Romania would lose its friend and de facto ally Serbia, and would have to reconsider its attitude towards the Triple Alliance; Bulgaria would undoubtedly join the Triple Alliance once Macedonia was awarded to it at Serbia's expense; Russian influence in the Balkans would be absolutely shattered; and, as was argued in an internal Ballhausplatz memorandum written on 6 July, even 'the arrogance of Italian imperialists' would be dampened by an Austro-Hungarian success against Serbia. Moreover, Burián recorded in his diary on 14 July that Albania could only be saved if Serbia was out of the way.[123]

Last, but not least, a successful war against Serbia would at the same time solve the Monarchy's South Slav question – or at least ensure that Serbia could no longer play a role in it because the country would either not exist at all or it would be too small to matter after being forced to cede territories to its neighbours. In short, smashing Serbia would make Austria-Hungary the unchallenged master of South Eastern Europe. It was a dazzling prospect.

While in Berlin, Hoyos had told the Germans about Vienna's plans for a 'full partition' of Serbia.[124] He may have done so without prior authorization from his boss Berchtold, but such talk did undoubtedly reflect the ideas circulating at the Ballhausplatz at the time. It is true that under Tisza's pressure the Ministerial Council which took place on 19 July agreed, though very reluctantly, to inform foreign powers at the beginning of the war that Vienna did not intend to annex Serbia. But the Council's reservations in this matter were very substantial, for it also agreed that a 'diminution' of Serbia through the incorporation of its territories by other states could not be ruled out. It also kept open the option that 'strategically necessary frontier corrections' could be made. On this occasion Berchtold argued for 'the greatest possible' transfers of Serbian territories to Bulgaria, Greece, Albania and possibly also Romania so that Serbia would 'no longer be dangerous'.[125] After the meeting on 19 July, Biliński revealed to Thálloczy that what the Council of Ministers called 'frontier corrections' would really be the incorporation by Austria-Hungary of the districts of Belgrade and Šabac. He added: 'If Romania wishes it, it will also get a piece; also Bulgaria; also Albania.'[126] And only three days earlier, commenting on a suggestion that Russia should be informed about Austria-Hungary's intention to respect the territorial integrity of Serbia, Forgách wrote privately to Ambassador Mérey in Rome: 'Incidentally, just what will happen after a hopefully successful war is, by the way, between you and me, another question.'[127]

Austria-Hungary's war aims concerning Serbia in July 1914 may not have been meticulously defined in a single policy paper, but they did not need to be. The objectives were blindingly obvious: crippling Serbia one way or another was meant to engender massive regional benefits. For the collapse of Serbia would entail Russia's political collapse in the Balkans. As Franz Joseph indicated in his letter to Wilhelm II, a hostile Balkan league would be nipped in the bud and an alternative one would be set up under the aegis of the Triple Alliance. These were the clear and eminently sensible war aims of Austria-Hungary. The key was, as Forgách predicted with admirable prescience, 'a hopefully successful war'. Anything could have been implemented thereafter. Hence it is difficult to agree with Norman Stone who argued, in an influential 1966 article, that in July 1914 'Austria-Hungary had in effect no policy, and she had to be supplied with one by Germany'.[128] F.R. Bridge, in his major study of Austro-Hungarian diplomacy, devotes only one sentence to Vienna's war aims in July 1914, but at least he gets it right: 'The Austrians were above all concerned to re-establish their position in the Near East by crushing Serbia and destroying the influence of Russia.'[129]

As for Germany, far from supplying Austria-Hungary with a policy, it had actually begun to accept and support policy proposals from Vienna. As noted in chapter thirteen, Wilhelm II had up to April 1914 been urging the Austrian statesmen to find a *modus vivendi* with Serbia. In this he had been backed by Bethmann Hollweg and the German Foreign Office. Anticipating as he always was a future war with Russia, his main concern in the Balkans was to secure the south-eastern flank. Impressed by Serbia's military performance in the recent Balkan Wars, he thought it far prefer-able to have it as a friend rather than an enemy drawing considerable resources away from the Russian front. Possibly under Tisza's influence, however, he changed his mind in May, only weeks before the Konopischt meeting with Franz Ferdinand, and adopted the Ballhausplatz standpoint that Austro-Serb differences were irreconcilable.

This, however, was not the only shift in Germany's Balkan policy. Highly significant, too, was its change of attitude towards Bulgaria. This became very evident over the question of the Bulgarian loan. Early in 1914, with its treasury depleted after the Balkan Wars, Bulgaria began looking for finance from abroad. Its pro-Austrian Radoslavov Government turned to Berchtold, requesting him to facilitate a big loan in Germany. Berchtold obliged, and with zeal – in order, as he explained, not to push Bulgaria into the arms of France and Russia.[130] As is well known, the German Emperor had a strong dislike for King Ferdinand of Bulgaria (and much fondness for King Carol of Romania). Yet, by the end of June the Bulgarians had completed negotiations for a massive, 500 million franc loan from Germany. The Bulgarians concluded that the loan was 'a triumph for Austrian diplo-macy'.[131] And so it really was: a stunning feat by the Ballhausplatz in Berlin. 'The conclusion of the Bulgarian loan in Berlin', declared a delighted Berchtold, 'fills me with the liveliest satisfaction.'[132]

'Poor Leopold'

The 'quick fait accompli' in the Balkans wished for by the German Chan-cellor Bethmann Hollweg never happened. In the evening hours of 8 July Berchtold told Conrad that the ultimatum would not be presented before the end of the harvest and the completion of the 'Sarajevo proceedings' – meaning the enquiry into the assassination. The ultimatum, Conrad was informed, would be delivered on 22 July. In the meantime, Berchtold suggested, it would be a good idea if Conrad and the War Minister were to go on holiday in order to keep up a pretence that nothing was afoot.[133]

As recounted earlier, the enquiry into the Sarajevo assassination was never going to be more than window-dressing, since the Ballhausplatz 'itinerary' had already been worked out. Historians have devoted much more attention to the issue of the summer harvest as a factor delaying Austria-Hungary's next moves against Serbia, namely the delivery of the ultimatum and mobilization. At this time the absence of many troops on harvest leave affected seven of the sixteen army corps districts, including three bordering Serbia. As early as 6 July Berchtold was pointing out to Conrad that 'the Monarchy would have to live from the harvest for one year'. Most of the troops on harvest leave were scheduled to return by 19 July, with some not due back until 25 July.[134] The Imperial Army would not be ready before 12 August. One can only speculate whether an earlier action would have made much difference. But given the speed of Serbia's mobilization after 25 July and the subsequent performance of its Army, it is difficult to believe that Austria-Hungary would have been able to bring about the 'quick fait accompli'.

In any case, Berchtold was under no illusion that capturing some Serbian territory would be of much use diplomatically. At their meeting on 8 July, Conrad told him in no uncertain terms that 'nothing' would be achieved by holding some territory. Success would not come until 'we have beaten the Serbian Army'.[135] The difference in tactical assumptions between Berlin and Vienna was thus very considerable. A further consideration regarding the timetable concerned the state visit by the French President to St Petersburg. It will be remembered that on 14 July Burián argued for delaying delivery of the ultimatum until Poincaré's departure from Russia. At first the Ballhausplatz believed that the visit would be from 20 to 25 July, and so Berchtold wrote to Franz Joseph that the ultimatum would be handed to the Serbian Government on Saturday, 25 July. On 15 July, however, the Austro-Hungarian Embassy in St Petersburg informed the Ballhausplatz that the visit would actually end on 23 July.[136] The ultimatum was therefore delivered on 23 July and Vienna declared war on 28 July. But this concern about the French President's presence in Russia reveals another, curious discrepancy between Austria-Hungary and Germany. Bethmann Hollweg appeared to believe that France, having recently incurred major financial losses in South America, would act 'in strongest terms' as a brake on any Russian ideas about war.[137] The thinking in Vienna was quite different. The whole point of delivering the ultimatum only after Poincaré had completed his visit was to have him out of the way – at sea, returning slowly to France. The idea was, as the Austro-Hungarian Ambassador to St Petersburg Fritz Szápáry recalled, to make a peace orientation easier for Russia. 'Rightly or wrongly', Szápáry wrote, 'there existed in Vienna greater confidence in Russia's love of peace than in that of Poincaré'.[138]

Nevertheless, policy-makers in Austria-Hungary, just like those in Germany, fully anticipated the possibility that Russia would not stay on the side-lines. This eventuality was, after all, the underlying reason for the Hoyos mission. On 8 July, at a time when he was still opposing the proposed settling of accounts with Serbia, Tisza wrote to Franz Joseph to warn him that it would provoke Russian intervention, invoke 'the world war', and make Romania's neutrality 'very questionable'.[139] Franz Joseph himself, when he read the text of the ultimatum to Serbia on 20 July, declared that a European war was 'certain', for Russia would find it 'impossible' to put up with such affront.[140] As War Minister Krobatin stated in January 1916, it had been reckoned, during the preparation of the action against Serbia in 1914, that an intervention by Russia was 'inevitable'.[141] Few, however, seemed to be particularly worried by this prospect. On 13 July Count Lützow talked to an unnamed younger official at the Ballhausplatz (probably Forgách) who astonished him with his nonchalance at the prospect of a world war: 'What great harm can come to us? If things go wrong, we shall only lose Bosnia and a piece of East Galicia!'[142] And on 15 July Josef Redlich recorded in his diary what Hoyos had told him on that day: 'If a world war breaks out, it is all the same to us.'[143]

On 19 July, at a meeting of the Joint Ministerial Council, the finishing touches to the ultimatum were applied and the date for its delivery decided. The Germans, in the meantime, had been growing increasingly nervous and were practically demanding Austria-Hungary's immediate military engagement in the Balkans.[144] At the Council meeting of 19 July, as discussed above, there was still some bickering over how much of Serbia would be annexed, but Tisza was by now firmly in the war camp. The die was cast. Yet even at this moment of imperial resolve an exchange between Tisza and Conrad revealed just how insecure the Habsburg leaders felt about the peoples they governed. Responding to Tisza's anxiety about the strength of the forces remaining in Transylvania in the event of a general mobilization, Conrad assured him that they would be sufficient to stall an advance by the Romanian Army. Those troops, he explained, were so selected that only a small percentage represented the Romanians of Hungary.[145]

In the end, the chief worry among the small circle of Habsburg statesmen, diplomats and soldiers making preparations for war was that Serbia might spoil the show by actually accepting the ultimatum in full. Thus Biliński 'agonised' on 23 July, that fateful day when the ultimatum was delivered, about what might happen if the Serbs did accept.[146] A Ballhausplatz legal expert, Alexander von Hold-Ferneck, prepared a memorandum, dated 25 July, to address this very question. It argued that if Serbia qualified its acceptance by any kind of protest, this could still result in a declaration of war because, for example, Serbia would thereby be breaching its note of March 1909. This was the document, it will be recalled, which ended the Bosnian annexation crisis and by which Serbia undertook to maintain friendly relations with the Habsburg Monarchy. Even if Serbia accepted the ultimatum across the board and without a protest, Hold-Ferneck continued, Austria-Hungary could still object on the grounds that the authorities in Belgrade had failed to carry out within the given time limit (*Frist*) those provisions containing such stipulations as 'immediately' or 'with utmost expedition'. The demand for the abolition of the *Narodna Odbrana* was suggested as a case in point.[147]

Of course, such jitters proved unfounded. However, they were fully understandable given that Habsburg officialdom perceived the moment as one of those now-or-never occasions, a matter of life and death. On 7 July, after the Joint Ministerial Council, Berchtold told Wladimir Giesl who was about to return to his post in Belgrade: 'Regardless of how the Serbs react, you have to break off relations and depart; it must come to war.'[148] The stress experienced by Berchtold during the hectic days of July must have been horrendous. He desperately wanted a war against Serbia. In October 1914 his wife related how 'poor Leopold could not sleep on the day he wrote his ultimatum to the Serbs, as he was so worried that they would accept it. Several times in the night he had got up and altered or added some clause, to reduce this risk.'[149]

17

Serbia in the July Crisis

Kosovo Day

SUNDAY, 28 JUNE 1914 was meant to be in the whole of Serbia, and for the Serbs everywhere, a day of solemn remembrance and great celebration. It was *Vidovdan* – St Vitus Day, sometimes also called the Kosovo day. St Vitus, who had died a martyr's death, was regarded by both Orthodox and Catholics as one of the fourteen holy helpers, 'with power against all injuries that beasts can do to men'.[1] In 1389, on 28 June, the remnants of what had been a powerful Serbian Empire put up a fight against the invading Ottoman army on the plain of Kosovo, 'the field of black birds'. The Serbs fought with some Balkan allies (the Bosnian King Tvrtko, identifying with the Serb cause, had sent a contingent) but assisted by no major power from Latin Europe – just as later, in 1453, it was the fate of the Orthodox Christian empire of Byzantium to be abandoned by the powers of the West. The battle of Kosovo ranks among the bloodier clashes in 14th century Europe. In military terms, no one really won on the day: what was left of the two armies immediately withdrew after a horrific carnage in which both Sultan Murad and the Serbian leader, Prince Lazar, perished. However, the Serbians and their allies had at least stopped the Ottoman advance, upon which news the bells of Notre Dame pealed out in Paris. It was to take the Ottomans another seventy years to bring Serbia under their total domination.

Yet 1389 was also the last occasion when the Serbs stood united in opposing the Turks. In retrospect, the Serbian medieval state indeed never recovered after Kosovo. In the centuries that followed, a myth was created by the Serbian Orthodox Church about the battle: that of a glorious defeat. It was glorious, so the legend went, because on the field of Kosovo the Serbs had chosen 'the Kingdom of Heaven'. This was the religious aspect of the Kosovo story, but there was also a rather earthly point: the defeat, the story said, was suffered as a result of treason from within Serbian ranks. At the same time popular ballads celebrated the self-sacrifice of Miloš Obilić, the Serbian nobleman who, after obtaining access to the Sultan by deceit, killed him and was himself then cut to pieces. Much of this epic tale is of course unverifiable. It had, however, had a powerful impact on the Serbs` historical memory. Non-Serbs have always found it slightly puzzling. Miško Jovanović, who was to be hanged for his part in assisting the Sarajevo assassins, was asked in court: 'Why do you Serbs celebrate the day of St Vitus?' He replied: 'He is a national saint, we celebrate him because on that day the Serbian Empire met its downfall.' So the next question naturally followed: 'How come a downfall is celebrated?' Jovanović explained simply: 'It is in remembrance of sorrow.'[2] Writing in 1916 about the Kosovo day for *The Daily News*, G.K. Chesterton drew attention to 'that particular spirit which remembers a defeat rather than a victory'.[3] In British images, for example, Kosovo would be the equivalent of Harold at Hastings, Shakespeare's history plays, Rorke's Drift, the Somme and Dunkirk rolled into one. For the Serbs, the battle of Kosovo symbolized the spiritual as well as the temporal, the perfidious as well as the heroic, the tragic as well as the glorious. The debacle allegedly suffered on the field of battle had thus been turned into a complex tale about a cataclysmic, yet glorious calamity.

This, however, is to perhaps misunderstand the totality of the event that Kosovo symbolised: it should be emphasised that once the Ottoman Empire returned some seventy years later and occupied the Serbian territories, the 1389 battle of Kosovo was over the coming centuries also to serve as a vivid reminder to a subsequently disenfranchised and downtrodden Serbian populace that they had previously had their own legitimate, functioning state (monarchy, national empire and rulers); and that Serbians were not intrinsically destined to be slaves to the manor born. So of paramount importance was not so much the defeat, but what had been defeated – the existence of a Serbian state. And that was no myth. This sense of self-perceived though undeniable tradition is perhaps the most important and least mythical aspect of the memory of Kosovo from the point of view of Serbian national consciousness. It is also one that through the centuries of Ottoman occupation kept alive the possibility of an alternative – the restoring of a legitimate Serbian/Slav self-rule, which was finally achieved through the battles of the nineteenth and twentieth centuries.

Gavrilo Princip may have felt empathy with such a struggle, but did he draw any inspiration from the date of the original battle in deciding to commit his act? A great deal has been made in many accounts of the Sarajevo assassination of the fact that Franz Ferdinand was parading himself and the Habsburg state precisely on 28 June. In 1925 Robert Seton-Watson wrote what became a characteristic interpretation in the works of later historians: 'It was thus peculiarly unfortunate that this day, of all days, should have been deliberately selected for the visit of one who personified

a foreign domination and was not unnaturally regarded as the most formidable obstacle to Serbian national expansion.'[4] Whether the day had been
'deliberately' selected is, however, very much open to question. Potiorek
had desperately wanted the Archduke's visit to be a success – his arrogance
notwithstanding, he would have been sensitive and sensible enough to
respond to any perceived local Serbian feeling concerning *Vidovdan*. It is
conceivable, however, that the drama which took place in Hotel Bosna in
the late hours of 27 June, when the Archduke very nearly decided to
abandon the visit to the city the following day, may well have played out
because someone in his entourage had realized the significance of the date.
And when, that night, Merizzi argued in favour of continuing the programme, his argument – apart from the offence which he said would be
caused to Potiorek if the visit did not take place – was that a cancellation
would be a snub to the city's loyal Catholic (Croat) population. Here,
Merizzi may well have been responding with a counter-argument to a
warning that Franz Ferdinand's presence in Sarajevo on *Vidovdan* would
provoke the local Serbs. This, of course, is speculation, but it is worth
asking why the Archduke even considered cutting short his trip before
deciding not to. Had precise intelligence about a plot to assassinate him
been presented to him on the evening of 27 June, he would probably never
have entered Sarajevo, and certainly not with his wife. If, on the other
hand, his attention had simply been drawn to the symbolism of *Vidovdan*,
this would have been sufficiently perturbing to make him think twice but
probably not enough to clinch the matter. Thus it was that Merizzi's
Catholics won out.

The *Vidovdan* fascination among historians has continued unabated for
a hundred years. The kind of emphasis placed on it has largely depended
on the subjective point of view of the writer. Serbian historians have by
now acquired the habit of citing A.J.P. Taylor on the subject: 'If a British
royalty had visited Dublin on St Patrick's day at the height of the Troubles,
he, too, might have expected to be shot at.'[5] Taylor's was of course a valid
point, but a purely academic one given that the assassins themselves had
attached no importance to 28 June as the day of the visit. In his memoirs
Ivan Kranjčević specifically rejected the idea that the assassination had
had anything to do with *Vidovdan*.[6] As has been seen, the decision to kill
Franz Ferdinand had been taken long before the exact date of his arrival
became known. It cannot be emphasized too strongly that *Vidovdan* 1914
and the Sarajevo assassination involved only an unexpected coincidence.
Yet in his recent study of the Sarajevo assassination, the Serbian historian
Radoš Ljušić devotes an entire chapter to attempting to convince the
reader that the Young Bosnia assassins – basically a group of atheists – had
been 'mesmerized by Vidovdan, the conscious sacrifice and the Kingdom
of Heaven'. The element of conscious sacrifice was certainly there, but

only as a measure to protect others involved in the conspiracy – certainly not in relation to any aspect of 'the Kingdom of Heaven' underpinning the *Vidovdan* myth. Trifko Grabež, the son of a priest and the only one among the assassins who had declared himself a believer in God, had failed abjectly to act. Ljušić, in any case, goes on to contradict himself by pointing out, correctly, that the assassins had initially not known the exact date of Franz Ferdinand's arrival in Bosnia.[7]

Although most accounts simply note the significance of *Vidovdan* and the coincidence of its anniversary with the day of the assassination, there are also those who see some of its elements as formative influences on the mindset of the assassins. Thus the Austrian writer Friedrich Würthle, in his influential 1975 work on the Sarajevo assassination, chose to dwell on the Miloš Obilić aspect of the *Vidovdan* tale: the assassination of the Sultan.[8] Rather more recently, in what has become another influential book on 1914, the legend of Kosovo is described in terms of 'assassination, martyrdom, victimhood and the thirst for revenge', and an attempt is made to portray Gavrilo Princip as a fanatical follower of Miloš Obilić.[9] To buttress this, Christopher Clark, author of the work in question, uses a report, dated 29 June 1914, from Wilhelm von Storck, a councillor at the Austro-Hungarian Legation in Belgrade with the reputation of a 'Slavophobe'.[10] Furious at the assassination in Sarajevo, Storck wrote about *die Obilić-Feier* (Obilić celebration – even though this was a description never used by Serbs themselves) in Serbia on 28 June and made sure his bosses in Vienna understood what Obilić was famous for.[11] It is entirely understandable that an ambitious Austro-Hungarian junior diplomat in Belgrade chose to interpret *Vidovdan* in this strident way on the day after the Habsburg Heir to the Throne was assassinated. What is interesting is that, a century later, a practically identical slant should be offered in one part of the historical scholarship on this issue. Furthermore, the tenets of the Kosovo legend, along with Obilić's act of assassination, are presented as something unique to the Serbs. Yet the Swiss, for example, have Wilhelm Tell, whose legend has similarly served to nourish national identity – for Tell, after all, is supposed to have ambushed and assassinated Albrecht Gessler, who was also a representative of tyrannical Austrian (indeed Habsburg) rule, thus inaugurating the struggle which eventually brought independence to the Swiss Confederacy.

What cannot be disputed is that the Serbs had longed to regain Kosovo. Their most famous churches and monasteries were there – as were their co-nationals. According to the Serbian geographer Jovan Cvijić, in 1912 the Serbians still outnumbered the Albanians in the so-called 'Old Serbia', i.e., Kosovo.[12] The aim of redeeming the province was finally achieved in the autumn of 1912 during the First Balkan War. A proper celebration of *Vidovdan*, however, could not be held in 1913 because of the tensions with

Bulgaria which had led to the Second Balkan War that summer. Therefore 28 June 1914, with Serbia finally at peace, was to be the first such commemoration – a memorial day of the first order – five hundred and twenty-five years after the event.

Belgrade had not seen such crowds 'for a very long, long time'. Many people arrived from the countryside to join the burgers of Belgrade, as had a lot of Serbs (and Croats) from outside Serbia. Reaching Belgrade a day earlier, on 27 June, they had received a cordial welcome from the large crowds waiting for them at the railway station.[13] The official celebrations began the next day, at ten in the morning on 28 June in an open space at Mali Kalemegdan below the city's old fortifications. First to arrive before the gaze of the crowd were the *Sokoli* – young men from Serbia's athletic societies, joined afterward by members of various singing ensembles and youth temperance associations, with Serbian Jewish singing and musical societies playing a prominent part. Also included on the official side of the celebration were representatives of the volunteers' alliance that had fought in the Balkan Wars of 1912 and 1913, and female high school pupils wearing national costumes from all parts of Serbdom. These participants formed a rectangle in two corners of which a poignant scene could be observed: on the left a group of young girls dressed in white dresses, on the right young boys in blue suits. These children, aged between three and twelve, had lost their fathers in the Balkan Wars.[14]

Followed from Belgrade's Cathedral Church of St Michael by an entourage of nineteen priests, Metropolitan Dimitrije then conducted the remembrance service. Thousands of people, bare-headed, stood in complete silence during the ceremony. Simultaneously, a separate service was held in the Church of the Assumption, with Regent Alexander, many dignitaries and high-ranking officers in attendance. After the ceremony at Mali Kalemegdan a procession moved from there through the main streets of Belgrade, preceded by four heralds on horses, blowing trumpets. Huge crowds lined the pavements. Oddly enough, this most Serbian of occasions had a very Yugoslavian character. First the Croatian anthem was sung as the procession entered the centre of the city. Then, at the Royal Palace, to which the Regent had already returned from the Church of the Assumption, the ensembles sang the Serbian anthem. Finally, as the procession passed the Officers' Club, the Slovenian anthem was sung. At midday, having ended in Slavija Square, the procession and the crowd began to disperse.[15]

By this time, of course, Franz Ferdinand and his wife had already been killed in Sarajevo. According to Dušan Lončarević, a journalist working in Belgrade for the Vienna *Telegraphen-Korrespondenz-Bureau*, it was approaching 3 p.m. when the Serbian Press Bureau received the first news of the assassination. Extra-editions of Belgrade papers were printed. Regent Alexander and Finance Minister Lazar Paču were informed immediately.

The latter was in charge of government as Prime Minister Pašić had left the city for Priština to start the election campaign in the south. In the evening Lončarević reported on the mood of the populace following the news from Sarajevo. He wrote that 'the impact everywhere was one of consternation' and that there was widespread sympathy for the old Emperor.[16] Julius von Griesinger, the German Minister in Belgrade, informed Berlin on 30 June that the assassination had made a deep impression in Serbia and that the mood was 'quite gloomy'.[17] Dayrell Crackanthorpe, the British Chargé d'Affaires in Belgrade, thought that the effect was 'rather of stupefaction than of regret'.[18]

The *Vidovdan* festivities had continued in the city after the main celebration in the morning, but the Government now ordered that they be stopped. All the restaurants and coffee houses were immediately shut down. All music, singing and entertainment in public places was also banned by the Interior Minister, Stojan Protić.[19] Nicholas Hartwig, the Russian Minister in Belgrade, informed St Petersburg that even without this order the various associations involved in the memorial day festivities had, following the assassination, spontaneously ended the celebrations on their own initiative.[20] When the special correspondent of the Budapest *Az est* arrived in the centre of the city late in the evening, he found everything in darkness and thought at first that there had been an electric failure. He reported that on the streets people 'debated quietly deep into the night', and that fears were being voiced that the fanatical act of an individual could be unjustly ascribed to the Serbian people as a whole.[21]

Lull Before the Storm

The news that Franz Ferdinand and his wife had been killed was given to Regent Alexander by his aide-de-camp, Major Panta Draškić. The Regent reacted with astonished and prolonged silence, finally commenting only briefly: 'Poor woman, at least her they could have spared.'[22] He ordered an eight-day Court mourning.[23] In his memoirs Draškić related that Alexander was a superstitious man – being much impressed after the Balkan Wars by a story about a Serbian soldier killed at the battle of Kumanovo whose spirit had begun soon thereafter to communicate with a family member, to prophesy a new war – 'the greatest war' – in which the whole country would suffer horrendously, but would ultimately prevail.[24] Certainly, a war of some kind now appeared to be a distinct possibility. Alexander's father, King Peter, was convinced of it. When his aide-de-camp, Lieutenant-Colonel Antonije Antić, told him about the assassination in Sarajevo, the news had 'an awfully depressing' effect on him. It was known straight away that the assassin was a Bosnian Serb. The King agreed with Antić that Austria-Hungary would blame Serbia and that war was inevitable.[25] In

Government circles, as Milan Stojadinović related in his memoirs, 'we felt immediately that Vienna would indict Serbia'.²⁶ On 28 June Ilija Pavlović, a prominent Serbian banker, commented bitterly about the event in Sarajevo: 'This is terrible! Only those who at this moment wish ill on Serbia could have carried this out!'²⁷

Pašić's reported reaction to the assassination on 28 June ('It is very bad. It will mean war.') may not be verifiable, but it is conceivable that such thoughts may have crossed his mind.²⁸ However, apart from asking Jovan M. Jovanović, the Serbian Minister in Vienna, to convey condolences on behalf of the Royal Serbian Government, Pašić did not send any specific instructions, adopting instead his characteristic wait-and-see attitude.²⁹ It is very difficult to find any credibility in the report by Heinrich Jehlitschka, the Austro-Hungarian Consul-General in Skopje, Macedonia, that Pašić had on 29 June held a confidential meeting in the city in which he allegedly said that 'certain political circles' would exploit the assassination in Sarajevo against Serbia. 'But the Serbs', the report claimed he had said, 'will know how to take up a stand and to fulfil their duty.'³⁰ It would surely have been far too early to make such a combative statement even in a closed meeting since Pašić could on 29 June have had little idea about what the official reaction in Vienna would be.³¹

In a series of telegrams from the Habsburg capital, however, Serbia's own Minister Jovanović soon began to warn Belgrade about the increasing tendency of the Austro-Hungarian press to link Serbia with the assassination in Sarajevo.³² He clearly acted without consulting Pašić when seeing Baron Karl Macchio at the Ballhausplatz on 30 June, to tell him that the Serbian Government vigorously condemned the Sarajevo assassination, but also to express his private opinion that the Government would deliver any conspirators should they be found in Serbia.³³ On 1 July Pašić himself finally reacted to the developing crisis, sending a circular telegram to Serbian legations abroad, in which he drew their attention to the accusations against Serbia rife in the Austrian press. 'At a moment when Serbia is doing its utmost to improve the relations with the neighbouring Monarchy and make them progressively friendlier', he wrote, 'it is absurd to think that it could tolerate acts such as this last one.' The legations were then merely informed, however, that Serbia would re-double its efforts to control any 'anarchist elements' on its territory and that the Government had already, before the dissolution of the country's Assembly, drafted a law on anarchists. The Prime Minister's tone was embittered, and he emphasized that his Government could not allow 'the Viennese press' to mislead European public opinion.³⁴

But Jovanović had not just been warning about the press of Austria-Hungary: in the telegrams that he sent at the end of June and early in July, he consistently pleaded with Pašić that 'the greatest attention' should be paid to what the Serbian newspapers were going to write.[35] This was always going to be a tricky business for Pašić, not least because the Austro-Hungarian press was itself hardly restrained in its speculations about where the likely originators of the Sarajevo assassination were to be found. Besides, the Serbian Constitution of 1903, just like that of 1888, declared that: 'The press is free.'[36] Whatever else may be said of Pašić, he was not a dictator. He could control only the organ of his own Radical Party, and indeed this paper, *Samouprava*, displayed great tact and moderation throughout the July Crisis. The suggestions made by historians that Pašić had not gagged the press because of the fear of nationalist reaction, especially that of the Army, miss a fundamental point: with the pogroms against the Bosnian Serbs after 28 June, and with the Austro-Hungarian press campaign against Serbia, *all* of Serbia had become nationalist – this was a country and a nation feeling itself to be under siege. Nevertheless, Pašić responded to Jovanović's urgings on 6 July and had the Government's chief of the Press Bureau summon the newspaper editors for 7 July. It is not known, however, what was said at that meeting.[37]

Signs of nervousness soon began to creep into the Prime Minister's language. On 4 July, responding to a telegram from Paris which was somewhat ambiguous about the fate of a Serbian order for 400,000 rifles, he demanded that the French Government should provide a precise and definitive answer, for 'we can no longer wait'.[38] The sorry state of Serbia's Army, especially the deficit with regard to rifles, is confirmed by a Serbian document from 6 July 1914 which reveals that Belgrade was at this time also engaged in secret talks for the procurement of rifles with the Vickers arms company in Britain.[39] Early in July, Pašić could perhaps draw some reassurance from a short telegram sent by Miroslav Spalajković, the Serbian Minister at St Petersburg, informing him that that the Russian Foreign Minister was not attaching any significance to the Austrian accusations – because Pašić, being at the head of the Government, represented a guarantee that Serbia was 'not a breeding ground for adventures'. Sazonov believed that Europe would show increased sympathy for Serbia in the light of the violence against the Bosnian Serbs, and he advised restraint and the calming of tempers, both in Serbia and Bosnia.[40] From Paris, the Serbian Minister Milenko Vesnić reported that the astonishment in France at the assassination of Franz Ferdinand had quickly subsided once it had been realized what 'danger to the peace of Europe' the Archduke had represented. René Viviani, the French Prime and Foreign Minister, had counselled Serbia to remain 'dispassionate and dignified'.[41]

On the other hand, Jovanović in Vienna was anything but sanguine. On 7 July, the exact day when the Austro-Hungarian Joint Ministerial Council was meeting, he warned of indications that Austria-Hungary would create out of the Sarajevo assassination an 'all-Serb, Yugoslav, pan-Slav conspiracy'.[42] On the same day, having become alarmed at the rise of Austrian press antagonism against Serbia, Sazonov telegraphed Hartwig in Belgrade with advice that the Serbian Government should 'exercise extreme caution' in order not to make the situation even worse.[43] On 9 July Hartwig replied that he had carried out the instruction, reporting Pašić as saying that the Government was fully aware of the need for prudence and was determined not to react to Austria's provocations – this telegram was sent the day before Hartwig died.[44]

Indeed, the Russian Minister at Belgrade had in the days after the Sarajevo assassination been concerned, as Strandtmann wrote in his memoirs, 'only about the state of his own health'. When Strandtmann returned from his Italian trip he noted 'Hartwig's almost total indifference to everything that was happening around us'.[45] Already on 30 June Hartwig had asked for a four-week holiday, pleading that everything was quiet in Serbia and that Pašić himself was preparing to go to Marienbad.[46] On 10 July at 9 p.m. he paid a visit to Baron Giesl who had that morning returned from a holiday in France. After less than half an hour of conversation, Hartwig, a very corpulent man, dropped dead in Giesl's study – the result, as the doctors established, of heart failure. Giesl, who described this scene in his book, also made the claim that, had Hartwig still been alive on the critical day of 25 July (when the deadline for the Serbian reply to the Austro-Hungarian ultimatum was due to expire), 'the world war would not have broken out'.[47] Giesl's cheek is truly admirable. On 22 July, a day before he was going to deliver the formidable Austro-Hungarian ultimatum to the Serbian Government, he descibed it to Strandtmann as a *'note anodine'*.[48] No doubt Hartwig, had he lived (and had he been in Belgrade on the critical day, which he would not have been as he had been planning to leave after 12 July) would have counselled extreme moderation to Pašić – he is reported to have said soon after the news had arrived about Franz Ferdinand's assassination: *'Au nom de Ciel, pourvu que ça ne soit pas un Serbe.'*[49] But as Mark Cornwall has argued, his supposed influence in Belgrade, generally assumed to have been almost divine, is something of a 'myth', promoted by Hartwig himself and ignoring the fact that Pašić was shaping his own, independent policy.[50]

The real impact of Hartwig's sudden death was that it worsened the already highly strained Austro-Serbian relations. As Jovanović was to report, the great pomp with which he had been buried in Belgrade (on 14 July) had not gone down well in Vienna.[51] But a far more serious issue had arisen before the funeral. Because he had died at the Austro-Hungarian Legation, wild rumours quickly spread in Belgrade that he had been poisoned. When Giesl saw Pašić on 11 July, the latter himself described the rumours as an 'absurdity' and said that he had ordered that they be countered where required.[52] But already on the next day Giesl sent a panicky telegram to

Vienna, passing on some information received from a confidant: 'Large scale demonstrations are planned at dusk against Austro-Hungarian subjects and property. Numerous *komitadjis* from the interior assigned, and bombs distributed among them. Neither life nor property will be spared'. In Vienna, even Berchtold was dismayed by this outburst of frenzy, reprimanding Giesl for attaching so much weight to a questionable source. But Giesl had on 12 July already presented Pašić with a *démarche* on this subject, so that strong gendarmerie units were now guarding the Austro-Hungarian Legation – and the press in Austria-Hungary was widely reporting on the supposed threat. The Austro-Hungarian colony in Belgrade, alarmed by their own Minister, had either fled across the border to Zemun (Semlin) or taken refuge at the Legation. No demonstrations of any kind, let alone bomb throwing, took place. Nevertheless, Giesl sent another telegram to Vienna on 13 July, giving information received from another 'confidant' that two Russian anarchists with explosives had arrived in Belgrade, with the task of blowing up ('*in die Luft zu sprengen*') the Austro-Hungarian Legation.[53]

One is left wondering about the sums that Giesl's Legation was paying to its spies for such 'information'. At any rate, following the grand Belgrade funeral accorded to Hartwig by the Serbian state, the Belgrade press zoomed in on Giesl. On 16 July, for example, the daily *Politika* devoted its front-page editorial to the Austro-Hungarian Minister. It reminded its readers that, after the Sarajevo assassination of Franz Ferdinand, a hunt of Serbian citizens had been staged across Vienna. 'Some were beaten up on the streets', the editorial recalled, 'some had been scolded and spat at, some had been thrown out of apartments, coffee houses and schools'. It emphasized that the Serbian Legation in Vienna had been 'under siege' for three days, but that the Serbs in Serbia, although they knew about all this, had remained calm and dignified. And then, 'Mr Giesl ran to Mr Pašić and sought the protection of the Serbian authorities because of demonstrations which were ostensibly being prepared ... but all along we in Belgrade knew nothing about it, for there were no demonstrations.' So, *Politika* asked, who was guilty? Of course, the paper lambasted Giesl who, as a diplomat, had been 'deceived' and, as a general, had been 'frightened'. But it reserved its main searching question for Pašić, asking him what he proposed to do to prevent such future 'comedies'.[54]

The Belgrade press, so often castigated by historians of the July Crisis, was at least on this occasion feeding off the remarkable ineptitude of Austro-Hungarian diplomacy. But some of Serbia's diplomats, serving in exposed positions, were inevitably more sensitive than their Government to foreign perceptions of the Serbian press. Thus Jovanović sent another two telegrams from Vienna on 10 July, renewing his call for press moderation at home.[55] Another Jovanović (Milutin), the Chargé d'Affaires in Berlin, drew Pašić's attention to the new situation of the time, in which, up to a point, the Serbian press had acquired world importance: 'Articles are being cited even from papers which are completely insignificant to us.'[56] With some justification, however, Pašić himself was by mid-July far more focused on the writings of the Austro-Hungarian press. Following Giesl's claims about an imminent threat to Austro-Hungarian subjects and property, Jovanović sent a telegram reporting that anxiety prevailed in Vienna and asking that the Belgrade Legation and Austro-Hungarian subjects should be protected 'without delay'. The Prime Minister's response was to fire off an angry telegram *en claire*: 'All the news being spread in Vienna and Budapest to the effect that disorder and excitement rule here – is untrue. The Austro-Hungarian Minister and the rest of the personnel move freely on the streets and no one is insulting them, still less that there are demonstrations at their houses. No one has been sworn at, or pushed or hit ... All such news is untrue, and it is *specifically spread* [emphases in the original] in order to excite public opinion in Austria-Hungary and turn it against Serbia.'[57]

And this little outburst was not enough for Pašić, for on the same day he sent a circular telegram to all Serbian legations on the same subject. His target was the Austro-Hungarian *Korrespondenz-Bureau* which was alarming public opinion in Europe 'with particular tendency', by incorrectly transmitting the reactions of the Belgrade press: 'It selects *especially the strongest phrases* from articles which carry responses to the offences, threats and tendentious untruths ... It cites the yellow press which no one reads in Belgrade because it is embarrassing to be seen reading such papers.' (Emphasis in the original.) Pašić also reminded his diplomats abroad – as if they did not know it already – that press freedom in Serbia was absolute, confiscation being possible only in the case of the King being insulted or calls for revolution being made. Serbia, he emphasized, had 'no such thing as preventive censorship', so that the Government had 'neither constitutional nor legal means to stop the press'. Finally, he made the point that 'no one in Europe' would have the faintest idea what the Serbian press was writing were it not for the slanderous *Korrespondenz-Bureau*.[58]

Soon, however, the Prime Minister's energies were directed to far more important matters. Until now, he might well have still harboured hopes for a peaceful outcome of the crisis – despite significant clues to the contrary, particularly the behaviour of the Austro-Hungarian press which had so annoyed him. On 14 July he told the Russian Chargé d'Affaires that he saw as a good sign the willingness of the Austro-Hungarian side to resume negotiations about the Eastern Railways (taken over by Serbia from Turkey after the Balkan Wars).[59] Around mid-July, however, speculation increased in European chancelleries that Vienna would soon take some kind of diplomatic step regarding Serbia. On 16 July the Serbian Minister in London Bošković reported that a 'fateful coercion' of Serbia was being prepared by

Austria-Hungary and that Henry Wickham Steed, the editor of *The Times*, also had information to that effect. Steed believed that Vienna was planning to 'humiliate' Serbia.[60] The next day, Pašić received the disturbing information from Rome that the Italian Foreign Minister had talked of a possible Austro-Hungarian measure which would go 'against the sovereign rights of Serbia'. Late at night another telegram was received from the Legation in Rome. It related the impression formed by Duke Avarna, the Italian Ambassador to Vienna, that, following a speech by the Hungarian Prime Minister Tisza (on 15 July), some Austrian action against Belgrade was inevitable and that the danger of an armed conflict existed if Serbia failed to give satisfaction.[61]

Indeed, Tisza's speech in the Hungarian Parliament (referred to in the previous chapter), hinting at the possibility of war, had been widely reported – not least in the Belgrade press.[62] Mark Cornwall considers that this was 'crucial evidence' for Pašić.[63] It most certainly was, although he waited three days before reacting. Exactly at midnight on 18/19 July Pašić sent a long and fairly dramatic circular telegram to the Serbian legations (excepting Vienna) in which he devoted much space to outlining the history of the Austro-Hungarian press campaign against Serbia in the wake of the Sarajevo assassination. He noted that those who had closely followed the polemics between the Austro-Hungarian and the Serbian press could have seen that the Belgrade papers had merely been responding to tendentious untruths, but surmised that foreign governments, busy with other important matters, could not have detected '*how the Austro-Hungarian press was with specific tendency alarming public opinion both home and abroad*'. (Emphasis in the original.) Pašić mentioned the possibility that the Serbian Government should expect some step to be taken by Austria-Hungary ('but we do not know in what form') and also the prospect of an armed conflict in the event that the Government could not give a categorical and satisfactory reply. The point of the circular was that friendly governments should 'take note of our sincere willingness to maintain friendly relations with Austria-Hungary'. Pašić, however, attached a caveat: 'But we could not meet demands which would be unacceptable to any state that guards its independence and dignity.'[64]

On the next day the Russian Chargé d'Affaires saw Pašić who looked to him 'very worried'. Tisza's speech in Budapest, Pašić said, had made 'a deep impression' on him. He also had reports about Austro-Hungarian military movements on Serbia's borders. However, in order to avoid dangerous entanglements, not 'a single' Serbian soldier had been moved, contrary to false statements in Vienna. Pašić also told Strandtmann that all available legal means were being applied to restrain the Serbian press. The Serbian Prime Minister was, Strandtmann emphasized in his telegram to Sazonov, conscious of the 'difficulty of his task'.[65] Indeed the old man needed a break at this point. In his memoirs, Strandtmann was to expand a little on this 19 July encounter with Pašić. The latter was leaving Belgrade the next day, officially to take part in the election campaign, 'but in fact to rest, since he had had to put off the cure in Marienbad'.[66]

The Prime Minister left for Negotin in north-eastern Serbia on 20 July. The day before, of course, the Austro-Hungarian Joint Ministerial Council had made its final decision for war. It was ironic, therefore, that on the day Pašić had left, Jovanović had from Vienna sent yet another telegram urging Pašić to try and make the Belgrade newspapers 'show more dignity and less admonition'.[67]

Ultimatum Delivered

A useful reconstruction of what took place in Belgrade during the momentous forty-eight hours of 23-25 July was provided in 1934 by Slavko Grujić, then Secretary-General of the Serbian Foreign Ministry, whose recollections of that period were published in four consecutive articles in the daily *Politika*.[68] Grujić writes that, after the initial turbulence surrounding the killing of Franz Ferdinand, days and weeks followed without any official move by Austria-Hungary. Opinion began to take hold as a result that the Austro-Serbian dispute would be solved 'in a peaceful, diplomatic way'. So it was that just before the presentation of the ultimatum 'calm had almost returned' with attention in Serbia mainly focused on the forthcoming elections, and Prime Minister Pašić and some other members of his cabinet campaigning away in the interior of the country. At 9 a.m. on the morning of 23 July, arriving for work at the Foreign Ministry, Grujić spotted a *fiaker* parked in front. Soon he met the Secretary of the Austro-Hungarian Legation who informed him that his boss, the Minister Baron Giesl, wished to see Mr Pašić at 4 p.m. This was highly unusual according to Grujić – although foreign representatives could request meetings outside the pre-arranged, fixed dates, they were not supposed to set the time of such appointments. Grujić explained that the Finance Minister Lazar Paču was deputizing for the absent Pašić and asked about the purpose of Giesl's proposed visit. '*Eine wichtige Mitteilung*', replied the Secretary – 'an important notification'.

Grujić immediately realized that a note with a time-limit would be delivered because the Austro-Hungarian request made in the morning for a meeting at 4 p.m. implied precisely that. With Pašić out of town, the man in charge in Belgrade was Laza Paču, the Finance Minister and now the acting Prime and Foreign Minister, hated in the Serbian Army for his 'energetic' opposition to military expenditure.[69] It was to him that Grujić predicted an Austrian ultimatum, suggesting that the time-limit for Serbia would be a short one. Paču disagreed: 'Fifteen days,' he said, 'maybe a whole month.' At first, he did not even share Grujić's hunch that Giesl's visit would have something to do with the Sarajevo assassination. For his part, Grujić took steps for Pašić to be informed of the development and called those Government Ministers still in Belgrade to assemble at the Foreign Ministry. However, at 4 p.m. it was not Giesl, but the Secretary of the Legation who appeared again, requesting that the meeting be postponed until 6 p.m. Little did the assembled Serbs know that the delay had been caused by the realization of Vienna, obsessed by the French, that the ultimatum would be best delivered at 6 p.m. – once the French President and his Prime Minister, following their meetings with the Tsar, were indeed safely on a warship leaving Russian waters. Pač1u, none too pleased, 'hesitated for while about whether to receive the Minister', before finally agreeing to do so. Promptly at 6 p.m. Giesl turned up and was received by Pačzu and Grujić in Pašić's office. The Austro-Hungarian Minister, sat down in an armchair and holding 'a big white envelope' announced in French that his government had instructed him to hand 'this note' to the Royal Serbian Government and to communicate verbally that, if the Serbian Government did not give satisfactory replies to all the points in the note by 6 p.m. on 25 July, he would together with the personnel of the Legation leave Belgrade.[70] Of course, this would be an unmistakeable pointer to the imminent breaking off of diplomatic relations.

Pačzu, a passionate smoker, was blowing thick rings of smoke as Giesl spoke. The latter placed the envelope on the table, but Pačzu refused to take it, saying, 'fairly indignantly', that, since the Prime Minister and several Ministers were out of Belgrade, he was not sure he would be able to convene them or to produce any kind of reply in such a short space of time. Whereupon Giesl remarked, 'smiling', that in this age of the telegraph, telephone and fast means of travel, distances did not exist. Pačzu merely shrugged his shoulders at that rejoinder and the whole meeting, Grujić observed, lasted barely two to three minutes.

After Giesl had left, Grujić and Pačzu returned to the conference room in the Ministry where, together with the assembled Ministers, they began to examine the eight-page, type-written ultimatum. It did not take them long to realize the significance of the document. 'Complete silence reigned for a while', Grujić writes, 'as if no one wished to be the first to state his opinion.' Finally, Ljuba Jovanović, the Education Minister who had been pacing up and down across the length of the conference room, stopped and declared: 'There is nothing left to do but die in battle!'[71] That evening, Pačzu sent a circular telegram to Serbia's legations abroad, informing them that the Government had not yet reached any decision regarding the Austro-Hungarian demands, but that those demands were 'such that no Serbian Government can accept them in entirety'.[72] Mark Cornwall has seen this attitude as a manifestation of a Serbian 'resistance that was not sheer bravado', and Annika Mombauer has written about 'the defiant mood' in

Belgrade on 23 July, curbed only by Pašić's return the following day.[73] In fact it would require Pašić's coolness and clear-headedness to stop actual panic in the ranks of his Government. For example, that same evening Paču ordered Dušan Stefanović, the War Minister, to lock up Major Vojislav Tankosić – which Stefanović duly did.[74] Thus, already on 23 July, Paču had single-handedly well-nigh accommodated point 7 in the Austro-Hungarian ultimatum which had demanded the arrest of Tankosić.

The truth was that the Austro-Hungarian ultimatum had had the effect of a thunderbolt in Belgrade. Ljuba Jovanović, in his famous 1924 article in *The Blood of Slavdom*, is quite misleading in describing the prevailing mood when he writes that 'among my colleagues and all other persons who on that evening and on the next day heard of the Austro-Hungarian step and immediately saw the true seriousness of it, I saw no one who showed fear, and still less, panic.'[75] He himself may have, as reported by Grujić, decided that war was inevitable, but that was not necessarily true of his colleagues. Indeed, at 6.20 p.m. – only twenty minutes after receiving the ultimatum – Paču had the Russian Chargé d'Affaires Strandtmann summoned by telephone to come urgently to the Foreign Ministry. Strandtmann, on arriving, began to read the ultimatum and, as he wrote: 'I could not believe my eyes' – so that he would re-read some passages in order to make sure that he really had read correctly. Paču requested Russia's protection, adding that no Serbian government could agree to the demands of the ultimatum. However, when the Finance Minister asked him what he thought, Strandtmann counselled that the note left a dismal impression, but that the Serbian Government, in its reply, was 'obliged to go to the extreme limits of complaisance'. Paču was quick to moderate his position: 'Yes, of course, we shall do so, and Pašić will find adequate phrases to add to our reply that agreeability with which we shall meet all of Vienna's legitimate demands.'[76] This, surely, hardly suggested a defiant stance on the part of Serbia.

Although, as has been seen, Pašić had in his telegram of 18 July to Serbia's legations already anticipated some kind of unpleasant Austro-Hungarian diplomatic action in Belgrade, the delivery of the ultimatum on 23 July had perhaps not been expected so soon. On that very day, the Belgrade daily *Politika* had speculated that Vienna would not act before the conclusion of its enquiry into the Sarajevo assassination.[77] Julius von Griesinger, the German Minister in Belgrade, reported to Berlin on 24 July that the 'energetic tone and the precise demands' of the Austro-Hungarian note had come to the Serbian Government 'completely unforeseen'. Griesinger also suggested, somewhat sensationally, that a 'military uprising' was feared in the event that the Government agreed to publish Serbia's apologies to Austria-Hungary as an order of the day by the Serbian King in the Army official bulletin – as demanded in the section of the ultimatum preceding the enumeration of ten further demands.[78] As it turned out, this demand was to be accepted by the Serbian Government pretty much in full – despite some hair-splitting over the wording on the part of the Ballhausplatz when it saw the Serbian reply.

However, so strong apparently was the shock of the ultimatum that on 24 July Oskar von Hranilović, the head of the *Evidenzbüro*, told Count Karl Kageneck, the German Military Attaché in Vienna, that a 'revolution' could possibly break out in Serbia. Again, such prognoses had been massively exaggerated. Hranilović had received this information from a confidant just arrived from Belgrade who had also reported, rather more accurately, that the impact of the Austro-Hungarian note had been one of 'downright consternation'.[79] Pašić, on his way back to the capital city from the south of Serbia after having been asked by the Regent to return, had been informed in advance by Grujić on the telephone about the contents of the ultimatum.[80] According to Crackanthorpe, the British Chargé d'Affaires in Belgrade, when the Prime Minister arrived early in the morning of 24 July he looked 'very anxious and dejected'.[81]

No less worried was Regent Alexander. At 10 p.m. on 23 July he suddenly appeared at the Russian Legation where Strandtmann had been hurriedly encrypting telegrams for St Petersburg – a work so demanding that he had had to enlist the help of his wife as well as that of the daughter of the late Minister Hartwig. The Regent, 'very excited', asked Strandtmann about the ultimatum and received from him the answer that Paču had already heard: even if the ultimatum could not be accepted in its entirety, it was 'indispensable to make even seemingly impossible concessions'. Strandtmann underlined the point by adding that 'Serbia's fate depends on it'. And like Paču before him, Alexander also agreed with the Russian diplomat's soft approach. 'You are right', he told Strandtmann, but he also asked what Russia would do. Strandtmann could only give his private opinion that Russia would 'give its say for your protection'. This rather vague answer could not have greatly encouraged the Regent, who then asked what Serbia should do. He was advised that a telegram requesting help should be sent to the Tsar, and another one to the King of Italy, Alexander's uncle, whose country was in the Triple Alliance but whose interests, Strandtmann argued, were not entirely in harmony with those of Austria-Hungary. Strandtmann's suggestion, placing Italy alongside Russia in the same rescue boat for Serbia, must have been enough to make Alexander greatly fear for the future of his country. All in all, the Regent could hardly have been reassured that concrete help would be forthcoming from Russia – pointedly reminding his host at the end of their conversation that Russia had still not delivered the 120,000 rifles it had promised Serbia. 'It seemed to me', Strandtmann wrote in his memoirs, 'that the Crown Prince had begun to have doubts about that delivery'.[82]

Strandtmann had all of a sudden become the most sought-after diplomat in Belgrade. The next day, 24 July, he was visited again, towards 9 a.m.,
this time by Prime Minister Pašić who had arrived in town around 5 a.m.
Looking 'exceptionally anxious, but collected and determined', Pašić had
already been acquainted with Strandtmann's advice as given to Paču and
the Regent. His first impression about the Austrian note, he told Strandtmann, was that it 'could be neither accepted nor rejected' – and that, what
was needed 'at any cost', was to 'gain time, so that the Great Powers could
have the possibility of taking matters into their hands'. And this, it may
be suggested, was absolutely the key frame of reference that was to guide
Serbia's response to the Austro-Hungarian ultimatum. The Serbian reply
on the next day was to be precisely what Pašić had intimated to Strandtmann: neither an acceptance nor a rejection. Faced with formidable
demands in the ultimatum and not many hours in which to reply, Pašić
knew that the only way to wriggle out was to play for time. Thus a full
Serbian acceptance of all the demands was never on the cards. On the
other hand, for such a stratagem to have any chance of success, the Serbian
Government would have to bend over backwards to swallow a very heavy
dose of the humiliation so carefully concocted and packaged in Vienna.[83]

It is important to note that this approach had been formulated by the
Serbian Prime Minister almost as soon as he had returned to Belgrade, and
it is also important to emphasize that at that point he had not even asked
Strandtmann what the attitude of Russia would be. Evidently, he did not
see Russia, as opposed to the Great Powers acting in concert, as being in
a position to stop the coming of the war. True, he did tell Strandtmann
that 'Russia alone could save Serbia', but this was no more than polite
artifice. As Mark Cornwall has argued, Pašić 'was unsure how Russia might
react'. Moreover, he informed Strandtmann: 'If war becomes unavoidable,
we shall fight, whatever the answer to the telegram which the Crown
Prince has sent to the Tsar.' What this meant was that he was not going to
place the fate of Serbia into the hands of the Tsar. Strandtmann also noted
that Pašić saw the future as 'extremely bleak'.[84]

The telegram which Regent Alexander sent to the Tsar on 24 July, with
its dramatic appeal for help, is mentioned in many accounts of the July
Crisis, but in fact played no role in the formulation of the Serbian reply to
the ultimatum because the Tsar only read it on 26 July – after the ultimatum had already expired – and his answer was seen by Pašić as late as
29 July – by which time Austria-Hungary had already declared war on
Serbia. It is, nevertheless, an important document in that it emphasized
the Serbian standpoint worked out by Pašić: 'We are willing to accept those
Austro-Hungarian demands which are consistent with the position of an
independent state'. True, Alexander did add that Serbia would also accept
those demands for which the Tsar might 'advise' them to concede.

However, in the light of Pašić's very clear words to Strandtmann that, if necessary, Serbia would fight irrespective of the Tsar's advice, Alexander's ostensible flexibility must be seen as an obligatory but empty deferential gesture towards a ruler being written to for help.[85]

Indeed, the anticipation of imminent war was so strong that nothing was being left to chance. In the course of 24 July, as Pašić and his colleagues feverishly conferred about the ultimatum, Grujić reported that they also found time to consider measures of evacuation from the capital: all the ministries and the more important government bureaus, the archives, the treasuries of the Ministry of Finance and the National Bank, etc., were to be moved into the interior. In the Foreign Ministry alone, over fifty boxes containing archival material and confidential administrative paper work were packed on 24 July. Significantly, Grujić was asked to appear in the conference room, where the Ministers were assembled, to confirm Giesl's verbal communication that he would leave Belgrade unless '*all the demands*' in the ultimatum received satisfactory replies – a sure indication that the Serbian Government was not contemplating to accommodate all of them.[86] At the same time the War Minister Stefanović was taking measures of his own – 'without the Prime Minister's knowledge', as he recalled. He asked the Army divisional commanders to look into the mobilization plans, and ordered that all the officers on leave or sick leave be recalled to their command posts. He also ordered some senior commanders, at the time outside Belgrade, to return immediately. 'There was a premonition that war was coming', Stefanović wrote later, 'and one had to prepare the essentials for that contingency.'[87] Late at night Grujić heard the clatter of horses and the wheeling of field guns and munitions carriages – the Belgrade artillery regiment was leaving the city, in accordance with the axiom long held by the Serbian Army that the capital, seated right on the border, would not, and could not, be defended in the event of a war with Austria-Hungary.[88]

Serbia Forsaken

How did the international position of Serbia look between 23 and 25 July? On the whole, the picture must have appeared fairly dismal to the Government in Belgrade – both regionally and continent-wide. In the regional Balkan context, only tiny Montenegro could be regarded as a reasonably reliable ally on account of its Serbian character in general, and the strength of its anti-Austrian public sentiment in particular. Thus, on 6 July, a meeting of solidarity with the Serbs of Bosnia-Herzegovina was held in the capital Cetinje. But when the crowd moved in the direction of the Austro-Hungarian Legation (shouting: 'Down!'), King Nicholas himself appeared, riding in a car, ordering the people to move back. The Montenegrin

Government subsequently forbade further demonstrations. The King's predicament in July 1914 was profound. Not only did he not wish to antagonize Austria-Hungary, but he also saw the leading demonstrators of 6 July as the advocates of a union with Serbia. As discussed in chapter eight, such a union was the last thing he wanted.

On the other hand, the King could not ignore the pro-Serbian feelings of his own people and it was no wonder that he complained to Gustav Hubka, the Austro-Hungarian Military Attaché, about 'my desperate position'.[89] In the end, the march of events left him with little choice. The ultimatum to Serbia had made 'a deep impression' on him, and on 24 July he openly admitted to Eduard Otto, the Austro-Hungarian Minister, his worry that Montenegro would be dragged into a war by 'public opinion'.[90] That evening, responding to Pašić's request to clarify its position, the Montenegrin Government held a session, presided over by Nicholas, following which it sent a message to Belgrade, suggesting that the Serbian Government should heed any Russian advice, and adding that the fate of Serbia 'is ours, too'. Petar Plamenac, the Montenegrin Foreign Minister, told the Serbian Minister in Cetinje: 'Serbia may count on the brotherly and unlimited support of Montenegro, both in this fateful moment for the Serbian people, and in any other.'[91]

Although even the Russian Minister in Cetinje had privately expressed to Nicholas his hope that Montenegro would be spared the 'disaster' of war, neutrality was not really an option for the King following the presentation of the Austro-Hungarian ultimatum.[92] Maintaining a detached line would almost certainly have resulted in the overthrow of both him and his dynasty. Almost until the last moment, however, he was fishing in troubled waters, telling Otto (on 22 July) that Austria-Hungary should back Montenegro's territorial expansion in north Albania – in which case the 'danger of the union with Serbia' would be removed and the Monarchy would on its southern border gain a friend upon whom it could 'count absolutely'.[93] Such, then, was the ruler of Serbia's ostensibly most dependable regional ally.

Elsewhere in the region, nothing could be expected from Bulgaria, the defeated foe of 1913, though Sofia, sitting carefully on the fence in the Austro-Serbian quarrel, did in fact already declare neutrality on 25 July.[94] The prospects of support from otherwise friendly Romania were hardly better. Interestingly, July 1914 witnessed incidents on the border between Romania and Bulgaria, with casualties on both sides.[95] Belgrade was prepared to act on Romania's side – in support of the Treaty of Bucharest which had ended the Balkan Wars. Late on 23 July, amid all the excitement following the presentation of the ultimatum, Paču found time to warn the Bulgarian Government, through the Serbian Minister in Sofia, that Serbia would 'not remain indifferent' in the event of a Bulgaro-Romanian conflict.[96] But it was illusory to expect Bucharest to offer a corresponding gesture to the Serbian Government in its hour of need – as long as the old Hohenzollern King Carol lived, Romania was not going to move against Austria-Hungary. Towards midnight on 24 July Pašić learned from Fotije Stanojević, the Secretary of the Serbian Legation in Bucharest, that the Romanian Foreign Minister was 'avoiding' stating how his country would react if Austria-Hungary attacked Serbia.[97]

Belgrade could conceivably hope for greater support from Greece since Article 1 of the Greco-Serbian Treaty of Alliance, concluded on 1 June 1913, obliged the signatories to come to each other's aid with their 'complete armed forces' in the event of unprovoked attack.[98] In mid-July Pašić had hoped to travel to Salonika for a meeting with the Greek Prime Minister Eleftherios Venizelos – precisely to remind the Greek side that *casus foederis* should come into operation if Austria-Hungary moved against Serbia. However, Venizelos prudently dodged the proposed meeting.[99] Astonishingly and uniquely, on 24 July his Germanophile Foreign Minister, Georgios Streit, maintained to the Serbian Minister in Athens that, while the Austro-Hungarian demands in the ultimatum were difficult and unacceptable, he thought that rejecting them would not entail for Serbia 'any heavy consequences' because Austria-Hungary 'cannot and dare not take any action'.[100]

Given that Pašić had in a circular telegram of 24 July to the Serbian legations in Montenegro, Greece and Romania specifically and urgently asked for clarification as to whether Serbia could count on support from those three neighbours, he could reasonably be expected to pay at least as much attention in his decision-making to information on the likely conduct of the potentially friendly Great Powers: Italy, Britain, France and, of course, Russia.[101] Interestingly, Serbian documents do not indicate a similarly fervent interest on his part in how those Powers – Russia included – might react in the rapidly developing crisis. Christopher Clark, however, writes that, on 24 July, Pašić 'had determined that no decision should be taken until the Russians had made their view known'.[102] This is a massive, yet unsubstantiated claim. For there is actually no evidence that he had done so, and his conversation with Strandtmann in the morning suggests that he was quite independent-minded even on the grave matter of war and peace. Further confirmation for this is provided by Grujić in his memoir, when he states that 'in principle, it had already been decided that not all of the Austro-Hungarian demands could be accepted'.[103] Clark, heavily committed to the opposite interpretation, also writes that Pašić 'cabled Spalajković, asking him to ascertain the views of the Russian government'.[104] But Pašić did nothing of the kind. The telegram which he sent to Spalajković on 24 July contains just these three sentences: 'I announced to the Russian Chargé d'Affaires that I shall submit, tomorrow, Saturday, by six o'clock, the answer to the Austro-

Hungarian ultimatum. I told him that the Serbian Government will request friendly states to protect the independence of Serbia. I added that, if war is inevitable, Serbia will wage it.'[105] In other words, as in his conversation with Strandtmann, Pašić did not even bother to raise the question of the Russian attitude. He was not asking the Russians to inform him, he was *informing them*, the retrospective claims of some modern historians notwithstanding.

It was clear even before the delivery of the ultimatum that, with regard to at least two of the conceivably benevolent Great Powers, Italy and Britain, Serbian diplomacy would be working in vain. Italy's policy during the July Crisis was run entirely by Foreign Minister Antonino di San Giuliano. This Sicilian had apparently warned the German Ambassador, on 10 July, that the Triple Alliance would be dead if Austria-Hungary moved to take the strategic Mount Lovćen in Montenegro, even threatening, in such an eventuality, that Italy would wage war against Austria-Hungary with the help of Serbia and Russia.[106] Around mid-July, however, once he fully realized that the danger of European war had become real, his policy was to urge restraint everywhere – Italy's military weakness pointing it towards neutrality rather than war.[107] Hence when Ljubomir Mihajlović, the Serbian Minister in Rome, saw San Giuliano on 22 July, he was told that Italy could help Serbia 'only diplomatically'. Even though he did not yet know the contents of the much rumoured-about Austro-Hungarian note to Serbia, San Giuliano advised amenability, even 'sacrifices', since the future 'belongs to Serbia' – one had to think, he said, about the history of Piedmont following Orsini's assassination attempt.[108]

From Britain, the Great Power least interested in the Balkan wrangle, Serbia could never expect a great deal. Foreign Secretary Sir Edward Grey, while anxious to secure a peaceful outcome of the Austro-Serbian crisis, had for most of the month of July pursued a policy of 'misplaced confidence in Berlin', believing that Germany would moderate the Austro-Hungarian position.[109] Grey's characterization of the Austro-Hungarian ultimatum ('the most formidable document I had ever seen addressed by one State to another') is of course well known.[110] But to him, as he put it on 20 July to the German Ambassador Prince Lichnowsky, the whole idea that Serbia could drag any of the Great Powers into a war was 'detestable'.[111] On 23 July Mateja Bošković, the Serbian Minister in London, saw Arthur Nicolson, the Permanent Under-Secretary at the Foreign Office, telling him that the Serbian Government was 'most anxious and disquieted'. Nicolson, as yet unacquainted with the contents of the Austro-Hungarian ultimatum, said that it was 'quite impossible to form an opinion', and so Bošković reported to Belgrade on 24 July that he had not been able to obtain any precise indication about the position of the British Government.[112] That night, having seen the ultimatum, Grey informed

Crackanthorpe in Belgrade that Bošković had 'implored' him (presumably through Nicolson) for a clarification of the British attitude, but not wishing to 'undertake responsibility', he could only advise the Serbian Government to give a favourable reply 'on as many points as possible within the limit of time and not to meet Austrian demand with a blank negative'. This, he believed, was 'the only chance' of averting Austrian military action.[113] Pašić, of course, had already reached practically the same judgement.

France's position *vis-à-vis* Serbia during those days offered somewhat more encouragement – notwithstanding the fact that Léon Descos, the French Minister in Belgrade, was nowhere to be seen. On 16 July Baron Giesl could not resist reporting to Vienna, in great detail, about the 'strange behaviour' of his French colleague who had not been seen for months and who had 'hermetically' sealed himself from the rest of the world. The view among many in the Belgrade diplomatic community was, Giesl reported, that Descos was 'insane'. The Austro-Hungarian Minister concluded triumphantly that: 'The Triple Entente is at the moment hardly represented in Belgrade. Mr Hartwig is dead, Mr Descos is reportedly mad, and the English Chargé d'Affaires is sickly and hence indifferent to political events.'[114] On 15 July, in a telegram to Sazonov, Strandtmann likewise commented at some length (as he was also to do in his memoirs) on the curious conduct of the French Minister (who would not answer phone calls or let anyone inside his Legation), noting that Regent Alexander himself had requested Pašić to intervene in France and secure a replacement for Descos.[115] In the meantime, on 23 July, the French President Raymond Poincaré and his Prime (and Foreign) Minister René Viviani had concluded their state visit to the Tsar at St Petersburg and were for the next few days travelling on battleship *France* – in some isolation from the July Crisis. Nevertheless, Pašić was able to glean some valuable information about the French attitude from Spalajković in St Petersburg. On 21 July the diplomatic corps was being presented to Poincaré at the Winter Palace. According to Maurice Paléologue, the French Ambassador, as Poincaré was shaking hands with ministers representing the minor powers, he only stopped to speak to Spalajković.[116] In a brief telegram to Belgrade, Spalajković reported that, when the President had asked him about the news from Serbia, he described the situation to him as 'very serious'. To which Poincaré said: 'We shall help you to improve it.'[117]

Such a statement of support contained nothing concrete, but it contrasted sharply with what must have been perceived in Belgrade as glaring British insouciance. Pašić had several other indications at this time that the French were sympathetic. Thus Milutin Jovanović, the Chargé d'Affaires in Berlin, reported on 24 July that Jules Cambon, the French Ambassador, had placed himself 'completely at our disposal'.[118] On the same day Fotije Stanojević sent a telegram from Bucharest, informing that he and the French Ambassador spent 'the whole day' trying to convince the Romanian Foreign Minister that Serbia's downfall would also be the downfall of Romania, and that Russia would not remain indifferent to Romania's attitude towards Serbia at such a critical time.[119] All of which, however, did not amount to a great deal. On the morning of 25 July Pašić also read a telegram from Milenko Vesnić, the Minister in Paris, which probably confirmed him in his belief that he had taken the right approach. For Vesnić referred to the Under-Secretary at the Quai d'Orsay as saying that Serbia, by swiftly accepting whatever it could in the ultimatum, might gain time and win support among the Great Powers.[120]

The French position was all the more important to Pašić because of the closeness of the Franco-Russian alliance. But how exactly was Russia going to react? The Bosnian annexation crisis had already shown the Serbians that Russia, though friendly, was an unreliable ally. Pašić, for one, was never likely to be starry-eyed about the big Slav brother. In the light of the experience of the Adriatic and Scutari crises in 1913, his lack of confidence in Serbia's supposed protector was well-founded. And it was not just Pašić among the leading Serbs who was wary about the Russians. Miroslav Spalajković, the new Serbian Minister at St Petersburg, 'complained bitterly' in January 1914 that there was little understanding in Russia for Serbian interests.[121] During the momentous days of the July Crisis Spalajković would have ample opportunity to test this assumption.

18

Critical Days in Belgrade

A Note With a Time-Limit: The Controversy

IN 2003 the American historian Richard C. Hall perceptively pointed out that, by themselves, the killings of Archduke Franz Ferdinand and his wife in Sarajevo had 'caused nothing' – that what brought the war about was 'the use made of this event', initially by Austria-Hungary. 'The key event', according to Hall, 'was the delivery of the Austro-Hungarian note to Serbia on 23 July.'[1] Officially, Vienna insisted on calling its note a '*démarche* with a time limit', but everyone else was to designate it as an 'ultimatum' precisely because of the forty-eight hour time limit that accompanied it. In internal discussions, both at the Ballhausplatz and elsewhere, moreover, it was invariably referred to as 'ultimatum'. Not least because of the conciliatory Serbian reply to it, this document was to become perhaps the most notorious in twentieth-century diplomatic history: a document designed to produce, indeed guarantee, a war against Serbia, it also led to a world war. Lord Vansittart, at the time a junior official at the Foreign Office, described the ultimatum as 'a real stinker which left little prospect of independence', and which 'no country with a spark of spirit could accept'.[2] Winston Churchill who, as the First Lord of the Admiralty had attended the British Cabinet meeting on 24 July which discussed the ultimatum, held much the same opinion: 'This note was clearly an ultimatum; but it was an ultimatum such as had never been penned in modern times. As the reading proceeded it seemed absolutely impossible that any State in the world could accept it'.[3] In Italy, the text of the ultimatum was on 24 July read together by Antonio Salandra, the Prime Minister, and San Giuliano, the Foreign Minister. Present, too, was Hans von Flotow, the German Ambassador. 'It is no exaggeration to say that our faces blanched', Salandra recalled. Even Flotow, who had turned 'pale', exclaimed: '*Vraiment! c'ést un peu fort!*'[4] Prince Bülow, the former German Chancellor, declared in 1916 that no land, 'not even the Republic of San Marino', could have accepted the contentious paragraphs of the ultimatum.[5]

The exacting nature of Austria-Hungary's final terms to Serbia are examined below. But could those terms, nonetheless, have been accepted unreservedly by the Government in Belgrade, thus halting Europe's descent into cataclysm? After all it seemed obvious even then, as international tensions grew rapidly following the presentation of the ultimatum on 23 July, that only an unequivocal Serbian acquiescence to its demands could stop the crisis from escalating. However, what was unknown to international opinion at the time, except to very small decision-making circles in Austria-Hungary and Germany, was that the ultimatum which Giesl was to deliver in Belgrade on 23 July was always intended to be a complete farce. Prince Friedrich Stolberg, the Councillor at the German Embassy in Vienna, had in mid-July asked Berchtold what would happen if Serbia accepted all the demands. 'With a smile ... the count had said he felt it most unlikely that even such a government as the Serbian would swallow the ultimatum whole. If, however, they did make up their mind to do it, the only other course, after all its exactions had been fulfilled, would be so to harry and injure Serbia that, in the end, she gave Austria pretext for invading her.'[6] Despite such evidence, some historians, from Albertini to the present day, have pursued what to them is not an academic question of why Serbia had not accepted all the demands in full. And while the ultimatum itself has certainly not been the subject of heated historiographical disputes, views on the evolution of the Serbian response present, if not a controversy as such, then at least very strange dichotomies among historians. Given a century-long academic debate on the origins of the war of 1914, fixated on the question of 'war-guilt', it is now necessary that some background be given here on how contemporaries and historians have treated the matter.

The Serbian Government, whatever its views on the possible European repercussions of the local Balkan ruckus, was at least supremely aware that Serbia could find itself suddenly standing first in the line of fire if it returned to Vienna anything other than a wholly satisfactory reply. Indeed, one account from 1928 by a contemporary on the spot in Belgrade in 1914 (the journalist Dušan Lončarević) suggested that the Serbs had been heading for complete capitulation, when a 'sensational turnabout' occurred in the afternoon hours of 25 July as a result of two telegrams that had arrived from St Petersburg.[7] In 1927 Giesl wrote in his memoirs that until midday on that 25 July it had looked as if the Serbs would give in; in the early afternoon hours, however, he had learnt of a long telegram which had just arrived from the Tsar for King Petar: 'Russia's entire might' had apparently been pledged to Serbia that she might resist the ultimatum; and Crown Prince Alexander, according to Giesl, brought the telegram to the officers' club where it was read to the assembled amid 'stormy demonstrations in favour of the war'.[8] In 1931 Alfred von Wegerer, the editor of *Berliner Monatshefte* and a key academic apologist for the Central Powers, wrote a whole book on the subject: in it, he argued that two telegrams from Russia – one from the Serbian Minister Spalajković, and one from the Tsar – had on 25 July decisively changed the outlook of the Serbian Government which had been about to surrender to the Austro-Hungarian ultimatum.[9] However, Wegerer supplied neither. In 1933 the French historian Jules Isaac assumed that the information arriving from St Petersburg had produced a new attitude in Belgrade – but he was careful not to claim any certainty on the matter.[10] The celebrated authority Luigi Albertini later elaborated on these contentions, arguing that, but for the 'assurances of full support' from St Petersburg, the Serbian reply would have contained 'full formal acceptance of the ultimatum', with a reservation on one point only (point 6) – but a reservation 'so skilfully worded' that it would have made it 'very difficult for Austria to construe it into a rejection'.[11]

'Full support' from St Petersburg? Did Russia, then, start World War One? And did Serbia, by embracing that alleged Russian support on 25 July and by not accepting at least one of the demands in the ultimatum (point 6, referring to the participation of Austro-Hungarian officials in a judicial enquiry on Serbian soil) play a full ancillary role in bringing about the war? These questions go right to the heart of the war guilt issue which has characterized so much of the historiographical discussion on the origins of the First World War. For if Russia had indeed advised the Serbian Government to resist the ultimatum, it must have willed the war.

Of course the converse also applies. But the question of exactly what information the Serbian Government received from St Petersburg after the delivery of the Austro-Hungarian ultimatum at 6 p.m. on Thursday, 23 July – and *before* the expiry of the time limit for Serbia to reply by 6 p.m. on Saturday, 25 July – has not been settled even after a hundred years. In his renowned 1983 study of Russia and the origins of the First World War, Dominic Lieven briefly tackled the subject and mentioned 'Russia's support' (communicated, according to Lieven, on 24 July by Foreign Minister Sazonov to Miroslav Spalajković, the Serbian Minister at St Petersburg) which, Lieven writes, 'came as music to the ears of Pasic and Prince-Regent Alexander'. Lieven even deferentially refers to Albertini's conclusion that Russian promises of support had resulted in the Serbian rejection of Point 6 of the ultimatum.[12] However, following the publication in 1980 of the relevant Serbian documents, the American historian Samuel R. Williamson rejected, in an essay from 1988, the earlier explanations that 'the Russians had acted to stiffen the Serbian will to resist', emphasizing that a 'hard-line position in Belgrade' had predated the ultimatum.[13] In 1995 the British historian Mark Cornwall, utilizing the same Serbian documents and a wealth of additional material, produced by far the most thorough account of Serbia's action and responses during the July Crisis. He addressed the subject of the St Petersburg telegrams head on, concluding that during those crucial forty-eight hours Serbia had 'remained almost isolated' and 'lacked suffi-cient backing even from the Russians'.[14] And yet, already in 1996, in his influential book on the July Crisis, the American historian William Jannen had gone back to the assumptions entertained by Albertini. Jannen sub-mitted that in the afternoon hours of 25 July a telegram from Spalajković, caused the Serbian Government not to agree to all ten demands in the ultimatum ('with minor reservations') and 'risk a firmer reply' instead.[15]

The bewildering discrepancies between various accounts of the Serbian reply to the Austro-Hungarian ultimatum have continued to this day. The Albertini school is certainly still very strong. In 2012 Christopher Clark essentially dismissed Mark Cornwall's research and relied on Albertini instead. 'It was probably the news from Russia', Clark writes, 'that dispelled the mood of fatalism in Belgrade and dissuaded the ministers from attempting to avoid war by acquiescing in the demands of the ultimatum.'[16] And in 2013, Margaret MacMillan wrote that a report had reached Belgrade on 25 July that Russia's key ministers and the Tsar had decided 'to go to the limit in defense of Serbia', and that this 'may well have encouraged' the Serbian Government as it formulated its final reply to the ultimatum.[17] In his book on the July Crisis, likewise from 2013, Sean McMeekin similarly writes that sometime in the afternoon of 25 July a new attitude had been formed in Belgrade – following the arrival of a telegram from Spalajković in which Sazonov had advised Pašić not to accept points 5 and 6 and that 'Serbia may count on Russian aid'.[18] In her 2014 study of the July Crisis, Annika Mombauer drew attention to Sazonov's view, expressed to Spalajković on 24 July, that no state could accept the points in the ultimatum 'without committing suicide'. While careful to emphasize that no blank cheque had been given by Russia to Serbia, Mombauer nevertheless writes: 'This counsel was fatal, for it implied an encouragement of Serbia not to accept all the Austrian terms, and to risk a war.'[19] In his updated, massive work on Austria-Hungary in World War One, Austria's leading authority Manfried Rauchensteiner repeated in 2013 the point he had already made in 1993: that the Serbian Government, in rejecting point 6 of the ultimatum, was 'confident of Russia's support'.[20]

On the other hand, three other experts who in 2014 published detailed books on the July Crisis have remained sceptical about such claims. Gerd Krumeich has explicitly rejected Clark's arguments, declaring himself a follower of Mark Cornwall's 'impressively clear analysis'.[21] T.G. Otte has remarked that Sazonov's advice to the Serbs 'appeared anything but hard-line', and that he did not wish Serbia 'to complicate matters by taking a provocative stance'.[22] Finally, Gordon Martel has argued that Russia, France and Britain had all urged the Serbs to go for maximum accommodation: 'No one promised military assistance.' Martel also pointed out that the British and French representatives in Belgrade both thought that 'Russia had been instrumental in convincing the Serbs to reply in such a conciliatory manner'.[23]

Clearly, then, a massive divergence of opinion still exists about what is arguably the most important single episode in the whole of the July Crisis. How so? Are the Serbian (and Russian) sources really so ambiguous as to allow of diametrically opposed interpretations? As will be shown below, the available evidence actually makes it abundantly clear that, far from encouraging the Serbian Government to defy any points in the Austro-Hungarian ultimatum, the information from St Petersburg which reached Belgrade on 25 July, before the expiry of the ultimatum, actually had the opposite effect, demonstrating to the Serbs that concrete Russian support for them was conspicuous only by its absence. The recently published memoirs of Vasily Strandtmann, the Russian Chargé d'Affaires in Belgrade, confirm that Russia had in fact engaged in a moderating effort. And although there is no final clarity as to the arrival time of one particular telegram from Spalajković, it will be seen from long-neglected Serbian evidence that the drafting of Serbia's reply to the ultimatum was in any case completed at around 11 a.m. on Saturday, 25 July. That is to say, contrary to the suggestions of numerous historians, there were in reality no further interventions that afternoon, i.e., before the expiry of the deadline at 6 p.m.

Miroslav Spalajković and the Crisis of 23-25 July

What information, then, about the likely conduct of Russia did Belgrade receive during the pivotal forty-eight hours, 23-25 July 1914? A central figure in the historiography of these famous days in the July Crisis, perhaps undeservedly, became Miroslav Spalajković, the Serbian Minister in St Petersburg. There are several reasons for Spalajković's fame or, rather, his infamy. In the first place, his unquestionably combative nature was always going to ruffle feathers and attract comment. In July 1914 even Sazonov reportedly thought of Spalajković as 'unbalanced [*déséquilibré*]'.[24] A few years later, with Spalajković still serving as the Serbian Minister in Russia, Lenin was to remark on his 'brutality of expression'. For in January 1918, at a meeting with Lenin and his associates, Spalajković produced a 'veritable tirade of accusation', calling them 'bandits' and announcing that 'he was spitting in their faces'.[25]

Secondly, Spalajković's notoriety was further guaranteed when Albertini reinforced the mystery (created initially in Germany by the aforementioned Wegerer) of a 'missing telegram' from him, which supposedly arrived in Belgrade in the afternoon of 25 July, and which allegedly contained Russia's recommendation to Serbia to reject points 5 and 6 of the ultimatum, coupled with the promise that Russia would vigorously support and defend Serbia.[26] As will be seen below, this reconstruction of events finds adherents even today. And, thirdly, Spalajković has been seen as an ardent, at times reckless, Serbian ultra-nationalist – mostly by post-war Austrian and German academics making the case for the Central Powers, and subsequently by the like-minded Anglo-Saxon 'new revisionists' of today. They were never able to forgive him, *inter alia*, for the highly effective role he had played during the Friedjung process in exposing the Austro-Hungarian forgeries. The fact that Spalajković was the son-in-law of Gligorije Jeftanović, the Bosnian Serb grandee from Sarajevo, is also taken as proof of his ultra-nationalism – notwithstanding the fact, pointed out in chapter nine, that Jeftanović and his political circle were quite happy to cooperate with the imperial Austro-Hungarian authorities in Bosnia-Herzegovina. In 1935 Alfred Rappaport von Arbengau wrote a long, malicious article for *Berliner Monatshefte*, devoted entirely to Spalajković.[27] Christopher Clarke has recently described Spalajković as the 'excitable Austrophobe'.[28]

It seems, however, that such adverse assessments of Spalajković have been exaggerated. Robert Seton-Watson wrote admiringly about him in 1911, commenting, in particular, on his self-restraint at the Friedjung trial.[29] Anatole Nekludov, Spalajković's Russian colleague when they were serving in Sofia, thought that his Serbian nationalism was tempered by sensitivity to wider Slavic solidarity.[30] And as for his bellicosity, even Count Friedrich Szápáry, the Austro-Hungarian Ambassador to St Petersburg, remarked that Spalajković appeared 'crestfallen' when Austria-Hungary declared war on Serbia.[31]

Be that as it may, Spalajković's role in the July Crisis has unfortunately been over-coloured by frequent references to his vibrant persona. Historically far more relevant, however, are the telegrams which he sent in the critical forty-eight hours following the ultimatum. It will be contended here that they have been invested with an importance out of all proportion to any impact they may have had. It will be further contended that they are in a sense more significant for what they omitted to say than for what they actually passed on.

What, then, had Spalajković been reporting from St Petersburg? There was an air of routine business about the dispatches he had sent to Belgrade just before the storm unleashed by the delivery of the Austro-Hungarian ultimatum in the early evening of 23 July. He had briefly notified Belgrade on 22 July that, since Sazonov was busy with the French President's visit, the contents of Pašić's circular telegram of 18 July had been sent to him in a letter.[32] The next telegram, sent on 23 July was similarly terse. It stated that the Russian Foreign Ministry had had no news from either Vienna or Belgrade, and that there had been no talk of an ultimatum. In the concluding sentence, Spalajković informed that Szápáry, who had recently returned from Vienna, had personally told him that there, in the Austrian capital, the relations with Serbia were being viewed 'with calm'.[33]

Of course, by the time this telegram had reached Belgrade, at 12:40 p.m. on 24 July, following the presentation of the ultimatum the day before, the Serbian Government had taken precisely the opposite view of the state of its relations with Austria-Hungary. Nevertheless, amid the turmoil in Belgrade, Pašić, the hardened political veteran, kept his nerve. He also kept his determination not to compromise Serbia's independence. It was seen in the preceding chapter that he had returned to Belgrade that morning and had been to see Strandtmann, whom he had told in no uncertain terms that, if necessary, Serbia would fight – whatever the Tsar might say. On the same day, Pašić asked Crackanthorpe to convey to London his hope that the British Government would work to moderate the Austrian demands, whilst adding that some of them were 'quite unacceptable'.[34] He then let the Serbian Legation in London know that he had spoken to the English Chargé d'Affaires, and concluded: 'I did not hide my concern about the events that might unfold.'[35]

Meanwhile, in St Petersburg, Spalajković had towards noon on the 24th received from the Foreign Ministry in Belgrade the full text (in French) of the Austro-Hungarian ultimatum. In 1934 he was to write a memoir of that day for a lecture delivered at the Société d'Histoire Générale et d'Histoire Diplomatique in Paris, subsequently published in *Revue d'Histoire Diplomatique*. In it, Spalajković writes that after 'the first moments of consternation' had passed, he telephoned the Russian Foreign Ministry, asking for an urgent meeting with Foreign Minister Sazonov. The meeting, according to Spalajković, was agreed for 4 p.m. at the Ministry, and he recalls arriving there shortly before the appointed hour.[36] However, it is most unlikely that he was able to see the Russian Foreign Minister at around that time: Sazonov had in the morning already talked to Szápáry who had shown him the note his country had presented to Serbia; he had then had luncheon at the French Embassy with the French and British Ambassadors to discuss the crisis; and afterwards attended the Russian Ministerial Council, which had been hastily convened for the same reason, starting at 3 p.m. Count Friedrich Pourtalès, the German Ambassador to St Petersburg, informed Berlin that the Ministerial Council session was still in progress at 5 p.m.[37] According to the official diary of the Russian Foreign Ministry for 24 July, Spalajković had an interview with Sazonov after the Ministerial Council had ended but before the arrival of Pourtalès, who was received around 7 p.m.[38]

The meeting of the Russian Ministerial Council on 24 July 1914, in response to the Austro-Serbian tension, is a famous benchmark in the history of the July Crisis, for it decided in principle (pending the Tsar's approval) to mobilize four Russian military districts as well as the Baltic and Black Sea fleets. As regards Serbia, the Council approved two proposals by Sazonov: '(1) In conjunction with the other Powers to request Austria to prolong the period which she had fixed for the receipt of a reply from

Serbia in order to afford the Powers time in which to acquaint themselves, in accordance with the proposal of Austria herself, with the results of the judicial enquiry into the Serajevo assassination; and (2) to advise Serbia not to enter into hostilities with Austro-Hungarian troops, but, withdrawing her own forces, to request the Powers to compose the quarrel that had arisen.' The diary of the Russian Foreign Ministry notes briefly that Sazonov, in his ensuing interview with Spalajković, had 'advised extreme moderation in respect of the Serbian reply to the Austrian note'.[39]

Sazonov's memoirs also make only brief mention of his talk with Spalajković. The latter was told that his Government 'should accept the Austrian demands, save those concerning the sovereign rights of Serbia'. Sazonov wrote that he had offered this advice 'from a practical point of view'.[40] He was clearly alluding to the idea that Serbia, and the Great Powers, might be able to gain time were there to be a conciliatory Serbian reply. As has been seen, Pašić had already received much the same advice from the Quay d'Orsay, and Grey had communicated to Crackanthorpe in Belgrade a similar suggestion that Serbia's only chance of averting Austrian military action was to accept as many demands as possible. In other words, all three Entente Powers viewed the question in essentially identical manner: that Serbia should comply to the last possible limit of concession. Their recommended tactical scenario – offering maximum concession in order to buy time – did not differ from the one envisaged by Pašić.

But the Sazonov-Spalajković meeting had lasted for about one hour.[41] What else had been said? Had Sazonov, contrary to his own and the official Russian Foreign Ministry's record, perhaps whispered words of encouragement to Spalajković, promising mother Russia's military support to little Slavic Serbia – as writers from Wegerer and Albertini to, more recently, Clark and McMeekin, have been more or less suggesting? Not according to Spalajković's recollections from 1934. After he and Sazonov had considered the various points raised in the Austro-Hungarian ultimatum, the Russian Foreign Minister said that it contained some clauses which a sovereign state could hardly accept 'without risking suicide'. But he then proposed that they should treat the matter as 'wise and practical people', following this up by asking: 'What should be our objective?' To which he himself answered: 'Avoiding the worst, which is war. Therefore one ought to accept as much as possible of what Austria demands.' Sazonov then went on to praise Pašić's wisdom, saying how certain he was that Pašić would be able to do the 'impossible', that he would 'even find the means not to refuse anything'. Pašić alone, Sazonov said, 'could make sacrifices which, probably, no one else would dare contemplate'.[42]

Sazonov, in other words, was more than hinting at the desirability of Serbia considering complete capitulation in its reply to the ultimatum. When Spalajković put it to him that 'the key to the solution' did not lie 'there' (i.e., in how Pašić would handle the matter), Sazonov agreed that whatever the Serbian response to the ultimatum, it would not be of 'capital importance' in the whole affair. This sounds strange in the light of the emphasis by Sazonov on the need for Serbia to make sacrifices in its response to the ultimatum. It will be explained below, however, that the Russian Foreign Minister was urging Serbia to adopt a submissive attitude only as the initial gambit in a desperately tight framework when time was of the essence.

Not everything is clear in Spalajković's account from 1934. Sazonov added, according to Spalajković, that he would immediately ask Nikolai Shebeko, Russia's Ambassador to Vienna, to demand a prolongation of the forty-eight hour limit for the Serbian reply.[43] But Shebeko was at that time on his way to St Petersburg and Sazonov must have known that – the Russian Embassy in Vienna was in Shebeko's absence being run by Prince Nikolai Kudashev, the Chargé d'Affaires.[44] Moreover, as has been seen, the Russian Ministerial Council had just taken the decision to seek a prolongation of the time-limit for the Serbian response – Sazonov, presumably, would have informed Spalajković of this development. There is a further oddity in Spalajković's 1934 memoir. He writes about how he had suggested to Sazonov that, for there to exist the slightest hope of averting war, Germany had to understand that the conflict could not be localised to Austria-Hungary and Serbia. And so he recommended that Russia should mobilize in those districts adjoining the border with Austria-Hungary. Sazonov, according to Spalajković, replied that he would talk to the Tsar.[45] Again, the Russian Ministerial Council had only a little while earlier decided in principle on such a mobilization. It is not inconceivable, on the other hand, that Sazonov deliberately withheld this information so as not to unduly encourage Spalajković who, as he knew, was about to report to Pašić.

It is of course also possible that Spalajković's memory, twenty years after the event, had left something to be desired. Be that as it may, the next section in his 1934 memoir contains undoubtedly authentic utterances from Sazonov because, as will be seen, the Serbian Minister would later that night pass on to Belgrade substantially the same information. Sazonov, aware that Spalajković's report from St Petersburg had to reach Pašić at the latest by midday the next day, 25 July, 'envisaged the eventuality of an Austro-Hungarian declaration of war on Serbia'. In such a case, he advised 'abstaining completely from any defence, any fight, any resistance.' He asked: 'What is the point?' Serbia, he thought, had been exhausted by the two Balkan Wars and could not defend itself without arms, ammunition and equipment. So, his advice was that Serbia, instead of resisting, make an appeal to all the nations, 'even Japan', that a small country numbering four million, attacked by a Great Power of over fifty million, desists to defend itself in such an unequal battle, and takes humanity as the witness of its martyrdom. 'And the world', Sazonov added, 'will soon revolt against the infamy of Austria-Hungary.' He then explained the practical aspect of his advice: 'Whilst, if no blood is being spilled, if Serbia does not resist, one gains time, one continues to negotiate, and finally, we'll see.'

Clearly, then, Sazonov had for his guidance to the Serbs conceived of two scenarios, both of which were all about gaining time. The first was to urge that Pašić should make sacrifices when responding to the ultimatum: that he do the 'impossible' and even find ways 'not to refuse anything'. Thus, unlike France and Britain, Russia was actually recommending complete surrender. Sazonov, however, had anticipated that not even such an abject submission would necessarily deter Vienna from launching war. His remark to Spalajković that the Serbian response would not be of 'capital importance' reflects his own scepticism on the matter, that is, his conviction that Austria-Hungary was determined on war. He had therefore thought a step further, prognosticating a second scenario (in effect a continuation of the first) whereby Austria-Hungary indeed declared war, in which event he begged Serbia not to resist but appeal to the Powers instead. Spalajković's comment is perhaps worth noting: 'Paradoxical as his thoughts may seem to us today, Sazonov was no less confident in July 1914 that, to get the most, Serbia had to momentarily renounce everything, and that through its imminent declaration of war, Austria-Hungary would offer Serbia a way to recover from this paradox.'[46]

Spalajković, however, was less than impressed by Sazonov's advice to Serbia not to oppose an attack. 'Mr Pašić', he told Sazonov, 'can do every-thing, even the impossible, except one thing ... I know him as well as I know myself and we both know our people. All defeatism is repugnant to the Serbian soul. How can you advise the most heroic among peoples a non-resistance which will be seen everywhere as an abdication of its honour, its independence, its glory? Anything, anything, even death, but not that! A people which does not defend itself hardly deserves that other peoples come to its aid.' Before he left Sazonov, Spalajković also reproached him by reminding him about the promise that had been made to Pašić to deliver much-needed Russian rifles to the Serbian Army. 'I did not wish to do it up to now', Sazonov replied revealingly, 'so that Russia could not be accused of arming Serbia against Austria.'[47]

Spalajković sent Pašić his report about the meeting with Sazonov in a telegram at midnight, 24/25 July. But this was only the first part of the telegram, the second part being sent at 1 a.m. on 25 July. The first part arrived in Belgrade at 4:17 in the morning of 25 July, and the second later that morning at 10. Thus both parts could be considered by the Serbian Government before the expiry of Vienna's deadline at 6 p.m.[48] The first part of Spalajković's telegram reads as follows:

The Russian Minister for Foreign Affairs condemns, with loathing, the Austro-Hungarian ultimatum. He tells me: there are demands within it which no state can accept without committing suicide. Report: we can undoubtedly count on Russia's support, but as yet he did not make himself clear in what shape that support will manifest itself, since the Tsar will have to decide on that and France will have to be asked; he has taken energetic steps in Vienna and Berlin. He has received a telegram from the Chargé d'Affaires in Belgrade that chaos has taken over there and that Serbia, for lack of weapons and ammunition, was not in a position to defend itself. If that is so, the Russian Minister for Foreign Affairs is giving this advice: to announce, immediately, to all the states that Serbia had condemned, with loathing, the crime in Sarajevo and it had been prepared to deliver to the Court any of its subjects about whom it had been proved that he had been a participant; the Serbian Government categorically rejects all the charges which stipulate that Serbia is responsible for that crime; towards Austria-Hungary, Serbia had loyally carried out all its obligations; and, generally, through its loyal conduct Serbia had in the last years won general recognition on all questions.

The second part of the telegram continued thus:

Hence Serbia is directing an appeal at the feeling of justice and humanity, declaring that it will not, and cannot, defend itself by arms against a Great Power like Austria-Hungary, which is eleven times the size of small Serbia. Accordingly, the Russian Minister for Foreign Affairs is advising us provisionally: if you cannot defend yourselves, then act like the Bulgarians did last year. That would cause the indignation of all the peoples against A.-Hungary. He has, to that effect, telegraphed the Chargé d'Affaires in Belgrade. I told him that his advice would be practical if we had the assurance that Austria-Hungary would invade only the border areas, but we cannot allow Austria-Hungary to devastate the whole of our country, and we would have to organize the defence somewhere in the interior and accept the fight. The Minister for Foreign Affairs replied to me that our decision has to depend on our defence capability, and we could transport the money and the rest to Greece, and retreat with the Army towards Greece. He has also telegraphed to Bucharest, for Romania's role will be of great significance. I said to the Minister: the only method of preventing war is for Russia to declare to Austria-Hungary and Germany that it will be forced to declare general mobilization should the Serbo-Austrian conflict not be submitted, as in 1909, for the deliberation of the Great Powers, as the declaration of the Serbian Government at the time was the work of the Great Powers which retain the exclusive right to assess whether or not Serbia had fulfilled its obligations from that declaration. This matter will be solved in the evening, and a communiqué will be issued. Spalajković[49]

The telegram makes no mention of the 24 July meeting and decisions of the Russian Ministerial Council, but it is an open question here as to how much, if anything at all, Sazonov had told Spalajković about the meeting from which he had just emerged. More strangely, perhaps, not a word was written here about Sazonov's urgings that Pašić do the 'impossible' and accommodate the Austro-Hungarian ultimatum – something which Spalajković himself admitted in his 1934 memoir that Sazonov had implored. Yet it would be difficult to argue that Spalajković was deliberately hiding anything from Pašić, or that he had contrived to present a picture rosier than the reality. For the telegram to Belgrade contained not a single greatly encouraging piece of news from St Petersburg. Spalajković did inform that Serbia could 'undoubtedly' count on Russian support, but he added that Sazonov had been unable to specify the nature of that support. And this, in conjunction with the mention of Sazonov's talk about taking 'energetic steps' in Vienna and Berlin, was just about the only moderately buoyant piece of news that Pašić could glean from Spalajković's telegram – not an altogether reassuring message.

Moreover, Sazonov's suggestion that Serbia's treasure should be sent to Greece, and that the Serbian Army should also be withdrawing towards Greece, could only be interpreted as a sure indication that Russia was not about to spring to Serbia's military defence. Sazonov's words, as reported by Spalajković, that Serbia should consider whether to fight in the light of its 'defence capability' carried the meaning that Serbia should not include Russia in any such calculation. As Mark Cornwall has argued, 'the implication was that, although Russia was working on Serbia's behalf, for the present the latter would be alone in its conflict with the Austrians'.[50]

Pašić wrote a short minute at the bottom of this telegram: 'Have taken note with gratitude.' But his gratitude could only have related to reading that Sazonov had assessed the ultimatum as containing demands which no state could accept without committing suicide. The Serbian Prime Minister could thus feel justified and confirmed in the course he had taken from the start: there would be no complete surrender to the ultimatum. Little did he know, owing to Spalajković's impressionistic telegram, that Sazonov had in fact recommended precisely such a suicide, i.e., that Pašić should fashion a way 'not to refuse anything'.

There followed a further, much shorter telegram from Spalajković, sent at 1.40 a.m. on 25 July, which may or may not have arrived in the course of the morning. Vladimir Dedijer and Života Anić, the editors of the relevant tome of Serbian documents, pointed out that the two-part telegram from St Petersburg was the only one to have arrived in Belgrade on 25 July before the expiry of the Austro-Hungarian deadline.[51] Mark Cornwall disagrees – according to him, the next telegram arrived at 11:30 a.m. on 25 July.[52] Be that as it may, this telegram should also be cited in full:

> The Russian Minister for Foreign Affairs told the Austro-Hungarian Ambassador that all of this represents a threat in the highest degree. The

general opinion is that Serbia cannot accept the demands of Austria-Hungary. The Ministerial Council has resolved to take energetic measures, even a mobilization. The Tsar's sanction is expected. An official communiqué will now be published, by which Russia is taking Serbia under protection. Spalajković[53]

As is well known, during the morning of 25 July there indeed took place another session of the Russian Ministerial Council, at Tsarskoe Selo, presided over by the Tsar. This meeting 'approved and further developed' the decisions of the Ministerial Council from the previous evening.[54] At long last, Spalajković had passed on to Belgrade that something was moving, or was about to move, at the highest levels in St Petersburg. But did this telegram, assuming that it had indeed reached Belgrade at 11:30 a.m. on 25 July, along with the two-part telegram which had indisputably arrived in the morning of 25 July, actually make any difference to Pašić and his colleagues as they were polishing off the Serbian reply to the ultimatum?

In the first place, it will be shown below that the drafting of the Serbian reply had in all probability already been completed around 11 a.m. – and undergone no subsequent addition or alteration. And secondly, the evidence from contemporaries, such as it is, also suggests that Belgrade had acted independently. Already in 1925 Robert Seton-Watson had 'learnt on first-hand authority at Belgrade' that the Serbian answer to the Austro-Hungarian ultimatum was 'the unaided work of the Belgrade Government'.[55] Also in 1925, Ljuba Jovanović told Hamilton Fish Armstrong of *Foreign Affairs* that it had been 'prepared entirely without communication with the Powers'.[56] The academic opinion, as has been seen, is mixed, but Mark Cornwall, the leading authority on the subject, is also on the whole convinced that the Serbian Government had behaved autonomously on that fateful 25 July. He considers that the 'messages from St Petersburg by midday on 25 July were still imprecise'. Sazonov's language, he writes, was 'too vague'. He maintains that, even taking into account the telegram hinting at Russian mobilization, 'it seems highly unlikely that ... Pašić was suddenly moved to stiffen the terms of the Serbian reply'. Cornwall concludes that it is 'quite probable ... that Russian advice had little effect on the framing of Serbia's note'.[57]

The 'Missing Telegram' from St Petersburg

Where, then, is Spalajković's 'suppressed' telegram from St Petersburg, speculated about and made famous by Luigi Albertini?[58] Where is the evidence on which Christopher Clark bases his musings that 'the steady crescendo of indications in Spalajković's cables must have sufficed to reassure the Serbian leadership that the Russians were on the track to intervene'?[59] And just where does Sean McMeekin find support for what he calls

'Sazonov's pledge' and 'Russian backing' – referring to an alleged report from Spalajković in which Sazonov had advised Pašić 'not to accept points 5 and 6'?[60] All these are major, indeed massive claims, for they depict the Serbian reply to the ultimatum as a last-minute modification of what is alleged to have previously been a draft note offering complete capitulation. The drift of their logic points to the conclusion that war broke out in 1914 because Russia had decisively encouraged Serbia not to accept the ulti-matum *in toto*. Such contentions, therefore, require to be addressed and examined, especially because, as will be shown, they stem from a fantastic concoction. And whereas Clark and McMeekin have only recently appeared with their contributions to the subject, Albertini has over many decades barely been challenged.

This book has already drawn attention to some problematic interpre-tations and claims advanced by Albertini, a journalist who had made his career with the Milan newspaper *Corriere della Sera*. Perhaps the most prob-lematic of all is his analysis of what took place in Belgrade on 23-25 July 1914. Here, Albertini relied heavily on what his friend and fellow Italian journalist Luciano Magrini had written after the war. In the autumn of 1915 Magrini was in Serbia as a journalist, joining the Serbian Army on its retreat south in October. His 1929 book on the origins of the war, *Il drama di Seraievo*, is especially interesting because it describes the events in Belgrade following the reception of the Austro-Hungarian ultimatum on 23 July. Magrini writes that in 1915 he obtained details about that period from Colonel Živko Pavlović, whose function in the Serbian Army in July 1914 he gives as 'Chief of Staff [*capo dello stato maggiore*]'. His account, certainly, makes for some arresting reading.

According to Magrini, the Serbian Government held a meeting on the evening of 23 July, presided over by Regent Alexander, and 'in the presence of Colonel Pavlović' as Chief of Staff. Everybody realized that 'if the Austrian note were not accepted in full, war would follow'. Pavlović too, along with the Ministers, was in favour of full acceptance of the ultimatum 'to avoid the worst' – so claims Magrini. But no decision was taken, not only because Pašić was absent, but also because the governments in London, Paris and St Petersburg would have to be consulted – 'especially the latter'. When Pašić returned the following day, a new cabinet meeting was held. 'The opinions were not different', Magrini writes, 'from those of the previous evening. The Chief of Staff categorically repeated that Serbia was not able to sustain an Austrian offensive.'[61]

There now follows the crucial part of Magrini's story: 'But in the after-noon [of 24 July] came a telegram from Spalajković, stating that Sazonov had told him that he considered the Austrian ultimatum unacceptable in its totality, and that Serbia, to demonstrate goodwill, should accept those parts which it considered compatible with its independence, but that if she wished to preserve its honour, she had to reject those impositions such as clauses 5 and 6, damaging the sovereign rights of Serbia. Russia could not remain indifferent to an Austrian attack against Slav interests and, taking up the Serb cause, would vigorously support and defend legitimate Serb interests.'[62]

A very excited Luigi Albertini makes a great deal in his book out of Magrini's startling revelations, citing large chunks of what his friend had written on this subject. 'The existence of this telegram from Spalaikovic', Albertini opines, 'vouched for by Colonel Pavlović, is not proved by the Serbian documents which have been made public, but that does not mean anything, because the Serbian diplomatic documernts of the period have never been published in full. This may well be due to the unwillingness of the Serbian Government to confess that Serbia would have accepted the ultimatum unconditionally if Russia had not advised her otherwise.' And more: 'This telegram proves that the Serbian Government had suppressed certain communications from its St Petersburg representative.'[63]

Not many people read Magrini these days, but Albertini's work on the origins of the war of 1914 is still seen as one of the most authoritative studies. Indeed, Christopher Clark's recent book directs its readers to Albertini's account of the impact of the telegrams from Russia, but it also – 'specifically on Sazonov's rejection of points 5 and 6 of the ultimatum' – cites page 206 of Magrini's work – the page which contains the story about the arrival of Spalajković's dramatic telegram in the afternoon of 24 July.[64] In his book on the July Crisis, Sean McMeekin wonders about the reasons why 'Serbia's prime minister decided not to comply with the Austrian ultimatum' and suggests an explanation whereby 'Pašić resolved to take a firmer line after reading Spalaiković's report from Petersburg, in which Sazonov had advised him not to accept points 5 and 6'.[65] Elsewhere in his book McMeekin insists on this explanation. 'Sazonov's advice was firm', he writes, Serbia must not 'accept articles 5 and 6'. Sazonov, according to McMeekin, sent a 'clear' message to Belgrade: 'Serbia should make a show of moderation but not yield. If it came to war, Russia would fight on her behalf.' The authority cited by McMeekin for these rather brave assertions is Albertini.[66]

And Albertini, as has been seen, had constructed his own relevant passages on the basis of what his friend Magrini had written. Yet despite a fanfare lasting many decades, the famous St Petersburg telegram of 24 July has stubbornly refused to surface – for in reality it never existed. Whereas Albertini could, at the time of writing his work, legitimately complain about the non-publication of relevant Serbian documents, later generations of historians have had every opportunity to look at them, as they were published in 1980. However, instead of then questioning the Magrini-Albertini thesis, as those documents seem to demand, these historians have actually lent it further support. Yet it can now be demonstrated in any case that the entire basis upon which Magrini, then Albertini, and now their modern followers, pronounced judgement on Serbia's reply to the ultimatum is a spurious one: a pure concoction. The latter concerns the whereabouts at key times of Colonel Živko Pavlović – the indispensable figure in Magrini's narrative.

Colonel Pavlović was not, as Magrini stated, the Serbian 'Chief of Staff'. He was the head of the operations section of the Serbian General Staff. As such, he was the first assistant to *Vojvoda* (Field Marshal) Radomir Putnik, who was the Chief of the General Staff. But that is not the problem – the problem is that Pavlović was not even in Belgrade at the time when Magrini makes him not just a witness, but also a player with a role in the deliberations of the Serbian Government which were held in Belgrade on 23-24 July. Yet Pavlović had been staying in Bad Reichenhall, Bavaria. Just like his boss Putnik, who had since late June been in Bad Gleichenberg, Styria, Pavlović was taking a cure at a time when July's major European events were taking place. A three-page letter by Pavlović, deposited in the archive of the Serbian Academy in Belgrade, reveals his exact movements. He wrote it in July 1931 to his friend Dušan Stefanović who had been the War Minister in 1914. Pavlović had already left Belgrade for Bad Reichenhall with his wife and son at the end of May. After the assassination in Sarajevo, feeling 'very uncomfortable' in the German environment and sensing that serious events were about to take place, he decided to cut short his stay and set off for Belgrade, which he reached via Salzburg and Zagreb towards midnight on 24 July (he writes: 'around 23:30').

In other words, Magrini's chief source Colonel Pavlović was actually travelling on a series of trains through Austria-Hungary at the time of his supposed personal involvement in the Belgrade conferences of the Serbian Government on 23 and 24 July. Concerning the ultimatum, Pavlović wrote that he had not had 'the foggiest idea' about it, and had learnt of it only after his return to Belgrade late on 24 July. On the next day, 25 July, he reported to Colonel Dušan Pešić at the General Staff where he found 'a terrible hubbub' as the General Staff were moving to Kragujevac. Nowhere in his letter does Pavlović hint that he may have been, even on 25 July, in any way consulted by the Serbian Government.[67] This is important to emphasize, because Albertini, in an obsessive attempt to prove the existence of a game-changing telegram from St Petersburg was forced to change the arrival day of this supposed telegram – from 24 July as cited by Magrini, to the following day, 25 July. Hence he wrote: 'Pavlović's statement that the telegram which changed the whole situation arrived on the afternoon of the 24th is evidently due to a slip of memory which has led him to confuse the 24th with the 25th.'[68] Of course, Albertini had to say this. Unlike Magrini, he knew his history and realized that Belgrade could not possibly have received such a telegram on the afternoon of 24 July since that day the Russian Ministerial Council had been in session until the evening. Even so, Albertini's retrospective change of date would still presuppose Pavlović's presence in the Foreign Ministry on 25 July – something which, if true, Pavlović would surely have mentioned in his detailed letter. Whereas Pavlović merely stated in that letter that on 25 July he had been called to the War Ministry by Minister Stefanović and confirmed in his position as head of the operations section.[69] Stefanović's own account makes it clear that this meeting took place as late as 9 p.m.[70] And given that Magrini has Pavlović allegedly participating in the earlier ministerial deliberations of 23 July – a claim Albertini does not question – the whole story, even when modified by the later change of date, is simply unsustainable because its chief protagonist Pavlović, despite being cited as the source, had clearly had nothing to do with it.

The accounts by Albertini and Magrini are thus baseless and fallacious. The more recent ones (Clark, McMeekin), relying on those two Italians, should now also be dismissed in the light of the available evidence. There is a telling little intervention by Albertini who demotes Pavlović to 'acting' Chief of Staff, whereas Magrini had promoted him to 'Chief of Staff'.[71] Even this correction by Albertini, incidentally, is false: in the absence of *Vojvoda* Putnik, his deputy, i.e., the acting Chief of Staff, was actually Colonel Dušan Pešić.[72] But Albertini, who had otherwise interviewed a great many participants of the events leading up to the outbreak of the war, had never interviewed Pavlović who was still alive in 1938.[73] Magrini may or may not have talked to Pavlović in 1915, but he certainly could not have heard from the latter's lips the sort of information which he subsequently put in his book.[74] It would be fruitless to wonder why he wrote his tale. Perhaps a more appropriate question to ask might be why some historians today still refer to a telegram which has never been seen and, in the light of published materials, is highly unlikely ever to have been sent.

25 July 1914: Morning or Afternoon?

Important circumstantial evidence – hitherto neglected – actually exists about the impact of at least some of the information from Spalajković in St Petersburg reaching Belgrade on the morning of 25 July. It is contained in the brief 1926 memoir of Jovan Nestorović, the editor of *Samouprava*. As this paper was the mouthpiece of Pašić's Radical Party, Nestorović was in daily touch with its leaders. He saw Pašić on the evening of Friday, 24 July, when the latter asked him to write an article for *Samouprava* in which the main message should be that 'Serbia will meet all the justified demands of its northern neighbour, but that there also exist in the submitted note such demands which infringe sovereign Serbia as an independent state'. Nestorović dutifully carried out this 'order', as he called it, and submitted the article to Pašić sometime that night. The piece was meant to appear the following day, Saturday, 25 July. Pašić read it and, though satisfied, asked Nestorović to bring him the article again in the morning – newspapers in Belgrade, it should be noted, appeared in the afternoon hours, so that Pašić would still have the time on the morning of 25 July to ask for revisions. Indeed, Nestorović thought to himself: 'He still hasn't made up his mind!'

At 'around' 10 a.m. on Saturday, 25 July, Nestorović arrived at the Foreign Ministry with the article, now already typeset. But Pašić was in a ministerial session, so Nestorović sent him the article via an employee at the Ministry. After 'several minutes' he was summoned inside and Pašić told him: 'Run just this first part, and cut the rest.' The first part, as Nestorović recalled, was only about a third of the original article and referred to Serbia's readiness to meet all the justified demands of Austria-Hungary. The rest, about Serbia's reservations with regard to the demands infringing its sovereignty, had been censored by Pašić. Nestorović unfortunately does not specify those reservations, but judging by his reaction to the fact that they had now been struck from his article one can safely assume that they were numerous. 'We have had it', he thought to himself, his knees trembling. 'With desperation in my heart', he recalled, 'I carried out the order.'[75]

He need not have worried, however, that Pašić was about to capitulate. Nevertheless, later in the day the *Samouprava* carried the truncated article on its front page under the title 'Serious Moments'. After introductory remarks about the delivery of the ultimatum, it stated:

> Serbia's Minister for Foreign Affairs has on several occasions already expressed his and his government colleagues' view that Serbia, in the name of its great and important interests, desires sincere and correct neighbourly relations with the Austro-Hungarian Monarchy. Permeated sincerely by this desire and the conviction about the necessity of such relations, the Government of the Kingdom of Serbia will compliantly meet all those demands of the Austro-Hungarian Government which aim at the elimination of criminal and disorderly acts in the neighbouring countries, because it sees this as the obligatory fulfilment of duty for any civilized state. Today, the Government of the Kingdom of Serbia continues, after the submission of the note, to adhere to that standpoint and will, in pursuit of that aim, do everything in its power to demonstrate the full sincerity of its aspiration to carry out, *vis-à-vis* Austria-Hungary, all the obligations of a good neighbour.[76]

The proposed acceptance here of 'all those demands' which aimed at 'the elimination of criminal and disorderly acts' had still left Pašić with plenty of space to reject any demand compromising Serbia's sovereignty. Now, by the time Pašić had bowdlerized most of the original article at some point after 10 a.m. on Saturday, 25 July, he may or may not have read the second part of Spalajković's telegram – which had arrived at 10 a.m., but may not have been deciphered in time for him to consider. That second part, it will be remembered, had passed on Sazonov's suggestion that, in the event of an Austro-Hungarian attack, Serbia's response should depend on its defence capability – about which the Russian Foreign Minister had obviously taken a dim view since he had also suggested that the Serbian Army should in such a situation retreat towards Greece. But Pašić would undoubtedly have read the first part of the telegram, which had arrived at 4.17 a.m. In that first part, it will also be remembered, Spalajković had related Sazonov's horror at the ultimatum ('there are demands within it which no state can accept without committing suicide'), and his assurance of Russian support for Serbia. But Spalajković had also commented on the basic ambiguity of that assurance, since Sazonov 'did not make himself clear in what shape that support will manifest itself'.

This piece of information alone would have been enough for Pašić to wish to moderate the public pronouncement of his position, about to be published in the *Samouprava*. In other words, his action in stopping Nestorović from printing what were no doubt hawkish parts of the original article had been influenced by information about Russian ambivalence. If Pašić had by this time also seen the second part of the telegram, his further conclusion could only have been that Sazonov's language betrayed meekness as well as ambivalence. Nestorović's evidence convincingly demonstrates that, contrary to Albertini's view about 25 July 1914, Pašić had, far from moving towards complete capitulation on 24 July and the morning of 25 July, in fact contemplated a tougher response than the one which his Government eventually submitted. It was Russian restraint, not Russian encouragement, that had begun to influence Pašić. At the same time there was never any doubt that, in the reply to the ultimatum, the Serbian Prime Minister would include objections or reservations regarding anything perceived as encroaching on Serbia's sovereignty. All his pronouncements and telegrams since his return to Belgrade early on 24 July had contained at least a shade of defiance.

Unfortunately, in his treatment of the events of 25 July in Belgrade, Luigi Albertini was not content to rely solely on Colonel Pavlović's supposed testimony. He also believed he had identified a document to which, to his surprise, 'so few historians have paid attention'. This is Pašić's circular telegram to Serbian legations of 25 July, which does not carry the time of dispatch, but whose context makes clear that it had been sent before the handing in of the Serbian reply to the ultimatum:

> A brief summary of the reply of the Royal Government was communicated to the representatives of the allied Governments at the Ministry for Foreign Affairs to-day. They were informed that the reply would be quite conciliatory on all points and that the Serbian Government would accept

the Austro-Hungarian demands as far as possible. The Serbian Government trust that the Austro-Hungarian Government, unless they are determined to make war at all costs, will see their way to accept the full satisfaction offered in the Serbian reply.

According to Albertini, in this telegram 'Pašić announces the accept-ance in principle of all the Austrian demands'. And he berates other histo-rians because they had failed to ask themselves how it came about that Pašić 'later in the final reply made reservations on many points and rejected one outright'.[77] Albertini uses here the English translation of the telegram which is included in the *Serbian Blue Book* and which forms part of the *Collected Diplomatic Documents*, published in London and New York in 1915. In the original Serbian publication from 1914, however, 'quite conciliatory on all points' is in fact 'quite conciliatory overall [*u svemu*]'. But this is a minor point – what is worrisome is Albertini's disregard of the ensuing caveat by Pašić that the Austro-Hungarian demands would be accepted 'as far as possible [*u meri u kojoj je to najviše mogućno učiniti*]'.[78] In other words, the telegram which is claimed by Albertini as corroborating his thesis about an imminent capitulation, contains the opposite message.

In the course of 25 July it was entirely clear to at least two diplomats in Belgrade that the reply of the Serbian Government was not going to embody a full acceptance of the demands. Crackanthorpe, having received from Grujić at the Foreign Ministry a brief summary of the reply, dis-patched a telegram to London at 12.30 p.m. informing that the demands would be met 'in as large measure as possible', and that the ten points 'are accepted with reserves'.[79] As Mark Cornwall has noted, the words 'in as large measure as possible' were really a euphemism for the rejection of those points violating Serbia's sovereignty.[80] The other diplomat on that day was Auguste Boppe, who had arrived in Belgrade only that morning to replace the increasingly demented Descos as the French Minister. Boppe had always dreamt of becoming the Minister in Belgrade – he had learnt Serbian as a student and had already served at the French Legation in Belgrade in a junior capacity.[81] But his old acquaintance Strandtmann, who had run into him at the railway station whilst putting his family on what turned out to be the last Orient Express train to Constantinople before war broke out, told him that the Government and the diplomatic corps would be leaving the city that very evening.[82] By 3 p.m. Boppe had found out enough about the situation to be able to send his first telegram to Paris. Having seen Pašić, he wrote to the Quai d'Orsay about the wide-ranging acceptance by the Serbian Government of the demands in the ultimatum – exceping one point: namely, regarding the participation of Austrian functionaries in the *enquête* on Serbian soil, the Government would ask for an explanation, and it would 'only take into consideration that which corresponds to international law or good neighbourly relations'. The fact that Boppe further reported Pašić's readiness – in the event of Austrian dissatisfaction with the Serbian government response – to hand the matter over to the Hague Tribunal or to the Great Powers, also heralded a less than absolutely conciliatory Serbian reply.[83]

Strandtmann, for his part, was convinced that the Serbs would fight. So much so that he chose not to convey to Pašić the contents of an urgent telegram he had received on the morning of 25 July from Sazonov in which the latter now repeated the advice he had already given to Spalajković: if Serbia's position was hopeless, it would perhaps be better for the Serbs to allow the country to be occupied without a fight and then make a solemn appeal to the Great Powers.[84] Even though, as has been seen, Strandtmann had otherwise been a veritable dove of peace in the advice he had been giving the Serbs ever since the arrival of the ultimatum, his encounters with Pašić and Regent Alexander had left him in 'no doubt about their determination to defend the fatherland'. So he ignored the telegram because he considered it impossible to give advice which, while it would not be taken, could be interpreted as 'a shameful incitement to lay down the weapons'.[85]

It is important, however, to point out another telegram from St Petersburg which Strandtmann did show to Pašić in the course of 25 July. This was Sazonov's circular of 24 July to the Russian embassies in Vienna, Berlin, Paris, London and Rome, and to the legations in Bucharest and Belgrade. Sazonov insisted that, since Austria-Hungary had only consulted the Powers twelve hours after the delivery of the ultimatum, the remaining short period did not suffice for them to undertake anything useful towards the settlement of the complications which had thereby arisen. It was thus necessary that Austria-Hungary should, 'above all', prolong the time-limit for the reply, and a failure to so would be contrary to 'international ethics'.[86] Again, what Pašić had learnt from this about Russian reaction to the ultimatum was that it seemed merely to consist of some diplomatic resistance to what Austria.Hungary was doing – not of any proposed Russian military steps. In his memoirs Strandtmann wrote that he had shown this telegram to Pašić before the completion of the Serbian reply.[87] Essentially, both telegrams seen by Pašić had it in common that neither was offering him concrete Russian support nor any encouragement for a hardline Serbian response.

But when exactly on 25 July had the Serbian reply to the ultimatum been completed? This is not some pointless academic question. For those historians painting a picture whereby 'Russian support stiffened Serbia's spine',[88] it is rather important to maintain that the reply had only been completed in the late afternoon hours – as more work had been required following the alleged receipt of information during the day about, so it is claimed, Russian encouragement. 'During the afternoon of Saturday 25 July', Christopher Clark writes, 'there were numerous drafts as the ministers took turns in adding and scratching out various passages.'[89] Recently, Clark has by no means been alone in suggesting that frenetic activity had been taking place in the Serbian Foreign Ministry in the few hours left before the expiry of the deadline. 'All Saturday afternoon', Sean McMeekin insists, 'Pašić and his advisers badgered poor Gruić with suggested changes', and the Serbian Prime Minister 'clearly sweated over his draft until the last minute'.[90] In fact, no drama of this kind had transpired.

The source used by Clark and McMeekin – and many others before them – to back up such vivid descriptions is once more that towering authority, Luigi Albertini. The latter, it has to be said, was a rather imaginative scenographer. In addition to hastening Colonel Pavlović's return from Bavaria and placing him in the very interesting role of a crown witness to the events in Belgrade from 23 to 25 July, he also succeeded in creating historiographically lasting images of a supposedly very hectic afternoon of 25 July in the Serbian Foreign Ministry. So what did Albertini do here? He claimed to have talked to Slavko Grujić, in 1914 the Secretary-General at the Serbian Foreign Ministry, who had 'narrated' to him (Albertini does not say when or where) that at 11 a.m. he had received 'the first text' of the Serbian reply for translation (into French). Without directly quoting Grujić, Albertini merely tells the following story:

> At many points the text was almost illegible, there were many sentences crossed out and many added. While the work of translation was proceeding, between noon and 5 p.m., the text was several times taken away and the Ministers, in continuous session in an adjoining large room, made many changes, additions and completions. At last after 4 p.m. the text seemed finally settled and an attempt was made to type it out. But the typist was inexperienced and very nervous and after a few lines the typewriter refused to work, with the result that the reply had to be written out by hand in hectographic ink, copies being jellied off. Towards 5 p.m. when the copying out of the translation was not yet quite finished, Gruić was summoned into the Cabinet room and asked for the first part of the Serbian text for the introduction of one more change. Gruić declared that it was not possible to make any fresh corrections or the text would never be ready in time. The last half-hour was one of feverish work. The reply was corrected by pen here and there. One whole phrase placed in parenthesis was crossed out in ink and made illegible. At 5.45 p.m. Gruić handed the text to Pašić in an envelope.[91]

It is truly surprising that the above account, used and relied on by so many historians, has never been challenged. For it becomes clear, on closer inspection, that Albertini had probably never talked to Grujić – but merely read him. Reference has been made, in this and especially in the previous chapter, to Grujić's 1934 memoir which had been published in four instalments by the Belgrade daily *Politika*. Albertini literally reproduced large chunks of the relevant part of Grujić's memoir while claiming that the material had been 'narrated' to him by Grujić. In 1935 the *Berliner Monatshefte* published the memoir in German – which is what Albertini must have read. Everything in Albertini's narration, from the contents of the sentences to the sequences in which they appear, and even the mispelling of Grujić's name, indicates not a conversation with Grujić, but rather a reading of his published memoir.[92] In this exercise, however, there was also a necessary modicum of adding – in order for an authentic testimony to be twisted to conform to Albertini's view of 25 July in Belgrade.

The key change which Albertini made to Grujić's published account relates to the time when the Serbian reply (in Serbian) had finally been completed. Grujić states very clearly that he received the text 'at around 11 a.m.' – he did not write that this was 'the first text' as Albertini would have it. He then began working on its translation into the French. While complaining about the difficulty of reading the original Serbian text, in which many parts were rubbed out and new sentences inserted, at no point does he say – as Albertini makes him say in the imagined rendition – that 'the text was several times taken away' so that the Ministers could make 'many changes, additions and completions'. There is nothing about that in Grujić's memoir. True, he writes (and Albertini repeats this) that around 5 p.m. he had been called into the Cabinet room and asked to bring back the first part of the Serbian text because a change needed to be made. Grujić had refused to go along with this because time had been pressing, but Albertini describes the episode not as a request for a change, but as a request for 'one more change'. Again, this is absent from Grujić's memoir, in which the firm impression is given that this had been the only attempt at changing anything in the six hours since 11 a.m.[93]

The fact that Grujić had been asked to bring back the first part of the Serbian reply is in itself quite revealing. For the first part of the Serbian reply to the ultimatum did not deal with any of the ten points raised in the ultimatum – those were dealt with in the second part. The first part was restricted to general remarks. In other words, whatever change the Serbian Ministers had wished to make towards 5 p.m., it could not have been related to a last-minute attempt to alter the substance of the draft reply as a result of any allegedly encouraging news coming from Spalajković in St Petersburg.

Attempting to maintain the credibility of his story that Colonel Pavlović had testified to the arrival of a supportive telegram from Russia in the afternoon of 25 July, Albertini thus had to do two things: firstly, to depict the drafting of the Serbian reply as running well into the afternoon and, secondly, in order to make this believable, he had to invent a first class witness. Given the structural likeness of his account to Grujić's published memoir, it seems clear that Albertini simply added to the latter a few crucial details – those concerning the allegedly incessant reworking of the reply late into the afternoon – and pretended that Grujić himself was the author of this revised narrative. Why, Grujić himself had told him so (Grujić had died in London in 1937 and was thus not able to comment). All the other details, for example the typewriter breaking down, were genuine and had been wisely retained by Albertini. But what the Italian journalist had in effect managed to achieve, in order to validate his own story, was to report Grujić as the source – in blatant contradiction, at least in crucial details, to the latter's own 1934 account. There is little point in dwelling on why Albertini crafted his falsification – except to say, perhaps, that people can get perversely obsessed with the question of how to persuade others to accept a scenario in which they themselves genuinely believe. Inventing small, key details when depicting events may seem to them a small price to pay. However, this crossing of the boundary between history and undeclared fiction is of course a step too far.

The fact that the Serbian reply had been completed well before 5 p.m. on 25 July is confirmed by Strandtmann in his memoirs. Strandtmann, otherwise quite taken up on that day with packing the archive of his Legation, nevertheless managed to see Pašić who told him that the text of the reply had been formulated and was being translated, and that he should 'come back after 5 o'clock in the afternoon' when he, Pašić, would be able to show him the reply in its final, translated form. Strandtmann does not state the time of this meeting with Pašić, but the context points towards late morning.[94] In any event, Pašić's words hardly suggest a continuous, feverish activity on re-wording the text of the reply until the last moment. Alexander Savinsky, who knew Strandtmann, and who in 1914 served as the Russian Minister in Sofia, later wrote that the text of the Serbian reply to the Austrian ultimatum had been established 'much earlier than the appointed hour' – one assumes that he had received this information from his Russian colleague in Belgrade.[95] According to the diary entry for 25 July of the Serbian politician Jovan Žujović, it had been known in Belgrade 'around midday' that Austria would not be satisfied with the reply to the ultimatum – this, again, suggests that the original Serbian version had been completed sometime late in the morning.[96]

Grujić wrote that the final French translation was handed to Pašić at 5.45 p.m.[97] The reason why it had taken so long to complete the work is fully explained in his article in *Politika*. He had initially been allocated another Ministry official, fluent in French, to carry out the work of translation. But soon Pašić had given this man some other task, so that Grujić had had to do it all alone. His writing was fairly illegible, necessitating that the whole text had to be written down again, with Grujić dictating his own translation. On top of that the work was constantly being interrupted by officials bringing in deciphered telegrams, as well as by foreign diplomats, hungry for news, crowding the ante chamber of the Ministry and 'physi-cally detaining' Grujić as he crossed it to enter the Cabinet room. Because the Ministry was being evacuated, Grujić, as its Secretary-General, had to deal at the same time with his officials seeking instructions.[98] It is remark-able that, in this chaotic environment, he had been able to complete his onerous task on time.

He may even have done it a little earlier than he himself suggested, i.e., before 5.45 p.m. For another contemporary source maintains that Pašić had emerged from the Foreign Ministry 'at exactly 5.40 p.m.' to take the reply to the Austro-Hungarian Legation.[99] Be that as it may, it should perhaps be noted here that the Prime Minister was not carrying some horribly messy collage of a document which, under Albertini's influence, many historians still believe was the case. The nine-page hand-written reply (plus Pašić's covering note) is available for inspection in Vienna's Haus-, Hof- und Staatsarchiv. It is very legible and contains only a few minor corrections – with one exception on page 6 where a whole sentence is blotted out.[100] This, indeed, is the page which the editors of the *Österreich-Ungarns Aussepolitik* chose to attach as a facsimile to their official collection of documents.[101]

As Pašić, sporting a black redingote and with a long white envelope under arm, stepped on to a carriage, he looked 'dignified' and wore on his face 'that eternal, light smile'. A crowd had already gathered at the Foreign Ministry. When they heard Pašić order the coachman to take him to the Austro-Hungarian Legation, many people ran to Krunska Street in order to await his departure from the Legation and attempt to judge the outcome by his demeanour and facial expression.[102] For his part, Baron Giesl knew in advance that the Serbian reply would not concede all the points because shortly before Pašić's arrival he had seen the Economy Minister Velizar Janković who had told him that the 'humiliating' demands had not been accepted. Giesl had in any case anticipated as much, having during the day packed everything in the Legation and got his personnel ready to catch the 6.30 train to Zemun, just across the river in Hungary. He must also have felt justified in his choice of attire for the day, which Janković described as 'a travelling suit' with 'short trousers'. Although Giesl subsequently denied it in his memoirs, other witnesses, not least Pašić, also reported him as wearing an informal outfit, which was most probably a suit with knee-length breeches.[103]

The meeting between Baron Giesl and Nikola Pašić at the Austro-Hungarian Legation was brief and devoid of any drama. Pašić arrived, according to Giesl, at 5.55 p.m., 'evidently aware of the importance of the moment'. His 'exceptionally clever' eyes betrayed a 'solemn gravity' of expression. When Giesl enquired about the contents of the reply, he said: 'We have accepted one part of your demands ... as for the rest, we place our hopes on the loyalty and chivalry of an Austrian General. We have always been content with you.' Pašić must have been gently poking fun with his flattering remarks addressed to Giesl, though the latter had apparently taken him seriously because in his 1927 memoir he wrote that Pašić could 'naturally not have known' that the decision had not depended on him, i.e., on Giesl. He promised Pašić an early response – he first had to compare the terms of the Serbian reply with his instructions. The two men then shook hands and the Prime Minister left the Legation.[104]

The Serbian Reply

The Serbian reply to the Austro-Hungarian ultimatum is one of the more famous documents of modern European history. A quick review, however, is called for, as the familiarity with it is only too often quite superficial. Described in many history books as a 'masterpiece', or 'brilliant', this document in fact represents a kind of hara-kiri by a sovereign state. On any detached reading of their reply, the Serbs had, as H.W. Wilson put it in 1928, 'bowed themselves in the dust'.[105] J.A.R. Marriott, another British historian, had been even more categorical: 'No submission', he wrote in 1918, 'could have been more complete and even abject.'[106] The exercise, to be sure, was consistent with Pašić's stratagem of gaining time. He knew, therefore, that a heavy price would have to be paid just to create a hope, however remote, that war could be averted. And he was prepared to pay such a price. Even the fact that the Government accepted the very first demand, preceding the ten specific points, that it publish on the front page of Serbia's official gazette a condemnation of supposed propaganda against Austria-Hungary already constituted a crushing blow to the country's sovereignty since such a condemnation was being dictated from Vienna. And so did the fact that the Government, acting in this instance on behalf of the King of Serbia, had simultaneously agreed to publish the same condemnation in the Army's official bulletin. Sidney Fay, the American historian, was later to speculate that Pašić would have been in danger of being overthrown by the Army and the officers around the Black Hand ('eager for war') if he had made concessions to the Monarchy and, especially, if he had agreed to publish a condemnation of anti-Austrian propaganda in the Army's official bulletin. The danger of an Army revolt was averted, according to Fay, only because mobilization soon followed.[107] Clearly, however, even if such fears concerning Army reactions had existed, Pašić had been fully prepared to leave them out of account.

On point 1, regarding the suppression of any publication inciting hatred against the Monarchy, the Serbian Government went as far as to promise a change in the Constitution (Article 22) in order to be able to confiscate publications expressing sentiment offensive to Austria-Hungary. Point 2, with its demand that the *Narodna Odbrana* and similar societies be dissolved, was also accepted entirely. The Government thereby violated Article 25 of the Constitution, which guaranteed freedom of association. With regard to point 3, about immediate elimination from Serbia's educational institutions of everything serving, or potentially serving, to foment propaganda against Austria-Hungary, the Government asked for facts and proofs of such propaganda. However, it accepted this point in principle and thereby agreed that the Monarchy was free to meddle in the educational system of a sovereign country. On point 4, which demanded the removal of officers and officials, named by the Imperial and Royal Government, who were guilty of propaganda against the Monarchy, Pašić had privately commented to Strandtmann, 'not without irony', that he himself could be affected by this point.[108] But The Serbian Government agreed to remove all those found guilty by judicial enquiry of deeds aimed against the territorial integrity of the Monarchy – if this sounded a little reserved, the Government actually asked the Austro-Hungarian side to supply it with the names of such officers and officials. As has been seen, it had promptly arrested Major Tankosić without waiting for any judicial enquiry.

Point 5 had apparently caused some puzzlement to the Serbian Government: what was 'the sense and the scope', it wondered, of the demand that Serbia accept the collaboration on its territory of the organs of the Imperial and Royal Government? Point 5 demanded collaboration in the suppression of subversive movements directed against the territorial integrity of the Monarchy – but was indeed quite vague in that it said nothing about the specifics of such a collaboration. The Ballhausplatz subsequently realized its blunder, because in its detailed remarks on the Serbian reply, dispatched to all its diplomatic missions on 28 July, it talked of a 'special arrangement' with Serbia which should allow for such an Austro-Hungarian activity – but point 5 had not mentioned such an arrangement.[109] Nevertheless, the Serbian Government declared its willingness to accept 'every cooperation' that would accord with the principles of international law and criminal procedure, as well as with good neighbourly relations. Did this amount to an acceptance or a rejection of point 5? The answer must be neither – a vague demand had been met with a vague answer. But the fact that the Austro-Hungarian demand had not been met with greater resistance testified to Pašić's readiness to crawl and grovel.

The Serbian Government only paused with this ceremonious self-abnegation at point 6. The latter, of course, is the famous demand by Austria-Hungary that Serbia should open *'une enquête judiciaire'* against persons on Serbian territory involved in the plot of 28 June, and that organs delegated by the Imperial and Royal Government would take part in the investigations. This demand was turned down. While the Serbian Government emphasized that it considered it its duty to open such an enquiry, it could not accept the participation of organs delegated by Austria-Hungary since this would constitute 'a violation of the Constitution and of the law on criminal procedure'. This, indeed, was the case, but Pašić himself explained in 1920 to the French historian Léon Savadjian the deeper reasons behind the rejection of point 6 and the reservations concerning point 5. The ultimatum, he said, stipulated 'nothing' about the 'form and extent' of the proposed Austro-Hungarian participation in the investigations in Serbia. Austria-Hungary, Pašić continued, 'would have sent us a whole horde of policemen and investigators with special privileges ... Who was supposed to be in charge of the enquiry? We or the Austrians? The terms of the ultimatum avoided to specify this. Certainly, however, Austria-Hungary would have appropriated all the rights for itself, and we would have found it difficult to resist had we accepted the ultimatum without any reserve.' The logic of accepting these provisions of the ultimatum, Pašić argued, would have led to Austria-Hungary arresting Serbian ministers, ransacking the ministries and public institutions, obtaining plans about the organization of the Serbian Army, etc. – with some kind of conflict inevitably ensuing, but with Serbia meanwhile rendered impotent while the Central Powers would have had supremacy in the Balkans.[110]

Point 6, however, was the only one to have been refused. On point 7, which had demanded the arrest of Tankosić and Ciganović, the Government replied that it had already arrested Tankosić and that it had not yet been possible to arrest Ciganović who was, it emphasized, 'a subject of the Austro-Hungarian Monarchy'. Those historians trying to prove the culpability of the Serbian Government in the Sarajevo assassination have argued, on the basis of practically no evidence, that the authorities had tucked Ciganović away in the countryside where he had been moving freely.[111] In fact, no one in the Serbian Government had initially known anything about Ciganović. When, early in July, the first news about his ties with the assassins had been carried by the Austro-Hungarian press, Pašić asked Minister Joca Jovanović 'who this official of his was'. Jovanović was the Minister for Public Works and so Ciganović, an employee at the Serbian state railways, was in his Ministry – but no one there knew of him. 'Under pressure from Pašić', however, 'they at last unearthed Ciganović in some small clerical post in the railway administration.' But he was nowhere to be seen. Joca Jovanović subsequently informed his colleagues that Ciganović 'had gone off somewhere out of Belgrade', suggesting that his exact whereabouts were not known to the Government.[112] Far from hiding Ciganović, it had already acted in the evening of 23 July when it issued a warrant for his arrest.[113]

Point 8, demanding that the Serbian authorities prevent the smuggling of explosives and weapons across the frontier and punish those officials who had helped the assassins cross the frontier, was accepted entirely by the Serbian Government. Point 9 merely reflected the petulance of the

Ballhausplatz: it demanded explanations with regard to 'the unjustifiable remarks' of high Serbian functionaries, given in 'hostile' tone towards the Austro-Hungarian Monarchy in press interviews following the assassination of 28 June. This, again, was something of a fuzzy demand, and the Serbian Government replied that it would 'readily' give explanations, but it also asked for the relevant passages from those interviews to be communicated to it. Point 9, in other words, had thus been accepted. Point 10, the last on the list, was just a demand that the Serbian Government should without delay inform the Imperial and Royal Government about the execution of the measures comprised in the preceding points. This demand, too, was accepted.

In their reply, Pašić and his Cabinet made one final appeasing gesture. In the event that the Imperial and Royal Government were not satisfied with the response, and considering that it was 'against the common interest to precipitate the question', the Serbian Government offered to refer its own response to the International Tribunal at the Hague, or to the Great Powers which had taken part in the working out of the declaration made by the Serbian Government on 31 March 1909.[114] That declaration of 1909 represented, of course, Serbia's capitulation in the Bosnian annexation crisis. Again, however, the idea was to play for time. When Pašić talked to Léon Savadjian in 1920, he said that Serbia 'would have accepted the decisions of the Hague Tribunal 'without any objection', but he also emphasized that by going to an international court 'one would have gained a few days of respite, during which period some miracle might have occurred to save peace.'[115]

Alexander von Musulin famously described the Serbian reply as 'the most brilliant example of diplomatic skill ever'.[116] Of course, he went on to fulminate against it – the grudging praise related to the document's perceived trickery. But that was the Ballhausplatz reaction. Elsewhere in Europe, the reception accorded to the Serbian reply was most positive. On 27 July Sazonov was predictably enthusiastic: 'The reply exceeds all our expectations through its moderation and the readiness to give Austria full satisfaction.' But he was still concerned: 'We cannot conceive that the Austrian demands could still be maintained, unless a pretext is sought for an expedition against Serbia.'[117] From Paris Vesnić reported to Belgrade the opinion of the Quay d'Orsay that Serbia 'could not have gone further'.[118] Indeed, the Austro-Hungarian Ambassador Count Miklós Szécsen had been told by Under-Secretary Philippe Berthelot that the Serbian reply was 'tantamount to complete capitulation'.[119] Jean-Baptiste Bienvenu-Martin, the acting French Foreign Minister, subsequently put it to Szécsen that, since Serbia had accepted so much, the remaining differences could be settled '*avec un peu de bonne volonté réciproque*'.[120] From Rome Mihajlović passed on the view of the Italian Foreign Ministry that the reply was 'good', and that it 'could not have been coined in any other way'.[121] Even Vasil

Radoslavov, the pro-Austrian and pro-German Prime Minister of Bulgaria, thought that the Serbian reply 'had made all possible concessions'.[122]

The most widely known reaction is that of Kaiser Wilhelm II. On 28 July he commented at the bottom of the Serbian reply: 'A brilliant performance for a time-limit of only 48 hours. This is more than one could have expected! A great moral success for Vienna; but with it every reason for war drops away, and Giesl might have remained quietly in Belgrade.'[123] Notwithstanding these remarks by the mercurial German Kaiser, the most objective assessment of the Serbian reply in the Europe of 1914 should be gauged by the reverberations in London, not Berlin. Britain, the Great Power least bound by the system of alliances, and with no stake in the Balkan mess except for the desire to avoid a general war, was always going to view the crisis more equitably than the others. According to Lord Vansittart, there was 'stupefaction' in the Foreign Office that Serbia had accepted most of the 'impossible' terms. 'We left the Foreign Office that evening', he wrote in his memoirs, 'with the hope that another crisis had been surmounted by submission.'[124] When he saw the Serbian reply, Arthur Nicolson wrote to Foreign Secretary Grey that it 'practically concedes all the Austrian demands'. And Eyre Crowe minuted: 'The Answer is reasonable. If Austria demands absolute compliance with her ultimatum it can only mean that she wants a war.'[125] Grey had shared these assessments. In a conversation on 27 July with Count Albert Mensdorff-Pouilly, the Austro-Hungarian Ambassador to London, he did not mince his words. It seemed to him, he told the Ambassador, that the Serbian reply already involved 'the greatest humiliation' that he had ever seen a country undergo, and it was very disappointing to him 'that the reply was treated by the Austrian Government as if it were as unsatisfactory as a blank negative.'[126]

Some current academic opinion, strangely, makes no mention of such evaluations of the Serbian reply made in the European chancelleries in late July 1914. Thus Christopher Clark sees the Serbian reply as 'a subtle cocktail of acceptances, conditional acceptances, evasions and rejections'. T.G. Otte employs very similar language when he describes the reply as 'a clever concoction of acceptance and equivocation, evasion and rejection, and all dressed up in accommodating language'.[127] Interestingly, Berchtold wrote something similar at the Ballhausplatz when, on 27 July, he pleaded with Franz Joseph to allow him to proceed with the drafting and sending of the telegram that would declare war on Serbia. For he had become panicked by the Serbian reply, anticipating that the Triple Entente Powers could still attempt to reach a peaceful settlement. He therefore described the reply as 'accommodating' and 'very skilfully composed', but 'quite worthless' in substance.[128] The manner in which this judgement is defended more than a century later is quite bizarre. Clark warns his readers about the 'profoundly misleading' claim made in 'general narratives' that the reply represented 'an almost complete capitulation'.[129] The whole matter, however, does not stem from any general narratives: as has been seen, the opinion that Serbia had practically capitulated was in fact an insider one, held in July 1914 by statesmen and professional diplomats across Europe.

There have been non-German and non-Austrian narratives, on the other hand, which have taken the side of Vienna in pronouncing the Serbian reply more conciliatory in form than in substance. One such is by Sidney Fay, but even he, anxious as he was to revise the verdict that Germany and her allies had been responsible for the Great War, rejected the Austrian claim that the Serbian reply had not given adequate guarantees of security. For 'it was not primarily guarantees which Austria aimed at in her ultimatum, but an excuse for weakening Serbia and putting an end to the Greater Serbia danger by making war on her.'[130] Bernadotte Schmitt, much less sympathetic to the Central Powers than Fay, but at least as great an authority, considered that Austria-Hungary, with 'nine-tenths' of the demands conceded, could have negotiated and demanded a rigid execution of the Serbian promises. An 'unassailable' diplomatic position would have been gained by Austria in default of Serbian performance. 'Unfortunately for her', Schmitt concluded, 'she had not expected so great a surrender on the part of Serbia, and she was determined not to accept a diplomatic solution.'[131]

This was the belief even in some Austrian establishment circles. Biliński, who had indeed argued for war, nevertheless wrote in his memoirs that Giesl, otherwise 'not known for excessive diplomatic talent', should not have left Belgrade after receiving significant concessions.[132] On 3 August, in Vienna's Hotel Imperial, Josef Redlich ran into Ernst von Plener, the distinguished elder statesman from the upper house of the *Reichsrat*. What the bellicose Redlich heard from Plener was not to his taste: Pašić's reply had conceded most points, Giesl had only superficially read the reply before rejecting it, the Austrian note was 'ill-fated', and there was a will to war without foreseeing a world war.[133] In 1921, Plener recalled: 'The note had been written in order to be rejected, hence our surprise was all the greater as the Serbs accepted, despite its humiliating tenor, most of the points, rejecting only a few, and proposing for the unresolved remainder a judicial or international diplomatic arrangement.'[134]

In 1914, one person in Austria-Hungary who was never likely to be profoundly misled by the Serbian reply was the retired, but otherwise quite active, esteemed diplomat Count Heinrich Lützow. He was not so naïve, he wrote later, to believe that Serbia would have abided by its obligations. However, he also saw the reply as a diplomatic success for Vienna, 'one can almost say a triumph', the like of which Austria had not had since its diplomatic defeat of Prussia at Ölmutz in 1850. The key point, in Lützow's view, was that at the time no one had yet begun to mobilize, at least not officially. After the war he met Berchtold in Switzerland and told him that, had he, Lützow, been the Minister in Belgrade, he would 'certainly' not have left the city after receiving the Serbian reply. 'What could have happened to me?', he asked Berchtold, 'after all, you would not have had my head chopped off!'[135]

Mobilization and War

Indeed, Baron Giesl had left Belgrade with extraordinary haste. He admitted in his book that he had only glanced at the Serbian reply, but it was 'quite clear' to him that it was not an unconditional reply.[136] Adhering strictly to his instructions, and only minutes after Pašić had left, he signed a pre-prepared letter, informing the Serbian Prime Minister that, in the light of the unsatisafactory reply, he was leaving Belgrade with the personnel of his Legation, and that the rupture of diplomatic relations between the Kingdom of Serbia and Austria-Hungary would assume '*le caractère d'un fait accompli*' with the receipt of the letter.[137] He then hurried to catch the 6.30 train to Zemun. Four carriages had been parked outside the Legation, one of them crammed with suitcases and baggage. Only a quarter of an hour after Pašić had emerged from the Legation, Giesl appeared with his Serbian wife and their son. In order to reach the railway station, the cortege of carriages had to drive past the Foreign Ministry building where a large number of people had gathered, congesting the street. In 'dead silence', the crowd moved in order to let Giesl through. 'Not a single voice', one witness reported, 'either threatening or scorning, was heard from the ranks of the people huddling here.'[138]

Pašić had asked Strandtmann to wait for him at the Foreign Ministry while he was at the Austro-Hungarian Legation delivering the Serbian Government's reply. When he returned, he began complaining to the Russian Chargé d'Affaires about what he thought was a suspect attitude to the ultimatum on the part of the Montenegrin King Nicholas. But soon thereafter Giesl's letter arrived, announcing the breaking off of diplomatic relations. 'Pašić', Strandtmann wrote to Sazonov, 'was deeply shocked by this news'. While fully retaining his composure, 'suddenly, he somehow wilted'.[139] On the other hand, the intuitive decision which the Serbian Government had already taken the previous day to evacuate itself south to the city of Niš had now been fully vindicated. Strandtmann, too, hurried to get on the train later that evening, departing from the small station at Topčider – because, given the prevailing expectation that an Austro-Hungarian attack could begin at any moment, the main railway station located in the border area close to the river Sava had been declared unsafe.[140]

But had Serbia already mobilized its Army in the early afternoon hours of 25 July, that is, before the Serbian reply to the ultimatum had been handed to Giesl? This is an apposite question: most non-Serbian accounts maintain that the Serbian mobilization was decreed at 3 p.m. on 25 July. Alfred von Wegerer claimed this in 1931 on the basis of hearsay evidence; Albertini later re-stated the 3 p.m. thesis on the basis of no evidence at all; Manfried Rauchensteiner likewise provides zero evidence for his claim that mobilization had begun 'hours' before the Serbian reply had been given; Sean McMeekin is slightly more guarded in suggesting that the mobilization was ordered at 3 p.m. on 25 July – 'although it was not yet made public'.[141] The idea here is of course to show that if the mobilization had been going on even before anyone in the Serbian Government had known how Austria-Hungary was going to react to its reply, then the whole exercise with that reply would have been, at least at some point on 25 July, somewhat spurious. Needless to say, the claims about an early Serbian mobilization contradict the claims that the Belgrade Government was ready to capitulate on 25 July before it allegedly received a Russian pledge of support, which made it change its mind – but then, even historians can lose sight of the implications of their arguments. In this instance, these two well-known hypotheses run in parallel, but contradict each other.

The remark which Count Lützow made in his memoirs that no official mobilization had been occurring at the time when Serbia had handed in its reply to the ultimatum is a very important one. Lutzow was referring to Russia and Serbia. It falls outside the scope of this book to consider the Russian mobilization. In the case of Serbia, however, one could only with some embroidery adduce any unofficial mobilization. As shown in the previous chapter, on the evening of 23 July War Minister Stefanović had on his own initiative begun to take some measures in anticipation of impending conflict with Austria-Hungary. Undoubtedly, there had been a fair amount of military and related activity in Belgrade. But it would be difficult to agree with Griesinger who, at 9.45 p.m. on Friday, 24 July, informed Berlin that the Serbian mobilization was 'in full swing'.[142] This was a massive overstatement since units and equipment were merely being moved out to bivouacs at Torlak, about ten kilometres south-east, given the capital city's vulnerability. It had also been decided to shift the main headquarters to the town of Kragujevac further south. Stefanović had in the night of 23 July instructed the Director of Serbian railways to get everything ready 'in case' troop transportation might be required.[143] Some of this activity may therefore be described in terms of precautionary mobilization measures – all of which, however, did not amount to mobilization.[144] Moreover the intent of such measures, far from being aggressive, was only to withdraw forces from possible areas where they might be attacked.

On the morning of 25 July Stefanović went to see Pašić. 'What are we going to do with the Army, Mr Prime Minister', he wondered, 'are we going to mobilize?' Pondering, his hand on his beard, Pašić replied: 'Do not touch anything for the time being. We shall know this evening.'[145] Of course, the evening was going to bring some kind of *dénouement* with regard to the ultimatum crisis – there would be no mobilization beforehand. The Serbian historian Mile Bjelajac has recently established that only at 7 p.m. on 25 July, i.e., after diplomatic relations had been severed, did War Minister Stefanović, together with Colonel Krsta Smiljanić, write the mobilization order, which was finally then given at 9 p.m., to begin on 26 July.[146] Crackanthorpe informed London at 10 p.m. that mobilization had been ordered.[147] Towards 11 p.m. the order was being read out in central Belgrade – accompanied, as was the custom in Serbia, by drumbeats.[148]

Austria-Hungary made its decision to mobilize at roughly the same time. Late on 24 July Conrad received a telegram from the 13th Corps in Zagreb to the effect that mobilization had been proclaimed at 4 p.m. in Šabac, the Serbian town close to the Bosnian border. The report was false, but Conrad immediately raised the alarm with Berchtold and on the following morning demanded of the War Minister Krobatin that the Austro-Hungarian mobilization be ordered that same day, 25 July, for 'we must not lag behind Serbia even a single day'.[149] Since the Serbian reply was due that evening, Krobatin was about to travel to Bad Ischl to meet with Franz Joseph. Berchtold was also going to be at the Emperor's summer residence. The Foreign Minister had on 24 July already been reminded by the increasingly hawkish Hungarian Prime Minister Tisza that, in the event of an unsatisfactory Serbian reply, the order for mobilization should ensue without fail. In a telegram of 25 July Tisza sent Franz Joseph the same message.[150]

The details of what was said at the meeting on 25 July in Kaiservilla, Bad Ischl, which Krobatin, too, attended, are sparse. But Margutti, Franz Joseph's adjutant, reported Berchtold as looking 'conspicuously strained'.[151] Meanwhile, Giesl reached Zemun, and spoke on the telephone with Tisza in Budapest. Tisza passed on the news of the conversation to Bad Ischl. His information was personally brought by Margutti to Emperor Franz Joseph, upon which the latter immediately summoned Berchtold.[152] Krobatin later recalled that they had been informed about Giesl leaving Belgrade, but also told that the Serbian Army mobilization had been 'well underway' since the early afternoon.[153] Conrad reported that the Emperor's own mobilization order had arrived at 9.23. p.m. – for partial mobilization, envisaged for '*Fall B*' (case B for Balkan, i.e., against Serbia and Montenegro), involving eight corps, and to begin on 28 July.[154] Interestingly, no one in Bad Ischl or Vienna had at this stage actually read the text of the Serbian reply. The first among Austria-Hungary's decision makers to be able to do so was Tisza, when he met Giesl at the Budapest railway station early on 26 July.[155] It is a remarkable lapse in the massive historiography of the origins of the First World War that this important little detail from the

July Crisis – namely the fact that Austria-Hungary mobilized against Serbia before its statesmen had even read the Serbian answer – is nowhere discussed, which is especially strange given the tendency of some to dwell on the idea that a more conciliatory Serbian answer might have avoided war.

In the course of the previous day, 25 July, there had already been considerable consternation in Vienna's leading circles, induced by growing conjecture that the Serbs would accept everything in the ultimatum and thus avoid punishment by war. The article in the *Samouprava*, discussed above, had been noted at the Ballhausplatz and its compliant tone had made Count Franz Kinsky 'distressed'.[156] Moreover, the evening edition of the *Neue Freie Presse* (which actually appeared in the afternoon) carried a front page report from its special correspondent in Belgrade, which declared that peace had been secured since the Serbian Government would accept the Austro-Hungarian note '*tel quel*'.[157] In his diary, Ludwig Thallóczy notes that the decision-making circles were 'nervous' that day. And some officials had indeed turned into nervous wrecks. In the Joint Finance Ministry, Paul Kuh-Chrobak declared that he would hang himself in the event that there were to be no war.[158] Hans Schlitter, the Director of the State Archive, was present in the Ballhausplatz during that critical evening period. He writes that the mood of the officials, Macchio and Forgách amongst them, was 'jittery', and 'the highest suspense' prevailed. When, at 7.15 p.m., Giesl got through on the telephone from Zemun, the jubilant shout went up: '*Abgebrochen!*', i.e., relations broken off. Everybody shook hands.[159] The British Ambassador to Vienna, when he subsequently reported to Grey on the events of 25 July, mentioned an initial 'moment of keen disappointment' as rumours began to spread that Serbia had unconditionally accepted the ultimatum. But, later, as it became known that Giesl had in Belgrade broken off diplomatic relations, 'Vienna burst into a frenzy of delight, vast crowds parading the streets and singing patriotic songs till the small hours of the morning'.[160] When Giesl finally made it back to Vienna, he was greeted 'with jubilation' at the Ballhausplatz. Referring to his military background, a high-ranked official told him: 'No one among us would ever have been able to accomplish this, only a soldier could have done it'.[161]

At some point during the evening/night of 25 July Pašić apprised all the Serbian legations abroad of the breakdown of diplomatic relations with Austria-Hungary and of the fact that the Regent had, on behalf of the King, issued the order for the mobilization of the Army. But he also emphasized that the Serbian reply had gone to 'the extreme limits' of what had been possible.[162] Serbia's capacity to yield had been exhausted. It was now, as Mark Cornwall observes, 'highly doubtful' that any further concessions would be made 'without extreme pressure from all the Powers'.[163] Moreover, over the next two days Pašić realized that, in fact, he may have gone too far in accommodating the Austro-Hungarian demands. The famous series of buoyant telegrams from Spalajković in St Petersburg began to arrive on Sunday, 26 July, by which time the only thing that they could influence was the mood of the Serbian Government. The first of them, which arrived at 9.40 a,m. on 26 July, talked of Russia's willingness to make any sacrifice in order to protect Serbia: 'All military measures have been undertaken. Indescribable enthusiasm has gripped all segments of the Russian people for the Tsar and the Government [and] for entering war.' The second telegram, which took almost twenty-four hours to arrive, reported 'favourable resolutions' reached on behalf of Serbia at the Russian Ministerial meeting that had been presided over by the Tsar on 25 July. The third telegram, based on a conversation between the Serbian Military Attaché and the Russian Chief of General Staff, was perhaps the most upbeat: 'The Military Council has displayed the greatest belligerence and has taken the decision to do utmost for the defence of Serbia, the Tsar in particular has surprised all by his determination'.[164]

Serbia, it now seemed reasonable to assume, did not stand alone. In the meantime Sazonov had on 25 July suggested to Strandtmann to plant the idea into Pašić's mind that, given 'England's' undoubted impartiality in the existing crisis, the Serbian Government should perhaps address a request to London for mediation.[165] But Strandtmann had only managed to decipher the telegram from Sazonov late on 25 July – on the train to Niš, where the Serbian Government and the diplomatic corps were being evacuated. He did not see Pašić again until the morning of 27 July.[166] Predictably, the Prime Minister was in the new circumstances not keen on mediation. He talked of 'England's insufficiently clarified position', but Strandtmann reported to Sazonov his own view that the Serbian Government in fact feared the possibility of having to make even more concessions. Besides, as Strandtmann noted, the Government was now under the influence of Spalajković's upbeat telegrams and did not wish to shift the focal point away from St Petersburg to some other European capital.[167]

All of which, however, should not be seen as reflecting blind new confidence in Russia on the part of Serbia. As Strandtmann elaborated in his memoirs, Pašić had also wondered why the delivery of Russian rifles to Serbia, long promised, had still not materialized. Nor had Pašić suddenly become complacent about the dangers still facing Serbia. He told Strandt-mann about his suspicions concerning possible Bulgarian incursions into Macedonia, and about his unhappiness regarding the behaviour of Romania and, in particular, Serbia's formal ally, Greece. At the same time he was under no illusion about Germany, describing the spirit in Berlin as 'belli-cose'.[168] The general situation was still highly precarious for Serbia. In fact, on that same day (27 July) in Niš, Pašić had sent his Finance Minister Lazar Paču to seek out Griesinger, the German Minister. The latter was told that it was now up to Austria-Hungary to state clearly which part of the Serbian reply it had found unsatisfactory, and then to make new demands. 'Do you not have', Paču asked Griesinger, 'any instructions to negotiate?'[169]

This approach by Paču may well have evinced, as Griesinger was later to opine, Pašić's wish to exhaust all the avenues before it came to war because of his uncertainty, dating back to the Bosnian annexation crisis, about Russia's willingness to come immediately to Serbia's aid.[170] Certainly, one cannot speak of a completely new atmosphere in the Serbian Government following the arrival of the otherwise reassuring news from St Petersburg. Nevertheless, a mixture of boldness and creeping optimism did begin to manifest itself. Early in the evening on 27 July Pašić minuted on a telegram that had arrived from Berlin: 'We have made our last concession – further we shall not go, nor shall we seek mediation, for that would indicate our readiness to yield still more. Russia is holding up excellently. Italy neutral.'[171] In late afternoon he had seen Stefan Chaprashikov, the Bulgarian Minister, and painted to him Serbia's international position: Russia resolved to protect Serbia; France in solidarity with Russia; Italy unhappy with Vienna because it had been kept in the dark during the crisis; and England wished to avoid war, but would not remain neutral if it broke out – as it turned out, Pašić had a fantastically accurate picture. He told Chaprashikov that, after the delivery of the reply to the ultimatum, Serbia had nothing to add – no more concessions. As Chaprashikov reported to Sofia, Pašić lamented that, had he known that he would be supported to this extent, he 'would not have, by any means, allowed the concessions that had been made'.[172]

Just this expression of regret by Pašić is evidence enough that he had not, before the expiry of the ultimatum's deadline on 25 July, received any game-changing support from Russia. By 27 July, moreover, the Serbs had still not received the Tsar's reply to the telegram sent to him by Regent Alexander on 24 July. The Tsar had seen this telegram, with its dramatic plea for Russian help, only on 26 July. He minuted at the bottom: 'Very humble and dignified telegram. How should one answer it?'[173] His reply, sent on 27 July, travelled more than twenty-four hours and reached Strandtmann late in the evening on 28 July. It assured the Regent that, even if efforts to avoid blood-letting were to be unsuccessful, 'Russia would under no circumstances remain indifferent to Serbia's fate'.[174] Coming from the highest quarter, here, finally, for the first time, Russia's commitment to Serbia had been spelled out. Strandtmann brought the telegram to Pašić early on 29 July. As he read it out to him, Pašić at first 'froze' and then, overcome with excitement, crossed himself, saying: 'Oh Lord, the Great, Merciful Russian Tsar.' Tears were pouring out of his eyes.[175]

By this time, of course, Serbia was already at war. Austria-Hungary had declared hostilities on 28 July. From the moment of Giesl's departure from Belgrade this outcome was hardly in serious doubt. Luigi Albertini goes to great lengths to present Berchtold between 25 and 28 July as willing, in the last analysis, to accept a peaceful solution.[176] Hugo Hantsch, Berchtold's otherwise generous biographer, makes no attempt in that direction.[177] For there is precious little contemporary evidence of any hesitation on Berchtold's part. On the contrary, on 26 July he sent a telegram to the Austro-Hungarian Embassies in Berlin, Rome, London and Paris, in which he spoke of the decision, reached after 'years of sufferance', to confront the Great Serbian agitation 'with the sword'.[178] It seems that the nature of the Serbian reply had created something of a fright at the Ballhausplatz. For also on 26 July, Hoyos wrote to Baron Franz Schiessl, Franz Joseph's cabinet secretary, that the Serbian reply, although it completely lacked in merit, could nevertheless be used against Austria-Hungary because it had been 'so skilfully composed'. Hoyos let Schiessl know that Berchtold intended to 'accelerate the matter' and have the war against Serbia declared on Tuesday, 28 July, 'to impede a possible intervention of third Powers or other incidents'.[179]

Indeed, on that same 26 July Grey launched the initiative for a Four-Power conference in London (Britain, Germany, France, Italy) to try and settle the Balkan crisis which had by now become a European problem of the first order. Hans Schlitter, who had heard in Vienna's journalist circles that negotiations would take place and war would be averted, met Hoyos in Volksgarten in the evening of 27 July and told him about it. Hoyos commented: 'Nonsense – no negotiations, but rather war!'[180] Berchtold himself wrote on that day to Franz Joseph that, in the light of the Serbian reply, it should not be ruled out that 'the Powers of the Triple Entente might yet make another attempt to achieve a peaceful settlement of the conflict unless a clear situation is created by a declaration of war'.[181] The Austrian historian Fritz Fellner considers this justification 'so monstrous' that it should have been sufficient to silence all debate about who had started the war.[182]

Berchtold, according to Samuel Williamson, 'was the one person who could have prevented the outbreak of war.' Peace would have been preserved, Williamson maintains, had Berchtold pursued 'militant diplomacy' instead of 'hostile, military confrontation'.[183] In fact, Franz Joseph was another person who could have halted the progression towards a bloody showdown. For his signature was of course required for the declaration of war on Serbia. The evidence about his mindset concerning war and peace during these days is rather mixed. Ludwig Thallóczy, who knew everybody in Vienna, remarked in his diary entry for 23 July on the Emperor's 'great bellicosity [*eine grosse Kampflust*]'.[184] On the other hand, some of his loyal servants who produced memoir accounts after the war painted a very reluctant Emperor. Krobatin, for example, wrote that on 25 July Franz Joseph had only after 'long hesitation', ordered him to proceed with mobilization. He then told him: 'Go now, I cannot do otherwise.'[185] And Margutti cited, also with regard to the events of 25 July, the Emperor's words that the rupture of diplomatic relations with Serbia did 'not necessarily mean conflict [*noch immer nicht*]'.[186] In 1917, however, Biliński, another loyalist, revealed a rather different Franz Joseph to the Viennese journalist Heinrich Kanner. Biliński, who had spent much of July 1914 in Bad Ischl, stated that the Emperor had during the crisis 'especially' reckoned with Russia's involvement in a great war. Franz Joseph is supposed to have told him after the delivery of the ultimatum to Serbia: 'Russia cannot possibly put up with it.'[187]

Be that as it may, in Bad Ischl on 28 July, July Franz Joseph duly signed the declaration of war on Serbia, as well as the manifesto to his peoples ('*An meine Völker*'). The latter was post-dated to 29 July, the day when it was to be published in the many languages of the Monarchy. Berchtold had on 27 July sent the Emperor the draft declaration of war and also informed him about a report that the Serbian troops had opened fire from 'Danube steamboats' on Austro-Hungarian troops at Temes-Kubin (Kovin) which had resulted in a 'big skirmish'.[188] The draft declaration of war included a reference to the Temes-Kubin incident, and it was this document which the Emperor signed.[189] Except that the big border skirmish never happened. All mention of it was dropped from the text of the declaration of war sent to Serbia, and Berchtold subsequently explained to Franz Joseph that he had eliminated it in the absence of corroborating evidence. Such retrospective integrity, however, was absent when he told the German Ambassador on 28 July that he saw the British mediation proposal as coming 'too late' because Serbia had opened hostilities and the declaration of war had ensued since.[190]

This whole charade ended with what initially appeared as a bad joke. The conventional way of declaring war was through a diplomatic representative on the ground, but Giesl and his personnel had of course left Belgrade. A telegram had to do – a most unusual step. But because direct wire connections between Austria-Hungary and Serbia had been cut, it was decided to send the telegram, *in claris*, via Czernowitz (today Chernivtsi in western Ukraine) and Bucharest.[191] And since no one in Vienna was sure whether the Serbian Government was in Niš or in Kragujevac (where in fact the Serbian General Staff had moved), the declaration of war was sent to both places. In Niš on 28 July, Pašić, his cabinet and the whole of the diplomatic corps were having lunch in the garden of the restaurant 'Evropa'. At around 2 p.m., a postman approached the Serbian Prime Minister and handed him a telegram from his bag. Pašić, sitting at a table with his wife and two daughters, read it, crossed himself, and handed it to Strandtmann who, together with the German Minister, sat at an adjoining table. The Russian Chargé d'Affaires then returned it to Pašić without a comment, before immediately getting up and rushing off to inform Sazonov. But soon a secretary from the Serbian Foreign Ministry arrived at Strandtmann's residence with a message from Pašić that an identical telegram had been received by the Army in Kragujevac. The suspicion was being entertained by Serbian Ministers that perhaps a 'provocation or mystification' was in play, aimed at getting the Serbs to make a careless move. An investigation was then ordered to determine the origin of the telegrams.[192]

A factor contributing to incredulity among the Serbs was that Griesinger, whom Pašić had questioned, knew nothing about a declaration of war – despite the fact that, before breaking off diplomatic relations, Giesl had entrusted the German Legation to look after the affairs of Austria-Hungary in Serbia. Touchingly in retrospect, Pašić told Griesinger that the whole affair was particularly suspect because at that moment international mediation was under way.[193] At 7.30 p.m., however, the Prime Minister informed the Serbian Legation in Cetinje that doubts about the authenticity of the telegrams had been removed.[194] Indeed, towards midnight the Austro-Hungarian river monitors from the Danube flotilla, the bulk of which had been concentrated at Zemun, started bombarding Belgrade.[195] The First World War, initially resembling a 'Third Balkan War', had begun, but within days it was to show itself as being in fact a European bloodbath of an extent never previously experienced.

A rather meagre Russian supply of military materials finally reached Serbia on 21 August – a little ammunition and still no rifles.[196] By this time the Serbian Army had already repelled an Austro-Hungarian invasion at the battle of Cer mountain. This marked the first Allied victory of the Great War. But, typically for the nationally discordant Habsburg Empire, the disaster at Cer was blamed on the Czech 8th Corps, some units of which were accused of 'cowardice and dereliction of duty', being at the same time unfavourably compared to the Austrian-German troops. The charges were iniquitous, the Czech soldiers were 'badly alienated' as a result, but even the 1930 official Austrian history of the war blamed the 'national causes' for the mishap in Serbia.[197] Potiorek, the commander-in-chief on the Balkan front, had led with the accusations against the Czechs. The *Feldzeugmeister*, as always, was utterly incapable of self-criticism. His military leadership in 1914, just like his management of Franz Ferdinand's visit to Sarajevo on 28 June, proved a monumental fiasco. Captain Alfred Jansa, who took part in the campaign against Serbia, recalled that Potiorek had been a 'couch potato [*Stubenhocker*]', a commander whom, isolated as he was between four walls and well away from the frontlines, his troops 'did not see a single time' during four and a half months of almost incessant fighting.[198] After his second failure to subdue Serbia, Potiorek was finally sacked and pensioned off in December 1914. But he was lucky. Thanks to his connections in Vienna, he is said to have retired on a double pension.[199] He lived in Klagenfurt until his death in 1933, in an apartment where his occasional visitors could see the Bosnian sofa on which Archduke Franz Ferdinand had died.

Conclusions

STUDENTS OF HISTORY wishing to understand the causes of the First World War invariably read in the relevant literature that the Balkans before 1914 were the 'powder keg of Europe'. This label, implying a region of intrinsic instability and tendency to violence, has been a most unhelpful and misleading explanatory tool. For historically, between the 1878 Congress of Berlin and the Balkan Wars of 1912-1913, there were only two conflicts, brief ones, between Balkan states. These were the Serbo-Bulgarian war of 1885 and the Greco-Turkish war of 1897, neither of which threatened anything. The progressive decrepitude of the Ottoman Empire did lead to insurrections, such as the Macedonian one in 1903, but these local disorders had little international impact. The First Balkan War, inaugurated in 1912 by an alliance of Balkan states to liquidate the remnants of Turkey in Europe, was not in itself a destabilizing event – this last phase of the 'Eastern Question' had been expected for decades in the chancelleries of the Great Powers. What did make it potentially dangerous was the fact that Austria-Hungary was unhappy with its results, resenting above all the emergence of Serbia on the Adriatic coast. With the exception of Italy, no other Great Power, not even Austria-Hungary's ally, Germany, had much interest in reversing the outcome. Then, after the Second Balkan War, only Austria-Hungary wished to revise the Treaty of Bucharest which wrapped up the new Balkan settlement in 1913.

The real powder keg of Europe, indeed, was the continued existence of an increasingly panic-stricken and yet assertive Habsburg Monarchy. Its internal frailty had previously been demonstrated in spectacular fashion during the 1848-1849 revolutions. Its Great Power ambitions had produced a war in 1859, against the Italians and the French, and another one in 1866, against the Prussians. After the Congress of Berlin, if one excludes the Franco-German clash over non-European Morocco in 1911, the greatest threat to European peace came in 1909, as a consequence of Austria-Hungary's formal annexation of Bosnia-Herzegovina in October 1908. In the end, a world war erupted in the wake of the assassination of Franz Ferdinand in Bosnia-Herzegovina's capital because Habsburg policy-makers, reckless and frenzied ever since the end of the Balkan Wars, hoped to massively shift the regional balance of power by destroying Serbia, and because this plan of theirs was backed by Germany, which saw it as a well-timed opportunity to wreck the unity of the Entente Powers and so open the path to German continental hegemony.

In 1972, in his famous essay on the origins of the First World War, Paul Schroeder argued that the decline of Austria was 'the central threat to the European system'.[1] The Habsburg Empire lived dangerously, internally and externally. Having been expelled from Italy and Germany, it reformed itself in 1867 in such a way as to make further significant reform to all intents and purposes impossible. The 'Dual Monarchy' established by the 1867 Compromise enshrined the pre-eminence of the two strongest groups, the Austro-Germans and the Hungarians. This arrangement, which left so many other nations dissatisfied, saved the Empire for the Habsburg dynasty, but also placed a large question mark over its long term viability. From the Czechs in the Austrian half, to the Croats in the Hungarian half, the disadvantaged nations expected and clamoured for reform that would accommodate their own national aspirations. As these objectives turned out to be illusory, ideas about a political existence outside the Dual Monarchy began to gain ground. Even the two ruling nations protested and challenged. Thus in 1897 the Austrian Germans responded with violent riots to Badeni's language laws. The Hungarians, not content with the supremacy that they had achieved in the lands under the crown of St Stephen, were themselves making separatist demands that brought the Empire to the brink of civil war in 1905. By the turn of the century at the latest, the Habsburg elites for their part were viewing the future in the most pessimistic terms.

The unresolved nationality problems of this Central European hotch-potch of a state would perhaps not have mattered so much if it had not insisted on the continuation of its Great Power status. Externally, the Habsburg Monarchy's room for manoeuvre was severely reduced by Bismarck's success in unifying Germany in 1871. But Emperor Franz Joseph, thirsty as he was for imperial aggrandizement, soon spotted a refreshing new oasis for his Empire, to the south-east, in Bosnia-Herzegovina. And so, in 1878, the 'sick man on the Danube' duly replaced the 'sick man on the Bosphorus' in the heart of the Balkan peninsula. The Austro-Hungarian occupation of Bosnia-Herzegovina was met with fierce local resistance, producing by far the bloodiest Balkan conflict in the period between the Congress of Berlin and the Balkan Wars. Apart from the routine and cavalier affectation about going into the provinces on a 'civilizing mission', the occupation was justified on the flimsy strategic grounds that Bosnia-Herzegovina was a hinterland to the Dalmatian coast, and accompanied by a blast of moral fanfare about the need to implement land reform in the provinces. Yet the new regime never built any railways to connect Dalmatia with its supposed hinterland, and it was not until 1914 that it even began to address the agrarian question. Serfs remained serfs. In fact, the real reason behind the occupation, as Foreign Minister Andrássy explained, was to open up 'the gates to the Orient'. At the same time, Austria-Hungary's military presence in the neighbouring Sanjak of Novi Pazar served to prevent the formation of a 'Slavonic great state', that is, a union of Serbia and Montenegro.

But it was precisely the Habsburgs' expansion to the south-east that made their concern about the ambitions of the small Slavonic neighbours a self-inflicted strategic predicament. In occupying Bosnia-Herzegovina, Austria-Hungary achieved the unique feat of increasing its insecurity by increasing its size. For given the expected natural loyalties of the large Serbian population living in the newly-acquired Balkan territory, the independent Serbian state next door gradually came to be seen as posing a challenge to the integrity of the Empire itself within its new borders. Hence the emergence of that aspect of the 'South Slav Question' which Habsburg officialdom equated with the Serbian question and described as an 'existential threat'.

Even before its occupation of Bosnia-Herzegovina, the Monarchy faced another and quite separate South Slav headache in the shape of Croat nationalism. The continued Hungarian suppression of the Croats may have made that into an intractable problem. The Croat Party of Right, for example, set out with the objective of complete independence, and Croats were the most persistent assassins in the Empire. With regard to Serbia and the Serbs, however, an early and permanent settlement might have been achieved. In autumn 1870 Consul-General Kállay presented the Serbian Government with Andrássy's suggestion that Bosnia-Herzegovina be divided between Austria-Hungary and Serbia: the frontier would run along the rivers of Vrbas and Neretva. This would have satisfied Serbian objectives in very large measure. Belgrade was suspicious, but in any case Andrássy dropped the proposal almost immediately because Bismarck's victory over France left Prussia dominant in Central Europe, meaning that the only area left for Habsburg Great Power posturing would be the Balkans.[2]

Accordingly, what determined the regional dynamics was the would-be imperialism of this declining Great Power. For its part, Serbia, largely preoccupied with itself and the antics of its Austrophile ruler Milan Obrenović, and unable to rely on Russia, became after 1878 a de facto vassal state of Austria-Hungary. However, the threat of a 'Great Serbia' was perceived by Austro-Hungarian foreign ministers from Andrássy to Gołu-chowski. The latter repeatedly made statements that a union between Serbia and Montenegro would not be permitted. Such a union, of course, was unwelcome because a strong South Slav state might come to seem a more attractive proposition to the South Slavs of the Habsburg Monarchy than the Empire itself. For this reason, despite their internal Croat problem, Habsburg statesmen used the terms 'South Slav state' and 'Great Serbia' almost interchangeably. Keeping Serbia weak thus became the fundamental axiom of Vienna's Balkan policy. Even at his very advanced age in 1914, Franz Joseph himself was determined to go to war rather than watch Serbia's emergence as a more robust regional rival.

One of the biggest myths about the late Dual Monarchy, enthusiastically promoted by legions of historians, is that the Habsburg elites, and Archduke Franz Ferdinand in particular, had seriously considered reforming the Empire in a way that would tackle both their internal South Slav question and the perceived external threat from independent Serbia. This supposed project of reform revolved around so-called 'Trialism', by which a third, South Slav, unit would be established with its centre in Zagreb, possessing such power of attraction as would neutralize anything that Belgrade could offer. It has to be said, however, that these were just balloons of fantasy visualized largely by nationalist Croats at the time. With the exception of Aehrenthal, no one of any consequence among the statesmen of the Monarchy had actually proposed Trialism. And even Aehrenthal quickly gave up on the idea. Franz Joseph was decidedly against it – his abortive experiment with Czech Trialism in 1871 had left him allergic to any structural reform of the Empire. Even more important was the Hungarian opposition to any imperial restructuring that would entail a loss of lands under the Crown of St Stephen.

Nor can the Heir to the Throne be described as an advocate of Trialism. He cannot, in fact, be seen as a champion of any meaningful reform. Such tentative sympathy as Franz Ferdinand may have had for Trialism related to his obsession with weakening Hungary and collapsed completely after the establishment in Croatia-Slavonia, in 1905, of the Croato-Serb alliance – an alliance favouring the ultra-nationalist Hungarians against Vienna. Both the Archduke and his associates then considered Trialism a dangerous idea, for they saw the South Slavs as unreliable. Against the evidence, many historians still speculate that only the assassination of Franz Ferdinand prevented the realization of his trialist plans concerning the South Slavs. Some even suggest that those plans had caused the assassination. Then there are others who write books in which the Archduke is keen to promote not Trialism, but rather federalism along national lines. Yet he never even remotely contemplated any kind of power-sharing system, let alone one based on the principle of nationality. His vision, in so far as he had one, was that of a strong centralized state in which historic Habsburg Crown Lands, not national units, would be allowed a degree of local autonomy. And although he had had many years in which to prepare for power, his one and only practical post-accession plan in 1914 was to destroy the hated dualist structure which enabled Budapest to deal with Vienna on an equal footing. The Hungarians had anticipated this and made known that they would defend the Constitution with force. What is equally important is the fact that the Archduke's military chancellery had likewise made provisions for a military showdown.

But Franz Ferdinand has long been a peg on which fanciful theories about an enlightened Habsburg Monarchy could be hung. Modern historians have queued up to hang their hats on this ill-suited peg. This is as baffling as it is farcical in the light of the available source materials which invariably show Franz Ferdinand as a die-hard paleoconservative. Historians have completed the apotheosis of the Archduke by attributing to him a peace-loving orientation. Yet he was a restless imperialist and militarist, as was illustrated by his support for Austria-Hungary's Albanian venture and his vigorous sponsorship of the Austro-Hungarian naval programme. Dreaming of a re-conquest of Venice and Lombardy, he yearned for a war against Italy just as much as Conrad did, and was more than ready to fight Serbia as well – in 1909, 1912, 1913 and, indeed, in June 1914. He absolutely detested not just the Serbs, but the Slavs in general. His flaming temper, massive prejudice and combative nature hardly squared with the retrospective depiction of him as a restrained and responsible future emperor. In 1969 C.A. Macartney expressed his puzzlement that Franz Ferdinand had been written down 'as a great statesman' by some writers. 'It is difficult', Macartney protested, 'to see the justification for these praises.'[3]

Another pertinent myth long in circulation concerns the Serbian origins of the First World War. Serbia has been seen as Austria-Hungary's docile satellite until the 1903 murder of King Alexander Obrenović. Thereafter, according to conventional interpretations, a sharp change of course took place with the arrival of a supposedly Russophile Karađorđević dynasty, bringing an increasingly assertive Serbia into collision with the Dual Monarchy. Stereotypically pejorative depictions of Serbia have gone hand in hand with these accounts. Recently, Serbia has been described as 'a turbulent and intermittently violent state' – as if other states did not experience political turbulence and occasionally resort to the use of force.[4] Another recent description of Serbia, typically jaundiced while analytically unhelpful, is that it was the Habsburg Empire's 'troublesome neighbour'.[5] The assassination of Franz Ferdinand in Sarajevo is normally portrayed in non-Serbian literature as the culmination of Serbia's relentless – indeed programmed – anti-Habsburg orientation.

Little if anything in this picture corresponds to historical truth. The basis of Serbia's presumed programme of expansion, the *Načertanije* of 1844, was a document inspired, and largely written, by a Paris-based Polish émigré organization scheming plots and building allies against Russia and Austria. Few in Serbia had read it, let alone followed it. It goes without saying that Belgrade wished to incorporate the Serbian-inhabited territories outside Serbia, but this was neither a systematically conducted enterprise, nor, with regard to Austria-Hungary, viewed as a very realistic aim or pursued at all. As for the 1903 regicide, its import has been vastly exaggerated. Almost all relevant historiography treats the subsequent clashes between Belgrade and Vienna as flowing from it, in effect endowing this event with a world-historical significance. But those clashes were also happening before the regicide, and therefore did not derive from it. Austro-Serbian relations had during the reign of Alexander Obrenović left much to be desired, as evidenced by a series of 'pig wars' launched by Vienna in order to keep Serbia economically weak. Serbia's 1881 secret convention with Austria-Hungary, which had placed the country in such a subservient position *vis-à-vis* its large neighbour, expired at the end of 1895 and would not be renewed. The 1903 conspiracy against King Alexander and Queen Draga was itself entirely divorced from any foreign policy agenda, although it so happened that its civilian organizers were Austrophiles who made sure of obtaining Vienna's backing before proceeding with the putsch.

Invariably, however, standard accounts present Serbia's post-1903 foreign policy as turning away from Austria-Hungary to Russia and even being directed by the latter. Such interpretations are entirely inaccurate. In the first place, long before the restoration of the House of Karađorđe-vić, which had otherwise enjoyed almost no support in the country, Serbia had tried to move closer to Russia. In the 1890s King Alexander had already allowed the Novaković and Simić governments to position themselves as Russophile. At that time, a basic consensus emerged across the Serbian political establishment that only Russia would conceivably assist Serbia in foreign policy. However, the Treaty of San Stefano had demonstrated in 1878 that Russia was principally interested in the eastern part of the Balkan peninsula; this was still the case thirty years later when, in the Bosnian annexation crisis, it showed that it only cared about the Straits. Thus there was no 'major realignment' of Serbia's foreign policy in the direction of St Petersburg after 1903. Nor could there have been such realignment in a situation where the regional Great Powers, Russia and Austria-Hungary, were consensually maintaining the Balkan *status quo*. In other words, there was nothing for Serbia to realign between. In truth, after 1903 the statesmen of Serbia knew they could not count on Russia in respect of any regional pretensions they may have desired to pursue. The Austro-Russian Balkan entente of 1897 held firm for a long time – until January 1908, when Aehrenthal destroyed it with his Sanjak of Novi Pazar railway project. Besides, defeat in the war against Japan and revolution at home had weakened Russia tremendously. When, in February 1908, the Serbian Government turned to Izvolsky for help to realize its Adriatic railway project as a counter to Aehrenthal's plans, it was the first occasion after 1903 that any significant request had been addressed by Serbia to St Petersburg.

Nor was the latter any more forthcoming than it had previously been. In one after another of the crises that followed, Serbia was left stranded by Russia. In 1908 the cynical Izvolsky first offered to Aehrenthal both Bosnia-Herzegovina and the Sanjak of Novi Pazar, and then, after the annexation of the former, left Serbia to Aehrenthal's tender mercies. In the First Balkan War Sazonov, who had tried to stop it, watched calmly as Vienna forced the Serbs to withdraw from the Adriatic coast; and, in the spring of 1913, he agreed that Scutari should go to Vienna's Albanian protégé. In October of that year, in a further Albanian crisis, he again failed to back the Serbs. Despite Belgrade's repeated pleas to St Petersburg for armaments, rifles in particular, Sazonov studiously ignored this, to Serbia, fundamentally important matter. As late as 24 July 1914 he was telling the Serbian Government to withdraw its Army towards Greece rather than fight Austria-Hungary. Russia's famous 'missing telegram' and St Petersburg's supposed encouragement of the Serbian Government on 24 and 25 July to resist the Austro-Hungarian ultimatum, exist only in the imagination of those historians obsessively advancing a thesis of Russian, and indeed Serbian, war guilt. Moreover, Russia's subsequent decision for war was certainly not made on Serbia's behalf, though it was, at long last, to Serbia's advantage. This is not to say that Russia had actually owed anything to Serbia, but it shows that their relationship in the decade before 1914 was not what it is made out to be in so many accounts looking to pigeonhole history. All of which demonstrates at the same time that Russia by its actions in the Balkans, or lack thereof, did not contribute to the pressures that triggered the world war in 1914 and indeed that it tried to defuse them.

Even the Austro-Hungarian Minister in Belgrade considered, in late 1904, that the Serbs had written Russia off for up to ten years. And indeed for most of this period Pašić was actually trying to get closer to Austria-Hungary. In the course of 1904 and later he repeatedly sought an accommodation with Vienna, but found his advances rebuffed. What Serbia got instead was a trade war imposed by a disdainful and waspish Dual Monarchy. At the Ballhausplatz, Gołuchowski would not tolerate any sign of autonomous conduct by Serbia, such as seeking to buy its artillery elsewhere in Europe, and concluding a customs union with Bulgaria. This was at a time, between 1904 and 1906, when Serbia was hoping to negotiate a new commercial treaty with Austria-Hungary, overwhelmingly its most important economic partner. However, Pašić got nowhere with his offer to buy Austrian guns in return for Habsburg support of Serbia's ambitions in Kosovo and Macedonia. The pragmatic Serbian Prime Minister fared no better even when he proposed to set up an Austrophile party in Serbia. 'No contract for guns – no Commercial Treaty', was Gołuchowski's candidly stated position. It was this high-and-mighty Polish aristocrat who hacked and butchered Austro-Serbian relations after 1903, but he was merely following Austria-Hungary's long-established policy of enfeebling the small Balkan neighbour. It backfired: the 'Pig War' that followed in July 1906 most unexpectedly helped Serbia to become economically independent. What is so compelling about all these developments, in the light of prevalent wisdom, is that they were in no way connected with the 1903 putsch in Belgrade, or with Russia, or for that matter with any Austro-Serbian issues over Bosnia-Herzegovina. In 1906, the downward spiral in the Balkans began as a result of Vienna's petty imperialism.

Serbia's foreign policy, in contrast to the way it has been depicted in much of the relevant historiography, had, before the annexation of Bosnia-Herzegovina, almost forgotten these lands. Aehrenthal's move to establish Habsburg sovereignty over these provinces may have related to plans for internally consolidating the Empire and even restructuring it, but he was at the same time signalling that Austria-Hungary was not especially interested in supporting the Balkan *status quo*. In any case, strange as it may sound, the storm caused by his act of annexation really concerned a peripheral issue in relations between Vienna and Belgrade. In steering Bosnia-Herzegovina towards the calm waters of Habsburg-controlled quasi-constitutionalism, Burián had managed to obtain the political co-operation of all the national groups. There had been no Great Serbian agitation in the provinces inspired or supported by the government in Belgrade. Previous to the crisis of 1908-1909 the main Austro-Serbian frictions had been well removed from Bosnia-Herzegovina. In addition to those connected with the 'guns question' that led to the tariff war, they concerned Serbian misgivings with regard to the Mürzsteg reform process and suspicions about an Austro-Hungarian '*Drang nach Saloniki*'. The primary aim of the Serbian Government before the annexation was to counter Aehrenthal's Sanjak railway with its own Danube-Adriatic project. After the annexation, Austro-Serbian wrangles again had nothing to do with Bosnia-Herzegovina: the issue of the Serbian Army's presence on the coast of Albania in winter 1912-1913; Scutari in spring of 1913; and Albania again in October 1913. At no point was Serbia threatening, or in a position to threaten, the integrity of the Habsburg Empire. Vienna's Balkan imperialism, by contrast, was relentlessly stifling Serbia's at every turn. At times, both Milovanović and Pašić, unable to whip up external support, toyed with the idea that Serbia should give up altogether as an independent state and submit to the Monarchy.

Some writers protest that Austria-Hungary had legitimate 'security imperatives' and that, like any Great Power, it 'possessed interests that it had the right robustly to defend'.[6] No one could quarrel with that, except that it is difficult to see how, for example, the 'Pig War' against Serbia was a defensive measure connected with security considerations. It is equally difficult to see how the creation of a puppet Albanian state was meant to defend the territorial integrity of the great Habsburg Empire – unless, of course, one extends the definition of 'security imperatives' to the point where the distinction between defence and aggression becomes utterly meaningless. For the purpose of setting up Albania, it should be recalled, was not only to deny the Serbs an Adriatic port but also to recruit a local army that would fight against them.

The remarkable fact about Austro-Serbian relations in the months before the Sarajevo assassination is that they were reasonably good. All tensions had subsided with the ending of the October 1913 crisis over Albania. The murders in Sarajevo, of course, immediately revived and dramatized the old antagonism. Yet the assassination of Franz Ferdinand succeeded only because of the self-obsession and incompetence of Bosnia-Herzegovina's *Landeschef* Oskar Potiorek. The story of 28 June 1914 is as much about the personal aspirations of this Austrian General as it is about an amateurish conspiracy against Franz Ferdinand. However, a dead Arch-duke now became a useful tool in Vienna's pursuit of pocket imperialism in the Balkans, expressed by Austria-Hungary's resolve to place Serbia in the dock. This despite the fact that the Ballhausplatz had no proof of the Serbian Government's complicity in the Sarajevo assassination and that its own investigator Wiesner had actually ruled out such complicity.

For more than a hundred years, generations of historians have likewise failed to provide any convincing evidence that official Belgrade was involved in the conspiracy to kill Franz Ferdinand. What they have invari-ably pointed to, ever since the publication of Professor Stanojević's unsourced pamphlet in 1923, is the involvement of Lieutenant-Colonel Apis, the head of Serbian military intelligence and also the leader of the so-called Black Hand organization. Apis's own confessions that he had organized the Sarajevo assassination – first revealed in Serbian memoir literature of the early 1930s and confirmed at his posthumous 1953 retrial – appeared to substantiate the view that official Serbia, albeit in the shape of a rogue officer heading a secret nationalist society, had stood behind the Sarajevo outrage.

And so the Black Hand story became the gospel truth even though Apis's various statements on the subject were contradictory as well as generally absurd. As this book has argued, Apis was a braggart and a liar. What is clear, however, is that he was sufficiently alarmed before the assassination to try and stop it once he learned that some youths loaded with weapons had been assisted to cross into Bosnia. He knew that Serbia was not ready for another war, let alone one against Austria-Hungary. Equally important was his realization that a major complication in relations with Austria-Hungary could fatally undermine the plan he was actively pursuing in May-June 1914 to take power in Serbia through a military putsch and with the cooperation of Serbia's opposition parties. The famous and to this day misunderstood Serbian warning to Vienna in June 1914 appears to have been his work. So why, then, if Apis had tried to prevent the assassination, did he later brag that he had put it all together? The answer is, of course, that a world war had intervened. In the middle of that conflict Apis happily took credit for what many Serbs viewed as the patriotic act of assassinating an Austrian Archduke. Moreover, at his 1917 Salonika trial, he thought he would save his skin by claiming responsibility for Sarajevo. Interestingly – and very tellingly – in his Salonika confidential report Apis failed to mention what he privately admitted in 1915: that he had actually taken steps to halt the assassins. In 1917, obviously, with his life at stake, Apis had to adjust his story to fit his reduced circumstances, for it was of no advantage to him to say, as he had been doing, that he had both organized the patriotic work of assassinating the Archduke and also that he had tried to stop it.

In 2011 Sean McMeekin concluded with a dose of pomposity that, since the 1920s, 'few informed observers have doubted Apis's – and thus semi-official Serbian – culpability in the crime. No serious historians do today.'[7] It should, however, be incumbent on serious historians to look closely at the foundations of established versions of history, especially those set in controversial contexts. Upon re-examination, the established thesis of Apis and the Black Hand organization as culpable for Sarajevo is shown to be a complete falsehood. For, rather than organizing the assassination, it is clear that Apis tried to prevent it.

Many of the tendentious evaluations that have associated official or semi-official Serbia with the Sarajevo assassination have then moved seamlessly on to the outbreak of the war, equally tendentiously presenting it as an inevitable consequence of the murders. Yet those historians who have argued in this manner have wrongly fused the question of who bore responsibility for the assassination with a second, separate question of what subsequently impelled the Habsburg decision-makers to react as they did. Certainly, Vienna was not weighing up any Black Hand linkage – if for no other reason than that no one was claiming that this organization was involved; nor indeed was such a claim made until long after the end of the Empire, becoming a theme only in 1923. For this reason the impact of Apis and his Black Hand on the Austro-Hungarian decision for war was nil, and any opposite contention is in fact a complete red herring. This matter was pointed out a long time ago with elegant simplicity by A.J.P. Taylor: 'Berchtold determined to force war on Serbia, though he had no proof of Serbian complicity and never found any ... The later evidence of Serbian complicity, even if accepted, is therefore irrelevant to the judgement of Berchtold's policy.'[8]

Yet some historians are stubbornly clinging to the thesis about Serbia's culpability for the assassination which they then use to account for

Habsburg decision-making in July 1914. In a major recent study of the Austro-Hungarian General Staff, Günther Kronenbitter explains Vienna's decision for war on the grounds of Serbia supposedly being a rogue state in the existing international system: 'Serbia', he writes, 'challenged the existential basis of the Habsburg Empire because, with regard to the Serbian propaganda, it dodged an inter-state resolution. The Belgrade Government was not ready to accept responsibility for the nationalist underground.'[9] Kronenbitter has apparently not studied the Serbian reply to the Austro-Hungarian ultimatum, nor does he seem aware of Berchtold's private admission in July 1914 of the difficulty of finding any Great Serbian propaganda material aimed against the Monarchy. Count Hoyos's own post-war confession that he did not, in July 1914, believe Belgrade guilty of the assassination, taken together with Serbia being cleared by Vienna's own investigator at the time, show that the Ballhausplatz knew Serbia's Government was innocent of assassinating the Archduke, and indeed of spreading propaganda. Thus Austria-Hungary was not acting on a misplaced assumption of Serbian guilt, but rather on the basis of its wider strategic self-interest. Its regional strategic ambition is clearly revealed in, among other documents, Franz Joseph's handwritten letter to Wilhelm II, delivered by Hoyos on 5 July 1914.

Equally noteworthy has been the general inability of Vienna-focused historians to distinguish between 'South Slav' and 'Great Serbian' concepts. The two are normally lumped together, as indeed they were at the Ballhausplatz. Yet there was not a great deal of interest in Serbia for the South Slav idea – this was a Croat nationalist construct which had evolved into a demand for Trialism, a different name for Great Croatia. To be sure, some Serbian intellectuals, such as Skerlić and Cvijić, were proponents of Yugoslav unity – though not under a Habsburg roof. Serbian politicians, on the other hand, were interested in a Great Serbia. But Bosnia-Herzegovina, a main building bloc of such a state, looked unattainable to them. Therefore, Serbian policy had focused on Kosovo and Macedonia long before the annexation, and it continued on that course after the annexation. Pašić was forever telling his Austro-Hungarian interlocutors that Serbia's perspective 'lay in the south' and that there was nothing it was hoping for in Bosnia-Herzegovina.

The South Slav issue, in truth, was entirely a domestic Habsburg affair. The Yugoslav ideology that reached Gavrilo Princip and his friends in Sarajevo did not come from Serbia. It was native to Austria and Hungary or, to be more precise, to their provinces of Dalmatia and Croatia. Representing a new variant of Yugoslavism, one that began to be associated with Croat students from the mid-1890s onward, it had nothing to do with Trialism or Great Croatia. It was a 'nationalist and revolutionary' movement asserting the existence of a single Serbo-Croat nation and calling for the overthrow of the Monarchy. Maintained by Hungarian misrule in Croatia and led by such able agitators as Tartaglia and Ujević, it attracted the support of both Croat and Serb students in Croatia and, more importantly, it had a very significant effect on high school students in Bosnia-Herzegovina. 'Young Bosnia' was born in 1912 of a student riot in Sarajevo that had been organized as a manifestation of solidarity with students in Croatia. Princip, one of the most active participants in the riot, was of Serbian birth, but to describe him, as is so often the case, as a 'Serbian nationalist' is to impute to him the antithesis of his actual political orientation. Princip and his fellow assassins, with one exception, were believers in Serbo-Croat unity and would actually call themselves 'nationalists', meaning by this 'Serbo-Croats' or 'Yugoslavs'. The exception was the one Muslim in their number, Mehmedbašić, whose loyalties were pro-Serbian rather than Yugoslavian. Otherwise, they were South Slav nationalists and Yugoslavs were to them a single nation that needed its state – but not within the Habsburg Monarchy.

The rationale for war against Serbia as a means of mending and reinvigorating the Empire internally runs like a red thread through the reasoning of Habsburg officialdom regarding the South Slav question. Important as this rationale is in the context of 1914, however, this book has also pointed out the wider regional considerations that guided Vienna's decision for war. On three occasions in 1912-1913 Austria-Hungary was on the brink of military intervention against Serbia over matters (in Albania) which had nothing to do with any South Slav issues – but had everything to do with projecting its Great Power status. It was only a question of time before Berchtold, Conrad and, indeed, Franz Ferdinand, decided to strike out. In July 1914, the necessity to act appeared all the more urgent because of the deterioration in the regional situation. In particular, Romania's apparent defection from the Triple Alliance set the alarm bells ringing in both Vienna and Budapest. Seldom had a little war looked more enticing: Serbia would basically disappear, Romania, Bulgaria and Albania would all be secured, and Russia would be dislodged from the region. Provided that Germany could ward Russia off, this war in the Balkans could be a game changer for the long-suffering Habsburg Empire. The strategy was risky, but quite irresistible.

Of course, it all ended with the break-up of the old Monarchy. The Austrian writer Anton Mayr-Harting opined that this was the predictable outcome, all in all, for a state which had been characterized by so much 'folly and malice'.[10] Its fate in 1918 is a reminder today to the elites of the European Union, ensconced in the European Commission in Brussels, of the possible hazards they face in trying to exert control over the continent's divergent national interests. There is a sense in which, however, the Empire lived on even after 1918, for at the conclusion of the Great War the Serbs created a large, multi-national 'Kingdom of the Serbs, Croats and Slovenes' – instead of setting up a nationally compact Great Serbia, which would have been an equitable and befitting end result of their enormous blood sacrifice since 1912. It was to prove the costliest mistake in their history. There is a tendency in Western writings to see the new state, ruled from Belgrade, as having in effect been a Great Serbia. But it was nothing of the kind. It inherited from Austria-Hungary the same problem that had plagued that empire: disaffected nationalism, in this case the Croat variety. In 1929, King Alexander changed the name of the country into 'Yugoslavia'. But no amount of camouflage could compensate for the absence of unity. In 1941, when Hitler invaded, Yugoslavia collapsed like a house of cards. Interestingly, in the horrendously bloody civil war of 1941–1945 that ensued, the opposing royalist *Četnik* and the communist Partisan forces both contained units named 'Gavrilo Princip'.[11]

In communist Yugoslavia nations and national minorities were sheltered and even pampered in a laudable federal system, and formerly non-recognized national groups became recognized nations. Soon after the death of its dictator Marshal Josip Broz Tito, however, Yugoslavia entered a period of vicious nationalist strife and then fragmented again in conditions of escalating violence. This time it would not be resurrected. One wonders how long a reformed, federated Habsburg state would have lasted had it ever been created along the national principle and even abstained from pursuing Balkan hegemony. In 1948, writing about the new Yugoslavia towards the end of his study of the Habsburg Monarchy, A.J.P. Taylor dwelt on the subject of common loyalty and reflected on what could appease national conflicts. He could not have foreseen at the time just how right he would turn out to be when he described Tito as 'the last of the Habsburgs'.[12]

Notes

Abbreviations

Prologue: Sick Man on the Danube

1 Karl Kraus, 'Franz Ferdinand und die Talente', *Die Fackel*, Wien, 10 July 1914, pp.2 and 4.

2 Josef Stürgkh, *Politische und militärische Erinnerungen*, Leipzig, 1922, p.5.

3 Cited in Viktor Bibl, *Von Revolution zu Revolution in Österreich*, Berlin-Leipzig-München, 1924, p.473.

4 Oskar von Wertheimer (ed.), *Graf Stefan Tisza. Briefe 1914-1918*, Berlin, 1928, vol.1., p.63.

5 Ottokar Czernin, *Im Weltkriege*, Berlin-Wien, 1919, pp.41-42.

6 See, in particular, Solomon Wank, 'Pessimism in the Austrian Establishment at the Turn of the Century' in Solomon Wank *et al.* (eds.), *The Mirror of History: Essays in Honor of Fritz Fellner*, Santa Barbara – Oxford, 1988, pp.295-314.

7 Fritz Fellner and Doris A. Corradini (eds.), *Schicksalsjahre Österreichs. Die Erinnerungen und Tagebücher Josef Redlichs 1869-1936*, Wien-Köln-Weimar, 2011, vol.1, p.517, diary entry for 2 December 1912, p.517. Redlich's diary was first published in 1953. All quotations given here are from the 2011 extended edition. Hereafter cited as Redlich, *Schicksalsjahre*.

8 Norman Stone, *Europe Transformed*, London, 1983, p.407.

9 L.B. Namier, 'The Downfall of the Habsburg Monarchy' in H.W.V. Temperley (ed.), *A History of the Peace Conference of Paris*, London, 1921, vol.4, p.59; A.J.P. Taylor, *The Habsburg Monarchy 1809-1918*, London, 1948, p.10.

10 Arthur J, May, *The Passing of the Habsburg Monarchy, 1914-1918*, Philadelphia, 1966, vol.1, Preface, p.6.

11 Carl J. Burckhardt, *Begegnungen*, Zürich, 1958, p.57.

12 Alan Sked, *The Decline and Fall of the Habsburg Empire, 1815-1918*, London-New York, 1989, p.187; Joachim Remak, 'The Healthy Invalid: How Doomed the Habsburg Empire?', *The Journal of Modern History*, vol.41, no.2 (June 1969), p,141; Hans Kohn, 'Was the Collapse Inevitable?', *Austrian History Yearbook*, vol.3, part 3 (1967), p.251; Taylor, *The Habsburg Monarchy*, p.228 and Preface, p.7.

13 Johannes Lepsius, Albrecht Mandelssohn Bartholdy and Friedrich Timme (eds.), *Die Grosse Politik der Europäischen Kabinette 1871-1914*, Berlin, 1927, vol.39, no. 15734, private letter Tschirschky to Jagow, 22 May 1914. Herafter cited as *GP*.

14 Karl Kautsky, Max Montgelas and Walter

Schücking (eds.), *Die Deutschen Dokumente zum Kriegsausbruch 1914*, Berlin, 1922, no.72, private letter Jagow to Lichnowsky, 18 July 1914. Hereafter cited as *DD*.

15 Karl Alexander von Müller, *Mars und Venus. Erinnerungen 1914-1919*, Stuttgart, 1954, p.36.

16 Take Jonescu, *Some Personal Impressions*, London, 1919, p.261.

17 Rudolf Sieghart, *Die letzten Jahrzehnte einer Grossmacht*, Berlin, 1932, p.211.

18 Günther Kronenbitter, 'Verhinderter Retter? Erzherzog Franz Ferdinand und die Erhaltung der Habsburgermonarchie' in Ulrich E. Zellenberg, *Konservative Profile. Ideen und Praxis in der Politik zwischen FM Radetzky, Karl Kraus und Alois Mock*, Graz-Stuttgart, 2003, p.275.

19 Franz Adlgasser and Margaret Friedrich (eds.), *Heinrich Friedjung. Geschichte in Gesprächen. Aufzeichnungen 1898-1919*, Wien-Köln-Weimar, 1997, vol.1, p.341. Hereafter cited as Friedjung, *Geschichte in Gesprächen*.

20 Seton-Watson's introduction to Karl Tschuppik, *The Reign of Emperor Francis Joseph 1848-1916*, London, 1930, p.xi.

21 Cited in Hans Kohn, *Pan-Slavism: Its History and Ideology*, Notre Dame, 1953, p.67.

22 Solomon Wank, 'Some Reflections on the Habsburg Empire and Its Legacy in the Nationalities Question', *Austrian History Yearbook*, vol. 28, 1997, p.135.

23 Robert A. Kann, *The Multinational Empire: Nationalism and National Reform in the Habsburg Monarchy, 1848-1918*, New York, 1950, vol.2, p.38. For the Kremsier draft of 1849 see also Rudolf Wierer, *Der Föderalismus im Donauraum*, Graz-Köln, 1969, pp.40-43.

24 Louis Eisenmann, *Le Compromis austro-hongrois de 1867: Études sur le dualisme*, Paris, 1904, p.208.

25 Franz Schnürer (ed.), *Briefe Kaiser Franz Josephs I. an seine Mutter 1838-1872*, München, 1930, p.301.

26 Jasna Turkalj, 'Starčevićeva misao o nužnosti samostalne hrvatske države' in Ivan Gabelica (ed.), *Starčević. Znanstveni kolokvij o 180. obljetnici rođenja*, Zagreb, 2004, p.37.

27 Kann, *The Multinational Empire*, vol.2, p.127.

28 Albert von Margutti, *Kaiser Franz Joseph. Persönliche Erinnerungen*, Wien-Leipzig, 1924, p.235 and pp.228-230 and 233.

29 A.J.P. Taylor, *Europe: Grandeur and Decline*, Harmondsworth, 1967, p.80.

30 Feldmarschall Conrad, *Aus meiner Dienstzeit 1906-1918*, Wien-Berlin-Leipzig-München, 1921, vol.1, p.49.

31 Milan Hodža, *Federation in Central Europe: Reflections and Reminiscences*, London, 1942, p.63.

32 Wank, 'Some Reflections on the Habsburg Empire and Its Legacy in the Nationalities Question', p.138.

33 F.R. Bridge, *From Sadowa to Sarajevo: The Foreign Policy of Austria-Hungary, 1866-1914*, London-Boston, 1972, pp.7-8.

34 Friedrich Prinz, 'Der österreichisch-ungarische Ausgleich von 1867 als historiographisches Problem' in *Bohemia*, Jahrbuch des Collegium Carolinum, vol.9, München 1968, p.350.

35 Erich Zöllner, *Geschichte Österreichs*, Wien, 1961, p.412.

36 Taylor, *The Habsburg Monarchy*, p.133.

37 Jean-Paul Bled, *Franz Joseph*, Oxford, 1994, p.149.

38 Robert A. Kann, 'The Austro-Hungarian Compromise of 1867 in Retrospect. Causes and Effect?' in Ľudovit Holotík (ed.), *Der österreichisch-ungarische Ausgleich 1867*, Bratislava, 1971, p. 24.

39 Cited in Bled, *Franz Joseph*, p.152.

40 Richard Charmatz, *Österreichs innere Geschichte von 1848 bis 1907*, Leipzig, 1911, p.76.

41 Cited in S. Harrison Thomson, *Czechoslovakia in European History*, Princeton, 1953, p.215.

42 Friedrich F.G. Kleinwaechter, *Der Untergang der Oesterreichisch-ungarischen Monarchie*, Leipzig, 1920, p.228.

43 Leon Biliński, *Wspomnienia i dokumenty*, Warszawa, 1924, vol.1, p.234.

44 Taylor, *The Habsburg Monarchy*, p.136.

45 Eisenmann, *Le Compromis austro-hongrois*, p.651.

46 Gerald Stourzh, 'The Multinational Empire Revisited: Reflections on Late Imperial Austria', *Austrian History Yearbook*, vol. 23, 1992, p.12.

47 Oscar Jászi, *The Dissolution of the Habsburg Monarchy*, Chicago, 1929, p.356.

48 Alexander Spitzmüller-Harmersbach, *Die letzte österreichisch-ungarische Ausgleich und der Zusammenbruch der Monarchie*, Berlin, 1929, pp.10-11.

49 Vojislav Vučković (ed.), *Politička akcija Srbije u južnoslovenskim pokrajinama habsburške monarhije 1859-1874*, Beograd, 1965, no.198, p.361.

50 Namier, 'The Downfall of the Habsburg Monarchy', p.66.

51 Rudolf Springer [Karl Renner], *Grundlagen und Entwicklungsziele der Österreichisch-Ungarischen Monarchie*, Wien-Leipzig, 1906, p.46.

52 Cited in Bled, *Franz Joseph*, p.149

53 Cited in Egon Caesar Corti, *Mensch und Herrscher. Wege und Schicksale Kaiser Franz Josephs I.*, Graz, 1952, p.386.

54 Jean Bérenger, *A History of the Habsburg Empire 1700-1918*, London-New York, 1997, p.214.

55 Baron von Falkenegg [Alois Paul Ledersteger], *Ungarn am Scheidewege. Politische Betrachtungen*, Berlin, 1905, p.14.

56 *GP*, vol.39, no.15736, annex, p.367.

57 Jászi, *The Dissolution of the Habsburg Monarchy*, p.109.

58 Piotr S. Wandycz, 'The Poles in the Habsburg Monarchy', *Austrian History Yearbook*, vol.3, part 2, 1967, p.278; Lothar Höbelt, *Franz Joseph I. Der Kaiser und sein Reich*, Wien-Köln-Weimar, 2009, p.66.

59 Carl Freiherr von Bardolff, *Soldat im alten Österreich. Erinnerungen aus meinem Leben*, Jena, 1938, p.156.

60 C.A. Macartney, *The Habsburg Empire 1790-1918*, London, 1969, p.576.

61 Spiridon Gopčević, *Österreichs Untergang – die Folge von Franz Josefs Mißregierung*, Berlin, 1920, p.242.

62 Ivo Goldstein, *Croatia: A History*, London, 1999, p.34.

63 Kann, *The Multinational Empire*, vol.1, p.239.

64 Cited in Ivo Perić, *A History of the Croats*, Zagreb, 1988, p.160.

65 Mario Strecha, 'Franjo Josip I. (1848-1916.)' in Neven Budak, Mario Strecha and Željko Krušelj, *Habsburzi i Hrvati*, Zagreb, 2003, pp.149-150.

66 'Die Kroaten – das sind Fetzen.' Cited in Josip Horvat, *Pobuna omladine 1911-1914*, Zagreb, 2006, p.34.

67 Ferdo Šišić, *Jugoslovenska misao*, Beograd, 1937, pp.247-248.

68 Friedjung, *Geschichte in Gesprächen*, vol.1, p.116.

69 Dalmatia was taken by Austria in 1797 when Napoleon put an end to the Venetian Republic.

70 Mirjana Gross, *Vladavina hrvatsko-srpske koalicije 1906-1907*, Beograd, 1960, p.17.

71 Namier, 'The Downfall of the Habsburg Monarchy', pp.87-88.

72 Zöllner, *Geschichte Österreichs*, p.440.

73 Margutti, *Kaiser Franz Joseph*, p.212.

74 R.W. Seton-Watson, *Transylvania: A Key-Problem*, Oxford, 1943, p.5.

75 Robert A. Kann, *A History of the Habsburg Empire 1526-1918*, Berkeley-Los Angeles-London, 1974, p.362.

76 Cited in Macartney, *The Habsburg Empire*, p.560.

77 Kann, *The Multinational Empire*, vol.1, p.135.

78 Arthur J. May, *The Habsburg Monarchy 1867-1914*, Cambridge, Massachusetts, 1965, p.83.

79 Kann, *A History of the Habsburg Empire*, p.336.

80 Dragutin Tadijanović (ed.), *Tin Ujević. Sabrana djela*, Zagreb, 1966, vol.10, p.28.

81 Albert Eberhard Friedrich Schäffle, *Aus meinem Leben*, Berlin, 1905, vol.1, pp.204-206.

82 *Ibid.*, p.208.

83 Macartney, *The Habsburg Empire*, p.582.

84 Friedrich Prinz, *Geschichte Böhmens 1848-1948*, München, 1988, p.145.

85 Schäffle, *Aus meinem Leben*, vol.2, p.43.

86 Alfred Payrleitner, *Österreicher und Tschechen*, Wien-Köln-Weimar, 1990, p.119.

87 Schäffle, *Aus meinem Leben*, vol.2, p.41

88 Thomson, *Czechoslovakia*, pp.217-218.

89 Karl Tschuppik, *Franz Joseph I. Der Untergang eines Reiches*, Hellerau bei Dresden, 1928, p.190.

90 Adolph Fischhof, *Österreich und die Bürgschaften seines Bestandes*, Wien, 1869, p.37.

91 *Ibid.*, p.139.

92 *Ibid.*, p.61.

93 *Ibid.*, p.108.

94 *Ibid.*, p.224.

95 Justus Freimund [Karl Eduard Müller], *Österreichs Zukunft entwickelt aus seiner Vergangenheit und Gegenwart*, Brüssel, 1867, pp.106, 41, 56-58, 56, 107 and 49.

96 Hugo Hantsch, *Die Nationalitätenfrage im alten Österreich*, Wien, 1953, p.61.

97 Kann, *A History of the Habsburg Empire*, p.281.

98 Macartney, *The Habsburg Empire*, p.610.

99 Bled, *Franz Joseph*, p.226.

100 Brigitte Hamann (ed.), *Kronprinz Rudolf. Geheime und private Schriften*, Wien-München, 1979, p.63.

101 Cited in Macartney, *The Habsburg Empire*, p.615.

102 William Alexander Jenks, *The Austrian Electoral Reform of 1907*, New York, 1950, p.106.

103 *Ibid.*, p.207.

104 Macartney, *The Habsburg Empire*, p.664.

105 Prinz, *Geschichte Böhmens*, p.175.

106 Fran Zwitter, *Nacionalni problemi v habsburški monarhiji*, Ljubljana, 1962, pp.163-164.

107 Cited in Gabor P. Vermes, 'South Slav Aspirations and Magyar Nationalism in the Dual Monarchy' in Ivo Banac, John G. Ackerman and Roman Szporluk (eds.), *Nation and Ideology: Essays in honour of Wayne S. Vucinich*, Boulder, 1981, pp.183-184.

108 Jörg K. Hoensch, *A History of Modern Hungary 1867-1994*, London-New York, 1996, p.27.

109 Kann, *A History of the Habsburg Empire*, p.362.

110 Gustav Erényi, *Graf Stefan Tisza*, Wien-Leipzig, 1935, p.112.

111 Anton Mayr-Harting, *Der Untergang. Österreich-Ungarn 1848-1922*, Wien-München, 1988, p.47.

112 Bibl, *Von Revolution zu Revolution*, p.392.

113 Kann, *The Multinational Empire*, vol.1, p.138.

114 See Kurt Peball and Gunther E. Rothenberg, 'Der Fall "U": Die geplante Besetzung Ungarns durch die k. u. k. Armee im Herbst 1905', *Schriften des Heeresgeschichtlichen Museums in Wien*, Militärwissenschaftliches Institut, Wien-München 1969.

115 Gunther E. Rothenberg, *The Army of Francis Joseph*, West Lafayette, 1976, p.135.

116 Ante Trumbić, *Suton Austro-Ugarske*, Zagreb, 1936, p.97.

117 Macartney, *The Habsburg Empire*, p.762.

118 Margutti, pp.238-239.

119 Macartney, *The Habsburg Empire*, p.686.

120 Jenks, *Austrian Electoral Reform*, p.207.

121 Macartney, *The Habsburg Empire*, p.794.

122 Ernst Plener, *Erinnerungen*, Stuttgart-Leipzig, 1921, vol.3, p.437.

1 Heir to the Throne

1 Friedjung, *Geschichte in Gesprächen*, vol.1, p.178.

2 Höbelt, *Franz Joseph*, p.157.

3 Tschuppik, *The Reign of the Emperor Francis Joseph*, p.336.

4 Nikitsch-Boulles, *Vor dem Sturm. Erinnerungen an Erzherzog Thronfolger Franz Ferdinand*, Berlin, 1925, p.67.

5 Alexander von Spitzmüller-Harmersbach, 'Franz Joseph und der Dualismus' in Eduard Ritter von Steinitz (ed.), *Erinnerungen an Franz Joseph I*, Berlin, 1931, p.111.

6 Rudolf Schlesinger, *Federalism in Central and Eastern Europe*, London, 1945, p.225.

7 Leopold Wölfling, *Als ich Erzherzog war*, Berlin, 1935, p.127.

8 Countess Marie Larisch, *My Past*, London, 1913, p.129.

9 *Tagebuch meiner Reise um die Erde 1892-1893*, Wien, 1895-96, 2 vols.

10 Victor Eisenmenger, *Erzherzog Franz Ferdinand*, Zürich-Leipzig-Wien, 1930, p.10.

11 Egon Caesar Corti and Hans Sokol, *Der alte Kaiser*, Graz-Wien-Köln, 1955, pp.200-201.

12 Lavender Cassels, *The Archduke and the Assassin*, London, 1984, p.33.

13 Fürstin Nora Fugger, *Im Glanz der Kaiserzeit*, Wien-München, 1980, p.318.

14 Rudolf Vierhaus (ed.), *Das Tagebuch der Baronin Spitzemberg*, Göttingen, 1960, p.351.

15 Haus-, Hof und Staatsarchiv, Wien (HHStA), Nachlass Erzherzog Franz Ferdinand, Karton 8, letter Franz Ferdinand to Max Wladimir Beck, 6 May 1897. Hereafter cited as NLEFF/8.

16 J. Alexander Mahan, *Vienna Yesterday and Today*, Vienna, 1933, p.30.

17 Comte de Saint-Aulaire, *François-Joseph*, Paris, 1945, p.329; Hanne Egghardt, *Habsburgs schräge Erzherzöge*, Wien, 2008, p.165. Empress Elisabeth, Franz Joseph's wife, even wrote a scolding poem about this scandal. See Brigitte Hamann (ed.), *Kaiserin Elisabeth. Das poetische Tagebuch*, Wien, 2008, pp.255-257.

18 Egghardt, *Habsburgs schräge Erzherzöge*, p.168; Saint-Aulaire, *François-Joseph*, p.328.

19 Corti and Sokol, *Der alte Kaiser*, pp.197-198.

20 Leopold Wölfling, *Habsburger unter sich*, Berlin-Wilmersdorf, 1921, p.147. According to the Austrian statesman Count Kielmansegg, Maria Josepha herself, not her sister, had been intended for Franz Ferdinand by his father, but the Archduke thought she was 'a big, blonde German girl, holding little allure'. See Erich Graf Kielmansegg, *Kaiserhaus, Staatsmänner und Politiker*, Wien-München, 1966, p.131.

21 Gopčević, *Österreichs Untergang*, p.145.

22 Kielmansegg, *Kaiserhaus*, p.141.

23 Emperor Karl (1887-1922) who succeeded Franz Joseph in 1916 has been seen, in stark contrast to his father Otto, as a saintly figure, declared 'Blessed' by Pope John Paul II in 2004.

24 Edmund Glaise-Horstenau, 'Erzherzog Franz Ferdinand', *Neue Österreichische Biographie*, Wien, 1926, p.11.

25 Maurice Muret, *L'archiduc François-Ferdinand*, Paris, 1932, p.68. Muret states that the Choteks were elevated to barons in 1566. But another French biographer, Thiériot, gives the year as 1702. See Jean-

Louis Thiériot, *François Ferdinand d'Autriche. De Mayerling à Sarajevo*, Paris, 2005, p.102.

26 Although the title of prince/princess (*Fürst/Fürstin*) ranked in Austrian nobility above that of count/countess, it was nevertheless not a royal title. The title of duke/duchess (*Herzog(Herzogin)* ranked higher, and Sophie was in fact given the title of Duchess (of Hohenberg) in 1909. Again, however, this only meant that she could be addressed as 'Serene Highness' – although she was now more formally included in the family, she was still not equal in rank to the Habsburg arch-duchesses and was ranked behind the youngest archduchess decorated with the Order of the Starry Cross. See Margit Silber, 'Obersthofmeister Alfred Fürst Montenuovo. Höfische Geschichte in den beiden letzten Jahrzenten der öster-reichisch-ungarischen Monarchie 1896-1916', Dissertation, Universität Wien, 1991, pp.615-617.

27 Margutti, *Kaiser Franz Joseph*, p. 132.

28 Wölfling, *Als ich Erzherzog war*, p.118; Heinrich Graf von Lützow, *Im diplomat-ischen Dienst der k.u.k. Monarchie*, Wien, 1971, p.159; Fugger, *Im Glanz der Kaiser-zeit*, p. 332.

29 Kielmansegg, *Kaiserhaus*, p.165.

30 Adalbert Graf Sternberg, *Warum Öster-reich zugrunde gehen musste*, Wien, 1927, pp.97-98.

31 Martina Winkelhofer, *'Viribus unitis'. Der Kaiser und sein Hof*, Wien, 2008, pp.236 and 210.

32 Silber, 'Obersthofmeister Alfred Fürst Montenuovo', pp.619-621.

33 For example: Hertha Pauli, *The Secret of Sarajevo: The Story of Franz Ferdinand and Sophie*, London, 1965; Gordon Brook-Shepherd, *Victims at Sarajevo: The Romance and Tragedy of Franz Ferdinand and Sophie*, London, 1984; Beate Hammond, *Habsburgs grösste Liebesgeschichte. Franz Ferdinand und Sophie*, Wien, 2001; Erika Bestenreiner, *Franz Ferdinand und Sophie von Hohenberg. Verbotene Liebe am Kaiserhof*, München, 2004.

34 Juliana von Stockhausen, *Im Schatten der Hofburg*, Heidelberg, 1952, p.218.

35 Cited in Margutti, *Kaiser Franz Joseph*, p.114.

36 Kielmansegg, *Kaiserhaus*, p.146.

37 Hans Rochelt (ed.), *Adalbert Graf Stern-berg 1868-1830. Aus den Memorien eines konservativen Rebellen*, Wien, 1997, p.106. Sternberg was quite close to Franz Ferdinand. He wrote a book, intended for private circulation, about the right of the Archduke's children to succeed him on the Habsburg throne. See Redlich, *Schicksalsjahre*, vol.1, diary entries for 6 June and 25 November 1912, pp.444 and 513.

38 Stockhausen, *Im Schatten der Hofburg*, pp.223 and 213.

39 Philipp Fürst zu Eulenburg-Hertefeld, *Erlebnisse an deutschen und fremden Höfen*, Leipzig, 1934, pp.307-308.

40 Various accounts are vague about the date when Franz Ferdinand and Sophie first met, whereas others fix the year 1894. Thiériot (*François Ferdinand*, p.102) locates a photograph from 1892 that shows Franz Ferdinand and Sophie together. Margutti (*Kaiser Franz Joseph*, p.127) recalled that Franz Ferdinand met Sophie for the first time at the 'beginning of the 1890s'. The latest research by Norbert Nemec also establishes the year 1892 as the most likely – see Norbert Nemec, *Erzherzogin Maria Annunziata (1876-1961). Die unbekannte Nichte Kaiser Franz Josephs I.*, Wien-Köln-Weimar, 2010, p.81.

41 Nikitsch-Boulles, *Vor dem Sturm*, p.27.

42 Eva-Marie Csáky (ed.), *Vom geachteten zum geächteten. Erinnerungen des k. und k. Diplo-maten und k. Ungarischen Außenministers Emerich Csáky 1882-1961*, Wien-Köln-Weimar, 1994, p.91. Bohuslav Chotek died in a madhouse. See Tanja Kraler, 'Gott schütze Österreich vor seinen *Staats-männern*, aber auch vor seinen *Freunden!*' Das Tagebuch von Hans Schlitter 1912-1927, Dissertation, Leopold-Franzens-Universität Innsbruck, 2009, diary entry for 24 April 1914, p.224. Hereafter cited as Kraler, 'Schlitter'.

43 Saint-Aulaire, *François-Joseph*, p.339.

44 Bestenreiner, *Franz Ferdinand und Sophie von Hohenberg*, pp.39-40.

45 Wölfling, *Als ich Erzherzog war*, p.122.

46 *Profil*, Wien, 9 September 2013, p.76.

47 HHStA, NLEFF/8, letter Franz Ferdi-nand to Beck, 8 August 1896.

48 HHStA, NLEFF/8, letter Franz Ferdi-nand to Beck, 22 December 1896.

49 Bestenreiner, *Franz Ferdinand und Sophie von Hohenberg*, p. 40.

50 HHStA, NLEFF/8, letter Franz Ferdi-nand to Beck, 6 May 1897.

51 See Brook-Shepherd, *Victims at Sarajevo*, p.41.

52 Friedjung, *Geschichte in Gesprächen*, vol.1, p.271.

53 Eulenburg-Hertefeld, *Erlebnisse*, p.280.

54 Fugger, *Im Glanz der Kaiserzeit*, pp.321-322.

55 HHStA, NLEFF/8, letter Franz Ferdinand to Beck, 25 August 1900.

56 Beate Hammond (*Habsburgs grösste Liebesgeschichte*) asserts (p.94) that Archduchess Isabella found out about the liaison already at the end of November 1898, but provides no evidence. Brook-Shepherd (*Victims at Sarajevo*) dates the outbreak of the scandal to June or July 1899 (p.62).

57 Karl Friedrich Nowak and Friedrich Thimme (eds.), *Erinnerungen und Gedanken des Botschafters Anton Graf Monts*, Berlin, 1932, letter Monts to Holstein, 2 November 1899, p.391. Hereafter cited as Monts, *Erinnerungen*.

58 Kielmansegg, *Kaiserhaus*, pp.147-148.

59 Corti and Sokol, *Der alte Kaiser*, p.253.

60 Sieghart, *Die letzten Jahrzehnte einer Grossmacht*, pp.54-55.

61 Fugger, *Im Glanz der Kaiserzeit*, p.326.

62 Eulenburg-Hertefeld, *Erlebnisse*, p.295.

63 Hellmut Andics, *Die Frauen der Habsburger*, Wien-München, 1986, pp.304-305.

64 Général Baron Albert de Margutti, *La tragédie des Habsbourg. Mémoires d'un aide de camp*, Paris-Vienne, 1923, p.80.

65 Johann Christoph Allmayer-Beck, *Ministerpräsident Baron Beck*, Wien, 1956, p.36.

66 Corti and Sokol, *Der alte Kaiser*, p.257.

67 Margutti, *Kaiser Franz Joseph*, pp.128-129.

68 Friedjung, *Geschichte in Gesprächen*, vol.1, p.343.

69 Lucian Meysels, *Die Verhinderte Dynastie. Erzherzog Franz Ferdinand und das Haus Hohenberg*, Wien, 2000, p.20.

70 Friedjung, *Geschichte in Gesprächen*, vol.1, p.443.

71 Kann, *A History of the Habsburg Empire*, p.59, n.7.

72 Redlich, *Schicksalsjahre*, vol.1, diary entry for 18 February 1912, p.425.

73 Marga Lammasch and Hans Sperl (eds.), *Heinrich Lammasch. Seine Aufzeichnungen, sein Wirken und seine Politik*, Wien-Leipzig, 1922, p.80.

74 Silber, 'Obersthofmeister Alfred Fürst Montenuovo', pp.608-609.

75 Cited in Corti and Sokol, *Der alte Kaiser*, p.254; Silber, 'Obersthofmeister Alfred Fürst Montenuovo', p.614.

76 [Albert Margutti], *Kaiser Franz Joseph I. und sein Hof*, Wien-Hamburg, 1984, p.169.

77 Kielmansegg, *Kaiserhaus*, p.170.

78 Redlich, *Schicksalsjahre*, vol.1, diary entry for 22 August 1914, p.636.

79 Günther Kronenbitter, 'Haus ohne Macht? Erzherzog Franz Ferdinand (1863-1914)

und die Krise der Habsburgermonarchie' in Wolfgang Weber (ed.), *Der Fürst. Ideen und Wirklichkeiten in der europäischen Geschichte*, Köln-Weimar-Wien, 1998, p.185; Viktor Bibl, *Thronfolger*, München, 1929, p.238.

80 Margutti, *Kaiser Franz Joseph*, pp.129-130.

81 Cited in Rudolf Agstner (ed.), *1914. Das etwas andere Lesebuch zum 1. Weltkrieg. Unbekannte Dokumente der österreichisch-ungarischen Diplomatie*, Wien, 2013, p.76.

82 Margutti, *Kaiser Franz Joseph*, p.135.

83 Redlich, *Schicksalsjahre*, vol.1, diary entry for 19 October 1912, p.487.

84 Andics, *Die Frauen der Habsburger*, p.319.

84 Gopčević, *Österreichs Untergang*, pp.136-137.

86 Silber, 'Obersthofmeister Alfred Fürst Montenuovo', pp.597-598.

87 Gopčević, *Österreichs Untergang*, p.133.

88 Silber, 'Obersthofmeister Alfred Fürst Montenuovo', p.624.

89 Bibl, *Thronfolger*, p.243.

90 Ursula Prutsch and Klaus Zeyringer (eds.), *Leopold von Andrian (1875-1951). Korrespondenzen, Notizen, Essays, Berichte*, Wien-Köln-Weimar, 2003, p.167.

91 Redlich, *Schicksalsjahre*, vol.1, diary entry for 2 July 1914, p.612.

92 Lützow, *Im diplomatischen Dienst*, p.110.

93 Kann, *The Multinational Empire*, vol.2, p.188.

94 Mayr-Harting, *Der Untergang*, pp.523 and 519.

95 Henri de Weindel, *The Real Francis-Joseph: The Private Life of the Emperor of Austria*, London, 1909, p.284.

96 Eugene Bagger, *Franz Joseph. Eine Persönlichkeits-Studie*, Zürich-Leipzig-Wien, n.d., p.530.

97 Rudolf Kiszling, *Erzherzog Franz Ferdinand von Österreich-Este. Leben, Pläne und Wirken am Schicksalsweg der Donaumonarchie*, Graz-Köln, 1953, p.14; Eisenmenger, *Erzherzog Franz Ferdinand*, p.140. See also Alfred Dumaine, *La dérniere ambassade de France en Autriche*, Paris, 1921. p.66. The French Ambassador wrote that the Archduke spoke French 'without fluency'.

98 Hodža, *Federation in Central Europe*, p.50.

99 Lammasch and Sperl, *Lammasch*, p.78.

100 HHStA, NLEFF/8, letter Franz Ferdinand to Beck, 23 February 1902.

101 Rainer Egger, 'Die Militärkanzlei des Erzherzog-Thronfolgers Franz Ferdinand und ihr Archiv im Kriegsarchiv Wien', *Mitteilungen des österreichischen Staatsarchivs*, 28, Wien, 1975, p.146.

102 Joh. Christoph Allmayer-Beck, 'Die Militärkanzlei des Erzherzog-Thronfolgers Franz Ferdinand' in Peter Broucek and Erwin A. Schmidl (eds.), *Joh. Christoph Allmayer-Beck. Militär, Geschichte und Politische Bildung. Aus Anlaß des 85. Geburtstages des Autors*, Wien-Köln-Weimar, 2003, p.361.

103 Eisenmenger, *Erzherzog Franz Ferdinand*, p.140.

104 Glaise-Horstenau, 'Erzherzog Franz Ferdinand', p.16; Gerd Holler, *Franz Ferdinand von Österreich-Este*, Wien-Heidelberg, 1982, p.40.

105 Redlich, *Schicksalsjahre*, vol.1, diary entry for 28 June 1914, p.610.

106 Theodor Brückler, *Thronfolger Franz Ferdinand als Denkmalpfleger*, Wien-Köln-Weimar, 2009, pp.78-81.

107 Holler, *Franz Ferdinand*, p.40.

108 Brückler, *Thronfolger Franz Ferdinand*, p.74.

109 Kraler, 'Schlitter', p.206, diary entry for 5 March 1914.

110 Bertha Zuckerkandl, *Österreich intim. Erinnerungen 1892-1942*, Wien-München, 1981, pp.105-106.

111 Friedrich Weissensteiner, *Franz Ferdinand. Der verhinderte Herrscher*, Wien, 2007, pp.57-58.

112 Holler, *Franz Ferdinand*, p.37.

113 HHStA, NLEFF/8, letter Franz Ferdinand to Beck, 30 March 1893.

114 Danilo Dimović, 'Poslednja večera. Politički ispad Franza Ferdinanda uoči sarajevskog atentata 27. juna 1914', *Pogledi na savremena pitanja*, Zagreb, 1, May 1934, p.17.

115 Rebecca West, *Black Lamb and Grey Falcon*, London, 1941, vol.1, p.340.

116 Glaise-Horstenau, 'Erzherzog Franz Ferdinand', p.10.

117 Eulenburg-Hertefeld, *Erlebnisse*, p.307.

118 Glaise-Horstenau, 'Erzherzog Franz Ferdinand', p.10.

119 Kielmansegg, *Kaiserhaus*, p.85.

120 Manfred Weigert, 'Die Militärkanzlei seiner k.u.k. Hoheit des durchl. Herrn General der Kavallerie Erzherzog Franz Ferdinand. Nebenregierung oder machtlose Opposition?', Diplomaarbeit, Universität Wien, 2001, p.42.

121 *Ibid.*, p.45.

122 Csáky, *Vom Geachteten zum Geächteten*, p.207.

123 Redlich, *Schicksalsjahre*, vol.1, diary entry for 10 November 1909, p.269.

124 Prutsch and Zeyringer, *Leopold von Andrian*, p.172.

125 Bardolff, *Soldat im alten Österreich*, p.123.

126 *Ibid.*, p.173.

127 Silber, 'Obersthofmeister Alfred Fürst Montenuovo', p.613.

128 Robert A. Kann, 'Heir Apparent Archduke Franz Ferdinand and His Stance on the Bohemian Question' in Stanley B. Winters (ed.), *Dynasty, Politics and Culture*, Boulder, 1991, p.154.

129 Friedjung, *Geschichte in Gesprächen*, vol.2, p.263.

130 Cited in Kann, 'Franz Ferdinand and His Stance on the Bohemian Question', p.172.

131 *Ibid.*, pp.172-173.

132 Friedjung, *Geschichte in Gesprächen*, vol.2, p.194.

133 Prutsch and Zeyringer, *Leopold von Andrian*, p.170.

134 Franz Adlgasser (ed.), *Die Aehrenthals. Eine Familie in ihrer Korrespondenz 1872-1911*, Wien-Köln-Weimar, 2002, vol.2, pp.805-806.

135 *Ibid.*, p.266.

136 Alfred Francis Pribram, *Austrian Foreign Policy, 1908-18*, London, 1923, p.60.

137 Jan Galandauer, *Franz Fürst Thun. Statthalter des Königreiches Böhmen*, Wien-Köln-Weimar, 2014, pp.128-131.

138 Friedjung, *Geschichte in Gesprächen*, vol.1, p.434.

139 Kielmansegg, *Kaiserhaus*, pp.133 and 155.

140 Unpublished, untitled and undated typescript by Andreas von Morsey, Schlossarchiv Artstetten (SArt), Personalia MO, p.45.

141 Bardolff, *Soldat im alten Österreich*, p.132.

142 *Ibid.*, pp.135-136.

143 Wilhelm Wühr (ed.), *Ludwig Freiherr von Pastor. Tagebücher-Briefe-Erinnerungen*, Heidelberg, 1950, p.540.

144 Conrad, *Aus meiner Dienstzeit*, vol.3, pp.435-436.

145 *Ibid.*, vol.1, p.328.

146 Margutti, *Kaiser Franz Joseph*, p.272.

147 Heinrich Kanner, *Kaiserliche Katastrophen-Politik*, Leipzig-Wien-Zürich, 1922, p.154.

148 Glaise-Horstenau, 'Erzherzog Franz Ferdinand', p.31.

149 Samuel R. Williamson, Jr., 'Influence, Power, and the Policy Process: The Case of Franz Ferdinand, 1906-1914', *The Historical Journal*, vol.17, no.2, June 1974. p.434.

150 Norman Stone, 'The power of the assassin', *The Sunday Times*, London, 21 April 1985.

151 Christopher Clark, *The Sleepwalkers: How Europe Went to War in 1914*, London, 2012, p.395.

152 Margaret MacMillan, *The War That Ended Peace: How Europe Abandoned Peace for the First World War*, London, 2013, p.xxvii.

153 Paul G. Halpern, *The Mediterranean Naval Situation 1908-1914*, Cambridge, Massachusetts, 1971, p.155.

154 Muret, *L'archiduc François-Ferdinand*, p.189.

155 Quoted in Friedrich Kiessling, *Gegen den 'grossen Krieg'? Entspannung in den internationalen Beziehungen 1911-1914*, München, 2002, p.129, n.254.

156 *Ibid.*, pp.129-130.

157 HHStA, NLEFF/8, letter Franz Ferdinand to Beck, 25 August 1900.

158 HHStA, NLEFF/8, letter Franz Ferdinand to Beck, 9 May 1907.

159 Conrad, *Aus meiner Dienstzeit*, vol.1, p.153; Peter Broucek (ed.), *Theodor Ritter von Zeynek: Ein Offizier im Generalstabskorps erinnert sich*, Wien-Köln-Weimar, 2009, p.136.

160 [Moritz] Auffenberg-Komarów, *Aus Österreichs Höhe und Niedergang*, München, 1921, p.223.

161 *Ibid.*, p.156.

162 Prutsch and Zeyringer, *Leopold von Andrian*, p.167.

163 Bogdan Graf von Hutten-Czapski, *Sechzig Jahre Politik und Gesellschaft*, Berlin, 1936, vol.2, pp.134-135.

164 *Dokumenti o spoljnoj politici Kraljevine Srbije*, Beograd, 1980, vol.7/2, no.293, Đorđević to the Foreign Ministry, Belgrade, 30 June 1914. Hereafter cited as *DSPKS*.

165 Carl von Bardolff, *Deutschösterreichisches Soldatentum im Weltkrieg*, Wien, 1937, p.16.

166 Conrad, *Aus meiner Dienstzeit*, vol.3, p.155.

167 Cited in Robert A. Kann, 'Archduke Franz Ferdinand and Count Berchtold During His Term as Foreign Minister, 1912-1914' in Stanley B. Winters (ed.), *Dynasty, Politics and Culture*, Boulder, 1991, pp.122-123; Robert A. Kann, *Erzherzog Franz Ferdinand Studien*, Wien, 1976, p.220.

168 Holger Afflerbach, *Der Dreibund. Europäische Grossmacht- und Allianzpolitik vor dem Ersten Weltkrieg*, Wien-Köln-Weimar, 2002, pp.597-598.

169 Kann, 'Heir Apparent Archduke Franz Ferdinand and His Stance on the Bohemian Question', p.153.

170 Günther Kronenbitter, *'Krieg im Frieden'. Die Führung der k.u.k. Armee und die Großmachtpolitik Österreich-Ungarns 1906-1914*, München, 2003., p.372.

171 Kiessling, *Gegen den 'grossen Krieg'?*, p.131.

172 Hodža, *Federation in CentralEurope*, pp.55-56 and 58-59.

173 Erwin Matsch (ed.), *November 1918 auf dem Ballhausplatz. Erinnerungen Ludwigs Freiherrn von Flotow*, Wien-Köln-Graz, 1982, p.303.

174 Vladislav Skarić, 'Sarajevo i njegova okolina od najstarijih vremena do austrugraske okupacije' in Milorad Ekmečić (ed.), *Vladislav Skarić. Izabrana djela*, Sarajevo, 1985, vol.1, pp.129-131

175 Solomon Wank (ed.), *Aus dem Nachlass Aehrenthal. Briefe und Dokumente zur österreichisch-ungarischen Innen- und Außenpolitik 1885-1912*, Graz, 1994, vol.2, no.467, p.624. In the light of this letter by Franz Ferdinand to Aehrenthal, it is interesting to read that 'Ferdinand had fervently opposed the annexation of Bosnia-Herzegovina by the dual monarchy as a needless provocation of the South Slavs, especially the Orthodox Serbs'. See Sean McMeekin, *July 1914*, New York, 2013, p.3.

2 Belvedere 'Reform' Plans

1 MacMillan, *The War That Ended Peace*, p.214.

2 Luigi Albertini, *The Origins of the War of 1914*, London 1952, vol.2, pp.11-12.

3 Kann, *The Multinational Empire*, vol.1, p.14. As such, the Crown Lands were according to Kann 'chief impediments to a successful conversion of the Habsburg lands either to complete centralism or to a federalist setup on ethnic lines.' The Crown Lands in the Austrian half of the Empire were as follows: Lower Austria, Upper Austria, Carinthia, Styria, Salzburg, Tirol, Voralberg, Bohemia, Moravia, Silesia, Galicia, Bukowina, Carniola, Dalmatia and Küstenland (Coastland). The latter was in fact made up of three units: Gorizia, Gradisca and Trieste. The Crown Lands in Hungary were just the Kingdom of Hungary itself, the Kingdom of Croatia-Slavonia, and Fiume (Rijeka) with environs.

4 Kraler, 'Schlitter', diary entry for 5 March 1914, p.206,

5 *Ibid.*, diary entry for 5 March 1914, p.207.

6 John W. Boyer, *Culture and Political Crisis in Vienna: Christian Socialism in Power, 1897-1918*, Chicago-London, 1995, pp.365 and 601, n.184.

7 Cited in Wilhelm Schüssler, *Österreich und das deutsche Schicksal. Eine historisch-politische Skizze*, Leipzig, 1925, p.70.

8 Cited in Margutti, *Kaiser Franz Joseph*, p.225.

9 Redlich, *Schicksalsjahre*, vol.1, diary entry for 18 February 1912, p.425.

10 Mayr-Harting, *Der Untergang*, p.517.

11 Macartney, *The Habsburg Empire*, p.805.

12 Kann, *The Multinational Empire*, vol.2, p.192.

13 Margutti, *Kaiser Franz Joseph*, p.125.

14 Jean-Paul Bled, *Franz Ferdinand. Der eigensinnige Thronfolger*, Wien-Köln-Weimar, 2013, p.208

15 Georg Franz, *Erzherzog Franz Ferdinand und die Pläne zur Reform der Habsburger Monarchie*, Brünn-München-Wien, 1943, p.77.

16 Taylor, *The Habsburg Monarchy*, p.197.

17 Cited in József Galántai, 'Francis Ferdinand and Hungary ', *Annales Universitatis Scientiarum Budapestinensis de Rolando Eötvös nominatae*, Budapest, vol.15, 1974, p.108.

18 Michael Károlyi, *Fighting the World: The Struggle for Peace*, London, 1924, p.48.

19 Margutti, *Kaiser Franz Joseph*, pp.115-116.

20 Franz Wolf, 'Aurel Constantin Popovici', *Österreich in Geschichte und Literatur*, Wien, no 10, 1964, p.480.

21 Aurel C. Popovici, *Die Vereinigten Staaten von Groß-Österreich. Politische Studien zur Lösung der nationalen Fragen und staatsrechtlichen Krisen in Österreich-Ungarn*, Leipzig, 1906, p.27.

22 *Ibid.*, pp.308-309.

23 *Ibid.*, p.10.

24 *Ibid.*, pp.11, 14 and 191.

25 *Ibid.*, pp.215-216.

26 *Ibid.*, p.185.

27 *Ibid.*, pp.189, 210, 187, 349 and 347.

28 *Ibid.*, p.321. According to Popovici's nationalities key, this mammoth imperial government would have the following make-up: Germans: ten; Hungarians: eight; Czechs: five; Romanians: four; Croats, Poles and Ukrainians: three each; Slovaks and Italians: two each; Slovenes and Serbs: one each.

29 *Ibid.*, pp.318-319 and 324-325.

30 Kann, *The Multinational Empire*, vol.2, p.205.

31 *Ibid.*, pp.324, 314-315 and 352.

32 Rochelt, *Adalbert Graf Sternberg*, p.84.

33 Popovici, *Groß-Österreich*, p.341.

34 Franz, *Erzherzog Franz Ferdinand*, p.73.

35 Albertini, *The Origins of the War of 1914*, vol. 2, p.12.

36 Theodor von Sosnosky, *Franz Ferdinand. Der Erzherzog-Thronfolger*, München-Berlin, 1929, pp.71-75.

37 Kann, *Erzherzog Franz Ferdinand Studien*, p.45.

38 Glaise-Horstenau, 'Erzherzog Franz Ferdinand', p.21.

39 Hodža, *Federation in Central Europe*, pp.26-30.

40 Ludwig Graf Creneville, 'Groß-Österreich?', Graz-Wien, 1908, pp.33-39; Alfons Graf Mensdorff-Pouilly, 'Österreich'. *Geschichtliche, politische und kulturelle Betrachtungen*, Wien, 1910, pp.85-90.

41 Mensdorff-Pouilly, 'Österreich', p.87.

42 Kiszling, *Erzherzog Franz Ferdinand*, p.325.

43 *Ibid.*, p.251.

44 See Rudolf Kiszling, 'Erzherzog Franz Ferdinands Pläne für den Umbau der Donaumonarchie', *Neues Abendland*, München, no.4, 1956, pp.364-365. Was this a retrospective realization on the part of Kiszling that he had pushed things too far? Needless to say, his biography of Franz Ferdinand has been read far more widely than his article on the Archduke's reform intentions.

45 Schlesinger, *Federalism in Central and Eastern Europe*, p.231.

46 Taylor, *The Habsburg Monarchy*, p.197.

47 Kann, *The Multinational Empire*, vol.2, p.133.

48 Cited in Kann, *Erzherzog Franz Ferdianand Studien*, p.116.

49 Boyer, *Culture and Political Crisis in Vienna*, pp.331 and 364.

50 Friedjung, *Geschichte in Gesprächen*, vol.2, p.452.

51 Fugger, *Im Glanz der Kaiserzeit*, p.298.

52 HHStA, NLEFF/8, letter Franz Ferdinand to Beck, 5 Sepetember 1899.

53 Kronenbitter, 'Verhinderter Retter?', p.274.

54 Cited in R.W. Seton-Watson, *Sarajevo: A Study in the Origins of the Great War*, London, 1925, p.84.

55 HHStA, NLEFF/8, letter Franz Ferdinand to Beck, 25 August 1900.

56 HHStA, NLEFF/8, letters Franz Ferdinand to Beck, 30 July 1901; 15 April 1902; 30 July 1904.

57 Kralek, 'Schlitter', diary entry for 5 March 1914, p.207.

58 G.P. Gooch and Harold Temperley (eds.), *British Documents on the Origins of the War 1898-1914*, London, 1933, vol.9/1, no.553, Buchanan to Grey, 24 February 1912, p.548. Hereafter cited as *BD*.

59 Kronenbitter, 'Haus ohne Macht?', p.196.

60 Cited in Edmund von Glaise-Horstenau, *Franz Josephs Weggefährte. Das Leben des Generalstabchefs Grafen Beck*, Zürich-Leipzig-Wien, 1930, p.405.

61 HHStA, NLEFF/8, letter Franz Ferdinand to Beck, 5 March 1905.

62 HHStA, NLEFF/8, letter Franz Ferdinand to Beck, 4 March 1904.

63 Friedjung, *Geschichte in Gesprächen*, vol.1, p.497.

64 Hodža, *Federation in Central Europe*, p.56.

65 Cited in Hilde Spiel, *Vienna's Golden Autumn 1866-1938*, London, 1987, p.197.

66 Leopold von Chlumecky, *Erzherzog Franz Ferdinands Wirken und Wollen*, Berlin, 1929, p.33.

67 Tschuppik, *Franz Joseph*, p.316.

68 Kronenbitter, 'Verhinderter Retter?', p.276; Allmayer-Beck, 'Die Militärkanzlei des Erzherzog-Thronfolgers Franz Ferdinand', p.359. Franz Ferdinand's patronage of the Catholic *Schulverein* was indeed straying into party politics as, by his own admission, he wanted thereby to 'express his sympathy' for the Christian Social movement led by Dr Karl Lueger. See Bardolff, *Soldat im alten Österreich*, p.134.

69 See Egger, 'Die Militärkanzlei des Erzherzog-Thronfolgers Franz Ferdinand', p.144.

70 Allmayer-Beck, 'Die Militärkanzlei des Erzherzog-Thronfolgers Franz Ferdinand', p.361.

71 Martha Sitte, 'Alexander Brosch, der Flügeladjutant und Vorstand der Militärkanzlei des Thronfolgers Franz Ferdinand', Dissertation, Universität Wien, 1961, p.6.

72 Allmayer-Beck, 'Die Militärkanzlei des Erzherzog-Thronfolgers Franz Ferdinand', p.362.

73 Redlich, *Kaiser Franz Joseph*, p.427.

74 Nikitsch-Boulles, *Vor dem Sturm*, p.61.

75 Cited in Chlumecky, *Erzherzog Franz Ferdinands Wirken und Wollen*, p.362.

76 Cited in Franz, *Erzherzog Franz Ferdinand*, pp.27-28.

77 *Ibid.*, p.26.

78 [Margutti], *Kaiser Franz Joseph und sein Hof*, p.165.

79 Williamson, 'Influence, Power and the Policy Process', p.419.

80 Prutsch and Zeyringer, *Leopold von Andrian*, p.173.

81 Johann Christoph Allmayer-Beck, 'Die bewaffnete Macht in Staat und Gesellschaft' in Adam Wandruszka and Peter Urbanitsch (eds.), *Die Habsburgermonarchie 1848-1918*, vol.5, *Die bewaffnete Macht*, Wien, 1987, p.131.

82 Allmayer-Beck, 'Die Militärkanzlei des Erzherzog-Thronfolgers Franz Ferdinand', pp.365-366.

83 Friedrich Funder, *Vom Gestern ins Heute. Aus dem Kaiserreich in die Republik*, Wien-München, 1971, pp.291-292.

84 *Ibid.*, p.303.

85 Franz, *Erzherzog Franz Ferdinand*, p.72, n.296.

86 Hodža, *Federation in Central Europe*, p.47.

87 Egger, 'Die Militärkanzlei des Erzherzog-Thronfolgers Franz Ferdinand', p.152; Allmayer-Beck, 'Die Militärkanzlei des Erzherzog-Thronfolgers Franz Ferdinand', p.365.

88 Sitte, 'Alexander Brosch', p.21.

89 Franz, *Erzherzog Franz Ferdinand*, pp.59-61.

90 Egger, 'Die Militärkanzlei des Erzherzog-Thronfolgers Franz Ferdinand', p.148.

91 Cited in Franz, *Erzherzog Franz Ferdinand*, p.27.

92 Sieghart, *Die letzten Jahrzente einer Grossmacht*, p.235.

93 Lammasch and Sperl, *Lammasch*, pp.81 and 77.

94 *Ibid.*, p.82.

95 *Ibid.*, pp.85-86.

96 'Franz Ferdinands Regierungsprogramm', *Neues Wiener Journal*, Wien, 30 December 1923, pp.7-10 and 1 January 1924, pp.7-9. Also printed in Franz, *Erzherzog Franz Ferdinand*, pp.123-149.

97 Sitte, 'Alexander von Brosch', pp.106 and 118.

98 Kann, *The Multinational Empire*, vol.2, p.190.

99 Franz, *Erzherzog Franz Ferdinand*, p.146.

100 *Ibid.*, p.126.

101 *Ibid.*, p.131.

102 *Ibid.*, pp.126-127.

103 *Ibid.*, p.128.

104 *Ibid.*, p.143.

105 *Ibid.*, p.145.

106 Plener, *Erinnerungen*, vol.3, p.322.

107 Taylor, *The Habsburg Monarchy*, p.225.

108 Edmund Steinacker, *Lebenserinnerungen*, München, 1937, p.226.

109 Cited in Robert A. Kann, 'Count Ottokar Czernin and Archduke Franz Ferdinand', *Journal of Central European Affairs*, vol.16, no.2, July 1956, pp.128 and 132. Emphases in the original.

110 Funder, *Vom Gestern ins Heute*, p.312.

111 Gabor Vermes, *István Tisza: The Liberal Vision and Conservative Statecraft of a Magyar Nationalist*, New York, 1985, p.133.

112 Wertheimer, *Tisza Briefe*, letter Tisza to Tschirschky, 6 October 1914, p.89.

113 Bardolff, *Soldat im alten Österreich*, p.162.

114 Peter Broucek (ed.), *Ein General im Zwielicht. Die Erinnerungen Edmund Glaises von Horstenau*, Wien-Köln-Graz, 1980, vol.1, p.235.

115 Lammasch and Sperl, *Lammasch*, pp.87, 85 and 91.

116 Franz, *Erzherzog Franz Ferdinand*, p.161.

117 Johannes Mende, 'Dr. Carl Freiherr von Bardolff', Dissertation, Universität Wien, 1984, p.59.

118 Prutsch and Zeyringer, *Leopold von Andrian*, pp.166-173.

119 *Ibid.*, p.172.

120 Allmayer-Beck, 'Die Militärkanzlei des Erzherzog-Thronfolgers Franz Ferdinand', p.369.

121 Bardolff, *Soldat im alten Österreich*, pp.116-117.

122 Egger, 'Die Militärkanzlei des Erzherzog-Thronfolgers Franz Ferdinand', p.156; Allmayer-Beck, 'Die Militärkanzlei des Erzherzog-Thronfolgers Franz Ferdinand', p.369.

123 Sieghart, *Die letzten Jahrzehnte einer Grossmacht*, p.241.

124 *Reichspost*, Wien, 28 March 1926, pp.1-3. The article is only partly reproduced in Franz, *Erzherzog Franz Ferdinand*, pp.150-155.

125 Franz, *Erzherzog Franz Ferdinand*, p.93.

126 Including, strangely, Georg Franz. See Franz, *Erzherzog Franz Ferdinand*, pp.89-94.

127 *Ibid.*, pp.90-91.

128 Egger, 'Die Militärkanzlei des Erzherzog-Thronfolgers Franz Ferdinand', p.157.

129 Clark, *The Sleepwalkers*, p.108.

130 Prutsch and Zeyringer, *Leopold von Andrian*, p.170.

131 Franz, *Erzherzog Franz Ferdinand*, p.94; Kiszling, 'Erzherzog Franz Ferdinands Pläne für den Umbau der Donaumonarchie', p.368.

3 Great Croatia: The Trialist Rainbow

1 Kann, *The Multinational Empire*, vol.1, p.257.

2 David Fromkin, *Europe's Last Summer: Why the World Went to War in 1914*, London, 2004, p.261.

3 Danilo Dimović, 'Grof Stevan Tisa', *Preporod*, Beograd, 10 September 1922, p.7.

4 HHStA, NLEFF/8, Letter Franz Fedinand to Beck, n.d., June-July, 1906.

5 Kann, 'Archduke Franz Ferdinand and Count Berchtold', p.121.

6 Glaise-Horstenau, 'Erzherzog Franz Ferdinand', p.14

7 Weissensteiner, *Franz Ferdinand*, p.186.

8 Thomson, *Czechoslovakia*, p.133.

9 Willy Lorenz, *Abschied von Böhmen*, Wien-München, 1973, p.40.

10 HHStA, NLEFF/8, letter Franz Ferdinand to Beck, 5 September 1899.

11 Letter reproduced in Sieghart, *Die letzten Jahrzente einer Grossmacht*, pp.462-463.

12 Alexander Spitzmüller, *'und hat auch Ursach, es zu lieben'*, Wien-München-Stuttgart-Zürich, 1955, p.96.

13 Hodža, *Federation in Central Europe*, p.45.

14 Jászi, *The Dissolution of the Habsburg Monarchy*, p.125.

15 Ernst Anrich, *Die Jugoslawische Frage und die Julikrise 1914*, Stuttgart, 1931, p.31.

16 Ernst Anrich, *Europas Diplomatie am Vorabend des Weltkrieges*, Berlin, 1937, p.35.

17 Albertini, *The Origins of the War of 1914*, vol.2, p.88.

18 Franz, *Erzherzog Franz Ferdinand*, p.82.

19 Clark, *The Sleepwalkers*, p.108.

20 Trpimir Macan, *Povijest hrvatskoga naroda*, Zagreb, 1999, 3rd edition, p.200.

21 Dušan Bilandžić, *Hrvatska moderna povijest*, Zagreb, 1999, p.26.

22 Chlumecky, *Erzherzog Franz Ferdinands Wirken und Wollen*, p.202.

23 [Alexander] Freiherr von Musulin, *Das Haus am Ballplatz. Erinnerungen eines österreich-ungarischen Diplomaten*, München, 1924, p.204.

24 Kann, *The Multinational Empire*, vol.1, pp.233-234.

25 Vaso Bogdanov, *Historija poličkih stranaka u Hrvatskoj*, Zagreb, 1958, p.652.

26 Jaroslav Šidak, *Studije iz hrvatske povijesti XIX stoljeća*, Zagreb, 1973, p.67.

27 Barbara Jelavich, *History of the Balkans: Eighteenth and Nineteenth Centuries*, Cambridge, 1983, vol.1, pp.304-305; Eisenmann, *Le Compromis austro-hongrois*, p.564.

28 Wayne S. Vucinich, 'Croatian Illyrism: Its Background and Genesis' in Stanley B. Winters and Joseph Held (eds.), *Intellectual and Social Developments in the Habsburg Empire from Maria Theresa to World War I*, Boulder, 1975, p.68.

29 M. Murko, 'Ko je stvorio Jugoslovene i Jugoslaviju.' *Nova Evropa*, Zagreb, vol.19, no.2, 26 January 1929, p.49.

30 Šidak, *Studije iz hrvatske povijesti XIX stoljeća*, pp.74.

31 Macartney, *The Habsburg Empire*, p.288.

32 Vucinich, 'Croatian Illyrism', p.100.

33 Cited in Turkalj, 'Starčevićeva misao o nužnosti samostalne hrvatske države', p.31.

34 Charles Jelavich, 'The Croatian Problem in the Habsburg Empire in the Nineteenth Century', *Austrian History Yearbook*, vol.3, part 2, 1967, p.97.

35 Vitomir Korać, *Hrvatski 'problem'*, Beograd, 1922, p.13.
36 Cited in Zlatko Hasanbegović, 'Islam i bosanski muslimani u djelima Ante Starčevića' in Ivan Gabelica (ed.), *Starčević. Znanstveni kolokvij o 180. obljetnici rođenja*, Zagreb, 2004, p.54.
37 Šidak, *Studije iz hrvatske povijesti XIX stoljeća*, p.54.
38 Macartney, *The Habsburg Empire*, p.739.
39 Cited in Ilija Jukić, *Pogledi na prošlost, sadašnjost i budućnost hrvatskog naroda*, London, 1965, p.44.
40 Cited in Mirjana Gross, *Povijest pravaške ideologije*, Zagreb, 1973, p.122.
41 'Jugoslovjenstvo' being the title under which Franjo Rački published a series of articles in *Pozor*, Zagreb, 21 October-3 November, 1860.
42 Šidak, *Studije iz hrvatske povijesti XIX stoljeća*, p.55.
43 Viktor Novak, *Franjo Rački*, Beograd, 1958, p.62.
44 Mirjana Gross, *Vijek i djelovanje Franje Račkoga*, Zagreb, 2004, p.58.
45 Cited in Filip Lukas, *Strossmayer i hrvatstvo*, Zagreb, 1926, p.29.
46 Mirjana Gross, 'Zur Frage der jugoslawischen Ideologie bei den Kroaten' in Adam Wandruszka, Richard G. Plaschka and Anna M. Drabek (eds.), *Die Donaumonarchie und die südslawische Frage von 1848 bis 1918*, Wien, 1978, p.22.
47 Gross, *Vijek i djelovanje Franje Račkoga*, p.499.
48 Vasilije Đ. Krestić, *Biskup Štrosmajer. Hrvat, velikohrvat ili Jugosloven*, Jagodina, 2006, pp.125-126.
49 Mirjana Gross and Agneza Szabo, *Prema hrvatskome građanskom društvu. Društveni razvoj u civilnoj Hrvatskoj i Slavoniji šezdesetih i sedamdesetih godina 19. stoljeća*, Zagreb, 1992, p.270.
50 F. Šišić (ed.), *Korespondencija Rački-Strossmayer*, Zagreb, 1930, vol.3, p.118.
51 Nikša Stančić, *Hrvatska nacija i nacionalizam u 19. i 20. stoljeću*, Zagreb, 2002, p.187.
52 Gross, *Vijek i djelovanje Franje Račkoga*, p.201.
53 Šidak, *Studije iz hrvatske povijesti XIX stoljeća*, pp.55-56.
54 Jukić, *Pogledi*, p.41.
55 Bilandžić, *Hrvatska moderna povijest*, p.31.
56 Jelavich, 'The Croatian Problem in the Habsburg Empire in the Nineteenth Century', p.108.
57 Šidak et al., *Povijest hrvatskog naroda*, p.96.
58 Jukić, *Pogledi*, p.43.
59 Mato Artuković, *Srbi u Hrvatskoj. Khuenovo doba*, Slavonski Brod, 2001, p.7
60 See table in Vasilije Krestić, *Istorija Srba u Hrvatskoj i Slavoniji 1848-1914*, Beograd, 1992, p.362.
61 Nicholas J. Miller, *Between Nation and State: Serbian Politics in Croatia before the First World War*, Pittsburgh, 1997, pp.42-43 and 37.
62 R.W. Seton-Watson, *The Southern Slav Question and the Habsburg Monarchy*, London. 1911, p.107.
63 Iso Kršnjavi, *Zapisci. Iza kulisa hrvatske politike*, Zagreb, 1986, vol.1, p.375.
64 Josip Horvat, *Politička povijest Hrvatske*, Zagreb, 1989, vol.1, p.215.
65 Kršnjavi, *Zapisci*, vol.1, p.273.
66 Šidak et al., *Povijest hrvatskog naroda*, p.130.
67 Strecha, 'Franjo Josip I. (1848.-1916.)', p.163.
68 Horvat, *Politička povijest Hrvatske*, vol.1, p.211.
69 *Ibid.*, p.212.
70 Josip Horvat, *Živjeti u Hrvatskoj. Zapisci iz nepovrata 1900-1941*, Zagreb, 1984, p.306.
71 Šidak et al., *Povijest hrvatskog naroda*, p.145.
72 Stančić, *Hrvatska nacija i nacuionalizam*, p.194; Strecha, 'Franjo Josip I. (1848.-1916.)', p.163.
73 Cited in Dušan Berić, *Hrvatsko pravaštvo i Srbi*, Novi Sad, 2005, vol.2, p.223.
74 Horvat, *Živjeti u Hrvatskoj*, p.306.
75 Cited in Mirjana Gross, *Izvorno pravaštvo*, Zagreb, 2000, p.781.
76 Horvat, *Politička povijest Hrvatske*, vol.1, pp.230 and 227.
77 Kann, *The Multinational Empire*, vol.1, p.255.
78 Šidak et al., *Povijest hrvatskog naroda*, p.147.
79 Jukić, *Pogledi*, p.46.
80 Šidak et al., *Povijest hrvatskog naroda*, p.148. See also Gross, *Izvorno pravaštvo*, pp.805-828.
81 Horvat, *Politička povijest Hrvatske*, vol.1, p.248.
82 Janko Ibler, *Hrvatska politika 1903.*, Zagreb, 1914, p.7.
83 Kršnjavi, *Zapisci*, vol.1, p.260.
84 Gross, *Povijest pravaške ideologije*, pp.326-327.
85 *Ibid.*, p.328.
86 Seton-Watson, *The Southern Slav Question*, p.114.
87 Wilhelm Schüssler, *Das Verfassungsproblem im Habsburgerreich*, Stuttgart-Berlin, 1918, p.146.
88 Gross, *Povijest pravaške ideologije*, p.328. Mirjana Gross also speculates (p.328) that a reason for the Serbian change of attitude was the murder of King Alexan-

der Obrenović in Serbia (June 1903) which returned the Karađorđević dynasty and set the previously pro-Austrian Serbia on a policy of relying on Russia in order to 'free itself from the economic *diktat* of the Monarchy.' In fact, no evidence exists for any of these suppositions. See chapter five on Serbia, below.

89 Friedjung, *Geschichte in Gesprächen*, vol.1, p.490.

90 *BD*, vol.9/1, no.553, Buchanan to Grey, 24 February 1912, p.548.

91 Mirjana Gross, 'Hrvatska politika velikoaustrijskog kruga oko prijestolonasljednika Franje Ferdinanda', *Časopis za suvremenu povijest*, Zagreb, vol.2, 1970, p.10.

92 Allmayer-Beck, *Ministerpräsident Baron Beck*, p.98.

93 *Ibid.*, p.91.

94 Cited in Trumbić, *Suton Austro-Ugarske*, p.87.

95 *Ibid.*, pp.92-93.

96 Seton-Watson, *The Southern Slav Question*, p.149.

97 Šidak *et al.*, p.221.

98 Jukić, *Pogledi*, p.51.

99 Rene Lovrenčić, *Geneza politike 'Novog kursa'*, Zagreb, 1972, p.15.

100 Gross, *Vladavina hrvatsko-srpske koalicije*, p.9.

101 Redlich, *Schicksalsjahre*, vol.1, diary entry for 3 May 1909, p.230,

102 Miller, *Between Nation and State*, pp.50 and 106.

103 Mark Biondich, *Stjepan Radić, the Croat Peasant Party, and the Politics of Mass Mobilization, 1904-1928*, Toronto-Buffalo-London, 2000, p.105.

104 Kosta Milutinović, 'Hrvatsko-srpska koalicija', *Istorija srpskog naroda*, Beograd, 1983, vol.6/1, p.432.

105 The view that 'an independent Yugoslav state' was the maximalist aim of the New Course is put forward in Šidak *et al*, p.221. However, no supporting argumentation is provided.

106 Cited in Jukić, *Pogledi*, p.52.

107 Kršnjavi, *Zapisci*, vol.2, p.64.

108 Cited in L. v. Südland [Ivo Pilar], *Die Südslawische Frage und der Weltkrieg*, Wien, 1918, p.658.

109 Miller, *Between Nation and State*, p.82.

110 Bilandžić, *Hrvatska moderna povijest*, p.35.

111 Šidak *et al.*, p.234.

112 Kiszling, *Erzherzog Franz Ferdinand*, pp.121-122.

113 Rudolf Kiszling, *Die Kroaten. Der Schicksalsweg eines Südslawenvolkes*, Graz-Köln, 1956, p.76.

114 Cited in Trumbić, *Suton Austro-Ugarske*, p.88.

115 Gross, *Vladavina hrvatsko-srpske koalicije*, p.219 and n.62 on the same page.

116 Galántai, 'Francis Ferdinand and Hungary', p.111.

117 Chlumecky, *Franz Ferdinands Wirken und Wollen*, p.45.

118 *Ibid.*, p.44.

119 Sosnosky, *Erzherzog Franz Ferdinand*, p.86.

120 Gross, *Vladavina hrvatsko-srpske koalicije*, p.120. In the nearby Trebinje, according to Gross who referred to a police report, people were paid 30 crowns to shout 'long live!' when the Archduke visited the town.

121 Gross, 'Hrvatska politika velikoaustrijskog kruga', p.53.

122 Cited in Robert Kann, 'William II and Archduke Francis Ferdinand in Their Correspondence', *The American Historical Review*, vol.57, no.2 (January 1952), p.334. See also Kiszling, *Erzherzog Franz Ferdinand*, pp.148-149.

123 Redlich, *Schicksalsjahre*, vol.1, diary entry for 26 November 1912, p.515.

124 Chlumecky, *Franz Ferdinands Wirken und Wollen*, p.201.

125 Gross, 'Hrvatska politika velikoaustrijskog kruga', p.39.

126 Sosnosky, *Erzherzog Franz Ferdinand*, p.86.

127 Franz, *Erzherzog Franz Ferdinand*, p.78; Albert von Margutti, *Vom alten Kaiser*, Leipzig-Wien, 1921, p.137. Margutti gave August 1913 as the date of his conversation with Franz Ferdinand.

128 Chlumecky, *Franz Ferdinands Wirken und Wollen*, p.335.

129 Paul Samassa, *Der Völkerstreit im Habsburgerstaat*, Leipzig, 1910, p.170.

130 Bardolff, *Soldat im alten Österreich*, p.152.

131 Theodor von Sosnosky, *Die Politik im Habsburgerreiche*, Berlin, 1913, vol.2, pp.385-389.

132 Chlumecky, *Franz Ferdinands Wirken und Wollen*, p.76.

133 Šidak *et al*, p.242.

134 Chlumecky, *Franz Ferdinands Wirken und Wollen*, p.178.

135 Gross, 'Hrvatska politika velikoaustrijskog kruga', pp.23 and 71.

136 Zwitter, *Nacionalni problemi v habsburški monarhiji*, p.203.

137 Vladimr Dedijer, 'Planovi nadvojvode Franje Ferdinanda o reorganizaciji Habsburške monarhije' in Vasa Čubrilović (ed.), *Jugoslovenski narodi pred Prvi Svetski Rat*, Beograd, 1967, p.194.

138 Gross, 'Hrvatska politika velikoaustrijskog kruga', p.20.

139 Cited in Kiszling, *Erzherzog Franz Ferdinand*, p.231.
140 Seton-Watson, *The Southern Slav Question*, pp.341 and 338.
141 Gross, 'Hrvatska politika velikoaustrijskog kruga', p.24, n.52.
142 Cited in Tihomir Cipek and Stjepan Matković (eds.), *Programatski dokumenti hrvatskih političkih stranaka i skupina 1842.- 1914.*, Zagreb, 2006, p.650.
143 Gross, 'Hrvatska politika velikoaustrijskog kruga', p.41. Crenneville's article is entitled 'Trialistische Bestrebungen', *Reichspost*, 7 February 1912.
144 Sidney B. Fay, *The Origins of the World War*, New York, 1966, vol.2, p.27.
145 Hermann Wendel, *Die Habsburger und die Südslawenfrage*, Belgrad-Leipzig, 1924, p.21.
146 Gross, 'Hrvatska politika velikoaustrijskog kruga', pp.11 and 71-72.
147 Sosnosky, *Erzherzog Franz Ferdinand*, p.75.

4   Bosnia-Herzegovina: The Gates to the Orient

1   Bernadotte E. Schmitt, *The Coming of the War 1914*, New York-London, 1930, vol.1, p.108.
2   Cited in Šidak *et al.*, *Povijest hrvatskog naroda*, p.95.
3   The fear of Slavs produced some drastic proposals. Thus the Styrian autonomists demanded in their 1868 programme that Galicia and Dalmatia be jettisoned to relieve the Germans of the Slavonic strain in the Austrian half of the Monarchy. See Andreas Moritsch, 'Dem Nationalstaat entgegen (1848-1914)' in Andreas Moritsch (ed.), *Alpen-Adria. Zur Geschichte einer Region*, Klagenfurt-Ljubljana-Wien, 2001, p.388.
4   Cited in Luka Đaković, *Položaj Bosne i Hercegovine u austrougarskim koncepcijama rješenja jugoslovenskog pitanja 1914-1918*, Tuzla, 1981, p.21.
5   Jelavich, *History of the Balkans*, vol.1, p.353.
6   Kann, *A History of the Habsburg Empire*, p.280.
7   Joseph M. Baernreither, *Fragments of a Political Diary*, London, 1930, p.19.
8   Ferdo Šišić, *Kako je došlo do okupacije a onda do aneksije Bosne i Hercegovine*, Zagreb, 1938, pp.15-17; Adolf Beer, *Die orientalische Politik Oestereichs seit 1774*, Prag-Leipzig, 1883, pp.435-436.
9   Beer, *Die orientalische Politik*, pp.747-748.
10 Theodor von Sosnosky, *Die Balkanpolitik Oesterich-Ungarns*, Stuttgart-Berlin, 1913,

vol.1, Appendix, p.290, memorandum Radetzky, 30 August 1856.
11 *Ibid.*, vol.2, p.18.
12 Glaise-Horstenau, *Franz Josephs Weggefährte*, p.204.
13 George Hoover Rupp, *A Wavering Friendship: Russia and Austria 1876-1878*, Philadelphia 1976, p.39.
14 Michael Hurst (ed.), *Key Treaties for the Great Powers 1814-1914*, Newton Abbot, 1972, vol.2, p.551.
15 Cited in Heinrich Friedjung, *Das Zeitalter des Imperialismus 1884-1914*, Berlin, 1919, vol.1, p.32.
16 Sosnosky, *Die Balkanpolitik Oesterich-Ungarns*, vol.2, pp.18-19.
17 Glaise-Horstenau, *Franz Josephs Weggefährte*, p.204
18 *Ibid.*, pp.184-185.
19 Plener, *Erinnerungen*, vol.2, p.91.
20 Anton Freiherr v. Mollinary, *Sechsundvierzig Jahre im österreich-ungarischen Heere 1833-1879*, Zürich, 1905, vol.2, p.287.
21 James Creagh, *Over the Borders of Christendom and Eslamiah. A Journey Through Hungary, Slavonia, Serbia, Bosnia, Herzegovina, Dalmatia, and Montenegro, to the North of Albania, in the Summer of 1875*, London, 1876, vol.2, p.184.
22 [Joseph Alexander] von Helfert, *Bosnisches*, Wien, 1879, pp.147-148.
23 Helmut Rumpler, 'Die Dalmatienreise Kaiser Franz Josephs 1875 im Kontext der politischen Richtungsentscheidungen der Habsburgermonarchie am Vorabend der orientalischen Krise' in Lothar Höbelt and Thomas G. Otte (eds.), *A Living Anachronism? European Diplomacy and the Habsburg Monarchy*, Wien-Köln-Weimar, 2010, p.162.
24 Cited in Corti, *Mensch und Herrscher*, p.487.
25 *Ibid.*, pp.490-491.
26 Glaise-Horstenau, *Franz Josephs Weggefährte*, pp.195 and 202.
27 Cited in Ludwig v. Przibram, *Erinnerungen eines alten Oesterreichers*, Stuttgart-Leipzig, 1912, vol.2, p.73.
28 Arthur J. Evans, *Through Bosnia and the Herzegovina on Foot During the Insurrection*, London, 1877, p.249.
29 Aleksa J. Popović-Sarajlija, *Hadži-Lojina buna u Bosni*, Beograd, 1897, pp.38-39 and 36.
30 Milorad Ekmečić, *Stvaranje Jugoslavije 1790-1918*, Beograd, 1989, vol.2, p.329.
31 Popović-Sarajlija, *Hadži-Lojina buna*, p.46.
32 Bridge, *From Sadowa to Sarajevo*, p.94.

33 John R. Schindler, 'Defeating Balkan Insurgency: The Austro-Hungarian Army in Bosnia-Hercegovina, 1878-82', *The Journal of Strategic Studies*, vol.27, no.3, September 2004, pp.530, 532 and 537.

34 Mihovil Mandić, *Povijest okupacije Bosne i Hercegovine 1878*, Zagreb, 1910, p.99.

35 Popović-Sarajlija, *Hadži-Lojina buna*, p.83ff; Mehmedalija Bojić, *Historija Bosne i Bošnjaka*, Sarajevo, 2001, p.131.

36 Przibram, *Erinnerungen eines alten Oester-reichers*, vol.2, p.81.

37 Cited in Hamdija Kapidžić, *Hercegovački ustanak 1882. godine*, Sarajevo, 1973, p.11.

38 Mustafa Imamović, *Historija Bošnjaka*, Sarajevo, 1997, p.373.

39 Ante Malbaša, *Hrvatski i srpski nacionalni problem u Bosni za vrijeme režima Benjamina Kallaya*, Osijek, 1940, p.23

40 Mirko Gjurkovečki, *Politička historija Bosne za okupacije*, Zagreb, 1920, p.7.

41 Hamdija Čemerlić (ed.), *100 godina ustanka u Hercegovini 1882. godine*, Naučni skup, Sarajevo, 1983, p.232, discussion statement by Božo Madžar.

42 Kapidžić, *Hercegovački ustanak 1882*, p.74.

43 Todor Kruševac, *Sarajevo pod austro-ugarskom upravom 1878-1918*, Sarajevo, 1960, p.271.

44 Risto Jeremić, 'Oružani otpor protiv Austro-Ugarske, od 1878-1882' in Pero Slijepčević (ed.), *Napor Bosne i Hercegovine za oslobođenje i ujedinjenje*, Sarajevo, 1929, p.73; Ekmečić, *Stvaranje Jugoslavije*, vol.2, p.413; Vladislav Skarić, Osman Nuri-Hadžić and Nikola Stojanović, *Bosna i Hercegovina pod austro-ugarskom upravom*, Beograd, 1938, p.23.

45 Grgur Jakšić and Vojislav J. Vučković, 'Pokušaj aneksije Bosne i Hercegovine (1882-1883)', *Glas Srpske Akademije Nauka*, CCXIV, Beograd, 1954, p.70.

46 Malbaša, *Hrvatski i srpski nacionalni problem u Bosni*, p.17.

47 Bridge, *From Sadowa to Sarajevo*, pp 91-92.

48 Ernst R. Rutkowski, 'Die Plan für eine Annexion Bosniens und der Herzegowina aus den Jahren 1882/83', *Mitteilungen des Oberösterreichischen Landesarchivs*, Graz-Köln, vol.5, 1957, p.121.

49 *Ibid.*, pp.124-126.

50 *Ibid.*, p.129.

51 *Ibid.*, p.134. Tisza put forward at the same time precise proposals for the division of Bosnia-Herzegovina. He wanted Hungary to be given the regions of Banja Luka and Bihać, leaving Travnik, Tuzla, Sarajevo and Mostar to Austria. As Rutkowski noted (p.135), 'Tisza had not selected the worst regions of Bosnia for his country.'

52 *Ibid.*, p.137.

53 HHStA, NLEFF/8, letter Franz Ferdinand to Beck, 14 April 1896.

54 Tomislav Kraljačić, *Kalajev režim u Bosni i Hercegovini 1882-1903*, Sarajevo, 1987, p.91.

55 Malbaša, *Hrvatski i srpski nacionalni problem u Bosni*, p.19; Kruševac, *Sarajevo pod austro-ugarskom upravom*, p.263.

56 Benjámin Kállay, *Geschichte der Serben*, Budapest-Wien, 1878.

57 Andrija Radenić (ed.), *Dnevnik Benjamina Kalaja 1868-1875*, Beograd-Novi Sad, 1976.

58 *Ibid.* Introduction by Andrija Radenić, p.XXVII.

59 Friedjung, *Geschichte in Gesprächen*, vol.1, p.487.

60 Mayr-Harting, *Der Untergang*, p.349.

61 Cited in the introduction by Ludwig von Thallóczy to Kállay's posthumously published work: *Die Geschichte des serbischen Aufstandes 1807-1810*, Wien, 1910, p.XXX.

62 Cited in *ibid.*, p.XXXV.

63 Benjamin v. Kállay, *Ungarn an den Grenzen des Orients und des Occidents*, Budapest, 1883, p.40.

64 *Ibid.*, p.47.

65 Robin Okey, *Taming Balkan Nationalism*, Oxford, 2007, p.75.

66 Đorđe Pejanović, *Stanovništvo Bosne i Hercegovine*, Beograd, 1955, p.46.

67 Kraljačić, *Kalajev režim u Bosni i Hercegovini*, p.106.

68 Kruševac, *Sarajevo pod austro-ugarskom upravom*, pp.272-273.

69 Mirko Maksimović, 'Crkvene borbe i pokreti' in Slijepčević, *Napor Bosne i Hercegovine*, p.81.

70 Kraljačić, *Kalajev režim u Bosni i Hercegovini*, p.333.

71 *Ibid.*, p.337.

72 Malbaša, *Hrvatski i srpski nacionalni problem u Bosni*, p.74.

73 Cited in Milorad Ekmečić, 'Društvo, privreda i socijalni nemiri u Bosni i Hercegovini', *Istorija srpskog naroda*, Beograd, 1983, vol.6/1, p.584.

74 Peter F. Sugar, *Industrialization of Bosnia-Hercegovina 1878-1918*, Seattle, 1963, pp.32-33.

75 Okey, *Taming Balkan Nationalism*, p.59.

76 Malbaša, *Hrvatski i srpski nacionalni problem u Bosni*, p.63.

77 *Ibid.*, p.74.

78 Mustafa Imamović, *Pravni položaj i unutrašnji politički razvitak Bosne i Hercegovine of 1878. do 1914.*, Sarajevo, 1976, p.129.

79 Emil von Laveleye, *Die Balkanländer*, Leipzig, 1888, vol.1, p.52.

80 Kraljačić, *Kalajev režim u Bosni i Herce-govini*, p.501.
81 Cited in Seton-Watson, *The Southern Slav Question*, p.236.
82 Kraljačić, *Kalajev režim u Bosni i Herce-govini*, p.504.
83 *Ibid.*, pp.506-507.
84 Malbaša, *Hrvatski i srpski nacionalni prob-lem u Bosni*, pp.102-104, n.220.
85 *Ibid.*, pp.102-103.
86 Ferdo Hauptmann, 'Privreda i društvo Bosne i Hercegovine u doba austro-ugarske vladavine (1878-1918)' in Enver Redžić (ed.), *Prilozi za istoriju Bosne i Hercegoine*, Sarajevo, 1987, vol.2, pp.140, 162 and 164-165.
87 Noel Malcolm, *Bosnia: A Short History*, London, 1994, p.141.
88 Clark, *The Sleepwalkers*, p.74.
89 Sugar, *Industrialization of Bosnia-Hercegov-ina*, p.36.
90 Moriz Graf Attems, *Bosnien einst und jetzt*, Wien, 1913, p.30.
91 Malbaša, *Hrvatski i srpski nacionalni prob-lem u Bosni*, pp.75-77.
92 Okey, *Taming Balkan Nationalism*, p.60.
93 *Ibid.*
94 Baernreither, *Fragments of a Political Diary*, p.17.
95 Kállay, *Geschichte der Serben*, p.21. It has frequently been asserted, not least by Serb historians, that Kállay had banned his own *History of the Serbs* in Bosnia-Herzegovina – as an afterthought. But Vojislav Bogićević showed that Kállay had done nothing of the kind and had in fact been puzzled by claims to that effect. Bogićević did also show, however, that Kállay's officials had banned the Serbian translation of the work – precisely because the author argued that the inhabitants of Bosnia-Herzegovina were Serbs. See Vojislav Bogićević, 'Da li je ministar Kalaj zabranio svoju *Istoriju Srba* na području Bosne i Hercegovine?', *Godišnjak istoris-kog društva Bosne i Hercegovine*, Sarajevo, 1955, pp.205-208.
96 Kraljačić, *Kalajev režim u Bosni i Herce-govini*, p.83.
97 Zoran Grijak, *Politička djelatnost vrhbosans-kog nadbiskupa Josipa Stadlera*, Zagreb, 2001, pp.123-124.
98 Luka Đaković, *Političke organizacije bosans-kohercegovačkih katolika Hrvata*, Zagreb, 1985, p.152.
99 Michael Boro Petrovich *A History of Mod-ern Serbia 1804-1918*, New York-London, 1976, vol.2, p.437.

100 Kraljačić, *Kalajev režim u Bosni i Herce-govini*, p.216.
101 *Ibid.*, p.226.
102 *Ibid.*, pp.196-197.
103 *Ibid.*, pp.234-235.
104 *Ibid.*, pp.211-213. The kings of Hungary had since 1135 (Bela II) carried *rex Ramae* in their titles.
105 Imamović, *Pravni položaj*, p.130.
106 Malbaša, *Hrvatski i srpski nacionalni prob-lem u Bosni*, p.122.
107 *Ibid.*, p.67, and Kruševac, *Sarajevo pod austro-ugarskom upravom*, p.286.
108 Imamović, *Pravni položaj*, pp.71-72.
109 Creagh, *Over the Borders of Christendom and Eslamiah*, vol.2, p.124, n.2.
110 Gino Bertolini, *Muselmanen und Slaven*, Leipzig, 1911, p.239.
111 Malbaša, *Hrvatski i srpski nacionalni prob-lem u Bosni*, pp.67-70.
112 Bojić, *Historija Bosne i Bošnjaka*, p.142.
113 Ivo Banac, *The National Question in Yugo-slavia*, Ithaca-London, 1984, p.365.
114 Nijaz Duraković, *Prokletstvo Muslimana*, Tuzla, 1998, p.112.
115 Šaćir Filandra, *Bošnjačka politika u XX. stoljeću*, Sarajevo, 1998, p.16.
116 Kruševac, *Sarajevo pod austro-ugarskom upravom*, p.308.
117 Nusret Šehić, *Autonomni pokret Muslimana za vrijeme austrougarske uprave u Bosni i Hercegovini*, Sarajevo, 1980, p.129.
118 Imamović, *Pravni položaj*, p.127.
119 *Ibid.*, p.73.
120 Okey, *Taming Balkan Nationalism*, p.61.
121 Mirjana Gross, 'Hrvatska politika u Bosni i Hercegovini od 1878. do 1914', *Historijski zbornik*, Zagreb, 1966-67, pp.15 and 18.
122 Malbaša, *Hrvatski i srpski nacionalni prob-lem u Bosni*, pp.19 and 10-13.
123 Petar Vrankić, *Religion und Politik in Bosnien und der Herzegowina 1878-1918*, Paderborn-München-Wien-Zürich, 1998, p.369.
124 Okey, *Taming Balkan Nationalism*, p.114.
125 Macartney, *The Habsburg Empire*, p.746.
126 Kraljačić, *Kalajev režim u Bosni i Herce-govini*, pp.316 and 313.
127 Berislav Gavranović, *Uspostava redovite katoličke hijerarhije u Bosni i Hercegovini 1881. godine*, Beograd, 1935, pp.199-201.
128 *Ibid.*, p.52.
129 Vrankić, *Religion und Politik in Bosnien und der Herzegowina*, p.444.
130 Kraljačić, *Kalajev režim u Bosni i Herce-govini*, p.318.
131 Okey, *Taming Balkan Nationalism*, pp.117 and 121.

132 Cited in Gross, 'Hrvatska politika u Bosni i Hercegovini', p.20.
133 Auffenberg-Komarów, *Aus Österreichs Höhe und Niedergang*, p.112.
134 Okey, *Taming Balkan Nationalism*, p.121.
135 Šehić, *Autonomni pokret Muslimana*, p.377.
136 Imamović, *Pravni položaj*, pp.121-122.
137 *Ibid.*, pp.122-123.
138 On Gavrila see Šehić, *Autonomni pokret Muslimana*, pp.137-140, and Milorad Ekmečić, 'Nacionalni pokret u Bosni i Hercegovini', *Istorija srpskog naroda*, Beograd, 1983, vol. 6/1, pp.626-629.
139 Božo Madžar, *Pokret Srba Bosne i Hercegovine za vjersko-prosvjetnu samoupravu*, Sarajevo, 1982, p.373.
140 *Ibid.* p.430.
141 *Ibid.*, pp.236-248.
142 Okey, *Taming Balkan Nationalism*, p.122.
143 *Ibid.*, p.254.
144 Macartney, *The Habsburg Empire*, p.743.
145 Stojan Kesić, *Radnički pokret u Bosni i Hercegovini i Hrvatskoj 1894-1914*, Beograd, 1990, pp.162-164.
146 Sugar, *Industrialization of Bosnia-Hercegovina*, pp.73-80.
147 [William Le Queux], *The Near East: The Present Situation in Montenegro, Bosnia, Servia, Bulgaria, Roumania, Turkey and Macedonia*, New York, 1907, pp.105 and 109.
148 Gjurkovečki, *Politička historija Bosne za okupacije*, p.11,
149 Imamović, *Pravni položaj*, p.129.
150 Baernreither, *Fragments of a Political Diary*, p.27.
151 Mitar Papić, *Školstvo u Bosni i Hercegovini za vrijeme austro-ugarske okupacije*, Sarajevo, 1972, p.11.
152 Nikola Stojanović, *Bosanska kriza 1908-1914*, Sarajevo, 1958, p.14.
153 Papić, *Školstvo u Bosni i Hercegovini*, p.51.
154 Šehić, *Autonomni pokret Muslimana*, p.132.
155 *DSPKS*, vol.I/1, no.80, telegram Hristić to the Foreign Ministry, Belgrade, 14 July 1903.
156 Redlich, *Shicksalsjahre*, vol.1, diary entry for 1 December 1909, p.273.
157 Stojanović, *Bosanska kriza*, p.21.
158 Danilo Dimović, 'Iz mojih uspomena', *Preporod*, Beograd, 7 Septemebr 1922, p.2.
159 Stephan Burián, *Austria in Dissolution*, London, 1925, p.279.
160 Okey, *Taming Balkan Nationalism*, pp.147-148.
161 Kruševac, *Sarajevo pod austro-ugarskom upravom*, p.325.
162 Imamović, *Pravni položaj*, pp.131-132.
163 Kruševac, *Sarajevo pod austro-ugarskom upravom*, pp.327-328.
164 Okey, *Taming Balkan Nationalism*, p.148.
165 Redlich, *Schicksalsjahre*, vol.1, entry for 7 January 1910, p.284.
166 Osman Nuri Hadžić, 'Muslimanska versko-prosvetna autonomija u Bosni i Hercegovini i pitanje Carigradskog Halifata', *Brastvo*, Beograd, vol.19, 1925, pp.231-232.
167 Imamović, *Pravni položaj*, p.143.
168 *Ibid.*, p.147.
169 *Ibid.*, pp.140-141.
170 Skarić, Nuri-Hadžić and Stojanović, *Bosna i Hercegovina pod austro-ugarskom upravom*, pp.115-116.
171 Imamović, *Pravni položaj*, p.162.
172 Veselin Masleša, *Mlada Bosna*, Sarajevo, 1945, p.90.
173 *Ibid.*, pp.48-50.
174 *Ibid.*, pp.36 and 91.
175 Hamdija Ćemerlić, 'Alibeg Firdus – borba Muslimana za vjersko-prosvjetnu autonomiju' in Vasa Čubrilović (ed.), *Jugoslovenski narodi pred Prvi svetski rat*, Beograd, 1967, p.879. In 1910 Firdus was named the first President of the new Bosnian Diet, but mortal illness prevented him from taking up the office.
176 *Ibid.*, pp.96-97.
177 Okey, *Taming Balkan Nationalism*, p.134 and n.66, p.292; Šehić, *Autonomni pokret Muslimana*, pp.133-140 and 126.
178 Amir Brka (ed.), *Adem-aga Mešić. Moj odgovor bezimenim klevetnicima*, Tešanj, 1998, p.71.
179 Imamović, *Pravni položaj*, p.127.
180 Gross, 'Hrvatska politika u Bosni i Hercegovini', p.21.
181 Okey, *Taming Balkan Nationalism*, p.148.
182 Grijak, *Politička djelatnost Josipa Stadlera*, p.204.
183 Cipek and Matković, *Programatski dokumenti*, pp.593-594. The chief HNZ ideologue was Dr Ivo Pilar, a lawyer from Tuzla, later the influential author (under the pseudonym L. v. Südland) of *Die südslawische Frage und der Weltkrieg*, Wien, 1918. In the Second World War the Croat *Ustaša* regime published the Croat translation under the title *Južnoslovensko pitanje. Prikaz cjelokupnog pitanja*, Zagreb, 1943.
184 Burián, *Austria in Dissolution*, pp.294-295.
185 Friedjung, *Geschichte in Gesprächen*, vol.2, p.89.
186 Burián, *Austria in Dissolution*, p.296.
187 Gross, 'Hrvatska politika u Bosni i Hercegovini', pp.32-33.
188 *Ibid.*, p.34; Kruševac, *Sarajevo pod austro-ugarskom upravom*, p.348;
189 Gross, 'Hrvatska politika u Bosni i Hercegovini', pp.34 and 40.

190 Imamović, *Pravni položaj*, p.190; Kruševac, *Sarajevo pod austro-ugarskom upravom*, p.348.

191 Ekmečić, 'Nacionalni pokret u Bosni i Hercegovini', p.637.

192 Stojanović, *Bosanska kriza*, pp.47-48. The document was published in Budapest: 'Proklamation der bosnischen Serben und Mohammedaner', *Pester Lloyd*, Budapest, 13 October 1908 (Morgenblatt), p.3.

193 Redlich, *Shicksalsjahre*, vol.1, diary entry for 7 January 1910, p.285.

194 Hamdija Kapidžić, *Bosna i Hercegovina pod austrougarskom upravom. Članci i rasprave*, Sarajevo, 1968, p.55.

195 Kapidžić, *Bosna i Hercegovina pod austro-ugarskom upravom*, p.58.

196 Horts Haselsteiner, *Bosnien-Hercegovina. Orientkrise und Südslawische Frage*, Wien-Köln-Weimar, 1996, p.102.

197 Imamović, *Pravni položaj*, pp.197-202.

198 Kruševac, *Sarajevo pod austro-ugarskom upravom*, p.354.

199 There were thus three kinds of citizenship in the Habsburg Monarchy: Austrian, Hungarian and 'Land' (*Landeszugehörigkeit*) that is, Bosnian-Herzegovinian. The often repeated assumption that Gavrilo Princip and his fellow assassins were Austro-Hungarian citizens is therefore incorrect as there was no such thing as Austro-Hungarian citizenship.

200 Dževad Juzbašić, *Nacionalno-politički odnosi u bosanskohercegovačkom saboru i jezičko pitanje 1910-1914*, Sarajevo, 1999, p.63.

201 Okey, *Taming Balkan Nationalism*, p.178.

202 Kapidžić, *Bosna i Hercegovina pod austro-ugarskom upravom*, pp.82-86.

203 Kann, *The Multinational Empire*, vol.1, pp.292 and 432, n.23.

204 Ekmečić, 'Nacionalni pokret u Bosni i Hercegovini', p.639. The Diet had 72 elected members and 20 appointed ones (*virilisti*). In the latter category each of the three confessions had five high ranking clergymen as members (there was also one Jewish member). This group of distinguished *ex officio* local heavyweights was seen as 'the state-building element' – a kind of upper house and a 'brake' to any reform tendency (Kapidžić, *Bosna i Hercegovina pod austrougarskom upravom*, pp.81-82). The 72 elected members were divided into three curias. In the first (18 mandates) were the big landowners (predominantly Muslims), big merchants, clergy and intelligentsia. The second (20 mandates) was basically the petit bourgeoisie. The third (34 mandates) was made up of the peasantry. The Orthodox had 31 mandates, the Muslims 24 and the Catholics 16. There was also one Jewish mandate among the 72.

205 Cited in Okey, *Taming Balkan Nationalism*, p.178.

206 Imamović, *Historija Bošnjaka*, p.440; Ekmečić, 'Nacionalni pokret u Bosni i Hercegovini', p.640.

207 Božo Cerović, *Bosanski omladinci i sarajevski atentat*, Sarajevo, 1930, p.47.

208 Vladimir Dedijer, *The Road to Sarajevo*, London, 1967, p.240.

209 General Varešanin, although unquestionably a Habsburg loylist, has perhaps unjustly been presented in the Yugoslav historiography in an entirely negative light. He was, in fact, a supporter of Serbo-Croat unity. 'Serbs and Croats', he said in 1909, 'are the same people which, unfortunately, has two names.' See Kršnjavi, *Zapisci*, vol.2, pp.581-582.

210 Dedijer, *The Road to Sarajevo*, p.243.

211 Drago Ljubibratić, *Vladimir Gaćinović*, Beograd, 1961, p.64.

212 Vojislav Bogićević, *Mlada Bosna. Pisma i prilozi*, Sarajevo, 1954, p.49.

213 Masleša, *Mlada Bosna*, p.108.

214 Todor Kruševac, 'Seljački pokret – štrajk u Bosni 1910. godine' in Vasa Čubrilović (ed.), *Jugoslovenski narodi pred Prvi svetski rat*, Beograd, 1967, p.397.

5 Serbia 1903: Bad King, Bad Blood

1 Wayne Vucinich, however, pointed out that it is simply not true that one of Serbia's ruling families (Karađorđević) had always leaned on Russia, while the other (Obrenović) on Austria – and that the reality was in fact quite mixed. See Wayne S. Vucinich, *Serbia Between East and West: The Events of 1903-1908*, Stanford, 1954, p.1. The German historian Walter Markov had already in 1934 argued much the same. He suggested that the idea of an allegedly Russophile Karađorđević dynasty on the one hand, and an Austorphile Obrenović dynasty on the other, amounted to a tendentious 'political-propagandist' exercise. See Walter M. Markov, *Serbien zwischen Österreich und Russland 1897-1908*, Stuttgart, 1934, p.81.

2 Alfred von Wegerer, *Der Ausbruch des Weltkrieges 1914*, Hamburg 1939, vol. 1, p.38.

3 Fay, *The Origins of the World War*, vol. 1, p.358.

4   He writes: 'A plot was organized by a Russophile military *camarilla* which included Captain Dragutin Dimitrievic and Second-Lieutenant Voja Tankosic, both of whom, eleven years later, were to play a large part in the crime of Sarajevo.' See Albertini, *The Origins of the War of 1914*, vol. 1, p. 138.

5   L.C.F. Turner, *Origins of the First World War*, London, 1970, p. 6; James Joll, *The Origins of the First World War*, London, 1992, 2nd edition, pp.10-11.

6   Holm Sundhaussen, *Geschichte Serbiens 19.-21. Jahrhundert*, Wien-Köln-Weimar, 2007, p.210.

7   Holger H. Herwig, 'Why Did It Happen?' in Richard F. Hamilton and Holger H. Herwig (eds.), *The Origins of World War I*, Cambridge 2003, p.443.

8   Hans Uebersberger, *Österreich zwischen Russland und Serbien*, Köln-Graz, 1958, p.8; Markov, *Serbien zwischen Österreich und Russland*, p.80; Roderich Gooß, *Das österreichisch-serbische Problem bis zur Kriegserklärung Österreich-Ungarns an Serbien, 28. Juli 1914*, Berlin, 1930, p.61; Friedjung, *Das Zeitalter des Imperialismus*, vol.1, p.163; Bridge, *From Sadowa to Sarajevo*, pp.261-262.

9   Lazar Vrkatic, *Pojam i bice srpske nacije*, Sremski Karlovci-Novi Sad, 2004, pp.168-69.

10   M.D. Stojanovic, *The Great Powers and the Balkans, 1875-1878*, Cambridge, 1939, p.278.

11   Article II of the Treaty stipulated that Serbia would not just keep hands off Bosnia and Herzegovina, but also steer clear of the *sanjak* of Novi Pazar, Turkish-held but with an Austro-Hungarian military presence in its garrisons. The Novi Pazar region separated Serbia from Montenegro. Similarly, Article VII specifically excluded Novi Pazar as an area where Vienna would tolerate a Serbian southward expansion. See Alfred Francis Pribram, *Die politischen Geheimverträge Österreich-Ungarns 1879-1914*, Wien-Leipzig 1920, vol.1, pp.18-20.

12   Slobodan Jovanovic, *Vlada Aleksandra Obrenovica*, Beograd, 1929-1931, vol.2, p.378.

13   Baernreither, *Fragments of a Political Diary*, p.116.

14   N.V. Tcharykow, *Glimpses of High Politics Through War and Peace 1855-1929*, New York, 1931, p.230.

15   Oskar Freiherr von Mitis, *Das Leben des Kronprinzen Rudolf*, Wien, 1971, p.263.

16   Brigitte Hamann, *Rudolf: Kronprinz und Rebell*, Wien, 1982, p.290.

17   Petrovich, *A History of Modern Serbia*, vol.2, pp.447-448.

18   *Ibid.*, p.249; R. Ljušic and S. Rajic, 'Aleksandar Obrenovic', *Srpski biografski rečnik*, Novi Sad, 2004, vol.1, p.96.

19   Constantin Dumba, *Dreibund- und Entente Politik in der Alten und Neuen Welt*, Zürich-Leipzig –Wien, 1931, p.163.

20   Dimitrije Đorđevic, 'U senci Austro-Ugarske', *Istorija srpskog naroda*, Beograd, 1983, vol.6/1, pp.109-110.

21   Jovanovic, *Vlada Aleksandra Obrenovica*, vol.2, p.85.

22   Jovan Đ. Avakumovic, *Memoari*, Sremski Karlovci-Novi Sad, 2008.

23   Samuel R. Williamson Jr. and Russel Van Wyk (eds.), *July 1914: Soldiers, Statesmen, and the Coming of the Great War. A Brief Documentary History*, Boston and New York, 2003, p.18.

24   William L. Langer, *The Diplomacy of Imperialism*, New York, 1951, p.374.

25   Cited in Živ. Živanovic, *Politička istorija Srbije u drugoj polovini devetnaestog veka*, Beograd, 1924, vol.3, pp.104-105.

26   Vasa Kazimirovic, *Nikola Pašic i njegovo doba 1845-1926*, Beograd, 1990, vol.1, p.503; Jovanovic, *Vlada Aleksandra Obrenovica*, vol.1, pp.83-84.

27   Đorđevic, 'U senci Austro-Ugarske', p.108.

28   Živanovic, *Politička istorija Srbije*, vol.3, p.107.

29   Jovanovic, *Vlada Aleksandra Obrenovica*, vol.1, pp.75-76.

30   Miodrag Jovičic (ed.), *Ustavi Kneževine i Kraljevine Srbije 1835-1903*, Beograd, 1988, p.128. Article 22 stipulated that newspapers and other printed material could be banned only if they contained insults against the King and the Royal House, or against foreign sovereigns and their houses, or if they called on citizens to rise up in arms.

31   Jovanovic, *Vlada Aleksandra Obrenovica*, vol.1, p.78.

32   Monts, *Erinnerungen*, p.126.

33   Kazimirovic, *Nikola Pašic*, vol.1, p.504.

34   Jovanovic, *Vlada Aleksandra Obrenovica*, vol.1, p.79.

35   Jonescu, *Some Personal Impressions*, p.31.

36   Branislav Vranešević, 'Die aussenpolitischen Beziehungen zwischen Serbien und der Habsburgermonarchie' in *Die Habsburgermonarchie 1848-1918*, vol.6/2: *Die Habsburgermonarchier im System der internationalen Beziehungen*, Wien, 1993, p.362.

37 Dimitrije Đorđević, *Carinski rat Austro-Ugarske i Srbije 1906-1911*, Beograd, 1962, p.16.

38 Nikola Vučo, *Privredna istorija naroda FNRJ do prvog svetskog rata*, Beograd, 1948, pp.260-261.

39 Wank, *Aus dem Nachlass Aehrenthal*, vol.1, no.43, letter Kálnoky to Aehrenthal, 14 December 1893, p.51.

40 Mihailo Vojvodić, *Srbija u međunarodnim odnosima krajem XIX i početkom XX veka*, Beograd, 1988, pp.52-53 and 69-72.

41 *Ibid.*, p.73.

42 *Ibid.*, pp.46-49.

43 Vrkatić, *Pojam i biće srpske nacije*, p.212.

44 Vojvodić, *Srbija u međunarodnim odnosima*, p.67.

45 *Ibid.*, pp.55-56.

46 *Ibid.*, pp.103-105.

47 *Ibid.*, p.106.

48 Vasa Čubrilović and V. Ćorović, *Srbija od 1858 do 1903 godine*, Beograd, n.d., pp.168-169.

49 Ana Stolić, *Đorđe Simić. Poslednji srpski diplomata XIX veka*, Beograd, 2003, pp.204 and 217.

50 Vojvodić, *Srbija u međunarodnim odnosima*, p.110.

51 Jovanović, *Vlada Aleksandra Obrenovića*, vol.2, p.65.

52 *Ibid.*, p.66.

53 Vojvodić, *Srbija u međunarodnim odnosima*, p.163.

54 Chedomille Mijatovich, *A Royal Tragedy*, London, 1906, pp.94 and 96.

55 Suzana Rajić, *Vladan Đorđević. Biografija pouzdanog obrenovićevca*, Beograd, 2007, pp.212-223.

56 Jovanović, *Vlada Aleksandra Obrenovića*, vol.2, pp.66-67.

57 *Ibid.*, pp.78-79.

58 Petrovich, *A History of Modern Serbia*, vol.2., p.502.

59 Milić Milićević, *Reforma vojske Srbije 1897-1900.*, Beograd, 2002, p.159.

60 Jovanović, *Vlada Aleksandra Obrenovića*, vol.2, pp.41-43.

61 Marco [Božin Simić], 'Pripremanje 29. Maja 1903', *Nova Evropa*, Zagreb, vol.15, no.2, 11 June 1927, pp.412-413.

62 Jovanović, *Vlada Aleksandra Obrenovića*, vol.2, p.64.

63 *Ibid.*, pp.80-81.

64 Mijatovich, *A Royal Tragedy*, pp.67-68.

65 Jovanović, *Vlada Aleksandra Obrenovića*, vol.2, p.132.

66 Vladan Đorđević, *Kraj jedne dinastije. Prilozi za istoriju Srbije od 11 oktobra 1897 do 8 jula 1900*, Beograd, 1906, vol.3, pp.685-691.

67 Ana Stolić, *Kraljica Draga Obrenović*, Beograd, 2009, pp.27-28.

68 A. Kutschbach, *Der Brandherd Europas. 50 Jahre Balkan-Erinnerungen*, Leipzig, 1929, p.116.

69 Stolić, *Kraljica Draga Obrenović*, p.35.

70 Jovanović, *Vlada Aleksandra Obrenovića*, vol.2, pp.162 and 211.

71 *Ibid.*, p.170.

72 Vladan Đorđević wrote in his memoirs that he had only later found out that King Alexander suffered from a condition called phimosis. This condition, according to Đorđević, had decisively convinced Alexander that 'he could be a man only with Draga.' Himself a medical doctor by training, Đorđević noted that the matter could have been solved by minor surgery, something that would have given Serbia's later history an entirely different shape. He lamented: 'A whole Kingdom for a phimosis!' (Đorđević, *Kraj jedne dinastije*, vol.3, pp.468-469.) Alexander's phimosis was well known to the Austro-Hungarian Legation in Belgrade. Baron Karl Heidler, the Minister, even opined privately in September 1900 that Alexander could accomplish coitus only with Draga. See Friedjung, *Geschichte in Gesprächen*, vol.1, p.349.

73 A. Savinsky, *Recollections of a Russian Diplomat*, London, 1927, p.33.

74 Stolić, *Kraljica Draga Obrenović*, p.27; Dumba, *Dreibund*, p.163.

75 Andrija Radenić, *Spoljna politika Srbije u kontroverznoj istoriografiji*, Beograd, 2006, p.74, n.31.

76 Živojin Aleksić (ed.), *Tasin dnevnik 1870-1906*, Beograd, 1991, p.380.

77 Mijatovich, *A Royal Tragedy*, pp.70-71.

78 Đorđević, *Kraj jedne dinastije*, vol.3, p.451.

79 Mijatovich, *A Royal Tragedy*, pp.68-69.

80 Vucinich, *Serbia Between East and West*, pp.5-12.

81 Vasa Kazimirović, *Crna Ruka. Ličnosti i događaji u Srbiji od prevrata 1903. do solunskog procesa 1917. godine*, Kragujevac, 1997, pp.41 and 49.

82 Jovanović, *Vlada Aleksandra Obrenovića*, vol.2, p.155, n.2.

83 Cited in Stolić, *Kraljica Draga Obrenović*, p.92.

84 Jovanović, *Vlada Aleksandra Obrenovića*, vol.2, p.155.

85 *Ibid.*, p.156. The Austro-Hungarian Legation in Belgrade was perfectly aware of

these exchanges between Alexander and Mansurov. See Friedjung, *Geschichte in Gesprächen*, vol.1, p.348.

86 Whether Milan genuinely believed that his son could continue the line is perhaps open to doubt. In December 1898 Alois von Aehrenthal, then the Austro-Hungarian Minister in Bucharest, stated privately that Milan considered Alexander to be 'impotent', and thought of adopting one of his illegitimate sons to be the Heir to the Throne. See Friedjung, *Geschichte in Gesprächen*, vol.1, p.209.

87 Chedomille Mijatovich, *The Memoirs of a Balkan Diplomatist*, London, 1917, p.170.

88 Vojvoda Gavro Vuković, *Memoari*, Cetinje, 1996, p.729.

89 Margutti, *Kaiser Franz Joseph*, p.366; Jovanović, *Vlada Aleksandra Obrenovića*, vol.2, p.255.

90 Ana Milićević-Lunjevica, *Moja sestra kraljica Draga*, Beograd, 1995, p.76.

91 Karl Gladt, *Kaisertraum und Königskrone. Aufstieg und Untergang einer serbischen Dynastie*, Graz-Wien-Köln, 1972, p.315.

92 Đorđević, *Kraj jedne dinastije*, vol.3, pp.595-596.

93 Dušan Savković, *Sekira. Povest Drage Mašin*, Zagreb, 1977, p.5.

94 Kazimirović, Nikola Pašić, vol.1, p.590."

95 Đorđević, *Kraj jedne dinastije*, vol.3, p.698.

96 Stolić, *Kraljica Draga Obrenović*, p.34.

97 Herbert Vivian, *The Servian Tragedy with Some Impressions of Macedonia*, London, 1904, p.70.

98 Radovan M. Drašković, *Pretorijanske težnje u Srbiji. Apis i 'Crna Ruka'*, Beograd, 2006, pp.20-21.

99 Đorđević, *Kraj jedne dinastije*, vol.3, p.626.

100 Avakumović, *Memoari*, p.415.

101 Harold W.V. Temperley, *History of Serbia*, London, 1919, p.278.

102 Đorđević, *Kraj jedne dinastije*, vol.3, p.644 and n.3 at the bottom of this page.

103 *Ibid.*, p.650.

104 Avakumović, *Memoari*, pp.423-430.

105 Jovanović, *Vlada Aleksandra Obrenovića*, vol.2, p.166.

106 *Ibid.*, p.144.

107 Đorđević, *Kraj jedne dinastije*, vol.3, p.642.

108 Živanović, *Politička istorija Srbije*, vol.4, p.215.

109 Jovanović, *Vlada Aleksandra Obrenovića*, vol.2, p.175.

110 Stolić, *Kraljica Draga Obrenović*, p.96.

111 West, *Black Lamb and Grey Falcon*, vol.1, p.572.

112 Miloš Trifunović, *Istorija Radikalne stranke*, Beograd, 1995, p.348.

113 Jovanović, *Vlada Aleksandra Obrenovića*, vol.2, p.159.

114 *Ibid.*, pp.168, 166 and 165, n.2.

115 Gladt, *Kaisertraum und Königskrone*, p.316.

116 Stolić, *Kraljica Draga Obrenović*, p.162.

117 *Ibid.*, p.161.

118 Jovanović, *Vlada Aleksandra Obrenovića*, vol.2, p.211.

119 *The Spectator*, London, 25 May 1901, p.1.

120 Jovanović, *Vlada Aleksandra Obrenovića*, vol.2, pp.209 and 211-212.

121 M. Edith Durham, *Twenty Years of Balkan Tangle*, London, 1920, p.72.

122 'Königin Draga', *Neue Freie Presse*, Wien, 22 May 1901, (Abendblatt), p.2.

123 Živanović, *Politička istorija Srbije*, vol.4, p.250.

124 Jovanović, *Vlada Aleksandra Obrenovića*, vol.2, pp.209-210.

125 *Ibid.*, p.212.

126 Stolić, *Kraljica Draga Obrenović*, p.139.

127 Vuković, *Memoari*, p.735.

128 Dumba, *Dreibund*, pp.165-166.

129 Jovanović, *Vlada Aleksandra Obrenovića*, vol.2, p.161.

130 *Ibid.*, p.162.

131 Tcharykow, *Glimpses of High Politics*, p.234.

132 Vojvoda Simo Popović, *Memoari*, Cetinje-Podgorica, 1995, pp.383-384.

133 Jovanović, *Vlada Aleksandra Obrenovića*, vol.2, p.174.

134 Albertini, *The Origins of the War of 1914*, vol.1, p.138.

135 Mihailo Vojvodić, *Petrogradske godine Stojana Novakovića*, Beograd, 2009, pp.13-14.

136 Markov, *Serbien zwischen Österreich und Russland*, p.33, n.155.

137 Tcharykow, *Glimpses of High Politics*, p.232.

138 *Ibid.*, pp.232-233.

139 Following her divorce from George in 1906, she married Grand Duke Nicholas in 1907. Her sister Milica was married to Grand Duke Peter, Nicholas's younger brother.

140 Popović, *Memoari*, pp.383-384.

141 Graf Witte, *Erinnerungen*, Berlin, 1923, p.140.

142 Jovanović, *Vlada Aleksandra Obrenovića*, vol.2, pp.157-158.

143 Vuković, *Memoari*, p.785.

144 Vojvodić, *Srbija u međunarodnim odnosima*, p.311.

145 Trifunović, *Istorija Radikalne stranke*, p.352.

146 Avakumović, *Memoari*, pp.433-434.

147 Živanović, *Politička istorija Srbije*, vol.4, pp.244-245.

148 Vojvodić, *Srbija u međunarodnim odnosima*, pp.308-309 and 336-337.
149 Markov, *Serbien zwischen Österreich und Russland*, p.41.
150 Vojvodić, *Srbija u međunarodnim odnosima*, pp.408-409.
151 *Ibid.*, pp.295-296.
152 Corti and Sokol, *Der alte Kaiser*, p.266; Jean de Bourgoing (ed.), *Briefe Kaiser Franz Josephs an Frau Katharina Schratt*, Wien, 1964, pp.345-346.
153 Jovanović, *Vlada Aleksandra Obrenovića*, vol.2, p.192.
154 Vojvodić, *Srbija u međunarodnim odnosima*, pp.316-317.
155 Wank, *Aus dem Nachlass Aehrenthal*, vol.1, no.183, letter Aehrenthal to Szögyény, 27 September 1901, p.245.
156 *Ibid.*, no.189, letter Gołuchowski to Aehrenthal, 29 December 1901, p.259.
157 *GP*, vol.18/1, no.5443, Eulenburg to Bülow, 6 January 1901.
158 *GP*, vol.18/1, no.5441, endnote on pp.113-114, referring to report by Kiderlen, Bucharest, to Chancellor Bülow, 27 February, 1901.
159 Markov, *Serbien zwischen Österreich und Russland*, p.32.
160 Tcharykow, *Glimpses of High Politics*, p.234.
161 Glaise-Horstenau, *Franz Josephs Weggefährte*, p.391.
162 Trifunović, *Istorija Radikalne stranke*, p.361.
163 Živanović, *Politička istorija Srbije*, vol.4, p.295; Markov, *Serbien zwischen Österreich und Russland*, p.41.
164 Jovanović, *Vlada Aleksandra Obrenovića*, vol.2, p.325; Vucinich, *Serbia between East and West*, p.39.
165 Dumba, *Dreibund*, p.173.
166 Glaise-Horstenau, *Franz Josephs Weggefährte*, pp.391-392.
167 Živanović, *Politička istorija Srbije*, vol.4, pp.318-319; Ognjan Topalović, *Đeneral Belimarković*, Vrnjačka Banja, 1998, p.239.
168 Vojvoda Živojin Mišić, *Moje uspomene*, Beograd, 1969, p.205.
169 Jovan Žujović, *Dnevnik*, Beograd, 1986, vol.1, p.138.
170 Jovanović, *Vlada Aleksandra Obrenovića*, vol.2, pp.332-336; Stolić, *Kraljica Draga Obrenović*, p.188.
171 HHStA, P.A. XIX, 47, report Dumba to Gołuchowski, 31 May 1903.
172 Jovanović, *Vlada Aleksandra Obrenovića*, vol.2, *pp.*276-278.
173 Vojvodić, *Srbija u međunarodnim odnosima*, p.407.
174 Jovanović, *Vlada Aleksandra Obrenovića*, vol.2, pp.325-326.
175 *Ibid*, p.215; Živanović, *Politička istorija Srbije*, vol.4, p.251.
176 Jovanović, *Vlada Aleksandra Obrenovića*, vol.2, pp.216-217 and 280.
177 Tcharykow, *Glimpses of High Politics*, p.234.
178 [Anon.], *Draga, Ivan-danski atentat i njezina trudnoća*, Beograd, 1903, p.28.
179 Cited in Lady Grogan, *The Life of J.D. Bourchier*, London, 1927, p.94.
180 Dragoljub R. Živojinović, *Kralj Petar I Karađorđević*, Beograd, 2009, vol.1, p.451; Stolić, *Kraljica Draga Obrenović*, p.167.
181 Jovanović, *Vlada Aleksandra Obrenovića*, vol.2, p.339.
182 David MacKenzie, *Apis: The Congenial Conspirator*, Boulder, 1989, p.31.
183 Sundhaussen, *Geschichte Serbiens*, p.205; McMeekin, *July 1914*, p.6; Clark, *The Sleepwalkers*, pp.11 and 15.
184 Milorad Ekmečić, 'Austro-ugarska obaveštajna služba i majski prevrat u Srbiji 1903. godine', *Istorijski časopis*, Beograd, vol.32, 1985, p.213.
185 Dragiša Vasić, *Devetsto treća*, Beograd, 1925, p.57; Antonije Antić, *Beleške*, Zaječar, 2010, p.71.
186 Drašković, *Pretorijanske težnje u Srbiji*, pp.28-29.
187 Antić, *Beleške*, p.72.
188 Drašković, *Pretorijanske težnje u Srbiji*, pp.22-23.
189 *Ibid.*, p.28.
190 Dragutin K. Mićić, 'Srpski oficiri. Njihova uloga i značaj u životu Srbije do ujedinjenja', p. 15, Arhiv Vojno-istorijskog instituta, Beograd, Popisnik 16.
191 Č. Popov, 'Đorđe A. Genčić', *Sprpski biografski rečnik*, Novi Sad, 2006, vol.2, pp.646-647; Vivian, *The Servian Tragedy*, p.92; Drašković, *Pretorijanske težnje u Srbiji*, pp.15-18; Aleksić, *Tasin dnevnik*, p.439.
192 Kazimirović, *Crna ruka*, p.89.
193 Markov, *Serbien zwischen Österreich und Russland*, p.37.
194 Clark, *The Sleepwalkers*, p.10. See Vranešević, 'Die aussenpolitischen Beziehungen zwischen Serbien und der Habsburgermonarchie', pp.361-362. Clark gives, incorrectly, the page numbers as 36-7.
195 Cited in Kazimirović, *Crna ruka*, p.87.
196 Drašković, *Pretorijanske težnje u Srbiji*, p.29.
197 Antić, *Beleške*, p.74; Jovanović, *Vlada Aleksandra Obrenovića*, vol.2, p.342.
198 D. Denda, 'Aleksandar J. Mašin', *Srpski biografski rečnik*, Novi Sad, 2014, vol.6, p.332.
199 Jovanović, *Vlada Aleksandra Obrenovića*, vol.2, pp.345-346.

200 Drašković, *Pretorijanske težnje u Srbiji*, p.48.

201 Vivian, *The Servian Tragedy*, p.131.

202 Antić, *Beleške*, p.109.

203 Mićić, 'Srpski oficiri', p.16.

204 *Ibid*; Drašković, *Pretorijanske težnje u Srbiji*, p.33.

205 Jovanović, *Vlada Aleksandra Obrenovića*, vol.2, p.349.

206 Vasić, *Devetsto treća*, p.77.

207 Dumba, *Dreibund*, p.175.

208 Tcharykow, *Glimpses of High Politics*, p.235.

209 Dumba, *Dreibund*, p.182.

210 Mićić, 'Srpski oficiri', p.16. This information was added in handwriting to the type-written memoir.

211 Jovan M. Jovanović Pižon, *Dnevnik 1896-1920*, Novi Sad, 2015, diary entry for 3 August 1917, p.321.

212 Drašković, *Pretorijanske težnje u Srbiji*, p.33.

213 Fritz von Reinhöl, 'Die angebliche Mitwissenschaft der österreichisch-ungarischen Regierung an der Verschwörung gegen König Alexander von Serbien im Jahre 1903', *Berliner Monatshefte*, May 1936.

214 Ekmečić, 'Austro-ugarska obavještajna služba i majski prevrat u Srbiji 1903. godine', pp.209-232.

215 Henry Wickham Steed, *Through Thirty Years*, London, 1924, vol.1, pp.203-204.

216 V. Ćorović, 'Misija Andre Đorđevića u Beču 1903 godine', *Srpski književni glasnik*, Beograd, vol.42, no.7, August 1934, pp.531-532.

217 Dumba, *Dreibund*, pp.175-176.

218 Peter Schuster, *Henry Wickham Steed und die Habsburger Monarchie*, Wien-Köln-Graz, 1970, pp.24-25.

219 M. Boghitschewitsch, *Kriegsursachen*, Zürich, 1919, pp.15-16.

220 M. Boghitschewitsch, *Die auswärtige Politik Serbiens 1903-1914*, Berlin, 1931, vol.3, p.198.

221 Živojinović, *Kralj Petar I*, vol.1, p.462.

222 Boghitschewitsch, *Die auswärtige Politik Serbiens*, vol.3, pp.7-8.

223 Jovanović Pižon, *Dnevnik*, diary entry for 15 August 1917, p.327.

224 Vojvodić, *Srbija u međunarodnim odnosima*, p.459.

225 Božo K. Maršićanin, *Tajne dvora Obrenovića. Upraviteljeve beleške*, Beograd, n.d., vol.2, p.122.

226 Triša Kaclerović, *Martovske demonstracije i majski prevrat 1903*, Beograd, 1950, pp.37-41.

227 *Ibid.*, p.73; Jovanović, *Vlada Aleksandra Obrenovića*, vol.2, pp.310-311.

228 Cited in Živanović, *Politička istorija Srbije*, vol.4, p.300, n.2.

229 *Ibid.*, pp.301-302.

230 Trifunović, *Istorija Radikalne stranke*, p.365.

231 Jovanović, *Vlada Aleksandra Obrenovića*, vol.2, pp.348-349.

232 Vasić, *Devetsto treća*, pp.73-74; Drašković, *Pretorijanske težnje u Srbiji*, p.31.

233 Kutschbach, *Der Brandherd Europas*, p.138; Vucinich, *Serbia Between East and West*, p.55; Suzana Rajić, 'The Russian Secret Service and King Alexander Obrenović of Serbia 1900-1903', *Balcanica*, Belgrade, vol.43 (2012), pp.164-165.

234 Jovanović, *Vlada Aleksandra Obrenovića*, vol.2, p.351; Maršićanin, *Tajne dvora Obrenovića*, vol.2, pp.159-160-

235 Jovanović, *Vlada Aleksandra Obrenovića*, vol.2, pp.351-352; Dumba, *Dreibund*, pp.173-174.

236 Drašković, *Pretorijanske težnje u Srbiji*, p.44.

237 Antić, *Beleške*, p.142.

238 *Ibid.*, p.124.

239 Vasić, *Devetsto treća*, p.90.

240 Jovanović, *Vlada Aleksandra Obrenovića*, vol.2, p.353.

241 Vasić, *Devetsto treća*, p.90.

242 *Ibid.*, pp.86-88 and 90.

243 *Ibid.*, p.89.

244 Vivian, *The Servian Tragedy*, p.106; Vasić, *Devetsto treća*, p.91.

245 Antić, *Beleške*, pp.169-173.

246 *Ibid.*, p.171; Mićić, 'Srpski oficiri', p.23; Vasić, *Devetsto treća*, pp.92-93.

247 A well-informed British book from 1903 speculated that Petrović, being assured that the conspirators desired only the King's abdication, had led them to Draga's wardrobe. See Mrs. Northesk Wilson, Belgrade: *The White City of Death*, London, 1903, p.96.

248 Vasić, *Devetsto treća*, p.93

249 *Ibid.*, pp.93-94.

250 Tcharykow, *Glimpses of High Politics*, pp.235-236

251 HHStA, P.A., XIX, 74, Dumba to Gołuchowski, 13 June 1903.

252 Vivian, *The Servian Tragedy*, p.109.

253 Antić, *Beleške*, p.173.

254 Vrkatić, *Pojam i biće srpske nacije*, p.214.

6   The Rise of Austro-Serbian Antagonism

1   Dumba, *Dreibund*, p.181.

2   Đorđević, *Carinski rat*, p.34, n.1.

3   Tcharykow, *Glimpses of High Politics*, p.236.

4   Boghitschewitsch, *Die auswärtige Politik*

Serbiens, vol.1, no.1, telegram, Franz Joseph to King Peter, 16 June 1903; Dumba, *Dreibund*, p.189.

5 Wendel, *Die Habsburger und die Südslawenfrage*, p.26.

6 Dušan A. Lončarević, *Jugoslaviens Entstehung*, Zürich-Leipzig-Wien, 1929, p.49.

7 Redlich, *Schicksalsjahre*, vol.1, diary entry for 27 January 1906, p.177.

8 See Alexander Hoyos, *Der deutschenglische Gegensatz und sein Einfluss auf die Balkanpolitik Österreich-Ungarns*, Berlin-Leipzig, 1922, pp.41-42; [Franz I. von und zu Liechtenstein], 'Der Kaiser und die Zaren' in Eduard Ritter von Steinitz (ed.), *Erinnerungen an Franz Joseph I*, Berlin, 1931, p.243; Lützow, *Im diplomatischen Dienst*, p.96.

9 See Bridge, *From Sadowa to Sarajevo*, p.262; Afflerbach, *Der Dreibund*, p.610. According to the Austrian historian Lothar Höbelt, the Russians had 'apparently almost invited' an Austro-Hungarian intervention in Serbia – 'tongue-in-cheek because they suspected the Austrians of having supported the coup d'état.' See Lothar Höbelt, 'Why did Austria-Hungary Decide for War in 1913-1914?' in Dragoljub R. Živojinović (ed.), *The Serbs and the First World War*, Belgrade, 2015, p.171, n.6.

10 Andrija Radenić (ed.), *Austro-Ugarska i Srbija 1903-1918. Dokumenti iz bečkih arhiva*, vol.1, 1903, Beograd, 1973, no.54, Aehrenthal to Gołuchowski, 2 July 1903. Hereafter cited as *DBA*. Most of the Austro-Hungarian documents relevant to relations with Serbia during the period 1903-1906 were published in this collection, in the original German, by the Historical Institute, Belgrade (volumes 1 and 2 in 1973; vol.3 in 1985; and vol.4 in 1989). Although envisaged to cover the period up to 1918, the collection stops at the end of 1906. The bulk of its diplomatic documents stems from Vienna's Haus-, Hof- und Staatsarchiv, where much material can be found in the political archive (Politisches Archiv) concerning Serbia, reference P.A. XIX.

11 *DBA*, vol.1, no.6, Aehrenthal to Gołuchowski, 13 June 1903.

12 *DBA*, vol.1, no. 4, Pomiankowski to the War Ministry, 12 June 1903; no 5, Pomiankowski to the War Ministry, 13 June 1903.

13 Vladimir Tržecjak, 'Jedan ruski savremeni dokumenat o 29. Maja', *Nova Evropa*, Zagreb, vol.16, no.7, 11 October 1927, p.229.

14 *BD*, vol.5, no.132, telegram Scott to Lansdowne, 18 June 1903.

15 HHStA, P.A. XIX, 74, telegram Pomiankowski, 13 June 1905, Präsidialbureau no.4006.

16 Živojinović, *Kralj Petar*, vol.1, p.5.

17 Drašković, *Pretorijanske težnje u Srbiji*, p.63.

18 Antić, *Beleške*, p.176.

19 Đ. Đurić, 'Jovan M. Žujović', *Srpski biografski rečnik*, Novi Sad, 2007, vol.3, p.817.

20 *DBA*, vol.1, no.14, Dumba to Gołuchowski, 16 June 1903.

21 Vojislav J. Vučković, 'Unutrašnje krize Srbije i Prvi svetski rat', *Istorijski časopis*, Beograd, vol.14-15, 1963-1965, p.177.

22 Antić, *Beleške*, p.187.

23 Drašković, *Pretorijanske težnje u Srbiji*, p.55.

24 According to several accounts, however, the ardent republican Jovan Žujović had abstained.

25 *Spomenica Jaše M. Prodanovića*, Beograd, 1958, p.185.

26 *DBA*, vol.1, no.7, Die Familie Karađorđević, 14 June 1903.

27 Avakumović, *Memoari*, pp.512-513; Živanović, *Politička istorija Srbije*, vol.4, pp.359-360.

28 Clark, *The Sleepwalkers*, p.15.

29 Žujović, *Dnevnik*, vol.1, p.114.

30 Jovičić, *Ustavi Kneževine i Kraljevine Srbije*, p.194.

31 Živojinović, *Kralj Petar*, vol.2, pp.27 and 42.

32 Cited in *ibid.*, p.199.

33 Clark, *The Sleepwalkers*, p.29.

34 Vrkatić, *Pojam i biće srpske nacije*, p.214.

35 Clark, *The Sleepwalkers*, p.21.

36 W.H. Zawadzki, *A Man of Honour: Adam Czartoryski as a Statesman of Russia and Poland 1795-1831*, Oxford, 1993, p.331; M. Kukiel, *Czartoryski and European Unity 1770-1861*, Princeton, 1955, p.246.

37 A.J.P. Taylor, *The Trouble Makers: Dissent over Foreign Policy 1792-1939*, London, 1957, p.46.

38 The memorandum is published in Marceli Handelsman, *La question d'Orient et la politique yugoslave du prince Czartoryski après 1840*, Paris, 1929.

39 The Zach Plan is published in Drag. Stranjaković, 'Kako je postalo Garašaninovo *Načertanije*', Srpska kraljevska akademija, Spomenik 91, Beograd, 1939.

40 Clark, *The Sleepwalkers*, p.21. See asterisk note at the bottom of the page.

41 Garašanin's *Načertanije* is published in Stranjaković, 'Kako je postalo Garašaninovo *Načertanije*', with its text printed in parallel with the text of the Zach Plan.

42 Radoš Ljušić, 'Ilija Garašanin o srpskoj državnosti' in Vladimir Stojančević (ed.), *Ilija Garašanin 1812-1874*, Beograd, 1991, pp.149 and 153.

43 Charles and Barbara Jelavich, *The Establishment of the Balkan National States, 1804-1920*, Seattle-London, 1977, p.63.

44 Clark, *The Sleepwalkers*, p.21.

45 Radenić, *Spoljna politika Srbije u kontroverznoj* istoriografij, p.10.

46 V. Karić, *Srbija i balkanski savez*, Beograd, 1893, p.20.

47 *DSPKS*, vol.1, 4/1, no.37, Proceedings of the conference of the diplomatic representatives abroad, held on 22-25 July (O.S.) 1905.

48 Clark, *The Sleepwalkers*, p.82.

49 *DSPKS*, vol.2, 2/2, no.416, report Petković, Budapest, 8 December 1906.

50 Conrad, *Aus meiner Dienstzeit*, vol.1, p.518.

51 Cited in Mile Bjelajac, *Diplomatija i vojska. Srbija i Jugoslavija 1901-1999*, Beograd, 2010, p.54.

52 HHStA, P.A. XIX, 74, report Mensdorff to Gołuchowski, 13 June 1903. For a detailed account of the role played by Edward VII see Aleksandar Rastović, *Velika Britanija i Srbija 1903-1914*, Beograd, 2005, pp.60-104.

53 Matsch, *November 1918 auf dem Ballhausplatz*, p.149.

54 Živojinović, *Kralj Petar*, vol.2, p.72.

55 *DBA*, vol.1, no.133, Dumba to Gołuchowski, 1 October 1903.

56 Živojinović, *Kralj Petar*, vol.2, p.236.

57 *DBA*, vol.1, no.155, Pomiankowski to Beck, 24 October 1903.

58 Živojinović, *Kralj Petar*, vol.2, pp.234-235.

59 Vasić, *Devetsto treća*, pp.171-172.

60 Drašković, *Pretorijanske težnje u Srbiji*, p.80.

61 Wank, *Aus dem Nachlass Aehrenthal*, vol.1, no.233, letter Mérey to Aehrenthal, 27 November 1903, p.316.

62 *DSPKS*, vol.1/1, no.67, report Spalajković, 8 July 1903; no.543, report Novaković, 25 February 1904.

63 *BD*, vol.5, no.122, memorandum Grey for the King, 23 May 1906.

64 Clark, *The Sleepwalkers*, p.80.

65 Bridge, *From Sadowa to Sarajevo*, p.263.

66 *DBA*, vol.1, no.65, report Dumba, 10 July 1903.

67 *Ibid.*, no.67, Gołuchowski to Aehrenthal, 17 July 1903; no.80, report Aehrenthal, 31 July 1903.

68 Živojinović, *Kralj Petar*, vol.2, p.256.

69 Antić, *Beleške*, pp.201-202.

70 Markov, *Serbien zwischen Österreich und Russland*, p.48.

71 Only two works of substance on Pašić are available in English: Count Carlo Sforza, *Fifty Years of War and Diplomacy in the Balkans: Pasbich and the Union of the Yugoslavs*, New York, 1940, and Alex N. Dragnich, *Serbia, Nikola Pašić, and Yugoslavia*, New Brunswick, 1974.

72 Clark, *The Sleepwalkers*, pp.62-63.

73 Kazimirović, *Nikola Pašić*, vol.1, p.20.

74 Thus Pašić's ethnic background is not explained by Kazimirović, *op.cit.*, in his otherwise very extensive two-volume study (see pp.150-151, vol.1), or by Đorđe Radenković in his *Pašić i Srbija*, Beograd, 1997, another large work (see pp.14-15).

75 Quoted in Žarko Milošević, 'Mladi Pašić – od rođenja do Ciriha (1845-1868)' in *Nikola Pašić: Život i delo*, Zbornik radova, Beograd, 1997, p.23.

76 T.J. Winnifrith, *The Vlachs: The History of a Balkan People*, London, 1987, remains the best scholarly treatment of this subject.

77 For the Cincars of Serbia, see D.J. Popović, *O Cincarima*, Beograd, 1937, 2nd edition, one of the rare accounts. Popović, himself a Cincar, compared his people to the Jews (p.77). His book is to this day the standard work on the Cincars of Serbia. It points out that the Cincars were very successful in Serbian society – indeed that they *were* Serbian society. At the time the first edition of this work was published (1929), it drew a heavy attack from an eminent Serb academic: see Jov. N. Tomić, *Referat o knjizi Dušana J. Popovića O Cincarima*, Beograd, 1929. In the 1920s, following the formation of the Kingdom of Serbs, Croats and Slovenes, the Cincars of Serbia were the object of a hate campaign by the Croat politicians who believed they ruled Belgrade. See also Pribislav B. Marinković, *Velikani – Znamenite ličnosti cincarskog porekla u istoriji Srba*, Beograd, 2005.

78 M. Bjelajac, 'Dragutin T. Apis Dimitrijević', *Srpski biografski rečnik*, Novi Sad, 2007, vol.3, p.223.

79 Topalović, *Đeneral Belimarković*, p.240.

80 Wladimir Giesl, *Zwei Jahrzehnte im Nahen Orient*, Berlin, 1927, p.269; Hamilton Fish Armstrong, *Peace and Counterpeace: From Wilson to Hitler*, New York, 1971, p.365; Dimitrije Popović, 'Nikola Pašić i Rusija', *Godišnjica Nikole Čupića*, Beograd, vol.46, 1937, p.144; Dumba, *Dreibund*, p.235.

81 Kosta Stojanović, *Slom i vaskrs Srbije*, Beograd, 2012, pp.108, 89, 201 and 88.

82 Kazimirović, *Nikola Pašić*, vol.1, p.9.
83 Redlich, *Schicksalsjahre*, vol.1, diary entry for 4 November 1912, p.496.
84 Žujović, *Dnevnik*, vol.1, p.146.
85 Dimitrije Đorđević, *Milovan Milovanović*, Beograd, 1962, p.71.
86 Jaša M. Prodanović, 'Nikola P. Pašić', *Srpski književni glasnik*, Beograd, vol.20, no.2, 16 January 1927, pp.125 and 129-130.
87 *Ibid.*, p.132.
88 *Spomenica Nikole P. Pašića, 1845.-1925.*, Beograd, 1926, p.7.
89 Marco [Božin Simić], 'Nikola Hartvig i Srbija', *Nova Evropa*, Zagreb, vol.26, no.6, 26 June 1933.
90 Andrew Rossos, *Russia and the Balkans*, Toronto-Buffalo-London, 1981, p.4.
91 Nadine Lange-Akhund, *The Macedonian Question, 1893-1908*, Boulder, 1998, pp.142-143.
92 *BD*, vol.5, p.66.
93 Steven W. Sowards, *Austria's Policy of Macedonian Reform*, Boulder, 1989, p.74.
94 *DSPKS*, vol.1/1, no.274, report Hristić (Constantinople), 8 October 1903.
95 *DSPKS*, vol.1/1, no.351, report Milovanović, 8 November 1903.
96 *DBA*, vol.1, no.179, Dumba to Gołuchowski, 23 November 1903.
97 *GP*, vol.22, no.7391, Wedel to Bülow, 18 February 1904.
98 *DSPKS*, vol.2, 2/1, report Vujić, 4 October 1906.
99 *DBA*, vol.2, no.293, private letter Dumba to Mérey, 9 December 1904.
100 *DBA*, vol.2, no.5, Pomiankowski to Beck, 14 February 1904.
101 *DBA*, vol.1, no.188, Pasetti to Gołuchowski, 1 December 1903.
102 *DBA*, vol.2, no.116, Kuhn to Gołuchowski, 25 March 1904.
103 *DBA*, vol.2, no.142, Forgách to Gołuchowski, 20 April 1904.
104 *DSPKS*, vol.1/1, no.532, report Hristić, Athens, 19 February 1904.
105 *DSPKS*, vol.1/2, no.615, report Milovanović, 27 December 1904.
106 *DBA*, vol.1, no.174, protocol of the meeting on 19 November 1903.
107 *DBA*, vol.1, no.132, record of a meeting between Minister Gołuchowski and Emperor Wilhelm, Vienna (dated 'end of September 1903').
108 Prince von Bülow, *Memoirs 1897-1903*, London-New York, 1931, p.615.
109 See, for example, *DBA*, vol.2, no.302, Gołuchowski to Braun, Sofia, 15 December 1904.
110 Živojinović, *Kralj Petar*, vol.2, p.186.

111 *DSPKS*, vol.1/1, no.387, Nikolić circular, 2 December 1903; no.434, Vuković to Grujić, 30 December 1903; no.502, letter Vujić to Pašić, 9 February 1904; no.518, report Milovanović, 14 February 1904.
112 *DSPKS*, vol.1/1, no.525, Pašić to the Serbian Legation, Constantinople, 16 February 1904.
113 *DSPKS*, vol.1/2, no.43, Pašić to Novaković, St Petersburg, 14 March 1904.
114 Savo Skoko, *Vojvoda Radomir Putnik*, Beograd, 1985, vol.1, pp.220-221.
115 Đorđević, *Carinski rat*, pp.47-48.
116 *Ibid.*, p.54; *DBA*, vol.2, no.183, private letter Dumba to Gołuchowski, 10 June 1904; Đorđević, *Carinski rat*, p.55.
117 Vladimir Ćorović, *Odnosi između Srbije i Austro-Ugarske u XX veku*, Beograd, 1992, p.92; Dumba, *Dreibund*, p.218.
118 Đorđević, *Carinski rat*, p.60.
119 Dumba, *Dreibund*, pp.206-207.
120 Đorđević, *Carinski rat*, p.61.
121 *Ibid.*, p.78; Dimitrije Boarov, *Dr Lazar Paču: legenda srpskih finansija*, Novi Sad, 2006, p.127.
122 Cited in Đorđević, *Carinski rat*, p.67.
123 Vrkatić, *Pojam i biće srpske nacije*, p.215.
124 Dumba, *Dreibund*, p.218.
125 Boarov, *Dr Lazar Paču*, p.123.
126 Đorđević, *Carinski rat*, pp.62-63; Dumba, *Dreibund*, p.220.
127 Cited in Đorđević, *Carinski rat*, p.72.
128 *DSPKS*, vol.1/3/1, no.64, report Vujić, 9 February 1905.
129 Živojinović, *Kralj Petar*, vol.2, p.193.
130 *Ibid.*, pp.194-195; Đorđević, *Carinski rat*, p.76; Ljiljana Aleksić-Pejković, *Odnosi Srbije sa Francuskom i Engleskom 1903-1914*, Beograd, 1965, p.106.
131 Dimitrije Đorđević, 'Sučeljavanje sa Austro-Ugarskom', *Istorija srpskog naroda*, Beograd, 1983, vol.6/1, p.138.
132 Jovo Bakić, *Ideologije jugoslovenstva između srpskog i hrvatskog nacionalizma 1918-1941*, Zrenjanin, 2004, p.128, n.80.
133 Dumba, *Dreibund*, p.230.
134 Đorđević, 'Sučeljavanje sa Austro-Ugarskom', p.153.
135 Lončarević, *Jugoslaviens Entstehung*, p.97.
136 *DBA*, vol.4, no.59, record of the meeting held in Vienna, 2 February 1906.
137 *DSPKS*, vol.1/1, no.540, record of the meeting between Pašić and Colonel Hesapchiev, 24 February 1904.
138 The text of the Traty of Alliance is in V. Ćorović, 'Pregovori o balkanskim savezima', *Godišnjica Nikole Čupića*, Beograd, vol.47, 1938, pp.1-24; Ernst Christian Helmreich, *The Diplomacy of the Balkan*

Wars 1912-1913, Cambridge, Mass., 1938, p.7.

139 Ćorović, 'Pregovori o balkanskim savez-ima', p.20.

140 *DSPKS*, vol.1/4/1, no.17, Ministry of Finance to the Ministry of Foreign Affairs, 22 July 1905, and Appendix 1; Lončarević, *Jugoslaviens Entstehung*, pp.98-99.

141 *DBA*, vol.4, no.29, Gołuchowski to Czikann, 17 January 1906.

142 *DSPKS*, vol.2/1/1, no.44, report Vujić, 23 January 1906.

143 Đorđević, *Carinski rat*, p.174.

144 *DSPKS*, vol.2/1/1, no.331, report Vujić, 5 April 1906; *DBA*, vol.4, no.152, 'Österreichisch-ungarische Erklärungen vom 5. April 1906'.

145 *BD*, vol.5, no.132, Thesiger to Grey, 19 April 1906.

146 Christopher H.D. Howard (ed.), *The Diary of Edward Goschen, 1900-1914*, London, 1980, diary entry for 11 April 1906, p.121.

147 *BD*, vol.5, no.134, Thesiger to Grey, 2 May 1906.

148 Živojinović, *Kralj Petar*, vol.2, pp.283-284; *BD*, vol.5, no.126, Grey to Goschen, 31 May 1906.

149 Đorđević, *Carinski rat*, pp.215-220.

150 Ljiljana Aleksić-Pejković, 'Pašić i opredeljivanje Srbije između dva bloka velikih sila' in *Nikola Pašić. Život i Delo*, Beograd, 1997, p.273.

151 See Živojinović, *Kralj Petar*, vol.2, pp.274-277.

152 Nastas N. Petrović, 'Pašić i Goluhovski', *Nova Evropa*, Zagreb, vol.13, no.12, 22 June 1926, pp.416-424.

153 Slobodan Jovanović, *Moji savremenici*, Windsor, Canada, 1962, pp.195-199; Đorđević, *Carinski rat*, pp.220-221; *DBA*, vol.4, no.181, Czikann to Gołuchowski, 1 May, 1906.

154 Živojinović, *Kralj Petar*, vol.2, pp.280-282; Antić, *Beleške*, p.201.

155 *DSPKS*, vol.2/1/2, no.508, minute Pašić, undated, circa 23 May 1906.

156 *DSPKS*, vol.2/1/2, no.500, Pašić circular, 22 May 1906.

157 *DSPKS*, vol.2/1/2, no.587, report Petković, 13 June 1906, and no.588, report Vujić, 14 June 1906.

158 Đorđević, *Carinski rat*, p.241.

159 *DSPKS*, vol.2/1/2, no.602, Pašić to Vujić, 20 June 1906, and Milićević to Jovanović, 14 June 1906.

160 Géza Andreas von Geyr, *Sándor Wekerle 1848-1921*, München, 1993, p.284.

161 *DSPKS*, vol.2/2/2, no.257, report Vujić, 22 October 1906.

162 *DSPKS*, vol.2/1/2, no.644, Czikann to Pašić, 30 June 1906; no.672, Pašić circular, 7 July 1906.

163 Jonescu, *Some Personal Impressions*, p.40.

164 Đorđević, *Carinski rat*, p.270.

165 Bridge, *From Sadowa to Sarajevo*, p.279.

166 Markov, *Serbien zwischen Österreich und Russland*, pp.68-69.

167 Đorđević, *Carinski rat*, p.383.

168 Vucinich, *Serbia Between East and West*, p.207.

7 From the Bosnian Annexation to the Balkan Wars

1 Afflerbach, *Der Dreibund*, p.616.

2 Vucinich, *Serbia Between East and West*, p.142.

3 Howard, *The Diary of Edward Goschen*, diary entry for 13 March 1907, p.140.

4 Solomon Wank, 'Varieties of Political Despair: Three Exchanges Between Aehrenthal and Goluchowski 1898-1906' in Stanley B. Winters and Joseph Held (eds.), *Intellectual and Social Developments in the Habsburg Empire from Maria Theresa to World War I*, Boulder, 1975, pp.203-239.

5 Jonescu, *Some Personal Impressions*, p.73.

6 Sieghart, *Die letzten Jahrzenten einer Grossmacht*, p.134.

7 Eurof Walters, 'Franco-Russian Discussions on the Partition of Austria-Hungary, 1899', *The Slavonic and East European Review*, vol.28, no.70, November 1949, p.191.

8 G.P. Gooch, *Before the War: Studies in Diplomacy*, London, 1936, vol.1, p.438.

9 *DSPKS*, vol.2/2/2, no.301, report Vujić, 3 November 1906; no.284, report Vujić, 30 October 1906.

10 Baernreither, *Fragments of a Political Diary*, p.36.

11 Đorđević, *Carinski rat*, p.546.

12 Friedjung, *Geschichte in Gesprächen*, vol.2, p.44.

13 István Diószegi, *Hungarians at the Ballhausplatz: Studies on the Austro-Hungarian Common Foreign Policy*, Budapest, 1983, p.203.

14 Friedjung, *Geschichte in Gesprächen*, vol.1, pp.342 and 485.

15 Baernreither, *Fragments of a Political Diary*, p.34.

16 Đorđević, *Carinski rat*, p.427.

17 Bridge, *From Sadowa to Sarajevo*, p.302.

18 Conrad, *Aus meiner Dienstzeit*, vol.1, p.528.

19 Baernreither, *Fragments of a Political Diary*, pp.44-45.
20 *ÖUA*, vol.1, no.32, Denkschrift, 9 August 1908.
21 Wank, *Aus dem Nachlass Aehrenthal*, vol.1, no.74, Denkschrift Aehrenthal, September 1895, p.94.
22 *GP*, vol.26/1, no.8927, von Schoen to Bülow, 5 September 1908.
23 Plener, *Erinnerungen*, vol.3, p.389.
24 Friedjung, *Geschichte in Gesprächen*, vol.2, pp.71, 76 and 124-125.
25 Conrad, *Aus meiner Dienstzeit*, vol.1, p.247.
26 Gross, *Vladavina hrvatsko-srpske koalicije*, pp.162-165.
27 Solomon Wank, 'Aehrenthal's Programme for the Constitutional Transformation of the Habsburg Monarchy: Three Secret *Mémoires*', *The Slavonic and East European Review*, vol.41, no.97, June 1963, pp.513-536.
28 *Ibid.*, p.523.
29 *Ibid.*, p.524.
30 *Ibid.*, p.527.
31 *Ibid.*, p.530.
32 *Ibid.*, p.529.
33 Gross, *Vladavina hrvatsko-srpske koalicije*, p.164.
34 Wank, 'Aehrenthal's Programme for the Constitutional Transformation of the Habsburg Monarchy', p.521.
35 *Ibid.*, p.522.
36 Plener, *Erinnerungen*, vol.3, pp.391-392.
37 Solomon Wank, 'Aehrenthal and the Sanjak of Novibazar Railway Project: a Reapprisal', *The Slavonic and East European Review*, vol.42, no.99, June 1964, p.355.
38 *Ibid.*, p.365 and 355.
39 Gooch, *Before the War*, vol.1, p.321.
40 Dimitrije Đorđević, 'Austro-srpski sukob oko projekta novopazarske železnice', *Istorijski časopis*, Beograd, vol.7, 1957, pp.224-225.
41 Felix Somary, *Erinnerungen aus meinem Leben*, Zürich, 1959, pp.68-69.
42 This is the view advanced by Robert Seton-Watson in his *Sarajevo*, p.29.
43 Gooch, *Before the War*, vol.1, p.382.
44 *DSPKS*, vol.3/1/3, no.74, report Popović, 6 February 1908.
45 *DSPKS*, vol.3/1/3, no.89, report Milovanović, Rome, 10 February 1908; no.106, report Milićević, London, 16 February 1908; *BD*, vol.5, no.247, Grey to Egerton, 5 March 1908.
46 Christer Jorgensen, 'Deadly Dilemma: Grey, Great Britain and the Great Bosnian Crisis, October 1908 – March

1909' in Rajko Kuzmanović (ed.), *Stogodišnjica aneksije Bosne i Hercegovine*, Banja Luka, 2009, p.223.
47 *DSPKS*, vol.3/3 and *DSPKS*, vol.3/4 which cover the period from 7 October 1908 to 13 April 1909.
48 For Serbia's Adriatic railway project see Vucinich, *Serbia Between East and West*, pp.210-230.
49 In retrospect, one can see certain parallels with Sarajevo 1914. Interestingly, the Serbian Minister in Cetinje at the time was Jovan Jovanović, the same diplomat who was the Minister in Vienna in 1914.
50 Nikola P. Škerović, *Crna Gora na osvitku XX vijeka*, Beograd, 1964, p.277.
51 L. Tomanović, 'Austrija i Crna Gora', *Nova Evropa*, Zagreb, vol.20, no.5, 26 August 1929, p.133.
52 *DSPKS*, vol.3/1/2, no.580, report Jovanović, Cetinje, 3 June 1908.
53 *DSPKS*, vol.3/1/2, no.591, report Jovanović, 5 June 1908.
54 Novica Rakočević, *Politički odnosi Crne Gore i Srbije 1903-1918*, Cetinje, 1981, p.72.
55 *DSPKS*, vol.2/3/2, no.444, telegram Milovanović, 29 April 1907, and Pašić minute, 30 April 1907.
56 *DSPKS*, vol.3/1/1, no.226, report Milojević, 11 March 1908.
57 See, for example, *DSPKS*, vol.2/4/2, no.444, report Ljubišić, Skopje, 20 November 1907.
58 T.G. Masaryk, 'Österreich und der Balkan' in M.J. Bonn (ed.), *Die Balkanfrage*, München-Leipzig, 1914, p.149.
59 *DSPKS*, vol.3/1/1, no.310, minute Pašić, 30 March 1908.
60 *DSPKS*, vol.3/1/1, no.500, report Popović, 12 December 1907; no.528, report Simić, 23 December 1907.
61 *DSPKS*, vol.3/1/2, no.581, report Simić, Sofia, 3 June 1908; no.586, report Simić, 4 June 1908; no.610, report Simić, 11 June 1908.
62 *DSPKS*, vol.3/2/1, no.22, report Popović, St Petersburg, 20 June 1908; no.19, report Simić, 20 June 1908.
63 MacMillan, *The War that ended Peace*, p.390. Macmillan gives C.A. Macartney as her source (*The Habsburg Empire*, p.774), but Macartney himself cites no sources for these extraordinary claims. 'Bands of Serb agents', he writes (p.774), 'roamed the provinces unrestricted.' One wonders how this was possible in Bosnia-Herzegovina, which under Habsburg rule had more police stations than schools.

64 Dževad Juzbašić, *Politika i privreda u Bosni i Hercegovini pod austrougarskom upravom*, Sarajevo, 2002, p.276, n.35.
65 Conrad, *Aus meiner Dienstzeit*, vol.1, p.569.
66 *Ibid.*, p.567.
67 Dragan Gasic, 'Die Presse Serbiens 1903-1914 und Österreich-Ungarn', Dissertation, Universität Wien, 1971, pp.181-197.
68 *DSPKS*, vol.2/4/2, no.473, report Simić, 4 December 1907; no.543, report Simić, 30 December 1907.
69 *DSPKS*, vol.3/1/2, no.499, report Popović, 13 May 1908.
70 *DSPKS*, vol.3/1/2, no.468, report Simić, 5 May 1908; no.507, report Simić, 14 May 1908.
71 *DSPKS*, vol.3/2/2, no.485, report Subotić, Rome, 11 September 1908.
72 *GP*, vol.26/1, no.8936, telegram Tschirschky, 28 September 1908.
73 Boarov, *Dr Laza Paču*, pp.154-156; Đorđević, *Carinski rat*, pp.416-417.
74 Jovanović, *Moji savremenici*, p.252.
75 Đorđević, *Milovan Milovanović*, p.128.
76 Jovanović, *Moji savremenici*, pp.233-234.
77 *Ibid.*, pp.252-253.
78 *DSPKS*, vol.3/2/2, no.406, report Balugdžić, 22 August 1908, and Milovanović minute.
79 *DSPKS*, vol.3/2/2, no.567, Milovanović to the Serbian Legation, Berlin, 4 October 1908.
80 Ludwig Bittner, Alfred Francis Pribram, Heinrich Srbik and Hans Uebersberger (eds.), *Österreich-Ungarns Aussenpolitik von der bosnischen Krise bis zum Kriegsausbruch 1914*, Wien-Leipzig, 1930, vol.1, no.78, record of a meeting with Milovanović, 14 September 1908. Hereafter cited as *ÖUA*. The relevant tome of the published Serbian documents, *DSPKS*, vol.3/2/2, does not contain a record of this meeting.
81 Dimitrije Popović, 'Milovan Milovanović i aneksija', *Srpski književni glasnik*, Beograd, vol.53, no.7, 1 April 1938, p.496. Popović was in 1908 Serbia's Minister in St Petersburg. The exact date of the Izvolsky-Milovanović meeting at Karlsbad is not given.
82 *ÖUA*, vol.1, no.9.
83 Friedjung, *Geschichte in Gesprächen*, vol.2, p.101. Aehrenthal related this to Friedjung on 6 October 1908.
84 W.M. Carlgren, *Iswolsky und Aehrenthal vor der bosnischen Annexionkrise*, Uppsala, 1955, p.313.
85 *BD*, vol.5, no.330, Grey to Goschen, 7 Octobr 1908.
86 *ÖUA*, vol.1, no.453, report Mensdorff, 30 October 1908.

87 Kršnjavi, *Zapisci*, vol.2, p.537.
88 Seton-Watson, *The Southern Slav Question*, p.178.
89 Georg Nastitsch, *Finale*, Budapest, 1908 – published in German.
90 Cited in Bakić, *Ideologije jugoslovenstva*, p.100.
91 Ćorović, *Odnosi između Srbije i Austro-Ugarske*, p.199.
92 Jv. Tvrtkovic, 'König Peter und die großserbische Bewegung', *Österreichische Rundschau*, Wien, vol.17, no.1, 1 October 1908, pp.1-13.
93 Heinrich Friedjung, 'Oesterreich-Ungarn und Serbien', *Neue Freie Presse*, Wien, 25 March 1909 (Morgenblatt).
94 Steed, *Through Thirty Years*, vol.1, p.309.
95 See T.G. Masaryk, *Vasić-Forgách-Aehrenthal*, Prag, 1911. The most exhaustive work in English on this subject remains that by Theodore V. Gjugjevic, 'The Friedjung and Vasic Trials in the Light of the Austrian Diplomatic Documents 1909-1911', University of Oxford D.Phil. thesis, 1956.
96 Seton-Watson, *The Southern Slav Question*, pp.263-271.
97 Baernreither, *Fragments of a Political Diary*, pp.103 and 105.
98 *ÖUA*, vol.1, nos.40 and 75.
99 Bridge, *From Sadowa to Sarajevo*, p.301.
100 Milorad Ekmečić, *Radovi iz istorije Bosne i Hercegovine XIX veka*, Beograd, 1997, p.381, n.37.
101 Đorđe Mikić, *Austro-Ugarska i Mladoturci 1908-1912*, Banjaluka, 1983, pp.89-90.
102 *ÖUA*, vol.1, no.66, telegram Pallavicini, 5 September 1908.
103 József Galántai, *Die Österreichisch-Ungarische Monarchie und der Weltkrieg*, Budapest, 1979, pp.70-71.
104 H.H. Fisher (ed.), *Out of My Past: The Memoirs of Count Kokovtsov*, Stanford, 1935, p.217; D.C.B. Lieven, *Russia and the Origins of the First World war*, London-Basingstoke, 1983, p.35.
105 Eugene de Schelking, *Recollections of a Russian Diplomat*, New York, 1918, p.183.
106 Bernadotte E. Schmitt, *The Annexation of Bosnia* Cambridge, 1937, pp.36 and 44; Albertini, *The Origins of the War of 1914*, vol.1, pp.220 and 225.
107 D.W. Sweet, 'The Bosnian Crisis' in F.H. Hinsley (ed.), *British Foreign Policy Under Sir Edward Grey*, Cambridge, 1977, pp.178-179.
108 H.H. Asquith, *The Genesis of the War*, London, 1923, p.40.
109 *GP*, vol.26/1, no.8992, Kaiser's marginalia

on telegram Bülow to Jenisch, 7 October 1908.

110 See, for example, Otto v. Pirch, *Reise in Serbien im Spätherbst 1829*, Berlin, 1830, vol.1, pp.6-7; R.G. Latham, *The Ethnology of Europe*, London, 1852, p.237; Johann Roškiewicz, *Studien über Bosnien und die Herzegovina*, Leipzig-Wien, 1868, p.81.

111 Maximilian Schimek, *Politische Geschichte des Koenigreichs Bosnien und Rama, vom Jahre 857 bis 1741*, Wien, 1787, pp.6 and 10.

112 Pejanović, *Stanovništvo Bosne i Hercegovine*, p.48.

113 Yovan Cvijić, *The Annexation of Bosnia and Herzegovina and the Serb Problem*, London, 1909, p.9.

114 Jovan Milićević, 'Javnost Beograda prema aneksiji Bosne i Hercegovine' in Čubrilović (ed.), *Jugoslovenski narodi pred Prvi Svetski Rat*, pp.553-557.

115 Jovanović, *Moji savremenici*, p.255.

116 *DSPKS*, vol.3/3, no.31, telegram Popović, 8 October 1908.

117 *DSPKS*, vol.3/2/2, no.586, report Vesnić, 5 October 1908.

118 Đorđević, *Milovan Milovanović*, p.94.

119 *DSPKS*, vol.3/3, no.69, report Grujić, London, 13 October 1908.

120 *DSPKS*, vol.3/3, no.38, report Petković, 9 October 1908.

121 *DSPKS*, vol.3/3, no.238, report Simić, 5 November 1908.

122 Schmitt,*The Annexation of Bosnia*, p.144.

123 *DSPKS*, vol.3/3, no.1. The note was submitted to Austria-Hungary, Germany, France, Great Britain, Russia and Italy.

124 Đorđević, *Milovan Milovanović*, pp.99-100 and 103-104.

125 *BD*, vol.5, no.374, report Whitehead, 13 October 1908.

126 *DSPKS*, vol.3/4, no.32, telegram Milovanović to the Serbian Legation, Paris, 22 January 1909.

127 *BD*, vol.5, no.421, report Nicolson, St Petersburg, to Grey, 31 October 1908; no.413, report Goschen to Grey, 28 October 1908.

128 *DSPKS*, vol.2/3/1, no.180, report Grujić, St Petersburg, 2 March 1907.

129 *DSPKS*, vol.3/3, no.186, telegram Pašić, 30 October 1908.

130 *DSPKS*, vol.3/3, no.244, telegram Pašić, 6 November 1908.

131 *DSPKS*, vol.3/3, no.52, report Simić, 10 October 1908.

132 Đorđević, *Carinski rat*, p.532.

133 *DSPKS*, vol.3/3, no.177, telegram Milovanović, 29 October 1908; *BD*, vol.5, no.416, Grey to Nicolson, 29 October 1908.

134 *DSPKS*, vol.3/3, no.125, telegram Milovanović, 21 October 1908.

135 *DSPKS*, vol.3/3, no.269, telegram Milovanović, 10 November 1908.

136 George Abel Schreiner (ed.), *Entente Diplomacy and the World*, New York-London, 1921, no.257, communication of the French Embassy at St Petersburg to the Imperial Russian Government, 26 February 1909. Herafter this collection of Russian documents is cited as *Siebert* – after B. de Siebert, the former Secretary of the Russian Embassy in London, who had collected the material and who had also spied for Germany.

137 *Siebert*, no.261, Izvolsky to the Russian Minister at Belgrade, 27 February 1909.

138 *DSPKS*, vol.3/4, no.298, telegram Popović, 16 March 1909.

139 *BD*, vol.5, no.623, Grey to Whitehead, 27 February 1909.

140 *BD*, vol.5, no.484, report Cartwright, Vienna, to Grey, 11 December 1908.

141 Schmitt,*The Annexation of Bosnia*, p.171; *Siebert*, no. 273, Izvolsky to the Russian Minister at Belgrade, 7 March 1909.

142 *Siebert*, no.268, the Russian Minister at Belgrade to Izvolsky, 3 March 1909.

143 Schmitt,*The Annexation of Bosnia*, pp.175 and 180; *DSPKS*, vol.3/3, no.278, report Simić, 12 March 1909.

144 *DSPKS*, vol.3/4, no.173, telegram Simić, 21 February 1909.

145 *DSPKS*, vol.3/4, no.292, telegram Popović, 15 March 1909.

146 *DSPKS*, vol.3/4, no.307, Milovanović circular, 17 March 1909.

147 *DSPKS*, vol.3/4, no.263, telegram Popović, 10 March 1909. See also M. Boghitschewitsch, *Die Auswärtige Politik Serbiens*, vol.1, no 65, telegram Košutić, special Serbian delegate at St Petersburg, 10 March 1909.

148 *DSPKS*, vol.3/4, no.239, telegram Popović, 4 March 1909.

149 *ÖUA*, vol.1, no.1185, telegram Berchtold, 11 March 1909.

150 Prince von Bülow, Memoirs 1903-1909, London-New York, 1931, p.388.

151 *GP*, vol.26/2, no.9441, Pourtalès, St Petersburg, to Bülow, 16 March 1909.

152 Schmitt,*The Annexation of Bosnia*, pp.191-192.

153 *Ibid.*, p.187; Ernst Jäckh, *Kiderlen-Wächter der Staatsmann und Mensch*, Berlin-Leipzig, 1924, vol.2, p.25.

154 Ralf Forsbach, *Alfred von Kiderlen-Wächter 1852-1912*, Göttingen, 1997, vol.1, pp.298-299.

155 Schmitt, *The Annexation of Bosnia*, p.194.
156 *Ibid.*, p.199.
157 *DSPKS*, vol.3/4, no.374, telegram Popović, 24 March 1909.
158 Text in both Serbian and French in *DSPKS*, vol.3/4, no.436.
159 *BD*, vol.5, no.807, n.1, private letter Sir Charles Hardinge to Sir A. Nicolson, 30 March 1909.
160 *DSPKS*, vol.3/4, no.417, telegram Popović, 27 March 1909.
161 *GP*, vol.26/2, no.9478, telegram Tschirschky, 26 March 1909.
162 Redlich, *Schicksalsjahre*, vol.1, entry for 26 March 1909, p.225.
163 For this episode see [Joseph] Baernreither, 'Aehrenthal und Milovanovich. Ein Tagebuchblatt', *Deutsche Revue*, Stuttgart-Leipzig, January 1922, pp.84-89, in particular pp.87-88.
164 Broucek, *Zeynek*, p.136.
165 *Ibid.*, p.137
166 *ÖUA*, vol.1, no.67, record of a meeting with the Italian Foreign Minister in Salzburg, 5 September 1908.
167 *ÖUA*, vol.3, no.2683, telegram Aehrenthal to Ambrózy, Rome, 1 October 1911.
168 *DSPKS*, vol.4/4/1, no.407, report Milojević, Sofia, 30 September 1911.
169 *DSPKS*, vol.4/4/1, no.128, report Spalajković, 27 July 1911.
170 *DSPKS*, vol.4/4/1, no.418, record of conversations with Hartwig held on 28, 29 and 30 Septemebr 1911, 1 October 1911.
171 *DSPKS*, vol.4/4/1, no.405, report Milojević, 30 September 1911.
172 *DSPKS*, vol.4/4/1, no.434, report Milojević, 4 October 1911.
173 *DSPKS*, vol.4/4/1, no.439, record of a meeting with Rizov, held on 3-4 October 1911, 4 October 1911.
174 *DSPKS*, vol.4/4/1, no.449, report Ristić, Bucharest, 6 October 1911.
175 *DSPKS*, vol.4/4/2, no.796, History of Negotiations for the Conclusion of Serbo-Bulgarian Agreement. This lengthy document, dated 13 April 1911 (31 March, old style) was written by Milovanović. The relevant citations here are on pages 1494 and 1508.
176 *DSPKS*, vol.5/1, no.134, report Popović, 1 March 1912.
177 *DSPKS*, vol.5/1, nos.168 and 328.
178 See, for a brief discussion of this issue, Helmreich, *The Diplomacy of the Balkan Wars*, pp.58-59.
179 *Siebert*, no.367, the Russian Chargé d'Affaires at Sofia to Sazonov, 8 April 1911.

180 *DSPKS*, vol.5/3, no.171, telegram Popović, 12 November 1912.
181 Helmreich, *The Diplomacy of the Balkan Wars*, pp.69-89.
182 *Siebert*, no.396, Sazonov to the Russsian Ambassador at London, 30 March 1912.
183 *DSPKS*, vol.5/2, no.277, report Spalajković, 1 September 1912.
184 Clark, *The Sleepwalkers*, p.260.
185 Edward, C. Thaden, *Russia and the Balkan Alliance of 1912*, Philadelphia, 1965, pp.131-133.
186 Đorđević, *Milovan Milovanović*, p.139.
187 *Ibid.*, pp.168-169.
188 Richard C. Hall, *The Balkan Wars 1912-1913: Prelude to the First World War*, London, 2000, p.12.
189 Clark, *The Sleepwalkers*, p.256.
190 *DSPKS*, vol.5/2, no.286, record of a conversation with the Bulgarian Minister A. Tošev 3 September 1912.
191 *DSPKS*, vol.5/2, no.375, Pašić to Vesnić, 17 September 1912.
192 See, for example, Clark, *The Sleepwalkers*, p.283.
193 *DSPKS*, vol.5/2, no.505, report Grujić, 30 September 1912.
194 Vansittart minute, 22 September 1912, cited in R.J. Crampton, *The Hollow Detente: Anglo-German Relations in the Balkans 1911-1914*, London, 1979, p.171.
195 *DSPKS*, vol.5/2, no.528, report Spalajković, 2 October 1912.
196 *DSPKS*, vol.5/3, no.9, telegram Popović, 19 October 1912.
197 *DSPKS*, vol.5/3, no.50, report Vesnić, 30 October 1912.
198 Steed, *Through Thirty Years*, vol.1, p.361.
199 Friedjung, *Geschichte in Gesprächen*, vol.2, p.380.
200 Kršnjavi, *Zapisci*, vol.2, p.682.
201 Steed, *Through Thirty Years*, vol.1, p.362.
202 Winston Churchill, *The World Crisis: The Eastern Front*, London, 1931, p.55.
203 *DSPKS*, vol.5/2, no.631, telegram Popović, 11 October 1912.
204 Halpern, *The Mediterranean Naval Situation 1908-1914*, pp.295-313.
205 Friedjung, *Geschichte in Gesprächen*, vol.2, p.381.
206 Redlich, *Schicksalsjahre*, vol.1, diary entries for 2, 4, 5 and 6 November 1912, pp.492-505. Pašić's account of his meeting with Redlich is in *DSPKS*, vol.5/3, no.120.
207 Redlich, *Schicksalsjahre*, vol.1, diary entry for 6 November 1912, p.507.
208 *GP*, vol.33, no.12393, report Kageneck, 18 November 1912; no.12402, report Tschirschky, 18 November 1912.

209 Kronenbitter, *'Krieg im Frieden'*, p.385.

210 *DSPKS*, vol.5/3, no.137, report Popović, 9 November 1912; no.158, report Popović, 11 November 1912.

211 Kokovtsov, *Out of My Past*, pp.344-347.

212 Clark, *The Sleepwalkers*, p.268.

213 *DSPKS*, vol.5/3, no.530, telegram Popović, 30 December 1912.

214 *DSPKS*, vol.5/3, no.558, telegram Popović, 2 January 1913.

215 Kronenbitter, *'Krieg im Frieden'*, p.388.

216 *Ibid.*, pp.396-397; Forsbach, *Alfred von Kiderlen-Wächter*, vol.2, pp.728-730; Fritz Fischer, *War of Illusions: German Policies from 1911 to 1914*, London, 1975, p.158.

217 Dimitrije Đorđević, *Izlazak Srbije na jadransko more i konferencija ambasadora u Londonu 1912*, Beograd, 1956, p.89.

218 *BD*, vol.9/2, no.328, Grey to Bertie, Paris, 4 December 1912.

219 Đorđević, *Izlazak Srbije na jadransko more*, p.122.

220 *BD*, vol.9/2, no.404, Grey to Paget, Belgrade, 20 December 1912, enclosure 1.

221 *DSPKS*, vol.6/1, telegram Popović, 9 February 1913.

222 Bardolff, *Soldat im alten Österreich*, pp.173-175.

223 *ÖUA*, vol.4, no.4559, telegram Szögyény, 22 November 1912; no.4571, telegram Franz Ferdinand, 22 November 1912.

224 Lammasch and Sperl, *Lammasch*, pp.92-94.

225 As related by Colonel Bardolff to Conrad. See Conrad, *Aus meiner Dienstzeit*, vol.3, p.127.

226 *Ibid.*, p.156.

227 Lawrence Sondhaus, *Franz Conrad von Hötzendorf: Architect of the Apocalypse*, Boston-Leiden-Cologne, p.106-107.

228 Hugo Hantsch, *Leopold Graf Berchtold. Grandseigneur und Staatsmann*, Graz-Wien-Köln, 1963, vol.1, pp.360-364.

229 Andrija P. Jovićević, *Dnevnik iz balkanskih ratova*, Beograd, 1996, pp.71-94.

230 *DSPKS*, vol.6/1, no.442, telegram Gavrilović, 5 April 1913; *ibid.*, no.457, telegram Popović, 6 April 1913.

231 *DSPKS*, vol.6/1, no.500, Pašić to Gavrilović, 10 April 1913.

232 Mihailo Vojvodić, *Skadarska kriza 1913. godine*, Beograd, 1970, p.139, n.16.

233 Friedjung, *Geschichte in Gesprächen*, vol.2, p.381.

234 *Ibid.*, p.275.

235 Wladimir Aichelburg, *Erzherzog Franz Ferdinand von Österreich-Este 1863-1914. Notizen zu einem ungewöhnlichen Tagebuch eines aussergewönlichen Lebens*, Wien, 2014, vol.2, p.1023.

236 *ÖUA*, vol.6, no.6870, record of the meeting held in Vienna on 2 May 1913.

237 Conrad, *Aus meiner Dienstzeit*, vol.3, p.272.

238 Robert Kann, *Kaiser Franz Joseph und der Ausbruch des Weltkrieges*, Wien, 1971, p.13.

239 Conrad, *Aus meiner Dienstzeit*, vol.3, p.160.

240 Baernreither, *Fragments of a Political Diary*, pp.146-147; Hantsch, *Leopold Graf Berchtold*, vol.1, p.370; Kanner, *Kaiserliche Katastrophen-Politik*, pp.110-113.

241 Thomas Garrigue Masaryk, *The Making of a State: Memories and Observations 1914-1918*, London, 1927, p.24.

242 Baernreither, *Fragments of a Political Diary*, pp.147-148.

243 Biliński, *Wspomnienia*, vol.1, pp.257-258.

244 Hantsch, *Leopold Graf Berchtold*, vol.1, p.371.

245 *GP*, vol.33, no.12487, report Tschirschky, 6 December 1912.

246 *DSPKS*, vol.5/3, no.110, telegram Crown Prince Alexander to Pašić, 6 November 1912 and Pašić's instruction below.

247 *ÖUA*, vol.4, no.4316, telegram Berchtold to Ugron, 8 November 1912.

248 Lončarević, *Jugoslaviens Entstegung*, p.460.

249 *DSPKS*, vol.5/3, no.255, report of the 3rd Army Commander, Prizren, 20 November 1912; no.351, report Rakić, Skopje, 1 December 1912.

250 *DSPKS*, vol.5/3, no.464, report Janković, 19 December 1912.

251 *ÖUA*, vol.4, no.4664, telegram von Heimroth, Skopje, 27 November 1912, containing Prochaska's report.

252 *DSPKS*, vol.5/3, no.351, report Rakić, Skopje, 1 December 1912.

253 Ćorović, *Odnosi između Srbije i Austro-Ugarske*, p.434.

254 'Wie lange noch ...', *Reichspost*, Wien, 19 November 1912 (Morgenblatt), pp.1-2.

255 *ÖUA*, vol.4, no.4625, telegram von Heimroth, 25 November 1912.

256 Robert A. Kann, *Die Prochaska-Affäre vom Herbst 1912*, Wien, 1977, pp.6 and 8-9. The full text of the Press Bureau's *communiqué* is in Sosnosky, *Die Balkanpolitik Österreich-Ungarns*, vol.2, pp.295-296.

257 *GP*, vol.33, no.12487, report Tschirschky, 6 December 1912; no.12494, report Tschirschky, 13 December 1912; no.12498, Kiderlen to Prince zu Stolberg, Vienna, 22 December 1912.

258 Kann, *Die Prochaska-Affäre*, p.14.

259 Baron J. von Szilassy, *Der Untergang der Donau-Monarchie. Diplomatische Erinnerungen*, Berlin, 1921, p.230.

260 See Tschirschky's comments on Baron Leo Chlumecky, the unofficial spokes-

man for Franz Ferdinand's circle: *GP*, vol.33, no.12494, report Tschirschky, 13 December 1912.

261 Hantsch, *Leopold Graf Berchtold*,vol.1, pp.368-369.

262 Baernreither, pp.154 and 196.

263 Clark, *The Sleepwalkers*, p.283.

264 See *ÖUA*, vol.4, no.4647, telegram von Heimroth, 26 November 1912 and no.4664, telegram von Heimroth, 26 November 1912, containing Prochaska´s report from Skopje.

265 Ratko Parežanin, *Mlada Bosna i Prvi svetski rat*, München, 1974, p.208. This Viennese detail from the Prochaska affair was related to Parežanin by Leopold Mandl, a well known publicist who was otherwise in close contact with the Ballhausplatz and authored several anti-Serbian pamphlets.

8   Quo vadis Austria?

1 Redlich, *Schicksalsjahre*, vol.1, diary entry for 20 October 1912, p.487.

2 Chlumecky, *Erzherzog Franz Ferdinands Wirken und Wollen*, letter Brosch to Chlumecky, New Year's Eve, 1912, p.160.

3 Kraler, 'Schlitter', diary entries for 3 and 5 January, and 9 February 1913, pp.123 and 128.

4 Conrad, *Aus meiner Dienstzeit*, vol,2, p.380, memorandum dated 14 December 1912.

5 Friedjung, *Geschichte in Gesprächen*, vol.2, p.375.

6 *Ibid.*, p.385.

7 Redlich, *Schicksalsjahre*, vol.1, diary entries for 31 January 1913 and 31 March/ 1 April 1913, pp.526 and 535.

8 *Ibid.*, diary entry for 26 November 1912, p.514.

9 Szilassy, *Der Untergang*, p.223.

10 *Ibid.*, p.265.

11 *ÖUA*, vol.7, no.8157, memorandum Berchtold, 1 August 1913.

12 Friedjung, *Geschichte in Gesprächen*, vol.2, p.385.

13 Franz Weinwurm, 'FZM Oskar Potiorek. Leben und Wirken als Chef der Regierung für Bosnien und der Herzegowina in Sarajevo – 1911-1914', Dissertation, Universität Wien, 1964´, p.366.

14 Redlich, *Schicksalsjahre*, vol.1, diary entry for 19 November 1912 p.512.

15 Conrad, *Aus meiner Dienstzeit*, vol.3, pp.443-444.

16 *ÖUA*, vol.7, no.8779, minutes of a meeting held in Vienna on 3 October 1913.

17 *ÖUA*, vol.7, no.9243, report Gellinek, 26 January 1914.

18 Ernest U. Cormons [Emanuel Urbas], *Schicksale und Schatten. Eine österreichische Autobiographie*, Salzburg, 1951, p.153.

19 Redlich, *Schicksalsjahre*, vol.1, diary entry for 22 July 1913, p.552.

20 *ÖUA*, vol.7, no.9463, report Czernin, 11 March 1914.

21 Conrad, *Aus meiner Dienstzeit*, vol.3, p.465.

22 Alexander Graf Hoyos, 'Zusammenhänge' in Eduard Ritter von Steinitz (ed.), *Rings um Sasonow*, Berlin, 1928, p.69.

23 Friedjung, *Geschichte in Gesprächen*, vol.2, p.449.

24 Czernin, *Im Weltkriege*, p.11.

25 Christopher Birdwood Thomson, *Old Europe's Suicide*, New York, 1922, p.78.

26 Conrad, *Aus meiner Dienstzeit*, vol.3, p.453.

27 *ÖUA*, vol.7, no.8708, record of a meeting with von Jagow in Berlin on 25 September 1913; Cinrad, *Aus meiner Dienstzeit*, vol.3, p.462.

28 Redlich, *Schicksalsjahre*, vol.1, diary entry for 15 October 1913, p.562.

29 *Ibid.*, diary entry for 2 November 1912, p.495.

30 *ÖUA*, vol.7, no.8157, memorandum Berchtold, 1 August 1913.

31 *ÖUA*, vol.7, no.9032, Berchtold to Czernin, 26 November 1913.

32 Alma Hannig, 'Austro-Hungarian foreign policy and the Balkan Wars' in Dominik Geppert, William Mulligan and Andreas Rose (eds.), *The Wars before the Great War: Conflict and International Politics before the Outbreak of the First World War*, Cambridge, 2015, p.246.

33 Fritz Fellner, 'Austria-Hungary' in Keith Wilson (ed.), *Decisions for War, 1914*, New York, 1995, p.13.

34 Jürgen Angelow, *Kalkül und Prestige. Der Zweibund am Vorabend des Ersten Weltkrieges*, Köln-Weimar-Wien, 2000, p.67.

35 Cited in Hantsch, *Leipold Graf Berchtold*, vol.1, p.291.

36 Keith Hitchins, *Rumania 1866-1947*, Oxford, 1994, p.144.

37 *Ibid.*, p.148.

38 *DSPKS*, vol.6/3, no.271, report Jovanović, 27 August 1913.

39 *DSPKS*, vol.6/3, no.296, report Ristić, 13 September 1913.

40 Baernreither, *Fragments of a Political Diary*, p.289.

41 *ÖUA*, vol.7, no.9463, report Czernin to Berchtold, 11 March 1914.

42 *ÖUA*, vol.7, no.9521, Berchtold to Czernin, 26 March 1914.

43 *DSPKS*, vol.6/3, no.472, report Bošković, 11 November 1913.
44 *GP*, vol.39, no.15811, report Waldthausen to Bethmann Hollweg, 1 January 1914.
45 *ÖUA*, vol.7, no.9600, report Czernin, 23 April 1914.
46 Conrad, *Aus meiner Dienstzeit*, vol.3, p.467.
47 Clark, *The Sleepwalkers*, p.279.
48 Samuel R. Williamson, Jr, *Austria-Hungary and the Origins of the First World War*, New York, 1991, p.171.
49 Otto Hoetzsch (ed.), *Die Internationale Beziehungen im Zeitalter des Imperialismu. Dokumente aus den Archiven der Zarischen und der Provisorischen Regierung*, Berlin, 1931-1934, vol.1/3, no.339, report Sazonov, 24 June 1914. Hereafter cited as *IBZI*.
50 *ÖUA*, vol.7, no.9544, report Czernin, 2 April 1914.
51 Paul Schroeder, 'Romania and the Great Powers before 1914', *Revue Roumaine d'Histoire*, Bucureşti, 1975 (1), p.47
52 Cited in Kann, 'Archduke Franz Ferdinand and Count Berchtold', p.143.
53 Jonescu, *Some Personal Impressions*, pp.86-87.
54 Vermes, *István Tisza*, pp.208-209.
55 Schroeder, 'Romania and the Great Powers before 1914', pp.46-47.
56 *ÖUA*, vol.5, no.6126, private letter Berchtold to von Jagow, 13 March, 1913.
57 *ÖUA*, vol.7, no.8157, instructions Berchtold to the Berlin Embassy, 1 August 1913.
58 *ÖUA*, vol.7, no. 8969, record of a meeting held on 6 November with King Ferdinand of Bulgaria, 8 November 1913. See also *GP*, vol.39, no.15799, report Tschirschky to Bethmann Hollweg, 6 November 1913.
59 *ÖUA*, vol.7, no. 8969.
60 *ÖUA*, vol.7, no.8946, telegram Szögyény, 2 November 1913.
61 *ÖUA*, vol.7, no.8948, telegram Berchtold, 3 November 1913.
62 *ÖUA*, vol.7, no.8951, private letter Szögyény to Berchtold, 4 November 1913.
63 *ÖUA*, vol.7, no.8960, telegram Szögyény, 6 November 1913.
64 *ÖUA*, vol.7 no.9032, Berchtold to Czernin, 26 November 1913.
65 Hantsch, *Leopold Graf Berchtold*, vol.2, pp.509-510.
66 *ÖUA*, vol.7, no.9009, private letter Szögyény to Berchtold, 19 November 1913.
67 *ÖUA*, vol.7, no.8934, Berchtold's account, dated 28 October 1913, of a conversation with Wilhelm II on 26 October 1913.
68 *BD*, vol.10/1, no.59, private letter Nicolson to Hardinge, 29 October 1913.

69 Herbert Adams Gibbons, *The New Map of Europe 1911-1914*, New York, 1915, pp.364-365.
70 *A Handbook of Serbia, Montenegro, Albania and Adjacent Parts of Greece*, Admiralty War Staff Intelligence Division, No. I.D. 1096, [London], 1916, pp.52-53.
71 Lützow, *Im diplomatischen Dienst*, pp.207 and 211.
72 Theodor Wolff, *The Eve of 1914*, New York, 1936, p.386.
73 Bogumil Hrabak, *Arbanaške studije*, Beograd, 2007, vol.5, p.185.
74 Sreten Draškić, *Evropa i albansko pitanje*, Beograd, 2000, p.227.
75 N. Petsalis-Diomidis, *Greece at the Paris Peace Conference 1919*, Thessaloniki, 1978, pp.22-23.
76 Edward Capps, *Greece, Albania and Northern Epirus*, Chicago, 1963, p.13.
77 See, in particular, Nicola Guy, *The Birth of Albania: Ethnic Nationalism, the Great Powers of World War I and the Emergence of Albanian Independence*, London, 2012, pp.55-61.
78 Hanns Christian Löhr, *Die Gründung Albaniens. Wilhelm zu Wied und die Balkan-Diplomatie der Grossmächte 1912-1914*, Frankfurt am Main, 2010, pp.154-155.
79 Draškić, *Evropa i albansko pitanje*, pp.232-234.
80 *GP*, vol.36/2, no.14452, telegram Flotow, Rome, 25 May 1914, Kaiser's marginal remarks.
81 Marie, Queen of Roumania, *The Story of my Life*, London, 1934, vol.2, p.295.
82 Jovanović, *Dnevnik*, entry for 25 July 1917, p.314.
83 Marie, *The Story of my Life*, vol.2, p.295.
84 Friedrich Wallisch, *Der Adler des Skanderbeg. Albanische Briefe aus dem Früjahr 1914*, Leipzig, 1914, p.57; Guy, *The Birth of Albania*, p.72.
85 *DSKPS*, vol.7/1, no.483, circular, 6 April 1914.
86 *ÖUA*, vol.7., no.9513, report Löwenthal, 25 March 1914.
87 *GP*, vol.36/2, no.14438, Nadolny to Bethmann Hollweg, 21 April 1914.
88 Draškić, *Evropa i albansko pitanje*, p.239.
88 Cited in Baernreither, *Fragments of a Political Diary*, p.278.
90 Draškić, *Evropa i albansko pitanje*, p.247.
91 Löhr, *Die Gründung Albaniens*, pp.210-211. Draškić casts doubts on Essad's alleged involvement with the rebels on the grounds that those same rebels later opposed him: *Evropa i albansko pitanje*, pp.247-248.

92 *DSKPS*, vol.7/2, no.30, telegram Balugdžić, Athens, 18 May 1914.

93 *DSKPS*, vol.7/2,no.50, report Gavrilović, 20 May 1914; no.59, report Gavrilović, 21 May 1914.

94 *GP*, vol.36/2, no.14482, report Nadolny to Bethmann Hollweg, 31 May 1914.

95 Guy, *The Birth of Albania*, p.79.

96 Conrad, *Aus meiner Dienstzeit*, vol.3, p.474.

97 *DSKPS*, vol.7/2, no.100, minute Pašić, 23 May 1914.

98 See *DSKPS*, vol.7/1, no.566, report Gavrilović, 27 April 1914, and Pašić's minute at the bottom of the report.

99 H. Charles Woods, *The Cradle of the War: The Near East and Pan-Germanism*, London, 1918, p.169.

100 *GP*, vol.36/2, no.14452, telegram Flotow, 25 May 1914.

101 Conrad, *Aus meiner Dienstzeit*, vol.3, pp.586-589.

102 Löhr, *Die Gründung Albaniens*, p.242.

103 The title of a memoir by Duncan Heaton-Armstrong, Wied's Irish private secretary, London, 2005.

104 *Austrian Red Book*: *Official Files pertaining to Pre-War History*, part 2, London, n.d., p.51.

105 *DSPKS*, vol.6/3, no.322, Serbian Foreign Ministry circular, 25 September 1913.

106 Draškić, *Evropa i albansko pitanje*, pp.217-219; Savo Skoko and Petar Opačić, *Vojvoda Stepa Stepanović u ratovima Srbije 1876-1918*, Beograd, 1979, p.310. For the Albanian incursion, see also Mirko Gutić, 'Oružani sukobi na srpsko-albanskoj granici u jesen 1913. godine', *Vojnoistorijski glasnik*, Beograd, vol.36, no.1, January-April 1985, pp.225-372, and Bogumil Hrabak, *Arbanaški upadi i pobune na Kosovu i u Makedoniji od kraja 1912. do kraja 1915. godine*, Vranje, 1988.

107 *ÖUA*, vol.7, no.8694, report Gellinek, 24 September 1913.

108 Dragoslav Janković, 'Stavovi sila Trojnog sporazuma prema nacionalnom pitanju Srbije i jugoslovenskih naroda uoči Prvog svetskog rata' in Vasa Čubrilović (ed.), *Velike sile i Srbija pred Prvi svetski rat*, Beograd, 1976, p.308.

109 *DSPKS*, vol.6/3, no.379, telegram Balugdžić, Corfu, 17 October 1913 and undated Pašić minute; no.310, circular Spalajković, 22 September 1913; no.318, report Jovanović, 23 September 1913.

110 *DSPKS*, vol.6/3, no.337, Serbian Foreign Ministry circular, 28 September 1913.

111 *DSPKS*, vol.6/3, no.406, report Vesnić, Paris, 20 October 1913; no.320, telegram Ristić, Athens, 24 September 1913; no.537, telegram Ristić, Bucharest, 9 December 1913.

112 *BD*, vol.10/1, no.20, Crackanthorpe to Grey, 25 September 1913.

113 *DSPKS*, vol.6/2, no.23, report Jovanović, 16 April 1913.

114 Conrad, *Aus meiner Dienstzeit*, vol.3, p.456.

115 Kronenbitter, 'Krieg im Frieden', p.408.

116 *GP*, vol.34/1, no.12709, report Kageneck, 17 January 1913.

117 Conrad, *Aus meiner Dienstzeit*, vol.3, pp.443-445.

117 *ÖUA*, vol.7, no.8779.

118 Conrad, *Aus meiner Dienstzeit*, vol.3, p.465.

120 Galántai, *Die Österreichisch-Ungarische Monarchie und der Weltkrieg*, pp.176-178.

121 *ÖUA*, vol.7, nos.8850 and 8859.

122 *ÖUA*, vol.7, no.8882, report Storck, 20 October 1913.

123 J. Galántai, 'Austria-Hungary and the War: The October 1913 Crisis – Prelude to July 1914' in *Etudes historiques hongroises 1980*, vol.2, Budapest, 1980, p.84; Conrad, *Aus meiner Dienstzeit*, vol.3, p.474.

124 *GP*, vol.36/1, no.14160, telegram Stolberg, 15 October 1913.

125 Conrad, *Aus meiner Dienstzeit*, vol.3, p.466.

126 Williamson, *Austria-Hungary and the Origins of the First World War*, p.155.

127 *GP*, vol.36/1, no.14160, telegram Stolberg, 15 October 1913.

128 Bridge, *From Sadowa to Sarajevo*, p.359.

129 Williamson, *Austria-Hungary and the Origins of the First World War*, p.151.

130 Clark, *The Sleepwalkers*, p.286.

131 *GP*, vol.36/1, no.14160, telegram Stolberg, 15 October 1913; no.14163, telegram Zimmermann, 16 October 1913.

132 *GP*, vol.36/1, no.14176, telegram Stolberg, 18 October 1913; Conrad, *Aus meiner Dienstzeit*, vol.3, p.470.

133 Fischer, *War of Illusions*, p.220.

134 R.J.B. Bosworth, *Italy, the Least of the Great Powers:Italian foreign policy before the First World War*, Cambridge, 1979, p.234.

135 Redlich, *Schicksalsjahre*, vol.1, diary entry for 16 October 1913, p.563.

136 *BD*, vol.10/1, no.38, minute Crowe, 16 October 1913; no.45, telegram Grey to Goschen, 18 October 1913; no.48, Grey to Goschen, 20 October 1915.

137 *DSKPS*, vol.6/3, no.432, report Popović to Pašić, 28 October 1913.

138 Conrad, *Aus meiner Dienstzeit*, vol.3, p.477.

139 Cited in Kann, 'Archduke Franz Ferdinand and Count Berchtold', pp.137-138. The emphasis is in the original. For the

German text see Kann, *Erzherzog Franz Ferdinand Studien*, pp.231-232.

140 Cited in Kann, 'Archduke Franz Ferdinand and Count Berchtold', p.132. Emphasis in the original.

141 *Ibid.*, p.138.

142 *Ibid.*, p.131. Emphases in the original.

143 *Ibid.*, p.129.

144 *Ibid.*, p.122.

145 *ÖUA*, vol.7, no.8813, record by Berchtold (undated) on the conversation with Pašić, held on 3 October 1913.

146 *ÖUA*, vol.7, no.8779.

147 *BD*, vol.10/1, no.8, Crackanthorpe to Grey, 7 September 1913.

148 As related by King Carol to Ristić, the Serbian Minister at Bucharest: *DSKPS*, vol.6/3, no.296, report Ristić, 13 September 1913.

149 *DSPKS*, vol.6/3, no.21, Pašić circular telegram, 17 July 1913.

150 *DSPKS*, vol.6/3, no.355, minute Pašić, undated, on or after 14 October 1913.

151 *DSPKS*, vol.6/3, no.414, telegram Ristić, 21 October 1913; draft reply by Pašić (undated).

152 *ÖUA*, vol.7, no.8201, telegram Fürstenberg, 3 August 1913.

153 *ÖUA*, vol.7, no.8240, telegram Berchtold, 6 August 1913.

154 Biliński, *Wspomnienia*, vol.1, pp.260 and 258.

155 Baernreither, *Fragments of a Political Diary*, p.95.

156 *DSPKS*, vol.6/1, no.500, telegram Pašić, 10 April 1913.

157 Carlo Sforza, *Makers of Modern Europe*, London, 1930, p.139.

158 *DSKPS*, vol.7/2, no.100, report Ristić, 26 May 1914, and Pašić minute, dated 23 May 1914 (old calendar).

159 *DSKPS*, vol.7/2, Pašić minute.

160 *ÖUA*, vol.7, no.8797, telegram Storck, 7 October 1913; no.9110, report Gellinek, 20 December 1913.

161 *ÖUA*, vol.7, no.9337, telegram Czernin, 11 February 1914.

162 *ÖUA*, vol.7, no.9418, report Giesl, 24 February 1914.

163 Giesl, *Zwei Jahrzehnte*, p.254.

164 *Ibid.*

165 Herbert Feis, *Europe the World's Banker 1870-1914*, New Haven, 1930, pp.296-311.

166 *DSPKS*, vol.7/2, no.1, Serbian Ministry for Foreign Affairs to Jovanović, 14 May 1914, and minute by Pašić (undated).

167 Dumba, *Dreibund*, p.159.

168 *GP*, vol.39, no.15716, telegram Treutler, 24 March 1914.

169 *ÖUA*, vol.7, no.8976, 10 November 1913.

170 B. von Siebert (ed.), *Graf Benckendorffs Diplomatischer Schriftwechsel*, Berlin-Leipzig, 1928, vol.3, no.1041, private letter Sazonov to Hartwig, Belgrade, 5 March 1914.

171 *GP*, vol.38, no.15539, Griesinger, Belgrade to Bethmann Hollweg, 11 March 1914, Kaiser's marginal remarks.

172 *DSPKS*, vol.6/3, report Mihailović, Rome, 6 November 1913.

173 Novica Rakočević, *Politički odnosi Crne Gore i Srbije 1903-1918*, Cetinje, 1981, pp.197-198.

174 *GP*, vol.38, no.15539, Griesinger, Belgrade to Bethmann Hollweg, 11 March 1914.

175 Novica Rakočević, 'Odnosi Crne Gore i Srbije 1903-1918' in *Crna Gora u međunarodnim odnosima*, Titograd, 1984, p.98.

176 Dimitrije-Dimo Vujović, *Ujedinjenje Crne Gore i Srbije*, Titograd, 1962, p.67.

177 Rakočević, *Politički odnosi Crne Gore i Srbije*, p.200.

178 *ÖUA*, vol.7, no.9486, report Otto, 18 March 1914, and editorial annotation under 'd'; Hans Heilbronner, 'The Merger Attempts of Serbia and Montenegro, 1913-1914', *Journal of Central European Affairs*, 18, October 1958, p.286.

179 Rakočević, *Politički odnosi Crne Gore i Srbije*, p.215.

180 Heilbronner, 'The Merger Attempts of Serbia and Montenegro', p.284.

181 Vujović, *Ujedinjenje Crne Gore i Srbije*, pp.68-69.

182 *Deutschland schuldig? Deutches Weissbuch über die Verantwortlichkeit der Urheber des Krieges*, Berlin, 1919, annex 26, pp.133-134.

183 The letter is reproduced in Rakočević, *Politički odnosi Crne Gore i Srbije*, pp.293-294.

184 *IBZI*, vol.1/2, no.169, Hartwig to Sazonov, 7 April 1914.

185 *GP*, vol.38, no.15537, Eckardt to Bethmann Hollweg, 25 February 1914.

186 The letter is reproduced in Rakočević, *Politički odnosi Crne Gore i Srbije*, p.295.

187 *IBZI*, vol.1/2, no.119, Hartwig to Sazonov, 30 March 1914. See also *IBZI*, vol.1/2, no.170, Hartwig to Sazonov, 7 April 1914.

188 *IBZI*, vol.1/2, no.412, Giers to Sazonov, 12 May 1914.

189 *ÖUA*, vol.8, no.9851, report Giesl, 13 June 1914.

190 *ÖUA*, vol.8, no.9564, report Giesl, 10 April 1914.

191 *ÖUA*, vol.8, no.9674, Berchtold to Szögyény, 16 May 1914, and enclosure containing Gellinek's report of 20 April 1914.

192 *ÖUA*, vol.7, no. 9532, 30 March 1914; no. 9543, 2 April 1914.
193 Vladan Georgevitch, *Quo vadis Austria?*, Leipzig, 1913, p.32. The translation is from the Serbian edition of this pamphlet: Vladan Djordjević, *Kuda si se uputila Austrijo?*, Beograd, 1913, pp.36-37.
194 As told by German Foreign Minister Jagow to Ludwig von Flotow, a counsellor at the Austro-Hungarian Embassy in Berlin: *ÖUA*, vol.7, no.8682, private letter Flotow, 23 September 1913.

9 General Oskar Potiorek

1 Broucek, *Zeynek*, p.143.
2 Redlich, *Schicksalsjahre*, vol.1, diary entry for 15 July 1914, p.614.
3 Sondhaus, *Franz Conrad von Hötzendorf*, p.79.
4 Broucek, *Zeynek*, p.122; Broucek, *Ein General im Zwielicht*, vol.1, p.211, n.238.
5 Glaise-Horstenau, *Franz Josephs Weggefährte*, p.438; Broucek, *Zeynek*, p.122; Conrad, *Aus meiner Dienstzeit*, vol.1, p.33.
6 Rudolf Jeřábek, *Potiorek: General im Schatten von Sarajevo*, Graz-Wien-Köln, 1991, p.27.
7 Edmund von Glaise-Horstenau, 'Feldzeugmeister Potiorek', *Berliner Monatshefte*, February 1934, p.144.
8 Auffenberg-Komarów, *Aus Österreichs Höhe und Niedergang*, p.145.
9 Jeřábek, *Potiorek*, pp.9 and 20; Vladimir Ćorović, *Istorija Srba*, Beograd, 1989, vol.3, p.217; Peter Broucek (ed.), *Ein österreichischer General gegen Hitler: Feldmarschalleutnant Alfred Jansa. Erinnerungen*, Wien-Köln-Weimar, 2011, p.198.
10 Jov. M. Jovanović, 'Odgovornost za svetski rat', *Srpski književni glasnik*, Beograd, August 1925, p.599.
11 Friedjung, *Geschichte in Gesprächen*, vol.1, pp.189-190.
12 Jeřábek, *Potiorek*, p.19.
13 Theodor von Lerch, 'Beck und Potiorek', *Österreichische Wehrzeitung*, Wien, 6 April 1934, p.3; Broucek, *Ein General*, p.268.
14 Cited in Kronenbitter, *'Krieg im Frieden'*, p.107.
15 Margutti, *Kaiser Franz Joseph*, p.438
16 Jeřábek, *Potiorek*, p.30.
17 Broucek, *Zeynek*, p.119; Jeřábek, *Potiorek*, p.20.
18 Kronenbitter, *'Krieg im Frieden'*, p.58; Peball and Rothenberg, 'Der Fall 'U': Die geplante Besetzung Ungarns durch die k. u. k. Armee im Herbst 1905', p.101.
19 Broucek, *Zeynek*, p.144.
20 *Ibid.*, p.124.
21 Rudolf Kiszling, 'Feldmarschall Franz Conrad von Hötzendorf (1852-1925)' in Hugo Hantsch (ed.), *Gestalter der Geschicke Österreichs*, Innsbruck-Wien-München, 1962, p.555; Jeřábek, *Potiorek*, p.32.
22 Conrad, *Aus meiner Dienstzeit*, vol. 1, p.38; Sondhaus, *Franz Conrad von Hötzendorf*, p.78.
23 Margutti, *Kaiser Franz Joseph*, p.270.
24 Wolfram Dornik, *Des Kaisers Falke. Wirken und Nach-Wirken von Franz Conrad von Hötzendorf*, Insbruck-Wien-Bozen, 2013, p.61.
25 'Thronfolger Erzherzog Franz Ferdinand', *Danzer's Armee-Zeitung*, Wien, 2 July 1914, p.3.
26 Margutti, *Kaiser Franz Joseph*, pp.271-276; Rothenberg, *The Army of Francis Joseph*, p.170.
27 Georg Markus, *Der Fall Redl*, Wien – München, 1984, p.258.
28 Weinwurm, 'FZM Oskar Potiorek', p.46.
29 Funder, *Vom Gestern ins Heute*, p.344.
30 Jeřábek, *Potiorek*, p.42.
31 *Ibid.*
32 Broucek, *Ritter von Zeynek*, p.127.
33 Jeřábek, *Potiorek*, p.42.
34 Karl Friedrich Nowak, *Der Weg zur Katastrophe*, Berlin, 1926, p.101.
35 Juzbašić, *Politika i privreda u Bosni i Hercegovini*, p.301.
36 Glaise-Horstenau, 'Feldzeugmeister Potiorek', p.144; Weinwurm, 'FZM Oskar Potiorek', pp.51-52.
37 Jeřábek, *Potiorek*, p.43.
38 *Ibid.*, pp.52-55; Auffenberg-Komarów, *Aus Österreichs Höhe und Niedergang*, p.144.
39 Conrad, *Aus meiner Dienstzeit*, vol.2, pp.42-43.
40 Jeřábek, *Potiorek*, p.42; Kronenbitter, *'Krieg im Frieden'*, p.59.
41 Jeřábek, *Potiorek*, p.77.
42 Weinwurm, 'FZM Oskar Potiorek', pp.59-60.
43 Kielmansegg, *Kaiserhaus*, p.90.
44 *Ibid.*, p.50.
45 Juzbašić, *Politika i privreda u Bosni i Hercegovini*, pp.301-303.
46 Hantsch, *Leopold Graf Berchtold*, vol.1, p.248; Galántai, *Die Österreichisch-Ungarische Monarchie und der Weltkrieg*, p.155.
47 Biliński, *Wspomnienia*, vol.1, p.240.
48 Chlumecky, *Erzherzogs Franz Ferdinands Wirken und Wollen*, p.98.
49 Weinwurm, 'FZM Oskar Potiorek', p.95.
50 Cited in *ibid.*, p.97, n.2.
51 *Ibid.*, p.84.

52 Juzbašić, *Politika i privreda u Bosni i Hercegovini*, pp.307-308.
53 *Ibid*, p.311.
54 Cited in Hamdija Kapidžić, 'Previranja u austro-ugarskoj politici u Bosni i Hercegovini 1912. godine', *Glasnik arhiva i društva arhivista Bosne i Hercegovine*, Sarajevo, 1961, Godina I. – Knjiga I, p.230.
55 Nowak, *Der Weg zur Katastrophe*, p.101.
56 Jeřábek, *Potiorek*, pp.46-47.
57 Weinwurm, 'FZM Oskar Potiorek', p.80; Jeřábek, *Potiorek*, p.49.
58 Juzbašić, *Politika i privreda u Bosni i Hercegovini*, p.309.
59 Cited in Kapidžić, 'Previranja', p.229, n.18a.
60 Kruševac, *Sarajevo pod austro-ugarskom upravom*, p.370; Imamović, *Pravni položaj*, p.253.
61 *Ibid.*, p. 19; *Slovenec*, Ljubljana, 7 July 1914, p.4.
62 Broucek, *Zeynek*, p.104, n.69 and p.119.
63 Broucek, *Jansa*, p.194.
64 *Ibid.*, p.225.
65 *Ibid.*, p.194 and pp.226, 205, 207 and 218; Jeřábek, *Potiorek*, pp.29-30.
66 Broucek, *Jansa*, p.194; *Alt-Neustadt*, Mitteilungsblatt 5, Wien, July 1964, p.5; Auffenberg-Komarów, *Aus Österreichs Höhe und Niedergang*, p.145; Fabius [Leopold Kann], *Mit Blitzlicht durch Kriegserotik, Generalstab u.a.*, Leipzig-Wien, n.d., p.73.
67 Broucek, *Jansa*, p.205; Jeřábek, *Potiorek*, pp.68, 70-71.
68 Jeřábek, *Potiorek* p.69.
69 Theodor von Lerch, 'Beck und Potiorek', *Österreichische Wehrzeitung*, Wien, 6 April 1934, p.3; 'Die letzten Monate im Armeeinspektorat Sarajevo', *Alt-Neustadt*, p.5.
70 Norman Stone, *World War One: A Short History*, London, 2007, p.43; Lerch, 'Beck und Potiorek', p.3.
71 Lützow, *Im diplomatischen Dienst*, p.237.
72 Jeřábek, *Potiorek*, pp.218-219.
73 Williamson, 'Influence, Power and the Policy Process: The Case of Franz Ferdinand', p.423.
74 Broucek, *Jansa*, p.201.
75 *Ibid.*, pp.201-202.
76 *Ibid.*, p.196.
77 Kielmansegg, *Kaiserhaus*, p.298.
78 Broucek, *Zeynek*, p.104; Peter Broucek, 'Merizzi', *Österreichisches Biographisches Lexikon 1815-1950*, Wien, 1975, vol.6, p.230.
79 Broucek, *Jansa*, p. 208.
80 Jeřábek, *Potiorek*, p.69.
81 'Die Manöver in Bosnien', *Bosnische Post*, Sarajevo, 19 May 1914, pp.5-6.

82 Gross, 'Hrvatska politika u Bosni i Hercegovini', p.37.
83 *Ibid.*, p.50.
84 Grijak, *Politička djelatnost Josipa Stadlera*, p.459.
85 *Ibid.*, p.460.
86 Grijak, *Politička djelatnost Josipa Stadlera*, p.462.
87 Imamović, *Pravni položaj*, p.230.
88 *Ibid.*, p.234.
89 Kruševac, *Sarajevo pod austro-ugarskom upravom*, p.359.
90 Imamović, *Pravni položaj*, p.244.
91 *Ibid.*, pp.242-243.
92 Kruševac, *Sarajevo pod austro-ugarskom upravom*, p.364.
93 Imamović, *Pravni položaj*, p.245, n.48.
94 *Ibid.*, p.245.
95 Gross, 'Hrvatska politika u Bosni i Hercegovini', p.45.
96 *Ibid.*, pp.50-51.
97 Cited in Imamović, *Pravni položaj*, p.246.
98 Gross, 'Hrvatska politika u Bosni i Hercegovini', p.49.
99 Weinwurm, 'FZM Oskar Potiorek', p.112.
100 Cited in Kruševac, *Sarajevo pod austro-ugarskom upravom*, p.367.
101 Broucek, *Jansa*, p.198.
102 Weinwurm, 'FZM Oskar Potiorek', pp.64-73.
103 Okey, *Taming Balkan Nationalism*, p.191.
104 Annika Mombauer (ed.), *The origins of the First World War: Diplomatic and military documents*, Manchester-New York, 2013, no.113, p.177.
105 Josef Brauner, 'Bosnien und Herzegowina. Politik, Verwaltung und leitende Personen vor Kriegsausbruch', *Berliner Monatshefte*, April 1929, pp.320 and 339; Weinwurm, 'FZM Oskar Potiorek', p.91, n.1.
106 Sieghart, *Die letzten Jahrzente einer Grossmacht*, p.29.
107 Jovanović, 'Odgovornost za svetski rat', p.602. Jovanović later repeated these points, almost word for word, in his *Stvaranje zajedničke države Srba, Hrvata i Slovenaca*, Beograd, 1928, vol.1, pp.52-53.
108 Brauner, 'Bosnien und Herzegowina', p.326.
109 Kapidžić, 'Previranja', p.224, n.1a.
110 Biliński, *Wspomnienia*, vol.1, pp.264 and 279.
111 Dedijer, *The Road to Sarajevo*, p.206.
112 Karl Kaser, 'Die serbischen politischen Gruppen, Organisationen und Parteien und ihre Programme in Bosnien und der Hercegovina 1903-1914', Dissertation, Karl-Franzens-Universität Graz, 1980, p.143.

113 Kruševac, *Sarajevo pod austro-ugarskom upravom*, pp.370-371; Kapidžić, 'Previranja', p.234; Ekmečić, 'Nacionalni pokret u Bosni i Hercegovini', p.641.

114 Kruševac, *Sarajevo pod austro-ugarskom upravom*, p.371.

115 Imamović, *Pravni položaj*, p.254.

116 Weinwurm, 'FZM Oskar Potiorek', p.173.

117 Biliński, *Wspomnienia*, vol.1, pp.248 and 268.

118 Weinwurm, 'FZM Oskar Potiorek', p.143.

119 Kapidžić, 'Previranja', p.237.

120 Weinwurm, 'FZM Oskar Potiorek', p.145.

121 Kapidžić, 'Previranja', pp.236-237.

122 Milan Gulić, 'Odjek balkanskih ratova u Dalmaciji' in Srđan Rudić and Miljan Milkić (eds.), *Balkanski ratovi 1912/1913: Nova viđenja i tumačenja*, Beograd, 2013, pp.362-363.

123 Cited in Richard Georg Plaschka, 'Serbien und die Balkankriege als Motivationselemente in der österreichisch-ungarischen Armee' in Čubrilović (ed.), *Velike sile i Srbija pred Prvi svetski rat*, p.83.

124 Igor Despot, *Balkanski ratovi 1912.-1913. i njihov odjek u Hrvatskoj*, Zagreb, 2013, p.207.

125 Kapidžić, 'Previranja', p.238; Kruševac, *Sarajevo pod austro-ugarskom upravom*, p.373.

126 Cited in Imamović, *Pravni položaj*, p.255.

127 Weinwurm, 'FZM Oskar Potiorek', pp.159 and 162.

128 Kapidžić, 'Previranja', pp.238-239.

129 Kaser, 'Die serbischen politischen Gruppen, Organisationen und Parteien', p.149.

130 Kapidžić, 'Previranja', pp.239-240.

131 Cited in Milorad Ekmečić, 'Impact of the Balkan Wars on Society in Bosnia and Herzegovina' in Béla K. Király and Dimitrije Djordjevic (eds.), *East Central European Society and the Balkan Wars*, Boulder, 1987, p.264.

132 Jeřábek, *Potiorek*, p.51.

133 Weinwurm, 'FZM Oskar Potiorek', p.176.

134 *Ibid.*, p.144-146; Redlich, *Shicksalsjahre*, vol.1., diary entry for 19 October 1912, p.487.

135 Weinwurm, 'FZM Oskar Potiorek', p.149.

136 *Ibid.*, pp.175 and 177.

137 Conrad, *Aus meiner Dienstzeit*, vol.2, pp.397-398.

138 Cited in Gina Gräfin Conrad von Hötzendorf, *Mein Leben mit Conrad von Hötzendorf*, Leipzig, 1935, p.66.

139 Hantsch, *Leopold Graf Berchtold*, vol.1, p.373; Kronenbitter, '*Krieg im Frieden*', p.403.

140 Rothenberg, *The Army of Francis Joseph*, p.168.

141 Bridge, *From Sadowa to Sarajevo*, p.350.

142 Kapidžić, *Bosna i Hercegovina pod austro-ugarskom upravom*, p.163.

143 *ÖUA*, vol.6, no.6870, pp.330-331 and 334.

144 Ekmečić, 'Impact of the Balkan Wars on Society in Bosnia and Herzegovina', p.271.

145 Weinwurm, 'FZM Oskar Potiorek', p.227.

146 Baernreither, *Fragments of a Political Diary*, p.244.

147 Đorđe Mikić, 'Balkanska kriza 1912-1913. godine i Bosanska Krajina' in Milorad Ekmečić (ed.), *Zbornik za istoriju Bosne i Hercegovine*, Beograd, 2008, vol.5, p.217.

148 Kapidžić, *Bosna i Hercegovina pod austro-ugarskom upravom*, p.182.

149 Weinwurm, 'FZM Oskar Potiorek', pp.229-232.

150 Cited in *ibid.*, p.233.

151 See Potiorek's report to Biliński, dated 4 June 1913, in Conrad, *Aus meiner Dienstzeit*, vol.3, pp.370-371.

152 Kaser, 'Die serbischen politischen Gruppen, Organisationen und Parteien', pp.171-172; Kruševac, *Sarajevo pod austro-ugarskom upravom*, pp.374-375; Imamović, *Pravni položaj*, p.256.

153 Okey, *Taming Balkan Nationalism*, p.228.

154 Redlich, *Schicksalsjahre*, vol.2, diary entry for 4 March 1915, p.24.

155 *Ibid.*, p.176.

156 Kaser, 'Die serbischen politischen Gruppen, Organisationen und Parteien', pp.167-168.

157 *Ibid.*, p.185.

158 Danilo Dimović, 'Iz mojih uspomena', *Preporod*, Beograd, 8 September, 1922, p.7.

159 Kaser, 'Die serbischen politischen Gruppen, Organisationen und Parteien', p.180.

160 Conrad, *Aus meiner Dienstzeit*, vol.3, pp.372 and 374.

161 Juzbašić, *Politika i privreda u Bosni i Hercegovini*, p.315.

162 Kruševac, *Sarajevo pod austro-ugarskom upravom*, p.376.

163 Juzbašić, *Nacionalno-politički odnosi*, p.188.

164 Kaser, 'Die serbischen politischen Gruppen, Organisationen und Parteien', p.193.

165 Okey, *Taming Balkan Nationalism*, pp.230 and 256.

166 Conrad, *Aus meiner Dienstzeit*, vol.3, p.372.

167 *Ibid.*, p.374; Weinwurm, 'FZM Oskar Potiorek', pp.196-197.

168 Dimović, 'Iz mojih uspomena', *Preporod*, Beograd, 8 September, 1922, p.7.

169 Imamović, *Pravni položaj*, p.257, n.14.

170 Okey, *Taming Balkan Nationalism*, p.228.

10 South Slav Student Nationalism

1 Arthur Polzer-Hoditz, *Kaiser Karl*, Zürich-Leipzig-Wien, 1929, p.220.
2 McMeekin, *July 1914*, p.6.
3 Albertini, *The Origins of the War of 1914*, vol.2, p.42.
4 The 100th anniversary of the Sarajevo assassination and the outbreak of the First World War has generated many popular accounts, but even academic works tend to perpetuate this fallacy. Thus Christopher Clark (*The Sleepwalkers*, p.51) writes: 'For all the assassins, Belgrade was the crucible that radicalized their politics and aligned them with the cause of Serb unification.' The eminent Austrian historian Manfried Rauchensteiner similarly writes that the Sarajevo assassins had been 'shaped and radicalised' by the 'Great Serbian movement' (*durch die großserbische Bewegung ... geprägt und radikalisiert*). See Manfried Rauchensteiner, *Der Erste Weltkrieg und das Ende der Habsburgermonarchie 1914-1918*, Wien-Kölm-Weimar, 2013, p.88. No supporting evidence or argumentation can be found in these interpretations.
5 Šidak *et al.*, *Povijest hrvatskog naroda*, p.152.
6 Horvat, *Politička povijest Hrvatske*, vol.1, p.223.
7 Mirjana Gross, 'Nacionalne ideje studentske omladine u Hrvatskoj uoči I svjetskog rata', *Historijski Zbornik*, Zagreb, vol.21-22, 1968-1969, p.76.
8 Branko Lazarević, 'Predsednik Masarik i jugoslovensko pitanje' in Dragutin Prohaska (ed.), *T.G. Masarik Zbornik*, Beograd-Praha, 1927, pp.9-10.
9 Mirjana Gross, 'Studentski pokret 1875-1914', *Spomenica u povodu proslave 300-godišnjice sveučilišta u Zagrebu*, Zagreb, 1969, p.459.
10 Okey, *Taming Balkan Nationalism*, p.203.
11 See Šidak *et al.*, *Povijest hrvatskog naroda*, pp.153-154.
12 Cited in Damir Agičić, *Hrvatsko-češki odnosi na prijelazu iz XIX. u XX. stoljeće*, Zagreb, 2000, pp.144 and 154.
13 Ivan S. Šajković, 'Nekoliko momenata iz omladinskoga pokreta . (Od 1893-1903 godine)', *Književni Sever*, Subotica, vol.5, July-August-September 1929, p.261.
14 Viktor Novak, 'Masarik i Jugosloveni', *Srpski književni glasnik*, Beograd, vol.29, no.6, 16 March 1930, p.449.
15 Pero Slijepčević, 'G. Masarik i predratna omladina', *Srpski književni glasnik*, Beograd, vol.29, no.6, 16 March 1930, p.467.

16 Srđan Budisavljević, *Stvaranje države Srba, Hrvata i Slovenaca*, Zagreb, 1958, pp.49-51; Dragoslav Janković, *Srbija i jugoslovensko pitanje 1914-1915. godine*, Beograd, 1973, p.36.
17 Gross, 'Nacionalne ideje', pp.80-81.
18 Cited in Bakić, *Ideologije jugoslovenstva*, p.100.
19 *Ibid.*, p.84.
20 Vasilije Krestić, 'Politički, privredni i kulturni život u Hrvatskoj i Slavoniji', *Istorija srpskog naroda*, Beograd, 1983, vol.6/1, p.420.
21 Edmund von Glaise-Horstenau, *Die Katastrophe, Die Zertrümmerung Österreich-Ungarns und das Werden der Nachfolgestaaten*, Zürich-Leipzig-Wien, 1929, p.179.
22 Gross, 'Nacionalne ideje', pp.76-77.
23 Wank, *Nachlass Aehrenthal*, vol.2, no.374, Aehrenthal to Franz Joseph, 25 June, 1907, p.515.
24 Gross, 'Nacionalne ideje', p.88.
25 Redlich, *Schicksalsjahre*, vol.1., diary entry for 11 February 1912, pp.422-423. Tomašić's wife was reputed to have 'the best pair of legs in the lands under St Stephen's crown'. In order to be able to marry her Tomašić converted to the Serbian Orthodox faith. See Horvat, *Pobuna omladine*, p.86.
26 R.W. Seton-Watson, *Absolutism in Croatia*, London, 1912, p.7.
27 Vice Zaninović, 'Mlada Hrvatska uoči I. svjetskog rata', *Historijski zbornik*, Zagreb, vol.11-12, 1958-1959, p.70.
28 Gross, 'Nacionalne ideje', p.91.
29 Horvat, *Pobuna omladine*, pp.132-135.
30 Arpad Lebl (ed.), *Politički lik Vase Stajića. Izabrani politički i ideološki spisi*, Novi Sad, 1963, p.159. The pressure of Croat public opinion did subsequently, however, lead to Jukić's death sentence being commuted to life imprisonment. He became a free man in 1918, after the collapse of the Habsburg Monarchy.
31 Dedijer, *The Road to Sarajevo*, p.272.
32 *Ibid.*, pp.273-274; Horvat, *Pobuna omladine*, p.256.
33 Dedijer, *The Road to Sarajevo*, p.311.
34 Gross, 'Nacionalne ideje', pp.98 and 102; Zaninović, 'Mlada Hrvatska', p.77.
35 Gross, 'Nacionalne ideje', p.97.
36 Okey, *Taming Balkan Nationalism*, p.213.
37 Horvat, *Pobuna omladine*, p.97.
38 Gross, 'Nacionalne ideje', p.111.
39 Zaninović, 'Mlada Hrvatska', pp.75 and 80.
40 Oskar Tartaglia, *Veleizdajnik*, Zagreb-Split, 1928, pp.16-17.
41 Šišić, *Jugoslovenska misao*, p.258.

42 Gross, 'Nacionalne ideje', p.107.

43 *Ibid.*, p.106 and n.43, pp.106-107.

44 *Ibid.*, p.103.

45 Cited in *ibid.*, p.119.

46 Niko Bartulović, 'Glose k Predratnoj Omladini', *Književni Sever*, Subotica, vol.5, July-August-September 1929, p.323.

47 Ivan Mužić, *Hrvatska politika i jugoslavenska ideja*, Split, 1969, pp.60 and 62.

48 Ljubibratić, *Vladimir Gaćinović*, p.82.

49 Gross, 'Nacionalne ideje', p.111.

50 Nationalist Bosnian Croats were completely against the proposals for establishing a university in Sarajevo, believing that there was no need for it when a university already existed in Zagreb, and seeing in the project a devious Hungarian scheme aimed against the Croat cultural and national idea. See Risto Besarović, *Iz kulturne i političke istorije Bosne i Hercegovine*, Sarajevo, 1966, pp.55-56, n.64.

51 Gross, 'Hrvatska politika u Bosni i Hercegovini', p.54, n.200.

52 Dragoslav Ljubibratić, *Mlada Bosna i sarajevski atentat*, Sarajevo, 1964, p.115. On 17 August 1914, during his last pre-trial interrogation, Gavrilo Princip was asked whether he knew anything about 'some 140 students' having been supposedly sent from Serbia to carry out the assassination. He replied that he knew nothing about that, adding that there were 'not even 50 students' from Bosnia and Austria attending high schools in Belgrade. (HHStA, Nachlass Erzherzog Franz Ferdinand, Karton 167, *Prozess in Sarajevo*, p.139.)

53 Slijepčević, 'Mlada Bosna', p.186.

54 Cvetko Popović, 'Prilog istoriji sarajevskog atentata', *Politika*, Beograd, 31 March 1928, p.2. Much later, Popović published a somewhat modified version of this memoir. See Cvetko Đ. Popović, *Sarajevski Vidovdan 1914*, Beograd, 1969. Šukrija Kurtović, a Bosnian Muslim student at Vienna University, had already written at the beginning of 1914 something very similar about the Muslim national-political traffic between the Serbs and Croats in Bosnia-Herzegovina. According to Kurtović, it was 'very often' the case that the Muslims would 'emigrate from the Croats to the Serbs and conversely – as if from one political party to another'. See Šukrija Kurtović, *O nacionalizovanju Muslimana*, Sarajevo, 1914, p.45.

55 Popović, 'Prilog istoriji', p.2.

56 Ante Malbaša, *Bosansko pitanje i Austro-Ugarska*, Sarajevo, 1933, p.57.

57 Ratko Parežanin, *Mlada Bosna i Prvi svetski rat*, München, 1974, p.56.

58 Popović, 'Prilog istoriji', p.2.

59 Redlich, *Schicksalsjahre*, vol.1, diary entry for 11 February 1912, p.422.

60 Horvat, *Pobuna omladine*, p.91.

61 Tadijanović, *Tin Ujević. Sabrana djela*, vol.10, p.14.

62 Zaninović, 'Mlada Hrvatska', p.83; Gross, 'Nacionalne ideje', p.117.

63 Tartaglia, *Veleizdajnik*, pp.19-20.

64 Ivan Kranjčević, *Uspomene jednog učesnika u sarajevskom atentatu*, Sarajevo, 1954, pp.33-34.

65 Ljubibratić, *Vladimir Gaćinović*, p.82.

66 Vojislav Bogićević (ed.), *Sarajevski atentat 28. VI 1914. Pisma i saopštenja*, Sarajevo, 1965, p.58. Hereafter cited as Bogićević, *Pisma i saopštenja*.

67 Vojislav Bogićević, *Sarajevski atentat. Izvorne stenografske bilješke sa glavne rasprave protiv Gavrila Principa i drugova, održane u Sarajevu 1914 g.*, Sarajevo, 1954, p.178. Hereafter cited as Bogićević, *Stenogram*.

68 Cited in Ljubibratić, *Gavrilo Princip*, p.131.

69 Slijepčević, 'Mlada Bosna', p.206.

70 Ljubibratić, *Gavrilo Princip*, p.46.

71 Bogićević, *Pisma i prilozi*, p.124.

72 Kranjčević, *Uspomene*, pp.35-37; Ferdo Behr, 'Oko sarajevskog atentata', *Pregled*, Sarajevo, vol.5, 1 September 1930, p.608.

73 Ljubibratić, *Gavrilo Princip*, p.45.

74 Behr, 'Oko sarajevskog atentata', p.607.

75 As testified by Bogoljub Konstantinović: Bogićević, *Pisma i saopštenja*, p.34.

76 Ljubibratić, *Mlada Bosna*, p.106.

77 Ilija Kecmanović, 'Jedna borbena omladinska generacija', *Pregled*, Sarajevo, March 1958, p.249.

78 Risto Radulović, *Izabrani radovi*, Sarajevo, 1988, p.176. Article in *Narod* is dated 21 February 1912.

79 Behr, 'Oko sarajevskog atentata', p.608; Gross, 'Nacionalne ideje', p.117.

80 Dedijer, *The Road to Sarajevo*, p.265.

81 Ljubibratić, *Gavrilo Princip*, p.45.

82 Bogićević, *Pisma i prilozi*, p.132.

83 *Ibid.*, pp.292-293.

84 Srećko M. Džaja, *Bosnien-Herzegowina in der österreichisch-ungarischen Epoche 1878-1918*, München, 1994, p.234.

85 Predrag Palavestra, *Dogma i utopija Dimitrija Mitrinovića. Počeci srpske književne avangarde*, Beograd, 1977, p.88.

86 Ljubibratić, *Mlada Bosna*, p.85.

87 Tartaglia, *Veleizdajnik*, p.22.

88 Janko Baričević, 'Zagrebački đaci u Srbiji 1912. godine', *Riječ*, Zagreb, 15 February 1930, p.3.

89 *ÖUA*, vol.4, no.3489, pp.136-137, report Ugron, 26 April 1912.

90 Ljubibratić, *Gavrilo Princip*, p.87. In his *Vladimir Gaćinović* (p.87), Ljubibratić repeated this point about the three texts forming the basic programme of the Yugoslav youth. Mirjana Gross ('Nacionalne ideje', p.121) considered only Ujević's and Mitrinović's texts as providing the programmatic framework.

91 Osvetnik, *Smrt jednog heroja*, Beograd, 1912. With minor modifications, *Death of a Hero* was reprinted under the title 'Bogdan Žerajić'in Todor Kruševac (ed.), *Vladimir Gaćinović. Ogledi i pisma*, Sarajevo, 1956, pp.117-132.

92 Popović, *Oko sarajevskog atentata*, p.229.

93 Bogićević, *Stenogram*, pp.55 and 314. According to Drago Ljubibratić, the foreword was written by Špiro Soldo, a Herzegovinian friend of both Žerajić and Gaćinović. See Ljubibratić, *Vladimir Gaćinović*, p.86.

94 Bogićević, *Stenogram*, p.85.

95 *Ibid.*, p.55.

96 Ljubibratić, *Vladimir Gaćinović*, p.64.

97 Popović, *Oko sarajevskog atentata*, pp.228-229.

98 *Smrt jednog heroja*, pp.16, 6, 12 and 14.

99 See the introductory essay on Gaćinović by Todor Vujasinović in Kruševac, *Vladimir Gaćinović*, pp.7-19.

100 *Smrt jednog heroja*, pp.9 and 12-13.

101 Clark, *The Sleepwalkers*, p.42.

102 Vujasinović in Kruševac, *Vladimir Gaćinović*, p.14.

103 See, for example, Wolf Dietrich Behschnitt, *Nationalismus bei Serben und Kroaten*, München, 1980, pp.215 and 306, n.343.

104 The article appeared in 1910 in 'Prosvjeta', Sarajevo, calendar for 1911. It was reprinted in Kruševac, *Vladimir Gaćinović*, pp.70-72. The name 'Young Bosnia', however, was first used by the Bosnian Serb writer and politician Petar Kočić in 1907. See Dedijer, *The Road to Sarajevo*, p.477, n.1. Dedijer suggested (p.178) that Gaćinović modelled the name on Mazzini's 'Giovane Italia'.

105 Radoslav Gaćinović, *Mlada Bosna*, Beograd, 2014, p.230.

106 Drago Ljubibratić, 'Mjesto Mlade Bosne u društveno-političkom razvoju Bosne i Hercegovine', *Pregled*, Sarajevo, February 1953, p.112; Vujasinović in Kruševac, *Vladimir Gaćinović*, p.15.

107 Popović, *Oko sarajevskog atentata*, pp.223 and 232-233. In the West Gaćinović's national position has hitherto been accurately represented in only one account. See Martha M. Čupić-Amrein, *Die Opposition gegen die österreichisch-ungarische Herrschaft in Bosnien-Hercegovina 1878-1814*, Bern-Frankfurt am Main-New York-Paris, 1987, pp.376-378.

108 Ljubibratić, *Vladimir Gaćinović*, p.90.

109 Slijepčević, 'Mlada Bosna (Ideologija)', p.61.

110 *Hrvatska u borbi za slobodu*, Beograd, 1912. The 15-page pamphlet was published anonymously. Mirjana Gross argued that Krešimir Kovačić was Ujević's co-author: Gross, 'Nacionalne ideje', p.121, n.23.

111 Gross, 'Nacionalne ideje', p.121.

112 *Hrvatska u borbi za slobodu*, pp.12-14.

113 *Ibid.*, pp.14-15.

114 Cited in Bakić, *Ideologije jugoslovenstva*, p.131.

115 Jovan Skerlić, 'Ante Starčević', *Srpski književni glasnik*, Beograd, vol.28, 1 February 1912, pp.215-216.

116 Bakić, *Ideologije jugoslovenstva*, pp.158-159.

117 Gross, 'Nacionalne ideje', p.132.

118 Although no one has seriously disputed Mitrinović's authorship of *National Unification*, various historians, including Mirjana Gross, have speculated that other student leaders were possibly involved. Predrag Palavestra, the leading authority on Mitrinović, has established that Mitrinović is the sole author. See Predrag Palavestra (ed.), *Dimitrije Mitrinović. Sabrana djela*, Sarajevo, 1990, vol.2, p.269.

119 Milo Borić, 'Od "napredne" do "nacionalističke" omladine', *Književni Sever*, Subotica, vol.5, July-August-September 1929, p.312.

120 Ljubibratić, *Gavrilo Princip*, p.101.

121 Andrew Rigby, *Initiation and Initiative: An Exploration of the Life and Ideas of Dimitrije Mitrinović*, Boulder, 1984.

122 Palavestra, *Mitrinović. Sabrana djela*, vol.1, p. 161.

123 *Ibid.*, pp.37-38, Foreword by Predrag Palavestra.

124 Rigby, *Initiation and Initiative*, p.9.

125 Palavestra, *Dogma i utopija Dimitrija Mitrinovića*, p.83; Gross, 'Nacionalne ideje', p.90.

126 Palavestra, *Mitrinović. Sabrana djela*, vol.2, pp.182-185. In addition to being printed in Mitrinović's collected works edited by Palavestra, the programme *National Unification* is also reproduced in the following: Tartaglia, *Veleizdajnik*, pp.61-64; Viktor Novak, *Antologija jugoslovenske misli i narodnog jedinstva*, Beograd, 1930, pp.637-640; Bogićević, *Pisma i prilozi*, pp.296-300; and Ljubibratić, *Princip*, pp.102-105.

127 Kecmanović, 'Jedna borbena omladinska generacija', pp.254-255.

128 Ljubibratić, *Mlada Bosna*, p.86.
129 Tartaglia, *Veleizdajnik*, pp.61 and 64.
130 Bogićević, *Pisma i prilozi*, p.133.
131 Cited in Ljubo Jandrić, *Sa Ivom Andrićem*, Beograd, 1977, p.384.
132 Palavestra, *Dogma i utopija Dimitrija Mitrinovića*, p.86.
133 Palavestra, Mitrinović. *Sabrana djela*, vol.2, pp.168-174.

11 Gavrilo Princip and Friends

1 Radovan Jovanović, 'Iz đačkih dana Gavrila Principa', *Književni Sever*, Subotica, 1 February 1928.
2 Dobroslav Jevđević, *Sarajevski atentatori*, Zagreb, 1934, pp.27 and 7.
3 See 'Gavrilo Princip: hero or villain?', *The Guardian*, London, 6 May 2014, for a useful summary of this debate.
4 MacMillan, *The War That Ended Peace*, pp.513-514.
5 Bogićević, *Stenogram*, p.62.
6 HHStA, Nachlass Erzherzog Franz Ferdinand, Karton 167, *Prozess in Sarajevo*, pp.132 and 136. Herafter cited as HHStA, NLEFF/167, *Prozess*. This is a major source for the genesis and the actual execution of the Sarajevo assassination, as related by the captured assassins and their helpers during a series of interrogations in the days and weeks after the assassination. Most of those in Archduke Franz Ferdinand's entourage, riding with him in the motorcade through the streets of Sarajevo on 28 June 1914, also deposited eywitness statements, as did several key witnesses from the public. *Prozess in Sarajevo* is a typewritten document, numbering 503 pages.
7 Bogićević, *Stenogram*, p.297.
8 Clark, *The Sleepwalkers*, p.56.
9 McMeekin, *July 1914*, p.7.
10 [Miloš] Boghitchévitch, *Le Procès de Salonique*, Paris, 1927, p.56.
11 David MacKenzie, *The 'Black Hand' on Trial: Salonika, 1917*, Boulder, 1995, p.46.
12 MacKenzie, *Apis: The Congenial Conspirator*, p.135.
13 Albertini, *The Origins of the War of 1914*, vol.2, p.42. A few pages below in his work (p.55), Albertini then writes as if Princip's membership of the Black Hand was thus a proven fact.
14 Tartaglia, *Veleizdajnik*, pp.35 and 48-49.
15 Albertini, *The Origins of the War of 1914*, vol.2, p.56.
16 Ljubibratić, *Gavrilo Princip*, pp.23-24 and 27; Božidar M. Tomić, 'Poreklo i detinjstvo

Gavrila Principa', *Nova Evropa*, Zagreb, vol.32, no.10, 26 October 1939, pp.328-330; Jevđević, *Sarajevski atentatori*, p.99.
17 Jevđević, *Sarajevski atentatori*, p.31.
18 Ljubibratić, *Gavrilo Princip*, pp.36-38 and 41-42; Jevđević, *Sarajevski atentatori*, p.30.
19 Bogićević, *Pisma i saopštenja*, p.87.
20 *Ibid.*, p.40.
21 *Ibid.*, p.53. As testified by Srećko Džamonja.
22 Bogićević, *Pisma i prilozi*, p.132.
23 Borivoje Jevtić, 'Vladimir Gaćinović u Sarajevu', *Spomenica Vladimira Gaćinovića*, Sarajevo, 1921, p.104.
24 Bogićević, *Pisma i prilozi*, p.134.
25 Jovan Kršić, 'Lektira sarajevskih atentatora', *Pregled*, Sarajevo, 26 June 1927, pp.6-7. An expanded version of this article by Kršić appeared in *Pregled* in the 1935 January-February issue, pp.115-119.
26 *Gavrilo Princips Bekenntnisse*, Wien, 1926, p.8.
27 Jevđević, *Sarajevski atentatori*, pp.18, 34 and 29.
28 HHStA, NLEFF/167, *Prozess*, p.99.
29 Vladimir Dedijer, *Sarajevo 1914*, Beograd, 1978, vol.1, pp.354-355.
30 Related subsequently by Džamonja himself in Bogićević, *Pisma i saopštenja*, pp.96-97.
31 Bogićević, *Pisma i prilozi*, pp.301-302.
32 Popović, *Sarajevski Vidovdan*, p.31.
33 Bora Ćosić, 'Wer schoss in Sarajevo?', *Neue Zürcher Zeitung*, Zürich, 28 June 2014, p.23.
34 Parežanin, *Mlada Bosna*, p.127.
35 Jevđević, *Sarajevski atentatori*, p.40.
36 Jevtić, *Sarajevski atentat*, p.24.
37 Ljubibratić, *Gavrilo Princip*, p.53.
38 HHStA, NLEFF/167, *Prozess*, p.157.
39 Jevđević, *Sarajevski atentatori*, p. 23.
40 *Ibid.* pp.64 and 55; Dedijer, *Sarajevo 1914*, vol.1, p.383.
41 Brook-Shepherd, *Victims at Sarajevo*, p.217.
42 Ljubibratić, *Gavrilo Princip*, p.59.
43 Jevđević, *Sarajevski atentatori*, p.42.
44 HHStA, NLEFF/167, *Prozess*, p.309.
45 Parežanin, *Mlada Bosna*, p.117.
46 *Ibid.*, pp.139-140.
47 HHStA, NLEFF/167, *Prozess*, p.142.
48 Jevtić, *Sarajevski atentat*, p.25.
49 Vojislav Bogićević, 'Poreklo isečka iz novina', *Pregled*, Sarajevo, November-December 1935, pp.626-628.
50 Palavestra, *Književnost Mlade Bosne*, vol.2, p.410.
51 Cited in *ibid.*, vol.1, p.199.
52 *Ibid.*, pp.228-229.
53 Cited in *ibid.*, p.261.

54 Jevtić, in his *Sarajevski atentat* (p.25), maintained that Pušara posted the cutting in Zenica 'the next day', which would have been on 18 March 1914.

55 HHStA, NLEFF/167, *Prozess*, p.104.

56 HHStA, NLEFF/167, *Prozess*, pp.187 and 191.

57 HHStA, NLEFF/167, *Prozess*, p.134.

58 Bogićević, *Stenogram*, pp.34 –35 and 85.

59 HHStA, NLEFF/167, *Prozess*, p.117.

60 Brigitte Hamann (ed.), *Die Habsburger. Ein biographisches Lexicon*, Wien, 1988, p.262.

61 'Fronleichnam', *Bosnische Post*, Sarajevo, 12 June 1914, p.3.

62 Popović, *Sarajevski Vidovdan*, p.32.

63 Nikola Trišić, 'Moje uspomene', *Pregled*, Sarajevo, February 1935, p.97.

64 HHStA, NLEFF/167, *Prozess*, pp.181 and 154.

65 HHStA, NLEFF/167, *Prozess*, p.306.

66 Bogićević, *Stenogram*, p.399.

67 Clark, *The Sleepwalkers*, p.49.

68 Clark uses the transcript of the trial in Albert Mousset, *Un drame historique: l'attentat de Sarajevo*, Paris, 1930, p.131. Compare with Bogićević, *Stenogram*, p.72, and Dolph Owings, Elizabeth Pribic and Nikola Pribic (eds.), *The Sarajevo Trial*, Chapel Hill, 1984, vol.1, p.68.

69 Bogićević, *Stenogram*, p.72.

70 Nikola Stojanović, 'Pogled na Bosansku Politiku od 1903. do 1914'. in Pero Slijepčević (ed.), *Napor Bosne i Hercegovine za oslobođenje i ujedinjenje*, Sarajevo, 1929, p.178.

71 Glaise-Horstenau, *Die Katastrophe*, p.21.

72 Ćorović, *Odnosi između Srbije i Austro-Ugarske*, pp.630-631.

73 *DSPKS*, vol.7/2, no.424, report Jovanović, 14 July 1914.

74 Bogićević, *Stenogram*, p.37.

75 HHStA, NLEFF/167, *Prozess*, p. 306.

76 HHStA, NLEFF/167, *Prozess*, p.186.

77 Bogićević, *Stenogram*, p.72.

78 See, for example, the determined questioning of Čabrinović by Viktor Ivasiuk on 3 July 1914: HHStA, NLEFF/167, *Prozess*, pp.152-153.

79 HHStA, NLEFF/167, *Prozess*, p.103.

80 HHStA, NLEFF/167, *Prozess*, p.152.

81 Bogićević, *Pisma i saopštenja*, pp.92-94.

82 Ljubibratić, *Mlada Bosna*, p.150.

83 HHStA, NLEFF/167, *Prozess*, p.150.

84 HHStA, NLEFF/167, *Prozess*, p.116.

85 Rakočević, *Politički odnosi Crne Gore i Srbije*, p.58.

86 HHStA, NLEFF/167, *Prozess*, p.103.

87 HHStA, NLEFF/167, *Prozess*, p.103.

88 HHStA, NLEFF/167, *Prozess*, p.116.

89 HHStA, NLEFF/167, *Prozess*, p.309.

90 HHStA, NLEFF/167, *Prozess*, pp-146-147.

91 Clark, *The Sleepwalkers*, pp.53-54. On p.54 Clark provides a photo of a person who he thinks is Milan Ciganović (as stated in the caption), but is in fact Đuro Šarac.

92 Milorad Belić, *Komitski vojvoda Vojislav Tankosić*, Valjevo, 2005, pp.70-71.

93 Jevđević, *Sarajevski atentatori*, pp.38-39.

94 M. Đerić, 'Jafetov program', *Razvitak*, Banja Luka, 1 December 1939, p.368-369.

95 Dušan Slavić, 'Djuro Šarac', p.1, MS, Matica Srpska, Novi Sad.

96 *Ibid.*, p.2.

97 Bogićević, *Stenogram*, pp.53-54.

98 HHStA, NLEFF/167, *Prozess*, p.133.

99 HHStA, NLEFF/167, *Prozess*, p.292.

100 HHStA, NLEFF/167, *Prozess*, pp.135, 190 and 314. According to Čabrinović, the only other person, apart from Šarac, to see the three assassins off on 28 May was one Risto Milićević, a lawyer, who had been told at the last moment about the intentions of those departing. This testimony by Čabrinović tallies with the account in the Dušan Slavić MS.

101 *Gavrilo Princips Bekenntnisse*, p.16.

102 Slavić, 'Djuro Šarac', pp.2-3.

103 However, Albertini relates (*The Origins of the War of 1914*, vol.2, p.72, n.2) that some Black Hand members considered Šarac to have been a 'spy' of the Serbian Prime Minister Nikola Pašić.

104 Ljubibratić, *Mlada Bosna*, pp.150-154; Dedijer, *The Road to Sarajevo*, pp.291-294.

105 Milovan Grba, 'Das Attentat gegen Franz Ferdinand und die Sarajevoer Polizei', *Prager Presse*, Prague, 29 July 1924 (Morgen Ausgabe), p.3.

106 *Tajna prevratna organizacija. Izveštaj sa pretresa u vojnom sudu za oficire u Solunu po beleškama vođenim na samom pretresu*, Solun, 1918, p.258.

107 Seton-Watson, *Sarajevo*, p.141.

108 Gradimir Nikolić, *Mirno spavaj Vojvodo*, Beograd, 2012, p.24.

109 Kazimirović, *Crna Ruka*, p.19.

110 Nikolić, *Mirno spavaj Vojvodo*, pp.34-35.

111 *Ibid.*, p.104.

112 *Ibid.*, p.9; Kazimirović, *Crna Ruka*, p.285.

113 Nikolić, *Mirno spavaj Vojvodo*, p.112.

114 Stojan Protić, *Jugoslavija protiv Srbije. Zapisi iz naše političke istorije*, Beograd, 2009, p.142.

115 Velimir Terzić (ed.), *Prvi balkanski rat 1912-1913*, Beograd, 1959, pp.425-426 and 465, n.118.

116 Marco [Božin Simić], 'Pred Kumanovsku Bitku', *Nova Evropa*, Zagreb, vol.15, no.10-11, 26 November 1927, pp.337-338.

117 Nikolić, *Mirno spavaj Vojvodo*, pp.140-141.
118 Bogićević, *Stenogram*, p.36.
119 HHStA, NLEFF/167, *Prozess*, p.309.
120 Bogićević, *Stenogram*, p.37.
121 HHStA, NLEFF/167, *Prozess*, pp.170 and 119.
122 HHStA, NLEFF/167, *Prozess*, p.345.
123 HHStA, NLEFF/167, *Prozess*, pp.112 and 119.
124 HHStA, NLEFF/167, *Prozess*, pp.309-310.
125 Dragoslav Ljubibratić, 'Nepoznati dokumenat o sarajevskom atenatatu', *Borba*, Beograd, 25 May 1960.
126 HHStA, NLEFF/167, *Prozess*, p.117.
127 HHStA, NLEFF/167, *Prozess*, p.112.
128 Slavić MS, p.4.
129 HHStA, NLEFF/167, *Prozess*, p.114.
130 HHStA, NLEFF/167, *Prozess*, p.311.
131 T.G. Otte, in his recent *July Crisis: The World's Descent Into War, Summer 1914*, Cambridge, 2014, appears to believe (p.20) that the assassins travelled from Belgrade to Šabac by train, having received 'free tickets' from Ciganović ('in his official capacity as a railway clerk'). Otte does not have a footnote to back up his story: there was no Belgrade-Šabac railway line in 1914, and one does not exist even to this day.
132 HHStA, NLEFF/167, *Prozess*, pp.315 and 114.
133 HHStA, NLEFF/167, *Prozess*, pp.319 and 346.
134 Fay, *The Origins of the World War*, vol.2, p.120.
135 HHStA, NLEFF/167, *Prozess*, pp.312 and 114-115.
136 Bogićević, *Stenogram*, p.66; Dedijer, *The Road to Sarajevo*, p.298.
137 HHStA, NLEFF/167, *Prozess*, pp.322-323.
138 Albertini, *The Origins of the War of 1914*, vol.2, p.58.
139 Bogićević, *Stenogram*, p.103.
140 Dedijer, *Sarajevo 1914*, vol.1, p.391.
141 Cited in Zdravko Antonić, *Čubrilovići 1914 i kasnije*, Beograd, 1999, p.79. The citation is from a long letter that Vaso Čubrilović, one of the six assassins on 28 June 1914, wrote from prison to his two sisters at the beginning of 1918. Milović himself had related this episode to Čubrilović in prison.
142 Bogićević, *Stenogram*, p.83.
143 HHStA, NLEFF/167, *Prozess*, p.455.
144 Bogićević, *Stenogram*, p.165.
145 HHStA, NLEFF/167, *Prozess*, p.381; Bogićević, *Stenogram*, p.204.
146 Bogićević, *Pisma i saopštenja*, p.126.
147 Borivoje Nešković, *Istina o solunskom procesu*, Beograd, 1953, p.277-278.
148 Bogićević, *Pisma i saopštenja*, p.130.
149 HHStA, NLEFF/167, *Prozess*, p.319.
150 HHStA, NLEFF/167, *Prozess*, pp.166-167.
151 Jevtić, *Sarajevski atentat*, p.25.
152 Clark, *The Sleepwalkers*, p.56.
153 Popović, *Oko sarajevskog atentata*, p.164.
154 *Gavrilo Princips Bekenntnisse*, p.16.
155 Bogićević, *Stenogram*, p.69.
156 Parežanin, *Mlada Bosna*, pp.141 and 146.
157 Trišić, 'Moje uspomene', p.97.
158 Jevtić, *Sarajevski atentat*, p.29.
159 HHStA, NLEFF/167, *Prozess*, pp.425-426.
160 HHStA, NLEFF/167, *Prozess*, p.426.
161 HHStA, NLEFF/167, *Prozess*, pp.416, 418 and 422.
162 HHStA, NLEFF/167, *Prozess*, p. 412.
163 They were: Marko Perin, Branko Zagorac, Ivan Kranjčević, Nikola Forkapić and Dragan Kalember.
164 Popović, *Sarajevski Vidovdan*, p.39
165 HHStA, NLEFF/167, *Prozess*, p.365.
166 Popović, *Sarajevski Vidovdan*, pp.14, 39, 25 and 41.
167 HHStA, NLEFF/167, *Prozess*, p.405.
168 HHStA, NLEFF/167, *Prozess*, pp.402-403.
169 Hajrudin Ćurić, 'Jedan nacionalni revolucionar iz Hercegovine', *Gajret Kalendar za god. 1939*, Sarajevo, 1938, pp.254-255 and 262.
170 HHStA, NLEFF/167, *Prozess*, p.246.
171 Cited in Nešković, *Istina o solunskom procesu*, p.281.
172 Trišić, 'Moje uspomene', p.87.
173 Ćurić, 'Jedan nacionalni revolucionar iz Hercegovine', pp.257-258.
174 *Ibid.*, pp.259-260. This particular episode has been somewhat distorted by Gordon Martel in his recent *The Month That Changed The World: July 1914*, Oxford, 2014. Martel writes (p.61) that not only Mehmedbašić, but also Golubić set off from Toulouse to kill Potiorek, and that Gaćinović had provided them with 'guns' which they then threw away for fear of being discovered by customs officials. Exactly how Martel is able to assert this is not clear as he adds no footnote. Golubić had of course stayed behind in Toulouse.
175 Albertini, *The Origins of the War of 1914*, vol.2, p.54.
176 HHStA, NLEFF/167, *Prozess*, pp.241-260.
177 Albertini, *The Origins of the War of 1914*, vol.2, pp.54-55.
178 *Ibid.*, p.73.
179 Nikola Trišić, 'Oko sarajevskog atentata', *Pregled*, Sarajevo, January-June, 1929, p.22.
180 Trišić, 'Moje uspomene', p.88.
181 HHStA, NLEFF/167, *Prozess*, p.246.

12 Black Hand – Red Herring

1 Dedijer, *The Road to Sarajevo*, pp.377-378.
2 Okey, *Taming Balkan Nationalism*, p.229.
3 N.M Potapov, *Dnevnik*, Podgorica-Moskva, 2003, vol.2, diary entry for 9 (22) December 1914, p.659.
4 Mombauer, *Diplomatic and Military Documents*, no.180, pp.292-293.
5 See Potiorek's telegrams in *ÖUA*, vol.8, no.9991, 2 July 1914, no.9993, 3 July 1914 and no.10023, 3 July 1914.
6 Barbara Jelavich, 'What the Habsburg Government Knew about the Black Hand', *Austrian History Yearbook*, vol.22, 1991, p.140.
7 Herbert Vivian, *Secret Societies: Old and New*, London, 1927, p.19.
8 Kazimirović, *Crna ruka*, pp.343 and 346.
9 Mićić, 'Srpski oficiri', p.43; Čed. A. Popović, 'Organizacija *Ujedinjenje ili smrt* ('Crna ruka')', *Nova Evropa*, Zagreb, vol.15, no.12, 11 June 1927, pp.403-404.
10 L.T. [Leon Trotsky], *Sarajevski atentat*, Wien, 1922, pp.8-9.
11 Kazimirović, *Crna ruka*, p.351. For the links between Freemasons and the Black Hand see Zoran D. Nenezić, *Masoni u Jugoslaviji 1764-1980*, Beograd, 1984, pp.300-327. Nenezić lists (p.313) the names of thirteen Black Hand members who were also, verifiably, Freemasons. These, with the exception of Jovanović-Čupa (and Milan Gr. Milovanović, one of the ten founding members) are not particularly prominent names. But Nenezić leaves open the possibility that Dragutin Dimitrijević Apis, Voja Tankosić and Milan Ciganović were likewise Freemasons (p.325).
12 Stephen Graham, *St. Vitus Day*, London, 1930, p.135.
13 Article 3 of the Rules of Procedure. The full texts of the statute and the rules of procedure can be found in Milan Ž. Živanović, *Pukovnik Apis. Solunski proces hiljadu devetsto sedamnaeste*, Beograd, 1955, pp.669-674.
14 Vivian, *Secret Societies*, p.110.
15 Borivoje Nešković, *Istina o solunskom procesu*, Beograd, 1953, p.18.
16 Vojislav J. Vučković, 'Unutrašnje krize Srbije i Prvi svetski rat', *Istorijski časopis*, vol.14-15, 1963-1965, p.180.
17 *DSPKS*, vol.5/1, no.28, report Đorđrvić, 29 January 1912.
18 Ćorović, *Odnosi između Srbije i Austro-Ugarske*, p.599; Vladimir Dedijer and Branko Pavićević, 'Dokazi za jednu tezu', *Nova misao*, Beograd, August 1953, p.229.

19 Kazimirović, *Crna ruka*, p.419.
20 *Ibid.*, pp.373, 401 and 389.
21 *ÖUA*, vol.3, no.2911, report Ugron, 12 November 1911; *ÖUA*, vol.4, no.3517, report Ugron, 11 May 1912.
22 Drašković, *Pretorijanske težnje u Srbiji*, p.145.
23 *ÖUA*, vol.4, appendix to no.3673, report Pflügl, Belgrade, 8 August 1912.
24 Jovanović, *Moji savremenici*, p.35.
25 MacKenzie, *Apis*, p.58.
26 Antić, *Beleške*, pp.246-247.
27 Vučković, 'Unutrašnje krize Srbije i Prvi svetski rat', p.181.
28 Branislav Gligorijević, *Kralj Aleksandar Karađorđević*, Beograd, 2010, vol.1, p.47.
29 Ćorović, *Odnosi između Srbije i Austro-Ugarske*, p.600; *Tajna prevratna organizacija*, p.373.
30 Samuel R. Williamson, Jr., 'July 1914 revisited and revised: The erosion of the German paradigm' in Jack S. Levy and John A. Vasquez (eds.), *The Outbreak of the First World War: Structure, Politics and Decision-Making*, Cambridge, 2014, p.40.
31 Kazimirović, *Crna ruka*, p.514.
32 Đorđević, *Milovan Milovanović*, pp.157-158.
33 Kazimirović, *Crna ruka*, p.526.
34 Dedijer, *The Road to Sarajevo*, pp.377-378.
35 Nešković, *Istina o solunskom procesu*, p.170.
36 *Tajna prevratna organizacija*, p.308; Čed. A. Popović, 'Sarajevski atentat i organizacija *Ujedinjenje ili Smrt*', *Nova Evropa*, Zagreb, vol.25, no.8, July 1932, p.400.
37 Kazimirović, *Crna ruka*, pp.543-544.
38 Mićić, 'Srpski oficiri', p.51; Kazimirović, *Crna ruka*, p.566.
39 Mićić, 'Srpski oficiri', p.51.
40 *BD*, vol.10/1, no.326, report Crackanthorpe to Grey, 17 January 1914.
41 Živojinović, *Kralj Petar*, vol.2, pp.515-516; *ÖUA*, vol.7, no.9260, report Hoflehner, Niš, 28 January, 1914; Velimir J. Ivetić, 'Politička uloga ministara vojnih Kraljevine Srbije od 1903. do 1914. godine' (doktorska disertacija, Univerzitet Beograd, 2013), pp.309-310.
42 Drašković, *Pretorijanske težnje u Srbiji*, pp.172-173.
43 Stojanović, *Slom i vaskrs Srbije*, p.121.
44 Mićić, 'Srpski oficiri', pp.51-52; Drašković, *Pretorijanske težnje u Srbiji*, p.174.
45 MacKenzie, *Apis*, p.108; Drašković, *Pretorijanske težnje u Srbiji*, p.176.
46 Kazimirović, *Crna ruka*, pp.574-575.
47 MacKenzie, *Apis*, p.109.
48 Mićić, 'Srpski oficiri', pp.52-53; Kazimirović, *Crna ruka*, p.577.
49 Dedijer, *The Road to Sarajevo*, p.386.

50 Mićić, 'Srpski oficiri', p.53; Kazimirović, *Crna ruka*, p.577.
51 Vučković, 'Unutrašnje krize Srbije i Prvi svetski rat', pp.185-186.
52 'Portret vladinog sluge', *Pijemont*, Beograd, 2 (15) May, 1914.
53 Cited in Albertini, *The Origins of the War of 1914*, vol.2, p.85.
54 Ivetić, 'Politička uloga ministara vojnih Kraljevine Srbije', p.319; Dedijer, *Sarajevo 1914*, vol.2, p.101.
55 Živojinović, *Kralj Petar I Karađorđević*, vol.2, pp.520-523.
56 Gligorijević, *Kralj Aleksandar Karađorđević*, vol.1, pp.61and 63.
57 Cited in Dedijer and Pavićević, 'Dokazi za jednu tezu', p.227. For the attitudes of the Serbian opposition parties towards the Black Hand, see Gjurgjevic, 'The Friedjung and Vasic Trials in the Light of the Austrian Diplomatic Documents', pp.376-378.
58 Janković, *Srbija i jugoslovensko pitanje*, p.87.
59 Vučković, 'Unutrašnje krize Srbije i Prvi svetski rat', p.191, n.53.
60 Žujović, *Dnevnik*, vol.2, diary entry for 14 (27) June, p.58.
61 Vučković, 'Unutrašnje krize Srbije i Prvi svetski rat', p.191.
62 Živojinović, *Kralj Petar*, vol.2, p.523; Jovanović, *Moji savremenici*, p.34.
63 *Tajna prevratna organizacija*, pp.272-273; Živanović, *Pukovnik Apis*, pp.218-219.
64 Jovanović, *Moji savremenici*, p.34.
65 Antić, *Beleške*, p.264. Apis's letter to Colonel Glišić does not seem to have survived.
66 *Tajna prevratna organizacija*, pp.174-175.
67 Drašković, *Pretorijanske težnje u Srbiji*, p.186.
68 Antić, *Beleške*, p.261.
69 Živojinović, *Kralj Petarć*, vol.2, p.530.
70 *Ibid*. pp.526-527.
71 Kazimirović, *Crna ruka*, p.565.
72 MacKenzie, *The 'Black Hand' on Trial*, p.395.
73 Nešković, *Istina o solunskom procesu*, pp.277-278. Also cited in Dedijer, *The Road to Sarajevo*, p.398, but the translation there is at times somewhat free.
74 Nešković, *Istina o solunskom procesu*, pp.280-281.
75 Popović, *Oko sarajevskog atentata*, p.219.
76 See Drašković, *Pretorijanske težnje u Srbiji*, pp.285-286.
77 Popović, 'Sarajevski Atentat i organizacija Ujedinjenje ili Smrt', pp.407-408.
78 *DSPKS*, vol.7/2, no.104, contained in report by Smiljanić (War Ministry, Belgrade) to Pašić, 26 May 1914.
79 Vučković, 'Unutrašnje krize Srbije i Prvi svetski rat', p.195.
80 Antić, *Beleške*, pp.338-339.
81 Bjelajac, *1914-2014. Zašto revizija?*, p.61.
82 Victor A. Artamonov, 'Erinnerungen an meine Militärattachézeit in Belgrad', *Berliner Monatshefte*, July/August 1938, p.594. A great deal of speculation is still being offered up about the role of Russia in the Sarajevo assassination and of Artamonov in particular. Luigi Albertini's seldom questioned but questionable authority is much to blame for this. He interviewed Artamonov after the war and wrote that during this encounter Artamonov did not succeed in giving him 'a convincing explanation of his departure from Belgrade precisely on the eve of the Austrian grand manoeuvres in Bosnia.' Albertini does not take into acccount the fact that the Serbian General Staff were not greatly concerned with the projected Austro-Hungarian manoeuvres and that, logically, Artamonov would likewise have been similarly unperturbed. Besides, as Artamonov explained to Albertini, he had not had any leave in the previous three years. This would indicate that he left when he felt the situation allowed, i.e., when things were quiet – Albertini's opposite contention submits no evidence in its own favour. Certainly, Artamonov denied that he had any foreknowledge of the plot to assassinate Franz Ferdinand. He also stated to Albertini that he and Apis had never discussed the Bosnian manoeuvres. (See Albertini, *The Origins of the War of 1914*, vol.2, pp.84-86.) In 2011 Sean McMeekin revisited the subject. 'There has always been something suspicious', he writes, 'about Russian denials of foreknowledge of the assassination plot.' He goes on to say that Artamonov's absence from Belgrade on 28 June gave him 'a convenient alibi' and that the Russians 'must have known that something was afoot.' Yet McMeekin produces not a shred of evidence to back up his claims. (See McMeekin, *The Russian Origins of the First World War*, p.47 and p.257, n.17.) More recently, Samuel Williamson has brought up the subject again, agreeing with Albertini that Artamonov 'probably knew' about the plot. Again, however, no evidence is submitted. (See Samuel R. Williamson, Jr., 'July 1914 revisited and revised', p.41.) Dealing in probablities is

of course allowed to historians, but they normally hypothesize on the basis of at least some relevant material. Artamonov, in any case, emerges from the memoirs of Vasily Strandtmann, the Russian Chargé d'Affaires in Belgrade, as a highly cautious, level-headed type. Thus on the eve of the First Balkan War he was appalled that Serbia would attack Turkey because of the possible complications for Russia. It is difficult to imagine that he would have been any less concerned in 1914. Strandtmann, from his personal knowledge of the man, makes the point that, had Artamonov been in any way involved in the assassination plot, he would have stayed in Belgrade and not gone on holiday. (See Vasilij Štrandman, *Balkanske uspomene*, Beograd, 2009, pp.181 and 262.) In his private diary, in the entry for 28 June 1914, Artamonov wrote: 'Extremely disturbing day for Serbia and Russia.' (See Ju. A. Pisarev, 'Rossijskaja kontrrazvedka i tajnaja serbskaja organizacija *Chernaja ruka*', VIZh., 1993, no.1, p.29).

83 There exists, in fact, a fourth narrative, albeit a very brief one and only in an indirect form. At the beginning of the war Slobodan Jovanović served together with Apis at the General Staff in Kragujevac. Serbia's great historian talked to him, among other things, about the Sarajevo assassination. Strangely for a historian, however, in an essay on Apis which he later wrote, Jovanović does not quote a single word related to him by Apis on this subject. He merely offers his own interpretation, based on what he had heard from Apis, that the latter did not expect a war to result from the assassination and that, on the contrary, it would prevent war. Apis, according to Jovanović, also feared that the enthusiasm of the 'Serbian revolutionary youth' would 'dwindle through inactivity'. (See Jovanović, *Moji savremenici*, pp.65-66.) If this is indeed what Apis said or implied to Jovanović, it is a further pointer to the conclusion that Apis was lying to everybody who asked him about the assassination. There were certainly less dangerous ways of maintaing the enthusiasm of the revolutionary youth than directing them to murder the Austro-Hungarian Heir to the Throne.

84 Milan M. Stojadinović, *Ni rat ni pakt*, Buenos Aires, 1963, p.65.

85 Apparently the only historian who mentioned, albeit very briefly, Milovan Grba's article in the *Prager Presse* was Hermann Wendel. In June-July 1925 Wendel published a series of articles in *Volksstimme* which were then re-published as a booklet under the title *Das Attentat von Sarajevo. Eine historisch-kritische Untersuchung*, n.p. and n.d., but probably Magdeburg, 1925. Wendel related here (p.12) only that part of Grba's article which pertained to the warning issued by Šarac and Ciganović to Apis, and moreover wrongly gave the date of the article in the *Prager Presse* as 25 July 1924, whereas the correct date is 29 July (morning edition). This may account for the fact that no specialist on Sarajevo 1914 appears ever to have read it.

86 Grba, 'Das Attentat gegen Franz Ferdinand', p.3.

87 *Tajna prevratna organizacija*, p.167.

88 Svetozar Pribićević, *Diktatura Kralja Aleksandra*, Beograd, 1952, p.299.

89 Stevan Zec, *Apisov tamničar*, Zemun, 1987, pp.86-87.

90 Drašković, *Pretorijanske težnje u Srbiji*, pp.146-149; Popović, 'Sarajevski Atentat i organizacija Ujedinjenje ili Smrt', p.400.

91 In 1918 Leopold Mandl, who had been very close to the Ballhausplatz, published a book in which the Black Hand officers are mentioned in the context of the training which some of the Sarajevo assassins ostensibly received with regard to throwing bombs and shooting from Browning pistols. Mandl, however, does not make a big deal out of the Black Hand and lays much more emphasis on alleging the involvement of the *Narodna Odbrana*. See Leopold Mandl, *Die Habsburger und die serbische Frage*, Wien, 1918, pp.146-147.

92 St. Stanojević, *Ubistvo austriskog prestolonaslednika Ferdinanda*, Beograd, 1923, pp.44-46.

93 Ćorović, *Odnosi između Srbije i Austro-Ugarske*, p.637.

94 Seton-Watson, *Sarajevo*, p.129; Schmitt, *The Coming of the War 1914*, vol.1, p.195.

95 Stanoje Stanojević, *Die Ermordung des Erzherzogs Franz Ferdinand*, Frankfurt a. M., 1923.

96 Uebersberger, *Österreich zwischen Russland und Serbien*, p.256.

97 Another Serbian work aimed at discrediting Apis was produced in 1935 by Dragiša Stojadinović who emphasized, *inter alia*, Apis's pro-German orientation and suggested, without any convincing evidence, that the assassination of Archduke Franz Ferdinand had been

coordinated with the Hungarian Prime Minister, Tisza. Stojadinović's rather messy manuscript was never published. See Dragiša M. Stojadinović, 'Srbija i Nemačka u Prvom svetskom ratu. Pokušaji za sklapanje zasebnog mira između Srbije i Nemačke za vreme od 1914 do 1918 god.', Beograd, 1935, deposited in Narodna Biblioteka, Beograd, P736/II/1.

98 Stanojević, *Ubistvo austriskog presto-lonaslednika Ferdinanda*, p.42.

99 Joachim Remak, *Sarajevo: The Story of a Political Murder*, London, 1959, p.50.

100 MacKenzie, *Apis*, pp.133-134. Slobodan G. Markovich, a noted Serbian expert, has also recently dismissed Stanojević's 'dubious pamphlet'. See his 'Anglo-American Views of Gavrilo Princip', *Balcanica*, Belgrade, vol.46, 2015, p.280.

101 Bogićević, *Pisma i saopštenja*, pp.90-91.

102 *Ibid.*, p.87.

103 Ivan Meštrović, *Uspomene na ljude i događaje*, Zagreb, 1993, p.24.

104 Pribićević, *Diktatura kralja Aleksandra*, p.299.

105 HHStA, NLEFF/167, *Prozess*, p.107.

106 See Ljubibratić, *Mlada Bosna*, p.160 and Dedijer, *The Road to Sarajevo*, p.309.

107 Popović, *Oko sarajevskog atentata*, p.209. Colonel Čedomir Popović related this to the Russian researcher Vladimir Lebedev.

108 HHStA, NLEFF/167, *Prozess*, p.249.

109 Bogićević, *Stenogram*, pp.99 and 103.

110 *Ibid.*, p.115.

111 HHStA, NLEFF/167, *Prozess*, p.330.

112 Bogićević, *Stenogram*, p.118.

113 *Ibid.*, p.70.

114 HHStA, NLEFF/167, *Prozess*, p.350.

115 Popović, *Oko sarajevskog atentata*, p.209.

116 Ljubibratić, *Mlada Bosna*, p.161; Bogićević, *Stenogram*, p.284.

117 Bogićević, *Pisma i saopštenja*, pp.126-127.

118 Ljubibratić, *Mlada Bosna*, p.161.

119 Dedijer, *Sarajevo 1914*, vol.2, p.140.

120 A. Ksjunjin (ed.), *Krv Slovenstva. Spomenica desetogodišnjice svetskog rata*, Beograd, 1924.

121 Ljuba Jowanowitsch, 'Nach dem Veitstage des Jahres 1914', *Die Kriegsschuldfrage*, February 1925, pp.68-82.

122 M. Ljuba Jovanović, *The Murder of Sarajevo*, London, 1925.

123 *Ibid.*, p.3.

124 Alfred von Wegerer, 'Die Mitwisserschaft der serbischen Regierung an der Ermordung des Erzherzogs Franz Ferdinand zugegeben', *Die Kriegsschuldfrage*, February 1925, p.68.

125 M. Edith Durham, *The Serajevo Crime*, London, 1925, p.129.

126 Fay, *The Origins of the World War*, vol.2, p.62.

127 Alberini, *The Origins of the War of 1914*, vol.2, p.101.

128 Clark, *The Sleepwalkers*, p.56.

129 Dedijer, *Sarajevo 1914*, vol.2, pp.102-104. The document was hastily published in 1945, in Vienna, as the Third Reich was about to collapse. See Ludwig Bittner, Alois Hajek and Hans Uebersberger (eds.), *Serbiens Aussenpolitik 1908-1918. Diplomatische Akten des serbischen Ministeriums des Äussern in deutscher Übersetzung*, Wien, 1945, 2nd Series, vol.3 (26 May to 6 August 1914). This slim volume contains German translations of Serbian documents taken during the war in Belgrade by the German forces and transported to Vienna. It is the only one that was actually published within the intended project.

130 Dedijer, *Sarajevo 1914*, vol.2, p.105.

131 *Ibid.*, p.106.

132 Ćorović, *Odnosi između Srbije i Austro-Ugarske*, pp.656-657.

133 *Ibid.*, p.651.

134 Hermann Kantorowicz, *Gutachten zur Kriegsschuldfrage 1914*, Frankfurt am Main, 1967, p.367.

135 *DSPKS*, vol.7/2, no.206, report Protić to Pašić, 15 June 1914.

136 *DSPKS*, vol.7/2, no.155, report Tucaković to Protić, 4 June 1914; no.199, telegram Stefanović to the Drina Division Headquarters, Valjevo, 14 June 1914.

137 *DSPKS*, vol.7/2, no.214, report Putnik, 18 June 1914.

138 See report to Protić by Tucaković in *DSPKS*, vol.7/2, no.206, contained in Protić's report to Pašić, 15 June 1914.

139 Dedijer, *Sarajevo 1914*, vol.2, p.112.

140 *DSPKS*, vol.7/2, no.230, report Dimitrijević, 21 June 1914.

141 Dedijer, *Sarajevo 1914*, vol.2, pp.114-115.

142 It is perhaps important to point out, in this connection, a recent attempt by Christopher Clark to represent Pašić before the assassination rather differently – as someone who, if he were sure of Russia, would be prepared to risk war against Austria-Hungary. Clark suggests that Pašić may have hoped for an assassination scenario in which Vienna would appear as an aggressor against innocent Serbia, for in such a scenario Serbia could count on Russian support. He writes: 'Such a scenario would fail, of course if the world were to construe the assassination plot itself as an act of Serbian aggression; but Pašić was certain that the

Austrians would be unable to establish any connection between the assassination (if it were to succeed) and the government of Serbia because, in his own mind, no such linkage existed.' (*The Sleepwalkers*, pp.62-63). Interestingly, Clark's footnote at the end of this sentence refers to the work of the well-known Serbian historian Đorđe Stanković, entitled *Nikola Pašić, saveznici i stvaranje Jugoslavije* (Nikola Pašić, the Allies and the Creation of Yugoslavia). Clark cites the second, popular edition of the book, despite its lack of footnotes, but this is a minor point. What is surprising to anyone familiar with Stanković's work is the implication that he would paint his hero Pašić as scheming to start a war against Austria-Hungary on the basis of some belief that Vienna would be unable to connect an imminent Archducal assassination with his own Serbian Government. Indeed, on reading what Stanković actually wrote, it becomes clear that Clark should never have invoked him in this manner. For Stanković writes as follows (on page 36 of the popular edition consulted and footnoted by Clark): 'Pašić believed, in the first place, that the Austrian authorities could not establish any connection between official Serbia and the event on the bank of the Miljacka.' Stanković's preceding sentence makes it clear that he was discussing Pašić's conduct during and not before the July crisis: 'Such understanding of events connected to the Sarajevo assassination also determined Pašić's entire conduct in the course of the July crisis in 1914.' Of course, his reference to the event on the bank of the Miljacka river (where the assassination of Franz Ferdinand took place) makes it doubly clear that Stanković, unlike Clark, is discussing Pašić's mindset in the aftermath of the murder, that is, he is addressing Pašić's conduct during the post-assassination, July crisis, not his conduct in the previous period. Hence Clark is wrong to footnote Stanković's passage in support of his own pre-assassination thesis, for Stanković's writing offers no such support. Yet Professor Clark continues in a similar vein with his next sentence: 'An attack from Austria-Hungary must therefore surely trigger support from Russia and her allies; Serbia would not stand alone.' (*The Sleepwalkers*, p.63). Once again, Clark has a footnote citing Stanković (taken from page 41 of the popular edition).

But what did Stanković actually write? Once more, the relevant passage in Stanković is about Pašić during the July crisis: '... it was therefore strange that Pašić did not seek protection from the allied Great Powers [i.e., the Entente] in a possible clash with the more powerful neighbouring Monarchy. Was Pašić consciously avoiding such an escape from uncertainty, or was he calculating that Serbia could in fact not remain alone, for its conflict with Austria-Hungary was not a matter of local Balkan test of strength?' This Stanković passage is cited by Clark as if it supports his claim that Pašić was certain that 'Serbia would not stand alone'. Yet, in contrast to Clark, it is for Stanković only a question, not an assertion. Moreover, Stanković's question is again about Pašić's thinking in the post-Sarajevo period – not the period being addressed by Clark. It is exceedingly difficult to see from all this how Clark could justifiably use Stanković's analyses of Pašić, post-Sarajevo, in the pre-Sarajevo context.

143 Jovan Jovanovic, 'Meine Warnung an den Erzherzog Franz Ferdinand', *Neues Wiener Tagblatt*, Wien, 28 June 1924, pp.3-4. In his 1927 article for the journal *Brastvo* Jovanović gave the precise date of the meeting: 23 May, which was the old calendar date, corresponding exactly to 5 June. See Jov. M. Jovanović, 'Sarajevski atentat i Srbija', *Brastvo*, Beograd, vol.21, 1927, p.33.

144 Albertini, *The Origins of the War of 1914*, vol.2, pp.98 and 100.

145 Clark, *The Sleepwalkers*, p.60.

146 'In Oesterreich', *Pester Lloyd*, Budapest, 29 June 1914 (Morgenblatt), p.6.

147 There were comparable reports elsewhere. Dedijer, who seemed unaware of the *Pester Lloyd* piece, cited one from the *New York Times*, dated 29 June, which carried a Vienna dispatch from the London *Daily Mail*: 'Before the Archduke went to Bosnia last Wednesday, the Serbian Minister here expressed doubts as to the wisdom of the journey, saying that the country was in a very turbulent condition and the Serbian part of the population might organize a demonstration against the Archduke.' See Dedijer, *The Road to Sarajevo*, p.506, n.99.

148 Seton-Watson, *Sarajevo*, p.153.

149 *DSPKS*, vol.7/2, no.293, 30 June 1914, p.429.

150 *DSPKS*, vol.7/2, no.331, 4 July 1914, p.468.

151 *DSPKS*, vol.7/2, no.334, 4 July 1914, p.470.
152 Dedijer, *The Road to Sarajevo*, p.507, n.100. Hans Uebersberger, in his utterly tendentious *Österreich zwischen Russland und Serbien*, is anxious to downplay the importance of the Biliński-Jovanović meeting and, taking Jovanović's guarded words to Pašić at face value, argues that Jovanović's reply to the enquiry from Belgrade about reports in newspapers is proof that he had not warned Biliński. Not quite content with this dismissal of the whole episode, Uebersberger also writes that Jovanović had in his postwar writings on 1914 'generated a lot of fantasy' and that he had found it 'interesting' to present himself as the person delivering the warning. See pp.259-261.
153 Williamson, 'July 1914 revisited and revised: the erosion of the German paradigm', p.41.
154 Otte, *July Crisis*, p.37.
155 Clark, *The Sleepwalkers*, p.61.
156 Martel, *The Month that changed the World*, p.67.
157 Paul Flandrak, 'Bilinskis Eingreifen in die auswärtige Politik. Die Warnungen des serbischen Gesandten Jovanovic', *Neues Wiener Journal*, Wien, 26 April 1925, pp.7-8.
158 See Biliński, *Wspomnienia*, vol.1, pp.277-278.
159 Jovanovic, 'Meine Warnung an den Erzherzog Franz Ferdinand'.
160 Biliński, *Wspomnienia*, vol.1, p.240.
161 A relative of Biliński's claimed in 1934 that the Joint Finance Minister had advised against the Archduke's trip but without success. See Ćorović, *Odnosi između Srbije i Austro-Ugarske*, p.653, n.3.
162 Nikola Đ. Trišić, *Sarajevski atentat u svjetlu bibliografskih podataka*, Sarajevo, 1964, p.222.
163 Hellmut Andics, *Der Untergang der Donaumonarchie. Österreich-Ungarn von der Jahrhundertwende bis zum November 1918*, München, 1980, pp.324-325, n.3.
164 Edmund Glaise-Horstenau, 'Der Thronfolgermord im Lichte der heutigen Geschichtskenntnis', *Neues Wiener Tagblatt*, Wien, 28 June 1924, pp.2-3.
165 *ÖUA*, vol.8, no.9952, note a.
166 John C.G. Röhl, 'The Curious Case of the Kaiser's Disappearing War Guilt: Wilhelm II in July 1914' in Holger Afflerbach and David Stevenson (eds.), *An Improbable War? The Outbreak of World War I and European Political Culture Before 1914*, New York-Oxford, 2007, p.79. See also

Röhl's essay 'Germany' in Keith Wilson (ed.), *Decisions for War, 1914*, New York, 1995, p.46, and *Wilhelm II. Der Weg in den Abgrund 1900-1941*, München, 2008, p.1074. In an interview about the responsibility of Kaiser Wilhelm II for the outbreak of the war, Röhl described the episode with Waldersee and the Saxon, Bavarian and Württembergian plenipotentiaries as an indication that 'something highly secret' had been going on – see Stephan Burgdorff and Klaus Wiegrefe (eds.), *Der Erste Weltkrieg. Die Ur-Katastrophe des 20. Jahrhunderts*, München-Hamburg, 2008, p.37.
167 Schmitt, *The Coming of the War 1914*, vol.1, p.244.
168 Fay, *Origins of the World War*, vol.2, p.163.
169 *Ibid.*, pp.163 and 166.
170 Elisabeth Kovács (ed.), *Kaiser und König Karl I. (IV). Politische Dokumente aus Internationalen Archiven*, Wien-Köln-Weimar, 2004, no.52, p.223.
171 *ÖUA*, vol. 3, no.3270, report Ugron, 6 February 1912.
172 Cited in Albertini, *The Origins of the War of 1914*, vol.2, p.106.
173 Gligorijević, *Kralj Aleksandar Karađorđević*, vol.1, p.61.
174 Dušan T. Bataković, 'Storm over Serbia: The Rivalry between Civilian and Military Authorities (1911-1914)', *Balcanica*, Belgrade, vol. 44, 2013, p.341.
175 Kazimirović, *Nikola Pašić*, vol.2, p.279.
176 Kazimirović, *Crna Ruka*, p.528.
177 Dedijer, *Sarajevo 1914*, vol.2, p.137.
178 Jovan M. Jovanović, *Odgovornost Srbije za svetski rat*, Beograd, 1927, pp.24-25.
179 *R. W. Seton-Watson and the Yugoslavs: Correspondence 1906-1941*, London-Zagreb, 1976, vol.2, no.135, letter Jovan M. Jovanović to R.W. Seton-Watson, 12 August 1925, p.139.
180 Jovanović, *Odgovornost Srbije za svetski rat*, p.27.

13 The Secrets of Konopischt

1 Lamasch and Sperl, *Lammasch*, p.81.
2 Hodža, *Federation in Central Europe*, pp.51-52.
3 Redlich, *Schicksalsjahre*, vol.1, diary entry for 6 May 1914, p.599.
4 *Ibid.*, diary entry for 13 May 1914, p.602.
5 Kraler, 'Schlitter', diary entry for 28 May 1914, p.228.
6 SArt, Morsey MS, Personalia MO, pp.53-54.
7 *Ibid.*, pp.55-56. In the 1920s and 1930s Morsey produced several versions of his

memoir, one of which was published in a drastically abridged form: 'Konopischt und Sarajewo. Erinnerungen', *Berliner Monatshefte*, June 1934.

8 Kraler, 'Schlitter', diary entries for 26 March 1914 and 2 April 1914, pp.131 and 145.

9 Christopher H.D. Howard, 'The Vienna Diary of Berta de Bunsen, 28 June-17 August 1914', *Bulletin of the Institute of Historical Research*, London, 51 (1978), p.222.

10 Boyer, *Culture and Political Crisis*, p.597, n.136 and p.365. Boyer criticizes Rudolf Kiszling, one of Franz Ferdinand's biographers, for skirting this issue. Rumours about Franz Ferdinand's health already began to emerge in the first half of 1913. At the beginning of April Count Hardegg told Schlitter, the Director of *Staatsarchiv*, that the Heir of the Throne was ill, but stated the cause of illness as tuberculosis. See Kraler, 'Schlitter', p.145, diary entry for 2 April 1913.

11 Schuster, *Henry Wickham Steed und die Habsburgermonarchie*, p.114. On Steed see also Harry Hanak, *Great Britain and Austria-Hungary During the First World War*, London, 1962.

12 Redlich, *Schicksalsjahre*, vol.2, diary entry for 14 January 1917, p.259.

13 *Ibid.*, vol.1, diary entry for 7 May 1914, p.599.

14 Kurt Sendtner, *Rupprecht von Wittelsbach. Kronprinz von Bayern*, München, 1954, pp.175-176,

15 SArt, Morsey MS, Personalia MO, p.40.

16 Seton-Watson, *Sarajevo*, p.100.

17 Kiszling, *Erzherzog Franz Ferdinand*, p.280.

18 G. von Jagow, *Ursachen und Ausbruch des Weltkrieges*, Berlin, 1919, p.101, n.2.

19 Prince Lichnowsky, *Heading for the Abyss: Reminiscences*, London, 1928, p.71.

20 Richard Bassett, *For God and Kaiser: The Imperial Austrian Army from 1619 to 1916*, New Haven-London, 2015, p.427.

21 Nikitsch-Boulles, *Vor dem Sturm*, p.82.

22 SArt, Morsey MS, Personalia MO, pp.48-49.

23 'Der Tag von Sarajevo. Konopischt', *Die Kriegschuldfrage*, Berlin, no.8, August 1925, p.562. The note by Tirpitz was dated 'mid-June 1914' and was first published in *Darmstädter Tageblatt* on 28 June 1925.

24 Wolff, *The Eve of 1914*, p.391.

25 *GP*, vol.39, no.15736, private letter Treutler to Zimmermann, 15 June 1914.

26 Karl-Heinz Janssen (ed.), *Die graue Exzellenz. Aus den Papieren Karl Georg von Treutlers*, Frankfurt/Main – Berlin, 1971, p.156.

27 See *ÖUA*, vol.8, nos. 9845, 9846, 9847, 9852 and 9863.

28 Redlich, *Schicksalsjahre*, vol.1, diary entry for 28 April 1914, p.597.

29 *Ibid.*, diary entry for 13 June 1914, p.606.

30 *GP*, vol.39, no.15736.

31 *Ibid.*

32 Conrad, *Aus meiner Dienstzeit*, vol.4, p.36.

33 *Ibid.*, pp.38-39.

34 Seton-Watson, *Sarajevo*, p.97, n.1.

35 Kantorowicz, *Gutachten*, p.223.

36 Alfred von Wegerer, *Die Widerlegung der Versailler Kriegsschuldthese*, Berlin, 1928, p.207.

37 *GP*, vol.39, no.15737, letter Tschirschky to Bethmann Hollweg, 17 June 1914.

38 Bardolff, *Soldat im alten Österreich*, p.179.

39 Sosnosky, *Erzherzog Franz Ferdinand*, p.166. Andreas Morsey was evidently also upset by Metzger's revelation and wrote that he then checked with several witnesses who, just like Morsey, were present in the Ilidža hotel on 27 June 1914. Those witnesses reassured him that it was all 'an absolute misunderstanding'. But Morsey does not inform his readers how it had come to such a misunderstanding, nor does he name his witnesses. See Morsey, 'Konopischt und Sarajewo', p.487.

40 Albertini, *The Origins of the War of 1914*, vol.2, pp.17-18.

41 Fay, *The Origins of the World War*, vol.2, n.49, p.41.

42 Schmitt, *The Coming of the War 1914*, vol.1, p.169.

43 H.W. Wilson, *The War Guilt*, London, 1928, p.169.

44 Kantorowicz, *Gutachten*, pp.225-226.

45 *ÖUA*, vol.7, no.8934, report Berchtold, dated 28 October 1913, on a conversation with the German Emperor held in Vienna, on 26 October 1913.

46 Cited in Fischer, *War of Illusions*, p.225. Emphases in the original.

47 *ÖUA*, vol.7, no.9009, private letter Szögyeny to Berchtold, 19 November 1913.

48 *ÖUA*, vol.7, no.9096, private letter Velics to Berchtold, 16 December 1913.

49 *ÖUA*, vol.8, no.9739, telegram Szögyény, 25 May 1914; *GP*, vol.38, no.15541, Bethmann Hollweg to Tschirschky, 6 April 1914.

50 In a recent essay Professor John Röhl argues that in November 1912 Wilhelm II gave Austria-Hungary a 'blank cheque' for a war of aggression against Serbia, and that, ever since, this was 'the settled policy of the entire Berlin leadership'. Röhl does not mention the German Kaiser's efforts in 1913 and 1914 to push

Vienna towards reaching a *rapprochement* with Serbia in order to ease the burden of the anticipated war with Russia. See John C.G. Röhl, '*Jetzt oder nie*. The Resurgence of Serbia and Germany's first 'blank cheque' of November 1912' in Dragoljub R. Živojinović (ed.), *The Serbs and the First World War*, Belgrade, 2015, pp.57-77.

51 *GP*, vol.39, no.15715, Tschirschky to Bethmann Hollweg, 23 March 1914; no, 15716, telegram Treutler, 24 March 1914.

52 Telegram Treutler, 5 April 1914, contained in *GP*, vol.38, no.15541, Bethmann Hollweg to Tschirschky, 6 April 1914.

53 *GP*, vol.39, no.15716, telegram Treutler, 24 March 1914.

54 Cited in Galántai, *Die Österreichisch-Ungarische Monarchie und der Weltkrieg*, p.197.

55 *ÖUA*, vol.7, no.9470, report Szögyény, 12 March 1914.

56 *ÖUA*, vol.7, no.8934, Berchtold's account, dated 28 October 1913, of a conversation with Wilhelm II on 26 October 1913.

57 *ÖUA*, vol.7, no.8708, record of a meeting in Berlin between Jagow and Forgách, 25 September 1913.

58 Kraler, 'Schlitter', diary entry for 17 January 1914, p.194.

59 Szilassy, *Der Untergang*, p.259.

60 Somary, *Erinnerungen*, p.113.

61 Nicolas de Basily, *Diplomat of Imperial Russia 1903-1917: Memoirs*, Stanford, 1973, p.90.

62 Conrad, *Aus meiner Dienstzeit*, vol.3, p.119.

63 Kraler, 'Schlitter', diary entry for 5 August 1914, p. 259.

64 SArt, Morsey MS, Personalia MO, pp.51-52.

65 Williamson, *Austria-Hungary and the Origins of the First World War*, p.164.

66 See, for example, Aleš Skřivan, *Schwierige Partner. Deutschland und Österreich-Ungarn in der europäischen Politik der Jahre 1906-1914*, Hamburg, 1999, pp.377-379. In his recent book on Franz Ferdinand, Jean-Paul Bled also dismisses the Konopischt meeting, arguing that the talks were mainly about Romania and that the subject of Serbia was hardly broached. See Bled, *Franz Ferdinand*, p.274.

67 Greg King and Sue Woolmans, *The Assassination of the Archduke: Sarajevo 1914 and the Murder that Changed the World*, London, 2013, p.151.

68 Hodža, *Federation in Central Europe*, p.58.

69 *Reichspost*, Wien, 28 March 1926, p.1.

70 István Diószegi (ed.), 'Aussenminister Stephan Graf Burián. Biographie und Tagebuchstelle', *Annales Universitatis Scientiarum Budapestinensis de Rolando Eötvös nominatae*, Sectio historica, vol.8, Budapest, 1966, diary entry for 17 June 1914, p.203.

71 Fischer, *War of Illusions*, p.419.

72 Graydon A. Tunstall, Jr., *Planning for War Against Russia and Serbia: Austro-Hungarian and German Military Strategies, 1871-1914*, Boulder, 1993, p.139.

73 Cited in Kann, 'Archduke Franz Ferdinand and Count Berchtold', pp.122-123.

74 Friedjung, *Geschichte in Gesprächen*, vol.2, p.449.

75 Diószegi, 'Burián. Biographie und Tagebuchstelle', diary entry for 8 June 1914, p.203.

76 Williamson, *Austria-Hungary and the Origins of the First World War*, p.165.

77 Galántai, *Die Österreichisch-Ungarische Monarchie und der Weltkrieg*, p.203.

78 Henry Wickham Steed, 'The Pact of Konopisht', *The Nineteenth Century and After*, vol.79, February 1916, pp.253-273.

79 Fay, *The Origins of the World War*, vol.2, p.36; Luigi Albertini, *The Origins of the War of 1914*, Oxford, 1952, vol.2, p.18, n.1; Dumaine, *La dérnière ambassade*, p.127. The United States diplomat Charles Vopicka, who served at the time as the envoy to Romania, Serbia and Bulgaria, provided in his memoirs a slight variation to the Konopischt story related by Steed (without mentioning Steed) in that he asserted Sophie's personal involvement in plotting with the Kaiser against Serbia and also discussing with him war with Russia. Unlikely as this sounds, one should nevertheless bear in mind Sophie's general interest in political matters as confirmed by Colonel Brosch and discussed in chapter one. See Charles J. Vopicka, *Secrets of the Balkans: Seven Years of a Dilomatist's Life in the Storm Centre of Europe*, Chicago, 1921, pp.46-47.

80 R.W. Seton-Watson, *German, Slav, and Magyar: A Study in the Origins of the Great War*, London, 1916, pp.111-112; Seton-Watson, *Sarajevo*, pp.98-99.

81 Schmitt, *The Coming of the War*, vol.1, p.170.

82 Steed, *Through Thirty Years*, vol.1, pp.396-399.

83 Strandman, *Balkanske uspomene*, pp.254-258.

84 At this point, it should perhaps be noted that Kaiser Wilhelm II did have a predilection for suggesting grand re-arrangements of the continental order. In March 1914 the European press was speculating about an interview given to *Novoe Vremya*

by an unnamed Russian source, generally assumed to have been Count de Witte, the former Finance Minister. The paper's interlocutor revealed a sensational plan which had been broached: the concluding of an alliance between Germany and Russia, to partition the Habsburg Empire, and the subsequent establishment of a political coalition of Russia, France, Germany and Britain as a guarantor of European peace and general disarmament. In fact, according to official Serbian documents, it was General Vladimir Sukhomlinov, the Russian War Minister, not de Witte, who had divulged this information to *Novoe Vremya*. And Sukhomlinov, in turn, had been told about the whole thing in 1913 by no less a person than Kaiser Wilhelm II. Spalajković, the Serbian Minister at St Petersburg, was informed in the editorial offices of *Novoe Vremya* that the Kaiser had suggested the following to Sukhomlinov: that the burgeoning armaments race was intolerable; that the conclusion of an alliance between Germany, Russia, France and Britain should put an end to it; and that this should be accompanied by a settlement of the Alsace-Lorraine question, as well as by a division of 'Austria' (i.e., the Habsburg Empire) between Russia, Germany, the Czech lands, Hungary and the 'Yugoslav states'. See *DSKPS*, vol.7/1, no.413, report Spalajković, 27 March 1914. For the reaction in Austria-Hungary see, for example, 'Die Wahrheit über die Enthüllungen der Nowoje Wremja', *Pester Lloyd*, Budapest, 29 March 1914 (Morgenblatt), p.1.

85 Lichnowsky, *Heading for the Abyss*, p.71.
86 Howard, *The Diary of Edward Goschen*, p.289.
87 SArt, Morsey MS, Personalia MO, p.52.
88 Hantsch, *Leopold Graf Berchtold*, vol.2, p.544.
89 *GP*, vol.39, no.15737, letter Tschirschky to Bethmann Hollweg, 17 June 1914.
90 Rauchensteiner, *Der erste Weltkrieg*, p.33.
91 Hantsch, *Leopold Graf Berchtold*, vol.2, p.545.
92 Fay, *The Origins of the World War*, vol.2, p.189; A.J.P. Taylor, *The Struggle for Mastery in Europe*, Oxford, 1954, p.516; Fritz Fischer, *Germany's Aims in the First World War*, New York, 1967, p.53.
93 *ÖUA*, vol.7, no.9482, memorandum Tisza, 15 March 1914.
94 Vermes, *István Tisza*, p.212.
95 *ÖUA*, vol.8, no.9627, memorandum Flotow, May 1914 – no exact date is given.

96 *ÖUA*, vol.8, no.9627.
97 Bridge, *From Sadowa to Sarajevo*, p.368; Hannig, 'Austro-Hungarian foreign policy and the Balkan Wars', pp.240-241.
98 *ÖUA*, vol.8, no.9918, memorandum Matscheko. The editors of *ÖUA* point out that the memorandum carries no date, but stipulate 'vor 24. Juni', i.e., before 24 June.
99 Schroeder, 'Romania and the Great Powers before 1914', pp.45-46.
100 *ÖUA*, vol.7, no.8945, private letter Haymerle to Berchtold, 1 November 1913; no.8961, private letter Hoyos to Haymerle, 6 November 1913.
101 *ÖUA*, vol.8, no.9918, memorandum Matscheko. A much abridged version of the Matscheko Memorandum is provided in English translation in Bridge, *From Sadowa to Satajevo*, pp.443-447.
102 Clark, *The Sleepwalkers*, p.115.
103 *ÖUA*, vol.8, appendix to no.9984.
104 H. Bertil A. Petersson, 'Das österreichisch-ungarische Memorandum an Deutschland vom 5. Juli 1914', *Scandia*, vol.30, no.1, 1964, pp.145, 157, 159 and 173.
105 Schroeder, 'Romania and the Great Powers before 1914', p.45.
106 *ÖUA*, vol.8, no.9926.
107 Petersson, 'Das österreichisch-ungarische Memorandum', p.154.
108 *ÖUA*, vol.8, no.9918. memorandum Matscheko.
109 *ÖUA*, vol.7, no.8498, address Berchtold to Franz Joseph, 28 August, 1913.
110 *ÖUA*, vol.8, no.9918, memorandum Matscheko.
111 Cited in Galántai, *Die Österreichisch-Ungarische Monarchie und der Weltkrieg*, p.202.
112 Schroeder, 'Romania and the Great Powers before 1914', p.46.
113 Baernreither, *Fragments of a Political Diary*, p.302.

14 Warnings, Misgivings and the Last Supper

1 *Almanach de Madame de Thèbes pour l`année 1914: conseils pour être heureux*, Paris, 1913.
2 'Kako se je prestolonaslednik vedno pripravljal, da stopi pripravljen pred svojega Stvarnika', *Slovenec*, Ljubljana, 8 July 1914, p.3.
3 Jagow, *Ursachen und Ausbruch des Weltkrieges*, p.95.
4 August Urbański von Ostrymiecz, 'Mein Beitrag zur Kriegsschuldfrage', *Die Kriegsschuldfrage*, February 1926, pp.84-85; August

Urbański v. Ostrymiecz, 'Conrad v. Hötzenforf und die Reise des Thronfolgers nach Sarajevo', *Berliner Monatshefte*, May 1929, p.468; August Urbański von Ostrymiecz, *Conrad von Hötzendorf. Soldat und Mensch*, Graz-Leipzig-Wien, 1938, p.213-214.

5 Conrad, *Aus meiner Dienstzeit*, vol.3, p.702. In her *The Archduke and the Assassin*, Lavender Cassels also claims that Conrad 'thought that the visit should be cancelled' (p.162), but supplies no evidence whatsoever. Albert Pethö, in his work on the Austro-Hungarian intelligence, *Agenten für den Doppeladler. Österreich-Ungarns geheimer Dienst im Weltkrieg*, Graz-Stuttgart, 1998, similarly asserts that Conrad was in favour of cancelling the visit (p.253) – and likewise provides no substantiation.

6 Generalmajor Max Ronge, *Kriegs- und Industrie-Spionage*, Zürich – Leipzig – Wien, 1930, p.86.

7 Broucek, *Jansa*, p.218.

8 Kronenbitter, '*Krieg im Frieden*'; Pethö, *Agenten für den Doppeladler*.

9 Verena Moritz, 'Spione am Werk' in Verena Moritz, Hannes Leidenger and Gerhard Jagschitz, *Im Zentrum der Macht. Die vielen Gesichter des Geheimdienstchefs Maximilian Ronge*, St Pölten – Salzburg, 2007, p.120.

10 Kronenbitter, '*Krieg im Frieden*'; pp.17-18; Broucek, *Zeynek*, pp.153-154.

11 Verena Moritz and Hannes Leidinger, *Oberst Redl*, St Pölten-Salzburg-Wien, 2012, p.108.

12 Conrad, *Aus meiner Dienstzeit*, vol.4, pp.14-15.

13 Moritz, 'Spione am Werk', p.120.

14 Conrad, *Aus meiner Dienstzeit*, vol.4, p.16.

15 Leo Ashley Nicoll, 'Anton Puntigam S.J. Leben und Wirken eines Jesuiten in Bosnien', Universität Wien Dissertation, 1970, p. 156.

16 Angster, *1914*, p.72.

17 Emil Seeliger, *Abendsonne über Habsburgs Reich*, Wien – Leipzig, 1935, pp.227-228; Biliński, *Wspomnienia*, vol.1, p. 273.

18 Dedijer, *The Road to Sarajevo*, p.407.

19 *Ibid.*, p.408.

20 Carl Collas, 'Auf den bosnischen Wegspuren der Kriegsschuldigen', *Die Kriegsschuldfrage*, January 1927, p.21.

21 Conrad, *Aus meiner Dienstzeit*, vol. 3, p.700, and vol. 4, p.37. It is not clear whether the Archduke's audience with the Emperor had actually taken place on 4 June or possibly a day or two earlier. In his *Victims at Sarajevo*, Gordon Brook-Shepherd states

(p.222) that the only reported audience involving the Archduke during this period was on 7 June.

22 Eisenmenger, *Erzherzog Franz Ferdinand*, p.178.

23 Wladimir Aichelburg, *Sarajevo 28. Juni 1914*, Wien, 1984, p.25.

24 J.A. Zibert, *Der Mord von Sarajewo und Tiszas Schuld an dem Weltkriege*, Laibach, 1919. The fascimile is between p.16 and p.17.

25 Holler, *Franz Ferdinand*, p.226.

26 Brook-Shepherd, *Victims at Sarajevo*, p.221.

27 King and Woolmans, *The Assassination of the Archduke*, p.170.

28 Aichelburg, *Sarajevo*, p.10.

29 Zdenko Radslav Graf Kinsky, *Zu Pferd und zu Fuß*, Wien-Rom, 1974, p.60.

30 Cited in Wühr, *Ludwig Freiherr von Pastor*, p.612.

31 Victor Naumann, *Dokumente und Argumente*, Berlin, 1928, p.3.

32 'Aus den letzten Tagen des Erzherzogs', *Reichspost*, Wien, 30 June 1914 (Nachmittagsausgabe), p.4.

33 Mende, 'Dr. Carl Freiherr von Bardolff', p.63.

34 Bardolff, *Soldat im alten Österreich*, p.181.

35 Cited in Mende, 'Dr. Carl Freiherr von Bardolff', p.62.

36 Broucek, *Zeynek*, pp.142 and 155.

37 Cited in Mende, 'Dr. Carl Freiherr von Bardolff', p.63.

38 Max Hastings, *Catastrophe: Europe Goes to War 1914*, London, 2013, p.xxxv.

39 Redlich, *Schicksalsjahre*, vol.1, diary entry for 28 June 1914, p.609.

40 Čerović, *Bosanski Omladinci i Sarajevski Atentat*, pp.225-226.

41 Biliński, *Wspomnienia*, vol.1, p.278.

42 Collas, 'Auf den bosnischen Wegspuren der Kriegsschuldigen', p.21.

43 Vladislav Glik, 'Sarajevo juna 1914 godine', *Politika*, Beograd, 17 November 1933, p.1.

44 Bogićević, *Pisma i saopštenja*, p.12.

45 Collas, 'Auf den bosnischen Wegspuren der Kriegsschuldigen', pp 21 and 17.

46 *Ibid.*, p.21.

47 *Ibid.*, p.22.

48 Vojislav Bogićević, 'Austriske vlasti i Sarajevski Atentat', *Nova Evropa*, Zagreb, vol.27, no.8, July 1934, p.270.

49 Władysław Gluck, *Sarajewo. Historja zamachu sarajewskiego*, Kraków, 1935, pp.136-137.

50 Vladislav Glik, 'Sarajevo juna 1914. godine', *Politika*, Beograd, 16 November 1933, pp.1-2.

51 Dedijer, *The Road to Sarajevo*, p.276.

52 *Österreichisch-ungarisches Rotbuch. Diplomatische Aktenstücke zur Vorgeschichte des Krieges 1914*, Wien, 1915, no.19, p.44.

53 Glik, 'Sarajevo juna 1914 godine', p.1.

54 Gluck, *Sarajewo*, pp.137-138.

55 Bogićević, *Pisma i saopštenja*, pp.105-106.

56 Biliński, *Wspomnienia*, vol.1, pp.275-276.

57 Milovan Grba, 'Das Attentat gegen Franz Ferdinand und die Sarajevoer Polizei', *Prager Presse*, Prag, 29 July 1924 (Morgen-Ausgabe), p.3.

58 Gluck, *Sarajewo*, pp.139-140.

59 Vojislav Bogićević, 'Austrijske policiske vlasti i sarajevski atentatori', *Pregled*, Sarajevo, vol.12, March 1936, p.152.

60 Dedijer, *Sarajevo 1914*, vol.2, p.157; Glik, 'Posle atentata na Franju Ferdinanda', *Politika*, Beograd, 19 November 1933, p.2.

61 Vladislav Glik, 'Kako su Poćorekovi oficiri sprečili da se spase život Franji Ferdinandu', *Politika*, Beograd, 18 November 1933, p.2.

62 Glik, 'Posle atentata na Franju Ferdinanda', p.2.

63 Kralek, 'Schlitter', diary entry for 25 April 1914, p.223.

64 Nikitsch-Boulles, *Vor dem Sturm*, p.211.

65 SArt, Morsey MS, Personalia MO, p.54.

66 *Ibid.*, pp.54-55.

67 Nikitsch-Boulles, *Vor dem Sturm*, p.210.

68 SArt, Morsey MS, Personalia MO, p.55; Paul Höger, 'Erinnerungen an die Todesfahrt', *Österreichische Wehrzeitung*, 27 June 1924, p.2

69 Halpern, *The Mediterranean Naval Situation, 1908-1914*, p.155.

70 Höger, 'Erinnerungen an die Todesfahrt'.

71 *Ibid.*

72 'Die Eröffnung des Franz Ferdinand-Bades in Mostar', *Bosnische Post*, Sarajevo, 4 June 1914 p.5; 'Der Besuch des Thronfolgers und Gemahlin', *Bosnische Post*, Sarajevo, 25 June 1914, p.5.

73 Heinrich Renner, *Durch Bosnien und die Hercegovina, kreuz und quer*, Berlin, 1897, p.110.

74 Conrad, *Aus meiner Dienstzeit*, vol.4, p.13.

75 Kranjčević, *Uspomene*, p.66. Other sources identify Potiorek as the person who had already on 24 June ordered the removal of Serbian and Croatian flags at Ilidža. See Pero Slijepčević, 'Mlada Bosna' in Slijepčević, *Napor Bosne i Hercegovine*, p.213, and Popović, *Oko sarajevskog atentata*, p.38. In his famous novel about the Sarajevo assassination, Bruno Brehm, however, has Franz Ferdinand, not Potiorek, ordering the removal of the flags. See Bruno Brehm, *Apis und Este. Ein Franz Ferdinand*

Roman, München, 1931, p.342. The story is also mentioned in Jevtić, *Sarajevski atentat*, p.32.

76 SArt, Morsey MS, Personalia MO, p.61.

77 'Wie der Thronfolger und seine Gemahlin in Ilidža wohnen werden', *Bosnische Post*, Sarajevo, 23 June 1914, pp.4-5.

78 'Der Besuch des Thronfolgers und Gemahlin', *Bosnische Post*, Sarajevo, 26 June 1914, p.2; Vlado Gluck, 'Sitne primedbe uz knjigu *Istraga u sarajevskom atentatu*', *Pregled*, Sarajevo, vol.14, October 1938, pp.652-653. Kabilio's bill, with item descriptions, is in Schlossarchiv Artstetten, Erzherzog Franz Ferdinand, Chronologie 14.6.1914 – 28.6.1914.

79 'Die Ermordung des Erzherzogs Franz Ferdinand. Unterredung mit dem Landeschef von Bosnien Feldzeugmeister Potiorek', *Neue Freie Presse*, Wien, 6 July 1914 (Nachmittagblatt), p.2.

80 Jevtić, *Sarajevski atentat*, p.33.

81 HHStA, NLEFF/167, *Prozess*, pp.99-140.

82 Clark, *The Sleepwalkers*, p.369. The story that the royal couple went to the Sarajevo bazaar (Baščaršija) was first introduced by Nikitsch-Boulles (*Vor dem Sturm*) when he wrote that the Archduke was surrounded by a crowd and his entourage was pushing the way from one shop to another 'with fists and elbows ' (p.213). Nikitsch-Boulles gives the date incorrectly as 26 June. In 1953 Rudolf Kiszling (*Erzherzog Franz* Ferdinand, p.292), repeated that the couple went to the *Čaršija* ('der Basare von Sarajevo'). In his *Sarajevo*, which is a book without footnotes, Joachim Remak, presumably following Nikitsch-Boulles, wrote that, 'at the famous Oriental bazaar', the officers from the entourage 'had to pave a way through the mass of people' (p.102). In *The Archduke and the Assassin* (another book without footnotes), Lavender Cassels is the most inventive in that she writes about Morsey and other members of the entourage 'sweating with fear' as they pushed and shoved 'to clear a path through the people who pressed in on them' (p.166). But there is nothing at all about this in the various accounts Morsey wrote, whether published or unpublished. Nor does Countess Lanjus, present during the shopping trip on 25 June, mention anything of the kind in her unpublished memoir. The Sarajevo newspapers likewise carried nothing about such ostensible scenes. Some of the confusion has perhaps to do with the inability of many

writers to differentiate between *čaršija* (town) and *Baščaršija* (the oriental bazaar in Sarajevo). In any case, no supporting evidence exists that the royal couple visited the bazaar or that they had had to struggle through crowds.

83 SArt, Morsey MS, Personalia MO, pp.61-62.

84 SArt, Vilma Kastner [Lanjus], 'Meine Erinnerungen an Erzherzog Franz Ferdinand und Herzogin Sofie von Hohenberg', n.d., Personalia LA, pp.14-15.

85 'Iz zadnjih nadvojvodovih dni', *Slovenec*, Ljubljana, 1 July 1914, p.3.

86 'Der Besuch des Thronfolgers und Gemahlin', *Bosnische Post*, Sarajevo, 26 June 1914, pp.2-3.

87 SArt, Morsey MS, Personalia MO, p.62.

88 Gluck, 'Sitne primedbe', p.652.

89 SArt, Morsey MS, Personalia MO, p.62.

90 Nicoll, 'Anton Puntigam S.J.', Appendix, p.60, n.2.

91 On security grounds the 11th Mountain Brigade of the 15th Corps was left in the lower Drina region (facing Serbia) during the manoeuvres, and the 14th Mountain Brigade of the 16th Corps was positioned in the Bay of Cattaro area (facing Montenegro). See Broucek, *Jansa*, p.215.

92 'Die Manöver in Bosnien', *Bosnische Post*, Sarajevo, 19 May 1914, p.6.

93 'Das gestrige Unwetter', *Bosnische Post*, Sarajevo, 24 June 1914, p.4.

94 'Die Thronfolgermanöver in Bosnien', *Bosnische Post*, Sarajevo, 26 June 1914, pp.2-3.

95 Broucek, *Jansa*, pp.219-220.

96 Rauchensteiner, *Der Erste Weltkrieg*, p.85.

97 Broucek, *Zeynek*, p.143.

98 Bardolff, *Soldat im alten Österreich*, pp.181-182.

99 Karl Schulda, 'Generaloberst Freiherr Arthur von Bolfras. Generaladjutant und Vorstand der Militärkanzlei Seiner Majestät Kaiser Franz Josephs I', Dissertation, Universität Wien, 1993, p.243.

100 But Gligorije Jeftanović, possibly the most prominent Serb in Bosnia-Herzegovina at the time, was struck off the list because he was considered too close to official Serbia. See Holler, *Franz Ferdinand*, p.274.

101 Safvet beg Bašagić-Redžepašić, *Kratka uputa u prošlost Bosne i Hercegovine*, Sarajevo, 1900, p.18.

102 Biliński, *Wspomnienia*, vol.1, pp.265-266.

103 Funder, *Vom Gestern ins Heute*, pp.345; 373.

104 Miroslav Prstojević, *Zaboravljeno Sarajevo*, Sarajevo-Wien, 2010, p.167.

105 Hafiz Muhamed Pandža, 'Merhum Džemaludin Čaušević' in Enes Karić and Mujo

Demirović (eds.), *Reis Džemaludin Čaušević. Prosvjetitelj i reformator*, Sarajevo, 2002, vol.1, p.170.

106 Moravský Zemský archiv (MZA), Brno, Harrach papers, G393/908/65/18, 'Musik-Programm für die Höchste Hoftafel am 27. Juni 1914 in Ilidža-Bad.'

107 MZA, G393/908/65/18, 'Dîner du 27 Juin 1914.'

108 Danilo Dimović, 'Kod Karla Habzburga. (Iz mojih uspomena.)', *Politika*, Beograd, 7 April 1922, p.1.

109 Aichelburg, *Sarajevo*, p.37; Conrad, *Aus meinerDienstzeit*, vol.4, p.15.

110 Funder, *Vom Gestern ins Heute*, p.374. Sunarić related this story to Friedrich Funder ten years after the event.

111 'Der Bürgermeister über das Attentat', *Bosnische Post*, Sarajevo, 3 July 1914, p.1.

112 Ivan Mužić, *Masonstvo u Hrvata*, Split, 2001, p.99, n.172.

113 'Zum Attentat', *Bosnische Post*, Sarajevo, 1 July p.3; 'Erzherzog Franz Ferdinand in Kupres', *Bosnische Post*, Sarajevo (Zweite Auflage), 15 July 1914, p.1.

114 Nikitsch-Boulles, *Vor dem Sturm*, pp.214-215.

115 'Die Rolle der Polizei von Sarajevo.', *Reichspost*, Wien, 30 June 1914 (Morgenblatt), p.4.

116 Jevđević, *Sarajevski atentatori*, p.96.

117 Bardolff, *Soldat im alten Österreich*, p.182.

118 Höger, 'Erinnerungen an die Todesfahrt'. The second part of Höger's short memoir appeared in the *Österreichische Wehrzeitung* on 4 July 1924.

119 Morsey, 'Konopischt und Sarajewo', p.491.

15 Assassins' Avenue: Sarajevo 28 June 1914

1 SArt, Morsey MS, Personalia MO, pp.66-67; Andreas Freiherrn v. Morsey, 'Der Schicksalstag von Sarajewo', *Reichspost*, Wien, 28 June 1924, p.1.

2 Paul Höger, 'Erinnerungen an die Todesfahrt', *Österreichische Wehrzeitung*, Wien, 4 July 1924, p.2.

3 SArt, Lanjus MS, Personalia LA, p.15.

4 West, *Black Lamb and Grey Falcon*, vol.1, p.355.

5 Ljubibratić, *Gavrilo Princip*, p.226.

6 Fritz Würthle, 'Franz Ferdinands letzter Befehl. Der verhängnisvolle Fahrirrtum von Sarajevo', *Österreich in Geschichte und Literatur*, Wien, June 1971, p.316.

7 Margutti, *Kaiser Franz Joseph*, p.106; Hans Seper, Martin Pfunder and Hans Peter Lenz, *Österreichische Automobilgeschichte*, Wien, 1999, p.93.

8   Chlumecky, *Erzherzog Franz Ferdinands Wirken und Wollen*, p.363.

9   'Der Bürgermeister über das Attentat', *Bosnische Post*, Sarajevo, 3 July 1914, p.1.

10   Kiszling, *Erzeherzog Franz Ferdinand*, p.297; Remak, *Sarajevo*, p.115; Dedijer, *The Road to Sarajevo*, p.11; Friedrich Würthle, *Die Spur führt nach Belgrad. Die Hintergründe des Dramas von Sarajevo 1914*, Wien-München-Zürich, 1975, p.11; Galántai, *Die Österreich-isch-Ungarische Monarchie und der Weltkrieg*, p.216; Aichelburg, *Sarajevo*, p. 42; Brook-Shepherd, *Victims at Sarajevo*, p.244; Cassels, *The Archduke*, p.173; Holler, *Franz Ferdinand*, pp.281-282; Bernd Sösemann, 'Die Bereitschaft zum Krieg. Sarajevo 1914' in Alexander Demandt (ed.), *Das Attentat in der Geschichte*, Köln-Weimar-Wien, 1996, p.300; Weissensteiner, *Franz Ferdinand*, p.26; Ružica Grgić, 'Mir scheint, wir werden heute noch einige Kugeln bekommen' in Michael Gehler and René Ortner (eds.), *Von Sarajewo zum 11. September. Einzelattentate un Massenterrorismus*, Insbruck-Wien-Bozen, 2007, p.31.

11   This is Robert J. Donia in his *Sarajevo: A Biography*, London, 2006, p.121. He writes about a 'three-car caravan'.

12   Fay, *The Origins of the World War*, vol.2, p.124; Schmitt, *The Coming of the War*, vol.1, p.256; Albertini, *The Origins of the War of 1914*, vol.2, p.35.

13   'Der Bürgermeister über das Attentat.', *Bosnische Post*, Sarajevo, 3 July 1914, p.1.

14   Vojislav Bogićević, 'Sećanja na Vidovdan-ski atentat 1914', *Pregled*, Sarajevo, vol.11, February 1935, p.79.

15   HHStA, NLEFF/167, *Prozess*, p.355. Bernstein, who saw the first assassination attempt on Appel Quay, assessed this distance to have been some 30 metres, whereas the distance between the second car and that of Franz Ferdinand behind it was, he believed, only some 15 metres.

16   Bogićević, *Stenogram*, p.299.

17   Würthle, 'Franz Ferdinands letzter Befehl.', p.319.

18   Dedijer, *The Road to Sarajevo*, p.11. See also Friedrich Würthle, *Dokumente zum Sarajevoprozeß. Ein Quellenbericht*, Wien, 1978, p.21, n.1.

19   'Die polizeiliche Untersuchung in Sarajevo.', *Neue Freie Presse*, Wien, 30 June 1914 (Morgenblatt), p.4.

20   MZA, Harrach diary, Appendix, G393/898, karton 54.

21   Photographic collection in Schlossarchiv Artstetten.

22   For the technical characteristics of the car see Holler, *Franz Ferdinand*, p.282.

23   M. Christian Ortner and Thomas Ilming, *Das Auto von Sarajevo. Der geschichts-trächtigste Oldtimer der Welt*, Schleinbach, 2014, p.86.

24   Würthle, *Dokumente*, pp.28-29, n.16.

25   As confirmed in letter by Prince Hohen-lohe, the *Obersthofmeister* to Emperor Karl, dated 9 July 1917: MZA, Harrach papers, G393/908/65/118.

26   Aichelburg, *Erzherzog Franz Ferdinand von Österreich-Este*, vol.3, p.8.

27   'Gespräch mit dem Chauffeur Franz Ferdinands.', *Neues Wiener Journal*, Wien, 9 June 1927, pp.4-5.

28   HHStA, NLEFF/167, *Prozess*, p.198.

29   MZA, Harrach papers, letter Robert Grein to Harrach, 18 July 1914, G393/908/65/118.

30   Aichelburg, *Sarajevo*, p.42. In his 2014 reconstruction, Aichelburg changes his mind and has Robert Grein's brother (whose Chistian name he does not know) as the chauffeur – though he still mistak-enly places this car in the no.7 position rather than no.6 – as he also did in his 1984 study. See Aichelburg, *Erzherzog Franz Ferdinand von Österreich-Este*, vol.3, p.8, and, below in this chapter, n.33.

31   HHStA, NLEFF/167, *Prozess*, p.285; Aichelburg, *Sarajevo*, p.42.

32   HHStA, NLEFF/167, *Prozess*, p.229.

33   Wladimir Aichelburg claims (*Erzherzog Franz Ferdinand von Österreich-Este*, vol.3, p.8) that Morsey, Pilz and Starch were in car no.6, and that Hüttenbrenner, Ditfurth, Erbach-Fürstenau and brothers Grein were in car no.7 – precisely the reverse of what this book maintains. Since Aichelberg provides no sources for his reconstruction, it is difficult to deter-mine how he reached his conclusion. Statements given by passengers in the motorcade (contained in *Prozess in Sara-jevo*, deposited with Franz Ferdinand's papers in the Haus-, Hof- und Staats-archiv, Vienna) tend to contradict Aichel-burg. Major Höger (who is in car no.5 in Aichelburg's 2014 reconstruction, and also placed in the same car by this study) declared that he was in 'the third car'; Erbach-Fürstenau (who is in car no.7 in Aichelburg's 2014 reconstruction, but in car no.6 in this study) stated that he was in 'the fourth car' – it is thus abundantly clear that they were counting the arch-ducal car as the first in the motorcade (i.e., discounting the two leading, local cars) and that Erbach-Fürstenau, as this book maintains, was in the car right behind

Höger's, that is, in car no.6. See HHStA, NLEFF/167, *Prozess*, pp.275 and 273.

34 Morsey, 'Konopischt und Sarajewo.', p.492; Andreas Freiherrn v. Morsey, 'Der Schicksalstag von Sarajewo', *Reichspost*, Wien, 28 June 1924, p.1.

35 Conrad, *Aus meiner Dienstzeit*, vol.4, p.20.

36 SArt, Lanjus MS, Personalia LA, p.16.

37 Dedijer, *The Road to Sarajevo*, p.11.

38 Dedijer gives as his source Biliński's memoirs, *Wspomnienia*, p.282, (vol.1), but Biliński writes (on p.280 rather than p.282 as indicated by Dedijer) as follows: 'The Archduke and his suite, having got off the train, immediately took up seats in the cars and moved on; but the police agents in their entourage – unnecessarily burdened with the Duchess' boxes of jewellery – should have gone in front and behind the Archduke's car to oversee matters, but no cars or carriages had been provided. They had to stay at the factory and, only when they heard the echo of exploded bombs, they rushed on foot to the place of the assassination which was by then already empty.' It is not clear how Dedijer came to draw something out of Biliński that was not there – for at no point does Biliński mention a 'chief officer', still less one who managed to get into the first car, and he makes no mention of three local detectives, either. In any event, the boxes of jewellery supposedly carried around by police agents on behalf of the Duchess render the Minister's account quite absurd and perhaps tendentious – were those agents in fact doubling as domestic servants and how much jewellery could the Duchess wear on a single day?

Among others, Gerd Holler (*Franz Ferdinand*, p.281), Gordon Brook-Shepherd (*Victims at Sarajevo*, p.244), Bernd Sösemann ('Die Bereitschaft zum Krieg', p.300), David James Smith (*One Morning in Sarajevo*, p.169) and Gordon Martel (*The Month That Changed the World*, p.78) have uncritically restated this episode more or less as depicted by Dedijer. In his *Sleepwalkers*, Christopher Clark also restates (p.369) this myth – without, however, acknowledging in any way its inventor Vladimir Dedijer. He writes: 'Even the special security detail was missing – its chief had mistakenly climbed into one of the cars with three local Bosnian officers, leaving the rest of his men behind at the railway station.' Clark gives Biliński as his source and also cites page 282 (the wrong page), thus replicating Dedijer's blunders all the way. Since he makes the same small mistake as Dedijer in his page reference to Biliński, and supports Dedijer's supererogatory discovery of detectives who have left no documentary trace, it would seem justifiable to assume that Clark's account of the matter comes from Dedijer, or some hypothetical third source, but not from Biliński. There is a further reason to suppose that this is the case. Dedijer writes (in the same passage where he conjures up the 'chief officer' of 'special security detectives' and the 'three local police officers') that the archducal party were met by General Potiorek 'at the Sarajevo station'. It was seen above in this chapter that the train had in fact brought the party to the area of the tobacco factory, near the *Philippoviclager* where a troop inspection was going to take place – not to the Sarajevo railway station. But Clark, like Dedijer before him (but not Biliński) postulates an imagined arrival at the Sarajevo railway station since he writes that the men of the special security detail (less their 'chief') were subsequently left 'behind at the railway station.' Yet in his memoirs, Biliński himself is very clear (and correct) on the question of the exact location where the archducal party had arrived in Sarajevo. He writes (pp.279-280), only a few sentences above the passage which Dedijer had got so wrong, that on that day, i.e., 28 June, the Archduke and his party travelled by train from Ilidža 'not to the Sarajevo railway station, but rather they got off at the western entrance to the city, near the tobacco factory'. It is of course possible that Clark fails to acknowledge Dedijer *per incuriam*, or that he relies on some other account perhaps based on Dedijer. But to submit that his source is Biliński is demonstrably false. Sir Christopher Clark is Regius Professor of History at the University of Cambridge and a Fellow of St Catherine's College. Another Professor, T.G. Otte, writes in his *July Crisis* (p.24) that 'owing to some confusion', the security detail 'were left behind at the station, and only their commanding officer travelled in the motorcade along with three local gendarmes.' Otte also gives Biliński as his source – page 282.

39 Ferdinand Hauptmann and Anton Prasch (eds.), *Dr. Ludwig Thallóczy – Tagebücher 23.VI.1914.-31.XII.1914*, Graz, 1981, entry

for 5 July 1914, p.31. Hereafter cited as
Thallóczy, *Tagebücher*.

40 [Władysław Gluck], 'Posle atentata na
Franju Ferdinanda', *Politika*, Beograd, 19
November 1933, p.2.

41 MZA, Harrach papers, letter Bardolff to
Harrach, 22 June 1914, RAH, G393, 908/
65/118.

42 Miroslav Prstojević, *Zaboravljeno Sarajevo*,
Sarajevo-Wien, 1999, p.II, preface to the
second edition. During the Second World
War Appel Quay became the Adolf Hitler
Quay.

43 Kraljačić, *Kalajev režim u Bosni i Hercegovini*, pp.76 and 231.

44 'Ein Aufruf des Bürgermeisters.', *Bosnische
Post*, Sarajevo, 24 June 1914, pp.3-4.

45 'Sarajevo in Erwartung des Thronfolgers',
Bosnische Post, Sarajevo, 27 June 1914, p.3.

46 Kranjčević, *Uspomene*, p.62.

47 Jeřábek, *Potiorek*, p.82.

48 [Anon.], *Zločin v Sarajevu. Tragična smrt
prestolonaslednika Fran Ferdinanda in njegove
soproge vojvodinje Hohenberg*, Ljubljana,
1914, p.10.

49 Jevđević, *Sarajevski atentatori*, p.105.

50 'Graf Boos-Waldeck über das erste Attentat', *Bosnische Post*, Sarajevo, 29 June 1914,
p.2; 'Die letzte Freude der Herzogin',
Bosnische Post, Sarajevo, 29 June 1914, p.2.

51 Bogićević, 'Sećanja', p.79; HHStA,
NLEFF/167, *Prozess*, p.279.

52 Jevtić, *Sarajevski atentat*, p.37.

53 Ćurić, 'Jedan nacionalni revolucionar iz
Hercegovine', p.261. This article contains
Mehmedbašić's recollections of his life up
to 1914, related to Hajrudin Ćurić in 1938.

54 Vojislav Gaćinović, *Kob revolucionarne
Mlade Bosne i njenih junaka*, Tunis, 1973, p.43.

55 HHStA, NLEFF/167, *Prozess*, p.216.

56 Bogićević, *Pisma i saopštenja*, p.138.

57 HHStA, NLEFF/167, *Prozess*, p.364.

58 HHStA, NLEFF/167, *Prozess*, pp.355-357.

59 HHStA, NLEFF/167, *Prozess*, pp.294 and
355.

60 Weissensteiner, *Franz Ferdinand*, p.27.

61 HHStA, NLEFF/167, *Prozess*, p.226.

62 Bogićević, 'Sećanja na Vidovdanski atentat
1914', p.82.

63 See Popović, *Oko sarajevskog atentata*, p.39.
The story first appeared in Sarajevo's
Hrvatski dnevnik on 29 June 1914.

64 'Die Waffen der Attentäter', *Neu Freie
Presse*, Wien, 29 June 1914 (Morgenblatt),
p.2.

65 Donia, *Sarajevo*, p.121.

66 Geoffrey Wawro, *A Mad Catastrophe: The
Outbreak of World War I and the Collapse of the
Habsburg Empire*, New York, 2014, p.105.

67 Remak, *Sarajevo*, pp.121-122.

68 HHStA, NLEFF/167, *Prozess*, pp.200 and
225, and pp.293-294.

69 Ljubibratić, *Gavrilo Princip*, pp.227 and 229.

70 HHStA, NLEFF/167, *Prozess*, pp.233 and
229.

71 Bogićević, 'Sećanja na Vidovdanski atentat
1914', p.79.

72 MZA, Harrach diary, Appendix, G393/898,
karton 54. See also Jaroslav Chramosta,
'Sarajevské události z deníku Františka
Harracha a Jaroslava Thuna' in Jan Galandauer *et al.*, *Od Sarajeva k velké válce – Ab
Sarajewo zum grossen Krieg*, Praha, 1995,
vol.1, p.40.

73 Bogićević, 'Sećanja na Vidovdanski atentat
1914', p.79.

74 *Ibid.*

75 HHStA, NLEFF/167, *Prozess*, p.238.

76 Bogićević, *Pisma i saopštenja*, p.138.

77 HHStA, NLEFF/167, *Prozess*, pp.355-356
and 226.

78 HHStA, NLEFF/167, *Prozess*, p.295. Mrs
Dimović herself was hit and sustained a
minor injury under her left eyebrow.

79 Popović, *Oko sarajevskog atentata*, p.114;
'Graf Boos-Waldeck über das erste Attentat', *Bosnische Post*, Sarajevo, 29 June 1914,
p.2.

80 Hans Fronius, *Das Attentat von Sarajevo*,
Graz-Wien-Köln, 1988, p.16.

81 Popović, *Oko sarajevskog atentata*, p.237.

82 'Flaschenbombe und Revolver. Die Waffen
der Attentäter.', *Reichspost*, Wien, 29 June
1914 (Nachmittagsausgabe), p.2.

83 Nikola Trišić, 'Uspomene na Muhameda
Mehmedbašića povodom desetogodišnjice smrti', *Pregled*, Sarajevo, July-August,
1953, p.58.

84 *Ibid.*

85 Popović, *Sarajevski Vidovdan*, p.45.

86 HHStA, NLEFF/167, *Prozess*, p.405.
Popović was not so frank in his subsequent recollections of the event. Thus he
insisted, in 1930, that 'Ferdinand's car
drove past, without me seeing it at all.'
He claimed this in a letter addressed to
Vojislav Bogićević who had stood near
him on the pavement. See Bogićević,
Pisma i saopštenja, p.140.

87 HHStA, NLEFF/167, *Prozess*, p.217.

88 HHStA, NLEFF/167, *Prozess*, pp.289-290;
'Die ärtzliche Hilfe für den Erzherzog
und seine Gemahlin', *Neue Freie Presse*,
Wien, 29 June 1914 (Morgenblatt), p.2.

89 HHStA, NLEFF/167, *Prozess*, p.356.

90 Popović, *Oko sarajevskog atentata*, p.77.

91 Ljubibratić, *Gavrilo Princip*, p.228; HHStA,
NLEFF/167, *Prozess*, p.229.

92 'Pogromi protiv Srba u Sarajevu', *Politika*, Beograd, 21 November 1933, p.2.

93 'Ein Augenzeuge des ersten Attentats.', *Pester Lloyd*, Budapest, 29 June 1914 (Morgenblatt), p.3; Bogićević, 'Sećanja na Vidovdanski atentat 1914', p.80.

94 Jeřábek, *Potiorek*, p.84.

95 Ljubibratić, *Gavrilo Princip*, p.228; HHStA, NLEFF/167, *Prozess*, p.225.

96 'Die Schilderung der Attentate durch einen Augenzeugen', *Pester Lloyd*, Budapest, 2 July 1914 (Morgenblatt), p.4.

97 Jeřábek, *Potiorek*, p.83.

98 HHStA, NLEFF/167, *Prozess*, p.276.

99 Würthle, *Dokumente*, p.29, n.16.

100 Morsey, 'Konopischt und Sarajewo', p.494; 'Die ärztliche Hilfe für den Erzherzog und seine Gemahlin', *Neue Freie Presse*, Wien, 29 June 1914 (Morgenblatt), p.2.

101 Dedijer, *The Road to Sarajevo*, p.13; Smith, *One Morning in Sarajevo*, p.183.

102 HHStA, NLEFF/167, *Prozess*, pp.233-235. Galántai is among those who ascribe to Rumerskirch this non-existent intervention: *Die Österreichisch-Ungarische Monarchie und der Weltkrieg*, p.221.

103 MZA, Harrach diary, Appendix, G393/898, karton 54.

104 HHStA, NLEFF/167, *Prozess*, p.100.

105 Kiszling, *Erzherzog Franz Ferdinand*, p.298; Remak, *Sarajevo*, p.129; Dedijer, *The Road to Sarajevo*, p.13; Holler, *Franz Ferdinand*, p.286.

106 'Vor und nach dem Attentate', *Bosnische Post*, Sarajevo, 2 July 1914, p.1.

107 http://www.iwm.org.uk/collections/item/object/1060023361

108 Bogićević, *Pisma i saopštenja*, p.142; Gluck, *Sarajewo*, p.152.

109 Holler, *Franz Ferdinand*, p.287.

110 Jevđević, *Sarajevski atentatori*, p.110.

111 'Razburjenje rajnega nadvojvode po prvem atentatu.', *Slovenec*, Ljubljana, 2 July 1914, p.2.

112 'Na, jetzt lassen Sie Ihre Rede vom Stapel.', Gluck, *Sarajewo*, p.152, and also in Ljubibratić, *Gavrilo Princip*, p.231.

113 'Der Bürgermeister über das Attentat.', *Bosnische Post*, Sarajevo, 3 July 1914, p.1; Jevđević, *Sarajevski atentatori*, p.112.

114 Jevđević, *Sarajevski atentatori*, p.112.

115 'Der Hergang der Attentate', *Neue Freie Presse*, Wien, 29 June 1914 (Morgenblatt), p.2.

116 Full texts of the two speeches are in *Neue Freie Presse*, Wien, 29 June 1914 (Morgenblatt), p.2, and in *Reichspost*, Wien, 29 June 1914 (Morgenblatt), p.3. The Serbo-Croat text of the concluding sentence is in Aichelburg, *Sarajevo*, p.49.

117 Chramosta, 'Sarajevské události', p.40.

118 Jevđević, *Sarajevski atentatori*, p.110.

119 West, *Black Lamb and Grey Falcon*, vol.1, p.353.

120 Danilo Dimović, 'Iz mojih uspomena', *Preporod*, Beograd, 10 September 1922, p.7.

121 SArt, Lanjus MS, Personalia LA, p.17.

122 'Zum Attentat. Die Herzogin von Hohenberg und die moslimischen Damen.', *Bosnische Post*, Sarajevo, 30 June 1914; 'Der Bürgermeister über das Attentat', *Bosnische Post*, Sarajevo, 3 July 1914, p.1; 'Herzogin und Beginica. Eine Szene in Sarajevoer Rathause', *Reichspost*, Wien, 2 July 1914 (Morgenblatt), p.4.

123 'Vor und nach dem Attentate. Eine Unterredung mit dem Abgeordneten Vizebürgermeister von Vancaš', *Bosnische Post*, Sarajevo, 2 July 1914, p.1.

124 Morsey, 'Konopischt und Sarajewo', p.494.

125 HHStA, NLEFF/167, *Prozess*, p.218.

126 Remak, *Sarajevo*, p.132.

127 'Die ärztliche Hilfe für den Erzherzog und seine Gemahlin', *Neue Freie Presse*, Wien, 29 June 1914 (Morgenblatt), p.2.

128 *Ibid.*

129 HHStA, NLEFF/167, *Prozess*, pp.303-304.

130 'Tretja žrtev sarajevskega atentata', *Slovenec*, Ljubljana, 3 July 1914, p.4.

131 'Die Untersuchung. Der Zustand des Oberstleutnants Merizzi.', *Pester Lloyd*, Budapest, 8 July 1914 (Morgenblatt), p.3.

132 Conrad, *Aus meiner Dienstzeit*, vol. 4, pp.20-21.

133 Aichelburg, *Sarajevo*, pp.8-9.

134 Lord Vansittart, *The Mist Procession*, London, 1958, pp.119-120.

135 Thallóczy, *Tagebücher*, pp.26-27.

136 SArt, Morsey MS, Personalia MO, p.70.

137 'Der Schicksalstag von Sarajewo.', *Reichspost*, Wien, 28 June 1924, pp.1-2; Morsey, 'Konopischt und Sarajewo', p.495.

138 SArt, Morsey MS, Personalia MO, p.70.

139 'Offizieller Bericht über das Attentat in Sarajevo', *Neue Freie Presse*, Wien, 30 June 1914 (Morgenblatt), p.3; *ÖUA*, vol.8, no.9949, pp.215-218.

140 L. Pfefer, *Istraga u sarajevskom atentatu*, Zagreb, 1938, p.47. This is the second, extended and amended, edition of Pfeffer's book.

141 Würthle, *Dokumente*, p.45.

142 Jeřábek, *Potiorek*, p.84.

143 HHStA, NLEFF/167, *Prozess*, pp.218-219.

144 Nikitsch-Boulles, *Vor dem Sturm*, p.216.

145 Sosnosky, *Erzherzog Franz Ferdinand*, p.207, n.2.

146 Chlumecky, *Erzherzog Franz Ferdinands Wirken und Wollen*, p.364.

147 Gluck, *Sarajewo*, pp.153-154.

148 *Ibid.*, pp.154-155.

149 Fritz Würthle seems to be the only writer who has discussed, albeit briefly, Gluck's revelation that Potiorek had ordered Gerde to continue from the Town Hall along the originally scheduled route. While not dismissing it, however, Würthle does not attach a great deal of importance to this evidence and even speculates that Potiorek may have 'misspoken'. He also writes that Potiorek's words were '*Planmäßige Route einhalten*', whereas Gluck gave this, in German, as '*Programmässigen Weg einhalten*' – which would suggest that Würthle was working on some secondhand interpretation of Gluck's book. See Würthle, 'Franz Ferdinands letzter Befehl', p.320.

150 HHStA, NLEFF/167, *Prozess*, p.234; 'Vor und nach dem Attentate. Eine Unterredung mit dem Abgeordneten Vizebürgermeister von Vancaš', *Bosnische Post*, Sarajevo, 2 July 1914, p.1.

151 Biliński, *Wspomnienia*, vol.1, pp.281-282.

152 Redlich, *Schicksalsjahre*, vol.1, diary entry for 6 August 1914, p.624; SArt, Lanjus MS, Personalia LA, p.17.

153 Broucek, *Zeynek*, p.159.

154 Trišić, 'Moje uspomene', p.95; Bogićević, *Stenogram*, p.71.

155 HHStA, NLEFF/167, *Prozess*, p.218.

156 Chramosta, 'Sarajevské události', p.40.

157 'Vor und nach dem Attentate.', *Bosnische Post*, Sarajevo, 2 July 1914, p.1.

158 HHStA, NLEFF/167, *Prozess*, p.227.

159 Jeřábek, *Potiorek*, p.84.

160 *ÖUA*, vol.8, no.9949, p.216; Morsey, 'Konopischt und Sarajewo', p.496.

161 Paul Höger, 'Erinnerungen an die Todesfahrt', *Österreichische Wehrzeitung*, Wien, 4 July 1924, p.3.

162 West, *Black Lamb and Grey Falcon*, vol.1, p.339.

163 Aichelburg, *Sarajevo.* pp.54 and 42.

164 Aichelburg, *Erzherzog Franz Ferdinand von Österreich-Este*, vol.3, pp.8 and 18.

165 *Ibid.*, p.8.

166 Bogićević, *Pisma i saopštenja*, p.142.

167 Bogićević, *Stenogram*, p.300.

168 Trišić, 'Moje uspomene', p.95.

169 It is virtually certain that Schneiberg was present because there exists a letter to Harrach from the Crown Equerry office in Vienna, dated 10 July 1914, asking him for clarification as to Schneiberg's exact positioning in the motorcade when the assassination took place. The letter asked whether Schneiberg had perhaps been seated in one of the 'government' cars, or whether he had been in the archducal car. Harrach was further asked whether Schneiberg, in case he was in Franz Ferdinand's car, was up front with the driver or whether he was standing on the running board. The letter is preserved among Harrach's papers in Moravský zemský archiv, Brno: G393/908/65/118. No doubt Schneiberg had wanted to extract some decoration or reward for being present on 28 June, and the Crown Equerry office was simply verifying his claims.

170 HHStA, NLEFF/167, *Prozess*, pp.330 and 332.

171 Jeřábek, *Potiorek*, p.85.

172 HHStA, NLEFF/167, *Prozess*, p.219; *ÖUA*, vol.8, no.9949, p.216.

173 MZA, Harrach diary, G393/898, Karton 54. Special entry entitled 'Am 28. Juni', written on two back pages of the diary book.

174 HHStA, NLEFF/167, *Prozess*, pp.200 and 235. The relevant passage of Lojka's testimony reads: 'Ich habe den Auftrag gehabt, immer dem Automobil des Bürgermeisters zu folgen, und so lenkte ich mein Automobil auch beim zweiten Attentat. Als wir zur Stelle kamen, wo das Attentat geschah, beauftragte mich der Landesbefehlshaber, nicht dem ersten Automobil zu folgen, sondern über eine Brükke einzubiegen. Ich hielt das Automobil an und als ich zurück wenden wollte und 2 Schritte vom Trottoir entfernt war, schoss wieder ein Jüngling einen Schritt vor mir und 2 Schritte vom Automobil entfernt, zweimal hintereinander.'

175 Bogićević, *Stenogram*, pp.426-427.

176 Würthle, 'Franz Ferdinands letzter Befehl', p.318.

177 HHStA, NLEFF/167, *Prozess*, p.234.

178 HHStA, NLEFF/167, *Prozess*, p.226.

179 Ferdo Ber, 'U času atentata', *Pregled*, Sarajevo, February 1935, p.104.; HHStA, NLEFF/167, *Prozess*, p.420.

180 Ber, 'U času atentata', p.104.

181 Bogićević, *Pisma i saopštenja*, p.139.

182 HHStA, NLEFF/167, *Prozess*, p.100; 'Die Mordinstrumente', *Pester Lloyd*, Budapest, 29 June 1914 (Morgenblatt), p.3; 'Die Untersuchung', *Pester Lloyd*, Budapest, 29 June 1914 (Abendblatt), p.1; Morsey, 'Konopischt und Sarajewo.', p.496.

183 HHStA, NLEFF/167, *Prozess*, p.100.

184 HHStA, NLEFF/167, *Prozess*, p.110.

185 HHStA, NLEFF/167, *Prozess*, p.100. It is almost beyond reasonable doubt that Princip's pistol was in fact a Browning 9 mm and not a 7.65 mm – as is sometimes claimed. The Heeresgeschichtliches Museum in Vienna has on display three 9 mm Brownings belonging to the assassins, but not Princip's: the whereabouts of his weapon are unknown. Some doubts about the calibre remain, however. The 9 mm version had a six-round magazine, whereas the 7.65 mm could hold seven rounds. The information provided by Princip that he had loaded the pistol with seven rounds is therefore confusing, though he could have loaded his 9 mm with six rounds and the seventh loaded in the chamber. But Baron Morsey reported that the examination of Princip's Browning revealed four rounds left in the magazine, the capacity of which was seven. He added that 'an eighth round' could be inserted into the barrel ('*in den Lauf*'): Morsey, 'Konopischt und Sarajewo', p.496. Morsey knew what he was talking about because he himself possessed a Browning. In the unpublished version of his memoir, he writes: 'I used to carry on a daily basis a loaded Browning pistol. Exceptionally, on 28 June I did not.' (SArt, Morsey MS, Personalia MO, p.75).

186 Trišić, 'Moje uspomene', p.95.

187 Bogićević, *Stenogram*, pp.71-72.

188 Jezdimir Dangić, 'S Gavrilom Principom, od Sarajeva do Terezina', *Nova Evropa*, Zagreb, vol.33, no.12, 26 November 1940, p.374.

189 Bogićević, *Stenogram*, p.278.

190 HHStA, NLEFF/167, *Prozess*, pp.197 and 228.

191 Holler, *Franz Ferdinand*, p.291.

192 'Neue Einzelheiten über den Hergang des Attentats.', *Neue Freie Presse*, Wien, 1 July 1914 (Morgenblatt), p.3; Morsey, 'Konopischt und Sarajewo.', p.496.

193 'Mitteilungen über den ärztlichen Befund bei den Leichen', *Neue Freie Presse*, Wien, 3 July 1914 (Morgenblatt), p.4.

194 Clive Ponting, *Thirteen Days – Diplomacy and Disaster: The Countdown to the Great War*, London, 2003, p.28. The creator of the fable about Mihajlo Pušara's allegedly decisive intervention was Borivoje Jevtić in his *Sarajevski atentat* (1924), p.39. In *The Road to Sarajevo* (1967) Vladimir Dedijer re-told the fantasy based on Jevtić ('... the intervention at the decisive moment of Mihajlo Pušara', p.321) even though he had all the materials which invalidate Jevtić. Among the writers who then followed Dedijer on this detail were Gerd Holler in his 1982 book (*Franz Ferdinand*, p. 293) and, in 1984, Gordon Brook-Shepherd, except that he baptized Mihajlo Pušara as 'Simon' Pušara: *Victims at Sarajevo*, p.250. Simon Pušara was in fact Mihajlo's relative. David James Smith, in his *One Morning in Sarajevo* (2008), correctly points out (p.191) that there is no evidence in the transcripts of the trial for Dedijer's account of this episode.

195 Bogićević, *Stenogram*, pp.277-278; Trišić, 'Moje uspomene', p.96.

196 Trišić, 'Moje uspomene', p.96; Bogićević, *Stenogram*, pp.278 and 71.

197 'Daniel Pusic über das Attentat', *Reichspost*, Wien, 2 July 1914 (Nachmittagsausgabe), p.3; 'Das Attentat.', *Bosnische Post*, Sarajevo, 2 July 1914, p.2; 'Ein Augenzeuge über die Verhaftung Prinzips', *Pester Lloyd*, Budapest, 2 July 1914 (Abendblatt), p.2; 'Das Attentat', *Bosnische Post*, Sarajevo, 4 July 1914, p.6. Bogićević also states that the people had begun to run away from the scene: *Pisma i saopštenja*, p.139.

198 Morsey, 'Konopischt und Sarajewo', p.497; HHStA, NLEFF/167, *Prozess*, pp.228 and 230-231; SArt, Morsey MS, Personalia MO, p.75; Ber, 'U času atentata', p.104.

199 Trišić, 'Moje uspomene', pp.96-97; Morsey, 'Konopischt und Sarajewo', p.497; 'Daniel Pusic über das Attentat', *Reichspost*, Wien, 2 July 1914 (Nachmittagsausgabe), p.3; Bogićević, *Pisma i saopštenja*, p.139; Jevđević, *Sarajevski atentatori*, p.119.

200 Bogićević, *Stenogram*, pp.288 and 278; Morsey, 'Der Schicksalstag von Sarajewo', *Reichspost*, Wien, 28 June 1914, p.2; 'Das Attentat', *Bosnische Post*, Sarajevo, 2 July 1914, p.2.

201 Remak, *Sarajevo*, p.135. During the war Harrach wrote patriotic poems, some of which he published privately in Sarajevo under the assumed name of Altgraf Erich. See his *Kriegsgedichte*, Sarajevo 1914-1915.

202 Würthle, 'Franz Ferdinands letzter Befehl', p.314.

203 MZA, Harrach diary, G393/898, Karton 54. Special entry entitled 'Am 28. Juni ', written on two back pages of the diary book.

204 HHStA, NLEFF/167, *Prozess*, p.228.

205 Holler, *Franz Ferdinand*, p.293; HHStA, NLEFF/167, *Prozess*, p.235; Jeřábek, *Potiorek*, p.85.

206 HHStA, NLEFF/167, *Prozess*, pp.219-220.

207 HHStA, NLEFF/167, *Prozess*, p.235.

208 'Der Burgermeister über das Attentat', *Bosnische Post*, Sarajevo, 3 July 1914, p.1.

209 HHStA, NLEFF/167, *Prozess*, pp.286 and 284.

210 Jevđević, *Sarajevski atentatori*, p.118.

211 Morsey, 'Konopischt und Sarajewo', p.497; HHStA, NLEFF/167, *Prozess*, pp.240, 279-280.

212 'Die letzten Minuten des Thronfolgerpaares', *Pester Lloyd*, Budapest, 1 July 1914 (Abendblatt), p.2.

213 HHStA, NLEFF/167, *Prozess*, pp.235, 240 and 221; [Morsey], 'Ein autentischer Bericht über das Attentat', *Reichspost*, Wien, 8 July 1914 (Morgenblatt), p.3; Biliński, *Wspomnienia*, vol.1, p.283.

214 Steed, *Through Thirty Years*, vol.1, p.400.

215 Paul Höger, 'Erinnerungen an die Todesfahrt', *Österreichische Wehrzeitung*, Wien, 4 July, p.3; 'Wie der Erzherzog starb', *Reichspost*, Wien, 29 June 1914 (Nachmittagsausgabe), p.1; Morsey, 'Konopischt und Sarajewo.', p.498.

216 'Die letzten Augenblicke des Thronfolgerpaares', *Neue Freie Presse*, Wien, 3 July 1914 (Morgenblatt), p.3.

217 Thallóczy, *Tagebücher*, diary entry for 4 July 1914, p.28.

218 For the denials, see 'Die Vorkehrungen nach dem Attentat', *Pester Lloyd*, Budapest, 4 July 1914 (Abendblatt) and 'Rücktritt des Landeschefs Potiorek', *Reichspost*, Wien, 7 July 1914 (Morgenblatt), p.3.

219 Redlich, *Schicksalsjahre*, vol.1, diary entry for 25 September 1914, p.669.

220 Aichelburg, *Sarajevo*, p.60; Jeřábek, *Potiorek*, p.86.

221 SArt, Morsey MS, Personalia MO, p.77; 'Wie der Erzherzog starb', *Reichspost*, Wien, 29 June 1914 (Nachmittagsausgabe), p.1.

222 SArt, Lanjus MS, Personalia LA, p.18; Paul Höger, 'Erinnerungen an die Todesfahrt'; *Österreichische Wehrzeitung*, Wien, 4 July 1924, p.3.

223 'Weitere Einzelheiten zu dem Attentate', *Reichspost*, Wien, 6 July 1914 (Mittagsausgabe), p.3; Morsey Mss., p.76.

224 Höger, 'Erinnerungen an die Todesfahrt', *Österreichische Wehrzeitung*, Wien, 4 July, p.3; 'Weitere Einzelheiten zu dem Attentate', *Reichspost*, Wien, 6 July 1914 (Mittagsausgabe), p.3; Morsey, 'Der Schicksalstag von Sarajewo', *Reichspost*, Wien, 28 June 1924, p.3.

225 Redlich, *Schichsalsjahre*, vol.1, entry for 12 July 1914, p.237; Aichelburg, *Sarajevo*, p.60.

226 Nicoll, 'Anton Puntigam S.J. ', Appendix, pp.59-60; SArt, Lanjus MS, Personalia LA, p.19; *Wiener Zeitung*, Wien, 29 June 1914, p.4. I am grateful to the Reverend Alan Walker for his assistance here.

227 Broucek, *Jansa*, pp.221-222; Pfefer, *Istraga*, p.35.

228 'Die bei dem Bombenattentate Verletzten', *Reichspost*, Wien, 30 June 1914 (Morgenblatt), p.4; 'Bevorstehender Rücktritt Potioreks', *Pester Lloyd*, Budapest, 30 June 1914 (Abendblatt), p.5.

229 Thallóczy, *Tagebücher*, diary entry for 5 July 1914, p.30.

230 See, for example: 'Der "Optimismus" Dr. von Bilinskis', *Reichspost*, Wien, 1 July 1914 (Morgenblatt), p.6, and 'Rücktritt des Landeschefs Potiorek?', *Reichspost*, Wien, 7 July 1914 (Morgenblatt), p.3.

231 Broucek, *Zeynek*, p.189, n.242.

232 Ljubibratić, *Gavrilo Princip*, p.238; Broucek, *Jansa*, p.223.

16 Austria-Hungary in the July Crisis

1 Kielmansegg, *Kaiserhaus*, pp.97-98.

2 Corti and Sokol, *Der alte Kaiser*, p.413.

3 Thallóczy, *Tagebücher*, diary entry for 29 June 1914 (addendum), p.13.

4 Margutti, *Kaiser Franz Joseph*, pp.138-139.

5 Silber, 'Obersthofmeister Alfred Fürst von Montenuovo', pp.780-781, 787 and 789.

6 Sieghart, *Die letzten Jahrzehnte einer Grossmacht*, p.242.

7 Muriel Gardiner (ed.), *The Wolf-Man and Sigmund Freud*, London, 1972, p.91. I am grateful to the Reverend Alan Walker for drawing my attention to this comment by Freud.

8 Thallóczy, *Tagebücher*, diary entry for 28 June 1914, p.6.

9 *Ibid.*, diary entry for 4 July 1914, p.29.

10 Stefan Zweig, *The World of Yesterday*, London, 1943, pp.168-169.

11 Danilo Dimović, 'Iz mojih uspomena: Grof Stevan Tisa', *Preporod*, Beograd, 10 September 1922, p.7; Kranjčević, *Uspomene*, p.62.

12 'Der heutige Tag in Sarajevo', *Neue Freie Presse*, Wien, 2 July 1914 (Abendblatt), p.2.

13 See reports in the *Neue Freie Presse*: 'Die Demonstrationen gegen die Serben in Wien', 2 July 1914 (Morgenblatt), p.6; 'Die Demonstrationen gegen die Serben in Wien', 3 July 1914 (Morgenblatt), pp.4-5.

14 Kraler, 'Schlitter', diary entry for 24 July 1914, p.252.

15 Hantsch. *Leopold Graf Berchtold*, vol.2, pp.551-552; Ernest U. Cormons [Emanuel Urbas], *Schicksale und Schatten. Eine österreichische Autobiographie*, Salzburg, 1951, p.157.

16 Robert A. Kann, *Kaiser Franz Joseph und der Ausbruch des Weltkrieges*, Wien, 1971, p.16.

17 Conrad, *Aus meiner Dienstzeit*, vol.4, p.36.
18 Jeřábek, *Potiorek*, p.95; Thallóczy, *Tage-bücher*, diary entry for 13 July 1914, p.44.
19 Conrad, *Aus meiner Dienstzeit*, vol.4, pp.33-34.
20 Redlich, *Schicksalsjahre*, vol.1, diary entry for 17 May 1913, p.543.
21 Kanner, *Kaiserliche Katastrophen-Politik*, pp.88-89.
22 Taylor, *Europe: Grandeur and Decline*, p.186.
23 Winston S. Churchill, *The Eastern Front*, London, 1931, p.53.
24 Prince von Bulow, *Memoirs 1909-1919*, London-New York, 1932, p.138.
25 Szilassy, *Der Untergang*, p.208.
26 *DSPKS*, vol.5/1, no.150, report Popović, 7 March 1912.
27 Solomon Wank, 'The Appointment of Count Berchtold as Austro-Hungarian Foreign Minister', *Journal of Central European Affairs*, vol.23, July 1963, pp.147-148; Hantsch, *Leopold Graf Berchtold*, vol.1, pp.246-248. Hantsch denies that Franz Ferdinand had directly tried to influence Berchtold to accept the post of Foreign Minister, but admits that Berchtold's name was not the first on the list of the contemplated successors to Aehrenthal (see p.242 and n.2 on pp.241-242). Karl von Macchio, who was under Berchtold the First Section Chief at the Ballhaus-platz, cast doubts as to whether Berch-told's name had been put forward by Aehrenthal in the first place. See Karl Freiherr von Macchio, 'Momentbilder aus der Julikrise 1914', *Berliner Monatshefte*, October 1936, p.768.
28 Ludwig Bittner, 'Graf Johann Forgách', *Berliner Monatshefte*, November 1935, pp.955-956.
29 Monts, *Erinnerungen*, p.249.
30 Thallóczy, *Tagebücher*, diary entry for 7 July 1914, p.36.
31 Redlich, *Schicksalsjahre*, vol.1, diary entry for 3 May 1914, p.599.
32 Jovanović, *Dnevnik*, diary entry for 31 August 1916, p.156. This episode was related to Jovanović by Alfred Dumaine, the French Ambassador in Vienna from 1912 to 1914.
33 Szilassy, *Der Untergang*, p.254.
34 Hutten-Czapski, *Sechzig Jahre Politik und Gesellschaft*, p.138.
35 *DSPKS*, vol.2/2/2, no.542, report Jova-nović, 13 January 1907.
36 Spitzmüller, *'und hat auch Ursach'*, p.114.
37 Macchio, 'Momentbilder aus der Julikrise 1914', p.731.
38 Cormons, *Schicksale und Schatten*, p.143.
39 It seems clear, however, that Musulin was by no means the only author of the ultimatum. Redlich recorded in his diary that Hoyos and Forgách were the prin-cipal contributors (*Schicksalsjahre*, vol.1, diary entry for 23-24 July 1914, p.615). Thallóczy, on the other hand, claims that the ultimatum was drafted 'entirely' by Burián (*Tagebücher*, diary entry for 23 July 1914, p.55). Circumstancial evidence suggests that Berchtold, too, had been involved. Musulin, certainly, would have translated the German draft into the French.
40 Fritz Fellner, 'Die Mission Hoyos' in Heidrun Maschl and Brigitte Mazohl-Wallnig (eds.), *Vom Dreibund zum Völker-bund*, München, 1994, p.135.
41 *ÖUA*, vol.8, no.10006, report Berchtold on a conversation with the German Ambassador, 3 July 1914.
42 Friedjung, *Geschichte in Gesprächen*, vol.2, p.196.
43 Fellner, 'Die Mission Hoyos'; John Leslie, 'Österreich-Ungarn vor dem Kriegs-ausbruch' in Ralph Melville, Claus Scharf, Martin Vogt and Ulrich Wengenroth (eds.), *Deutschland und Europa in der Neuzeit. Festschrift für Karl Otmar Freiherr von Aretin zum 65. Geburtstag*, Stuttgart, 1988, vol.2.
44 Fellner, 'Austria-Hungary', pp.11-12; John Leslie, 'The Antecedents of Austria-Hungary's War Aims' in Elisabeth Springer and Leopold Kammerhofer (eds.), *Wiener Beiträge zur Geschichte der Neuzeit*, vol.20, Archiv und Forschung, München, 1993, p.309.
45 Leslie, 'Österreich-Ungarn vor dem Kriegsausbruch', p.680; Cormons, *Schick-sale und Schatten*, p.163.
46 Cited in Fellner, 'Austria-Hungary', p.14. The text of Andrian-Werburg's memoir is appended to Leslie, 'Österreich-Ungarn vor dem Kriegsausbruch', pp.675-684.
47 *ÖUA*, vol.8, no.9978.
48 *ÖUA*, vol.8, no.9984. Both documents are included under this number.
49 Fellner, 'Die Mission Hoyos', p.126.
50 Konrad H. Jarausch, *The Enigmatic Chan-cellor: Bethmann Hollweg and the Hubris of Imperial Germany*, New Haven-London, 1973, p.156.
51 *ÖUA*, vol.8, no.10058, telegram Szögyény, 5 July 1914.
52 Karl Kautsky, Max Montgelas and Walter Schücking (eds.), *Die Deutschen Dokumente zum Kriegsausbruch 1914*, Berlin, 1922, no.7, marginal comments by Wilhelm II

on report Tschirschky to Bethmann Hollweg, 30 June 1914. Emphases in the original. The Kaiser wrote his comments on 4 July. Hereafter cited as *DD*.

53 Egmont Zechlin, *Krieg und Kriegsrisiko. Zur deutschen Politik im Ersten Weltkrieg*, Düsseldorf, 1979, p.69.

54 Th. von Bethmann Hollweg, *Betrachtungen zum Weltkriege*, Berlin, 1919, vol.1, pp.135-136.

55 *ÖUA*, vol.8, no.10076, telegram Szögyény, 6 July 1914.

56 Hoyos, *Der deutsch-englische Gegensatz*, p.79.

57 Fellner, 'Die Mission Hoyos', p.138.

58 Albertini, *The Origins of the War of 1914*, vol.2, p.145. Hoyos also told Albertini that he had composed the telegram of 6 July, sent to Vienna after the meeting with Bethmann Hollweg.

59 Jarausch, *The Enigmatic Chancellor*, p.176.

60 Fritz Fischer, *Germany's Aims in the First World War*, New York, 1967, pp.103-106.

61 Frederick Maurice, *The Life of Viscount Haldane of Cloan*, London, 1937, vol.1, pp.349-352. Hoyos wrote the letter to Haldane around 15 July, but intended it to be delivered on the day of the war declaration on Serbia. See Redlich, *Schicksalsjahre*, vol.1, diary entry for 15 July 1914, p.613.

62 *GP*, vol.34/1, no.12818, private letter Bethmann Hollweg to Berchtold, 10 February 1913.

63 Dietrich Erdmann (ed.), *Kurt Riezler. Tagebücher, Aufsätze, Dokumente*, Göttingen, 2008, diary entry for 7 July 1914, p.182. Hereafter cited as Riezler, *Tagebücher*.

64 Müller, *Mars und Venus*, p.35.

65 Riezler, *Tagebücher*, diary entry for 8 July, 1914, p.184.

66 Müller, *Mars und Venus*, p.37.

67 V.R. Berghahn, *Germany and the Approach of War in 1914*, New York, 1993, p.200.

68 J.J. Ruedorffer [Kurt Riezler], *Grundzüge der Weltpolitik in der Gegenwart*, Stuttgart-Berlin, 1914, pp.214-216, 219 and 221.

69 Riezler, *Tagebücher*, diary entries for 7 and 8 July, 1914, pp.183-184.

70 Müller, *Mars und Venus*, p.38.

71 Bernd Sösemann (ed.), *Theodor Wolff. Tagebücher 1914-1919*, Boppard am Rhein, 1984, vol.1, diary entry for 19 July 1917, pp.521-522. Hereafter cited as Wolff, *Tagebücher*.

72 *Ibid.*, diary entry for 24 May 1916, p.385.

73 *Ibid.*, diary entry for 7 July 1914, p.183.

74 Wolff, *Tagebücher*, vol.2, letter Riezler to Wolff, 21 March 1930, pp.950-951.

75 Riezler, *Tagebücher*, diary entry for 11 July 1914, p.185.

76 *Ibid.*, diary entry for 14 July 1914, p.185.

77 Fellner, 'Die Mission Hoyos', p .137.

78 Clark, *The Sleepwalkers*, pp.519-520.

79 Clark writes in his Conclusion (*ibid*, p.561): 'The outbreak of war in 1914 is not an Agatha Christie drama at the end of which we will discover the culprit standing over a corpse in the conservatory with a smoking pistol.'

80 John C.G. Röhl, *Wilhelm II: Into the Abyss of War and Exile 1900-1941*, Cambridge, 2014, p.1026.

81 Hew Strachan, *The Outbreak of the First World War*, Oxford, 2004, p.91.

82 Wilhelm Fraknói, *Die ungarische Regierung und die Entstehung des Weltkrieges*, Wien, 1919, pp.60-61.

83 Vermes, *István Tisza*, p.230.

84 Danilo Dimović, 'Iz mojih uspomena: Grof Stevan Tisa', *Preporod*, Beograd, 10 September 1922, p.7.

85 Ludwig Windischgraetz, *My Memoirs*, London, 1921, p.49.

86 Thallóczy, *Tagebücher*, diary entry for 3 July 1914, p.22.

87 Josef Galántai, 'Stefan Tisza und der Erste Weltkrieg', *Österreich in Geschichte und Literatur*, Wien, vol.10, 1964, pp.465-477.

88 *ÖUA*, vol.8, no.9978.

89 *ÖUA*, vol.7, no.8779.

90 Galántai, 'Stefan Tisza und der Erste Weltkrieg', pp.473 and 476.

91 Vermes, *István Tisza*, p.220.

92 *ÖUA*, vol.8, no.10118.

93 Galántai, 'Stefan Tisza und der Erste Weltkrieg', p.475.

94 *ÖUA*, vol.8, no.10272, Berchtold to the Emperor, 14 July 1914; Galántai, *Die Österreichisch-Ungarische Monarchie und der Weltkrieg*, p.273.

95 Leslie, 'The Antecedents of Austria-Hungary's War Aims', pp.342-343.

96 *DD*, no.50, report Tschirschky to Bethmann Hollweg, 14 July 1914; no.49, report Tschirschky to Bethmann Hollweg, 14 July 1914.

97 Marvin Benjamin Fried, 'A Life and Death Question: Austro-Hungarian War Aims in the First World War' in Holger Afflerbach (ed.), *The Purpose of the First World War: War Aims and Military Strategies*, Berlin-Boston, 2015, p.119.

98 Erényi, *Graf Stefan Tisza*, p.112.

99 Dimović, 'Iz mojih uspomena: Grof Stevan Tisa', *Preporod*, Beograd, 10 September 1922, p.7.

100 Kraler, 'Schlitter', diary entry for 11 July 1914, p.247.

101 Galántai, *Die Österreichisch-Ungarische*

Monarchie und der Weltkrieg, pp.267 and 274; Diószegi, 'Burián. Biographie und Tagebuchstelle', diary entries for 8 and 14 July 1914.

102 *DD*, no.49, Tschirschky to Bethmann-Hollweg, 14 July 1914.

103 'Die Interpellationen über Serbien und Bosnien', *Pester Lloyd*, Budapest, 16 July 1914 (Morgenblatt), p.3.

104 Thallóczy, *Tagebücher*, diary entry for 13 July 1914, p.43.

105 Friedrich Ritter von Wiesner, 'Meine Depesche vom 13. Juli 1914' in Eduard Ritter von Steinitz (ed.), *Rings um Sasonow*, Berlin, 1928, pp.173 and 175-176; Friedrich Ritter von Wiesner, 'Das Mémoire Österreich-Ungarns über die großserbische Propaganda und deren Zusammenhänge mit dem Sarajevoer Attentat', *Die Kriegsschuldfrage*, June 1927, p.499.

106 The translation is taken from Friedrich R. von Wiesner, 'The Forged and the Genuine Text of the *Wiesner Documents*', *Die Kriegsschuldfrage*, October 1925, p.653. Full text of the report is included in this article which is also published in German ('Die verfälschte und der echte Text des *Dokument* Wiesner') in the same issue of *Die Kriegsschuldfrage*, pp.641-648. The 13 July 1914 Wiesner report from Sarajevo likewise appears in *ÖUA*, vol.8, no.10252 and no.10253 (its continuation and end).

107 Wiesner, 'The Forged and the Genuine Text of the *Wiesner Documents*', pp.653-654.

108 Hoyos, *Der deutsch-englische Gegensatz*, p.77.

109 Williamson, *Austria-Hungary and the Origins of the First World War*, p.193. Williamson, admittedly, has a long footnote (n.9, p.246), but the sources he lists deal with the Sarajevo assassination plot and do not provide any backing whatsoever for his assertion about the involvement of 'some elements of the Serbian government'.

110 Hantsch, *Leopold Graf Berchtold*, vol.2, p.590. Hantsch mentions Wiesner's trip to Sarajevo, but not the report.

111 Rauchensteiner, *Der Erste Weltkrieg*, p.106.

112 McMeekin, *July 1914*, p.120.

113 Fay, *The Origins of the World War*, vol.2, p.239.

114 Clark, *The Sleepwalkers*, p.454.

115 Conrad, *Aus meiner Dienstzeit*, vol.4, p.83.

116 Schmitt, *The Coming of the War 1914*, vol.1, p.363.

117 *ÖUA*, vol.8, no.9976, note Berchtold to the Chief of General Staff, 1 July 1914.

118 *ÖUA*, vol.8, no.9995, note by Chief of General Staff, 2 July 1914.

119 Otte, *July Crisis*, p.57.

120 Williamson, *Austria-Hungary and the Origins of the First World War*, p.195.

121 *ÖUA*, vol.8, appendix to no.9984.

122 *ÖUA*, vol.8, no.9984.

123 Solomon Wank, 'Desperate Counsel in Vienna in July 1914: Berthold Molden's Unpublished Memorandum', *Central European History*, vol.26, no.3 (Autumn 1993), p.309; Diószegi, 'Burián. Biographie und Tagebuchstelle', diary entry for 14 July 1914, p.206.

124 *DD*, no.18, telegram Tschirschky, 7 July 1914.

125 *ÖUA*, vol.8, no.10393, record of a meeting of the Ministerial Council in Vienna, held on 19 July 1914.

126 Thálloczy, *Tagebücher*, diary entry for 19 July 1914, p.49.

127 Fritz Fellner, 'Zwischen Kriegsbegeisterung und Resignation – ein Memoransum des Sektionchefs Graf Forgách vom Jänner 1915' in Hermann Wiesflecker and Othmar Pickl (eds.), *Beiträge zur allgemeinen Geschichte*, Graz, 1975, p.154.

128 Norman Stone, 'Hungary and the Crisis of July 1914', *Journal of Contemporary History*, vol.1, no.3, July 1966, p.170.

129 Bridge, *From Sadiwa to Sarajevo*, p.378.

130 *ÖUA*, vol.7, no.9522, telegram Berchtold to Mérey, 26 March 1914.

131 Richard C. Hall, *Bulgaria's Road to the First World War*, Boulder, 1996, pp.269-270.

132 *ÖUA*, vol.8, no.10107, telegram Berchtold to Tarnowski, Sofia, 7 July 1914.

133 Conrad, *Aus meiner Dienstzeit*, vol.4, p.61.

134 John R. Schindler, *Fall of the Double Eagle: The Battle for Galicia and the Demise of Austria-Hungary*, Lincoln, 2015, p.101; Conrad, *Aus meiner Dienstzeit*, vol.4, p.40; Sondhaus, *Franz Conrad von Hötzendorf*, pp.142-143.

135 Conrad, *Aus meiner Dienstzeit*, vol.4, p.62.

136 *ÖUA*, vol.8, no.10272, Berchtold to Franz Joseph, 14 July 1914; no.10291, telegram Otto Czernin, 15 July 1914.

137 Müller, *Mars und Venus*, p.38.

138 Friedrich Graf Szápáry, 'Das Verhältnis Österreich-Ungarns zu Rußland' in Eduard Ritter von Steinitz (ed.), *Rings um Sasonow*, Berlin, 1928, pp.103-104.

139 Conrad, *Aus meiner Dienstzeit*, vol.4, p.57.

140 Kann, *Kaiser Franz Joseph und der Ausbruch des Weltkrieges*, p.12.

141 Miklós Komjáthy (ed.), *Protokolle des Gemeinsamen Ministerrates der Österreichisch-Ungarischen Monarchie 1914-1918*, Budapest, 1966, minutes of the Joint Ministerial Council meeting held in Vienna on 7 January 1916, p.370.

142 Lützow, *Im diplomatischen Dienst*, pp.219-219.
143 Redlich, *Schicksalsjahre*, vol.1, diary entry for 15 July 1914, p.613.
144 See, for example, *ÖUA*, vol.8, no.10215, report Szögyény, 12 July 1914.
145 *ÖUA*, vol.8, no.10393.
146 Thallóczy, *Tagebücher*, diary entry for 23 July 1914, p.53.
147 *ÖUA*, vol.8, no.10706. See also Seton-Watson, *Sarajevo*, pp.264-265.
148 Cited in Rauchesteiner, *Der erste Weltkrieg*, pp.103-104.
149 Michael Karolyi, *Faith Without Illusion*, London, 1956, p.56.

17 Serbia in the July Crisis

1 Elizabeth Hill, *The Spirit of Kossovo*, London, 1945, p.3.
2 Bogićević, *Stenogram*, pp.172-173.
3 Article reproduced in F.W. Harvey *et al.*, *The Lay of Kossovo: Serbia's Past and Present, 1389-1917*, n.p., 1917, p.32.
4 Seton-Watson, *Sarajevo*, p.101.
5 Taylor, *The Struggle for Mastery in Europe*, p.520, n.2. For this Taylor quotation employed recently by Serbian historians see, for example: Miloš Ković, 'Srbija u borbi za opstanak' in Čedomir Popov, Dragoljub R. Živojinović and Slobodan G. Marković (eds.), *Dva veka moderne srpske diplomatije*, Beograd, 2013, p.156; Mira Radojević and Ljubodrag Dimić, *Srbija u velikom ratu 1914-1918*, Beograd, 2014, p.73; Mile Bjelajac, *Zašto revizija? Stare i nove kontroverze o uzrocima Prvog svetskog rata*, Beograd, 2014, p.68.
6 Kranjčević, *Uspomene*, p.66.
7 Radoš Ljušić, *Princip Gavrilo (1895-1918). Ogled o nacionalnom heroju*, Beograd, 2014, pp.49 and 173.
8 Würthle, *Die Spur*, pp.21-22.
9 Clark, *The Sleepwalkers*, pp.23 and 51.
10 Štrandman, *Balkanske uspomene*, p.261.
11 *ÖUA*, vol.8, no.9943, p.211.
12 Dimitrije Bogdanović, *Knjiga o Kosovu*, Beograd, 1986, p.166.
13 Aleksandar-Aca Pavlović, *1914. Ljudi i događaji, ideje i ideali*, Beograd, 2002, p.7.
14 The descriptions here are based on the articles about the *Vidovdan* celebration in Belgrade ('Na Vidovdan' and 'Vidovdan u Beogradu') printed in the Belgrade daily *Pijemont*, 15 (28) June, p.2, and 16 (29) June 1914, p.3.
15 *Pijemont*, Beograd, 16 (29) June 1914, p.3.
16 Lončarević, *Jugoslaviens Enstehung*, pp.546-548.
17 *DD.*, vol.1, no.10, Griesinger to Bethmann Hollweg, 30 June 1914.
18 *BD*, vol. 11, Crackenthorpe to Grey, 2 July 1914, p.19.
19 Dejvid Mekenzi, *Stojan Protić srpski novinar i državnik*, Beograd, 2008, p.105.
20 *IBZI.*, vol.1/4, no.35, Hartwig to Sazonov, 30 June 1914, p.42
21 As reported in *Balkan*, Beograd, 20 June (3 July) 1914, article under the title 'Pogibija F. Ferdinanda', p.1.
22 Panta M. Draškić, *Moji memoari*, Beograd, 1990, p.76.
23 *Politika*, Beograd, 17 (30) June 1914, p.3.
24 Draškić, *Moji memoari*, pp.74-75.
25 Antić, *Beleške*, p.265-266.
26 Stojadinović, *Ni rat ni pakt*, p.67.
27 Vasilije Trbić, *Memoari*, Beograd, 1996, vol.2, p.41.
28 Cited in Hamilton Fish Armstrong, 'Three Days in Belgrade: July, 1914', *Foreign Affairs*, 5:1/4 (1926/1927), p.267.
29 *DSPKS*, vol.7/2, no.279, telegram Pašić, 28 June 1914.
30 *ÖUA*, vol.8, no.9973, report Jehlitschka, 1 July 1914.
31 In his *Sleepwalkers* Christopher Clark does not question (p.389) the reliability of this report and describes Pašić's alleged statement as 'an extraordinary gesture' – so soon after the Sarajevo assassination. Mark Cornwall, in his authoritative essay on Serbia during the July Crisis, is far more guarded and writes that Pašić 'appears to have made a speech in Skopje'. See Mark Cornwall, 'Serbia' in Keith Wilson (ed.), *Decisions for War 1914*, New York, 1995, p.56.
32 *DSPKS*, vol.7/2, nos.286 (29 June 1914), 287 (29 June 1914) and 294 (30 June 1914).
33 *DSPKS*, vol.7/2, no.296, telegram Jovanović, 30 June 1914.
34 *DSPKS*, vol.7/2, no.299, telegram Pašić, 1 July 1914.
35 *DSPKS*, vol.7/2, no.286, telegram Jovanović, 29 June 1914. See also nos. 294 (30 June), 303 (1 July) and 344 (6 July).
36 Jovičić, *Ustavi Kneževine i Kraljevine Srbije*, p.202.
37 See minute by Slavko Grujić in *DSPKS*, vol.7/2, no.344.
38 *DSPKS*, vol.7/2, no.312, draft telegram Pašić, 4 July 1914, and no.361, telegram Vesnić, 8 July 1914.
39 *DSPKS*, vol.7/2, no.347, confidential dispatch from the Foreign Ministry, Belgrade, to the War Ministry, Belgrade, 6 July 1914.
40 *DSPKS*, vol.7/2, no.332, telegram Špalajković, 4 July 1914.

41 *DSPKS*, vol.7/2, no.337, telegram Vesnić, 4 July 1914.

42 *DSPKS*, vol.7/2, no.355, telegram Jovanović, 7 July 1914.

43 *IBZI*, vol.1/4, telegram Sazonov to Hartwig, 7 July 1914.

44 *IBZI.*, vol.1/4, telegram Hartwig to Sazonov, 9 July 1914.

45 Štrandman, *Balkanske uspomene*, pp.260 and 262.

46 *IBZI.*, vol.1/4, letter Hartwig to Trubetskoi, 30 June 1914.

47 Giesl, *Zwei Jahrzente*, p.260.

48 Štrandman, *Balkanske uspomene*, p.291.

49 *ÖUA*, vol.8, appendix to no.10235, report Storck to Giesl, 12 July 1914. A similar version of Hartwig's reaction is in *DD.*, vol.1, no.10, letter Griesinger to Bethmann Hollweg, 30 June 1914.

50 Cornwall, 'Serbia', pp.60 and 68.

51 *DSPKS*, vol.7/2, no.435, report Jovanović, 15 July 1914.

52 *ÖUA*, vol.8, no.10191, telegram Giesl, 11 July 1914.

53 *ÖUA*, vol.8, no.10213, telegram Giesl, 12 July 1914; no.10230, telegram Berchtold, 13 July 1914; no.10231, telegram Giesl, 13 July 1914.

54 'G. general Gizl', *Politika*, Beograd, 3 (16) July 1914, p.1.

55 *DSPKS*, vol.7/2, nos. 379 (10 July 1914) and 380 (10 July 1914).

56 *DSPKS*, vol.7/2, no.390, report Mulutin Jovanović, 11 July 1914.

57 *DSPKS*, vol.7/2, no.396, telegram Pašić, 14 July 1914.

58 *DSPKS*, vol.7/2, no.415, telegram Pašić, 14 July 1914.

59 *IBZI.*, vol.1/4, no.238, letter Strandtmann to Sazonov, 15 July 1914.

60 *DSPKS*, vol.7/2, no.449, telegram Bošković, 16 July 1914.

61 *DSPKS*, vol.7/2, nos.450 and 451, telegrams Mihajlović, 17 July 1914.

62 'Tisin odgovor', *Politika*, Beograd, 3 (16) July 1914.

63 Cornwall, 'Serbia', p.69.

64 *DSPKS*, vol.7/2, no.462, telegram Pašić, 18 July 1914.

65 *IBZI.*, vol.1/4, no.286, telegram Strandtmann to Sazonov, 19 July 1914.

66 Štrandman, *Balkanske uspomene*, p.286.

67 *DSPKS*, vol.7/2, no.463, telegram Jovanović, 20 July 1914.

68 Slavko Grujić, 'Od austro-ugarskog ultimatuma do objave rata Srbiji', *Politika*, Beograd, 22, 23, 24 and 25 July 1934.

69 Mićić, 'Srpski oficiri', p.40.

70 Grujić, 'Od austro-ugarskog ultimatuma do objave rata Srbiji', *Politika*, Beograd, 22 July 1934.

71 *Ibid.*, 23 July 1934.

72 *Diplomatska prepiska o srpsko-austrijskom sukobu*, Niš, 1914, no.33. Only the Serbian Legation in Vienna had been excepted from this circular.

73 Cornwall, 'Serbia', p.73; Mombauer, *Diplomatic and military documents*, pp.307-308.

74 Dušan P. Stefanović, 'Pred buru' in Slobodan Ž. Vidaković (ed.), *Agonija Beograda u svetskom ratu 1914-1915*, Beograd, 1931, pp.3-4.

75 Jovanović, 'The Murder of Sarajevo', p.14.

76 Štrandman, *Balkanske uspomene*, pp.293-294.

77 'Austrijska nota', *Politika*, Beograd, 10 (23) July 1914, p.2.

78 *DD.*, vol.1, no.159, telegram Griesinger, 24 july 1914.

79 Günther Kronenebitter, 'Die Macht der Illusionen. Julikrise und Kriegsausbruch 1914 aus der Sicht des deutschen Militärattachés in Wien', *Militärgeschichtliche Mitteilungen*, Oldenbourg, 57 (1998) 2, p.536.

80 Grujić, 'Od austro-ugarskog ultimatuma do objave rata Srbiji', *Politika*, Beograd, 23 July, 1934, p.2.

81 *BD.*, vol.11, no.92, telegram Crackanthorpe to Grey, 24 July 1914.

82 Štrandman, *Balkanske uspomene*, pp.299-301.

83 *Ibid.*, p.302.

84 *IBZI.*, vol.1/5, Beilage 8, p.354; Cornwall, 'Serbia', p.75; Štrandman, *Balkanske uspomene*, p.302. Strandtmann communicated the official version of his encounter with Pašić in a telegram to Sazonov: *IBZI*, vol. 1/5, no.35, Strandtmann to the Foreign Minister, 24 July 1914. The contents of the telegram do not differ in essential details from those in Strandtmann's memoir, except that Pašić's words: '... whatever the answer to the telegram which the Crown Prince has sent to the Tsar' are not included.

85 *IBZI.*, vol.1/5, no 37, personal telegram Regent Alexander to Nicholas II, 24 July 1914.

86 Grujić, 'Od austro-ugarskog ultimatuma do objave rata Srbiji', *Politika*, Beograd, 24 July 1934, p.1.

87 Stefanović, 'Pred buru', p.4.

88 Grujić, 'Od austro-ugarskog ultimatuma do objave rata Srbiji', *Politika*, Beograd, 24 July 1934, p.1.

89 Novica Rakočević, *Crna Gora u Prvom svjetskom ratu 1914-1918*, Cetinje, 1969, pp.26-27 and 30.

90 *ÖUA*, vol.8, no.10594, telegram Otto, 24 July 1914.

91 Rakočević, *Crna Gora u Prvom svjetskom ratu*, pp.32-33.

92 *IBZI.*, vol.5/1, no.77, telegram Giers to Sazonov, 25 July 1914.

93 *ÖUA*, vol.8, no.10486, report Otto, 22 July 1914.

94 Hall, *Bulgaria's Road to the First World War*, p.287.

95 *Ibid.*

96 *DSPKS*, vol.7/2, no.488, telegram Paču to Čolak-Antić, 23 July 1914.

97 *DSPKS*, vol.7/2, no.518, telegram Stanojević to Pašić, 24 July 1914.

98 Miladin Milošević, *Srbija i Grčka 1914-1918*, Zaječar, 1997, appendix 1, p.306.

99 *Ibid.*, pp-21-22.

100 *DSPKS*, vol.7/2, no.534, telegram Balugdžić to Pašić, 25 July 1914.

101 *DSPKS*, vol.7/2, no.500, telegram Pašić, 24 July 1914.

102 Clark, *The Sleepwalkers*, p.461. Clark provides no source for this assertion.

103 Grujić, 'Od austro-ugarskog ultimatuma do objave rata Srbiji', *Politika*, Beograd, 24 July 1934.

104 Clark, *The Sleepwalkers*, p.461. Again, Clark has not attached a footnote here.

105 *DSPKS*, vol.7/2, no.501, telegram Pašić to Spalajković, 24 July 1914.

106 *GP*, vol.38, no.15555, Flotow to Bethmann Hollweg, 10 July 1914.

107 Bosworth, *Italy, the Least of the Great Powers*, pp.377-394.

108 *DSPKS*, vol.7/2, no.483, telegram Mihajlović, 22 July 1914.

109 Keith Wilson, 'Britain' in Keith Wilson (ed.), *Decisions for War 1914*, New York, 1995, p.183.

110 *BD*, vol.11, no.91, Grey to de Bunsen, 24 July 1914.

111 *BD*, vol.11, no.68, Grey to Rumbold, 20 July 1914.

112 *DSPKS*, vol.7/2, no.536, telegram Bošković, 24 July 1914.

113 *BD*, vol.11, no.102, telegram Grey to Crackanthorpe, 24 July 1914.

114 *ÖUA*, vol.8, no.10294, report Giesl, 16 July 1914.

115 *IBZI.*, vol.1/4, no.238, letter Strandtmann to Sazonov, 15 July 1914; Štrandman, *Balkanske uspomene*, pp.273 and 281.

116 Maurice Paléologue, *An Ambassador's Memoirs*, London, 1925, vol.1, p.19.

117 *DSPKS*, vol.7/2, no.484, telegram Spalajković, 22 July 1914. At this reception in St Petersburg, Poincaré had spoken quite sharply to Count Friedrich Szápáry, the Austro-Hungarian Ambassador. As they touched on the subject of Serbia, Szápáry said that the judicial enquiry was proceeding, whereupon Poincaré remarked: 'Of course I'm anxious about the results of this enquiry, *Monsieur l'Ambassadeur*. I can remember two previous enquiries which did not improve your relations with Serbia ... Don't you remember ... the Friedjung affair and the Prochaska affair?' For good measure, he added: 'Serbia has some very warm friends in the Russian people. And Russia has an ally, France.' See Paléologue, *An Ambassador's Memoirs*, vol.1, pp.18-19.

118 *DSPKS*, vol.7/2, no.513, telegram Jovanović, 24 July 1914.

119 *DSPKS*, vol.7/2, no.518, telegram Stanojević, 24 July 1914.

120 *DSPKS*, vol.7/2, no.529, telegram Vesnić, 24 July 1914.

121 *ÖUA*, vol.7, no.9279, report Otto Czernin, 30 January 1914. Otto Czernin, serving at the Austro-Hungarian Embassy in St Petersburg, should not be confused with his more famous elder brother Ottokar Czernin.

18 Critical Days in Belgrade

1 Richard C. Hall, 'Serbia' in Richard F. Hamilton and Holger H. Herwig, *The Origins of World War I*, Cambridge, 2003, p.110.

2 Vansittart, *The Mist Procession*, p.123.

3 Winston S. Churchill, *The World Crisis 1911-1914*, London, 1923, p.193.

4 Antonio Salandra, *Italy and the Great War: From Neutrality to Intervention*, London, 1932, pp.49-50.

5 Wolff, *Tagebücher*, vol.1, entry for 31 January 1916, p.342.

6 Bulow, *Memoirs 1909-1919*, p.205.

7 Lončarević, *Jugoslaviens Enstehung*, p.608.

8 Giesl, *Zwei Jahrzente*, pp.267-268. Giesl repeated these points in 'Konnte die Annahme der serbische Antwortnote den Ausbruch des Weltkrieges verhindern?', *Berliner Monatshefte*, May 1933, p.465.

9 Alfred von Wegerer, *Der entscheidende Schritt in den Weltkrieg*, Berlin, 1931. See, in particular, pp.44-53.

10 Jules Isaac, *Un débat historique. Le problème des Origins de la Guerre*, Paris, 1933, pp.122-124.

11 Albertini, *The Origins of the War of 1914*, vol.2, pp.360-361. In 1933 an interview with Berchtold was published, in which he claimed that the Serbs were on the

12 Lieven, *Russia and the Origins of the First World War*, p.144.

13 Samuel R. Williamson, Jr., 'The Origins of World War I', *The Journal of Interdisciplinary History*, vol.18, no.4, Spring 1988, p.811.

14 Cornwall, 'Serbia', p.84.

15 William Jannen Jr., *The Lions of July: Prelude to War, 1914*, Novato, 1996, p.100.

16 Clark, *The Sleepwalkers*, p.463 and n.35, p.649.

17 MacMillan, *The War That Ended Peace*, p.537.

18 McMeekin, *July 1914*, pp.198-199.

19 Annika Mombauer, *Die Julikrise. Europas Weg in den Ersten Weltkrieg*, München, 2014, p.65.

20 Rauchensteiner, *Der Erste Weltkrieg*, p.118; Manfried Rauchensteiner, *Der Tod des Doppeladlers. Österreich-Ungarn und der Erste Weltkrieg*, Graz-Wien-Köln, 1997, p.85.

21 Gerd Krumeich, *Juli 1914. Eine Bilanz*, Paderborn-München-Wien-Zürich, 2014, p.128.

22 Otte, *July Crisis*, pp.238-239.

23 Martel, *The Month That Changed the World*, pp.204-205.

24 *ÖUA*, vol.8, no.10461, telegram Szápáry, 21 July 1914.

25 George F. Kennan, *Russia Leaves the War*, Princeton, 1956, p.336.

26 Albertini, *The Origins of the War of 1914*, vol.2, pp.352-353.

27 Alfred Rappaport von Argenbau, 'Staatsmänner und Diplomaten der Vorkriegszeit. Spalajković', *Berliner Monatshefte*, July 1935, pp.555-576.

28 Clark, *The Sleepwalkers*, p.359.

29 Seton-Watson, *The Southern Slav Question*, pp.263-271.

30 Nekludoff, *Diplomatic Reminiscences*, p.53.

31 *ÖUA*, vol.8, no.10999, telegram Szápáry, 29 July 1914.

32 *DSPKS*, vol.7/2, no.477, telegram Spalajković, 22 July 1914. In fact, it was in the form of an aide-mémoire that Spalajković notified Sazonov, on 22 July, about Pašić's circular of 18 July. See *IBZI.*, vol.1/4, no.319.

33 *DSPKS*, vol.7/2, no.496, telegram Spalajković, 23 July 1914.

34 *BD*, vol.11, nos. 92 and 94, Crackanthorpe to Grey, 24 July 1914.

35 *DSPKS*, vol.7/2, no.502, telegram Pašić, 24 July 1914.

36 M. Spalaïkovitch, 'Une journée du Ministre de Serbie à Pétrograd. Le 24 juillet 1914', *Revue d'histoire diplomatique*, Paris, April-June 1934, p.138.

37 *DD*, vol.1, no.148, telegram Pourtalès, 24 July 1914. The conversations at the French Embassy had begun 'at noon', according to Sir George Buchanan, the British Ambassador. See George Buchanan, *My Mision to Russia and Other Diplomatic Memories*, London, 1923, vol.1, p.192. Paléologue, the French Ambassador, writes that Sazonov had left at 'three o'clock' to go to Ielaguin Island, where the Ministerial Council meeting was going to be held. See Paléologue, *An Ambassador's Memoirs*, vol.1, p.32.

38 *IBZI.*, vol.1/5, no.25. Albertini asserts that on 24 July 'Spalajković saw Sazonov or his representative twice before the Cabinet meeting', i.e., before he saw him for the third time in the evening. Based on Sazonov's timetable for 24 July, it is impossible to see just when, before the evening, he could have received Spalajković. The latter may well have seen a representative of Sazonov in the afternoon hours as he waited for the Cabinet meeting to come to an end. But it seems most unlikely that Spalajković was sending any telegrams to Belgrade that afternoon – another claim made by Albertini. Indeed, the Serbian documents do not contain any telegrams from him sent before midnight on 24/25 July. See Albertini, *The Origins of the War of 1914*, vol.2, p.354.

39 The citations are from the English translation of the relevant passages in the diary of the Russian Foreign Ministry. See *How the War Began in 1914*, London, 1925, pp.30-31.

40 Serge Sazonov, *Fateful Years 1909-1916*, London, 1928, p.177.

41 Cornwall, 'Serbia', p.79.

42 Spalaïkovitch, 'Une journée', p.139.

43 *Ibid.*, pp.139-140.

44 N. Schebeko, *Souvenirs. Essai historique sur les origines de la guerre de 1914*, Paris, 1936, p.218.

45 Spalaïkovitch, 'Une journée', p.140.

46 *Ibid.*, pp.140-141.

47 *Ibid.*, pp.142-143.

48 See the note by the editors of the relevant volume of Serbian documents, *DSPKS*, vol.7/2, no.527, n.1, p.649.

49 *DSPKS*, vol.7/2, no.527, telegram Spalajković. The dispatch date and time of this telegram are given as 24 July 1914 at 12 a.m. – '24. VII 1914. u 12 sati – min. pre

podne'. This is clearly a mistake as Spalajković was reporting on his 24 July talk with Sazonov – the correct date is 25 July, that is, around midnight on 24/25 July.

50 Cornwall, 'Serbia', p.80.

51 See the note by the editors, *DSPKS*, vol.7/2, no.527, n.1, p.649.

52 Cornwall, 'Serbia', p.80 and p.94, n.149.

53 *DSPKS*, vol.7/2, no.503, telegram Spalajković, 25 July 1914. Mark Cornwall points out that this telegram is incorrectly dated as 24 July, Cornwall, 'Serbia', p.94, n.152. Since it was sent at 1:40 a.m. (received at 11:30), and since it clearly refers to the events of 24 July, its date of dispatch can indeed only be 25 July.

54 *IBZI.*, vol.1/5, no.51.

55 Seton-Watson, *Sarajevo*, p.257 and n.4 on the same page.

56 Armstrong, *Peace and Counterpeace*, p.363.

57 Cornwall, 'Serbia', pp.80-81.

58 Albertini, *The Origins of the War of 1914*, vol.2, p.353.

59 Clark, *The Sleepwalkers*, p.649, n.35.

60 McMeekin, *July 1914*, pp.199-200.

61 Luciano Magrini, *Il drama di Seraievo. Origini e responsabilità della guerra europea*, Milano, 1929 pp.203-205.

62 *Ibid.*, p.206.

63 Albertini, *The Origins of the War of 1914*, vol.2, p.353.

64 Clark, *The Sleepwalkers*, p.649, n.35.

65 McMeekin, *July 1914*, p.199.

66 *Ibid.*, pp.185-186 and p.414, n.12 to 'Notes to Chapter 14'.

67 Arhiv SANU, 8701, Dnevnici i hartije ministra vojnog Dušana Stefanovića, letter Pavlović to Dušan Stefanović, 16 July 1931.

68 Albertini, *The Origins of the War of 1914*, vol.2, p.356.

69 Arhiv SANU, 8701, letter Pavlović to Dušan Stefanović, 16 July 1931.

70 Stefanović, 'Pred buru', p.7.

71 *Ibid.*, p.352.

72 Stefanović, 'Pred buru', p.4; Rudolf Kißling, 'Die serbische Mobilmachung im Juli 1914', *Berliner Monatshefte*, July 1932, p.678.

73 Mile S. Bjelajac, *Generali i admirali Kraljevine Jugoslavije 1918-1941*, Beograd, 2004, p.239.

74 Pavlović was an altogether serious officer and also, after the war, a noted military historian, publishing a major study of the battles between Serbia and Austria-Hungary during August 1914. See Živko G. Pavlović, *Bitka na Jadru avgusta 1914 god.*, Beograd, 1924.

75 Jovan V. Nestorović, 'Prisebnost' in *Spomenica Nikole P. Pašića 1845-1925*, Beograd, 1926, p.123.

76 'Ozbiljni trenutci', *Samouprava*, Beograd, 12 (25) July 1914, p.1.

77 Albertini, *The Origins of the War of 1914*, vol.2, pp.358-359.

78 *Diplomatska prepiska o srpsko-austrijskom sukobu*, no.38, telegram Pašić, 12 (25) July 1914. This telegram is also in *DSPKS*, vol.7/2, no.537.

79 *BD.*, vol.11, no.114, telegram Crackanthorpe to Grey.

80 Cornwall, 'Serbia', p.81.

81 *DSPKS*, vol.7/2, no.495, report Vesnić, 23 July 1914.

82 Štrandman, *Balkanske uspomene*, p.306.

83 *Documents diplomatiques français*, Paris, 1936, 3rd series, vol.11, no.63, telegram Boppe to Bienvenu-Martin, 25 July 1914. Hereafter cited as *DDF*.

84 *IBZI.*, vol.1/5, no.22, telegram Sazonov to Strandtmann, 24 July 1914.

85 Štrandman, *Balkanske uspomene*, pp.309-310.

86 *IBZI.*, vol.1/5, no.23, Sazonov circular, 24 July 1914.

87 Štrandman, *Balkanske uspomene*, p.309.

88 Paul Ham, *1914: The Year the World Ended*, London, 2013, p.306.

89 Clark, *The Sleepwalkers*, p.463.

90 McMeekin, *July 1914*, p.200.

91 Albertini, *The Origins of the War of 1914*, vol.2, pp.363-364.

92 Slavko Gruić, 'Persönliche Erinnerungen aus der Julikrisis 1914', *Berliner Monatshefte*, July 1935 pp.576-597. Grujić's surname is spelled in the *Berliner Monatshefte* without the letter 'j', which is how Albertini also spells it. Had he really talked to Grujić, he would have received from him a *carte de visite* with the correct spelling. Interestingly, Albertini does not include this article in his bibliography.

93 Grujić, 'Od austro-ugarskog ultimatuma do objave rata Srbiji', *Politika*, Beograd, 24 July 1934, p.1-2.

94 Štrandman, *Balkanske uspomene*, p.308.

95 Savinsky, *Recollections*, p.238.

96 Žujović, *Dnevnik*, vol.2, p.58.

97 Grujić, 'Od austro-ugarskog ultimatuma do objave rata Srbiji', *Politika*, Beograd, 24 July 1934, p.2.

98 *Ibid.*, p.1.

99 Pavlović, *1914: Ljudi i događaji*, p.64.

100 HHStA, P.A. I/811.

101 *ÖUA*, vol.8, attachment to no.10648.

102 Pavlović, *1914: Ljudi i događaji*, p.64.

103 Velizar Janković, 'Jedna tendenciozna

kampanja', *Politika*, Beograd, 10 July 1931, p.2; Giesl, *Zwei Jahrzente*, p.268; Stefanović, 'Pred buru', p.7.

104 Giesl, *Zwei Jahrzente*, pp.268-269.

105 Wilson, *The War Guilt*, p.317.

106 J.A.R. Marriott, *The European Commonwealth: Problems Historical and Diplomatic*, Oxford, 1918, p.294.

107 Fay, *The Origins of the World War*, vol.2, pp.341-342.

108 Strandman, *Balkanske uspomene*, p.314.

109 *ÖUA*, vol.8, no.10860, circular to Athens and all the other missions, 28 July 1914. Even Roderich Gooß, a postwar academic defender of Austria-Hungary, admitted that point 5 of the ultimatum had failed to specify the manner and, 'in particular', the duration of the collaboration with the Austro-Hungarian authorities on Serbian soil. See Gooß, *Das österreichisch-serbische Problem*, p.280.

110 Léon Savadjian, *Les origines et les responsabilités de la guerre mondiale*, Paris, 1933, p.59.

111 See, for example, Friedrich von Wiesner, 'Milan Ciganović', *Die Krigsschuldfrage*, November 1927, p.1046. Joachim Remak (*Sarajevo*, p.208) states that it was 'absolutely essential' to keep Ciganović from talking to the Austrians. Christopher Clark (*The Sleepwalkers*, p.465) accepts the theory about Ciganović being protected by the Serbian authorities. Ciganović's fame grew considerably greater after the war. In 1925 Miloš Bogićević, the ex-Serbian diplomat turned apostate, published an article where he alleged that Ciganović had 'introduced' the assassins to Lieutenant-Colonel Dimitrijević and Major Tankosić, but also that he had at the same time been a 'confidant' (*Vertrauensmann*) of the Serbian Government. See [Miloš] Boghitschewitsch, 'Weitere Einzelheiten über das Attentat von Sarajevo', *Die Kriegsschuldfrage*, July 1925, p.440. Though unsubstantiated, this was great news for German and Austrian propagandists. Friedrich von Wiesner, the Ballhausplatz legal expert famous for his July 1914 report to Vienna in which he could not point at the complicity in the assassination of the Serbian Government, described Ciganović in his 1927 article as 'the actual organizer of the assassination' (p.1045). More important, Wiesner followed Bogićević in suggesting that Ciganović had also worked for the Serbian Government as its spy in the ranks of the Black Hand. Thus, according to Wiesner, the Serbian Government knew about the Sarajevo assassination because its man Ciganović had – amazingly – organized the whole enterprise with its knowledge and on behalf of the Black Hand. In Wiesner's interpretation, therefore, the Serbian Government and the Black Hand appear to have acted in cahoots to eliminate Franz Ferdinand. The question why, then, if the Black Hand was such a good ally there should be a need to spy on it in the first place was of course not tackled by Wiesner. The problem for all the proponents of the theory about a large Serbian conspiracy behind the Sarajevo assassination, is their desire to have it both ways: to insist that the Black Hand, or the nationalist circles in the Serbian military, represented an independent power factor, constantly threatening Pašić and his Government; and yet to also suggest, not least by highlighting the case of Ciganović, that the two would have been quite happy to cooperate in such a sensitive matter as had been the preparation of the assassination in Sarajevo.

112 Jovanović, *The Murder of Sarajevo*, p.7.

113 Andrej Mitrović, *Serbia's Great War 1914-1918*, London, 2007, p.46.

114 The text of the ultimatum can be found, *inter alia*, in *ÖUA*, vol.8, no.10395; the Serbian reply is in *ÖUA*, vol.8, no.10648; the remarks of the Ballhausplatz on the individual points in the Serbian reply are in *ÖUA*, vol.8, no.10860, as well as in *BD*, vol.11, Appendix B.

115 Savadjian, *Les origines et les responsibilités de la guerre mondiale*, p.60.

116 Musulin, *Das Haus am Ballplatz*, p.241.

117 *IBZI.*, vol.1/5, no.119, circular telegram Sazonov to Paris, London, Vienna, Rome, Constantinople and Berlin, 27 July 1914.

118 *DSPKS*, vol.7/2, no.586, telegram Vesnić, 27 July 1914.

119 *ÖUA*, vol.8, no.10739, telegram Szécsen 26 July 1914.

120 *DDF*, vol.11, no.147, circular telegram Bienvenu-Martin to Berlin, London, St Petersburg, Vienna and Rome, 27 July 1914.

121 *DSPKS*, vol.7/2, no.594, telegram Mihajlović, 27 July 1914.

122 *DSPKS*, vol.7/2, no.562, telegram Čolak-Antić, 26 July 1914.

123 Imanuel Geiss (ed.), *July 1914. The Outbreak of the First World War: Selected Documents*, New York, 1974, p.222; *DD*, no.271,

Antwortnote der serbischen Regierung auf das österreichisch-ungarische Ultimaatum.

124 Vansittart, *The Mist Procession*, p.124.

125 *BD*, vol.11, no.171, Nicolson to Grey; 27 July 1914; minute Crowe, 28 July 1914.

126 *BD*, vol.11, no.188, Grey to de Bunsen, 27 July 1914.

127 Clark, *The Sleepwalkers*, p.466; Otte, *July Crisis*, p.282.

128 *ÖUA*, vol.8, no.10855, Berchtold to Franz Joseph, 27 July 1914.

129 Clark, *The Sleepwalkers*, p.465.

130 Fay, *The Origins of the World War*, vol.2, p.348.

131 Schmitt, *The Coming of the War 1914*, vol.1, p.539.

132 Biliński, *Wspomnienia*, vol.1, p.292.

133 Redlich, *Schicksalsjahre*, vol.1, diary entry for 3 August 1914, p.620.

134 Plener, *Erinnerungen*, vol.3, p.438.

135 Lützow, *Im diplomatischen Dienst*, p.227.

136 Giesl, *Zwei Jahrzente*, p.270.

137 *DSKPS*, vol.7/2, no.539.

138 Pavlović, *1914: Ljudi i događaji*, p.64.

139 *IBZI.*, vol.1/5, Appendix 8, telegram Strandtmann to Sazonov, 6 August 1914; Štrandman, *Balkanske Uspomene*, p.314.

140 Štrandman, *Balkanske Uspomene*, p.314.

141 Wegerer, *Der entscheidende Schritt*, p.44; Albertini, *The Origins of the War of 1914*, vol.2, p.363. n.2; Rauchensteiner, *Der erste Welkrieg*, p.118; McMeekin, *July 1914*, pp.200-201.

142 *DD*, vol.1, no.158, telegram Griesinger, 24 July 1914.

143 Stefanović, 'Pred buru', p.6.

144 One of the wildest claims made by a historian about the Serbian mobilization is that by Graydon Tunstall, who writes that 'Serbia had commenced full mobilization measures three hours prior to receipt of the Austro-Hungarian note.' That would make it at 3 p.m. on 23 July. No supporting evidence whatsoever is given. See Graydon A. Tunstall, Jr., 'Austria-Hungary' in Richard F. Hamilton and Holger H. Herwig (eds.), *The Origins of World War I*, Cambridge, 2003, p.142.

145 *Ibid.*

146 Bjelajac, *Zašto revizija?*, p.179.

147 *BD*, vol.11, no.130, telegram Crackanthorpe to Grey, 25 July 1914.

148 Lončarević, *Jugoslaviens Entstehung*, pp.609-610.

149 Conrad, *Aus meiner Dienstzeit*, vol.4, pp.109-110.

150 Roderich Gooss, *Das Wiener Kabinet und die Entstehung des Weltkrieges*, Wien, 1919,

p.216; *ÖUA*, vol.8, no.10708, Tisza to Franz Joseph, 25 July 1914.

151 Margutti, *Kaiser Franz Joseph*, p.413.

152 *ÖUA*, vol.8, no.10646; Galántai, *Die Österreichisch-Ungarische Monarchie ind der Weltkrieg*, p.344; Margutti, *Kaiser Franz Joseph*, pp.413-415.

153 Alexander von Krobatin, 'Aus meinen Erinnerungen an den Kaiser' in Steinitz, *Erinnerungen an Franz Joseph I*, p.325.

154 Conrad, *Aus meiner Dienstzeit*, vol.4, p.122.

155 Galántai, *Die Österreichisch-Ungarische Monarchie und der Weltkrieg*, p.346.

156 Redlich, *Schicksalsjahre*, vol.1, diary entry for 26 July 1914, p.616.

157 'Die Nachricht unseres Spezialkorrespondenten', *Neue Freie Presse*, Wien, 25 July 1914 (Abendblatt), p.1.

158 Thallóczy, *Tagebücher*, diary entry for 25 July 1914, pp.57 and 59.

159 Kraler, 'Schlitter', diary entry for 25 July 1914, p.253.

160 *BD*, vol.11, no.676, report de Bunsen to Grey, 1 September 1914.

161 Szilassy, *Der Untergang*, p.266.

162 *DSPKS*, vol.7/2, no.540, Pašić circular, 25 July 1914. The time of dispatch of this telegram is not given.

163 Cornwall, 'Serbia', p.82.

164 *DSPKS*, vol.7/2, no.556, telegram Spalajković, 26 July 1914, dispatched at 2.55 a.m.; no.559, telegram Spalajković, 25 July 1914, dispatched at 3.22 p.m., received at 2.40 a.m. on 26 July; no.570, telegram Spalajković, 25 July 1914, dispatched at 8 p.m., received on 26 July, but no exact time is given. Christopher Clark wrongly gives the number of this last telegram (no.570) as no.556, and although he states correctly that it had been dispatched at 8 p.m. on 25 July, he seems to treat it in the context of what he explains as the 'steady crescendo' of Spalajković's cables which had encouraged the Serbian Government to stiffen its attitude before composing its reply to the ultimatum. See Clark, *The Sleepwalkers*, pp.462-463 and p.649, n.33 and n.35.

165 *IBZI*, vol.1/5, no.49, telegram Sazonov to Strandtmann, 25 July 1914.

166 Štrandman, *Balkanske uspomene*, pp.318 and 321-322.

167 *IBZI*, vol.1/5, no.149, telegram Strandtmann to Sazonov, 27 July 1914.

168 Štrandman, *Balkanske uspomene*, pp.323-324.

169 Freiherr von Griesinger, 'Die kritischen Tage in Serbien', *Berliner Monatshefte*, September 1930, p.843.

170 *Ibid.*, p.844.
171 *DSPKS*, vol.7/2, no. 588, minute Pašić, 27 July 1914.
172 'Die Bulgarischen Dokumenten zum Kriegsausbruch 1914', *Die Kriegsschuldfrage*, March 1928, pp.244-245, Tschapraschikow to the Bulgarian Foreign Minister, 27 July 1914.
173 *IBZI*, vol.1/5, no.37.
174 *IBZI*, vol.1/5, no.120, telegram Nicholas II to Crown Prince Alexander, 27 July 1914. Also in *DSPKS*, vol.7/2, no.604, which has the text of the Tsar's telegram in French.
175 Štrandman, *Balkanske uspomene*, pp.327-328.
176 Albertini, *The Origins of the War of 1914*, vol.2, pp.376-389.
177 See Hantsch, *Leopold Graf Berchtold*, vol.2, pp.612-616.
178 *ÖUA*, vol.8, no.10714, circular telegrram, 26 July 1914.
179 *ÖUA*, vol.8, no.10772, private letter Hoyos to Schiessl, 26 July 1914.
180 Kraler, 'Schlitter', diary entry for 27 July 1914, p.254.
181 *ÖUA*, vol.8, no.10855, Berchtold to Franz Joseph, 27 July 1914.
182 Fellner, 'Austria-Hungary', p.16.
183 Samuel R. Williamson, Jr., 'Leopold Count Berchtold: The Man Who Could Have Prevented the Great War' in Günter Bischof and Fritz Plasser (eds.), *From Empire to Republic: Post-World War I Austria*, New Orleans and Innsbruck, 2010, p.24.
184 Thallóczy, *Tagebücher*, diary entry for 23 July 1914, p.55.
185 Krobatin, 'Aus meinen Erinnerungen an den Kaiser', p.325.
186 Margutti, *Kaiser Franz Joseph*, p.415.
187 Kann, *Kaiser Franz Joseph und der Ausbruch des Weltkrieges*, p.16.
188 *ÖUA*, vol.8, no.10855, Berchtold to Franz Joseph, 27 July 1914.
189 Gooss, *Das Wiener Kabinett*, pp.218-219.
190 *ÖUA*, vol.8, no.11015, Berchtold to Franz Joseph, 29 July 1914; *DD*, no.313, telegram Tschirschky 28 July 1914.
191 Gooss, *Das Wiener Kabinett*, p.220.
192 Štrandman, *Balkanske uspomene*, p.327.
193 Griesinger, 'Die kritischen Tage in Serbien', pp.846-847;
194 *DSPKS*, vol.7/2, no. 629, telegram Pašić, 28 July 1914.
195 Olaf Richard Wulff, *Die österreichisch-ungarische Donauflotille im Weltkriege 1914-1918*, Wien-Leipzig, 1934, p.32.
196 Nikola B. Popović, *Srbija i carska Rusija*, Beograd, 2007, p.137.
197 John R. Schindler, 'Disaster on the Drina: The Austro-Hungarian Army in Serbia, 1914', *War in History*, 2002, 9:159, p.177; Edmund Glaise-Horstenau (ed.), *Österreich-Ungarns letzter Krieg 1914-1918*, Wien, 1930, vol.1, p.151, n.1.
198 Broucek, *Jansa*, pp.232 and 246.
199 Lützow, *Im diplomatischen Dienst*, p.237.

Conclusion

1 Paul W. Schroeder, 'World War I as Galloping Gertie: A Reply to Joachim Remak', *The Journal of Modern History*, vol.44, no.3 (September 1972), p.345
2 Jov. Ristić, *Spoljašnji odnošaji Srbije novijeg vremena*, Beograd, 1901, vol.3, pp.140-146; Vasa Čubrilović, *Bosanski ustanak 1876-1878*, Beograd, 1930, pp.179-181.
3 Macartney, *The Habsburg Empire*, p.805.
4 Clark, *The Sleepwalkers*, p.559.
5 David Reynolds, *The Long Shadow: The Great War and the Twentieth Century*, London, 2013, p.xix.
6 Clark, *The Sleepwalkers*, pp.356 and 558.
7 McMeekin, *The Russian Origins of the First World War*, p.42.
8 Taylor, *The Struggle for Mastery in Europe*, p.521 and n.1 on the same page.
9 Kronenbitter, 'Krieg im Frieden', p.528.
10 Mayr-Harting, *Der Untergang*, p.918.
11 S.M. Štedimlija, *Auf dem Balkan*, Zagreb, 1943, p.56.
12 Taylor, *The Habsburg Monarchy*, pp.260-261.

Bibliography

UNPUBLISHED SOURCES

Arhiv Srpske akademije nauka i umetnosti, Beograd
Haus-, Hof- und Staatsarchiv (HHStA), Wien
Matica Srpska, Novi Sad
Moravský Zemský archiv, Brno
Narodna biblioteka, Beograd
Schlossarchiv (SArt), Artstetten
Vojno-istorijski institut, Beograd

PUBLISHED COLLECTIONS OF DOCUMENTS

Official diplomatic pertaining to:

1 AUSTRIA-HUNGARY
   Österreichisch-ungarisches Rotbuch. Diplomatische Aktenstücke zur Vorgeschichte des Krieges 1914 (Wien, 1915).
   BITTNER, Ludwig, PRIBRAM, Alfred Francis, SRBIK, Heinrich and UEBERS-BERGER, Hans, *Österreich-Ungarns Aussenpolitik von der bosnischen Krise bis zum Kriegsausbruch 1914* (Wien-Leipzig, 1930), 8 vols.

2 FRANCE
   Documents diplomatique français (1871-1914). 3ᵉ série (1911-1914), vols.10 and 11 (Paris, 1936).

3 GERMANY
   Deutschland schuldig? Deutches Weissbuch über die Verantwortlichkeit der Urheber des Krieges (Berlin, 1919).
   KAUTSKY, Karl, MONTGELAS, Max and SCHÜCKING, Walter (eds.), *Die Deutschen Dokumente zum Kriegsausbruch 1914* (Berlin, 1922), 4 vols.
   LEPSIUS, Johannes, MANDELSSOHN BARTHOLDY, Albrecht and TIMME, Friedrich (eds.), *Die Grosse Politik der Europäischen Kabinette 1871-1914* (Berlin, 1922-1927), vols. 18, 22, 26, 33, 34, 36, 38 and 39.

4 GREAT BRITAIN
   GOOCH, G.P. and TEMPERLEY, Harold (eds.), *British Documents on the Origins of the War 1898-1914* (London, 1926-1938), vols. 5, 9, 10 and 11.

5 RUSSIA
   How the War Began in 1914 (London, 1925) – 'Being the Diary of the Russian Foreign Office from the 3rd to the 20th (Old Style) of July, 1914'.
   HOETZSCH, Otto (ed.), *Die Internationalen Beziehungen im Zeitalter des Imperialismus. Dokumente aus den Archiven der Zarischen und der Provisorischen Regierung* (Berlin, 1931-1934), vols. 1/1, 1/2, 1/3, 1/4 and 1/5 (14 January-4 August 1914).

6 SERBIA
   Diplomatska prepiska o srpsko-austrijskom sukobu (Niš, 1914).
   DEDIJER, Vladimir *et al.* (eds.), *Dokumenti o spoljnoj politici Kraljevine Srbije 1903-1914* (Beograd, 1980-2015), 42 vols.

Unofficial Compilations:

AGSTNER, Rudolf (ed.), *1914. Das etwas andere Lesebuch zum 1. Weltkrieg. Unbekannte Dokumente der österreichisch-ungarischen Diplomatie* (Wien, 2013).

BITTNER, Ludwig, HAJEK, Alois and UEBERSBERGER, Hans (eds.), *Serbiens Aussenpolitik 1908-1918. Diplomatische Akten des serbischen Ministeriums des Äussern in deutscher Übersetzung* (Wien, 1945), 2nd Series, vol.3 (26 May to 6 August 1914).

BOGHITSCHEWITSCH, M., *Die auswärtige Politik Serbiens 1903-1914* (Berlin, 1928-1931), 3 vols.

GEISS, Imanuel (ed.), *July 1914. The Outbreak of the First World War: Selected Documents* (New York, 1974).

KOMJÁTHY, Miklós (ed.), *Protokolle des Gemeinsamen Ministerrates der Österreichisch-Ungarischen Monarchie 1914-1918* (Budapest, 1966).

KOVÁCS, Elisabeth (ed.), *Kaiser und König Karl I. (IV.). Politische Dokumente aus Internationalen Archiven* (Wien-Köln-Weimar, 2004),

MOMBAUER, Annika (ed.), *The origins of the First World War: Diplomatic and military documents* (Manchester-New York, 2013).

PERIŠIĆ, Miroslav (ed.), *Sarajevski atentat. Povratak dokumentima* (Andrićgrad-Višegrad, 2014).

PRIBRAM, Alfred Francis, *Die politischen Geheimverträge Österreich-Ungarns 1879-1914* (Wien-Leipzig 1920), 2 vols.

RADENIĆ, Andrija (ed.), *Austro-Ugarska i Srbija 1903-1918. Dokumenti iz bečkih arhiva* (Beograd, 1973-1989), 4 vols.

SCHREINER, George Abel (ed.), *Entente Diplomacy and the World* (New York-London, 1921).

SIEBERT, B von (ed.), *Graf Benckendorffs Diplomatischer Schriftwechsel* (Berlin-Leipzig, 1928), 3 vols.

VUČKOVIĆ, Vojislav (ed.), *Politička akcija Srbije u južnoslovenskim pokrajinama habsburške monarhije 1859-1874* (Beograd, 1965).

WILLIAMSON, Samuel R. Jr. and WYK, Russel Van (eds.), *July 1914: Soldiers, Statesmen, and the Coming of the Great War. A Brief Documentary History* (Boston and New York, 2003).

SARAJEVO TRIAL 1914, TRANSCRIPTS

BOGIĆEVIĆ, Vojislav, *Sarajevski atentat. Izvorne stenografske bilješke sa glavne rasprave protiv Gavrila Principa i drugova, održane u Sarajevu 1914 g.* (Sarajevo, 1954).

MOUSSET, Albert, *Un drame historique: l'attentat de Sarajevo* (Paris, 1930).

OWINGS, Dolph, PRIBIC, Elizabeth and PRIBIC, Nikola (eds.), *The Sarajevo Trial* (Chapel Hill, 1984), 2 vols.

SALONIKA TRIAL 1917

NEŠKOVIĆ, Borivoje, *Istina o solunskom procesu* (Beograd, 1953).

Tajna prevratna organizacija. Izveštaj sa pretresa u vojnom sudu za oficire u Solunu po beleškama vođenim na samom pretresu (Solun, 1918).

DIARIES, PAPERS AND LETTERS

ADLGASSER, Franz and FRIEDRICH, Margret (eds.), *Heinrich Friedjung. Geschichte in Gesprächen. Aufzeichnungen 1898-1919* (Wien-Köln-Weimar, 1997), 2 vols.

ADLGASSER, Franz (ed.), *Die Aehrenthals. Eine Familie in ihrer Korrespondenz 1872-1911* (Wien-Köln-Weimar, 2002), 2 vols.

ALEKSIĆ, Živojin (ed.), *Tasin dnevnik 1870-1906* (Beograd, 1991).

BOGIĆEVIĆ, Vojislav (ed.), *Mlada Bosna. Pisma i prilozi* (Sarajevo, 1954).

BOGIĆEVIĆ, Vojislav (ed.), *Sarajevski atentat 28. VI 1914. Pisma i saopštenja* (Sarajevo, 1965).

BOURGOING, Jean de (ed.), *Briefe Kaiser Franz Josephs an Frau Katharina Schratt* (Wien, 1964).

CHLUMECKY, Leopold von, *Erzherzog Franz Ferdinands Wirken und Wollen* (Berlin, 1929).

CONRAD [von Hötzendorf, Franz], Feldmarschall, *Aus meiner Dienstzeit 1906-1918* (Wien-Berlin-Leipzig-München, 1921-1925), 5 vols.

DIÓSZEGI, István (ed.), 'Außenminister Stephan Graf Burián. Biographie und Tagebuchstelle', *Annales Universitatis Scientiarum Budapestinensis de Rolando Eötvös nominatae*, Sectio historica, vol.8 (Budapest, 1966).

ERDMANN, Dietrich (ed.), *Kurt Riezler. Tagebücher, Aufsätze, Dokumente* (Göttingen, 2008), new edition.

FELLNER, Fritz and CORRADINI, Doris A. (eds.), *Schicksalsjahre Österreichs. Die Erinnerungen und Tagebücher Josef Redlichs 1869-1936* (Wien-Köln-Weimar, 2011), 2 vols.

HAMANN, Brigitte (ed.), *Kronprinz Rudolf. Geheime und private Schriften* (Wien-München, 1979).

HAUPTMANN, Ferdinand and PRASCH, Anton (eds.), *Dr. Ludwig Thallóczy – Tagebücher 23.VI.1914-31.XII.1914* (Graz, 1981).

HITCHENS, Keith (ed.), *The Nationality Problem in Austria-Hungary: The Reports of Alexander Vaida to Archduke Franz Ferdinand's Chancellery* (Leiden, 1974).

HOWARD, Christopher H.D., 'The Vienna Diary of Berta de Bunsen, 28 June-17 August 1914', *Bulletin of the Institute of Historical Research* (London), 51 (1978).

HOWARD, Christopher H.D. (ed.), *The Diary of Edward Goschen 1900-1914* (London, 1980).

JANSSEN, Karl-Heinz (ed.), *Die graue Exzellenz. Aus den Papieren Karl Georg von Treutlers* (Frankfurt/Main – Berlin, 1971).

JEDLICKA, Ludwig, 'Alexander Brosch von Aarenau und Moritz von Auffenberg-Komarów. Dokumente einer Freundschaft', in FRANZEL, Emil (ed.), *Virtute fideque. Festschrift für Otto von Habsburg zum fünfzigsten Geburtstag* (Wien-München, 1965).

JOVANOVIĆ, Jovan M. Pižon, *Dnevnik 1896-1920* (Novi Sad, 2015).

JOVIĆEVIĆ, Andrija P., *Dnevnik iz balkanskih ratova* (Beograd, 1996).

KRUŠEVAC, Todor (ed.), *Vladimir Gaćinović. Ogledi i pisma* (Sarajevo, 1956).

POTAPOV, N.M, *Dnevnik* (Podgorica-Moskva, 2003), vol.2.

PRUTSCH, Ursula and ZEYRINGER, Klaus (eds.), *Leopold von Andrian (1875-1951). Korrespondenzen, Notizen, Essays, Berichte* (Wien-Köln-Weimar, 2003).

SCHNÜRER, Franz (ed.), *Briefe Kaiser Franz Josephs I. an seine Mutter 1838-1872* (München, 1930).

SETON-WATSON, Hugh et al. (eds.), *R.W. Seton-Watson and the Yugoslavs: Correspondence 1906-1941* (London-Zagreb, 1976), 2 vols.

ŠIŠIĆ, F. (ed.), *Korespondencija Rački-Strossmayer* (Zagreb, 1930), vol.3.

SÖSEMANN, Bernd (ed.), *Theodor Wolff. Tagebücher 1914-1919* (Boppard am Rhein, 1984), 2 vols.

STOJANOVIĆ, Nikola, *Mladost jednog pokoljenja (Uspomene 1880-1920. – Dnevnik od godine 1914. do 1918.* (Beograd, 2015).

VIERHAUS, Rudolf (ed.), *Das Tagebuch der Baronin Spitzemberg* (Göttingen, 1960).

WALLISCH, Friedrich, *Der Adler des Skanderbeg. Albanische Briefe aus dem Früjahr 1914* (Leipzig, 1914).

WANK, Solomon (ed.), *Aus dem Nachlaß Aehrenthal. Briefe und Dokumente zur österreichisch-ungarischen Innen- und Außenpolitik 1885-1912* (Graz, 1994), 2 vols.

WERTHEIMER, Oskar von (ed.), *Graf Sefan Tisza. Briefe 1914-1918*, (Berlin, 1928), vol.1.

WÜHR, Wilhelm (ed.), *Ludwig Freiherr von Pastor 1854-1928. Tagebücher-Briefe-Erinnerungen* (Heidelberg, 1950).

ŽUJOVIĆ, Jovan, *Dnevnik* (Beograd, 1986), 2 vols.

MEMOIR LITERATURE

ANTIĆ, Antonije, *Beleške* (Zaječar, 2010).
ANTIĆ, Jovan, *Zapažanja* (Zaječar, 2014).
ARMSTRONG, Hamilton Fish, *Peace and Counterpeace: From Wilson to Hitler* (New York, 1971).
ASQUITH, H.H., *The Genesis of the War* (London, 1923).
AUFFENBERG-KOMARÓW [Moritz von], *Aus Österreichs Höhe und Niedergang. Eine Lebensschilderung* (München, 1921).
AVAKUMOVIĆ, Jovan Đ., *Memoari* (Novi Sad, 2008).
BAERNREITHER, Joseph M., *Fragments of a Political Diary* (London, 1930).
BARDOLFF, Carl von, *Deutschösterreichisches Soldatentum im Weltkrieg* (Wien, 1937).
BARDOLFF, Carl Freiherr von, *Soldat im alten Österreich. Erinnerungen aus meinem Leben* (Jena, 1938).
BASILY, Nicolas de, *Diplomat of Imperial Russia 1903-1917* (Stanford, 1973).
BATTHYÁNY, Theodor Graf, *Für Ungarn gegen Hohenzollern* (Zürich-Leipzig-Wien, 1930).
BETHMANN HOLLWEG, Th. von, *Betrachtungen zum Weltkriege* (Berlin, 1919), 2 vols.
BILIŃSKI, Leon, *Wspomnienia i dokumenty* (Warszawa, 1924), vol.1.
BROUCEK, Peter (ed.), *Ein General im Zwielicht. Die Erinnerungen Edmund Glaises von Horstenau* (Wien-Köln-Graz, 1980), vol.1.
BROUCEK, Peter (ed.), *Theodor Ritter von Zeynek: Ein Offizier im Generalstabskorps erinnert sich* (Wien-Köln-Weimar, 2009).
BROUCEK, Peter (ed.), *Ein österreichischer General gegen Hitler. Feldmarschalleutnant Alfred Jansa. Erinnerungen* (Wien-Köln-Weimar, 2011).
BUCHANAN, Sir George, *My Mission to Russia and other Diplomatic Memories* (London, 1923), 2 vols.
BÜLOW, Prince von, *Memoirs* (London-New York, 1932), 4 vols.
BURCKHARDT, Carl J., *Begegnungen* (Zürich, 1958).
BURIÁN, Count Stephan, *Austria in Dissolution* (London, 1925).
ČEROVIĆ, Božo, *Bosanski Omladinci i Sarajevski Atentat* (Sarajevo, 1930).
CHURCHILL, Winston S., *The World Crisis 1911-1914* (London, 1923).
CORMONS, Ernest U. [Emanuel Urbas], *Schicksale und Schatten. Eine österreichische Autobiographie* (Salzburg, 1951).
CRAMON, A. von and FLECK, Paul, *Deutschlands Schicksalsbund mit Österreich-Ungarn. Von Conrad von Hötzenforf zu Kaiser Karl* (Berlin, 1932).
CSÁKY, Eva-Marie (ed.), *Vom geachteten zum geächteten. Erinnerungen des k. und k. Diplomaten und k. Ungarischen Außenministers Emerich Csáky 1882-1961* (Wien-Köln-Weimar, 1994), 2nd edition.
CZERNIN, Ottokar, *Im Weltkriege* (Berlin-Wien, 1919).
ĐORĐEVIĆ, Vladan, *Kraj jedne dinastije. Prilozi za istoriju Srbije od 11 oktobra 1897 do 8 jula 1900* (Beograd, 1905-1906), 3 vols.
DRAŠKIĆ, Panta M., *Moji memoari* (Beograd, 1990).
DUMAINE, Alfred, *La dérniere ambassade de France en Autriche* (Paris, 1921).
DUMBA, Constantin, *Dreibund- und Entente-Politik in der Alten und Neuen Welt* (Zürich-Leipzig-Wien, 1931).
EISENMENGER, Victor, *Erzherzog Franz Ferdinand* (Zürich-Leipzig-Wien, 1930).
EULENBURG-HERTEFELD, Philipp Fürst zu, *Erlebnisse an deutschen und fremden Höfen* (Leipzig, 1934).
FABIUS [Leopold Kann], *Mit Blitzlicht durch Kriegserotik, Generalstab u.a.*, (Leipzig-Wien, n.d.).
FISHER, H.H., (ed.), *Out of My Past: The Memoirs of Count Kokovtsov* (Stanford, 1935).
FRONIUS, Hans, *Das Attentat von Sarajevo* (Graz-Wien-Köln, 1988).
FUGGER, Fürstin Nora, *Im Glanz der Kaiserzeit* (Wien-München, 1980).

FUNDER, Friedrich, *Vom Gestern ins Heute. Aus dem Kaiserreich in die Republik* (Wien-München, 1971), 3rd edition.

GIESL, Wladimir, *Zwei Jahrzehnte im Nahen Orient* (Berlin, 1927).

GLUCK, Władysław, *Sarajewo. Historja zamachu sarajewskiego* (Kraków, 1935).

GREY, Viscount, Twenty-Five Years 1892-1916 (London, 1925), 2 vols.

HODŽA, Milan, *Federation in Central Europe: Reflections and Reminiscences* (London, 1942).

HORVAT, Josip, *Živjeti u Hrvatskoj. Zapisci iz nepovrata 1900-1941* (Zagreb, 1984).

HÖTZENDORF, Gina Gräfin Conrad von, *Mein Leben mit Conrad von Hötzendorf* (Leipzig, 1935).

HOYOS, Alexander, *Der deutsch-englische Gegensatz und sein Einfluß auf die Balkanpolitik Österreich-Ungarns* (Berlin-Leipzig, 1922).

HUTTEN-CZAPSKI, Bogdan Graf von, *Sechzig Jahre Politik und Gesellschaft* (Berlin, 1936), vol.2.

JAGOW, G. von, *Ursachen und Ausbruch des Weltkrieges* (Berlin, 1919).

JANDRIĆ, Ljubo, *Sa Ivom Andrićem* (Beograd, 1977).

JEVĐEVIĆ, Dobroslav, *Sarajevski atentatori* (Zagreb, 1934).

JEVTIĆ, Borivoje, *Sarajevski atentat. Sećanja i utisci* (Sarajevo, 1924),

JONESCU, Take, *Some Personal Impressions* (London, 1919).

JOVANOVIĆ, M. Ljuba, *The Murder of Sarajevo* (London, 1925).

JOVANOVIĆ, M.S. (ed.), *Nikola P. Pašić. Povodom desetogodišnjice Pašićeve smrti* (Beograd, 1937).

JOVANOVIĆ, Slobodan, *Moji savremenici* (Windsor, Canada, 1962).

KACLEROVIĆ, Triša, *Martovske demonstracije i majski prevrat 1903* (Beograd, 1950).

KAMBEROVIĆ, Husnija (ed.), *Bosna i Hercegovina u 'Uspomenama' Leona Bilińskog* (Sarajevo, 2004).

KÁROLYI, Count Michael, *Fighting the World: The Struggle for Peace* (London, 1924).

KAROLYI, Michael, *Faith Without Illusion* (London, 1956).

KIELMANSEGG, Erich Graf, *Kaiserhaus, Staatsmänner und Politiker* (Wien-München, 1966).

KINSKY, Zdenko Radslav Graf, *Zu Pferd und zu Fuß* (Wien-Rom, 1974).

KLEINWAECHTER, Friedrich F.G., *Der Untergang der Österreichisch-ungarischen Monarchie* (Leipzig, 1920).

KRANJČEVIĆ, Ivan, *Uspomene jednog učesnika u sarajevskom atentatu* (Sarajevo, 1954).

KRŠNJAVI, Iso, *Zapisci. Iza kulisa hrvatske politike* (Zagreb, 1986), 2 vols.

KSUNJIN, A. (ed.), *Krv Slovenstva. Spomenica desetogodišnjice svetskog rata* (Beograd, 1924).

KUTSCHBACH, A., *Der Brandherd Europas. 50 Jahre Balkan-Erinnerungen* (Leipzig, 1929).

LAMMASCH, Marga and SPERL, Hans (eds.), *Heinrich Lammasch. Seine Aufzeichnungen, sein Wirken und seine Politik* (Wien-Leipzig, 1922).

LARISCH, Countess Marie, *My Past* (London, 1913).

LENSEN, George Alexander (ed.), *Revelations of a Russian Diplomat: The Memoirs of Dmitrii I. Abrikossow* (Seattle, 1964).

LICHNOWSKY, Prince, *Heading for the Abyss: Reminiscences* (London, 1928).

LONČAREVIĆ, Dušan A., *Jugoslaviens Entstehung* (Zürich-Leipzig-Wien, 1929).

LÜTZOW, Heinrich Graf von, *Im diplomatischen Dienst der k.u.k. Monarchie* (Wien, 1971).

MADOL, Hans Roger, *Gespräche mit verantwortlichen* (Berlin, 1933).

MARGUTTI, Albert von, *Vom alten Kaiser* (Leipzig-Wien, 1921).

MARGUTTI, Général baron Albert de, *La tragédie des Habsbourg. Mémoires d'un aide de camp* (Paris-Vienne, 1923).

MARGUTTI, Albert Freiherr von, *Kaiser Franz Joseph. Persönliche Erinnerungen* (Wien-Leipzig, 1924).

[MARGUTTI, Albert], *Kaiser Franz Joseph I. und sein Hof* (Wien-Hamburg, 1984).

MARIE, Queen of Roumania, *The Story of my Life* (London, 1934), 3 vols.

MARŠIĆANIN, Božo K., *Tajne dvora Obrenovića. Upraviteljeve beleške* (Beograd, n.d.), 2 vols.

MASARYK, Thomas Garrigue, *The Making of a State: Memories and Observations 1914-1918* (London, 1927).

MATSCH, Erwin (ed.), *November 1918 auf dem Ballhausplatz. Erinnerungen Ludwigs Freiherrn von Flotow* (Wien-Köln-Graz, 1982).

MEŠTROVIĆ, Ivan, *Uspomene na ljude i događaje* (Zagreb, 1993).

MIJATOVICH, Chedomille, *A Royal Tragedy* (London, 1906).

MIJATOVICH, Chedomille, *The Memoirs of a Balkan Diplomatist* (London, 1917).

MILIĆEVIĆ-LUNJEVICA, Ana, *Moja sestra kraljica Draga* (Beograd, 1995).

MIŠIĆ, Vojvoda Živojin, *Moje uspomene* (Beograd, 1969).

MOLLINARY, Anton Freiherr v., *Sechsundvierzig Jahre im österreich-ungarischen Heere 1833-1879* (Zürich, 1905), vol.2.

MÜLLER, Karl Alexander von, *Mars und Venus. Erinnerungen 1914-1919* (Stuttgart, 1954).

MUSULIN, [Alexander], Freiherr von [Gomirje], *Das Haus am Ballplatz. Erinnerungen eines österreich-ungarischen Diplomaten* (München, 1924).

NAUMANN, Victor, *Dokumente und Argumente* (Berlin, 1928).

NEKLUDOFF, A., *Diplomatic Reminiscences: Before and During the World War, 1911-1917* (New York, 1920).

NIKITSCH-BOULLES, Paul, *Vor dem Sturm. Erinnerungen an Erzherzog Thronfolger Franz Ferdinand* (Berlin, 1925).

NOVAKOVIĆ, Stojan, *Dvadeset godina ustavne politike u Srbiji 1883-1903* (Beograd, 1912).

NOWAK, Karl Friedrich and THIMME, Friedrich (eds.), *Erinnerungen und Gedanken des Botschafters Anton Graf Monts* (Berlin, 1932).

PALÉOLOGUE, Maurice, *An Ambassador's Memoirs* (London, 1925), vol.1.

PAVLOVIĆ, Aleksandar-Aca, *1914. Ljudi i događaji, ideje i ideali* (Beograd, 2002).

PFEFER, L., *Istraga u sarajevskom atentatu* (Zagreb, 1938), 2nd edition.

PLENER, Ernst, *Erinnerungen* (Stuttgart-Leipzig, 1921), vols. 2-3.

POLZER-HODITZ, Arthur, *Kaiser Karl* (Zürich-Leipzig-Wien, 1929).

POMIANKOWSKI, Joseph, *Der Zusammenbruch des Ottomanischen Reiches. Erinnerungen an die Türkei aus der Zeit des Weltkrieges* (Graz, 1969).

POPOVIĆ, Cvetko Đ., *Sarajevski Vidovdan 1914. Doživljaji i sećanja* (Beograd, 1969).

POPOVIĆ, Dimitrije, *Izvoljski i Erental. Diplomatske uspomene iz aneksione krize* (Beograd, 1927).

POPOVIĆ, Dimitrije, *Balkanski ratovi 1912-1913* (Beograd, 1993).

POPOVIĆ, Vojvoda Simo, *Memoari* (Cetinje-Podgorica, 1995).

PRIBIĆEVIĆ, Svetozar, *Diktatura Kralja Aleksandra* (Beograd, 1952).

[PRINCIP, Gavrilo], *Gavrilo Princips Bekenntnisse* (Wien, 1926).

[PRODANOVIĆ, Jaša M], *Spomenica Jaše M. Prodanovića* (Beograd, 1958).

PRZIBRAM, Ludwig v., *Erinnerungen eines alten Oesterreichers* (Stuttgart-Leipzig, 1912), vol.2.

ROCHELT, Hans (ed.), *Adalbert Graf Sternberg 1868-1830. Aus den Memorien eines konservativen Rebellen* (Wien, 1997).

RONGE, Generalmajor Max, *Kriegs- und Industrie-Spionage* (Zürich-Leipzig-Wien, 1930).

SALANDRA, Antonio, *Italy and the Great War: From Neutrality to Intervention* (London, 1932).

SAVINSKY, A., *Recollections of a Russian Diplomat* (London, 1927).

SAZONOV, Serge, *Fateful Years 1909-1916* (London, 1928).

SCHÄFFLE, Albert Eberhard Friedrich, *Aus meinem Leben* (Berlin, 1905), 2 vols.

SCHEBEKO, N., *Souvenirs. Essai historique sur les origines de la guerre de 1914* (Paris, 1936).

SCHELKING, Eugene de, *Recollections of a Russian Diplomat* (New York, 1918).

SEELIGER, Emil, *Abendsonne über Habsburgs Reich* (Wien-Leipzig, 1935).

SFORZA, Carlo, *Makers of Modern Europe* (London, 1930).

SFORZA, Count Carlo, *Fifty Years of War and Diplomacy in the Balkans: Pashich and the Union of the Yugoslavs* (New York, 1940).

SIEGHART, Rudolf, *Die letzten Jahrzente einer Grossmacht. Menschen, Völker, Probleme des Habsburger-Reichs* (Berlin, 1932).

SOMARY, Felix, *Erinnerungen aus meinem Leben* (Zürich, 1959).

SPITZMÜLLER, Alexander, '*und hat auch Ursach, es zu lieben*' (Wien-München-Stuttgart-Zürich, 1955).

SPITZMÜLLER-HARMERSBACH, Alexander, *Die letzte österreichisch-ungarsiche Ausgleich und der Zusammenbruch der Monarchie* (Berlin, 1929).

STEED, Henry Wickham, *Through Thirty Years* (London, 1924), vol.1.

STEINACKER Edmund, *Lebenserinnerungen* (München, 1937).

STEINITZ, Eduard Ritter von (ed.), *Erinnerungen an Joseph I.* (Berlin, 1931).

STERNBERG, Adalbert Graf, *Warum Österreich zugrunde gehen musste* (Wien, 1927).

STOCKHAUSEN, Juliana von, *Im Schatten der Hofburg* (Heidelberg, 1952).

STOJADINOVIĆ, Milan M., *Ni rat ni pakt* (Buenos Aires, 1963).

STOJANOVIĆ, Kosta, *Slom i vaskrs Srbije* (Beograd, 2012).

ŠTRANDMAN, Vasilij N., *Balkanske uspomene* (Beograd, 2009).

STÜRGKH, Josef, *Politische und militärische Erinnerungen* (Leipzig, 1922).

SZILASSY, Baron J. von, *Der Untergang der Donau-Monarchie. Diplomatische Erinnerungen* (Berlin, 1921).

TARTAGLIA, Oskar, *Veleizdajnik. Moje uspomene iz borbe protiv crno-žutog orla* (Zagreb-Split, 1928).

TCHARYKOW, N.V., *Glimpses of High Politics Through War and Peace 1855-1929* (New York, 1931).

TRBIĆ, Vojvoda Vasilije, *Memoari* (Beograd, 1996), vol.2.

TRUMBIĆ, Ante, *Suton Austro-Ugarske* (Zagreb, 1936).

URBAŃSKI, August von Ostrymiecz, *Conrad von Hötzendorf. Soldat und Mensch* (Graz-Leipzig-Wien, 1938).

VANSITTART, Lord, *The Mist Procession* (London, 1958).

VIDAKOVIĆ, Slobodan Ž. (ed.), *Agonija Beograda u svetskom ratu* (Beograd, 1931).

VOPICKA, Charles J., *Secrets of the Balkans: Seven Years of a Dilomatist's Life in the Storm Centre of Europe* (Chicago, 1921).

VUKOVIĆ, Vojvoda Gavro, *Memoari* (Cetinje, 1996).

WINDISCHGRAETZ, Ludwig, *My Memoirs* (London, 1921).

WITTE, Graf, *Erinnerungen* (Berlin, 1923).

WÖLFLING, Leopold, *Habsburger unter sich* (Berlin-Wilmersdorf, 1921).

WÖLFLING, Leopold, *Als ich Erzherzog war* (Berlin, 1935).

ZEC, Stevan, *Apisov tamničar* (Zemun, 1987).

ŽIVKOVIĆ, Petar, *Sećanja 1903-1946* (Zaječar, 2016).

ZUCKERKANDL, Bertha, *Österreich intim. Erinnerungen 1892-1942* (Wien-München, 1981).

ZWEIG, Stefan, *The World of Yesterday* (London, 1943).

BOOKS AND PAMPHLETS

AFLERBACH, Holger, *Der Dreibund. Europäische Großmacht- und Allianzpolitik vor dem Ersten Weltkrieg* (Wien-Köln-Weimar, 2002).

AGIČIĆ, Damir, *Hrvatsko-češki odnosi na prijelazu iz XIX. u XX. stoljeće* (Zagreb, 2000).

AICHELBURG, Wladimir, *Sarajevo 28. Juni 1914* (Wien, 1984).

AICHELBURG, Wladimir, *Erzherzog Franz Ferdinand von Österreich-Este 1863-1914. Notizen zu einem ungewöhnlichen Tagebuch eines aussergewönlichen Lebens* (Wien, 2014), 3 vols.

ALBERTINI, Luigi, *The Origins of the War of 1914* (London, 1952), 3 vols.

ALEKSIĆ-PEJKOVIĆ, Ljiljana, *Odnosi Srbije sa Francuskom i Engleskom 1903-1914* (Beograd, 1965).

ALLMAYER-BECK, Johann Christoph, *Ministerpräsident Baron Beck* (Wien, 1956).

ANDICS, Hellmut, *Der Untergang der Donaumonarchie. Österreich-Ungarn von der Jahrhundertwende bis zum November 1918* (München, 1980).

ANDICS, Hellmut, *Die Frauen der Habsburger* (Wien-München, 1986).
ANGELOW, Jürgen, *Kalkül und Prestige. Der Zweibund am Vorabend des Ersten Weltkrieges* (Köln-Weimar-Wien, 2000).
[Anon.], *Draga, Ivan-danski atentat i njezina trudnoća* (Beograd, 1903).
[Anon.], *Zločin v Sarajevu. Tragična smrt prestolonaslednika Fran Ferdinanda in njegove soproge vojvodinje Hohenberg* (Ljubljana, 1914).
ANRICH, Ernst, *Die Jugoslawische Frage und die Julikrise 1914* (Stuttgart, 1931).
ANRICH, Ernst, *Europas Diplomatie am Vorabend des Weltkrieges* (Berlin, 1937).
ANTONIĆ, Zdravko, *Čubrilovići 1914 i kasnije* (Beograd, 1999).
ARTUKOVIĆ, Mato, *Srbi u Hrvatskoj. Khuenovo doba* (Slavonski Brod, 2001).
ATTEMS, Moriz Graf, *Bosnien einst und jetzt* (Wien, 1913).
BAGGER, Eugene, *Franz Joseph. Eine Persönlichkeits-Studie* (Zürich-Leipzig-Wien, n.d.).
BAKIĆ, Jovo, *Ideologije jugoslovenstva između srpskog i hrvatskog nacionalizma 1918-1941* (Zrenjanin, 2004).
BANAC, Ivo, *The National Question in Yugoslavia* (Ithaca-London, 1984).
BARTULOVIĆ, Niko, *Od Revolucionarne Omladine do Orjune. Istorijat jugoslovenskog omladinskog pokreta* (Split, 1925).
BAŠAGIĆ-REDŽEPAŠIĆ, Safvet beg, *Kratka uputa u prošlost Bosne i Hercegovine* (Sarajevo, 1900).
BASSETT, Richard, *For God and Kaiser: The Imperial Austrian Army from 1619 to 1916* (New Haven-London, 2015).
BAZDULJ, Muharem (ed.), *Mlada Bosna* (Čačak, 2010).
BEER, Adolf, *Die orientalische Politik Oesterreichs seit 1774* (Prag-Leipzig, 1883).
BEHSCHNITT, Wolf Dietrich, *Nationalismus bei Serben und Kroaten 1830-1914. Analyse und Typologie der nationalen Ideologie* (München, 1980).
BELIĆ, Milorad, *Komitski vojvoda Vojislav Tankosić* (Valjevo, 2005).
BÉRENGER, Jean, *A History of the Habsburg Empire 1700-1918* (London-New York, 1997).
BERGHAHN, V.R., *Germany and the Approach of War in 1914* (New York, 1993).
BERIĆ, Dušan, *Hrvatsko pravaštvo i Srbi* (Novi Sad, 2005), 2 vols.
BERTOLINI, Gino, *Muselmanen und Slaven* (Leipzig, 1911).
BESAROVIĆ, Risto, *Iz kulturne i političke istorije Bosne i Hercegovine* (Sarajevo, 1966).
BESTENREINER, Erika, *Franz Ferdinand und Sophie von Hohenberg. Verbotene Liebe am Kaiserhof* (München, 2004).
BIBL, Viktor, *Von Revolution zu Revolution in Österreich* (Berlin-Leipzig-München, 1924).
BIBL, Viktor, *Thronfolger* (München, 1929).
BILANDŽIĆ, Dušan, *Hrvatska moderna povijest* (Zagreb, 1999).
BIONDICH, Mark, *Stjepan Radić, the Croat Peasant Party, and the Politics of Mass Mobilization, 1904-1928* (Toronto-Buffalo-London, 2000).
BJELAJAC, Mile S., *Generali i admirali Kraljevine Jugoslavije1918-1941* (Beograd, 2004).
BJELAJAC, Mile, *Diplomatija i vojska. Srbija i Jugoslavija 1901-1999* (Beograd, 2010).
BJELAJAC, Mile, *1914-2014. Zašto revizija? Stare i nove kontroverze o uzrocima Prvog svetskog rata* (Beograd, 2014).
BLED, Jean-Paul, *Franz Joseph* (Oxford, 1994).
BLED, Jean-Paul, *Franz Ferdinand. Der eigensinnige Thronfolger* (Wien-Köln-Weimar, 2013).
BOAROV, Dimitrije, *Dr Laza Paču. Legenda srpskih finansija* (Novi Sad, 2006).
BOECKH, Katrin, *Von den Balkankriegen zum Ersten Weltkrieg. Kleinstaatenpolitik und ethnische Selbstbestimmung auf den Balkan* (München, 1996).
BOGDANOV, Vaso, *Historija poličkih stranaka u Hrvatskoj* (Zagreb, 1958).
BOGDANOVIĆ, Dimitrije, *Knjiga o Kosovu* (Beograd, 1986).
BOGHITCHÉVITCH, [Miloš], *Le Procès de Salonique. Juin 1917* (Paris, 1927).
BOGHITSCHEWITSCH, M., *Kriegsursachen* (Zürich, 1919).
BOJIĆ, Mehmedalija, *Historija Bosne i Bošnjaka* (Sarajevo, 2001).
BOSWORTH, R.J.B., *Italy, the Least of the Great Powers: Italian foreign policy before the First World War* (Cambridge, 1979).

BOYER, John W., *Culture and Political Crisis in Vienna: Christian Socialism in Power, 1897-1918* (Chicago-London, 1995).
BREHM, Bruno, *Apis und Este. Ein Franz Ferdinand Roman* (München, 1931).
BRIDGE, F.R., *From Sadowa to Sarajevo: The Foreign Policy of Austria-Hungary, 1866-1914* (London-Boston, 1972).
BRKA, Amir (ed.), *Adem-aga Mešić* (Tešanj, 1998).
BROOK-SHEPHERD, Gordon, *Victims at Sarajevo: The Romance and Tragedy of Franz Ferdinand and Sophie* (London, 1984).
BRÜCKLER, Theodor, *Thronfolger Franz Ferdinand als Denkmalpfleger* (Wien-Köln-Weimar, 2009).
BUDAK, Neven, STRECHA, Mario and KRUŠELJ, Željko, *Habsburzi i Hrvati* (Zagreb, 2003).
BUDISAVLJEVIĆ, Srđan, *Stvaranje države Srba, Hrvata i Slovenaca* (Zagreb, 1958).
BURGDORFF, Stephan and WIEGREFE, Klaus (eds.), *Der Erste Weltkrieg. Die Ur-Katastrophe des 20. Jahrhunderts* (München-Hamburg, 2008).
CANIS, Konrad, *Die bedrängte Großmacht. Österreich-Ungarn und das europäische Mächtesystem 1866/67-1914* (Paderborn, 2016).
CAPPS, Edward, *Greece, Albania and Northern Epirus* (Chicago, 1963).
CARLGREN, W.M., *Iswolsky und Aehrenthal vor der bosnischen Annexionkrise* (Uppsala, 1955).
CASSELS, Lavender, *The Archduke and the Assassin* (London, 1984).
ĆEMERLIĆ, Hamdija (ed.), *100 godina ustanka u Hercegovini 1882. godine*, Naučni skup (Sarajevo, 1983).
CHARMATZ, Richard, *Österreichs innere Geschichte von 1848 bis 1907* (Leipzig, 1911).
CHURCHILL, Winston, S., *The World Crisis: The Eastern Front* (London, 1931).
CIPEK, Tihomir and MATKOVIĆ, Stjepan (eds.), *Programatski dokumenti hrvatskih političkih stranaka i skupina 1842.-1914.* (Zagreb, 2006).
CLARK, Christopher, *The Sleepwalkers: How Europe Went to War in 1914* (London, 2012).
ĆOROVIĆ, Vladimir, *Odnosi između Srbije i Austro-Ugarske u XX veku* (Beograd, 1992).
ĆOROVIĆ, Vladimir, *Istorija Srba* (Beograd, 1989), vol.3.
CORTI, Egon Caesar, *Mensch und Herrscher. Wege und Schicksale Kaiser Franz Josephs I.* (Graz, 1952).
CORTI, Egon Caesar and SOKOL, Hans, *Der alte Kaiser* (Graz-Wien-Köln, 1955).
CRAMPTON, R.J., *The Hollow Detente: Anglo-German Relations in the Balkans 1911-1914* (London, 1979).
CREAGH, James, *Over the Borders of Christendom and Eslamiah. A Journey Through Hungary, Slavonia, Serbia, Bosnia, Herzegovina, Dalmatia, and Montenegro, to the North of Albania, in the Summer of 1875* (London, 1876), vol.2.
CRENEVILLE, Ludwig Graf, *'Groß-Österreich?'*, (Graz-Wien, 1908).
ČUBRILOVIĆ, Vasa, *Bosanski ustanak 1876-1878* (Beograd, 1930)
ČUBRILOVIĆ, Vasa and ĆOROVIĆ, V., *Srbija od 1858 do 1903 godine* (Beograd, n.d.).
ČUPIĆ-AMREIN, Martha M., *Die Opposition gegen die österreichisch-ungarische Herrschaft in Bosnien-Hercegovina 1878-1914* (Bern-Frankfurt am Main-New York-Paris, 1986).
CVIJIĆ, Yovan, *The Annexation of Bosnia and Herzegovina and the Serb Problem* (London, 1909).
ĐAKOVIĆ, Luka, *Položaj Bosne i Hercegovine u austrougarskim koncepcijama rješenja jugoslovenskog pitanja 1914-1918* (Tuzla, 1981).
ĐAKOVIĆ, Luka, *Političke organizacije bosanskohercegovačkih katolika Hrvata* (Zagreb, 1985).
DEDIJER, Vladimir, *The Road to Sarajevo* (London, 1967).
DEDIJER, Vladimir, *Sarajevo 1914* (Beograd, 1978), 2 vols., 2nd edition.
DESPOT, Igor, *Balkanski ratovi 1912.-1913. i njihov odjek u Hrvatskoj* (Zagreb, 2013).
DIÓSZEGI, István, *Hungarians at the Ballhausplatz: Studies on the Austro-Hungarian Common Foreign Policy* (Budapest, 1983).
DONIA, Robert J., *Sarajevo: A Biography*, (London, 2006).

ĐORĐEVIĆ, Dimitrije, *Izlazak Srbije na jadransko more i konferencija ambasadora u Londonu 1912* (Beograd, 1956).

ĐORĐEVIĆ, Dimitrije, *Carinski rat Austro-Ugarske i Srbije 1906-1911* (Beograd, 1962).

ĐORĐEVIĆ, Dimitrije, *Milovan Milovanović* (Beograd, 1962).

DORNIK, Wolfram, *Des Kaisers Falke. Wirken und Nach-Wirken von Franz Conrad von Hötzendorf* (Innsbruck-Wien-Bozen, 2013).

DRAGNICH, Alex N., *Serbia, Nikola Pašić, and Yugoslavia* (New Brunswick, 1974).

DRAŠKIĆ, Sreten, *Evropa i albansko pitanje* (Beograd, 2000).

DRAŠKOVIĆ, Radovan M., *Pretorijanske težnje u Srbiji. Apis i 'Crna ruka'* (Beograd, 2006).

DURAKOVIĆ, Nijaz, *Prokletstvo Muslimana* (Tuzla, 1998).

DURHAM, M. Edith, *Twenty Years of Balkan Tangle* (London, 1920).

DURHAM, M. Edith, *The Serajevo Crime* (London, 1925).

DŽAJA, Srećko M., *Bosnien-Herzegowina in der österreichisch-ungarischen Epoche 1878-1918* (München, 1994).

EGGHARDT, Hanne, *Habsburgs schräge Erzherzöge* (Wien, 2008).

EISENMANN, Louis, *Le Compromis austro-hongrois de 1867: Études sur le dualisme* (Paris, 1904).

EKMEČIĆ, Milorad, *Ratni ciljevi Srbije* (Beograd, 1973).

EKMEČIĆ, Milorad (ed.), *Vladislav Skarić. Izabrana djela* (Sarajevo, 1985), vol.1.

EKMEČIĆ, Milorad, *Stvaranje Jugoslavije 1790-1918* (Beograd, 1989), 2 vols.

EKMEČIĆ, Milorad *et al.*, *Politički procesi Srbima u BiH 1914-1917* (Laktaši, 1996).

EKMEČIĆ, Milorad, *Radovi iz istorije Bosne i Hercegovine XIX veka* (Beograd, 1997).

ERÉNYI, Gustav, *Graf Stefan Tisza* (Wien-Leipzig, 1935).

EVANS, Arthur J., *Through Bosnia and the Herzegovina on Foot During the Insurrection* (London, 1877).

FALKENEGG, Baron von [Alois Paul Ledersteger], *Ungarn am Scheidewege. Politische Betrachtungen* (Berlin, 1905).

FAY, Sidney B., *The Origins of the World War* (New York, 1966), 2 vols., 2nd edition.

FEIS, Herbert, *Europe the World's Banker 1870-1914* (New Haven, 1930).

FILANDRA, Šaćir, *Bošnjačka politika u XX. stoljeću* (Sarajevo, 1998).

FISCHER, Fritz, *Germany's Aims in the First World War* (New York, 1967).

FISCHER, Fritz, *War of Illusions: German Policies from 1911 to 1914* (London, 1975).

FISCHHOF, Adolph, *Österreich und die Bürgschaften seines Bestandes* (Wien, 1869).

FORSBACH, Ralf, *Alfred von Kiderlen-Wächter 1852-1912* (Göttingen, 1997), 2 vols.

FRAKNÓI, Wilhelm, *Die ungarische Regierung und die Entstehung des Weltkrieges* (Wien, 1919).

FRANZ, Georg, *Erzherzog Franz Ferdinand und die Pläne zur Reform der Habsburger Monarchie* (Brünn-München-Wien, 1943).

FREIMUND, Justus [Karl Eduard Müller], *Österreichs Zukunft entwickelt aus seiner Vergangenheit und Gegenwart* (Brüssel, 1867).

FRIEDJUNG, Heinrich, *Das Zeitalter des Imperialismus 1884-1914* (Berlin, 1919-1922), 3 vols.

FROMKIN, David, *Europe's Last Summer: Why the World Went to War in 1914* (London, 2004).

GABRIĆ, Nenad P., *Jovan Jovanović Pižon i evropska diplomatija Srbije 1913-1918* (Beograd, 2011).

[GAĆINOVIĆ, Vladimir], *Smrt jednog heroja* (Beograd, 1912).

GAĆINOVIĆ, Vojislav, *Kob revolucionarne Mlade Bosne i njenih junaka* (Tunis, 1973).

GAĆINOVIĆ, Radoslav, *Mlada Bosna* (Beograd, 2014).

GALANDAUER, Jan, *Franz Fürst Thun. Statthalter des Königreiches Böhmen* (Wien-Köln-Weimar, 2014).

GALÁNTAI, József, *Die Österreichisch-Ungarische Monarchie und der Weltkrieg* (Budapest, 1979).

GARDINER, Muriel (ed.), *The Wolf-Man and Sigmund Freud* (London, 1972).

GAVRANOVIĆ, Berislav, *Uspostava redovite katoličke hijerarhije u Bosni i Hercegovini 1881. godine* (Beograd, 1935).

GEORGEVITCH, Vladan, *Quo vadis Austria?* (Leipzig, 1913).

GEYR, Géza Andreas von, *Sándor Wekerle 1848-1921* (München, 1993).

GIBBONS, Herbert Adams, *The New Map of Europe 1911-1914* (New York, 1915).

GJURKOVEČKI, Mirko, *Politička historija Bosne za okupacije* (Zagreb, 1920).

GLADT, Karl, *Kaisertraum und Königskrone. Aufstieg und Untergang einer serbischen Dynastie* (Graz-Wien-Köln, 1972).

GLAISE-HORSTENAU, Edmund von, *Die Katastrophe. Die Zertrümmerung Österreich-Ungarns und das Werden der Nachfolgestaaten* (Zürich-Leipzig-Wien, 1929).

GLAISE-HORSTENAU, Edmund von, *Franz Josephs Weggefährte. Das Leben des Generalstabchefs Grafen Beck* (Zürich-Leipzig-Wien, 1930).

GLAISE-HORSTENAU, Edmund (ed.), *Österreich-Ungarns letzter Krieg 1914-1918*, (Wien, 1930),vol.1.

GLIGORIJEVIĆ, Branislav, *Kralj Aleksandar Karađorđević* (Beograd, 2010), 3 vols.

GODSEY, William D. Jr., *Aristocratic Redoubt: The Austro-Hungarian Foreign Office on the Eve of the First World War* (West Lafayette, 1999).

GOLDSTEIN, Ivo, *Croatia: A History* (London, 1999).

GOOCH, G.P., *Before the War: Studies in Diplomacy* (London, 1936), 2 vols.

GOOSS, Roderich, *Das Wiener Kabinet und die Entstehung des Weltkrieges* (Wien, 1919).

GOOß, Roderich, *Das österreichisch-serbische Problem bis zur Kriegserklärung Österreich-Ungarns an Serbien, 28. Juli 1914* (Berlin, 1930).

GOPČEVIĆ, Spiridon, *Österreichs Untergang – die Folge von Franz Josefs Mißregierung* (Berlin, 1920).

GRAHAM, Stephen, *St. Vitus Day* (London, 1930).

GRIJAK, Zoran, *Politička djelatnost vrhbosanskog nadbiskupa Josipa Stadlera* (Zagreb, 2001).

GROGAN, Lady, *The Life of J.D. Bourchier* (London, 1927).

GROSS, Mirjana, *Vladavina hrvatsko-srpske koalicije 1906-1907* (Beograd, 1960).

GROSS, Mirjana, *Povijest pravaške ideologije* (Zagreb, 1973).

GROSS, Mirjana, *Izvorno pravaštvo* (Zagreb, 2000).

GROSS, Mirjana, *Vijek i djelovanje Franje Račkoga* (Zagreb, 2004).

GROSS, Mirjana and SZABO, Agneza, *Prema hrvatskome građanskom društvu. Društveni razvoj u civilnoj Hrvatskoj i Slavoniji šezdesetih i sedamdesetih godina 19. stoljeća* (Zagreb, 1992).

GUY, Nicola, *The Birth of Albania: Ethnic Nationalism, the Great Powers of World War I and the Emergence of Albanian Independence* (London, 2012).

HALL, Richard C., *Bulgaria's Road to the First World War* (Boulder, 1996).

HALL, Richard C., *The Balkan Wars 1912-1913: Prelude to the First World War* (London-New York, 2000).

HALPERN, Paul G., *The Mediterranean Naval Situation 1908-1914* (Cambridge, Massachusetts, 1971).

HAM, Paul, *1914: The Year the World Ended* (London, 2013).

HAMANN, Brigitte, *Rudolf: Kronprinz und Rebell* (Wien, 1982).

HAMANN, Brigitte (ed.), *Die Habsburger. Ein biographisches Lexikon* (Wien, 1988).

HAMANN, Brigitte (ed.), *Kaiserin Elisabeth. Das poetische Tagebuch* (Wien, 2008).

HAMMOND, Beate, *Habsburgs grösste Liebesgeschichte. Franz Ferdinand und Sophie* (Wien, 2001).

HANAK, Harry, *Great Britain and Austria-Hungary During the First World War* (London, 1962).

HANDELSMAN, Marceli, *La question d'Orient et la politique yugoslave du prince Czartoryski après 1840* (Paris, 1929).

HANNIG, Alma, *Franz Ferdinand. Die Biografie* (Wien, 2013).

HANTSCH, Hugo, *Die Nationalitätenfrage im alten Österreich* (Wien, 1953).

HANTSCH, Hugo, *Leopold Graf Berchtold. Grandseigneur und Staatsmann* (Graz-Wien-Köln, 1963), 2 vols.

HARVEY, F.W., *et al.*, *The Lay of Kossovo: Serbia's Past and Present, 1389-1917* (n.p., 1917).
HASELSTEINER, Horts, *Bosnien-Hercegovina. Orientkrise und Südslawische Frage* (Wien-Köln-Weimar, 1996).
HASTINGS, Max, *Catastrophe: Europe Goes to War 1914* (London, 2013).
HEATON-ARMSTRONG, Duncan, *The Six Month Kingdom* (London, 2005).
HELFERT, [Joseph Alexander] von, *Bosnisches* (Wien, 1879).
HELMREICH, Ernst Christian, *The Diplomacy of the Balkan Wars 1912-1913* (Cambridge, Massachusetts, 1938).
HEYROWSKY, Adolf, *Neue Wege zur Klärung der Kriegsschuld* (Berlin, 1932).
HILL, Elizabeth, *The Spirit of Kossovo* (London, 1945).
HITCHENS, Keith, *Rumania 1866-1947* (Oxford, 1994).
HÖBELT, Lothar, *Franz Joseph I. Der Kaiser und sein Reich* (Wien-Köln-Weimar, 2009).
HOENSCH, Jörg K., *A History of Modern Hungary 1867-1994* (London-New York, 1996).
HÖGLINGER, Felix, *Ministerpräsident Heinrich Graf Clam-Martinic* (Graz-Köln, 1964).
HOLLER, Gerd, *Franz Ferdinand von Österreich-Este* (Wien-Heidelberg, 1982).
HORVAT, Josip, *Politička povijest Hrvatske* (Zagreb, 1989), 2 vols.
HORVAT, Josip, *Pobuna omladine 1911-1914* (Zagreb, 2006).
HRABAK, Bogumil, *Arbanaški upadi i pobune na Kosovu i u Makedoniji od kraja 1912. do kraja 1915. godine* (Vranje, 1988).
HRABAK, Bogumil, *Arbanaške studije* (Beograd, 2007), vol.5.
HURST, Michael (ed.), *Key Treaties for the Great Powers 1814-1914* (Newton Abbot, 1972), vol.2.
IBLER, Janko, *Hrvatska politika 1903.* (Zagreb, 1914).
IMAMOVIĆ, Mustafa, *Pravni položaj i unutrašnji politički razvitak Bosne i Hercegovine od 1878. do 1914.* (Sarajevo, 1976).
IMAMOVIĆ, Mustafa, *Historija Bošnjaka* (Sarajevo, 1997).
ISAAC, Jules, *Un débat historique. Le problème des Origins de la Guerre* (Paris, 1933).
JÄCKH, Ernst, *Kiderlen-Wächter der Staatsmann und Mensch* (Berlin-Leipzig, 1924), 2 vols.
JANKOVIĆ, Dragoslav, *Srbija i jugoslovensko pitanje 1914-1915. godine* (Beograd, 1973).
JANNEN, William Jr., *The Lions of July: Prelude to War, 1914* (Novato, 1996).
JARAUSCH, Konrad H., *The Enigmatic Chancellor: Bethmann Hollweg and the Hubris of Imperial Germany* (New Haven-London, 1973).
JÁSZI, Oscar, *The Dissolution of the Habsburg Monarchy* (Chicago, 1929).
JELAVICH, Charles and Barbara, *The Establishment of the Balkan National States, 1804-1920* (Seattle-London, 1977).
JELAVICH, Barbara, *History of the Balkans: Eighteenth and Nineteenth Centuries* (Cambridge, 1983), 2 vols.
JENKS, William Alexander, *The Austrian Electoral Reform of 1907* (New York, 1950).
JEŘÁBEK, Rudolf, *Potiorek: General im Schatten von Sarajevo* (Graz-Wien-Köln, 1991).
JOLL, James, *The Origins of the First World War* (London, 1992), 2nd edition.
JOVANOVIĆ, Jovan M., *Odgovornost Srbije za svetski rat* (Beograd, 1927).
JOVANOVIĆ, Jov. M., *Stvaranje zajedničke države Srba, Hrvata i Slovenaca* (Beograd, 1928), vol.1.
JOVANOVIĆ, Slobodan, *Vlada Aleksandra Obrenovića* (Beograd, 1929-1931), 2 vols.
JOVIČIĆ, Miodrag (ed.),*Ustavi Kneževine i Kraljevine Srbije 1835-1903* (Beograd, 1988).
JUKIĆ, Ilija, *Pogledi na prošlost, sadašnjost i budućnost hrvatskog naroda* (London, 1965).
JUZBAŠIĆ, Dževad, *Nacionalno-politički odnosi u bosanskohercegovačkom saboru i jezičko pitanje 1910-1914* (Sarajevo, 1999).
JUZBAŠIĆ, Dževad, *Politika i privreda u Bosni i Hercegovini pod austrougarskom upravom* (Sarajevo, 2002).
KÁLLAY, Benjámin, *Geschichte der Serben* (Budapest-Wien, 1878).
KÁLLAY, Benjámin v., *Ungarn an den Grenzen des Orients und des Occidents* (Budapest, 1883).
KÁLLAY, Benjámin von, *Die Geschichte des serbischen Aufstandes 1807-1810* (Wien, 1910).
KANN, Robert A., *The Multinational Empire: Nationalism and National Reform in the Habsburg Monarchy, 1848-1918* (New York, 1950), 2 vols.

KANN, Robert, *Kaiser Franz Joseph und der Ausbruch des Weltkrieges* (Wien, 1971).
KANN, Robert A., *A History of the Habsburg Empire 1526-1918* (Berkeley-Los Angeles-London, 1974).
KANN, Robert A., *Erzherzog Franz Ferdianand Studien* (Wien, 1976).
KANN, Robert A., *Die Prochaska-Affäre vom Herbst 1912* (Wien, 1977).
KANNER, Heinrich, *Kaiserliche Katastrophen-Politik* (Leipzig-Wien-Zürich, 1922).
KANTOROWICZ, Hermann, *Gutachten zur Kriegsschuldfrage 1914* (Frankfurt am Main, 1967).
KAPIDŽIĆ, Hamdija, *Bosna i Hercegovina pod austrougarskom upravom. Članci i rasprave* (Sarajevo, 1968).
KAPIDŽIĆ, Hamdija, *Hercegovački ustanak 1882. godine* (Sarajevo, 1973).
KARIĆ, V., *Srbija i balkanski savez* (Beograd, 1893).
KAZIMIROVIĆ, Vasa, *Nikola Pašić i njegovo doba 1845-1926* (Beograd, 1990), 2 vols.
KAZIMIROVIĆ, Vasa, *Crna ruka. Ličnosti i događaji u Srbiji od prevrata 1903. do solunskog procesa 1917. godine* (Kragujevac, 1997).
KENNAN, George F., *Russia Leaves the War* (Princeton, 1956).
KESIĆ, Stojan, *Radnički pokret u Bosni i Hercegovini i Hrvatskoj 1894-1914* (Beograd, 1990).
KIESSLING, Friedrich, *Gegen den 'großen Krieg'? Entspannung in den internationalen Beziehungen 1911-1914* (München, 2002).
KING, Greg and WOOLMANS, Sue, *The Assassination of the Archduke: Sarajevo 1914 and the Murder that Changed the World* (London, 2013).
KISZLING, Rudolf, *Erzherzog Franz Ferdinand von Österreich-Este. Leben, Pläne und Wirken am Schicksalsweg der Donaumonarchie* (Graz-Köln, 1953).
KISZLING, Rudolf, *Die Kroaten. Der Schicksalsweg eines Südslawenvolkes* (Graz-Köln, 1956).
KOHN, Hans, *Pan-Slavism: Its History and Ideology* (Notre Dame, 1953).
KORAĆ, Vitomir, *Hrvatski 'problem'* (Beograd, 1922).
KRALJAČIĆ, Tomislav, *Kalajev režim u Bosni i Hercegovini 1882-1903* (Sarajevo, 1987).
KRESTIĆ, Vasilije, *Istorija Srba u Hrvatskoj i Slavoniji 1848-1914* (Beograd, 1992).
KRESTIĆ, Vasilije Đ., *Biskup Štrosmajer. Hrvat, velikohrvat ili Jugosloven* (Jagodina, 2006).
KRONENBITTER, Günther, *'Krieg im Frieden'. Die Führung der k.u.k. Armee und die Großmachtpolitik Österreich-Ungarns 1906-1914* (München, 2003).
KRUMEICH, Gerd, *Juli 1914. Eine Bilanz* (Paderborn-München-Wien-Zürich, 2014).
KRUŠEVAC, Todor, *Sarajevo pod austro-ugarskom upravom 1878-1918* (Sarajevo, 1960).
KUKIEL, M., *Czartoryski and European Unity 1770-1861* (Princeton, 1955).
KURTOVIĆ, Šukrija, *O nacionalizovanju Muslimana* (Sarajevo, 1914).
LANGE-AKHUND, Nadine, *The Macedonian Question, 1893-1908* (Boulder, 1998).
LANGER, William L., *The Diplomacy of Imperialism* (New York, 1951).
LATHAM, R.G. *The Ethnology of Europe* (London, 1852).
LAVELEYE, Emil von, *Die Balkanländer* (Leipzig, 1888), vol.1.
LAZAREVITSCH, Dobrivoi, *Die Schwarze Hand* (Lausanne, 1917).
LEBL, Arpad (ed.), *Politički lik Vase Stajića. Izabrani politički i ideološki spisi* (Novi Sad, 1963).
LIEVEN, D.C.B., *Russia and the Origins of the First World War* (London-Basingstoke, 1983).
LJUBIBRATIĆ, Drago, *Gavrilo Princip* (Beograd, 1954).
LJUBIBRATIĆ, Drago, *Vladimir Gaćinović* (Beograd, 1961).
LJUBIBRATIĆ, Dragoslav, *Mlada Bosna i sarajevski atentat* (Sarajevo, 1964).
LJUŠIĆ, Radoš, *Princip Gavrilo (1895-1918). Ogled o nacionalnom heroju* (Beograd, 2014).
LÖHR, Hanns Christian, *Die Gründung Albaniens. Wilhelm zu Wied und die Balkan-Diplomatie der Grossmächte 1912-1914* (Frankfurt am Main, 2010).
LORENZ, Willy, *Abschied von Böhmen* (Wien-München, 1973).
LOVRENČIĆ, Rene, *Geneza politike 'Novog kursa'* (Zagreb, 1972).
L.T. [Leon Trotsky], *Sarajevski atentat* (Wien, 1922).
LUKAS, Filip, *Strossmayer i hrvatstvo* (Zagreb, 1926).

LYON, James, *Serbia and the Balkan Front, 1914: The Outbreak of the Great War* (London, 2015).

MACAN, Trpimir, *Povijest hrvatskoga naroda* (Zagreb, 1999), 3rd edition.

MACARTNEY, C.A., *The Habsburg Empire 1790-1918* (London, 1969).

MACKENZIE, David, *Apis: The Congenial Conspirator. The Life of Colonel Dragutin T. Dimitrijević* (Boulder, 1989).

MACKENZIE, David, *The 'Black Hand' on Trial: Salonika, 1917* (Boulder, 1995).

MACKENZIE, David, *Serbs and Russians* (Boulder, 1996).

MACKENZIE, David, *The Exoneration of the 'Black Hand' 1917-1953* (Boulder, 1998).

MACMILLAN, Margaret, *The War That Ended Peace: How Europe Abandoned Peace for the First World War* (London, 2013).

MADŽAR, Božo, *Pokret Srba Bosne i Hercegovine za vjersko-prosvjetnu samoupravu* (Sarajevo, 1982).

MAGRINI, Luciano, *Il drama di Seraievo. Origini e responsabilità della guerra europea* (Milano, 1929).

MAHAN, J. Alexander, *Vienna Yesterday and Today* (Vienna, 1933).

MALBAŠA, Ante, *Bosansko pitanje i Austro-Ugarska* (Sarajevo, 1933).

MALBAŠA, Ante, *Hrvatski i srpski nacionalni problem u Bosni za vrijeme režima Benjamina Kallaya* (Osijek, 1940).

MALCOLM, Noel, *Bosnia: A Short History* (London, 1994).

MANDIĆ, Mihovil, *Povijest okupacije Bosne i Hercegovine 1878* (Zagreb, 1910).

MANDL, Leopold, *Die Habsburger und die Serbische Frage. Geschichte des staatlichen Gegensatzes Serbiens zu Österreich-Ungarn* (Wien, 1918).

MARINKOVIĆ, Pribislav B., *Velikani – Znamenite ličnosti cincarskog porekla u istoriji Srba* (Beograd, 2005).

MARKOV, Walter M., *Serbien zwischen Österreich und Russland 1897-1908* (Stuttgart, 1934).

MARKUS, Georg, *Der Fall Redl* (Wien-München, 1984).

MARRIOTT, J.A.R., *The European Commonwealth: Problems Historical and Diplomatic* (Oxford, 1918).

MARTEL, Gordon, *The Month That Changed The World: July 1914* (Oxford, 2014).

MASARYK, T.G., *Vasić-Forgách-Aehrenthal* (Prag, 1911).

MASLEŠA, Veselin, *Mlada Bosna* (Sarajevo, 1945).

MAURICE, Frederick, *The Life of Viscount Haldane of Cloan* (London, 1937), vol.1.

MAY, Arthur J., *The Habsburg Monarchy 1867-1914* (Cambridge, Massachusetts, 1965).

MAY, Arthur J., *The Passing of the Habsburg Monarchy, 1914-1918* (Philadelphia, 1966), 2 vols.

MAYR-HARTING, Anton, *Der Untergang. Österreich-Ungarn 1848-1922* (Wien-München, 1988).

MCMEEKIN, Sean, *The Russian Origins of the First World War* (Cambridge, Massachusetts-London, 2011).

MCMEEKIN, Sean, *July 1914: Countdown to War* (New York, 2013).

MEKENZI, Dejvid, *Milovan Milovanović. Srpski diplomata i državnik* (Beograd, 2007).

MEKENZI, Dejvid, *Stojan Protić. Srpski novinar i državnik* (Beograd, 2008).

MENSDORFF-POUILLY, Alfons Graf, *'Österreich'. Geschichtliche, politische und kulturelle Betrachtungen* (Wien, 1910).

MEYSELS, Lucian, *Die Verhinderte Dynastie. Erzherzog Franz Ferdinand und das Haus Hohenberg* (Wien, 2000).

MIKIĆ, Đorđe, *Austro-Ugarska i Mladoturci 1908-1912* (Banjaluka, 1983).

MILIĆEVIĆ, Milić, *Reforma vojske Srbije* (Beograd, 2002).

MILLER, Nicholas J., *Between Nation and State: Serbian Politics in Croatia before the First World War* (Pittsburgh, 1997).

MILOŠEVIĆ, Miladin, *Srbija i Grčka 1914-1918* (Zaječar, 1997).

MITIS, Oskar Freiherr von, *Das Leben des Kronprinzen Rudolf* (Wien, 1971).

MITROVIĆ, Andrej, *Prodor na Balkan. Srbija u planovima Austro-Ugarske i Nemačke 1908-1918* (Beograd, 1981).

MITROVIĆ, Andrej, *Serbia's Great War* (London, 2007).

MOMBAUER, Annika, *Die Julikrise. Europas Weg in den Ersten Weltkrieg* (München, 2014).

MORITZ, Verena and LEIDINGER, Hannes, *Oberst Redl* (St Pölten-Salzburg-Wien, 2012).

MURET, Maurice, *L'archiduc François-Ferdinand* (Paris, 1932).

MUŽIĆ, Ivan, *Hrvatska politika i jugoslavenska ideja* (Split, 1969).

MUŽIĆ, Ivan, *Masonstvo u Hrvata* (Split, 2001).

NASTITSCH, Georg, *Finale* (Budapest, 1908).

NEMEC, Norbert, *Erzherzogin Maria Annunziata (1876-1961). Die unbekannte Nichte Kaiser Franz Josephs I.* (Wien-Köln-Weimar, 2010).

NENEZIĆ, Zoran D., *Masoni u Jugoslaviji 1764-1980* (Beograd, 1984).

NIKIFIROV, Konstantin Vladimirovič, *'Načertanije' Ilije Garašanina i spoljašna politika Srbije 1842-1853* (Beograd, 2016).

NIKOLIĆ, Gradimir, *Mirno spavaj Vojvodo* (Beograd, 2012).

NINTCHITCH, Momtchilo, *La crise bosniaque (1908-1909) et les puissances européennes* (Paris, 1937), 2 vols.

NOVAK, Viktor, *Antologija jugoslovenske misli i jedinstva* (Beograd, 1930).

NOVAK, Viktor, *Franjo Rački* (Beograd, 1958).

NOWAK, Karl Friedrich, *Der Weg zur Katastrophe* (Berlin, 1926).

OKEY, Robin, *Taming Balkan Nationalism: The Habsburg 'Civilizing Mission' in Bosnia, 1878-1914* (Oxford, 2007).

ORTNER, M. Christian and ILMING, Thomas, *Das Auto von Sarajevo. Der geschichtsträchtigste Oldtimer der Welt* (Schleinbach, 2014).

PALAVESTRA, Predrag, *Književnost Mlade Bosne* (Sarajevo, 1965), 2 vols.

PALAVESTRA, Predrag, *Dogma i utopija Dimitrija Mitrinovića. Počeci srpske književne avangarde* (Beograd, 1977).

PALAVESTRA, Predrag (ed.), *Dimitrije Mitrinović. Sabrana djela* (Sarajevo, 1990-1991), 3 vols.

PAPIĆ, Mitar, *Školstvo u Bosni i Hercegovini za vrijeme austro-ugarske okupacije* (Sarajevo, 1972).

PAREŽANIN, Ratko, *Mlada Bosna i Prvi svetski rat* (München, 1974).

PAULI, Hertha, *The Secret of Sarajevo: The Story of Franz Ferdinand and Sophie* (London, 1965).

PAVLOVIĆ, Živko G., *Bitka na Jadru avgusta 1914 god.* (Beograd, 1924).

PAYRLEITNER, Alfred, *Österreicher und Tschechen* (Wien-Köln-Weimar, 1990).

PEJANOVIĆ, Đorđe, *Stanovništvo Bosne i Hercegovine* (Beograd, 1955).

PERIĆ, Ivo, *A History of the Croats* (Zagreb, 1988).

PETHÖ, Albert, *Agenten für den Doppeladler. Österreich-Ungarns geheimer Dienst im Weltkrieg* (Graz-Stuttgart, 1998).

PETROVICH, Michael Boro, *A History of Modern Serbia* (New York-London, 1976), 2 vols.

PETSALIS-DIOMIDIS, N., *Greece at the Paris Peace Conference 1919* (Thessaloniki, 1978).

PIRCH, Otto v., *Reise in Serbien im Spätherbst 1829* (Berlin, 1830), 2 vols.

PONTING, Clive, *Thirteen Days – Diplomacy and Disaster: The Countdown to the Great War* (London, 2003).

POPOVIĆ, Cvetko Đ., *Oko sarajevskog atentata* (Sarajevo, 1969).

POPOVIĆ, D.J., *O Cincarima* (Beograd, 1937), 2nd edition.

POPOVIĆ, Nikola B., *Srbija i carska Rusija* (Beograd, 2007), 2nd edition.

POPOVIĆ-SARAJLIJA, Aleksa J., *Hadži-Lojina buna u Bosni* (Beograd, 1897).

POPOVICI, Aurel C., *Die Vereinigten Staaten von Groß-Österreich. Politische Studien zur Lösung der nationalen Fragen und staatsrechtlichen Krisen in Österreich-Ungarn* (Leipzig, 1906).

PRIBRAM, Alfred Francis, *Austrian Foreign Policy, 1908-18* (London, 1923).

PRINZ, Friedrich, *Geschichte Böhmens 1848-1948* (München, 1988).

PROHASKA, Dragutin (ed.), *T.G. Masarik Zbornik* (Beograd-Praha, 1927).
PROTIĆ, Stojan, *Jugoslavija protiv Srbije. Zapisi iz naše političke istorije* (Beograd, 2009).
PRSTOJEVIĆ, Miroslav, *Zaboravljeno Sarajevo* (Sarajevo-Wien, 2010).
[QUEUX, William le], *The Near East: The Present Situation in Montenegro, Bosnia, Servia, Bulgaria, Roumania, Turkey and Macedonia* (New York, 1907).
RADENIĆ, Andrija, *Spoljna politika Srbije u kontroverznoj istoriografiji* (Beograd, 2006).
RADENKOVIĆ, Đorđe, *Pašić i Srbija* (Beograd, 1997).
RADOJEVIĆ Mira and DIMIĆ Ljubodrag, *Srbija u velikom ratu 1914-1918* (Beograd, 2014).
RADULOVIĆ, Risto, *Izabrani radovi* (Sarajevo, 1988).
RAHTEN, Andrej, *Prestolonaslednikova smrt. Po sledeh slovenskih interpretacij sarajevskega atentata* (Ljubljana, 2014).
RAJIĆ, Suzana, *Vladan Đorđević. Biografija pouzdanog obrenovićevca* (Beograd, 2007).
RAJIĆ, Suzana, *Aleksandar Obrenović. Vladar na prelazu vekova. Sukobljeni svetovi* (Beograd, 2011).
RAKOČEVIĆ, Novica, *Crna Gora u Prvom svjetskom ratu 1914-1918* (Cetinje, 1969).
RAKOČEVIĆ, Novica, *Politički odnosi Crne Gore i Srbije 1903-1918* (Cetinje, 1981).
RAUCHENSTEINER, Manfried, *Der Erste Weltkrieg und das Ende der Habsburgermonarchie 1914-1918* (Wien-Köln-Weimar, 2013).
REDLICH, Joseph, *Kaiser Franz Joseph von Österreich. Eine Biographie* (Berlin, 1928).
REMAK, Joachim, *Sarajevo: The Story of a Political Murder* (London, 1959).
RENNER, Heinrich, *Durch Bosnien und die Hercegovina, kreuz und quer* (Berlin, 1897).
REYNOLDS, David, *The Long Shadow: The Great War and the Twentieth Century* (London, 2013).
RIGBY, Andrew, *Initiation and Initiative: An Exploration of the Life and Ideas of Dimitrije Mitrinović* (Boulder, 1984).
RISTIĆ, Jov., *Spoljašnji odnošaji Srbije novijeg vremena* (Beograd, 1901), vol.3.
RÖHL, John C.G., *Wilhelm II. Der Weg in den Abgrund 1900-1941* (München, 2008).
RÖHL, John C.G., *Wilhelm II: Into the Abyss of War and Exile 1900-1941* (Cambridge, 2014).
ROŚKIEWICZ, Johann, *Studien über Bosnien und die Herzegovina* (Leipzig-Wien, 1868).
ROSSOS, Andrew, *Russia and the Balkans: Inter-Balkan Rivalries and Russian Foreign Policy 1908-1914* (Toronto-Buffalo-London, 1981).
ROTHENBERG, Gunther E., *The Army of Francis Joseph* (West Lafayette, 1976).
RUEDORFFER, J.J. [Kurt Riezler], *Grundzüge der Weltpolitik in der Gegenwart* (Stuttgart-Berlin, 1914).
RUPP, George Hoover, *A Wavering Friendship: Russia and Austria 1876-1878* (Philadelphia 1976).
SAINT-AULAIRE, Comte de, *François-Joseph* (Paris, 1945).
SAMASSA, Paul, *Der Völkerstreit in Habsburgerstaat* (Leipzig, 1910).
SAVADJIAN, Léon, *Les origines et les responsabilités de la guerre mondiale* (Paris, 1933).
SAVKOVIĆ, Dušan, *Sekira. Povest Drage Mašin* (Zagreb, 1977).
SCHIMEK, Maximilian, *Politische Geschichte des Koenigreichs Bosnien und Rama, vom Jahre 857 bis 1741* (Wien, 1787).
SCHINDLER, John R., *Fall of the Double Eagle: The Battle for Galicia and the Demise of Austria-Hungary* (Lincoln, 2015).
SCHLESINGER, Rudolf, *Federalism in Central and Eastern Europe* (London, 1945).
SCHMITT, Bernadotte E., *The Coming of the War 1914* (New York-London, 1930), 2 vols.
SCHMITT, Bernadotte E., *The Annexation of Bosnia 1908-1909* (Cambridge, 1937).
SCHÜSSLER, Wilhelm, *Das Verfassungsproblem im Habsburgerreich* (Stuttgart-Berlin, 1918).
SCHÜSSLER, Wilhelm, *Österreich und das deutsche Schicksal. Eine historisch-politische Skizze* (Leipzig, 1925).
SCHUSTER, Peter, *Henry Wickham Steed und die Habsburgermonarchie* (Wien-Köln-Graz, 1979).

ŠEHIĆ, Nusret, *Autonomni pokret Muslimana za vrijeme austrougarske uprave u Bosni i Hercegovini* (Sarajevo, 1980).

SENDTNER, Kurt, *Rupprecht von Wittelsbach. Kronprinz von Bayern* (München, 1954).

SEPER, Hans, PFUNDER, Martin and LENZ, Hans Peter, *Österreichische Automobilgeschichte* (Wien, 1999).

SETON-WATSON, R.W., *The Southern Slav Question and the Habsburg Monarchy* (London 1911).

SETON-WATSON, R.W., *Absolutism in Croatia* (London, 1912).

SETON-WATSON, R.W., *German, Slav, and Magyar: A Study in the Origins of the Great War* (London, 1916).

SETON-WATSON, R.W., *Sarajevo: A Study in the Origins of the Great War* (London, 1925).

SETON-WATSON, R.W., *Transylvania: A Key-Problem* (Oxford, 1943).

ŠIDAK Jaroslav, *Studije iz hrvatske povijesti XIX stoljeća* (Zagreb, 1973).

ŠIDAK, Jaroslav, GROSS, Mirjana, KARAMAN, Igor and ŠEPIĆ, Dragovan, *Povijest hrvatskog naroda g.1860-1914* (Zagreb. 1968).

ŠIŠIĆ, Ferdo, *Jugoslovenska misao* (Beograd, 1937).

ŠIŠIĆ, Ferdo, *Kako je došlo do okupacije a onda do aneksije Bosne i Hercegovine* (Zagreb, 1938).

SKARIĆ, Vladislav, NURI-HADŽIĆ, Osman and STOJANOVIĆ, Nikola, *Bosna i Hercegovina pod austro-ugarskom upravom* (Beograd, 1938).

SKED, Alan, *The Decline and Fall of the Habsburg Empire, 1815-1918* (London-New York, 1989).

ŠKEROVIĆ, Nikola P., *Crna Gora na osvitku XX vijeka* (Beograd, 1964).

SKOKO, Savo, *Vojvoda Radomir Putnik* (Beograd, 1985), 2.vols.

SKOKO, Savo and OPAĆIĆ, Petar, *Vojvoda Stepa Stepanović u ratovima Srbije 1876-1918* (Beograd, 1979).

SKŘIVAN, Aleš, *Schwierige Partner. Deutschland und Österreich-Ungarn in der europäischen Politik der Jahre 1906-1914* (Hamburg, 1999).

SLIJEPČEVIĆ, Pero (ed.), *Napor Bosne i Hercegovine za oslobođenje i ujedinjenje* (Sarajevo, 1929).

SMITH, David James, *One Morning in Sarajevo: 28 June 1914* (London, 2008).

SONDHAUS, Lawrence, *Franz Conrad von Hötzendorf: Architect of the Apocalypse* (Boston-Leiden-Cologne, 2000).

SOSNOSKY, Theodor von, *Die Balkanpolitik Österreich-Ungarns seit 1866* (Stuttgart-Berlin, 1912-1913), 2 vols.

SOSNOSKY, Theodor von, *Die Politik im Habsburgerreiche* (Berlin, 1912-1913), 2 vols.

SOSNOSKY, Theodor von, *Franz Ferdinand. Der Erzherzog-Thronfolger* (München-Berlin, 1929).

SOWARDS, Steven W., *Austria's Policy of Macedonian Reform* (Boulder, 1989).

SPALAÏKOVITCH, M.J., *La Bosnie et l'Herzégovine. Étude d'histoire diplomatique et de droit international* (Paris, 1899).

SPIEL, Hilde, *Vienna's Golden Autumn 1866-1938* (London, 1987).

SPRINGER, Rudolf [Karl Renner], *Grundlagen und Entwicklungsziele der Österreichisch-Ungarischen Monarchie* (Wien-Leipzig, 1906).

STANČIĆ, Nikša, *Hrvatska nacija i nacuionalizam u 19. i 20. stoljeću* (Zagreb, 2002).

STANKOVIĆ, Đorđe Đ., *Nikola Pašić, saveznici i stvaranje Jugoslavije* (Beograd, 1984).

STANKOVIĆ, Đorđe, *Nikola Pašić, saveznici i stvaranje Jugoslavije* (Zaječar, 1995), 2nd edition.

STANOJEVIĆ, St., *Ubistvo austriskog prestolonaslednika Ferdinanda. Prilozi pitanju o početku svetskog rata* (Beograd, 1923).

STANOJEVIĆ, Stanoje, *Die Ermordung des Erzherzogs Franz Ferdinand* (Frankfurt a. M., 1923).

STEED, H.W., *The Habsburg Monarchy* (London, 1913).

STOJANOVIĆ, M.D., *The Great Powers and the Balkans, 1875-1878* (Cambridge, 1939).

STOJANOVIĆ, Nikola, *Bosanska kriza 1908-1914* (Sarajevo, 1958).

STOLIĆ, Ana, *Đorđe Simić. Poslednji srpski diplomata XIX veka* (Beograd, 2003).
STOLIĆ, Ana, *Kraljica Draga Obrenović* (Beograd, 2009).
STONE, Norman, *Europe Transformed* (London, 1983).
STONE, Norman, *World War One: A Short History* (London, 2007).
STRACHAN, Hew, *The Outbreak of the First World War* (Oxford, 2004).
SÜDLAND, L. v. [Ivo Pilar], *Die südslawische Frage und der Weltkrieg* (Wien, 1918).
SUGAR, Peter F., *Industrialization of Bosnia-Hercegovina 1878-1918* (Seattle, 1963).
SUNDHAUSSEN, Holm, *Geschichte Serbiens 19.-21. Jahrhundert* (Wien-Köln-Weimar, 2007).
SZÁNTO, Alexander, *Apis. Der Führer der Schwarzen Hand* (Berlin, 1928).
TADIJANOVIĆ, Dragutin (ed.), *Tin Ujević. Sabrana djela* (Zagreb, 1966), vol.10.
TAYLOR, A.J.P., *The Habsburg Monarchy 1809-1918: A History of the Austrian Empire and Austria-Hungary* (London, 1948).
TAYLOR, A.J.P., *The Struggle for Mastery in Europe* (Oxford, 1954).
TAYLOR, A.J.P., *The Trouble Makers: Dissent over Foreign Policy 1792-1939* (London, 1957).
TAYLOR, A.J.P., *Europe: Grandeur and Decline* (Harmondsworth, 1967).
TEMPERLEY, Harold W.V., *History of Serbia* (London, 1919),
TERZIĆ, Velimir (ed.), *Prvi balkanski rat 1912-1913* (Beograd, 1959).
THADEN, Edward C., *Russia and the Balkan Alliance of 1912* (Philadelphia, 1965).
THIÉRIOT, Jean-Louis, *François Ferdinand d'Autriche. De Mayerling à Sarajevo* (Paris, 2005).
THOMSON, Christopher Birdwood, *Old Europe's Suicide* (New York, 1922).
THOMSON, Harrison, *Czechoslovakia in European History* (Princeton, 1953).
TODOROVA, Maria, *Imagining the Balkans* (New York-Oxford, 1997).
TOPALOVIĆ, Ognjan, *Đeneral Belimarković* (Vrnjačka Banja, 1998).
TRIFUNOVIĆ, Miloš, *Istorija Radikalne stranke* (Beograd, 1995).
TRIŠIĆ, Nikola Đ., *Sarajevski atentat u svjetlu bibliografskih podataka* (Sarajevo, 1964).
TSCHUPPIK, Karl, *Franz Joseph I. Der Untergang eines Reiches* (Hellerau bei Dresden, 1928).
TSCHUPPIK, Karl, *The Reign of Emperor Francis Joseph 1848-1916* (London, 1930).
TUNSTALL, Graydon A. Jr., *Planning for War Against Russia and Serbia: Austro-Hungarian and German Military Strategies, 1871-1914* (Boulder, 1993).
TURNER, L.C.F., *Origins of the First World War* (London, 1970).
UEBERSBERGER, Hans, *Österreich zwischen Russland und Serbien* (Köln-Graz, 1958).
[UJEVIĆ, Tin], *Hrvatska u borbi za slobodu* (Beograd, 1912).
VASIĆ, Dragiša, *Devetsto treća (majski prevrat). Prilozi za istoriju Srbije od 8. jula 1900. do 17. januara 1907.* (Beograd, 1925).
VERMES, Gabor, *István Tisza: The Liberal Vision and Conservative Statecraft of a Magyar Nationalist* (New York, 1985).
VEROSTA, Stephan, *Theorie und Realität von Bündnissen. Heinrich Lammasch, Karl Renner und der Zweibund 1897-1914* (Wien, 1971).
VIVIAN, Herbert, *The Servian Tragedy with some Impressions of Macedonia* (London, 1904).
VIVIAN, Herbert, *Secret Societies: Old and New* (London, 1927).
VOJVODIĆ, Mihailo, *Skadarska kriza 1913. godine* (Beograd, 1970).
VOJVODIĆ, Mihailo, *Srbija u međunarodnim odnosima krajem XIX i početkom XX veka* (Beograd, 1988).
VOJVODIĆ, Mihailo, *Petrogradske godine Stojana Novakovića* (Beograd, 2009).
VRANKIĆ, Petar, *Religion und Politik in Bosnien und der Herzegowina 1878-1918* (Paderborn-München-Wien-Zürich, 1998).
VRKATIĆ, Lazar, *Pojam i biće srpske nacije* (Sremski Karlovci-Novi Sad, 2004).
VUCINICH, Wayne S., *Serbia Between East and West: The Events of 1903-1908* (Stanford, 1954).
VUČO, Nikola, *Privredna istorija naroda FNRJ do prvog svetskog rata* (Beograd, 1948).
VUJOVIĆ, Dimitrije-Dimo, *Ujedinjenje Crne Gore i Srbije* (Titograd, 1962).
WANK, Solomon, *In the Twilight of Empire: Count Alois Lexa von Aehrenthal (1854-1912) Imperial Habsburg Patriot and Statesman* (Wien-Köln-Weimar, 2009), vol.1.

WAWRO, Geoffrey, *A Mad Catastrophe: The Outbreak of World War I and the Collapse of the Habsburg Empire* (New York, 2014).

WEGERER, Alfred von, *Die Widerlegung der Versailler Kriegsschuldthese* (Berlin, 1928).

WEGERER, Alfred von, *Der entscheidende Schritt in den Weltkrieg* (Berlin, 1931).

WEGERER, Alfred von, *Der Ausbruch des Weltkrieges 1914* (Hamburg 1939), 2 vols.

WEINDEL, Henri de, *The Real Francis-Joseph: The Private Life of the Emperor of Austria* (London, 1909).

WEISSENSTEINER, Friedrich, *Franz Ferdinand. Der verhinderte Herrscher* (Wien, 2007).

WENDEL, Hermann, *Die Habsburger und die Südslawenfrage* (Belgrad-Leipzig, 1924).

WENDEL, Hermann, *Das Attentat von Sarajewo. Eine historisch-kritische Untersuchung* (n.d., n.p.).

WERTHEIMER, Eduard von, *Graf Julius Andrássy. Sein Leben und seine Zeit* (Stuttgart, 1910-1913), 3 vols.

WEST, Rebecca, *Black Lamb and Grey Falcon* (London, 1941), vol.1.

WIERER, Rudolf, *Der Föderalismus im Donauraum* (Graz-Köln, 1969).

WILLIAMSON, Samuel R., Jr, *Austria-Hungary and the Origins of the First World War* (New York, 1991).

WILSON, H.W., *The War Guilt* (London, 1928).

WILSON, Northesk Mrs., *Belgrade: The White City of Death* (London, 1903).

WINKELHOFER, Martina, *'Viribus unitis'. Der Kaiser und sein Hof* (Wien, 2008).

WINNIFRITH, T.J., *The Vlachs: The History of a Balkan People* (London, 1987).

WOLFF, Theodor, *The Eve of 1914* (New York, 1936).

WOODS, H. Charles, *The Cradle of the War: The Near East and Pan-Germanism* (London, 1918).

WULFF, Olaf Richard, *Die österreichisch-ungarische Donauflotille im Weltkriege 1914-1918* (Wien-Leipzig, 1934).

WÜRTHLE, Friedrich, *Die Spur führt nach Belgrad. Die Hintergründe des Dramas von Sarajevo 1914* (Wien-München-Zürich, 1975).

WÜRTHLE, Friedrich, *Dokumente zum Sarajevoprozeß. Ein Quellenbericht* (Wien, 1978).

ZAWADZKI, W.H., *A Man of Honour: Adam Czartoryski as a Statesman of Russia and Poland 1795-1831* (Oxford, 1993).

ZECHLIN, Egmont, *Krieg und Kriegsrisiko. Zur deutschen Politik im Ersten Weltkrieg* (Düsseldorf, 1979).

ŽIBERT, J.A., *Der Mord von Sarajewo und Tiszas Schuld an dem Weltkriege* (Laibach, 1919).

ŽIVANOVIĆ, Milan Ž., *Pukovnik Apis. Solunski proces hiljadu devetsto sedamnaeste. Prilozi za proučavanje političke istorije Srbije od 1903 do 1918 god.* (Beograd, 1955).

ŽIVANOVIĆ, Živ., *Politička istorija Srbije u drugoj polovini devetnaestog veka* (Beograd, 1923-1925), 4 vols.

ŽIVOJINOVIĆ, Dragoljub R., *Kralj Petar I Karađorđević* (Beograd, 2009), 3 vols.

ZÖLLNER, Erich, *Geschichte Österreichs* (Wien, 1961).

ZWITTER, Fran, *Nacionalni problemi v habsburški monarhiji* (Ljubljana, 1962).

ARTICLES AND ESSAYS

ALEKSIĆ-PEJKOVIĆ, Ljiljana, 'Pašić i opredeljivanje Srbije između dva bloka velikih sila', in *Nikola Pašić. Život i Delo* (Beograd, 1997).

ALLMAYER-BECK, Johann Christoph, 'Die bewaffnete Macht in Staat und Gesellschaft' in WANDRUSZKA, Adam and URBANITSCH, Peter (eds.), *Die Habsburgermonarchie 1848-1918*, vol.5, *Die bewaffnete Macht* (Wien, 1987).

ALLMAYER-BECK, Joh. Christoph, 'Die Militärkanzlei des Erzherzog-Thronfolgers Franz Ferdinand' in BROUCEK, Peter and SCHMIDL, Erwin A. (eds.), *Joh.Christoph Allmayer-Beck. Militär, Geschichte und Politische Bildung. Aus Anlaß des 85. Geburtstages des Autors* (Wien-Köln-Weimar, 2003).

ARGENBAU, Alfred Rappaport von, 'Staatsmänner und Diplomaten der Vorkriegszeit. Spalajković', *Berliner Monatshefte*, July 1935.

ARMSTRONG, Hamilton Fish, 'Three Days in Belgrade: July, 1914', *Foreign Affairs*, 5:1/4 (1926/1927).

ARTAMONOV, Victor A., 'Erinnerungen an meine Militärattachézeit in Belgrad', *Berliner Monatshefte*, July-August 1938.

BAERNREITHER, [Joseph], 'Aehrenthal und Milovanovich. Ein Tagebuchblatt', *Deutsche Revue* (Stuttgart-Leipzig), January 1922.

BARTULOVIĆ, Niko, 'Glose k Predratnoj Omladini', *Književni Sever* (Subotica), vol.5, July-August-September 1929.

BATAKOVIĆ, Dušan T., 'Storm over Serbia: The Rivalry between Civilian and Military Authorities (1911-1914)', *Balcanica* (Belgrade), vol. 44, 2013.

BEHR, Ferdo, 'Oko sarajevskog atentata', *Pregled* (Sarajevo), vol.5, 1 September 1930.

BER, Ferdo, 'U času atentata', *Pregled* (Sarajevo), February 1935.

BITTNER, Ludwig, 'Graf Johann Forgách', *Berliner Monatshefte*, November 1935.

BJELAJAC, M., 'Dragutin T. Apis Dimitrijević', *Srpski biografski rečnik* (Novi Sad, 2007), vol.3.

BOGHITSCHEWITSCH, [Miloš], 'Weitere Einzelheiten über das Attentat von Sarajevo', *Die Kriegsschuldfrage*, July 1925.

BOGIĆEVIĆ, Vojislav, 'Austriske vlasti i Sarajevski Atentat', *Nova Evropa* (Zagreb), vol.27, no.8, 26 July 1934.

BOGIĆEVIĆ, Vojislav, 'Sećanja na Vidovdanski atentat 1914', *Pregled* (Sarajevo), vol.11, February 1935.

BOGIĆEVIĆ, Vojislav, 'Austrijske policiske vlasti i sarajevski atentatori', *Pregled* (Sarajevo), vol.12, March 1936.

BOGIĆEVIĆ, Vojislav, 'Da li je ministar Kalaj zabranio svoju *Istoriju Srba* na području Bosne i Hercegovine?', *Godišnjak istoriskog društva Bosne i Hercegovine* (Sarajevo), 1955.

BORIĆ, Milo, 'Od 'napredne' do 'nacionalističke' omladine', *Književni Sever* (Subotica), vol.5, July-August-September 1929.

BRAUNER, Josef, 'Bosnien und Herzegowina. Politik, Verwaltung und leitende Personen vor Kriegsausbruch', *Berliner Monatshefte*, April 1929.

BROUCEK, Peter, 'Merizzi', *Österreichisches Biographisches Lexikon 1815-1950* (Wien, 1975), vol.6.

BURZ, Ulfried, 'Austria and the Great War: Official Publications in the 1920s and 1930s', in WILSON, Keith (ed.), *Forging the Collective Memory: Government and International Historians Through Two World Wars* (Providence-Oxford, 1996).

ĆEMERLIĆ, Hamdija, 'Alibeg Firdus – borba Muslimana za vjersko-prosvjetnu autonomiju' in ČUBRILOVIĆ, Vasa (ed.), *Jugoslovenski narodi pred Prvi svetski rat* (Beograd, 1967).

CHRAMOSTA, Jaroslav, 'Sarajevské události z deníku Františka Harracha a Jaroslava Thuna' in GALANDAUER, Jan *et al.*, *Od Sarajeva k velké válce – Ab Sarajewo zum grossen Krieg* (Praha, 1995), vol.1.

COLLAS, Carl, 'Auf den bosnischen Wegspuren der Kriegsschuldigen', *Die Kriegsschuldfrage*, January 1927.

CORNWALL, Mark, 'Serbia' in WILSON, Keith (ed.), *Decisions for War 1914* (New York, 1995).

ĆOROVIĆ, V., 'Misija Andre Đorđevića u Beču 1903 godine', *Srpski književni glasnik* (Beograd), vol.42, no.7, August 1934.

ĆOROVIĆ, V., 'Pregovori o balkanskim savezima', *Godišnjica Nikole Čupića* (Beograd), vol.47, 1938.

ĆURIĆ, Hajrudin, 'Jedan nacionalni revolucionar iz Hercegovine', *Gajret Kalendar za god. 1939* (Sarajevo, 1938).

DANGIĆ, Jezdimir, 'S Gavrilom Principom, od Sarajeva do Terezina', *Nova Evropa* (Zagreb), vol.33, no.12, 26 November 1940.

DEDIJER, Vladimir and PAVIĆEVIĆ, Branko, 'Dokazi za jednu tezu', *Nova misao* (Beograd), August 1953.

DEDIJER, Vladimir, 'Planovi nadvojvode Franje Ferdinanda o reorganizaciji Habsburške monarhije' in ČUBRILOVIĆ, Vasa (ed.), *Jugoslovenski narodi pred Prvi Svetski Rat* (Beograd, 1967).

DENDA, D., 'Aleksandar J. Mašin', *Srpski biografski rečnik* (Novi Sad, 2014), vol.6.

DIMOVIĆ, Danilo, 'Poslednja večera. Politički ispad Franza Ferdinanda uoči sarajevskog atentata 27. juna 1914', *Pogledi na savremena pitanja* (Zagreb), 1, May 1934.

ĐORĐEVIĆ, Dimitrije, 'Austro-srpski sukob oko projekta novopazarske železnice', *Istorijski časopis* (Beograd), vol.7, 1957.

ĐORĐEVIĆ, Dimitrije, 'U senci austro-ugarske', *Istorija srpskog naroda* (Beograd, 1983), vol.6/1.

ĐORĐEVIĆ, Dimitrije, 'Sučeljavanje sa austro-ugarskom', *Istorija srpskog naroda* (Beograd, 1983), vol.6/1.

ĐURIĆ, Đ., 'Jovan M. Žujović', *Srpski biografski rečnik* (Novi Sad, 2007), vol.3.

EGGER, Rainer, 'Die Militärkanzlei des Erzeherzog-Thronfolgers Franz Ferdinand und ihr Archiv im Kriegsarchiv Wien', *Mitteilungen des österreichischen Staatsarchivs*, 28, Wien, 1975.

EKMEČIĆ, Milorad, 'Društvo, privreda i socijalni nemiri u Bosni i Hercegovini', *Istorija srpskog naroda* (Beograd, 1983), vol.6/1.

EKMEČIĆ, Milorad, 'Nacionalni pokret u Bosni i Hercegovini', *Istorija srpskog naroda* (Beograd, 1983), vol.6/1.

EKMEČIĆ, Milorad, 'Austro-ugarska obavještajna služba i majski prevrat u Srbiji 1903. godine', *Istorijski časopis* (Beograd), vol.32, 1985.

EKMEČIĆ, Milorad, 'Impact of the Balkan Wars on Society in Bosnia and Herzegovina' in KIRÁLY, Béla K. and DJORDJEVIC, Dimitrije (eds.), *East Central European Society and the Balkan Wars* (Boulder, 1987).

FELLNER, Fritz, 'Zwischen Kriegsbegeisterung und Resignation – ein Memorandum des Sektionchefs Graf Forgách vom Jänner 1915' in WIESFLECKER, Hermann and PICKL, Othmar (eds.), *Beiträge zur allgemeinen Geschichte* (Graz, 1975).

FELLNER, Fritz, 'Die Mission Hoyos' in MASCHL, Heidrun and MAZOHL-WALLNIG, Brigitte (eds.), *Vom Dreibund zum Völkerbund* (München, 1994).

FELLNER, Fritz, 'Austria-Hungary' in WILSON, Keith (ed.), *Decisions for War, 1914* (New York, 1995).

FRIED, Marvin Benjamin, 'A Life and Death Question: Austro-Hungarian War Aims in the First World War' in AFFLERBACH, Holger (ed.), *The Purpose of the First World War: War Aims and Military Strategies* (Berlin-Boston, 2015).

GALÁNTAI, Josef, 'Stefan Tisza und der Erste Weltkrieg', *Österreich in Geschichte und Literatur*, vol.10, 1964.

GALÁNTAI, József, 'Francis Ferdinand and Hungary', *Annales Universitatis Scientiarum Budapestinensis de Rolando Eötvös nominatae* (Budapest), vol.15, 1974.

GALÁNTAI, J., 'Austria-Hungary and the War: The October 1913 Crisis – Prelude to July 1914', *Etudes historiques hongroises 1980* (Budapest, 1980), vol.2.

GIESL, Wladimir von, 'Konnte die Annahme der serbische Antwortnote den Ausbruch des Weltkrieges verhindern?', *Berliner Monatshefte*, May 1933.

GLAISE-HORSTENAU, Edmund, 'Erzherzog Franz Ferdinand 1863 bis 1914', *Neue Österreichische Biographie 1815-1918* (Wien, 1926).

GLUCK, Vlado, 'Sitne primedbe uz knjigu Istraga u sarajevskom atentatu', *Pregled* (Sarajevo), vol.14, October 1938.

GRGIĆ, Ružica, 'Mir scheint, wir werden heute noch einige Kugeln bekommen' in GEHLER, Michael and ORTNER, René (eds.), *Von Sarajewo zum 11. September. Einzelattentate un Massenterrorismus* (Insbruck-Wien-Bozen, 2007).

GRIESINGER, Freiherr von, 'Die kritischen Tage in Serbien', *Berliner Monatshefte*, September 1930.

GROSS, Mirjana, 'Hrvatska politika u Bosni i Hercegovini od 1878. do 1914', *Historijski zbornik* (Zagreb), 1966-67.

GROSS, Mirjana, 'Nacionalne ideje studentske omladine u Hrvatskoj uoči I svjetskog rata', *Historijski zbornik* (Zagreb), vol.21-22, 1968-1969.

GROSS, Mirjana, 'Studentski pokret 1875-1914', *Spomenica u povodu proslave 300-godišnjice sveučilišta u Zagrebu* (Zagreb, 1969).

GROSS, Mirjana, 'Hrvatska politika velikoaustrijskog kruga oko prijestolonasljednika Franje Ferdinanda', *Časopis za suvremenu povijest* (Zagreb), vol.2, 1970.

GROSS, Mirjana, 'Zur Frage der jugoslawischen Ideologie bei den Kroaten' in WANDRUSZKA, Adam, PLASCHKA, Richard G. and DRABEK, Anna M. (eds.), *Die Donaumonarchie und die südslawische Frage von 1848 bis 1918* (Wien, 1978).

GRUIĆ, Slavko, 'Persönliche Erinnerungen aus der Julikrisis 1914', *Berliner Monatshefte*, July 1935.

GULIĆ, Milan, 'Odjek balkanskih ratova u Dalmaciji' in RUDIĆ, Srđan and MILKIĆ, Miljan (eds.), *Balkanski ratovi 1912/1913: Nova viđenja i tumačenja* (Beograd, 2013).

GUTIĆ, Mirko, 'Oružani sukobi na srpsko-albanskoj granici u jesen 1913. godine', *Vojnoistorijski glasnik* (Beograd), vol.36, no.1, January-April 1985.

HALL, Richard C., 'Serbia' in HAMILTON, Richard F. and HERWIG, Holger H. (eds.), *The Origins of World War I* (Cambridge, 2003).

HANNIG, Alma, 'Austro-Hungarian foreign policy and the Balkan Wars' in GEPPERT, Dominik, MULLIGAN, William and ROSE, Andreas (eds.), *The Wars before the Great War: Conflict and International Politics before the Outbreak of the First World War* (Cambridge, 2015).

HANTSCH, Hugo, 'Erzherzog-Thronfolger Franz Ferdinand und Graf Leopold Berchtold' in HANTSCH, Hugo, VOEGELIN, Eric and VALSECCHI, Franco (eds.), *Historica. Studien zum geschichtlichen Denken und Forschen* (Wien-Freiburg-Basel, 1965).

HASANBEGOVIĆ, Zlatko, 'Islam i bosanski muslimani u djelima Ante Starčevića' in GABELICA, Ivan (ed.), *Starčević. Znanstveni kolokvij o 180. obljetnici rođenja* (Zagreb, 2004).

HAUPTMANN, Ferdo, 'Privreda i društvo Bosne i Hercegovine u doba austro-ugarske vladavine (1878-1918)' in REDŽIĆ, Enver (ed.), *Prilozi za istoriju Bosne i Hercegovine* (Sarajevo, 1987), vol.2.

HEILBRONNER, Hans, 'The Merger Attempts of Serbia and Montenegro, 1913-1914', *Journal of Central European Affairs*, vol.18, October 1958.

HERWIG, Holger H., 'Why Did It Happen?' in HAMILTON, Richard F. and HERWIG, Holger H. (eds.), *The Origins of World War I* (Cambridge 2003).

HÖBELT, Lothar, 'Why did Austria-Hungary Decide for War in 1913-1914?' in ŽIVO-JINOVIĆ, Dragoljub R. (ed.), *The Serbs and the First World War* (Belgrade, 2015).

HOYOS, Alexander Graf, 'Zusammenhänge', in STEINITZ, Eduard Ritter von (ed.), *Rings um Sasonow* (Berlin, 1928).

JAKŠIĆ, Grgur and VUČKOVIĆ, Vojislav J., 'Pokušaj aneksije Bosne i Hercegovine (1882-1883)', *Glas Srpske Akademije Nauka*, CCXIV (Beograd, 1954).

JANKOVIĆ, Dragoslav, 'Stavovi sila Trojnog sporazuma prema nacionalnom pitanju Srbije i jugoslovenskih naroda uoči Prvog svetskog rata' in ČUBRILOVIĆ, Vasa (ed.), *Velike sile i Srbija pred Prvi svetski rat* (Beograd, 1976).

JELAVICH, Barbara, 'What the Habsburg Government Knew about the Black Hand', *Austrian History Yearbook*, vol.22, 1991.

JELAVICH, Charles, 'The Croatian Problem in the Habsburg Empire in the Nine-teenth Century', *Austrian History Yearbook*, vol.3, part 2, 1967.

JEREMIĆ, Risto, 'Oružani otpor protiv Austro-Ugarske, od 1878-1882' in SLIJEPČE-VIĆ, Pero (ed.), *Napor Bosne i Hercegovine za oslobođenje i ujedinjenje* (Sarajevo, 1929).

JEVTIĆ, Borivoje Jevtić, 'Vladimir Gaćinović u Sarajevu', *Spomenica Vladimira Gaćinovića* (Sarajevo, 1921).

JORGENSEN, Christer, 'Deadly Dilemma: Grey, Great Britain and the Great Bosnian

Crisis, October 1908-March 1909' in KUZMANOVIĆ, Rajko (ed.), *Stogodišnjica aneksije Bosne i Hercegovine* (Banja Luka, 2009).

JOVANOVIĆ, Jov. M., 'Odgovornost za svetski rat', *Srpski književni glasnik* (Beograd), August 1925.

JOVANOVIĆ, Jov. M., 'Sarajevski atentat i Srbija', *Brastvo* (Beograd), vol.21, 1927.

JOVANOVIĆ, Radovan, 'Iz đačkih dana Gavrila Principa', *Književni Sever* (Subotica), 1 Febraury 1928.

JOWANOWITSCH, Ljuba, 'Nach dem Veitstage des Jahres 1914', *Die Kriegsschuldfrage*, February 1925.

KANN, Robert, 'William II and Archduke Francis Ferdinand in Their Correspondence', *The American Historical Review*, vol.57, no.2 (January 1952).

KANN, Robert A., 'Count Ottokar Czernin and Archduke Franz Ferdinand', *Journal of Central European Affairs*, vol.16, no.2, July 1956.

KANN, Robert A., 'The Austro-Hungarian Compromise of 1867 in Retrospect. Causes and Effect' in HOLOTIK, Ľudovit (ed.), *Der österreichisch-ungarische Ausgleich 1867* (Bratislava, 1971).

KANN, Robert A., 'Archduke Franz Ferdinand and Count Berchtold During His Term as Foreign Minister, 1912-1914' in WINTERS, Stanley B. (ed.), *Dynasty, Politics and Culture* (Boulder, 1991).

KANN, Robert A., 'Heir Apparent Archduke Franz Ferdinand and His Stance on the Bohemian Question' in WINTERS, Stanley B. (ed.), *Dynasty, Politics and Culture* (Boulder, 1991).

KAPIDŽIĆ, Hamdija, 'Previranja u austro-ugarskoj politici u Bosni i Hercegovini 1912. godine', *Glasnik arhiva i društva arhivista Bosne i Hercegovine* (Sarajevo, 1961), Godina I. – Knjiga I.

KECMANOVIĆ, Ilija, 'Jedna borbena omladinska generacija', *Pregled* (Sarajevo), March 1958.

KIßLING, Rudolf, 'Die serbische Mobilmachung im Juli 1914', *Berliner Monatshefte*, July 1932.

KISZLING, Rudolf, 'Erzherzog Franz Ferdinands Pläne für den Umbau der Donaumonarchie', *Neues Abendland* (München), no.4, 1956.

KISZLING, Rudolf, 'Feldmarschall Franz Conrad von Hötzendorf (1852-1925)' in HANTSCH, Hugo (ed.), *Gestalter der Geschicke Österreichs* (Innsbruck-Wien-München, 1962).

KOHN, Hans, 'Was the Collapse Inevitable?', *Austrian History Yearbook*, vol.3, part 3 (1967).

KOVIĆ, Miloš, 'Srbija u borbi za opstanak' in POPOV, Čedomir, ŽIVOJINOVIĆ, Dragoljub R. and MARKOVIĆ, Slobodan G. (eds.), *Dva veka moderne srpske diplomatije* (Beograd, 2013).

KRESTIĆ, Vasilije, 'Politički, privredni i kulturni život u Hrvatskoj i Slavoniji', *Istorija srpskog naroda* (Beograd, 1983), vol.6/1.

KROBATIN, Alexander von Krobatin, 'Aus meinen Erinnerungen an den Kaiser' in STEINITZ, Eduard Ritter von (ed.), *Erinnerungen an Franz Joseph I* (Berlin, 1931).

KRONENBITTER, Günther, 'Nur los lassen. Österreich-Ungarn und der Wille zum Krieg' in BECKER, Josef, KRAUß, Henning and WIATER, Werner (eds.), *Lange und kurze Wege in den Ersten Weltkrieg* (München, 1996).

KRONENBITTER, Günther, 'Haus ohne Macht? Erzherzog Franz Ferdinand (1863-1914) und die Krise der Habsburgermonarchie' in WEBER, Wolfgang (ed.), *Der Fürst. Ideen und Wirklichkeiten in der europäischen Geschichte* (Köln-Weimar-Wien, 1998).

KRONENBITTER, Günther, 'Die Macht der Illusionen. Julikrise und Kriegsausbruch 1914 aus der Sicht des deutschen Militärattachés in Wien', *Militärgeschichtliche Mitteilungen* (Oldenbourg), 57 (1998) 2.

KRONENBITTER, Günther, 'Verhinderter Retter? Erzherzog Franz Ferdinand und die Erhaltung der Habsburgermonarchie', in ZELLENBERG, Ulrich E. (ed.),

Konservative Profile. Ideen und Praxis in der Politik zwischen FM Radetzky, Karl Kraus und Alois Mock (Graz-Stuttgart, 2003).

KRŠIĆ, Jovan, 'Lektira sarajevskih atentatora', *Pregled* (Sarajevo), 26 June 1927.

KRUŠEVAC, Todor, 'Seljački pokret – štrajk u Bosni 1910. godine' in ČUBRILOVIĆ, Vasa (ed.), *Jugoslovenski narodi pred Prvi svetski rat* (Beograd, 1967).

LAZAREVIĆ, Branko, 'Predsednik Masarik i jugoslovensko pitanje' in PROHASKA, Dragutin (ed.), *T.G. Masarik Zbornik* (Beograd-Praha, 1927).

LESLIE, John, 'Österreich-Ungarn vor dem Kriegsausbruch' in MELVILLE, Ralph, SCHARF, Claus, VOGT, Martin and WENGENROTH, Ulrich (eds.), *Deutschland und Europa in der Neuzeit. Festschrift für Karl Otmar Freiherr von Aretin zum 65. Geburtstag* (Stuttgart, 1988), vol.2.

LESLIE, John, 'The Antecedents of Austria-Hungary's War Aims' in SPRINGER, Elisabeth and KAMMERHOFER, Leopold (eds.), *Wiener Beiträge zur Geschichte der Neuzeit*, vol.20, Archiv und Forschung (München, 1993).

LJUBIBRATIĆ, Drago, 'Mjesto Mlade Bosne u društveno-političkom razvoju Bosne i Hercegovine', *Pregled* (Sarajevo), February 1953.

LJUŠIĆ, Radoš, 'Ilija Garašanin o srpskoj državnosti' in STOJANČEVIĆ, Vladimir (ed.), *Ilija Garašanin 1812-1874* (Beograd, 1991).

LJUŠIĆ, R. and RAJIĆ, S., 'Aleksandar Obrenović', *Srpski biografski rečnik* (Novi Sad, 2004), vol.1.

MACCHIO, Karl Freiherr von, 'Momentbilder aus der Julikrise 1914', *Berliner Monatshefte*, October 1936.

MARCO [SIMIĆ, Božin] 'Pripremanje 29. Maja 1903', *Nova Evropa* (Zagreb), vol.15, no.2, 11 June 1927.

MARCO, [SIMIĆ, Božin], 'Pred Kumanovsku Bitku', *Nova Evropa* (Zagreb), vol. 15, no. 10-11, 26 November 1927.

MARCO, [SIMIĆ, Božin], 'Nikola Hartvig i Srbija', *Nova Evropa* (Zagreb), vol.26, no.6, 26 June 1933.

MARKOVICH, Slobodan, G., 'Anglo-American Views of Gavrilo Princip', *Balcanica* (Belgrade), vol.46, 2015.

MASARYK, T.G., 'Österreich und der Balkan' in BONN, M.J. (ed.), *Die Balkanfrage* (München-Leipzig, 1914)

MIKIĆ, Đorđe, 'Balkanska kriza 1912-1913. godine i Bosanska Krajina' in EKMEČIĆ, Milorad (ed.), *Zbornik za istoriju Bosne i Hercegovine* (Beograd, 2008), vol.5.

MILIĆEVIĆ, Jovan, 'Javnost Beograda prema aneksiji Bosne i Hercegovine' in ČUBRILOVIĆ, Vasa (ed.), *Jugoslovenski narodi pred Prvi Svetski Rat* (Beograd, 1967).

MILOŠEVIĆ, Žarko, 'Mladi Pašić – od rođenja do Ciriha (1845-1868)' in *Nikola Pašić: Život i delo,* Zbornik radova (Beograd 1997).

MILUTINOVIĆ, Kosta, 'Hrvatsko-srpska koalicija', *Istorija srpskog naroda*, (Beograd, 1983), vol.6/1.

MORITSCH, Andreas, 'Dem Nationalstaat entgegen (1848-1914)' in MORITSCH Andreas (ed.), *Alpen-Adria. Zur Geschichte einer Region* (Klagenfurt-Ljubljana-Wien, 2001).

MORITZ, Verena, 'Spione am Werk' in MORITZ, Verena, LEIDENGER, Hannes and JAGSCHITZ, Gerhard, *Im Zentrum der Macht. Die vielen Gesichter des Geheimdienstchefs Maximilian Ronge* (St Pölten-Salzburg, 2007).

MORSEY, Andreas Freiherr von, 'Konopischt und Sarajewo. Erinnerungen', *Berliner Monatshefte*, June 1934.

MURKO, M., 'Ko je stvorio Jugoslovene i Jugoslaviju', *Nova Evropa* (Zagreb), vol.19, no.2, 26 January 1929.

NAMIER, L.B., 'The Downfall of the Habsburg Monarchy' in TEMPERLEY, H.W.V., (ed.), *A History of the Peace Conference of Paris* (London, 1921), vol.4.

NESTOROVIĆ, Jovan V., 'Prisebnost' in *Spomenica Nikole P. Pašića 1845-1925* (Beograd, 1926).

NOVAK, Viktor, 'Masarik i Jugosloveni', *Srpski književni glasnik* (Beograd), vol.29, no.6, 16 March 1930.

NURI HADŽIĆ, Osman, 'Muslimanska versko-prosvetna autonomija u Bosni i Hercegovini i pitanje Carigradskog Halifata', *Brastvo* (Beograd), vol.19, 1925.

PANDŽA, Hafiz Muhamed, 'Merhum Džemaludin Čaušević' in KARIĆ, Enes and DEMIROVIĆ, Mujo (eds.), *Reis Džemaludin Čaušević. Prosvjetitelj i reformator* (Sarajevo, 2002), vol.1.

PEBALL, Kurt and ROTHENBERG, Gunther E., 'Der Fall "U": Die geplante Besetzung Ungarns durch die k. u. k. Armee im Herbst 1905', *Schriften des Heeresgeschichtlichen Museums in Wien*, Militärwissenschaftliches Institut, (Wien-München 1969).

PETERSSON, H. Bertil A., 'Das österreichisch-ungarische Memorandum an Deutschland vom 5. Juli 1914', *Scandia*, vol.30, no.1, 1964.

PETROVIĆ, Nastas N., 'Pašić i Goluhovski', *Nova Evropa* (Zabreb), vol.13, no.12, 22 June 1926.

PISAREV, Ju. A., 'Rossijskaja kontrrazvedka i tajnaja serbskaja organizacija *Chernaja ruka*', VIZh., 1993, no.1.

PLASCHKA, Richard Georg, 'Serbien und die Balkankriege als Motivationselemente in der österreichisch-ungarischen Armee' in ČUBRILOVIĆ, Vasa (ed.), *Velike sile i Srbija pred Prvi svetski rat* (Beograd, 1976).

POPOV, Č., 'Đorđe A. Genčić', *Sprpski biografski rečnik* (Novi Sad, 2006), vol.2.

POPOVIĆ, Čed. A., 'Organizacija *Ujedinjenje ili smrt* ('Crna ruka')', *Nova Evropa* (Zagreb), vol.15, no.12, 11 June 1927.

POPOVIĆ, Čed. A., 'Sarajevski atentat i organizacija *Ujedinjenje ili Smrt*', *Nova Evropa* (Zagreb), vol.25, no.8, July 1932.

POPOVIĆ, Dimitrije, 'Nikola Pašić i Rusija', *Godišnjica Nikole Čupića* (Beograd), vol.46, 1937.

POPOVIĆ, Dimitrije, 'Milovan Milovanović i aneksija', *Srpski književni glasnik* (Beograd), vol.53, no.7, 1 April 1938.

PRINZ, Friedrich, 'Der österreichisch-ungarische Ausgleich von 1867 als historiographisches Problem' in *Bohemia,* Jahrbuch des Collegium Carolinum, vol. 9 (München 1968).

PRODANOVIĆ, Jaša M., 'Nikola P. Pašić', *Srpski književni glasnik* (Beograd), vol.20, no.2, 16 January 1927.

RAJIĆ, Suzana, 'The Russian Secret Service and King Alexander Obrenović of Serbia 1900-1903', *Balcanica*, Belgrade, vol.43 (2012).

RAKOČEVIĆ, Novica, 'Odnosi Crne Gore i Srbije 1903-1918' in *Crna Gora u međunarodnim odnosima* (Titograd, 1984).

REDŽIĆ, Enver, 'Omladinski pokret i sarajevski atentat', *Prilozi za istoriju Bosne i Hercegovine* (Sarajevo, 1987), vol.2.

REINHÖL, Fritz von, 'Die angebliche Mitwissenschaft der österreichisch-ungarischen Regierung an der Verschwörung gegen König Alexander von Serbien im Jahre 1903', *Berliner Monatshefte*, May 1936.

REMAK, Joachim, 'The Healthy Invalid: How Doomed the Habsburg Empire?', *The Journal of Modern History*, vol.41, no.2 (June 1969).

RÖHL, John C.G., 'Germany ' in WILSON, Keith (ed.), *Decisions for War, 1914* (New York, 1995).

RÖHL, John C.G., 'The Curious Case of the Kaiser's Disappearing War Guilt: Wilhelm II in July 1914' in AFFLERBACH, Holger and STEVENSON, David (eds.), *An Improbable War? The Outbreak of World War I and European Political Culture Before 1914* (New York-Oxford, 2007).

RÖHL, John C.G., '*Jetzt oder nie*. The Resurgence of Serbia and Germany's first 'blank cheque' of November 1912' in Dragoljub R. Živojinović (ed.), *The Serbs and the First World War* (Belgrade, 2015).

RUMPLER, Helmut, 'Die Dalmatienreise Kaiser Franz Josephs 1875 im Kontext der politischen Richtungsentscheidungen der Habsburgermonarchie am Vorabend der orientalischen Krise' in HÖBELT, Lothar and OTTE, Thomas G. (eds.), *A Living Anachronism? European Diplomacy and the Habsburg Monarchy* (Wien-Köln-Weimar, 2010).

RUTKOWSKI, Ernst R., 'Die Plan für eine Annexion Bosniens und der Herzegowina aus den Jahren 1882/83', *Mitteilungen des Oberösterreichischen Landesarchivs* (Graz-Köln), vol.5, 1957.

ŠAJKOVIĆ, Ivan S., 'Nekoliko momenata iz omladinskoga pokreta. (Od 1893-1903 godine)', *Književni Sever* (Subotica), vol.5, July-August-September 1929.

SCHINDLER, John R., 'Defeating Balkan Insurgency: The Austro-Hungarian Army in Bosnia-Hercegovina, 1878-82', *The Journal of Strategic Studies*, vol.27, no.3, September 2004.

SCHINDLER, John R., 'Disaster on the Drina: The Austro-Hungarian Army in Serbia, 1914', *War in History*, 2002, 9:159.

SCHROEDER, Paul, 'World War I as Galloping Gertie: A Reply to Joachim Remak', *The Journal of Modern History*, vol.44, no.3 (September 1972).

SCHROEDER, Paul, 'Romania and the Great Powers before 1914', *Revue Roumaine d'Histoire* (Bucureşti), 1975 (1).

SKARIĆ, Vladislav, 'Sarajevo i njegova okolina od najstarijih vremena do austrougraske okupacije' in EKMEČIĆ, Milorad (ed.), *Vladislav Skarić. Izabrana djela* (Sarajevo, 1985), vol.1.

SKERLIĆ, Jovan, 'Ante Starčević', *Srpski književni glasnik* (Beograd), vol.28, 1 February 1912.

SLIJEPČEVIĆ, Pero, 'Mlada Bosna' in SLIJEPČEVIĆ, Pero (ed.), *Napor Bosne i Hercegovine za oslobođenje i ujedinjenje* (Sarajevo, 1929).

SLIJEPČEVIĆ, Pero, 'Mlada Bosna (Ideologija)', *Pregled* (Sarajevo), August 1929.

SLIJEPČEVIĆ, Pero, 'G. Masarik i predratna omladina', *Srpski književni glasnik* (Beograd), vol.29, no.6, 16 March 1930.

SÖSEMANN, Bernd, 'Die Bereitschaft zum Krieg. Sarajevo 1914' in DEMANDT, Alexander (ed.), *Das Attentat in der Geschichte* (Köln-Weimar-Wien, 1996).

SPALAÎKOVITCH, M., 'Une journée du Ministre de Serbie à Pétrograd. Le 24 juillet 1914', *Revue d'histoire diplomatique* (Paris), April-June 1934.

SPITZMÜLLER-HARMERSBACH, Alexander von, 'Franz Joseph und der Dualismus' in STEINITZ, Eduard Ritter von (ed.), *Erinnerungen an Franz Joseph I.* (Berlin, 1931).

STEED, Henry Wickham, 'The Pact of Konopisht', *The Nineteenth Century and After*, vol.79, February 1916.

STEFANOVIĆ, Dušan P., 'Pred buru' in VIDAKOVIĆ, Slobodan Ž. (ed.), *Agonija Beograda u svetskom ratu 1914-1915* (Beograd, 1931).

STOJANOVIĆ, Nikola, 'Pogled na Bosansku Politiku od 1903. do 1914.' in SLIJEP-ČEVIĆ, Pero (ed.), *Napor Bosne i Hercegovine za oslobođenje i ujedinjenje* (Sarajevo, 1929).

STONE, Norman, 'Hungary and the Crisis of July 1914', *Journal of Contemporary History*, vol.1, no.3, July 1966.

STOURZH, Gerald, 'The Multinational Empire Revisited: Reflections on Late Imperial Austria', *Austrian History Yearbook*, vol. 23, 1992.

STRANJAKOVIĆ, Drag., 'Kako je postalo Garašaninovo *Načertanije*', Srpska kraljevska akademija, Spomenik 91 (Beograd, 1939).

STRECHA, Mario, 'Franjo Josip I. (1848-1916.)' in BUDAK, Neven, STRECHA, Mario and KRUŠELJ, Željko, *Habsburzi i Hrvati* (Zagreb, 2003).

SWEET, D.W., 'The Bosnian Crisis' in HINSLEY, F.H. (ed.), *British Foreign Policy Under Sir Edward Grey* (Cambridge, 1977).

SZÁPÁRY, Friedrich Graf, 'Das Verhältnis Österreich-Ungarns zu Rußland' in STEINITZ, Eduard Ritter von (ed.), *Rings um Sasonow* (Berlin, 1928).

TOMANOVIĆ, L., 'Austrija i Crna Gora', *Nova Evropa* (Zagreb), vol.20, no.5, 26 August 1929.

TOMIĆ, Božidar M., 'Poreklo i detinjstvo Gavrila Principa', *Nova Evropa* (Zagreb), vol.32, no.10, 26 October 1939.

TRIŠIĆ, Nikola, 'Oko sarajevskog atentata', *Pregled* (Sarajevo), January-June, 1929.

TRIŠIĆ, Nikola, 'Moje uspomene', *Pregled* (Sarajevo), February 1935.

TRIŠIĆ, Nikola, 'Uspomene na Muhameda Mehmedbašića povodom desetogodišnjice smrti', *Pregled* (Sarajevo), July-August 1953.

TRŽECJAK, Vladimir, 'Jedan ruski savremeni dokumenat o 29. Maja', *Nova Evropa* (Zagreb), vol.16, no.7, 11 October 1927.

TUNSTALL, Graydon A., Jr., 'Austria-Hungary' in HAMILTON, Richard F. and HERWIG, Holger H. (eds.), *The Origins of World War I* (Cambridge 2003).

TURKALJ, Jasna, 'Starčevićeva misao o nužnosti samostalne hrvatske države' in GABELICA, Ivan (ed.), *Starčević. Znanstveni kolokvij o 180. obljetnici rođenja* (Zagreb, 2004).

TVRTKOVIC, Jv., 'König Peter und die großserbische Bewegung', *Österreichische Rundschau* (Wien), vol.17, no.1, 1 October 1908.

URBAŃSKI, August von Ostrymiecz, 'Mein Beitrag zur Kriegsschuldfrage', *Die Kriegsschuldfrage*, February 1926.

URBAŃSKI, August v. Ostrymiecz, 'Conrad v. Hötzenforf und die Reise des Thronfolgers nach Sarajevo', *Berliner Monatshefte*, May 1929.

VERMES, Gabor P., 'South Slav Aspirations and Magyar Nationalism in the Dual Monarchy', in BANAC, Ivo, ACKERMAN, John G. and SZPORLUK, Roman (eds.), *Nation and Ideology: Essays in honour of Wayne S. Vucinich* (Boulder, 1981).

VRANEŠEVIĆ, Branislav, 'Die aussenpolitischen Beziehungen zwischen Serbien und der Habsburgermonarchie' in *Die Habsburgermonarchie 1848-1918*, vol.6/2: *Die Habsburgermonarchier im System der internationalen Beziehungen* (Wien, 1993).

VUCINICH, Wayne S., 'Croatian Illyrism: Its Background and Genesis' in WINTERS, Stanley B. and HELD, Joseph (eds.), *Intellectual and Social Developments in the Habsburg Empire from Maria Theresa to World War I* (Boulder, 1975).

VUČKOVIĆ, Vojislav J., 'Unutrašnje krize Srbije i Prvi svetski rat', *Istorijski časopis* (Beograd), vol.14-15, 1963-1965.

WALTERS, Eurof, 'Franco-Russian Discussions on the Partition of Austria-Hungary, 1899', *The Slavonic and East European Review*, vol.28, no.70, November 1949.

WANDYCZ, Piotr S., 'The Poles in the Habsburg Monarchy', *Austrian History Yearbook*, vol.3, part 2, 1967.

WANK, Solomon, 'Aehrenthal's Programme for the Constitutional Transformation of the Habsburg Monarchy: Three Secret *Mémoires*', *The Slavonic and East European Review*, vol.41, no.97, June 1963.

WANK, Solomon Wank, 'The Appointment of Count Berchtold as Austro-Hungarian Foreign Minister', *Journal of Central European Affairs*, vol.23, July 1963.

WANK, Solomon, 'Aehrenthal and the Sanjak of Novibazar Railway Project: a Reappraisal', *The Slavonic and East European Review*, vol.42, no.99, June 1964.

WANK, Solomon, 'Varieties of Political Despair: Three Exchanges Between Aehrenthal and Goluchowski 1898-1906' in WINTERS, Stanley B. and HELD, Joseph (eds.), *Intellectual and Social Developments in the Habsburg Empire from Maria Theresa to World War I* (Boulder, 1975).

WANK, Solomon, 'Pessimism in the Austrian Establishment at the Turn of the Century' in WANK, Solomon *et al.* (eds.)., *The Mirror of History: Essays in Honor of Fritz Fellner* (Santa Barbara-Oxford, 1988).

WANK, Solomon, 'Desperate Counsel in Vienna in July 1914: Berthold Molden's Unpublished Memorandum', *Central European History*, vol.26, no.3 (Autumn 1993).

WANK, Solomon, 'Some Reflections on the Habsburg Empire and Its Legacy in the Nationalities Question', *Austrian History Yearbook*, vol. 28, 1997.

WEGERER, Alfred von, 'Die Mitwisserschaft der serbischen Regierung an der Ermordung des Erzherzogs Franz Ferdinand zugegeben', *Die Kriegsschuldfrage*, February 1925.

WIESNER, Friedrich R. von, 'The Forged and the Genuine Text of the *Wiesner Documents*', *Die Kriegsschuldfrage*, October 1925.
WIESNER, Friedrich Ritter von, 'Das Mémoire Österreich-Ungarns über die groß-serbische Propaganda und deren Zusammenhänge mit dem Sarajevoer Attentat', *Die Kriegsschuldfrage*, June 1927.
WIESNER, Friedrich von, 'Milan Ciganović', *Die Krigsschuldfrage*, November 1927.
WIESNER, Friedrich Ritter von, 'Meine Depesche vom 13. Juli 1914' in STEINITZ, Eduard Ritter von (ed.), *Rings um Sasonow* (Berlin, 1928).
WILLIAMSON, Samuel R. Jr., 'Influence, Power, and the Policy Process: The Case of Franz Ferdinand, 1906-1914', *The Historical Journal*, vol.17, no.2, June 1974.
WILLIAMSON, Samuel R., Jr., 'The Origins of World War I', *The Journal of Interdisciplinary History*, vol.18, no.4, Spring 1988.
WILLIAMSON, Samuel R., Jr., 'Leopold Count Berchtold: The Man Who Could Have Prevented the Great War' in BISCHOF, Günter and PLASSER, Fritz (eds.), *From Empire to Republic: Post-World War I Austria* (New Orleans and Innsbruck, 2010).
WILLIAMSON, Samuel R., Jr., 'July 1914 revisited and revised: The erosion of the German paradigm' in LEVY, Jack S. and VASQUEZ, John A. (eds.), *The Outbreak of the First World War: Structure, Politics and Decision-Making* (Cambridge, 2014).
WILSON, Keith, 'Britain' in WILSON, Keith (ed.), *Decisions for War 1914* (New York. 1995).
WOLF, Franz, 'Aurel Constantin Popovici', *Österreich in Geschichte und Literatur* (Wien), no. 10, 1964.
WÜRTHLE, Fritz, 'Franz Ferdinands letzter Befehl. Der verhängnisvolle Fahrirrtum von Sarajevo', *Österreich in Geschichte und Literatur* (Wien), June 1971.
ZANINOVIĆ, Vice, 'Mlada Hrvatska uoči I. svjetskog rata', *Historijski zbornik* (Zagreb), vol.11-12, 1958-1959.

UNPUBLISHED DISSERTATIONS AND THESES

GASIC, Dragan, 'Die Presse Serbiens 1903-1914 und Österreich-Ungarn' (Dissertation, Universität Wien, 1971).
GJURGJEVIC, Theodore, V., 'The Friedjung and Vasic Trials in the Light of the Austrian Diplomatic Documents' (D.Phil. thesis, St Antony's College, University of Oxford, 1956).
IVETIĆ, Velimir J., 'Politička uloga ministara vojnih Kraljevine Srbije od 1903. do 1914. godine' (doktorska disertacija, Univerzitet Beograd, 2013).
KASER, Karl, 'Die serbischen politischen Gruppen, Organisationen und Parteien und ihre Programme in Bosnien und der Herzegovina 1904-1914' (Dissertation, Karl-Franzens-Universität Graz, 1980).
KRALER, Tanja, 'Gott schütze Österreich vor seinen *Staatsmännern*, aber auch vor seinen *Freunden*!' Das Tagebuch von Hans Schlitter 1912-1927 (Dissertation, Leopold-Franzens-Universität Innsbruck, 2009).
MENDE, Johannes, 'Dr. Carl Freiherr von Bardolff' (Dissertation, Universität Wien, 1984).
NICOLL, Leo Ashley Jr., 'Anton Puntigam S.J. Leben und Wirken eines Jesuiten in Bosnien' (Dissertation, Universität Wien, 1970).
SCHULDA, Karl, 'Generaloberst Freiherr Arthur von Bolfras. Generaladjutant und Vorstand der Militärkanzlei Seiner Majestät Kaiser Franz Josephs I' (Dissertation, Universität Wien, 1993).
SILBER, Margit, 'Obersthofmeister Alfred Fürst von Montenuovo. Höfische Geschichte in den beiden letzten Jahrzenten der österreichisch-ungarischen Monarchie 1896-1916' (Dissertation, Universität Wien, 1991).
SITTE, Martha, 'Alexander von Brosch, der Flügeladjutant und Vorstand der Militärkanzlei des Thronfolgers Franz Ferdinand' (Dissertation, Universität Wien, 1961).

WEIGERT, Manfred, 'Die Militärkanzlei seiner k.u.k. Hoheit des durchl. Herrn General der Kavallerie Erzherzog Franz Ferdinand. Nebenregierung oder machtlose Opposition?' (Diplomaarbeit, Universität Wien, 2001).

WEINWURM, Franz, 'FZM Oskar Potiorek. Leben und Wirken als Chef der Regierung für Bosnien und der Herzegowina in Sarajevo – 1911-1914' (Dissertation, Universität Wien, 1964).

Index

Bath & North East
Somerset

4 3 0001664 8

A & H   14-Nov-2017

940.31   £27.95

BNBL

5567394

THE HABSBURG EMPIRE 1914